Dictionary of Behavioral Assessment Techniques

(PGPS-147)

Pergamon Titles of Related Interest

PERGAMON GENERAL PSYCHOLOGY SERIES
EDITORS
Arnold P. Goldstein, *Syracuse University*
Leonard Krasner, *Stanford University and SUNY
at Stony Brook*

Dictionary of Behavioral Assessment Techniques

Edited by

Michel Hersen
*University of Pittsburgh
School of Medicine*

Alan S. Bellack
*Medical College of Pennsylvania
at Eastern Pennsylvania
Psychiatric Institute*

PERGAMON PRESS
New York · Oxford · Beijing · Frankfurt
São Paulo · Sydney · Tokyo · Toronto

U.S.A.	Pergamon Press, Inc., Maxwell House, Fairview Park, Elmsford, New York 10523, U.S.A.
U.K.	Pergamon Press plc, Headington Hill Hall, Oxford OX3 0BW, England
PEOPLE'S REPUBLIC OF CHINA	Pergamon Press, Room 4037, Qianmen Hotel, Beijing, People's Republic of China
FEDERAL REPUBLIC OF GERMANY	Pergamon Press GmbH, Hammerweg 6, D-6242 Kronberg, Federal Republic of Germany
BRAZIL	Pergamon Editora Ltda, Rua Eça de Queiros, 346, CEP 04011, Paraiso, São Paulo, Brazil
AUSTRALIA	Pergamon Press Australia Pty Ltd., P.O. Box 544, Potts Point, N.S.W. 2011, Australia
JAPAN	Pergamon Press, 5th Floor, Matsuoka Central Building, 1-7-1 Nishishinjuku, Shinjuku-ku, Tokyo 160, Japan
CANADA	Pergamon Press Canada Ltd., Suite No 271, 253 College Street, Toronto, Ontario, Canada M5T 1R5

Copyright © 1988 Pergamon Press Inc.

First edition 1988

Library of Congress Cataloging in Publication Data

Dictionary of behavioral assessment techniques.
(Pergamon general psychology series)
Includes index.
1. Behavioral assessment — Dictionaries.
I. Hersen, Michel. II. Bellack, Alan S. III. Series.
[DNLM: 1. Mental Disorders — diagnosis — handbooks.
2. Personality Assessment. 3. Psychological Tests — methods — handbooks. WM 141 D554]
BF176.5.D53 1987   150'.28'7   86–25352

British Library Cataloguing in Publication Data

Dictionary of behavioral assessment techniques.
(Pergamon general psychology series).
1. Man. Behaviour. Assessment
I. Hersen, Michel. II. Bellack, Alan S.
152.8
ISBN 0–08–031975–0

Printed in Great Britain by A. Wheaton & Co. Ltd., Exeter

Contents

CONTENTS

CONTENTS

CONTENTS

CONTENTS

Preface

A few years ago, when we edited the *Dictionary of Behavior Therapy Techniques,* it became clear to us that the field of behavior therapy had expanded to such a considerable extent that it was impossible, even for the so-called experts, to be knowledgeable about all of the strategies carried out by our colleagues on a day-to-day basis. We therefore concluded that a dictionary, incorporating clear descriptions of major and minor techniques, would be of value to the field. In the process of selecting suitable entries for that *Dictionary,* we researched our own libraries, made lists of techniques, and obtained feedback from our colleagues about these lists. We then invited the leading exponents and practitioners of the particular behavior therapy techniques to share their expertise with us, eventuating in the *Dictionary of Behavior Therapy Techniques.*

While working on that project, it became apparent that it was even more difficult to identify assessment procedures than treatment procedures. We realized that there was an equal need, if not more so, for a *Dictionary of Behavioral Assessment Techniques.* Although a good number of scholarly books are available on the theoretical and practical aspects of behavioral assessment (some of which have been perpetrated by the current editors), none of these provides the quick reference guide for researchers and clinicians alike needed for the multitude of assessment devices used in widely diverse problems and disorders in children, adolescents, adults, and the geriatric population. Moreover, we found that there are numerous instruments repeatedly used by behavioral assessors that often may not be associated by workers in the field as being within the province of the behavioral endeavor.

In our search for both frequently and infrequently used behavioral assessment tools, we were impressed with the wide range of modalities that behaviorists use to evaluate their clients, patients, and subjects. These include, but are not limited to, behavioral observations, self-reports, parent ratings, staff ratings, sibling ratings, judges' ratings, teacher ratings, therapist ratings, nurses' ratings, physiological assessment, biochemical assessment, biological assessment, structured interviews, semistructured interviews, and analogue tests.

We also found that a number of our behavioral assessment strategies have dual modality components. That is, some of the assessment strategies may include both behavioral observation and self-report or perhaps behavioral observation and physiological assessment.

In presenting each of the definitions of behavioral assessment techniques, we asked our contributors to follow a standard outline that includes the following: Description, Purpose, Development, Psychometric Characteristics, Clinical Use, and Future Directions. We followed this format to facilitate the work of both our *clinical and research* colleagues in the field. In addition, we have provided a Users' Guide, in which the focus of assessment (e.g., anxiety, depression, and unassertiveness) is listed in alphabetical order in the first column. In the second column, titles of assessment devices subsumed under these disorders or problems are listed; and in the third column the assessment modality is specified (e.g., behavioral observation and self-report).

Many persons have participated in the laborious job of gathering and presenting the information in this *Dictionary.* First of all, we thank and compliment our contributors for their willingness to share their expertise with us. Second, we are most appreciative of the remarkable effort by our respective administrative assistants, Mary Newell and Florence Levito, for learning a new computer language and word processing the rough manuscript into a viable presentation. Finally, once again, we thank Jerry Frank, our editor at Pergamon, for his enthusiasm, encouragement, firm guidance, and understanding.

Michel Hersen, Ph.D.
Alan S. Bellack, Ph.D.

Sources of Entries

ENTRIES	SOURCE
Abnormal Involuntary Movement Scale	Jeste, D.V., & Wyatt, R.J. (1982). Scale *Understanding and treating tardive dyskinesia* (pp. 301-303). New York: Guilford Press.
Activities of Daily Living - Modular Assessment	Mr. David A. Eberly Dept. of Aging & Mental Health Florida Mental Health Institute 13301 N. 30th Street Tampa, Florida 33612
Activity Measure	Mr. James Mansell Institute of Social and Applied Psychology University of Kent at Canterbury Beverley Farm Canterbury Kent CT1 7LZ United Kingdom
Addiction Severity Index	ASI Reprint Fund (P.E.R.F.) c/o A. Thomas McLellan, Ph.D. Psychiatry Department University of Pennsylvania 319 Blockley Hall 419 Service Drive Philadelphia, Pennslyvania 19104
Adelaide Version of Conners' Parent Rating Scale	Peter H. Glow, Ph.D. University of Adelaide Department of Psychology GPO Box 498 Adelaide, South Australia 5001
Adelaide Version of Conners' Teachers Rating Scale	Peter H. Glow, Ph.D. University of Adelaide Department of Psychology GPO Box 498 Adelaide, South Australia 5001

Adjusted Weight Measure for Children	Edwards, K.A. (1978). An index for assessing weight change in children: Weight/height ratios. *Journal of Applied Behavior Analysis, 11,* 421-429.
Adolescent Problems Inventory	Barbara Jane Freedman, Ph.D. 4130 Cherokee Drive Madison, Wisconsin 53711
Adult Diagnostic Interview Schedules	Barry Edelstein, Ph.D. Department of Psychology West Virginia University Morgantown, West Virginia 26506
Adult Self-Expression Scale	Adult Self-Expression Scale P. O. Box 220174 Charlotte, North Carolina 28222
Agoraphobic Cognitions Questionnaire	Dianne L. Chambless, Ph.D. Department of Psychology The American University 4400 Massachusetts Avenue, N.W. Washington, DC 20016
AlcEval	Robert S. Davidson, Ph.D. Miami VA Hospital NW 16th Street Miami, Florida 33125
Alcohol Beliefs Scale	Gerard J. Connors, Ph.D. Research Institute on Alcoholism 1021 Main Street Buffalo, New York 14203
Analogue Communications Assessment	Stephen N. Haynes, Ph.D. Department of Psychology Illinois Institute of Technology Chicago, Illinois 60616
Anger Expression Scale	Charles Spielberger, Ph.D. Department of Psychology University of South Florida Tampa, Florida 33620-8200
Antidepressive Activity Questionnaire	Vicky Rippere, Ph.D. Department of Psychology Institute of Psychiatry De Crespigny Park Denmark Hill London, SE5 8AF England
Anxiety Disorders Interview Schedule - Revised	David H. Barlow, Ph.D. Center for Stress and Anxiety Disorders 1535 Western Avenue Albany, New York 12203

Assertion Inventory

Eileen Gambrill, Ph.D.
University of California
School of Social Welfare
120 Haviland Hall
Berkeley, California   94720

Assertion Self-Statement
Test-Revised

Richard G. Heimberg, Ph.D.
Center for Stress and Anxiety Disorders
State University of New York at Albany
1535 Western Avenue
Albany, NY   12203

Assertion Situations

Cynthia Gallois, Ph.D.
Department of Psychology
University of Queensland
St. Lucia
Queensland, Australia   4067

Assertiveness Self-Statement
Test

Robert M. Schwartz, Ph.D.
Western Psychiatric Institute
  and Clinic
Department of Psychiatry
University of Pittsburgh
  School of Medicine
3811 O'Hara Street
Pittsburgh, Pennsylvania   15213

Assessment of Self-Care Skills
of Mentally Retarded Individuals

American Association on
Mental Deficiency
1719 Kalorama Road, N.W.
Washington, DC   20015

Automated Matching Familiar
Figures Test

Peter H. Glow, Ph.D.
University of Adelaide
Department of Psychology
GPO Box 498
Adelaide, South Australia   5001

Automatic Thoughts
Questionnaire

Philip C. Kendall, Ph.D.
Psychology-Weiss Hall
Temple University
Philadelphia, Pennsylvania   19122

Beck Depression Inventory

The Psychological Corporation
c/o Yolanda Aguero
5555 Academic Court
San Antonio, Texas   78204-9990

Behavior Profile Rating Scale

Barbara G. Melamed, Ph.D.
Department of Clinical Psychology
University of Florida
Box J-165 JHMHC
Gainesville, Florida   32610

Behavioral Assertiveness   Richard M. Eisler, Ph.D.
Test - Revised   Department of Psychology
                                             Virginia Polytechnic Institute
                                               and State University
                                             Blacksburg, Virginia   24061

Behavioral Assertiveness Test   Educational Testing Service
for Children   Princeton, New Jersey   08541

Behavioral Assessment of Bruxism   Michael S. Rosenbaum, Ph.D.
                                             West Mobile Psychology Center
                                             4325 Midmost Drive - Suite B
                                             Mobile, Alabama   36609

Behavioral Assessment Procedure   Vicky Rippere, Ph.D.
for Food Addiction   Department of Psychology
                                             Institute of Psychiatry
                                             De Crespigny Park
                                             Denmark Hill
                                             London, SE5 8AF
                                             England

Behavioral Avoidance Slide   Donald J. Levis, Ph.D.
Test   Department of Psychology
                                             University Center at Binghamton
                                             Binghamton, New York   13901

Behavioral Avoidance Test   F. Dudley McGlynn, Ph.D.
                                             University of Florida
                                             J. Hillis Miller Health Center
                                             Box J-404
                                             Gainesville, Florida   32610

Behavioral Checklist for Mildly   Carden Smith, L.K., & Fowler, S.A.
Handicapped Children   (1984). Positive peer pressure: The
                                             effects of peer monitoring on children's
                                             disruptive behavior. *Journal of
                                             Applied Behavior Analysis, 17,*
                                             213-227.

Behavioral Conversational   Frances M. Haemmerlie, Ph.D.
Measures   Department of Psychology
                                             University of Missouri-Rolla
                                             Rolla, Missouri   65401

Behavioral Eating Test   D. Balfour Jeffrey, Ph.D.
                                             Department of Psychology
                                             University of Montana
                                             Missoula, Montana   59812

Behavioral Measures of   Williams, J.G., Barlow, D.H.,
Severe Depression   & Agras, W.S. (1972). Behavioral
                                             measurement of severe depression.
                                             *Archives of General Psychiatry,
                                             27,* 330-333.

Behavioral Role-Playing Assertion Test	Richard M. McFall, Ph.D. Department of Psychology Indiana University Bloomington, Indiana 47405
Behavioral Situations Test	Billy A. Barrios, Ph.D. College of Liberal Arts Department of Psychology University of Mississippi University, Mississippi 38677
Behavioral Visual Acuity Test	Frank L. Collins, Ph.D. Department of Psychology Rush Medical College Rush Presbyterian St. Luke's Medical Center 1753 West Congress Parkway Chicago, Illinois 60612
Behavioral Walk	S.Lloyd Williams, Ph.D. Department of Psychology 17 Lehigh University Bethlehem, Pennsylvania 18015
Behaviorally Referenced Rating System of Intermediate Social Skills	Jan S. Wallander, Ph.D. Sparks Center University of Alabama at Birmingham 1720 Seventh Avenue South Birmingham, Alabama 35233
Binge Eating Scale	Gormally, J., Black, S., Daston, S., & Rardin, D. (1982). The assessment of binge eating severity among obese persons. *Addictive Behaviors, 7,* 47-55.
Binge Scale Questionnaire	Aubrey J. Yates, Ph.D. Department of Psychology The University of Western Australia Nedlands, Western Australia 6009
Blood Alcohol Level	Luckey Laboratories, Inc. San Bernardino, California 92404
Blood Pressure Assessment	B. Kent Houston, Ph.D. Department of Psychology The University of Kansas 426 Fraser Hall Lawrence, Kansas 66045-2160
Blood Pressure Reactivity	C. Barr Taylor, M.D. Department of Psychiatry Stanford University School of Medicine Stanford, California 94305

Body Mass Index

Thomas, A.E., McKay, D.A., & Cutlip, M.B. (1976).Nomograph for Body Mass Index (KG/M²).*American Journal of Clinical Nutrition, 29,*   302-304.

Body Sensations Questionnaire

Dianne L. Chambless, Ph.D.
Department of Psychology
The American University
4400 Massachusetts Avenue, N.W.
Washington, DC   20016

Brief Psychiatric Rating
Scale

John E. Overall, Ph.D.
Department of Psychiatry
University of Texas Medical School
P. O. Box 20708
Houston, Texas   77225

Bulimia Test

Aubrey J. Yates, Ph.D.
Department of Psychology
The University of Western Australia
Nedlands, Western Australia   6009

Callner-Ross Assertion
Questionnaire

Callner, D.A., & Ross, S.M. (1976).The reliability and validity of three measures of assertion in a drug addict population. *Behavior Therapy, 7,* 659-667.

Cardiotachometry

Geary S. Alford, Ph.D.
Dept. of Psychiatry and Human Behavior
The University of Mississippi Medical
   Center
2500 North State Street
Jackson, Mississippi   39216-4505

Checklist of Appropriate
Speaking Behaviors

W. L. Marshall, Ph.D.
Department of Psychology
Queen's University
Kingston, Canada
K7L 3N6

Child Behavior Checklist and
Related Instruments

Thomas M. Achenbach, Ph.D.
Department of Psychiatry
University of Vermont
1 South Prospect Street
Burlington, Vermont   05401

Child Depression Scale

Psychological Assessment Resources
P. O. Box 998
Odessa, Florida   33556

Child Development Questionnaire

Barbara G. Melamed, Ph.D.
Department of Clinical Psychology
University of Florida
Box J-165 JHMHC
Gainesville, Florida   32610

Child Diagnostic Interview
Schedules

Barry A. Edelstein, Ph.D.
Department of Psychology
West Virginia University
Morgantown, West Virginia   26506

Children's Action Tendency Scale

Robert H. Deluty, Ph.D.
University of Maryland
Baltimore County
Baltimore, Maryland   21228

Children's Assertive Behavior
Scale

Michelson, L., & Wood, R. (1982).
Development and psychometric properties
of the Children's Assertive Behavior
Scale. *Journal of Behavioral Assessment, 4,* 3-13.

Children's Assertiveness
Inventory

Thomas H. Ollendick, Ph.D.
Department of Psychology
Virginia Polytechnic Institute
  and State University
Blacksburg, Virginia   24061

Children's Depression Inventory

Maria Kovacs, Ph.D.
Western Psychiatric Institute
  and Clinic
Department of Psychiatry
University of Pittsburgh
  School of Medicine
3911 O'Hara Street
Pittsburgh, Pennsylvania   15213

Children's Interpersonal
Behavior Test

Vincent B.Van Hasselt, Ph.D.
Department of Psychiatry
  and Human Behavior
University of California
  at Irvine
101 City Drive South
Orange, California   92668

Client Resistance Coding System

Chamberlain, P., Patterson, G.R., Reid,
J.B., Kavanagh, K., & Forgatch, M.S.
(1984).Observation of client
resistance. *Behavior Therapy,*
15, 144-155.

Clinical Dementia Rating

Hughes, C.P., Berg, L., Danziger, W.L.,
Cohen, L.A., & Martin, R.L. (1982).
A new clinical scale for the staging of
dementia. *British Journal of*
Psychiatry, 140,   566-572.

Clinical Frequencies Recording
System

Gordon L. Paul, Ph.D.
System (CFRS) Department of Psychology
University of Houston/University Park
Houston, Texas   77004

Code for Instructional Structure
and Student Academic Response

Juniper Gardens Children's Project
1614 Washington Blvd.
Kansas City, Kansas   66102

Cognitive Bias Questionnaire

Constance Hammen, Ph.D.
Department of Psychology
University of California at Los Angeles
405 Hilgard Avenue
Los Angeles, California   90024

Cognitive-Somatic Anxiety
Questionnaire

Schwartz, G.E., Davidson, R.J., &
Coleman, D.J. (1978). Patterning of
cognitive and somatic processes in the
self-regulation of anxiety: Effects of
meditation versus exercise.
Psychometric Medicine, 40,   321-328.

Cold Pressor Test

Jeffrey J. Dolce, Ph.D.
Department of Medicine
Division of General and Preventive
  Medicine
The University of Alabama
University Station
Birmingham, Alabama   35294

College Self-Expression Scale

Galassi, J.P., DeLo, J.S., Galassi, M.D.,
& Bastien, S. (1974). The College
Self-Expression Scale: A measure of
assertiveness. *Behavior Therapy,*
5, 165-171.

College Women's Assertion
Sample

MacDonald, M.L. (1975). A behavioral
assessment methodology applied to the
measurement of assertion.
Dissertation Abstracts International,
35, 6101B. (University Microfilms
No. 75-11, 819).

Combat Exposure Scale

Foy, D.W., Sipprelle, R.C., Rueger, D.B.,
& Carroll, E.M. (1984). Etiology of
posttraumatic stress disorder in Vietnam
veterans: Analysis of premilitary,
military, and combat exposure of
influences. *Journal of Consulting
and Clinical Psychology, 52,* 79-87.

Communication Satisfaction
Questionnaire

Stephen N. Haynes, Ph.D.
Department of Psychology
Illinois Institute of Technology
Chicago, Illinois   60616

Communications Skills Assessment
for the Mentally Ill Elderly

David A. Eberly, M.S.
Dept. of Aging & Mental Health
FMHI/USF
13301 N. 30th Street
Tampa, Florida   33612

Community Interaction Checklist

Robert G. Wahler, Ph.D.
Child Behavior Institute
University of Tennessee, UTK
Knoxville, Tennessee   37996-0900

Community Members' Rating Scale

Arthur L. Robin, Ph.D.
Children's Hospital of Michigan
1901 Beaubien Blvd.
Detroit, Michigan   48201

Compliance Measures

Glen A. Martin, Ph.D.
Student Development and
Counseling Center
Nash Hall 032A
University of North Carolina
Chapel Hill, North Carolina   27514

Compliance Test

Mark W. Roberts, Ph.D.
Psychology Department
Box 8112
Idaho State University
Pocatello, Idaho   83209

Comprehensive Drinker Profile

Marlatt, G. A., & Miller, W.R. (1984).
Comprehensive drinker profile.
Odessa, Florida: Psychological
Assessment Resources, Inc.

Compulsive Activity Checklist

Gail Steketee, Ph.D.
Boston University
School of Social Work
264 Bay State Road
Boston, Massachusetts   02215

Conflict Behavior Questionnaire

Arthur L. Robin, Ph.D.
Children's Hospital of Michigan
1901 Beaubien Blvd.
Detroit, Michigan   48201

Conflict Inventory

Gayla Margolin, Ph.D.
Department of Psychology
University of Southern California
Seely G. Mudd Bldg., 923
Los Angeles, California   90089-1061

Conners' Teacher Rating Scales

Conners, C.K. (1969). A teacher rating
scale for use in drug studies with
children. *American Journal of
Psychiatry, 126,* 884-888.

Consumer Satisfaction
Questionnaire

Forehand, R.L., & McMahon, P.J. (1981).
Helping the noncompliant child.
New York: Guilford Press.

Conversation Probe

Vincent B.Van Hasselt, Ph.D.
Department of Psychiatry and Human Behavior
University of California at Irvine
101 City Drive South
Orange, California   92668

Cooking Methods Test	Anthony J. Cuvo, Ph.D. Office of the Dean College of Human Resources Southern Illinois University Carbondale, Illinois 62901-4322
Coping Strategies Scales	Ernest Edward Beckham, Ph.D. Department of Psychiatry and Behavioral Sciences Oklahoma University Health Sciences Center P. O. Box 26901 Oklahoma City, Oklahoma 73190
Corah Dental Anxiety Scale	Norman L. Corah, Ph.D. Department of Behavioral Sciences University at Buffalo Squire Hall Buffalo, New York 14214
Daily Child Behavior Checklist	Rex Forehand, Ph.D. Psychology Department University of Georgia Athens, Georgia 30602
Daily Sleep Diary	Lacks, P. (1987).*Behavioral treatment for persistent insomnia.* New York: Pergamon Press.
Dating Behavior Assessment Test	Carol R. Glass, Ph.D. Department of Psychology The Catholic University of America Washington, DC 20064
Del Greco Assertive Behavior Inventory	Linda Del Greco, Ed.D. 21 Bloomingdale Road White Plains, New York 10605
Dental Fear Survey	Kleinknecht, R.A., Klepac, R.K., & Alexander, L.T. (1973).Origins and characteristics of fear of dentistry. *Journal of the American Dental Association, 86,* 842-848.
Dental Operatory Rating Scale	Ronald A. Kleinknecht, Ph.D. Department of Psychology Western Washington University Bellingham, Washington 98225
Dental Subscale of the Children's Fear Survey Schedule	Barbara G. Melamed, Ph.D. Department of Clinical Psychology University of Florida Box J-165 JHMHC Gainesville, Florida 32610
Derogatis Sexual Functioning Inventory	Clinical Psychometric Research P. O. Box 425 Riderwood, Maryland 21139

Derogatis Symptom Checklist 90-R	Clinical Psychometric Research P. O. Box 425 Riderwood, Maryland 21139
Diabetes Assertiveness Test	Gross, A.M., & Johnson, W.G. (1981). Diabetes assertiveness test: A measure of social coping skills in preadolescent diabetics. *The Diabetes Educator*, *7*, 26-27.
Dieter's Inventory of Eating Temptations	David G. Schlundt, Ph.D. Department of Psychology 234 Wesley Hall Vanderbilt University Nashville, Tennessee 37240
Dining Room Manners	*Behavior Assessment Record.* Robert D. Sanders, Ph.D., Editor Partlow State School & Hospital P. O. Box 1730 Tuscaloosa, Alabama 35403-1730
Direct Behavioral Observation	Spence, S.H., & Marzillier, J.S. (1981). Social skills training with adolescent male offenders. II. Short-term, long- term and generalized effects. *Behaviour Research and Therapy*, *19*, 349-368.
Dyadic Adjustment Scale	Spanier, G.B., & Filsinger, E.E. (1983). The Dyadic Adjustment Scale.In E. E. Filsinger (Ed.), *Marriage and family assessment:A sourcebook for family therapy* (pp. 155-168).Beverly Hills: Sage Publications.
Dyadic Prestressor Interaction Scale	Joseph Bush, Ph.D. Scale Department of Psychology VCU Box 2018 Richmond, Virginia 23284-0001
Dysfunctional Attitude Scale	Oliver, J., & Baumgart, E.P. (1985). The Dysfunctional Attitude Scale: Psychometric properties and relation to depression in an unselected adult population. Cognitive Therapy and Research, 9, *161-167.*
Eating Attitudes Test	Garner, D.M., Olmsted, M.P., Bohr, Y., & Garfinkel, P.E. (1982).The eating attitudes test: Psychometric features and clinical correlates. *Psychological Medicine, 12,* 871-878.
Eating Disorder Inventory	Psychological Assessment Resources, Inc. P. O. Box 98 Odessa, Florida 33556

Eating Problems Questionnaire

Aubrey J. Yates, Ph.D.
Department of Psychology
The University of Western Australia
Nedlands, Western Australia   6009

Eating Questionnaire

Aubrey J. Yates, Ph.D.
Department of Psychology
The University of Western Australia
Nedlands, Western Australia   6009

Eating Self-Efficacy Scale

Shirley M. Glynn, Ph.D.
Camarillo-UCLA Research Center
Box A
Camarillo, California   93011

Electrocardiography

Michael E. Thase, M.D.
Western Psychiatric Institute
  and Clinic
Department of Psychiatry
University of Pittsburgh
  School of Medicine
3811 O'Hara Street
Pittsburgh, Pennsylvania   15213

Electroencephalography

Michael E. Thase, M.D.
Western Psychiatric Institute
  and Clinic
Department of Psychiatry
University of Pittsburgh
  School of Medicine
3811 O'Hara Street
Pittsburgh, Pennsylvania   15213

Electromyography

David F. Peck, Ph.D.
Department of Psychiatry
Royal Edinburgh Hospital
Morningside Park
Edinburgh, EH10 5HF
England

Experience Sampling Method

Aubrey J. Yates, Ph.D.
Department of Psychology
The University of Western Australia
Nedlands, Western Australia   6009

Expired Air Carbon Monoxide
Measurement

CO Analyzer
Energetics Science, Inc.
Elmsford, New York   10523

Eyberg Child Behavior Inventory

Forehand, R.L., & McMahon, R.J. (1981).
Helping the noncompliant child.
  New York: The Guilford Press.

Eysenck Personality Inventory

EDITS
P. O. Box 7234
San Diego, California   92107

Eysenck Personality Questionnaire	EDITS P. O. Box 7234 San Diego, California 92107
Fagerstrom Tolerance Questionnaire	Karl Olov Fagerstrom, Ph.D. Leo Research Laboratory and Medicine Clinic Helsingborg Hospital Sweden
Family Interaction Coding System	J. B. Reid, Ph.D. Oregon Social Learning Center 207 E. 5th Suite 207 Eugene, Oregon 97401
Family Ratings of Program Behaviors	Beverly Sandifer, Ph.D. Psychological Services, P. A. 105 Asbury Circle Hattiesburg, Mississippi 39401
Fear of Negative Evaluation	Watson, D., & Friend, R. (1969). Measure of social-evaluative anxiety. *Journal of Consulting and Clinical Psychology, 33,* 448-457.
Fear Survey Schedule I	Akutagawa, D.(1956). A study in construct validity of the psychoanalytic concept of latent anxiety and a test of a projection distance hypothesis. Unpublished doctoral thesis, University of Pittsburgh. Langley Library, University of Pittsburgh, 217 Langley Hall, Pittsburgh, Pennsylvania 15213
Fear Survey Schedule III	Wolpe, J., & Lang, P.J. (1964). A fear survey schedule for use in behavior therapy. *Behaviour Research and Therapy, 2,* 27-30.
Fear Survey Schedule for Children-Revised	Thomas H. Ollendick, Ph.D. Department of Psychology Virginia Polytechnic Institute and State University Blacksburg, Virginia 24061
Fear Thermometer	Lang, P.J., & Lazovik, A.D. (1963). Experimental desensitization of a phobia.*Journal of Abnormal and Social Psychology, 66,* 519-525.
Feinstein Weight Reduction Index	Feinstein, A.R. (1959).The measurement of success in weight reduction: An analysis of methods and a new index. *Journal of Chronic Diseases, 10,* 439-456.

Fire Emergency Behavioral Situations
Scale

Russell T. Jones, Ph.D.
Department of Psychology
Virginia Polytechnic Institute
  and State University
Blacksburg, Virginia   24061

Fire Emergency Dialing Checklist

Russell T. Jones, Ph.D.
Department of Psychology
Virginia Polytechnic Institute
  and State University
Blacksburg, Virginia   24061

Frequency Interaction Recording
System

Educational Achievement Systems
513 North West 48th Avenue
Delray Beach, Florida   33445

Fully Faceted Type A Survey for
Students

Paul R. Yarnold, Ph.D.
Department of Medicine
Northwestern University Medical School
250 E. Superior Street
Suite 296
Chicago, Illinois   60611

General Happiness Rating

Dirk Revenstorf, Ph.D.
Psychology Institute of the
University of Tubingen
Gartenstrabe 29D-7400 Tubingen
West Germany

Generalized Expectancy for
Success Scale

Fibel, B., & Hale, W.D. (1978). The
generalized expectancy for success
scale--a new measure. *Journal of
Consulting and Clinical Psychology,
46,* 924-931.

Georgia Court Competency
Test - Revised

Wildman, R.W. II, Moore, J.T., Nelson,
F.R., Thompson, L., Batchelor, E.S.,
de Laosa, M., & Patterson, M.E. The
Georgia Court Competency Test: An
attempt to develop a rapid quantitative
measure of fitness for trial.
Unpublished manuscript, Forensic Services
Division, Central State Hospital,
Georgia, 1978.

Geriatric Assessment Inventory

John H. Schnelle, Ph.D.
Box 438
Middle Tennessee State University
Murfreesboro, Tennessee   37170

Global Deterioration Scale

Reisberg, B., Ferris, S.H., de Leon,
M.J., & Crook, T. (1982). The global
deterioration scale for assessment of
primary degenerative dementia.
American Journal of Psychiatry, 139,
1136-1139.

Goal Attainment Scaling

Thomas J. Kiresuk, Ph.D.
Program Evaluation Resource Center
501 Park Avenue South
Minneapolis, Minnesota 55415

Height Avoidance Test

S.Lloyd Williams, Ph.D.
Department of Psychology 17
Lehigh University
Bethlehem, Pennsylvania 18015

Heterosocial Skills Behavior
Checklist for Males

Barlow, D.H., Abel, G.G., Blanchard,
E.B., Bristow, A.R., & Young, L.D.
(1977). Heterosocial skills behavior
checklist for males. *Behavior Therapy, 8,* 229-239.

Home Accident Observations

Allen Marchetti, Ph.D.
Department of Mental Health
and Mental Retardation
200 Interstate Park Drive
P.O. Box 3710
Montgomery, Alabama 36193-5001

Home Accident Prevention Inventory

Tertinger, D.A., Greene, B.F., &
Lutzker, J.R. (1984). Experimental
validation of a program to reduce safety
hazards in the homes of abused and
neglected children. *Journal of
Applied Behavior Analysis, 17,* 159-174.

Home/Clinic Coding System

Rex Forehand, Ph.D.
Psychology Department
University of Georgia
Athens, Georgia 30602

Home Report

Arthur L. Robin, Ph.D.
Department of Pediatrics/Psychology Div.
Wayne State University School of Medicine
3901 Beaubien Blvd.
Detroit, Michigan 48201

Hopelessness Scale

Beck, A.T., Weissman, A., Lester, D., &
Trexler, L. (1974).The measurement of
pessimism: The Hopelessness Scale.
*Journal of Consulting and Clinical
Psychology, 42,* 861-865.

Hospital Fears Rating Scale

Barbara G. Melamed, Ph.D.Department of Clinical
Psychology
University of Florida
Box J-165 JHMHC
Gainesville, Florida 32610

Hostility and Direction of
Hostility Questionnaire

Caine, T.M., Foulds, G.A., & Hope,
K. (1967). Manual of the Hostility and
Direction of Hostility Questionnaire (HDHQ).
London, England: University of
London Press.

Impact of Event Scale

Mardi. J. Horowitz, M.D.
Department of Psychiatry
University of California
  School of Medicine
401 Parnassus Street
San Francisco, California   94143

Individualized Behavioral
Avoidance Test

David H. Barlow, Ph.D.
Phobia and Anxiety Disorders Clinic
1535 Western Avenue
Albany, New York   12203

Instruments to Measure Knowledge
of Behavioral Principles as
Applied to Children

O'Dell, A.L., Tarler-Benlolo, L.,
& Flynn, J.M. (1979).An instrument to
measure knowledge of behavioral
principles as applied to children.
*Journal of Behavior Therapy and
Experimental Psychiatry, 10, 29-34.*

Interaction Coding System

Kurt Hahlweg, Ph.D.Max-Planck-Institute for Psychiatry
Psychologische Abteilung
Kraepelinstrabe 10
8000 Munchen 40
West Germany

Interpersonal Attraction Inventory

Terence M. Keane, Ph.D.Chief, Psychology Service
VA Medical Center
Boston, Massachusetts   02130

Interpersonal Behavior Construct
Scale

Kogan, K.L., & Gordan, B.M. (1979).
Interpersonal behavior constructs:
A revised approach to defining dyadic
interaction styles. *Psychological
Reports, 36, 835-846.*

Interpersonal Evaluation Inventory

Jeffrey A. Kelly, Ph.D.
Department of Psychiatry and
Human Behavior
University of Mississippi Medical Center
2500 North State Street
Jackson, Mississippi   39216-4505

Intervention Rating Profile

Joseph C.Witt, Ph.D.
Psychology Department
Louisiana State University
Baton Rouge, Louisiana   70803-5501

Interview Assessment of Adolescent
Male Offenders

Spence, S.H. (1981).Validation of
social skills of adolescent males in an
interview conversation with a previously
unknown adult. *Journal of Applied Behavior Analysis, 14,*
159-168.

Interview Schedule for Children

Maria Kovacs, Ph.D.
Western Psychiatric Institute
  and Clinic
Department of Psychiatry
University of Pittsburgh
  School of Medicine
3811 O'Hara Street
Pittsburgh, Pennsylvania   15213

In Vivo Cognitive Assessment

Steven D. Hollon, Ph.D.
Department of Psychology
Vanderbilt University
134 Wesley Hall
Nashville, Tennessee   37240

In Vivo Measurement of Agoraphobia

Emmelkamp, P.M.G. (1982).*Phobic and
obsessive-compulsive disorders*.
New York:Plenum Press.

IOWA-Conners Teacher Rating Scale

Loney, J., & Milich, R. (1982).
Hyperactive inattention, and aggression
in clinical practice. In M. Wolraich &
D. Routh (Eds.), *Advances in
developmental and behavioral pediatrics,
(Vol. 3)* (pp. 113-147). Greenwich,
CT: JAI Press.

Irrational Beliefs Inventory

Lynn Alden, Ph.D.
Department of Psychology
University of British Columbia
Vancouver, B.C.Canada
V6T1Y

Issues Checklist

Arthur L. Robin, Ph.D.
Dept. of Pediatrics/Psychology Div.
Wayne State University School of Medicine
3901 Beaubien Blvd.
Detroit, Michigan 48201

Jenkins Activity Survey:
Student Version (Form T)

Kenneth E. Hart, Ph.D.
Department of Psychology
Hofstra University
Hempstead, New York 11550

Job Interview Assessment

Jeffrey A. Kelly, Ph.D.
Department of Psychiatry and
Human Behavior
University of Mississippi Medical Center
2500 North State Street
Jackson, Mississippi 39216-4505

Kiddie-Schedule for Affective
Disorders and Schizophrenia
in Present Episode

Joaquim Puig-Antich, M.D.
Western Psychiatric Institute
  and Clinic
Department of Psychiatry
University of Pittsburgh
  School of Medicine
3811 O'Hara Street
Pittsburgh, Pennsylvania 15213

Large Scale Integrated Sensor

Mr. Gary Matthews
Western Psychiatric Institute
  and Clinic
Department of Psychiatry
University of Pittsburgh
  School of Medicine
3811 O'Hara Street
Pittsburgh, Pennsylvania 15213

Lehrer-Woolfolk Anxiety Symptom
Questionnaire

Paul M. Lehrer, Ph.D.
Department of Psychiatry
University of Medicine and
Dentistry of NJRW Johnson Medical School
Piscataway, New Jersey 08854

Leyton Obsessional Inventory

Cooper, J. (1970). The Leyton
Obsessional Inventory.*Psychological
Medicine, 1,* 48-64.

Likert Scaling

Likert, R., Roslow, S., & Murphy, G.
(1934). A simple and reliable method of
scoring the Thurstone Attitude Scale.
Journal of Social Psychology, 5,
228-238.

Marital Interaction Coding
System

Robert L. Weiss, Ph.D.
Oregon Marital Studies Program
Psychology Department
University of Oregon
Eugene, Oregon 97403

Marks and Mathews Fear Questionnaire

Isaac M. Marks, M.D.
The Section of Experimental Psychopathology
Maudsley Hospital
99 Denmark Hill
London, England SE5 8AZ

Maudsley Obsessional-Compulsive
Inventory

Rachman, S., & Hodgson, R.J. (1980).
Obsessions and compulsions. Englewood
CLiffs, New Jersey: Prentice Hall.

McGill Pain Questionnaire

Ronald Melzack, Ph.D.
Department of Psychology
McGill University
1205 Dr. Penfield Avenue
Montreal, Quebec Canada H3A 1B1

Measurement of Chronic Aggression:
Direct Quantitative Methods

Larry A. Doke, Ph.D.
P. O. Box 3087
Las Vegas, New Mexico 87701

Michigan Alcoholism Screening Test

Selzer, M. (1971).The Michigan
Alcoholism Screening Test: The quest
for a new diagnostic instrument.
American Journal of Psychiatry,
127, 89-94.

Mini-Mental State Exam

Folstein, M.F., Folstein, S.F., &
McHugh, P.R. (1975)."Mini-Mental
State": A practical method for
grading the cognitive state of patients
for the clinician. *Journal of
Psychiatric Research, 12,* 189-198.

Minnesota Multiphasic Personality
Inventory

Professional Assessment Service System
P. O. Box 1416
Minneapolis, Minnesota 55440

Mobility Inventory for Agoraphobia

Chambless, D.L., Caputo, G.C., Jasin,
S.E., Gracely, E.J., & Williams, C
(1985).The Mobility Inventory for
Agoraphobia. *Behaviour Research and
Therapy, 23,* 35-44.

Modified Fear Survey

Dean G. Kilpatrick, Ph.D.
The Crime Victims Research and
 Treatment Center
Department of Psychiatry and
Behavioral Sciences
Medical University of South Carolina
Charleston, South Carolina 29425-0742

Motivation Assessment Scale

V. Mark Durand, Ph.D.
Department of Psychology
SUNY at Albany
1400 Washington Avenue
Albany, New York 12222

Multiple Affect Adjective
Check List-Revised

Zuckerman, M., & Lubin, B.(1985). Check
Manual for the Revised Multiple Affect
Adjective Check List. San Diego,
California: Educational and Industrial
Testing Service.

Munroe Daily Sleep
Questionnaire-Revised

Munroe, L.J. (1967).Psychological
and physiological differences between
good and poor sleepers. *Journal of Abnormal Psychology, 72,*
255-264.

Musical Performance Anxiety
Self-Statement Scale

Michael G. Craske, Ph.D.
Department of Psychology
University of British Columbia
2075 Wesbrook Mall
Vancouver, B.C. Canada V6T 1W5

Novaco Provocation Inventory

Raymond W. Novaco, Ph.D.
Program in Social Ecology
University of California
Irvine, California 92717

Observational System for Assessing Mealtime Behaviors in Children and Associated Parent Behavior	Klesges, R.C., Coates, T.J., Brown, G., Sturgeon-Tillisch, J., Moldenhauer Moldenhauer-Klesges, L.M., Holzer, B., Woolfrey, J., & Vollmer, J. (1983). Parental influences on children's eating behavior and relative weight. *Journal of Applied Behavior Analysis, 16,* 371-378.
Observational System to Quantify Social, Environmental, and Parental Influences on Physical Activity in Children	Klesges, R.C., Coates, T.J., Moldenhauer, L.M., Holzer, B., Gustavson, J., & Barnes, J. (1984).The FATS: An observational system for assessing physical activity in children and associated parent behavior. *Behavioral Assessment, 6,* 333-345.
Observer Rating Scale of Anxiety	Barbara G. Melamed, Ph.D. Department of Clinical Psychology University of Florida Box J-165 JHMHC Gainesville, Florida 32610
Observational Record of Inpatient Behavior	Alexander J. Rosen, Ph.D. Psychology Department University of Illinois at Chicago Chicago, Illinois 60680
Open Middle Inventory	Karen Marchione Department of Psychiatry University of Pittsburgh School of Medicine, 3811 O'Hara St, Pittsburgh Pa. 15213
Pain Assessment Questionnaire	Steven H. Sanders Pain Control & Rehabiliation Institute of Georgia 350 Winn Way Decatur, Georgia 30030
Pain Behavior Observation	Francis J. Keefe, Ph.D. Box 3926 Duke Medical Center Durham, North Carolina 27710
Pain Behavior Rating Scales	Mary Lou Kelley, Ph.D. 236 Audubon Psychology Department Louisiana State University Baton Rouge, Louisiana 70803-5501
Pain Cuff	Dr. Ernest G. Poser 4517 West 4th Avenue Vancouver, B.C. V6R 1R4

Pain Observation

Paul M. Cinciripini, Ph.D.
Department of Psychiatry and Behavioral Sciences
The University of Texas
Medical Branch at Galveston
Galveston, Texas 77550

Panic Attack Questionnaire

G. R. Norton
Department of Psychology
The University of Winnipeg
515 Portage Avenue,
Manitoba, Canada R3B 2E9

Parent-Adolescent Interaction
Coding System

Arthur L. Robin, Ph.D.
Psychiatry/Psychology Director
Children's Hospital of Michigan
3901 Beaubien
Detroit, Michigan 48201

Parent's Consumer Satisfaction
Questionnaire

Marc S. Atkins, Ph.D.
Forehand, R., & McMahon, R.J.
(1981). *Helping the
Noncompliant Child: A
Clinician's Guide to Parent
Training* (Appendix A, pp. 175-182).
New York: Guilford Press.

PFB Partnership Questionnaire

Dr. Kurt Hahlweg
Max-Planck-Institute of Psychiatry
Kraepelinstr. 2
8000 Munich,
West Germany

Peer and Self-Rating Scale

Peter H. Glow, Ph.D.
Psychology Department
University of Adelaide
GPO Box 498
ADELAIDE, 5001
South Australia

Penile Volume Responses

Neil McConaghy, M.D.
Penile Volume Changes to
Moving Pictures of Male &
Female Nudes in Heterosexual
and Homosexual Males.
(1967) *Behaviour Research
& Therapy, 5* 43-48.

Personal Beliefs Inventory

Ricardo F. Munoz
University of California,
San Francisco,
San Francisco General
Hospital-7M
1001 Potrero Avenue
San Francisco, California 94110

Personal Questionnaire Rapid Scaling Technique	Stan Lindsay and D. Mulhall The Personal Questionnaire Rapid Scaling Technique Published by NFER -Nelson, Darville House, 2 Oxford Road East Windsor SL4 1DF England
Personal Report of Confidence as a Performer	Michael G. Craske, Ph.D. Kenneth D. Craig, and Margaret J. Kendrick The University of British Columbia Department of Psychology 2075 Wesbrook Mall Vancouver, B.C. Canada V6T 1W5
Personal Report of Confidence as a Speaker	Paul, G.L. (1966). *Insight versus Desensitization in Psychotherapy* Stanford, CA: Stanford University Press.
Pittsburgh Initial Neuropsychological Testing System	Goldstein, G., Tarter, R.E., Shelly, C. & Hegedus, A.(1983) Pints: A neuropsychological screening battery for psychiatric patients. *Journal of Behavioral Assessment, 5* 227-238.
Pleasant Events Schedule	Peter M. Lewinsohn, Ph.D. Oregon Research Institute 1899 Willamette Street Eugene, Oregon 97401
Plethysmography	Paul Cinciripini, Ph.D. Department of Psychiatry and Behavioral Sciences University of Texas Medical School Galveston, Texas 77550
Probability Ratings and Liking Category Ratings	Charlene Muehlenhard Department of Psychology Texas A & M University College Station, Texas 77843
Problem Identification Checklist	Bergan, J.R., & Kratochwill, T.R. (in press). *Behavior Consultation in Applied Settings.* New York: Plenum.

Problem List	Dr. Kurt Hahlweg Max-Planck-Institute of Psychiatry Kraepelinstr. 2 8000 Munich, West Germany
Procrastination Assessment Scale—Students	Esther D. Rothblum, Ph.D. Department of Psychology University of Vermont Burlington, Vermont 05405
Psychophysiological Assessment of Electrodermal Activity	Carlos F. Mendes de Leon & Paul M. Cinciripini, (1980) I. Martin & P.H. Venables (Eds.) *Technique & Psychophysiology* New York: John Wiley & Sons.
Psychosocial Adjustment to Illness Scale	Clinical Psychometric Research 1228 Wine Spring Lane Towson, Maryland 21204
Pupil Evaluation Inventory	E.G. Pekarik, R.J. Prinz, D.E. Liebert, S. Weintraub, J.M. Neale, (1976). The Pupil Evaluation Inventory: A sociometric technique for assessing children's social behavior. *Journal of Abnormal Child Psychology* 4 83-97.
Rape Aftermath Symptom Test	The Crime Victims Research and Treatment Center Department of Psychiatry and Behavioral Sciences Medical University of South Carolina Charleston, SC 29425-0742
Rational Behavior Inventory	Shorkey T. Clayton, 3.104 Social Work Building University of Texas Austin, Texas 78712
Real-Time Data Acquisition	David Felce British Institute of Mental Handicap Wolverhampton Road, Kiddeminster Worcestershire DY10 3PP, England
Reinforcement Survey Schedule	J.R. Cautela, (1977). *Behavior Analysis Forms for Clinical Intervention*, p.45 Champaign, Illinois: Research Press.

Relaxation Assessment Device

Timothy J. Hoelscher, Ph.D.
Box 2908
Duke University Medical Center
Durham, North Carolina 27710

Reprimand Assessment Scale

Ron Van Houten, Ph.D.
The Behavior Analysis Family Centre
17 John Brenton Drive
Dartmouth, Nova Scotia
B2X 2V5

Resident Disruptive Behavior

Vineland Adaptive
Behavior Scale
American Guidance
Service, Inc
Circle Pines, Minnesota
55014-1796

Restraint Scale: Assessment
of Dieting

Janet Polivy, Ph.D.
Department of Psychology
University of Toronto
Windale Campus
3359 Mississuaga Rd
Mississuaga, Ontario
L51 1C6, Canada

Reward Computation Worksheet

W.G. Johnson, & P.M.Stalonas
(1981). *Weight No
Longer,*
Gretna, LA: Pelican.

Reynolds Adolescent Depression
Scale

William M. Reynolds, Ph.D.
Psychological Assessment
Resources
P.O. Box 998
Odessa, Florida 33556

Riboflavin Tracer Technique for
Assessment of Medication Compliance

Patricia A. Cluss, Ph.D.
Staunton Clinic
Sewickley Valley Hospital
Sewickley Valley, PA 15143

Role-Playing Assessment Instruments

Stephen B. Fawcett
Department of Human Development
University of Kansas
Lawrence, Kansas 66045

Rosenbaum's Self-Control Schedule

Michael Rosenbaum, Ph.D.
Department of Psychology
Tel-Aviv University
Tel-Aviv 69978, Israel

S-R Inventory of Anxiousness

Thomas W. Lombardo
N.S. Endler, J.McV. Hunt,
A.J. Rosenstein, (1962). An
S-R Inventory of Anxiousness.
Psychological Monographs,
76, (Whole No. 536) 1-31.

Scale for Suicide Ideation	Robert A. Steer, Ed.D. University of Medicine and Dentistry of New Jersey School of Osteopathic Medicine 401 Haddon Avenue Camden, New Jersey 08107
Self-Control Questionnaire	Lynn P. Rehm, Ph.D. Department of Psychology University of Houston 4800 Calhoun Houston, Texas 77004
Self-Control Rating Scale	Philip C. Kendall, Ph.D. Psychology-Weiss Hall Temple University Philadelphia, Pennsylvania 19122
Self-Efficacy Scale	A. Bandura, N.E. Adams, & J. Beyer, (1977). Cognitive processes mediating behavioral change. *Journal of* *Personality and Social* *Psychology, 35,* 125-139.
Self-Injurious Behavior Assessment	Johannes Rojahn, Ph.D. The Nisonger Center Ohio State University 1581 Dodd Drive Columbus, Ohio 43210-1205
Self-Monitoring Analysis System	David G. Schlundt, Ph.D. Assistant Professor Department of Psychology 134 Wesley Hall Vanderbilt University Nashville, Tennessee 37240
Self-Monitoring of Cognitions	P.C. Kendall, & S.D. Hollon (1981). Assessing self-referent speech: Methods in the measurement of self statements. In P.C. Kendall & S.D. Hollon (Eds.) *Assessment Strategies for* *Cognitive Behavioral* *Interventions* New York: Academic Press.
Self-Reinforcement Questionnaire	Elaine M. Heiby, Ph.D. Department of Psychology University of Hawaii Honolulu, Hawaii 96822

Self-Schema in Depression

Dr. Nicholas A. Kuiper
Department of Psychology
University of Western Ontario
London, Ontario
CANADA N6A 5C2

Self-Statement Assessment
via Thought Listing

Elizabeth M. Altmaier
356 Lindquist Center
The University of Iowa
Iowa City, Iowa 52242

Semantic Differential of Sex Roles

R. Julian Hafner, M.D.
Director
Dibden Research Unit
Glenside Hospital
226 Fullarton Road
EASTWOOD S.A. 5063
AUSTRALIA

Sensation Scale

Stephen A. Maisto, Ph.D.
Butler Hospital
345 Blackstone Blvd.
Providence, Rhode Island 02906

Sensation Seeking Scale - Form VI

Marvin Zuckerman Ph.D.
Department of Psychology
University of Delaware
Newark, Delaware 19716

Sexual Experience Scales

Walter Everard
Department of Clinical
Psychology
Psychotherapy & Prevention
University of Utrecht
Trans 4
3512 JK Utrecht
The Netherlands

Situation Role-Play Assessment

Paul E. Bates, Ph.D.
Professor
Department of Special Education
Southern Illinois University
Carbondale, Illinois 62901

Situational Self-Statement and
Affective State Inventory

Thomas H. Harrell
The School of Psychology at
Florida Institute of Technology
150 W. University Boulevard
Melbourne, Florida 32901

Skill Survey

A.P. Goldstein, R.P. Sprafkin,
& N.J. Gershaw (1976).
*Skill Training for Community
Living: Applying Structured
Learning Therapy.*
New York:
Pergamon Press.

Skinfolds

Patricia M. Dubbert
Acting Chief, Psychology Service
VA Medical Center
1500 East Woodrow Wilson Dr.
Jackson, Mississippi 39216
Harpendon Calipers obtained:
Quinton Instruments
2121 Terry Avenue
Seattle, Washington 98121

Social Adjustment Scale—
Self-Report

Myrna M. Weissman, Ph.D.
Professor of Epidemiology
in Psychiatry
College of Physicians and
Surgeons of Columbia
University
722 West 168th Street
New York, New York 10032

Social Avoidance and Distress
Scale and Fear of Negative
Evaluation Scale

D. Watson, & R.Friend (1969).
Measurement of social evaluative
anxiety. *Journal of
Consulting and Clinical Psychology,
33* 448-457.

Social Interaction Test

P. Trower, B. Bryant, &
M. Argyle (1978). *Social
Skills and Mental Health.*
Pittsburgh: University of
Pittsburgh Press.

Social Reaction Inventory
Revised

J.P. Curran, D.P. Corriveau,
P.M. Monti, & S.B. Hagerman,
(1980). Social skill and social
anxiety: Self-report measurement
in a psychiatric population.
Behavior Modification, 4
493-512.

Social Skills Test for Children

Donald A. Williamson, Ph.D.
Department of Psychology
Louisiana State University
Baton Rouge, Louisiana 70803

Sociometric Measures

Samuel L. Odom
Indiana University
Developmental Training Center
2853 East Tenth Street
Bloomington, Indiana

Spouse Observation Checklist

R.L. Weiss, & B.A. Perry.
(1974). *Assessment &
Treatment of Marital
Dysfunction*
Eugene: Oregon: Marital
Studies Program.

Spouse Verbal Problem Checklist

Stephen Haynes, Ph.D.
Professor and Director
of Graduate Studies in
Clinical Psychology
Illinois Institute of Technology
Chicago, Illinois 60616

Staff Behavior Observation

A.M. Delamater, C.K. Conners,
& K.C. Wells, K.C. (1984).
A comparison of staff training
procedures: Behavioral
applications in the child
psychiatric inpatient setting.
Behavior Modification, 8
39-58.

Staff-Resident Interaction
Chronograph

Research Press
Box 3177, Dept. 58
Champaign, Illinois 61821

Standardized Observation Codes

Robert G. Wahler, Ph.D.
Child Behavior Institute
University of Tennessee,
UTK, Knoxville, Tennessee
37996-0900

Standardized Walk

Dr. Chris Adler
Phobia & Anxiety Disorder Clinic
1535 Western Avenue
Albany, New York 12203

State-Trait Anger Scale

PAR, Inc.
P.O. Box 998
Odessa, Florida 33556

State-Trait Anxiety Inventory
(Form Y)

PAR, Inc.
P.O. Box 998
Odessa, Florida 33556

Strain Gauge

J.H.J. Bancroft, H. Gwynne Jones,
& B.R. Pullan (1966). A Simple
Transducer for Measuring Penile
Erection. *Behaviour Research
and Therapy, 4* 239-241.

Structured Observation System

Karen S. Budd, Ph.D.
Associate Professor of
Psychology
Illinois Institute of Technology
Chicago, Illinois 60616

Student Version of the
Jenkins Activity Survey

D.S. Krantz, D.C. Glass,
& M.L. Snyder, (1974).
Helplessness stress levels,
and the coronary-prone behavior
pattern. *Journal of
Experimental Social
Psychology, 10* 284-300.

Subjective Anxiety Scale	Joseph Wolpe (1982). *The Practice of Behavior Therapy* (3rd edition), Pergamon Press.
Subjective Probability of Consequences Inventory	Decky E. Fiedler, Ph.D. Pacific Luthern University Tacoma, Washington 98447
Suicidal Ideation Questionnaire	Psychological Assessment Resources P.O. Box 998 Odessa, Florida 33556
Suinn Text Anxiety Behavior Scale	Rocky Mt. Behavioral Sciences Institute P.O. Box 1066 Ft. Collins, Colorado 80523
Survey of Heterosexual Interactions	SHI (Males) C. Twentyman, T. Boland, & R.M. McFall, (1981). Heterosocial avoidance in college males: Four studies. *Behavior Modification,* 5, 523-552
	SHI (Females) Dr. Carolyn L. Williams University of Minnesota School of Public Health Program in Health Education Box 197 Mayo Memorial Bldg. Minneapolis, Minnesota 55455
System for Observing Social-Interpersonal Behavior	Stephen W. Armstrong Special Education Department Jacksonville State University Jacksonville, Alabama 36265
Target Behaviors in Compliance Training	Dr. Macon Parrish 32 Oak Shadows Ct. Baltimore, Maryland 21228
Target Problems	The Section of Experimental Psychopathology Maudsley Hospital 99 Denmark Hill London, SE5 8AZ
Taste Test Assessments	P.M. Miller, M. Hersen, R.M. Eisler, & T.E. Elkin. (1974). A retrospective analysis of alcohol consumption on laboratory tasks as related to therapeutic outcome. *Behaviour Research and Therapy, 12,* 73-76.

Test Anxiety Inventory

PAR, Inc.
P.O. Box 998
Odessa, Florida 33556

Test Meals in the Assessment of
Bulimia Nervosa

James C. Rosen, Ph.D.
Department of Psychology
University of Vermont
Burlington, Vermont 05405

Thought-Listing Procedure

Cynthia G. Last. Ph.D.
Department of Psychiatry
University of Pittsburgh
School of Medicine
3811 O'Hara Street
Pittsburgh Pa. 15213

Three-Area Severity of Depression
Scales

Dr. Allen Raskin, Ph.D.
Director, Psychology Division
Lafayette Clinic
951 East Lafayette
Detroit, Michigan 48207

Time-Line Drinking Behavior
Interview

L.C. Sobell, & M.D. Sobell,
Clinical Institute
Addiction Research Foundation
33 Russell Street
Toronto, Ontario
Canada M5S 2S1

Timeout Assessment

Mark W. Roberts
Associate Professor
Department of Psychiatry
Idaho State University
Pocatello, Idaho 83209-0009

Time-Sample Behavioral Checklist

Research Press
Box 3177
Champaign, Illinois 61821

Training Proficiency Scale -
Parent Version

Alan Hudson
Phillip Institute of
Technology
Plenty Road
Bundoora 3083
AUSTRALIA

Treatment Evaluation Inventory

Alan E. Kazdin, Ph.D.
Department of Psychiatry, University of
Pittsburgh School of Medicine
3811 O'Hara Street
Pittsburgh, Pennsylvania 15213

Type A Structured Interview

Dr. Meyer Friedman
Director, Harold Brunn Institute
Mount Zion Hospital Medical
Center
San Francisco, California 94120

Unpleasant Events Schedule	Peter M. Lewinsohn, Ph.D. Oregon Research Institute 1899 Willamette Street Eugene, Oregon 97401
Visual Analogue Scale	Olof Nyren, M.D., D.M.Sc. Department of Surgery University Hospital S-751 85 Uppsala, Sweden
Willoughby Personality Schedule	Gail Steketee, Ph.D. Boston University School of Social Work 264 Bay State Road Boston, Massachusetts 02215
Written Assertiveness Knowledge Test	Monroe A. Bruch, Ph.D. Department of Counseling Psychology, ED 217 SUNY at Albany Albany, New York. 12222
Zung Self-Rating Anxiety Scale	William W.K. Zung, M.D. Professor of Psychiatry Duke University Medical Center Veterans Administration Medical Center 508 Fulton Street Durham, North Carolina. 27705
Zung Self-Rating Depression Scale	CIBA Pharmaceutical Co. Division of CIBA-GEIGY Corporation, 556 Morris Ave Summit, New Jersey. 07901

User's Guide

In the *Users' Guide* the Focus of Assessment (e.g., Acrophobia, Aggression, Anxiety, Depression, and Unassertiveness) is listed in alphabetical order in the first column. Titles of assessment devices subsumed under these disorders or problems are listed (e.g., Height Avoidance Test for Acrophobia and Cognitive-Somatic Anxiety Questionnaire and Lehrer-Woolfolk Anxiety Symptom Questionnaire for Anxiety) in the second column. In the third column the Assessment Modality is specified (e.g., teacher rating, staff rating, behavioral observation, self-report, structured interview, permanent product measure, physiological, or biological).

FOCUS OF ASSESSMENT	TITLE	ASSESSMENT MODALITY
Acceptability of Classroom Intervention	Intervention Rating Profile	Teacher Rating
Accident Prevention	Home Accident Prevention Inventory	Staff Rating
Acrophobia	Height Avoidance Test	Behavioral Observation
Adolescent Activity	Experience Sampling Method	Self-Report
Adult Psychopathology	Minnesota Multiphasic Personality Inventory	Self-Report
Affect and Mood	Multiple Affect Adjective Checklist-Revised	Self-Report
Aggression	Hostility and Direction of Hostility Questionnaire	Self-Report
Aggression	Measurement of Chronic Aggression: Direct Quantitative Methods	Behavioral Observation
Aggression in Children	Iowa-Conners' Teacher Rating Scale	Teacher Rating
Aggressiveness	Children's Action Tendency Scale	Self-Report

Agoraphobia	Agoraphobic Cognitions Questionnaire	Self-Report
Agoraphobia	Behavioral Walk	Behavioral Observation
Agoraphobia	In Vivo Measurement of Agoraphobia	Behavioral Observation
Agoraphobia	Mobility Inventory for Agoraphobia	Self-Report
Agoraphobia	Standardized Walk	Self-Report, Behavioral Observation, Physiological
Alcoholism	Addiction Severity Index	Structured Interview, Self-Report
Alcoholism	AlcEval	Self-Report Independent Observation
Alcoholism	Alcohol Beliefs Scale	Self-Report
Alcoholism	Blood Alcohol Level	Biochemical
Alcoholism	Comprehensive Drinker Profile	Structured Interview
Alcoholism	Michigan Alcoholism Screening Test	Structured Interview
Alcoholism	Sensation Scale	Self-Report
Alcoholism	Taste Test Assessment	Self-Report
Alcoholism	Time Line Drinking Behavior Interview	Semi-Structured Interview
Alzheimer's Disease	Clinical Dementia Rating Scale	Staff Rating
Alzheimer's Disease	Global Deterioration Scale	Staff Rating
Anger	Novaco Provocation Inventory	Self-Report
Anger	State-Trait Anger Scale	Self-Report
Anorexia Nervosa	Eating Attitudes Test	Self-Report
Anorexia Nervosa	Eating Disorder Inventory	Self-Report
Anxiety	Anxiety Disorders Interview Schedule-Revised	Structured Interview

Anxiety	Body Sensations Questionnaire	Self-Report
Anxiety	Cognitive-Somatic Anxiety Questionnaire	Self-Report
Anxiety	Lehrer-Woolfolk Anxiety Symptom Questionnaire	Self-Report
Anxiety	Marks and Mathews' Fear Questionnaire	Self-Report
Anxiety	Panic Attack Questionnaire	Self-Report
Anxiety	Personal Questionnaire Rapid Scaling Technique	Self-Report
Anxiety	Personal Report of Confidence as a Performer	Self-Report
Anxiety	Personal Report of Confidence as a Speaker	Self-Report
Anxiety	Psychophysiological Assessment of Electrodermal Activity	Physiological
Anxiety	Rational Behavior Inventory	Self-Report
Anxiety	Reinforcement Survey Schedule	Self-Report
Anxiety	S-R Inventory of Anxiousness	Self-Report
Anxiety	State-Trait Anxiety Inventory	Self-Report
Anxiety	Subjective Anxiety Scale	Self-Report
Anxiety	Thought-Listing Procedure	Self-Monitoring
Anxiety	Zung Self-Rating Anxiety Scale	Self-Report
Anxiety in Children	Observer Rating Scale of Anxiety	Behavioral Observation
Arousal	Psychophysiological Assessment of Electrodermal Activity	Physiological
Arousal and Stress	Plethysmography	Physiological
Assertiveness	Children's Action Tendency Scale	Self-Report

Assertiveness	Subjective Probability of Consequence Inventory	Self-Report
Assertiveness	Written Assertiveness Knowledge Test	Self-Report
Aversive Conditioning	Pain Cuff	Biological, Self-Report
Behavioral Consultation	Problem Identification Checklist	Semistructured Interview
Binge Eating	Binge Eating Scale	Self-Report
Bruxism	Behavioral Assessment of Bruxism	Self-Report
Bulimia	Binge-Scale Questionnaire	Self-Report
Bulimia	Bulimia Test	Self-Report
Bulimia	Eating Disorder Inventory	Self-Report
Bulimia	Eating Problems Questionnaire	Self-Report
Bulimia	Experience Sampling Method	Self-Report
Bulimia	Test Meals in the Assessment of Bulimia Nervosa	Behavioral Observation, Self-Report
Cardiac Functioning	Blood Pressure Assessment	Physiological
Cardiac Functioning	Blood Pressure Reactivity	Physiological
Cardiac Functioning	Cardiotachometry	Physiological
Cardiac Functioning	Electrocardiography	Physiological
Cardiovascular Disease	Type A Structured Interview	Structured Interview
Child Behavior Problems	Adelaide Version of Conners' Parent Rating Scale	Parent Rating
Child Behavior Problems	Adelaide Version of Conners' Teachers Rating Scale	Teacher Rating

Child Behavior Problems	Child Behavior Checklist and Related Instruments	Peer Rating, Teacher Rating, Youth Self-Report, Behavioral Observation
Child Behavior Problems	Conners' Teacher Rating Scales	Teacher Rating
Child Behavior Problems	Daily Child Behavior Checklist	Parent Rating
Child Behavior Problems	Eyberg Child Behavior Inventory	Self-Report
Child Behavior Problems	Home/Clinic Coding System	Behavioral Observation
Child Behavior Problems	Self-Control Rating Scale	Rating Scale
Child Behavior Problems	Social Competence	Peer Rating, Self-Report
Child Behavior Problems	Structured Observation System	Behavioral Observation
Child Fear of Hospital and Medical Concerns	Hospital Fears Rating Scale	Self-Report
Child Psychopathology	Interview Schedules for Children	Semistructured Interview
Children's Eating Behavior	Behavioral Eating Test	Behavioral Observation
Chronic Illness	Psychosocial Adjustment to Illness Scale	Semistructured Interview, Self-Report
Chronic Psychiatric Inpatients	Clinical Frequencies Recording System	Behavioral Observation
Cigarette Smoking	Expired Air Carbon Monoxide Measurement	Biochemical
Cigarette Smoking	Fagerstrom Tolerance Questionnaire	Self-Report
Classroom Behavior	Code for Instructional Structure and Student Academic Response	Behavioral Observation
Classroom Interaction	Peer and Self Rating Scales	Self-Report, Peer Rating
Client Resistance in Treatment	Client Resistance Coding System	Behavioral Observation
Cognition	Self-Monotitoring of Cognitions	Self-Report
Cognition	Self-Statement Assessment via Thought Listing	Self-Report

Cognition	Situational Self-Statement and Affective State Inventory	Self-Report
Cognition	Thought-Listing Procedure	Self-Monitoring
Cognition	Automatic Thoughts Questionnaire	Self-Report
Cognitive Impairment	Mini-Mental State Exam	Structured Interview
Compliance in Treatment	Compliance Measures	Self-Report, Behavioral Observation, Physiological, Permanent Product
Conduct Disorder	Parent Adolescent Interaction Coding System	Behavioral Observation
Conduct Disorder	Parent Consumer Satisfaction Questionnaire	Self-Report
Conduct Disorder	Standardized Observation Codes	Behavioral Observation
Conduct Disorder	Timeout Assessment	Behavioral Observation
Conduct Disorder	Target Behaviors in Compliance Training	Behavioral Observation
Consumer Satisfaction with Treatment	Treatment Evaluation Inventory	Self-Report
Coping Ability	Coping Strategies Scales	Self-Report
Coronary Disease	Student Version of the Jenkins Activity Survey	Semistructured Interview, Behavioral Observation
Coronary Prone Behavior in Students	Fully Faceted Type A Survey for Students	Self-Report
Dating Skills	Dating Behavior Assessment Test	Behavioral Observation
Dementia	Global Deterioration Scale	Staff Rating
Dental Fear	Corah Dental Anxiety Scale	Self-Report
Dental Fear	Dental Fear Survey	Self-Report

Expectancies	Subjective Probability of Consequence Inventory	Self-Report
Extraversion-Introversion	Eysenck Personality Inventory	Self-Report
Family Communication	Interaction Coding System	Behavioral Observation
Family Interaction	Family Interaction Coding System	Behavioral Observation
Family Interaction	Standardized Observation Codes	Behavioral Observation
Fear	Body Sensations Questionnaire	Self-Report
Fear	Fear Survey Schedule-I	Self-Report
Fear	Fear Survey Schedule-II	Self-Report
Fear	Fear Thermometer	Self-Report
Fear in Children	Child Development Questionnaire	Parent Rating
Fear in Children	Fear Survey Schedule for Children-Revised	Self-Report
Fear in Home	Individualized Behavioral Avoidance Test	Therapist Rating Behavioral Observation
Food Addiction	Behavioral Assessment Procedure for Food Addiction	Self-Report
Heterosocial Anxiety	Behavioral Conversational Measures	Behavioral Observation
Heterosocial Anxiety	Behavioral Situations Test	Behavioral Observation, Physiological
Heterosocial Skills	Dating Behavior Assessment Test	Behavioral Observation
Heterosocial Skills	Survey of Heterosexual Interactions	Self-Report
Heterosocial Skills in Males	Hetersocial Skills Checklist for Males	Behavioral Observation
Hyperactivity	Conners Teacher Rating Scales	Teacher Rating

Hypertension	Student Version of the Jenkins Activity Survey	Semistructured Interview, Behavioral Observation
Hypertension	Type A Structured Interview	Structured Interview
Hostility	Hostility and Direction of Hostility Questionnaire	Self-Report
Impulsiveness in Children and Adults	Automated Matching Familiar Figures Test	Analogue Test
Inpatient Evaluation	Time-Sample Behavioral Checklist	Behavioral Observation
Inpatient Geriatric Behavior	Geriatric Assessment Inventory	Nurses' Ratings
Insomnia	Daily Sleep Diary	Self-Report
Insomnia	Munroe Daily Sleep Questionnaire-Revised	Self-Report
Interpersonal Sensitivity	Willoughby Personality Schedule	Self-Report
Irrational Beliefs	Irrational Beliefs Inventory	Self-Report
Job Interview Skills	Job Interview Assessment	Behavioral Observation
Learned Helplessness	Generalized Expectancy for Success Scale	Self-Report
Life Events	Unpleasant Events Schedule	Self-Report
Likert-Scaling	Visual Analogue Scale	Self-Report
Marital Adjustment	Semantic Differential of Sex Roles	Self-Report
Marital Conflict	Conflict Inventory	Self-Report
Marital Distress	Analogue Communications Assessment	Behavioral Observation
Marital Distress	Communications Satisfaction Questionnaire	Self-Report
Marital Distress	Dyadic Adjustment Scale	Self-Report
Marital Distress	Marital Interaction Coding System	Behavioral Observation

Marital Distress	PFB Partnership Questionnaire	Spouse Rating
Marital Distress	Problem List	Spouse Rating
Marital Distress	Spouse Observation Checklist	Spouse Rating, Behavioral Observation
Marital Distress	Spouse Verbal Problem Checklist	Spouse Rating
Marital Satisfaction	General Happiness Rating Scale	Self-Report
Mental Competence to Stand Trial	Georgia Court Competency Test–Revised	Structured Interview
Mental Retardation	Activity Measure	Behavioral Observation
Mental Retardation	Assessment of Self-Care Skills of Mentally Retarded Individuals	Staff Rating, Behavioral Observation
Mental Retardation	Dining Room Manners	Behavioral Observation
Mental Retardation	Home Accident Observations	Behavioral Observation
Mental Retardation (Mild and Moderate)	Cooking Methods Test	Behavioral Observation
Mildly Handicapped Children	Behavioral Checklist for Mildly Handicapped Children	Staff Rating, Peer Rating
Mother-Child Interaction in Stressful Situations	Dyadic Prestressor Interaction Scale	Behavioral Observation
Muscle Tension	Electromyography	Physiological,
Music Performance Anxiety	Musical Performance Anxiety Self-Statement Scale	Self-Report
Myopia	Behavioral Visual Acuity Test	Behavioral Observation
Neurological Activity	Electroencephalography	Physiological
Neuroticism	Eysenck Personality Inventory	Self-Report
Nicotine Dependence	Fagerstrom Tolerance Questionnaire	Self-Report
Noncompliant Children	Timeout Assessment	Behavioral Observation

Overweight	Dieter's Inventory of Eating Temptations	Self-Report
Overweight	Eating Questionnaire	Self-Report
Overweight	Eating Self-Efficacy Scale	Self-Report
Pain	Cold Pressor Test	Behavioral Observation
Pain	McGill Pain Questionnaire	Self-Report
Pain	Pain Assessment Questionnaire	Self-Report
Pain	Pain Behavior Observation	Behavioral Observation
Pain	Pain Observation	Self-Monitoring, Behavioral Observation
Pain - Children	Pain Behavior Rating Scales	Self-Report, Staff Rating, Parent Rating
Pain Tolerance	Pain Cuff	Biological Self-Report
Parent-Adolescent Conflict	Community Member's Rating Scale	Judges' Ratings
Parent-Adolescent Conflict	Conflict Behavior Questionnaire	Self-Report
Parent-Adolescent Conflict	Issues Checklist	Self-Report
Parent-Adolescent Conflict	Parent Adolescent Interaction Coding System	Behavioral Observation
Parent-Adolescent Interactions	Home Report	Parent and Sibling Rating
Parent Behavior	Reprimand Assessment Scale	Behavioral Observation
Parent Behavior	Training Proficiency Scale-Parent Version	Behavioral Observation
Parent-Child Conflict	Parent Adolescent Interaction Coding System	Behavioral Observation
Parent-Child Interactions	Family Interaction Coding System	Behavioral Observation
Parent-Child Interactions	Interpersonal Behavior Construct Scale	Behavioral Observation

Parent-Child Interactions	Structured Observation System	Behavioral Observation
Parental Satisfaction with Therapy	Consumer Satisfaction Questionnaire	Semistructured Interview Self-Report
Parental Understanding of Behavioral Principles	Instruments to Measure Knowledge of Behavioral Principles as Applied to Children	Self-Report
Parents of Behaviorally Disordered Children	Community Interaction Checklist	Semistructured Interview
Performance Anxiety	Musical Performance Anxiety Self-Statement Scale	Self-Report
Phobia	Fear Survey Schedule I	Self-Report
Phobia	Fear Survey Schedule III	Self-Report
Phobia	Fear Thermometer	Self-Report
Phobia	Marks and Mathews Fear Questionnaire	Self-Report
Phobia	Target Problems	Self-Report, Behavioral Observation
Phobia in Children	Fear Survey Schedule for Children-Revised	Self-Report
Physical Activity	Large Scale Integrated Sensor	Electronic Assessment
Posttraumatic Stress Disorder	Combat Exposure Scale	Self-Report
Posttraumatic Stress Disorder	Impact of Event Scale	Self-Report
Posttraumatic Stress Disorder	Rape Aftermath Symptom Test	Self-Report
Preschool Child's Compliance with Parents	Compliance Test	Behavioral Observation
Preschool Reciprocal Interaction	Frequency Interaction Recording System	Behavioral Observation
Problem Solving - Children	Open Middle Inventory	Cognitive Task
Procrastination	Procrastination Assessment Scale-Students	Self-Report

Program Evaluation	Goal Attainment Scaling	Staff Rating
Psychiatric Diagnosis	Adult Diagnostic Interview Schedules	Structured Interview
Psychiatric Diagnosis	Child Diagnostic Interview Schedules	Structured Interview
Psychiatric Evaluation	Brief Psychiatric Rating Scale	Staff Rating
Psychiatric Patients	Observational Record of Inpatient Behavior	Behavioral Observation
Psychiatric Patients	Time-Sample Behavioral Checklist	Behavioral Observation
Psychiatric Symptoms	Derogatis Symptom Checklist 90-R	Self-Report
Psychoticism	Eysenck Personality Questionnaire	Self-Report
Public Speaking	Checklist of Appropriate Speaking Behaviors	Behavioral Observation
Punitiveness	Hostility and Direction of Hostility Questionnaire	Self-Report
Rape	Rape Aftermath Symptom Test	Self-Report
Rape-Induced Fear	Modified Fear Survey	Self-Report
Relationship of Antecedents, Behaviors, and Consequences	Self-Monitoring Analysis System	Self-Report (Computerized Program)
Schizophrenia	Eysenck Personality Questionnaire	Self-Report
Schizophrenia	Observational Record of Inpatient Behavior	Behavioral Observation
Schizophrenia	Time-Sample Behavioral Checklist	Behavioral Observation
Schizophrenia in Children	Kiddie-Schedule for Affective Disorders and Schizophrenia-Present Episode	Semistructured Interview
School Behavior Problems	Pupil Evaluation Inventory	Peer Rating, Sociometric
Self-Control	Rosenbaum's Self-Control Schedule	Self-Report
Self-Efficacy	Self-Efficacy Scale	Self-Report

Self-Injury	Self-Injurious Behavior Assessment	Behavioral Observation
Self-Reinforcement in Children	Self-Reinforcement Questionnaire	Self-Report
Sensation Seeking	Sensation Seeking Scale	Self-Report
Sex Role Orientation	Semantic Differential of Sex Roles	Self-Report
Sexual Arousal	Strain Gauge	Biological Physiological
Sexual Assault Victims	Social Adjustment Scale-Self-Report	Self-Report
Sexual Disorders	Strain Gauge	Biological Physiological
Sexual Dysfunction	Derogatis Sexual Functioning Inventory	Self-Report
Sexual Dysfunction, Male	Penile Volume Response	Physiological
Sexual Experience	Sexual Experience Scale	Self-Report
Sleep Disorder	Munroe Daily Sleep Questionnaire-Revised	Self-Report
Social Adjustment	Social Adjustment Scale-Self-Report	Self-Report
Social Anxiety	Fear of Negative Evaluation	Self-Report
Social Anxiety	Social Avoidance and Distress Scale and Fear of Negative Evaluation Scale	Self-Report
Social Anxiety	Survey of Heterosexual Interactions	Self-Report
Social Behavior, Children	System for Observing Social-Interpersonal Behavior	Behavioral Observation
Social Competence	Sociometric Measures	Peer Rating (Sociometrics)
Social Perception	Interpersonal Attraction Inventory	Self-Report
Social Phobia	Willoughby Personality Schedule	Self-Report
Social Skills	Behavioral Role-Playing Assertion Test	Behavioral Observation

Social Skills	Behaviorally Referenced Rating System of Intermediate Social Skills	Behavioral Observation, Judge's Rating
Social Skills	Direct Behavioral Observation	Behavioral Observation
Social Skills	Interpersonal Evaluation Inventory	Staff Rating
Social Skills	Role-Playing Assessment Instruments	Behavioral Observation
Social Skills	Situation Role-Play Assessment	Behavioral Observation
Social Skills	Skill Survey	Therapist Rating, Staff Rating, Self-Report
Social Skills	Social Interaction Test	Behavioral Observation
Social Skills	Social Reaction Inventory-Revised	Self-Report
Social Skills	Written Assertiveness Knowledge Test	Self-Report
Social Skills in Children	Children's Interpersonal Behavior Test	Behavioral Observation
Social Skills in Children	Conversation Probe	Behavioral Observation
Social Skills in Children	Social Skills Test for Children	Behavioral Observation
Social Skills in Male Adolescents	Adolescent Problems Inventory	Behavioral Observation, Self-Report
Social Skills of Male Offenders	Interview Assessment of Adolescent Male Offenders	Behavioral Observation
Social Status	Sociometric Measures	Peer Rating (Sociometrics)
Specific Fears	Behavioral Avoidance Slide Test	Behavioral Observation
Specific Fears	Behavioral Avoidance Test	Behavioral Observation
Staff Behavior	Staff Behavior Observation	Behavioral Observation

Staff Behavior	Staff-Resident Interaction Chronograph	Behavioral Observation
Submission in Children	Children's Action Tendency Scale	Self-Report
Suicidal Ideation	Hopelessness Scale	Self-Report
Suicidal Ideation	Scale for Suicide Ideation	Self-Report
Suicidal Ideation	Suicidal Ideation Questionnaire	Self-Report
Symptom Severity	Likert Scaling	Self-Report
Tardive Dyskinesia	Abnormal Involuntary Movement Scale	Behavioral Observation
Teacher Behavior	Reprimand Assessment Scale	Behavioral Observation
Test Anxiety	Suinn Test Anxiety Behavior Scale	Self-Report
Test Anxiety	Test Anxiety Inventory	Self-Report
Therapy Evaluation	Treatment Evaluation Inventory	Self-Report
Thought Content and Process	In Vivo Cognitive Assessment	Judges' Rating
Treatment Compliance	Relaxation Assessment Device	Permanent Product, Mechanical
Treatment Compliance (Medication)	Riboflavin Tracer Technique for Assessment of Medication Compliance	Biological, Permanent Product, Mechanical
Type A Behavior	Jenkins Activity Survey: Student Version (Form T)	Self-Report
Unassertiveness	Adult Self-Expression Scale	Self-Report
Unassertiveness	Assertiveness Self-Statement Test	Self-Report
Unassertiveness	Assertion Self-Statement Test-Revised	Self-Report
Unassertiveness	Assertion Situations	Behavioral Observation
Unassertiveness	Assertion Inventory	Self-Report
Unassertiveness	Behavioral Assertiveness Test-Revised	Behavioral Observation

Unassertiveness in Children	Behavioral Assertiveness Test for Children	Behavioral Observation
Unassertiveness in Children	Children's Assertive Behavior Scale	Self-Report
Unassertiveness in Children	Children's Assertiveness Inventory	Self-Report
Unassertiveness in College Students	College Self-Expression Scale	Self-Report
Unassertiveness in College Students	College Women's Assertion Sample	Behavioral Observation
Unassertiveness in College Students	Del Greco Assertive Behavior Inventory	Self-Report
Unassertiveness in Diabetics	Diabetes Assertiveness Test	Behavioral Observation
Unassertiveness in Drug Addicts	Callner-Ross Assertion Questionnaire	Self-Report
Weight Loss	Family Ratings of Program Behaviors	Behavioral Observation
Weight Loss	Feinstein Weight Reduction Index	Permanent Product Measure (Mathematical)

Abnormal Involuntary Movement Scale

William M. Glazer

Description

The Abnormal Involuntary Movement Scale (AIMS) is a clinical instrument that includes 10 items (each coded zero to 4 in order of increasing severity); seven items assess the level of involuntary movements in different anatomic areas and three global items assess general severity, incapacitation, and patient awareness of the condition. A total AIMS score is compiled by adding the seven anatomic scores. The global severity score is computed by comparing the movements of the patient examined to those of all other patients seen. In addition, there are two items that deal with dental status because of its apparent relationship to oral dyskinesia.

Purpose

The purpose of the AIMS is to measure the occurrence and severity of involuntary movements associated with tardive dyskinesia (T.D.), a late onset disorder occurring in psychiatric patients exposed to neuroleptic medications.

Development

The early scales for T.D. were designed by Crane and were multi-item in nature. In the early 1970s, as part of the Psychopharmacology Research Branch's Collaborative Study of Long-Acting Fluphenazine Decanoate, the AIMS was developed out of a need for a global scale for involuntary movements. This scale focused globally on movement within body areas, as opposed to movements thought to be specific for T.D., such as the "bon bon sign." Particular attention was paid to the mouth area because: (a) the diagnosis of T.D. was thought to depend on the occurrence of buccolingual masticatory movements; (b) buccolingual masticatory movements were judged more frequent than movements of the upper and lower extremities and trunk; and (c) the tongue was believed to be the earliest part affected in T.D.

Since the development of the AIMS, two modifications have occurred. First, the scale no longer includes the convention that scores movements occurring on activation 1 less than those occurring

spontaneously. Second, removal of shoes and socks is not part of the AIMS examination.

Psychometric Characteristics

Because there is no valid marker for T.D., there is no way to assess accurately the validity of the AIMS. The AIMS has good content validity because all anatomic areas affected by T.D. are rated. It could be argued that the three nonorofacial items should be subdivided into more detail, such as rating the toes, ankles, and knees separately instead of as one. However, orofacial movements occur more frequently than nonorofacial movements, and some investigators believe that the former but not the latter movements are necessary in making the diagnosis of T.D.

Studies of the interrater reliability of the AIMS have focused mainly on interrater agreement for the total AIMS score using the Pearson correlation coefficient. Lane, Glazer, Hansen, Berman, and Kramer (1985) described interrater reliability among four psychiatrists, two experienced and two inexperienced, over a 10-month period. Intraclass correlations comparing all four raters were significant ($p < .001$) and ranged from a low of 0.50 (trunk) to a high of 0.79 (total AIMS score). Experienced raters showed consistently higher intraclass correlation scores compared with those of inexperienced raters. However, inexperienced raters showed improved intraclass correlation scores over time, whereas experienced rater scores stayed constant over time.

After performing AIMS examination in 228 patients with T.D, we measured the internal consistency of the scale using Cronbach's alpha, which provides an index of the extent to which the seven anatomic items measure the same symptom complex. Coefficient alpha was 0.23, suggesting that the internal consistency of the AIMS is low. Factor analysis on the seven anatomic items indicated that orofacial movements separated from nonorofacial movements. This finding replicates the work of a number of investigators. Applying mathematical modeling techniques to determine whether these factors were associated with clinical variables, we found that severe orofacial movements are associated with increasing age, a diagnosis of schizoaffective or affective disorder, and living alone, whereas severe nonorofacial movements are associated with the current neuroleptic medication dose, living alone, and the absence of psychiatric medication other than neuroleptics.

1

Richardson and Craig (1982) compared the AIMS with the Simpson Abbreviated Dyskinesia Scale (ADS) and demonstrated significant inter-scale correlations on total scores, total facial/oral, and total extremity subscales. Pearson correlations were 0.96, 0.98, and 0.87, respectively. Several investigations reported a lack of association between total AIMS scores and frequency counts of selected involuntary movements. These data are disturbing in that they suggest that global scales such as the AIMS are not measuring all aspects of the disorder.

There is difficulty assessing the intrarater reliability of the AIMS because of the variability of the movements within a given patient. This variation in ratings is due to such factors as anxiety, time of day, medication, and posture. Solutions to this problem will be addressed under Future Directions.

Clinical Use

The AIMS is used in psychiatric patients who have been exposed to neuroleptic medications. Schooler and Kane (1982) developed a classification scheme that establishes three prerequisites for the diagnosis of T.D.: (a) at least 3 months of cumulative neuroleptic exposure; (b) a minimum AIMS score of either 3 for one anatomic area or 2s; and (c) the absence of differential diagnoses. The AIMS examination is applicable to patients meeting criteria for T.D., but it does not distinguish patients manifesting other neuroleptic-induced movement disorders, such as tremor, dystonia, or akathisia. It is not applicable to other movement disorders of known or unknown etiology.

The AIMS can be used for research or clinical purposes or both. Because the scale fits on a single page, it can be included in the patient's medical record to document the examination for T.D. and to follow its course over time.

The AIMS takes about 5 minutes to complete. It is accompanied by a set of instructions that structure the administration of the examination. The examination begins with a general observation of the patient, and it then focuses on various anatomic areas, particularly the mouth region. The patient is observed sitting, standing, and walking. It is best to seat the patient in a chair without arms to allow maximum observation of extremity movements. An important component of the examination is the *elicitation* of movements, which consists of giving the patient a distracting motoric exercise, for

example, touching fingers to thumb repetitively, and observing the occurrence of T.D. movements. We have omitted the prescribed convention of subtracting 1 point for movements observed only with the elicitation exercise because in our experience such patients continue to manifest T.D. movements over time. Adherence to this convention could therefore result in underdiagnosis of T.D. Patients wearing dentures are best observed with them in place because teeth provide the jaw with a source of support. Toe movements may be missed if shoes and socks are not removed.

We have developed a number of conventions that help define the use of the AIMS more clearly (Lane et al., 1985). In assessing the severity of movements, we consider their quality, amplitude, and frequency. Movements in T.D. are choreic in quality. The extremes of movement frequency (an approximate range of less than one per minute to greater than two per second) determine whether or not a movement is consistent with T.D. A movement amplitude of less than 1 cm may or may not indicate T.D., but above this level, greater amplitude is associated with greater severity. Other conventions assist in rating specific anatomic areas, such as distinguishing jaw from lip movements and rating tongue and upper extremity movements.

In assessing the patient with the AIMS, it is best to include an examination for neuroleptic-induced parkinsonism. Separate consideration of parkinsonian signs insures against confusing T.D. with tremor and akathisia. Furthermore, because neuroleptic-induced parkinsonism can potentially mask T.D., it is important to assess both disorders separately over time.

Future Directions

Future questions for the AIMS relate to its reliability and validity. Because differences between raters do not appear to be the primary explanation for observed intrapatient variability, other approaches to assess measurement error should be employed. For example, test-retest reliability coefficients and stability coefficients can be computed from a set of three or four serial measures (e.g., from the first three or four equally spaced AIMS examinations). In this procedure, intraperson variability can be separated into two components: that are due to measurement error (unreliability) and that are due to true changes in T.D. severity (instability). To demonstrate that the orofacial-nonorofacial subtypes are clinically meaningful, individual patients must be assigned to one of these categories to see if these clinical groupings demonstrate the same predictors just mentioned. Furthermore, it will be necessary to follow such patients longitudinally to see if the course of the T.D. varies between the two groups.

Lane et al.'s (1985) guidelines need to be tested to see if they lead to better interrater reliability. However, more explicit conventions are most needed when the rater has had relatively little exposure to patients with T.D. or when unusual manifestations of T.D. must be rated. Although instructional videotapes are useful, the utility of this approach is limited if guidelines for the ratings cannot be put into words. The difficulty in developing conventions for AIMS ratings is that the movements themselves are extremely complex and therefore difficult to describe and gradate. Lane et al. (1985) described limited success in verbally formulating additional specific guidelines, and this may represent an inherent limitation of any scale that attempts to quantitatively capture complex clinical phenomena. However, any further improvements in the reliability of the AIMS will facilitate clinical care and research on the phenomenon of T.D. itself.

References

Lane, R.D., Glazer, W.M., Hansen, T.E., Berman, W.H., & Kramer, S.I. (1985). The assessment of tardive dyskinesia using the abnormal involuntary movement scale. *Journal of Nervous and Mental Disease, 173*, 1-5.

Richardson, M.A., & Craig T.J. (1982). Tardive dyskinesia: Inter- and intra-rating scale comparisons. *Psychopharmacology Bulletin, 18*, 4-7.

Schooler, N.R., & Kane, J.M. (1982). Research diagnoses for tardive dyskinesia. *Archives of General Psychiatry, 39*, 486-487.

Activities of Daily Living - Modular Assessment

Roger L. Patterson

Description

The Activities of Daily Living (ADL I) is designed to measure whether a subject can perform routine grooming and self-feeding behaviors independently and in an acceptable manner. Major areas are Oral Hygiene (one item), Bathing and Dressing (five items), Nail Care (two items), and Eating Behavior (two items). A set of instructions for administering the scale as a whole and each item individually is part of the assessment. The eight grooming items are scored by asking subjects if they perform the particular item routinely and independently. The self-report is verified by inspection. For example, if subjects say that they perform oral hygiene daily, the teeth are examined for evidence that the self-report is true. If there is reason to suspect that the particular activity may have been performed for the subject (e.g., those who are or have been in institutions recently), then the subject is asked to actually demonstrate the activity independently. For rating eating behavior, the subject is observed eating a regular meal. For each of the 10 items, independent, correct performance is scored 1; otherwise, a zero is given.

Purpose

This scale was developed to provide a rapid, easily administered assessment of the basic personal hygiene skills of ambulatory elderly mental health clients in *any* setting in which there are full bathroom and eating facilities. It gives a total score, identifies specific deficits, and may be repeated frequently to observe changes in behavior.

Development

The items on this scale were those that an occupational therapist, nursing staff, geropsychologist, and others agreed were necessary for elderly ambulatory mental health clients to be able to perform in order to live in noninstitutional settings or without receiving institutional-type care at home. Before being evaluated psychometrically, the scale was informally tested for general usefulness and ease of administration in a residential unit for ambulatory, mentally ill, elderly persons and a day-treatment center for similar clients.

Psychometric Characteristics

Reliability. Interrater reliability was established by having two raters observe a videotape of the assessment of six clients. These ratings agreed in 93% of the items (exact agreement method). A minimal estimate of test-retest reliability of the total scores for 16 subjects over a period of 4 weeks was 0.53. The reason this latter figure is *only* a low estimate is that all subjects were in treatment, which required that their personal hygiene and eating behaviors improve during the 4-week test-retest interval.

Validity. Patterson, Eberly, Harrell, and Penner (1983) evaluated the validity of the ADL I scale which was established by means of a multi-trait, multi-method correlation matrix as described by Campbell and Fiske (1959). In this study, the ADL I Modular Assessment correlated $r = 0.43$ with a widely used behavioral rating scale of personal hygiene. In general, the ADL I scale met most of the criteria for acceptable convergent and discriminant validity as established by Campbell and Fiske (1959). Of great significance, the *change* scores on the ADL I scale correlated with the change scores on the behavior rating scale, $r = 0.53$ (Patterson et al., 1982).

Clinical Use

The scale may be used by a variety of professionals and paraprofessionals in various settings including: (a) needs assessment; (b) identification of specific deficits; (c) monitoring clinical progress; and (d) evaluation of programs designed to correct such deficits. Obviously, training is required to insure reliability.

Future Directions

The scale was developed for use with a specific elderly population, although it can be used with other populations having deficits in personal hygiene. The author also recently added two items pertaining to the use of an automatic washing machine and dryer. Separate task analyses also were developed relating to most items in the scale. Therefore, the scale may be administered, areas of deficits identified, and more specific deficient behavior pinpointed.

References

Campbell, D.T., & Fiske, D.W. (1959). Convergent and discriminant validation by the multitrait-multimethod matrix. *Psychological Bulletin, 56,* 81-105.

Patterson, R.L., Dupree, L.W., Eberly, D.A., Jackson, G.M., O'Sullivan, M.J., Penner, L.A. & Dee-Kelley, C. (1982). *Overcoming deficits of aging: A behavioral treatment approach.* New York: Plenum Press.

Patterson, R.L., Eberly, D.A., Harrell, T.L., & Penner, L.A. (1983). Behavioral assessment of intellectual competence, communication skills, and personal hygiene skills of elderly persons. *Behavioral Assessment, 5,* 207-218.

Activity Measure

James Mansell

Description

The Activity Measure is an observational measure of individual activity designed for program evaluation studies in residential and day-care services for mentally retarded people.

Subjects in a group are observed in sequence at 1-minute intervals. The person's behavior at the moment of observation is recorded (i.e., the measure is a time sample); the observer also uses observation from 3 seconds before to 3 seconds after the moment of observation to determine how the behavior should be coded.

The data sheet consists of a grid for each client in which each column represents an observation. For each subject, there are five rows in which the observer records the room the person is in and his or her behavior (in four classes) for each observation. In this way, a single data sheet can hold up to 4 hours of observation. The room code is preassigned a letter or number. The activity codes are grouped in four major classes: contact (interaction and other social behavior), engaged (purposeful adaptive behavior), neutral, and inappropriate behaviors. Within these classes particular activities are coded by number.

Definitions of Contact. *Interaction*: speaking to, gesturing at, listening to, looking at, or touching a person who is doing one of these behaviors in return. Code C1 is for interaction with the client and C2 for interaction with any other person.

Initiates: speaking to, gesturing at, or touching a person (C3 for client, C4 for other person) who is not doing one of these behaviors in return (unless loud or intrusive in which case code 15 or 16 is used). Includes speaking to persons in a group in which a person is not apparent, for example, "Let's go to lunch." When the person to whom the client apparently initiates is the observer, asterisk the box (C4*).

Being Attended To: a person is speaking to the client at the moment of observation, or has spoken in the preceding 3 seconds and continues to direct attention to the client (C5).

Being Held or Guided: does not include simple touching (e.g., client and person seated holding hands), but does include any physical guidance, however subtle (C6).

Codes C1 to C4 can be used without an ENI code. C5 cannot be coded with C1 or C2 because attention is subsumed in interaction.

Definitions of Engagement. *Leisure (E1):* using recreational or leisure materials purposefully or participating in an activity that does not involve touching materials (e.g., dance). Includes getting out or putting away leisure materials, switching radio and the like on or off, and carrying materials between place of storage and place of use.

Personal (E2): getting ready for or doing a self-help or personal activity (getting materials, carrying them to place of use, or putting them away). Includes eating (not from floor or other person's plate), washing, dressing, grooming (including wiping or blowing nose with tissue or handkerchief), looking at clock or watch, taking medicines, and so forth. Also, minor movement to furniture in the act of sitting down or standing up, winding watch, serving self, handling money or sweets, and putting on or taking off prostheses. If in doubt about whether materials handled are personal, code as domestic (except money and sweets).

Domestic (E3): getting ready to do or doing housework. Includes serving others, decorating, moving furniture (other than E2), opening and closing doors and windows, and operating light switches.

Gardening (E4): getting ready to do or doing gardening and clearing away afterwards (indoor gardening is *leisure*; putting on boots is *personal*; and laying table for meal in garden is *domestic*). Includes sniffing flowers, and arranging garden furniture.

Engaged behaviors can be coded together (watching television and drinking tea simultaneously are coded 1 and 2); enter both codes in the box.

Definitions of Neutral Behavior. *Passive:* sitting, standing, walking, or lying (or transitions between these) only; if person moves furniture out of the way, this is E2. Wheeling one's own or another's wheelchair or just holding materials is included. If simply *walking carrying materials*, code as engaged (e.g., walking carrying teapot is E3). If just *walking* at moment of observation, wait 3 seconds to see whether behavior is fetching. If client picks up object within 3 seconds, code as engaged (e.g., walk and turns on radio). Code N1 for passive eyes open and N2 for passive eyes closed.

Unpurposeful (N3): manipulating materials to no apparent end; minor self-manipulation. Includes fiddling with clothing, tapping pencil, wiping nose on hand or sleeve, thumbsucking, nail biting, nose picking, and talking quietly to oneself.

Smoking (N4): manipulating smoking materials (do not have to be lit). Usually, it is appropriate to rule that N1 and N3 cannot be coded with any Engaged or Inappropriate codes in a study. Therefore, if a client is chewing and tapping pencil, code E2 personal only.

Definitions of Inappropriate Behavior. *Self-Stimulation, Stereotypes (I1):* movements must be repeated in the 6-second period or, if a complex ritual, must continue throughout the period. Partial or single movements that are within the range of normal body movements (e.g., stretching neck and tapping fingers on face) should be coded as neutral. If in doubt code under a neutral category. Do not code grinding teeth, as it cannot be reliably distinguished from chewing.

Aggression to Self (I2): any activity that directly harms another person (e.g., hitting, kicking, pinching, pushing, and spitting on someone, but threatening is I6).

Damages Property (I4): any activity that directly damages, overturns, or disarranges property.

Inappropriate Vocalization (I5): verbal threats, shouting, and the like. Includes talking loudly to self (talking quietly to oneself is N3), laughing hysterically, and verbal interruption, but disagreeing (e.g., saying no) is not in itself coded as inappropriate.

Other (I6): any other inappropriate behavior, including the act of elimination in public, public masturbation or intercourse (but not minor kissing or petting), pestering, and interrupting by touch. Thumb sucking, nail biting, and nose picking should be coded as unpurposeful (N3).

For I2 and I4, code the act of hitting, and the like, if the person does it in the 6-second period (e.g., if person bangs table in 3 seconds before observation point and has arm raised at moment of observation, shaking with rage, code I4).

More than one inappropriate code can be entered (enter second code in gap below I row) and inappropriate codes can be entered with other categories except N1 and N3.

Purpose

This measure was developed specifically to enable systematic observation of severely and profoundly mentally handicapped people living in ordinary houses. None of the available measures exactly met the requirement for a measure that would produce *individual* rather than *group* scores and would include *activities* as well as *behaviors*.

Development

An earlier evaluation of community-based facilities for severely and profoundly mentally handicapped persons used a measure of client engagement in activity throughout a 12-hour day as one of a battery of measures in the study (Felce, Kushlick, & Mansell, 1980). However, group scores did not adequately reflect the effect of service interventions when moving from group comparison studies to applied work (Mansell, Felce, de Kock, & Jenkins, 1982), in which individual differences were of more interest. The Client Behavior Measure (Porterfield, Evans, & Blunden, 1981), which has been used in hostel and day care settings for mentally handicapped persons, was therefore investigated. This is an individual measure and has the advantage of including classes of activity (such as educational/recreational, looking/listening, and personal).

However, the categories were revised to reflect interest in housework rather than recreational activity and to include more detailed classification of where people were, what staff contact they received, and what their inappropriate behaviors were. In addition, the coding forms were modified so that instead of recording 5-minute data per sheet, 4 hours of observation could be combined on one sheet, yielding a graph of the main classification for each individual without further analysis.

Psychometric Characteristics

No studies of validity have been carried out, although the categories have face validity in giving feedback to staff in care settings.

Estimates of interobserver reliability were obtained in a study of activity levels of six severely or profoundly retarded persons in ordinary housing (Mansell, Jenkins, Felce, & de Kock, 1984). For the major behavior code and the room code, the number of observations in which both observers entered the same code was divided by the total number of pairs of observations for each person each day. Mean agreement across subjects was 91% for behavior (81 to 100%) and 99% for room (97 to 100%). For the specific engagement code, the number of observations in which both observers entered the same engaged behavior was divided by

the number of observations in which they entered different engaged codes or in which one entered an engaged code and the other entered a neutral or inappropriate code. Mean agreement was 89% (67 to 100%). This level of agreement reflected disagreement between personal and neutral codes for one person in which the observers were unable to reliably distinguish chewing from passive behavior.

Clinical Use

The measure has been used to study the activity of severely and profoundly mentally handicapped adults living in ordinary housing with full staff support (Mansell et al., 1984), in undergraduate teaching in psychology, and in methodological studies of time-sampling (Mansell, in press).

Future Directions

Recent developments in microcomputer technology have led to the prospect of replacing clipboard-and-stopwatch methods with hand-held micros running data capture programs. The Activity Measure definitions can be used in this way, with the added facility that real-time continuous event recording as well as time-sampling can easily be undertaken.

References

Felce, D., Kushlick, A., & Mansell, J. (1980). Evaluation of alternative residential facilities for the severely mentally handicapped in Wessex: Client engagement. *Advances in Behaviour Research and Therapy, 3,* 13-18.

Mansell, J. (1985). Time sampling and measurement error: The effect of interval length and sampling pattern. *Journal of Behavior Therapy and Experimental Psychiatry, 16,* 245-251.

Mansell, J., Felce, D., de Kock, U., & Jenkins, J. (1982). Increasing purposeful activity of severely and profoundly mentally handicapped adults. *Behaviour Research and Therapy, 20,* 593-604.

Mansell, J., Jenkins, J., Felce, D., & de Kock, U. (1984). Measuring the activity of severely and profoundly mentally handicapped adults in ordinary housing. *Behaviour Research and Therapy, 22,* 23-29.

Porterfield, J., Evans, G., & Blunden, R. (1981). *The client behavior measure and staff behavior measure: Manual for time-sampling procedures.* Cardiff: Mental Handicap in Wales, Applied Research Unit, unpublished.

Addiction Severity Index

A. T. McLellan

Description

The Addiction Severity Index (ASI) is a structured, 40-item clinical research interview designed to assess problem severity in seven commonly affected areas in substance abusers: medical condition, employment, drug use, alcohol use, illegal activity, family relations, and psychiatric condition. In each area, objective questions are asked to measure the number, extent, and duration of problem symptoms in the patient's lifetime and in the past 30 days. The patient also supplies a subjective report of the recent (past 30 days) severity and importance of each problem area. The design and rationale for the ASI have been described elsewhere (McLellan, Luborsky, & O'Brien, 1980; McLellan, Luborsky, & Cacciola, 1985).

Two types of summary measures result from the collected data in each problem area: severity ratings and composite scores.

Severity Ratings. One important measure within each problem area is a 10-point (0-9) *interviewer rating* of problem severity. Within the ASI, severity is considered as the "need for additional treatment" and is measured by the problem symptoms. Although severity ratings are ultimately subjective, the ASI is designed to maximize the use of the objective information in formulating these ratings. Both the rating method and the data on which the ratings are based are standardized, thereby reducing interrater variation. An Instruction Manual detailing the administration procedure is available from the senior author.

Composite Scores. The second measure available from the ASI is the mathematically derived composite score. These composite scores are developed from sets of interrelated items within each problem area that are standardized and summed to produce a mathematical estimate of a patient's status in each problem area. The composite scores are strongly related to the severity ratings (average correlation .88), but they offer a more empirical evaluation of patient change and treatment effectiveness (McLellan et al., 1985; McLellan, Luborsky, & O'Brien, 1982).

Purpose and Development

The Addiction Severity Index (ASI) was introduced in 1979 as a comprehensive, clinical/research instrument designed to assess the multiple problems seen in alcohol- and drug-dependent persons seeking treatment. The instrument was developed to produce information that would be relevant for both clinical and research evaluations. Therefore, the interview was designed for use within a variety of alcohol and drug treatment settings, for administration by a trained technician in less than 1 hour, and for repeat administrations at posttreatment and follow-up evaluations. Information resulting from ASI interviews has been used by clinical staff for the initial intake evaluation, treatment planning, and referral decisions. Because the ASI is computer coded and provides quantitative, time-based assessments of patient status in several areas, researchers have used the ASI to evaluate patient improvement following treatment (McLellan, Luborsky, Woody, & O'Brien, 1983; McLellan, Woody, Luborsky, O'Brien, & Druley, 1983).

Psychometric Characteristics

The ASI is quite reliable. Trained technicians serving as interviewers can estimate the severity of patients' problems with an average reliability of .89. Further, this level of reliability was uniformly high in each of the seven problem areas and in subgroups of the patient population divided on the basis of age, race, sex, primary drug problem, and treatment center. The consistency of the patient self-report data over a 3-day, test-retest interval was also very reliable. Paired statistical comparisons of the composite measures and severity ratings showed no significant differences ($p > 0.10$), even when different technicians performed the repeat inverviews (McLellan et al., 1980, 1985).

Both the severity ratings and the composite scores are valid. Comparisons of these ASI measures with a battery of previously validated test results indicate clear evidence of concurrent and discriminant validity. This discriminant validity was again found in subgroups of patients on the basis of age, race, sex, primary drug problem, and treatment center. There is also evidence of predictive validity with the ASI (McLellan et al., 1982, 1983), and these findings complement the validity reports on the ASI from two independent studies.

Taken together, these data suggest that the instrument may be used with confidence across a range of substance abuses and treatment centers.

Clinical Use and Future Directions

During the past 6 years, the ASI has been used extensively to evaluate and compare different forms of alcohol and drug abuse treatments and to explore methods of "matching" the patient to the most effective treatment available. More recently, other investigators have used the ASI in individual treatment evaluation examinations of patient subgroups and in collaborative, multicenter studies of substance abuse treatments.

Despite the satisfactory level of reliability and validity, cautions are associated with the use of the ASI. First, the instrument has been designed with the minimum number of items possible in each problem area. Therefore, it is a screening instrument rather than a detailed evaluation. Several investigators have added items or even supplemental instruments to augment the evaluation.

The ASI was designed as an interview and not a questionnaire. Because of reduced reliability and serious problems with many patients' reading comprehension, we do not endorse the use of the ASI when administered as a questionnaire or through a computer terminal.

Three subgroups of substance abusers appear to be inappropriate for evaluation with the ASI. Some older substance abuse patients (generally alcoholic addicts) presenting overt evidence of cognitive impairment are sometimes unable to analyze the individual problem areas separately. They may confuse the distinctions between different questions, thereby reducing the validity of the information.

A second subgroup of substance abusers with whom we have had little success is a small but significant group of younger, generally drug-addicted, patients often with a history of criminal involvement. Many of these patients deliberately misrepresent their objective answers and subjective patient ratings. We have been able to detect this pattern through verification of objective items and through built-in consistency checks within the ASI. Approximately 5% of all interviews have been discarded for invalid information, and less than 3% of interviews have been poorly comprehended by the patient.

Younger adolescents (under 16), supported by their families, form a third group of patients for whom the ASI is not an adequate evaluation. The ASI was designed for adult or older adolescent populations. Many individual items within the interview assume at least the capacity for self-support and adult relationships. We encourage interested parties to adapt the design and items of the ASI to more effective use with younger populations.

There is not, and will not be, a totally satisfactory instrument to assess what is arguably a most complex health care problem: substance dependence. However, the ASI is now widely used in both clinical and research applications, and despite its limitations, we are encouraged by its potential advantages in examining important issues, such as predicting treatment outcome, comparing different forms of treatment, and "matching" the patient to treatment.

References

McLellan, A.T., Luborsky, L., & O'Brien, C.P. (1980). An improved evaluation instrument for substance abuse patients: The Addiction Severity Index. *Journal of Nervous and Mental Disease, 168,* 26-33.

McLellan, A.T., Luborsky, L., & Cacciola, J. (1985). New data from the Addiction Severity Index: Reliability and validity in three centers. *Journal of Nervous and Mental Disease, 173,* 412-413.

McLellan, A.T., Luborsky, L., & O'Brien, C.P. (1982). Is treatment of substance abuse effective? *Journal of the American Medical Association, 247,* 1423-1427.

McLellan, A.T., Luborsky, L., Woody, G.E., & O'Brien, C.P. (1983). Predicting response to alcohol and drug abuse treatment: Role of psychiatric severity. *Archives of General Psychiatry, 40,* 620-625.

McLellan, A.T., Woody, G.E., Luborsky L., O'Brien, C.P., & Druley, K.A. (1983). Increased effectiveness of substance abuse treatment: A prospective study of patient-treatment "matching." *Journal of Nervous and Mental Disease, 170,* 597-605.

Adelaide Version of Conners' Parent Rating Scale

Roslyn A. Glow and Peter H. Glow

Description

The Adelaide Version of the Conners' Parent Rating Scale (APRS) is a 96-item behavior rating scale of children's behavior completed by parents. The items are derived from Conners' (1973) instrument, except that negatives and American vernacular have been eliminated and three items added. Each item is rated on a 4-point frequency-severity scale (0 = no problem, 3 = severe or frequent problem). The APRS is available in Italian and Greek, and there is a draft version in Serbo-Croatian. A profile form to aid clinical use is available. The APRS is organized into 12 factorially derived scales: P1 Conduct Problem, P2 Immature-Inattentive, P3 Hyperactive-Impulsive, P4 Shy-Sensitive, P5 Self-gratification-Hostility, P6 Antisocial, P7 Sleeping Difficulties, P8 Perfectionist-Compulsive, P9 Psychosomatic Problems, P10 Feeding Problems, P11 Tearful-Dependent, and P12 Temperamental. A 13th measure, P13, is the number of nonsyndromic problems (i.e., the number of non-scale items with non-zero scores).

Purpose

The APRS is designed to assist in the assessment of children (roughly aged 5 to 13) with behavior problems, notably but not exclusively the attention deficit disorder (ADD).

Development

A stratified random sample of elementary school cohorts was selected. Parents were contacted through school and replied anonymously. Return rates (70% overall) showed some variability with school and child factors, but the sample, $N = 1919$, was representative of elementary school children from English-speaking homes. (Non-English-speaking parents had higher nonreturn rates.) Analyses of speed of response showed little effect of subject self-selection on questionnaire variables except that fast respondents rated their children as higher on P8 Perfectionist-Compulsive. Thus, subject self-selection does not bias the norms for the other scales, and the effect on P8 is small. Items were organized into scales on the basis of principal factor and item analyses.

Psychometric Characteristics

Scale reliabilities range from alpha .63 to .85 (higher for scales with most items). P13 has an alpha of .53, reflecting its miscellaneous content. Stability over a 1-year period ranged from non-significant for P6 Antisocial to $r = .68$ for P2 Immature-Inattentive, whereas P13 for nonsyndromic problems was relatively stable, $r = .71$ ($N = 155$).

Correlations between APRS ratings and peer rating on related characteristics were moderately high for observable troublesome behavior (P6 Antisocial correlated $r = .77$ with peer rating "Bully"), but low for less observable (neurotic) behavior. Absence of a 1:1 correspondence between the behavioral constructs being measured contributed to the low correlations. Correlations between APRS ratings and teacher ratings of related traits were modest. APRS ratings vary slightly with age and sex, but the size of each effect is small. Boys were rated slightly higher than girls on most of the scales of troublesome behavior. Age effects were variable across the scales. Family and data-source (school) variables accounted for little variance in ratings. Attenders in a child psychiatric facility were rated much higher than the normative group in all 13 APRS measures (Glow, Glow, & White, 1983). A group of hospital attenders in general medical and respiratory clinics were very like the normative sample except that asthmatic children, especially girls, tended to be rated higher than unselected children on P7 Sleeping Difficulties. Comparisons among children within the psychiatry facility showed that those attending only for treatment of nocturnal enuresis were more like the normative group than the psychiatric group. Psychiatry attenders with neurological disorders had high ratings on APRS variables.

Although there was reasonable agreement between APRS ratings and crude diagnostic categories (disordered/not disordered, and presence or absence of troublesome behavior disorders), agreement at finer levels of classification was negligible, due in part to unreliability of clinical diagnosis and the lack of a 1:1 correspondence between APRS categories and diagnostic conceptualization. Despite the lack of fine-grained diagnostic agreement, the APRS gives realistic prevalence estimates for major child disorders. Factorial study of psychiatric attenders ($N = 305$) replicated the first seven APRS factors and partly replicated five of the remainder. The factor solution and scale composition based on the normative study has to be preferred on the grounds of its greater representativeness and the stability of the factors found due to the large sample.

Clinical Use

The APRS is a valuable aid to clinical diagnosis in that it allows a systematic and organized appraisal of the parent's view of the child's problematic behavior. This is a contribution to clinical diagnosis and an aid to monitoring treatment efforts. Additionally, presentation of the APRS profile to the parent rater can be used by the clinician to assist the parents in clarifying their understanding of the child's behavior. This helps toward the formation of a therapeutic alliance. When the child's behavior is a focus of marital conflict, independent parent ratings on the APRS can be used to clarify areas of agreement and disagreement, whereas joint completion of the APRS is an appropriate task for some couples in marital or family therapy. Initial ratings on the APRS tend to be higher than subsequent ratings. This finding must be kept in mind when the APRS is used to monitor treatment and management efforts.

The APRS is a useful addition to description of subjects in research studies, particularly of cognitive characteristics of behavior problem or learning disabled children. Such instruments will aid the cumulativeness of data. The APRS has potential as a nonintrusive monitoring instrument for children at risk, such as those placed in foster homes or residential care situations. When used to select individuals, the APRS is best conceptualized as a measuring rater as well as a rater of child characteristics, that is, high ratings can indicate shared distress as well as objectively disordered behavior. Such rater effects are less important when the APRS is used to describe groups (e.g., research studies) than to select individuals. Algorithms for categorization of children into discrete groups have been developed to aid the use of the APRS in systematic child psychopathology and epidemiological studies. The use of the APRS as a screening device in child health settings (e.g., enuresis clinics) to select children for mental health evaluation is likely to be efficient and effective.

Future Directions

The APRS was developed to help disentangle processes whereby a child acquires the label "hyperactive" and to assist in anchoring experimental studies of the performance characteristics of children considered to be attention disordered. The use of multidimensional assessment techniques and multiple data sources is an advance in both clinical work and child psychopathology research over the use of single diagnostic classification and informal data collection from relevant observers. Research in child psychopathology will be most cumulative when it makes use of multivariate designs and the same subject descriptors in many studies. The APRS is suitable for this purpose as well as having high parent acceptance in clinical settings.

References

Conners, C.K. (1973). Rating scales for use in drug studies with children. *Psychopharmacology Bulletin: Special Issues on Pharmacotherapy of Children*, 24-84.

Glow, R.A., Glow, P.H., & White, M. (1983). *A clinical validation of the Adelaide Parent Rating Scale of Children's Behavior Problems*. Report prepared for the Department of Health, Canberra, University of Adelaide, South Australia.

Adelaide Version of Conners' Teachers Rating Scale

Roslyn A. Glow and Peter H. Glow

Description

The Adelaide Version of Conners' (1973) Teachers Rating Scale (ATRS) is a 39-item behavior rating scale in which the teacher rates the child on each behavior characteristic on the basis of frequency (0 = not at all, 3 = very much). The items are organized into seven scales for interpretation (Glow, Glow, & Rump, 1982). In addition to the individual child rating form, there is a class group form in which up to 20 children are rated on each side of a single document. A profile sheet is available to aid interpretation by a clinician. The items are the same as those in Conners' TRS, but their organization into scales differs. The scales are T1 Conduct Problem, T2 Hyperactive-Inattentive, T3 Unforthcoming-Unassertive, T4 Socially Rejected, T5 Antisocial, T6 Depressed Mood, and T7 Anxious to Please.

Purpose

The ATRS is designed to assist in the assessment of children roughly aged 5 to 13 years with behavior problems, notably but not exclusively the attention deficit disorder (ADD).

Development

A stratified sample of age cohorts within the Adelaide elementary school system was selected and each child ($N = 2475$) was rated by the homeroom teacher. The return rate was 100%. The items were organized into seven scales on the basis of principal component and item analyses.

Psychometric Characteristics

Reliabilities range from a = .58 to .91 (N = 2475), highest for the scales with most items. Teacher agreement for children with two teachers is adequate, r = .38 to .70 (from worst to best scale). However, when many teachers rate the same child, agreement declines probably because of the different educational contexts in which the children are taught by specialist teachers (e.g., teacher-librarian and physical education teacher). Stability over a 1–year period varied from nonsignificant to r = .57, but notably all students were rated by a different teacher on the second occasion. Stability over a shorter period and when the rater is constant is higher. Agreement between teacher and peer ratings of similar behavior is substantial (e.g., T2 Hyperactive-Inattentive correlated r = .93 with peer-perceived hyperactivity).

Agreement between teacher and parent ratings is modest, due at least in part to the differing contexts in which behavior is observed and the absence of a 1:1 correspondence between the behavioral constructs being measured. Therefore, T2 Hyperactive-Inattentive on the ATRS correlated as strongly (r = .30) with P1 Conduct Problem on the Adelaide Parent Rating Scale (APRS) as it did with P3 Hyperactive-Impulsive (r = .29) on the APRS, and the correlation with P2 Immature-Inattentive (r = .38) was not significantly higher (N = 256). Multifactor-Multitrait Factor Analysis showed meaningful relationships between parent (APRS) and ATRS ratings. Ratings vary as a function of child age and sex and of school background characteristics, but these factors account for only a small proportion of variance. Boys were generally more disordered, the strongest sex difference being on T2 Hyperactive-Inattentive. Generally, younger children were rated as more disordered.

Clinical Use

The ATRS is a useful part of the clinical assessment of children referred for treatment of developmental and behavioral disorders (Glow et al., 1982). It is invaluable in monitoring treatment, although it is important to note an apparent trend toward lower ratings on the second rater occasion of ATRS use. The ATRS is a very descriptive device for characterizing children used in experimental studies, notably the ADD, but also for any cognitive performances believed to be related to behavioral development. The ATRS is a potentially useful screening device for selecting children for further study, with a view towards giving extra support to classroom teachers, and may have value in resource allocation within educational systems.

Future Directions

The ATRS was developed to refine the assessment and diagnosis of children with ADD in order to carry out systematic work in experimental child psychopathology. Clinical diagnosis of ADD is as yet too unreliable to ensure the rapid accumulation of research results in which groups of disordered children are compared with nondisordered peers. The use of multivariate designs in which child performance is related to numerous child characteristics will be more fruitful than the traditional comparison of disordered with nondisordered children. The use of instruments that take a multitrait view of the child's behavior, such as the ATRS, can assist the cumulativeness of empirical efforts in child psychopathology.

References

Conners, C.K. (1973). Rating scales for use in drug studies with children. *Psychopharmacology Bulletin: Special Issue, Psychopharmacotherapy with Children*, 24-84.

Glow, R.A., Glow, P.H., & Rump, E.E. (1982). The stability of child behavior disorders: A one year test-retest study of Adelaide versions of the Conners' Teacher and Parent Rating Scales. *Journal of Abnormal Child Psychology, 10*, 33-59.

Adjusted Weight Measure for Children

Daniel S. Kirschenbaum

Description

Because children grow at a substantial rate every year, researchers in childhood obesity and other weight-related phenomena cannot report a simple weight measure when describing the results of their interventions with children over time. If a child grows several inches every year, his or her weight would naturally increase. Therefore, when intervening with obese children, the natural increase in weight that will occur even over a relatively brief period (e.g., several months) due simply to growth in height must be considered. The adjusted weight measure for children corrects for this growth factor and allows researchers to report a simple pound or kilogram measure of weight. The formula for the adjusted weight measure for children is as follows: adjusted weight equals current weight plus initial weight minus (initial weight x [100% + normal % weight gain]).

Purpose

Edwards (1978) has shown that it is necessary to adjust for children's growth (height) when reporting weight changes in treatment programs for childhood obesity. Guthrie (1975) reported that girls grow 5.8 to 7.8 cm each year from age 4 to 13. The rate of growth then decreases progressively until age 18 when they normally stop growing. Boys increase in height at a rate of 7 cm during the fourth year and then annually from 5 to 8.6 cm to age 16, with increases of 2.3 and 1 cm during the 17th and 18th years, respectively. A corresponding increase in weight for both girls and boys is associated with these increases in height. The amount of weight gained as a function of increases in height is available in tables developed by researchers and groups including Guthrie (1975).

Edwards (1978) developed the following weight index for children which takes growth rates into account: weight index equals actual weight/actual height minus normative weight/normative height; height and weight in this formula are measured in inches and pounds, respectively, and the normative data can refer to the 50th percentile for particular age cohorts (Guthrie, 1975, appendix E, pp. 499-500).

Development

Kirschenbaum, Harris, and Tomarken (1984) developed the adjusted weight measure for children so that they could report a weight measure that would be easily interpreted (paralleling the weight measure used in adult research) when they described the outcome of their behavioral treatment program for obese children. A number of methodologists (e.g., Wilson, 1978) have argued that it is helpful to include weight measures in addition to measures of percent overweight or other indices when reporting results of treatment outcome studies for obesity. Accordingly, Kirschenbaum et al. (1984) used Edwards' weight index to derive an adjusted weight measure. The problem with weight indices is that they are not readily understood by most readers. Simple weight measures (or in this case an adjusted weight measure) offers the advantage of being easily understood by any readership.

Clinical Use

Clinical use of the adjusted weight measure for children can be illustrated by describing an example from Kirschenbaum et al. (1984). The average child in their treatment study's parent plus child group at the beginning of treatment was a 10.4-year-old girl who weighed 123 pounds and was 5 ft. 7 in. tall. Relative to the girl at the 50th percentile in terms of the weight index (Edwards, 1978) this girl was 58% overweight. If a researcher or clinician wanted to know this girl's results at the end of a 1-year follow-up, an adjusted weight measure for this child would have to be calculated. Referring back to the adjusted weight measure formula, in this study the typical or average girl treated for this condition at 1-year follow-up was an 11.4-year-old girl who weighed 135 pounds. This 12-pound increase from the pretreatment weight of 123 pounds might at first look like a treatment failure. However, using the adjusted weight measure, it becomes clear that this child lost a clinically significant amount of weight (Kirschenbaum et al., 1984). The average 11.4-year-old girl would have grown approximately 3 in. from the time she was 10.4 years old, and the 50th percentile weight/height index for an 11.4-year-old girl is 1.5. Therefore, in this case, adjusted weight equals current weight (135), plus initial weight (123), minus initial weight (123), times 100% plus normal percent weight gain equals 16.4. When this formula is computed for this example, the resulting adjusted weight is 115 pounds. Therefore, although this child's actual weight was 135 pounds after treatment, it would be misleading to simply report 135 pounds as the weight. Instead, using the adjusted weight measure for children, it can be seen that 1 year after treatment her adjusted weight was 115 pounds, which compares favorably with her pretreatment weight of 123 pounds.

Psychometric Characteristics

Because this is a mathematically adjusted index derived from a biologic measure, psychometric characteristics are more straightforward than psychological indices of various kinds. However, it could be argued that both the weight index and the adjusted weight measure for children are based on a difference score. As Edwards (1978) noted, some statisticians argue that difference scores are somewhat less reliable than alternative measures. For example, a covariate-adjusted measure could use the normed score as the covariate and produce a similar measure of adjusted weight. This procedure may be somewhat more reliable, although much more cumbersome to use for most practitioners. Because practical factors are very important for many practitioners and for researchers, the potential for unreliability of this measure is not so great as to warrant the use of a much more cumbersome mathematical approach to deriving it.

Future Directions

Primary future directions for this technique are in treatment studies pertaining to weight in children. It could be applied not only to studies of obesity but also to studies of anorexia and related weight disorders in children. The benefit of using a growth- or height-adjusted measure when dealing with children's weight is such that absolute weights should no longer be used when measures are taken over time or even when measures are used at one point in time, because heights among children are so variable.

References

Edwards, K.A. (1978). An index for assessing weight change in children: Weight/height ratios. *Journal of Applied Behavior Analysis, 11,* 421-429.

Guthrie, H.A. (1975). *Introductory nutrition.* St. Louis: C.V. Mosby.

Kirschenbaum, D.S., Harris, E.S., & Tomarken, A.J. (1984). Effects of parental involvement in behavior weight loss therapy for pre-adolescence. *Behavior Therapy, 15,* 485-500.

Wilson, G.T. (1978). Methological considerations in treatment outcome research on obesity. *Journal of Consulting and Clinical Psychology, 46,* 68-702.

Adolescent Problems Inventory

W. La Vome Robinson and Leonard A. Jason

Description

The Adolescent Problems Inventory (API) is an empirically developed assessment inventory of social-behavioral skills for adolescent boys. The API may be administered as a behavioral role-playing test as well as a multiple choice inventory; each form of the API consists of 44 items. A rater's manual for each form of the API is available; item-specific responses are assigned values on a 5-point scale corresponding to explicit competence criteria. Concurrent discriminant studies support both forms of the API as valid measures of delinquency for teenage boys.

Purpose

Two forms of the API were developed to assess the social-behavioral assets and deficits of adolescent boys. Behavioral role-playing tasks assess the adolescent's skills at *generating* competent responses to problem interpersonal situations, whereas the multiple choice format of the API assesses the adolescent's skills at *recognizing* competent responses in comparable problem interpersonal situations.

Development

A theorized relationship between social-behavioral skills and interpersonal/legal difficulties (i.e., delinquency) among adolescent boys guided the development of the API. Initially identified were 90 problem situations that, if mishandled, could get a teenage boy into trouble. These situations were identified using various methods: (a) examination of the sociological and psychological literature relating the etiology of delinquency; (b) case records of institutionalized delinquents; (c) an open-ended self-report index administered to 22 institutionalized delinquent adolescent boys; (d) systematic interviews with nondelinquent adolescent boys; and (e) interviews with forensic psychologists, social workers, teachers, and youth counselors (Freedman, Rosenthal, Donahue, Schlundt, & McFall, 1978).

Following the situational analysis of problems likely encountered by adolescent boys, the problem situations were transformed into test items in the form of narrative descriptions. The item narratives were then presented to adolescent boys (12 institutionalized delinquents and 6 noninstitutionalized nondelinquents). The items were presented in individual sessions 1.5 to 2.5 hours in duration. After each item presentation, the teens were queried as to how they would handle each problem if they themselves were in the situation. In addition, veteran adult delinquency workers served as special consultants and gave what they believed to be the best solution for teenage boys in each problem situation. These procedures resulted in a range of socially competent responses to the 90 item narratives. The participants responded orally to a verbal presentation of each problem situation; their responses were recorded and later evaluated.

To evaluate the competence of the responses given by the participants for each of the item narratives, judges were employed. Using typed transcripts, each judge rated between 22 and 90 responses to test items; each test item were rated by 8 to 13 judges, with a median of 11. The responses given to each judge were randomized and the order of the test items was counterbalanced to minimize possible order effects. Four men and nine women ($N = 13$) who were either advanced undergraduate psychology majors, clinical psychology interns, or professional psychologists served as the judges; they were volunteers and naive as to the hypotheses under investigation.

Considering interjudge agreement and item difficulty, the original 90 item narratives of problem situations were subsequently abridged to 44 items, constituting the final version of the free response form of the API, a behavioral role-play test. The judges' ratings of the item narratives were also used to formulate a rater's manual for the API. The responses to the 44 items are rated on a 5-point scale of competence (i.e., very competent to very incompetent). Response examples representing a multiplicity of competence levels are included in the manual.

In brief, five successive steps were followed in developing the free response form of the API: "(a) situational analysis, (b) item development, (c) response enumeration, (d) response evaluation, and (e) construction of the inventory and rater's manual" (Freedman et al., 1978, p. 1949).

To determine whether API performance scores truly represented social/interpersonal skill competencies or whether the scores were actually influenced by the instructional set of the open-ended, free response instrument, a second form of the API was developed. The second form of the API, a multiple choice form, was developed by formulating corresponding response options for each item in accordance with the 5-point rating scale originally developed to score the free response form of the API. Forty institutionalized delinquents and 40 noninstitutionalized nondelinquents participated in the development of the multiple choice format of the API. The youths were Caucasian boys and matched within each group; they were not significantly different in age or social class standing. However, the nondelinquents did score significantly higher on the IQ measures administered to them.

Psychometric Characteristics

A series of evaluative studies for the free-response form of the API were conducted. Study 1 was a concurrent discriminant validity study that compared the social competencies of a group of institutionalized delinquent boys against two groups of teacher-nominated noninstitutionalized delinquent boys against two groups of teacher–nominated noninstitutionalized nondelinquent teenage boys, "good citizens and leaders" (Freedman et al., 1978, p. 1452). Each group consisted of 20 Caucasian boys ($N = 60$). The mean age of the teens in each group ranged from 16.4 to 16.8 years. The institutionalized delinquents and the good citizens were members of the working class. However, the social class standing of the leaders was significantly higher; the leaders mainly belonged to the upper middle class.

Using audiotaped presentations of the 44 test items, each participant was examined individually in sessions lasting 1 hour. The oral responses of the participants were recorded and later independently rated by two trained judges; the judges were naive as to the hypotheses under investigation. Interrater reliability was very high ($r = .99$).

Using total API scores, planned group comparisons indicated that the responses of the leaders were generally superior to those of the good citizens, $F(1,57) = 19.63, p < .001$. Also, the responses of the good citizens were generally superior to those of the delinquents, $F(1,57) = 217.71, p < .001$. Nonetheless, these significant F's do not reveal the API's ability to discriminate between the groups. Considering the hazards of truly identifying a population (i.e., delinquents) with a very low base rate (Meehl & Rosen, 1955), Freedman and her colleagues proposed using set base rates, solution ratios, and costs of misclassification as a means of determining the API's ability to discriminate between groups. Using these procedures, the API discriminates between delinquents and nondelinquents in a remarkable fashion.

Although factor analyses were inappropriate for this study, four hierarchical cluster-analytic techniques were performed to possibly group the test items using the similarity of the participants' competence in responding as the criterion. Generally, the clusters were not interpretable and the test items themselves were only moderately correlated. The lack of interpretability and relatedness here suggests that the API scores are highly situationally specific and are a poor measure for constructing a situational taxonomy. However, the internal consistency of the API appears high (coefficient alpha = .966).

Although IQ estimates for each participant were available, the precise relationship between participants' IQs and their API scores was impossible to determine. Regrettably, the IQ estimates for the participants were based on three different instruments, and also the question remains as to how representative the participants were of their parent groups. Nonetheless, attempts to match IQs per group and then examine API scores suggest that API scores may be influenced somewhat by IQ level, but more so the API appears to differentiate some skill above and beyond intelligence.

The purpose of the second concurrent discriminant study was to determine the API's (free response form) ability to distinguish between adolescents representing lesser extremes than those in Study 1. In particular, two groups of institutionalized delinquents were examined in Study 2; each group consisted of 15 male youths ($N = 30$). The teens were grouped on the basis of their history of disruptive behavior within the institution. In one group, the teens frequently engaged in disruptive behaviors (i.e., assault, drug or contraband possession, and running away), resulting in 25 days' stay or longer in the institution's security cottage for the preceding 6 months. The second group of teens was much less disruptive, having spent less than 5 days in the institution's security cottage for the preceding 6 months. The age of the adolescents ranged from 14 to 17 years. The social class differences for the two groups (Classes IV and V) were not statistically significant.

The examining procedure used for Study 2 was the same as that for Study 1; the two raters were 100% reliable for 93.5% of their ratings of the participants' individual responses to the 44 test items. The low-disruptive group earned significantly higher total scores on the API than did the high-disruptive group, $F(1,28) = 5.92, p <.025$. Also, the low-disruptive group scored higher on 32 of the 44 items, chi square (1) = 8.64, $p <.01$.

The multiple choice form of the API was evaluated by comparing it against the free response form of the API. Two separate ANOVAs were performed for the multiple choice items and the free response items. The ANOVAs revealed significant performance differences between the delinquents and nondelinquents: free response, $F(1,64) = 21.68, p <.001$ and multiple choice, $F(1,64) = 10.59, p <.005$. Both delinquents and nondelinquents performed better on the multiple choice items than the free response items; also, the instructional set given (i.e., would do versus best to do) appeared as inconsequential for the multiple choice form of the API but not for the free response form.

Clinical Use

The API may be used to identify, measure, and interpret social-behavioral deficiencies particular to delinquency in Caucasian boys. The precision of the assessment offered by the API favors the formulation of efficacious social skills training programs for delinquent boys.

Future Directions

Although an instrument similar in form to the free response version of the API, the Problem Inventory for Adolescent Girls (PIAG: Gaffney & McFall, 1981) was developed to measure delinquency in adolescent girls; applicability of the API is limited to social-behavioral concerns of Caucasian adolescent boys. Because of the limited samples used to date to examine the utility of the API, the relevance of the API for a broad sample of adolescents representing the various racial/ethnic groups as well as the differing socioeconomic groups remains.

The consistency shown by judges in rating and evaluating the competency of responses to the API is impressive. However, because these competency ratings have not been based on actual observed consequences to behavior, the scoring manual for the API as well as the response options for the multiple choice form of the API are somewhat suspect. A more empirical analysis of competence per se would be very worthwhile for future investigators.

Whether the role-play responses of participants in the API actually correlated with their responses in vivo has not yet been determined. This determination is critical to establishing the external validity of the API.

Theoretically and conceptually, the underpinnings used to distinguish delinquents from nondelinquents using the API might be extended to distinguish among other clinical behaviors as well (i.e., depression and substance abuse).

References

Freedman, B.J., Rosenthal, L., Donahue, C.P., Jr., Shlundt, D.G., & McFall, R.M. (1978). A social-behavioral analysis of skill deficits in delinquent and nondelinquent adolescent boys. *Journal of Consulting and Clinical Psychology, 46,* 1448-1462.

Gaffney, L.R., & McFall, R.M. (1981). A comparison of social skills in delinquent and nondelinquent adolescent girls using a behavioral role-playing inventory. *Journal of Consulting and Clinical Psychology, 49,* 959-967.

Meehl, P.E., & Rosen, A. (1955). Antecedent probability and the efficiency of psychometric signs, patterns, and cutting scores. *Psychological Bulletin, 52,* 194-216.

Adult Diagnostic Interview Schedules

Barry Edelstein, Gregory Alberts, and Sharon Estill

Description

The clinical assessment of an individual involves some form of data-gathering procedure that enables relevant information to be elicited for descriptive and diagnostic purposes. A diagnostic interview schedule is one such assessment tool that guides the clinician or researcher in questioning for information necessary for making an accurate diagnosis.

A diagnostic interview schedule is characterized by the following: (a) a list of questions, behaviors, symptoms, and/or areas of inquiry, (b) a procedure or set of rules for conducting the interview, and (c) a procedure or rules for recording or rating the interviewee's responses. These schedules may vary in a number of dimensions, one of these being the degree of structure. Highly structured schedules specify all questions and probes to be used and may include a response classification or symptom-scoring system by which to rate the client's response. A less structured interview schedule supplies statements, probes, or an outline for questioning to be used at the option of the interviewers. This less restrictive format allows the interviewer more flexibility in determining what to ask and how to phrase the questions. Schedules also vary according to the amount of clinical inference and decision making required of the interviewer. Typically, as the instrument increases in structure, the inferential role of the clinician is minimized. Further, schedules vary in the amount of clinical training required of the interviewer, ranging from schedules that may be administered by lay persons to those requiring the experienced judgment and skills of a trained clinician. Finally, schedules vary in length and time requirements, period of client history covered, and diagnostic coverage. Several diagnostic interviews were constructed to be used with a particular set of diagnostic criteria (e.g., DSM-III and Research Diagnostic Criteria). Some schedules can be used with several different diagnostic criteria.

Purpose

The primary purpose of an interview schedule is to increase the likelihood of obtaining an accurate diagnosis. The clinical utility of the instrument is related to the extent to which the selection of an effective treatment is guided by an accurate diagnosis. Several schedules are time-consuming to administer, and the relative advantages of ensuring an accurate diagnosis must be weighed against the disadvantages of the additional time that may be required in using an interview schedule. Structured interviews have been criticized as being stilted, which could interfere with either the establishment or the maintenance of rapport with the client. The efficacy of the interview schedule is ultimately tied to the use of the diagnosis (e.g., treatment outcome, evaluation, research, and sentencing by courts).

Development

The development of the diagnostic interview schedule was stimulated by the need to enhance reliability and validity in the diagnosis of psychological disorders. This was accomplished by reducing the variance inherent in the "free-flowing" format by which clinicians/researchers typically conducted diagnostic interviews. A systematic approach to gathering patient information was advocated to control for differences among clinicians' methodologies, training, and biases that contribute to low interrater agreement. Additionally, the construction of diagnostic schedules was facilitated by the development of more operationally defined diagnostic criteria and by the increasing comprehensiveness of the various classification systems. These advancements added to the concern for the valid and reliable separation diagnosis of patients.

Psychometric Characteristics

The psychiatric interview was standardized to control for the effect that differences among interviewers (e.g., theoretical orientation, style, and question content) have on the unreliability of psychiatric diagnoses. Studies that have evaluated the psychometric properties of structured interview schedules are varied. Differences in the design of these studies are typically a function of the type of reliability (e.g., interrater and test-retest) or validity (e.g., procedural and discriminant) being assessed. Design differences may include the nature of the population under study, the medium from which the data are collected, the level of training of the interviewers, or the time frame of the test-retest interval, to name a few. Data have been collected in vivo from taped interviews and from written case vignettes. Some studies have employed psychiatrists, psychologists, or lay observers, or any combination of the three to assess diagnostic concordance. The temporal stability of diagnoses has been investigated in test-retest studies of both long-interval (e.g., 1 month) and short-interval (e.g., 24 hours) designs.

The validation of structured interviews may rely on an assessment of the "fact" or content validity of the interview or, more stringently, on its ability to discriminate between different psychiatric populations. The criterion validity of the interview has been evaluated by assessing the extent to which the instrument yields results similar to those of a previously established diagnostic procedure (e.g., free-flowing interviews) that serve as the criterion or "yardstick."

An additional consideration regarding the psychometric integrity of interview schedules involves the concepts of sensitivity (rate of true-positive diagnoses) and specificity (rate of true negative diagnoses). These two values summarize the criterion validity of the diagnostic procedure and are influenced by the base rate of the particular diagnosis in the population under study. Although it cannot be argued that interview schedules, together with explicit diagnostic criteria and rigorous training of raters, have caused major advances in the magnitude of reliability in psychiatric diagnosis in the last decade, comparisons among different instruments indicate a wide range of reliability. In general, diagnostic reliability for major diagnostic categories (e.g., major depression) is greater than that for subtype diagnoses and "milder" types of pathology (e.g., hypomania). For several of the major schedules, the range of reliability coefficients in test-retest designs is .16 to 1.00. Differences in time intervals or changes in symptoms over time may contribute to this variability. Likewise, interrater reliability coefficients show a considerable range with values from .26 to 1.00 for pairs of raters on total score or diagnosis and values of .00 to .97 for individual items. Estimates of sensitivity for various schedules have ranged from 41 to 100% across diagnostic categories, whereas estimates of specificity have ranged from 75 to 100%.

Given the variety of methods and indices related to the psychometric performance of interview schedules, and considering that empirical research on diagnosis is relatively rare, valid comparisons among different interviews are difficult to make. Several instruments that have been studied are the Diagnostic Interview Schedule (DIS), Present State Examination (PSE), Schedule of Affective Disorders and Schizophrenia-Current (SADS-C), and the Renard Diagnostic Interview (RDI). (See Matarazzo, 1983, for references and a review.)

Future Directions

Although the substantial utility of diagnostic interview schedules for researchers is acknowledged, some authors question whether diagnostic interview schedules will ever be used widely by clinicians. Clinicians must operate under circumstances different from those of researchers. Time is at a premium for the clinician, and the need for an extremely accurate diagnosis may be outweighed by the need to move on to other activities. Some interview schedules are cumbersome to use and may require considerable practice before being mastered to a degree that warrants their use. The structure imposed by interview schedules may also limit the flexibility desired by interviewers for establishing and maintaining rapport with the client. Deviations from the schedule when interesting data are forthcoming may not be allowed, leading to some interviewer frustration and what some might consider a formal, stilted interview style.

Despite the possible disadvantages associated with their use, adult diagnostic interview schedules are here to stay. They emerged out of the need by clinical researchers and epidemiologists for diagnostic precision. This need will undoubtedly continue as long as two interviewers can disagree on a diagnosis.

References

Matarazzo, J. (1983). The reliability of psychiatric and psychological diagnosis. *Clinical Psychology Review, 33*, 103-145.

Adult Self-Expression Scale

John P. Galassi and Merna D. Galassi

Description

The Adult Self-Expression Scale (ASES) is a 48-item, self-report measure of assertiveness generally designed for use with adults. An initial report about the scale was published by Gay, Hollandsworth, and Galassi (1975). A sample copy of the scale with a self-scoring answer sheet may be obtained from ASES, PO Box 220174, Charlotte, NC 28222.

The scale items utilize a 5-point Likert format (0 to 4). To minimize the response set, 23 of the items require reverse scoring (e.g., 4=0 and 3=1). Scores on the 48 items are added to yield a total score for the ASES. The higher the total score, the greater the assertiveness.

The majority (39) of items include both a specific type of verbal assertive behavior and a specific interpersonal situation. That is, the items involve verbalizing one of seven types of behavior: expressing opinions, refusing unreasonable requests, taking the initiative in conversations and in dealing with others, expressing positive feelings, standing up for legitimate rights, expressing negative feelings, and asking favors in one of five interpersonal situations with authority figures, friends, parents, in intimate relationships, and in public contact with strangers, salespersons, and the like. The other nine items involve one of the seven types of assertive behaviors, but they lack a specific situational referent.

Purpose

The ASES was constructed because, at the time, no assertiveness scale that was developed and validated on an adult population and that covered a broad range of assertive behaviors and situations was available. The ASES was designed to serve three major purposes. First, it was intended for assertion training research and practice and as a dependent variable in other assertion-related research. Second, based on the total ASES score, it was seen as a broad global index and screening measure of an individual's general level of assertion skills. Finally, its individual items could be used as an efficient means of identifying assertion-deficient areas of behavior across a broad variety of interpersonal situations.

Development

The ASES was developed through doctoral dissertation research by Gay and Hollandsworth supervised by Galassi. Development was guided by a situation-specific approach to assessment. Some items were drawn or modified from the College Self-Expression Scale (CSES) to be appropriate for an adult population; others were written specifically for the ASES.

A two-dimensional (6 x 7) descriptive model of assertiveness was designed as a 2-way specification table for item development. The first dimension consisted of the five interpersonal situation types already described plus a sixth undifferentiated or global situation. The second was comprised of the seven types of verbal assertive behaviors described previously.

Psychometric Characteristics

Item Analyses. The initial item pool of 106 items consisted of all 50 original CSES items, rewritten CSES items, and other items, all of which were constructed in accordance with the criteria just specified. These items were administered to 194 community college adults aged 18 to 54 years with a mean age of 24.5. Item analyses consisted of item frequency distributions, item-total score correlations, and original versus rewritten item correlations. Based on these analyses, at least 1 item was retained in 40 of the 42 cells of the model. The final 48-item ASES includes four original CSES items, 29 items rewritten from the CSES, and 15 new items.

Reliability and Norms. Test-retest correlations of .88 and .91 were reported for 2- and 5-week intervals by Gay et al. (1975). Hollandsworth, Galassi, and Gay (1977) reported 1-week test-retest reliabilities of .81 and .87 for two samples of adult students, .89 for psychiatric inpatients, and .92 for male prisoners. Based on several studies in North Carolina (Gay et al., 1975; Hollandsworth et al., 1977), mean total scores on the ASES for normal adults typically fall in the 112 to 120 range with standard deviations of 18 to 23. Mean scores of 117, 102, and 105 have been reported for groups of male prisoners, outpatients, and psychiatric inpatients, respectively.

Validity. Validity data are available for the ASES, and complete citations for the studies to be discussed are provided by Beck and Heimberg (1983), Galassi, Galassi, and Vedder (1981), and Galassi, Galassi, and Fulkerson (1984).

In the original study, Gay et al. (1975) presented several indices of construct validity. As with the CSES, the ASES correlated appropriately with selected scales from the Gough Adjective Checklist. In addition, discriminant analysis showed that groups of low and high assertive results on the ASES were differentiated by two of three measures (manifest anxiety and self-confidence, but not locus of control).

In a subsequent study, Hollandsworth et al. (1977) used a mutitrait-multimethod validation strategy with several samples (adult students, prisoners, and psychiatric patients), three traits (dominance, abasement, and aggression), and three methods (self-report, reports by others, and criminal records). The results of this stringent evaluation of the ASES indicated moderately strong convergent validity and moderate discriminant validity.

The ASES (Gay et al., 1975; Hollandsworth et al., 1977) can detect differences between clinical populations (i.e., outpatients and psychiatric inpatients) and normal subjects. Also, more subtle differences were found between outpatients who were judged clinically to be in need of assertion training and an undifferentiated group of outpatient clients (Hollandsworth et al., 1977).

The ASES is significantly related to other measures of assertion. It correlates .79 and .85 with the CSES (Gay et al., 1975) and minus .78 with the Gambrill and Richey Assertion Inventory (Hollandsworth, 1979).

Several studies provide data about the concurrent validity of the ASES. Kirchner, Kennedy, and Draguns (1979) correlated total ASES scores and positive- and conflict-related items with three role-play measures (assertion, positive expression, and aggression) and two paper-and-pencil measures of aggression and anxiety for black and white offenders and nonoffenders. Behavioral and self-report measures of assertion were significantly correlated among white nonoffenders. The ASES showed little relationship to self-report and behavioral measures of aggression except for the Buss-Durkee Hostility scale in the black nonoffender group. Bourque and Landouceur (1979) reported significant correlations between item combinations on the ASES and behavioral measures of role-playing performance.

The ASES, in addition, has been used as an outcome measure in several treatment studies. For example, it has been sensitive to change in alcoholic addicts following assertion training (Ferrell & Galassi, 1981) and in agoraphobic persons following cognitive restructuring (Emmelkamp & Mersch, 1982).

Factor Structure. The ASES has been the subject of several factor analytic investigations including one study with American Indians (LaFramboise, 1983). The studies have shown the instrument to be multifactored, with data by Gay et al. (1975) indicating that it contains both behavior and situational factors, thereby supporting the two dimensional model from which its items were constructed.

Clinical Use

The ASES can be used in a number of ways. First, because a variety of clinical populations achieve mean scores of 1 or more standard deviations below the ASES mean, such scores suggest that a more thorough assessment of a client's assertion skills may be in order. Second, all but nine of the items contain both behavior and situational components. As a result, an inspection of the ASES items for those on which low scores (especially scores of 0 and 1) have been obtained can readily indicate the types of behaviors and/or situations for which assertion skills are problematic for a client. In addition to screening for global and specific assertion deficits, the ASES can be used to monitor change and maintenance. Depending on the focus of treatment, the clinician may track changes in total score or in scores of clusters of items or factors over time.

Future Directions

Although experimentation on the ASES is no longer being conducted by its originators, literature about the instrument continues to accumulate. As is true for many other self-report assertion scales, collection of data about correspondence with actual behavioral indices of assertion, both in the laboratory and in vivo, will probably be of increasing importance in the future.

References

Beck, J.G., & Heimberg, R.G. (1983). Self-report assessment of assertive behavior. *Behavior Modification, 7,* 451-487. Bourque, P., & Landouceur, R. (1979). Self-report and behavioral measures in the assessment of assertive behavior. *Journal of Behavior Therapy and Experimental Psychiatry, 10,* 287–292.

Emmelkamp, P.M.G., & Mersch, P.P. (1982). Cognition and exposure in vivo in the treatment of agoraphobia: Short-term and delayed effects. *Cognitive Therapy and Research, 6,* chl 77-88.

Ferrell, W.L., & Galassi, J.P. (1981). Assertion training and human relations training in the treatment of chronic alcoholics. *The International Journal of the Addictions, 16,* 957–966.

Galassi, J.P., Galassi, M.D., & Fulkerson, K. (1984). Assertion training in theory and practice: An update. In C.M. Franks (Ed.), *New developments in practical behavior therapy: From research to clinical application* (pp. 319-376). New York: Haworth Press.

Galassi, J.P., Galassi, M.D., & Vedder, M.J. (1981). Perspective on assertion as a social skills model. In J.D. Wine & M.D. Smye (Eds.), *Social competence* (pp. 287-345). New York: Guilford Press.

Gay, M.L., Hollandsworth, J.G., Jr., & Galassi, J.P. (1975). An assertive inventory for adults. *Journal of Counseling Psychology, 22,* 340-344.

Hollandsworth, J.G., Jr., Galassi, J.P., & Gay, M.L. (1977). The Adult Self–Expression Scale: Validation by the mulitrait-multimethod procedure. *Journal of Clinical Psychology, 33,* 407–415.

Hollandsworth, J.G., Jr. (1979). Self–report assessment of social fear, discomfort, and assertive behavior. *Psychological Reports, 44,* 1230.

Kirchner, E.P., Kennedy, R.E., & Draguns, J.G. (1979). Assertion and aggression in adult offenders. *Behavior Therapy, 10,* 452–571.

LaFramboise, T. (1983). Validity of the Adult Self-Expression Scale with American Indians. *Educational and Psychological Measurement, 43,* 547–555.

Agoraphobic Cognitions Questionnaire

Dianne L. Chambless

Description

The Agoraphobic Cognitions Questionnaire (ACQ: Chambless, Caputo, Bright, & Gallagher, 1984) is a 14-item self-report questionnaire in which clients are asked to rate on a scale of 1 (never occurs) to 5 (always occurs) how frequently each thought occurs when they are anxious. The items all reflect catastrophic thinking about the consequences of anxiety and load on one of two factors, accounting for 46% of the variance: physical consequences (e.g., "I'm going to have a heart attack") or social/behavioral consequences (e.g., "I will not be able to control myself"). The ACQ has been translated into French (Canadian) and Dutch.

Purpose

The ACQ along with its companion measure, the Body Sensations Questionnaire (BSQ), was devised to assess "fear of fear" (Goldstein & Chambless, 1978) among persons with agoraphobia. Agoraphobics' fear of panic is supported by numerous maladaptive thoughts about what will happen to the victim of an attack. The ACQ, as a self-report instrument, is an easily administered, inexpensive measure of this aspect of agoraphobia for use in clinical work as well as research. While phrased to inquire about general thought patterns, it may be altered to request information about a client's thoughts during a specific session for use in process research.

Development

The ACQ items were developed on the basis of clients' reports about their concerns in interviews, in vivo exposure sessions, and imaginal flooding sessions. Validational studies were carried out on a sample of 175 outpatients with a diagnosis of agoraphobia with panic attacks, 194 clients with other neurotic disorders, and 23 normal control subjects. The initial version of the ACQ had nine items; after subsequent additions and deletions, the final scale contains 14 items averaged to yield a total scale score. The initial and final versions are highly correlated (Spearman rho = .96).

Psychometric Characteristics

The 14-item scale is somewhat positively skewed with a mean of 2.32 (SD = 0.07). Correlations with the BSQ of .34 and .67 have been obtained.

Reliability. The ACQ is internally consistent (alpha = .80) and is reliable over time (median 31-day test-retest r = .75; 8-day r = .86).

Validity. The ACQ was stable over the pretreatment reliability period, showing neither a significant decline nor a significant increase, but the decrease was significant with in vivo exposure plus cognitive coping strategies. Therefore, the scale is sensitive to changes with treatment. Validity was assessed further in two ways, First, the scale's relationships with measures of psychopathology predicted to correlate with fear of fear were examined. The ACQ, as hypothesized, correlated positively with depression, trait anxiety, neuroticism, avoidance behavior, and panic frequency, but not to the extent that it seemed to duplicate these other measures. It was significantly related to a theoretically unrelated measure of psychopathology (the psychoticism scale of the Eysenck Personality Questionnaire), indicating that the ACQ does not reflect a simple tendency to report greater psychological problems. Scores were not affected by age or socioeconomic status. Second, the ACQ's ability to discriminate agoraphobic clients from a normal control group and from other clinical samples was examined (Chambless et al., 1984; Chambless, 1985). The ACQ significantly discriminated agoraphobic from normal persons, depressed persons, and clients with other anxiety disorders (obsessive-compulsive disorder, generalized anxiety disorder, and social phobia). Items concerning physical consequences more consistently discriminated than did those reflecting social/behavioral concerns. Clients receiving a diagnosis of panic disorder had similar scores, suggesting that fear of fear is high in clients who have or have had frequent panic attacks, but not as prevalent in those with other anxiety problems.

Clinical Use

The ACQ is useful before intake to elicit important concerns which are then discussed during the interview. Assessment of maladaptive cognitions provides a good opportunity for education about the actual effects of anxiety (e.g., that one will not "go crazy" as the result of a panic attack). Such education is critical in obtaining the client's compliance with an in vivo exposure program. Additionally, the scale facilitates discussion of the role of cognitions in creating and maintaining anxiety. It may be periodically readministered during treatment to check for progress; change on cognitions typically lags somewhat behind change on avoidance.

Future Directions

The ACQ is less cumbersome and more reliable than other cognitive measures used with agoraphobic clients, such as tape-recording thoughts that clients are requested to repeat aloud during in vivo assessments. Nonetheless, in vivo assessment has considerable face validity, and it would be desirable to assess the relationship of the ACQ with such measures.

References

Chambless, D.L. (1985). Specificity of fear of fear among neurotic clients. Manuscript submitted for publication.

Chambless, D.L., Caputo, G.C., Bright, P., & Gallagher, R. (1984). Assessment of fear of fear in agoraphobics: The Body Sensations Questionnaire and the Agoraphobic Cognitions Questionnaire. *Journal of Consulting and Clinical Psychology, 52,* 1090-1097.

Goldstein, A.J., & Chambless, D.L. (1978). A reanalysis of agoraphobia. *Behavior Therapy, 9,* 47-59.

AlcEval

Robert S. Davidson

Description

The AlcEval is a clinical and research instrument of 110 items designed to assist in the evaluation of alcohol drinking problems. Multiple choice, scaled, and fill-in items assess demographic, social, family, religious, and leisure areas, drinking history, current drinking rate and pattern, antecedents and consequences of drinking, psychological and vocational adjustment areas, as well as motivation for treatment. Forty-one continuous and 33 discontinuous items are available for statistical research study as well as clinical application. Continuous items have been phrased to enable statistical analysis by parametric tests such as the Pearson product-moment correlation coefficient and analysis of variance. Continuous items include formats such as, "What is your age?," "How often do you go out socially (for example, to dinner or to the movies) in an average month?," and "How much do you like your work? (on a scale of 0 to 100)."

Discontinuous items are yes/no, multiple choice, or fill-in items. Examples of each are: "Is your goal to stop drinking completely?" (yes/no), "How do you usually drink? (at home, at work, on the street, in the car, in bars, in other places [where?])," "What has been your occupation during most of your adult life?," and "List below up to 10 reasons why you drink (from most to least important)." Discontinuous items are most often analyzed by nonparametric statistics such as chi square or point biserial.

Purpose

The purpose of the AlcEval is to provide reliable and valid information on persons with alcohol drinking problems or to rule out such problems.

Because of the range of information elicited, a completed AlcEval is as useful in treatment planning as it is in research or diagnostic evaluation. The AlcEval lends itself particularly well to broad-range therapy, because it taps motivational, social, religious, family birth order, and vocational areas in addition to strictly behavioral assessment. The latter is done through self-report of specific behaviors such as drinking alone versus drinking with others, where and when drinking occurs, discontinuous (binge) versus continuous drinking, controlled versus uncontrollable drinking, consequences of drinking (e.g., blackouts, hangovers, delirium tremens, days of work lost, and jobs lost), type of alcohol consumed, motivation to drink (relaxation, depression, and getting high), and motivation to quit drinking alcohol. Names and addresses of three corroborative witnesses and permission to contact witnesses are requested. Cooperative witnesses can supply independent objective verification or disconfirmation of patient report data or both.

Development

The AlcEval has grown out of a 15-year data-based program of experimental assessment and treatment of alcoholic patients. Treatment has been primarily behavioral, including relaxation, assertion training, covert sensitization, biofeedback, aversive and exercise training, multiple risk factor reduction, and multimodal combinations of the foregoing.

The AlcEval has been revised as research from our own and other programs has suggested variables that were important predictors of differential response to treatment, noncompliance, and/or dropping out before completion of the treatment program. The current version of the AlcEval (copyright 1980) is the fourth revision based on empirical data and clinical judgment. The number of items has grown from 56 in the first version to 110 in the current revision.

Psychometric Characteristics

An early study (Davidson & Stein, 1982) established the reliability of 15 of the 35 continuous items in the first (56-item) version of the AlcEval. Pearson product-moment correlation coefficients on each of the items were studied in 50 male volunteer chronic alcoholic patients enrolled in the behavioral treatment program. The questionnaire was administered by a psychologist or social worker

7 to 10 days after admission to the hospital (after any necessary detoxification) and then repeated an average of 7 days later.

Correlations greater than .90 were found in self-reported age, number of children, years of education, number of siblings, birth order, drinking to relax, and age at first intoxication. Correlations greater than .80 were found in reported father's heavy drinking, duration of last job, average number of days of continued drinking, previous delirium tremens, number of times a lawyer had been seen, reported age at first drink, and number of years drinking had been a problem.

Inter-item correlations were generally low and not significant, suggesting that these items were measuring different areas. Three item pairs that reached highly significant correlations (all above .50) made logical sense. They were correlations between: age at first drink and age at first intoxication (.678), age and the number of years drinking had been a problem (.518), and birth order and the reported number of siblings (.735). The magnitude of the latter indicates that these patients tended to be last born. This supports previous reports that alcoholic addicts may be interpersonally dependent within the family structure before developing dependence on alcohol.

In a later study, the discriminant validity of the AlcEval items was studied by comparing matched groups of 20 alcoholic patients, social drinkers, and teetotalers (Davidson, 1985). The subjects were matched empirically by age, education, marital status, months of employment on last job, months unemployed, income, size of family, and number of persons currently living together. The groups were not significantly different in any of these variables. However, all three groups differed significantly in the number of consecutive days they reported going without a drink as well as the number of consecutive days they continued drinking once begun, the number of days they missed work because of drinking, the number of reported hangovers, the number of ounces of beer consumed per day, the number of times help was sought, the age at first drink, the number of years drinking had been a problem, and the number of years the person reported being an alcoholic addict.

Most of these differences occurred between the pooled nondrinkers and social drinkers compared with the alcoholic addicts. In many of these cases (as in days of missed work because of drinking, days of consecutive drinking, number of hangovers, number of years of alcoholism, and number of years of reported drinking problems), the teetotalers and social drinkers responded alike with zero or near-zero responses. Differences among all three groups were found in days without drinking, days of continuous drinking, number of beers per day, and age at first intoxication.

These two studies together support the reliability and validity of the AlcEval. Current studies are replicating these findings on larger and different groups undergoing treatment. A follow-up version of the AlcEval has also been developed to measure differences between the initial AlcEval responses and those due to treatment.

Clinical Use

The AlcEval was designed to be a research-based instrument for use with alcoholic patients in treatment. Most recently, it is being used in a computer-based patient tracking system which stores the data and can rapidly locate patients according to the following keys: name, case number, social security number, geographical location (address), date tested, and tests administered. This information has been of great value in designing treatment tailored to the individual. For example, it suggests a different type of treatment for an older alcoholic addict who has an intact social and family life, job, and the like than for a younger person who has lost all the same as a result of drinking.

In one study, data from the AlcEval were used to predict attrition (Davidson & Baker, 1985). The data were used in a discriminant function analysis of the differences between 48 alcoholic patients who completed versus 48 who dropped out before completion of a behavioral treatment program for alcoholism. The following 13 AlcEval variables accounted for 40% of the variance between the two groups and correctly classified 80% of the patients (variance accounted for by each variable alone in parentheses): age (9%), number of previous hospitalizations (4.9%), preference for hard liquor (4%), binging versus daily drinking patterns (3.8%), number of persons living with patient (3.1%), drinking helps to relax (2.7%), number of court convictions for drunk and disorderly conduct (2.6%), reporting employment at time of admission (1.8%), drinking mostly in bars (1.8%), age at first intoxication (1.4%), drinking alone (1.3%), reporting prior job(s) lost because of drinking (1.3%), and reporting that the mother died before the patient was 16 years of age (1%).

Most of these variables, with the exception of the last, have been predictive of attrition in previous studies. The alcoholic addict most likely to complete treatment based on this study is an older patient who drinks primarily hard liquor in a binge-drinking, periodic pattern, who says drinking is mainly to relax and mainly in bars, who lives with a number of persons, who may drink alone, who was employed on admission, and who has not lost a job because of drinking or been hospitalized previously for drinking problems.

In future treatment programs, patients may be selected on the basis of such variables. Such screening may produce patients who show better prospects of remaining in a treament program to its completion, thus increasing the cost effectiveness as well as the efficacy of the program.

Future Directions

One new direction will be to include the AlcEval in a battery of psychological tests specifically tailored for treatment planning with alcoholic patients. Such a battery now being used in our laboratory includes the Minnesota Multiphasic Personality Inventory (MMPI), the Millon Clinical Multiaxial Inventory (MCMI), the Shipley Institute of Living Scale, the AlcEval, and the Goal Assessment Profile (GAP). The MCMI is of special value because it often supplements or complements the MMPI, and it has specific drug and alcohol abuse scales. The Shipley is a screening test of intelligence. The GAP, a new multiscale test under development in our laboratory, will measure skill development (or deficits) in 24 important areas including relaxation, assertiveness, social skills, physical fitness, family relations, emotional self-control, rational thinking, cognitive self-control, flexibility, systematic problem solving, self-assessment, values and philosophy, working through past problems, money management, time management, behavioral self-control, motivation and attitude, persistence, goal setting, causes and antecedents of alcoholism, control and prevention of alcoholism, treatment of alcoholism, motivation to drink and to quit, and motivation for treatment.

The next step will be to program the entire test battery so that it may be administered entirely by an on-line computer. The AlcEval has been programmed in branching logic to run over an extended BASIC and disk-operating system (DOS), both by North Star (Bremser & Davidson, 1978). It is anticipated that this entire battery will take an average of 3 to 4 hours for administration once completed and programmed. The challenge for the future will be to make maximal use of all the information generated by this superbattery in the design of individually tailored therapy packages based on the specific needs, strengths, weaknesses, and skill deficits indicated by the tests.

The next logical step after tailoring treatment to individuals based on empirical test data will be to repeat the test battery (or some parts of it) after treatment to evaluate the effectiveness of the program. Once reliable and valid criteria of successful treatment outcome are determined, the AlcEval and other tests may be used in studies to determine the predictability of treatment outcome from initial measures. One such initial attempt has been encouraging (McMahon & Davidson, 1985).

References

Bremser, R.F., & Davidson, R.S. (1978). Microprocessor-assisted assessment in the clinical laboratory. *Behavior Research Methods and Instrumentation, 10,* 582-584.

Davidson, R.S., & Stein, S. (1982). Reliability of self-report of alcoholics. *Behavior Modification, 6,* 107-109.

Davidson, R.S. (1985). Self-reported differences between chronic alcoholics, social drinkers, and teetotalers (non-drinkers). Unpublished manuscript.

Davidson, R.S., & Baker, M.P. (1985). Prediction of attrition from an inpatient behavioral treatment program for alcoholism. Unpublished manuscript.

McMahon, R.C., & Davidson, R.S. (1985). Personality characteristics, symptom patterns, and treatment outcomes for heavy daily drinkers versus binge drinkers. Unpublished manuscript.

Alcohol Beliefs Scale

Gerard J. Connors and Stephen A. Maisto

Description

The Alcohol Beliefs Scale (ABS) is a two-part, 48-item questionnaire used to collect dose-related data on drinkers' expectancies regarding alcohol's effects and usefulness. On Part A (26 items) of the scale, subjects indicate the extent to which three different amounts of alcohol (one to three standard drinks, four to six standard drinks, and "when drunk") increase or decrease behaviors and feelings, such as judgment, problem solving, depression, aggression, stress, and group interaction. A standard drink is defined as 1 ounce of 90-proof liquor or its equivalent of beer or wine. The ratings are made on an 11-point scale ranging from

−5 (strong decrease in the behavior or feeling) to 5 (strong increase in the behavior or feeling); a rating of zero is used to indicate no change in the behavior or feeling. Four domains of effects have been derived from the items contained on Part A of the questionnaire: control issues, sensations, capability issues, and social issues. On Part B (22 items) of the scale, drinkers rate how useful the consumption of each of the three doses of alcohol would be for a variety of reasons (e.g., to relax, to become more popular, to become uninhibited, to relieve depression, and to forget worries). These estimates are made on an 11-point scale ranging from "not at all useful" to "very useful." The factors derived from Part B have been labeled as: useful in feeling better, useful for being in charge, and useful for alleviating aversive states.

Purpose

Clinical researchers have been focusing increasingly on the role of cognitive factors in decisions to drink and in drinkers' responses to alcohol. One such cognitive factor is the expectancy regarding alcohol's effects (Donovan & Marlatt, 1980; Maisto, Connors, & Sachs, 1981). The construct *expectancy* generally refers to cognitive representations of an individual's past direct or indirect experiences with alcohol. These representations are hypothesized to determine anticipated outcomes in using alcohol.

Because not all individuals have the same experiences with alcohol, the specification of an individual's beliefs and expectations about alcohol's effects becomes a critical factor in understanding the drinking behavior. This information also may be helpful in developing treatment strategies designed to alter or modify the alcohol abusers' alcohol expectations and to substitute more adaptive or realistic cognitions and behaviors. The ABS was developed to help identify these expectancies by assessing (a) the expectancies about the effects of alcohol on different feelings and behaviors, (b) the usefulness of drinking for different reasons or desired outcomes, and (c) how expectancies vary with the amount of alcohol.

Development

The ABS was developed by Connors, Maisto, and Watson (1982). The items comprising the scale were generated through two main sources. The first and primary source was previous research, especially survey studies, which provided information on alcohol effects and reasons for drinking. The second source involved the perceptions provided by the authors' patients, many of whom presented with problems in their use of alcohol.

Clinical Use

The ABS is primarily used generally to assess the domains and strengths of a drinker's expectations regarding the use of alcohol. In addition, information is generated on how these expectancies vary as a function of different amounts of alcohol. Information on the alcohol abuser's general and dose-specific expectancies helps to evaluate those beliefs that most strongly mediate decisions to drink and responses to alcohol. This type of assessment also may assist in developing more individualized treatment approaches and permits more efficient tailoring of treatment options to client needs.

Psychometric Characteristics

Psychometric evaluation of the ABS has been conducted by Connors, O'Farrell, Cutter, and Logan (1984), who administered the ABS to 260 alcoholic addicts, 79 problem drinkers, and 81 nonproblem drinkers. Separate factor analyses on Parts A and B were performed on subjects' ratings for each dose. These analyses yielded four factors common to each dose level on Part A and three factors in common on Part B. The factors derived from Part A (and associated questionnaire items) were *control issues* (feeling in control of a situation, judgment, feeling powerful, and problem solving); *sensations* (depression, light-headedness, nonsocial anxiety, and head spinning); *capability issues* (ability to drive a car, decision making, stress, estimating time, thinking clearly, and reaction speed); and *social issues* (interacting in groups, courage, and elation). The three factors derived on Part B of the ABS were as follows: *useful in feeling better* (feel more control, be more sociable, get in a better mood, feel happy, and become uninhibited); *useful for being in charge* (increase courage, attract attention, increase the effects of other drugs, and be aggressive); and *useful for alleviating aversive states* (relieve depression, forget worries, and escape stress).

Subsequent analyses were performed to assess differences in subjects' factor scores as a function of drinker type (alcoholic addict, problem drinker, and nonproblem drinker) and dose (one to three

standard drinks, four to six standard drinks and "when drunk"). Results showed that on Part A factors, subjects expected themselves to be in less control and less capable "when drunk" than after consuming one to three or four to six standard drinks. On the social issues factor, the greatest positive endorsement was attributed to the moderate (four to six standard drinks) dose. Group effects generally showed that the nonproblem drinkers expected greater impairment on the control issues and capability issues factors than did the problem drinkers, who in turn reported more impairment than did the alcoholic subjects.

Analyses on Part B of the scale, which pertained to the expected usefulness of different amounts of alcohol, yielded significant interactions between the drinker population and dose. On the useful in feeling better factor, alcoholic addicts scored higher in endorsing this expected effect at each dose; in addition, all subjects rated the four to six standard drinks dose higher than the "when drunk" dose, which in turn was rated higher than the one to three standard drinks dose. On the factor labeled useful for being in charge, endorsements were positively correlated with dose. Further, the nonproblem drinkers scored significantly lower than the problem drinkers and alcoholic addicts, who did not differ. Finally, on the factor of useful for alleviating aversive states, alcoholic addicts on each dose scored higher than problem drinkers, who in turn scored higher than the nonproblem drinkers. The ratings provided by each drinker population also were positively correlated with dose.

In summary, these data suggest that the ABS effectively discriminates between nonproblem drinkers, problem drinkers, and alcoholic populations, and provides information on the strength and domains of expectancies attributed to different amounts of alcohol.

Future Directions

Efforts to assess alcohol expectancies and to apply such information to clinical practice are in an early stage of development. Additional work is needed in scale development and assessment of alcohol expectancies among a wider range of alcohol consumers. Longitudinal research also should focus on the development of expectations regarding alcohol's effects. Additional research is needed to demonstrate the relation between expectations and decisions to drink, to assess the concordance between these expected effects and those actually experienced, and to determine the relationship between alcohol expectancies and treatment outcome.

References

Connors, G.J., Maisto, S.A., & Watson, D. (1982). *The Alcohol Beliefs Scale*. Unpublished data.

Connors, G.J., O'Farrell, T.J., Cutter, H.S.G., & Logan, D. (1984). *Beliefs regarding alcohol effects: Dose-related data from three populations of drinkers*. Paper presented at the annual meeting of the Association for Advancement of Behavior Therapy, Philadelphia, PA.

Donovan, D.M., & Marlatt, G.A. (1980). Assessment of expectancies and behaviors associated with alcohol consumption: A cognitive-behavioral approach. *Journal of Studies on Alcohol, 41*, 1153-1185.

Maisto, S.A., Connors, G.J., & Sachs, P.R. (1981). Expectation as a mediator in alcohol intoxication: A reference level model. *Cognitive Therapy and Research, 5*, 1-18.

Analogue Communications Assessment

Kathy Sexton-Radek and Stephen N. Haynes

Description

The Analogue Communication Assessment (ACA) is a procedure for the observation of couples' verbal communication behaviors: (a) a sociometric structure for the communication sample, (b) instructions to couples, (c) a method of selecting discussion topics, and (d) behavioral sampling and observation methods. Couples are instructed to sit in a comfortable chair several feet from each other at a 90-degree angle in a room (clinic or home) that is free from distraction. After the rationale is provided (to help the assessor identify the positive and negative aspects of the couples' communication methods), a topic is selected based on the highest mean dissatisfaction rating on items from a marital satisfaction questionnaire (e.g., handling money, expressing affection). Couples are instructed to discuss the topic "as you would at home" and to continue until told to stop (they are stopped after 10 minutes). The interactions are recorded on video- or audiotape and later scored by trained observers. Observers record the occurrence or nonoccurrence of each of six behaviors in the coding system every 15 seconds. The codes are categorized as positive (agree, approve, and humor) and negative (disagree, complain, and interrupt), although a larger number of codes (e.g., eye contact, command) have also been used (Haynes, Chavez, & Samuel, 1984; Haynes, Jensen, Wise, & Sherman, 1981).

Purpose

The purpose of the ACA is to efficiently measure marital interaction in a problem-solving context, utilizing an analogue situation that is conducive to valid and reliable behavioral measurement. This assessment method is designed primarily to measure verbal communication behaviors for research purposes. Because of the time required for scoring and the limited number of behaviors scored, it is less useful for nonresearch clinical situations.

Development

The specific behaviors targeted in this assessment procedure were extracted from the Marital Interaction Coding System (Hops, Wills, Weiss, & Patterson, 1972) on the basis of previous studies demonstrating their discriminant or other criterion-related validity. Specific instructions and other variables (position of spouses, duration of sample, and method of selecting topics) were based on the results of several pilot studies.

Psychometric Characteristics

The ACA has shown satisfactory criterion-related validity (Haynes, Follingstad, & Sullivan, 1979; Haynes et al., 1981, 1984). The Locke-Wallace Marital Adjustment Scale scores were significantly related to eye contact, $r(25) = -.36, p < .07$, criticism, $r(25) = -.43, p < .05$, and disagreement, $r(25) = -.53, p < .01$. Stuart's overall marital satisfaction score was related to eye contact, $r(25) = -.47, p < .01$, interruption, $r(25) = -.58, p < .01$, disagreement, $r(25) = -.48, p < .01$, agreement, $r(25) = .43, p < .05$, and criticism, $r(25) = -.55, p < .01$. Negative behaviors were significantly correlated with (N = 380) the Dyadic Adjustment Scale ($r = -.16, p < .01$), the Spouse Verbal Problems Checklist ($r = .14, p < .05$), and the Communication Satisfaction Questionnaire ($r = .15, p < .05$). The correlation between these scales and positive behaviors only approximated statistical significance ($p < .07$). Interobserver agreement, from random samples, following 16 hours of training never fell below .80 for 175 samples.

Clinical Use

The formal application of the procedures just outlined is time-consuming and consequently useful primarily for research applications. However, informal and qualitative observation of marital interaction in the situation described can provide a rich source of hypotheses concerning the communication patterns of married clients.

References

Haynes, S.N., Chavez, R.E., & Samuel, V. (1984). Assessment of marital communication and distress. *Behavioral Assessment, 6,* 315-321.

Haynes, S.N., Follingstad, D.R., & Sullivan, J.C. (1979). Assessment of marital satisfaction and interaction. *Journal of Consulting and Clinical Psychology, 47,* 789-791.

Haynes, S.N., Jensen, B.J., Wise, E., & Sherman, D. (1981). The Marital Intake Interview: A multimethod criterion validity assessment. *Journal of Consulting and Clinical Psychology, 49,* 379-387.

Hops, H., Willis, T., Weiss, R., & Patterson, G.R. (1972). *Marital interaction coding system (MICS).* Unpublished manuscript. University of Oregon and Oregon Research Institute.

Anger Expression Scale

Charles D. Spielberger

Description

In assessing anger, it is important to distinguish between the experience and the expression of angry feelings. The Anger Expression (AX) Scale is a 24-item, self-report psychometric inventory with three subscales for assessing individual differences in the expression, suppression, and control of anger. The AX Scale yields four different scores. The Anger Expression (AX/EX) score is based on all 24 items and provides a general index of the frequency with which anger is expressed irrespective of the direction of expression. The three AX subscales assess individual differences in tendencies to: (a) express anger toward other people or objects in the environment (AX/Out); (b) experience but hold in (suppress) angry feelings (AX/In); and (c) control the experience and expression of anger (AX/Con). In responding to each AX scale item ("I argue with others"), subjects rate themselves on the following 4-point *frequency* scale: (a) almost never; (b) sometimes; (c) often; and (d) almost always.

Purpose

The AX Scale was designed to assess individual differences in the degree to which angry feelings are directly expressed in behavior, inhibited, or controlled. Anger-out refers to the tendency to express angry feelings overtly and directly in behavior ("I say nasty things"). Anger-in refers to individual differences in how often feelings of anger are experienced but held in or suppressed ("I boil inside, but don't show it"). People also differ in the extent to which they endeavor to control angry feelings ("I calm down faster than most other people") and to control the expression of anger ("I keep my cool").

Development

In assessing individual differences in the expression of anger as a personality trait, we originally intended to develop a unidimensional, bipolar scale, with anger-in and anger-out as opposite poles of this dimension. A pool of items was assembled in accordance with the working definitions of anger-expression just described. This preliminary version of the AX Scale was administered during regular class periods to 1,114 high school students (634 males, 480 females) enrolled in health science courses (Johnson, 1984; Spielberger et al., 1985).

Factor analyses of the items in the preliminary AX Scale suggested that the anger-in and anger-out items were tapping two relatively independent underlying dimensions. This finding was clearly reflected in the simple structure of the factor analyses for both males and females, in which most items had strong loadings on either the anger-in or anger-out factor, with negligible loadings on the other. Given the clarity and strength of the anger–in and anger–out factors, the striking similarity (invariance) of these factors in separate analyses for males and females, and the large heterogeneous samples on which these analyses were based, the test construction strategy was subsequently modified to develop two distinct scales for measuring anger-in and anger-out as independent dimensions.

In further analyses to identify homogeneous subsets of items to comprise the anger–in and anger–out subscales, items with small loadings (below .35) on both factors for either males or females were eliminated, reducing the total items in the final version of the AX Scale to 20. On the basis of the results of separate factor analyses of these items for males and females, items with uniformly high loadings on the same factor for both sexes and negligible loadings on the second factor were selected for the 8-item anger–in and anger–out subscales.

Three items ("Control my temper," "Keep my cool," and "Calm down faster than others") had moderate negative loadings on *both* the anger–in and the anger–out factors; the content of these items appeared to be related to the control of anger or resistance to becoming angry or both, which logically cuts across both modes of anger expression. In research with college students, additional evidence of an "anger control" factor has emerged (Pollans, 1983). With the three items as a nucleus, additional anger control items were written, and factor analyses of these items identified a strong anger control factor. Items with the highest loadings on this factor and the largest item-remainder correlations were selected for the 8-item experimental AX/Con subscale.

Psychometric Characteristics

Normative data are available for the AX Scale for high school and college students and working adults. The internal consistency of the 8-item AX/In, AX/Out, and AC/Con subscales is surprisingly high as reflected in the item-remainder correlations and alpha coefficients for the normative samples. The alphas ranged from .72 to .89 and were somewhat higher for older subjects (college students and working adults).

Evidence of the convergent and divergent validity of the AX and its subscales may be found in correlations with other anger and personality measures. The AX/Out subscale is moderately correlated with T-Anger and the T-Angry/Temperament subscale of the *State-Trait Personality Inventory* (Spielberger, Jacobs, Russell, & Crane, 1983), suggesting that persons who experience more anger are more likely to express it toward other persons and objects in the environment. The AX/Out and AX/In subscales both correlate positively with the STPI T-Angry/Reaction subscale, suggesting that persons who often experience angry reactions seem equally likely to express or suppress their anger. Small positive correlations of the AX/In and Ax/Out subscales with the STPI T-Anxiety Scale suggest that anxiety inhibits the expression of anger in persons with high AX/In scores, and is associated with apprehension about anticipated retaliation in persons high in anger-out. Essentially zero correlations of the AX Scales with the STPI Curiosity Scales provides evidence of divergent validity.

Clinical Use

A major goal in constructing the AX Scale was to develop a measure that could be used to investigate the role of anger expression in the origin of hypertension and coronary heart disease. Research has shown that high school students with high Anger/Out scores have lower blood pressure, and those with high AX/In scores have higher blood pressure than students with low to average scores (Johnson, 1984). Moreover, black students have higher AX/In scores and higher blood pressure than Caucasian students (Johnson, 1984), and hypertensive patients have significantly higher AX/In scores and lower AX/Out scores than do patients with normal blood pressure (Hartfield, 1985). There is also suggestive evidence that Type A coronary-prone persons who develop heart disease are high in both the expression and suppression of anger.

The AX Scale is currently being used in patients with chronic pain and other psychosomatic and behavioral disorders, and in assessing persons incarcerated in prison for various offenses. Because the scale provides information on individual differences in the extent to which people express anger directly in behavior, suppress anger, and/or withdraw from situations that provoke it, and attempt to control anger when it is experienced, it should prove useful to counselors and psychotherapists who work with a variety of patients. The AX Scale may also be used as an outcome measure in counseling, psychotherapy, and behavioral treatment research.

Future Directions

Counselors and psychotherapists should find the AX Scale useful in diagnosing and evaluating patient progress in psychotherapy. Given the observed empirical relationships between the AX Scale, elevated blood pressure, hypertension, and coronary heart disease, the scale can be used to identify persons at risk for heart disease for preventive programs and as an outcome measure in evaluating therapeutic intervention studies. The AX Scale may also be used in evaluating participants in stress management workshops in terms of how they express anger as compared with others.

References

Hartfield, M.T. (1985). *Appraisals of anger situations and subsequent coping responses in hypertensive and normotensive adults: A comparison.* Unpublished doctoral dissertation, University of California, San Francisco.

Johnson, E.H. (1984). *Anger and anxiety as determinants of blood pressure in black and caucasian adolescents.* Unpublished doctoral dissertation, University of South Florida, Tampa.

Pollans, C.H. (1983). *Convergent and divergent validity of the Anger Expression Scale.* Unpublished master's thesis, University of South Florida, Tampa.

Spielberger, C.D., Jacobs, G.A., Russell, S.F., & Crane, R. (1983). Assessment of anger: The State-Trait Anger Scale. In J.N. Butcher & C.D. Spielberger (Eds.), *Advances in personality assessment* (Vol. 2). Hillsdale, NJ: Lawrence Erlbaum Associates.

Spielberger, C.D., Johnson, E.H., Russell, S.F., Crane, R.S., Jacobs, G.A., & Worden, T.J. (1985). The experience and expression of anger. In M.A. Chesney & R.H. Rosenman (Eds.), *Anger and hostility in behavioral medicine.* New York: Hemisphere/McGraw-Hill.

Antidepressive Activity Questionnaire

Vicky Rippere

Description

The Antidepressive Activity Questionnaire (AAQ) is an empirically derived 100-item rating schedule for antidepressive behavior (Rippere, 1974, 1976). Respondents are asked to circle the numbers of any items on the list that describe their own usual antidepressive activity and are invited to add any personally relevant activities not included on the list. They then rate each designated item on two 3-point qualitative scales to indicate how often they use the method and how helpful they usually find it. The scale points for frequency are "rarely," "sometimes," and "quite often," and those for helpfulness are "not very," "moderately," and "very" helpful.

The items include both everyday methods of dealing with feeling depressed, such as seeing or talking to a friend, going for a walk, distracting oneself, or keeping busy, and various forms of professional help-seeking, (e.g., seeing a therapist and taking prescribed drugs). There are also items pertaining to self care, particular forms of distraction and busyness, and general strategies of self-management ("Avoid things I know will make me feel worse") and self-presentation ("Try to act as if I

weren't feeling depressed"). Cognitive ("Try to get my situation into perspective") as well as behavioral stances are represented.

The 5-page questionnaire is self-administering, but it may also be given as a semi-structured interview. Its intended purpose is to describe rather than to evaluate behavior. The instrument yields three measures and a qualitative list of self-help behaviors. The measures are: (a) the number of items circled and added (ni), (b) the number of items rated (moderately and very) helpful (nh); and (c) the percentage of items rated helpful (%h).

Purpose

The AAQ was originally devised as a research instrument for comparing the antidepressive behavior of depressed and nondepressed psychiatric patients and normal subjects in a systematic and descriptive manner (Rippere, 1974, 1976). Subsequently, it has been used to compare the antidepressive activities of other groups of patients (Jackson, 1978), and it may also be used clinically to assess and treat individual cases.

Development

Most items in the AAQ resulted from a pilot study in which 50 English-speaking normal subjects were asked, "What's the thing to do when you're feeling depressed?," and their responses were content analyzed and frequency counted (Rippere, 1977). The most frequently mentioned items were included in the questionnaire. To these were added several more items concerning the different types of therapist a patient might conceivably find it helpful to see.

Because the AAQ is intended as a descriptive rather than a classificatory device, elaborate development, such as item analysis, was not undertaken. There is no à priori reason why items should differentiate depressed from other patients or from normal subjects, so there is no reason for items that do not differentiate between these groups to be eliminated from such a measure. Factor analysis also was not done because people engage in behaviors and activities rather than in factors.

The present form of the instrument is not, however, intended to be definitive. If the item content were empirically derived in the manner described or in some other sensible manner, other investigators would be perfectly justified in devising alternative versions with locally relevant content. Other versions might be more appropriate for use with, for example, elderly or handicapped clients or members of other social classes or ethnic groups.

Psychometric Characteristics

Retest reliability for items at an interval of 7 to 10 days was determined with a sample of 16 normal subjects (8 men, 8 women; mean age of men, 24.6 years, of women, 23.5 years). Acceptable agreement was found for the measure under these conditions (r men = + .77, p <.05; r women = + .95, p <.01, combined r = + .89, p <.01). The reliability of the frequency and helpfulness ratings is still to be determined for normal subjects and both of these and item reliability for other groups.

Validation of the measure, such as it is, has been against the self-report of subjects in the original comparative study. All subjects, whether normal subjects or patients, circled at least six items. Very few additional items were written in the space provided. From these findings it was concluded that the list of items in the questionnaire probably does describe the antidepressive activities of persons in the groups sampled. All items were circled by at least one respondent.

The mean number of items circled in the validation study was 32 (SD 18), the mean number rated helpful was 22 (SD 14), and the mean percentage rated helpful was 72 (SD 22).

Clinical Use

The main clinical use of the AAQ to date has been to structure discussions with patients about their own antidepressive activities and to gather systematic information about the content, range, and helpfulness of their antidepressive repertoire, when this information is considered to be worth knowing. Because depression is such a common symptom among psychiatric patients, they need not be clinically depressed for the approach to be possibly relevant. If patients are clinically depressed, it is best to undertake an evaluation after biological treatment has had some effect. The procedure is not recommended for patients who are either acutely psychotic or in extreme states of depressive agitation or stupor, but for those who recover some degree of insight and psychomotor normality, it may have a place in their management.

There is no established procedure for the clinical use of data derived from this assessment. In using the information clinically, however, it is essential to avoid the pitfall of assuming that if some antidepressive behavior is good, more of the same must necessarily be better. Patients should not be encouraged to do more of what they find helpful. Some repertoires, such as having a good cry, having a drink, crawling away on one's own, and wallowing in one's feelings of depression, if increased too greatly in frequency, might render the patient less rather than more able to cope.

In some cases, the list of activities generated by the questionnaire has provided a useful basis for a self-monitoring schedule designed to increase feelings of self-efficacy and to reduce helplessness ("I'm not doing anything about the state I'm in, I'm doing something constructive to make myself feel better, and there is actually something I can do about the way I feel").

In other cases, patients have complained that this procedure interferes with their efforts to be spontaneous and is not particularly helpful. The way the information is used needs to be negotiated with the patient.

Future Directions

Future work with the original AAQ or with locally relevant variants might usefully compare and contrast the antidepressive behavior of different groups of patients. In particular, the approach might clarify the differences between a normal depressed mood and clinical depression either between or, perhaps even more interestingly, within individuals studied longitudinally over an extended period. Spontaneous comments by depressed patients suggest that some individuals distinguish their own different states of depression according to the degree of effectiveness of their antidepressive activities. If they cannot distract or cheer themselves up, they know it is time to see their doctor.

Developmental aspects of antidepressive behavior might also be fruitful to study, although versions of the AAQ suitable for younger children and adolescents would need to be developed for this research to be possible. In this context, it would be especially interesting to consider the respective roles of trial and error, didactic teaching, and informal social or observational learning in the development of young people's antidepressive repertoires.

References

Jackson, M. (1978). *Locus of control, antidepressive behavior and epileptic handicap*. M. Phil. thesis; University of London.

Rippere, V. (1974). *Antidepressive behavior*. M. Phil thesis; University of London.

Rippere, V. (1976). Antidepressive behavior: A preliminary report. *Behaviour Research and Therapy, 14,* 289-299.

Rippere, V. (1977). "What's the thing to do when you're feeling depressed?": A pilot study. *Behaviour Research and Therapy, 15,* 185-191.

Anxiety Disorders Interview Schedule-Revised

Janet S. Klosko, Peter A. Di Nardo, and David H. Barlow

Description

The Anxiety Disorders Interview Schedule-Revised (ADIS-R; Di Nardo et al., 1985) is a structured interview designed to provide differential diagnosis among anxiety disorders according to DSM-III and DSM-III-R criteria. The interview protocol, which is organized around the DSM-III anxiety disorder categories, includes criteria for anxiety and affective disorders and screening questions for psychosis, substance abuse, and somatoform disorders.

The organization of the ADIS-R permits an integrated interview. Suggested phrasing of questions appears in bold italic print. To assist the interviewer, the ADIS-R provides brief descriptions of DSM-III and DSM-III-R criteria. Several sections begin with a general screening question which the patient answers with a "yes" or "no." A negative response permits the interviewer to skip the section dealing with that disorder. Rows of stars set apart skip instructions from the text of the interview.

The ADIS-R provides detailed symptom ratings, particularly of symptoms of panic and generalized anxiety, and of phobic avoidance and interference in functioning. The interview includes the Hamilton Anxiety Scale (Hamilton, 1959) and the Hamilton Depression Scale (Hamilton, 1960). The scales are presented adjacent to one another so that items similar in content can be rated at the same time. The interviewer may choose to omit the Hamilton scales, because the interview itself provides sufficient information to establish diagnostic criteria and make differential diagnoses.

Purpose

The primary purpose of the ADIS-R is to provide diagnoses of DSM-III and DSM-III-R anxiety disorders, to assess for affective disorders, and to screen for psychosis, substance abuse, and somatoform disorders. The ADIS-R permits the interviewer to arrive at primary and additional diagnoses and to rate the severity of all diagnoses. In addition, the ADIS-R assesses situational and cognitive factors that influence anxiety, and provides information for functional analyses of anxiety disorders. Because depression is commonly part of the clinical picture in anxiety disorders, several questions assess the relation between anxiety and depressive symptoms. Finally, it includes several questions on psychiatric and psychological history and demographic variables.

As a research instrument, the ADIS has been used to collect data that address issues in diagnosing anxiety disorders (Cerny, Himadi, & Barlow, in press) including multiple anxiety disorders and other Axis I disorders (Barlow, Di Nardo, Vermilyea, Vermilyea, & Blanchard, in press), and the phenomenon of panic across DSM-III anxiety disorders (Barlow, Vermilyea, Blanchard, Vermilyea, Di Nardo, & Cerny, 1985). The Hamilton scales permit thorough assessment of symptoms of anxiety and depression and yield scores that can be used to compare populations within and across clinical settings.

Development

Both the ADIS and the ADIS-R were developed over a period of years by staff of the Phobia and Anxiety Disorders Clinic, Albany, New York. The clinic is funded by the National Institute of Mental Health to study the classification and treatment of anxiety disorders. The content, wording, and sequence of questions evolved over 3 years of experience interviewing clinic patients and diagnosing them using DSM-III and, more recently, DSM-III-R criteria.

Psychometric Characteristics

Initial studies indicate good reliability for DSM-III diagnoses with the ADIS (Di Nardo, O'Brien, Barlow, Waddell, & Blanchard, 1983). Within anxiety disorders, reliability tests of the ADIS in 125 subjects using Kappa coefficients were conducted for agoraphobia with panic attacks ($Kappa = .845, N = 41$), social phobia ($Kappa = .905, N = 19$), simple phobia (*Kappa* = .558, *N* = 7), panic disorder (*Kappa* = .651, *N* = 17), generalized anxiety disorder (*Kappa* = .571, *N* = 12), and obsessive compulsive disorder (*Kappa* = .825, *N* = 6) (Barlow, 1984).

Clinical Use

The ADIS-R is to be used as a clinical interview rather than a symptom checklist. A number of questions require elaboration by the patient, and clinical judgment is required to evaluate these responses. An instruction manual explains the administration, scoring, and diagnostic procedures. Skilled interviewers average 2 hours to complete the ADIS-R, including the Hamilton scales.

The ADIS-R primarily is designed for detailed examination of the anxiety disorder and assessment of depressive symptoms. Although it includes screening questions for other disorders, it is not intended to be a general diagnostic interview for use in outpatient clinics or in broad-based research efforts covering all DSM-III disorders. Other structured interviews are now available that cover a wider range of disorders, although they provide considerably less detail concerning anxiety disorders.

Future Directions

Studies currently are in progress to determine the reliability of DSM-III-R anxiety categories using the ADIS-R.

References

Barlow, D.H. (1984). The dimensions of anxiety disorders. In A.H. Tuma & J.D. Maser (Eds.), *Anxiety and the anxiety disorders*. Hillsdale, NJ: Lawrence Erlbaum Associates.

Barlow, D.H., Di Nardo, P.A., Vermilyea, B.B., Vermilyea, J., & Blanchard, E.B. (in press). Co-morbidity and depression among the anxiety disorders: Issues in diagnosis and classification. *Journal of Nervous and Mental Disease*.

Barlow, D.H., Vermilyea, J., Blanchard, E.B., Vermilyea, B.B., Di Nardo, P.A., & Cerny, J.A. (1985). The phenomenon of panic. *Journal of Abnormal Psychology*.

Cerny, J.A., Himadi, W.G., & Barlow, D.H. (in press). Issues in diagnosing anxiety disorders. *Journal of Behavioral Assessment*.

Di Nardo, P.A., Barlow, D.H., Cerny, J.A., Vermilyea, B.B., Vermilyea, J.A., Himadi, W.G., & Waddell, M.T. (1985). *Anxiety Disorders Interview Schedule-Revised (ADIS-R)*. Albany, NY: Center for Stress and Anxiety Disorders.

Di Nardo, P.A., O'Brien, G.T., Barlow, D.H., Waddell, M.T., & Blanchard, E.B. (1983). Reliability of DSM-III anxiety disorder categories using a new structured interview. *Archives of General Psychiatry, 40*, 1070-1078.

Hamilton, M. (1959). The assessment of anxiety states by rating. *British Journal of Medical Psychology, 32*, 50-55.

Hamilton, M. (1960). A rating scale for depression. *Journal of Neurology, Neurosurgery, and Psychiatry, 23*, 56-62.

Assertion Inventory

Eileen Gambrill and Cheryl Richey

Description

The Assertion Inventory (AI) is a 40-item, self-report questionnaire (Gambrill & Richey, 1975). For each item, the respondent indicates: (a) the degree of discomfort on a 5-point scale ranging from 1 (none) to 5 (very much); (b) the probability of displaying the behavior if presented with the situation on a 5-point scale ranging from 1 (always do it) to 5 (never do it); and (c) the situations in which the respondent would like to be more assertive. Selected demographic information is collected at the end.

Purpose

The purpose of the AI is to provide an overview of discomfort and response probability in a variety of social situations. Additional information can be gathered from clients or subjects concerning specific situations in which high discomfort or a low likelihood of responding, or both, is reported.

The distinction between discomfort and behavior is important because different combinations of these two factors may require different interventions. For example, a person might experience high discomfort but engage in appropriate social behavior dispite this, or such discomfort may result in response inhibition and avoidance of related situations. If, despite high discomfort, behaviors are followed by positive consequences, it is likely that the repertoire of appropriate behavior exists. If, however, assertion does not occur, behavior, affective, or cognitive surfeits or deficits may exist. An individual may have inaccurate perceptions of goals that can be effectively pursued in specific social situations or inaccurately assess social risks. Examining both discomfort and response probability and how they interact permits a description of possible inter-group differences, such as males versus females and treatment versus nontreatment populations.

Development

A list of potential items was derived from a variety of sources, including reports from students and clients, as well as a review of the literature to determine frequently occurring assertion difficulties. The 40 items included fell into the following categories: (a) turning down requests; (b) expressing personal limitations such as admitting ignorance in some areas; (c) initiating social contacts; (d) expressing positive feelings; (e) handling criticism; (f) differing with others; (g) asserting oneself in service situations; and (h) giving negative feedback. Because it was recognized that behavior may vary according to the relationship between the persons involved, that is, whether they are strangers, acquaintances, or intimates, and this dimension was built into many of the items. However, to keep questionnaire completion within realistic time boundaries (the AI takes about 20 minutes to complete), the degree of specificity was limited.

Psychometric Characteristics

Total discomfort and probability scores are computed by adding responses in each dimension. Difference scores can be determined by subtracting discomfort from response probability. Normative data collected from 608 undergraduates at the University of California at Berkeley, aged 18 to 27 years (M = 22 years), yielded an overall mean discomfort score of 93.92 (SD = 20.93), a response probability score of 103.80 (SD = 16.18), and a mean difference score of 10.05 (SD = 18.69). Four profiles, created by using normative mean scores to generate high and low discomfort and response probability values, include "assertive," "unassertive," "anxious performer," and "doesn't care."

Stability of the AI was assessed by having a sample of 49 University of Washington students complete the measure at two different times 5 weeks apart. Pearson correlations between test periods were .87 for discomfort and .81 for response probability, indicating high stability of scores over time. The modest correlation of .47 between response probability and discomfort (Furnham & Henderson, 1984) supports the assumption that many persons may act assertively despite feeling uncomfortable.

Factor analysis of the discomfort scores for the 1983 California sample of 313 persons generated 11 factors accounting for 61% of the variance. Each factor accounted for 3.9 to 7%. The emergence of relatively equally weighted factors supports the situational specificity of social behavior. Factors included: (a) initiating interactions; (b) confronting others; (c) giving negative feedback; (d) responding to criticism; (e) turning down requests; (f) handling service situations; (g) resisting pressure to alter one's consciousness; (h) engaging in "happy talk"; (i) complimenting others; (j) admitting personal deficiencies; and (k) handling a bothersome situation.

Additional validity is provided by comparing clinical and normative samples. For example, before training, a mean discomfort score of 109.9 (SD 19.20) for 68 women aged 22 to 58 years (M 32.5 years), was significantly higher than the mean discomfort score for the nonclinical sample, t (742) = 5.37, p <.001. Similarly, the average pretraining response probability score of 110.73 (SD 19.45) for the clinical group was significantly higher than the average nonclinical score, indicating a lower response probability, t (742) = 3.11, p <.001. The clinical group also decreased significantly in both discomfort (M 86.57, SD 21.68) and response probability (M 91.08, SD 22.12) following training, t (134) = 5.40, p <001. Further validation of the AI is required, especially in view of evidence that responses on the AI may be confounded with social desirability (McNamara & Delamater, 1984).

Clinical Use

The AI can be used to screen for high social discomfort and low response probability in clinically relevant situations. The treatment implications for respondents reporting high discomfort and low response probability may be different than those for respondents reporting high discomfort and a high response probability (anxious performers). In the latter case, self-critical thoughts or worries about negative social evaluation may cue arousal, which disrupts an otherwise adequate behavioral performance. Helping people to alter their thoughts might be more useful than concentrating on specific verbal skills and nonverbal components of effective social behavior. In the former, greater emphasis on developing and refining specific verbal and nonverbal skills may be necessary to correct behavior deficits. More information is needed on individuals who report very low social anxiety as well as low response probability. Clinical observations indicate that persons who have a "don't care" profile may feel "burnt out," depressed, or "helpless," may not believe that assertive responding is socially correct or polite, or may control their arousal levels by avoiding stressful situations. One limitation of the AI is in identifying individuals who respond aggressively. Although highly speculative, clinical observations suggest that such persons may score as "super-assertive" on the AI, with very low anxiety and probability scores.

The AI can provide one source of feedback on progress in training programs designed to enhance effective social behavior. Gains would be expected only on items related to the focus of intervention. Gains on nonrelated items would not necessarily be expected given the lack of generalization found among different types of social behavior. However, the AI could be used to check for maintenance of treatment gains over time and generalization of skills to nontreatment situations.

Responses on the AI do not necessarily reflect behavior in real-life situations. Some studies (Furnham & Henderson, 1981) have not found a correlation between behavioral measures and self-reported discomfort and response probability. This finding may be due to the inappropriate expectation that intervention aimed at one kind of social behavior should have generalized effects on others and the possibility that high discomfort may not correspond to a low response probability (some people are "anxious performers").

Future Directions

Greater use of scores on the 11 factors revealed by factor analysis offers more refined information than do overall discomfort or response probability scores and discourages a "trait" approach to social behavior. For example, significant differences on two factor scores for discomfort were found in a comparison of college students with and those without a visible physical disability (Gambrill, Florian, & Splaver, 1985). Students with disabilities reported less discomfort in situations involving initiating interactions and turning down requests. Other studies have explored gender differences in relation to specific situations. For instance, Furnham and Henderson (1984) report that British women have greater difficulty with negative behavior (giving and receiving criticism), whereas British men have difficulty with positive behavior (giving and receiving compliments).

Exploration of the relationship between the degree of social discomfort and the likelihood of response and other variables such as self-esteem and attribution would be valuable. One recent study found significant correlations between greater discomfort and lower the likelihood of assertive response and higher self-reported loneliness and lower perceived control over the quality of social life (Gambrill, Florian, & Splaver, 1985).

Further research is also needed to determine the conditions under which scores on the AI are indeed predictive of behavior in real-life situations. Finally, additional normative data are needed to aid the assessment of other groups of individuals, for example, the elderly, adolescents, and ethnic minority populations.

References

Furnham, A., & Henderson, M. (1981). Sex differences in self-reported assertiveness. British Journal of Clinical Psychology, 20, 227-238.

Furnham, A., & Henderson, M. (1984). Assessing assertiveness: A content and correlational analysis of five assertiveness inventories. Behavioral Assessment, 6, 550-561.

Gambrill, E.D., & Richey, C.A. (1975). An assertion inventory for use in assessment and research. Behavior Therapy, 6, 550-561.

Gambrill, E., Florian, V., & Splaver, G. (1985). Assertion, loneliness and perceived control among students with and without physical disabilities. Submitted to Rehabilitation Counseling Bulletin.

McNamara, J.R., & Delamater, R.J. (1984). The Assertion Inventory: Its relationship to social desirability and sensitivity to rejection. Psychological Reports, 55, 719-724.

Assertion Self-Statement Test-Revised

Richard G. Heimberg

Description

The Assertion Self-Statement Test-Revised (ASST-R) is a 24-item questionnaire that measures the frequency of self-statements related to assertive behavior. Items (self-statements) are phrased in a general way so as to be relevant to a variety of assertive behavior situations. Twelve items describe positive self-statements (i.e., a self-statement that may facilitate assertive self-expression), whereas the remainder describe negative self-statements (i.e., a self-statement that may hinder or inhibit assertive self-expression). The subject rates the frequency with which each self-statement occurred to him or her during an immediately preceding behavioral role-play test. Ratings vary from 1 (hardly ever) to 5 (very often) and may be summed to provide separate scores for the frequency of positive and negative self-statements (range 12 to 60).

Purpose

The ASST-R was developed by Heimberg, Chiauzzi, Becker, and Madrazo-Peterson (1983) to assess the typical pattern of self-statements among assertive and unassertive psychiatric patients, normal adults, and college students. It is an offspring of the Assertion Self-Statement Test originally developed by Schwartz and Gottman (1976). However, that device was judged inappropriate for our purposes, as it is geared specifically to the assessment of self-statements about the refusal of unreasonable requests in a collegiate environment. It was necessary to devise a similar instrument which cast generalized self-statements so that each statement would be relevant to a variety of assertive behavioral situations.

Development

Schwartz and Gottman's questionnaire provided the item pool for the development of the ASST-R. Each item was recast in more general terms. For example, the item, "I was thinking that I would get embarrassed if I refused," became "I was thinking that I would become embarrassed if I let my feelings be known." The list of 32 new statements was then submitted to two panels of student evaluators (nine doctoral students participating in the author's seminar on social skills training and nine advanced undergraduate students who served on the author's research team and were familiar with research on assertive behavior). Self-statements were retained if, and only if, eight students from each panel independently and correctly categorized them as positive or negative. Eight items failed this test, leaving 12 positive and 12 negative self-statements on the final version of the ASST-R.

Psychometric Characteristics

Heimberg et al. (1983) reported the results of the ASST-R in samples of psychiatric patients, normal adults, and college students. Before administration of the ASST-R, each subject role-played 24 situations derived from the Behavioral Assertiveness Test-Revised (Eisler, Hersen, Miller, & Blanchard, 1975) and completed the Revised Wolpe-Lazarus

Assertiveness Schedule (Hersen et al., 1979). Subjects were assigned to assertive and unassertive groups on the basis of their Wolpe-Lazarus test scores.

Assertive versus Unassertive Subjects. Unassertive subjects reported significantly more frequent negative self-statements during the role-played situations than did assertive subjects. Positive self-statement scores of the two groups did not differ.

Patients, Adults, and Students. Patients reported significantly more negative self-statements than did subjects in the other two groups. They also reported fewer positive self-statements than did the college students. Patients were the only group whose mean negative self-statement score exceeded their mean positive self-statement score.

Clinical Use

The ASST-R has not yet been systematically utilized in a clinical setting. However, the finding that it discriminates between assertive and unassertive subjects drawn from three distinct population groups (including a sample of patients diagnosed as schizophrenic or depressed) suggests that it may be a useful clinical tool for (a) identifying self-statements that may inhibit or interfere with the expression of assertive behavior so that they may be targeted during training, and (b) measuring the change in cognitive style that may result from cognitive-behavioral assertion training. It may be useful in any group of patients who experience generalized difficulties with assertive behavior.

Future Directions

Although available data support the validity of the ASST-R, much remains to be done in the area of psychometric development. Administration of the ASST-R to larger homogeneous samples of patients or clients will allow for the determination of scale reliability, internal consistency, and the like, for the development of meaningful normative data, and for the conduct of factor analytic studies. As these data are collected, the ASST-R may be used to answer questions about the relationship of self-statements, affect, and assertive behavior. It will be important to assess how positive and negative self-statements relate to performance in various assertive behavior situations, whether these relationships are specific to certain diagnostic groups, or whether they change as external contingencies for assertive behavior vary.

References

Eisler, R.M., Hersen, M., Miller, P.M., & Blanchard, E.B. (1975). Situational determinants of assertive behavior. *Journal of Consulting and Clinical Psychology, 43*, 330-340.

Heimberg, R.G., Chiauzzi, E.J., Becker, R.E., & Madrazo-Peterson, R. (1983). Cognitive mediation of assertive behavior: An analysis of the self-statement patterns of college students, psychiatric patients, and normal adults. *Cognitive Therapy and Research, 7*, 455-464.

Hersen, M., Bellack, A.S., Turner, S.M., Williams, M.T., Harper, K., & Watts, J.G. (1979). Psychometric properties of the Wolpe-Lazarus Assertiveness Scale. *Behaviour Research and Therapy, 17*, 63-69.

Schwartz, R.M., & Gottman, J.M. (1976). Toward a task analysis of assertive behavior. *Journal of Consulting and Clinical Psychology, 44*, 910-920.

Assertion Situations

Cynthia Gallois and L. Keithia Wilson

Description

Assertion situations consist of a series of video-taped vignettes illustrating positive and negative assertive messages with close and distant referents. An audiotape version of the videotapes has also been prepared. The assertion situations are based on the factor structure of a paper-and-pencil measure, the Difficulty in Assertion Inventory, developed by Leah, Law, and Snyder (1978). This factor structure, subsequently confirmed by Firth and Snyder (1979), identifies two referent classes (close and distant) and two response classes (positive and negative). Close referents include friends, spouse or date, and parents. Distant referents include strangers along with persons in authority and persons in a business or service role. Positive assertive responses include initiating interactions, expressing agreement and positive feelings, and asking favors (in general, behaviors that strengthen a relationship). Negative assertive responses include expression of criticism, disagreement and negative feelings, as well as refusing requests (behaviors that risk weakening a relationship).

Each vignette contains a short voice-over narrative passage that sets the scene, followed by an assertive message delivered by a sender to a receiver. A full list of situations can be obtained from the first author. In addition, filler items have been prepared which use the same narration and words as the target vignettes, but the message is accompanied by aggressive or submissive nonverbal behavior.

We currently have compiled a set of videotaped vignettes using two basic formats. In one format, the narrator identifies both sender and receiver and their relationship (e.g., "a customer and a shop assistant"), and the sender speaks to a person whose back is visible to the camera. Both male and female senders and receivers are used. In this case, listeners react as observers. In the second format, the narrator refers to the listener as "you," and the message is delivered directly to the camera. Listeners react to the tape as if they were the receivers. Alternative narration casts the sender as a close referent (e.g., "a good friend of yours") or as a distant referent (e.g., "a student whom you don't know"). Audiotaped versions of each format can easily be dubbed.

By dubbing the vignettes, tapes can mix positive and negative messages or close and distant referents or keep them separate. Wilson and Gallois (1985) found that positive and negative messages produce a dramatically different impact on the listener, which can overwhelm other effects; therefore, it is probably advisable to keep these response classes separate. Normally, the tapes are dubbed so that about 30% of the vignettes are fillers. Subjects evaluate each vignette using a 6-point rating scale on assertiveness, social appropriateness, attractiveness, and so forth, or write down their reaction to the messages.

Purpose

Recent research indicates that assertiveness is not a unitary response domain. Rather, clients often report difficulties with some, but not all, assertion situations. In addition, the impact of assertive responses on receivers and observers varies depending on the type of assertion and the social context. The set of situations described here is intended to provide a comprehensive measure of the impact of assertive messages.

The advantage of videotaped vignettes over paper-and-pencil measures is that the vignettes provide a more lifelike and immediate message. In addition, videotaped messages allow realistic scripting of voice quality and other nonverbal behaviors. When videotapes seem inappropriate (because, for example, of the type of referent being studied; see Lewis & Gallois, 1984), audiotapes provide a reasonable intermediate medium.

Development

The first set of vignettes we developed dealt with positive and negative assertive messages from distant referents, in which subjects reacted as observers (Wilson & Gallois, 1985). The assertive messages and situations were initially drawn from the literature (including especially Leah et al., 1978) to obtain a systematic representation of response classes and referents. Narration, messages, and scripts for nonverbal behavior (including voice quality) were evaluated by two groups: assertion trainers and psychologists specializing in the study of nonverbal communication. These raters evaluated the scripts on assertiveness, aggressiveness-submissiveness, realism, and naturalness, as well as giving specific suggestions for improvement. Revised scripts were then rated by groups of male and female undergraduate students using four scales already mentioned. The final scripts were all rated as clearly assertive, realistic, and natural.

Several male and female actors recorded each vignette. All of the actors, aged 20 to 35 years, were experienced in the theater, in assertion training, or in both. All scripts were carefully rehearsed before taping, and several recordings were made of each vignette. Actors were casually dressed and were placed in full view of the camera in front of a neutral background; the camera framed the top half of the sender's body and the receiver's back. The narrator was not visible on camera.

The second set of vignettes (Lewis & Gallois, 1984) involved audiotapes of negative assertive situations with close and distant referents. The third set (Harris, 1984) used videotapes of positive and negative messages with distant referents. Subjects reacted as receivers in all of these situations. Procedures for pilot-testing the scripts and selecting the actors were the same as those for the first set of situations. After taping and selecting the final scripts, master tapes were prepared for all these sets of situations, from which dubbing can now be done.

Psychometric Characteristics

The assertion situations are intended mainly as a research instrument to measure the impact of different assertive messages delivered by senders in same-sex and mixed-sex interactions who vary in relationship to the subject. As a result, we have neither developed norms for the situations nor conducted studies of reliability and validity.

The pilot research described, however, showed that the scripts were perceived by both assertion trainers and naive raters as natural and assertive. In addition, studies using the vignettes found clear differences in the reactions of receivers and observers to positive and negative messages (Harris, 1984; Wilson & Gallois, 1985) as well as to different message types within each response class, such as refusing a request or expressing negative feelings (Harris, 1984; Lewis & Gallois, 1984). In addition, negative messages from friends were evaluated differently from messages from strangers (Lewis & Gallois, 1984). Sex of the sender, receiver, and observer interacted in determining an evaluation of the messages (Harris, 1984; Lewis & Gallois, 1984; Wilson & Gallois, 1985). Finally, early results suggest some differences in the impact of the messages as a function of the subject's locus of control and difficulty in assertion (Harris, 1984), although these effects are weaker than those mentioned earlier.

Clinical Use

Although primarily for the researcher, this instrument has a number of training applications. First, the situations can be used to assess specific deficits in clients in assertion training programs, because the vignettes are based directly on the domain tapped by the Difficulty in Assertion Inventory (Leah et al., 1979) as well as by other assertion inventories. The assertion situations, in conjunction with the filler items, can be used to test a trainee's ability to discriminate between assertive, aggressive, and submissive behaviors, a major problem for many clients. Both verbal and nonverbal components of messages and the extent to which they are congruent can be explored. The assertive situations can also be used to elicit a trainee's judgment of the appropriateness of assertive behaviors in mixed-sex and same-sex interactions. This information can provide useful discussion material about a trainee's perceptions of sex role-appropriate behavior. Finally, these situations can be used as a stimulus to explore a trainee's expectations or self-statements about the positive or negative consequences of assertiveness.

Future Directions

The vignettes represent situations common to young middle-class Australians, and they were pilot-tested with that group. Nonetheless, the methodology makes it relatively easy to extend the situations to other cultures, ages, or classes. The situations can also be extended to examine reactions to empathic or nonempathic assertion or to vary the nonverbal components of the message. In summary, these assertion situations provide a flexible and systematic way of examining the many relationship and situational aspects of assertive messages in either a research or a clinical context.

References

Firth, P.M., & Snyder, C.W. (1979). Three-mode factor analysis of self-reported difficulty in assertiveness. *Australian Journal of Psychology, 31,* 125-135.

Harris, B. (1984). Perceptions of positive and negative assertion: The influence of gender, sex-role orientation, and locus of control. Unpublished bachelor of arts (Hons) thesis, University of Queensland, Australia.

Leah, J.A., Law, H.G., & Snyder, C.W. (1978). The structure of self-reported difficulty in assertiveness: An application of three-mode common factor analysis. *Multivariate Behavioral Research, 14,* 443-462.

Lewis, P.N., & Gallois, C. (1984). Disagreements, refusals, or negative feelings: Perception of negatively assertive messages from friends and strangers. *Behavior Therapy, 15,* 353-368.

Wilson, L.K., & Gallois, C. (1985). Perceptions of assertive behavior: Sex combination, role appropriateness, and message type. *Sex Roles, 12,* 125-141.

Assertiveness Self-Statement Test

Robert M. Schwartz

Description

The Assertiveness Self-Statement Test (ASST) is a self-report inventory consisting of 16 positive (PSSs) and 16 negative (NSSs) self-statements relevant to the refusal of unreasonable requests. The positive-negative dichotomy was conceptualized by Schwartz and Gottman (1976) in terms of the *functional impact* of cognitions on coping with a situationally specific threat. The PPSs are defined as statements that *facilitate* or "make it easier to refuse" the request (e.g., "I am perfectly free to say no" and "This request is an unreasonable one"), and NSSs are those that *interfere* or "make it harder to refuse" (e.g., "I was worried what the other person would think about me if I refused" and "The other person might be hurt or insulted if I refused").

After responding to refusal situations, individuals are asked to indicate on a scale of 1 (hardly ever) to 5 (very often) how frequently these SSs

characterized their thoughts, yielding separate maximum scores of 80 for the PSS and NSS scales. An additional item assesses which of four *sequences* characterized their thought processes: (a) coping (+ −): at first negative and later positive; (b) unshaken doubt (− −): at first negative and later negative; (c) unshaken confidence (+ +); (d) giving up (+ −): at first positive and later negative. The inventory takes between 5 and 10 minutes to complete.

Purpose

The ASST is an objective measure of the frequencies of PSSs and NSSs for empirical investigations of the role of cognition in assertion-related problems. To avoid potential problems in assessing covert processes, cognition was operationalized as "self-statements" or statements to oneself; the inventory was designed to be situationally specific rather than global; and responses were obtained while cognitions were active in short-term memory to minimize distortion and postperformance rationalization. The ASST was designed to investigate group differences in PSSs and NSSs between functional and dysfunctional groups and to measure cognitive change in response to psychotherapy with nonassertive persons.

Development

As part of a "task analysis" of assertive behavior (Schwartz & Gottman, 1976), the ASST was developed to assess the cognitive component of nonassertiveness, the specific focus being problematic situations involving unreasonable requests. Based on these situations, self-statements were generated from the responses of a pilot sample of undergraduate subjects and from a rational analysis of the *internal dialogue* of persons faced with unreasonable demands. This analysis yielded five categories of cognitive response: self-sufficiency versus the need for approval, expectancy of gain versus punishment, rational versus irrational problem evaluation, autonomy versus guilt and shame, and self-directed versus other-directed responses. For each of these categories, five PSSs and five NSSs were included in an initial pool of items. These 50 SSs were consensually validated on an independent sample of 37 college students. Items that obtained 90% agreement as to whether they facilitated (positive) or interfered (negative) with refusal behavior were included in the final inventory.

Psychometric Characteristics

The internal consistency, *reliability,* of the ASST has been established at .78 (Bruch, Haase, & Purcell, 1984). Norms and test-retest reliability are currently lacking. The construct *validity* of the instrument continues to grow from studies that: (a) consistently demonstrate that functional and dysfunctional groups differ in the frequency of PSSs and NSSs, and (b) show predictable changes in SSs (primarily a reduction in negative) as a function of psychotherapy. For example, Schwartz and Gottman (1976) found that low assertive persons reported significantly more NSSs and fewer PSSs than did moderate or highly assertive persons, with a stronger effect on the negative dimension. Intragroup differences revealed that highly assertive persons had significantly more PSSs than NSSs (1.6:1 ratio); low assertive persons did not differ in the frequency of PSSs and NSSs (1:1 ratio), suggesting that unassertive persons are characterized by an "internal dialogue of conflict." A similar pattern of differences was established in replication studies with undergraduates and was extended to psychiatric populations, including those with schizophrenia, acute psychotic episodes, and affective disorders. Although psychotherapy outcome studies have yielded changes in both PSSs and NSSs, the effect has been more pronounced for NSSs. This is seen most clearly in Derry and Stone's (1979) study of cognitive-behavioral treatments of unassertive persons, which resulted in significant decreases in NSSs without corresponding increases in PSSs. The ASST has been related predictably to other cognitive variables, obtaining a correlation of −.40 between NSSs and a measure of cognitive complexity, −.31 between NSS and scores on the Irrational Beliefs Test, and .36 between PSSs and self-efficacy scores.

Bruch, Haase, and Purcell's (1984) factor analysis of the ASST resulted in the following *factor structure:* Factor 1 (19.0%): incurring negative emotional and interpersonal reactions when refusing; Factor 2 (16.0%): examination of the rationality and justification of refusing unreasonable requests; Factor 3 (8.6%): underlying theme of morality and guilt. Only Factors 1 and 2 made signficant, unique contributions to a regression analysis on an independent measure of assertive response.

Clinical Use

The ASST can be used to assess unassertive persons' level of cognitive functioning before treatment and to track changes in PSSs and NSSs as a function of psychotherapy. Diagnostically, the ASST can be used to determine whether an individual client is deficient in PSSs, excessive in NSSs, or both. The instrument also provides specific information about the content of the client's dysfunctional thinking. For example, one person may be overly concerned about negative evaluation, whereas another might exhibit irrational thinking in considering the reasons for refusal. Therefore, the ASST provides information about the nature of a given client's assertion-related cognitive deficit, which allows increased specificity in the therapeutic intervention. Because the ASST is easy to administer and score, it can be used by clients to periodically self-monitor their internal dialogue throughout the course of treatment.

Future Directions

Although the validity of the ASST continues to be strengthened by its use in group contrast and psychotherapy outcome studies, psychometric studies are needed to establish norms, test-retest reliability, and relative freedom from bias and demand. Psychotherapy studies have used the ASST to establish pre- to posttreatment cognitive changes as a function of therapy. More attention might be given to using the ASST to promote client self-monitoring and to increase the specificity of cognitive interventions. Lastly, the ASST (as have related self-statement inventories) has typically treated the positive and negative dimensions of thought separately. Schwartz and Garamoni (1986) developed a structural model of positive and negative states of mind that demonstrates the value of a new construct - *state of mind (SOM)* - that focuses on the *balance* between positive (P) and negative (N) cognitions of $P/(P + N)$. Functional individuals (including highly assertive persons) demonstrate a SOM proportion equal to .618 (*Positive Dialogue*), whereas persons with mild dysfunction (including unassertive persons) exhibit a SOM proportion equal to .500 (*Internal Dialogue of Conflict*). This balance measure allows the comparison of obtained SOM proportions to specific theoretical values and should therefore be adopted in any future applications of the ASST.

References

Bruch, M.A., Haase, R.F., & Purcell, M.J. (1984). Content dimensions of self-statements in assertive situations: A factor analysis of two measures. *Cognitive Therapy and Research, 8,* 173-186.

Derry, P.A., & Stone, G.L. (1979). Effects of cognitive-adjunct treatments on assertiveness. *Cognitive Therapy and Research, 3,* 213-221.

Schwartz, R.M., & Garamoni, G.L. (1986). A structural model of positive and negative states of mind: Asymmetry in the internal dialogue. In P.C. Kendall (Ed.), *Advances in cognitive-behavioral research and therapy.* New York: Academic Press.

Schwartz, R.M., & Gottman, J.M. (1976). Toward a task analysis of assertive behavior. *Journal of Consulting and Clinical Psychology, 44,* 910-920.

Assessment of Self-Care Skills of Mentally Retarded Individuals

Patrick W. McGuffin

Description

The assessment of self-care skills in mentally retarded individuals is of concern both to determine the level of impairment and to aid in planning educational programming to address the impairment. The American Association on Mental Deficiency Adaptive Behavior Scale (ABS) provides scores for 10 discrete categories of adaptive behavior. Since its development, the ABS has become one of the most popular adaptive behavior scales for use with mentally retarded individuals (Spreat, 1982).

The ABS is divided into two major sections: Adaptive Behavior and Maladaptive Behavior. These two sections function independently, and an individual's score on one part does not influence the score on the other. Only Part 1 (Adaptive Behavior) will be discussed, as Part 2 (Maladaptive Behavior) does not measure adaptive skill levels. Part 1 of the ABS is made up of 10 subareas or domains. Scores for each of these 10 domains are determined by an individual's scores on the performance of specific skills assessed within each domain. A total of 66 specific skills are measured within Part 1 of the ABS (with a range of 3 to 21 skills measured within each of the 10 domains). Each of these 66 skills is made up of more specific skills necessary to produce the skill being measured (for example, the "Use of Table Utensils" is made up of seven subskills, including "uses knife and fork correctly and neatly," "uses table knife for cutting or spreading," "feeds self with spoon neatly," and "feeds self with fingers or must be fed").

Purpose

Although severely mentally retarded individuals generally display a wide range of adaptive skill deficits, this knowledge by itself is not sufficient to develop training programs designed to improve adaptive functioning. Information on the specific deficits an individual displays is necessary for thorough assessment and program planning. The ABS provides specific measures of adaptive skills. Because of the 10 domain scores provided by the ABS (as opposed to one total score) and the specific skills listed in determining an individual's score in each of the 10 domains, the ABS is thought to provide "a better operational definition of the concept of adaptive behavior" (Roszkowski, 1980) than that in assessments. The specificity of the operational definition allows the ABS to be used in developing training programs to address the skill deficiencies of the individuals being assessed. Additionally, the ABS can be used for on-going assessment of adaptive functioning, thereby providing information on the efficacy of training programs.

Development

The ABS was developed because of the limited specificity of other measures of adaptive behavior. The Vineland Social Maturity Scale (Doll, 1937) had previously been recommended by the American Association on Mental Deficiency (AAMD) as the best measure of adaptive behavior. The Vineland, however, produces a single score of adaptive functioning, which limits its ability to measure specific areas of skill deficit, thereby decreasing its ability to be used as a tool in developing training programs to address these deficits. The ABS was normed on institutionalized mentally retarded individuals aged 3 to 69 years representing all levels of mental retardation (mild, moderate, severe, and profound). It produces percentile scores related to the normative sample.

As the ABS provides information on a wide range of adaptive skills, it can give a clear picture of the functioning level of the person being assessed. Studies of the ABS have given evidence of the instrument's ability to distinguish among children in different classroom settings (educable, trainable, and regular classroom children) and other groups "which possess different behavioral characteristics" (Spreat, 1982, p. 54). Spreat (1982) also reports that, "Part 1 domains reliably discriminated among different behavioral categories [and] significantly discriminated between mentally retarded patients residing in five different types of homogeneous residential units" (p. 53).

Psychometric Characteristics

A review article of psychometric findings regarding the ABS (Spreat, 1982) showed test-retest correlations for Part 1 domains to range from .85 to .97, with a mean of .91, and interrater correlations to range from .71 to .93, with a mean of .86. Two factors were found to account for most of the variance in Part 1 of the ABS, one reflecting basic self-care skills and the other reflecting "some sort of motivational aspect of personality" (Spreat, 1982, p. 51.).

Evaluation of the data indicates that the ABS is both a reliable and valid assessment of adaptive skills in mentally retarded individuals. Test-retest, interrater, and internal consistency studies show the ABS to have adequate reliability. Additionally, the ABS appears to "tap relevant dimensions of human behavior" (Spreat, 1982, p. 54).

Although the ABS has been a reliable and valid measure of adaptive functioning in mentally retarded individuals, some problematic areas in the scale have been seen. For example, ABS ratings do not always agree with direct observations of behavior (Spreat, 1982). Although a possible flaw in the assessments might exist, other explanations for the disagreement are possible. One possibility is that there might be "some sort of an approximation of a normal distribution of error" (Spreat, 1982, p. 52). It has also been postulated that direct observation does not adequately assess overall adaptive behavior, as the ABS rating is designed to do.

The ABS has also been susceptible to arithmetic errors and errors in applying the scoring rules, which would result in differences between observations and assessed skill levels. Although this finding does not point to any inherent shortcomings in the ABS as an assessment instrument, it does point out an area of concern that needs to be considered when evaluating the validity of an individual use of the ABS.

Clinical Use

As stated, mentally retarded individuals generally display adaptive skill deficits. Assessment of these deficits is necessary to develop training programs and to evaluate their effectiveness. The ABS, by its specificity, provides this necessary information. It is appropriate for both children and adults and can be administered by nonprofessionals. It can also be administered as a third party assessment, with the administrator questioning a person familiar with the behavior of the person being assessed. The individual administering the ABS can also be the informant, provided that she or he is sufficiently familiar with the person being assessed to answer all of the items on the ABS.

Future Directions

The ABS has been useful in assessing the adaptive functioning of mentally retarded individuals. Its one limitation is the occurrence of scoring errors. Future research should be directed at this problem.

References

Doll, E.A. (1937). *The management of social competence: A manual for the Vineland Social Maturity Scale*. Minneapolis, MN: Educational Publishers.

Roszkowski, M. (1980). Concurrent validity of the Adaptive Behavior Scale as assessed by the Vineland Social Maturity Scale. *American Journal of Mental Deficiency, 85,* 86-89.

Spreat, S. (1982). The AAMD Adaptive Behavior Scale: A psychometric review. *Journal of School Psychology, 20,* 45-56.

Automated Matching Familiar Figures Test

Peter H. Glow and Roslyn A. Glow

Description

The Automated Matching Familiar Figures Test (MFFT) is a computer-administered version of Kagan's MFFT (Kagan, Rosman, Day, Albert, & Phillips, 1964) available in two parallel forms for adults and preschool and elementary forms. It is designed to assess cognitive tempo (reflectiveness-impulsiveness), an aspect of cognitive style. The subject sits at a 16-panel screen. A target figure appears in one of the panels of the top row and up to eight comparison figures are simultaneously displayed in the bottom two rows. The subject's task is to touch the bottom of the correct comparison figure's panel. There are 12 items in each version of the test. The latency to the first response to each item and the total number of errors made (incorrect items are readministered) until each item receives a response are the basic data. From these two measures are computed impulsiveness-reflectiveness (z-score latency minus z-score errors) and efficiency-inefficiency (z-score latency plus z-score errors). In this type of task, speed and accuracy of performance are negatively correlated.

Purpose

In situations of high response uncertainty, individuals differ in the direction in which they play off speed and accuracy of responding. Kagan et al. (1964) considered this to be an important cognitive style variable that might explain performance in a variety of settings. The purpose of automating the MFFT is to increase accuracy of measurement and to facilitate wide-scale study of this cognitive style variable.

Development

A parallel version of the adult MFFT was prepared and used in addition to the original MFFT figures. Studies with prisoners (Lange, 1982) showed little difference in performance when instructions, feedback on correctness, and order of administration of failed items were changed. Computer administration was highly acceptable to prisoners, university students, and elementary school children.

Psychometric Characteristics

The internal consistency of each of the adult forms is high for impulsiveness-reflectiveness ($r = .91$, and .89 Forms I and II, respectively) and acceptable for efficiency-inefficiency ($r = .70$ and .73 Forms I and II, respectively). Repeated (parallel-forms) measures reliabilities were $r = .83$ and .63 for impulsiveness-reflectiveness and efficiency-inefficiency, respectively. There were no sex differences in undergraduates (Glow, Lange, Glow, & Barnett, 1981). Lange (1982) gives data on mean latency and total errors for prisoners, undergraduates, and police cadets, ranging from 32.41 and 20.71 for prisoners (latency and errors, respectively) to 45.66 and 14.89 for undergraduates. Correlations between mean latency and total errors range from $-.57$ to $-.68$. The relationships between MFFT performance and various other measures show modest correlations (.21 to .45) between impulsiveness and various other adult characteristics, such as self-description as an impulsive, lively, and risk-taking person, questionnaire acquiescence, Peabody Picture Vocabulary Test and Porteus Maze Performance, and (negatively) rated conscientiousness. Efficiency was related to performance in a university examination. Prisoners were more impulsive than other adults, but correlations between various performance and real-life measures were not large, and detailed analyses suggested that the MFFT errors score is as valid as the impulsiveness-reflectiveness measure when external criteria are used. The impulsiveness-reflectiveness measure is more stable, however, than the errors measure.

Clinical Use

Because impulsiveness is a symptom of the attention deficit disorder (ADD) (with and without hyperactivity), the automated MFFT may provide a means for assessing large numbers of children with suspected ADD or learning disability. In children, cognitive tempo appears to be modifiable with special training, and socially significant improvement in cognitive performance may result. Selection for such training could be speeded by the use of the automated MFFT.

Future Directions

The use of a portable, automated MFFT is practical, effective, and acceptable to subjects, but the efficiency of assessment increases only when large numbers of individuals are assessed. Cognitive impulsiveness is relatively specific, and relationships to socially significant behavior are modest, especially when variance due to general intellect (correlated with MFFT errors) is removed. Nevertheless, MFFT impulsiveness is quite stable over changed instructions and task exposure, suggesting a relatively robust characteristic with trait-like properties that is worthy of further study in applied settings.

References

Glow, R.A., Lange, R.V., Glow, P.H., & Barnett, J.A. (1981). The measurement of cognitive impulsiveness: Psychometric properties of two automated adult versions of the matching Familiar Figures Test. *Journal of Behavioral Measurement, 3*, 415-429.

Kagan, J., Rosman, B.L., Day, D., Albert, J., & Phillips, W. (1964). Information processing in the child: Significance of analytic and reflective attitudes. *Psychological Monographs, 78*, 1 (Whole No. 578).

Lange, R.V. (1982). *Cognitive and behavioural impulsivity among prisoners and comparison groups*. Unpublished doctoral dissertation, University of Adelaide, South Australia.

Automatic Thoughts Questionnaire

Philip C. Kendall and Rebecca C. Hays

Description

The Automatic Thoughts Questionnaire (ATQ) is a 30-item inventory in which clients are asked to indicate, on a scale of 1 (not at all) to 5 (all the time), how frequently the listed "thoughts" have occurred to them in the past week (Hollon & Kendall, 1980). The items for endorsement include such thoughts as, "I feel like I'm up against the world" and "I'm so disappointed in myself."

Purpose

There has been increasing interest in the role of cognition in the etiology, maintenance, and treatment of various types of psychopathology. Stemming from Beck's cognitive model of depression, research has frequently been concerned with automatic thoughts and related self-statements as well as the relationship between the modification of such self-statements and behavior. The ATQ was developed (a) to examine the extent of negative cognitions associated with depression, and (b) to use as an independent measure of cognitive change associated with either laboratory manipulations or clinical interventions.

Development

The items for the ATQ were generated by a college student population ($n = 788$) who were asked to record the thoughts that "popped" into their heads when considering a depressing time in their lives. These items were organized and condensed into a 100-item pool and administered to another group of students ($n = 312$). These students were simultaneously administered the Beck Depression Inventory (BDI), the Minnesota Multiphasic Personality Inventory Depression Scale (MMPI-D), and the State-Trait Anxiety Inventory. Depressed and nondepressed subjects were then psychometrically identified on the basis of dual criteria of scoring within the depressed range on both the BDI and MMPI-D. The 30 "automatic thought" items that significantly differentiated these groups then constituted the ATQ. The ATQ was then cross-validated on another sample of psychometrically defined groups of depressed and nondepressed subjects.

Psychometric Characteristics

In the original ATQ study, both split-half (.97) and alpha (.96) reliability coefficients were determined to be significant at the .001 level, demonstrating sufficient reliability (Hollon & Kendall, 1980). Cross-validation also demonstrated that persons in the depressed group scored significantly higher on the ATQ than did those in the nondepressed group. Correlations between the ATQ, BDI, and MMPI-D were also statistically significant ($p < .01$). Finally, all item-to-total correlations for the ATQ were significantly at or beyond the .001 level.

Since the original study, additional research has further demonstrated the reliability and validity of the ATQ. Ross and Gottfredson (1983) examined the ATQ, MMPI-D, and BDI of clinically defined samples and reported that the means, standard deviations, and intercorrelations were similar to those reported by Hollon and Kendall (1980), who used a psychometrically defined student population. Dobson and Breiter (1983) examined the ATQ, Dysfunctional Attitude Scale, and Interpersonal Inventory and reported good internal reliability, with the ATQ noticeably higher. Harrell and Ryon (1983) also administered the ATQ to a clinical population and reported that it differentiated between depressed and nondepressed groups. These authors also reported that the ATQ correlated positively with the therapist ratings, MMPI-D, and BDI scores. Most recently, in research employing diagnostically distinct groups of clinical outpatients, the ATQ demonstrated greater specificity for levels of syndrome depression than did the Dysfunctional Attitudes Scale (Hollon, Kendall, & Lumry, in press).

Clinical Use

Different areas must be assessed to diagnose syndrome depression, including changes in eating, sleeping, and fatigue patterns. The ATQ can successfully be used in such an assessment to evaluate the cognitive component of depression. Additionally, both the clinician and researcher may find the ATQ useful before and after treatment to evaluate gains made by clients. Simons, Garfield, and Murphy (1984) used the ATQ to measure treatment outcomes for clients assigned to either cognitive therapy or pharmacotherapy and reported that the outcomes of both treatments were reflected by changes in the ATQ. Finally, the ATQ may be used as a "homework" assignment or session-to-session process measure, in which each individual client's responses on the ATQ may be an area for therapeutic discussion and focus.

Future Directions

Interesting questions remain, one of which concerns the qualitative aspects of client's endorsements of self-statements. An area being examined at this time is the *meaning* of the self-statement for the individual. Both the value that persons place on the self-statement and the degree to which they believe the content of the statement are clearly important information for our understanding of the role of cognitions. Another consideration is the *sequence* of self-statements, such that the extent to which positive and negative self-statements are followed by retorts and qualifiers and the relative predictiveness of separate versus sequences of self-talk may be examined. Further research may center on the examination of whether the ATQ can offer incremental validity to predictions of treatment outcome. Finally, the ATQ may shed light on the etiological role of cognitions in syndrome depression. Recent research suggests that the cognitions associated with depression are state-dependent rather than evidence of a trait-like pattern (Hollon, Kendall, & Lumry, in press).

References

Dobson, K.S., & Breiter, H.J. (1983). Cognitive assessment of depression: Reliability and validity of three measures. *Journal of Abnormal Psychology, 92,* 107-109.

Harrell, T.H., & Ryon, N.B. (1983). Cognitive-behavioral assessment of depression: Clinical validation of the automatic thoughts questionnaire. *Journal of Consulting and Clinical Psychology, 51,* 721-725.

Hollon, S.D., & Kendall, P.D. (1980). Cognitive self-statements in depression: Development of an automatic thoughts questionnaire. *Cognitive Therapy and Research, 4,* 383-395.

Hollon, S.D., Kendall, P.D., & Lumry, A. (in press). The specificity of depressotypic cognitions in clinical depression. *Journal of Abnormal Psychology.*

Simons, A.D., Garfield, S.L., & Murphy, G.E. (1984). The process of change in cognitive therapy and pharmacotherapy of depression: Changes in mood and cognition. *Archives of General Psychiatry, 41,* 45-51.

Beck Depression Inventory

Robert A. Steer and Aaron T. Beck

Description

The Beck Depression Inventory (BDI) (Beck, Ward, Mendelsohn, Mock, & Erbaugh, 1961) is one of the most widely used instruments not only for assessing the intensity of depression in psychiatrically diagnosed patients, but also for detecting patients in normal populations (Steer, Beck, & Garrison, in press). According to the files of the Center for Cognitive Therapy at the University of Pennsylvania's Medical School, which acts as a clearinghouse for BDI research, it has been used in over 1,500 different research studies. There have been a number of comprehensive reviews about the psychometric properties (Beck & Beamesderfer, 1974) and appropriate applications of the instrument (Steer, Beck, & Garrison, in press) over the last 26 years. The following brief description of the BDI draws heavily upon information presented within the two aforementioned reviews.

The BDI was derived from clinical observations about the attitudes and symptoms frequently displayed by depressed psychiatric patients (Beck et al., 1961). The clinical observations were systematically consolidated into 21 symptoms and attitudes that could be rated from 0 to 3 in terms of intensity. The items were chosen to assess the intensity of depression and not reflect a particular theory of depression. The 21 symptoms and attitudes were: (a) mood, (b) pessimism, (c) sense of failure, (d) lack of satisfaction, (e) guilt feelings, (f) sense of punishment, (g) self-dislike, (h) self-accusations, (i) suicidal wishes, (j) crying, (k) irritability, (l) social withdrawal, (m) indecisiveness, (n) distortion of body image, (o) work inhibition, (p) sleep disturbance, (q) fatigability, (r) loss of appetite, (s) weight loss, (t) somatic preoccupation, and (u) loss of libido.

Although the BDI was initially designed to be administered by trained interviewers, today it is most often self-administered. When self-administered, the instrument generally takes 5 to 10 minutes to complete and is scored by summing the ratings for each of the 21 items.

In 1970 a revised version of the BDI, which was eventually copyrighted in 1978 (Beck & Steer,

1984), was introduced. An abbreviated 13-item version has been used widely. Currently, several computerized administration and interpretation versions of the BDI exist. It has been translated into over 30 languages.

Although Beck and Beamesderfer (1974) urged that cutoff scores for the BDI should be based on the clinical decisions for which the instrument was being employed, the Center for Cognitive Therapy distributes the following cutoff-score guidelines for using the BDI with patients diagnosed as having affective disorders: (a) none or minimal depression is <10; (b) mild to moderate depression is 11 to 17; (c) moderate depression is 18 to 29; and (d) severe depression is 30 to 63. The mean BDI scores for minimal, mild, moderate, and severe classifications according to Beck (1967, pp. 196) are 10.9 (SD 8.1), 18.7 (SD 10.2), 25.4 (SD 9.6), and 30.0 (SD 10.4).

The BDI was not developed as a screening instrument to detect depressive syndromes in normal adult populations, but over the years there has been considerable interest in using this instrument for such purposes (Steer et al., in press). Although considerable debate exists over what cutoff scores to use for detecting depression in adult normal populations, the current consensus is that scores >18 are indicative of possible depressive symptomatology.

Development

Symptoms on the BDI were derived from clinical observations as previously stated. Conducting psychotherapy with patients, Beck made systematic observations and records about the characteristics, attitudes, and symptoms of his depressed patients. He selected a group of attitudes and symptoms that appeared to be specific for depression and were consistent with the descriptions of depression contained in the psychiatric literature. From this procedure, 21 symptoms and attitudes were identified and each was described by four or five statements indicating increasing severity. Numerical values from 0 to 3 were assigned to each statement to indicate the degree of severity. For some symptoms, two alternative statements were presented for a given level of severity and were assigned the same numerical rating. The equivalent statements were labeled A and B in the 1961 version to indicate that they were at the same level. The equivalent statement system was eventually eliminated in the 1970 version.

Psychometric Characteristics

A substantial number of studies have been conducted about the psychometric characteristics in the BDI with a diverse sample of both psychiatrically diagnosed patients and normal adult populations (Beck & Beamesderfer, 1974; Steer et al., in press). With respect to the internal consistency of the BDI, the mean coefficient alpha for psychiatric populations has been reported as .87, whereas the mean coefficient alpha for normal populations also appears to be .87 (Steer, Beck, & Garrison, in press). The BDI's test-retest reliability is highly dependent on the time spans being measured. For pre- and posttest administrations from covering insured intervals to pure short-time syncratic intervals such as a week, the mean pre- and posttest correlations are within the .80s for both psychiatric and nonpsychiatric populations.

The validity of the BDI can be judged by five different criteria: (1) content, (2) concurrent, (3) discriminant, (4) construct, and (5) factorial. Although as previously mentioned the BDI is one of the most frequently used instruments for measuring depression, Edwards et al. (1984) recently criticized the BDI for containing only six of the nine DSM-III criteria. For example, the BDI does not ask about gains in weight or increases in appetite. However, Beck (1967, p. 34) reported that increased appetite occurred so frequently in normal populations that its addition to the BDI would result in a spuriously high number of nondepressed persons.

With respect to the concurrent validity of the BDI, it demonstrates high positive correlations with other psychiatric self-report and clinical rating scales. Its mean correlations with the Hamilton Psychiatric Scale for Depression, the Zung Depression Scale, the MMPI-D Scale, and the SCL-09R D factor are typically in the .60s for psychiatric patients.

The BDI was developed not to discriminate between depressive and other disorders or among the subtypes of depressive patients manifesting different depressive disorders, but to measure the intensity of the dimensions of depression across all psychiatric disorders. Because the intensity of depressive symptomatology is higher in persons with depressive disorders than in normal subjects and generally higher than that in persons with other disorders, such as schizophrenia, it offers a rough guide to diagnosis but is no substitute for a clinical evaluation. Its construct validity has been demonstrated numerous times, as evidenced by the BDI's positive relationship with constructs, such as hopelessness, dysfunctional thoughts or attitudes, and suicidal behavior, which should theoretically be related to depression.

There are a number of factor analytic studies with the BDI across a wide spectrum of psychiatric and nonpsychiatric populations (Steer et al., in press). The number of factors ranges from three to seven in psychiatric samples and one to five in non-psychiatric samples. Although shift of symptoms across factors depends on samples drawn, there appear to be three primary depression factors representing (1) negative attitudes toward self, (2) performance difficulties, and (3) somatic complaints.

Clinical Use

The BDI is appropriate for persons who are older than 13 years of age and have at least a sixth grade education. In clinical practice, the instrument is useful for quantifying the intensity of depression in both psychiatric inpatients and outpatients. The instrument may detect depressive symptoms in normal adult populations when cutoff scores >18 are employed.

The BDI is not appropriate for differentiating between patients diagnosed with different types of depression. Its accuracy in estimating the severity of depression in medical patients or in those whose symptoms may be attributable to causes other than depression is also guarded. For example, the intensity of depression in alcoholic addicts as estimated by the BDI may be inflated because a number of the somatic symptoms that alcoholic addicts describe, such as loss of appetite, are also shared by those with a diagnosis of depression.

The BDI is very effective for detecting changes in depression associated with psychotherapy and psychotropic medication as compared with other instruments for assessing depression. Edwards et al. (1984) reported a meta-analysis in which the BDI proved to be more conservative than the Hamilton Psychiatric Rating Scale for Depression in detecting changes in depression associated with psychotherapy, especially those related to psychotropic medication.

Future Directions

Although the BDI was not developed to differentiate between types of depression, some clinicians are attempting to modify the BDI's content and scoring scheme to be more consonant with DSM-III criteria. Studies are also under way to evaluate the present form's ability to differentiate between various depressive disorders, such as major affective and dysthymic disorders. There is also a need to develop a definitive set of factor scores for the BDI so that symptom dimensions attributable to other disorders can be isolated and then eliminated in determining whether a patient is depressed. Finally, several computerized administration and interpretation programs for the BDI have recently emerged, and the reliability and validity of the computerized versions need to be established.

References

Beck, A.T. (1967). *Depression: Causes and treatment.* Philadelphia, PA: University of Pennsylvania Press.

Beck, A.T., & Beamesderfer, A. (1974). Assessment of depression: The Depression Inventory. In P. Pichot (Ed.), *Modern problems in pharmacopsychiatry* (pp. 151-169). Basel, Switzerland: S. Karger.

Beck, A.T., & Steer, R.A. (1984). Internal consistencies of the original and revised Beck Depression Inventories. *Journal of Clinical Psychology, 40*, 1365-1367.

Beck, A.T., Ward, C.H., Mendelsohn, M., Mock, J., & Erbaugh, J. (1961). An inventory for measuring depression. *Archives of General Psychiatry, 4*, 561-571.

Edwards, B.C., Lambert, M.J., Moran, P.W., McCully, T., Smith, K.C., & Ellington, A.G. (1984). A meta-analytic comparison of the Beck Depression Inventory and the Hamilton Rating Scale for Depression as measures of treatment outcome. *British Journal of Clinical Psychology, 23*, 93-99.

Steer, R.A., Beck, A.T., & Garrison, B. (in press). In N. Sartorius & T.A. Ban (Eds.), *Assessment of depression.* Geneva, Switzerland: World Health Organization.

Behavior Profile Rating Scale

Barbara G. Melamed and Mark A. Lumley

Description

The Behavior Profile Rating Scale (BPRS) is an observational instrument employed to assess the frequency of specific behaviors often associated with fear during dental treatment. The BPRS is designed for use with children, and it attempts to obtain an accurate representation of the child-dentist interaction by dividing the entire dental treatment session into 3-minute intervals. The observer records only the presence or absence of each behavior during each interval, regardless of its frequency during that interval. The BPRS allows for the recording of 27 child behaviors, including four pertaining to the child's separation from the mother: (1) cries, (2) clings to mother, (3) refuses to leave mother, (4) is carried in bodily; and the other 23 pertaining to the office visit, per se including, (5) inappropriately closes mouth, (6) chokes, (7) will not sit back, (8) attempts to dislodge instrument, (9) complains verbally, (10) overreacts to pain, (11) has white knuckles, (12) is negative, (13) keeps eyes closed, (14) cries at injection, (15) gives verbal message to terminate, (16) refuses to open mouth, (17) assumes rigid posture, (18) cries, (19) dentist uses loud voice, (20) requires restraints, (21) kicks, (22) stands up, (23) rolls over, (24) dislodges instrument, (25) refuses to sit in chair, (26) faints, and (27) leaves chair. Each category in the scale is weighted by a factor from 1 to 5 that indicates the degree of disruption (as determined by dentists' ratings). These two groups of 4 and 23 behaviors are listed here in order of increasing disruption. All behaviors are functionally defined on a separate sheet. The total score can be obtained by multiplying the frequency of occurrence of the behavior in each category by its weighted factor and then adding all of the categories. This score is then divided by the number of 3-minute intervals observed to give a score that reflects the frequency of disruptive behaviors per 3-minute interval. Additionally, it may be desirable to note the interval in which injection or drilling, or both, occurs if applicable, so as to provide additional information that may be useful at some point. The BPRS was described by Melamed, Weinstein, Hawes, and Katin-Borland (1975b).

Purpose

The assessment of children's fears and anxieties in particular situations is needed to determine the type and extent of treatment indicated as well as to evaluate the outcome of any intervention. A complete assessment of anxiety ideally includes self-report or cognitive as well as physiological recordings in addition to behavioral observations. Therefore, the BPRS is designed to be one instrument in a battery of tools needed to completely evaluate a child's anxiety or fear in the dental situation. The Dental Subscale of the Children's Fear Survey Schedule (DS of the CFSS) (Cuthbert & Melamed, 1982), for example, can be used to measure the self-report modality of fear in this setting. If possible, obtaining physiological measures using instruments such as the Palmar Sweat Index (PSI) would also be advantageous. The BPRS, therefore,

measures just one dimension of a child's anxiety in the dental situation. It can be used as part of a research protocol (Melamed, Hawes, Heiby, & Glick, 1975a) or as a therapeutic assessment tool for a child being treated for excessive fear of the dental situation.

Development

Melamed, Weinstein, Hawes, and Katin-Borland (1975) were studying the use of filmed modeling on the reduction of children's dental-fear-related behavior problems and required an observational scale that was specific to a child in the dental setting. They developed the BPRS by listing behaviors that are fear-related reactions to the dental setting. Ten pediatric dentists and 200 third-year dental students were asked to rate each of these behaviors on a 1 to 5 scale according to the degree to which it would disrupt the examination and treatment of a child. These weighting factors were incorporated into the final score. The scale was standardized by having four undergraduate students compare their independent observations made using the BPRS; this yielded a Spearman rank correlation coefficient of the interrater reliability of 0.977.

Psychometric Characteristics

As with other observational scales, data provided by the BPRS will be valid only if the behaviors recorded are products solely of a child's anxiety and fear of the dental situation. The less specific the behaviors are to anxiety alone, and the greater the variety of settings in which these behaviors occur, the less able one is to use this scale validly as intended. Klorman, Ratner, King, and Sveen (1977) showed that dentists' ratings of a child's fear of dentistry are positively correlated with the child's subsequent BPRS scores. Melamed, Hawes, Heiby, and Glick (1975a) found that the BPRS was able to differentiate a filmed modeling group from a control group ($p < .006$). Similar findings were reported by Melamed, Weinstein, Hawes, and Katin-Borland (1975) and by Melamed, Yurcheson, Fleece, Hutcherson, and Hawes (1978).

The interrater reliability for the BPRS was reported in several studies. Melamed et al. (1975b) reported a correlation coefficient of 0.977 derived during standardization of the scale. Melamed et al. (1975a) reported an interrater reliability of .99 between the dentist and an independent observer. The use of functionally defined behaviors and the ease of reporting only the presence or absence of a behavior during a 3-minute interval probably are responsible for such high reliabilities.

Clinical Use

The BPRS can be used as an observational assessment device to measure the state anxiety levels of children displaying varying degrees of dentally fearful behavior. Measurement can be made both before and after any treatment or intervention as one tool in the complete assessment of a child's anxiety. It has been employed in several studies of filmed modeling interventions designed to reduce fearful behavior of children in a dental situation. Presumably, it can be used to assess a single child in the clinical setting when not part of a research protocol. With individual children, it would be helpful to measure the child's trait anxiety to determine how specific the anxiety is to the dental setting. The BPRS can therefore be used as both a research and a clinical tool for dentally fearful children.

Future Directions

The device needs to be refined to see if all 27 behaviors are indicative of anxiety and if the weight given to each is valid. Moreover, it may be appropriate to include in the scale a scoring of the dentist's behavior as being neutral, positive, or aversive and either contingent or noncontingent on the child's behavior. This would allow for a consideration of the type of approach used by the dentist and its effect on the child.

References

Cuthbert, M.I., & Melamed, B.G. (1982). A screening device: Children at risk for dental fears and management problems. *Journal of Dentistry for Children, 49,* 432-436.

Klorman, R., Ratner, J., King, J.B., Jr., & Sveen, O.B. (1977). Pedodontic patient's uncooperativeness and maternal anxiety. *Journal of Dental Research, 56,* 432.

Melamed, B.G., Hawes, R.R., Heiby, E., & Glick, J. (1975a). Use of filmed modeling to reduce uncooperative behavior of children during dental treatment. *Journal of Dental Research, 54,* 797-801.

Melamed, B.G., Weinstein, D., Hawes, R., & Katin-Borland, M. (1975b). Reduction of fear-related dental management problems with use of filmed modeling. *Journal of the American Dental Association, 90,* 822-826.

Melamed, B.G., Yurcheson, R., Fleece, E.L., Hutcherson, S., & Hawes, R. (1978). Effects of film modeling on the reduction of anxiety related behaviors in individuals varying in level of previous experience in the stress situation. *Journal of Consulting and Clinical Psychology, 46,* 1357-1367.

Behavioral Assertiveness Test-Revised

Richard M. Eisler

Description

The Behavioral Assertiveness Test-Revised (BAT-R; 1975) is a 32-item role–play measure of assertiveness behavior. The test consists of narrated descriptions of interpersonal situations or scenarios and "prompts" that typically require an assertive response. The role-played responses can be scored from videotape or actual observation of the interaction. Both global ratings of assertiveness and specific verbal and nonverbal components of assertiveness are used in scoring.

The test is designed to tap both positive and negative expressions of assertiveness in a variety of interpersonal contexts to persons of both sexes including employer, friend, spouse, stranger, and the like. For example, half the items tap the assertive expression of feelings of anger or irritation associated with the individual's ability to "stand up for his or her rights" (negative assertion). Sixteen additional items relate to the person's ability to express "commendatory" feelings of admiration, appreciation, or affection (positive assertion). The scenarios are further arranged so that half require responses to a male and half to a female. Finally, familiarity or the degree of intimacy was varied by having half of the scenes about a person the individual relates to frequently, such as a spouse or employer (familiar), and half about a person the individual does not interact with regularly, such as a stranger or waitress (unfamiliar). Thus, the 32 scenarios of the BAT-R consist of eight categories of interpersonal situations, with four scenes per category (i.e., positive or negative assertion expressed toward a male or female individual who is either familiar or unfamiliar to the subject).

In most applications of the BAT-R, an audiovisual record of the interactions between the subject and a role-playing confederate is made by videotaping the 32 scenarios. Assertiveness variables and procedures for scoring them were described by Eisler, Hersen, Miller, and Blanchard (1975). The response measures may be broadly categorized as: (a) nonverbal assertiveness behaviors, (b) positive and negative assertive content, and (c) global ratings of assertiveness. The subject's behavior is quantified by timed measures, such as the duration of response, and by frequency of occurrence measures, such as smiles, plus observer ratings, such as the degree of appropriate affect shown. Depending on the purpose, investigators have used different combinations of these and additional scoring systems.

Purpose

The BAT-R (Eisler et al., 1975) was originally developed to provide a behavioral, as contrasted to a self-report, measure of assertive skills in clinically impaired individuals. It has been used in methodological research on assertiveness and clinically oriented investigations of the effectiveness of assertiveness training with various clinical populations (e.g., depressed or anxious individuals and schizophrenic, antisocial, or hyperaggressive persons).

Although the BAT-R scenarios were originally developed for a psychiatric population of adult men, it has been used successfully with adult female populations (Hersen, Bellack, & Turner, 1978). This measure has also been employed in both single case and group outcome research designed to assess the effectiveness of various assertiveness training techniques, including behavior rehearsal, modeling, coaching, and feedback. Because of many published studies with the BAT-R, its results in future research may be compared with those in the existing literature.

Development

The original role-play scenarios constructed for the BAT-R were based on Wolpe and Lazarus' (1966) definitions of "hostile" and "commendatory" assertion. An effort was made to select scenarios representative of real-life daily social encounters. Systematically varied in scene selection was the sex of the respondent and the degree of familiarity with the respondent. Research by the authors showed that responses to the scenarios selected differentiated high from low assertive individuals on the Wolpe-Lazarus Assertiveness Questionnaire and global ratings of overall assertiveness.

The scoring system for the BAT-R was based on variables typically chosen for social psychological research, including nonverbal speech characteristics, speech content, and global ratings of

demeanor. The specific variables for rating assertiveness were initially selected on their face validity; for example, assertive individuals should speak longer and sound more forceful than unassertive individuals. Measures found to differentiate high from low assertive individuals on concurrent self-report and observer ratings of assertiveness were retained in the final version of the BAT-R.

Psychometric Characteristics

Obtaining interrater reliability in scoring the BAT-R is highly dependent on the use of highly trained observers experienced in rating social interaction from videotape replays. Eisler et al. (1975) found that for frequency of occurrence measures, raters were able to obtain interjudge agreement of over 90%. For continuous measures, interobserver agreement based on correlation coefficients was over .94. Subsequent studies employing the BAT-R have reported reliability figures in a lower range, although still acceptably high.

A factor analytic study by Pachman, Foy, Massey, and Eisler (1978) examined the relationships between the verbal and nonverbal specific measures of assertiveness of the BAT-R and global ratings of assertiveness for the negative scenarios. The results showed that all speech measures, with the exception of reply latency, correlated significantly with the global assertiveness of ratings. Additionally, all measures with the exception of reply latency loaded on a single factor of assertiveness.

Support for the convergent validity of the BAT-R comes from studies that demonstrate significant correlations between self-reported assertiveness and expert clinical judgments of assertiveness with BAT-R scores. Further, evidence for the construct validity of the BAT-R comes from a relatively large number of studies that examine before and after changes on the BAT-R associated with assertiveness training. However, as with many role-play measures of behavior, several studies have questioned the external validity of the BAT-R in predicting assertive behavior in the natural environment. For example, Bellack, Hersen, and Turner (1978) found that although BAT-R scores were related to mental health experts' ratings of response effectiveness, they were not related to assertiveness ratings in a structured interview or group therapy situation.

Clinical Use

Many clinical research studies have employed the BAT-R to investigate assertiveness training and social skill deficits associated with a variety of clinical syndromes. For example, significant social skill deficits have been found with diverse populations, including schizophrenic, alcoholic, depressive, and aggressive-explosive individuals. In addition, individuals with anxiety inhibition or sexual dysfunction have benefited from assertiveness training using the BAT-R as both a behavioral assessment device and an aid to training.

For clinical purposes, the time and personnel required to administer and score all the BAT-R scenarios and measures would probably not be cost effective. However, unpublished reports from mental health centers and outpatient clinics indicate that shortened versions of the BAT-R have been employed with less formal scoring procedures to clinically assess and treat individuals with deficits in assertiveness. Typical procedures for the clinical use of the BAT-R have been: (a) to select 5 to 10 scenarios from the 32 items that target assertiveness deficits for the particular client, such as problems with male authority figures or unassertiveness in marital conflict; (b) to choose measures from the BAT-R that reflect the assessment of the client's deficits such as lack of eye contact or inability to make assertive requests. The relevant BAT-R scenarios are then employed in behavior rehearsal training for the targeted deficits. The global measure of assertiveness is typically used as a measure of training outcome or effectiveness.

Future Directions

Further development work is needed to facilitate the clinical use of the BAT-R. One major obstacle to that end is the current lack of normative data on both nonclinical populations and different clinical populations. Additionally, scenarios that discriminate among different assertiveness problems need to be identified with fewer scenes per problem area. Finally, a more refined, clinically useful scoring system should be developed that uses fewer but more clinically relevant ratings.

References

Bellack, S.S., Hersen, M., & Turner, S.M. (1978). Role-play tests for assessing social skills: Are they valid? Behavior Therapy, 9, 448-461.

Eisler, R.M., Hersen, M., Miller, P.M., & Blanchard, E.B. (1975). Situational determinants of assertive behaviors. Journal of Consulting and Clinical Psychology, 43, 330-340.

Hersen, M., Bellack, A.S., & Turner, S.M. (1978). Assessment of assertiveness in female psychiatric patients: Motor and autonomic measures. Journal of Behavior Therapy and Experimental Psychiatry, 9, 11-16.

Pachman, J.S., Foy, D.W., Massey, F., & Eisler, R.M. (1978). A factor analysis of assertive behavior. Journal of Consulting and Clinical Psychology, 46, 347.

Wolpe, J., & Lazarus, A.A. (1966). Behavior therapy techniques. New York: Pergamon Press.

Behavioral Assertiveness Test for Children

Mitchell R. Bornstein

Description

The Behavioral Assertiveness Test for Children (BAT-C) is a structured role-play behavioral assessment procedure consisting of a series of interpersonal situations requiring assertive responses by the child. The interpersonal encounters were designed to elicit assertion of one's rights, expression of anger, or the communication and/or reception of positive affect with other children.

The BAT-C is administered within a role-play format. After the narrator presents one interpersonal situation, the child responds to the assistant's prompts (standard lead-ins). Behavioral analysis of the child's responses is conducted to establish which verbal and nonverbal component behaviors of assertiveness appear with disproportionate frequency. Assessments of the overall level of assertiveness are also obtained.

Purpose

The BAT-C is intended to provide an accurate representation of a child's assertiveness within a laboratory/therapy setting. Ratings of overall assertiveness are conducted to enable the BAT-C to serve as a screening device for differentiating children with varying degrees of assertiveness. Children manifesting deficits in assertiveness are identified as potential candidates for social skills training. Ratings of verbal and nonverbal component behaviors of assertiveness permit the development of individualized treatment objectives for each child. Specific situations involving different kinds of assertiveness as well as specific behavioral deficiencies and excesses can be delineated.

The BAT-C is also intended as a medium for social skills training. The therapist can help the child recognize social skills deficits by reviewing responses to interpersonal situations. New, effective social skills can be acquired and maintained by directing treatment (i.e., instructions, modeling, and behavior rehearsal) to the targeted behaviors while the child responds to the situation. The impact of training can be ascertained through additional administrations of the BAT-C. Finally, the degree of generalization of training effects within the training setting can be evaluated with the BAT-C. Transfer of training gains can be assessed by the introduction of novel interpersonal encounters, extended interactions, or novel assistants or settings. Therefore, the BAT-C may be used for assessment, training, and treatment outcome evaluation.

Development

The BAT-C was developed as part of an effort to extend the application of social skills training to children. This interest stems from the recognition that the lack of appropriate social skills places a child at a severe interpersonal and academic disadvantage. Furthermore, inadequate social competency in a child may set the stage for ineffective interpersonal functioning as an adult, accentuating the potential for psychiatric disorder.

Bornstein, Bellack, and Hersen (1977, 1980) investigated the efficacy of social skills training on improving behavioral components of assertiveness in a nonclinical population of socially withdrawn children and a psychiatrically hospitalized population of highly aggressive children. The BAT-C was developed for this research. The Behavioral Assertiveness Test-Revised (Eisler, Hersen, Miller, & Blanchard, 1975) served as the model for the BAT-C. Eisler et al.'s (1975) research with adult psychiatric patients demonstrated that the overall level of assertiveness and component behaviors could be reliably identified on the basis of role-played responses to a series of standard interpersonal situations. The Behavioral Assertiveness Test-Revised was modified and adapted for use with children. Bornstein et al. (1977, 1980) found the BAT-C to be effective in identifying specific excesses and deficits in verbal and nonverbal behavioral components of assertiveness and the overall level of assertiveness in clinical and nonclinical populations of children globally described as low in interpersonal skill. The BAT-C also served as an effective vehicle for conducting training and assessing treatment outcome.

Psychometric Characteristics

The interpersonal situations included in the BAT-C were generated through naturalistic observations and interviews with professionals involved with the children such as teachers or staff on an inpatient psychiatric unit. Evaluations of the validity of role-play techniques in assessing children's social skills have yielded mixed results. Findings have ranged from none to moderate relationships evident between specific behaviors or ratings of overall assertiveness to criterion measures. Van Hasselt, Hersen, and Bellack (1981) assessed the external validity of the Children's Interpersonal Behavior Test (a slightly modified version of the BAT-C) and found statistically significant, albeit modest correlations between responses to the role-play test and sociometric data or teacher ratings.

Bornstein et al. (1980) found that the behavioral excesses and deficits identified through the BAT-C were similarly identified through naturalistic behavioral ratings. Williamson, Moody, Granberry, Lethermon, and Blouin (1983) argue that the simple correlational procedures used in most studies are inadequate to evaluate the relationship between the complex set of behaviors involved in social skills with molar measures of social competence. Employing a multivariate statistical approach, these authors found significant correlations between role-played assessment of children's social skills and criterion variables. Further investigation is clearly necessary to more fully establish the reliability and validity of the BAT-C.

Clinical Use

The BAT-C can be effectively and appropriately administered to children manifesting almost any childhood disorder. The only exceptions are children who have not yet developed role or perspective taking or who are so severely cognitively impaired as to preclude effective participation in the role-play format. Children manifesting severe clinical symptoms (e.g., hyperkinesia or psychosis) may require medication to attend to the BAT-C procedures.

The BAT-C is useful in identifying the overall level of assertiveness, deficits in behaviors requisite for socially skilled responses, as well as excesses in behaviors inappropriate for socially competent response. The BAT-C format lends itself to a wide range of interpersonal issues. Conversational ability, friendship development, positive and negative assertion, and interpersonal problem-solving represent a sampling of such issues.

The BAT-C can be administered in an experimental setting or less structured therapy session. Treatment modalities might include individual, group, or family therapy contexts.

Future Directions

There are many, as yet, unanswered questions with respect to the identification of social skills deficits in children. The lack of an agreed upon, precise definition of social competence in children represents a major stumbling block. Delineation of requisite skills and competencies must occur within an age-specific context. A developmental framework is critical because children's levels of cognitive, affective, and language development result in very different norms for appropriate, interpersonal behavior.

A clear-cut definition of social competence will allow determination of the extent to which positive and negative assertion (as measured in the BAT-C) represents important social behavior for different age groups. The validity of the BAT-C role-play format can be more accurately assessed once more precise criterion measures are developed. The findings of Williamson et al. (1983) suggest that future investigations of validity should include a multivariate evaluation of combinations of specific component behaviors against criterion measures. There is also a need for further demonstration of the reliability of the BAT-C. Once reliability and validity are more clearly established, research attention should be directed towards refining and standardizing administrative and scoring aspects of behavioral role-play assessments of social skills.

Several investigators (Van Hasselt et al., 1981) have attempted to overcome the current limitations in assessing social competence by suggesting the use of the multiple method assessment. Thus, the BAT-C would be administered along with sociometric measures and naturalistic observations. It would be important to determine the relative contribution of each assessment technique.

The demonstration of the BAT-C as a psychometrically sound assessment device is important because role-play evaluation of social skills represents a powerful, useful tool. Behavioral enactment of a skill is far preferable to a rating or perception of the skill. Furthermore, role play permits evaluation of the components of social skills that may occur with low frequency in the environment. The simulated setting can be controlled such that response to specific interpersonal stimuli can be evaluated in a systematic manner.

References

Bornstein, M.R., Bellack, A.S., & Hersen, M. (1977). Social skills training for unassertive children: A multiple baseline analysis. *Journal of Applied Behavior Analysis, 10,* 183-195.

Bornstein, M.R., Bellack, A.S., & Hersen, M. (1980). Social skills training for highly aggressive children: Treatment in an inpatient psychiatric setting. *Behavior Modification, 4,* 173-186.

Eisler, R.M., Hersen, M., Miller, P.M., & Blanchard, E.B. (1975). Situational determinants of assertive behavior. *Journal of Consulting and Clinical Psychology, 43,* 330-340.

Van Hasselt, V.B., Hersen, M., & Bellack, A.S. (1981). The validity of role play tests for assessing social skills in children. *Behavior Therapy, 12,* 202-216.

Williamson, D.A., Moody, S.C., Granberry, W.W., Lethermon, V.R., & Blouin, D.C. (1983). Criterion-related validity of a role play social skills test for children. *Behavior Therapy, 14,* 466-481.

Behavioral Assessment of Bruxism

Michael S. Rosenbaum

Description

Bruxism is a dental disorder involving "a nonfunctional gnashing and grinding of the teeth" (Glaros & Rao, 1977), which may also include teeth clenching (Shepherd & Price, 1971). Most individuals are usually unaware of exhibiting this habit disorder (Mikami, 1977), which can result in such symptomatic effects as abnormal wear to the teeth, structural damage around the teeth, facial pain, headache, loss of teeth, and temporomandibular joint pain (Glaros & Rao, 1977; Melamed & Mealiea, 1978; Shepherd & Price, 1971). Bruxism has been treated by occlusal adjustment or acrylic occlusal appliances, insight-oriented psychotherapy, and behavior therapeutic techniques (e.g., massed practice, relaxation, hypnosis, and biofeedback); however, most research studies fail to include data attesting to the effectiveness of the procedure(s) used, thereby resembling anecdotal reports. Using habit reversal to treat bruxism, Rosenbaum and Ayllon (1981) developed a self-report measure of this habit disorder to provide ongoing assessment of its occurrence before and after treatment.

Purpose and Development

The assessment of bruxism was based on a portable method with which clients could report the daily frequency of this habit across settings. Bruxism, as a habit, was conceptualized as automatic in nature, with the client being unaware when he was engaging in this behavior. Therefore, a method was needed that would enable the client to become aware of this behavior, so he or she could monitor it. During an interview, the client was asked to describe verbally and demonstrate physically the habit (e.g., teeth grinding or teeth clenching) and was instructed to record the frequency of this behavior on a daily basis. A 3 by 5 inch index card was divided into columns corresponding to the days of the week, and a slash mark was recorded each time the habit occurred. Because of its portability, the index card could be carried easily throughout the entire day, and each instance of the habit could be recorded.

Clinical Use

This assessment technique is applicable for clients who engage in bruxism during some part of their waking hours. Initially, the client and therapist need to develop a response definition before self-monitoring, so that the client is aware of what to record. For example, in the Rosenbaum and Ayllon (1981) study, teeth grinding for one client consisted of closing the mouth, biting the teeth together, and moving the jaw back and forth, thereby grinding the teeth surfaces against each other. Teeth clenching for another client consisted of biting the teeth together for a least 5 seconds, thereby producing muscular tension primarily in the masseter muscles. Bringing the teeth together for eating was not included in the response definition. The assessment method just described is not applicable for those individuals who engage in nocturnal bruxism only.

Psychometric Characteristics

In the Rosenbaum and Ayllon (1981) study, reliability of the assessment technique was obtained by changes noted in other behaviors associated with bruxism. For one client, a decrease in his self-reported teeth grinding was accompanied by a cessation in medication use for jaw pain following treatment. Another client reported a decrease in pain accompanying a decrease in self-reported teeth clenching.

Future Directions

As pointed out by Rosenbaum and Ayllon (1981), many clients may not be accurate in self-reports of bruxism because of their unawareness of many occurrences of this behavior. This fact has been substantiated by electromyographic recordings indicating the presence of electrical activity associated with bruxism in the absence of client self-reports of the behavior. Therefore, an additional component to the assessment of bruxism might be a portable biofeedback apparatus to signal the onset of this behavior, followed by the client recording the occurrence on an index card. This component could also extend the assessment of bruxism through self-recording to include nocturnal occurrences of this behavior.

References

Glaros, A.G., & Rao, S.M. (1977). Bruxism: A critical review. *Psychological Bulletin, 84*, 767-781.
Melamed, B.G., & Mealiea, W.L. (1978). Behavioral interventions in pain related problems in dentistry. In C.B. Taylor & J. Ferguson (Eds.), *Advances in behavioral medicine.* New York: Plenum Press.
Mikami, D.B. (1977). A review of psychogenic aspects and treatment of bruxism. *Journal of Prosthetic Dentistry, 37*, 411-419.
Rosenbaum, M.S., & Ayllon, T. (1981). Treating bruxism with the habit-reversal technique. *Behaviour Research and Therapy, 19*, 87-96.
Shepherd, R.W., & Price, A.S. (1971). Bruxism: The changing situation. *Australian Dental Journal, 16*, 243-248.

Behavioral Assessment Procedure for Food Addiction

Vicky Rippere

Description

This procedure is an objective, quantitative method for analyzing diet diaries for patterns of repetitive exposure to basic foods, which may indicate the presence of unsuspected food addiction (Randolph, 1956, 1976). Such a procedure is needed because there are currently no valid biological tests for food addiction. The method assumes that food addicts must be regularly exposed to their addictions (normally at intervals of less than 4 days) and that they are likely to present for treatment not when they are in a relatively symptom-free, adapted state but rather when their adaptation to their addictant foods has broken down. The two characteristics of this state are a steep increase in the frequency of consumption of addictants as sufferers try to ward off the increasingly prompt onset of withdrawal symptoms and, because these efforts are bound to fail, a polysymptomatic state, commonly with multiple system involvement.

If so, a complete record of everything a patient with multiple unexplained symptoms consumes within a 4- to 7-day period, when following his or her habitual diet, should permit the detection of any addictive eating patterns (if the diary is analyzed according to the frequency of consumption of basic food constituents) (such as wheat, cow's milk, yeast, and eggs). Rank-ordered frequency counts of food exposure in this period show the dietary range and the presence and identity of any foods consumed unusually frequently relative to the consumption of the other foods in the same individual's dietary. These very high frequency foods are hypothesized to be addictants. This hypothesis may be tested clinically.

A clinical example illustrates the method. A 33-year-old man who, after being successfully relieved of a situational phobia by in vivo exposure, continued to complain of feeling nervous, lightheaded, depressed, panicky, and intermittently tense for much of the time. Although he did not spontaneously report multiple other symptoms, they could readily be elicited. He had insomnia, a slow start in the morning, abdominal bloating, frequency of micturition, bowel disturbances, particularly constipation, generalized itching, rashes, headaches, dopiness, and myalgia. He was also somewhat, although not seriously, overweight. Because of chronic symptoms, he had become dependent on diazepam, which he had been prescribed for the last 6 years.

To analyze such a diary, the basic foods consumed are listed in a column in order of occurrence. Then a check is recorded against a food each time it is consumed, except if it is consumed in more than one form at a single sitting, in which case, it is checked the first time and the check crossed each subsequent time it is consumed at that sitting. Thus, a meal consisting of a cheese sandwich on white bread with butter, glass of milk, and a pot of fruit yoghurt would get a check for milk that would be crossed three times. The tally of checks represents the total number of individual exposures to the basic food rather than the number of dietary sources. The column may also contain synthetic

categories such as additives, caffeine, citrus, or processed and refined foods, if their inclusion serves a particular purpose.

Each day of the diary is analyzed in this manner, the counts for the days are summed, and the foods are listed in rank order from most to least frequently consumed. Our patient's 4-day totals consist of relatively few foods that tend to be eaten repetitively; 80% are consumed more than once in the 4 days. Of these, sugar (42 exposures) and coffee (33 exposures) stand out clearly above the rest in frequency of consumption. If coffee (33) and tea (7) are combined to form a synthetic "caffeine" category, the frequency rises to 40 exposures, giving an average for both sugar and coffee of around 10 exposures per day, as compared with an average of 2.5 exposures per day for the next most frequently consumed foods. Although 2.5 exposures per day is higher than once in 4 days, it is what might be expected of an ordinary dietary staple. Ten exposures per day is greatly in excess of such an expectation. Behavioral assessment, therefore, identifies sugar and caffeine as most likely to be addictant in this case.

The ranked data may be represented as a bar graph. The summed frequencies for the period may also be used to construct a ratio of nonnutritive to nutritive food exposures. To do this, all foods are divided into one or other of these categories, the exposure frequencies within each category are summed, and the ratio is found. In our patient's case, the nonnutritive foods (defined as those that contain either no nutrients or fewer nutrients than those needed for their metabolism) are sugar, coffee, tea, fruit, squash, alcohol, chocolate, and tonic water, and their ratio to nutritive exposures is 2:1. Such a ratio commonly suggests the need for nutritional supplementation.

Purpose

The procedure was devised to provide an inexpensive, noninvasive, objective, reproducible, systematic, and quantitative means of identifying hypothesized addictant foods in the absence of a definitive biological test. A secondary purpose is to provide data that may help convince defensively incredulous patients that certain foods have an unusual hold on their eating behavior.

Development

The method was developed more or less intuitively in the light of observations in the clinical ecology literature that were confirmed in the writer's own clinical experience. No elaborate development was necessary, because the method is essentially a variant of an established technique: content analysis. Moreover, the method is intended to generate rather than to test hypotheses, so that validation is clinical rather than psychometric.

Psychometric Characteristics

As the procedure is ipsative rather than normative, there are no standardized norms. However, the reliability of the findings may be ascertained within individual subjects. Split half reliability may be examined by dividing a 4-day diary in half and computing the rank order correlations of the total within-day frequencies (minus foods eaten only once) for the two groups of 2 days. Retest reliability can be ascertained by obtaining two diaries or sets of diaries from the same individual at some given time interval and finding the correlation between the total frequencies, assuming that the subject has not made dietary changes in the interim. Intrascorer reliability may be determined by having the same scorer analyze the same diary at a given time interval and interscorer reliability by having two or more persons analyze the same diary and computing appropriate correlations. For everyday clinical purposes, however, these methodological refinements are likely to be superfluous.

Validation of the hypotheses derived from data analysis is of greater interest. Currently, the sole criterion against which the hypotheses can be legitimately validated is the individual's clinical response to adequate dietary elimination and adequate challenge. This is obviously not the place for a treatise on what makes an elimination diet and challenge procedure adequate, but it should be noted that clinical testing of these hypotheses must be carried out by clinicians who are extremely knowledgeable about these procedures and how they can go wrong. It is especially important that foods with which the suspects might cross-react be eliminated at the same time as the suspects and that all traces of the suspected food be eliminated. Other dietary and environmental maneuvers suggested by the history and results of other investigations also need to be instituted for optimum response. However, assuming that many possible pitfalls have been avoided, it is possible to describe the expected response to the procedures.

If the hypothesis of food addiction is correct and the addictant foods have all been eliminated, the patient can experience a transient but commonly severe exacerbation of existing symptoms (and the possible emergence of new symptoms, such as headaches, a flulike state, or rhinitis) during the first 5 to 10 days of withdrawal, followed by extensive and often dramatic improvement. During this time, an appreciable amount of weight may be lost rapidly as waterlogged tissues shed stored fluid. A partial response commonly suggests either the presence of other environmental agents that are affecting the patient adversely or some other form of concurrent pathology, somatic or psychological. In some disorders, withdrawal may take longer than 5 to 10 days.

Once the patient's improvement has reached asymptote, the identity of the hypothesized addictants may be tested by reintroducing them, one at a time in normal-sized portions at least once and preferably up to three times a day for 1 week. If any unmistakably adverse reaction occurs, the food should be stopped and the patient should be allowed to recover fully before testing the next food. Each food that causes a reaction the first time it is tested should be tested again at a later time to verify that it was the food and not a concurrent event that caused the symptoms. Under some circumstances, double-blind testing may be desirable; however, often after having made themselves sick several times already while testing foods on an open basis, patients may be understandably reluctant to run the risk of being sick again.

If reintroducing the food in the dose schedule and dose level suggested does not produce a recurrence of some of the banished symptoms after 1 week, the hypothesis that the food is addictant may be discounted. However, with foods that contain drugs, such as coffee and tea, it may be necessary to reinstate the pretreatment dose level for an adequate period before drawing conclusions. A patient who has been poisoning himself with gram doses of caffeine may not react adversely to a single cup or even three cups of coffee daily but may become ill again when he or she goes back to 10 cups a day. Foods that do not cause symptoms on adequate reintroduction may be restored to the diet.

Clinical Use

The main use of the procedure is to generate hypotheses about whether food addiction is likely to be present in a given patient and, if so, which foods are likely to be involved. The main category of patient in whom the technique is relevant is the patient with multiple unexplained chronic and/or fluctuating symptoms, somatic and psychological, especially those who have failed to obtain a diagnosis from various medical specialists that has led to effective treatment. Patients who have at least two of the following are especially likely to fall into this group: persistent fatigue not helped by rest, a weight problem in either direction or a history of fluctuating weight, occasional puffiness of the face, hands, abdomen, or ankles, palpitations, especially during or after meals, and excessive sweating unrelated to exercise (Mackarness, 1976). Patients with migraines, unattributable panic attacks, an irritable bowel, and unattributable rashes seem particularly likely to come into this group, especially if they have other symptoms. The more unexplained symptoms affecting the bodily systems a patient has, especially if young and ostensibly fit, the more likely a food addiction is to be present. The symptoms in question may appear nonspecific, such as red, itchy eyes, generalized itching, pains in chest, abdomen, muscles, or joints, irritability, a "dopey" feeling, or inability to think clearly, eating binges, or a flulike state that never becomes flu. However, when several occur in the same person, they are virtually pathognomonic.

Several cautions must be mentioned, however. Food addiction may not be the only environmental problem present. Patients with one form of environmental intolerance commonly have other forms of environmental intolerance (Rippere, 1983). In addition, food addicts may have chemical sensitivity or organic inhalant allergies or addictions to nicotine, benzodiazepines, or various over-the-counter medications, or several of these at once. These problems may need to be dealt with before a valid test of the food addiction hypothesis is possible. Furthermore, patients with concurrent nutrient deficiencies and hypoglycemia, both of which may result from addictive eating of a nutrient-depleted refined food diet (Philpott & Kalita, 1980), will require additional dietary manipulations and supplementation. The method must be used in connection with other diagnostic approaches for a complete evaluation of a given patient's environmental sensitivities. Finally, the presence of environmental intolerance does not exclude concurrent organic or true psychological disorder, but patients may be easier to diagnose when the organic or psychogenic symptoms are not obscured by those of environmental origin.

Future Directions

It is hoped that the main future direction of the procedure will be in the increased frequency of use by conventional practitioners faced with treatment-resistant, polysymptomatic patients. Many unconventional practitioners are already considering food addiction as a possibility in their polysymptomatic patients *before* they have been fruitlessly subjected to years or decades of inappropriate routine investigations and treatments.

References

Mackarness, R. (1976). *Not all in the mind*. London: Pan.
Philpott, W., & Kalita, D.K. (1980). *Brain allergies: The psycho-nutrient connection*. New Cannan, CT: Keats Publishing Company.
Randolph, T.G. (1956). The descriptive features of addictive eating and drinking. *Quarterly Journal of Studies in Alcohol, 17,* 198-224.
Randolph, T.G. (1976). Stimulatory and withdrawal levels and the alternation of allergic manifestations. In L.D. Dickey (Ed.), *Clinical Ecology*. Springfield, IL: Charles C Thomas.
Rippere, V. (1983). *The allergy problem: Why people suffer and what should be done*. Wellingborough: Thorsons.

Behavioral Avoidance Slide Test

Donald J. Levis

Description

The Behavioral Avoidance Slide Test (BAST) consists of 11 visual pictures of a phobic stimulus ordered on the dimension of size from small (far) to large (close) or on the dimension of focus from out of focus (unclear) to in focus (clear). A press of a button by a subject advances the slide along the dimension being tested. Ten presses completes the series. The subject can avoid the slide content by either delaying the button press or refusing to press. A behavioral index of avoidance (latency of button presses) and a distance measure (number of presses) serve as the main dependent measure.

The typical procedure for presenting the BAST involves sitting the subject 2.36 meters in front of a projection screen. The subject is told that a slide of the phobic stimulus will be projected on the screen and that his task is to increase the view of the slide by pressing a button located in front of the subject. The slide test is discontinued for a given series if the subject makes 10 presses, if the subject requests to stop, or if a 180-second button press latency occurs at any point in the series. Each slide produces an image approximately 50 cm wide by 70 cm high. If the size dimension is used, the first slide in the series produces the smallest image (3.9 cm by 5.7 cm) and the last slide the largest (46.6 cm by 68.9 cm). Each intervening slide in the series results in an image approximately 30% greater than the preceding slide, as measured by image length. If the focus dimension is used, the slides are graded in visual clarity from out of focus (first slide) to in focus (last slide). The attainment of 10 increasingly equivalent degrees of subjective clarity is achieved by varying the F stop control. A 4-second delay period follows each button press to allow time for recording response latencies and other data, such as autonomic and self-report measures that can be recorded throughout testing.

Purpose

One major contribution of the behavior therapy movement has been its emphasis on targeting objective behavior for treatment modification and for determining therapy effectiveness. Without objective assessment procedures and treatment goals, the field of psychotherapy will remain in its current state of flux and impotency. Although the behavioral movement has made considerable gains in objectifying the response side of behavior, more work is needed to assess the stimulus content responsible for eliciting maladaptive fears and symptoms. Problematic in this quest to determine the lawful stimulus-response contingencies associated with a given maladaptive behavior is the difficulty in objectifying the stimulus dimension. Even when the eliciting stimulus is externalized (e.g., fear of flying), it is unclear whether other more aversive stimulus elements are associated with this content (e.g., fear of bodily injury or death). Furthermore, patients report many fears that are difficult to assess directly and objectively either because of the nature of the stimulus content or because they are internalized and avoided. Examples of the foregoing include fear of disease, punishment, emotional contact, and expressing anger, and sexually related fears. Verbal report of such fears is usually limited in stimulus characteristics and rarely specified to the point that the stimulus-response contingency can be readily assessed in terms of accuracy of content and magnitude of fearfulness. Yet, it is precisely in these areas that a paramount need exists for the development of behavioral assessment procedures.

The BAST is an attempt to achieve the aforementioned objective by permitting the assessment of stimulus content areas that do not readily lend themselves to a direct in vivo analysis. The procedure is designed to eliminate the problematic concerns associated with solely relying on verbal report by increasing the stimulus saliency of a given content area through visual presentations and by providing objective behavior measures of the subject's fearfulness and avoidance tendencies.

Development

The BAST procedure, first reported by Burchardt and Levis (1977), involves an extension of the Phobic Test Apparatus (PTA) procedure developed by Levis (1969). The PTA was designed to measure human avoidance behavior to small objects (e.g., a rat or snake) frequently used as target behaviors in analogue research. The apparatus consists of an 11-foot metal track 3.5 inches wide and 2.5 feet high. Each foot of the track is demarcated by alternating black and white patches. At one end of the track, fastened to a movable platform, is a clear Plexiglas box designed to hold the phobic-test stimulus. The distance from the opposite end of the track to the front edge of the box is 10 feet. A push button is mounted at the base of the track at the end opposite the box. The subject is seated directly in front of the push button and instructed to bring the phobic stimulus as close as possible by pressing the button. Each press of the button moves the phobic stimulus 1 foot closer to the subject. Ten presses put the phobic stimulus directly in front of the subject.

The PTA was designed to improve the typically used procedure of requiring the subject to enter a room and physically approach the phobic-test stimulus. Besides providing a distance and a contact-noncontact dependent measure, the PTA introduced the sensitive behavior index of latency to press. The use of a non-approach or delayed response latency at both the infrahuman and human level has a lengthy documented history of providing a sensitive index of emotional responding. In addition, the procedure allows for continuous monitoring of self-report and physiologic responding. These same advantages in measurement are incorporated into the BAST procedure.

Psychometric Characteristics

The psychometric characteristics of the PTA upon which BAST is based have undergone research scrutiny. Subjects who were divided into high and low fear groups on the basis of their responses to the rat or snake item on the Fear Survey Schedule II were reliably differentiated in terms of response topography on each of the behavior indices, which include the distance measure (number of presses), latency to press, and contact-noncontact measure. Furthermore, self-report indices such as the Fear Thermometer and the Affect Adjective Check List taken during or at the end of testing, as well as autonomic measures such as the Galvanic Skin Response, were found to appropriately separate high and low fear subjects. However, the latency to press measure proved to be a particularly sensitive index. Discriminating response gradients across the 10 button presses were obtained between subjects who could touch the phobic stimulus and those who could not. The former gradients were flat across the 10 presses with response times being quick (around 1 second). Conversely, those subjects who could not make contact generated progressively increasing steep gradients, supporting the notion that inverse relationships exist for the noncontact subjects between the latency of each button press and the distance of the phobic stimulus from the subject. Time between button presses progressively increased as the number of button presses increased (Craighead, 1973; Levis, 1969; Burchardt & Levis, 1977). The psychometric characteristics of the 10 discrete steps of the PTA runway were also analyzed by using Stevens' magnitude estimation procedure. Support was found for the assumption that a gradient of fear (from low to high) exists for fearful subjects across the 10 demarcated sections of the apparatus (Levis & Plunkett, 1979).

It is recognized that one of the best methods of separating subjects into high and low fear groups is to determine whether they can make contact with the phobic test stimulus. The strong relationship between the button-press measure and the contact measure suggests that the response-latency index may be substituted for contact measures when the latter is not readily assessible. Burchardt and Levis (1977) provided a direct comparison between the PTA and the BAST procedures using subjects who reported extreme fear of a rat stimulus. The slide procedure reliably discriminated between contact and noncontact subjects on the latency to press measure and on self-report and autonomic measures. No differences were found between the size and focus methods of slide presentation.

Peterson and Levis (1985) extended the use of the BAST to assess fear of bodily injury. The primary behavior index, response latency between button presses, reliably discriminated between preselected, high and low fear subjects and between a bodily injury and control slides. Support for the contention that the behavior avoidance measure was reflecting differences in fear level was obtained from the results provided by the autonomic and self-report measures. The slide test was administered 1 week later to assess the reliability of the measure. Good test-retest results were obtained. High correlations were found between sessions for the button press latency data and for self-report data, and moderate reliable correlations were found for autonomic measures (skin conductance response frequency data and heart rate change scores). Further analysis of their data suggests that defining a subject's fearfulness on the basis of a pre-selection inventory is problematic. They found that the behavioral latency measure was considerably more sensitive in defining an individual subject's fear level. For defining high fear subjects, they recommend using a criterion of failure to make 10 presses or an average response latency of 10 seconds or greater.

Clinical Use and Future Directions

The BAST procedure is still in the initial stages of experimental development. The procedure, which is easy to administer, is ultimately intended for clinical use. For example, slide material could be used to analyze fears of aggression, bodily injury, affection, sexual activity, rejection, death, and punishment. The long-term objective is to develop a battery of slide material representing different stimulus-content areas. Such an assessment battery could aid the clinician in isolating sensitive areas in need of further exploration. A battery of slides could also be assembled to assess a specific content area in detail. The sexual area readily lends itself to this kind of analysis. Slides depicting various sexual behaviors could easily be assembled (e.g., masturbation, nudity, homosexuality, oral sex, intercourse, and even fear of incest). The advantage of using such slide material is that a behavioral measure of fearfulness can be obtained in an area in which verbal report is difficult and unreliable.

The BAST can also be useful in outcome research both as a method for assessing a subject's fear level and as target behavior for assessing treatment effectiveness. The method may eventually prove useful in establishing a relationship between a given symptom and a specific, avoided stimulus-content area. If such a relationship can be established, considerable theoretical and assessment advances can be made. One final note concerning future development is in order. For slide material that may not be very arousing, it may prove useful to supplement the slide presentation with a detailed verbal description of the feared content.

References

Burchardt, C.J., & Levis, D.J. (1977). The utility of presenting slides of a phobic stimulus in the context of a behavioral avoidance procedure. *Behavior Therapy, 8,* 340-346.

Craighead, W.E. (1973). The assessment of avoidance responses on the Levis phobic test apparatus. *Behavior Therapy, 4,* 235-240

Levis, D.J. (1969). The phobic test apparatus: An objective measure of human avoidance behavior to small objects. *Behaviour Research and Therapy, 7,* 309-315.

Levis, D.J., & Plunkett, W.J. (1979). The use of subjective magnitude estimation technique to validate procedures for pre-selecting "phobic" subjects. *Behavioral Assessment, 1,* 191-201.

Peterson, D.A., & Levis, D.J. (1985). The assessment of bodily injury fears via the behavioral avoidance slide-test. *Behavioral Assessment, 7,* 172-184.

Behavioral Avoidance Test

F. Dudley McGlynn

Description

Motoric approach/avoidance of a feared stimulus can be assessed in contrived and naturalistic settings. This description is about assessment in contrived settings.

The behavioral avoidance test or behavioral approach test (BAT) is an assessment strategy, not a specific instrument or exact set of procedures. In general, a targeted fear stimulus (e.g., snake, rat, or spider) is caged at the end of a 10- to 20-foot walkway along which distances to the cage are indicated. Typically, performance aids such as a pointer and gloves are placed close to the cage. Frequently, the patient or subject is provided with a behavioral checklist that describes a number of discrete acts that are called for in the assessment. He or she is then shown to the far end of the walkway and given instructions to perform the activities on the list. The literature shows significant variations in the timing, delivery modes, and contents of BAT instructions, and in the locations and activities of therapists or experimenters during the tests. Variations also exist in what is recorded (e.g., degree of approach, latency to touch the feared stimulus, and

other fear behaviors during the task) (Bernstein & Nietzel, 1973).

Purpose

Early behavior therapists learned the dual process fear-mediation theory of phobic avoidance. According to this view, anxiety serves as an aversive drive state whose contingent removal or reduction negatively reinforces instrumental escape/avoidance of the cues that produce it. Given the direct connection between fear and avoidance, the original purpose of the BAT was to "measure fear objectively." Recently, behavior therapists have abandoned the dual-process theory of avoidance and adopted instead the three response-channel view according to which private/cognitive fear behaviors, physiological arousal behaviors, and locomotor escape/avoidance behaviors are largely separate features of complex fearful displays. Hence, the contemporary purpose of the BAT is to measure the motoric dimension of the three-channel construct.

Development

The BAT dates to the early work of Lang and his colleagues. In the original procedure (Lang & Lazovik, 1963) women who reported fear of snakes were asked to enter a room that contained a harmless, caged snake. While the subject remained at the door, the experimenter walked to the cage, removed the top, and invited her to observe, to touch, and to hold the snake. In the absence of compliance, each invitation was repeated once. The subject's behavior was scored according to "look, touch, hold" categories.

The BAT assessment strategy became popular during the late 1960s and early 1970s when pretreatment to posttreatment BAT improvements were used routinely to evaluate the effects of experimental therapies, such as systematic desensitization and modeling. Programmatic research towards developing valid BAT protocols was undertaken during this period, primarily by Bernstein and his colleagues. Widespread use of the approach, however, ultimately spawned procedural diversity, and no standard or consensually endorsed BAT protocol emerged.

Psychometric Characteristics

Approach/avoidance in a BAT walkway is influenced by several factors that, if not taken into account, will introduce noise into "fear" interpretations of BAT performance. Bernstein and Nietzel

(1973) reported that snake aversant subjects exposed to "fear assessment" in a clinic context showed longer touch latencies and more overt fear behaviors than did equally aversant subjects exposed to "physiological assessment" in a laboratory context. They also reported that subjects who received face-to-face BAT instructions approached the snake more closely and touched it more frequently than did subjects who received tape-recorded BAT instructions. Feist and Rosenthal (1973) reported that a BAT using a live snake produced more avoidance and more rated fear than did a BAT using an inert specimen. They also reported that subjects accompanied during the BAT were less avoidant and less fearful than were unaccompanied subjects, although this result interacted with several other variables. In brief, BAT performance mirrors the operation of a variety of factors that interact with the subject's or patient's fear. (For a review, see Bernstein, 1973.) The degree to which such contextual and procedural factors are influential probably is an inverse function of fear intensity.

Clinical Use

The BAT strategy is not restricted to patients who fear stimuli such as snakes, rats, and spiders. For claustrophobia, for example, patients were asked to sit in a small, dark, closed chamber for 10 minutes, or until they became sufficiently uncomfortable to terminate the test. For acrophobia, patients were asked to climb a standard stairway with an assistant. Use of the approach with fearful patients is limited only by the availability of stimuli and the inventiveness of the clinician.

Contrived BATs should be used for clinical work mainly as precursors to naturalistic assessment or when naturalistic assessment is not conveniently possible. This is so for several reasons. For one, there are known instances of demonstrably poor prediction from contrived fear assessment to naturalistic fear behavior. For another, content valid behavioral assessment requires representative sampling of the patient's actions, sampling not typically permitted by contrived assessment contexts. For a third, the behavioral assessor's concept of situational specificity more or less mandates naturalistic assessment to the extent that it is taken seriously. (For a cogent discussion of external validity and related issues in a contrived behavioral avoidance test, see Lick & Unger, 1977.) When contrived BATs are used *appropriately* in clinical work, they can provide valuable information. Fear behavior in a contrived setting is not discontinuous from fear behavior in the natural environment.

Future Directions

The programmatic research of Bernstein and others has shown how contextual, procedural, and instructional variables influence BAT performance among fearful college populations confronted with harmless animals. The early work also can serve as a model for programmatic investigation of nonfear determinants of contrived BAT performances among clinic populations interacting with other feared stimuli. Research toward "artifact-free," standardized protocols for BAT assessment of clinical populations is desirable given the relatively greater observational control available in contrived settings and the goal of a cumulative body of knowledge.

There is a related need for research concerning the contextual, procedural, and instructional aspects of contrived BATs that do and do not vitiate applicability of the assessment results to the task of predicting clinically relevant fear behavior. Trustworthy procedures for assessment in the clinic would be valued for convenience and cost effectiveness.

Because of its relative potential for observational control, the contrived BAT affords an important avenue to empirically fleshing out the three-channel fear construct. The confluence of ambulatory psychophysiological recording, computer management of real-time data, and statistical methods such as time-series analysis affords reason for optimistic research along such lines.

References

Bernstein, D.A. (1973). Behavioral fear assessment: anxiety or artifact? In H. Adams & P. Unikel (Eds.), *Issues and trends in behavior therapy*. Springfield, IL: Charles C Thomas.

Bernstein, D.A., & Nietzel, M.T. (1973). Procedural variation in behavioral avoidance tests. *Journal of Consulting and Clinical Psychology, 2*, 165-174.

Feist, J.R., & Rosenthal, T.L. (1973). Serpent versus surrogate and other determinants of runway fear differences. *Behaviour Research and Therapy, 11*, 483-490.

Lang, P.J., & Lazovik, A.D. (1963). Experimental desensitization of a phobia. *Journal of Abnormal and Social Psychology, 66*, 519-525.

Lick, J.R., & Unger, T.E. (1977). The external validity of behavioral fear assessment: The problem of generalizing from the laboratory to the natural environment. *Behavior Modification, 1*, 283-306.

Behavioral Checklist for Mildly Handicapped Children

Lisa Carden-Smith and Susan Fowler

Description

A simple behavioral checklist was developed for mildly handicapped children to use in rating their behavior (or their peer's behavior) during classroom transition times (i.e., classroom cleanup, using the bathroom, and a short waiting time). The checklist consisted of three pictures representing the three transition activities. The pictures were: children picking up materials, children washing their hands, and children seated on floor mats. Next to each picture was a space in which the child, teacher, or classroom observer could make a plus sign to indicate the child had behaved in an appropriate manner during the activity or a minus sign to indicate unsatisfactory performance. Rules for assigning plus and minus signs included: (a) A plus was assigned if the child completed the actions required by the transition acitivity. These included: (1) picking up materials during cleanup, (2) walking to and from the bathroom and washing hands while in the bathroom, and (3) selecting a book to look at and sitting quietly on a floor mat until the next learning activity began. (b) A minus was assigned if the child did not participate in the activity (when instructed to do so) or if the child engaged in the following inappropriate behaviors: (1) using aggressive behavior against a teacher or peer, (2) grabbing materials from a peer, (3) misusing materials, (4) leaving the room without permission or not returning directly from the bathroom, (5) using inappropriate language (e.g., name calling and swearing), (6) taking more than 30 seconds to begin compliance with an instruction, and (7) running or crawling in place of walking.

Purpose

The checklist was developed to record child participation (+) or nonparticipation/disruption (−) during ordinary classroom transition periods. The checklist has been used by teachers and by children (aged 5 and 6, evidencing mild handicaps).

Development and Psychometric Characteristics

Interobserver agreement was obtained on the rating scale by having a second observer simultaneously and independently complete the rating scales on all children at the end of the transition period approximately once every 5 days. Agreement was calculated by dividing the sum of observer agreements on the rating scale by the sum of observer disagreements and multiplying by 100. Mean agreement between adult observers with 19 children ranged from 87 to 100%.

For three children in each classroom, the checklist ratings were compared daily with a 5-second continuous interval recording system. Child behaviors recorded with the coding system were defined as: (a) Participation was scored if the child was engaged in the three transition activities. The behaviors included picking up materials, putting them in bins or on shelves, and looking for materials to pick up. Participation was also scored if the child was walking to the restroom, directing other children to the restroom, putting out the mats and materials for a large group, sharing a book in the waiting area, or sitting quietly in the waiting area waiting for the teacher to begin working with a large group. (b) Disruption was scored when a child broke a classroom rule. Disruptive behaviors included noncompliance with teacher instructions, continued use of learning center materials, verbal negatives, running, shouting, fighting, throwing, or misusing any classroom materials. Because ratings were based on the three transition activities, children could receive a rating of 0%, 33%, 67%, or 100% for a given day. The ratings of acceptable performance per baseline and treatment conditions obtained with the checklist correlated positively with the ratings of participation obtained with the interval recording system. However, checklist ratings provided a more stringent assessment of performance than did the 5-second continuous scoring system; one infraction of a classroom rule during an activity (e.g., running down the hallway) produced a rating of unacceptable performance for the activity in which it occurred.

Clinical Use

The checklist was used as part of a peer-monitoring treatment package designed to reduce disruption and nonparticipation during classroom transition activities. Thus far, it has been used successfully with 28 children (Carden-Smith & Fowler, 1984). During peer monitoring, children took turns serving as team captains. The team captains monitored each member of their team and awarded points (pluses) at the end of the transition activities to teammates who participated appropriately. The captains also self-awarded points for appropriate participation. During the initial phases of peer monitoring, teacher feedback was provided on the accuracy of the team captain's point awards. Points were exchanged later for recess privileges. Children who were awarded three points were eligible to attend recess, to vote for the recess activity, and to have their name placed in the drawing pool for team captain. Children who earned two points attended recess but were not eligible to vote or to be team captain. Children who received only one point missed the first 5 minutes of recess and children who received no points were excluded from recess.

To determine if children could award points accurately, reliability checks were conducted between peer awards and an adult observer, who also completed the checklist on the team captain and teammates before the team captain's administration of point awards. Analysis of the point awards indicates that peer monitors consistently awarded points that were earned. However, when corrective feedback from the teacher was withdrawn, the peers consistently awarded points that were not earned (i.e., they rarely gave a minus).

Future Directions

Additional, simple checklists could be developed to assist children in monitoring their behavior during classroom activities in which nonparticipation or disruption has been a problem.

Reference

Carden-Smith, L.K., & Fowler, S.A. (1984). Positive peer pressure: The effects of peer monitoring on children's disruptive behavior. *Journal of Applied Behavior Analysis, 17,* 213-227.

Behavioral Conversational Measures

Frances M. Haemmerlie

Description

Heterosocial/heterosexual anxiety, or anxiety experienced in social interactions involving members of the opposite sex, is an important problem for several reasons. It has been considered important because of its role in development during the adolescent years, as an antecedent of social problems in later life, as a clinically relevant target

behavior for analogue outcome research, and as a significant problem for college students (Galassi & Galassi, 1979). Although a number of self-report measures have been developed to measure heterosocial anxiety, attempts to develop behavioral measures have not been as successful. Although the ultimate goal of behavioral measures is to obtain direct measurement of behavior in a natural setting, a variety of practical problems have led most clinicians and researchers to use staged interactions in a laboratory or clinic setting (Bellack, 1979). Additionally, men have been studied much more frequently than have women. The behavioral assessment approach to be described involves a "natural interaction" between a subject and a confederate in a laboratory setting. Furthermore, it has been successfully used to evaluate treatment outcome in a study with male (Haemmerlie & Montgomery, 1982) and female (Haemmerlie, 1983) heterosocially anxious college students.

Subjects report to an experimental room where they initially read and sign a consent form, stating that at various points throughout the experiment their behavior will be directly monitored. When finished, the subject is taken by a research assistant to another room where an opposite sexed confederate (presented as another subject) is sitting at a table filling out some forms. The subject is told to be seated and is handed some forms to complete. The confederate previously was instructed to complete the forms before the subject is finished in order to be available for conversation during a 3-minute period after the subject finishes filling out the forms. The confederate also was told not to initiate conversation and to respond with only two- or three-word answers to questions. The conversation is audiotaped by a hidden tape recorder and is subsequently scored along a number of dimensions by a naive scorer.

After the 3-minute conversation period is over, the research assistant comes back into the room, hands the confederate an additional form to complete, and takes the subject to another room where additional instructions (depending upon the nature of the experiment) are given.

Purpose

The procedure is designed to obtain direct behavioral measures of heterosocial anxiety in an unobtrusive manner that closely approximates a natural social interaction between individuals of the opposite sex. Although administered in a laboratory setting, it involves the use of a minimally trained confederate who appears to be in the same situation as the subject and thus incorporates some aspects of an in vivo observational situation (Bellack, 1979).

Development

This behavioral assessment procedure was used by Haemmerlie (1983) to assess levels of heterosocial anxiety in college women before and after treatment. A 3-minute conversation audiotape was scored for the number of initiations of conversation made by the subject (a question asked of the confederate or an independent comment made after a 3-second period) and the percentage of conversational silence during the 3-minute period. Haemmerlie and Montgomery (1982) evaluated changes in the anxiety levels of college men who had been exposed to a therapeutic intervention. The 3-minute audiotapes obtained in this study were scored with regard to both the number of initiations of conversation and the number of personal statements (use of the pronoun "you" in a question or statement).

Psychometric Characteristics

Interrater reliability was assessed in the Haemmerlie (1983) and Haemmerlie and Montgomery (1982) studies by having a naive second scorer rate the audiotapes along the same dimensions as did the initial naive scorer. In the study with college women, Pearson product-moment correlation coefficients between these two raters who rated all tapes ranged from .9910 to .9996, indicating nearly perfect agreement for the number of initiations and the percent of conversational silence measures. In the Haemmerlie and Montgomery (1982) study of college men, a randomly selected subset of 25% of the audiotapes was rescored by a naive second rater. The correlation coefficients between these two raters were .83 for the personal attention measure and .89 for the initiation of conversation measure.

Evidence of test-retest reliability was obtained in the Haemmerlie and Montgomery (1982) study. A group of 13 control, nontreated subjects was reassessed 3 weeks after the initial assessment. Pearson test-retest reliability coefficients were .83 for the conversation initiations measure and .90 for the personal statements measure.

Evidence of validity in both studies is provided by the significant reductions in anxiety after treatment that occurred on some of the behavioral measures in both studies of heterosocially anxious college students. In the Haemmerlie (1983) study, results of an ANOVA with repeated measures showed that between pre- and posttreatment assessment, women significantly reduced the amount of conversational silence, $F(1,18) = 6.76$, $p:LT.05$, that occurred during the 3-minute audiotaped conversation period. In the Haemmerlie and Montgomery (1982) study, results of 2 x 2 (Treatment versus control group X pre- versus posttreatment assessment) ANOVAs with repeated measures, showed significant increases in the number of personal remarks, $F(1,24) = 38.50$, $p < .001$, and the number of initiations of conversation, $F(1,24) = 10.66$, $p < .001$, by the heterosocially anxious men during the 3-minute conversation period after the therapeutic intervention. Additionally, some evidence of construct validity was provided in this study with college men, because the number of personal statements for both treated and untreated groups of subjects before treatment correlated significantly with two self-report measures that were also used in this study. A correlation of $-.42$ $(p < .05)$ was obtained with the *Situation Questionnaire* and $-.35$ $(p < .05)$ with the *Fear of Negative Evaluation Scale*. (See Arkowitz [1977] for a review of these inventories.) These correlations suggest that high levels of self-reported anxiety in heterosocially anxious male subjects are associated with low numbers of personal statements and low numbers of initiations of conversation.

Clinical Use

To date, this conversational assessment procedure has been used only with heterosocially anxious college students in a laboratory setting. Therefore, its use with other populations or in nonlaboratory settings remains untested. It could easily be adapted to a clinic "waiting" or "testing room" setting, and it could be administered by either a technician or a secretary. Furthermore, as long as the client can remain in the presence of an individual of the opposite sex for several minutes, it could conceivably be used with any client who evinces a heterosocial interaction problem.

Future Directions

The behavioral assessment procedure described in this section is brief and relatively simple to arrange. Scoring, however, depending on what dimensions are evaluated, may be time consuming. The procedure approximates a natural conversation situation and it can be administered by a minimally trained assistant. It further allows for a wide variety of interactional dimensions to be scored, including component behaviors at the molecular (e.g., speech duration and voice volume), intermediate (e.g., conversational content and structure), and/or molar (e.g., global ratings of skills) levels of response specificity. However, like most in vivo and/or naturalistic observational procedures, it suffers from possible problems with restricted sampling of the behavioral domain and from the acting abilities or actions of the confederate. Although changes in the behavioral measures of heterosocial anxiety after treatment were obtained in two studies, the particular behaviors within which the changes occurred were different in the two studies. This finding may simply reflect differences in how heterosocially anxious men and women behave, or it might yet be another instance of the difficulty in identifying sets of molecular behaviors that relate to heterosocial anxiety. Future directions would include more research on the nature and extent of these problems and also could include the use of videotaped conversations.

References

Arkowitz, H. (1977). Measurement and modification of minimal dating behavior. In M. Hersen, R.M. Eisler, & P.M. Miller (Eds.), *Progress in behavior modification: Vol. 5* (pp. 1-61). New York: Academic Press.

Bellack, A.S. (1979). Behavioral assessment of social skills. In A.S. Bellack & M. Hersen (Eds.), *Research and practice in social skills training* (pp. 75-104). New York: Plenum Press.

Galassi, J.P., & Galassi, M.D. (1979). Modification of heterosocial skill deficits. In A.S. Bellack & M. Hersen (Eds.), *Research and practice in social skills training* (pp. 131-187). New York: Plenum Press.

Haemmerlie, F.M. (1983). Heterosocial anxiety in college females: A biased interactions treatment. *Behavior Modification, 7,* 611-623.

Haemmerlie, F.M., & Montgomery, R.L. (1982). Self-perception theory and unobtrusively biased interactions: A treatment for heterosocial anxiety. *Journal of Counseling Psychology, 29,* 362-370.

Behavioral Eating Test

Gregory L. Wilson and D. Balfour Jeffrey

Description

The Behavioral Eating Test (BET) is an assessment strategy that measures food and beverage consumption (Bridgwater, Jeffrey, Walsh, Dawson, & Peterson, 1984; Jeffrey et al., 1980a). Unlike self-report measures that often correlate poorly with actual eating behavior, the BET was designed as a nonintrusive, nonreactive behavioral assessment technique that attempts to limit expectancy or attitudinal factors. Empirical studies employing the BET have focused on children's consumption of pro-nutrition and low-nutrition foods and beverages (Jeffrey, McLellarn, & Fox, 1982; Peterson, Jeffrey, Dawson, & Bridgwater, 1984).

Specifically, the test consists of serving foods and beverages to subjects in 12 transparent, equal-sized cups placed on a tray. In these 12 cups are placed six familiar pro-nutrition (e.g., cheese, carrots, grapes, apples, milk, and orange juice) and low-nutrition foods (e.g., Hershey bars, Fritos, Chips Ahoy, Honeycombs, Pepsi, and Kool-Aid). All foods are prepared immediately before presentation to insure equal freshness. Additionally, all foods are presented in approximately equal-sized units, and placement of cups on the tray is randomly determined for each subject. Subsequent to presenting the tray, instructions are given that direct each subject to taste the different foods and beverages so that "you can tell me what you think of them." Each subject is further instructed to "eat as much of anything as you want" and "if there are foods you don't like, you don't need to eat them." Finally, questions are answered and the examiner leaves the testing room. During the consumption period (i.e., typically 8 minutes in length), subjects are unobtrusively observed to guard against procedural confounding (e.g., spillage and hoarding) as well as to provide additional qualitative data (Jeffrey et al., 1980a).

The BET measurement consists of weighing each food in grams or determining the volume of each beverage in milliliters. Interobserver reliability checks are easily completed, and interrater agreement estimates are calculated using the formula: (number of agreements/total agreements plus disagreements) x 100. All quantity data are then converted to caloric equivalents to provide a measure more directly related to obesity and to facilitate combining the data from both foods and beverages.

Methodological refinements (Jeffrey, McLellarn, & Fox, 1980b; Bridgwater et al., 1984) of the original BET procedures include: (a) adding a familiarization session before testing to allow subjects to feel more relaxed and better acquainted with the procedures; (b) reducing the number of foods from 12 to 6 and increasing the eating time from 8 to 10 minutes to increase the number of subjects tasting each food; and (c) selecting foods similar to one another in weight and in calories per gram within the pro-nutrition and low-nutrition categories to insure that individual foods would be weighted more equally in the composition of total scores.

Purpose

Research with the BET shows the test to be a feasible and economical laboratory procedure for assessing a child's eating behaviors. In addition, the BET demonstrates its potential as a method for assessing hypotheses related to eating behavior. Because previous studies employing the BET and food attitude scales indicated low order and inconsistent correlations between the behavioral and self-report measures, the different assessment techniques appear to be tapping different dimensions of eating behavior. Such results underscore the importance of including multidimensional measures in assessing complex behavior like eating.

Development

Because of concerns among health professionals over the dietary habits and resultant health problems of the American public (i.e., six leading causes of death in the United States are directly related to the two basic nutritional problems of obesity and excessive intake of fat and sugar), considerable attention has been directed towards investigating and modifying the develpment of poor nutritional practices in children. Whereas a number of factors have been suggested to influence a child's food preference and caloric consumption, critics of current nutritional practices have long argued that television and the promotion of low-nutrition foods have a significant impact on children's health problems. Unfortunately, much research in this area has been nonexperimental and has relied on surveys or self-report measures. To create a procedure for measuring actual food consumption, thereby attempting to avoid the limitations of earlier research, the BET was originally developed as a method for assessing the impact of television on the eating behavior of children (Jeffrey et al., 1980a).

Psychometric Characteristics

For Individual Food Scores, the original BET standard deviations were characteristically larger than the means. Conversely, the Total Score variable patterns revealed less relative variability and moderately high test-retest stabilities, ranging from +.51 to +.85 with a mean of +.67 (Jeffrey et al., 1980a). Similar findings were noted in other studies (Jeffrey et al., 1982). Methodological refinements of the BET have produced less skewed distributions and means that are more representative of group consumption. In addition, the number of outlying data points for each food have been reduced. These factors have, in turn, produced Individual Food Scores that are less variable and more temporally stable (Bridgwater et al., 1984).

Taken as a whole, each subsequent study on the BET has revealed small incremental improvements in the psychometric characteristics of the measure. In addition, there has been some external validation of the BET, in that children who eat a higher proportion of pro-nutrition calories on the test in the laboratory eat fewer low-nutrition foods at home. However, there still remain continuing problems with proportionally large standard deviations and relatively moderate test-retest stability coefficients on the Individual Food Scores. It now appears that these psychometric limitations probably reflect reality, in that actual food consumption is a highly complex response that is influenced by momentary variables. Therefore, it may be unrealistic to expect a measure of actual food consumption to be any more stable or sensitive, whether for children or for adults (Bridgwater et al., 1984).

Clinical Use

In addition to being used as a laboratory measure to evaluate the effects of television on children's food consumption, the BET could be considered as part of a multidimensional assessment package in assessing differences in consumptive patterns of obese and normal weight children (Jeffrey et al., 1980a). Also, the BET may aid in the measurement of treatment effects from programs designed for overweight children. For consistent patterns in food consumption to emerge, it might be necessary to have subjects eat a greater variety of foods over a period of days (Bridgwater et al., 1984).

Future Directions

Additional research is needed to evaluate further the generality of results to broader eating patterns outside the experimental paradigm. Clinicians and researchers interested in using this test with different foods and in different situations may want to develop alternative forms or analyze the internal consistency of the measure (Jeffrey et al., 1980a). Further refinements of the BET may have to work within the context of the psychometric limitations mentioned earlier (Bridgwater et al., 1984).

References

Bridgwater, C.A., Jeffrey, D.B., Walsh, J.A., Dawson, B., & Peterson, P. (1984). Measuring children's food consumption in the laboratory: A methodological refinement of the behavioral eating test. *Behavioral Assessment, 6,* 357-364.

Jeffrey, D.B., Lemnitzer, N.B., Hickey, J.S., Hess, M.S., McLellarn, R.W., & Stroud, J.M. (1980a). The development of a behavioral eating test and its relationship to a self-report food attitude scale in young children. *Behavioral Assessment, 2,* 87-89.

Jeffrey, D.B., McLellarn, R.W., & Fox, D.J. (1980b). *A methodological refinement of a behavioral eating test and a food attitude scale for young children.* Paper presented at the meeting of the Association for Advancement of Behavior Therapy, New York.

Jeffrey, D.B., McLellarn, R.W., & Fox, D.J. (1982). The development of children's eating habits: The role of television commercials. *Health Education Quarterly, 9,* 174-189.

Peterson, P., Jeffrey, D.B., Dawson, B., & Bridgwater, C.A. (1984). The effects of pro-nutrition ads on children's eating habits. *Developmental Psychology, 20,* 55-63.

Behavioral Measures of Severe Depression

Jeffrey E. Cassisi and Christopher Starratt

Description

Direct observation and ratings of the motoric correlates of severe depression can be made by nursing and other ward personnel on a time-sampling basis. Ratings are made in terms of the presence or absence of behaviors in three categories: (a) Talking, (b) Smiling, and (c) Other Motor Activity. Another category of Time in Room is also rated. The four categories are defined on daily tally sheets. Additionally, the list of alternate behaviors (possible activities on the ward) under the Other Motor Activity category is provided. Ratings are made, on the average, every half hour and summed to produce a single daily score.

Purpose

Depression is a multifaceted disorder that can affect verbal, physiological, and motoric behavior. Considerable attention has been directed towards the evaluation of the cognitive and affective correlates of depression, largely through self-report. Objective measurement of motoric or activity changes associated with depression has been less systematically investigated. The Behavioral Measures of Severe Depression serves this function within a multimodal assessment paradigm.

Development

Williams, Barlow, and Agras (1972) developed a system to measure depression behaviorally, with the goals that it would be easily learned, lend itself to relatively continuous use, and yet not be demanding of staff time. This system was studied in relation to two other methods of assessment in 10 severely depressed inpatients. Serial assessments were made using the Hamilton Rating Scale for Depression (a rating scale based on structured interviews) and the Beck Depression Inventory (a self-report inventory). All three methods correlated significantly, but the behavioral measures test appeared to better predict posttreatment adaptation.

Psychometric Characteristics

Williams et al. (1972) argue that a high concordance between the four categories (Talking, Smiling, Other Motor Behavior, and Time in Room) justifies combining the daily observations into a single total. Indeed, Kendall's coefficient of concordance was significant ($w = .70$, $p < .01$). After weighted Fisher's z-transformations were made, the overall Pearson product-moment correlation between the Hamilton scale and the behavioral measures test was $r = .71$, and the correlation between the Beck scale and the behavioral measures test was $r = .67$. Both of these mean correlations are statistically significant at the .05 level. No other studies on concurrent validity were found.

Implementation of this system, as with any behavioral rating system, requires special consideration to ensure consistency between raters. Appropriate interrater reliability checks must be made to detect observer drift and bias (Hartmann, 1977). Interrater reliability checks must be made frequently enough to minimize its effect on observers' vigilance. Covert interrater reliability checks may be useful to minimize observer reactivity.

Interrater reliability checks were made on at least 20 observations from each patient in the study by Williams et al. (1972). An interrater agreement of 96% was reported. Therefore, evidence that this system can be used reliably was presented.

Although this system correlates with other assessment devices, it is not intended to be a diagnostic instrument. Its discriminant validity is limited, because there are many psychiatric disorders with correlates of lowered activity. The original intention of the system was to provide a measure of the "depth" and course of depression, once a diagnosis has been made.

Clinical Use

The Behavioral Measures of Severe Depression test provides a measure of overt motoric behavior for inpatients diagnosed as suffering from an affective disorder. Use of this system is justified only when imbedded in a multimodal assessment approach. Such a procedure must include other objective diagnostic instruments. Although it is widely cited as exemplifying a behavioral alternative for measuring depression, only a handful of empirical investigations have actually used this instrument. One clinical report used this system to monitor the effects of a token economy on three depressed patients (Hersen, Eisler, Alford, & Agras, 1973). Contingent reinforcement for work assignments, occupational therapy, and personal hygiene resulted in marked diminution in observed depression relative to baseline in and A-B-A design.

Future Directions

The use of this system as a face valid measure of general activity level seems promising. Ongoing research in the Cognitive Rehabilitation Unit of the Veterans Administration Medical Center in Pittsburgh is using this system to measure activity in elderly and brain-damaged patients. Along with neuropsychological measures, the effectiveness of a pharmacological agent for dementia is being determined. This system may prove to be valuable in the evaluation of other psychopharmacological interventions (Alford & Williams, 1980).

Additional psychometric evaluation of the Behavioral Measure of Severe Depression test is essential. Concurrent validity studies with other methods of measuring activity, such as mechanical transduction and self-monitoring, are needed. Adaptations and changes in the activity list may be required in diverse settings. The effect this has on the psychometric characteristics of the system

should be determined. The incremental validity this system provides to decision-making processes within a multimodal behavioral assessment paradigm should be established.

If statistical analyses are required to evaluate data obtained from this system, an attempt should be made to partition out the effects of serial dependency by using sequential or time series analysis (Hartmann et al., 1981).

References

Alford, G.S., & Williams, J.G. (1980). The role and uses of psychopharmacological agents in behavior therapy. In M. Hersen, R.M. Eisler, & P.M. Miller (Eds.), *Progress in behavior modification: Vol. X*. New York: Academic Press.

Hartmann, D.P. (1977). Considerations in the choice of interobserver reliability estimates. *Journal of Applied Behavior Analysis, 10,* 103-116.

Hartmann, D.P., Gottman, J.M., Jones, R.R., Gardner, W., Kazdin, A.E., & Vaught, R.S. (1981). Interrupted time-series analysis and its application to behavioral data. *Journal of Applied Behavior Analysis, 14,* 111-120.

Hersen, M., Eisler, R.M., Alford, G.S., & Agras, W.S. (1973). Effects of token economy on neurotic depression: An experimental analysis. *Behavior Therapy, 4,* 392-397.

Williams, J.G., Barlow, D.H., & Agras, S.W. (1972). Behavioral measurement of severe depression. *Archives of General Psychiatry, 27,* 330-333.

Behavioral Role-Playing Assertion Test

Janet St. Lawrence

Description

The Behavioral Role-Playing Assertion Test (BRAT) (McFall & Lillesand, 1971) initiated a trend toward role-play assessment in social skills research, which continues to the present time. The BRAT is an audiotape, analogue procedure for assessing assertive competence in refusal situations. Originally employed to provide a sample of a subject's behavior in simulated refusal situations and to evaluate specific therapy techniques for training assertive refusal behavior, the BRAT stimulated the development of many similar measures.

Subjects are instructed to respond aloud to nine prerecorded stimulus situations, and their responses are audiotaped for later rating. The text for the BRAT's stimulus situations is available from the senior author upon request.

In the original study, subjects were seated alone in an experimental room while the experimenter was in an adjacent room where he could observe through a one-way window, operate the stimulus tape recorder, and record the subject's responses. Tape recordings of the subject's responses were later rated by two judges using a 5-point Likert scale. Judges in the original study were essentially untrained, having received only a one-page scoring manual that provided several examples for each scoring category.

Purpose

The BRAT is a highly specific role-play measure originated for use in experimental studies of specific therapy techniques. Rather than cover a broad, heterogeneous class of assertion situations, the BRAT concentrates on a limited, homogeneous subset of assertions, containing eight situations that involve the ability to refuse an unreasonable request and a ninth situation that calls for a different type of assertive response (i.e., asking the landlord to make promised repairs). Approximately half of the BRAT items were employed during training and used as a direct measure of treatment-related change. The other half were untrained items used to assess generalization from trained to unfamiliar refusal situations. The single nonrefusal item was employed to assess the extent to which training in assertive refusal would generalize to an unrelated response class.

Development

The first seven BRAT situations are refusal items adapted from the Conflict Resolution Inventory (CRI), developed by McFall and Lillesand following extensive pilot work to identify refusal situations that were actually problematic for college students. The eighth refusal situation was taken from an earlier study (McFall & Marston, 1970), and the ninth situation, included as a measure of generalization, called for a different type of assertive response (asking a landlord to make promised repairs). Unfortunately, the measure itself was not developed very systematically or empirically but originated specifically for an experimental study. However, it perpetuated a flood of assertion research which followed initial reports of its use.

Psychometric Characteristics

It is difficult to make a general statement about the psychometric properties of the BRAT because of the inconsistency with which it is implemented.

Although the BRAT is frequently borrowed for research use, it is so often modified that it is impossible to compare results across studies. As a result, adequate validational support has yet to be established.

McFall and Lillesand reported a significant positive correlation between assertive scores on the CRI and ratings of their refusal behavior on the BRAT (pretest: $r = .69$; posttest: $r = .63$). The concordance between the two measures offered some support for the validity of the CRI and the BRAT. Indirect validation was also demonstrated by a change in assertiveness ratings from pre- to post-treatment. The BRAT's test-retest reliability, computed by the authors over a 2-week period for subjects in an untreated control group, was .76 (McFall & Lillesand, 1971). Interrater reliabilities in the original study were high: .92 for pretest ratings and .95 for posttest ratings, indicating the measure could be reliably scored by even untrained raters.

Clinical Use

The BRAT developed for a specific experimental treatment paradigm with no expectation that it would be used as a general test of assertion. Therefore, the instrument was never intended for general clinical applications and is made available with the explicit request that its use be confined to research contexts. Indeed, the authors never intended the instrument to be a general assertion measure, although that is how many investigators have used it (McFall, 1985).

Future Directions

McFall's research helped bring into focus the critical issues involved in using such analogue methods for behavioral assessment. As a result, many of the suggestions that follow are applicable to behavioral role-play assessment and are not specific to the BRAT alone. The BRAT, or more often some variation of the BRAT, has been used extensively by different investigators in a number of assertion training experiments. Although the BRAT seems to be a significant improvement over previous measures, several major limitations remain to be addressed. One problem is that the BRAT was designed for use in a specific study and has not been cross-validated by other laboratories where it has been used with both similar and different subject populations. Although the BRAT is often borrowed, it is so frequently modified that it is impossible to compare results across studies. Because adequate validational support has not been published, the instrument requires more careful assessment of its psychometric properties before its real value can be determined.

Performance on the BRAT has not been shown to relate systematically to behavior in the natural environment, leaving questions about external validity unresolved. Given the frequency with which the BRAT and other role-play methods are employed in social skills research, assessment of external validity would make a contribution. In addition, because the BRAT's content is appropriate only with college students, its findings may not generalize to different clinical populations.

The usual procedure of scoring the BRAT by summing ratings over the individual situations to arrive at a total test score for each subject is a holdover from the days of trait measures (McFall, 1977). There is an implicit assumption of response additivity in such a scoring procedure, which is logically inconsistent with a situation-specific view of behavior. A scoring system that preserves the identity of individual responses while retaining the test data in a manageable form needs to be developed. McFall (1977) suggests that a performance profile analysis, similar to the type used on the Wechsler intelligence tests, may be a possible solution to the scoring problem. This possibility deserves to be explored.

Furthermore, the usual method of assessing interrater agreement by computing the intercorrelation between the total test scores given to an individual subject by different raters may not be appropriate. To be consistent with a situation-specific analysis of behavior, interrater agreement should reflect the intercorrelations for each individual response, not just for total scores (McFall, 1977). McFall (1977) suggests comparing ratings on a response by response basis and reporting the overall percent-agreement between raters. It would also be useful to examine interrater agreement on each of the individual test items for suggestions on which items warrant refinement or revision.

Another weakness in the BRAT is that it imposes an artificial constraint by allowing only one brief verbal response to each test situation. This constraint enables experimental rigor, but at the expense of realism. Unfortunately, efforts to develop more life-like role-playing measures, in which the subject is permitted to engage in un-structured interactions, encounter methodological problems, such as the difficulty of exercising control over relevant stimuli in such interactions.

The audiotape administration limits the BRAT results to an analysis of verbal content alone and does not enable more finely grained evaluation of the nonverbal and verbal components of an assertive refusal response. Because nonverbal behavior may be even more important in determining others' reactions than what is actually said (St. Lawrence, 1982), audiotape assessment may be too limited a paradigm to produce clinically useful information.

In addition, any role-play approach is limited by the subject's ability to enact a simulated situation. Many subjects find this kind of situation both difficult and atypical. Thus, role-play analogues may not be equally desirable for all subjects. To date, there has been no research that identifies differential subject characteristics with role-play ability. Given the extensive use of role-play assessment in social skills research, such research could well make a contribution.

References

McFall, R.M., & Lillesand, D.B. (1971). Behavior rehearsal with modeling and coaching in assertion training. *Journal of Abnormal Psychology, 77,* 313-323.

McFall, R.M., & Marston, A.R. (1970). An experimental investigation of behavior rehearsal in assertive training. *Journal of Abnormal Psychology, 76,* 295-303.

McFall, R.M. Personal communication, April 10, 1985.

McFall, R.M. (1977). Analogue methods in behavioral competence. In J. Cone & R. Hawkins (Eds.), *Behavioral assessment: New directions in clinical psychology.* New York: Brunner/Mazel Publishers.

St. Lawrence, J.S. (1982). Validation of a component model of social skills with a clinical outpatient population. *Journal of Behavioral Assessment, 4,* 15-27.

Behavioral Situations Test

Billy A. Barrios

Description

The Behavioral Situations Test uses a role-play format to assess anxiety in relation to heterosocial interactions, specifically the responses of men to initial encounters with women. Comprised of 12 items, that are actually vignettes of encounters with an unfamiliar woman, the Behavioral Situations Test serves as a vehicle for gathering multiple measures of motoric, subjective, and physiological responses. Drawn from the Survey of Heterosocial Interactions (Twentyman, Boland, & McFall, 1981), each of the 12 items is presented to the subject, followed by a request to role-play with an unfamiliar woman his reaction to the just-described situation. The subject is given 30 seconds to prepare for the encounter, asked to begin, and allowed to interact for a maximum of 3 minutes. Throughout these encounters, the woman is pleasant, polite, and compliant.

Purpose

Anxiety is a central or ancillary feature of most clinical disorders. The prevailing conceptualization of anxiety is that of a multidimensional construct comprised of overt motoric, subjective, and physiological responses. Therefore, any potentially content valid assessment of anxiety must gather measures of each of the three types of responses. Most assessments of anxiety in relation to heterosocial encounters have not gathered such measures; those that have gathered such measures have tended to gather them at different points in time. The Behavioral Situations Test is a paradigm for assessing heterosocial anxiety that allows for the near concurrent measurement of motoric, subjective, and physiological responses.

Development

From each of the Behavioral Situations Test's 12 role-play encounters, multiple measures of overt motoric, subjective, and physiological responses are collected. The role-play performances are audiotaped and subsequently scored for the frequency of the following motoric responses: approach behavior (i.e., eliciting the woman's attention, introducing oneself, engaging in small talk, and requesting a future meeting), avoidance behavior (i.e., refusal to role-play the situation with the woman), coping behavior (i.e., repeated requests for a future meeting on those role-play scenes in which the woman has been instructed to be noncompliant), speech duration, words spoken speech dysfluencies (i.e., a transformed score derived by dividing the number of words spoken into the number of dysfluencies), and silences (i.e., a period of 10 seconds of no verbal behavior).

Several measures of subjective reactions to each role-play scene are collected. Before role-playing a scene, the subject completes a rating of the level and strength of his self-efficacy expectations in relation to the four approach behaviors already described (i.e., the subject indicates which of the four approach behaviors he expects to perform and rates on a 0- to 100-point scale the strength or certitude of each one of those expectations). At the conclusion of all 12 interactions, the subject completes three questionnaires: the Survey of Heterosocial Interactions, the Social Avoidance and Distress Scale (Watson & Friend, 1969), and a modified version of the S-R Inventory of Anxiousness (Endler, Hunt, & Rosenstein, 1962) that consists of five stimulus situations, all of which overlap with those posed by the Behavioral Situations Test.

Heart rate and skin conductance level are monitored throughout the role-play assessments. Peak values are taken from two points in the preparation period: the 10 seconds following the scene description and the 10 seconds preceding the commencement of role-playing. From these values and basal level values (i.e., lowest activity during the 1-minute period before the scene description), 26 measures of heart rate and skin conductance response are computed; 12 measures of heart rate and 14 measures of skin conductance. Half of these measures are derived from the 10-second period following scene description, the other half from the 10-second period preceding the commencement of role-playing. The six heart rate measures for each 10-second interval are: Peak Heart Rate (i.e., maximum heart rate during the 10-second period), Heart Rate Difference (i.e., maximum heart rate during the 10-second period minus basal level), Heart Rate Standardized Difference (i.e., maximum heart rate and basal level are converted into Z scores and the latter are then subtracted from the former), Heart Rate Percentage Change (i.e., basal level is subtracted from maximum heart rate during the 10-second period and then divided by the basal level and multiplied by 100), Heart Rate Autonomic Lability Score (i.e., the difference between maximum heart rate during the 10-second period and heart rate predicted from the linear regression between the maximum and basal levels; this value is converted into a standardized score with a mean of 50 and a standard deviation of 10), and Heart Rate Range Score (i.e., maximum heart rate during the 10-second period minus the basal level divided by the range of possible heart rate responding). The seven skin conductance measures for each 10-second interval are: Peak Skin Conductance (i.e., maximum skin conductance during the 10-second period), Skin Conductance Difference (i.e., maximum skin conductance during the 10-second period minus the basal level),

Log Skin Conductance Difference (i.e., log of maximum skin conductance during the 10-second period minus basal level, then added to the constant 10), Difference Log Skin Conductance (i.e., log of maximum skin conductance during the 10-second period minus the log of basal level), Log Skin Conductance Change (i.e., log of the maximum skin conductance minus basal level divided by the basal level; this value is added to the constant 50), Skin Conductance Autonomic Lability Score (i.e., the difference between maximum skin conductance during the 10-second period and skin conductance predicted from the linear regression between maximum and basal levels; this value is converted into a standardized score with a mean of 50 and a standard deviation of 10), and Skin Conductance Range Score (i.e., maximum skin conductance during the 10-second period minus the basal level divided by the range of possible skin conductance levels).

Psychometric Characteristics

To date only three studies have examined the basic psychometric properties of the aforementioned measures. In the Barrios (1983) study, 10 white men aged 20 to 50 years and having less than one heterosocial contact within the 6 months before the investigation served as the subjects. In Experiments I and III of the Barrios, Mitchell, Bosma, and Thacker (1982) study, the participants were four white men aged 20 to 40 years and six white men aged 17 to 21 years. All 10 reported fewer than one heterosocial contact before their participation in their respective experiments. With respect to their reliability, the motoric and physiological measures have been found to be of acceptable levels of interrater reliability (estimates range from .78 to .99, with a mean of .94 for the motoric measures; .74 to .98, with a mean of .86 for the physiological measures). Estimates of internal consistency for the motoric and physiological measures also were found to be consistently high (range for the motoric measures .82 to .92, with a mean of .90; for the physiological measures, .82 to .92, with a mean of .86). Coefficient alphas obtained for the two self-efficacy measures were slightly lower, but still on the average within the borders of acceptable levels (range of .64 to .93, with a mean of .80). The temporal stability of the measures has yet to be determined.

Evidence relevant to the content validity of the measures comes from three sources: estimates of the measures' internal consistency, convergence among measures purported to assess the same response dimension, and fluctuations in the measures as a function of exposure to a presumably active treatment. Support has accrued from all three sources for the content validity of the motoric and subjective measures. As already stated, the motoric and subjective measures were found to be internally consistent and also to correlate highly with their companion measures (i.e., other measures purported to tap the same response system). Furthermore, they were shown to change on exposure to imaginal desensitization and participant modeling, two presumably effective treatments for heterosocial anxiety. Support for the content validity of the physiological measures was not so uniform. Although the measures were internally consistent and fluctuated in accord with our treatments for heterosocial anxiety, the heart rate and skin conductance scores did not correlate well with one another. Examinations of the measures' construct validity have been limited to examinations of their convergence. Marked convergence among the various motoric and subjective measures was consistently obtained. However, neither set of measures correlated reliably with any of the physiological indices to any appreciable degree.

Clinical Use

Assessment data are drawn upon for guidance in carrying out the clinical tasks of problem identification, treatment planning, and treatment evaluation. Although much is not known of the psychometric properties of the measures derived from the Behavioral Situations Test, what is known suggests that the measures can be of some service to the clinician. Because measures of subjective, motoric, and physiological responses are collected, the clinician can look to the data for help in identifying which of the response components need alteration and which do not. By pinpointing the aspects of the anxiety reaction that need modification, the clinician is now in a position to develop an efficient treatment, one that has as its targets those responses judged to be either excessive or deficient. Given that the measures fluctuate in accord with exposure to purportedly active treatments, they can also be used to evaluate the efficacy of our clinical interventions.

Future Directions

In summary, the Behavioral Situations Test exhibits promise as a useful paradigm for assessing heterosocial anxiety. Empirical support exists for the fundamental soundness (i.e., reliability and content validity) of all three sets of measures derived from the test-motoric, subjective, and physiological. The support, however, is more compelling for the motoric and subjective measures than the physiological ones. Evidence also exists attesting to the construct validity of the motoric and subjective measures; evidence is lacking for the construct validity of the physiological indices. Obvious foci for future research are the development of sensitive physiological measures, the establishment of norms, and the estimation of other psychometric properties such as diagnostic utility and validity.

References

Barrios, B.A. (1983). The role of cognitive mediators in heterosocial anxiety: A test of self-efficacy theory. *Cognitive Therapy and Research, 7,* 543-554.

Barrios, B.A., Mitchell, J.E., Bosma, B.M., & Thacker, W. (1982). *Perceived self-efficacy and physiological responsivity: The importance of individual difference variables.* Paper presented at the meeting of the Southeastern Psychological Association, New Orleans.

Endler, N., Hunt, J. McV., & Rosenstein, A. (1962). An S-R inventory of anxiousness. *Psychological Monographs, 76* (17 Whole No. 536).

Twentyman, C., Boland, T., & McFall, R.M. (1981). Heterosocial avoidance in college males: Four studies. *Behavior Modification, 5,* 523-552.

Watson, D., & Friend, R. (1969). Measurement of social-evaluative anxiety. *Journal of Consulting and Clinical Psychology, 33,* 448-457

Behavioral Visual Acuity Test

Frank L. Collins, Jr.

Description

The Behavioral Visual Acuity Test (BVAT) provides a measure of recognition visual acuity. The test was introduced by Epstein, Collins, Hannay, and Looney (1978) as the primary dependent measure used to evaluate the effectiveness of fading feedback training for improving visual acuity in myopic adults. Since that time, the BVAT has been used extensively in our research program (see Collins & Gil, 1984a, for a review) and by other investigators (Matson, Helsel, & LaGrow, 1983) to measure visual acuity in myopes.

Although several modifications of the BVAT have been reported, all share certain characteristics. Alphabetic letters are presented at different distances, one letter at a time. The subject is asked to identify the letter, and feedback is provided regarding the correctness or incorrectness of the response. The size of the stimulus letters should approximate those used on Snellen Letter Charts to estimate 20/20 visual acuity. Specifically, the total height of the letter should subtend a visual angle of min arc at 20 feet. The details of the letter should be one fifth this distance. This can be approximated with dry transferable presstype letters (Helvetica 1321-36 CLN) 10 mm high with 2 mm details.

In most research, letters have been presented at four distances: 5, 10, 15, and 20 feet. One study used five distances (34, 72, 108, 144, & 180 inches), whereas another used three distances: 9, 12, and 15 feet. Given the number of studies using four distances, it is recommended that 5, 10, 15, and 20 feet be used to increase comparison across studies.

Purpose

The BVAT was developed to provide more sensitive estimates of visual acuity than can be obtained using standard ophthalmic tests. Standardized assessment provides an evaluation of visual acuity at either 20 feet or 6 meters. This distance has been chosen as a standard because light rays that originate from such a distant source are parallel as they enter the eye. In a healthy eye, parallel rays can be refracted so that a clear image is formed on the retina. In myopia, the eye has excessive refraction; therefore, parallel rays are focused in front of the retina, resulting in blurred vision for distant objects. As an object is brought closer to the eye, it becomes clearer. For each myope, there is a finite distance called the far point, whereby the object is presented at this distance or closer. This concept is critical for an accurate behavioral assessment of myopia, because myopes do not have "poor visual acuity." Rather, they have poor visual acuity for stimuli presented beyond their far point. The further away past the far point, the poorer the visual acuity.

Likewise, improvements in visual acuity appear to be sensitive to specific distances. For example, Epstein et al. (1978; Experiment II: Subjects 1 and 2) found improvements on the BVAT at 5 feet when training occurred between 2 and 5 feet, and no improvement on the BVAT as measured at 10 feet. However, as training was provided at a farther distance (hypothetically training resulted in an improvement in the myope's far point), improvements were seen at 10 feet. Assessment at 20 feet using the BVAT did show this improvement. Therefore, use of the BVAT, with incorporation of all four testing distances, documents training effectiveness.

Development

The BVAT has gradually evolved. Early use of this measure did not control for the amount of time the subject spent viewing the test stimuli. Rather, the subject was given "approximately" 5 seconds. However, some subjects were slower and some faster. Gil, Collins, and Odom (1986) demonstrated that such variability may be a problem. In this study, subjects were assessed using the BVAT at three distances. However, rather than presenting the stimuli on cards, the letters were mounted in the center of 2 by 2 inch slides and presented using an automated vision trainer. The BVAT slides were placed in slide carousels so that every other slide contained a randomly selected letter with a blank slide between letter slides. Letters were then presented either for 2 or 8 seconds, and the subjects were instructed to view the slide for the whole presentation time, then to respond during the blank slide presentation (always 5 seconds). Subjects consistently identified significantly more letters during the 8-second presentation mode than during the 2-second presentation. Thus, the amount of time that the subject views the stimulus has an effect on performance. Care should be taken to control for the subject's viewing time. A computer program that presents letters through a Commodore 64 computer and television screen was recently developed. This mode of presentation allows for controlled presentations and greatly enhances the standardization of the assessment.

Psychometric Characteristics

Test-retest reliability for the measure appears very high. We recently found a correlation of .94 for untrained subjects who were retested using the BVAT after 6 weeks. No other formal psychometric evaluations have been reported.

Clinical Use

Perhaps the most important use of the BVAT is to provide feedback that is sensitive to changes in visual acuity at different distances. This is particularly important when evaluating the effectiveness of training programs designed to modify the far point for myopes.

Future Directions

There is some debate as to the exact nature of the values obtained with the BVAT. Matson et al. (1983) argue that assessments such as this merely measure visual efficiency and not visual acuity; that is, the BVAT provides an estimation of how well a person can identify the stimulus presented, not how clear the stimulus is. The problem with this argument is that visual acuity is, by definition, a *measure* of the precision by which an individual is able to see fine details of a stimulus. Furthermore, recognition visual acuity is measured by presenting stimuli that are familiar to the individual and asking the person to identify the item. Thus, the BVAT does provide an accurate estimate of visual acuity for different distances (Collins & Gil, 1984b).

There is very little information regarding the extent to which the BVAT actually assesses visual clarity. Initially, it was assumed that subjects were seeing "clearer" if they performed better; however, this may not be the case. Gil et al. (1986) reported data that suggest clarity is partly assessed with the BVAT. Subjects were asked not only to identify the letter, but also to rate how "clear" the letter appeared and how "confident" they were with their response. Training improved confidence, correctness, and clarity. Therefore, it appears that the BVAT may be assessing more than the ability of an individual to identify blurred objects. However, even in the absence of data to show that the BVAT is sensitive to changes in clarity, the use of the BVAT to measure an individual's ability to identify blurred stimuli is important for behavioral researchers and clinicians working with visual disorders.

As noted earlier, myopia results in poor distant visual acuity because the eye has excessive refraction. Significant improvements on the BVAT have been reported, with no corresponding change in refraction as measured by streak retinoscopy. Thus, an improvement in BVAT performance does not indicate an improvement in myopia. Rather, it is possible that visual acuity can be improved regardless of change in refraction. It is difficult to explain the processes involved in improved visual acuity in the absence of refraction change, and future research is needed to clarify this point.

References

Collins, F.L., & Gil, K.M. (1984a). Behavioral approaches to visual disorders. In S. Rachman (Ed.), *Contributions to medical psychology: Vol. 3* (pp. 55-92). New York: Pergamon Press.

Collins, F.L., & Gil, K.M. (1984b). Critical issues in the evaluation of behavioral training for myopia: A reply to Matson, Helsel, and LaCrow. *Behaviour Research and Therapy, 19,* 265-268.

Epstein, L.H., Collins, F.L., Hannay, H.J., & Looney, R.L. (1978). Fading and feedback in the modification of visual acuity. *Journal of Behavioral Medicine, 1,* 273-287.

Gil, K.M., Collins, F.L., & Odom, J.V. (1986). The effects of behavioral vision training on multiple aspects of visual functioning in myopic adults. *Journal of Behavioral Medicine, 1,* 373-387.

Matson, J.L., Helsel, W.J., & LaCrow, S.J. (1983). Training visual efficiency in myopic persons. *Behaviour Research and Therapy, 21,* 115-118.

Behavioral Walk

S. Lloyd Williams

Description

The behavioral walk is a behavioral avoidance (or approach) test of phobias of walking alone along a street (e.g., Bandura, Adams, Hardy, & Howells, 1980) or through a shopping mall (Telch, Agras, Taylor, Roth, & Gallen, 1985). The test is typically used to assess severity of agoraphobic disability. The agoraphobic person is instructed to walk along a clearly specified route as far as possible and to return immediately when unable to go farther, while the assessor waits at the start of the route. Performance on the test is verified by having the subject leave a mark, such as a distinctive piece of tape, at the farthest point reached (Telch et al., 1985). The tester's instructions do not embody limitations on how anxious the subject becomes, but simply state that the person should walk as far as he or she can. Otherwise, the test confounds behavioral capabilities with emotional responses. Often the tester will ask the person to rate his or her anxiety at various points along the walk to determine how anxiety provoking the person finds the situation. Walking approach behavior is scored as the distance or percentage of the route walked.

Purpose

The purpose of the behavioral walk is to obtain a precise estimate of how far an agoraphobic person can walk alone. This information is useful primarily as a basis for evaluating behavioral progress in a program of agoraphobia treatment and for evaluating scientific hypotheses in which the experimenter needs an objective measure of agoraphobic disability. The popularity of the behavioral walk as a measure of agoraphobia derives in part from its ease of administration and the straightforward scaling of walking performance in this type of test.

Development

The behavioral walk has been used in case studies of agoraphobia and group experimental designs. The procedures currently used for such tests are essentially the same as those used with the earliest behavioral walks developed in the late 1960s.

Psychometric Characteristics

The psychometric characteristics of the behavioral walk have not been studied extensively. However, the behavioral walk, like all behavioral avoidance tests, possesses a high degree of face validity as a measure of a person's behavioral capabilities for specifically defined activities. The validity of the behavioral walk as a test of agoraphobic disability is open to some question because walking phobia is only one of many kinds of phobic responses characteristic of agoraphobia (Williams, 1985). In addition, it is widely recognized that phobic avoidance behavior is only modestly correlated with subjective and physiological indices of phobia. Although test-retest reliability data on the behavioral walk are rarely reported, it seems likely that the behavioral walk would yield test-retest reliability coefficients comparable to those of other behavioral tests, which usually demonstrate very high stability when there is no intervening treatment.

Clinical Use

As just described, the behavioral walk has clinical applications just as behavioral tests generally do: to obtain objective and precise measurements of phobic behavior in the natural environment. Perhaps the most important clinical use of behavioral tests, in addition to their value as a measure of behavioral capabilities, is that of providing a context for sampling the thoughts and feelings that arise in phobic clients as they attempt to cope in real life with their fears (Williams, 1985).

Future Directions

Although the behavioral walk will undoubtedly continue to be widely used in research and practice with phobic individuals, its straightforward nature suggests that its basic format and procedures are unlikely to undergo much change.

References

Bandura, A., Adams, N.E., Hardy, A.B., & Howells, G.N. (1980). Tests of the generality of self-efficacy theory. *Cognitive Therapy and Research, 4,* 39-66.

Telch, M.J., Agras, W.S., Taylor, C.B., Roth, W.T., & Gallen, C.G. (1985). Combined pharmacological and behavioral treatment for agoraphobia. *Behaviour Research and Therapy, 23,* 325-335.

Williams, S.L. (1985). On the nature and measurement of agoraphobia. *Progress in Behavior Modification, 19,* 109-144.

Behaviorally Referenced Rating System of Intermediate Social Skills

Jan L. Wallander

Description

The Behaviorally Referenced Rating System of Intermediate Social Skills (BRISS) is a set of observational rating scales intended to be used by judges in evaluating the appropriateness of the male adult's social skills from videotaped role-play interactions. It consists of 11 scales, representing five nonverbal (Use of Head, Facial Expression, Eyes, Arms & Hands, and Overall Body & Legs) and six verbal (Language, Speech Delivery, Conversation Structure, Conversation Content, Personal Conversation Style, and Partner-Directed Behavior) component behaviors of social skills. Each is rated on a 7-point Likert-type scale from very inappropriate (1) to very appropriate (7). Each scale, moreover, has an average of 15 unique subdimensions (e.g., Personal Conversational Style: Self-disclosed affect, gave opinion, and used humor), each of which in turn consists of between one and five behavioral referents (e.g., for "gave opinion": no even when should, no, once, and several times). A referent indicates a behavior or an effect that may occur in a brief initial interaction. Each referent is associated with a specific scale value on the aforementioned 7-point scale. This scale value thus indicates the degree to which a referent is associated with a very inappropriate to a very appropriate display of the component behavior for which it is a referent. One scale with its behavioral referents can be seen in the report by Wallander, Conger, and Conger (1985, p. 141).

The judge's task is therefore to observe the interaction, note the display of any behavioral referents, consult the rating scale for the scale values suggested by each, integrate these values, and arrive at one component behavior rating for the specified interval.

Purpose

The BRISS was developed in response to the problems inherent in the strong reliance of social skills assessors on very global or highly specific measures. The BRISS provides an alternative by defining social skills components at an *intermediate* level of specificity, thereby capitalizing on the strengths of both global and specific approaches. For example, it allows raters to evaluate elements of interactions, such as timing and sequencing of behaviors, and situational context. At the same time it provides more detailed information than global ratings by focusing on fairly specific behavioral domains often needed for treatment planning.

It is intended for both research and clinical use whenever social skills components can be beneficially assessed at an intermediate level of specificity. The behaviors on the BRISS are most appropriately observed in brief, initial interactions as opposed to long interactions with a familiar person.

Development

Age peers viewed videotaped heterosocial interactions of college men and generated the behavioral cues they used in arriving at judgments about the subjects' social skills. Their 900 response examples were then systematized into a four-level hierarchy consisting of 60 components (Conger, Wallander, Mariotto, & Ward, 1982). Eleven of these components were selected as the component behaviors of the BRISS. A modified Thurstone Scaling Procedure was conducted to provide referents that would define behaviorally each of the 11 scales. To this end, 162 subdimensions and over 400 behavioral referents defining these subdimensions were generated. These referents were then scaled by 22 judges who assigned ratings to each on a 7-point scale. The BRISS was subsequently psychometrically evaluated in two samples of college students, one sample of college clinic volunteers, two samples of VA psychiatric patients, and one sample of nonpsychiatric, noncollege adults, for a total of 153 men. Details are provided in Wallander et al. (1985) and Farrell, Rabinowitz, Wallander, and Curran (1985).

Psychometric Characteristics

Normative data in the form of descriptive sample statistics are provided in Wallander (1981). Reliability analysis using generalizability theory indicates that BRISS components have good to excellent generalizability across judges and observation intervals regardless of sample composition. The BRISS ratings also appear free of interjudge drift over evaluation periods as long as 7 weeks. There is typically a moderate interrelationship among component behaviors. Yet a completely replicable factor structure has not been found across samples and judges. Nonetheless, principal components representing conversation behaviors, facial expressions and paralinguistic behaviors, and nonverbal behaviors related to body position and movement account for over 80% of the variance in the BRISS scales.

A variety of concurrent validity relationships have been investigated, using global social skills ratings, specific observation measures of social skills components, and self-reports as criteria for the different samples. In the vast majority of these cases, the BRISS ratings collectively accounted for a large and significant portion of the variance in the criterion measures, typically upwards of 80%. Individual BRISS component ratings typically were significantly correlated with all global criterion measures as well and with those specific measures that would be expected on the basis of shared operational definitions. The BRISS also was found to discriminate well between college clinic and nonclinic subjects, although individual classification of clinic volunteers is not satisfactory. Other construct validity information, such as treatment change sensitivity, is still lacking.

Clinical Use

The BRISS has thus far only been employed in a research context in part because of its recent development and need for technical evaluation. However, the fact that several samples in these evaluations consisted of patient volunteers in different settings (college clinic, VA day hospital, and VA inpatient unit) suggests its clinical application. It has by now been employed with enough of a range of male subjects and patients to suggest its application to almost any male adult sample or patient. It should be emphasized that both same- and opposite-sex interactions have been evaluated with the BRISS with similarly satisfactory psychometric

outcomes. However, no data exist on its applicability in female subjects. As a matter of fact, some of the referents included in the BRISS refer to expected male social behavior, at least as traditionally defined. Similarly, there is no reason to assume that the BRISS is applicable in the assessment of children.

Consequently, the BRISS may be used beneficially to assess a variety of adult male patients who appear to have social interaction difficulties. A role–play situation can be set up in the clinic with a confederate, selecting a situation representing an initial interaction suited to the patient's background and problem. The therapist can then observe, unobtrusively behind a one-way mirror, and rate the patient's social behavior in a series of intervals. Deficits and strengths can thus be delineated to aid treatment planning through judicious use of component behavior ratings and attention paid the particular referents that represent the subject's behavior. Changes noted across intervals may also be illuminating.

Future Directions

Several future directions are suggested. It is most important to evaluate the actual use of the BRISS for treatment planning and evaluation, adapt it for use with women, and simplify its use still more. To the latter end, Farrell et al. (1985) have taken the concepts and methods introduced through the BRISS and developed the Intermediate-Level Social Skills Assessment Checklist (ILSSAC), which simply is a set of checklists requiring the judge only to note the occurrence of behaviors. Empirically derived scale values are then used to summarize this information quantitatively. The ILSSAC has shown good psychometric properties as well. Finally, the methodology represented by both the BRISS and the ILSSAC could and should be employed for purposes other than social skills assessment. The techniques represented by these instruments promise to provide many benefits in behavioral assessment.

References

Conger, A.J., Wallander, J.L., Mariotto, M.J., & Ward, D. (1982). Peer judgments of heterosexual-social anxiety and skill: What do they pay attention to anyhow? *Behavioral Assessment, 2,* 243-260.
Farrell, A.D., Rabinowitz, J.A., Wallander, J.L., & Curren, J.P. (1985). Evaluation of two formats for intermediate-level assessment of social skills.

Behavior checklist vs. rating system. *Behavioral Assessment, 7,* 155-171.

Wallander, J.L. (1981). Development and evaluation of a behaviorally referenced, multicomponent rating system for heterosocial skills. *Dissertation Abstracts International, 42,* 2091B (University Microfilms No. DDJ81-2371).

Wallander, J.L., Conger, A.J., & Conger, J.C. (1985). Development and evaluation of a behaviorally referenced rating system for heterosocial skills. *Behavioral Assessment, 7,* 137-153.

Binge Eating Scale

Marsha Marcus

Description

The Binge Eating Scale (BES) (Gormally, Black, Datson, & Rardin, 1982) is a self-report measure designed to assess the extent and severity of binge eating problems in the obese. It consists of 16 sets of four statements relating to binge eating behavior. The individual is asked to endorse the one of each set of four statements that best describes his or her eating behavior.

Following the DSM-III criteria for bulimia, the BES includes statements that assess the behavioral (e.g., overeating to the point of nausea, overly strict dieting between binges, and eating in secret), cognitive (e.g., preoccupation with food), and affective (e.g., guilt and shame with regard to eating behavior) components of binge behavior.

Although there are few data that elucidate factors that determine severity of binge eating, Gormally et al. (1982) reasoned that the amount of food eaten, the frequency of binges, and the degree of emotional upset before and after a binge episode would be useful in discriminating levels of binge severity. The four statements included in each of the 16 items of the BES reflect a range of binge severity from no problem to serious problem.

Purpose

The BES was developed to provide a reliable and valid self-report assessment measure of the severity of binge eating. Available data indicate that binge eating is a common problem among applicants to behavioral weight control programs (Gormally et al., 1982; Marcus, Wing, & Lamparski, 1985). Furthermore, binge eating is negatively associated with treatment success in standard behavioral weight loss programs (Keefe, Wyshogrod, Weinberger, & Agras, 1984; Marcus, Wing, & Hopkins, 1985). Therefore, the assessment of binge severity is important for screening applicants to standard behavioral programs, planning new or individualized interventions for obese bingers, and as an impetus to further research on binge eating among the obese.

Development

Gormally and colleagues (1982) first created a list of 16 characteristics of binge eating based on their extensive clinical experience and the DSM-III diagnosis for bulimia. Next, four statements reflecting the range of severity for each characteristic were developed and independently weighted from 0 to 3 (0 = no problem, 3 = severe binge eating problems). Differences in item weighting among the investigators were resolved by discussion. Finally, Gormally et al. (1982) designed a structured interview to determine binge severity. The interview included an assessment of the ability to control eating urges, food preoccupations, emotions related to overeating, eating in secret, night eating, and physical discomfort associated with overeating.

Two samples of 65 and 47 middle–class, overweight individuals seeking behavioral treatment for obesity participated in the research. The first sample was comprised of women who averaged 39.3 years of age (*SD* = 8.1) and 34.6% were overweight (*SD* = 12.0). The second sample included 32 women and 15 men who averaged 41.2 years of age (*SD* = 11.6) and were 48.9% overweight.

All subjects completed the BES and participated in an interview conducted by a clinician who was blind to subjects' BES scores. Interviewers rated subjects as having no binge problems, moderate problems (episodic to frequent binges with a degree of self-control and a moderate level of negative emotion consequent to a binge), or severe problems (frequent episodes, lack of self control, large amount of food consumed, and strong negative emotion following an episode). Half of the subjects were independently rated by a second interviewer; interrater reliability was excellent.

The BES scores of the two samples did not differ (*M* = 2.8, *SD* = 8.4; *M* = 21.4, *SD* = 9.2). Furthermore, BES scores did not vary as a function of sex or percent overweight. Binge eating problems were prevalent among Gormally et al.'s (1982) subjects. Of these subjects 55% were judged to have moderate problems, 22% little or no problems, and 23% serious problems with binge eating.

Furthermore, the BES was highly effective in discriminating levels of binge severity. One-way analyses of variance with interviewer-determined level of binge severity (none, moderate, and severe) as the between group factor and BES score as the dependent measure were conducted for each sample. Results indicated a highly significant association between independently assessed binge status and scores on the BES for both samples ($F[2,62] = 13.5, p < .001; F[2,44] = 25.1, p < .001$).

Psychometric Characteristics

The BES appears to have adequate internal consistency. The scores for each individual item of the BES were compared with total BES scores for the 65 subjects of the first sample using Kruskal-Wallis analyses of variance for ranked data. Results indicated that higher ranked scores of all 16 individual items were strongly associated with higher total scores on the BES. There are no available test-retest reliability data on the BES.

The BES has been effective in distinguishing mild, moderate, and severe levels of binge eating severity among obese individuals as validated by independently conducted clinical interviews.

Currently, there are no conventions with regard to the range of scores for the three severity levels of binge eating. Gormally et al. (1982) observed a weighted mean BES score of 30 + 7 among individuals assessed as having a serious binge problem and weighted mean of 14 + 6.7 for individuals assessed as having little or no problem. In a subsequent study, Marcus, Wing, and Hopkins (1985) found that a BES cutoff score of 27 or higher reliably selected serious binge eaters, as corroborated by an independent semi-structured clinical interview based on DSM-III criteria for bulimia.

Clinical Use

Serious problems with binge eating are reported by 23 to 46% (Gormally et al., 1982, Marcus, Wing, & Lamparski, 1985) of applicants to behavioral weight control programs. Furthermore, recent data suggest that the treatment outcome for obese binge eaters in behavioral programs is poor (Keefe et al., 1984; Marcus et al., 1985). Therefore, the availability of an easy to administer, self-report measure of binge eating severity is important for screening purposes. Although a diagnosis of serious binge problems cannot be made on the basis of self-report data, the BES can be used to target individuals for further assessment. Serious binge eaters are likely

to require additional or alternate treatment for obesity. The BES includes items that assess the affective, cognitive, and behavioral components of binge eating. Therefore, BES data can be used to develop an individualized behavioral program for an obese individual (Marcus, 1985). Finally, BES data in conjunction with other information about obese individuals seeking treatment (e.g., weight and diet history, mood, and demographic data) may enhance our understanding of obesity as well as the factors involved in treatment outcome.

Future Directions

Marcus et al. (1985) found that BES scores of obese binge eaters decreased significantly after a standard behavioral weight control program and at 1-year follow-up. These decreases may reflect an amelioration of binge behavior. However, in the absence of test-retest reliability data on the BES, this finding is difficult to interpret. The decreases in BES scores may represent a regression to the mean or a demand characteristic of the treatment situation. Thus, test-retest reliability data may enhance the scope of BES utility.

To date, the BES has been largely confined to use in obese individuals seeking behavioral treatment for obesity. The BES data from obese individuals who are not seeking treatment may clarify the prevalence of binge eating problems among the obese. Finally, research utilizing the BES with non-obese populations may provide information on the continuity of eating attitudes and behavior among normal weight and obese individuals.

References

Gormally, J., Black, S., Datson, S., & Rardin, D. (1982). The assessment of binge eating severity among obese persons. *Addictive Behaviors, 7,* 47-55.

Keefe, P.H., Wyshogrod, D., Weinberger, E., & Agras, W.S. (1984). Binge eating and outcome of behavioral treatment of obesity: A preliminary report. *Behaviour Research and Therapy, 22,* 319-321.

Marcus, M.D. (1985). Behavior therapy in a case of obesity complicated by binge eating. In M. Hersen & C.G. Last (Eds.), *Behavior therapy casebook.* New York: Springer.

Marcus, M.D., Wing, R.R., & Hopkins, J. (1985). Obese binge eaters: Affects, cognitions, and response to behavioral weight control. Manuscript submitted for publication.

Marcus, M.D., Wing, R.R., & Lamparski, D.M. (1985). Binge eating and dietary restraint in obese patients. *Addictive Behaviors, 10,* 163-168.

Binge Scale Questionnaire

Aubrey J. Yates

Description

The Binge Scale Questionnaire (BS or BSQ) is a nine-item forced-choice questionnaire (maximum possible score 27) developed by Hawkins and Clement (1980).

Purpose

The questionnaire was designed "to measure the behavioral and attitudinal parameters of bulimia" (Hawkins & Clement, 1980, p. 221).

Development

The questionnaire was administered by Hawkins and Clement (1980) to two samples of normal weight men and women and one sample of over-weight women. Mean scores of 1.90 (SD 2.55), 5.63 (SD 4.37), and 8.42 (SD 4.76) were obtained for the samples of normal body weight men and women and for overweight women, respectively.

Psychometric Characteristics

In the Hawkins and Clement (1980) study, internal consistency was .68 (Cronbach's alpha), whereas test-retest reliability over 1 month was +.88. A principal components factor analysis identified a factor defined as "guilt" and "concern" about binging.

Clinical Use

A group of 24 female patients meeting strict criteria for bulimia nervosa were found by Yates and Sambrailo (1984) to have a mean BSQ score of 17.39 (SD 3.19), much higher than that of any of the groups tested by Hawkins and Clement (1980). Smith and Thelen (1984) gave the BSQ to 89 normal control subjects and 20 persons with bulimia. The point-biserial r (total score with group membership) was +.79 (p <.0001). Using a cutting score of 9 and an admission of at least one binge per week, 1 of 20 bulimic persons and 10 of 89 normal control subjects were misclassified. The BSQ correlated at a rate of +.93 (p <.001) with BULIT. The nine-item BSQ is reprinted in the article by Hawkins and Clement (1980, p. 221).

References

Hawkins, R.C., & Clement, P.F. (1980). Development and construct validation of a self-report measure of binge eating tendencies. *Addictive Behaviors, 5,* 219-226.

Smith, M.C., & Thelen, M.H. (1984). Development and validation of test for bulimia. *Journal of Consulting and Clinical Psychology, 52,* 863-872.

Yates, A.J., & Sambrailo, F. (1984). Bulimia nervosa: A descriptive and therapeutic study. *Behaviour Research and Therapy, 22,* 503-517.

Blood Alcohol Level

James Langenbucher and Timothy J. O'Farrell

Description

Blood alcohol level (BAL) or its equivalent term, blood alcohol concentration, is not a unique measure of scale but is rather a physical property of the body. It can be measured directly within fine tolerances, and BAL scores that are highly reliable, valid, and appropriately scaled for any statistic can be economically and conveniently achieved.

The notation used to quantify and communicate these scores is not uniform; rather, it varies widely between scholars and among disciplines. Scores may be reported in terms of milligrams of alcohol per deciliter of blood, grams of alcohol per kilogram of body weight, and others. Also various are the methods by which BAL can be estimated. Current methods of assay include analysis of blood and urine, but it is alveolar breath analysis, the "Breath-alyzer test," that is most familiar to clinical, research and forensic personnel. Highly accurate breath-testing equipment remains costly; however, even the cheap, disposable "Mobats" (Sobell & Sobell, 1975) or breath-test ampules available at a local pharmacy can provide rough estimates of BAL.

Purpose

Although now of frequent interest to psychologists, the concept of blood alcohol level first acquired currency in our allied disciplines of medicine and law. The purpose of measuring BAL was originally a forensic one, this being to provide, in the form of unambiguous physical evidence, a standard of comparison by which cases of intoxication and, particularly, intoxicated driving could be adjudicated. Following introduction of the first testing devices and the correlation of obtained BAL scores with clinical symptoms of intoxication, statutory standards, defined in terms of BAL, of the term *intoxicated* were written into law. In most states, a BAL of 100 mb/% or .10 g/kg constitutes this statutory standard.

However, because of the sedative-hypnotic properties and ubiquitous use of beverage alcohol, the construct of BAL has also been of interest to medical researchers, who have studied the effects of various BAL's on a variety of physical and mentational processes. In psychology, although the purpose of BAL measurement, to provide an unambiguous and physical standard of intoxication, remains the same, the ends achieved are broad. Clinical uses include the documentation of sobriety, methods for training in controlled drinking, and others. In research, paired with behavioral (e.g., body sway) and self-report measures (e.g., ratings of subjective intoxication), quantification of BAL constitutes the physiological component of a comprehensive measurement strategy in human alcohol research.

Development

Chemical assay of BAL dates to the turn of this century and the early work of Widmark and others. Originally relied on were samples of raw blood and, later, urine. Both of these methods are still in general forensic and clinical use. The convenience and nonintrusive nature of breath-testing, however, and the gradual perfection of instruments based on chromatographic analysis of captured breath, have made breath-testing progressively more dominant since its first introduction as the "Drunkometer" in 1937. Currently, the standard field device, the Smith and Wesson Breathalyzer, has experienced inroads by other manufacturers. Now available are highly accurate hand-held models based on microchip technology, and these compete for a sizable clinical, research, and forensic market.

Also made available recently are wallet-sized "alco-calculators" or nomographic tables that permit rough calculation of the BAL by reference to appropriate body weights, consumption totals, and length of the drinking episode. However, these figures make no allowances for individual factors, such as age, sex, and obesity, related to the amount of stored body fluids, nor for the presence of food in the stomach, all of which co-determine the BAC time curve and peak concentrations. Nomographic tables have not fared well against chemical assays in field trials.

Psychometric Characteristics

The BAL is a scalar variable of the interval type. Methods of BAL analysis vary in accuracy and therefore in reliability and validity, but most provide scores that are highly reliable and accurate to within 5 mb/%. Results are appropriate for any form of statistical analysis.

Although BAL analysis is not fakeable, it is subject to machine calibration errors and other sources of unintentional bias. In breath testing, results will be biased by the presence of ambient alcohol in the throat or mouth and by changes in the temperature of these tissues induced by recent smoking or by swallowing hot or cold beverages.

Clinical Use

Quantification of the BAL serves a number of clinical uses. Most frequently, the BAL is taken as part of a treatment protocol to ensure the sobriety of alcoholic patients during office visits (Sobell, Sobell, & VanderSpek, 1979). When such a patient's veracity is in doubt, BAL measures taken contemporaneously with self-reports are useful in confronting the posture of denial and minimization. In conjoint treatment, equipment of the patient's spouse or a significant other with a supply of disposable breath-test ampules, with instructions to administer them when drinking is suspected, helps both to monitor and reinforce treatment compliance and to reduce suspicion following the patient's unsupervised time.

Another particular use of BAL measurement is in training controlled drinking skills by teaching subjects to self-titrate alcohol intake to acceptable levels (e.g., Lansky, Nathan, & Lawson, 1978). Of some service to public safety are the methods for providing BAL feedback to potential intoxicated drivers, developed by Meier, Brigham, and Handel (1984). Finally, BAL data combined with observations of physical and mental status are a necessary component of inpatient and outpatient management in alcohol withdrawal.

Future Directions

Future uses of blood alcohol level assessment in psychological practice center on the greatly enhanced availability of highly reliable and accurate devices at reasonable cost, leading to their greater involvement in clinical, especially outpatient, care. Commercial use of breath-testing equipment (e.g., the installation of an "Alcohol

Guard" chromatograph in the neighborhood tavern) is a trend that has already been anticipated by several pilot projects. Self-administration of a breath test using a disposable ampule is another promising development; prototypes of breath-test ampules with acceptable accuracy are currently in development, and their use in self-control training in alcoholism treatment may be projected.

References

Lansky, D., Nathan, P.E., & Lawson, D.M. (1978). Blood alcohol level discrimination by alcoholics: The role of internal and external cues. *Journal of Consulting and Clinical Psychology, 46,* 953-960.

Meier, S.E., Brigham, T.A., & Handel, G. (1984). Effects of feedback on legally intoxicated drivers. *Journal of Studies on Alcohol, 45,* 528-533.

Sobell, M.B., & Sobell, L.C. (1975). A brief technical report on the MOBAT: An inexpensive portable test for determining blood alcohol concentration. *Journal of Applied Behavioral Analysis, 8,* 117-120.

Sobell, M.B., Sobell, L.C., & VanderSpek, R. (1979). Relationships among clinical judgment, self-report, and breath-analysis measures of intoxication in alcoholics. *Journal of Consulting and Clinical Psychology, 47,* 204-206.

Blood Pressure Assessment

B. Kent Houston

Description

Blood pressure within the arteries varies throughout the cardiac cycle from a maximum (systolic blood pressure) associated with the contraction of the heart (systole) to a maximum (diastolic blood pressure) associated with the relaxation of the heart (diastole). Usually, both measurements are presented together in the form of systolic blood pressure "over" diastolic blood pressure. The units of measurement are millimeters of mercury, abbreviated mm Hg.

Blood pressure has been measured by direct and indirect procedures. (See Geddes, 1970, for a technical description.) Blood pressure may be measured directly with a pressure–sensitive device inserted into an artery. Such a procedure is uncomfortable, causes apprehension in many individuals, and involves some medical risks. Consequently, most blood pressure monitoring involves procedures that are noninvasive (i.e., they do not enter an artery and therefore are indirect measures of blood pressure).

Most indirect methods of measuring blood pressure rely on the observation that when circulation in an artery is constricted, the pulse in the artery can be detected with a stethoscope or microphone pressed on it. The sounds produced by the pulse wave passing through the constricted artery are referred to as Korotkoff sounds. Typically, an inflatable cuff is wrapped around the upper arm, and the cuff is inflated to a pressure that shuts off or occludes the circulation in the brachial artery. The cuff is then slowly deflated until the first Korotkoff sound can be detected; this occurs when the pressure in the cuff is equal to the systolic pressure in the artery. The pressure in the cuff at this point is taken as the systolic blood pressure. The cuff continues to be deflated until the Korotkoff sounds cease to be detected. The pressure in the cuff at the last Korotkoff sound is typically taken as the diastolic blood pressure.

The standard equipment for measuring blood pressure is a mercury sphygmomanometer, the basic blood pressure measuring device that employs a mercury column for indicating pressure, a manually inflated cuff, and a stethoscope. Several variations of this standard equipment are also used. For instance, a cuff pump may be used to inflate the cuff, and systolic and diastolic blood pressure may be displayed by digital output or tracings on a polygraph. In some equipment, a microphone or other sound-sensitive device replaces the stethoscope for detecting Korotkoff sounds. In other equipment, rather than the Korotkoff sounds, ultrasonics are used to detect the movement of an artery wall beneath a cuff. In this approach two small devices are attached to the bottom of an inflatable cuff. One device generates ultrahigh frequency sound, and the other device detects reflected sound. The characteristics of the reflected sound vary as a function of pressure in an artery whose circulation is constricted, thereby allowing determination of systolic and diastolic blood pressure. Because the procedure employing the mercury sphygmomanometer is typically regarded as the standard for noninvasive measurement, it is desirable to check readings obtained from any of the variant devices against those obtained with the mercury sphygmomanometer.

Blood pressure measurements are usually taken during a period of stimulation, either naturally occurring or experimentally induced, during a period of rest, or both. Several recordings of blood pressure should be taken during either period because blood pressure is a continuous, potentially variable phenomenon, although typically it is only intermittently measured when noninvasive procedures are employed. Care must be taken when trying to obtain resting levels of blood pressure to eliminate arousal due to preceding, concurrent, or anticipated events.

Purpose

There are three major purposes of blood pressure measurement. One is to assess individual differences in resting levels. Unusually high or low resting levels are of interest for health reasons. Another purpose is to assess individual differences in blood pressure responses to stimulus events. Unusual blood pressure responsivity has been studied for its implications for physical health. Another purpose is to use resting blood pressure or blood pressure responsivity as a dependent variable. For example, levels of aerobic exercise, relaxation training, nicotine ingestion, personality variables, or emotion may be assessed for their relations to resting blood pressure or blood pressure responsivity, or both.

Development

Direct measurement of blood pressure is traced back to Hales who early in the 18th century inserted a brass pipe connected to a glass tube, into an artery in a horse's leg. Furthermore, Hales noted that the pressure of the blood caused the blood in the glass tube to rise to a height of over 8 feet (Geddes, 1970). In early indirect measurement of blood pressure, an individual's limb was placed in a water-filled container and the pressure of the water increased to occlude arterial circulation, at which point the skin turned pale. The pressure of the fluid at which color (blood flow) returned to the limb was taken as the systolic level. Around the turn of the 20th century, inflatable cuffs began to be used to apply pressure to occlude arterial circulation in a limb.

Psychometric Characteristics

Noninvasive techniques for measuring blood pressure have been found to misrepresent both systolic and diastolic blood pressure as assessed by direct arterial measurements by as much as 10 mm Hg (Hassett, 1978). Therefore, using direct, arterial assessment as the criterion, noninvasive techniques suffer some in concurrent validity.

Clinical Use

The primary clinical use of blood pressure measurement is to identify and treat adults and children with elevated blood pressure levels. For clinical (as well as research) purposes, it is important to use the correct cuff size. There are special cuffs for individuals with large upper arms (e.g., corpulent and very muscular adults), and special cuffs for individuals with small upper arms (e.g., children). Note that blood pressure levels in women may vary as a function of phase of the menstrual cycle and the use of oral contraceptives.

Future Directions

The most prominent future direction is the measurement and recording of blood pressure throughout the individual's day by means of ambulatory blood pressure monitoring equipment (Chesney, 1984). Very lightweight devices for measuring blood pressure are attached to the individual's body, and the information from these devices is entered on a recorder that the individual wears. Invasive ambulatory monitoring equipment that measures arterial blood pressure directly is available. Noninvasive ambulatory blood pressure monitoring equipment typically involves an inflatable cuff, an instrument to monitor Korotkoff sounds, and a device to inflate the cuff. Because of the problems of invasive blood pressure measurement, noninvasive approaches to ambulatory blood pressure monitoring will likely dominate in the immediate future.

References

Chesney, M.A. (1984). Noninvasive ambulatory blood pressure monitoring. In J.A. Herd, A.M. Gotto, P.G. Kaufmann, & S.M. Weiss (Eds.), Proceedings of the working conference on applicability of new technology to biobehavioral research (pp. 79-94). (NIH Publication No. 84-1654). Washington, DC: U.S. Department of Health and Human Services.

Geddes, L.A. (1970). The direct and indirect measurement of blood pressure. Chicago: Year Book Medical Publishers.

Hassett, J. (1978). A primer of psychophysiology. San Francisco: W.H. Freeman.

Blood Pressure Reactivity

C. Barr Taylor

Description

Blood pressure reactivity, sometimes referred to as blood pressure responsivity, refers to changes in blood pressure to various stimuli. In humans, the predominant measure of reactivity is the absolute change in blood pressure from baseline resting levels (Krantz & Manuck, 1984). Related to the concept of blood pressure reactivity are blood pressure lability and variability. Blood pressure lability is a clinical term, defined as the change in resting blood pressure from one measurement session to another, each session separated by a day or longer. Blood pressure variability is defined as the intrinsic variation in blood pressure expressed in such units as standard deviation or log standard deviation of the mean systolic, diastolic, or mean blood pressure or in comparison of one time of the day to another.

Purpose

Blood pressure reactivity is measured: (a) to detect individuals at risk of developing hypertension (Keys et al., 1971), (b) to evaluate the effects of psychological treatment procedures (Chesney & Jacobs, 1984), and (c) to investigate behavioral or psychosocial antecedents that might lead to hypertension.

Development

The observation that psychological states affect blood pressure was noted soon after indirect blood pressure measurement became possible in the late 19th century. In the 1930s psychosomatic researchers began to study the effects of various exogenous and endogenous stimuli on blood pressure changes and to relate these changes to personality variables, interpersonal behavior, conflict, and many other variables (Taylor & Fortmann, 1983). In a landmark study, Keys et al. (1971) measured blood pressure response to a cold pressor stimulus in 279 men aged 45 to 55. A blood pressure response greater than 20 mm Hg was one of the best predictors of cardiovascular illness measured 20 years later. This study implied that reactivity may have been a direct contributor to disease or a marker of correlated pathogenic processes, or both. In recent years, reactivity has received particular attention in relationship to borderline essential hypertension, defined, depending on the source, as blood pressure in the range of 140 to 160 systolic and 90 to 100 mm Hg diastolic. Many patients with borderline hypertension develop essential hypertension. Some of these patients have blood pressure elevations caused by increased cardiac output and only develop increased resistance later. Investigating the autonomic mechanisms that might be related to borderline hypertension evolving into

essential hypertension has been a focus of blood pressure reactivity studies. Numerous studies have shown that hypertensive individuals show greater reactivity to standard laboratory stimuli than do normotensive control subjects.

Research in Type A behavior (also called Coronary Prone Behavior) has stimulated much current interest in reactivity. Many studies have shown greater reactivity, including greater blood pressure reactivity during stressful circumstances among Type A subjects compared to Type B subjects. Some groups of Type A individuals may be particularly reactive to tasks that involve challenge and demand and that are stressful.

Psychometric Characteristics

Reliable measurement of blood pressure reactivity requires attention to test situation, baseline measurement, the task characteristics, measurement of response, and subject variables. A 5- to 20-minute resting baseline is commonly used, but other researchers argue that basal hemodynamic states cannot be made in the same session at which stressful stimuli are presented because of anticipatory arousal (Obrist, 1981). A lack of standardization of tasks used to elicit reactivity has confounded the literature. Different laboratory tasks produce different blood pressure responses in the same individual, and blood pressure increases are specific to the situation. Most investigators use tasks that last 5 to 15 minutes each, although the cold pressor, a commonly used measure of reactivity, requires only that the subject's extremity enter cold water. Most reactivity studies have been performed in homogeneous or case-controlled studies, and there is little known about the interaction between such variables as age, sex, race, and blood pressure reactivity.

Systolic blood pressure responsivity is reasonably stable and reproducible in some populations. The relationship between laboratory and ambulatory reactivity has not been well clarified.

Clinical Use

Blood pressure reactivity has, as yet, no standard place in clinical practice. Blood pressure responses greater than 20 mm Hg to cold pressor in men aged 45 to 55 may predict future cardiovascular disease. Labile hypertensive subjects are more prone to develop hypertension. So-called Type A patients may have greater cardiovascular reactivity than

Type Bs. Such increased reactivity has been hypothesized as an important pathogenic link between Type As and the development of cardiovascular disease.

Future Directions

New developments in ambulatory blood pressure measures will facilitate the investigation of laboratory and clinical measures and natural blood pressure levels. Standardized procedures for evaluating reactivity will be necessary to permit comparison across populations and clinical problems. Introduction to reactivity measures in ongoing prospective epidemiologic studies of cardiovascular disease would help determine the risk of reactivity for producing subsequent cardiovascular disease. The role of reactivity in identifying Type A subgroups prone to coronary heart disease or hypertension and in promoting hypertension or heart disease will be a major research issue in the 1980s.

References

Chesney, M.A., & Jacobs, R.G. (1984). Stress management for cardiovascular reactivity. *Behavioral Medicine Update, 6*, 23-27.

Keys, A., Taylor, H.L., Blackburn, H., Brozek, J., Anderson, J.T., & Somonson, E. (1971). Mortality and coronary heart disease among men studied for 23 years. *Archives of Internal Medicine, 128*, chl 201-214.

Krantz, D.S., & Manuck, S.B. (1984). Acute psychophysiologic reactivity and risk of cardiovascular disease: A review and methodologic critique. *Psychological Bulletin, 96*, 435-464.

Obrist, P.A. (1981). *Cardiovascular psychophysiology*. New York: Plenum Press.

Taylor, C.B., & Fortmann, S.P. (1983). Essential hypertension. *Psychosomatics, 24*, 433-488.

Body Mass Index

Gregory L. Wilson and D. Balfour Jeffrey

Description

The Body Mass Index (BMI, weight/height) is an assessment strategy that has proven useful in obesity treatment programs and epidemiological research. The ratio of weight divided by height squared provides a quick and accurate estimate of clinical obesity. Moreover, Thomas, McKay, and Cutlip (1976) have developed a nomograph to calculate BMI which allows for the determination of a range of acceptable weight. Thus, the BMI nomograph provides a continuous quantitative scale of acceptable weight ranges for various heights.

Purpose

Broadly defined, obesity represents an excess of stored body fat from caloric intake that is greater than the caloric expenditure required for physical acitivity, somatic maintenance, and growth. Behavioral approaches to the assessment of obesity often include measures of percentage over ideal weight and the weight-reduction index (Jeffrey, Dawson, & Wilson, in press). However, a major difficulty in assessment strategies employing ideal weight estimates concerns the estimation of frame size in height-weight charts. Currently, there is no quantifiable method for determining frame size, and the practitioner is forced to make a subjective estimate. Alternatives to utilizing such charts in estimating ideal weight and obesity are to employ ratios of weight relative to specific powers of height. The BMI represents the best such ratio (Thomas et al., 1976).

Development

The BMI nomograph uses life insurance data as population norms in specifying a range of acceptable weight. Whereas this method provides a continuous scale of acceptable weight ranges for different heights, it does not require an estimation of frame size to determine the acceptable range. An advantage of the nomograph is that, for all heights, obesity is defined as the point at which the BMI is equal to 30, and this point corresponds closely with 20% overweight. Whereas the criteria of obesity employed in behavioral research typically range from 10 to 20% over ideal weight, epidemiological research demonstrates no significant increase in medical disorders in individuals under 30% over ideal weight. However, beyond this point, there is a rapid rise in disorders related to obesity, with every percentage of increase over ideal weight (Bray, 1978). Thus, clinicians and researchers may prefer to employ cutoff scores greater than 30 on the BMI.

Psychometric Characteristics

The BMI correlates between .70 and .80 with more direct measures of body fat, thereby providing the lowest correlations with height independent of weight (Bray, 1978). Conversely, the nomograph has some weaknesses similar to those of the height-weight charts. Specifically, the BMI nomograph, like the height-weight charts, uses insurance data in defining population norms. Because these data are based on a sample of insurance customers and are not necessarily representative of the entire population in terms of physical, racial, ethnic, and socioeconomic factors, the tables may not accurately reflect the true norms. Another weakness is that the norms presented are based on samples from the 1950s and may well be outdated for today's population. Certainly, a lack of current, representative weight norms hinder both treatment and research.

Clinical Use

The BMI nomograph offers considerable advantages for clinicians and researchers. Besides eliminating the necessity of estimating frame size, the nomograph specifies particular BMI values for clinical obesity (i.e., equal to or greater than 30) and also allows an exact specification of ideal weight. A practitioner can choose a BMI within the acceptable range (e.g., 23) and then determine an exact ideal weight value for clients of differing heights. This procedure provides superior data for use in calculations concerning percentage over ideal weight and the weight-reduction index (Jeffrey & Knauss, 1981). Moreover, in contrast to caliper measurements of skin fold, the BMI nomograph provides more reliable and convenient data.

Future Directions

Development of representative weight norms and appropriate nomograph revision is needed. However, the utility of the BMI nomograph seems clear. Multidimensional assessment strategies that incorporate BMI procedures with measures of absolute weight, eating habits, physical activities, and other relevant dimensions seem most prudent (Jeffrey et al., in press; Jeffrey & Katz, 1977).

References

Bray, G.A. (1978). Definition, measurement, and classification of the syndromes of obesity. *International Journal of Obesity, 2*, 99-112.

Jeffrey, D.B., Dawson, B., & Wilson, G.L. (in press). Assessment of eating disorders: Adult obesity, childhood obesity, anorexia nervosa, and bulimia. In G.A. Marlatt & D.M. Donovan (Eds.), *Assessment of addictive behaviors: Behavioral, cognitive, and physiological procedures.* New York: Guilford.

Jeffrey, D. B., & Katz, R.C. (1977). *Take it off and keep it off: A behavioral program for weight loss and healthy living.* New York: Prentice-Hall.

Jeffrey, D.B., & Knauss, M.R. (1981). The etiologies, treatments, and assessments of obesity. In S.M. Haynes & L. Gannon (Eds.), *Psychosomatic disorders: A psychophysiological approach to etiology and treatment.* New York: Praeger.

Thomas, A.E., McKay, D.A., & Cutlip, M.B. (1976). Nomograph for body mass index (KG/M). *American Journal of Clinical Nutrition, 29,* 302-304.

Body Sensations Questionnaire

Dianne L. Chambless

Description

The Body Sensations Questionnaire (BSQ: Chambless, Caputo, Bright, & Gallagher, 1984) is a 17-item self-report questionnaire in which clients are asked to rate on a scale of 1 (not frightened) to 5 (extremely frightened) how frightening they find particular body sensations that are common during high anxiety (e.g., heart palpitations). The BSQ has been translated into French (Canadian) and Dutch.

Purpose

The BSQ along with its companion measure, the Agoraphobic Cognitions Questionnaire (ACQ), was devised to assess "fear of fear" (Goldstein & Chambless, 1978) among persons with agoraphobia. It has often been stated that persons with agoraphobia are afraid of the situations they avoid because they dread having panic attacks in places from which escape is difficult or in which help cannot easily be obtained. They become hyperalert to, and afraid of, any sensations that portend or are associated with panic (e.g., dizziness and derealization). These sensations then become themselves triggers for spiraling anxiety, maintaining a destructive cycle in which anxiety becomes the signal for even greater anxiety. The BSQ is designed to measure this aspect of fear of fear: the fear of one's own physical responses to anxiety cues.

Development

The ACQ and BSQ items were developed on the basis of clients' reports about their concerns during interviews, in vivo exposure sessions, and imaginal flooding sessions. Validational studies were carried out on a sample of 175 outpatients with a diagnosis of agoraphobia with panic attacks, 194 clients with other neurotic disorders, and a group of 23 normal control subjects.

Psychometric Characteristics

Scores for the BSQ are normally distributed around a mean of 3.05 (SD = 0.86). Responses to the individual items are averaged to yield the total score. Correlations with the ACQ of .34 and .67 have been obtained.

Reliability. The BSQ is internally consistent (alpha = .87) and is moderately reliable over time (median 31-day test-retest r = .67; 8-day r = .66).

Validity. The BSQ was found to be stable over the pretreatment reliability period, showing neither a significant decline nor increase, but decreased significantly with in vivo exposure plus cognitive coping strategies. Therefore, the scale is sensitive to changes with treatment.

Validity was assessed in two further ways. First, the scale's relationships with measures of psychopathology predicted to correlate with fear of fear were examined. The BSQ, as hypothesized, was positively correlated with depression, trait anxiety, neuroticism, avoidance behavior, and panic frequency, but not to the extent that it seemed to duplicate these other measures. It was not significantly related to a theoretically irrelevant measure of psychopathology, the Psychoticism scale of the Eysenck Personality Questionnaire, indicating that the BSQ does not reflect a simple tendency to report psychological problems. Scores were not affected by age or socioeconomic status.

Second, the BSQ's ability to discriminate agoraphobic clients from a normal control group and from other clinical samples was examined (Chambless et al., 1984; Chambless, 1985). The BSQ significantly discriminated agoraphobic from normal subjects, depressed clients, and clients with other anxiety disorders (obsessive-compulsive disorder, generalized anxiety disorder, and social phobia). Clients receiving a diagnosis of panic disorder had similar scores (although there was a trend for agoraphobic persons to have higher scores), suggesting that fear of fear is high in clients who have or have had frequent panic attacks, but not as prevalent in those with other anxiety problems.

Clinical Use

In clinical use, the BSQ may be administered to clients before intake to elicit important concerns and then discussed during the interview. Identification of the client's particular distressing symptoms aids in developing effective coping strategies for these symptoms and provides the therapist with the opportunity to educate the clients about the origins of such symptoms (e.g., dizziness may be caused by hyperventilation, not a brain tumor as the client may fantasize). Such education is critical in obtaining the client's compliance with an in vivo exposure program. The BSQ may be periodically readministered during treatment to check for progress; change on this measure typically lags somewhat behind change on avoidance.

References

Chambless, D.L. (1985). *Specificity of fear of fear among neurotic clients.* Manuscript in preparation.

Chambless, D.L., Caputo, G.C., Bright, P., & Gallagher, R. (1984). Assessment of fear of fear in agoraphobics: The Body Sensations Questionnaire and the Agoraphobic Cognitions Questionnaire. *Journal of Consulting and Clinical Psychology, 52,* 1090-1097.

Goldstein, A.J., & Chambless, D.L. (1978). A reanalysis of agoraphobia. *Behavior Therapy, 9,* 47-59.

Brief Psychiatric Rating Scale

John E. Overall

Description

The Brief Psychiatric Rating Scale (BPRS) has been the most widely used, general purpose, psychiatric rating scale in the decade of the 1970s and 1980s. It consists of 18 symptom constructs, each rated for severity on a 7-point scale ranging from "not present" to "extremely severe." Five factor scores obtained by summing ratings on related items provide composite measures of thinking disturbance, anxious depression, hostile suspiciousness, withdrawal retardation, and agitation excitement. Typical profile patterns for psychiatric patients tend to conform to one of eight phenomenologic types: florid thinking disorder, withdrawn disorganized thinking disturbance, paranoid hostile suspiciousness, agitation excitement, anxious depression, agitated depression, retarded depression, or hostile depression. Profile analysis methods can be used to operationalize the assignment of individual patients among these phenomenological types. Although the BPRS is not a diagnostic instrument, it provides good discrimination between major diagnostic classes, such as schizophrenia and depressive disorders. Its most extensive use has been in the evaluation of treatment response in controlled clinical drug trials, but it has been used in a wide range of other types of investigations, including epidemiologic studies and cross-cultural comparisons of diagnostic concepts. It is useful in characterizing patient populations seen in clinical practice.

The BPRS provides a symptom profile characterizing the essential features of manifest psychopathology for most types of patients in the general psychiatric population. It is designed to provide simplicity and parsimony in the quantitative description of manifest psychopathology for individual patients, to assess treatment response in clinical research, and to investigate differences among relevant psychiatric populations.

Development

First published in 1962 as a 16-item scale, the symptom constructs of the BPRS were chosen to represent relatively independent dimensions of manifest psychopathology identified in factor analyses of large item pools available from early psychiatric drug studies conducted within the Veterans Administration hospital system (Overall & Gorham, 1962). The initial intended use of the instrument was to provide more efficient assessment of treatment response in clinical psychopharmacology research; however, the BPRS was readily adapted to other uses.

Early investigations included empirical work in diagnosis, classification, and drug–prescribing practices. This work, particularly that concerned with diagnosis and classification, revealed deficiencies in characterizing agitation and dementia states, which resulted in addition of two items of "excitement" and "disorientation" in 1966. This rounded out the 18-item version of the BPRS that has been used for the last 20 years. A facsimile of the 18-item BPRS has been reproduced in numerous publications, and single copies suitable for reproduction can be obtained from the authors without cost (J.E. Overall, Ph.D., Department of Psychiatry, University of Texas Medical School, P. O. Box 20708, Houston, TX 77225).

Psychometric Characteristics

Numerous factor analyses of BPRS symptom ratings have been undertaken. Earlier analyses accomplished on the initial 16-item version consistently produced four factors described as thinking disturbance, withdrawal retardation, hostile suspiciousness, and anxious depression (Overall, Hollister, & Pichot, 1967). A score for

each of these factors is derived from the sum of ratings on three related items. With the addition of "excitement" as a rating construct, a diad of tension and excitement emerged as a fifth relatively independent dimension. The authors prefer the balance and clear interpretation achieved by defining each factor (except the last) in terms of only three items. An alternative factor scoring described in the NIMH-ECDEU Manual included items that have lower loadings on these primary factors in an attempt to sue all 18 items in the definition of factor scores. Had those authors considered only the three highest loading items for each factor, the more balance and more clearly interpretable factor scoring preferred by the authors of the BPRS would have emerged. The best review of psychometric characteristics of the BPRS is contained in an article by Hedlund and Vieweg (1980), which unfortunately is not widely available. Among 300 articles surveyed, those authors identified 22 reliability studies. Of 13 studies that used Pearson product moment correlation coefficients to assess interrater reliability, 10 reported reliability coefficients of .80 or greater for the BPRS total score (sum of ratings of the 18 items). Interrater reliability coefficients for individual items ranged from .63 to .83, with overall median reliability of .75 for the items.

As noted, the BPRS symptom ratings combine to define four factor scores, each based on the sum of ratings on three related items plus one diad factor described as agitation/excitement. Published studies that have reported reliability for the composite factor scores have found interrater reliability to range from .77 to .97 for the factor scores.

Increased reliability can be achieved by summing or averaging independent ratings by two trained observers. Item reliability coefficients for combined ratings by two raters have been reported to range from .73 to .95, and two-rater composite reliabilities for the four factor scores have been reported to range from .87 to .95. Reliability estimates have not been reported for the agitation/excitement diad, which was added to the factor scoring relatively recently.

Validity of the BPRS is best discussed in terms of its clinical uses, which are recounted briefly in the following section. In using BPRS profile data to illustrate various different methods of multivariate analysis, Overall and Klett (1983) have provided in one volume a comprehensive collection of validity studies relating to diagnosis, classification, drug treatment indications, and background characteristics of psychiatric patients.

Clinical Use

Validity of the BPRS has been demonstrated in hundreds of double-blind controlled studies of efficacy of drug treatment of psychiatric disorders. A majority of these studies have involved antipsychotic or antidepressant drugs in schizophrenia or depressive disorder, although the rating scale has successfully documented the effects of other types of drugs in other patient populations, such as alcoholic addicts and persons with senile dementia. Other forms of treatment that have been investigated formally using the BPRS to assess outcome have been ECT, psychotherapy, and behavioral and cognitive therapy.

In addition to research involving formal experimental designs, the BPRS has been used to evaluate treatment programs, to develop data bases for retrospective research in natural clinic settings, and to examine relationships of manifest psychopathology to history and background characteristics of patients. Validity of the BPRS has been examined with respect to choice of treatment for individual patients, and the instrument has been found to discriminate well between patients who are treated by doctor's choice with different major classes of drugs (e.g., antidepressant, antipsychotic, and antianxiety drugs). The BPRS has also been used to investigate patient symptom characteristics that relate to psychiatrist's decisions to treat with a particular drug within the major drug classes. This resulted in recognition that the activation/retardation dimension of patient behavior is the primary determinant of choice between drugs within both antidepressant and antipsychotic classes.

Although the BPRS is not intended as a diagnostic instrument, diagnosis in psychiatry is largely based on manifest signs and symptoms. The BPRS discriminates well among the major diagnostic populations of schizophrenia, depressive disorder, and anxiety-related disorders. Mania is reasonably well distinguished from acute schizophrenia, although the two groups share in common florid psychotic symptoms. The BPRS does not distinguish well among nonpsychotic conditions other than depression. Alcoholism, various personality disorders, and drug abuse are distinguishable from the major psychiatric syndromes just mentioned by the absence of notable pathology in the BPRS profiles, but they are not distinguishable among themselves.

Because both diagnosis and choice of treatment are largely symptom based in psychiatry, the BPRS has been used to develop quantitative and geometric models depicting similarities and differences among populations and treatment groups. Profile analysis algorithms based on these models can be used to document the appropriateness of clinical decisions relative to actuarial norms from BPRS data bases.

Empirical classification research is a final area of application that should be mentioned. An alternative to discriminating among clinically defined diagnostic groups is the empirical approach of identifying naturally occurring profile types. All possible BPRS profile patterns do not occur with equal frequency in nature. Some patterns occur with substantial frequency, whereas others are not represented at all in large data bases. Cluster analysis and related methodologies have been used to identify the most representative distinct BPRS profile patterns in the general adult psychiatric population. The profiles for most patients can be adequately described as belonging to one of eight types: florid thinking disorder, withdrawn-disorganized thinking disturbance, paranoid hostile suspiciousness, agitation-excitement, anxious depression, agitated depression, retarded depression, and hostile depression (Overall & Rhoades, 1982). Profile analysis algorithms and objective target-symptom decision rules have been offered for classification of individual patients among the descriptive categories on the basis of their BPRS symptom profiles. Such phenomenological classification cuts across major diagnostic lines and appears useful in stratifying patient samples in clinical research.

Future Directions

The BPRS has long been in the public domain. As a consequence, future directions will be determined by its many users. Evaluation of treatment response in clinical research will continue to be one primary use. Previous results in phenomenological classification of patients are likely to become more important as a means of stratifying behaviorally heterogeneous diagnostic groups for research purposes.

The BPRS is increasingly used to serve administrative and documentation needs other than clinical research per se. In several states, the BPRS is routinely used to document the justification for diagnosis and treatment in public hospital facilities. In at least one instance, the BPRS is used by a regional insurance audit to document the clinical condition of patients treated for psychiatric disorder. Such uses will likely increase as requirements for accountability increase for the health care delivery system. The BPRS provides a simple, quick, and efficient way of describing individual patients in a standard format that facilitates both administrative and research uses.

References

Hedlund, J.L., & Vieweg, B.W. (1980). The brief psychiatric rating scale (BPRS): A comprehensive review. *Journal of Operational Psychiatry, 11*, 48–65.

Overall, J.E., & Gorham, D.R. (1962). The brief psychiatric rating scale. *Psychological Report, 10*, 799-812.

Overall, J.E., Hollister, L.E., & Pichot, P. (1967). Major psychiatric disorders: A four dimensional model. *Archives of General Psychiatry, 16*, 146-151.

Overall, J.E., & Klett, C.J. (1983). *Applied Multivariate Analysis.* (Reprinted Edition) Malabar, FL: Krieger.

Overall, J.E., & Rhoades, H.M. (1982). Refinement of phenomenological classification in clinical psychopharmacology research. *Psychopharmacology, 76*, 251-257.

Bulimia Test

Aubrey J. Yates

Description

The Bulimia Test (BULIT) is a 32-item forced-choice questionnaire (maximum possible score, 160) developed by Smith and Thelen (1984).

Purpose

The questionnaire was designed to discriminate bulimic individuals from individuals with other eating disorders and from normal eaters; to distinguish between subgroups of bulimic individuals if these exist; and to identify these different eating problems in individuals who have never sought treatment.

Development

The test was developed in four stages: (a) application of a 75-item preliminary form of the test to 18 female bulimic subjects (meeting DSM-III criteria) and 119 female control subjects; (b) application of a 32-item scale to 22 bulimic and 99 normal control subjects, and to 14 subjects diagnosed as having anorexia nervosa (all female); (c) application of the 32-item scale to 652 college women; (d) application of the 32-item scale to 28 of the 652 women who scored above 102 on the scale. All of these subjects were independently rated for bulimic symptoms.

Psychometric Characteristics

The final version of the scale discriminated clinically diagnosed bulimic subjects (mean score, 124.0) and normal control subjects (mean score, 60.3) ($p < .0001$), with 30 of the 32 items producing a significant difference. The point-biserial correlation (total score/group membership) was $+ .82$ ($p < .0001$). Using a cutting score of 102, only one bulimic and two normal subjects were misclassified. Sensitivity, specificity, and positive and negative predictive values all exceeded .90. Six of the anorexic subjects scored in the bulimic range, whereas eight scored in the normal range. The bulimic anorexic persons were readily distinguishable as having anorexia on the basis of other characteristics such as menstrual cycle irregularity. Test-retest reliability (2 months) on normal subjects scoring above or just below the cutoff point was $+ .87$ ($p < .0001$). Total scores from the retest significantly differentiated between subjects the raters judged to be normal (mean 74.7) ($p < .0001$).

Factor analysis of the scale revealed seven factors (binging behavior and fear of losing control; feelings after a binge; vomiting behavior; preferred food for binge; laxative and diuretic abuse; weight fluctuations; and menstrual regularity). Multivariate analyses were also carried out. The BULIT was found to correlate $+ .93$ with the Body Sensations Questionnaire.

Clinical Use

The primary use of the test is to identify cases of bulimia nervosa. Discrimination of such cases from cases of anorexia nervosa cannot be made reliably on the basis of scores on this test.

Future Directions

The clinical usefulness of the test will depend on the demonstration of its construct validity in relation to the scores of other clinical groups with eating disorders.

Reference

Smith, M.C., & Thelen, M.H. (1984). Development and validation of test for bulimia. *Journal of Consulting and Clinical Psychology, 52*, 863-872.

Callner-Ross Assertion Questionnaire

Robert T. Ammerman and Vincent B. Van Hasselt

Description

The Callner-Ross Assertion Questionnaire (CRAQ: Callner & Ross, 1976) is a 40-item inventory measuring assertion in male substance abusers. The CRAQ is divided into five subscales of six items each as well as a 10-item General Assertion category. The five subscales are: (1) heterosexual, which involves dating, expression of affection, and starting a conversation with a female; (2) authority, consisting of statements regarding authority figures (e.g., bosses and the police); (3) positive feedback, involving accepting and communicating praise and appreciation; (4) negative feedback, involving giving and responding to criticism; and (5) drugs, dealing with turning down drugs in a variety of drug-related situations.

Each item is endorsed using a 4-point Likert scale denoting lack of assertion (-1, -2) or increased assertion ($+1$, $+2$). Therefore, the total score ranges from -80 to $+80$. Five of the subscales range from -12 to $+12$, whereas the General Assertion subscale ranges from -20 to $+20$. A sample CRAQ item is: "When it comes to drugs, I have a hard time turning them down, even when I really want to" (Drugs subscale).

Purpose

Studies indicate that many substance abusers exhibit social skills deficits, particularly in the area of assertion (Van Hasselt, Hersen, & Milliones, 1978). However, there is paucity of psychometrically sound measurement instruments of interpersonal skills in substance abusers. The CRAQ was developed to partially address this need.

Development

The CRAQ was developed following examination of several commonly employed assertion inventories (e.g., Wolpe-Lazarus Assertion Scale). Items and subscale categories were derived using face validity criteria.

Psychometric Characteristics

Callner and Ross (1976) examined the psychometric properties of the CRAQ. They used a sample of 16 male veteran drug addicts aged 18 to 25 years and 16 age-matched nonabusers. Using a 7-day interval, the CRAQ demonstrated a test-retest reliability of .86. Likewise, Ammerman, Van Hasselt, and Hersen (1986) examined the psychometric characteristics of the CRAQ using a sample of 137 male alcoholic addicts. To yield finer distinctions between subjects, they used a 9-point (rather than a 4-point) Likert scale format. After a 1-month interval, the CRAQ had a somewhat lower test-retest correlation of .63. In addition, it displayed good internal reliability (Cronbach's alpha = .86).

Ammerman et al. (1986) examined the factor structure of the CRAQ. Using a varimax rotation, four factors were derived, each of which accounts for at least 5% of the variance (total variance accounted for was 38.5%). Factor labels are: General Expressiveness (19.9%), Drugs (7.2%), Positive Heterosexual Situations (5.7%), and Taking the Initiative (5.7%). These factors moderately correspond to Callner and Ross' (1976) original subscale categories.

Callner and Ross (1976) examined the validity of the CRAQ by comparing the inventory to a role-play test. Role-play scenes were divided equally in content among the five subscale categories (e.g., Drugs, Authority, and the like). The role-play test included one prompt, and an audiotaped voice served as the "confederate." Responses were audiotaped and rated on 5-point Likert scales for duration, fluency, and affect. In addition, following the role-play, subjects were asked to rate themselves on how assertive they were in the role-play. A multitrait-multimethod matrix was derived by computing correlations between each of the measures. On the whole, correlations were moderate to high (ranging from .71 to .95), demonstrating adequate convergent validity. Correlations between subscale scores and other measures also were relatively high, indicating poor discriminant validity in this instance. The latter finding is consistent with Ammerman et al.'s (1986) factor analysis which provided little support for the CRAQ's original subscale structure.

Despite the Callner and Ross (1976) study, questions about the CRAQ's validity remain. First, the sample employed was limited to young male veteran substance abusers, and generalizability to other substance abuse populations must be made with caution. Second, use of a brief role-play test as a comparison instrument is questionable. Indeed, the validity of role-play tests is uncertain (e.g., Bellack, Hersen, & Turner, 1978). Therefore, further investigation of the CRAQ's psychometric properties is required.

Clinical Use

The CRAQ is the only assertion inventory specifically designed for substance abusers. As such, it can be a valuable clinical tool in the assessment of social skills in this population. Because of its questionable validity, however, caution must be applied when using the instrument in clinical settings.

Future Directions

The CRAQ has not had wide application because of the uncertainty surrounding its validity and generalizability. Additional research examining the psychometric characteristics of the CRAQ is necessary before the instrument's utility can be determined.

References

Ammerman, R.T., Van Hasselt, V.B., & Hersen, M. (1986). Assessment of assertion in alcoholics. Unpublished manuscript, University of Pittsburgh School of Medicine, Pittsburgh.
Bellack, A.S., Hersen, M., & Turner, S.M. (1978). Role-play tests for assessing social skill. Are they valid? *Behavior Therapy*, 9, 448-461.
Callner, D.A., & Ross, S.M. (1976). The reliability and validity of three measures of assertion in a drug addict population. *Behavior Therapy*, 7, 659-667.
Van Hasselt, V.B., Hersen, M., & Milliones, J. (1978). Social skills training for alcoholics and drug addicts: A review. *Addictive Behaviors*, 3, 221-223.

Cardiotachometry

Geary S. Alford

Description and Development

A cardiotachograph is an electrophysiological monitoring device that, as the name implies, measures and displays or "writes" (prints out) heart rate. There are a variety of such instruments ranging from very simple models that provide only a visual digital display indicating heart beats per minute, through standard electrocardiograph versions, to more complex, computerized instrumentation capable of analyzing wave characteristics, graphing average transients, and detecting very slight variations in electrophysiologic signals. Although more sophisticated assessment involves placing transduction electrodes on the surface of the subject's or patient's chest and extremities, recent, portable models are available in the form of 'wrist-watches' that reflect heart rate by using surface sensors to measure pulse rate from fingers or wrist. Technically, cardiotachometry refers only to measuring heart rate.

The relation between heart rate and psychological phenomena has a long history dating as far back as the second century A.D. when, Galen noted that a patient's heart rate significantly increased whenever the man she was in love with approached. Common expressions such as "heart throb," "heart breaking," and "heart stopping" have physiological bases. Heart rate has long been one of the multichannel components in the polygraphic "lie-detector." Although the validity of lie-detector tests with respect to detecting *deception* remains controversial, it is generally accepted that multichannel polygraphic measures can reliably reflect autonomic "emotional" arousal. In general, heart rate usually accelerates with increasing emotional arousal. However, heart rate also accelerates upon physical exertion. It is therefore necessary to control for physical exertion whenever cardiotachometry is employed as a measure of emotional behavior. This is usually accomplished by having patients or subjects remain in a sitting or even reclining position during testing. However, it is possible to examine emotion-related heart rate changes even when individuals are engaged in some physical activity. This requires the systematic establishment of base rates for a given activity, such as walking or manipulation of some object, then carefully maintaining or matching the physiokinetic activity while new independent variables are introduced. By way of simple example, base heart rates can be taken for a rodent-phobic patient's walking toward a table. Then, heart rate is monitored as the patient approaches that same table on which a caged rat has been placed. Establishment of activity-specific base rates can be crucial even when patients or subjects remain stationary. If a clinician or researcher is interested in heart rate changes that occur as a patient discusses certain emotionally loaded topics, it is necessary to determine each individual's heart rates when he or she is discussing neutral material because the act of talking itself accelerates heart rate in most people.

Purpose and Psychometric Characteristics

Interpretation of heart rate changes with respect to emotionality is a complex and difficult enterprise. Aside from the effects of skeletal muscular-physical exertion or possibly physical illness, increased heart rate at best reflects only changing levels of autonomic arousal. The particular class of emotion such as "anxiety," "anger," or "elated excitement" cannot be determined from the cardiotachograph itself. This determination must largely be made by reference to the subject's or patient's self-report, although certain other overt behaviors, such as avoidant, escape, or approach behaviors, provide additional data upon which inferences about the qualitative as well as quantitative aspects of emotional reactions can be based. Under controlled conditions, heart rate alone can reflect increased or changing levels of emotional arousal, but as a single measure of emotional state, reliability, validity, and hence utility are limited. Instead, if autonomic arousal or emotional behaviors are targets of behavioral assessment-treatment, cardiotachometrics are best employed in conjunction with multichannel measures, especially respiratory rate and depth, electromyography (muscle tension), and galvanic skin responses (skin conductance).

Clinical Use

Heart rate was one of the first physiological events to which biofeedback procedures were experimentally and subsequently clinically applied. Here, cardiographic instrumentation is utilized to provide feedback to subjects or patients regarding acceleration or deceleration of heart rate either by directly displaying ongoing recordings or by triggering some signal or presentation of a potential reinforcer contingent on attainment of criterion heart rates.

More recently, cardiotachometry has been commonly employed in behavioral medicine procedures designed to enhance physical, particularly cardiovascular, fitness. In addition to providing continuous monitoring of heart rate during physical exertion-exercises, a subject's different heart rates during baseline, exercise-exertion, and post-exertion recovery are computed within a standard formula, the results of which are combined with blood pressure and other measures providing a test of "cardiovascular fitness." Therefore, psychologists working with cardiologists and sports-medicine physicians use cardiotachometry along with other physiological tests to assess the effects and effectiveness of various behavioral training procedures intended to improve physical conditioning including cardiovascular function.

Future Directions

The future of cardiotachographic measurement in behavioral assessment is largely linked to the future direction of behavioral psychology and the behavior therapies. Having begun to confront, legitimize, incorporate, and expand the domains of human cognition, behavioral assessments and therapies are now entering an era of increasing interest in broader and more complex human emotionality. In this regard, the cardiotachograph, in conjunction with other psychophysiological instrumentation, will provide an objective measure of physiologic events that closely parallel and perhaps subserve various emotional phenomena. With the advent of computer-assisted electrophysiologic analysis, it may eventually be possible to reliably discriminate differential multichannel activation patterns associated with differing subjective emotional sensations. Such development would allow more objective electrophysiologic determination and assessment of the qualitative nature of emotional phenomena in addition to the present rather gross quantitative measurement of autonomic arousal. Likewise, cardiotachometry will continue to play a central assessment role in those behavioral medicine, health, and sports psychology procedures that involve the cardiovascular system.

Checklist of Appropriate Speaking Behaviors

W. L. Marshall and H. E. Barbaree

Description

The Checklist of Appropriate Speaking Behaviors (CASB) contains 19 items that describe three categories of overt behaviors displayed by competent public speakers. The three categories describe general behaviors, specific speech behaviors, and particular body movements. Within each category there are items describing specific behavioral displays, and each of these items is checked by an observer for its presence across three observation periods, each of which is 30 seconds long. These observations are made while the speaker gives a 5-minute talk, with the first observation period commencing after 1 minute of the speech and an interobservation interval of at least 30 seconds. For most accurate results, a preassessment practice period for the observer (observing six or more public speakers) is essential. The observer checks only the *presence* of the behaviors, and the final score is simply the sum of all the checked items totaled across the three observation periods, giving a possible range of 0 to 57.

Purpose

The purpose of the CASB is to provide a behavioral description of public speakers, which permits a score to be derived indicating the degree of skill displayed by the speaker. It is valuable both for research and for evaluating the effects of training public speakers.

Development

The scale was originally developed (Marshall, Cooper, & Parker, 1979) on the basis of a thorough appraisal of the literature describing effective public speakers. This literature is essentially anecdotal, so that subsequent refinements were made through application of the scale to the continuous flow of clients in our public speaking training program. We originally had 30 items in the scale but dropped 11 because either they were too difficult to infer when observing speakers or they failed to be manifest in more than a few component speakers. The final form was first described by Marshall, Parker, and Hayes (1982), who showed it to be valuable in analysis of the effectiveness of certain aspects of our training program.

The CASB was developed because although the literature on the behavioral analysis of public speaking was replete with measures indicating the incompetence of poor speakers, there was no index of gains made from training in the display of com-

petencies. Although it is true that poor speakers are readily distinguishable from good speakers in terms of bad speaking habits and signs of distress, good speakers not only fail to show these negative signs, but also display attractive features that capture the attention and interest of their audience. Adequate training should not only eliminate negative features, but also instill these attractive behaviors in the trainees.

Psychometric Characteristics

We have approached the psychometric evaluation of the CASB in several ways. Because the validity of a scale is not relevant until it can be shown that scores on the scale can be derived reliably, our first goal was to evaluate reliability. Given that the CASB score is derived from an observer's notes, we wanted to determine influences arising from observer characteristics. We also were interested in the stability of the observations over time in the absence of any intervention. This latter form of reliability (test-retest) was most crucial if the scale was employed as an index of training effectiveness; for these reasons we chose a 6-week test-retest interval.

Our reliability data indicate that two observers produced almost identical scores in assessing 40 good and 40 poor public speakers (interobserver reliability: $r = .99$). These observers were trained to identify the behaviors accurately in the scale before the experiment by practice observations of six speakers concomitant with discussions with the trainer. Similarly, in observations of these 40 good and 40 poor speakers, test-retest reliabilities over a 6-week interval were very high for each observer ($r = .99$ for both observers).

In terms of validity, our first step (criterion validity) was to examine the differences between both the 40 good and the 40 poor speakers and to evaluate changes in poor speakers resulting from demonstrably effective training. The good speakers were either active and successful members of the university debating team, members of the local Toastmasters Club, who were judged by fellow members to be exemplary speakers, or university professors who had received excellence ratings from students over each of the last 4 years. Poor speakers were selected from volunteers for our training program on the basis of both describing themselves as being anxious when speaking before an audience and being unable to identify the features of good speakers. Statistical analyses of scores on the CASB revealed highly significant differences between good and poor speakers ($F(1,78) = 898.76; p < .001$), with the good speakers (mean = 49.5; SD = 6.5) obtaining higher scores than the poor speakers (mean = 9.4; SD − 5.5). Similarly, in five studies (Marshall, Presse, & Andrews, 1976; Marshall, Stoian, & Andrews, 1977) evaluating the contribution of variance elements in our demonstrably effective training program, poor speakers showed statistically significant benefits from training on the CASB as well as on other well-established measures of public speaking performance (Hayes & Marshall, 1984; Marshall et al., 1982). After treatment, 77 poor speakers scored much the same (mean = 50.5; SD = 6.6) as did the good speakers.

The construct validity of the CASB was evaluated by examining the relationship between scores on this measure and other measures of public speaking, which have been employed by researchers for many years and for which validity data are available. Scores on the CASB are negatively related to scores on the Behavioral Checklist ($r = -.83$), which describes the inappropriate features of poor speakers. Scores on the CASB are also significantly negatively related to subjects' estimates of how anxious they felt (Fear Thermometer) when giving the evaluated speech ($r = -.92$), with the subjects' ratings of how anxious they anticipated they would be in various hypothetical speaking situations ($r = -.75$) and with the scale developed by Paul (1966) called the Personal Report of Communication Apprehension ($r = -.85$).

Clinical Use

We routinely use the CASB, along with the Behavior Checklist and the Fear Thermometer, as the standard assessment battery in our training program for public speakers. Accurate use of the measure as a clinical tool requires little experience by the observers (no more than practice with six speakers) and has the distinct advantage of describing the actual behaviors targeted in all of those training programs that provide sufficient details to determine the goals of treatment.

Future Directions

We believe the CASB has been sufficiently refined to represent a valuable index of the skills of public speakers and is therefore not in need of further refinement. However, in our most recent evaluation of our training program (Hayes & Marshall, 1984) we found that speaking performance, as appraised by our usual methods including the CASB, demonstrated marked generalization to other speaking situations and also to performance in other social situations. The latter observation suggests that personal performance across social situations may lie along a continuum. Recently, Hayes (personal communication) expanded this observation and demonstrated that enhancing public speaking skills in persons with social phobia markedly reduces their interpersonal fears in conversational encounters. These observations suggest that with little modification, the CASB may be valuable in assessing a broad range of problems common to people with social phobia. Indeed, we found supportive evidence in our most recent research (Hayes & Marshall, 1984).

References

Hayes, B.J., & Marshall, W.L. (1984). Generalization of treatment effects in training public speakers. *Behaviour Research and Therapy, 22,* 519-533.

Marshall, W.L., Cooper, C., & Parker, L. (1979). Skills training and anxiety management in producing effective public speakers. Paper presented at the 13th Annual Convention of the Association for Advancement of Behavior Therapy, San Francisco.

Marshall, W.L., Parker, L., & Hayes, B.J. (1982). Treating public speaking problems: A study using flooding and the elements of skills training. *Behavior Modification, 6,* 147-170.

Marshall, W.L., Presse, L., & Andrews, W.R. (1976). A self-administered program for public speaking anxiety. *Behaviour Research and Therapy, 14,* 33-40.

Marshall, W.L., Stoian, M., & Andrews, W.R. (1977). Skills and training and self-administered desensitization in the reduction of public speaking anxiety. *Behaviour Research and Therapy, 15,* 115-117.

Child Behavior Checklist and Related Instruments

Thomas M. Achenbach

Description

There are four versions of the Child Behavior Checklist for which extensive reliability and validity data have been obtained: The Child Behavior Checklist (CBCL) is designed to be filled out by parents and parent surrogates of children aged 4 through 16. It consists of 20 social competence items and 118 behavior problem items that can be reported and rated by most parents with a minimum of inference. It is scored on the Child Behavior Profile, which consists of social competence and behavior problem scales. The social competence scales reflect participation in sports, nonsports activities, organizations, jobs and chores, friendships, relations with other people, and school functioning. The behavior problem scales were derived through factor analyses of parents' ratings of 2,300 clinically referred children and were normed on 1,300 randomly selected non-referred children. To reflect age and sex differences in the patterning and prevalence of problems, factor analyses were performed separately for each sex at ages 4 to 5, 6 to 11, and 12 to 16. The resulting factors were used to construct scoring profiles standardized separately for each of these groups.

Profiles are available in hand-scored and computer-scored versions that display scores for all items, raw scores, and standard scores for all competence and syndrome scales, scores for broad-band internalizing and externalizing groupings, and total scores. Cluster analyses have identified profile types that can be used to classify children according to their overall patterns of syndrome scores. The computer-scored versions of the profile yield intraclass correlations that indicate the degree of similarity between a child's profile and each of the profile types identified for his or her age and sex.

The Teacher's Report Form (TRF) of the CBCL is designed to obtain teachers' ratings in a format similar to that of the CBCL for parents' ratings. It has many of the same behavior problem items as the CBCL, but adds some that are more appropriately rated by teachers, while omitting those that teachers would not be in a position to judge. In place of the social competence items rated by parents, teachers rate children's academic performance and four aspects of adaptive functioning, that is, how hard the child is working, how appropriately he or she is behaving, how much he or she is learning, and how happy he or she is. Like the CBCL, the TRF can be scored by hand or computer on profiles that display behavior problem scales derived empirically through factor analyses of data for clinically referred children and normed on large samples of randomly selected nonreferred children. Scoring profiles are standardized separately for each sex at ages 6 to 11 and 12 to 16

The Youth Self-Report (YSR) of the CBCL is designed to obtain self-ratings from youngsters aged 11 to 18 in a format like that of the CBCL. It has most of the same social competence and behavior problem items as the parent version of the CBCL, but omits those that would be inappropriate for adolescents. It can be scored on profiles analogous to those for the CBCL and TRF.

The Direct Observation Form (DOF) of the CBCL is designed to record observations of children in classrooms and other group situations. The observer writes a narrative description of the child's ongoing behavior over a 10-minute period, scores on-task behavior at the end of each minute, and then scores 96 problem items based on the 10 minutes of observation. Because problem behavior is often variable from one occasion to another, it is recommended that scores be averaged over six 10-minute samples taken on different occasions (e.g., mornings and afternoons of several days). It is also recommended that the target child's scores be compared with those obtained on the same occasions by two control children of the same sex observed in the same situation. Reliability and validity data have been published (Achenbach & Edelbrock, 1983), but it is not yet known whether standardized scoring profiles will be feasible for the variety of conditions in which the DOF is applicable.

Purpose

The purpose of the four versions of the CBCL is to obtain standardized reports of child and adolescent behavior in everyday environments, as judged by different informants. The empirically derived and normed scoring scales are designed to compare children with normal age–mates in terms of clinically significant syndromes and competencies. The profiles also provide a quantified picture of the relative degree of a child's reported deviance in each area, a basis for test-retest comparisons and outcome assessments, and a basis for grouping children according to similarities in their profile patterns. The empirically derived syndromes have a heuristic value in revealing age, sex, and informant differences in the patterning of perceived problems. The broad-band internalizing and externalizing groupings reveal relations between narrow-band syndromes and can be used to view children's problems in terms of global distinctions that subsume the more differentiated, narrow-band profile scales. The assessment procedures are intended to provide a common language for clinical, epidemiologic, and research use across diverse settings and populations.

Development

The CBCL and related instruments have been developed over more than a decade of work with numerous clinical and nonclinical populations. They draw on broad samples from many settings chosen to be representative of larger populations relevant to diverse clinical and research contexts. Further development, refinement, applications, and correlates are reported in forthcoming publications by the authors and other workers.

Psychometric Characteristics

Psychometric details are reported in the references listed with this entry and in other publications. Norms are based on large, randomly selected samples of nonreferred children. Pearson correlations for test-retest reliability are generally in the high .80s and .90s, with minimal changes in mean scores over the test-retest reliability periods. Sensitivity to longer-term change in treated children has been evident in significant declines in problem scores over periods of 3, 6, and 18 months. Pearson correlations for interrater reliabilities between observers simultaneously scoring children on the DOF are in the .90s. Pearson correlations for agreement between mothers and fathers and between teachers in the same classroom are in the .60s and .70s. Discriminant validity has been demonstrated by significant differences between item and scale scores for demographically matched, referred and nonreferred children. Item analyses have been reported that show the magnitude of significant effects associated with clinical status, socioeconomic status, age, sex, and ethnic group.

Clinical Use

The instruments are designed for easy use in diverse clinical contexts. Because the CBCL, TRF, and YSR are completed by unpaid informants and scored on-site by computer or clerical workers, they are economical and require little professional time. They can be read aloud to informants whose reading skills are below the sixth grade level. The DOF can be used by nonprofessional assistants and school personnel, such as special educators and school psychologists. The instruments are designed to contribute to initial clinical evaluations. They can also be used for periodic reassessments of functioning, outcome evaluations, follow-ups, and communication about individual cases. They can be used administratively for needs assessment and for documenting existing clinical case loads.

The normative data were obtained on non-retarded and nonhandicapped children, although such children can be assessed if the user wishes to compare them with each other or with normative groups of age–mates. Translations into 17 languages are available. The procedures are not designed to tap extremely rare or idiosyncratic behaviors, such as those displayed by severely autistic, retarded, or handicapped children.

Future Directions

Several research programs are in progress to advance the empirically based approach to assessment. A standardized clinical interview has been developed to assess 6- to 11-year-old children in ways that mesh with the CBCL, TRF, YSR, and DOF. Cluster analyses of profiles have been used to develop typologies whose correlates are now being tested. A version of the CBCL for 2- and 3-year-old children will soon be available. Long-term outcome studies will test the predictive correlates of the scale scores and profile patterns. Numerous studies of clinical, epidemiological, and research applications of the assessment procedures are underway in several countries.

Reference

Achenbach, T.M., & Edelbrock, C. (1983). *Manual for the Child Behavior Checklist and Revised Child Behavior Profile*. Burlington, VT: University of Vermont, Department of Psychiatry.

Child Depression Scale

William M. Reynolds

Description

The Child Depression Scale (CDS: Reynolds, in press) is a self-report measure of depressive symptoms designed for use with children 8 through 13 years of age. The CDS consists of 30 items, 29 of which relate to clinically defined symptoms of depression. Children respond to items by endorsing how often they have experienced the specific symptom during the last 2 weeks. The last item is a global dysphoric mood-state rating, consisting of five "smiley type" faces ranging from sad to happy, to which the child responds by placing an x over the face that shows how she or he feels. The 29 symptom-related items use a 4-point "almost never" to "all the time" response format. Items are worded in the present tense to elicit current symptom status. Seven items are inconsistent with depression and are reverse keyed so that a negative response is indicative of psychopathology. The inclusion of reverse-keyed items requires that the child pay more attention to each individual item and also allows for a check of dissimulation, for example, marking "all the time" to all items.

To date, the CDS has been used with over 1,500 children in studies by the author and other investigators. It has been used as an outcome measure in several treatment studies (Roseby & Deutsch, 1985; Stark, Reynolds, & Kaslow, in press), in psychometric investigations (Reynolds, Anderson, & Bartell, 1985), studies of descriptive psychopathology, and several group comparison studies. One study has examined differences in depression between gifted and nongifted children (Bartell & Reynolds, 1986), and another is a cross-cultural comparison study between children in Puerto Rico and those in the United States, using a Spanish translation of the CDS.

Item content on the CDS reflects depressive symptoms delineated by primary sources including: the Diagnostic and Statistical Manual of Mental Disorders (DSM-III) for major depression and dysthymic disorder, Research Diagnostic Criteria, and symptoms specified by the Weinberg Criteria. Symptoms include evaluation of somatic, behavioral, cognitive, mood, and vegetative components of depression. The CDS requires approximately 10 minutes to complete and can be individually or group administered. When used with younger children aged 8 and 9, it is suggested that the CDS be orally presented to avoid potential confounding of reading ability, particularly in poor readers.

Purpose

The CDS is designed to assess the severity of depressive symptoms in children. It can be used in schools and clinical settings for individual assessment as well as for large group screening. The CDS, as with most paper-and-pencil self-report measures of depression, does not provide a formal diagnosis of childhood depression, but rather it assesses the severity of depression as a more global clinical manifestation. Currently there are relatively few measures designed to evaluate self-reported depressive symptoms in children.

Depression is an internalized disorder and, as such, presents difficulties for accurate evaluation by significant others such as teachers and parents. Substantial data suggest that children are reliable reporters of their own affective status. The CDS provides a symptom-specific format for children's reports of their affect, behavior, and feelings that relate to the currently accepted clinical symptoms of depression. The availability of the CDS as a reliable and valid measure of depression provides a basis for the systematic study of this disorder in children.

Development

Initial development of the CDS began in 1980 with a 33-item form and subsequent field testing with children in school settings. Item content includes symptoms of depression specified by: Weinberg Criteria; The Diagnostic and Statistical Manual of Mental Disorders (third edition) for major depression and dysthymic disorder; and Research Diagnostic Criteria as found in the Schedule of Affective Disorders and Schizophrenia for School-Age Children (Kiddie-SADS). On the basis of the results of item analyses with 166 children, three items were eliminated because of low item and total score correlations. These items dealt with anger at parents, self-isolation, and not feeling hungry when it is time to eat. Of these items, the last is most commonly identified as symptomatic of depression. However, it is interesting that appetite disturbance is often the least endorsed symptom in depressed children.

After field testing, the 30-item version was administered to another sample of 470 children 8 to 13 years of age in grades 3 through 6. Racially, this sample consisted of 64% white, 33% black, and 3% Asian and Hispanic children. Data analyses confirmed the internal consistency of the CDS. A grade by gender by race (white/black) three-way analysis of variance indicated a significant main effect for race ($p < .01$). There were no significant differences between grades or between boys and girls, nor were there any significant interactions.

There is also a Spanish version of the CDS. In a cross-cultural investigation involving 181 children in the United States and 180 children in Puerto

Rico (using a Spanish translation of the CDS), no significant differences were found between children in each country. Consistent with previous investigations, gender differences were non-significant.

Psychometric Characteristics

The CDS has demonstrated high internal consistency reliability with samples of normal and depressed children from the United States, with coefficient alpha's ranging from .86 to .91 (Bartell & Reynolds, 1986; Reynolds et al., 1985). In an experimental treatment study of 30 moderately to severely depressed children, Stark et al. (in press) reported an internal consistency reliability of .88 on the CDS. In the aforementioned cross-cultural study, the internal consistency of the Spanish version of the CDS was .83.

Child depression measures need to demonstrate both content and construct validity. Content validity of the CDS is illustrated by the overlap of CDS item content with symptoms of depression specified by DSM-III, Research Diagnostic Criteria (as operationalized by the Kiddie-SADS), and the Weinberg Criteria (Reynolds, in press). The construct validity of the CDS has been demonstrated in a number of investigations and established by correlations with other self-report measures of depression and related constructs in children. In addition, correlations between the CDS and a formal clinical interview for depression in children and teachers' ratings of children's depression also support the validity of the CDS.

In investigations with normal children, correlations between the CDS and the Children's Depression Inventory (CDI) ranging from .68 to .72 were found. In the Stark et al. (in press) study of depressed children, a correlation of .79 was found between subjects' pretest scores on the CDS and those on the CDI. The CDS also correlates significantly with teacher's global ratings of children's depression ($r = .33 - .40$). Significant correlations were found between the CDS and measures of self-concept ($r = -.58$ to $-.67$), locus of control ($r = .33$), and anxiety ($r = .61$ to $.67$).

Of critical importance to the determination of validity of paper-and-pencil self-report measures of depression is their correspondence with formal clinical interviews for depression. In a study of 81 children using the Children's Depression Rating Scale-Revised (CDRS-R) by Poznanski and colleagues (an individually administered clinical interview), a correlation of .64 was found between the

CDRS-R and the CDS. Given the method variance difference, the correlation between the CDRS-R and CDS is considered very good and supportive of the validity of the CDS. Factor analytic and multivariate studies have also been conducted and support the validity of the CDS.

Clinical Use

The CDS is designed to measure the severity of depressive symptoms in children. In this regard the CDS is useful in school-wide screening for depression, in individual assessment, and as a measure of depression in treatment and clinical research. It is important to note that the CDS does not provide a formal diagnosis of depression as delineated by DSM-III or Research Diagnostic Criteria. It does provide a relatively brief (10-minute) measure of clinically relevant depressive symptoms associated with depression in children. When group administered by a teacher, it allows for the economic evaluation and identification of children at risk.

Future Directions

Currently there are few measures of depression for children. A growing body of research literature is being developed on the CDS. The psychometric characteristics of the CDS are very good, especially given the difficulties often involved in the assessment of young children. Given the recent surge in clinical interest in childhood depression by clinical, school, and counseling psychologists as well as the paucity of reliable and valid measures of this affective domain, the CDS is viewed as useful for clinical as well as research purposes.

References

Bartell, N., & Reynolds, W.M. (1986). Depression and self-esteem in academically gifted and nongifted children: A comparison study. Journal of School Psychology, 24, 55-61.

Reynolds. W.M. (in press). Child Depression Scale. Odessa, FL: Psychological Assessment Resources.

Reynolds, W.M., Anderson, G., & Bartell, N. (1985). Measuring depression in children: A tripartite assessment approach. Journal of Abnormal Child Psychology, 13, 513-526.

Roseby, V., & Deutsch, R. (1985). Children of separation and divorce: Effects of social role-taking group intervention on fourth and fifth graders. Journal of Clinical Child Psychology, 14, 55-60.

Stark, K., Reynolds, W.M., & Kaslow, N. (in press). A comparison of the relative efficacy of self-control therapy and behavior therapy for the reduction of depression in children. *Journal of Abnormal Child Psychology*.

Child Development Questionnaire

Barbara G. Melamed and Mark A. Lumley

Description

The Child Development Questionnaire (CDQ) contains 14 items that are completed by parents. It is designed to assess a child's reinforcement history in various fearful situations. The 14 items on the CDQ represent hypothetical situations in which children often become fearful and refuse to engage in the feared act. These 14 situations include the following: (a) having a (1) haircut, (2) injection, (3) operation, and (4) tooth drilled; (b) approaching (5) a puppy, (6) water, and (7) a dark closet; and (c) fears of (8) thunder and lightening, (9) being teased, (10) presenting before a class, (11) bad dreams, (12) going to summer camp, (13) being left overnight at a friend's house, and (14) falling off a bicycle. Each parent is asked to select from among five listed alternatives the technique that he or she would presently employ to deal with the child if the child were in that particular feared situation. A sixth alternative, labeled "other," is available for parents who need to write separately their own disciplinary technique for handling the situation. Each of the five listed alternatives for every given item is based on five distinct learning principles. These five principles, which are operationally defined, include positive reinforcement, punishment, force, reinforcement of dependency, and modeling and reassurance. Responses given for the "other" alternative are classified into one of these five categories. Five final scores are obtained by counting the frequency with which a parent used each of the techniques representing the five categories. The magnitude of these scores represents the degree to which a parent used each of the five learning principles with his or her child when in a feared situation. The CDQ is published in a paper by Zabin and Melamed (1980).

Purpose

There is a general consensus in the literature that parental attitudes, behaviors, and disciplinary techniques have a great influence on the development of a child's dependent (fearful) or independent (coping) behavior. Early researchers attempted to order a variety of child-rearing variables with respect to several dimensions, such as warmth-hostility and control-autonomy. The CDQ was developed to determine the techniques and behaviors employed and exhibited by parents to their child in accordance with learning principles. Specifically, fearful situations were chosen because of their relation to a child's anxiety and coping behavior. The CDQ, therefore, allows for a determination of the relations between general parental disciplinary techniques (as described in learning terminology) and child variables of interest (e.g., anxiety, approach-avoidance, and coping skills).

Development

The 14 situational items used in the CDQ were formulated from several lists of the most common fears of children (Hagman, 1932; Jersild, Markey, & Jersild, 1933). The five alternative disciplinary techniques relating to each situation were developed by Zabin and Melamed (1980) and were checked for their reliability by having 35 undergraduate psychology students code them as being representative of one of the five major categories of learning principles. Categories were revised until there was 88% interrater agreement.

Psychometric Characteristics

Zabin and Melamed (1980) present data that show a high level of predictive validity for the CDQ. Such validity was determined by measuring the anxiety levels of 36 children, aged 4 to 12 years, who had been hospitalized for elective surgery (Melamed & Siegel, 1975). The parents of these children had been given the CDQ after the children's hospitalization. Correlations between the various measures of child anxiety (Palmar Sweat Index, Hospital Fears Rating Scale, and Observer Rating Scale of Anxiety) and each of the five categories of parental disciplinary techniques were calculated. Maternal use of force correlated positively ($p < .05$) with the mother's verbal reports of their children's behavior problems and the children's posthospitalization anxiety. Maternal reports of the use of positive reinforcement for approaching the fearful situation were inversely related to the rated anxiety of their children during hospitalization. The reported use of punishment, force, and reinforcement of dependency were negatively correlated with the use of modeling and reinforcement

(p <.025). These results show significant predictive validity between child anxiety and behavior problems and the type of parental disciplinary technique employed.

A study by Bush, Melamed, Sheras, and Greenbaum (1986) examined the predictive validity of the CDQ by observing the behavior of mothers toward their children in the hospital waiting room. Mothers who reported the use of positive reinforcement tended to use distraction (p <.01) and restraint (p <.05) with their children, particularly with children who showed distress. Additionally, these mothers were less likely to ignore these distressed children. Conversely, mothers who reported the frequent use of punishment increased their use of ignoring, particularly when the child showed distress or exhibited socially affiliative behaviors.

The reliability of the five alternatives for each of the 14 situations was determined to see how representative were the alternatives of the five categories of learning principles utilized. Thirty-six undergraduates achieved an interrrater agreement of 88%. The split-half reliability coefficient in this study was .67.

Clinical Use

In light of CDQ's predictive validity, it is possible to determine the anxiety levels of children facing elective surgery based on parental scores. Presumably, anxiety in stressful situations, other than facing surgery, can also be predicted. Moreover, it is conceivable that the CDQ can be used, for example, as an assessment device for parents being instructed in disciplinary techniques, although this use has not been systematically examined.

A major use of the CDQ is as a research tool in determining the types of parental disciplinary techniques used and their relation to a variety of child variables, only one of which is anxiety and coping in a fearful setting.

Future Directions

Further validation of the CDQ with child variables other than anxiety and coping responses in a presurgery setting needs to be undertaken. It is probable that a wide range of child behaviors and attitudes can be related to the types of parental disciplinary techniques used in feared situations.

References

Bush, J.P., Melamed, B.G., Sheras, P.L., & Greenbaum, P.E. (1986). Mother-child patterns of coping with anticipatory stress. *Health Psychology, 5,* 137–157.

Hagman, R.R. (1932). A study of fears of children of preschool age. *Journal of Experimental Education, 1,* 110-130.

Jersild, A.T., Markey, F.U., & Jersild, C.L. (1933). Children's fears, dreams, wishes, daydreams, likes, dislikes, pleasant and unpleasant memories. *Child Development Monographs,* No. 12.

Melamed, B.G., & Siegel, L.J. (1975). Reduction of anxiety in children facing hospitalization and surgery by use of filmed modeling. *Journal of Consulting and Clinical Psychology, 6,* 31-35.

Zabin, M.A., & Melamed, B.G. (1980). Relationship between parental discipline and children's ability to cope with stress. *Journal of Behavioral Assessment, 2,* 17-38.

Child Diagnostic Interview Schedules

Barry Edelstein, Sharon Estill, and Gregory Alberts

Description

Diagnostic interview schedules developed for use with children and adolescents are similar in many respects to their counterparts in adults. Many child interview schedules are modified versions of the adult forms. Child interview schedules are diagnostic tools for clinicians and researchers which characteristically take the form of a list of behaviors, symptoms, and events to be covered in a prescribed manner. Instructions for conducting the interview as well as a method for recording the data elicited from the interviewee are also contained in the schedule.

The technical features of child interview schedules may differ from one another in several respects. Like the adult forms, child interview schedules vary in the degree of structure. The degree of structure of the schedule determines the extent to which the interviewer is allowed flexibility in conducting the interview. As the structure decreases, more flexibility is afforded the interviewer with respect to the order of questions, wording of questions, and recording of responses. Consequently, the role of clinical judgment and interpretation required of the interviewer increases as the amount of structure decreases. Interviews also vary in terms of the amount of training required of the interviewer, administration time, diagnostic coverage, and age of interviewee. Most schedules directly involve questioning the child about his or her own behavior, although some are used to interview the parent regarding the child's behavior. In some cases there is also a parallel version of the same interview schedule for use with the parent.

Purpose and Clinical Use

The primary purpose of an interview schedule is to increase the likelihood of obtaining an accurate and reliable diagnosis. Data obtained from an interview schedule are presumably more objective and quantifiable than those obtained from unstructured interviews. Interview schedules might also yield a more comprehensive picture of the individual by eliciting information from a broad range of areas. Adequate coverage of critical areas of functioning is important because research shows that clinicians form their diagnostic impressions early in the interview. These early diagnostic biases can influence future questions as well as the client's behavior to which the interviewer attends. The diagnostic and clinical information derived from the interview can also be used in the selection of treatments as well as in the evaluation of treatment outcomes.

Development

The development of the child diagnostic interview schedule is both a function of advances in interview methodology that have been achieved with adults and the relatively recent trend to utilize the child as a source of information regarding his or her own behavior. Methods for the direct interview of the child or parent for diagnostic purposes have also been influenced by the development of a more differentiated taxonomy of child and adolescent disorders.

Psychometric Characteristics

Because child interview schedules are a relatively recent development, only a few reliability and validity studies have been conducted and these have taken a variety of forms. Some differences between these studies include the medium in which the data are collected, who performs the ratings, the type of reliability or validity assessed, and the type of statistics used. Data have been collected in vivo, from taped interviews, and from written case summaries. Some studies use psychiatrists or psychologists as judges or raters, others employ lay observers, whereas still others employ a combination of all three types of observers or raters. The various forms of reliability studied include interrater reliability, test-retest reliability, parent-child agreement, and internal consistency. Different statistics such as Kappa, Pearson product-moment correlation, and percent agreement have been used to calculate the various forms of reliability and validity. Because of the wide variety of measures and procedures, results across studies are difficult to compare.

Some child interview schedules studied are the Child Assessment Schedule (CAS), Diagnostic Interview Schedule for Children (DISC), Mental Health Assessment Form (MHAF), Diagnostic Interview for Children and Adolescents (DICA), Interview Schedule for Children (ISC), and the children's or "Kiddie" version of the Schedule for Affective Disorders and Schizophrenia (K-SADS). (See Edelbrock and Costello, 1984, for references and reviews.)

These studies have evaluated various facets of reliability and validity, but few individual interview schedules have been thoroughly evaluated in terms of all forms of reliability and validity. Very few studies have assessed test-retest reliability, and the results have varied (correlational coefficients ranging from .09 to .90), possibly because of the varying intervals between test and retest among studies as well as other procedural differences. Some investigators have argued that diagnostic symptoms change over time. More attention has been given to interrater reliability, with correlation coefficients ranging from .40 to .96 for total score and from .43 to 1.0 for individual items. For those schedules that can be used with both parent and child, parent-child agreement on individual items has ranged from .02 to .95.

Validity has generally been assessed through measures of sensitivity (percent true positives) and specificity (percent true negatives), although some studies have examined correlations of the results of the diagnostic interview with other inventories. Studies evaluating criterion validity (i.e., sensitivity and specificity) have the problem of initially establishing the "true" diagnosis or criterion. Sensitivity has ranged from .72 to .78, and specificity from .76 to .84.

The reliability and validity might be expected to increase as the structure (and therefore objectivity) of the schedule increases; however, this relationship has not always been demonstrated. More studies are needed to address the strength of this assumption.

Future Directions

The increasing emphasis on the child as a major source of diagnostic information and the further differentiation of diagnostic criteria will probably stimulate increased use of child interview schedules. In contrast to adult interview schedules, the child diagnostic interview schedules will probably become more specialized as subtypes of various diagnostic groups are identified by researchers. Similarly, we can expect the content of interview schedules to change as diagnostic systems evolve. This further refinement will hopefully lead to increased reliability as well as sensitivity to changes in client status over time and the course of treatment.

The extent to which diagnostic interview schedules are used by clinicians will probably be determined on the basis of their use in formulating intervention programs, although that is certainly not the only use to which they would be put. Some investigators have suggested that the currently available interview schedules will never be used widely because they are time consuming to administer and sometimes cumbersome to use in the interview.

The clinical researcher and epidemiologist will continue to find the child diagnostic interview schedules invaluable. The practicing clinician must weight its accuracy and reliability against the additional time and effort it requires.

Reference

Edelbrock, C., & Costello, A. (1984). Structured psychiatric interviews for children and adolescents. In C. Goldstein & M. Hersen (Eds.), *Handbook of psychological assessment* (pp. 276-290). New York: Pergamon Press.

Children's Action Tendency Scale

Donald A. Williamson and Sandra J. McKenzie

Description

The Children's Action Tendency Scale (CATS) is a self-report measure of aggressiveness, assertiveness, and submissiveness in children (Deluty, 1979). The scale consists of 10 conflict situations

for which three pairs of response alternatives are provided. Specifically, for each situation the child must choose between an aggressive and assertive response, an aggressive and submissive response, and an assertive and submissive response. The child is instructed to choose the response he or she actually "would" do, not "should" do in the situation. This type of forced-choice format allows for assessment of the relative strength of each type of response and eliminates the possibility of choosing only the socially desirable response.

Purpose

Although aggressive and submissive behaviors have been successfully modified in children (Patterson, 1972), an instrument to identify those children in need of assertiveness training has been lacking. The CATS was designed to assess the level of assertiveness and may be useful in identifying children with preclinical levels of aggressiveness and submissiveness who might benefit from such training. In addition, the CATS may be useful in evaluating the efficacy of assertion training with children.

Development

The development of the CATS was based on a behavioral-analytic model. The conflict situations and response alternatives were chosen on the basis of an empirical analysis of relevant problem situations and probable responses of the population being studied. The first stage of development consisted of a situational analysis in which a group of children were asked to complete the following three statements: (1) I get angry when . . .; (2) I feel like giving up when . . .; and (3) I stand up for my rights when . . . The relevant conflict situations were derived from the most popular aggression-, assertion-, and submission-eliciting situations. The second stage of development consisted of response enumeration, in which children were asked to indicate what they "might" do if they were in each situation. The most popular responses for each situation were selected for use in the response evaluation state of the questionnaire's development. Four distinct groups of individuals were asked to rate the responses as aggressive, assertive, or submissive in this final stage. The groups consisted of: (a) psychology faculty and graduate students, (b) parents of school-age students, (c) grade school teachers, and (d) fifth grade students. An aggressive response was defined as "a hostile act that involves expressing one's rights and feelings at the expense of others." An assertive response was defined as "a nonhostile act that involves self-expression and self-enhancement without violating the rights and feelings of others." A submissive response was defined as "a nonhostile, unassertive act that involves considering the feelings, power, or authority of others while denying one's own rights and feelings" (Deluty, 1979). The responses chosen to be included were those most frequently rated by most evaluator groups.

Psychometric Characteristics

Spearman-Brown reliability coefficients were computed for three subscales of the CATS to determine the internal consistency of each scale (Deluty, 1979). Ten odd and 10 even items were available for each scale as a result of the paired-comparisons format. Positive correlations were found for all three subscales. The reliability coefficients for the Aggressiveness, Assertiveness, and Submissiveness subscales were .77, .63, and .72, respectively.

Test-retest reliability over a 4–month period was also assessed (Deluty, 1979). Significant positive correlations between the first and second administrations were found for each subscale: Aggressiveness (.48), Assertiveness (.60), and Submissiveness (.57).

Criterion-related validity of the CATS was also evaluated by Deluty (1979). Correlations between the CATS subscale scores and self-esteem scores on the Coopersmith Self-Esteem Inventory were computed. Although CATS aggressiveness did not correlate with Coopersmith Self-Esteem scores, CATS submissiveness scores correlated negatively with self-esteem scores (−.37).

The Children's Social Desirability Questionnaire (Crandall, Crandall, & Katkovsky, 1965) was also administered in Deluty's study. Scores on this questionnaire correlated positively with submissiveness scores (.57) and negatively with aggressiveness scores (−.44).

Correlations between scores on the CATS subscales and peer and teacher-report ratings were also computed. Ratings included physical aggression, assertiveness, and submissiveness for both peers and teachers. In addition, both groups were asked to rate the five most aggressive individuals and the five least aggressive individuals in the classroom. This procedure was used to rate individuals on assertiveness and submissiveness as well. Positive correlations were found between: (a) CATS aggressiveness scores and peer physical aggression scores, teacher verbal aggression scores, and peer and teacher ratings of most aggressive individuals, (b) CATS assertiveness scores and teacher ratings of assertiveness, and (c) CATS submissiveness scores and peer and teacher ratings of submissiveness.

Clinical Use

Deluty (1979) administered the CATS to 17 hyperaggressive boys aged 8 to 15 years to ascertain the scale's ability to differentiate normally from clinically aggressive children. As expected, the hyperaggressive boys had significantly higher aggressiveness scores and significantly lower assertiveness scores. Submissiveness scores did not differ significantly between the two groups.

The CATS has been used to categorize children as highly aggressive, highly assertive, and highly submissive in a study of cognitive problem-solving ability (Deluty, 1981) and in an investigation of children's evaluations of aggressive, assertive, and submissive behavior. In both instances, the CATS was used as an independent variable for group classification. Williamson, Moody, Granberry, Lethermon, and Blouin (1983) used the CATS as a criterion variable in a study of the validity of a role-play social skills test for children. Canonical correlations between the CATS total scale score and additional measures of social skill (e.g., fluency, eye contact, and teacher ratings) were consistently low. Pearson product–moment correlations between the aggressiveness and assertiveness subscales of the CATS and the other criterion variables were also low with the exception of the aggressiveness scale and teacher rating (Williamson, 1985). Furthermore, the assertiveness and submissiveness subscales were positively correlated.

Future Directions

Currently, limited data are available for general use of the CATS. Although Deluty (1979) does report means and standard deviations for school-age children from parochial and public schools, these data are based on a limited population, thereby making generalization to a broader population difficult. The development of norms from nonclinical as well as clinical populations would be useful in the use of this assessment instrument. Moreover, this assessment instrument would be of greater utility if norms were developed for specific diagnostic subgroups relative to both childhood and adolescent populations. Further refinement of the CATS would allow not only for greater sensitivity in clinical assessment but also potentially for predictive assessment as well.

References

Crandall, V.C., Crandall, V.J., & Katkovsky, W. (1965). A children's social desirability questionnaire. *Journal of Consulting Psychology, 29,* 27-36.

Deluty, R.H. (1979). Children's action tendency scale: A self-report measure of aggressiveness, assertiveness, and submissiveness in children. *Journal of Consulting and Clinical Psychology, 47,* 1061-1071.

Deluty, R.H. (1981). Alternative-thinking ability of aggressive, assertive, and submissive children. *Cognitive Therapy and Research, 5,* 309-312.

Patterson, R.L. (1972). Time-out and assertive training for a dependent child. *Behavior Therapy, 3,* 466-468.

Williamson, D.A. (1985). The SST-C revisited. A reply to Dr. Deluty and presentation of new data. *Behavior Therapy, 16,* 244-246.

Williamson, D.A., Moody, S.C., Granberry, S.W., Lethermon, V.R., & Blouin, D.C. (1983). Criterion-related validity of a role-play social skills test for children. *Behavior Therapy, 14,* 466-481.

Children's Assertive Behavior Scale

Larry Michelson

Description

The Children's Assertive Behavior Scale (CABS) is a 27-item self-report instrument for children that measures general and specific social skills and covers many socially relevant situations that are problematic for children. Response categories for each CABS item were designed to vary along the scrambled continuum of passive-assertive-aggressive answers. For each item, there are five possible responses which represent very passive, passive, assertive, aggressive, and very aggressive dimensions. This continuum provides information as to the type of nonassertive behaviors (i.e., passive-aggressive) used for various content areas. Scoring for each item is determined by the extent to which the chosen response is socially appropriate. A very passive response is scored as -2, partially passive response as -1, an assertive response is 0, a partially aggressive response as $+1$, and a very aggressive response is $+2$. An initial total score is calculated by summing the absolute value of the items of the scale. The greater the score (maximum 54), the greater the child's level of unassertiveness and conversely, the lower the score, the greater the child's

assertiveness. In addition, separate passive and assertive scores are determined by totaling the absolute value of minus and plus scores independently. These two scores represent the severity and directionality of the subject's nonassertive responses, which provides important information as to whether the child is deficient in assertive responses due to either passive or aggressive behavior.

Purpose

The primary objective of developing the CABS was to provide a self-report measure of knowledge of social skills, social perception, and self-perception of interpersonal abilities for elementary school children. In addition, to assess large numbers of children to determine levels of social functioning, it may be more efficient to employ self-report measures or questionnaires than to assess subjects on a one-to-one basis. Although self-report measures represent a convenient, quantifiable, and economical means of collecting data on how children perceive and report their social behavior, the subjectivity of self-report responses, in conjunction with their lack of demonstrated external validity in previous scales, has resulted in their limited development and use. Therefore, the CABS was constructed in accordance with behavioral-analytic test development procedures to ensure adequate reliability and external validity. Wood, Michelson, and Flynn (1978) developed the CABS to measure assertive behavior in children. Item categories consisted of assertive content areas dealing with a variety of situations and behaviors, such as giving and receiving compliments, empathy, requests, refusals, and initiating, maintaining, and terminating conversations. Assessing these areas provides important information regarding content knowledge and social perception of the children. Because social skills training is becoming more widespread in both clinical and educational settings, an instrument that can reliably and accurately assess social adjustment of children would have obvious clinical and research utility. Moreover, if effective training programs are going to be developed and implemented, accurate and reliable measurement devices must be applied.

Development

The CABS, originated by Wood et al. (1978) and Michelson and Wood (1982), contains item categories consisting of content areas dealing with assertive behavior that are identified as being socially relevant for elementary school children. After reviewing existing scales related to the social adjustment of children, potential items were included for critical analysis and examined by independent raters and expert judges to ensure they represented salient dimensions of children's social adjustment. In addition, ratings provided by "blind" judges assessed the validity of the continuum of the responses for each item. The results from the "blind" ratings yielded a mean interrater reliability of 94%. The CABS was pretested and socially validated with an independent group of fourth graders. Response categories for CABS items were designed to vary along a continuum of passive-assertive-aggressive answers. For each item, there are five possible replies, one of which is selected by the child to best represent his or her typical behavior in that specific situation.

Psychometric Characteristics

Wood et al. (1978), Michelson, Andrasik, Vucelic, and Coleman (1979), and Michelson and Wood (1982) reported on the psychometric properties of the CABS. In the Wood et al. (1978) study, the CABS was administered to 149 fourth-grade elementary school children in Florida. Additionally, CABS scores were compared with behavioral observations and teacher ratings of social skills. Behavioral observations correlated .38 with the CABS total score, whereas teacher ratings showed significant, although somewhat variable, correlations. Test-retest reliability conducted over a 4-week period of time was .87. Factor analyses using both principal components and varimax rotations yielded a homogeneous factor structure. No significant correlations were obtained between the CABS and potential moderator variables, including sex, intelligence, or social desirability.

Michelson et al. (1979) investigated the stability and generality of the original findings using 90 fourth, fifth, and sixth grade elementary school children. Employing a comprehensive assessment strategy, Michelson et al. (1979) compared the CABS responses with peer, parent, and teacher ratings of social competence, popularity, and overall social skills. Significant correlations were obtained between these measures, demonstrating good convergent validity. Once again, no significant correlations were obtained between the CABS and sex, intelligence, or social desirability measures, and factor analyses revealed a homogeneous factor structure.

Michelson and Wood (1980) found that the CABS possessed good discriminant validity and could accurately differentiate among 80 fourth-grade elementary school children who had received social skills training from those receiving only ecology discussions. Moreover, teachers who were blind to treatment conditions rated children in the social skills group significantly more socially competent using the teacher's version of the CABS. The CABS also exhibited pre- posttreatment differences on both the self-report and teacher's versions, indicating that it was sensitive to treatment effects. The KR20 measure of internal consistency was .78 for the Wood et al. (1978) study and .80 for the Michelson et al. (1979) report, indicating the scale is internally consistent. The CABS shows appropriate psychometric properties for clinical and research use. Internal reliability, test-retest reliability, item-total correlation, and its factor analytic structure indicate that the instrument possesses acceptable reliability. Significant, although occasionally moderate, correlations with teacher, parent, and peer ratings indicate that the CABS has good external validity.

Clinical Use

The CABS is an acceptable instrument for clinical and research use with regard to such applications as: (a) examining developmental changes of social competency across time; (b) screening children for prevention and early intervention programs; (c) screening at-risk or maladjusted elementary school children; (d) evaluating pre- and posttreatment changes; (e) conducting normative evaluations of elementary school populations; (f) providing a behavioral-analytic strategy for identifying deficits that can then be targeted for social skills training; and (g) examining the relationship of social competence, as measured by the CABS, with peer, parent, and teacher measures of social adjustment.

Future Directions

Research is needed to examine the relationship between the CABS and behavioral observations in the natural environment to provide additional information regarding its external validity. Normative data of the CABS across varying grades, geographic regions, and socioeconomic levels would be desirable. Similarly, normative data for racial-ethnic populations await and merit further study. Research examining the CABS with regard to interpersonal problem-solving, self-esteem, anxiety, locus of control, and related constructs could yield interesting conceptual and clinical insights. The association between the CABS and direct measures of interpersonal performance and adjustment would also provide important data. Finally, although self-report measures such as the CABS can provide valuable information regarding social perception and content knowledge, they are subject to a number of limitations (cf., Michelson, Sugai, Wood, & Kazdin, 1983). Hence, self-report strategies such as the CABS are optimally employed as part of a larger, more comprehensive evaluation strategy that incorporates multiple dimensions, situations, and sources of social assessment.

References

Michelson, L., Andrasik, F., Vucelic, I., & Coleman, D. (1979). *Concurrent predictive, and external validity of the Children's Assertive Behavior Scales; Teacher, parent, peers and self-report measures of social competencies in elementary school children.* Unpublished manuscript. University of Pittsburgh, Department of Psychiatry, School of Medicine.

Michelson, L., & Wood, R. (1980). Behavioral assessment and training of social skills for children and adolescents. In M. Hersen, P.M. Milleer, & R.M. Eisler (Eds.), *Progress in behavior modification: Vol. 9.* New York: Academic Press.

Michelson, L., & Wood, R. (1982). Development and psychometric properties of the Children's Assertive Behavior Scale. *Journal of Behavioral Assessment, 4,* 3-13.

Michelson, L., Sugai, D.P., Wood, R.P., & Kazdin, A.E. (1983). *Social skills assessment and training the children: An empirically-based handbook.* New York: Plenum Press.

Wood, R., Michelson, L., & Flynn, J. (1978, December). Assessment of assertive behavior in elementary school children. Paper presented at the meeting of the Association for Advancement of Behavior Therapy, Chicago, IL.

Children's Assertiveness Inventory

Thomas H. Ollendick

Description

The Children's Assertiveness Inventory (CAI) is a self-report instrument for the asssessment of assertiveness in children aged 6 to 12 years (Ollendick, 1981, 1984). It consists of 14 yes-no items. Seven items assess assertive response in positive situations (initiating interactions, giving a compliment, and accepting a compliment) and seven items assess assertive response in negative situations (refusing an unreasonable request and standing up for one's own rights). Representative items include, "When you meet someone your age, do you start talking with them?" and "When someone your age tells you they want to play a game but you don't feel like it, do you play with them?" A two-factor solution, accounting for 71% of the variance associated with responding to these items, has been reported. The two factors reflect assertive responding in positive and negative situations. A total score as well as separate scores for assertive behavior in positive and negative situations can be obtained.

Purpose

The CAI was designed to measure the child's own report of assertive responding in diverse social situations. As a self-report instrument, it possesses limitations attendant to all self-report inventories (Finch & Rogers, 1984). Nonetheless, as will be evident shortly, the instrument is potentially reliable, valid, and useful. The instrument currently appears to be particularly useful as a normative instrument for selecting unassertive children for study and as a pre- and posttreatment measure to evaluate therapeutic intervention. It also appears useful as an ipsative instrument to identify specific social situations that are problematic for individual children.

Development

The development of the CAI combined aspects of the theoretical-conceptual approach for test development and the behavioral-analytic method for validating selection of specific test items. Initially, a definition of assertive responding was formulated. Essentially, assertiveness was defined as the ability to express thoughts and feelings, both positive and negative, so that the person obtains his or her desired goals without violating the rights of others. Defined in this manner, assertive responding was determined to be involved in a variety of situations, including standing up for one's own rights, refusing unfair requests of others, giving compliments and praise to others, and accepting compliments from others. Given this conceptual framework, children were asked to generate specific situations that represented these conceptually based themes (e.g., "Telling someone I did good at school," "Having someone ask me to play when I really want to do something else," and

"Having someone take something of mine without my permission").

From this list of situations, the 20 most frequently cited situations were compiled and submitted to criterion review by four "expert" judges. These judges reviewed the items for clarity and duplicity of content; furthermore, on an a priori basis they excluded all items involving adult interactions. This process yielded 14 items, all of which depicted social situations involving peers of the same age and embodying the basic tenets of assertive responding. The items were worded so that a "yes" response indicated assertiveness for eight of the items and a "no" response reflected assertiveness for the remaining six. Accordingly, scores on the instrument range from 0 to 14, with higher scores reflecting increasing levels of assertiveness.

Initially, the instrument was examined on 57 boys and 42 girls, 8 to 11 years of age, who resided in a semirural, middle-class midwestern community (Ollendick, 1981). All children were Caucasian and were enrolled in the third and fourth grades; children with previous mental health contacts, special education placements, or both were excluded. Results indicated that mean assertiveness scores were similar for boys and girls ($M = 10.56, SD = 2.18$ for boys; and $M = 9.95, SD = 2.25$ for girls). In a subsequent standardization study with 51 boys and 67 girls, also 8 to 11 years of age and Caucasian but from a southeastern, semirural, middle-class community (Ollendick, 1984), similar mean scores were obtained ($M = 10.82, SD = 2.27$ for boys; $M = 10.23, SD = 2.02$ for girls). In this same study, an additional 71 boys and 56 girls between 7 and 12 years of age were also evaluated. Children in this sample resided in a large southeastern urban community and were from lower socioeconomic levels than were those in the two earlier samples; furthermore, about 50% of the children were black. Nonetheless, analyses indicated comparable levels of overall assertiveness ($M = 10.48, SD = 2.15$ for girls; $M = 10.21, SD = 2.05$ for boys) and, importantly, a significant developmental trend. Children in the sixth grade scored significantly higher ($M = 11.02$) than did children in the fourth grade ($M = 10.00$) or second grade ($M = 9.64$), who did not differ from one another.

Collectively, these findings indicate similarity in responding across semirural and urban, middle and lower socioeconomic class, midwestern, and southeastern communities. Furthermore, they indicate that assertiveness, as measured by this instrument, is similar for boys and girls but that it increases with age.

Psychometric Characteristics

Reliability of the CAI was determined in three ways: internal consistency, test-retest reliability, and stability of scores over 1-week and 3-month intervals. The internal consistency (KR20) ranges from .20 to .44 (Ollendick, 1984; Scanlon & Ollendick, 1985). These low estimates, although statistically significant, are not unexpected because the instrument consists of a set of heterogeneous situations involving assertiveness with peers. A greater homogeneity of items would be required to obtain higher internal consistency. A better indication of the reliability of the instrument can be found in its test-retest reliability which ranges from .76 for a 1-week interval to .61 for a 3-month interval. Scores over these intervals were also found to be highly stable, varying by no more than a half point. Therefore, although the instrument does not possess high internal consistency, it is reliable and stable over time, at least for normal samples of children. Reliability estimates have not been determined for clinical samples of children.

The validity of the CAI has been examined in two primary ways: correlations with other self-report, role-play, and behavioral measures and a comparison of a matched control group to an identified sample of socially withdrawn children (Ollendick, 1981; Scanlon & Ollendick, 1985). The CAI is moderately and positively related to other measures of assertiveness (.28 to .38), self-concept (.54 to .63), role-play assertiveness (.29), and positive social interaction with peers (.35). Furthermore, it is inversely related with trait anxiety ($-.21$ to $-.25$), external locus of control ($-.32$ to $-.61$), and social withdrawal as rated by teachers ($-.45$). Collectively, these relationships argue for a considerable degree of convergent and discriminant validity.

The validity of the CAI is further demonstrated by significant differences between teacher-nominated socially withdrawn ($M = 6.65, SD = 2.06$) and normal control children ($M = 10.45, SD = 2.35$). In fact, only 4 of 25 scores from socially withdrawn children overlapped with those of 25 normal control children. Clear discrimination of groups was evident. Recently, the validity of the instrument with socially aggressive children was questioned (Schneider, Ledingham, Poirier, Oliver, & Byrne, 1984). Essentially, these investigators reported that the expected relationships between the instrument and other measures of social behavior were not obtained for a sample of conduct disordered and attention deficient children who displayed high rates of aggressive behavior. This finding is consistent with Ollendick's (1984) admonition that the CAI in its present form fails to "unbind" aggression from assertion. A child who responds *"no"* to the item, "When someone your age takes something that is yours, do you let them take it?" would be scored as assertive on this instrument. An assertive and aggressive child might respond similarly; yet, they would be predicted to behave differently in this and similar situations.

Clinical Use

As noted earlier, the CAI appears most useful as an ipsative instrument to identify specific social situations involving assertiveness that are problematic for individual children and as a normative instrument for selecting unassertive children for treatment and evaluating therapeutic outcome. In this regard, it is probably best used with shy, anxious, and withdrawn children as noted by Scanlon and Ollendick (1985). The instrument is less useful with aggressive children (Schneider et al., 1984). It may be that the CAI does a better job of differentiating submissive behavior from assertive behavior, whereas other instruments, such as Deluty's (1981) Children's Action Tendency Scale and Michelson and Wood's (1982) Children's Assertive Behavior Scale, do a better job of "unbinding" aggressive from assertive behavior. Early findings by Scanlon and Ollendick (1985) support this claim.

The CAI also seems useful in the study of the development of assertiveness over age and in the examination of levels of assertiveness across diverse cultural and socioeconomic groups. Because it is developmentally sensitive, yet consistent across diverse socioeconomic and cultural groups (at least in the United States), it seems admirably suited for this purpose.

Finally, although the instrument has not been examined carefully with specific clinical populations, it would seem especially useful for disorders involving anxiety and depression. Such children are known to display shy and withdrawn behaviors. As noted by Scanlon and Ollendick (1985), such children frequently display low levels of assertiveness.

Future Directions

In addition to studies confirming the reliability and validity of the CAI as well as its factor structure, future research should be directed toward establishing the instrument's utility with diverse clinical groups. In particular, more research is needed to determine if the instrument is useful with aggressive children. Tentative unpublished findings suggest that agggressive children are less assertive in positive, commendatory situations than in situations requiring standing up for their own rights or refusing unreasonable requests. These situations parallel those tapped by the positive and negative assertion scenes on the CAI. One line of research might examine whether the responses of aggressive, withdrawn, and assertive children vary across the two factors of positive and negative assertion. It might be predicted that aggressive children would respond like assertive children on the negative assertion factor (stand up for rights and refuse unfair requests), but like withdrawn, unassertive children on the positive assertion factor (initiate contacts and give and receive compliments).

A second major area of future development concerns the practical utility of the instrument in making important clinical decisions related to assessment and treatment. As a screening instrument, the CAI seems eminently justified. However, whether it actually helps streamline and focus the assessment/treatment process remains open for empirical verification. Nonetheless, initial findings suggest that the instrument is a welcome tool in the clinician's armamentarium, especially in working with shy, anxious, and withdrawn children who may be unassertive.

References

Deluty, R.H. (1981). Children's Actions Tendency Scale: A self-report measure of aggressiveness, assertiveness, and submissiveness in children. *Journal of Consulting and Clinical Psychology, 47*, 1061-1071.

Finch, A.J., & Rogers, T.R. (1984). Self-report instruments. In T.H. Ollendick & M. Hersen (Eds.), *Child behavioral assessment; Principles and procedures.* New York: Pergamon Press.

Michelson, L., & Wood, R. (1982). Development and psychometric properties of the Children's Assertive Behavior Scale. *Journal of Behavioral Assessment, 4*, 3-13.

Ollendick, T.H. (1981). Assessment of social interaction skills in school children. *Behavioral Counseling Quarterly, 1*, 227-243.

Ollendick, T.H. (1984). Development and validation of the Children's Assertiveness Inventory. *Child and Family Behavior Therapy, 5*, 1-15.

Scanlon, E.M., & Ollendick, T.H. (1985). Children's assertive behavior: The reliability and validity of three self-report measures. *Child and Family Behavior Therapy, 7,* 9–21.

Schneider, B.H., Ledingham, J.E., Poirier, C.A., Oliver, J., & Byrne, B.M. (1984). Self-reports of children in treatment: Is assertiveness in the eyes of the beholder? *Journal of Clinical Child Psychology, 13,* 70-73.

Children's Depression Inventory

Conway Fleming Saylor

Description

Kovacs' Children's Depression Inventory (CDI) is a self-report paper-and-pencil measure that is a downward extension of the Beck Depression Inventory (BDI) for adults (Kovacs, 1983). It consists of 27 items that describe a variety of depressive symptoms, including sad mood, hopelessness, self-depreciation, suicidal ideation, neurovegetative signs of depression, sleep and eating disturbances, and poor school performance. Each item consists of three statements describing the extent to which the child feels he or she displays a given symptom. For example, the child is asked to endorse one of the following: "I am sad once in a while," "I am sad many times," and "I am sad all the time," as a way of describing how he or she has felt in the last 2 weeks. Items are scored on a scale of 0 to 2, with 2 representing the most depressed response and 0 representing the absence of depression.

The CDI was designed to be administered on an individual basis to children and adolescents from 8 to 17 years of age. Items generally are read aloud to children, but adolescents who show proficiency in reading over the first three or four items can be allowed to complete the inventory themselves without an adult reading each item so that rapport may be maintained (Kovacs, 1983). Although individual administration has been recommended, all of the normative data collected with normal subjects have been obtained in group administration in a classroom situation. Saylor et al. (1984) demonstrated that there was no significant difference in scores with individual administration versus group administration.

Purpose

Kovacs describes the inventory as having multiple purposes. By providing an indicator of the severity of depressive symptoms, it allows for an objective means of describing a child's clinical state, classifying research subjects, assisting in proper diagnosis, and monitoring treatment progress over extended periods. As mentioned in subsequent sections, empirical questions still exist regarding the usefulness of the CDI in differential diagnosis and in monitoring treatment progress through repeated administration.

Development

Kovacs and her colleagues drafted the first version of the CDI in March of 1975 by incorporating the suggestions of a small group of "normal" 10- to 15-year-olds, who were asked to give advice on how the items of the BDI could be worded to be "clear to kids." The resulting 25-item scale subsequently underwent a second major revision in February 1976, and it was this version of the inventory that was administered to thirty-nine 8- to 13-year-old guidance center admissions, 20 "normal" 8- to 13-year-olds, and 127 fifth and sixth grade 10- to 13-year-olds in the Toronto public school system. After these data were collected, the CDI was again revised yielding the May 1977 version which was pilot tested and more broadly distributed. The final version of the CDI, released in July 1977, has remained intact except for one revision. In August 1979 the numerical symbols under each item choice were removed. Saylor et al. (1984) demonstrated no significant difference between CDI scores using the early version of the CDI with the numerical symbols and the revised version without numerical symbols; therefore, data collected since 1977 are held to be applicable to the current version of the CDI.

Psychometric Characteristics

Kovacs (1983) reported a mean of 9.28 (SD = 7.30) in a sample of 860 8- to 14-year-old Toronto school children who completed an early version of the CDI, and a mean of 9.72 (SD = 7) for 630 12- to 15-year-old Pennsylvania school children. The most recent published normative data collected by Finch, Saylor, and Edwards (1985) yielded a similar overall CDI mean of 9.65 and a standard deviation of 7.3. Their data also suggested that scores may differ slightly for the two genders, with female subjects reporting fewer depressive symptoms than male subjects (female mean = 9.01, SD = 6.97; male mean = 10.33, SD = 7.59). Finch et al. (1985) also noted some subtle variation in scores as a function of age, with very young children (e.g., second and third graders) tending to report fewer symptoms than did older groups (e.g., seventh and eighth graders).

Three types of reliability have been investigated by multiple researchers. (For review, see Saylor, Finch, Spirito, & Bennett, 1984.) Kuder-Richardson reliability has been investigated in both normal and emotionally disturbed populations by the Saylor/Finch group and Kovac's group. Alpha coefficients have ranged from .80 to .94. Investigations of split–half reliability have yielded coefficients ranging from .57 to .74, depending on the type of split (even/odd versus first half/second half) and the population (normal versus emotionally disturbed). All coefficients have been statistically significant and suggest good internal consistency for the CDI.

More confusing findings have emerged from numerous studies examining the test-retest reliability of the CDI. Kovacs initially reported a 4-week test-retest reliability coefficient of .82 in a sample of 29 subjects with juvenile diabetes, but obtained this number by dropping two outliers from the sample of 29, changing the coefficient from its original level of .43. The .43 coefficient is similar to that of .38 obtained by Saylor et al. in 69 normal school children over a 1-week interval. In normal populations, test-retest correlations have been higher over longer intervals, with Kovacs reporting a significant correlation of .84 over a 9-week interval in 90 normal Canadian students. Test-retest reliability is higher for emotionally disturbed populations regardless of the test interval. Saylor et al., for example, obtained a 1-week test-retest coefficient of .87 for 30 emotionally disturbed children, and a 6-week test-retest coefficient of .59 for 24 emotionally disturbed children. Similarly, Kovacs cited research in which a test-retest correlation of .72 over a 9- to 13–week interval was obtained with 28 children whose test data suggested they were depressed. Kazdin, Esveldt-Dawson, Unis, & Rancurello (1983) similarly found a 6-week test-retest reliability of .50 for 37 psychiatric inpatient children. Unpublished data by Finch, Saylor, and their colleagues examine this question more systematically and suggest 2-week test-retest reliability of .82, 4-week test-retest reliability of .66, and 6-week test-retest reliability of .67 using a sample of 108 normal school children.   Questions surrounding the CDI's validity have also been addressed by multiple investigators using a variety of procedures. As reviewed by Saylor, Finch, Spirito, and Bennett (1984), one consistent finding is that the CDI can differentiate general populations of emotionally disturbed children from normal school children. The ability of the CDI to discriminate depressed and nondepressed children has been supported by Kovacs (1983), reporting that the CDI discriminated 27 children with a major depressive disorder from normal school children and 12 children in partial remission from depressive disorders, and by Kazdin et al. finding significantly higher CDI scores in children diagnosed as depressed on the DSM-III. Conversely, Saylor et al. failed to find differences in CDI scores between depressed and nondepressed groups. Multitrait-multimethod investigations of the discriminant and conversion validity of the CDI and other depression measures have consistently yielded high method variance and low trait variance, suggesting that the CDI may correlate with other self-report measures of other constructs (e.g., anxiety and anger), but may not consistently correlate with others' reports of the child's depressive symptoms.

Investigations reviewed by Saylor et al. (1984) suggest that contrary to Kovacs' initial suggestion that the CDI measured a single factor construct, it may, in fact, measure a construct that has multiple factors. Studies conducted with both normal and clinical populations have yielded two or three significant factors depending on the populations and statistical packages employed. A consistent finding across studies is a factor that Cantwell and colleagues described as "poor self-image" and that could be described as "fatigability and sense of failure." At this time, the CDI factors are not considered to be clinically useful.

Clinical Use

The CDI is subject to the same limitations as are all self-report measures; that is, it assesses only subjective information and is subject to bias in either a negative or positive direction. Furthermore, it may provide information that is at odds with that provided by outside observers. Despite these limitations the CDI is thought to be a useful indicator of a child's subjective experience of depressive symptoms. It should be combined with other means of assessment if it is to be used for assignment, diagnosis, or evaluation of treatment. As indicated in the validity literature, caution must be exercised in interpreting a high CDI score as a definite indication of an affective disorder. It may be that the CDI reflects general distress more so than a "pure" construct of depression. Because it only takes 5 to 10 minutes to administer and samples a variety of symptoms, the CDI can be a useful screening measure. A clinician might also be able to gain information by studying the specific pattern of items endorsed. For example, some children will respond selectively to items reflecting experiences of neurovegetative symptoms or to items suggesting a sense of being in trouble or failing in school.

Future Directions

Investigation of CDI's psychometric properties has already been conducted with both clinical and normal populations. In this respect, the CDI can be distinguished from most other self-report inventories in the area of childhood depression. Attention to sex and age differences should be part of subsequent investigations. The CDI's test-retest reliability in both clinical and normal populations also needs to be further explored more systematically. At this point, it is difficult to interpret changes in the CDI over brief and lengthy intervals of time because these data are so inconsistent. Failure of the CDI to consistently measure a distinct syndrome of depression needs further investigation, but it may reflect a limitation of current diagnostic categories. Future studies of the CDI should examine its uses with "special" populations, such as the developmentally delayed, handicapped, and pediatric populations. Finally, the applicability of the CDI in the clinical setting and its usefulness as a measure of treatment outcome or as a diagnostic tool need to be empirically examined with clinical populations.

References

Finch, A.J., Saylor, C.F., & Edwards, G.L. (1985). Children's Depression Inventory: Sex and grade norms for normal children. *Journal of Consulting and Clinical Psychology, 53*, 424.

Kazdin, A.E., Esveldt-Dawson, K., Unis, A.S., & Rancurello, M. (1983). Child and parent evaluations of depression and aggression in psychiatric inpatient children. *Journal of Abnormal Psychology, 11*, 401-413.

Kovacs, M. (1983). *The Children's Depression Inventory: A self-rated depression scale for school-aged youngsters.* Unpublished manuscript, University of Pittsburgh School of Medicine, Pittsburgh.

Saylor, C.F., Finch, A.J., Baskin, C.H., Saylor, C.B., Darnell, G., & Furey, W. (1984). Children's Depression Inventory: Investigation of procedures and correlates. *Journal of the American Academy of Child Psychiatry, 23*, 626-628.

Saylor, C.F., Finch, A.J., Spirito, A., & Bennett, B. (1984). Systematic Evaluation of the Children's Depression

Inventory. *Journal of Consulting and Clinical Psychology, 52*, 955-967.

Children's Interpersonal Behavior Test

Vincent B. Van Hasselt and Robert T. Ammerman

Description

The Children's Interpersonal Behavior Test (CIBT; Van Hasselt, Hersen, & Bellack, 1981) is a role-play test measuring social skills in children. It was derived from the Behavioral Assertiveness Test for Boys (Reardon, Hersen, Bellack, & Foley, 1979) and the Behavioral Assertiveness Test for Children (Bornstein, Bellack, & Hersen, 1977). In contrast to these earlier devices that were specifically designed to measure assertion, the CIBT was constructed to examine more broadly the concept of social skills in children. Specifically, the CIBT is composed of six role-play situations, which are enacted with a confederate. After three interchanges between the subject and the confederate, the test proceeds to the next situation.

Purpose

With increased interest in social functioning and social competence in children, a need developed for measures that provide a fine-grained analysis of interpersonal behavior. Role-play tests of social skills, which differ from more global assessment instruments by providing information about specific components of social behavior, partly satisfied this need.

Development

Role-play items were designed to be typical of social encounters children are likely to have in their real environments. Teacher input and feedback regarding scene content were obtained during item construction. One half of the scenes in the CIBT involve a male role–play partner, whereas the other half involve a female role–play partner. The following is an example of a scene from the CIBT involving a male prompt. (Copies of the entire CIBT are available from the author upon request.) Narrator: Your teacher has asked you and a group of your classmates to meet together to discuss current event topics of interest to the group members.

Your teacher comes over to your group and asks you: *Prompt 1*: "What would you like to talk about?" (Subject's Response 1)

Unlike the Behavioral Assertion Test (Eisler, Hersen, & Miller, 1973) or current behavioral assertiveness tests for children in which termination of the subject's response to the prompt serves as a cue for the experimenter to present the next situation, the role–play partner in the CIBT follows the subject's initial response with a series of prearranged counter–responses to allow for an extended interchange. Additional role–model prompts are determined by their: (a) ability to maintain the flow of conversation, (b) applicability to the situation irrespective of the subject's previous statements, and (c) logical sense given the particular scene narrative and preceding prompt(s).

In the example of the CIBT scene just presented, the role–play partner's additional responses are as follows: *Prompt 2*: "Are there things of greater interest to you that you would rather talk about in the group?" (Subject's Response 2) *Prompt 3*: "How do you like these group discussions?" (Subject's Response 3) Therefore, the subject's initial response (Subject's Response 1) is followed by a prearranged counter-response from the confederate (Prompt 2), which serves as a stimulus for another response by the subject (Subject's Response 2). This is followed by a final counter-response by the confederate (Prompt 3), which serves as a stimulus for the subject's final response (Subject's Response 3). Although some variation in prompt content occasionally is necessary, role–play partners are instructed to stay within the framework of the prearranged responses as closely as possible. The present format extends the interaction and potentially makes CIBT items more similar to real-life encounters that often are longer than the interactions possible with the one-line prompts and responses on instruments such as the BAT-R (Eisler, Hersen, Miller, & Blanchard, 1975).

Subject's responses to CIBT items typically are videotaped and subsequently rated on behavioral components of social skills identified by Eisler et al. (1973) and Eisler, Hersen, Miller, and Blanchard (1975). Some of these include: eye contact, smiles, physical gestures, speech duration, response latency, speech disturbances, and voice intonation. In addition, an independent set of judges rates each scene for Overall Friendliness on a 5-point scale from 1 (very unfriendly) to 5 (very friendly). All behaviors except the latter are rated for each of the three prompts. The mean of the three ratings for each scene is calculated for data analysis. Overall Friendliness ratings are based on observations of responses to entire scenes rather than individual prompts.

Such behaviors generally have been selected because of their use in many social skills investigations with adult populations as well as in parallel research with children (e.g., Bornstein et al., 1977; Reardon et al., 1979).

Psychometric Characteristics

Van Hasselt, Hersen, and Bellack (1981) examined the reliability and validity of the CIBT for assessing social skills in children. Twenty-two male and 20 female elementary school children aged 8 to 10 years were administered the CIBT. Other assessment strategies also were used including: (a) sociometric ratings, (b) naturalistic observations, and (c) teachers' ratings. Results of correlational analyses failed to support the validity of this measure. Specifically, although statistically significant relationships were found between responses on the CIBT and criterion social situations, these were of low magnitude. Also, test-retest reliability (at a 1–week interval) yielded highly variable correlation coefficients on rated skill components (range .06 to .91). Coefficients for only two components (smiles and response latency) were .80 greater. Van Hasselt et al. (1981) concluded that test-retest reliability of the CIBT was unacceptable.

Clinical Use

The CIBT was primarily designed for research use. However, the use of role playing in the clinical treatment of socially maladjusted children is highly recommended. The CIBT can be so employed as an initial screening of social skills in children in clinical settings.

Future Directions

Since the development of the CIBT, additional role–play test variations have been designed for use with children. However, psychometric properties of these measures have yet to be firmly established. It is expected that the CIBT and similar measures will continue to be employed as both clinical and research tools in the assessment of social skills in children. However, future research clearly is needed to construct a strategy with adequate parametric properties.

References

Bornstein, M.R., Bellack, A.S., & Hersen, M. (1977). Social skills training for unassertive children: A multiple baseline analysis. *Journal of Applied Behavior Analysis, 10,* 183-195.

Eisler, R.M., Hersen, M., & Miller, P.M. (1973). Effects of modeling on components of assertive behavior. *Journal of Behavior Therapy and Experimental Psychiatry, 4,* 1-6.

Eisler, R.M., Hersen, M., Miller, P.M., & Blanchard, E.B. (1975). Situational determinants of assertive behaviors. *Journal of Consulting and Clinical Psychology, 43,* 330-340.

Reardon, R.C., Hersen, M., Bellack, A.S., & Foley, J.M. (1979). Measuring social skill in grade school boys. *Journal of Behavioral Assessment, 1,* 87-105.

Van Hasselt, V.B., Hersen, M., & Bellack, A.S. (1981). The validity of role play tests for assessing social skills in children. *Behavior Therapy, 12,* 202-216.

Client Resistance Coding System

Patricia Chamberlain

Description

The Client Resistance Code (CRC) is an observational method designed to measure client behavior during treatment sessions. Each client verbalization is classified as being either cooperative with the direction set by the therapist or resistant, falling into one of eight categories that describe various types of client resistance: (a) challenge/disagree, (b) hopeless/blaming, (c) defending self/others, (d) own agenda/sidetracking, (e) answering for another, (f) not answering or not responding, (g) disqualifying previous statements, and (h) attacking other family members. Data are recorded in the sequence in which they occur throughout the session. A separate observation system is used to describe the content of the therapist's behavior. When the client response follows the direction set by the therapist's prior verbalization, cooperation is recorded. When the client's response diverts or impedes the direction set by the therapist, one of the eight resistance categories is used.

Videotapes of treatment sessions are dubbed using a date/time generator that records the passage of time in minutes and seconds on the tape. Data are recorded using a hand-held electronic computer that records the code categories onto a tape that is later transferred to the main computer for analysis. The duration of each entry as well as the sequence of therapist/client interactions is recorded. Each coded entry for clients and therapists consists of five digits: the first digit identifies who is speaking, the second and third describe the content of the verbalization, the fourth describes the valence of the client or therapist verbalization, and the fifth identifies the qualifier code (e.g., laughs and interrupts).

Purpose

The CRC was designed to quantify client resistance in the context of a parent training treatment approach for families of children and adolescents referred for oppositional or conduct disorders. Previous work shows that therapists rate 70% of such families as being at least somewhat resistant (O'Dell, 1982) to the parent training approach. Over the last 5 years, the role of therapist clinical, or "soft," skills in the successful implementation of parent training approaches has received increased attention in the literature (Griest et al., 1982; Patterson, 1984). Previous studies examining these variables may have been hampered by, as their primary data source, a reliance on global rating scales that group impressions.

Given the feasibility of measuring client resistant behaviors on a moment-to-moment or session-to-session basis, it is possible to examine empirically the relationship between various therapist activities and client resistance (e.g., the extent to which sessions are characterized by high densities of therapist educational statements associated with increased client resistance and the extent to which therapist supportive or affiliative remarks are associated with decreased client resistance). Because the sequence of behaviors is recorded in the CRC, it is possible to examine social interactional issues in the therapeutic process (e.g., do certain immediate reactions of the therapist to resistant client behaviors increase or decrease the probability that a sequence of resistant behaviors will continue?).

Development

The code was developed as an outgrowth of our interest in the question: "What determines the individual differences among families in their responses to treatment?" After viewing hundreds of hours of videotapes of our failure cases, the pivotal construct was thought to be client resistance, both within the session (e.g., client disagreements with the therapist blocking the direction in which the therapist was moving) and between sessions (e.g., client failure to attempt homework assignments). Our stance is that client resistance to parent training reflects the outcome of two variables: one is brought to the session by the client and the other by the therapist.

The circumstances surrounding the family's referral for treatment plus other social and personal factors, such as the level of deviancy of the child, are thought to determine the family's initial level of resistance in treatment. As treatment proceeds, the therapist's efforts to teach new skills or to try abandoned skills produce increased resistance. Within our general model, these forces are thought to be partially mitigated by the therapist's ability to reframe the problem, thereby reducing parental resistance. Reframing issues, such as the child's behavioral intent or what seems to have been a parental failure in the past, allows parents to become involved in the supervised training of parenting skills. It was towards the end of studying this process that the CRC and accompanying Therapist Behavior Code were developed.

Psychometric Characteristics

In a recently completed study using the CRC, Chamberlain, Patterson, Reid, Kavanagh, and Forgatch (1984) demonstrated that it is feasible to formulate a client total resistance score as a reliably observable event in therapy. Of the videotapes of a sample of 27 families, 28% were coded independently by two observers. Two indices of reliability were employed. The mean level of exact agreement (number of agreements divided by number of agreements plus disagreements) was .75 ($SD = .22$). Correlational analyses comparing the scores of the observer pairs across tapes were also conducted, indicating $r(33) = .09, p < .001$.

In an analysis of the stability of the resistance score within a given session, treatment sessions were coded for eight families. Each session was divided into three 15-minute segments. Data were analyzed for mothers only. The mean rates per minute of maternal resistant behavior for the first, second, and third 15-minute segments were .10, .12, and .10, respectively. The analysis of variance for repeated measures was not significant ($F = .50$, $df - 2.7$), indicating a similarity in resistance rates for each segment.

As its name implies, the CRC was designed to measure client behaviors that indicate or portray resistance to therapy. The results of a series of comparative analyses aimed at assessing the concurrent and construct validity of the CRC are briefly reviewed here. For 27 families referred for child management problems, families with high levels of initial resistance were more likely to drop out of treatment at an early stage. For the remaining families, it was hypothesized that in routine or successful cases, the average rate per minute of client resistance would vary systematically as a function of the stage of treatment. During the first sessions, when therapy is focused on information gathering and forming a relationship, resistance is expected to be low. During midtreatment, when therapy is focused on teaching the parents strategies for directly intervening in their child's problem behaviors, resistance is expected to be high. Toward the end of treatment, family members would have integrated changes, and resistance is expected to be low. The average rate per minute of observed parental resistance varied with the stage of treatment, with the highest rate during the midtreatment sessions ($F[2, 34] = 3.44, p < .05$). Differences in resistance levels from early to midtreatment were statistically significant ($F[1, 17] = 6.53$, $p < .03$); those from midtreatment termination approached statistical significance ($F[1, 17] = 3.33$, $p < .09$).

A related question was the extent to which a client's initial level of resistance is related to subsequent levels of resistance in later stages of therapy. Resistance scores from the early sessions were correlated with those observed at midtreatment. Despite the significant difference in the mean levels of resistance from early to midtreatment, clients tended to maintain their ordinal rankings: Early resistance was related to resistance at midtreatment ($rs[16] = .73, p < .01$). Curiously, no relationship was found between midsession and late session scores ($rs[16] = .04$). Self-referred clients are typically assumed to be more motivated for treatment than are agency-referred clients. Initial resistance levels were higher in agency-referred families than in self-referred families ($p < .004$).

When the relationship between client resistance and therapists' ratings of case outcome was analyzed, a positive correlation was found between client resistance at the end of treatment and therapists' posttreatment ratings of the success or failure of therapy. Cases rated as being more successful had lower levels of observed resistance at the end of treatment ($R[16] = .48, p < .05$). A related finding was that the therapists' ratings of successful outcome correlated with decreases in the rate per minute of client resistance from mid- to late treatment (Rpb[16] = .68, p <.01). As expected, there was also a correlation between therapists' ratings of success in treatment and reductions in client resistance from initial to termination sessions (Rpb[16] = .48, p <.05).

The relationships between the rates of observed client resistance to phase of treatment, client status (i.e., dropouts versus those who complete treatment), and referral source support the construct validity of the system. The relationship between observed client resistance and therapists' ratings of outcome status suggests that the observational system may have predictive value.

Clinical Use

The CRC has been used to code families of antisocial children and adolescents participating in parent training treatment. The reliability and validity of the system for other populations and therapies have not been examined. In a current study, the CRC is being used to study the same population receiving a structural family therapy treatment.

Future Directions

The use of observation coding systems to describe client-therapist interactions in terms of their content and process will allow better understanding of the active ingredients of treatment for various populations. The short-term impact of a given intervention can be studied within the context of the session. For example, Patterson and Forgatch (1985) found that therapists' teaching and confronting statements elicited reliably more resistance in the next client verbalization than did supportive or facilitative statements.

The findings of Chamberlain et al. (1984) should be verified in a replication. The issue of whether in-session resistance is counterproductive to the achievement of therapeutic goals needs study. Future research is needed to determine the relationship of independent measures of client behavior (e.g., missing sessions and completing assignments) to the transactions observed within the sessions and to assess the relationships of those transactions to more global factors (e.g., the degree to which the therapist and client share the same values and the client's attitudes towards therapy). Finally, the relationship between this observational measure of resistance and multiple

measures of treatment outcome must be established before this measurement system is taken seriously by students of the therapeutic process.

References

Chamberlain, P., Patterson, G.R., Reid, J.B., Kavanagh, K., & Forgatch, M.S. (1984). Observation to client resistance. *Behavior Therapy, 15,* 144-155.

Griest, D.L., Forehand, R., Rogers, T., Breiner, J., Furey, W., & Williams, C.A. (1982). Effects of parent enhancement therapy on the treatment outcome and generalization of a parent training program. *Behaviour Research and Therapy, 15,* 217-223.

O'Dell, S. (1982). Enhancing parent involvement training: A discussion. *The Behavior Therapist, 5,* 9-13.

Patterson, G.R. (1984). Beyond technology: The next stage in the development of parent training. In L. L'Abate (Ed.), *Handbook of psychology and psychotherapy.* New York: Dow Jones.

Patterson, G.R., & Forgatch, M.S. (1985). Therapist behavior as a determinant for client resistance: A paradox for the behavior modifier. *Journal of Consulting and Clinical Psychology, 6,* 846-851

Clinical Dementia Rating

Christopher Starratt and Robert B. Fields

Description

The Clinical Dementia Rating (CDR) scale is a global rating device to evaluate the level of functional impairment of individuals carefully screened for senile dementia of the Alzheimer's type (SDAT). A CDR rating of 0 (no impairment), .5 (questionable dementia), 1 (mild dementia), 2 (moderate dementia), or 3 (severe dementia) is assigned on the basis of information derived from a standardized 90-minute structured interview, the Initial Subject Protocol (ISP: Hughes, Berg, Danziger, Coben, & Martin, 1982). The ISP includes interview information derived from the subject as well as a collateral source that covers family, medical, and psychiatric history as well as social, educational, and cultural background. In addition, several cognitive screening tests are administered including the Blessed Dementia Scale, the Short Portable Mental Status Questionnaire, the Face-Hand Test as well as portions of the Boston Diagnostic Aphasia Exam and the Hamilton Depression Scale. (See Hughes et al., 1982, for details.) Based on the aforementioned information, subjects are rated on their current cognitive abilities and their past level of functioning. Ratings are made in: memory, orientation, judgment and problem solving, community affairs, home and hobbies, and personal care. A rating of 0, .5, 1, or 2 is given in each category. Overall CDR rating is based on the pattern of function across each area, with memory regarded as the primary rating category.

Purpose

It has long been recognized that the primary symptoms associated with dementing disorders such as Alzheimer's disease are cognitive and behavioral. Recent investigations have also highlighted the necessity and difficulty of diagnosing Alzheimer's disease during its early stages. The current scale was developed to derive a reliable means of quantifying the extent of dementia, especially during its early stages, when differentiating between dementia and presumed nonpathological age-related cognitive and behavioral changes is most difficult. It was assumed that the best way to arrive at this distinction was to evaluate both cognitive and behavioral functions believed to be related to SDAT as reported by prior research and clinical experience.

Development

The CDR and ISP were developed by the Dementia Study Group of Washington University to establish explicit clinical diagnostic criteria for SDAT to be used in a longitudinal study of mild dementia versus healthy aging. The CDR was modeled after the Crichton Geriatric Behavioral Rating Scale (Robinson, 1961) but offers more detailed evaluation of level of function, especially within the realm of cognitive status.

Initial reliability and validity data were derived from a sample of community-dwelling demented elderly and normal elderly volunteers recruited through public announcement in the St. Louis metropolitan area who have been followed longitudinally.

Psychometric Characteristics

Based on a pilot investigation (Hughes et al., 1982), adequate interrater reliability values were obtained (r = .89). As expected, during the initial development study, overall CDR rating correlated significantly with all of the individual cognitive screening measures used to formulate that rating. Nine-month follow-up of 90 subjects with a rating

between 0 and 1 was conducted. None of the nondemented subjects (CDR 0) progressed to a more impaired rating. None of the mildly demented subjects (CDR 1) obtained a rating indicating less dementia (CDR 0 or CDR .5); they all either remained at the same level or became more impaired. Three progressively declining subjects came to autopsy, and the presence of Alzheimer's disease was confirmed.

Additional investigation was conducted by the Washington University group regarding the psychometric and physiological differences between nondemented and mildly demented elderly subjects as staged by the CDR. Storandt, Botwinick, Danziger, Berg, and Hughes (1984) administered a large battery of neuropsychological tests to subjects with ratings of CDR 0 or CDR 1. A discriminant function analysis resulted in four brief neuropsychological tests that correctly classified 98% of the subjects on cross-validation. Longitudinally, subjects rated as demented declined in psychometric test performance, whereas nondemented subjects remained stable upon reevaluation at a 2.5-year follow-up (Storandt, Botwinick, & Danziger, 1986). Finally, physiological differences between groups have been reported as well. Subjects rated as demented have higher platelet MAO activity than do subjects rated as nondemented (Alexopoulos, Leiberman, & Young, 1984). Longitudinal evaluation of electroencephalographic activity also significantly differentiates subjects rated as nondemented versus demented based on the CDR.

Clinical Use

Although a relatively new rating scale, investigation to date by the parent research group suggests that the CDR shows promise as a reliable and valid method of systematically collecting and rating physical, cognitive, and behavioral information relevant to the diagnosis of Alzheimer's type dementia. It is intended to be most sensitive to discrimination of dementia during the early phases of the disease. The use of the ISP and derived CDR rating requires knowledge of or access to additional measures such as the Blessed Dementia Rating Scale and the Boton Diagnostic Aphasia Exam. Given the difficulty of early diagnosis, such comprehensiveness may be needed. The CDR is most relevant during the early stages of dementia. It does not differentiate levels during later stages of dementing processes as does the Global Deterioration Scale.

Future Directions

The CDR shows promise as a structured procedure for rating the level of functional impairment related to a dementing disorder, especially during the early phases of the disease. Continued effort directed at evaluating which components of the ISP weigh most heavily in CDR ratings would be of benefit. Although the CDR has been designed specifically to evaluate dementias of the Alzheimer type, long-term follow-up of patients with other dementing disorders would be helpful in determining if CDR staging is specific for SDAT.

References

Alexopoulos, G.S., Leiberman, K.W., & Young, R.C. (1984). Platelet MAO activity in primary degenerative dementia. *American Journal of Psychiatry, 141,* 97-99.

Hughes, C.P., Berg, L., Danziger, W.L., Coben, L.A., & Martin, R.L. (1982). A new clinical scale for the staging of dementia. *British Journal of Psychiatry, 140,* 566-572.

Robinson, R.A. (1961). Some problems of clinical trials in elderly people. *Gerontologia Clinica, 3,* 247-257.

Storandt, M., Botwinick, J., Danziger, W.L., Berg, L., & Hughes, C.P. (1984). Psychometric differentiation of mild senile dementia of the Alzheimer type. *Archives of Neurology, 41,* 497-499.

Storandt, M., Botwinick, J., & Danziger, W.L. (1986). Longitudinal changes: Patients with mild SDAT and matched healthy controls. In L.W. Poon (Ed.), *Handbook for the clinical memory assessment of older adults* (pp. 277-284). New York: American Psychiatric Association.

Clinical Frequencies Recording System

Gordon L. Paul and Mark H. Licht

Description

Compiled-multivariate Direct Observational Coding (DOC) systems, of which the Clinical Frequencies Recording System (CFRS) is a prototype, constitute the second of three central strategies in the comprehensive assessment paradigm designed to provide all of the common information needed on adult clients, staff, and programs to maximize the quality and rationality of clinical, administrative, professional/legal, and scientific decision-making in hospitals and other residential treatment facilities for the mentally and emotionally disabled (Paul, 1986). Like the core strategy of the paradigm (see the TSBC/SRIC System, Licht & Paul, this volume; Paul & Licht, this volume), the CFRS is a multiple-occasion DOC method, but one applied by indigenous clinical staff on event-sampling schedules in contrast to the core DOC system's application by independent observers on time-sampling schedules. Compiled-multivariate DOC strategies are the only cost-effective way to supplement the core DOC system for the assessment of client and staff functioning in areas in which the complete enumeration of performances and transitory events is needed: namely, assessment of totally setting-dependent behavior and low frequency critical events.

Unlike the core TSBC/SRIC System which can be overlaid on any existing treatment program, the compiled-multivariate DOC strategy requires the introduction of structure on programs and staff duties, with parallel structure over units/facilities if data are to be totally comparable over time and within/across programs. Similar introduction of structure is also required for the third central strategy of the paradigm (structured interviews and sequential interactive single-occasion assessments by clinical staff with clients and their significant others). Large segments of data from compiled-multivariate DOC systems are consequently program dependent such that complete generalizable systems have not been developed independently of particular treatment structures and populations. The CFRS is the only complete system that has been applied over more than one type of treatment program (Paul & Lentz, 1977; Redfield, 1979). The CFRS forms and application procedures are only available for its use with the comprehensive Social-Learning Program, which has been established as the treatment of choice for institutionalized mental patients (Paul & Shelite, in preparation). However, the CFRS could be adapted to most units and populations with few changes, if the accompanying program structure were adopted as well.

No ongoing cost increase is entailed as CFRS training/observations/recordings are completely integrated with the clinical/administrative duties of staff as part of the proper conduct of treatment programs. The CFRS is composed of many different noncomplex DOC instruments, arranged on 35 time-place-situation specific forms (recording protocols) to provide continuous coverage of clients and scheduled staff, 24 hours/day 7 days/week. Single forms are used by staff at any given time, with predetermined responsibilities for directly

transcribing immediate observations of inappropriate acts or specific setting-dependent actions,
interactions, and/or states of individual clients and
staff members' consequent reactions, and of staff
application of biomedical treatments. Direct entry
of tokens earned/spent on Social Learning Program
forms provides continuous accounting within the
token-economy part of the program as well as a permanent record of relevant events. The CFRS
forms are formatted to provide legal documentation of actions, when necessary, as well as hour-
by-hour monitoring of particular staff actions and
successive levels of specified client performance/
subtargets by visual inspection. The latter formats,
combined with daily processing of forms and
cumulative summaries for each client every Mon-
day through Sunday by night-shift staff, allow
instant determination of any client's performance
of situationally defined appropriate/inappropriate
behavior from a 10-minute period through 1 or
more days in a current week for consistent clinical
programming. The weekly cumulative frequency
summaries for each client, along with schedules
denoting the opportunities to perform specified
events, are entered into computer files each week.
Computer programs compile observations over
instruments and occasions (situations and times)
for each client to provide printed summaries of
higher-order CFRS scores indexing broader classes
of performance for individuals and for the entire
client group on each unit (means and standard
deviations).

Within Paul's nomenclature for DOC encoding
devices (Paul, 1986), the CFRS is a standardized
compiled-multivariate system with subsets of
component instruments specifically tailored to limited aspects of client and/or staff functioning and
individually applied on 100% event-sampling
schedules. For low-frequency critical events, performance of the acts of interest determine the
occasions of recording; for setting-dependent
behavior, observational sessions are determined by
an environmental event signifying the start of a
behavior setting that provides the opportunity for
phenomena of interest to occur (announcement,
program schedule, and entry to a location). Single-
target protocols for each client are used with all
instruments applied to low-frequency critical
events. Multiple-target client protocols are used
with instruments applied to setting-dependent
behavior, with a separate protocol for each
behavior setting and/or functional location in the
treatment program/environment. Component

instruments employ elemental category structure
to define units of observation, and coding formats/
notational schemes to define units of measurement
in single-element, checklist, or sequential concur-
rent-component forms; discrete-momentary or
continuous-chronographic observing-coding techniques are used as appropriate to the focal content.

Collateral categories for all protocols, and/or pre-
printed information, specify the facility, unit, shift,
and time (date, day, and clock time) of every discrete observational sessions as well as aspects of the
behavior setting and functional content (location
and activity) and the staff member responsible for
clinical tasks/observations/recordings.

Content categories specify a single or limited
class of focal client or staff behavior for each instrument or both. Those directed to low-frequency
critical events cover staff administration of psychotropic drugs and restrictive procedures (e.g., token
fines, time out, or seclusion) as well as client intolerable behavior (e.g., assaults and fire-setting) with
consequent staff actions. Two instruments cover
client setting-dependent behavior that is inappropriate to scheduled activities (inappropriate time/
location, and up during the night). Subsets of protocols focus on client use of resources, including the
time periods of facilities/services utilization (e.g.,
TV viewing and passes) and the acquisition of consumable items (e.g., cigarettes and snacks). Most
CFRS instruments/protocols focus on situationally
defined appropriate client functioning within each
focal setting, including the presence/absence of on-
time arrival and demonstration of component
levels of competence in targeted performance (e.g.,
on-task in classes, participation in meetings, and
bathing skills) or products of performance (e.g.,
appearance and clean and orderly personal living
area). Each of the latter protocols for recording
component levels of competence also combines the
discrete components to indicate the achievement
of "terminal-level performance" for the total
activity period or behavior setting (i.e., indistinguishable from "normal" functioning), and
jointly records specified staff responses.

The units of measurement on each protocol
allow hourly/daily monitoring of specific staff and
client performance/subtargets. Night-shift daily
summaries compile cumulative frequencies for
each client over instruments/occasions in 2 classes
of inappropriate behavior, 19 classes of facilities/
services use, 4 classes of consumable use, and 22
classes of appropriate setting-dependent behavior.
The computer-generated units of analysis (scores)

further compile the week's cumulative frequencies over instruments, observations, and classes of performance for each client, based on a hierarchical-cumulative measurement model, to provide rates per opportunity that index broader areas of functioning. Higher-order indices are provided for: Total Inappropriate Behavior and Intolerable Behavior as a component; Total Appropriate Behavior and components for Self-Care, Interpersonal Skills, and Instrumental Role Performance; Utilization of Consumables; Facilities and Services Utilization and their Stereotype/Variability.

Purpose

The CFRS is designed to provide continuous and comparable time- and situation-specific data on low frequency critical events and totally setting-dependent behavior of clients and staff in residential treatment settings in sufficient detail for moment-to-moment concurrent monitoring of planned psychosocial and biomedical clinical programming. It is also designed to provide the most trustworthy data on the use of resources, situationally defined competencies/deficits, and intolerable excesses of individual clients and groups and on biomedical treatments and critical responses by individual and aggregate clinical staff for placement/disposition decisions, problem identification/description, staff development/utilization, program evaluation, legal-ethical regulation/documentation, and specific research questions. (For decision problems and information needed in rational operations, see Paul, 1986.)

Development

The CFRS was introduced in a long-term comparative treatment study as a cost-effective integration of record keeping, differential clinical programming, and critical assessments. Over 7 years, research and development resulted in effective staff training methods, empirical selection of component instruments/reordered categories, and computer programs, forms, and procedures for widespread implementation/dissemination with the Social-Learning Program.

Psychometric Characteristics

The interobserver reliabilities (phi coefficients) of trained clinical staff on component CFRS instruments are regularly high. For example, over a period of more than 4 years, the average raw-recording replicabilities of 147 professional/preprofessional staff pairs ranged from phi .94 to phi .97 on 15.8 mean recordings per pair. The CFRS data have been free to drift, bias, and differential staff reactivity. Validity evidence has been obtained for all categories of decisions for which it is designed; however, the data base is limited to structured treatment programs in which the TSBC/SRIC are concurrently implemented and, to date, to chronic mental patient populations. Large sample norms are not yet available, as CFRS data require parallel program structures for total comparability. Absolute interpretations are possible (% of opportunities), demonstrating remarkable sensitivity to intended and unintended change in individual clients and groups with psychosocial and biological interventions. Discriminations among individual clients reflect differences in normal competencies ranging from weekly rates of 0% to 100%. Convergent and discriminant validities for CFRS higher-order indices account for most of the reliable variance from concurrently obtained ward ratings and structured interviews; appropriate (r's in the .60's and .80's) and inappropriate indices (r's in the .40's) also correlate with TSBCs. The CFRS indices predict performance on a variety of tasks, including ex-client level of functioning up to 18 months after discharge (r's in the .50's and .60's). Local setting-specific norms can be developed.

Clinical Use

In addition to the purposes just described with "hard evidence," the CFRS has been used in many ways, including teaching staff to subdivide performances for shaping/chaining; convincing fund givers of the need for specific resources; and convincing employers to hire clients.

Future Directions

After the TSBC/SRIC System is available (Paul, in press), publication of CFRS materials will allow proper dissemination of the integrated Social-Learning Program to research and service facilities (Paul & Shelite, in preparation). This will allow continuing improvements in clinical, administrative, and research utility and expansion of the data base. The CFRS will also be adapted to other populations and programs as part of the comprehensive assessment paradigm.

References

Paul, G.L. (Ed.). (1986). *Principles and methods to support cost-effective quality operations: Assessment in residential treatment settings, Part 1*. Champaign, IL: Research Press.

Paul, G.L. (Ed.). (in press). *Observational assessment instrumentation for service and research: The TSBC/SRIC System implementation package. Assessment in residential treatment settings, Part 5*. Champaign, IL: Research Press.

Paul, G.L., & Lentz, R.J. (1977). *Psychosocial treatment of chronic mental patients: Milieu versus social-learning programs*. Cambridge, MA: Harvard University Press.

Paul, G.L., & Shelite, I. (in preparation). The Clinical Frequency Recording System (CFRS): Social-Learning Program Forms. Supplement to G.L. Paul & R.J. Lentz (Eds.), *Psychosocial treatment of chronic mental patients* (2nd ed.). Champaign, IL: Research Press.

Redfield, J.P. (1979). Clinical Frequencies Recording Systems: Standardizing staff observations by event recording. *Journal of Behavioral Assessment, 1*, 211-219.

Code for Instructional Structure and Student Academic Response

Charles R. Greenwood and Joseph C. Delquadri

Description

The Code for Instructional Structure and Student Academic Response (CISSAR) is a 53-item direct observation system that allows recording of ecological and behavioral events within classroom settings (Greenwood, Delquadri, & Hall, 1984; Stanley & Greenwood, 1983). The codes are organized into five ecological categories (activity, task, structure, teacher position, and teacher behavior) and three student behavior categories (academic response, task management, and competing, inappropriate behavior). The codes, their definitions, and observational procedures are described in a manual for observers (Stanley & Greenwood, 1981).

Recording of ecological and student behavior events is accomplished using a momentary time-sampling procedure. Observers record events immediately following auditory cues, which regularly occur 10 seconds apart. Auditory cues are signaled by an electronic timer attached to a clipboard or by an auditory tape player.

Observations using CISSAR can be as long as an entire school day or as short as required by the questions being addressed. The system is designed to account for each moment of a child's educational experience. In the event that a child leaves the classroom, stop codes are used to account for why the student left and the time absent.

Purpose

The purpose of the CISSAR is to provide an intensive analysis of an individual student's behavior and the situational events temporally related to that behavior. In contrast to many classroom observation codes, the CISSAR system samples the situational contexts of a student's behavior as frequently as the behavior is evaluated. The system requires sustained assessment of a single child to produce a rich ecobehavioral record. It does not allow for simultaneous or nearly simultaneous samplings of many students within the classroom.

The CISSAR was designed primarily to address questions relating to classroom instruction and student academic behavior (e.g., writing, reading aloud, academic talk, answering questions, and the like). A secondary purpose is its use in behavior change studies in which behavioral intervention procedures have been used to manage children's behavior.

Development

The CISSAR system was developed to provide a process measure of classroom instruction. The system was developed at the Juniper Gardens Children's Project at the University of Kansas. The development of the CISSAR included: (a) a review of existing classroom-based observation systems, (b) a review of the literature, (c) an initial design, development, and tryout (Hall, Delquadri, Greenwood, & Thurston, 1982), (d) empirical validation (Greenwood, Delquadri, & Hall, 1984), (e) revision and refinement, (f) use in several major investigations (Greenwood et al., 1984; Greenwood, Schulte, Dinwiddie, Kohler, & Carta, 1986), and (g) dissemination to and use by other investigators.

Psychometric Characteristics

The psychometric characteristics of the CISSAR system include many features of a standardized instrument (Greenwood, Schulte, Dinwiddie, Kohler, & Carta, 1986) including standard administration and observer training procedures and data from studies of the instrument's validity and reliability. Social comparison data from inner-city and suburban student samples in Kansas City,

Kansas, are also available for the first, second, and fourth grades.

The CISSAR procedures for observer training and management of quality data collection are described in a manual (Stanley & Greenwood, 1981) used by the trainer as the basis for conducting a training workshop. Codes, definitions, and procedures are contained in the manual, as are mastery exercises and tests for observers. The final aspect of observer training is the production of reliable records in the classroom setting before the onset of actual data collection activities. Observers can be trained to use the code in 2 weeks at 4 hours per day.

The hypothesis that lower achieving, inner-city students, when compared with higher achieving, suburban students of the same age and grade, would also engage significantly less in observed academic responding during a typical school day was confirmed within a fourth grade sample (Greenwood, Delquadri, & Hall, 1984). This finding has recently been replicated with a first grade sample. The difference is on the order of 11 to 13 minutes or 5% per day between groups.

Ecological variables also differed across contrast groups formed by socioeconomic and achievement variables (Greenwood, Delquadri, & Hall, 1984). For example, instructional tasks used significantly more frequently by inner-city teachers included media (e.g., overhead projectors), whereas suburban teachers used reader tasks significantly more often.

The simple correlation of the CISSAR composite academic response score to a composite reading and mathematics achievement score was .42 (df = 92, p = .01) for a fourth grade sample. This correlation was .34 (df = 43, p = .05) and .39 (df = 46, p = .01) for inner city and suburban groups, respectively.

Several studies have demonstrated that the CISSAR ecological and student behavior scores are sensitive to instructional interventions. In single-subject designs, Greenwood et al. (1984) demonstrated in three studies that the use of classwide peer tutoring, in comparison with teacher instructional procedures, increased, and specific ecological and behavioral variables decreased. For example, the use of paper-and-pencil tasks and worksheets increased coincidentally with student's writing of spelling words and academic talk between tutors and tutees as errors were corrected. In comparison with teacher procedures, teacher/student discussion was a more frequent task when the teacher taught spelling and the student paid more attention to the teacher. This study clearly demonstrated that students performed best on Friday spelling tests when they had used the peer tutoring procedures. Therefore, the validity of the ecological and behavioral changes produced was supported by achievement gain outcomes.

In studies of eco-behavioral interaction, in which sequential analysis methods were used, student behavior scores were significantly dependent on variations in ecological variables (Greenwood, Delquadri, Stanley, Terry, & Hall, 1985).

The reliability of the CISSAR code has generally been high, particularly for a multicategory, multicode system. In a recent study, percentage agreement scores ranged from 79.8 to 98.5% across all 53 variables (Greenwood et al., 1984). The average agreement was 88.2% (SD = 4.2). A Pearson r based on 53 separate code proportion scores (not interval agreements) averaged .77 (SD = .24). Agreement figures have also been reported for eco-behavioral sequences formed from CISSAR data (Greenwood, Schulte, Dinwiddie, Kohler, & Carta, 1986).

Test-retest correlations 1 month apart ranged from .35 to .93 across CISSAR code scores. Twelve codes (23%) produced significantly different values at retest (Greenwood, Schulte, Dinwiddie, Kohler, & Carta, 1986).

Clinical Use

To date, the clinical applications of the code have been directed at the development and analysis of classroom instructional procedures in regular and special education settings. This has included monitoring of the effects of behavioral interventions with individual students (Greenwood, Schulte, Dinwiddie, Kohler, & Carta, 1986). Questions investigated have ranged from the very molar (e.g., amount of time spent in reading instruction during the day or the proportion of time a student engages in composite academic responding) to the very molecular (e.g., in reading during small group instruction, what was the effect on writing behavior given a change in task from paper/pencil to teacher/student discussion).

Because of the code's complexity and reliance on computerization for data-base management and analysis, it may be limited somewhat to the aforementioned specific applications. The possible features of the code lie in its use in detailed studies of ecological and behavioral processes in relation to outcome variables (e.g., achievement gain). The system is applicable to problems addressing classroom setting events and stimulus control.

Future Directions

The CISSAR code is currently in use in several studies being conducted by the author and his colleagues concerning instruction with inner-city students. Two variations of the code have been developed and are being evaluated in additional projects. One variation includes additional ecological variables to more fully assess situation factors in special education programs for moderately to severely handicapped students. A second code was written for use in preschool programs for handicapped and nonhandicapped children. These applications are designed to increase the ability to assess dimensions of setting events, stimulus control, and eco-behavioral interaction processes.

References

Greenwood, C.R., Delquadri, J.C., & Hall, R.V. (1984). Opportunity to respond and student academic performance. In W. Heward, T. Heron, D. Hill, & J. Trap-Porter (Eds.), Behavior analysis in education (pp. 58-88). Columbus, OH: Charles E. Merrill Publishing Co.

Greenwood, C.R., Delquadri, J.C., Stanley, S.O., Terry, B., & Hall, R.V. (1985). Assessment of eco-behavioral interaction in school settings. Behavioral Assessment, 7, 331–347.

Greenwood, C.R., Dinwiddie, G., Terry, B., Wade, L., Stanley, S., Thibadeau, S., & Delquadri, J. (1984). Teacher- versus peer-mediated instruction: An eco-behavioral analysis of achievement outcomes. Journal of Applied Behavior Analysis, 17, 521-538.

Greenwood, C.R., Schulte, D., Dinwiddie, G., Kohler, F., & Carta, J. (1986). Assessment and analysis of eco-behavioral interaction. In R. Prinz (Ed.), Advances in behavioral assessment of children and families: Vol. 2 (pp. 69–98). Greenwich, CT: JAI Press, Inc.

Hall, R.V., Delquadri, J.C., Greenwood, C.R., & Thurston, L. (1982). The importance of opportunity to respond to children's academic success. In E. Edgar, N. Haring, J. Jenkins, & C. Pious (Eds.), Serving young handicapped children: Issues and research (pp. 107-140). Baltimore, MA: University Park Press.

Stanley, S.O., & Greenwood, C.R. (1981). Code for instructional structure and student academic response (CISSAR): Observers' manual. Kansas City, KS: Juniper Gardens Children's Project, Bureau of Child Research, University of Kansas.

Stanley, S.O., & Greenwood, C.R. (1983). Assessing opportunity to respond in classroom environments through direct observation: How much opportunity to respond does the minority, disadvantaged student receive in school? Exceptional Children, 49, 370-373.

Cognitive Bias Questionnaire

William H. Norman and Ivan Miller

Description

The Cognitive Bias Questionnaire (CBQ: Hammen & Krantz, 1976; Krantz & Hammen, 1979) is a situation-specific cognitive task developed to assess depressive distortion as described by Beck (1976). The CBQ consists of six brief stories about problematic life situations, followed by four multiple choice questions pertaining to the central character's thoughts and feelings. The four response options after each situation are coded according to two dichotomous and crossed dimensions: depressed versus nondepressed and distorted versus nondistorted, yielding four response alternatives: (a) depressed-distorted, (b) depressed-nondistorted, (c) nondepressed-distorted, and (d) nondepressed-nondistorted.

Purpose

The CBQ is a global measure of Beck's (1976) construct of cognitive distortion. The depressed-distorted (DD) dimension of the CBQ is used to index the presence or absence of characteristic types of negative cognitions that Beck attributes to depressed persons: arbitrary inference, selective abstraction, and maximization of negative events.

Development

In a series of studies designed to test Beck's hypothesis that depressed individuals characteristically engage in distorted interpretations of events, Hammen and Krantz (1976) developed the CBQ to assess the extent to which depressed individuals, when compared with nondepressed individuals, would engage in distorted interpretations.

From an initial set of eight stories consisting of problematic situations common to college students, the four response options for each story were rated as to their depressed versus nondepressed tone and distorted versus nondistorted responses by 10 raters blind to the purpose of the study. Instances of cognitive errors such as arbitrary inference, selective abstraction, and overgeneralization were also rated by the independent raters. Using 80% interrater agreement as the criterion to gauge content validity, 6 stories and a total of 23 response items were retained in the final CBQ version. However, raters were unable to distinguish reliably among the categories of cognitive errors. The version of the CBQ used with clinical samples (Krantz & Hammen, 1979; Norman, Miller, & Klee, 1983) is based on the original items, with only minor content changes to reflect situations more appropriate to nonstudent populations, such as employer-employee problems.

Psychometric Characteristics

Of the four CBQ response options for each story, reports of the scale's psychometric characteristics have been limited to the depressed-distorted (DD) dimension. In Krantz and Hammen's (1979) student sample, the internal consistency estimates of the DD subscale ranged from .62 to .69. Item total correlations ranged from .12 to .5, with an average mean correlation of the 23 DD items with total scores of .34. Test-retest reliability over an 8-week period was moderate ($r = .62, p < .001$). With respect to concurrent validity of the DD subscale, depressed subjects were found to reveal higher mean level depressed-distorted scores than did nondepressed subjects in samples of college students (Krantz & Hammen, 1979; Blaney, Behar, & Head, 1980) and psychiatric inpatients (Krantz & Hammen, 1979; Norman, Miller, & Klee, 1983; Miller & Norman, 1986). Correlations with the Beck Depression Inventory (Beck, 1976) among mixed depressed and nondepressed college students and clinically depressed patient samples ranged from .39 to .52 (Krantz & Hammen, 1979; Blaney et al., 1980; Norman et al., 1983).

Clinical Use

The CBQ appears to be an adequate measure of cognitive distortion. As such, it may be useful clinically in a number of ways, especially to therapists utilizing cognitive approaches. First, it may be used diagnostically to assess the presence and severity of cognitive distortion. For difficult diagnostic cases, this assessment may be useful in determining if a particular patient manifests the cognitive features of depression. Second, the CBQ can be used in treatment planning. High scores on the CBQ may indicate the appropriateness of cognitive interventions. Finally, the CBQ may be used as an outcome measure to assess the degree of change in underlying cognitive distortions after a course of treatment.

Future Directions

Future research with the CBQ needs to progress in several directions. First, because the CBQ is one of several instruments developed to assess cognitive distortion as described by Beck, studies assessing the overlap between these instruments need to be conducted. Second, the relationship of the CBQ to depressive symptoms needs to be clarified. Are high scores on the CBQ simply another symptom of depression or do high levels of cognitive distortion predate the onset of depressive symptoms or continue after remission of symptoms or both? Third, the relationship of the CBQ with other parameters of depressive disorders needs to be studied. Are elevations on the CBQ associated with particular diagnostic, social, or biological variables? Fourth, more attention needs to be focused on the use of the CBQ, along with other measures of cognitive distortion, to identify subgroups of "high distorting" depressed patients who differ from other depressed patients in clinical characteristics, course of illness, or response to treatment.

References

Beck, A.T. (1976). Cognitive therapy and the emotional disorders. New York: International Universities Press.

Blaney, P.H., Behar, V., & Head, R. (1980). Two measures of depressive cognitions: Their association with depression and with each other. Journal of Abnormal Psychology, 89, 678-682.

Hammen, C.L., & Krantz, S. (1976). Effect of success and failure on depressive cognitions. Journal of Abnormal Psychology, 85, 577-586.

Krantz, S., & Hammen, C.L. (1979). Assessment of cognitive bias in depression. Journal of Abnormal Psychology, 88, 611-619.

Miller, I.W., & Norman, W.H. (1986). Persistence of depressive cognitions within a subgroup of depressed inpatients. Cognitive Therapy and Research, 10, 211-224.

Norman, W.H., Miller, I.W., & Klee, S.H. (1983). Assessment of cognitive distortion in a clinically depressed population. Cognitive Therapy and Research, 7, 133-140.

Cognitive-Somatic Anxiety Questionnaire

G. R. Norton

Description

The Cognitive-Somatic Anxiety Questionnaire (CSAQ; Schwartz, Davidson, & Goleman, 1978) consists of 14 statements that are subdivided into two 7–item subscales: Cognitive Anxiety (e.g., "I worry too much over something that doesn't really matter") and Somatic Anxiety (e.g., "I feel tense in my stomach"). The statements are responded to on 5-point Likert-type scales of 1 (not at all) to 5 (very much so), producing three scores: cognitive anxiety, somatic anxiety, and total anxiety. Each subscale has a range of 7 to 35 points.

Purpose

The CSAQ was designed to test the hypothesis (Davidson & Schwartz, 1976) that people experience anxiety in different ways and that the different forms of anxiety respond to different types of treatment (Schwartz et al., 1978; Norton & Johnson, 1983).

Development

Factor analyses of anxiety questionnaires and psychophysiological research have identified two separate dimensions of anxiety: (a) cognitive/subjective, and (b) somatic/bodily anxiety reactions. In a major theoretical article based on psychometric and psychophysiological research, Davidson and Schwartz (1976) developed a psychobiological model of anxiety in which they hypothesized that: (a) the two dimensions are relatively different ways in which people experience anxiety, (b) the two dimensions might be separately influenced by different environmental stimuli, and (c) different procedures used in the reduction of anxiety differ in the degree to which they affect the two systems. Schwartz et al. (1978) developed the CSAQ to test these hypotheses. They selected items from well-known questionnaires that three independent judges unanimously agreed represented cognitive or somatic anxiety. The final form of the CSAQ consisted of seven items measuring cognitive anxiety and seven measuring somatic anxiety.

Psychometric Characteristics

Several studies support the validity of the CSAQ. In the first, Schwartz et al. (1978) administered the CSAQ to 44 persons who regularly exercised and 33 who regularly practiced meditation. Based on the Davidson and Schwartz (1976) psychobiological model of anxiety, they predicted that the subjects who meditated would show lower cognitive anxiety scores and the subjects who exercised would show lower somatic scores. Their results

generally confirmed their predictions, but several confounding factors, such as differences in the proportion of women in the two groups, rendered the results inconclusive. More recently, Norton and Johnson (1983) divided snake-anxious subjects into cognitive anxious and somatic anxious groups based on their scores on the CSAQ. Half of each group received four sessions of an abbreviated form of progressive muscle relaxation and the other half received an equal number of sessions of training in Agni Yoga. Following training, each subject was asked to approach and, if possible, pick up a snake. During the approach test, the heart rate, approach distance, and subjective measures of anxiety/fear were obtained. The results showed that somatically anxious subjects who received progressive muscle relaxation training were significantly less anxious than were those who received Agni Yoga training. A similar trend indicated that cognitively anxious subjects who received Agni Yoga training were less anxious than were those who received progressive muscle relaxation.

Norton, Rhodes, Hauch, and Kaprowy (1985) showed that the CSAQ not only is useful in predicting who will benefit from relaxation training procedures designed to reduce cognitive and somatic anxiety, but also can help predict which subjects will experience a paradoxical increase in anxiety during relaxation training. Not all data support Davidson and Schwartz's (1976) model, however. Borkovec, Robinson, Pruzinsky, and DePree (1983) showed that persons who reported worrying 50% or more of each day scored significantly higher on both the cognitive and the somatic subscales than did nonworriers.

There is some evidence that men and women differ significantly in their scores on the CSAQ. Edwards, Zeichner, and Greene (1984) administered the CSAQ to 49 male and 74 female undergraduate students. The female students scored significantly ($p < .02$) higher on the cognitive subscale and marginally higher ($p < .08$) on the somatic subscale.

Clinical Use

The CSAQ has been effective in identifying persons who experience relative differences in cognitive and somatic anxiety. Norton and his coworkers (Norton & Johnson, 1983; Norton et al., 1985) further demonstrated that persons who primarily experience cognitive anxiety benefit more from relaxation training based on meditational procedures than those based on progressive muscle relaxation. Persons who experience somatic anxiety benefit more from progressive muscle relaxation than meditational procedures, however.

Future Directions

Future research should focus on the relationship between subscale scores on the CSAQ and clinical features of patients with different anxiety disorders. For example, recent evidence suggests that patients with panic disorder (PD) differ from those with generalized anxiety disorder because they experience more somatic symptoms. The CSAQ may help differentiate these disorders and others. In addition, the CSAQ may be useful in identifying which patients will benefit from different types of relaxation training procedures. For example, patients with panic disorders may benefit more from progressive muscle relaxation than would patients with generalized anxiety disorder. Finally, it is of interest why some persons show paradoxic anxiety reactions to relaxation training procedures. The CSAQ may help to identify these persons, and in doing so may help to identify some of the environmental factors associated with anxiety reactions.

References

Borkovec, T.D., Robinson, E., Pruzinsky, T., & DePree, J.A. (1983). Preliminary exploration of worry: Some characteristics and process. *Behaviour Research and Therapy, 21*, 9-16.

Davidson, R.J., & Schwartz, G.E. (1976). The psychobiology of relaxation and related states: A multi-process theory. In D.I. Mostofsky (Ed.), *Behavior control and modification of physiological activity* (pp. 399–442). Englewood Cliffs: Prentice-Hall.

Edwards, P.W., Zeichner, A., & Greene, P. (1984). Gender differences on the Cognitive-Somatic Anxiety Questionnaire. *Psychological Reports, 55*, 123-124.

Norton, G.R., & Johnson, W.E. (1983). A comparison of two relaxation procedures for reducing cognitive and somatic anxiety. *Journal of Behavior Therapy and Experimental Psychiatry, 14*, 209-214.

Norton, G.R., Rhodes, L., Hauch, J., & Kaprowy, E.A. (1985). Characteristics of subjects experiencing relaxation and relaxation induced anxiety. *Journal of Behavior Therapy and Experimental Psychiatry, 16*, 211–216.

Schwartz, G.E., Davidson, R.J., & Goleman, D.J. (1978). Patterning of cognitive and somatic processes in the self-regulation of anxiety: Effects of meditation and exercise. *Psychosomatic Medicine, 40*, 321-328.

Cold Pressor Test

Jeffrey J. Dolce and J. Kevin Thompson

Description

In its most basic format, the cold pressor test involves the submersion of some part of the body, usually the hand or hand/forearm, into a container of ice water. The apparatus may be any type of tank (standard ice chests are commonly used) that has been divided into two sections by a wire or plastic screen. The container is filled with water, and ice is placed in one side to cool the liquid. The hand is submerged in the ice-free section. During extended exposure, the water immediately surrounding the hand can be warmed by body temperature; therefore, it is necessary to circulate the water pump (as in an aquarium) to maintain a constant temperature during testing.

The hand or forearm, or both, may be placed in a sling or cradle with a mechanically operated timing device to facilitate procedural consistency. The authors have also had success with a simple instructional protocol, requiring subjects to submerge the forearm to the elbow joint and timing with a standard stopwatch. Interobserver agreement for this procedure ranges from .95 to .98. The instructions provided to the subject will vary, depending on the purpose of the research. Subjects may be asked to tolerate the water for "as long as possible" or a standard time interval may be used. Water temperature may also vary, given experimental design, from 0 to 18 degrees C (most researchers use 0 to 2 degrees C).

Purpose

The cold pressor test is used primarily in research on experimental pain induction and as an aversive stimulus for assessing psychological and physiological reactions to stress (Lovallo, 1975). It may be used to establish both pain thresholds and tolerance levels in laboratory settings. Verbal or visual analogue ratings of subjective pain intensity may be obtained during or after submersion. Cross modality matching procedures have also been used to assess clinical pain (Syrjala & Chapman, 1984).

Development

The physiologic impact of submerging various body parts into cold water has been well established (Kunkle, 1949; Lovallo, 1975; Wolfe &

Hardy, 1941). Exposure to water colder than 18 degrees C produces a continuous deep aching pain that is nonpulsatile (Wolfe & Hardy, 1941). This sensation is described as different from the experience of "cold" and has been labeled "cold pain." At colder temperatures the onset of cold pain occurs temporally earlier and the peak intensity is rated more intense. The peak intensity occurs after approximately 60 seconds of exposure to water colder than 18 degrees C. The deep aching pain that is felt at this time gradually subsides into the sensation of "pins and needles." Wolfe and Hardy (1941) noted that the intensity of "cold pain" does not vary as a function of the amount of tissue submerged (i.e., finger versus hand). The occurrence of a "second cold pain," similar in quality to initial "cold," has been reported after 10 minutes of submersion at a temperature below 5 degrees C (Kunkle, 1949). "Second cold pain" has been related to a reactive vasodilation response (Kunkle, 1949; Lovallo, 1975), whereas "cold pain" is associated with vasoconstriction in the skin (Wolfe & Hardy, 1941). Vasoconstriction, however, has not been determined to be the source of "cold pain" because pain may result from tissue damage or the release of metabolites (Kunkle, 1949).

A variety of psychophysiological changes occur during submersion. Exposure stimulates pain and temperature fibers, which ascend to cortical and subcortical regions, where the body's physiological responses are modulated to maintain homeostasis (Lovallo, 1975). The initial physiologic changes include increases in heart rate, skin conductance, pulse volume, respiration, and blood pressure (Lovallo, 1975), with a reduction in cutaneous temperature (Wolfe & Hardy, 1941). Skin conductance, respiration rate, and cutaneous temperature return to baseline during lengthy exposure, whereas the cardiovascular system displays a more prolonged response (Lovallo, 1975). Systolic and diastolic blood pressure increases 10 to 20 mm Hg following submersion. However, the elevation is only temporary, as baroreceptors function to restore homeostasis (Lovallo, 1975). Blood pressure elevations are proportional to the intensity of "cold pain" and water temperature (Wolfe & Hardy, 1941).

Psychometric Characteristics

Little research has emerged on psychometric properties of the cold pressor test. Most available data indicate that the procedure is highly reliable in individuals with intact sympathetic nervous systems. Persons with sympathectomy show an exaggerated pain response to the task (Wolfe & Hardy, 1941). Naturally occurring psychophysiologic properties (response stereotypy, individual response specificity, and law of initial values) have also been found with the cold pressor test (Lovallo, 1975). Social demand characteristics may similarly affect psychologic reactions and the perception of pain (Spanos, Hodgins, Stam, & Gwynn, 1984). Finally, sex effects have been inconsistently observed throughout investigations.

One of us (J.D.) noted a markedly skewed frequency distribution of pain tolerance in college students. These subjects were required to submerge the dominant hand in water at 2 degrees C for as long as possible. The subjects' tolerance to the task ranged from 14 to 480 seconds (experimentally imposed ceiling), with a mean of 46. The frequency distribution roughly paralleled the pain intensity curve plotted for water at 2 degrees C in Wolfe and Hardy's (1941) sample. It appeared that many subjects terminated exposure while pain was still increasing to its peak intensity. Subjects who persisted past the point of peak intensity where "cold pain" subsides were able to display greater tolerance durations. It is interesting that subjective pain ratings (0 to 10 scale) did not significantly correlate with pain tolerance times ($r = .07$). These results indicate that subjects may have terminated submersion because of factors other than their subjective pain experience, such as demand characteristics or coping expectancies.

Clinical Use

The cold pressor test has been used as a stressor in differentiating psychophysiologic responses in a variety of disorders, including hypertension, manic depression, anxiety disorders, and schizophrenia. Reliable differences between groups generally have not eventuated (Lovallo, 1975). The procedure has also been used to assess pain disorders for which cross-modality matching is used. Clients are asked to match a level of experimentally induced pain to their clinical pain. A maximum tolerance to experimental pain is also obtained, and a ratio of matched pain to pain tolerance is derived. Unfortunately, efforts to apply this ratio as a measure of clinical pain have not fared well (Syrjala & Chapman, 1984). In addition, the test can be employed as a practice stressor for biofeedback and pain coping skills training. The length of exposure and temperature may be varied to provide a graded series of stressful tasks to refine skills and build client confidence.

The cold pressor test appears to be a safe procedure for submersions of 8 to 10 minutes. Exposure times of 2 hours have been reported (Kunkle, 1949), but the potential for tissue damage increases substantially. Subjects with cardiovascular disease and peripheral circulatory system problems may be at higher risk for adverse reactions than are asymptomatic populations.

Future Directions

Research aimed at developing the cold pressor test as a training procedure for teaching pain coping skills is currently underway. Studies on cortical lateralization and dominant/nondominant hand submersion are also needed. More assessment of cross-modality matching to clinical pain problems is indicated. One promising avenue involves cross-modality matching of psychophysiologic data to descriptors rank ordered on scales of sensation, affect, and intensity (Syrjala & Chapman, 1984). Finally, the cardiovascular effects of the cold pressor test make it an excellent tool for research dealing with cardiovascular reactivity and the Type A behavior pattern.

References

Kunkle, E.C. (1949). Phasic pains induced by cold. *Journal of Applied Physiology, 1,* 811-824.

Lovallo, W. (1975). The cold pressor test and autonomic function: A review and integration. *Psychophysiology, 12,* 268-282.

Spanos, N.P., Hodgins, D.C., Stam, H.J., & Gwynn, M. (1984). Suffering for science: The effects of implicit social demands on responses to experimentally induced pain. *Journal of Personality and Social Psychology, 46,* 1162-1172.

Syrjala, K.L., & Chapman, C.R. (1984). Measurement of clinical pain: A review and integration of research findings. In C. Benedetti, C.R. Chapman, & G. Moricco (Eds.), *Advances in pain research and therapy: Vol.7.* (pp. 71-101). New York: Raven Press.

Wolfe, S., & Hardy, J.D. (1941). Studies on pain: Observations on pain due to local cooling and on factors involved in the cold pressor effect. *Journal of Clinical Investigations, 20,* 521-533.

College Self-Expression Scale

John P. Galassi and Merna Dee Galassi

Description

The College Self-Expression Scale (CSES) (Galassi, DeLo, Galassi, & Bastien, 1974) is a commonly used self-report measure of assertion, which was named a Citation Classic by *Current Contents* because of the frequency with which it has been cited in the social sciences literature. The inventory contains 50 items using a 5-point Likert format (0 to 4 scale). To minimize the possibility of a subject response set, 29 items are worded so that they require reverse scoring. (In the original article, it was incorrectly reported that item 47 should be reverse scored. Item 47 should *not* be reverse scored, e.g., 4 = 0, 3 = 1, etc.). Scores on the 50 items are summed to yield a total score, with higher total scores indicating more assertion. The items are concerned with three aspects of assertion: positive assertion, negative assertion, and self-denial. Positive assertion consists of expressing feelings of love, affection, admiration, approval, and agreement. Negative assertion involves expressing justified feelings of anger, disagreement, dissatisfaction, and annoyance, whereas self-denial includes overapologizing, excessive interpersonal anxiety, and exaggerated concern for the feelings of others. Scale items also are concerned with assertion with a variety of role occupants: strangers, authority figures, roommates, business relations, family and relatives, and same and opposite sex peers.

Purpose

The CSES was one of the earliest assertion self-report measures to be developed. It was designed as a standardized measure of a broad range of assertion behaviors in the population (college students) with which we were working at the time. The instrument was to serve both as a global measure of change following assertion training and as an assessment/screening tool to indicate specific areas and situations of deficient assertive behaviors for a given client.

Development

Development of the CSES was guided primarily by a population and situation-specific approach to assessment. Specifically, we wanted to construct an instrument that would incorporate a variety of assertion situations relevant to college students. The ability to act assertively was seen as being greatly influenced by the type of behavior to be expressed (e.g., love versus annoyance) and the situational context or person (e.g., parents or stranger). As a result, most items specify not only the behavior to be expressed but also the person or situational context. Some items were derived or modified from those provided by Lazarus and Wolpe, whereas others were written by our original research team.

Psychometric Characteristics

Considerable data about the psychometric characteristics, reliability, and validity of the CSES have accumulated. Many of those data and their references are contained in three sources that review the assertion literature more generally: Galassi, Galassi, and Vedder (1981), Galassi, Galassi, and Fulkerson (1984), and Galassi and Galassi (1978). The complete references for any citation mentioned in this section is contained in one of the three references just noted.

Galassi et al. (1974) reported test-retest reliability coefficients of 0.89 and 0.90 for two samples of students over a 2-week interval. Normative data for the CSES was collected on over 5000 students enrolled in college and university classes in West Virginia, North Carolina, and New York. Mean scores for the various groups typically fall in the 117 to 128 range, with standard deviations of 14 to 23.

A variety of construct validity data for the CSRS are available. In the original validational study, Galassi et al. (1974) predictably reported significant correlations between the CSES and selected scales of the Gough Adjective Check List (ACL). Moreover, Galassi et al. (1974) and Galassi and Galassi (1978) showed that the CSES shares little or no variance with such paper-and-pencil measures of aggression as the Buss Durkee Inventory and the aggression scale of the ACL.

The ability of the CSES to detect differences between intact groups that presumably differ in assertiveness was demonstrated in a study by Galassi and Galassi (1978). Students who sought personal adjustment counseling scored significantly lower (less assertive) on the CSES than did students who either did not seek counseling or sought only vocational-educational counseling.

The CSES was also shown to be significantly related to other self-report measures of assertiveness. Correlations between the CSES and Rathus Assertiveness Schedule (RAS) have ranged between .52 and .84 in six studies. A correlation of .72 was reported between the CSES and the Conflict Resolution Inventory and .59 between the CSES and the Gambrill-Richey Assertion Inventory.

Studies have also reported concurrent validity data for the CSES. Among these are low to moderate but significant correlations between self and supervising teacher ratings of assertion (Galassi et al., 1974) and between residence hall counselor and self-ratings of asssertion.

At least eight studies have provided data about the relationship between total and/or partial scores on the CSES and behavioral performance in laboratory or role-played situations. For example, Kirschner and Galassi (1983) reported that the role-play performance of high and low scores on the CSES was differentiated by a linear combination of three dependent variables (affect, content, and response duration) commonly used to measure assertion and by two of the variables (not response duration) separately. A previous study had shown that high and low assertive responses on the CSES were differentiated on a linear combination of four variables including content, eye contact, subjective anxiety, and response latency, with content and eye contact providing significant univariate results as well.

In addition to the studies just cited, the CSES has been widely used in assertion training and other counseling/psychotherapy outcome research (Galassi et al., 1981; Galassi et al., 1984; Galassi & Galassi, 1978). The measure has routinely been sensitive to change following therapeutic intervention.

The CSES has been the subject of several factor analytic investigations, including one study with Israeli subjects. The measure has routinely been shown to be multidimensional. For example, Galassi and Galassi (1979) factor analyzed the CSES using four samples of college students drawn from three different colleges and universities. The analyses yielded four to seven factors, which generally reflected the major behavioral dimensions (positive assertion, negative assertion, and self-affirmation) in accordance with which the CSES was constructed. The factor structure was relatively stable for men and women within the same population. Sex differences generally influenced the factor structure less than did population differences.

In a subsequent study, Galassi and Galassi (1980) compared the factor structure of the CSES with that of the Rathus Assertiveness Schedule (RAS) using a common population. The CSES contained several factors that the RAS did not. However, results from a combined analysis indicated that those factors provide the clinician with a more precise and situationally specific assessment of assertion than do the factors of either inventory alone.

Clinical Use

The CSES may be used clinically as a global screening measure of assertion deficits. We have found that students who seek personal adjustment counseling score about 1 standard deviation below the mean of the scale. As such, scores that are approximately 1 or more standard deviations below the CSES mean would suggest the need for a more thorough assessment concerning whether assertion training might benefit the client either as a primary intervention/focus of treatment or as a secondary or auxiliary focus.

In addition, inspection of individual item scores or factor scores can provide the clinician with information about specific situations in which a client is experiencing difficulty in being assertive. As will be recalled, the items on the CSES typically include references to both specific behaviors (e.g., expressing love and affection) and persons (e.g., members of the opposite sex). By inspecting low item scores (especially scores of 0 and 1), and then noting whether they tend to occur with particular behaviors or persons, or both, a clinician can begin to identify assertion troublespots for the client.

The CSES can also be used as a self-report measure to assess and monitor change and maintenance. The clinician can assess global change in assertion skills by noting changes in CSES total score. Suggestive indications of change in more restricted areas might also be assessed by noting changes in factor scores or scores on a group of items of interest.

Future Directions

Although we are currently not involved in further research and development of the CSES, research into the instrument's strengths and limitations continues to accumulate in the literature. One type of datum that is especially important to collect for both the CSES and other assertion instruments is how well scores on the CSES and on homogeneous clusters of its items or factors predict corresponding behavior in actual in vivo (in addition to role playing) situations.

References

Galassi, J.P., DeLo, J.S., Galassi, M.D., & Bastien, S. (1974). The College Self-Expression scale: A measure of assertiveness. *Behavior Therapy, 5*, 165-171.

Galassi, J.P., & Galassi, M.D. (1979). A comparison of the factor structure of an assertion scale across sex and population. *Behavior Therapy, 10*, 117-128.

Galassi, J.P., Galassi, M.D., & Fulkerson, K. (1984). Assertion training in theory and practice: An update. In C.M. Franks (Ed.), *New developments in practical behavior therapy: From research to clinical application* (pp. 319-376). New York: Haworth Press.

Galassi, J.P., Galassi, M.D., & Vedder, M.J. (1981). Perspective on assertion as a social skills model. In J.D. Wine & M.D. Smye (Eds.), *Social competence* (pp. 287-345). New York: Guilford Press.

Galassi, M.D., & Galassi, J.P. (1978). Assertion: A critical review. *Psychotherapy: Theory, Research and Practice, 15*, 16-29.

Galassi, M.D., & Galassi, J.P. (1980). Similarities and differences between two assertion measures: Factor analysis of the College Self-Expression Scale and the Rathus Assertiveness Schedule. *Behavioral Assessment, 2*, 43-47.

Kirschner, S,M., & Galassi, J.P. (1983). Person, situational, and interactional influences on assertive behavior. *Journal of Counseling Psychology, 30*, 355-360.

College Women's Assertion Sample

Marian L. MacDonald

Description

The College Women's Assertion Sample (CWAS) is a standardized role-play measure of assertion. The test includes 52 items, each of which describes an interpersonal encounter involving an infringement on one's rights. Test items and instructions are audiotaped and are presented aurally. Subjects, who are individually tested, respond by stating what they would say or do if they were actually experiencing each rights-infringement situation as they hear it. Responses are recorded verbatim by a trained examiner for later scoring.

Each CWAS item describes an interpersonal encounter representing one of six distinct types of rights-infringement situations: (a) encounters in which someone is placing an unwanted demand on the woman; (b) encounters in which the woman's felt needs are not being met; (c) encounters in which the woman has been insulted; (d) encounters in which someone is asking the woman for an inconvenient favor; (e) encounters with individuals who have been inconsiderate to the woman in the past; and (f) encounters in which someone is being inconsiderate to the woman in the present. Four of the 52 CWAS items describe rights-infringement situations that college women judge as morally warranting subjugation of the woman's rights for the benefit of another person; these items comprise a seventh scale, sensitivity to discriminating the appropriateness of assertion.

Responses to CWAS items are scored on the basis of a standardized content analytic procedure. Detailed scoring instructions are available by Mac-Donald (1978). In brief, scoring involves three phases. First, because responses with identical topographies can have markedly different impacts on different kinds of situations, one of the six distinct types of rights-infringement situations that provided the interpersonal context for the response is identified. Second, the critical topographic features of the response are identified. Finally, an empirically derived score is assigned to the response, as a joint function of the response's topography and its interpersonal/situational context. Scores for each situational context-response topography combination are reported by MacDonald (1975); these scores may be used for either ordinal or interval scaling.

Eight scores may be derived from the CWAS. The first is a global assertion score, representing a woman's mean score across all of the 48 rights-infringement situations judged as calling for assertion. Six situation type, or subscale, scores may also be derived, with each representing a woman's mean score across all of the situations warranting assertion within each distinct type of rights-infringement situation. Finally, a score reflecting a woman's ability to discriminate rights-infringement situations in which assertion is judged to be appropriate may be computed by calculating the difference between a woman's mean score across the four rights-infringement situations judged *not* to warrant assertion and her global assertion score.

Purpose

The CWAS was designed to measure assertion, defined as "the open expression of preferences, through words or actions, in a manner which causes others to take them into account; any act which serves to maintain one's rights" (MacDonald, 1975, p. 32). The instrument has four purposes: (a) to provide a good dependent variable for outcome research; (b) to provide a sensitive diagnostic and teaching tool for clinicians; (c) to provide a source of observational data for building theory about

social skills; and (d) to provide a carefully constructed, standardized role-play instrument for evaluating role-play assessment methodologies.

Development

The CWAS was developed through a series of some five studies involving more than 1,000 subjects (MacDonald, 1975, 1978). Test construction involved: (a) deriving a definition for the behavior construct of assertion; (b) generating an original item pool of situational items by asking women to record descriptions of situations they encountered in which "assertion was, or would have been, the most appropriate way to react;" (c) reducing the size of the original item pool by selecting items to retain on the basis of certain desirable test item properties (e.g., clarity, realism, and moderate difficulty level) as established through unidimensional ratings; (d) identifying clusters of distinct situation types marked by shared situational properties, as designated through a multidimensional scaling procedure; (e) eliciting response pools for each of the retained test items to demonstrate response variability and to identify response range; (f) isolating categories of topographically similar and presumably, therefore, functionally equivalent responses within each item's response pool; (g) designating scoring weights to assign to each response category within situation types, on the basis of unidimensional ratings; (h) fixing the test instructions, item order, and item presentation in a standardized audiotape format; and (i) evaluating the instrument's psychometric properties including structural fidelity, scorer and temporal reliability, and convergent and discriminant (i.e., construct) validity through cross-validation.

Psychometric Characteristics

Structural properties of the CWAS have repeatedly conformed to what would be expected on the basis of a situational specificity notion of assertion. Factor analyses typically yield at least four independent dimensions. Corrected item-total correlations within scales are typically significantly greater than corrected item-total correlations with the global CWAS score, and mean scores across the four rights-infringement situations judged *not* to warrant assertion are typically significantly lower than CWAS global scores. Interrater agreement, generally reported as better than 90%, has ranged from 96 to 81%. The CWAS global scores (i.e., overall means) have fallen between 4.53 and 5.56, with standard deviations ranging from .33 to .58. (*Note.* The CWAS scores can range from 1.00 to 9.00.) Mean scores on the four rights-infringement situations judged as *not* warranting assertion have ranged from 6.30 to 6.67 (*SD* range, .85 to .95).

Test-retest reliability coefficients were reported as .85 over 1 week, .84 over 4 weeks, and .57 over 2.5 months. The CWAS scores were repeatedly found to correlate significantly with a variety of self-report assertion measures such as the Conflict Resolution Inventory, the College Self-Expression Scale, and the Rathus Assertiveness Schedule, and to be independent of self-report and observational measures of anxiety and self-report measures of social desirability.

Further evidence of construct validity has been reported. The CWAS scores correlated significantly with relevant scales from carefully constructed personality measures such as the Personality Research Form and with global self-ratings of assertion. The CWAS scores evidenced significant correlations with masculine sex-role endorsement, as assessed by the Bem Sex-Role Inventory. Moreover, CWAS scores correlated significantly and in predicted directions with measures of cognitive complexity. For additional details on CWAS psychometric properties, the reader should refer to the following: Bruch, Heisler, and Conroy (1981); Kern and MacDonald (1980); Macdonald (1975, 1978); MacDonald and Tyson (1984); and Nix, Lohr, and Mosesso (1984).

Clinical Use

The CWAS has three primary clinical applications. First, it is useful as a diagnostic aid, particularly when it is suspected that a college female client may be behaving unassertively in only a restricted range of rights-infringement situations, or when it is suspected that a college female client may be insensitive to those occasions when assertion is regarded as inappropriate despite rights infringement. Second, the CWAS is useful as a training device, because the scoring manual identifies properties of appropriate responses and the instrument itself presents 52 situations that can be used for behavior rehearsal. Finally, the CWAS provides a good index of the effectiveness of a therapeutic intervention.

Future Directions

The growing mutual fascination between clinical psychologists and researchers in communication studies and information processing implies a particularly important role for assessment devices that require subjects to generate their own responses, which are later content analyzed (see especially Bruch et al., 1981); future research with the CWAS may well exploit this interface.

For quick assessments in which only a global assertion score is of interest, a shorter version of the CWAS would be most useful. A promising short-form of the original CWAS, developed as an experimental measure, will generally be available as soon as its psychometric properties have been confirmed through cross-validation. A special version of the experimental short form, adapted so as to be appropriate for older business and professional rather than college women samples, is currently under development.

The CWASs standardized format is quite robust: when the procedure as specified is followed, there are no significant effects of examiner gender or comport (i.e., professional versus casual). Anecdotal accounts indicate that it may be useful under certain circumstances (i.e., when large numbers of individuals must be tested with limited resources) to instruct subjects to write rather than verbalize their own responses. Although this departure from standard procedure does transform the test from a direct observational to a self-observational, or perhaps even self-report, one, it has the advantage of allowing group test administration.

References

Bruch, M.A., Heisler, B.D., & Conroy, C.G. (1981). Effects of conceptual complexity on assertive behavior. *Journal of Counseling Psychology, 28,* 377-385.

Kern, J.M., & MacDonald, M.L. (1980). Assessing assertion: An investigation of construct validity and reliability. *Journal of Consulting and Clinical Psychology, 48,* 532-534.

MacDonald, M.L. (1975). A behavioral assessment methodology applied to the measurement of assertion. *Dissertation Abstract International, 35,* 6101B. (University Microfilms No. 75-11, 819.)

MacDonald, M.L. (1978). Measuring assertion: A model and method. *Behavior Therapy, 9,* 889-899.

MacDonald, M.L., & Tyson, P.A. (1984). The College Women's Assertion Sample (CWAS): A cross-validation. *Journal of Educational and Psychological Measurement, 44,* 405-412.

Nix, J., Lohr, J.M., & Mosesso, L. (1984). The relationship of sex-role characteristics to self-report and role-play measures of assertiveness in women. *Behavioral Assessment, 6,* 89-93.

Combat Exposure Scale

David W. Foy and Kim T. Mueser

Description

The Combat Exposure Scale (CES) is an interview-based assessment designed to measure the extent of combat involvement experienced by an individual who has served in the military forces in the Vietnam era (1965 to 1975). The scale consists of seven items, ranging from "stationed in Vietnam" (score = 1) to "served third tour of duty in Vietnam" (score = 7). Individuals are assigned a combat exposure score based on their highest scale score, following a Guttman scalogram procedure.

Purpose

The CES assesses the degree of combat exposure a person has had in order to determine the possible role of traumatic war experiences in the development of combat-related Posttraumatic Stress Disorder (PTSD). A second purpose is to obtain clinically relevant information about the nature of an individual's traumatic experiences to facilitate treatment planning for that person. The use of a Guttman scale (assigning the highest scale score) to assess perceived trauma is designed to reduce the effect of post hoc reporting bias to which additive rating scales are susceptible.

Development

Subjects participating in the development of the scale were 43 Vietnam-era veterans applying for psychiatric services at a Veterans Administration Medical Center in Southern California. Individuals with primary psychotic or substance abuse diagnoses were not included in the sample. A detailed structured interview was used to elicit information about the individual's premilitary, military, and postmilitary history. Included in the military history section were 13 specific questions about the individual's participation in stressful combat-related activities. The questions were cast so that the responses could be dichotomously categorized. Content of the combat-related stressors was derived from clinical experience and by asking combat veterans to identify potentially stressful events for such a scale. A more detailed description of the procedures used in the development of the scale are available elsewhere (Foy, Sipprelle, Rueger, & Carroll, 1984; Lund, Foy, Sipprelle, & Strachan, 1984).

Psychometric Characteristics

Two indicators specific to Guttman scaling were calculated. First, reliability was assessed by a coefficient of reproducibility, which is a measure of correspondence between the ideal response pattern and the actual response patterns obtained. The CES coefficient of reproducibility was .93, which indicated that 93% of the cases used fit the ideal patterning of responses. This result exceeds the accepted standard of .90 for an indication of a reliable Guttman scale. A second indicator calculated was a coefficient of scalability, an indication of the scale's construct validity. The coefficient obtained was .76, which exceeds the standard of .60 as an indication of unidimensionality and the scale's cumulative nature.

A principal components factor analysis with a varimax rotation also indicated that the scale items loaded on a single factor, which accounted for 79% of the variance (Carroll, Rueger, Foy, & Donahoe, 1985). Criterion-related validity of the scale has been assessed by examining the correlation between the subject's PTSD intensity scores and the CES scores. Correlations in the .30 to .40 range were obtained (Foy et al., 1984).

Cross-validation of self-report military history data elicited in the CES showed correspondence with the discharge papers in over 80% of the cases examined (Carroll et al., 1985). Therefore, it appears that combat veterans give valid reports of the experiences assessed in the scale.

Clinical Use

Assessment of possible combat-related psychological sequelae is complicated in Vietnam veterans by the fact that the traumatic stressors were actually experienced over 10 years ago. This time gap makes it essential for the clinician or researcher to inquire directly about specific combat stressors that the individual may have experienced, rather than to treat combat exposure as a dichotomous variable with nonspecific dimensions. In our experience the probability of serious psychological sequelae (i.e., diagnosable PTSD) is highest in combat veterans who have been wounded. This experience produces a score of 5 on the CES. Below this score the probability of a positive PTSD diagnosis is less than 50% in a psychiatric help-seeking population.

Knowing the risk category that a particular individual belongs to by virtue of his CES score can be helpful to the mental health professional responsible for conducting clinical screening interviews. In many cases, individuals who have been traumatized by exposure to a severe stressor do not know that their discomfort is related to that experience. Therefore, the intake professional must "ask the right questions" to determine the probable relationship between presenting symptoms and probable antecedents. Information obtained on the CES can be used as a "foot in the door" to obtain more detailed information about the particular stressors that the individual experienced. The clinician can assess this material with the CES, which serves as an important beginning basis of therapy.

Future Directions

Although the apparent successful Guttman scaling of the CES suggests that stress leading to combat-related PTSD may be cumulative, this is by no means the final word in the matter. Neither is it clear that the apparent relationship between cumulative stress and the development of PTSD found in combat-related PTSD will be found in other kinds of trauma (e.g., natural disasters, transportation accidents, and criminal assaults). One future line of inquiry would be to use a similar Guttman scaling approach with other kinds of trauma exposure. Other work stemming from the CES could include the use of the instrument with a combat-exposed population that has not yet been thoroughly studied, such as non-help-seekers, those seeking help for physical problems only, and veterans of wars other than the Vietnam conflict.

Perhaps the primary contribution of the work in which the CES was developed is to cast trauma exposure as a continuous variable. Moving conceptually from issues of whether a trauma was experienced to operationalizing how much exposure and to what specific events seems to have been a major step forward. It may be that similar steps can be taken in the study of other types of trauma.

References

Carroll, E.M., Rueger, D.B., Foy, D.W., & Donahoe, C.P. (1985). Vietnam combat veterans with posttraumatic stress disorder: Analysis of marital and cohabitating ajustment. *Journal of Abnormal Psychology, 94,* 329-337.

Foy, D.W., Sipprelle, R.C., Rueger, D.B., & Carroll, E.M. (1984). Etiology of posttraumatic stress disorder in Vietnam veterans: Analysis of premilitary, military, and combat exposure influences. *Journal of Consulting and Clinical Psychology, 52,* 79-87.

Lund, M., Foy, D.W., Sipprelle, R.C., & Strachan, A. (1984). The Combat Exposure Scale: A systematic assessment of trauma in the Vietnam War. *Journal of Clinical Psychology, 40,* 1323-1328.

Communication Satisfaction Questionnaire

Kathy Sexton-Radek and Stephen N. Haynes

Description

The Communication Satisfaction Questionnaire (CSQ) is a scale measuring each spouse's satisfaction with marital communication during discussions or disagreements. The initial scale consisted of four items: (a) satisfaction with frequency of conversations, (b) compliments exchanged, (c) how disagreements are expressed, and (d) being listened to. Additional items have been added. Responses are indicated on a 10–point scale (1 = extremely satisfied, 10 = extremely dissatisfied).

Purpose

The purpose of the CSQ is to measure satisfaction with marital (dyadic) communication during discussions or disagreements.

Development

The scale was developed as part of the Marital Attitudes Questionnaire to measure various aspects of satisfaction with marital communication. Initial items reflected dimensions of communication reported by couples in pilot assessments and items included in other questionnaires. Items were added later as a function of additional data derived from assessment research.

Psychometric Characteristics

On a sample of 60 married subjects, internal consistency (Chronbach's alpha) was found to be $r =$ .90 (Phillips & Haynes, 1985). On the same sample, communication satisfaction was significantly correlated with the Dyadic Adjustment Scale ($r = .50$, $p < .01$) and with the Marital Satisfaction Inventory ($r = .35$, $p < .02$). On a sample of 360 married individuals (Haynes, Chavez, & Samule, 1984), the

CSQ was significantly correlated with the Spouse Verbal Problems Checklist ($r = -.59$, $p <.001$), with the Dyadic Adjustment Scale ($r - .74$, $p <.001$), and with negative behaviors emitted in an analogue communication situation ($r = -.15$, $p <.05$).

Clinical Use

The scale is useful in clinical and research situations in which dyadic communication satisfaction is an important dependent or independent variable, as in cases of marital distress or dyadic social skill difficulties. It can be used to measure therapy outcome and to identify problem areas in dyadic communication.

Future Directions

The questionnaire is currently in use in the assessment of other populations (i.e., outpatient adults) in which dyadic communication may be problematic.

References

Haynes, S.N., Chavez, R.E., & Samule, V. (1984). Assessment of marital communication and distress. *Behavioral Assessment, 6,* 315-321.

Phillips, J., & Haynes, S.N. (1985). Assessment of maritally distressed individual outpatients. Unpublished manuscript.

Communications Skills Assessment for the Mentally Ill Elderly

Roger L. Patterson

Description

This behavior rating scale consists of seven items. Three verbal behaviors (content, loudness, and voice feeling quality) and three nonverbal behaviors (facial expression, which includes eye-contact; body position; and gestures) are each rated on a 6-point scale. Also included is an overall rating of effectiveness. The ratings range from 1, indicating a behavior that is extremely inadequate or inappropriate, through 6, indicating full attainment of the appropriate target behavior.

Purpose

The scale was developed for use in conjunction with a simplified, basic social skills training program designed to overcome apathy, passivity, and/or complaining behavior of ambulatory elderly clients of a mental health treatment program. It is used to assess initial deficits, progress during training sessions, and outcome (Patterson et al., 1982).

Development

The social skills assessment developed by Liberman, King, DeRisi, and McCann (1975) served as an initial model. The Communications Scale is simpler than the earlier scale and uses a different scoring system.

Psychometric Characteristics

Interobserver reliability was determined by having four raters simultaneously rate videotapes of 21 clients role-playing scenes in which they enacted positive and negative assertion. The mean correlation between the six pairings of these ratings (total scores; correlation converted to Fisher's Z scores) was $r = 0.88$ (range 0.82 to 0.92). A minimal estimation of test-retest reliability was obtained by correlating total scores before and after 4 weeks of social skills training. This correlation for a group of 76 subjects was substantial ($r = 0.60$).

Patterson, Eberly, Harrell, and Penner (1983) validated the communications assessment using the multitrait, multimethod matrix of Campbell and Fiske (1959). It was found that the Communications Assessment correlated ($r = 0.41$) with the Social Competence subscale of the Nurse's Observation Scale for Inpatient Evaluation (NOSIE-30; Honigfeld, Gillis, & Klett, 1966). The Communications Assessment generally met most of the criteria for convergent and discriminant validity established by Campbell and Fiske.

Clinical Use

The target population consists of ambulatory, elderly mental health clients, including residential, day-treatment, and outpatients, who have difficulty expressing themselves. Patterson et al. (1982) have used the scale in conjunction with training such persons to express themselves in two major situations: (a) expressing affection or gratitude, or both, to others; and (b) expressing displeasure to others, along with requests for behavior change.

The assessment is used during training to provide information both to group leaders and to the trainee clients. A useful application is to have a large replica of the assessment located on the wall of the training room, easily visible and accessible to all. The trainee can obtain effective feedback by charting his or her own deficiencies and progress toward overcoming them by moving cardboard or magnetic markers according to the ratings given by the official rater.

Future Directions

Patterson et al. (1982) reported experimental and quasiexperimental program evaluation data indicating the usefulness of the assessment and the training associated with this scale in relatively simple social situations. It would be very useful if such an easily used and comprehended assessment could be applied to more complex, real-time social situations found in the residences and community living situations of the elderly. Specific deficits (e.g., insufficient volume and poor speech content) in such situations could be identified, and progress toward eliminating them could be reliably assessed.

References

Campbell, D.T., & Fiske, D.W. (1959). Convergent and discriminant validation by the multitrait-multimethod matrix. *Psychological Bulletin, 56,* 81-105.

Honigfeld, G., Gillis, R.D., & Klett, C.J. (1966). The nurses' observation scale for inpatient evaluation. *Journal of Consulting Psychology, 21,* 69-77.

Liberman, R.P., King, L.W., DeRisi, W.J., & McCann, M. (1975). *Personal effectiveness.* Champaign, IL: Research Press.

Patterson, R.L., Dupree, L.W., Eberly, D.A., Jackson, G.M., O'Sullivan, M.J., Penner, L.A., & Dee-Kelley, C. (1982). *Overcoming deficits of aging: A behavioral treatment approach.* New York: Plenum Press.

Patterson, R.L., Eberly, D.A., Harrell, T.L., & Penner, L.A. (1983). Behavioral assessment of intellectual competence, communication skills, and personal hygiene skills of elderly persons. *Behavioral Assessment, 5,* 207-218.

Community Interaction Checklist

M. Angeles Cerezo

Description

The Community Interaction Checklist (CIC), devised by Wahler, Leske, and Rogers (1979) is an interview format checklist for parents of behaviorally disordered children. The CIC requires parents to specify the quantity and quality of their social and extrafamily contact patterns with adults during a preceding 24-hour time frame. Every social contact reported is specified in terms of its interactor, initiator, location, duration, topic, and presence and absence of criticism between the interacting parties. The valence of each interchange is assigned according to a 7-point scale, which may be scored from -3 (aversive) to $+3$ (pleasant). A similar rating for the overall day is obtained as well.

This multiple category instrument has two parts. One is designed to check the adults' social contacts in the community, and the other is aimed at gathering information about spousal (or significant other) interactions.

The checklist is administered at home to both parents in separate interviews, each usually taking no longer than 15 minutes. The procedure is simple; each parent is asked to recall all community contacts and spousal contacts during the last 24 hours within the framework of several of the aforementioned categories.

Purpose

The main purpose of the CIC is to classify the mother (or other primary caretaker) of conduct-disordered children who have been referred for treatment as "insular" or "noninsular."

Several studies report the role of "insularity" as a relevant predictor in the maintenance of behavioral parent training benefits (Wahler, 1980; Wahler & Graves, 1983; Webster-Stratton, 1985). Insular mothers are relatively isolated in their communities, and a high proportion of their interactions tend to be coercive in nature.

A parent's social status derived from the CIC has led to socially and scientifically relevant findings in the study of deviant parent–child interactions. The use of the CIC implies a way of considering the social setting (i.e., the extrafamily environment) in which child caretaking interactions take place. As the results show, the mother–child exchanges can be better understood when their community contacts are assessed at the same time (Wahler & Dumas, in press).

Development

Wahler and colleagues found in their work contacts with clinic referrals that the mothers of conduct-disordered children who did not profit from parent training differed in their adult interpersonal problems from those who did show sustained changes. That is, the former mothers reported more instances of coercive adult contacts than did the latter parents.

Such initial findings led these researchers to study the community social contacts reported by mothers who were considered "failure cases" versus "success cases." Through informal interviews, the two sets of mothers evidenced different views on interpersonal problems related to child rearing. Therefore, although all the mothers reported similar problems at home (not only with the target child but also with other family members), they presented a different picture of their social community contacts. The failure cases reported few social contacts and viewed most of these as negative in valence. Additionally, these isolated mothers were generally from low socioeconomic levels.

The CIC was developed over a period of more than 1 year as an attempt to quantify the differences seeming to characterize the mothers who dropped out of parent training programs or failed to maintain their therapeutic changes. The data from the CIC largely verified those interview impressions. Mothers from middle income families report higher frequencies of contacts, usually with friends, and rate them as gratifying. The isolated mothers, however, rate their limited community contacts, usually with "kinsfolk" or "helping agency representatives," as aversive experiences or neutral in valence.

The first pool of data obtained through CIC was reported by Wahler et al. (1979). However, the instrument has been administered routinely with the families of aggressive children referred to the Child Behavior Institute since 1976.

Psychometric Characteristics

Because the CIC was primarily aimed at assessing the clinically relevant variable, "insularity," the reliability issue was oriented to test the stability or temporal consistency of "insularity" scores. Clinical and research experience led the CBI investigators to specify a mother's insular status as based on one of two criteria: (a) to report at least twice as many of her daily contacts with kinsfolk and/or helping agency representatives as with friends, and (b) to report one third or more of her contacts as neutral or negative (score of 0 to − 3).

Dumas and Wahler (1983) evaluated the reliability of CIC on two samples of mothers with oppositional children. Forty-nine mothers were the subjects of the original study and 18 participated in a replication study. All families were either self- or other-referred for psychological help with their conduct-disordered children. In the original study, the mother's mean age was 29.45 years ($SD = 4.46$) and 88% were white and 12% black. The children (25% female) ranged in age from 14 months to 12 years ($M = 6.55$; $SD = 2.42$). The statistics for mothers in the replication study were similar in that the age mean was 29.32 years ($SD = 4.32$), and 94% were white and 6% black. The children (25% female) ranged in age from 2 to 11 years ($M = 6.44$; $SD = 2.38$). The reliability of the CIC was evaluated by computing the intraclass correlation coefficient as an index of internal consistency. The checklist was administered on five occasions to each mother during baseline phase. After applying the insularity decision criteria just described, each occasion received either a noninsular or an insular score. The resulting data matrix was subjected to repeated analysis of variance. Therefore, the reliability of the insularity index was .81 F (48, 196) = 5.38, p <.0001 in the larger sample and .79, F (17, 72) = 4.83, p <.001 in the smaller group.

In another study by Wahler and Dumas (1983), the same index of insularity reached a reliability in terms of an intraclass correlation coefficient of .94, F (5, 48) = 15.63, p <.001. The measure was based on nine checklists administered across different phases of treatment to six mothers who participated in the study. As the authors pointed out, "since no direct intervention efforts were aimed at changing their maternal contact patterns, they were expected to remain stable throughout the study" (p. 23). According to the data, the insularity index that can be obtained from CIC tends to be a very stable measure.

The initial study involving the CIC (Wahler et al., 1979) reported dramatic differences in the daily rates of social contacts and content features of those community interchanges between so-called low-risk (parent training successes) and high-risk (parent training failures) mothers. In fact, the daily contact rate averaged 9.5 versus 2.6, respectively. Seventy-one percent were self-initiated contacts by low-risk mothers versus 38% by high-risk mothers. The identity of interactors differed markedly from one group to another. The low-risk mothers primarily reported contact with friends rather than helping agency representatives or relatives outside their nuclear families. However, the high-risk mothers presented exactly the opposite picture. Finally, the community contacts of high-risk mothers were judged to be more aversive than those experienced by low-risk mothers.

Supporting data were presented for the scores derived from the CIC as a predictor of mother's inconsistency in responding to her child's demand and prosocial behavior. Applying the insularity decision rules just mentioned, a clinic-referred sample of 52 mothers was divided in two groups, 21 noninsular and 31 insular. As expected by the authors' theoretic arguments, the insular mothers were more likely to respond adversely to any child behavior than were their noninsular counterparts. These findings show that the scores of insularity are significantly related to indiscriminate caretaking displayed by the mothers of aggressive-oppositional children.

Clinical Use

The insularity index obtained from CIC scores is a significant predictor of treatment outcome in families with oppositional children. In fact, Dumas and Wahler (1983) reported that a two-variable model derived from the results of an initial stepwise discriminant analysis model with seven socioeconomic measures and insularity as independent variables accounted for 49% of the variance in the two independent studies ($R2 = .492$, $F (2,46) = 22.23$, $p <.001$; $R2 = .490$, $F (2, 15) = 7.20$, $p <.01$). The model correctly classified 40 of the 49 families (82%) in the second group. It should be pointed out that each variable contributed a significant amount of unique variance, particularly the insularity index which accounted for 16% of the variance ($p <.0005$) in study 1 and 20% of the unique variance ($p <.05$) in study 2. One other study has obtained similar results (Webster-Stratton, 1985).

The practical implications of these findings in the clinical use of CIC lead us to recommend the instrument for diagnostic and prognostic purposes. Its usefulness may be improved when other ecological variables, such as social disadvantage, are considered as well.

As a diagnostic aid, the level of a troubled mother's community isolation and coercive patterns of social interaction should guide the therapist in devising the most appropriate treatment. Specifically, parent training as a singular form of therapy with insular disadvantaged families not only is insufficient for most of them, but also may become another aversive experience to be avoided

(by dropping out) or merely tolerated. Supplementary therapeutic efforts addressing the larger social interaction problem must also be implemented.

In conclusion, the CIC is appropriate for mothers and primary caretakers who seek help for child oppositional behavior. It also may be administered across treatment and follow-up phases to guide the clinician.

Future Directions

As long as use of the CIC is widespread, new data can be added and contrasted to those already existing. However, some further research steps are needed as follows: (a) The spousal and other caretaker reports on the number, topic, and valences of mutual interchanges within the family should be studied, because most multidistressed mothers (insular disadvantaged mothers) represent single-parent families. (b) The treatment validity of the CIC should be examined. This form of validity concerns the potential contribution of the measure to improved outcome in therapy. It can be tested by comparing the effectiveness of two intervention programs identical in every way except that one includes CIC reported data whereas the other does not.

References

Dumas, J.E., & Wahler, R.G. (1983). Predictors of treatment outcome in parent training: Mother insularity and socioeconomic disadvantaged. *Behavioral Assessment, 5,* 301-313.

Dumas, J.E., & Wahler, R.G. (1985). Indiscriminate mothering as a contextual factor in aggressive-oppositional child behavior: "Damned if you do and damned if you don't." *Journal of Abnormal Child Psychology, 13,* 1-17.

Wahler, R.G. (1980). The insular mother: Her problems in parent-child treatment. *Journal of Applied Behavior Analysis, 13,* 207-219.

Wahler, R.G., & Dumas, J.E. (1983). *Stimulus class determinants of mother-child coercive interchanges in multidistressed families: Assessment and intervention.* Paper presented at the Vermont Conference on the Primary Prevention of Psychopathology. Bolton Valley Winter/Summer Resort, Vermont, June.

Wahler, R.G., & Graves, M.G. (1983). Setting events in social networks: Ally or enemy in child behavior therapy? *Behavior Therapy, 16,* 19-36.

Wahler, R.G., Leske, G., & Rogers, E.S. (1979). The insular family: A deviance support system for oppositional children. In L.A. Hamerlynck (Ed.), *Behavioral systems for the developmentally disabled: I. School and family environments.* New York: Brunner/Mazel.

Webster-Stratton, C. (1985). Predictors of treatment outcome in parent training for conduct disordered children. *Behavior Therapy, 16,* 223-243.

Community Members' Rating Scale

Arthur L. Robin and William Canter

Description

The Community Members' Rating Scale (CMRS) consists of 24 seven-point Likert items tapping global impressions of parent–adolescent audiotaped interactions. The items assess the degree of conflict, effectiveness of problem solving, positiveness of communication, and the degree to which 21 specific problem-solving or communication habits characterize an audiotaped interaction. These include: accepting responsibility, agreement, approval, assent, command, complaint, compromise, denying responsibility, disagreement, evaluation, humor, interruption, laughter, negative solution, no response, positive solution, problem description, put down, question, specification of the problem, and talk. Brief, written definitions accompany each item. Several coders rate each audiotaped interaction, and the mean of their ratings on each item serves as the measure of parent-adolescent relations.

Purpose

The CMRS is designed to provide global-impressionistic ratings of general conflict, problem solving, and communication as well as specific aspects of problem solving and communication. Clinicians and researchers can employ the CMRS as a parsimonious, cost-efficient alternative to detailed frequency–based codes in situations in which subjective summary impressions of parent-adolescent relations provide sufficient information for assessment and treatment planning.

Development

The 23 categories of the Modified Marital Interaction Coding System (MICS), a frequency-based microscopic code classifying every utterance into mutually exclusive categories (Robin & Weiss, 1980), were translated into 7-point Likert ratings with brief definitions. Two categories (compliance and noncompliance) were omitted because of near-zero frequencies in normative data. Three global categories (conflict, problem solving, and communication) were added.

Psychometric Characteristics

The reliability and validity data on the CMRS were derived from the Robin and Canter (1984) comparison of the CMRS and Modified MICS. Four groups of untrained community members (15 mothers, fathers, and adolescents, and 13 mental health professionals) rated 16 audiotaped discussions of mothers and sons resolving specific disputes collected in an earlier investigation (Robin & Weiss, 1980). Eight dyads were in treatment for relationship problems (distressed) whereas eight were satisfied with their relationships and were not in treatment (nondistressed). All of the tapes were also coded with the Modified MICS.

Because the mean of a group of raters is the dependent measure, reliability of each mean score is computed by: (a) computing the average interrater correlation for all possible pairs of raters, and (b) correcting the average interrater correlations with the Spearman–Brown formula to estimate reliability with multiple raters (Prinz & Kent, 1978; Wiggins, 1973). Reliability exceeded .90 on all of the ratings of conflict, communication, and problem solving, but it was considerably more variable on the specific items. Of the reliability coefficients, 19% fell below .70. Ratings of evaluation, negative solution, problem description, question, specification of the problem, and talk evidenced the poorest reliability.

Assessment of discriminant validity revealed that distressed dyads received significantly higher scores than did nondistressed dyads on composite scores of conflict, communication, and problem solving as well as a composite of the more specific ratings. The pattern of significant differences was similar across the four groups of raters whose mean scores were intercorrelated strongly (mean $r = .93$).

Evidence for the construct validity of the CMRS emerged from correlations with the Modified MICS. Conflict, communication, and problem-solving scores on the CMRS correlated .81, .89, and .90 with a composite problem-solving communication score on the Modified MICS. There were moderate relationships (mean $r = .61$) between composite CMRS scores and MICS scores for 10 categories: agreement, assent, command, compromise, disagreement, denying responsibility, interruption, laughter, put-down, and question.

Clinical Use

The clinician can use the CMRS to obtain a rough, subjective impression of the overall degree of conflict, communication, and problem-solving deficits, as well as some useful suggestions about which specific aspects of communication and problem solving to examine further. It is generally appropriate for coding audiotaped interactions when the task has been to resolve a conflict or discuss an issue of disagreement. If a detailed frequency-based analysis of the occurrence of specific positive or negative behaviors is required, the Modified MICS or Parent Adolescent Interaction Coding System (Robin & Fox, 1979) should be used instead of the CMRS. Because the reliability and validity of the CMRS were obtained from the mean scores of groups of 13 to 15 coders, it cannot be assumed that the results would be comparable with a single clinician as the coder. Therefore, the clinician must gather a group of colleagues to obtain psychometrically sound data with the CMRS.

Future Directions

The reliability, discriminant, criterion-related, and construct validity of the CMRS need to be replicated because there has only been a single study using this system. Furthermore, its ability to identify behaviors that, if changed, lead to improved parent–adolescent relations needs to be established. Finally, even though the families and professionals who coded tapes with the CMRS to date have shown a high degree of correspondence in their perceptions, future studies need to establish parametrically the effects of using different groups of coders with global-impressionistic systems such as the CMRS.

References

Prinz, R.J., & Kent, R. (1978). Recording parent–adolescent interactions without the use of frequency or interval-by-interval coding. *Behavior Therapy, 9*, 602-604.

Robin, A.L., & Canter, W. (1984). A comparison of the Marital Interaction Coding System and community ratings for assessing mother–adolescent problem solving. *Behavioral Assessment, 6,* 303-313.

Robin, A.L., & Fox, M. (1979). *The parent-adolescent interaction coding system: Coding Manual.* Unpublished manuscript: University of Maryland Baltimore County.

Robin, A.L., & Weiss, J. (1980). Criterion-related validity of behavioral and self-report measures of problem-solving communication skills in distressed and nondistressed parent–adolescent dyads. *Behavioral Assessment, 2,* 339-352.

Wiggins, J.S. (1973). *Personality and prediction: Principles of personality assessment.* Reading, MA: Addison-Wesley.

Compliance Measures

Glen A. Martin

Description

A measure of compliance is any technique used to determine the extent to which a client has carried out a task assigned in counseling. Measures of compliance are as diverse as the tasks therapists devise and assign to their clients. They may be grouped into the following categories: self-report, observation by others, mechanical or electronic device, clinical outcome, permanent product, and interview (Dunbar, 1979; Shelton & Levy, 1981).

Self-report measures rely on the client to accurately record the extent of compliance with an assignment. Often this is an extension of the behavioral assessment, that is, the initial assessment indicated that some behaviors were occurring too frequently, at inappropriate times, or in an unskilled manner. The assignment, after appropriate training, is to correct the error. Self-monitoring continues as during the baseline assessment period but with a different goal: that of monitoring behavior change rather than assessing the presenting problem. Examples of self-report procedures include diary entries in which the client records not only whether the assignment is completed, but also the attitudes, emotions, and thoughts surrounding completion of the assignment for discussion in the next session. Another type of self-report compliance measure is a checklist that includes an assignment for each day that simply needs to be checked off on completion. Checklists have an advantage over diary entries in that they require less effort to complete, increasing the accuracy of the record and the likelihood that it will be kept up to date, but at the cost of information such as the immediate subjective impressions of the client as the assignment is completed. If the assignment is to study 60 minutes each day, talk with two strangers per day, be assertive once before the next session, and the like, a simple frequency count might be an adequate compliance measure. With more subjective assignments, such as monitoring thoughts and feelings during assertive interactions, a diary entry may be a more appropriate compliance measure.

Compliance may be assessed by others who directly observe the client. This procedure may be particularly appropriate with clients who would be poor self-observers, such as children. It is also often used in marital and family counseling. Family members may be used to observe the extent to which other family members comply with the therapeutic directives. The advantages of having others rate compliance include relieving the client of the chore of self-recording and increasing the likelihood of compliance by adding social pressure to comply. However, just as accuracy is a concern with self-monitoring, accuracy of observation remains a problem when others are used as observers. Some tasks are not readily assessed by outside observers either because the tasks are not likely to be performed in their presence or because the tasks cannot be seen by others. For example, assignments to increase positive self-thoughts would be difficult for someone other than the client to monitor. Observation by others may be a particularly reactive method of assessing compliance. In one case study, a client's spouse recorded the number of minutes the client worked on his dissertation each day. The client came to resent his spouse when work on the dissertation did not go well. In another case, a child whose assignment was to decrease the number of obscenities uttered daily actually increased the number of obscenities. This apparently was his reaction to the involuntary nature of the assignment, the method of assessing compliance, and the punishing consequences of not complying with the assignment. These examples suggest that when this method of assessing compliance is used, both the assignment and the observer should be chosen with care.

Some compliance measures use mechanical or electronic devices. For more accurate frequency counts, clients can use golf-counters or beaded wrist bands. Cognitive-behavioral assignments might make use of a portable tape recorder to record in vivo reactions to new coping self-statements. Portable blood pressure monitors might be used to assess the degree to which a client is practicing coping strategies for stress on the job. In addition, microelectronic devices have been used to record compliance with instructions to practice relaxation daily (Hoelscher, Lichstein, & Rosenthal, 1984). This type of measure may become increasingly useful as advances in technology make the devices more sophisticated, automated, and readily available.

An indirect method of assessing compliance is clinical outcome, that is, if a client loses weight, the therapist concludes that the client is complying with the assignment of eating less. If a client's grades improve, the therapist assumes he or she is complying with the assignment to increase study time. In most cases clinical outcome measures do not give the counselor or the client information on the progress of counseling from week to week that is needed to tailor homework assignments to the client's immediate concerns. Also, improvement in the desired direction is not necessarily related to therapeutic compliance. Clients may lose weight or get improved grades for reasons unrelated to the therapeutic homework. For these reasons, clinical outcome is of limited value as a measure of compliance with weekly assignments.

Another way to assess compliance is to assign a task that has a permanent product that can be shown to the counselor. A client with poor grooming habits may be assigned the task of bathing and changing clothes more frequently. A nonassertive client may be given the assignment of returning a defective shirt, with instructions to bring in a due bill as evidence of completion of the task. A sexually naive college student could be assigned the task of checking out books on sexual behavior. In a variation of this idea, Martin, Collins, Hillenberg, Zabin, and Katell (1981) provided clients with a series of relaxation tapes that contained differing numbers of brief, audible tones. The tapes were arranged in an order by the therapist to be played in sequence by the client, one tape for each day between sessions. The client self-monitored the number of tones heard on each tape. This practice provided the therapist with a permanent product, a list of the number of tones heard each day, which could be compared with the therapist's master list.

Perhaps the most common method of assessing compliance used by practitioners is to ask the client about the assignment at the beginning of the session following a homework assignment. The accuracy of this approach is suspect, but it may be adequate providing the therapist does not require detailed information. For example, if the assignment was to practice relaxation, the client could answer the question, "Did you practice?" with high accuracy. If the therapist asked for more specific information, such as how long and how many times was relaxation practiced or how effective was it in decreasing ambient stress levels, the accuracy of the responses to these questions would be much lower. It is likely that just as medical patients underestimate poor compliance and overestimate compliance to medical regimens (Dunbar, 1979), so do psychologists' clients underestimate lack of compliance and overestimate the degree of compliance to therapeutic assignments when asked to give such estimates during a clinical interview.

Purpose

The usual purpose of measuring compliance is to determine whether the client is carrying out the homework assignment. Compliance measures provide information to the counselor that is necessary for making decisions regarding future treatment interventions. If the client is making satisfactory progress, the counselor can continue on with the next assignment, building on the previous assignment until the desired behavior is obtained. If the client is not complying with the assignment, the therapist usually seeks the reason for noncompliance and reassigns a less difficult task or an entirely different assignment. Noncompliance, for example, may indicate that the wrong problem is being addressed and may lead the therapist to reassess the presenting problem.

Compliance measures may also be used to increase the client's awareness of the importance of a task or to provide the client with an opportunity to experience success.

Development

The development of compliance measures to be used with psychological treatment is in its infancy. Most of what is known about assessing compliance with therapeutic homework assignments can be attributed to research conducted on behavioral assessment and compliance with medical treatments. A notable exception is recent research on compliance with relaxation training assignments (Hoelscher et al., 1984).

Psychometric Characteristics

Few compliance measures are standardized. They are usually created as needed for a particular homework assignment. As a result, information on norms, reliability, and validity of a specific technique is seldom available. However, the following guidelines, based on research on behavioral assessment and self-monitoring, may enhance the accuracy of compliance assessment: (a) providing training in compliance assessment through behavioral

rehearsal, modeling, and role playing; (b) periodically assessing the accuracy of recording and reinforcing accurate compliance assessment; (c) assigning tasks that are readily observable and positively valued; (d) recording compliance as soon as it occurs; (e) using a simple recording system.

Despite such efforts, self-report compliance data will yield only a rough approximation of the actual compliance rate. Taylor, Agras, Schneider, and Allen (1983) found that 71% of their participants reported compliance with their assignment to practice relaxation daily while listening to tape-recorded instructions. A microprocessor that surreptitiously monitored the number of times the tape was actually played indicated that only 39% of the participants had actually listened to the tape daily. Hoelscher et al. (1984), using a similar microelectronic device and homework assignment, reported that participants overestimated their actual practice an average of 126%. Among the participants, 79% reported that they had practiced relaxation daily, but the automated estimate of compliance indicated that only 25% had practiced daily. Furthermore, self-report and automated estimates of compliance significantly correlated for the first 2 weeks of treatment, but not for the last 2 weeks of the 4-week treatment phase of the study. Clearly, self-report data on compliance rates are subject to error. The therapist should interpret such information cautiously, with knowledge that both the client and the therapist more frequently err in the direction of overestimating the rate of compliance.

A characteristic of most compliance measures is reactivity. Reactivity is a concern when the process of measuring compliance interferes with compliance or is so aversive that it contributes to premature termination from counseling. The foregoing guidelines for increasing the accuracy of compliance measures seem applicable to decreasing these types of reactivity of compliance measures, but there is little research in this area to guide the therapist.

Clinical Use

Compliance measures are appropriate for any problem for which homework is assigned. Such problems include anxiety, depression, marital problems, addictive behaviors, obesity, chronic operant pain, parenting skills, sexual dysfunction, and social skills (Shelton & Levy, 1981). Self-assessment of compliance may be contraindicated with clients who are actively psychotic, mentally retarded, or brain damaged. These clients may have trouble understanding the assignment and the compliance assessment procedures. Compliance measures also may be contraindicated in involuntary clients, clients with an unexpressed motive (a "hidden agenda") for seeking treatment, and clients who reject a behavioral approach to therapy. Such clients are likely to be poor monitors of their behavior and also may react with anger and distrust to behavioral assignments and compliance measures. Finally, compliance measures may be contraindicated when the reactivity of the measure interferes with the therapist's intent with the homework. For example, paradoxical assignments may call for different approaches to measuring compliance than might nonparadoxical assignments.

Future Directions

The literature on measures of compliance with psychological treatment greatly needs psychologists to begin reporting compliance rates with their assignments. Shelton and Levy (1981), in a survey of 500 articles concerning outpatient treatment published between January 1973 and January 1980 in eight behavior therapy journals, reported that 68% used assigned homework to promote treatment gains. Among these articles, only 5% reported compliance rates. Research reports that include compliance rates along with treatment outcome are needed if we are to understand the value of at home practice in psychological treatment.

Research is also needed to identify how therapists might capitalize on the reactivity of compliance measures to enhance compliance with homework assignments. It would be helpful to identify the types of monitoring that increase the likelihood of compliance with a homework assignment.

Finally, new ways of assessing compliance that are less subject to bias would be helpful. Microelectronics may offer much help in this direction, as demonstrated by Taylor et al. (1983) and Hoelscher et al. (1984). However, even without new technology, methods of compliance assessment can be developed that increase compliance and decrease errors in monitoring as demonstrated by Martin et al. (1981).

References

Dunbar, J. (1979). Issues in assessment. In S.J. Cohen (Ed.), *New directions in patient compliance*. Lexington, MA: D.C. Health.

Hoelscher, T.J., Lichstein, K.L., & Rosenthal, T.L. (1984). Objective vs. subjective asssessment of relaxation compliance among anxious subjects. *Behaviour Research and Therapy, 22,* 187-193.

Martin, J.E., Collins, F.L., Jr., Hillenberg, J.B., Zabin, M.A., & Katell, A.D. (1981). Assessing compliance to home relaxation: A simple technology for a critical problem. *Journal of Behavioral Assessment, 3,* 193-198.

Shelton, J.L., & Levy, R.L. (Eds.). (1981). *Behavioral assignments and treatment compliance.* Champaign, IL: Research Press.

Taylor, C.B., Agras, W.S., Schneider, J.A., & Allen, R.A. (1983). Adherence to instructions to practice relaxation exercises. *Journal of Consulting and Clinical Psychology, 51,* 952-953.

Compliance Test

Mark W. Roberts

Description

The Compliance Test (Day & Roberts, 1983) is a direct observation procedure performed in a clinic analogue to evaluate the probability of child compliance with parental instructions. Parent and child interact in a clinic playroom stocked with four sets of instruction-designated toys (animals, cars, blocks, and dolls), three containers (box, house, and bus), and distractor toys. Parents wear a Farrell Instruments "bug-in-the-ear" device to receive radio messages from a clinician/observer located behind a one-way window. A tape recorder provides the observer with a 5-second signal, marking the postinstruction interval. All parental behavior is controlled by the observer. After a brief warm-up period, parents are prompted to say: "(Name), I have some things for you to do now. It's important to me that you do these things right away, just like when we have to pick up our toys at home." The parent then issues instructions, points to instruction-designated toys and containers, and otherwise silently watches the child. Thirty standardized instructions are presented at approximately 15-second intervals. All instructions are of the form, "Put this (toy) in this (container)." The observer prompts the parent to give each instruction, starts the tape recorder, codes child behavior, rewinds the tape recorder, and prompts the next instruction. Toy/container pairings are completely arbitrary. If the child initiates a continuous motor response within the 5-second postinstruction interval that terminates in grasping the instruction-designated toy, the clinician codes the child's reaction as compliant. All other behavior is coded as noncompliant. A compliance ratio is derived by dividing the number of compliant responses by 30, the number of instructions issued during the assessment. A list of the 30 instructions is available from the author on request.

Purpose

The Compliance Test is designed to measure a preschool child's current level of compliance with parental requests. By providing repetitive, similar, chore-like instructions, the probability of child compliant responding can be estimated on a continuous scale from 0 to 100%. Such data can be used to describe a child's pretreatment problem level and to evaluate the effects of treatment.

Development

The Compliance Test was constructed to evaluate the treatment components of Forehand's compliance training program (Forehand & McMahon, 1981). Previous research suggested that the parental instructions (i.e., the test "items") to be used in the analogue should be controlled, explicit, and not subsequently interrupted by other parental verbiage for at least 5 seconds. Uncontrolled parental instruction giving had yielded compliance ratios that were reactive to demand effects (Green, Forehand, & McMahon, 1979). Furthermore, Roberts, McMahon, Forehand, and Humphreys (1978) demonstrated that compliance ratios were significantly influenced by instruction type. Therefore, the standardized instructions of the Compliance Test were controlled by the researcher, made explicit, and followed by parental silence. To further protect the interpretability of the obtained compliance ratios, parents were not permitted to interact with the child other than to issue instructions. The potential for differential social reinforcement by the parents of high compliant responders, relative to the parents of low compliant responders, was thereby precluded. Chore-like instructions were selected for us in the Compliance Test, because parents frequently reported that chore requests elicited defiance. As a result of the preceding decisions, compliance ratios generated by the Compliance Test can be interpreted as an unconfounded index of a child's compliance probability, given parental chore-like instructions in an analogue setting. The number of instructions to be given during the test was determined empirically. Twenty-seven subjects were administered 40 instructions each. Part-whole correlations were then computed between the total test score (based on 40 instructions) and the first 10, the first 20, and the first 30 instructions. The part-whole correlations obtained were .83, .94, and .99, respectively. Because compliance ratios based on the first 30 instructions predicted 97% of the total test variance, test length was established at 30 instructions.

Clinical Use

The Compliance Test is designed for children between the ages of 2 and 7 years. The test is not appropriate for infants, elementary school children, or children with significant delays in receptive language. The compliance ratios obtained from the test can be used to confirm parental interview or questionnaire data or both. The data describe a child's current problem level qualified only by the analogue setting and instruction type. Using the 60% cutoff level defined by Forehand (1977), a clinician can empirically discriminate clinical from normal levels of noncompliance. Such pretreatment data can be integrated with interview information, questionnaire data, and parent-collected home data to justify the more general diagnostic label of Conduct Disorder. During treatment the Compliance Test can be used repeatedly as a practice format for parental use of contingent praise, warnings, and chair timeouts recommended by the Forehand group for remediation of noncompliance (Forehand & McMahon, 1981). Posttreatment samples of child compliance can also be obtained to confirm interview information and home data collected by the parent.

Psychometric Characteristics

Compliance Test data have yielded consistently high interobserver agreement ratios (Day & Roberts, 1983). Agreement ratios reported in the six published studies using the Compliance Test ranged from 97.4 to 99.1%, and averaged 98.1%. Compliance ratio data have reacted quickly and predictably to treatment effects. For a summary of treatment component analyses, see the report by Day and Roberts (1983).

Unpublished data from 231 clinic referrals and 31 nonclinic recruits were analyzed specifically for the Dictionary of Behavioral Assessment Techniques to describe several characteristics of the Compliance Test. A test-retest reliability coefficient (r) of .73 was determined for 45 subjects who were retested, typically after a 1-week interval. The standard error of measurement was 16.7, indicating that a child's compliance ratio plus or minus 16.7 points defines a 68% confidence interval for his or her current performance. The internal consistency of the test was evaluated by the Kuder-Richardson formula. The analysis yielded a KR20 value of .99, indicating that the Compliance Test items (i.e., instructions) are homogeneous. Correlational analyses with demographic data indicated a strong relationship with child age ($r = .47$, $p < .001$), but no association with child sex ($r = -.12$) or family socioeconomic status ($r = -.01$). In summary, the Compliance Test accurately measures child compliance with chore-like instructions in an analogue setting. The obtained compliance ratios are reasonably consistent over brief temporal periods, but change readily with a standardized treatment for noncompliance. Furthermore, the compliance ratio appears to measure a single behavioral dimension that is clearly age correlated.

Future Directions

Any lengthy set of chore-like instructions would hypothetically elicit child behavior similar to that with the Compliance Test. Alternate forms of the Compliance Test will therefore be constructed and tested for correspondence with the original test. Criterion measurements need to be obtained in the home to validate the Compliance Test against concurrent settings. Home collected compliance ratios, however, are highly influenced by instruction and demand effects. Therefore, it is anticipated that Compliance Test scores will be only modestly associated with home setting compliance ratios. Correspondence between compliance ratios and other indices of conduct disorder (e.g., questionnaire scores and other overt forms of deviance) must be evaluated for evidence of convergent validity. Compliance Test associations with child behavior evoked by parental instructions to inhibit action (i.e., "Stop doing X!") or to perform tasks other than picking up toys (e.g., "Wash your hands! ") will also be evaluated. Finally, the Compliance Test needs to be normed on large, representative samples of nonclinic children from different age groups. Subsequently, clinic-referred children could be compared with an appropriate age group rather than be evaluated by the single standard (i.e., the 60% cutoff) currently in use for all preschool children.

References

Day, D.E., & Roberts, M.W. (1983). An analysis of the physical punishment component of a parent training program. *Journal of Abnormal Child Psychology, 11,* 141-152.

Forehand, R.L. (1977). Child noncompliance to parent commands: Behavioral analysis and treatment. In M. Hersen, R.M. Eisler, & P.M. Miller (Eds.), *Progress in behavior modification: Vol. 5.* New York: Academic Press.

Forehand, R.L. & McMahon, R.J. (1981). *Helping the noncompliant child: A clinician's guide to parent training.* New York: Guilford Press.

Green, K.D., Forehand, R.L., & McMahon, R.J. (1979). Parental manipulation of compliance and noncompliance in normal and deviant children. *Behavior Modification, 3,* 245-266.

Roberts, M.W., McMahon, R.J., Forehand, R.L., & Humphreys, L. (1978). The effect of parental instruction-giving on child compliance. *Behavior Therapy, 9,* 793-798.

Comprehensive Drinker Profile

G. Alan Marlatt and William R. Miller

Description

The Comprehensive Drinker Profile (CDP) is a 1- to 2-hour structured interview for the assessment of drinking behavior and alcohol–related problems. It is appropriate for both male and female clients as a pretreatment assessment with a wide range of intervention approaches in either outpatient or inpatient settings.

The complete CDP kit includes the interview booklet, a 79-page test manual, and eight reusable card sets. Because of its clear structure, the CDP can be administered by a broad range of professionals and paraprofessionals.

The card sorting tasks are techniques for the rapid initial assessment of areas with a large universe of possible responses: related life problems, drinking situations, beverage preferences, and emotional correlates of drinking behavior. The sorting tasks usually prove less threatening than verbal questioning, and initial information gained through the card sorts can be pursued in clinical sessions.

Answers to open-ended questions can be quantified through a series of content analysis rules provided in the manual, which also contains a sample computer coding format for those who wish to apply the CDP in research programs.

Purpose

The interview focuses on information relevant to the selection, planning, and process of treatment. It is predicated on the assumption that alcohol abuse is not a single, homogeneous disorder but rather a complex addictive behavior that must be understood within a larger social and motivational context. In addition to basic demographics, interview content traces the family history and development of drinking habits and problems, current levels of alcohol-related problems and dependence, a functional analysis of drinking behavior, relevant medical history, behavioral correlates including other addictive behaviors, and motivational aspects of drinking and change. Because it is designed for research as well as clinical applications, the CDP also yields quantitative indices of many of these dimensions, including alcohol consumption and dependence, other drug use, a range of beverages and drinking situations, family history, life problems, and emotional factors related to alcohol.

The original purpose of the CDP was to provide a consistent pretreatment data base useful for individualizing alcoholism treatment. The CDP provides an efficient structure to be used in the intake process. Whereas a typical clinical intake may consume 1 to 2 hours and yield only an unstructured case note, the CDP within the same time provides a range of information and indices useful in differential diagnosis and treatment planning.

The CDP can also be used to provide quantitative intake indices in treatment outcome research. Parallel follow-up measures are available to assess change over the course of intervention. The CDP can therefore be used simultaneously for clinical assessment and evaluative research purposes.

Development

Development of the CDP began in 1971, and an earlier version of the current instrument was described 5 years later as "The Drinking Profile" (Marlatt, 1976). The profile progressed through a series of revisions based on experience with its use in clinical and research settings.

Selzer's (1971) Michigan Alcoholism Screening Test, a widely used assessment of alcohol-related problems, was incorporated into the revision, and an alcohol dependence scale was added.

The method for assessing alcohol consumption was also modified in favor of a two-level system for quantifying steady and periodic drinking. The current approach employs a 1-week grid to specify drinking during a typical week and separate specification of the quantity and frequency of other drinking episodes.

Psychometric Characteristics

Normative data for an outpatient sample (N = 103) are provided in an appendix to the test manual. Because problem-drinking populations vary widely, however, individual scores are probably better compared with norms for the specific group from which they come.

Components of the CDP have been subjected to reliability and validity evaluations. The procedure for quantifying drinking behavior from self-report, for example, has been checked against collateral informant reports and found to yield variable but generally high coefficients of convergence (Miller, Crawford, & Taylor, 1979). The Michigan Alcoholism Screening Test, which is incorporated in the interview, has been subjected to item and factor structure analyses. Marlatt (1976) has reported interrater agreement in excess of 80% with the content coding system for open-ended questions.

Clinical Use

Clinically the CDP is used primarily as a comprehensive intake assessment for treatment planning. The interview produces information regarding the degree of physical dependence (and hence of likely need for detoxification), a survey of other life problems and addictive behaviors (providing clues to the need for additional problem-focused treatment), and a functional analysis of drinking behavior helpful in constructing strategies for behavior change. Detailed information, such as beverage preferences and drinking situations, can be useful in conducting specific behavioral interventions such as aversion therapies or self-control training.

We also have found that the CDP has considerable value as a motivational feedback tool (Miller, 1983). During the structured interview, the client confronts (sometimes for the first time) the actual extent and pattern of drinking, his or her level of dependence on alcohol, and the interrelationships of drinking with other life problems. Combined with other reactive procedures such as self-monitoring, this intake assessment can increase the motivation for behavior change.

The interview is designed to be applicable with a wide variety of problem-drinking populations, ranging from those with early problem development (e.g., drunk driving offenders and troubled employees) to inpatients receiving treatment for chronic alcoholism. Because the instrument focuses heavily on drinking and alcohol abuse, it is appropriate only when problem drinking may be a significant part of the clinical picture. The CDP is appropriate for multiple (polydrug) abusing populations, because problematic use of other substances is a frequent concomitant of alcohol abuse.

Future Directions

A shortened version of the CDP, the "Brief Drinker Profile," is being prepared for use in settings in which a more abbreviated assessment is appropriate and desired. This version eliminates some of the more "clinical" open-ended aspects of the interview and focuses heavily on quantitative information helpful in evaluation research. A parallel "Follow-up Profile Interview" is also being designed to parallel the content of the intake interview.

At the University of New Mexico we are now employing the profile as part of a "Drinker's Checkup," a test intended for individuals who wish to determine whether their use of alcohol is creating problems or the risk of problems. The intent of this checkup procedure is to increase awareness of risk potential and to increase motivation for change. The vast majority of persons who seek such an assessment already manifest substantial evidence of problem drinking, and the checkup appears to be an important part of intervention to alter their high-risk drinking patterns.

We also continue to employ the CDP and parallel follow-up profile as pre- and posttreatment assessment devices in evaluating treatment effectiveness (Miller, Taylor, & West, 1980). This assessment package provides information for screening out inappropriate referrals, evaluating the magnitude of change over the course of treatment, and examining individual difference predictors of differential outcome.

References

Marlatt, G.A. (1976). The drinking profile: A questionnaire for the behavioral assessment of alcoholism. In E.J. Mash & L.G. Terdal (Eds.), Behavior therapy assessment: Diagnosis, design, and evaluation. New York: Springer.

Miller, W.R. (1983). Motivational interviewing with problem drinkers. Behavioral Psychotherapy, 11, 147-172.

Miller, W.R., Crawford, V.L., & Taylor, C.A. (1979). Significant others as corroborative sources for problem drinkers. Addictive Behaviors, 4, 67-70.

Miller, W.R., Taylor, C.A., & West, J.C. (1980). Focused versus broad-spectrum behavior therapy for problem drinkers. Journal of Consulting and Clinical Psychology, 48, 590-601.

Selzer, M.L. (1971). The Michigan Alcoholism Screening Test: The quest for a new diagnostic instrument. American Journal of Psychiatry, 127, 1653-1658.

Compulsive Activity Checklist

Blanche Freund, Gail Steketee, and Edna B. Foa

Description

The original form of the Compulsive Activity Checklist (CAC) contained 62 items that described specific daily activities (Hallam, reported by Philpott, 1975). Each behavior was rated by an assessor on a 4-point Likert-like scale of severity. Repeated changes in the name of this instrument were noted in the literature. The original name, "Obsessive Compulsive Interview Checklist," was altered to "Compulsion Checklist" (Marks, Stern, Mawson, Cobb, & McDonald, 1980) and finally to "Compulsive Activity Checklist" (Mawson, Marks, & Ramm, 1982). Concurrent with these name changes, the checklist was shortened by Marks and his colleagues to a 37-item self-rated form that was later adapted by Foa and her colleagues as an assessor-rated 38-item version.

The checklist items in the later versions describe actions, such as "using toilet to urinate," "touching door handles," and "locking or closing doors or windows," which refer to stimulus situations for obsessive fears, as well as behaviors such as "retracing steps," "washing hands and face," or "checking electrical appliances," which refer more directly to compulsive rituals. Each item is rated for either duration, frequency, or avoidance according to the following scale: 0 = does not need to repeat or avoid it; 1 = activity takes about twice as long and has to repeat twice or tends to avoid it; 2 = activity takes about three times as long and has to repeat it three or more times or usually avoids it; and 3 = is unable to complete or attempt activity. To date the checklist appears to be the most behavior-specific standardized assessment technique for obsessive and compulsive symptoms.

Purpose

The purpose of this instrument is to assess quantitatively the degree of difficulty an individual has with common behaviors and situations that are likely to prove problematic for obsessive-compulsive persons. Ratings of 2 or 3 on items are indicative of considerable impairment and can be used to identify specific target areas for treatment as well as to assess the degree of improvement following therapy. Because this instrument includes items that describe a variety of feared situations and activities, observation of the clustering of responses with high ratings may be employed to identify categories of obsessions and rituals (i.e., washer, cleaner, checker, repeater, and mixed).

Psychometric Characteristics

Relatively little psychometric information about the CAC was available until recently (Freund, Steketee, & Foa, 1985). With respect to reliability, Marks et al. (1980) reported a high correlation coefficient of .95 for two raters conducting separate interviews, as well as a high correlation for physician and patient ratings ($r = .83$). By contrast, Freund et al. (1985) found only a moderate inter-rater correlation before treatment ($r = .62$). Because of this relatively low interrater correlation, test-retest reliability was examined by correlating the CAC scores taken on two occasions before treatment. This was done separately for the two independent raters. Coefficients were .63 and .84 over an average of 36.8 days. A comparison of mean scores at test and retest indicated no significant difference. Therefore, although this instrument appears to be reliable over time, some variability due to raters can be expected.

To study the construct and content validity of the CAC, Freund et al. (1985) conducted a factor analysis. Two factors were identified: a washer/cleaner factor (60% of the variance) and a checking/repeating one (37% of the variance). The alpha coefficients exceeded .89 for the CAC total score as well as for the washing and checking subscales.

Findings regarding the convergent validity (i.e., the similarity of the CAC to other measures of obsessive-compulsive symptoms) were variable. Low correlations (range .30 to .34) were obtained between the CAC, the Maudsley Obsessive-Compulsive Inventory (MOCI), and global rating scales of obsessions and compulsions. Somewhat higher correlations (range .35 to .56) were found with assessor-rated functioning (sex, family, home, and work); such a relationship would be expected in view of the focus of the CAC on daily activities. Compulsive Activity Checklist subscales were correlated moderately with the corresponding MOCI scales (.55 for washing and .44 for checking). Surprisingly, assessor-rated time spent ritualizing correlated poorly with the CAC despite the number of items on the latter that refer specifically to compulsive activity. Divergent validity was evident in the nonsignificant correlations of the CAC with measures of depression, anxiety, and neuroticism.

The CAC was sensitive to change in obsessive-compulsive symptoms following a behavioral treatment intervention (i.e., exposure and response prevention), but it was only mildly predictive of outcome of obsessive-compulsive behavior as measured by the MOCI (.28 after treatment and .23 at follow-up). Such a lack of relationship between pretreatment severity of symptoms and outcome has been observed in different studies using other measures (e.g., Foa, Steketee, Grayson, & Doppelt, 1983).

Clinical Use

The CAC is currently the only standardized instrument that uses a Likert-like scale to measure the functioning of obsessive-compulsive patients in specific daily activities. Like the MOCI, it can be administered quickly (10 to 15 minutes): unlike other standardized measures of obsessive-compulsive symptoms (e.g., the Leyton Obsessional Inventory, Lynfield Obsessional/Compulsive Questionnaire, and Sandler-Hazari Obsessional Inventory), it does not include items that refer to compulsive personality traits. Perusal of patients' responses to items on this instrument may assist the clinician in identifying specific feared stimuli or compulsive activities not reported during evaluation interviews. Scores on the two subscales as well as on total symptoms can be used to assess treatment efficacy.

Future Directions

In view of the aforementioned psychometric data, it is suggested that when the CAC is rated by an independent assessor, preliminary training in the use of the four response categories be provided. In future research on the CAC, an additional factor analysis with a larger sample is needed. Comparison of CAC scores of obsessive-compulsive persons with those of normative populations and other psychiatric patients is also needed to increase confidence in its utility as a measure of obsessive-compulsive symptoms. It is further recommended that the CAC be employed along with the MOCI in studies of treatment outcome with obsessive-compulsive disorder and that identical forms be used across centers to allow comparison of findings.

References

Foa, E.B., Steketee, G.S., Grayson, J.B., & Doppelt, H.G. (1983). Treatment of obsessive-compulsives: When do we fail? In E.B. Foa & P.M.G. Emmelkamp (Eds.), *Failures in behavior therapy* (pp. 10-34). New York: John Wiley & Sons.

Freund, B., Steketee, G.S., & Foa, E.B. (1985). *Compulsive Activity Checklist (CAC): Psychometric analysis with obsessive-compulsive disorder*. Unpublished manuscript.

Marks, I.M., Stern, R.S., Mawson, D., Cobb, J., & McDonald, R. (1980). Clomipramine and exposure for obsessive-compulsive rituals: I. *British Journal of Psychiatry, 136,* 1-25.

Mawson, D., Marks, I.M., & Ramm, L. (1982). Clomipramine and exposure for chronic obsessive-compulsive rituals: II. Two year follow-up and further findings. *British Journal of Psychiatry, 140,* 11-18.

Philpott, R. (1975). Recent advances in the behavioral measurement of obsessional illness: Difficulties common to these and other instruments. *Scottish Medical Journal, 20,* 33-40.

Conflict Behavior Questionnaire

Arthur L. Robin and Sharon L. Foster

Description

The Conflict Behavior Questionnaire (CBQ) is a self-report inventory assessing perceived communication and conflict between parents and adolescents. Parents and adolescents complete parallel versions of the CBQ, rating their interactions over the preceding 2 or 3 weeks. The parent version contains 75 true/false statements, 53 on the parents' appraisal of their adolescent's behavior (e.g., "My child sulks after an argument") and 22 on their perceptions of their interactions with the adolescent (e.g., "We joke around often"). The adolescent version contains 73 items, 51 on the adolescent's appraisal of the parent's behavior (e.g., "My mom doesn't understand me") and 22 identical to the parent form, tapping the adolescent's perception of interactions with the parent.

Separate scores are obtained for each member's appraisal of: (a) the other's behavior, and (b) the

dyadic interaction. In two-parent families, adolescents complete the CBQ separately for relations with mothers and fathers. Scoring is readily accomplished by constructing transparent overlays following an item key or using machine-scorable optimal scanning answer sheets.

Purpose

The CBQ gives a broad-based estimate of how much conflict and negative communication parents and adolescents experience in their relations. Items reflect general arguments, misunderstanding, inability to resolve disputes, and specific verbal and nonverbal communication deficits.

Development

The CBQ developed by Prinz, Foster, Kent, and O'Leary (1979) is based on an item pool initially generated by eighth-grade students, clinical psychologists, and research assistants. A sample of 91 college students and 40 mothers responded to the pilot items based on their recall of earlier parent-adolescent relations. Respondents also rated the overall quality of the relationship they were evaluating, and these ratings were used to split the samples into subgroups indicating generally "good" versus "poor" relationships. Items that discriminated between the groups formed the final version.

Subsequently, a short 20-item form was constructed through item analysis by retaining those items that correlated most highly with the total scores and maximally discriminated distressed from nondistressed families. The short form yields a single summary score that correlates .96 with scores from the longer original CBQ.

Psychometric Characteristics

The internal consistency of the CBQ (long form), assessed with alpha coefficients, was .90 and above for mothers and adolescents (Prinz et al., 1979), but was not examined for fathers. Combined data from waitlist control groups in two outcome studies provided preliminary estimates of test-retest reliability over 6- to 8-week intervals for small samples. Correlations for maternal appraisal of the adolescent and dyad were .57 and .61 ($N = 19$), respectively; for paternal appraisal of the adolescent and dyad, .84 and .85 ($N = 15$), respectively; for adolescent appraisal of the mother and dyad, .37

and .68 ($N = 19$), respectively; and for adolescent appraisal of the father and dyad, .84 and .85 ($N = 15$), respectively.

The interrater reliability of the CBQ, assessed by computing percentage agreement between parents and adolescents on the 22 identical items, averaged 67% for distressed and 84% for nondistressed dyads.

Three studies found evidence for the discriminant/criterion-related validity of the CBQ by contrasting responses of clinic-referred and nonclinic families with 10- to 18-year-old male and female adolescents (Prinz et al., 1979; Robin & Foster, 1984; Robin & Weiss, 1980). Clinic-referred mothers, fathers, and adolescents reported significantly more negative appraisals of the other members and of the dyadic relationship, with maternal scores explaining the greatest degree of the variance (48%) in distress status. Data from these studies were pooled with preassessment data from two treatment studies to product-aggregated normative data for 137 clinic-referred and 68 nonclinic families (Robin & Foster, 1984).

The CBQ reports also showed significant decreases in parent and adolescent scores following both behavioral and nonbehavioral family interventions (Foster, Prinz, & O'Leary, 1983; Robin, 1981). In addition, the CBQ correlates moderately ($- .52$) with problem-solving communication behavior coded from audiotaped interaction tasks and with the Dissatisfaction with Childrearing scale of the Marital Satisfaction Inventory (.55) (Robin & Foster, 1984), yielding evidence for construct validity.

Clinical Use

The CBQ can supplement interview and direct observation data in determining the degree of perceived conflict and negative communication in a parent-adolescent relationship (e.g., how distressed the family is). The short form, which takes approximately 5 minutes to complete, makes an excellent waiting-room screening measure. The clinician can estimate severity of conflict by plotting CBQ scores on T score profiles, which provide visual and quantitative comparisons with normative data from clinic and nonclinic families. By comparing the relative degrees of conflict within each dyad, the clinician can localize relationship problems and supplement the interview for forming hypotheses about family structure.

The CBQ is appropriate for parents and children aged 10 to 19 years. It has been used primarily to screen and quantify overt conflict, disputes, and negative interaction in families with adolescents experiencing externalizing behavior disorders (conduct disorders, attention deficit disorders, and delinquency). It was not designed for families in which the adolescent is experiencing internalizing behavior disorders, schizophrenia, or mental retardation. When conflict is avoided or denied despite basic disagreements between members, family members' scores on the CBQ may be artificially low and difficult to differentiate from a nondistressed profile.

Future Directions

The correspondence between perceived communication and conflict reported on the CBQ and actual conflict and negative communication assessed through direct observation is unclear. The CBQ correlates moderately with observations of conflict in samples of communication, but further investigations using more naturalistic observational and self-monitoring measures are needed. The discrepancies between different family members' scores on identical items raise additional questions about the accuracy of CBQ reports.

The normative data have been collected primarily with white, middle-class urban and suburban families. Further investigations exploring the responses of older adolescents and more heterogeneous racial and ethnic populations are sorely needed.

Finally, the use of the CBQ in discriminating between a broader range of family types needs further investigation, because research to date has focused on adolescents with externalizing behavior disorders.

References

Foster, S.L., Prinz, R.J., & O'Leary, K.D. (1983). Impact of problem-solving communication training and generalization procedures on family conflict. *Child and Family Behavior Therapy, 5,* 1-23.

Prinz, R.J., Foster, S.L., Kent, R.N., & O'Leary, K.D. (1979). Multivariate assessment of conflict in distressed and nondistressed mother–adolescent dyads. *Journal of Applied Behavior Analysis, 12,* 691-700.

Robin, A.L. (1981). A controlled evaluation of problem-solving communication training with parent–adolescent conflict. *Behavior Therapy, 12,* 593-609.

Robin, A.L., & Foster, S.L. (1984). Problem solving communication training: A behavioral-family systems approach to parent–adolescent conflict. In P. Karoly & J.J. Steffen (Eds.), *Adolescent behavior disorders: Foundations and contemporary concerns* (pp 195-240). Lexington, MA: D.C. Heath.

Robin, A.L., & Weiss, J. (1980). Criterion-related validity of behavioral and self-report measures of problem-solving communication skills in distressed and non-distressed parent–adolescent dyads. *Behavioral Assessment, 2,* 339-352.

Conflict Inventory

Gayla Margolin

Description

The Conflict Inventory (CI) was designed as an easily administered, cost-efficient measurement of marital conflict. The CI contains 26 items reflecting typical ways that couples express and react to conflict. Twenty-one of the 26 items fall into the three scales of Problem Solving, Withdrawal, and Aggression. Representative items for Problem Solving include: "Initiate a discussion to air your different points of view," or "State your position clearly." Items for Withdrawal include: "Try to hide the tension you feel and act as though nothing is wrong," or "Leave the room or walk away from your partner in the middle of a discussion." Items for Aggression include: "Insult your partner or call him/her names," and "Hit, push, or slap your partner."

The same 26 items reappear in five separate sections, which ask: (a) How often do you exhibit the behavior?, (b) How often would you like to exhibit the behavior?, (c) How often does your partner exhibit the behavior?, (d) How often would you like your partner to exhibit the behavior?, and (e) How often would your partner like you to exhibit the behavior? The 7-point rating, ranging from never (0%) to almost always (90%), is used for each of the five sections. Matching responses between real and ideal ("How often do you" versus "How often would you like to") ratings provides a measure of spouses' satisfaction with themselves and one another. Matching responses between the two partners ("How often I do each behavior" in comparison with "How often my partner thinks I do each behavior") offers a measure of perceptual accuracy.

Purpose

The purpose in designing the CI was to develop a measurement that evaluates the typical ways in which couples handle conflict in their natural environment, that separates the construct of conflict from the related but more general construct of overall satisfaction, that measures couples' conflict behaviors as well as couples' satisfaction with their conflict patterns, and that does not require the resources of direct observation. The instrument is based on a definition of conflict that includes all incompatibilities or antagonisms between the spouses, whether overt or covert. As such, it was designed to assess the frequency of a diverse range of conflict behaviors, many of which are inaccessible through direct observation. This instrument also is based on the wide variety of couples' conflict styles, with no one style necessarily being constructive or destructive. Therefore, dysfunction is assessed in terms of a couples' satisfaction with themselves and with one another, rather than by comparing them to an arbitrary external standard. As opposed to the Conflict Tactics Scale (CTS; Straus, 1979), which focuses exclusively on behavioral frequencies, the CI assesses psychological phenomena such as perceptual accuracy and satisfaction with marital conflict.

Development

The CI was patterned after LoPiccolo and Steger's (1974) Sexual Interaction Inventory. The initial 26 items were generated through discussions with a wide range of couples about how they respond to conflict. On the basis of 67% agreement among a group of clinicians, items were assigned to the three scales.

Psychometric Characteristics

The psychometric properties of the CI were examined in two studies. Margolin, Fernandez, Gorin, and Ortiz (1982) administered the scale to 73 couples, 19 distressed and 54 nondistressed. Alpha coefficients measuring the internal consistency of the three scales, from spouses' ratings of one another, were .82 for Problem Solving, .85 for Aggression, and .82 for Withdrawal. Construct validity was examined by looking for differences between distressed and nondistressed couples on the occurrence of each item, in ideal versus real discrepancies, and in discrepancies between spouses. Analyses of spouses' self-reports showed significant differences between distressed and non-distressed couples in 18 of the 26 items. The same analyses on spouses' reports of one another showed significant differences in 20 of the 26 items. Collapsing across items into the three scales revealed a similar picture. According to their own reports, distressed couples engage in less problem-solving, more aggression, and more withdrawal than do nondistressed couples. The between–group differences were somewhat larger when spouses rated their partners, as opposed to when they rated themselves. Comparisons between how often a behavior is exhibited and how often the spouse would like the behavior exhibited offer a dissatisfaction index, which was computed for spouses' reports of self and also for one another. Distressed compared with nondistressed spouses were more dissatisfied with their own and their partner's behavior. Concurrent validity was examined by correlating the CI with the Dyadic Adjustment Scale (DAS), a measurement of general marital adjustment, and with the Conflict Tactics Scale, a measurement of physical violence, verbal/symbolic aggression, and reasoning. As expected, the DAS score correlated positively with CI Problem Solving and negatively with CI Aggression and Withdrawal. The CI Problem Solving scale also showed a significant correlation with the CTS Reasoning scale. Conflict Inventory Aggression correlated with the CTS measure of Verbal Aggression and Violence.

In unpublished research by the author, 82 couples were examined who, on the basis of DAS and CTS scores, were classified as physically abusive, verbally abusive, withdrawn, and non-distressed-nonabusive. Item analyses showed significant group differences for 16 items based on self-reports and 18 items based on spouse reports. The three scale scores also showed significant group differences for self–reports and spouse reports. In addition to differences between the three distressed groups and the nondistressed group, the data reveal different patterns among the three distressed groups. Based on wives' reports, the physically aggressive husbands exhibit the highest percentage of withdrawing behaviors. On the basis of husbands' scores, however, wives in the physically aggressive couples have the highest percentages of aggressive and withdrawing behaviors. The dissatisfaction indices also showed significant group differences, with physically aggressive spouses having the highest overall dissatisfaction for self and for spouse. Using the CI, Kahn, Coyne, and Margolin (1985) showed that the scale scores also are sensitive to the conflict processes that occur between depressed spouses and their partners.

Clinical Use

Although the CI has been used primarily for research, it was developed to fill a void in our clinical instruments for measuring conflict. The instrument was designed as a systematic way for the spouses to communicate perceptions of their current conflict process as well as what that process would be ideally. Treatment goals are derived from the discrepancies between spouses' real and ideal ratings, not from comparisons with an "average" or "normal" sample. Rating oneself and the spouse helps each person to operationalize treatment targets for himself or herself and to articulate desired changes for the partner. The observed discrepancies between the two persons also provide a basis for discussing and reevaluating misperceptions about the conflict process. The section, "how often would your partner like you to exhibit the following behaviors," examines spouses' accuracy in predicting what would please the partner and helps to correct well-intentioned but misguided efforts in the conflict process.

Future Directions

As a relatively new instrument, the CI still needs further evaluation regarding its psychometric properties. Test-retest reliabilities are needed. Examination of the use of this instrument as a measurement of treatment outcome is warranted. Most importantly, however, more work on the validity of this instrument is recommended. Comparisons between CI data and behavioral samples (from either the laboratory or home setting) would help to determine how closely spouses' perceptions match a more objective evaluation of the couples' conflict styles. The predictive validity of this instrument also is an untapped area: How well do patterns on the CI predict the long-range accumulation of unresolved conflicts and an escalating pattern of destructive conflict? Finally, more research is needed to determine if the CI can be used to identify various broad conflict patterns (e.g., a pattern of withdrawal, aggression, or combined withdrawal and aggression, which then could be linked to specific intervention strategies).

References

Kahn, J., Coyne, J., & Margolin, G. (1985). Depression and marital disagreement: The social construction of despair. *Journal of Social and Personal Relationships, 2,* 447–461.

LoPiccolo, J., & Steger, J.C. (1974). The Sexual Interaction Inventory: A new instrument for assessment of sexual dysfunction. *Archives of Sexual Behavior, 3,* 585-595.

Margolin, G., Fernandez, V., Gorin, L., & Ortiz, S. (1982, November). *The Conflict Inventory: A measurement of how couples handle marital tension.* Paper presented at the 16th Annual Meeting of the Association for the Advancement of Behavior Therapy, Los Angeles.

Straus, M.A. (1979). Measuring intrafamily conflict and violence: The Conflict Tactics (CT) Scales. *Journal of Marriage and the Family*, *41*, 75-88.

Conners Teacher Rating Scales

Esther Deblinger and Marc S. Atkins

Description

The original Conners Teacher Rating Scale (CTRS) consists of 39 brief descriptors of negative child behaviors grouped into three categories: classroom behavior (e.g., daydreaming, and disturbing other children), group participation (e.g., appears easily led and has no sense of fair play), and attitude toward authority (e.g., submissive or defiant). The scale was developed by Conners (1969) to provide a standard measure for the evaluation of pharmacological interventions in children with behavior problems. Ten of these items comprise the Abbreviated Conners Teacher Rating Scale (ACTRS), also known as the Hyperkinesis Index, to provide a scale more suitable for repeated use (Conners, 1973). The 10 ACTRS items are those most frequently marked on CTRS ratings of hyperactive children and remain the most common rating scale used to identify hyperactive children in both clinical and research settings. Teachers respond to each item using a 4-point scale with the following levels: 0 = not at all; 1 = just a little; 2 = pretty much; and 3 = very much. Normative data provided by Werry, Sprague, and Cohen (1975) indicate that an ACTRS score of 15 out of a possible 30 would identify those children 2 standard deviations above the mean. The score is commonly considered the cutoff for classifying a child as hyperactive. The scales have been used by parents as well, and normative data for both teachers and parents by child's age and sex are available for the United States, Australia, and Canada.

Purpose and Development

Conners contributed significantly to the study of hyperactivity with his development of standardized rating scales to identify behavioral symptoms associated with hyperactivity. In addition, by designing a rating scale for teachers, Conners acknowledged the special role teachers can play in the assessment of deviant child behavior. As a result of their demonstrated sensitivity to drug effects, the scales have been used in numerous drug trials as pre and post measures. Researchers have most often relied on the ACTRS because of its ease of administration and scoring. In fact, the ACTRS was officially recommended by the National Institute of Mental Health's Early Clinical Drug Evaluation Unit for use in treatment outcome studies of hyperactive children. The CTRS has been revised twice to increase item clarity and response efficiency (Conners, 1973). However, the various scales are used interchangeably despite these item changes.

Psychometric Characteristics

The first factor analysis of the CTRS was undertaken by Conners (1969) on a sample of behavior problem children resulting in a five factor solution: Conduct Disorder, Daydreaming-Inattentive, Anxious-Fearful, Hyperactivity, and Sociable-Cooperative. Subsequently, the CTRS was factor analyzed with both large normative samples (e.g., Werry et al., 1975) and clinical populations, each deriving factor structures similar to the original analysis by Conners. Although all factors (with the exception of the Anxious-Fearful factor) have been shown to differentiate hyperactive children from normative control subjects and are responsive to drug effects, researchers have frequently chosen to use the Hyperactivity factor alone as a dependent measure. This factor consists of six items (teases other children, impulsive, excitable, restless or overactive, constantly fidgeting, and hums and makes other odd noises) that collect about 20% of the variance accounted for by all factors. One month test-retest reliability ranged from $r = .91$ for the Conduct Disorder factor to $r = .72$ for the Daydreaming-Inattentive factor and $r = .84$ for the Hyperactivity factor. Across-factor correlations range from $r = .03$ (Conduct Disorder-Anxious Fearful) to $r = .84$ (Conduct Disorder-Hyperactivity) for the original scale (Conners, 1969). Goyette, Conners, and Ulrich (1978) reported similar across-factor correlations for their revised version. Scores from the two most frequently used versions of the scales, the Conners (1969) Hyperactivity factor and the ACTRS, were found to correlate highly ($r = .93$) in a normative sample (Werry et al., 1975). Support for the validity of the Conners scales is based on the scales' relationship to alternative ratings of children's classroom behavior and on the correspondence of the CTRS ratings to observations of classroom behavior (Werry et al., 1975).

Clinical Use

Because of the numerous revisions of the original CTRS, clinicians and researchers must be cautious in identifying the version selected for use in order to avoid confusion in scoring and interpretation (Ullmann, Sleator, & Sprague, 1985). As noted previously, the CTRS Hyperactivity factor or the ACTRS have been used predominantly to identify hyperactive children and to monitor their responsiveness to pharmacological treatment. By contrast, the other factors derived from the original scale do not appear helpful clinically in differential diagnosis. However, hyperactive children's attentional changes may not be reflected by CTRS or ACTRS scores (Ullmann et al., 1985). Furthermore, despite the high correlation between the CTRS Hyperactivity factor and the ACTRS, the two scores are not interchangeable. Given the way in which scores on these scales are obtained, high correlations can result even when differences exist in the samples on the core symptoms of hyperactivity. That is, children manifesting symptoms of aggressive behavior but not overactive or inattentive behavior, and children manifesting symptoms of overactive and inattentive behavior but not aggressive behavior could both receive a diagnosis of hyperactivity based on scores on the ACTRS.

Future Directions

Recent research in hyperactivity is focused on attentional deficits as the core symptoms of the disorder, with increased activity levels considered secondary to difficulties in impulse control and distractibility. This shift in focus from prior definitions of this disorder is reflected by the DSM-III diagnostic criteria for attention deficit disorder with hyperactivity, which share only one attention characteristic in common with ACTRS items. Therefore, the use of the CTRS and ACTRS in the current assessment of hyperactivity and attention deficit disorder has been called into question (Ullmann et al., 1985). Similarly, neither the CTRS Hyperactivity factor nor the ACTRS has been found to discriminate hyperactivity from aggression. This distinction is important given the evidence for the independence of hyperactive and aggressive symptoms and the poorer prognosis of hyperactive children with aggressive symptoms as compared with those without aggressive symptoms (Loney & Milich, 1982). Therefore, Loney and Milich (1982), in a series of empirical evaluations,

developed the IOWA-Conners Teacher Rating Scale, a revised version of the ACTRS, to facilitate the differential diagnosis of attention deficit disorder and conduct disorder. Because of its ability to discriminate inattention-overactivity from aggression and because of the empirical support for the scale's validity, the IOWA-Conners scale appears to be superior to the CTRS and the ACTRS for clinical as well as research applications.

References

Conners, C.K. (1969). A teacher rating scale for use in drug studies with children. *American Journal of Psychiatry, 126,* 884-888.

Conners, C.K. (1973). Rating scales for use in drug studies with children. Pharmacotherapy of children (Special Issue). *Psychopharmacology Bulletin,* 24-84.

Loney, L., & Milich, R. (1982). Hyperactivity, inattention, and aggression in clinical practice. In M. Wolraich & D.K. Routh (Eds.), *Advances in behavioral pediatrics:* Vol. 2 (pp. 113-147). Greenwich, CT: JAI Press.

Ullmann, R.K., Sleator, E.K., & Sprague, R.L. (1985). A change of mind: The Conners Abbreviated Rating Scales reconsidered. *Journal of Abnormal Child Psychology, 13,* 553-565.

Werry, J.S., Sprague, R.L., & Cohen, M.N. (1975). Conners' Teacher Rating Scale for use in drug studies with children: An empirical study. *Journal of Abnormal Child Psychology, 3,* 217-229.

Consumer Satisfaction Questionnaire

Carolyn Webster-Stratton

Description

The Consumer Satisfaction Questionnaire was developed by Forehand and McMahon (1981) and adapted by Webster-Stratton (1984) to evaluate parents' satisfaction with individual or group therapy and parent training. It consists of 40 items with a 7-point Likert scale response format. Responses are transformed into scores of 1 to 7, with 7 being the most positive. There are six subscales that measure parents' perceptions about the following: child behavior improvement after treatment (11 items); format of treatment difficulty (5 items); and usefulness (5 items), such as live modeling, role playing, rehearsals, use of videotapes, and group discussion; difficulty (7 items) and usefulness (7 items) of specific parenting content and skills taught such as ignore, timeout, play skills, and commands; and attitudes towards the therapists (5 items).

Purpose

This comprehensive measure is used to assess consumer satisfaction with parent training programs. It not only evaluates parent satisfaction with treatment outcome and the therapist but also elicits detailed feedback about the usefulness and difficulties of specific treatment procedures and teaching format as well as the different areas of content and parenting skills taught.

Development

The measure was developed by Forehand and McMahon (1981) and Forehand, Wells, and Griest (1980) to determine the usefulness and difficulties of various parenting skills taught in their treatment program for child noncompliance. It was adapted by Webster-Stratton (1984) also to evaluate specific teaching formats, such as videotape modeling, live role-modeling, group discussion, lectures, homework, use of manuals, and self–administered videotape programs.

Psychometric Characteristics

Internal consistency of the six subscales ranged from .71 to .90. Positive scores on consumer satisfaction also correlated with positive changes on independent observations of child and parent behaviors in the home (Webster-Stratton, 1984).

Clinical Use

Typically, consumer satisfaction measures have been confined to evaluating treatment outcome and attitudes towards the therapist. This measure is particularly useful for the clinician because it also evaluates the content of therapy as well as the techniques used. Therefore, this measure can be used to evaluate components of parent training, for example, the usefulness and acceptability of treatment procedures, such as timeout versus ignore technique, or the format of teaching, such as live role-playing versus didactic teaching. This measure may also be administered at long-term follow-up assessments as well as immediately after treatment. When using this measure, it is important to minimize subjective response bias by having someone other than the therapist conduct the

assessment of consumer satisfaction. Consumer satisfaction measures should be basic to every therapist's assessment battery.

Future Use

More research is needed to develop reliable and valid consumer satisfaction inventories. Once these are refined and accepted, therapists across the country can use the same standardized measures and compare their respective treatment program results. In addition, it is important to develop measures that evaluate the children's satisfaction with treatment. This is rarely done in parent training research.

References

Forehand, R.L., & McMahon, R.J. (1981). *Helping the noncompliant child: A clinician's guide to parent training.* New York: Guilford Press.

Forehand, R.L., Wells, K.C., & Griest, D.L. (1980). An examination of the social validity of a parent training program. *Behavior Therapy, 11,* 448-502.

Webster-Stratton, C. (1984). Randomized trial of two parent-training programs for families with conduct-disordered children. *Journal of Consulting and Clinical Psychology, 52,* 666-678.

Conversation Probe

Vincent B. Van Hasselt and Robert T. Ammerman

Description

The Conversation Probe (CONPROBE) is an extended interaction role-play assessment of social skills in children. Specifically, the child is asked to simulate a social situation with a confederate. After a scene description is read, the child is required to initiate and maintain a conversation for 1 minute. Should the child fail to respond, the confederate delivers facilitating statements to elicit responding. Videotaped responses are retrospectively rated on a variety of components of social skill.

Purpose

The CONPROBE was designed to provide a role-play paradigm for extended interactions. Such an approach provides information about a type of interaction (e.g., conversation) that is not measured in traditional role-play assessments.

Development

The CONPROBE consists of six interpersonal situations that are similar to those found in the Children's Interpersonal Behavior Test (CIBT) (Van Hasselt, Hersen, & Bellack, 1981). However, the CONPROBE enables the subject to engage in prolonged (1-minute) conversations with the role-play partner. Also, with the CONPROBE, the confederate does not deliver a prompt. Rather, it is incumbent upon the child to initiate and maintain an interaction following description of an interpersonal situation. Confederates are directed to respond to subjects in a facilitating, nondominating manner and are asked to break silences of longer than 5 seconds by the introduction of a brief, facilitative question. An example of a CONPROBE scene is provided below.

Narrator. There is a new boy in your class and this is his first day at school. He does not know anyone and looks lonely. You wish he felt happier. He sits down near you and looks at you.

Videotapes of CONPROBE items are subsequently rated on behavioral components of social skill which also are rated on the CIBT. However, additional components of social skill examined by Whitehill, Hersen, and Bellack (1980) include the use of Open-Ended Questions and Informative Statements.

The administration of the CONPROBE follows in part from the procedure developed by Eisler et al. (1973), which has been adopted by most investigators in the area of social skills assessment with children (e.g., Bornstein, Bellack, & Hersen, 1977; Reardon, Hersen, Bellack, & Foley, 1979). First, each child is seated in a videotape studio. Then, the experimenter, from an adjoining room, reads instructions and presents a practice scene through the intercom. If it appears that the instructions are clear to the subject, he or she is then read a test scene. After the experimenter reads the narration for a scene, an experimental assistant seated next to the subject delivers a prompt, and the child responds as though the situation were actually occurring in his or her real environment.

Psychometric Characteristics

Van Hasselt et al. (1981) examined the test-retest reliability (1-week interval) and validity of the CONPROBE. Twenty-two male and 20 female elementary school children (8 to 10 years of age)

were administered this measure and completed sociometric ratings. Data from naturalistic behavioral observations and teachers' ratings also were obtained. Results of correlational analyses showed a range of coefficients on social skill components of .54 to .94. However, values for only three (eye contact, response latency, and overall friendliness) of nine rated behaviors exceeded .80. Therefore, reliability of the CONPROBE was considered unacceptable. With regard to the validity of the measure, some evidence of transitional consistency was found. For example, ratings of several social skill components (eye contact, speech duration, speech disturbances, and open-ended questions) on the CONPROBE were significantly correlated with scores on parallel categories in a more naturalistic setting. Therefore, there appears to be moderate support for the validity of this instrument.

Clinical Use

The CONPROBE was designed primarily for use in research with socially maladjusted children. Extended role-play interactions can easily be adapted to clinical settings. Pending further psychometric evaluation of the CONPROBE, however, clinicians should be cautious in using this assessment instrument.

Future Directions

Since the first report of the CONPROBE, variations of such role-play procedures for assessing social skills in children have been developed. Furthermore, assessment conditions and variables affecting parametric properties and skills performance on these measures have been the focus of increased study over the last few years (Kazdin, Esveldt-Dawson, & Matson, 1983). It is expected that with the increased investigative attention to children's social functioning, strategies such as the CONPROBE will continue to enjoy widespread application. However, additional research is required before any definitive conclusions concerning psychometric characteristics of this instrument and its variants can be confidently drawn.

References

Bornstein, M.R., Bellack, A.S., & Hersen, M. (1977). Social skills training for unassertive children: A multiple baseline analysis. *Journal of Applied Behavior Analysis, 10,* 183-195.

Eisler, R.M., Miller, P.M., & Hersen, M. (1973). Components of assertive behavior. *Journal of Clinical Psychology, 29,* 295-299.

Kazdin, A.E., Esveldt-Dawson, K., & Matson, J.L. (1983). The effects of instructional set on social skills performance among psychiatric inpatient children. *Behavior Therapy, 14,* 413-423.

Reardon, R.C., Hersen, M., Bellack, A.S., & Foley, J.M. (1979). Measuring social skill in grade school boys. *Journal of Behavioral Assessment, 1,* 87-105.

Van Hasselt, V.B., Hersen, M., & Bellack, A.S. (1981). The validity of role play tests for assessing social skills in children. *Behavior Therapy, 12,* 202-216.

Whitehill, M.B., Hersen, M., & Bellack, A.S. (1980). A conversation skills training program for socially isolated children: An analysis of generalization. *Behaviour Research and Therapy, 18,* 217-225.

Cooking Methods Test

Anthony J. Cuvo

Description

The Cooking Methods Test is comprised of six subtests. Each subtest consists of the mandatory steps to be performed from the task analyses for preparing two foods, each using three different cooking operations: boiling an egg, boiling vegetables, baking cornbread, baking biscuits, broiling hot dogs, and broiling English muffins. Subjects are given access to cooking materials and recipes for each subtest, and asked to cook the food using the designated cooking operation. The six subtests are presented sequentially in random order and are independent of each other. Testing is terminated when subjects cease performing relevant cooking behavior and respond affirmatively to the question: "Are you finished showing me what you know?" If the subject omits or incorrectly performs a mandatory step of the task analysis involving safety, the tester asks the subject to leave the room, changes the stimulus conditions to restore safety, and resumes testing. The assessment is discontinued when the subject omits or incorrectly performs the mandatory steps necessary to achieve the terminal behavior. Prompting, performance feedback, and response consequences are not provided during testing. Each method is scored separately for percentage of mandatory steps of the task analysis performed correctly without assistance.

Purpose

The purpose of the Cooking Methods Test is to assess whether the subject can perform three basic cooking operations with simple foods.

Development

The Cooking Methods Test was constructed as the principal dependent variable in an experiment to validate procedures to teach basic cooking skills to mildly retarded adults (Johnson & Cuvo, 1981). Similar methodology was used subsequently to develop task analytic assessments of preparing complex meals by moderately and severely retarded adults (Martin, Rusch, James, Decker, & Trtol, 1982).

Psychometric Characteristics

Selection and Social Validation of Cooking Responses. The content and social validity of food items and cooking responses assessed on the Cooking Methods Test were established using various criteria. Several cookbooks as well as individuals in the community with personal cooking skills suggested simple cooking methods and food items. Also, parents of workshop clients were surveyed to determine their home cooking processes and food preferences. A university professor of home economics who had experience teaching developmentally disabled students aided in the selection of cooking methods. A graduate student in nutrition specified a variety of foods appropriate for each method chosen, and the family food preference norms were examined for compatibility with this list. The six foods were selected by imposing restrictions based on preparation length, complexity, and economy. As a result of these social validation processes, the following cooking responses and food items were selected: boiling (eggs and vegetables), baking (cornbread and biscuits), and broiling (hot dogs and English muffins).

Task Analysis and Content Validation. The response components necessary for performing the aforementioned six cooking subtasks were identified by task analysis, and the content validity was established by the use of expert information. Preliminary task analyses were written based on observation of two graduate students and the experimenter performing the tasks. Written preliminary task analyses and a videotape of the experimenter performing the cooking responses were then presented to a home economist for critical evaluation. These recommendations and feedback led to revised task analyses that were then reviewed by a second home economist for a validity check.

Task analyses for baking, boiling, and broiling items yielded several response chains: (a) systematically using recipes; (b) gathering materials; (c) combining ingredients; (d) stirring; (e) discriminating stove dials and using the stove to boil, bake, and broil; (f) using a kitchen timer; (g) cleaning counter area and storing remaining food materials; (h) using pot holders; (i) turning foods; (j) turning handles away from stove edges; and (k) preheating oven and broiler.

Pilot work led to the development of the analyses for each subtask. The Cooking Methods Test task analyses listed only those steps mandatory for the safe, successful completion of the subtasks. These were responses that had to be performed correctly in a prescribed order to obtain the edible food product without endangering the participants' safety.

Response Recording and Reliability Checks.

The primary dependent variable was the percentage of steps performed with no help on the six task analyses of the Cooking Methods Test. Each response on the test was mandatory for the successful completion of cooking tasks. Responses were scored as either performed correctly without assistance or not performed correctly.

The reliability of scoring was assessed by having a second individual independently and concurrently observe performance on 10 (21%) sessions for all subjects. Checks were made for each subject during each of the six subtasks and four testing sessions. Observer agreement was calculated by dividing the number of agreements by the number of disagreements plus agreements and multiplying by 100%. The mean percent agreement averaged 93% with a range of 66 to 100%.

In addition to measuring agreement on performance of cooking responses, the edibility of the terminal food product also was socially validated. Edibility was based on the experimenter and secondary observer's assessment of visual desirability of the food. Agreement on this measure was 100%.

Clinical Use

The Cooking Methods Test is applicable with clinical populations that are mildly to moderately impaired with respect to their adaptive behavior. Clinical populations that may lack basic cooking operations include persons with mental retardation, autism, psychoses, brain injury, and related disorders. The Cooking Methods Test is generally not applicable to populations that are not impaired with respect to basic daily living skills.

Future Directions

Future research should incorporate a larger number of cooking operations and other foods to assess a wider repertoire of cooking skills. The assessment should be employed with additional clinical populations, and the procedures modified to accommodate more severely handicapped persons.

References

Johnson, B.F., & Cuvo, A.J. (1981). Teaching mentally retarded adults to cook. *Behavior Modification, 5,* 187-202.

Martin, J.E., Rusch, F.R., James, V.L., Decker, P.J., & Trtol, K.A. (1982). The use of picture cues to establish self-control in the preparation of complex meals by mentally retarded adults. *Applied Research in Mental Retardation, 3,* 105-119.

Coping Strategies Scales

Ernest Edward Beckham and Russell L. Adams

Description

The Coping Strategies Scales (COSTS) is a self-report psychological inventory consisting of 142 multiple choice items. The instructions ask subjects to indicate whether they have performed a particular behavior or had a particular thought in the last 2 weeks. After each item, subjects may check that they engaged in the behavior and felt better afterwards; that they engaged in the behavior and felt worse; that they engaged in the behavior and felt the same; or that they did not perform the behavior in the last 2 weeks.

Purpose

Although instruments have been developed to examine how persons typically cope (Andrews, Tennant, Hewson, and Vaillant, 1978) and function under stress (Ilfeld, 1980), there have been only a few published self-report instruments to measure coping style under stress (Folkman & Lazarus, 1980; Sidle, Moos, Adams, & Cady, 1969; Billings & Moos, 1981). These have been limited, however, by measuring only a few dimensions of coping responses. Moreover, there have been few published data on their reliability and validity among clinically depressed populations. The Coping Strategies Scales (COSTS) were designed to measure a variety of coping responses with sufficient items to insure high reliability for each scale.

Development

Items for the COSTS were drawn from a variety of sources: Rippere's studies of how persons cope with depression; studies of how persons cope with physical disability and illness; studies of how persons cope with death and grieving; the general literature on coping and adaptation; and current psychotherapeutic advice on how to overcome depression.

For purposes of maximal inclusiveness, "coping behaviors" were defined in the broadest possible way. They included behaviors and thoughts typically seen as coping attempts by mental health professionals as well as depressive symptoms that may or may not serve a coping function at times (e.g., avoiding aversive situations). For example, measures of blame and passivity were included because of evidence that these too may be ways of dealing with stressful situations, even though such behaviors may be ineffective or even ultimately pathogenic.

Coping responses drawn from the aforementioned sources formed an initial pool of 143 items. Ten categories of coping behaviors were defined to be inclusive of the greatest possible number of items: Blame, Emotional Expression, Emotional Containment, Social Support/Dependency, Religious Support, Philosophical/Cognitive Restructuring, General Activity, Avoidance/Denial, Problem Solving, and Passivity. Five clinical psychologists, one psychiatrist, and two social workers from the Academy of Certified Social Workers were given these definitions, and they assigned items to the 10 scales. Items with a 75% level of agreement or better (six of eight raters in agreement) were kept. One hundred and eight items passed this criterion. Because some scales were unacceptably short, 34 additional items were generated. These were rated by five of the original eight clinicians. Twenty-five of these items achieved 80% agreement and were retained.

The next step was to conduct a study of the internal reliability of the scales. Subjects were in psychotherapy and either had a primary diagnosis of nonpsychotic depression or were judged by their therapist to have depression as a significant part of their problem. Subjects were from a psychiatric

outpatient clinic, an inpatient hospital psychiatric ward, and a day hospital. These settings were chosen to provide a wide cross-section of depressed patients. Patients included both low income clinic patients and middle and high income private patients. There were 53 women and 47 men, aged 18 to 71 years, with an average Beck Depression Inventory (BDI) score in the moderate range (21.0). A replication sample contained data for 42 women and 22 men drawn from similar sources.

Three items did not correlate at the .25 level with the scale on which they were placed, and these were dropped. Nine of the 10 scales had Kuder-Richardson internal reliability coefficients above an acceptable level of .70 and four of these had reliability coefficients above .80. The internal reliability of the scales for patients who had not yet received treatment was generally higher than that for patient groups as a whole.

To produce scales of greater length and therefore greater reliability, three scales were derived from the entire item pool. A principal components factor analysis was performed on the 10-scale scores using a Varimax method of rotation. The first three factors accounted for 68% of the variance. Three scales closely approximated the orthogonal axes: Emotional Expression, Emotional Containment, and General Activity. The entire pool of items was correlated with each of these scales, and items correlating above the .25 level were used in forming three revised scales. This process was repeated three more times until a stable item assignment was achieved. One of the three factor scales represents an attempt to help oneself by engaging in a variety of activities (Individual Coping); one represents emotional containment and passivity (Containment/Passivity); and one represents emotional expression to elicit social support (Emotional Expression/Social Support). Internal reliability of these three factorially derived scales is higher than that of the original 10 scales, being between .86 and .91. Reliability statistics derived from the replication sample were only slightly lower.

Psychometric Characteristics

Internal reliability coefficients have just been reported. Also, several scales correlated significantly with the BDI. For example, the amount of blame that individuals experienced (both toward themselves and others) was correlated positively with the BDI. The subset of items regarding self-blame only correlated even higher with the BDI

(r = .45). General Activity correlated negatively with the BDI (r = − .34), and Passivity increased with higher levels of depression (r = .26). Finally, Emotional Expression correlated positively with the BDI (r = .23). These results provide evidence of construct validity for the COSTS, in that it is part of the clinical picture of depression to evince decreased activity, increased self-blame, and increased emotional expression. Other correlations between the BDI and coping scales suggest that with increased depression, subjects made less use of cognitive restructuring and religious coping strategies. Norms have been developed based on 164 depressed outpatients and inpatients.

Clinical Use

Without further research, clinical use of the COSTS must be tentative. Nevertheless, the scales may be very useful in generating hypotheses about coping styles by use of the norms gathered on depressed patients. It is hoped that in the future, scale patterns can be used to predict which patients may be responsive to psychotherapy, which persons experiencing trauma will have the greatest difficulty adjusting, and so on. Scale norms are applicable mainly to depressed populations, but nevertheless the scales are likely to be useful for other populations as well.

Future Directions

Further validation studies of the COSTS are needed to establish the relationship of COSTS scales to other measures of coping. Most needed are studies comparing COSTS scales with observer-rated measures of coping (such as those on an inpatient ward). Another method of validation would be to demonstrate differences in coping patterns of different types of personality disorders.

The COSTS has a variety of possible research applications. Questions that might be addressed include how coping syles vary with different subtypes of depression, how patients with different coping styles may differentially respond to psychotherapy for depression, and how prognosis for persons with specific coping styles may be estimated. Moreover, the COSTS should provide useful data on patient change in coping style in psychotherapy outcome research. Finally, the COSTS may prove helpful by allowing clinicians to pinpoint specific areas of coping to be targeted in psychotherapy.

References

Andrews, G., Tennant, C., Hewson, D.M., & Vaillant, G.E. (1978). Life event stress, social support, coping style, and risk of psychological impairment. *Journal of Nervous and Mental Disease, 166,* 307-316.

Billings, A.G., & Moos, R.H. (1981). The role of coping responses and social resources in attenuating the stress of life events. *Journal of Behavioral Medicine, 4,* 139-157.

Folkman, S., & Lazarus, R.S. (1980). An analysis of coping in middle-aged community sample. *Journal of Health and Social Behavior, 21,* 219-239.

Ilfeld, F.W. (1980). Coping styles of Chicago adults: A description. *Journal of Human Stress, 6,* 2-10.

Sidle, A., Moos, R., Adams, J., & Cady, P. (1969). Development of a coping scale. *Archives of General Psychiatry, 20,* 226-232.

Corah Dental Anxiety Scale

Norman L. Corah

Description

The Dental Anxiety Scale is a four-item multiple choice trait-anxiety scale (Corah, 1969). Because the scale is brief, it is reproduced here. The subject or patient is asked to check the alternative to each item that most closely matches his or her other feelings. (1) If you had to go to the dentist tomorrow, how would you feel about it? (a) I would look forward to it as a reasonably enjoyable experience. (b) I wouldn't care one way or the other. (c) I would be a little uneasy about it. (d) I would be afraid that it would be unpleasant and painful. (e) I would be very frightened of what the dentist might do.

(2) When you are waiting in the dentist's office for your turn in the chair, how do you feel? (a) Relaxed. (b) A little uneasy. (c) Tense. (d) Anxious. (e) So anxious that I sometimes break out in a sweat or almost feel physically sick.

(3) When you are in the dentist's chair waiting while he gets his drill ready to begin working on your teeth, how do you feel? (Same alternatives as number 2.).

(4) You are in the dentist's chair to have your teeth cleaned. While you are waiting and the dentist is getting out the instruments that he will use to scrape your teeth around the gums, how do you feel? (Same alternatives as number 2.)

Points are assigned for each choice with one point for an (a) choice to five points for an (e) choice. Total scores are the sum of the item scores and range from 4 to 20. If the scale is to be administered in a dental office before a treatment procedure, the wording of the first items is altered to read: "Before you came to the dental office today, how did you feel about it?" The verbs in the five alternatives are changed to past tense.

Purpose

The original purpose of the scale was to identify subjects with high and low anxiety levels and dental patients for research study. It was predicated on the assumption that most measures of general trait anxiety are measures of neuroticism and that to be useful a trait measure required an object. In this case, the object was anxiety concerning dental treatment.

Development

The scale was developed by selecting a list of dentally related experiences that were common to most persons. The four items selected included the broadest possible dental experiences in the population. The original large scale group used for standardization included 1,232 undergraduate college students.

Psychometric Characteristics

The psychometric characteristics of the scale have been established from several studies (Corah, 1969; Corah, Gale, & Illig, 1978). First, the scale shares characteristics with other anxiety measures in that the score distribution is positively skewed and women obtain slightly higher scores than do men. An appropriate estimate of the population mean (based on over 3,000 cases) would be 9.00 with a standard deviation of 3.00.

Reliability of the scale has been estimated for both internal consistency and stability over time. A coefficient alpha of .86 was obtained for a sample of 313 college students. This coefficient is reasonably high for a 4-item test. Test-retest stability was obtained from 171 subjects with 3 months intervening between test administrations. The correlation coefficient was .82. Predictive validity was obtained from several samples in which the criterion is the dentist's rating of patient anxiety in the operatory. Correlations between Dental Anxiety Scale (DAS) scores and the dentist rating in private practice range from .40 to .50. Correlations in hospital clinic settings where the dentist

is less familiar with his or her patients range from .30 to .40.

Attempts to relate the DAS to State-Trait measures of anxiety indicate a consistent relationship between the scale and State anxiety measures but not with other Trait anxiety measures (Weisenberg, Krundler, & Schachat, 1974). This finding reinforces the author's aforementioned bias concerning Trait measures of anxiety. The DAS generally accounts for 20 to 25% of the variance in State measures used to assess anxiety response to dental treatment.

Clinical Use

Although the DAS was originally developed for research, it has been used extensively in recent years to identify dental patients who are extremely anxious. We have recommended that a score of 13 or 14 on the scale should alert the dentist to the fact that he or she is dealing with an anxious patient (Corah, Gale, & Illig, 1978). A score of 15 or more indicates a highly anxious patient. Although some of these patients are able to cooperate in receiving dental treatment, their inner distress should be dealt with by the dentist. Independently identified dental phobics score between 14 and 20 on the DAS. We are aware of a number of dentists who routinely use the DAS in their offices to screen their patients before treatment.

Future Directions

We assume that future directions for the DAS will follow from work already completed. Modifications of the DAS, developed for use with young teenagers, permit parents to respond to the questions on behalf of their children (Keys, 1978). The scale has also been translated into several languages and used successfully by investigators in other countries (Ayer & Corah, 1984). Some writers have suggested cross-cultural comparisons of anxious patients and their treatment. The DAS will continue to be used as a major independent variable in behavioral dental research.

References

Ayer, W.A., & Corah, N.L. (1984). Behavioral factors influencing dental treatment. In L.K. Cohen & P.S. Bryant (Eds.), *Social sciences and dentistry: Vol. II* (pp. 267-322). London, England: Quintessence.
Corah, N.L. (1969). Development of a dental anxiety scale. *Journal of Dental Research, 48,* 596.

Corah, N.L., Gale, E.N., & Illig, S.J. (1978). Assessment of a dental anxiety scale. *Journal of the American Dental Association, 97,* 816-819.

Keys, J. (1978). Detecting and treating dental phobic children: Part I, detection. *Journal of Dentistry for Children, 45,* 296-300.

Weisenberg, M., Krundler, M., & Schachat, R. (1974). Relationship of the dental anxiety scale to the state-trait anxiety inventory. *Journal of Dental Research, 53,* 946.

Daily Child Behavior Checklist

William Furey and Rex Forehand

Description

The Daily Child Behavior Checklist (DCBC) (Furey & Forehand, l983) is a 65-item checklist of pleasing and displeasing behaviors that may or may not have occurred in the preceding 24 hours. There are 37 pleasing child behaviors and 28 displeasing child behaviors. The checklist is completed by parents and is used for children aged 2 to 8 years who are not severely disturbed (e.g., autistic or retarded). Three scores may be derived from the DCBC: (1) a total for the number of pleasing behaviors checked; (2) a total for the number of displeasing behaviors checked; and (3) a total child behavior score derived by subtracting the number of displeasing behaviors from the number of pleasing behaviors.

Purpose

The DCBC is designed to be a parent-completed child behavior checklist that (a) includes both positive and negative behaviors; (b) might be used on a daily basis; (c) uses specific and objective terminology; and (d) emphasizes factual events rather than parental attitudes, feeling states, or child-rearing practices. Furthermore, its purpose is to assess the existence of child behavior problems and to measure the change that occurs with treatment.

Development

With child behavior problems the parents are an important source of information. Concern with the reliability and validity of parental reports has been documented frequently. Various factors have been implicated in fostering inconsistencies between observed child behaviors and a parent's perception of the behavior. For example, increasing the time over which behavior is reported leads to inaccuracy, unpleasant events distort recall, social impression management influences the accuracy of data, and the clarity of the definition of problems influences reliability. The current checklist was developed because of weaknesses in these areas in the child behavioral checklists most frequently used and referred to in the literature (Wells, 1981). Items for the DCBC came from several existing instruments (e.g., the Child Behavior Checklist, Achenbach & Edelbrock, 1981), as well as numerous items from the authors.

Psychometric Characteristics

Furey and Forehand (1983) reported on the content, statistical conclusion, discriminant, and concurrent validities of the DCBC as well as its reliability. They reported a minimum of 90% agreement among two groups (clinical graduate students and mothers of children aged 2 to 8 years), sorting the items on the checklist into pleasing or displeasing categories. They (Furey & Forehand, 1984a) further reported the checklist to be sensitive to change with treatment of child behavior problems. The intercorrelation between pleasing and displeasing scores was nonsignificant (Furey & Forehand, 1984b; Furey & Forehand, 1985). The three scores derived from the checklist also were shown to discriminate between mothers who refer their children for psychological treatment of behavior problems and mothers who do not (Furey & Forehand, 1983). Significant correlations between each measure of the DCBC (pleasing, displeasing, and total behavior scores) and the four measures of the Parent Attitude Test (Cowen, Huser, Beach, & Rappaport, 1970) also were demonstrated.

Test-retest reliability for each subscale of the DCBC was assessed by computing a stability coefficient for nonclinic mothers over a 2-week interval between completions. The test-retest correlations for the three scales were -0.189 ($p > 0.05$) for DCBC-pleasing, 0.5930 ($p < 0.01$) for DCBC-displeasing, and 0.6646 ($p < 0.01$) for DCBC-total.

Clinical Use

The DCBC is designed primarily to assess behavior problems in the home with children aged 2 to 8 years. It appears most applicable for problems of noncompliance. Given its attempts to minimize, by research-proven procedures, the sources of bias and error to which parental reports are susceptible, the DCBC should be attractive to both clinicians and researchers. Furthermore, the checklist requires less than 5 minutes to complete and is easy to score.

Because of the lack of published normative data, the instrument appears to be limited in its applicability for diagnosing behavior problems. However, it is an excellent measure of change that occurs with treatment. Moreover, mothers participating in parent training for noncompliance of their child also report that it is a source of ideas for increasing the number of pleasant interactions with the child (e.g., shared pleasant activities).

Future Directions

More data on the DCBC are needed. Norms need to be established for clinic and nonclinic populations as well as numerous subgroups (e.g., male and female subjects, racial groups, and age groups). Replication of the treatment sensitivity of the checklist should be completed with a larger sample. The test-retest reliability of the DCBC, particularly the pleasing subscale, needs to be examined further. Data from fathers as well as the relationship between mother- and father-completed checklists are needed. Finally, factor analysis of the items on the checklist needs to be completed to determine whether the behaviors may be categorized along different dimensions and to determine the relative importance of various content categories.

References

Achenbach, T.M., & Edelbrock, C.S. (1981). Behavioral problems and competence reported by parents of normal and disturbed children aged four through sixteen. *Monographs of the Society for Research in Child Development, 46* (1, Serial No. 188).

Cowen, E.L., Huser, J., Beach, D.R., & Rappaport, J. (1970). Parental perceptions of young children and their relation to indexes of adjustment. *Journal of Consulting and Clinical Psychology, 34,* 97-103.

Furey, W., & Forehand, R. (1983). The daily child behavior checklist. *Journal of Behavioral Assessment, 5,* 83-95.

Furey, W., & Forehand, R. (1984a). Maternal satisfaction with clinic-referred children: Assessment by use of single-subject methodology. *Journal of Behavioral Assessment, 5,* 345-355.

Furey, W., & Forehand, R. (1984b). An examination of predictors of mothers' perceptions of satisfaction with their children. *Journal of Social and Clinical Psychology, 2,* 230-243.

Furey, W., & Forehand, R. (1986). What factors are associated with mothers evaluations of their clinic-referred children? *Child and Family Behavior Therapy, 8,* 21-42.

Wells, K.C. (1981). Assessment of children in outpatient settings. In M. Hersen & A.S. Bellack (Eds.), Behavioral assessment: A practical handbook (pp. 484-533). New York: Pergamon Press.

Daily Sleep Diary

Patricia Lacks

Description

The major dependent variable in most insomnia treatment outcome research (Bootzin, Engle-Friedman, & Hazelwood, 1981; Borkovec, 1982) is the subjective estimate of time to fall asleep or *sleep onset latency* (SOL) as collected on a sleep diary each morning. Individuals are asked to record, soon after awakening, their estimate in minutes of their SOL the previous night. Most sleep diaries also request estimates of the number and length of awakenings during the night and the total amount of sleep for the night. Typically, participants are asked to rate on a scale ranging from 5 to 9 points items such as: difficulty falling asleep, level of physical tension at bedtime, level of mental activity at bedtime, restedness, quality of sleep, and quality of daytime functioning. Sometimes a question about the amount and kind of sleep-inducing medication is included; however, most behavior therapy researchers require insomniacs to be drug free during treatment.

Purpose

The Daily Sleep Diary is used to monitor continuously the subjective *complaint* of insomnia. The Diary provides an inexpensive, nonintrusive, and efficient method of measuring the experiential component; that is, the element that serves as the usual impetus for the insomniac to seek medical treatment.

Development

The exact origin of this particular sleep diary format is unknown; however, insomnia researchers seem to have switched from retrospective reports to continuous daily monitoring in the early 1970s. The content for many of the questions derives to a large extent from Monroe (1967). Content and format have been remarkably consistent since then, enabling researchers to build a data base and to compare results across investigations. A more recent development, to ensure monitoring on a daily basis and to eliminate the possibility of retrospective estimates, is to require subjects to complete the Diary upon awakening and to mail it every day during baseline, treatment, and follow-up. The author has used this Diary successfully with hundreds of subjects and has not had problems with their understanding it or with client compliance in returning the Diary every morning (Lacks, Bertelson, Gans, & Kunkel, 1983).

Psychometric Characteristics

Normative studies have established clearcut SOL differences between insomniacs and good sleepers. In eight studies of good sleepers totaling 134 cases, SOL ranged from 9.4 to 14.4 minutes (mean 12.6) when the person slept at home and from 15.3 to 38.1 minutes (mean 24.6) when the person slept in the lab. Insomniacs in seven sleep laboratory studies with 217 cases had an SOL from 37 to 81.4 minutes (mean 56.7). In a 1978 review of seven treatment studies of clinical cases of insomnia the mean SOL was 82 minutes. Little is known about other aspects of sleep for good sleepers, but two studies have reported these figures for insomnia sufferers: 66.8 minutes awake after sleep onset (WASO) and 329.5 minutes of total sleep.

Besides the mean values of sleep diary items, behavior therapists should be aware of the high night-to-night variability of the sleep of insomnia sufferers. Total sleep diary variance for good sleepers exceeds considerably the variance for good sleepers. In fact, many sleep researchers believe that it is this variability that is the major source of the insomniac's complaint of daytime dysphoria rather than short sleep per se. Because of such variability, it is important to ensure sufficient sampling over time of the insomniac's sleep behavior.

Even though there are many potential sources of bias with such a self–report, research on the subjective estimate as recorded on a specific–item morning sleep diary has generally been favorable, in marked contrast to results with more global or retrospective sleep questionnaires or both. Test-retest reliability is high. In one study the average test-retest reliability for SOL was .86. In another it was .93 for poor sleepers and .58 for good sleepers. Agreement over three nights was .98 for SOL, .88 for the number of arousals, and .84 for WASO.

Measures of validity are equally encouraging. Subjective estimates of SOL from insomniacs correlate very highly with spouse or roommate observer estimates (r's = .84 to .99). Although no correlation coefficients were given, in one study good correspondence also was found between the insomniac self-report of SOL, observer estimates, and a clock that insomniacs activated with a switch in bed (r = .94 between subjective WASO and this device for nine insomniacs). This parallel relationship between the subjective sleep diary and the clock only occurred during the second week of the experiment after a significant reduction occurred in subjective SOL between the first and second weeks. Insomniacs may need a week of practice to develop consistency in estimating SOL. Using students who were poor sleepers, other researchers found the correlation between subjective estimate and EEG to increase from .37 on the second night in the laboratory to .75 by the fourth night. These studies indicate that insomniacs should be given 1 week to develop estimation accuracy before baseline figures are collected in the second week. In fact, converging evidence indicates that insomniacs are better estimators of the phenomenology of sleep than are good sleepers, perhaps because they have many years of experience of observing the target behavior.

Researchers have verified with all-night polysomnography (EEG) insomniacs' subjective reports of improvement following therapy. The SOL has also been found to correlate highly with EEG estimates (r's = .62 to .99), with the higher values occurring when more conservative criteria for sleep onset are used. Correlations between EEG and other diary items are generally lower: for number of arousals (r's = .27 to .63) and for WASO r's = .83 and .88.

Much of the criticism of subjective SOL is that these estimates are an overestimate of awake time compared with the EEG and with observers. Studies show a very consistent and constant 10 to 25 minutes' subjective overestimation of time to fall asleep using the EEG as the objective criterion, so that self-reports provide a reliable and valid relative index of SOL. However, because the correlations between the sleep diary and the EEG are substantial, this systematic error should not disqualify the sleep diary as a useful outcome measure. Both instruments appear to be assessing the same underlying dimension.

Recent research offers some understanding of the insomniac's overestimation of SOL when compared with the EEG. The traditional EEG objective marker for sleep onset has been the first sleep spindle or K complex. Evidence exists that for insomniacs the experience of sleep onset actually occurs at a later time during the EEG-assessed transition from waking to sleeping. In one study (Hauri & Olmstead, 1983) good sleepers were found to be very accurate in estimating sleep onset using the standard EEG criterion, whereas insomniacs consistently overestimated sleep onset. However, if the criterion for sleep onset was the first 15 minutes of stage 2 sleep, which was not interrupted by epochs scored as awake or stage 1, then insomniacs were extremely accurate (from 1 to 6 minutes) in their subjective estimates. During sleep onset, the insomniac experiences frequent alterations between stage 2 and wakefulness. Studies lend corroboration by finding that insomniacs usually report being awake when aroused during stage 1 and about half the time during the first onset of stage 2. Good sleepers typically report that they were asleep if aroused at these times.

Subjective reports of sleep improvement may be attributed to demand characteristics such as social acquiescence or the expectation of improvement. However, one study found no significant correlation between the sleep diary and the Marlow-Crowne Social Desirability Scale.

Clinical Use

This behavioral assessment technique is intended for sleep onset or sleep maintenance insomnia sufferers screened to eliminate those whose sleep problem is secondary to serious painful medical conditions (e.g., arthritis), psychopathology, or organic sleep pathology (e.g., apnea). The Daily Sleep Diary has been used successfully with persons of all age groups from 16 through 85, but it generally has only been tested on those with at least average intelligence. Well functioning older adults have no difficulty completing this measure.

Future Directions

The Daily Sleep Diary for monitoring sleep behaviors is a practical, inexpensive tool that has stood the test of time. As such, this measure is unlikely to undergo many future changes. A possible addition may be several questions that would tap the sense of self-efficacy or the individual's confidence in his or her ability to control sleep problems. Research has shown dramatic increases in self-efficacy after behavior therapy for insomnia.

References

Bootzin, R.R., Engle-Friedman, M., & Hazelwood, L. (1983). Insomnia. In P.M. Lewinsohn & L. Teri (Eds.), *Clinical geropsychology: New directions in assessment and treatment.* New York: Pergamon Press.
Borkovec, T.D. (1982). Insomnia. *Journal of Consulting and Clinical Psychology, 6,* 880-895.
Hauri, P., & Olmstead, E. (1983). What is the moment of sleep onset for insomniacs? *Sleep, 6,* 10-15.
Lacks, P., Bertelson, A.D., Gans, L., & Kunkel, J. (1983). The effectiveness of three behavioral treatments for different degrees of sleep onset insomnia. *Behavior Therapy, 14,* 593-605.
Monroe, L. (1967). Psychological and physiological differences between good and poor sleepers. *Journal of Abnormal Psychology, 72,* 255-264.

Dating Behavior Assessment Test

Carol R. Glass

Description

The Dating Behavior Assessment Test (DBAT) was developed by Glass, Gottman, and Shmurak (1976) to assess a change in a therapy outcome study comparing response acquisition (social skills training) and cognitive self-statement modification approaches for heterosocially anxious college men. The DBAT consists of 24 problematic social situations, presented on audiotape, involving interactions with members of the opposite sex. After a description of each situation, given by a male voice, a female voice supplies a leading statement and the subject is asked to role-play a response. For example: "You have called up a girl to ask her for a Saturday night date. She says 'Gee, I'm really sorry, but I'm busy Saturday night.' You say..."

Subjects' responses are taperecorded, transcribed, and rated according to specific adequacy criteria for each situation derived from judges' rationales for effective social behavior. A score of 0, 1, or 2 is given for each situation according to whether the subject meets none, some, or all of the criteria of a competent response. Therefore, the total score for all 24 situations can range from 0 to 48.

Purpose

The DBAT is an empirically developed laboratory role–play measure of men's social competence in dating situations. It was initially employed by Glass et al. (1976) to assess the outcome of various treatment programs for heterosocially anxious men.

Because 11 of the 24 situations were included as part of the therapy program, improvement in the 13 assessment-only situations provided evidence for the generalization of therapy change. The DBAT can therefore be used both in therapy and to assess change.

Development

The DBAT was based on Goldfried and D'Zurilla's (1969) behavioral-analytic method for creating assessment devices.

Identification of Problem Situations.

In a pilot study, undergraduates were interviewed and asked to recall difficult social situations and the key times when they experienced the most difficulty. In addition, the empirically derived situations from Goldsmith and McFall's (1975) study with socially unskilled psychiatric inpatients were rewritten to be more appropriate for a college population. This initial list of 75 situations was reduced to 41 through the elimination of redundant or idiosyncratic situations, those not dealing directly with dating problems, and situations concerning long-standing or ongoing relationships that were not immediately relevant for the therapy participants.

Identification of Competent Responses.

Competent responses to each of the 41 problematic dating situations were obtained in the following manner: (a) Six students previously identified as socially skilled responded to each situation as if they were actually involved. (b) These responses were given to five judges, who selected the most and least effective responses to each situation and also provided a rationale for their choices. (c) Responses were considered eligible for use in the assessment and therapy programs if four of the five judges agreed on a given competence or incompetence rating. Forty of the original 41 situations had a least one response that met this criterion. In addition, 23 situations and previously determined competent responses based on the work of Watkins (1972) were added to the pool.

Construction of the DBAT.

The final version of the DBAT consists of 24 of these 63 eligible situations chosen because they most clearly described key points of difficulty (i.e., they put the person "on the spot") and covered a range of difficulty, as determined by an additional pilot study. Scoring criteria for rating audiotaped responses to each

situation were based on adequacy criteria derived from judges' responses and rationales for competency. The rationales for the 11 situations used in therapy also served as the basis for the material presented in social skills training. An additional pilot study asked undergraduates to write down what their immediate thoughts and feelings would be in each problem situation, and how self-confident they would feel in each one. These thoughts were used to construct cognitive modeling material for use in the self-statement modification condition.

Psychometric Characteristics

Interrater reliabilities for DBAT scoring in the treatment study ranged from .75 to .92, with a mean of .83. The DBAT can be considered a content valid measure, because items and scoring criteria were derived from the population for which it was intended. Subjects who participated in one therapy program also demonstrated significant change in the DBAT, especially in the situations employed in treatment. Additional validity data have not been collected.

Pretreatment total scores on the DBAT for the 80 socially anxious male undergraduate and graduate students who volunteered for the program averaged 18.88 (11 situations employed in therapy mean = 7.64; 13 untrained situations mean = 11.24). For the 50 subjects who were assigned to a treatment group and completed one therapy program, posttreatment DBAT scores averaged 29.16 (trained situations mean = 14.54; untrained situations mean = 14.62). (Higher scores indicate greater social skill.)

Clinical Use

As previously described, the DBAT can be used as an outcome measure reflecting increases in social skills as a function of therapy intervention. In addition, the situations can be used as part of a therapy program itself. For social skills training, clients can practice responding to problematic dating situations and can learn more appropriate ways to handle conversations based on the response criteria developed. In cognitive restructuring, the situations can be employed to elicit negative self-statements from clients, who can then practice becoming aware of these self-defeating patterns, disputing and challenging their maladaptive thoughts, and substituting more positive, coping cognitions. For the assessment, it is important to recall that DBAT situations were obtained and selected for their relevance in a university population of heterosocially anxious men. Therefore, it may be inappropriate for socially anxious women, and its generalizability to a general adult population is unknown.

Future Directions

Future research on the DBAT should attempt to remedy some of these potential limitations. It would be valuable to develop a more general measure that could be used to assess heterosocial skills of both men and women in a wider age range. In both measure development and therapy intervention design, Goldfried and D'Zurilla's (1969) empirical approach is especially important. Obtaining norms on the DBAT for socially anxious and competent men would also allow therapists to evaluate if by the end of therapy clients had increased their social skills to the level of their socially competent peers.

References

Glass, C.R., Gottman, J.M., & Shmurak, S.H. (1976). Response acquisition and cognitive self-statement modification approaches to dating skills training. *Journal of Counseling Psychology, 23,* 520-526.

Goldfried, M.R., & D'Zurilla, T.J. (1969). A behavioral-analytic model for assessing competence. In C.D. Spielberger (Ed.), *Current topics in clinical and community psychology: Vol. 1* (pp. 151-196). New York: Academic Press.

Goldsmith, J.B., & McFall, R.M. (1975). Development and evaluation of an interpersonal skill-training program for psychiatric inpatients. *Journal of Abnormal Psychology, 84,* 51-58.

Watkins, B.R. (1972). The development and evaluation of a transductive learning technique for the treatment of social incompetence. *Dissertation Abstracts International, 33,* 286lB. (University Microfilms No. 72-78,199).

Del Greco Assertive Behavior Inventory

Linda Del Greco

Description

The Del Greco Assertive Behavior Inventory (DABI) is an 86-item questionnaire designed to measure assertive, aggressive, nonassertive, and passive aggressive behavior in college dormitory students. The self-administered questionnaire takes approximately 30 minutes to complete and yields four separate scores, one for each of the aforementioned behaviors. Each question is answered and scored using a Likert scale in which Almost Never, Seldom, Sometimes, Often, and Almost Always are awarded 1, 2, 3, 4, and 5 points, respectively.

Purpose

The DABI measures assertion (AS), aggression (AG), nonassertion (NA), and passive aggression (PA). Previous measures of assertion were based on a unidimensional model, where NA and AS make up the two ends of a continuum or where AS is the midpoint between NA and AG. Such scales yielded a single imprecise global score. Previous scales were further limited by the fact that the target behaviors were not well defined but were simply illustrated. In addition, passive aggressive behavior, which has received considerable interest in psychological and psychiatric inquiry, was not addressed at all.

The present inventory is based on a two-dimensional model first proposed by DeGiovanni (1979), which places the behaviors at fixed points along two continua: coercive versus noncoercive and overt versus covert. Aggressive behavior is defined as behavior that is both overt and coercive. Passive aggressive behavior is both covert and coercive. Assertive behavior is covert but not coercive. Nonassertive behavior is covert as well as noncoercive.

The two dimensions are critical because they combine both modes of communication (overt or covert) with intention (coercive or noncoercive). Without the benefit of the second dimension, overt behavior on a unidimensional scale (whether AS or AG) would be classified as assertive. Similarly, all covert behavior (whether PA or NA) would be classified as nonassertive. Therefore, the global unidimensional scores are at best incomplete and at worst inaccurate. The DABI yields four distinct scores, allowing for more precise interpretation.

Development

All subjects were dormitory students at the State University of New York at Buffalo during the Spring of 1979. The development was divided into four separate components to be discussed.

Item Generation. Situations involving any of the four target behaviors were generated by 121 students. Situations were restricted to those pertaining to the present milieu and peer group excluding significant others.

Item Evaluation. The 605 situations generated were collapsed into 142 items which were rated by 12 graduate students working and living in the dormitories.

Reliability Testing and Item Analysis. The preliminary form of the DABI was distributed to 500 randomly selected students. A correlation matrix of each item with each of the four scales was completed. The results showed that for all but six items, the highest positive correlation was with the correct scale. Four of these items were revised and the remaining two eliminated. Other items were eliminated because they were repeatedly left blank or initiated complaints from the subjects. Following this, the coefficient alphas for the four scales were: AS = 0.83 (mean = 72.8, SD = 12.8), AG = 0.91 (mean = 33.7, SD = 12.0), PA = 0.90 (mean = 39.1, SD = 11.9), and NA = 0.85 (mean = 55.2, SD = 12.5). This implies good reliability. Each of these alphas has a p value <0.001.

A principal-components plot was constructed using the correlation between each item and all other items representing the same behavior, corrected for attenuation. The best two-dimensional representation of the target behaviors resulted in four distinct clusters, which is quite similar to DeGiovanni's model (1979). This indicates that the relationship among the target behaviors is not random, but that assertion, in fact, fits a two-dimensional model.

Validity Testing. During the validity testing phase, each of 500 randomly selected dormitory students received the revised copy of the DABI, the College Self-Expression Scale (CSES), and three scales of the Buss-Durkee Aggression Inventory (BDI). These additional scales were used as measures of convergent and discriminant validity.

Psychometric Characteristics

Because a number of items had been removed or revised following the reliability testing phase, the internal consistency of the DABI was reexamined. The coefficient alphas for the AS, AG, PA, and NA scales were 0.83, 0.87, 0.87, and 0.82, respectively. The coefficient alphas for the CSES was 0.91 (all p values <0.001). Finally, the coefficient alphas for

the Buss-Durkee Inventory's Indirect Aggression, Assault, and Verbal Aggression Scales were 0.59, 0.73, and 0.62, respectively (all p values <0.001). The coefficient alphas indicate that both the DABI and the CSES have good internal consistency. The BDI scales were fair except for the Indirect Aggression Scale, which was weak.

The BDI Indirect Aggression Scale was unsuitable for convergent validity testing of the DABI PA Scale because of the BDI's low internal consistency and because the DABI PA Scale evolved in such a way that it no longer fit the BDI definition of indirect aggression. For the same reason, the BDI Indirect Aggression Scale was unsuitable as an indicator of the discriminant validity of the DABI AS Scale. However, the negative correlation between the DABI PA and AS Scales is indicative of the expected discrimination between these two behaviors. Negative correlations between the DABI NA Scale and the BDI Assault and Verbal Aggression Scales were achieved, supporting the DABI's validity.

Because the CSES was not comprised of separate scales for AS and NA, simple correlations could not be used to examine the convergent and discriminant validity of the DABI AS and NA Scales. However, because the CSES was made up of an approximately equal number of AS and NA items, a two-dimensional geometric representation of the correlations among the CSES, DABI, AS, and DABI NA Scales, corrected for attenuation, was examined.

The most efficient two-dimensional view of the configuration of the DABI AS and NA Scales and the CSES was constructed. The vector patterns produced by the CSES AS and projected negative NA items supported the convergent validity of the DABI AS and NA Scales. Similarly, the discriminant validity of the DABI AS and PA Scales had to be determined by examining the correlation pattern among the DABI AG and PA Scales and the CSES. The configuration shows a separation of the DABI AG and PA Scales from the CSES AS and projected negatively scored NA items.

In conclusion, the reliability of the AS, AG, NA, and PA Scales of the DABI using coefficient alpha is good. Convergent and discriminant validity in most cases turned out as expected. Unfortunately, the BDI Indirect Aggression Scale was not useful, leaving some question regarding the convergent and discriminant validity of the DABI PA and AS Scales, respectively. However, the DABI PA and AS Scales did cluster and were negatively correlated with each other as expected. A more detailed discussion of these results can be found in Del Greco (1983).

Clinical Use

Although the DABI's validity and reliability were established with a college dormitory population, its applications are not necessarily restricted to this population. Because the DABI is concerned with behavior that occurs in a group living situation, it can be used in any such setting regardless of the age of the respondents. This would include inpatient psychiatric hospitals, half-way houses, camps, and senior citizen communities. Indeed, it can be useful in any situation in which persons live together and strife may occur.

The DABI provides information on not only the mode of communication but also the intent of communication. It may be useful when either one or both of these factors are at issue. It is possible to collapse data along either of the two continua. Therefore, in studies in which the interest is only on coercion, the PA and AG scales as well as the AS and NA scales can be collapsed. Similarly, if the overt quality of communication is the focus of interest, the appropriate scales can be collapsed.

Therefore, the DABI may be useful for diagnosis, population description, and assessment of intervention techniques that have as their goal understanding or modification of behavior in group living situations, or both.

Future Directions

Most research concerned with AG, NA, and AS has to date concentrated on a unidimensional model and has therefore ignored important aspects of these behaviors, including PA. In fact, assertion training programs may inadvertently produce undesired behaviors. For example, a passive aggressive person (covert and coercive) may become more overt as a result of such training instead of becoming less coercive, resulting in AG behavior. Such discrepancies may explain some of the inconsistent results obtained with Assertiveness Training. Future researchers would do well to adapt a two-dimensional model for these behaviors and structure their intervention techniques accordingly.

The DABI is most applicable for persons living together in groups. It also may be useful in family situations, which may be thought of as a special case of group living. Minor modifications of the DABI could be made, and family dynamics may be

explicable in light of the two-dimensional model. Similar adaptations of the DABI may also be made so that it may be useful in situations in which people interact but do not live together (e.g., offices and schools) and in which the mode and intent of communication are important issues.

References

DeGiovanni, I.S. (1979). Development and validation of an assertiveness scale for couples. *Dissertation Abstracts International, 39*(9-B), 4573.
Del Greco, L. (1983). The Del Greco Assertive Behavior Inventory. *Journal of Behavioral Assessment, 5*, 49-63.

Dental Fear Survey

F. Dudley McGlynn

Description

The Dental Fear Survey (DFS) is a 20-item Likert-type questionnaire that prompts five-point ratings of dental avoidance, of somatovisceral arousal during dental treatment, and of fear during the naturalistic and clinical interactions included in seeking and receiving dental care. There is a global rating for fear of dentistry. The item stems are: (a) put off making an appointment, (b) canceling or failing to appear, (c) muscle tenseness, (d) increased breathing rate, (e) perspiration, (f) nausea, (g) faster heart beat, (h) making an appointment, (i) approaching dental office, (j) sitting in the waiting room, (k) sitting in dental chair, (l) smell of dental office, (m) seeing the dentist, (n) seeing the anesthetic needle, (o) feeling the anesthetic needle, (p) seeing the drill, (q) hearing the drill, (r) feeling the drill, (s) having teeth cleaned, and (t) overall fear of dentistry.

Purpose

In concert with the behavior therapy movement, psychologic thinking about fear and avoidance of dentistry shifted away from psychoanalytic formulations toward learning models of the problem. In one way or another, the learning models uniformly were couched in Stimulus–Response (S–R) terms. Therefore, a need existed for assessment methods that were in tune with S–R thinking. The twofold purpose of the 20-item DFS is to sample the various actual stimuli that might occasion fear or avoidance, or both, and to describe the examinee's specific and unique responses to these stimuli.

Development

Self-report measures of fear often have been obtained using single items imbedded in omnibus fear inventories. Single item self-assessments of dental fear are of limited value because they provide no information about concrete aspects of dentistry (instruments, settings, procedures, and dentist demeanors) that function as prominent fear cues. Corah (1969) improved on single item self-assessment by providing his Dental Anxiety Scale. However, Corah included only four items in his scale, thus restricting sharply its potential for representative content sampling (content validity) within both the stimulus and response dimensions. Kleinknecht, Klepac, and Alexander (1973) addressed the content validity problem in self-assessment of dental fear by developing a 27-item questionnaire. It was comprised of two items about dental avoidance, six items about perceived physiological arousal during dentistry, 14 items about the degree of fear prompted by various components of dental practice, one item about overall fear of dentistry, and four items about reactions to dentistry among family and friends. A cursorily reported test-retest reliability study, performed using the 27-item scale, yielded median correlation coefficients of 0.74 for items across 106 respondents and 0.73 for the respondents across 27 items. The 27-item scale was then administered to 322 college students, 86 high school students, and 79 junior high school students from Western Washington State College and the Bellingham, Washington school system. The mean and standard deviation for each item was computed for the group as a whole, for each sex, and for each sample group. The 20-item DFS is the final result of this work.

Psychometric Characteristics

Kleinknecht, Thorndike, McGlynn, and Harkavy (1984) reported a factor analysis of DFS scores obtained from 518 dental patients in Washington and from 415 introductory psychology students in Florida. Several criteria (e.g., Kaiser, scree, and inspection of residuals) led to a decision to retain three factors in both data sets. Several methods of principal axis factoring for three factors showed them to be highly stable within data sets. Correlations between factor score variables for Washington and Florida respondents showed the factors to be highly stable across geographically and demographically different populations. The first factor includes items about dental avoidance and private fear behaviors associated with the early steps in keeping a dental appointment. The second factor is about private fear behaviors associated with specific dental stimuli and restorative procedures. The third factor represents reported physiological arousal during dental treatment.

McGlynn and McNeil (1985) reported on the test-retest reliability and internal consistency of the DFS among introductory psychology students. Pearson product-moment correlations between first-test and second-test scores obtained 8 to 13 weeks later were robust for both total scores and three subscale scores defined by the Kleinknecht et al. factor analysis. Cronbach's alpha coefficients also were uniformly high within total scores and subscale scores from each administration.

Kleinknecht and Bernstein (1978) reported on the predictive validity of the DFS total scores. High scorers differed as expected from low scorers with regard to cancelled appointments, waiting room activity levels, pain reports during treatment, and patterns of palmar sweating.

Adequate normative data are not available for the scale, for its individual items, or for its factor analytically derived subscales. The psychometric work to date portrays the DFS as reliable and internally consistent. More validity work is needed for the entire scale and its three subscales.

Clinical Use

There is enough information on the DFS to justify its routine use now with dentally fearful patients and nonclinical research subjects. Kleinknecht et al. (1984) suggested that, at some point, scores on the three–factor analytically derived subscales might be used to match treatment with the patients. For example, fearful patients who score high on the first factor might be treated with "cognitive restructuring...to eliminate catastrophic thinking or introduce...coping strategies." (p. 61).

Future Directions

There is a need for item-by-item normative data from the general population and nonclinical research populations are needed. Additional validity studies are needed in which total scores and subscale scores predict clinically or experimentally relevant private, motoric, or physiologic fear behavior or a combination of these (Kleinknecht & Bernstein, 1978). Given indications of predictive validity in terms of adaptively relevant fear and/or avoidance, studies would be valuable in which sub-scale scores on the DFS are crossed with representative forms of the major treatments available for anxiety disorders.

References

Corah, N.L. (1969). Development of dental anxiety scale. *Journal of Dental Research, 48, 596.*

Kleinknecht, R.A., & Bernstein, D.A. (1978). The assessment of dental fear. *Behavior Therapy, 9, 626-634.*

Kleinknecht, R.A., Klepac, R.K., & Alexander, L.T. (1973). Origins and characteristics of fear of dentistry. *Journal of the American Dental Association, 86, 842-848.*

Kleinknecht, R.A., Thorndike, R.M., McGlynn, F.D., & Harkavy, J. (1984). Factor analysis of the dental fear survey with cross validation. *Journal of the American Dental Association, 108, 59-61.*

McGlynn, F.D., McNeil, D.W., Gallagher, S.L., & Vrana, S. (1987). Factor structure, stability, and internal consistency of the Dental Fear Survey. *Behavioral Assessment, 9, 57-66.*

Dental Operatory Rating Scale

Ronald A. Kleinknecht and Douglas A. Bernstein

Description

The Dental Operatory Rating Scale (DORS) is a time-sampling behavioral observation scale for recording the overt motor behavior of patients receiving dental treatment (Kleinknecht & Bernstein, 1978). The DORS focuses on 46 behaviors, categorized into three general areas: (a) postural status (sitting, reclining, gripping chair arms, and crossing legs), (b) general activity (reading, talking, and closing eyes), and (c) specific activity (standing up, tapping feet, biting nails, gaging, turning head away from dentist, and negative verbalizing).

Each category is coded on a time-sampling basis (5-second observation, 25-second recording) throughout a dental appointment and converted to a frequency-per-observation-interval. For each recording interval, notation is made of what treatment is occurring and who is present (e.g., dentist present and treating, patient alone, and dentist using drill). Thus, a full range of patient behavior is quantified along with the conditions under which it occurs.

Purpose

The DORS was designed to quantify the motoric component of fear behavior in patients undergoing dental treatment. This scale, along with a companion scale for quantifying patients' waiting room behavior, was developed as one component of a comprehensive dental fear assessment package (Kleinknecht & Bernstein, 1978) and as an outcome measure to evaluate dental fear reduction procedures (Bernstein & Kleinknecht, 1982).

Development

The format of the DORS was patterned after Paul's (1966) Timed Behavioral Checklist, but it was adapted to codify behaviors specific to the dental treatment setting. Behaviors to be included were based on a perusal of dental fear assessment literature and the authors' observations of numerous video recordings of patients undergoing treatment. The final set of behaviors selected appeared to reflect motoric fear components that could reliably be defined and coded by observers.

Psychometric Characteristics

The DORS is highly reliable in terms of interobserver agreement. Pairs of trained observers rating behavior from videotapes of routine dental appointments showed correlations ranging from .76 to .97; the mean across observer pairs and categories was .90. Coding of treatment status was the most reliable (1.0), whereas specific activities was the least (mean .76).

Validity of the DORS is more difficult to evaluate. In one study of 128 dental patients, the frequency of coded behaviors did not differentiate dental patients who reported themselves to be fearful from those reporting fearlessness. However, frequency of behaviors in each category differed as a function of treatment status. While the dentist was treating, all patients were essentially immobile. When alone in the operatory, they moved a great deal. In a subsequent study using only 16 subjects, fearful patients moved significantly less than did nonfearful patients when they were alone in the operatory (Kleinknecht & Bernstein, 1978). Although nonsignificant, this same trend was seen in the previous study. The lower frequency of operatory movement contrasts with that seen in the waiting room, where fearful patients move more than do those reporting little fear (Kleinknecht & Bernstein, 1978). Thus, the DORS is able to reliably capture movement throughout treatment, but its ability to differentiate patients with high-level and low-level fear has not been clearly established.

Clinical Use

The DORS was designed as a research instrument, and its current form does not lend itself to general clinical use. Because of its complex nature and requirement of considerable rater training, it is most appropriate as a research tool.

Future Directions

Future users of the DORS should seek to identify specific motor behaviors most clearly indicative of dental fear. Delineation of specific behaviors should simplify this scale and allow for a tighter focus on a smaller set of fear signs. Development and validation of a simplified version of the DORS could provide dentists and dental assistants with a useful assessment/diagnostic tool for early identification of fearful patients. Such an instrument should also prove valuable in the clinical training of dental students.

Such efforts presume that there is a class of clinically meaningful behaviors related to dental fear. Discussions with practicing dentists indicate that they do exist. Our minimal success in identifying such behaviors may have resulted from observing mildly to moderately fearful patients who actually appear for appointments. Use of the DORS with more clearly phobic patients should help determine if such discriminating signs do exist. We believe that such investigations are warranted.

References

Bernstein, D.A., & Kleinknecht, R.A. (1982). Multiple approaches to the reduction of dental fear. *Behavior Therapy and Experimental Psychiatry, 13,* 287-292.

Kleinknecht, R.A., & Bernstein, D.A. (1978). The assessment of dental fear. *Behavior Therapy, 9,* 626-634.

Paul, G. (1966). *Insight versus desensitization in psychotherapy: An experiment in anxiety reduction.* Stanford, CA: Stanford University Press.

Dental Subscale of the Children's Fear Survey Schedule

Barbara G. Melamed and Mark A. Lumley

Description

The Dental Subscale (DS) of the Children's Fear Survey Schedule (CFSS) is a set of 15 stimuli related to the dental situation and presumed to elicit fear and anxiety in the dental patient. The 50-item CFSS, which contains the 15 items specific to the dental situation, is a self-report measure administered to a child by an adult. The 15 items of the DS include the following: (1) dentists, (2) doctors, (3) persons in white uniforms, (4) injections (shots), (5) choking, (6) having somebody examine your mouth, (7) having somebody look at you, (8) having somebody put instruments in your mouth, (9) having a stranger touch you, (10) having the nurse clean your teeth, (11) having to go to the hospital, (12) having to open your mouth, (13) the dentist drilling, (14) the sight of the drill, and (15) the noise of the dentist drilling. The CFSS and therefore the DS are designed to be administered to children who are young, generally aged 4 to 12 years. This 5-point Likert type scale measures the intensity of a child's fear by asking the child to rate how afraid he or she is of each specific stimuli. The scale ranges from 1 (not at all afraid) to 5 (very afraid). To assist children in responding, a visual aid, the Fear Thermometer, can be used. The child points to one of five positions on the thermometer that corresponds to his or her level of fear of the given stimulus. A final score can be calculated by totaling either the ratings of all 50 items, yielding an overall score of the CFSS, or only the 15 dental items for a specific dental fear score. The DS is reprinted in an article by Cuthbert and Melamed (1982).

Purpose

Dental fear is a well-recognized problem in the general population. Because many of these fears can be learned in childhood, it is of interest to study the distribution and origin of dental fears among children as a group. Moreover, the individual child often needs to be assessed for her or his level of dental-related fear to be effectively handled in the dental setting. Because fear or anxiety is considered a multiple-dimensional construct comprising the behavioral, self-report, and psychophysiological modalities, a complete assessment of fear ideally involves tripartite measurement. The Behavior Profile Rating Scale (BPRS) is an observational tool designed especially for monitoring the verbal and motoric behavior of children in the dental setting. Numerous physiological recording devices exist that also can be used in the assessment of fear and anxiety.

Development

The CFSS is a modification of the Scherer and Nakamura (1968) Fear Survey Schedule for Children, an 80-item self-report measure composed of

10 factor-analyzed subscales of fears. One of these, the Medical Fears subscale, contains only a few items that are related to the dental situation. Kleinknecht and associates developed a dental fear scale to identify fear stimuli and measure patients' reactions, but it is intended for use with older children, from grade 6 through college. Melamed, Weinstein, Hawes, and Katin-Borland (1975) were interested in using the CFSS on younger children who were being prepared for dental work. To examine their reported fear of the dental situation itself, a modified version of the CFSS was developed containing a subscale of 15 items of high face validity. Cuthbert and Melamed (1982) conducted a large-scale study of the DS by presenting it alone to obtain normative data. This modified version of the CFSS has been used in several studies that have examined methods of preparing children for dental treatment. Self-reported fears have been examined both for the CFSS overall and for the DS in particular.

Psychometric Characteristics

Melamed and Cuthbert (1982) had the parents of 603 children aged 5 to 14 years present to their children the DS without the other CFSS items. Findings included the following: fear scores decreased with age ($r = .20, p < .001$); children 5 to 8 years of age reported more fears than did those 9 to 13 years old ($p < .001$); no overall sex differences in self-reported fear were found, but higher fear reports were presented by girls of particular ages (6, 7, 8, 9, and 13 years); the 15 items were ranked similarly by both boys and girls as to their fearful properties, with "choking" receiving the highest ranking, followed by "injections" and "the dentist drilling."

At least two studies show the DS to be a good predictor of the CFSS full-scale score, with correlations of .82 and .87 ($p < .001$) (Melamed, Yurcheson, Fleece, Hutcherson, & Hawes, 1978; Klingman, Melamed, Cuthbert, & Hermecz, 1984). Melamed et al. (1978) found the DS to be positively correlated with the independent behavioral measures of the BPRS, to be significantly correlated with the Behavior Problem Checklist and a parental questionnaire reporting general behavior problems ($r = .28, p < .05$), and also to be correlated with the Palmar Sweat Index (PSI), a measure of physiological activation ($r = .31, p < .01$). Klingman et al. (1984) found that the DS of the CFSS differentiated two groups of children (a symbolic modeling group and a participant modeling group)

from preinstructional film to the postinstructional film ($p < .02$) and to posttreatment time ($p < .04$). Klingman et al. (1984) found the test-retest reliability of the DS to be .86 ($p < .001$).

Clinical Use

The DS of the CFSS is an assessment device designed to evaluate a child's self-reported fear of the dental situation. As such, it can be used to screen those children with high dental fears in order to implement treatment. Moreover, assessment of intervention outcomes can be accomplished, as in the several studies mentioned. It appears that the DS score can be used to predict the full-scale score for the CFSS.

Future Directions

Several steps now need to be taken. First, studies with children in a nondental situation should be undertaken to further examine the predictive validity of the DS of the full-scale CFSS. Second, an attempt can be made to convert the DS into a separate self-report measure that can be used alone, as done with the Hospital Fears Rating Scale. If this were done, a logical next step would be to determine if this newly developed scale applies to adults as well as children.

References

Cuthbert, M.I., & Melamed, B.G. (1982). A screening device: Children at risk for dental fears and management problems. *Journal of Dentistry for Children, 49,* 431-436.

Klingman, A., Melamed, B.G., Cuthbert, M.I., & Hermecz, D.A. (1984). Effects of participant modeling on information acquisition and skill utilization. *Journal of Consulting and Clinical Psychology, 54,* 414-422.

Melamed, B.G., Weinstein, D., Hawes, R., & Katin-Borland, M. (1975). Reduction of fear-related dental management problems with use of filmed modeling. *Journal of the American Dental Association, 90,* 822-826.

Melamed, B.G., Yurcheson, R., Fleece, E.L., Hutcherson, S., & Hawes, R. (1978). Effects of film modeling on the reduction of anxiety-related behaviors in individuals varying in level of previous experience in the stress situation. *Journal of Consulting and Clinical Psychology 46,* 1357-1367.

Scherer, M.W., & Nakamura, C.Y. (1968). A fear survey schedule for children (FSS-FC): A factor analytic comparison with manifest anxiety (CMAS). *Behaviour Research and Therapy, 6,* 173-182.

Derogatis Sexual Functioning Inventory

Leonard R. Derogatis

Description

The Derogatis Sexual Functioning Inventory (DSFI) is a multidimensional, self-report, omnibus measure of sexual functioning designed to specifically reflect the *current* level of sexual functioning of the *individual* respondent. The DSFI is comprised of 10 principal domains that are scored as distinct subtests and also includes two global indices of sexual functioning (Derogatis & Melisaratos, 1979). The test was originally published in 1975 and subsequently revised consistent with its present form (Derogatis, 1978).

The DSFI was developed as a multidimensional test consistent with the posture that human sexual functioning is multiply determined and cannot be adequately represented along a simple unidimensional continuum (Derogatis, 1980). The individual respondent was selected as the unit of measurement, both because it represents the simplest and most straightforward unit and because ultimately the quality of the sexual experience must be judged by an individual.

The 10 domains of sexual behavior measured by the DSFI are: (1) Information, (2) Experience, (3) Drive, (4) Attitude, (5) Psychological Symptoms, (6) Affects, (7) Gender Role Definition, (8) Fantasy, (9) Body Image, and (10) Sexual Satisfaction. Two global measures, the psychometrically determined Sexual Functioning Index and the subjectively rated Global Sexual Satisfaction Index, complete the measurement provided by the DSFI.

It is worth noting that two of the subtests of the DSFI are themselves independent psychometric instruments: the *Symptoms* subtest is the Brief Symptom Inventory (BSI) (Derogatis & Melisaratos, 1983), whereas the *Affects* subtest is defined by the Affects Balance Scale (ABS) (Derogatis, 1976). The former, a short form of the SCL-90-R (Derogatis, 1977, 1983a) is a 53-item multidimensional symptom inventory, whereas the latter is an adjective mood scale that assesses both positive and negative affect states. Although for DSFI scoring only a single global score is derived for each subtest, the complete multidimensional profile for each instrument may be scored and displayed.

Psychometric Characteristics

Concerning psychometric characteristics, gender-keyed norms for men and women (in terms of area-T scores) are available, and each individual's DSFI record may be plotted on normative score/profile forms. Both internal consistency and test–retest forms of reliability are available for the instrument (Derogatis, 1980; Derogatis & Melisaratos, 1979).

Clinical Use

The DSFI has been used most extensively in the evaluation of individuals with *general sexual dysfunction* (Derogatis & Meyer, 1979a), although it has also been used in assessing *partners* of individuals presenting with sexual dysfunction (Derogatis & Meyer, 1979b), *retarded ejaculators* (Derogatis, 1983b), and *male* (Derogatis, Meyer, & Vazquez, 1978) and *female* (Derogatis, Meyer, & Boland, 1982) *gender dysphorias*. In addition, the DSFI has been employed to evaluate the sexual functioning of patients with neoplastic diseases (Anderson & Hacker, 1983) as well as patients with other medical disorders (Collins & Kinder, 1984). An investigation also showed several subtests of the DSFI to have discriminative capacity regarding biogenic versus psychogenic etiologies in impotence (Derogatis, Meyer, & Dupkins, 1976); however, the study sample was small and these findings have not been replicated.

Future Directions

In a recent review of self-report measures of sexual functioning (Conte, 1983), the DSFI was among the instruments assessed and received a positive evaluation by the reviewer. Future directions involve the completion of a short form of the instrument, and its publisher, Clinical Psychometric Research (Baltimore, MD), will soon be offering microcomputer software for both the administration and the scoring of the DSFI.

References

Anderson, B.L., & Hacker, N.F. (1983). Treatment for gynecological cancer: A review of the effects on female sexuality. *Health Psychology, 2,* 203–221.

Collins, G.F., & Kinder, B.N. (1984). Adjustment following implantation of a penile prosthesis: A critical overview. *Journal of Sex and Marital Therapy, 10,* 255-271.

Conte, H.P. (1983). Development and use of self-report techniques for assessing sexual functioning: A review and critique. *Archives of Sexual Behavior, 12,* 555-576.

Derogatis, L.R. (1976). The Affect Balance Scale (ABS). Baltimore, MD: Clinical Psychometric Research.

Derogatis, L.R. (1977). *SCL–90–R: Administration, scoring, and procedures manual* (Ed. I). Baltimore, MD: Clinical Psychometric Research.

Derogatis, L.R. (1978). Derogatis Sexual Functioning Inventory (DSFI) Preliminary Scoring Manual. Baltimore, MD: Clinical Psychometric Research.

Derogatis, L.R. (1980). Psychological assessment of psychosexual functioning. In J.K. Meyer (Ed.), *Psychiatric Clinics of North America: Vol. 3*, 113-131.

Derogatis, L.R. (1983a). *SCL–90–R: Administration, scoring, and procedures manual (Ed. II)*. Baltimore, MD: Clinical Psychometric Research.

Derogatis, L.R. (1983b). A psychological profile of the retarded ejaculator. In J.K. Meyer, C.W. Schmidt, & T. W. Wise (Eds.), *Clinical management of sexual disorders (2nd ed.)* (pp. 334-339). Baltimore, MD: Williams and Wilkins.

Derogatis, L.R., & Melisaratos, N. (1979). The DSFI: A multidimensional measure of sexual functioning. *Journal of Sex and Marital Therapy, 5*, 244-281.

Derogatis, L.R., & Melisaratos, N. (1983). The Brief Symptom Inventory (BSI): An introductory report. *Psychological Medicine, 13*, 595-605.

Derogatis, L.R., & Meyer, J.K. (1979a). A psychological profile of the sexual dysfunctions. *Archives of Sexual Behavior, 8*, 201-223.

Derogatis, L.R., & Meyer, J.K. (1979b). The invested partner in sexual disorders. *American Journal of Psychiatry, 12*, 1545-1549.

Derogatis, L.R., Meyer, J.K., & Boland, P. (1982). A psychological profile of the transsexual: II. The female. *Journal of Nervous and Mental Diseases, 169*, 157-168.

Derogatis, L.R., Meyer, J.K., & Dupkin, C.N. (1976). Discrimination of organic versus psychogenic impotence with the DSFI. *Journal of Sex and Marital Therapy, 2*, 229-239.

Derogatis, L.R., Meyer, J.K., & Vazquez, F. (1978). A psychological profile of the transsexual: I. The male. *Journal of Nervous and Mental Diseases, 166*, 234-254.

Derogatis Symptom Checklist 90-R

Andrea L. Seidner and Dean G. Kilpatrick

Description

The Derogatis Symptom Checklist 90–R (SCL-90-R; Derogatis, 1977) is a 90-item self-report inventory designed to reflect psychologic symptom patterns of psychiatric and medical patients. Respondents rate each item on a 5-point scale of discomfort ranging from "none" to "extreme" on the basis of their experience of each symptom during the previous week. Scores are obtained for nine primary symptom dimensions and three global indices of distress. The nine symptom dimensions are somatization, obsession-compulsion, interpersonal sensitivity, depression, anxiety, hostility, phobic anxiety, paranoid ideation, and psychoticism. The three global indicators are global severity index (reflecting the number and intensity of symptoms), positive symptom distress index (a pure intensity measure), and positive symptom total (reflecting the number of symptoms).

Purpose

The purpose of the SCL-90-R is to provide a brief, psychometrically sound self-report inventory that accurately reflects the pattern of psychological distress currently being experienced by psychiatric and medical patients. It is intended for research and clinical applications.

Development

The SCL-90-R is historically related to the Hopkins Symptom Checklist (HSCL). It was developed to address the limitations of this instrument, particularly the HSCL's exclusivity as a research instrument. To develop the SCL-90-R (Derogatis, 1977), core items from the HSCL were retained, others were dropped, and 45 new items were added. The intensity rating was expanded from a 4-point to a 5-point scale, and administration procedures were revised and standardized. Item phrasing was kept as basic as possible (i.e., the simplest word that retained meaning), and vocabulary levels across dimensions were equated.

Psychometric Characteristics

The psychometric properties of the SCL-90-R have been described in a number of studies. Internal consistency reliability, as measured by alpha coefficients, ranged from .77 to .90 for the nine symptom dimensions (Derogatis, 1977), and a value of .95 was reported for the overall measure (Edwards, Yarvis, Mueller, Zingale, & Wagman, 1978). The test-retest reliability of the measure ranged from .78 to .90 for a 1-week interval (Derogatis, 1977), and values of .81 to .94 were reported by Edwards et al. (1978) for several different time intervals.

Factor analytic studies confirmed the clinically derived structure of the measure. Factorial invariance across gender was demonstrated. Sensitivity to change and convergent and discriminant validity also were favorably demonstrated. Published norms exist for at least four groups: psychiatric outpatients, psychiatric inpatients, nonpatient normal adults, and nonpatient normal adolescents (Derogatis, 1977). In short, data supporting the positive psychometric characteristics of this measure are extensive and growing rapidly. The reader should consult a recent review by Derogatis (1983) for a complete summary of reliability and validity information on the SCL-90-R.

Clinical Use

The SCL-90-R is useful with a broad range of psychiatric and medical populations. It has been extensively used in depression, sexual disorders, pharmacologic research, and stress disorders. However, our focus here is on the use of this measure with sexual assault victims. Rape victims have significantly more symptoms than do nonvictims for at least 4 years after the rape (Kilpatrick, Resick, & Veronen, 1981; Kilpatrick & Veronen, 1984a; Kilpatrick, Veronen, & Resick, 1979). Specifically, Kilpatrick and Veronen (1984a) reported that the SCL-90-R significantly differentiated symptoms of rape victims from those of nonvictims at the .01 level on all nine symptom dimensions and on all three global indices for 1 year after the assault. The sample consisted of 204 recent adult rape victims (aged 16 or older, 6 to 21 days after the assault at the initial assessment) and a matched comparison group of nonvictims who completed the SCL-90-R as part of a larger study in which individuals were assessed at 6 to 21 days, 1 month, 3 months, 6 months, 1 year, 18 months, 2 years, 3 years, and 4 years after the assault. Beyond the 1-year assessment, the SCL-90-R still differentiated victims from nonvictims in some of the individual dimensions and indices, with the phobic anxiety dimension reaching statistical significance most often. This finding is consistent with those attained with assessment instruments that specifically tap fear and anxiety in rape victims (see Modified Fear Survey entry in this volume), suggesting that these particular difficulties are the most persistent in rape victims. The SCL-90-R also was used by Kilpatrick and Veronen (1984a) in an investigation of the efficacy of cognitive-behavioral treatment for rape-induced anxiety and it was able to detect the impact of treatment.

Future Directions

Three future directions should enhance the value of the SCL-90-R as an assessment tool for victims of sexual assault and other crimes. One is to extend the use of the scale to victims of other types of crime. The SCL-90-R was used in a study of the psychological impact on women of several types of crime, including aggravated assault, burglary, robbery, and sexual assault (Kilpatrick & Veronen, 1984b). Preliminary analyses of SCL-90-R data collected in that study suggest that the scale can detect the psychological impact of other types of crime as well as sexual assault. A second promising future direction is to use the individual SCL-90-R items rather than subscale scores to provide finer-grained information about the most frequent postcrime symptoms. A third promising direction for the SCL-90-R is to explore computer administration and scoring.

References

Derogatis, L.R. (1977). *SCL-90-R: Administration, scoring, and procedures manual I.* Baltimore, MD: Clinical Psychometrics Research.

Derogatis L.R. (1983). *Description and bibliography for the SCL-90-R and other instruments of the psychopathology rating scale series.* Baltimore, MD: Johns Hopkins University School of Medicine.

Edwards, D.W., Yarvis, R.M., Mueller, D.P., Zingale, H.C., & Wagman, W.J. (1978). Test-taking and the stability of adjustment scales. *Evaluation Quarterly, 2,* 275-291.

Kilpatrick, D.G., Resick, P.A., & Veronen, L.J. (1981). Effects of a rape experience: A longitudinal study. *Journal of Social Issues, 37,* 105-122.

Kilpatrick, D.G., & Veronen, L.J. (1984a). Treatment of fear and anxiety in victims of rape (Final Report, Grant No. R01 MH 29602). Rockville, MD: National Institute of Mental Health.

Kilpatrick, D.G., & Veronen, L.J. (1984b). The psychological impact of crime (Grant No. 84-IJ-CX-0039). Washington, DC: National Institute of Justice.

Kilpatrick, D.G., Veronen, L.J., & Resick, P.A. (1979). The aftermath of rape: Recent empirical findings. *American Journal of Orthopsychiatry, 49,* 658-669.

Diabetes Assertiveness Test

Alan M. Gross

Description

The Diabetes Assertiveness Test (DAT; Gross & Johnson, 1981) is a behavioral role-play test particular to social interactions involving diabetes. The DAT includes eight items covering areas that are potentially problematic for youngsters who have insulin-dependent diabetes. These include such topics as embarrassing questions from peers, refusing diet-inappropriate foods, teasing, and parent-child medical management conflicts. Each item consists of a description of a diabetes-related problematic social situation and a prompt.

Administration of the instrument requires a subject and two experimenters. The subject is informed that he or she will hear a verbal description of a social situation followed by a prompt statement from the experimenter. Subjects are instructed to respond verbally to the prompt as realistically as possible. During administration of the DAT the subject sits opposite an experimenter. The second experimenter stands off to the side and reads the scene descriptions.

Subject responses to the DAT are videotaped. Generally, placing the camera behind the experimenter facing the subject facilitates scoring. Responses can be scored on a wide variety of behaviors considered to be components of social skills including eye contact, duration of speech, verbal content, speech latency, affect, loudness of voice, fluency of speech, requests for new behaviors from interpersonal partners, and refusals of unreasonable requests. The scoring of role-play responses identifies social skills behaviors that are occurring at deficit levels.

Methods for scoring social skills component behaviors are the same as those commonly observed in the general social skills literature (duration of speech = time talking). Particular criteria for appropriate verbal content may be developed by the experimenter; however, general criteria have been established. In all scenes concerning peers and teachers, an appropriate verbal response consists of the child explaining that he or she has diabetes, that therefore he or she has difficulty eating or digesting certain foods, that a specific diet must be followed, and that as long as dietary and medical requirements are adhered to, he or she can do everything anyone else can do. Appropriate verbal content includes the child explaining to the parent that dietary restrictions were not violated, and that on occasion diabetes control is off for other reasons (e.g., growth and stress). Lastly, one item involves the youngster telling the parent how he or she will explain to a supervising adult the signs of a hypoglycemic reaction as well as what to do if one should occur.

Purpose

Of the many problems experienced by youngsters with diabetes, perhaps the most prominent occur in their relationships with peers. Attempts to maintain a taxing medical regimen and normal interpersonal relationships place a large burden on a child. The daily regimen of insulin administration, monitoring urine ketones and blood glucose, and activity limitations clearly distinguishes the child with diabetes from his or her nondiabetic peers. These medical restrictions coupled with the young diabetic patient's desire for social approval among peers who may not understand the nature of diabetes set the stage for significant social conflict and stress. Children with diabetes frequently are confronted with numerous questions from peers about their illness and its required medical treatment, as well as teasing about behavioral restrictions because of the diabetes. At times it will be difficult for the child with diabetes to meet the demands of conformity and to keep the diabetes in check. Unfortunately, few youngsters with diabetes have peer models to observe who demonstrate effective social skills for coping with these disease-related situations. As such, some of the reported interpersonal problems associated with youngsters who have diabetes may be a function of poorly developed social skills.

Similar to the difficulties with peers experienced by all children, youngsters with diabetes are also subject to numerous social conflicts with parents and significant others such as teachers. Common parental reactions to their child's disease include overconcern, compulsive behavior, overindulgence, and outright denial. The management requirements of the illness set the stage for continuing parent–child conflict revolving around adolescent independence, so that parent–child conflict may far exceed that experienced by nondiabetic teenagers.

Various social problems have been suggested as a function of poorly developed social skills. In the absence of such skills, a child may have difficulty learning the complex behavioral repertoire necessary for effective social interaction. As already noted herein, the social and medical demands of a child with diabetes, along with the relative absence of age-appropriate peer models of successful social coping behavior, place children with diabetes at high risk for developing social skills deficits. The purpose of the DAT is to help identify youngsters with diabetes who have inadequately developed social skills for coping with disease-related social stresses. The DAT is also useful in social coping skills training (Gross, Johnson, Wildman, & Mullett, 1981; Gross, Heimann, Shapiro, & Schultz, 1983; Johnson, Gross, & Wildman, 1983).

Development

The development of the DAT involved interviewing individuals aged 21 to 30 years who experienced the onset of diabetes as young children. They were asked to describe disease-related social situations that had been stressful when they were youngsters. From these interviews a list of 20 situations was obtained and written in question format. The questionnaire was then administered to 30 adults who experienced adolescence with insulin-dependent diabetes. They were asked to rate each scene retrospectively on a scale of 1 to 5 (1 = very; 5 = not at all) on the frequency of occurrence and how problematic the situation was experienced. From the responses of these subjects the eight most common and problematic scenes were selected and used in the DAT.

Psychometric Characteristics

To date, the DAT has been used to evaluate social skills deficits in 30 young diabetic patients. Although no formal statistical analyses have been performed to determine its test-retest reliability, multiple baseline data collected over a 10-week period indicate consistently stable responding to these items on the component social skills behaviors before intervention (Gross et al., 1981; Gross et al., 1983).

Clinical Use and Future Directions

The clinical usefulness of the DAT involves treating young diabetic patients aged 8 to 14 years who are experiencing social adjustment problems related to their disease. In particular, the DAT can identify social coping skills deficits and serve as a tool in the eradication of these problems. The scenes from the DAT are useful in social skills training. Subjects can role–play these situations and receive coaching and feedback on their performance. The continual assessment of subject performance on the DAT across training also provides multiple baseline data on skill acquisition. Studies have successfully used the DAT in this capacity.

The DAT is also useful in prompting groups of children with diabetes to discuss potential problems they experience in their social lives. Acquainting parents with the DAT also increases their awareness and sensitivity to social issues faced by their children (Gross, Magalnick, & Richardson, 1985).

Future directions for the DAT include expanding it to encompass disease-related social difficulties particular to diabetic adolescents and young adults (e.g., informing a boyfriend or girlfriend about having diabetes). Moreover, developing items relevant to parent concerns may also be a fruitful direction in which to extend this instrument.

References

Gross, A.M., Heimann, L., Shapiro, R., & Schultz, R. (1983). Social skills training and hemoglobin Alc levels in young diabetics. *Behavior Modification, 7,* 151-164.

Gross, A.M., & Johnson, W.G. (1981). Diabetes assertiveness test: A measure of social coping skills in preadolescent diabetics. *The Diabetes Educator, 7,* 26-27.

Gross, A.M., Johnson, W.G., Wildman, H.E., & Mullett, N. (1981). Copings skills training with young diabetics. *Child Behavior Therapy, 3,* 141-153.

Gross, A.M., Magalnick, L., & Richardson, P. (1985). Self-management training with families of insulin dependent diabetic children: A long term controlled investigation. *Child and Family Behavior Therapy, 7,* 35-50.

Johnson, W.G., Gross, A.M., & Wildman, H.E. (1983). Developing coping skills in juvenile diabetics. *Corrective and Social Psychiatry, 29,* 116-120.

Dieter's Inventory of Eating Temptations

David G. Schlundt

Description

The Dieter's Inventory of Eating Temptations (DIET) is a 30-item self-report competence inventory that samples behavior in six situations related to weight control: overeating, resisting temptation, food choice, positive social interactions, negative emotions, and exercise. Each item describes a specific situation related to caloric energy balance and presents a competent response that minimizes caloric intake or maximizes caloric expenditure. Subjects are instructed to imagine themselves in the situation and to rate the percentage of the time they would engage in the described response.

Purpose

Individuals who wish to control or lose weight are faced with the behavioral task of emitting some responses and omitting others in a variety of eating and activity-related situations. The purpose of the

DIET is to measure a subject's prediction of competence in handling a relevant sample of energy balance situations. The result is a profile that measures a subject's competence in each of the six situations. The DIET's purpose is to identify areas in which a subject needing help in controlling or losing weight would benefit from skill training.

Development

Four psychologists experienced in conducting weight reduction programs generated a pool of 50 descriptions of situations that weight loss subjects find difficult to handle. An initial 40-item version of the DIET was developed and administered to 21 overweight and 23 normal weight subjects. Items that were rated lower by overweight persons were retained. Additional items were written to replace unclear items and to balance the number of items sampled per class of situations. The DIET was then administered to 373 subjects recruited from a variety of sources. Twenty subjects were administered the DIET on two occasions between 1 and 2 weeks apart. Forty subjects participating in behavioral weight reduction programs took the DIET questionnaire before starting the program and self-monitored their eating behavior during the program (Schlundt & Zimering, 1983, 1985).

Psychometric Characteristics

Test-retest coefficients for the six situational types ranged from 0.81 to 0.96. Coefficient alpha, computed for each scale using the data from the 373 subjects, ranged from 0.68 to 0.86. Each DIET scale score correlated significantly with several parameters of eating behavior as measured by self-monitoring records. Stepwise multiple regression analyses using 12 measures of eating style derived from the self-monitoring records accounted for 34, 34, 53, 22, 16, and 36% of the variance in overeating, resisting temptation, food choice, positive social, negative emotions, exercise, and total DIET scores, respectively. The 168 overweight subjects scored significantly lower than did the 205 normal weight subjects on the overeating, negative emotions, exercise, and total DIET score scales.

Clinical Use

The DIET questionnaire is administered to subjects on entering a weight control program. The profile is examined and used to identify a subject's areas of strength and weakness. Behavioral training

techniques can be used to help a subject increase competence in the situations identified as problems on the DIET.

Future Directions

Studies need to be conducted to show that an assessment of weight control competence can be used to improve treatment outcome in weight loss therapy. Weight control programs consisting of modules need to be developed, each module devoted to training in how to handle each situation. The DIET could be used to determine which training modules are needed for each person. The DIET might also be useful in predicting the type of situation that induces a relapse after successful treatment.

References

Schlundt, D.G., & Zimering, R.T. (1983). *Exercise and affect induced overeating as possible problem situations for the overweight.* Paper presented at the Association for the Advancement of Behavior Therapy, Washington, DC.

Schlundt, D.G., & Zimering, R.T. (1985). *The Dieter's Inventory of Eating Temptations: A measure of weight control competence.* Unpublished manuscript, Vanderbilt University, Nashville, Tennessee.

Dining Room Manners

Allen Marchetti

Description

"Dining room manners" refers collectively to a number of independent, self-help skills rather than to a unitary skill to be taught and mastered. Therefore, evaluation incorporates assessment of each skill individually and may include assessment of a sequence of skills that are incorporated into a more comprehensive target behavior. Target behaviors included in this sequence may vary considerably depending on individual client characteristics (i.e., physical and/or sensory impairments), on the nature of the dining situation (i.e., individual versus family-style dining), and on the nature of the dining setting (i.e., institution, cafeteria, or public restaurant). Research in the area of dining skills training has begun to focus on more advanced mealtime skills. Behaviors that have been targeted have progressed from the simple use of utensils to such skills as independent dining in public restaurants (Van Den Pol et al., 1981). A variety of assessment and training techniques have been used in developing complex dining behaviors that require more advanced social skills. Such techniques have been used during role-playing in contrived settings, during actual dining, and using "mini-meals," which incorporate smaller portions served throughout the day (Azrin & Armstrong, 1973).

Purpose

Since the early 1960's, when studies focusing on the application of behavioral strategies for teaching self-feeding skills first appeared in the general research literature, a considerable body of research in the area of teaching more complex dining behaviors has been reported. Continued emphasis on placement of mentally retarded individuals into community settings has necessitated the development of strategies to assess and train these more complex social skills to facilitate such placements. Expanded vocational and leisure opportunities have increased social interaction and have necessitated that mentally retarded individuals use public facilities. Dining room manners are a necessary prerequisite if public dining facilities are to be used. Such utilization requires assessment, training, and generalization in a variety of settings.

Development

Early research of self-feeding strategies focused on the acquisition of a single dining skill such as eating with a spoon or fork. Teaching such skills, using operant conditioning, was considered fairly simple because the task involved simple chaining and was inherently reinforcing (i.e., edibles were involved in the program). After these initial investigations, inquiry in this area focused on acquisition strategies to teach more complex dining skills, deceleration strategies to decrease socially unacceptable mealtime behaviors, or both acceleration and deceleration strategies simultaneously (Reid, 1983) as in the case of dining room manners.

More recently, such research has been expanded to include a broader range of more complex dining skills (Matson, Ollendick, & Adkins, 1980) and has included dining in a variety of settings, including public dining facilities (Van Den Pol et al., 1981). Procedures used to teach dining behaviors such as manners have also incorporated less labor-intensive strategies, including self-evaluation, self-reinforcement, reinforcement of peers, and input

into some aspects of program design (Matson et al., 1980).

A review of the literature pertaining to dining room manners reflects no standardization of behaviors that are included in such a training program. Such behaviors vary considerably based on the nature of the dining setting and individual client characteristics. Matson et al. (1980) included 26 mealtime target behaviors in a comprehensive training program targeting dining manners. These target behaviors included: (1) picks up all utensils; (2) appropriate noise level; (3) appropriate line behavior; (4) stays seated during meals; (5) finishes eating before leaving table; (6) returns tray and utensils properly; (7) leaves dining room when finished eating; (8) chews food before swallowing; (9) takes small bites; (10) swallows before next bite; (11) drinks properly, glass in one hand; (12) eats at normal pace, not too fast; (13) uses spoon appropriately; (14) uses fork appropriately; (15) uses knife appropriately; (16) holds utensils properly; (17) eats neatly; (18) wipes up spilled food; (19) uses napkin; (20) talks with mouth empty; (21) has good posture; (22) eats at normal pace; (23) chews with mouth closed; (24) elbows off table; (25) hand in lap; and (26) pushes chair in.

Assessment instruments that provide extensive inventories of self-help skills, including complex dining behaviors, are available; however, the majority of these instruments do not report reliability or validity data. The Behavior Assessment Record (Sanders, 1978) and the Global Baseline Assessment Checklist (Watson, 1975) are examples of comprehensive inventories that are available.

Psychometric Characteristics

Early research in training independent dining skills to mentally retarded persons focused primarily on acquisition of a single target behavior; therefore, assessment was fairly straightforward. However, early training procedures were not well documented, and research methodology was not as rigorous as current applied research studies, thereby making such procedures difficult to replicate.

Later research has focused on more complex dining behaviors such as the dining manners sequence. Successful acquisition of this target behavior involves mastery of numerous independent dining skills, which must be assessed independently, as well as the sequence as a whole. Adding to the complexity of such assessments is the number of settings in which such tasks must be performed, thereby necessitating generalization to varied settings. Training procedures have also increased significantly in complexity since the early studies that only incorporated simple chaining procedures. Although reliability data reported in a number of these studies are within acceptable limits, it is extremely difficult to replicate more recent studies because of the varied training procedures used. Matson et al. (1980) included 26 target behaviors in their "comprehensive dining program" and individualized the training procedures to include in vivo modeling, peer social reinforcement, and self-evaluation.

Few empirical studies target a comprehensive dining manners sequence, and there is little agreement concerning what should comprise such a program. While Matson et al. (1980) targeted 26 individual dining behaviors, other researchers have targeted a more limited number of inappropriate dining skills (Favell, McGimsey, & Jones, 1980). Reliability between trained observers has been consistently high in these studies; however, it is difficult to make a specific statement concerning reliability across studies because the comprehensiveness of the studies and procedures used in these studies varied considerably.

Clinical Use

Assessment of basic and more advanced dining behaviors is useful in all mentally retarded individuals regardless of the level of retardation or handicapping condition. Those individual dining skills that are prioritized for assessment and training may vary depending on the client's level of retardation, physical and/or sensory impairment, and setting in which such skills will be used. Emphasis on serving mentally retarded persons in the least restrictive environment has resulted in significant numbers of mentally retarded individuals residing in community settings. As opportunities for utilization of community facilities, including dining facilities, have increased, so has the necessity for training more advanced dining skills such as dining room manners. Development of such skills is a necessary prerequisite if mentally retarded individuals are to continue to gain social acceptance in a variety of community settings.

Future Directions

Trends in the research literature reflect continued emphasis on training mentally retarded persons in more advanced dining behaviors and using more sophisticated training methodology in a variety of training procedures. Research in this area should continue to focus on expanding both the number and type of skills that are to be included in a comprehensive dining program. In addition, it is critical to evaluate skill generalization in various settings.

Further research is also needed in feeding instructions for persons with physical and/or sensory handicaps that interfere with independent feeding. The research literature is scant in this area. Additionally, further research is needed to validate the use of a variety of treatment strategies. Recent studies have only begun to explore novel training procedures such as self-evaluation, self-monitoring, and in vivo instruction. Assessment of dining skills in actual settings (public facilities) in which these skills are to be employed will significantly improve the validity of these assessment techniques.

References

Azrin, N.H., & Armstrong, P.M. (1973). The "mini-meal." A method for teaching eating skills to the profoundly mentally retarded. *Mental Retardation, 11,* 9-13.

Favell, J.E., McGimsey, J.F., & Jones, M.L. (1980). Rapid eating in the retarded: Reduction by nonaversive procedures. *Behavior Modification, 4,* 481-492.

Matson, J.L., Ollendick, T.H., & Adkins, J. (1980). A comprehensive dining program for mentally retarded adults. *Behaviour Research and Therapy, 18,* 107-112.

Reid, D.H. (1983). Trends and issues in behavioral research on training feeding and dressing skills. In J.L. Matson & F. Andrasik (Eds.), *Treatment issues and innovation in mental retardation.* New York: Plenum Press.

Sanders, R. (1978). *Behavior assessment record.* Tuscaloosa: Partlow State School.

Van Den Pol, R.A., Iwata, B.A., Ivanicic, M.T., Page, T.J., Neff, N.A., & Whitley, F.P. (1981). Teaching the handicapped to eat in public places: Acquisition, generalization, and maintenance of restaurant skills. *Journal of Applied Behavioral Analysis, 14,* 61-69.

Watson, L.S. (1975). *Global Baseline Assessment Checklist.* Illinois: BMT, Inc.

Direct Behavioral Observation

Susan H. Spence

Description

This direct behavior observation technique measures the frequency or duration of 13 specific, basic social skills. Each response requires the observer to be thoroughly familiar with these definitions before the onset of observation. The observer is then able to decode information from videotaped interviews, conversations, or interactions for each of the 13 social skills. An event recorder is used to measure the occurrence of the discrete behavioral events such as frequency of smiling or questions asked (number per minute of interaction), whereas a cumulative stopwatch is used to measure continuous behavioral data such as duration of eye contact or amount spoken (seconds per minute of interaction). This method, which is generally limited to videotaped situations, allows the observer to replay interactions to decode information about each skill. Such detailed analysis is not usually feasible with in vivo observations, because the simultaneous measurement of frequency and duration of many responses becomes too complex.

An initial 5-minute period of interaction generally is allowed before the onset of direct behavioral observation to allow participants to habituate to the presence of the video equipment. The social task selected should be made as realistic and naturalistic as possible to maximize the probability that the behavior observed is representative of the subject's real-life social behavior. The content of the social task is structured in advance according to the purpose of the assessment, to cover a set range of topics and prompts. The subject or client is then filmed from a position behind the interviewer or confederate to include a full torso picture. Throughout the process of decoding, the observer's data are subjected to regular reliability checks. To enhance accuracy, the observer should be unaware of which tapes will undergo this process.

Purpose

The purpose of this direct behavioral observation method is to provide a reliable measure of the frequency or duration of specific social skills for research or clinical use. From a research perspective, it allows the collection of baseline data against which future performance can be compared in order to demonstrate the effects of intervention. It is suitable for both group comparison and single case, multiple baseline design methodologies. In addition, the information provided facilitates identification of areas of basic social skills deficits, although the absence of any normative data for specific client groups or social tasks means that

such judgment depends on the subjective evaluation of the assessor.

Development

This technique was initially developed to evaluate the effectiveness of a social skills training program with youth offenders. The behaviors selected were based on responses shown in previous studies to be important in influencing the outcome of social interactions among adolescents (Minkin et al., 1976). Other responses suggested to be important social skills but less amenable to objective measurement (e.g., posture, voice volume, or tone of voice) were not included. Overall, the data produced by the observations were designed as an adjunct to various self–report and "others" report measures of social skills performance.

Clinical Use

This type of direct behavioral observation is time-consuming and requires suitable videotape equipment. Its use in many clinical settings may not be feasible, and practitioners may prefer subjective rating scales of the type outlined by Spence (1980) to measure specific social skills, rather than collecting actual frequency or duration data. Such detailed information is much more sensitive than rating scale information and is valuable in assessing behavior change following intervention.

The original technique was applied to a youth offender population, but given that the skills involved are frequently a focus of social skills training programs with other client groups, the method should prove useful in a variety of populations. Additional sources of information should be used during clinical assessment, in order that data concerning more complex social skills and other determinants of social competence (e.g., social anxiety) can also be explored. Similarly, the assessor should check the validity of the direct behavioral observation data as being representative of the client's "real-life" behavior.

Psychometric Characteristics

The interobserver reliability of this technique has been established to be good for each target behavior (Spence & Marzillier, 1981). In the original study, checks were carried out between one main observer and an independent observer on ten 5-minute videotaped interactions. The main observer was unaware of which of the 40 tapes were to be checked, as the 10 tapes were randomly selected. The independent observer was familiarized with the behavioral definitions and was given two initial, nonexperimental tapes with which to practice. Measures were then made for each of the 13 behavior variables. The independent observer was unaware of the true purpose of the exercise. The interrater reliabilities of the behavioral measures were found to be highly reliable, using a Pearson product–moment correlation coefficient. All measures were correlated at a statistically acceptable level of significance ($p < .01$).

The data produced by this type of direct behavioral observation have been sensitive to change in both group design and single case, multiple baseline evaluations of social skills training with youth offenders deficient in the skills concerned (Spence & Marzillier, 1981). The social validity of the behaviors included, with the exception of gestures, gross body movements, and attention feedback responses, was supported in a study by Spence (1981a). Performance in the skills observed was found to influence adults' judgments of videotaped conversations between adolescent male offenders and a previously unknown adult, in terms of ratings of friendliness, social skills performance, and social anxiety. Furthermore, in a subsequent study, the observed level of eye contact, head movements, amount spoken, fiddling movements, and gross body movements differed significantly between a youth offender group and their nonconvicted counterparts (Spence, 1981b). This finding supports the suggestion that the behaviors considered in this technique are associated with at least one index of behavioral functioning.

Future Directions

Research is needed with other populations and other social tasks in order to establish the validity of the specific, basic social skills considered herein. There is also a need to explore the importance of other responses not incorporated in this technique, that are likely to have important influences on judgments of a person's social competence. As techniques of indirect behavioral observation become more sophisticated, it may also be possible to research the importance of patterns of responses in the area of social skills, rather than to focus purely on individual response levels. This may then facilitate our understanding of the determinants of social competence.

References

Minkin, N., Braukmann, C.J., Minkin, B.L., Timbers, G.D., Timbers, B.J., Fixsen, D.L., Phillips, E.L., & Wolf, M.M. (1976). The social validation and training at conversation skills. Journal of Applied Behaviour Analysis, 9, 127-139.

Spence, S.H. (1980). Social skills training with children and adolescents: A counselor's manual. Windsor: NFER Publishing Co.

Spence, S.H. (1981a). Validation of social skills of adolescent males in an interview conversation with a previously unknown adult. Journal of Applied Behavior Analysis, 14, 159-168.

Spence, S.H. (1981b). Differences in social skills performance between institutionalized juvenile male offenders and a comparable group of boys without offence records. British Journal of Clinical Psychology, 20, 163-171.

Spence, S.H., & Marzillier, J.S. (1981). Social skills training with adolescent male offenders. II. Short-term, long-term and generalized effects. Behaviour Research and Therapy, 19, 349-368.

Dyadic Adjustment Scale

Gary R. Birchler

Description

The Dyadic Adjustment Scale (DAS) is a self-administered, self-report, paper-and-pencil, dyadic relationship assessment instrument that consists of 32 checkmark type items. Typewritten, it is about two pages in length. The scale is easily scored and produces a total scale score and scores for four subscales that may be of interest to the clinician.

Purpose

The DAS is designed most specifically to provide a standardized measure of marital adjustment, but the items are written in such a way that unmarried couples also may respond to them appropriately. Spanier and Cole (1976) reviewed the literature on the conceptualization of instruments available to measure marital adjustment. Based on this review, they determined the need to develop a revised instrument that would meet contemporary conceptual and methodological standards. They proposed a conceptual model according to which "marital adjustment is a process, the outcome of which is determined by the degree of: (1) troublesome marital differences; (2) interspousal tensions and personal anxiety; (3) marital satisfaction; (4) dyadic cohesion; and (5) consensus of matters of importance to marital functioning" (Spanier & Cole, 1976, pp. 127-128).

Development

First, using the foregoing definition of marital adjustment as a reference point, three judges reviewed 300 items for "goodness of fit." This initial pool of items was obtained from all available existing instruments, and new items were added to represent previously ignored areas of adjustment. Second, a questionnaire containing 225 items was administered to three different groups in Pennsylvania: a sample of 218 married persons; a sample of 94 recently divorced persons; and a small sample of unmarried cohabitating couples (whose data were not used in scale construction). Based on the frequency distributions of the items, all items with low variance and high skewness were eliminated. The variables that remained were first subjected to a t test for significance of the difference between the means of the married and divorced groups and then a factor analysis to determine the presence of hypothesized components of the model. Ultimately, 32 items were retained as the DAS (Spanier, 1976).

Psychometric Characteristics

Both the original factor analysis (Spanier, 1976) and a subsequent factor analytic study of 204 separated and divorced couples (Spanier & Thompson, 1982) indicated the presence of four dimensions in the DAS: "Dyadic Consensus (the degree to which the couple agrees on matters of importance to the relationship); Dyadic Cohesion (the degree to which the couple engages in activities together); Dyadic Satisfaction (the degree to which the couple is satisfied with the present state of the relationship and is committed to its continuance); and Affectional Expression (the degree to which the couple is satisfied with the expression of affection and sex in the relationship)" (Spanier & Filsinger, 1983, p. 157). The range of scores for the DAS subscales is 0 to 65 for Dyadic Consensus, 0 to 24 for Dyadic Cohesion, 0 to 50 for Dyadic Satisfaction, and 0 to 12 for Affectional Expression, providing a total scale score range of 0 to 151. The original group criterion means, which have been replicated fairly consistently in subsequent studies, were 114.8 and 70.7 for the married and divorced samples, respectively. Concerning the reliability and validity of the DAS, Spanier (1976) reported

the following internal consistency reliability coefficients: for Dyadic Adjustment, .96; for Dyadic Consensus, .90; for Dyadic Cohesion, .86; for Dyadic Satisfaction, .94; and for Affectional Expression, .73. Subsequent studies have reported similar numbers. Content validity of the DAS was established by judges' consensus on retaining certain items in the scale. Criterion-related validity was supported by the ability of the scale to discriminate between married and divorced samples. Construct validity was established by the fact that the factor analytic studies produced dimensions related to the original theoretical structure.

Clinical Use

As an easily obtainable measure of marital or dyadic relationship adjustment, the DAS may be administered to individuals or couples at any time. Results can be used diagnostically at intake or in the early stages of various modes of therapy. For example, the extent, severity, and kind of marital problems may be determined for the individual in psychotherapy, for the couple in marital therapy, and for the marital subsystem in the context of family therapy. Moreover, the effectiveness of the treatment of dyadic relationships, in particular, can be assessed by administering the DAS both before and after therapeutic intervention.

To date, some limitations exist in the interpretation of both subscale and total scale scores. Spanier and Filsinger (1983) indicate that too few studies of currently distressed and nondistressed couples have been done to allow for a reliable fixed cutoff point for determining the level of marital distress. In a clinical setting, it is recommended that interpretations of DAS scores be made in the context of having gathered several other sources of data. These sources of information might well include other self-report assessment questionnaires, clinical interviews, and clinic, home, or laboratory observation of marital or family interaction.

Future Directions

The DAS meets its objectives of providing an updated, practical, reliable, and valid measure of an individual's perception of his or her relationship adjustment. Solid normative data exist for general samples of white, middle-class marriages, and to a lesser extent for recently divorced couples. However, as Spanier and Filsinger (1983) suggest, definitive interpretations of total scale scores and the four subscale scores await further research. More normative data are needed from distressed couples seeking therapy, from well-functioning, nondistressed couples, and from any number of selected socioeconomic, ethnic, and otherwise special populations.

References

Spanier, G.B. (1976). Measuring dyadic adjustment: New scales for assessing the quality of marriage and similar dyads. *Journal of Marriage and the Family, 38,* 15-28.

Spanier, G.V., & Cole, C.L. (1976). Toward clarification and investigation of marital adjustment. *International Journal of Sociology of the Family, 6,* 121-246.

Spanier, G.B., & Filsinger, E.E. (1983). The dyadic adjustment scale. In E.E. Filsinger (Ed.), *Marriage and family assessment: A sourcebook for family therapy* (pp. 155-168). Beverly Hills, CA: Sage Publications.

Spanier, G.V., & Thompson, L.A. (1982). A confirmatory analysis of the Dyadic Adjustment Scale. *Journal of Marriage and the Family, 44,* 731-738.

Dyadic Prestressor Interaction Scale

Barbara G. Melamed and Joseph P. Bush

Description

An observational interaction scale was developed for the descriptive analysis of parent-child interaction in stressful situations. Four classes of functionally related child behaviors (attachment, distress, exploration, and prosocial behaviors) are defined by subclassed definitions reflecting motoric behavior, verbal expression, nonverbal affect, and physical or covert contact with the parent. Parent categories consist of six dimensions of parenting suggested by past research as being predictive of children's adjustment in stressful situations. The classes were: informing, distracting, reassuring, ignoring, restraining, and agitation. Four constituent behaviors for each class reflect motoric, verbal, and nonverbal communication patterns. The coding is done by videotape or on-line analysis of the global category as to its presence or absence at each 5-second sample during the anticipation of a medical examination. This scale is published in two chapters (Melamed & Siegel, 1975; Melamed & Bush, 1985).

Purpose

An observational scale (Dyadic Prestressor Interaction Scale, DPIS) of mother-child interactions in the outpatient medical setting was developed to extend the attachment and separation/stranger anxiety literature (Bretherton & Ainsworth, 1974) and to validate behavioral components of self-reported parent behaviors found to predict children's coping in stressful medical situations (Zabin & Melamed, 1980). Children between 4 and 10 years of age were expected to differ in their degree of dependence on the mothering strategy and on their expression of fear-related behaviors in anticipation of a pediatric diagnostic examination. The scale was expected to relate to self-reported maternal state anxiety, as crisis parenting suggests that parents who are under stress are not as effective in providing facilitation of their children's coping during periods of distress.

Development

The children's behavior categories selected were relevant to Bretherton and Ainsworth's (1974) functional systems of behavior in a strange situation. To adapt these categories to an extended age range (4 to 10 years), four new face-valid constituent items were constructed for each class of child behavior based on objective observability, regularity of occurrence, and representation of verbal and nonverbal behavior modalities. The parent behaviors represent dimensions of parenting suggested by previous research to be related to children's coping abilities (Melamed & Bush, 1985). Four constituent behaviors for each class, developed in the same manner as the child behaviors, were operationally defined. "Informing" was restricted to providing information relevant to the current medical situation; "distracting" was defined as engaging the child in an interaction that precluded focusing on the medical situation; and "ignoring" included maternal behavior that would require the child to interrupt her to get her attention. Reliability and validity were obtained for 65 mother-child dyads in the treatment room of outpatient pediatric clinics in a university hospital. The data may be analyzed to reflect the frequency of occurrence of the different behaviors and to provide a data base for computing conditional probabilities of the parent-child interactive sequences of responding over time.

Psychometric Characteristics

The videotaped observation period included at least 5 minutes of uninterrupted interaction, up to a maximum of 10 minutes. A time-date generator was used to superimpose an elapsed-time digital clock onto the tapes without obscuring the visibility of the subjects. Observers then used this clock to make instantaneous scale ratings of the 10 DPIS categories every 4 seconds. The response-class approach was used, in that the behavior was scored as having occurred if any of its four specific constituent behaviors was observed at the scan points. The specific constituent behaviors were not scored separately so that the instrument could easily be adapted by observers at the time of assessment in future studies. The 5-second interval was chosen so as to minimize the frequency of scorable behaviors occurring but not being scored because of onset and offset between scan points.

Interobserver reliability yielded significant coefficients between .77 and .99 for all categories except "restraint," using optimized and nonoptimized selection (highest agreement and randomly selected coding of three raters). The restraining category yielded an optimized coefficient of .60 and is less likely to be reliable because of its low relative occurrence and short duration. Relative frequencies, calculated as total frequency divided by the number of scan points, were used instead of observational periods. Intersubject variability was found among the 10 categories when relative frequency and standard deviation were examined. The child behaviors measured by the DPIS were relatively independent except for "distress," which correlated inversely with tendency to engage in exploration of the medical setting ($r = .28, p < .05$) and with prosocial activity ($r = -.34, p < .05$). Among the parent categories, ignoring was inversely related to the other parent categories: reassuring, distracting, restraining, and informing (all $p < .05$ or better). Ignoring was scored when mother was actively engaged in activity precluding her attending to the child. Ignoring was positively related to agitated behaviors of the parent ($r = .31$, $p < .05$). There was a strong correlation between mother's use of distraction and the child's engagement in prosocial behavior ($r = .77, p < .05$). Maternal information provision and child exploring were also correlated positively ($r = .57$, $p < .005$). Maternal reassurance and child attachment also correlated significantly ($r = .56$, $p < .005$). Both maternal agitation and reassurance

covaried positively with children's distress, whereas distraction was associated with children exhibiting less distress. Children were less likely to engage in prosocial or exploratory behavior if their mothers were ignoring them. Canonical analysis of the data indicated that the combination of parents' behaviors predicting children's behaviors could account for over 49% of the variance in observed child behaviors, whereas child behaviors accounted for 36% of the variance in the six parent behavior categories (Bush, Melamed, Sheras, & Greenbaum, 1986). Age-related findings indicated that children between 4 and 5 years and 9 months were most influenced by maternal use of informing and reassurance. Mothers tend to ignore younger children less and to distract them more. The only sex difference was the greater use of restraint with girls than with boys ($r = .27, p < .05$).

The reactivity of the measure when questionnaire data are also collected was evaluated by comparison of relative frequencies of the categories in an additional sample of 15 dyads receiving no questionnaires, compared with 50 already obtained from dyads involved in measurement of self-reported distress and coping. No significant differences were observed. Therefore, the observational tool is not situation specific and does seem sensitive to age-related changes in parenting tendencies.

The Child Development Questionnaire, which is a self-report of mother's use of different reinforcement strategies, correlated with what mothers actually tended to do with their children. Mothers who reported the use of positive reinforcements used distraction ($p < .01$) and restraint ($p < .05$) with their children, particularly with those showing distress. Additionally, they were less likely to ignore these distressed children. Conversely, mothers who reported high use of punishment were more likely to ignore distressed children (Bush, Melamed, Sheras, & Greenbaum, 1986).

Clinical Use

This measure is currently being evaluated as to its predictive validity with children's actual behaviors during the subsequent stressor (examination, venipuncture, or hospitalization). Sequential analysis shows that it is possible to determine whether the influence is from the child or mother. State anxious mothers exhibit agitation that leads to their children's distress, whereas mothers low on state anxiety respond to their children's distress.

Future Directions

When the normative data are accumulated across situations and age groups, it will be possible to use this interactional measure to pinpoint patterns of mother–child interaction that lead to maladaptive coping and to teach mothers more successful coping strategies.

The ability to predict the children who are at risk for difficulty in adjusting to environmental stressors should advance the knowledge of parenting influences in development of fear or competence in children's coping. In addition, the physician observing the dysfunctional patterns can refer families for preventive intervention. The relationship between this observational scale and children's temperament, as it predicts adjustment to hospitalization, return to school, and future health care behaviors, is underway.

References

Bretherton, I., & Ainsworth, M.D.S. (1974). Responses of one-year olds to a stranger in a strange situation. In M. Lewis & L.A. Rosenblum (Eds.), *The origins of fear*. New York: John Wiley & Sons.

Bush, J.P., Melamed, B.G., Sheras, P.L., & Greenbaum, P.E. (1986). Mother–child patterns of coping with anticipatory medical stress. *Health Psychology, 5*, 137-157.

Melamed, B.G., & Bush, J.P. (1985). The role of the family in acute illness. In D. Turk & R. Kearns (Eds.), *Health, illness, and families: A life span perspective*. New York: John Wiley & Sons.

Melamed, B.G., & Siegel, L.J. (1985). Children's reactions to medical/dental stressors: An ecological approach to the study of anxiety. In A.H. Tuma & J.D. Maser (Eds.), *Anxiety and the anxiety disorders*. New Jersey: Erlbaum.

Zabin, M., & Melamed, B.G. (1980). Relationship between parental discipline and children's ability to cope with stress. *Journal of Behavioral Asssessment, 2*, 17-38.

Dysfunctional Attitude Scale

Brian F. Shaw

Description

The Dysfunctional Attitude Scale is a self-report inventory appearing in three forms. The original 100-item inventory (DAS-T) is occasionally employed. Two 40-item parallel forms (DAS-A and DAS-B) were derived from the original scale, with the former being most common in use. Patients indicate the degree to which they agree or disagree with statements on a 7-point scale. Scores on the DAS-T range from 100 to 700, whereas on the DAS-A and DAS-B the total scores range from 40 to 280.

The scale items are typically stated as contingencies concerning approval from others, prerequisites for happiness, or perfectionistic standards. Sample items include: "It is difficult to be happy unless one is good looking, intelligent, rich and creative," "People will probably think less of me if I make a mistake," and "If someone disagrees with me, it probably indicates he does not like me."

Purpose

The DAS was originally designed by Weissman and Beck (Weissman, 1979) to identify a set of relatively stable attitudes associated with depressive disorders, although it is now clear that it is relevant to a range of psychopathological conditions. As certain dysfunctional attitudes may reflect prepotent self-schemas, the DAS has been proposed as one measure of cognitive vulnerability to major depressive disorder. The cognitive theory posits that individuals who maintain extreme, rigid assumptions about themselves and the events in their life are prone to emotional disorders. As a risk factor, dysfunctional attitudes are thought to interact with other factors, such as stressful life events, low levels of social support, and/or genetic makeup to precipitate a depressive or anxiety disorder.

Development

Weissman (1979) developed the DAS on a sample of college students, and more recently, Oliver and Baumgart (1985) completed a psychometric study of the three forms on a sample of adult hospital workers and their spouses. Testing with a nonselected normative sample remains to be completed. The DAS has been widely researched on patients with affective disorders.

Psychometric Characteristics

The mean score on the DAS-T was 296 (SD = 75) with selected adult volunteers. Students had a mean total score of 117.7 (SD = 26.8), using either the DAS-A or the DAS-B. Moderately depressed patients typically receive scores of 150 (SD = 40). Both the DAS-A and the DAS-B have good internal consistency and stability over time. With college students, coefficient alphas ranged from .89 to .92, with a test-retest correlation of .84 over an 8-week period (Weissman, 1979). Oliver and Baumgart (1985) reported alpha coefficients of .90, .85, and .81 for the DAS-T, DAS-A, and DAS-B, respectively. Their 6-week test-retest reliability for the DAS-T was .73 (sample = 43). As will be discussed, the stability of DAS scores in samples of depressed patients is an area of controversy, with some investigators reporting a relatively stable pattern, whereas others find a marked change in scores.

The construct validity of the DAS has been tested in several studies, but notably there have been few evaluations of concurrent validity. It would be expected that the DAS correlates moderately with measures of depressive severity and with measures of negative automatic thoughts, or cognitive distortions. In several clinical studies (Hamilton & Abramson, 1983; Dobson & Shaw, 1986) the DAS correlations with the Beck Depression Inventory were in the moderate range of .40 to .65. Similarly, the relation between DAS total scores and other cognitive measures is in the moderate range. For example, the DAS correlates .52 with the Cognitive Bias Questionnaire and the Automatic Thoughts Questionnaire, both of which are state-dependent measures of depressive cognitions.

Although the DAS can discriminate between groups of depressed and psychiatric control patients, it is not specifically associated with major depressive disorder. Patients with conditions such as generalized anxiety disorder, anorexia nervosa, panic disorder, and dysthymia may evidence abnormal DAS scores. Even more relevant are the findings that approximately 25% of depressed patients do not have abnormally high (i.e., at least 1 SD above the mean) scores (Hamilton & Abramson, 1983).

The DAS has been employed by various research groups that wanted to evaluate hypothesized cognitive changes that were a function of cognitive therapy. Several studies have found the DAS to be sensitive to clinical improvement. Simons, Garfield, and Murphy (1984) reported that the DAS scores change following treatment. Whether the DAS scores of depressed patients return to normal when the depression remits is a matter of considerable controversy. Eaves and Rush (1984) and Dobson and Shaw (1986), among others, have observed a reduction in DAS scores associated with a reduction in depressive symptoms. However, they found the remitted depressed patients to have abnormally high scores. Other

investigators (Hamilton & Abramson, 1983; Simons et al., 1984; Silverman, Silverman, & Eardley, 1984) have found the opposite. They noted that the DAS scores returned to normal as the condition remitted. Part of the difference in these results may be accounted for by the definition of remission and the time of retesting, but future work is obviously needed. In any event, it is clear that dysfunctional attitudes abate with a wide range of treatments (i.e., a change in DAS scores is by no means specific to cognitive therapy).

The DAS has been shown in two investigations to be a useful instrument to predict future depressive symptoms in previously depressed patients. In addition, the DAS has been used in several studies as an independent variable, purportedly tapping a cognitive vulnerability to depression.

Several factor analytic studies have been completed in addition to Weissman's (1979) original factor analysis designed to devise the two parallel short forms. Oliver and Baumgart (1985) reported four factors from both the DAS-A and DAS-B. Unfortunately, the factor structure differed for the two forms, with the exception of a need for approval factor. This factorial incongruence led these authors to conclude that the shortened forms cannot replace the DAS-T.

Clinical Use

The DAS has been used to assess change as a function of treatment, to differentiate depressed patients from patients with other psychiatric disorders, and to predict the outcome of various treatments. More studies are needed to provide conclusive indications for use for the scale.

The DAS is typically administered in a period of 15 to 20 minutes. The clinician should be mindful of the patient's biases in responding to the items, as evaluations of either acquiescence or social desirability have not been built into the test. We have observed several patients who differentiate between their "emotional responses" and their "intellectual responses" when completing the DAS. The former test-taking set is typically associated with a more extreme endorsement of dysfunctional attitudes.

Future Directions

Several conceptual questions are relevant to the use of the DAS. First, are dysfunctional attitudes actually experienced as such or are they simply approximate translations of an internal cognitive structure? Second, what is the most theoretically meaningful method of scoring the DAS? Weissman (1979) proposed the total score from either 40-item short form of the test as the best way to quantify the severity of dysfunctional attitudes endorsed by the individual. As these attitudes are hypothesized to serve as one source of influence on a person's behavior, it is expected that everyone will endorse some dysfunctional attitudes to various degrees. Is it more meaningful to consider the total score on the DAS or some other metric, such as the proportion of attitudes that are held in an extreme (presumably rigid) fashion? Clinically, an individual who holds few dysfunctional attitudes to an extreme and inflexible degree may be more vulnerable or more difficult to treat or both. We currently have little information on the relation between dysfunctional attitudes and vulnerability to psychopathology. For this reason, we cannot be certain about the best method of scoring the test. Third, how stable are the total scores on the DAS and how stable are the specific items of the test? Theoretically, dysfunctional attitudes are predicted to be more stable than other measures of cognition, such as the frequency of negative automatic thoughts or the probability of negatively biased recall of information. Nevertheless, during an episode of major depression it has generally been observed that most patients exhibit abnormally high scores on the DAS (i.e., greater than 140). A more controversial question is whether these DAS scores remain abnormal once the episode has remitted.

In summary, the DAS is a useful research tool to measure the attitudes associated with various emotional disorders. Future research will determine its applicability as a measure of change or a measure of vulnerability to future psychopathology or both.

References

Dobson, K.S., & Shaw, B.F. (1986). Cognitive assessment of major depressive disorder. *Cognitive Therapy and Research, 10*, 13-29.

Eaves, G., & Rush, A.J. (1984). Cognitive patterns in symptomatic and remitted unipolar major depression. *Journal of Abnormal Psychology, 93*, 31-40.

Hamilton, E.W., & Abramson, L.Y. (1983). Cognitive patterns and major depressive disorder: A longitudinal study in a hospital setting. *Journal of Abnormal Psychology, 92*, 173-184.

Oliver, J., & Baumgart, E.P. (1985). The Dysfunctional Attitude Scale: Psychometric properties and relation to depression in an unselected adult population. *Cognitive Therapy and Research, 9*, 161-167.

Silverman, J.S., Silverman, J.A., & Eardley, D.A. (1984). Do maladaptive attitudes cause depression? *Archives of General Psychiatry, 41*, 28-30.

Simons, A.D., Garfield, S.L., & Murphy, G.E. (1984). The process of change in cognitive therapy and pharmacotherapy of depression. Changes in mood and cognition. *Archives of General Psychiatry, 41*, 45-51.

Weissman, A. (1979). The Dysfunctional Attitude Scale: A validation study. Unpublished dissertation, University of Pennsylvania. *Dissertation Abstracts International, 40*, 1389-1390b.

Eating Attitudes Test

David M. Garner and Marion P. Olmsted

Description

The Eating Attitudes Test (EAT) is a measure of the attitudinal and behavioral symptoms of anorexia nervosa. The EAT is a self-report instrument designed to be economical in both administration and scoring time. The original version of the EAT (Garner & Garfinkel, 1979) consisted of 40 6-point forced choice items that were summed to yield one global index of the symptoms of anorexia nervosa. Respondents rate whether each item applies always, very often, often, sometimes, rarely, or never. A revised version of the EAT (Garner, Olmsted, Bohr, & Garfinkel, 1982) includes only 26 of the 40 original items and consists of three factor scores measuring: (a) dieting: the degree of avoidance of fattening foods and preoccupation with being thinner; (b) bulimia and food preoccupation: the presence of intrusive thoughts about food and the symptoms of bulimia, and (c) oral control: the degree of self-control around eating and the perception of pressure from others to gain weight. The abbreviated version of the EAT also includes a total score that is the sum of the 26 composite items and is highly correlated ($r = .98$ for anorexia nervosa patients and $r = .97$ for female college students) with the 40-item EAT total score.

Purpose

The EAT was developed primarily as a standardized, self-report assessment of symptoms common in patients with anorexia nervosa. It is intended as a viable prognostic and outcome measure for anorexia nervosa and bulimia. The EAT has also been successfully employed to identify eating disturbances in nonclinical samples. In several recent epidemiological studies of college students and dancers, the incidence of "probable" anorexia nervosa or bulimia was established on the basis of EAT scores without confirmation of diagnosis by clinical interview. Although the EAT may be employed as a screening instrument to identify individuals with a higher risk of formal eating disorder, it must be emphasized that the test should not be used as the sole means of arriving at a diagnosis of anorexia nervosa or bulimia. On statistical grounds alone, it is unreasonable to assume that the EAT can be used as a diagnostic instrument with any degree of accuracy. It is virtually impossible to achieve acceptable sensitivity, specificity, and positive predictive value for a test given the relatively low base rates for eating disorders in nonclinical populations.

Development

From a survey of the clinical literature, 35 preliminary items were generated and administered to 34 female college women (FC) and 32 female anorexia nervosa (AN) patients who met standard diagnostic criteria. Items were considered useful if they significantly differentiated the two groups. Of the 35 preliminary items, 23 were retained and the remainder were either reworded or discarded. Several new items were also developed, for a total of 40 items. The revised EAT was administered to fresh samples of 33 AN patients and 59 FC women. Validity for the 40-item EAT (EAT-40) was established on the basis of the second independent subject samples.

More recently, an abbreviated 26-item EAT (EAT-26) has been proposed (Garner et al., 1982). Factor analysis of the 40 EAT items, based on 160 female patients with anorexia nervosa, yielded three factors comprised of 26 of the 40 original items. The EAT-26 total score was highly correlated with the EAT-40 total score, indicating that the 14 eliminated items were redundant with the 26 retained items. The three factors of the EAT-26 represent more specific symptom clusters that may prove useful as potential predictors of outcome.

Psychometric Characteristics

For the EAT-40, a validity coefficient of 0.87 was obtained by correlating the total score with group membership (AN or FC). Male controls, obese subjects, and a small group of clinically recovered anorexia nervosa patients also demonstrated scores that were low and in the range of scores for female college women. Convergent and discriminant validity for the EAT-40 and the EAT-26 and its three factors was obtained by correlating these scores with clinical features and other psychometric measures that are relevant to anorexia nervosa (Garner et al., 1982). The EAT-26 consistently maintains as robust a correlation with clinical and psychometric variables as the EAT-40.

Because the first factor (dieting) of the EAT-26 is highly correlated ($r = 0.93$) with the total EAT-26, it may be an economical substitute for the total scale in some circumstances. The second factor (bulimia and food preoccupation) is positively related to the symptom of bulimia and a heavier body weight, two features that have been associated with poor outcome, whereas the third factor (oral control) is inversely related to weight and bulimia. Consequently, it has been postulated that low scores on factor two and high scores on factor three may be better predictors of favorable outcome than the total scale score.

For anorexia nervosa patients, standardized Cronbach's alphas for the EAT-40, EAT-26, and the three factors range from .83 to .92. For female college students, similar reliabilities range from .46 to .86 with only the coefficients for factors two and three being less than .80. Item-factor correlations for the three EAT-26 factors range from .44 to .71 for anorexia nervosa patients; only items that had factor loadings after oblique rotation of greater than .40 were retained.

Normative data for anorexia nervosa patients and female college women for the EAT-40, EAT-26, and the three factors are reported by Garner et al. (1982). Garner and Garfinkel (1979) note that a cutoff score of 30 on the EAT-40 would correctly classify all anorexia nervosa patients and misclassify 13% of the female college women. On clinical interview it was determined that the college women who scored over 30 were experiencing significant concerns about their weight. A cutoff score of 20 on the EAT-26 correctly classifies a similar proportion of anorexia nervosa patients and female college women.

Clinical Use

Within clinical populations, the EAT (40 or 26) provides a global index of the symptoms of anorexia nervosa. The three factors of the EAT-26 are indices of more specific symptom clusters; among anorexia nervosa patients, there is variability in the pattern of scores obtained across the three factors.

The EAT may be used to explore the relationships among symptom areas and clinical features, prognostic indicators, and outcome in anorexia nervosa. The EAT also represents a convenient and standardized method of assessing changes in symptoms as a result of treatment or other interventions.

In nonclinical populations, the EAT has been used as a screening instrument to identify individuals who are more likely than average to have disturbed eating patterns. Although most of the individuals who are identified as being at risk do not meet the criteria for a diagnosis of anorexia nervosa, they generally do have significant concerns about their weight (Garner, Olmsted, Polivy, & Garfinkel, 1984).

Future Directions

Although it has been postulated that the EAT may be a useful predictor of outcome, this hypothesis has not yet been tested. Also, it may be useful in identifying individuals who are at high risk for developing either anorexia nervosa or bulimia within nonclinical samples.

References

Garfinkel, P.E., & Garner, D.M. (1982). Anorexia nervosa: A multidimensional perspective. New York: Brunner/Mazel.

Garner, D.M., & Garfinkel, P.E. (1979). The Eating Attitudes Test: An index of the symptoms of anorexia nervosa. Psychological Medicine, 9, 273-279.

Garner, D.M., Olmsted, M.P., Bohr, Y., & Garfinkel, P.E. (1982). The Eating Attitudes Test: Psychometric features and clinical correlates. Psychological Medicine, 12, 871-878.

Garner, D.M., Olmsted, M.P., Polivy, J., & Garfinkel, P.E. (1984). Comparison between weight-preoccupied women and anorexia nervosa. Psychosomatic Medicine, 46, 255-266.

Eating Disorder Inventory

David M. Garner and Marion P. Olmsted

Description

The Eating Disorder Inventory (EDI) was constructed to assess a number of psychological and behavioral traits common in anorexia nervosa and bulimia. The EDI is a 64-item, self-report measure that consists of eight subscales assessing: (a) drive for thinness: reflects excessive concern with dieting, preoccupation with weight, and entrenchment in an extreme pursuit of thinness; (b) bulimia: indicates the tendency toward episodes of uncontrollable overeating (binging) as well as the impulse to engage in self-induced vomiting; (c) body dissatisfaction: reflects the belief that specific parts of the body associated with shape change or increased "fatness" at puberty are too large (e.g., hips, thighs, and buttocks); (d) ineffectiveness: assesses feelings of general inadequacy, insecurity, worthlessness, and the feeling of not being in control of one's life; (e) perfectionism: indicates excessive personal expectations for superior achievement; (f) interpersonal distrust: reflects a sense of alienation and a general reluctance to form close relationships; (g) interoceptive awareness: indicates perceived impairment in recognizing and accurately identifying emotions and sensations of hunger or satiety; (h) maturity fears: measures the desire to retreat to the security of the preadolescent years because of the overwhelming demands of adulthood.

The first three subscales focus on behaviors and attitudes concerning shape, weight, and eating, whereas the latter five subscales are relevant to psychological dimensions associated with ego strength and interpersonal functioning. The 64 EDI items have 6-point forced choice response categories. The respondent must rate whether each item applies always, usually, often, sometimes, rarely, or never. Brief demographic and weight history information are requested on the cover page of the EDI test booklet.

Purpose

Although recent measures permit standardized assessment of the behavioral/symptom parameters of anorexia nervosa and bulimia, they do not tap psychological dimensions that have been postulated to be more fundamentally related to these disorders. Bruch (1973) has described the entrenchment in an extreme pursuit of thinness, body image disturbance, a pervasive sense of ineffectiveness, perfectionistic achievement standards, and a deficiency in interoceptive labeling as central features of anorexia nervosa. A more detailed account of the clinical sources from which the EDI constructs were derived is presented in the EDI Manual (Garner & Olmsted, 1984). The objective assessment of the psychopathology typical in anorexia nervosa and bulimia is particularly important given the growing recognition that these are multidimensional disorders with considerable psychological variability across the heterogeneous patient population. (See Garfinkel & Garner, 1982, for a review.)

The EDI may also be used as a screening instrument in nonclinical populations; however, scores on the EDI should not be used as the sole basis for diagnostic formulations.

Development

The EDI was fully developed by 1983, and the first report was published in the same year (Garner, Olmsted, & Polivy, 1983). The most recent and most comprehensive report of the EDI, including updated psychometric information, is presented in the EDI Manual (Garner & Olmsted, 1984).

Validation of the EDI was based on three independent subsamples of female, primary anorexia nervosa (AN) patients (sample = 129) and three independent female comparison (FC) subsamples of university students (sample = 770). The AN patients met the diagnostic criteria described by Garfinkel and Garner (1982), and both "restricting" and "bulimic" subtypes were represented. Items retained from the original item pool had to display criterion validity (by significantly differentiating between the AN and FC groups) and internal consistency (by being more highly correlated with their intended subscale than with any other subscale). The final version of each subscale was required to have a coefficient of internal consistency (Cronbach's alpha) above .80 for the AN samples.

Although development of the EDI was based on AN patients, more recent work indicates that patients with the syndrome of bulimia or bulimia nervosa display levels of psychopathology on the EDI that are similar to those of patients with AN (Garner, Garfinkel, & O'Shaughnessy, 1985). The EDI is currently used as an assessment measure for both patient groups.

Psychometric Characteristics

Reliability. For AN patients, standardized Cronbach's alphas for the eight EDI subscales range from .83 to .93, standard errors of measurement for the subscales range from 1.9 to 2.9, and item-subscale correlations range from .23 to .79 with only three less than .40. For example, in college women, standardized Cronbach's alphas range from .72 to .92, with only two less than .80. Standard errors of measurement range from 1.3 to 2.3, and item-subscale correlations range from .25 to .79, with only three less than .40.

Validity. The EDI was constructed to differentiate between AN patients and female college students. Additional criterion validity was obtained by: (a) correlating AN patients' subscale scores with clinicians' ratings of the patients along the dimensions tapped by the EDI subscales; (b) demonstrating that a small group of *recovered* AN patients had scores on each subscale that were significantly lower than those for anorexia nervosa patients and not significantly higher than those for female college students; and (c) demonstrating that the *bulimia* subscale differentiated restricting AN patients from those with the complication of bulimia. Convergent and discriminant validity was provided by the obtained pattern of correlations among EDI subscales and a number of other psychological tests that have some conceptual overlap with specific subscales.

Interpretation of Scores. The EDI items are scored so that the most "anorexic" response receives the highest score; subscale scores are simply the sum of item scores. The EDI has been constructed to maximize ease of use and can be hand-scored quickly. Raw scores for each subscale must be interpreted with respect to the norms for that subscale. Normative data are available for AN patients, female college students, female high school students, and male college students (Garner & Olmsted, 1984).

The EDI subscales are not measures of independent constructs, and there are significant intercorrelations among the subscales. Even conceptually, there is overlap among the dimensions assessed by EDI subscales. No subscale, however, is completely redundant with some combination of the other subscales.

Clinical Use

Within the clinical populations, the EDI may be useful in identifying subtypes of AN and bulimia. Given the heterogeneity of the patient population, the EDI profile of a particular patient may provide the therapist with valuable clinical information relevant to treatment. Similarly, the EDI can be employed to assess change as a result of treatment.

In nonclinical populations, the EDI may be used as a screening instrument to indicate which individuals are likely to be very preoccupied with their weight and which individuals are likely to have serious ego deficits. Individuals who have high scores on all subscales may be a high risk group for

AN or bulimia. However, the EDI is *not* a diagnostic instrument, and formal diagnoses must be made on the basis of clinical interviews by qualified clinicians. Specific cutoff scores for EDI subscales have not been recommended. Rather, normative data have been published that allow test users who require cutoff points to make rational decisions about what scores would best serve the current purpose. Every opportunity has been taken to stress that there is no EDI score that provides conclusive evidence regarding diagnosis.

Respondents can generally complete the EDI independently in less than 20 minutes. The EDI appears to be appropriate for use with any population capable of understanding the items and responding honestly to them. Like all self-report instruments, the EDI is vulnerable to distortion because of response style bias, inaccurate reporting, and denial.

Future Directions

Because the EDI is a relatively new test, much of the research involving it has not yet reached the publication stage. Validity studies are currently in progress, and the ultimate utility of this instrument in identifying meaningful subgroups of AN and bulimia patients as well as predicting response to treatment is still in the early stages. Although the EDI has been used outside North America, formal cross-cultural comparisons have not yet been published.

Finally, the EDI does not represent an exhaustive sampling of the pathological characteristics of AN and bulimia. Measures of other psychological dimensions of functioning may complement the EDI in assessing patients with eating disorders.

References

Bruch, H. (1973). *Eating disorders: Obesity, anorexia nervosa and the person within.* New York: Basic Books.

Garfinkel, P.E., & Garner, D.M. (1982). *Anorexia nervosa: A multidimensional perspective.* New York: Brunner/Mazel.

Garner, D.M., & Olmsted, M.P. (1984). *The eating disorder inventory manual.* Odessa, FL: Psychological Assessment Resources.

Garner, D.M., Garfinkel, P.E., & O'Shaughnessy, M. (1985). The validity of the distinction between bulimia with and without anorexia nervosa. *American Journal of Psychiatry, 142,* 581-587.

Garner, D.M., Olmsted, M.P., & Polivy, J. (1983). Development and validation of a multidimensional eating disorder inventory for anorexia nervosa and bulimia. *International Journal of Eating Disorders, 1,* 15-34.

Eating Problems Questionnaire

Aubrey J. Yates

Description

This questionnaire was developed by Johnson, Stuckey, Lewis, and Schwartz (1982). It is not included in the paper, but a copy of it may be obtained from the authors. The form of the questionnaire is not stated.

Purpose

The questionnaire is designed to provide "descriptive information regarding current binging and purging behavior, history of weight and eating difficulties, and treatment experience" as well as "attitudes and medical difficulties associated with the eating disorder" and "other habits such as drug, alcohol, and cigarette use" (Johnson et al., 1982, p. 5).

Development

No information is available as to how the questionnaire was developed.

Psychometric Characteristics

The psychometric characteristics of the questionnaire have not been reported.

Clinical Use

The questionnaire was used by Johnson et al. (1982) to classify as probably bulimic 316 (67%) of 454 female subjects, who had requested information on bulimia after reading articles published by the authors in popular journals and whose responses to the questionnaire indicated that they met DSM-III criteria for bulimia. However, the reliability and validity of such classification have not been established. At present, the clinical uses of the test have not been established.

Future Directions

Because the questionnaire is not readily available, its development has not yet been described, and it has only been used in one study, it seems unlikely that it will be at all widely used until the authors make it more available and provide essential psychometric data.

Reference

Johnson, C.L., Stuckey, M.K., Lewis, L.D., & Schwartz, D.M. (1982). Bulimia: A descriptive survey of 316 cases. *International Journal of Eating Disorders, 2,* 3-16.

Eating Questionnaire

Aubrey J. Yates

Description

The Eating Questionnaire (EQ) is a 51-item questionnaire (36 true/false; 25 forced choice) developed by Stunkard and Messick (1985).

Purpose

The questionnaire measures three dimensions of human eating behavior: cognitive restraint of eating; disinhibition of eating; and hunger.

Development

The initial version of the questionnaire was administered to 18 male and 60 female "restrained" eaters ("dieters"), 22 male and 40 female "unrestrained" eaters ("nondieters"), and three other groups of men and women falling between these extremes in eating habits. The combined sample totaled 220 persons (97 men and 123 women), aged 17 to 77 years. The resultant data were factor analyzed. The same procedures were followed with a revised form of the questionnaire.

Psychometric Characteristics

In its final version, the first two dimensions (cognitive restraint of eating and disinhibition of eating) discriminated significantly between restrained and unrestrained eaters, but the third (hunger) did not. Coefficient alpha reliabilities for all scales for both groups were satisfactory, ranging from 0.79 to 0.92. Male and female subjects tend to respond differently to the scales, but the differences are reduced when height differences are controlled. Criterion validity and good test-retest reliability have been reported in unpublished studies.

Clinical Use

The clinical use of the test has not yet been reported. It should prove useful for assessment of eating behaviors in various clinical conditions such as anorexia nervosa, bulimia nervosa, and obesity.

Future Directions

Studies of construct validity are urgently needed. The relationship of the test to other measures of eating problems is required. The factorial structure of the test should enable theoretical analyses of different kinds of eating attitudes and behavioral patterns to be pursued more successfully.

Reference

Stunkard, A.J., & Messick, S. (1985). The three-factor Eating Questionnaire to measure dietary restraint, disinhibition and hunger. *Journal of Psychomatic Research, 29,* 71-83.

Eating Self-Efficacy Scale

Shirley M. Glynn and Audrey J. Ruderman

Description

Bandura (1977) proposes that psychotherapy achieves its effects by increasing clients' expectations that they can adequately perform behaviors to bring about desired goals. These expectations have been termed "self-efficacy." Many researchers in the addictive disorders (Condiotte & Lichtenstein, 1981) have established that efficacy expectancies are powerful predictors of relapse and therefore may merit specific attention during the therapeutic process. To date, little emphasis has been placed on developing reliable, valid, psychometrically sound instruments for use in assessing self-efficacy with regard to specific addictive disorders. One scale that has been developed with careful attention to its psychometric qualities is the Eating Self-Efficacy Scale (ESES) (Glynn & Ruderman, 1986). The ESES is a 25-item self-report questionnaire designed to assess self-efficacy with regard to controlling eating. Respondents are asked to indicate their degree of difficulty controlling their overeating in a variety of situations (e.g., "when angry" or "around holiday time"), using a scale of 1 (no difficulty controlling eating) to 7 (most difficulty controlling eating). Responses are then summed to yield total scores and two factor scores, one indicating difficulty when experiencing negative affect (NA) and one when in socially acceptable circumstances (SAC). High scores on the ESES indicate less eating self-efficacy.

Purpose

The ESES is designed to assess individuals' perceptions that they will be able to control possible urges to overeat when in situations that might increase these urges (e.g., "when there is tempting food available"). According to Bandura (1977), these perceptions should have a strong influence on actual behavior when individuals are experiencing such urges.

Development

A pool of 79 potential eating situations was generated by modifying applicable situations from Condiotte and Lichtenstein (1981) and adding any mentioned by at least 2 of the 25 college undergraduates asked to identify eating situations. This pool of items was reduced to 25 by administering the score to two samples of over 300 undergraduates each and by eliminating all items that did not reliably load with at least two other items on a single factor. This procedure yielded a 25-item scale, with 15 items loading on the NA subscale and 10 loading on the SAC subscale.

Psychometric Characteristics

The psychometric properties of the ESES have been examined most thoroughly with female undergraduates. Among this group, the ESES had a mean of 80.92, a median of 80, and a standard deviation of 26.50. The mean of the 15-item NA subscale was 42.15 (SD = 20.03) and the median was 39. The mean of the 10-item SAC subscale was 38.92 (SD = 11.47) and the median was 40. The two subscales were positively correlated and significant (r = .39). Self-reported dieters scored significantly higher (mean = 87.2) than did nondieters (mean = 74.1), but there was no significant difference between the scores of normal weight and obese subjects. Cronbach's coefficient alpha (Cronbach, 1951) was .92 for the entire scale, .94 for the NA subscale, and .85 for the SAC subscale. The test-retest reliability of the ESES over a 7-week period was .70. The ESES scores were significantly positively correlated with percentage overweight (r = .15), dietary restraint as measured by the Restraint Scale (Herman & Polivy, 1980) (r = .47), self-reported previous dieting (r = .23), and self-reported current dieting (r = .24). The ESES scores were significantly negatively correlated with self-esteem (r = to .51). Laboratory study revealed that NA subscale scores significantly predicted food consumption irrespective of the respondent's self-reported mood. Among adult participants in behaviorally oriented weight reduction programs, weight losses were significantly correlated with increases in ESES scores, but absolute levels of ESES scores were not related to weight or weight change. This finding indicates that individuals anchor the scale differently, but that within an individual, the ESES is sensitive to changes over time.

Preliminary psychometric evaluation of the ESES among male subjects indicates that they score significantly less (mean = 74.24) than do female subjects. Coefficient alpha for the scale and subscales was high (>.88) among this group, and an ESES factor structure similar to that of female subjects was established. The ESES were again significantly positively related to percentage overweight (r = .30) and restraint scores (r = .40). Self-reported dieters scored significantly higher than did nondieters.

Clinical Use

The ESES is intended for use with individuals indicating difficulty controlling their overeating or weight. As currently developed, it is not intended for use with anorexic or bulimic individuals, but for individuals contemplating or participating in weight loss regimens (i.e., obese individuals). It can be used as a pretreatment assessment instrument to identify dieters or weight loss program participants whose self-perceived control of eating habits is so low that postponing treatment until this perception can be improved might be warranted. It also can be used to identify potential dropouts and treatment failures early in treatment. The ESES scores significantly increase during treatment, typically during the first few weeks of dieting. Participants who do not exhibit an increase in ESES scores within 3 to 6 weeks of the beginning of treatment are unlikely to lose weight and are at high risk for dropping out of treatment. They may benefit from remedial work.

Future Directions

Further investigations with the ESES are required in three areas. First, a full investigation of the psychometric properties of the scale with adult, noncollege men and women must be conducted to assure that the scale accurately represents these groups. Second, the predictive ability of the scale with individuals in weight-reducing programs needs to be examined and confirmed in a large scale sample. Finally, the applicability of the scale to individuals with other eating disorders (e.g., anorexia nervosa and bulimia) might profitably be assessed.

References

Bandura, A. (1977). Self-efficacy: Toward a unifying theory of behavior change. *Psychological Review, 84*, 191-215.

Condiotte, M., & Lichtenstein, E. (1981). Self-efficacy and relapse in smoking cessation programs. *Journal of Consulting and Clinical Psychology, 49*, 648-658.

Cronbach, L. (1951). Coefficient alpha and the internal structure of tests. *Psychometrika, 16*, 297-334.

Glynn, S.M., & Ruderman, A.J. (1986). The development and validation of an eating self-efficacy scale. *Cognitive Therapy and Research, 10*, 403-420.

Herman, C.P., & Polivy, J. (1980). Restrained eating. In A.B. Stunkard (Ed.), *Obesity*. Philadelphia: Saunders.

Electrocardiography

Michael E. Thase

Description

The electrocardiogram (ECG or EKG) is a non-invasive method for recording the electrical rhythm and conduction patterns of the heart. An electrocardiographic recording is an amplified and graphically represented tracing of a series of consecutive heart beats. The electrical activity recorded corresponds to changes in the membrane potential of cardiac cells during depolarization and repolarization (Hurst & Myerburg, 1973). Such cardiac cells can be divided into two types on the basis of their electrical activity: specialized conducting cells and more ordinary muscle tissue (Hurst & Myerburg, 1973). The former cells make up the cardiac conduction system, which includes the sinoatrial node, the His-Purkinje tracts, and the atrioventricular (AV) node. Conducting cells are specialized for the purpose of initiating an electrical impulse. These cells propagate an electrical impulse (normally initiated in the sinoatrial node) that triggers contraction of the cardiac muscle in the atria and ventricles of the heart.

An ECG is recorded through a series of electrodes, including electrodes attached to each limb and six electrodes affixed to the chest wall (precordium). The electrode placed on the right leg alway serves as an inactive ground. In current practice, a 12-lead system is used, with each lead representing the change in electrical potential between either two electrodes or one electrode and a combination of several others (Hurst & Myerburg, 1973). The resultant display includes three standard limb leads (I, II, and III), three unipolar limb leads (aVR, aVL, and aVF), and six precordial leads (V1 through V6). The 12 leads reflect different regions of cardiac electrical activity and can be arranged as vectors in a hexaxial frontal plane to ascertain the mean electrical activity of the heart beat. Recordings are standardized such that a stylus deflection of 1 MUmm represents an electrical change of 0.1 MUmV and that 1 second of cardiac activity is captured over 25 MUmm of electrocardiographic paper (Hurst & Myerburg, 1973).

The characteristic sequence of depolarization and repolarization during the cardiac conduction cycle is composed of the P wave (atrial depolarization), the QRS complex (ventricular muscle depolarization), and the T wave (ventricular repolarization). Depending on the heart rate (which is readily determined by the distance between successive R waves), this orderly sequence normally repeats itself 1 to 2 times each second. The normal, regular pattern of cardiac conduction is referred to as a sinus rhythm.

Clinical interpretation of electrocardiographic recordings is based on the shape, amplitude, duration, and intervals of these wave forms. For example, the interval from the onset of the P wave to the onset of the R wave (PR interval), normally 0.12 to 0.20 second, reflects AV conduction time (Hurst & Myerburg, 1973). Values greater than .20 second indicate delayed conduction (i.e., heart block) in this system. The duration of the QRS complex, normally 0.04 to 0.10 second, indicates the time necessary for ventricular depolarization (Hurst & Myerburg, 1973). Delayed conduction in the His-Purkinje tracts or ventricular muscle damage may prolong the QRS interval. The QT interval corresponds to the refractory period of the ventricles during which depolarization is not possible. Structural damage to the heart may be reflected by alterations in the shape (i.e., amplitude or duration, or both) of specific wave forms, deviant electrical axis determinations, and/or abnormal amplitude of components of the QRS complex (Hurst & Myerburg, 1973). Premature or ectopic heart beats are detected by the QRS complex occurring either out of sequence or in a distorted fashion, or both.

Purpose

The ECG is a standard part of medical assessments of adults and an essential element in the assessment and longitudinal monitoring of all persons with heart disease. Behavioral researchers and clinicians treating individuals with cardiac disorders have used serial ECGs as an outcome measure and as a source of visual feedback in efforts to modify the cardiac conduction cycle (Bensen, Alexander, & Feldman, 1975; Engel, & Bleecker, 1974). An ECG also is a standard component of polygraphic recordings.

Development

The ECG has been in use in clinical medicine for over 60 years. More recent developments have included application of computer software to enable automated scoring of electrocardiographic strips and use of portable, telemetric devices to conduct longitudinal, in vivo assessment of more paroxysmal cardiac dysrhythmias.

Psychometric Characteristics

Electrocardiographic profiles can be read with a high degree of interrater reliability (Bensen et al., 1975). Although such interpretations generally are made by cardiologists, more basic electrocardiographic readings can be mastered by nearly all physicians in training and many other health care professionals. Automated scoring methods similarly have high "interrater" reliability with expert judges (Bensen et al., 1975).

Test-retest reliability of electrocardiographic tracings are limited by the state-dependent nature of many cardiac abnormalities. For example, a cardiac conduction defect secondary to metabolic derangement or drug toxicity will not be present when the underlying problem has been corrected. Tachycardia (extremely rapid heart rate) associated with exertion, anxiety, or drug ingestion certainly may not be present upon repeat testing. Similarly, episodic forms of cardiac dysrhythmia may be detected on some occasions, but not others. Electrocardiographic changes associated with acute, structural heart damage also may evolve over time. As a result, an electrocardiographic profile suggestive of myocardial infarction is strongly suggestive but not definitive in the absence of clinical evidence and other laboratory studies (i.e., cardiac muscle enzyme levels) (Hurst & Myerburg, 1973). Conversely, electrocardiographic evidence of an old, clinically "silent" (undetected) myocardial infarction is sometimes detected in apparently normal individuals.

Clinical Use

Behavioral assessments using the ECG have been most prominent in studies attempting to modify cardiac disorders through biofeedback or relaxation training (Bensen et al., 1975; Engel & Bleecker, 1974). Such efforts, generally reported in the literature as single case studies or small group investigations, have been most successful in aiding subjects to control premature heart beats and sinus tachycardia. An effective training program for sinus tachycardia generally includes feedback-assisted training to develop voluntary (operant) control over acceleration and deceleration of the heart rate. An ECG also could be used to determine pulse rate as an indicator of general arousal level, although there are simpler and equally reliable alternative methods available.

Future Directions

The ECG will remain an essential component for assessment of cardiac disorders for the foreseeable future. Its application as a behavioral assessment tool should rise or fall in conjunction with the efficacy of behavioral interventions to modify cardiac disturbances.

References

Bensen, H., Alexander, S., & Feldman, C.L. (1975). Decreased premature contractions through use of the relaxation response in patients with stable ischaemic heart-disease. Lancet, 2, 380-382.

Engel, B.T., & Bleecker, E.R. (1974). Application of operant conditioning techniques to the control of cardiac arrhythmias. In P.A. Obrist, A.H. Black, J. Brener, & L.V. DiCara (Eds), Cardiovascular psychophysiology. Chicago: Aldine.

Hurst, J.W., & Myerburg, R.J. (1973). Introduction to electrocardiography: 2nd ed. New York: McGraw-Hill.

Electroencephalography

Michael E. Thase

Description

Electroencephalography is a method of graphically recording the electrical activity of the cerebral cortex. Cerebral electrical activity is recorded by electrodes attached to the scalp and represents the postsynaptic potentials of neurons of the cerebral cortex. The electroencephalogram (EEG) records the sum of inhibitory and excitatory potentials of millions of neurons (Kiloh, McComas, & Osselton, 1972). Amplification of such electrical potentials is necessary for recording. The amplitude of the waking electroencephalographic rhythm in a normal adult generally averages only 50 to 75 MUmV.

In current practice, an electroencephalographic is obtained by attachment of 16 electrodes, symmetrically placed at standardized positions on the scalp (Kiloh et al., 1972). Additional reference electrodes are placed on the ears and at the vertex of the scalp. An electroencephalographic tracing usually is derived from a 16-channel polygraph, which records the difference in electrical potential between selected pairs of scalp electrodes. These channels correspond to various regions of the brain (i.e., temporal, parietal, or occipital regions). Following amplification, electrical impulses are translated into the movements of a lightweight stylus, which graphically records the EEG on paper. The tracing is calibrated such that a wave amplitude of 50 MUmV corresponds to a pen deflection of 7 mm.

Clinical interpretation of EEGs focuses on the frequency, form, and amplitude of waves, as well as the rhythmicity and location of wave forms (Kiloh et al., 1972). Electroencephalographic wave forms oscillate in sinusoidal patterns. Normal adult waking electroencephalographic activity has a periodicity of 8 to 13 cycles per second (Hz) and is termed the alpha rhythm. Faster wave forms (i.e., 14 to 20 Hz) are referred to as beta activity. Beta activity is sometimes seen in normal states of alertness or arousal. However, intermittent or focal beta activity is associated with epilepsy. Theta waves have a slower frequency of 4 to 7 Hz and very slow (i.e., <4 Hz) sinusoidal waves are named delta activity. Generalized slow wave activity during a waking state often denotes a pathologic cerebral process of structural or metabolic origin. Seizure activity is identified on an electroencephalographic tracing by an abrupt discharge or change in electrical potential, reflected as spike or spike and wave forms. For example, grand mal epilepsy is associated with paroxysmal bursts of high voltage spike and slow wave activity. Petit mal epilepsy is characterized by a pattern of bilateral, synchronous 3-per-second spike and slow wave activity.

Clinical use of routine electroencephalographic studies is enhanced by several techniques designed to accentuate abnormal wave forms or to provoke latent seizure activity. Such techniques routinely include photic (i.e., stroboscopic) stimulation, hyperventilation, and sleep tracings. When clinically indicated, more elaborate procedures may be employed, including sleep deprivation, longitudinal telemetric recording, administration of epileptigenic agents (e.g., metrazol), and deep electrode placement (Kiloh et al., 1972).

Purpose

The EEG primarily is used in neurology and psychiatry as a diagnostic aid as part of a comprehensive evaluation of suspected brain dysfunction. The foremost indication for an EEG is for evaluation of convulsive (epileptic) disorders. The EEG also is useful in the evaluation of altered mental states (i.e., delirium or dementia). As will be discussed, behavioral researchers have used electroencephalographic technology in the treatment of specific forms of epilepsy and to assist induction of relaxation.

Development

Electroencephalographic technology has been used in clinical practice for over 50 years. Electroencephalographic laboratories are now present in almost all hospitals and many neurology clinics. Refinements in technique and improved standardization of scoring methodology have led to greater comparability of results across research centers. However, initial hopes that waking electroencephalographic studies could be used to discriminate between various psychopathological states have not been realized. More recent research efforts involving computer-assisted electroencephalographic mapping of brain regions, spectral analysis, or stimulus-evoked electroencephalographic potentials have shown some degree of diagnostic sensitivity and specificity for schizophrenia and affective disorders.

Psychometric Characteristics

Identification of specific electroencephalographic wave forms can be achieved with extremely high interrater reliability (Kiloh et al., 1972). Interpretation of the clinical significance of an entire electroencephalographic study, however, requires the electroencephalographer to scan pages of tracings, that is, to develop a Gestalt impression derived from at least hundreds of wave forms. The effects of age and psychoactive drug use also must be taken into consideration. Interpretation of the EEG is therefore in part subjective.

Recent studies indicate considerable interrater variability in interpretation of the clinical significance of EEGs, particularly in "borderline" studies. (See for example Williams, Luders, Brickner, Goormastic, & Klass, 1985.) Test-retest reliability similarly is problematic, because electroencephalographic profiles are state dependent. Diagnostic confidence of "abnormal" and "normal" tracings also is limited. At least 10 to 15% of the normal population have electroencephalographic abnormalities (usually diffuse beta or theta wave activity), and essentially normal electroencephalographic profiles are recorded in up to one third of individuals with dementia or convulsive disorders (when based on a single electroencephalographic tracing) (Kiloh et al., 1972).

Clinical Use

Clinical applications of the EEG for diagnosing and monitoring seizure disorders and other organic states have just been briefly discussed. Behavioral researchers have successfully used electroencephalographic feedback to aid individuals with convulsive disorders to reduce the frequency of seizure episodes (Sterman, Macdonald, & Stone, 1974). Several groups also report favorable changes in electroencephalographic rhythms following intensive biofeedback training to increase alpha activity or 12 to 16 Hz sensorimotor rhythms (Lynch, Paskewitz, & Orne, 1974). Unfortunately, such efforts generally have been limited to either single case reports or small, uncontrolled studies.

Potential clinical implications of biofeedback training to enhance generation of alpha activity were extensively studied in the 1970s. In particular, the "alpha state" was postulated to correspond to a quasi-meditational state similar to that seen in yoga (Lynch et al., 1974). In these studies, visual or auditory feedback typically was provided when alpha rhythm was detected in occipital electroencephalographic leads. Concurrent biofeedback training with electromyography (EMG) sometimes was included. Although such studies generally found that the alpha rhythm could be brought under voluntary (operant) control, the meditational "alpha state" was more dependent on instructional set and subject expectancies.

Future Directions

The EEG will continue to play a prominent role in neurodiagnostic evaluation, particularly in the form of computer-assisted techniques. Applications for behavioral assessment appear much more limited at this time, however. Further study of the use of behavioral methods to modify abnormal electroencephalographic rhythms in persons with convulsive disorders merits further investigation, particularly for those individuals who do not respond to, or do not desire to take, anticonvulsant medications.

References

Kiloh, L.G., McComas, A.J., & Osselton, J.W. (1972). *Clinical electrocephalography (3rd Ed.)*. London: Butterworth & Co.

Lynch, J.J., Paskewitz, D.A., & Orne, M.T. (1974). Some factors in the feedback control of human alpha rhythm. *Psychosomatic Medicine, 36,* 399-410.

Sterman, M.B., Macdonald, L.R., & Stone, R.K. (1974). Biofeedback training of the sensorimotor electroencephalogram rhythm in man: Effect of epilepsy. *Epilepsia, 15,* 395-416.

Williams, G.W., Luders, H.O., Brickner, A., Goormastic, M., & Klass, D.W. (1985). Interobserver variability in EEG interpretation. *Neurology, 35,* 1714-1719.

Electromyography

David F. Peck

Description

Electromyography, or EMG, refers to the recording of electrical activity generated by the muscles. There are three kinds of muscle in the human body: (1) smooth muscle (also called visceral or involuntary), often very small, attached to blood vessels and internal organs such as the bladder; (2) cardiac muscle, attached to the walls of the heart; (3) striated muscle (also called skeletal or voluntary), attached to the skeleton and responsible for gross body movement. The striated muscles are of particular interest in behavioral assessment, and the remainder of this entry will refer only to this muscle type.

Muscle consists of an extended mass of tissue comprising thousands of individual fibers running together in bundles (fasciculi). The fasciculi are themselves surrounded by touch connective tissue and large numbers of them together form the muscle mass. The basic element in muscle activity is the single motor unit (SMU), which consists of a single nerve cell body, its axon and terminal branches, and a group of muscle fibers. The number of muscle fibers per SMU varies considerably, mainly according to the precision of muscle movement required. Large slow muscles (e.g., those in the thigh) have approximately 2,000 to 3,000 muscle fibers per SMU, whereas bicep muscles have approximately 150, and small muscles around the eye may have as few as 10.

Muscles produce movement by contracting and relaxing, thereby moving that part of the skeleton to which they are attached. Contractions are of two types: isotonic, or constant steady contraction, and isometric, or tension of constant muscle length against some kind of resistance. Most muscle contractions are a blend of both. Gross muscle contraction is in effect the summation of thousands of independent twitches of individual SMUs, each of which lasts just a few milliseconds, followed by a brief period of relaxation, followed in turn by a further twitch when the impulse arrives from the nerve fiber. The SMU twitches occur asynchronously, and it is this asynchrony that permits muscles to move steadily and smoothly rather than in an "all-or-none" fashion. Each SMU can twitch at a rate of up to 50 per second, and a small electrical potential is produced with each twitch. Even when at rest, muscles are not completely relaxed, but are always in a state of tonus, or slight tension.

The electrical activity of the muscle is picked up by electrodes, normally attached to the skin above the muscle. Muscles are not separate and discrete, but there is a great deal of anatomical overlap. Electrodes on the surface of the body cannot normally pick up activity from a single muscle; rather, the recordings will reflect the activity of a group of muscles. If very accurate and discrete recordings are required, needle electrodes precisely implanted into the muscle can be used. For behavioral assessment, surface electrodes will normally be sufficient. Being noninvasive, they produce less disruption and stress in the subject and may therefore be preferable. Three electrodes are required: one reference electrode and two active electrodes. The activity is measured by a "balanced" electronic amplifier, which detects the differences between each active electrode and the reference, and amplifies the resulting difference between electrode leads. Potential differences of less than 10 MUmV (millionths of a volt) peak to peak are obtained from smaller muscles at rest, but larger muscles at work can produce potentials of several hundred millivolts (thousandths of a volt). Amplification of the order of 100,000 times the original voltage may be required. The frequency of the signal will vary widely, but amplifiers that are sensitive to a range of 10 to 1,000 Hz (cycles per second) will be satisfactory for use in behavioral assessment. This range of frequencies and the degree of amplification required present difficulties in that many other biological signals may be picked up and contaminate the electromyographic recording.

Once the signal has been amplified, it can be displayed on a simple voltmeter, or, in addition, a permanent record is commonly kept using a pen recorder, magnetic tape, or a floppy disc. One difficulty in recording electromyographic signals arises from the very high frequency just noted. Pen recorders, for example, could not produce a clear trace with the pen crossing the recording paper 1,000 times in a second; important information could be obscured amid the abundance of activity. Electromyographic signals are normally "smoothed out" or integrated before the final recording stage. There are various techniques for achieving this. One uses a procedure similar to that of a cumulative recorder, in which the pen deflections are cumulative and proportional to the level of muscle tension; the pen resets when a set level of accumulated activity has been achieved. A second method entails electronic averaging, producing a highly smoothed curve. Basmajian (1979) has provided an excellent detailed description of muscle activity and its measurement.

Purpose

The purpose of EMG is to obtain an ongoing record of muscle activity. As with most psychophysiological measures, basal (resting) level and response to a stimulus are analyzed. These measures can be used to monitor changes over time, to assess whether a treatment intervention (e.g., relaxation training) has produced changes in the resting muscle tension level; and to permit comparisons across groups (e.g., whether one group of anxious patients differs from another in terms of electromyographic changes in response to an anxiety-provoking stimulus). A further purpose of EMG is to provide a measure of activity that can be converted into a signal to be fed back to subjects, to provide them with up-to-date and accurate information about muscle tension levels, thereby permitting additional control (i.e., electromyographic biofeedback).

It is seldom possible to make valid comparisons of precise electromyographic levels across studies. Because of the degree of signal processing that occurs during amplification and integration, any observed differences across studies may be due to different instrument characteristics or to other procedural variations.

Development

Electromyography did not develop from within the tradition of behavioral assessment, but from electrophysiology and physiotherapy. It is a technique in common use in a variety of medical specialties such as neurology, orthopedics, and physical rehabilitation. Psychology has played little part in the development of EMG, except for the pioneering work of Budzynski and Stoyva (1969), whose early report on the conversion of electromyographic activity into an auditory feedback signal stimulated the more widespread clinical application of electromyographic biofeedback.

Psychometric Characteristics

Reliability. A common way of assessing reliability is to see how far a device provides consistent results when measuring the same characteristics under similar circumstances; an example is repeated testing over time. Recent studies have examined reliabilty of human frontalis and tricep muscle activity within and between subjects. High levels of reliability (up to + 0.98) were obtained for most subjects, particularly when EMG was sampled at short intervals. However, it would appear that reliability may be lower at other sites (e.g., forearm). High reliability, using fine wire electrodes, has also been reported from animal studies.

Validity.   One way of examining validity is to see how far electromyographic recordings from one muscle group are contaminated by other biological activity, such as artifacts from eye blinks, cardiac activity, electrical mains interference, and movements of the electrode leads. Fortunately, the frequencies of such sources of contamination are often known, and the use of filters of appropriate band width can normally eliminate the interference. Interference from nearby muscle groups (e.g., frontalis recordings are very prone to contamination from swallowing and jaw clenching) requires a different solution because similar frequencies are generated. One popular solution is to record simultaneously activity from likely sources of interference so that this influence can be determined.

A related question is how far activity in a particular muscle group may be taken as a valid indication of general muscle tension. It was originally and naively assumed that tension in the frontalis muscle was an accurate and valid reflection of muscle activity throughout the body, and that reductions in frontalis activity would be associated with similar reductions in the general muscle system and the autonomic nervous system. Evidence suggests that this is not so. Typically, the correlation of activity levels across muscle groups is low to moderate. Although electromyographic biofeedback has been associated with changes in other indices of arousal, these changes are similar to those obtained with simple relaxation training.

Similarly, the relationship between frontalis electromyographic activity and subjective ratings of anxiety are normally zero or of small magnitude. Certainly, electromyographic recordings alone cannot be regarded as a valid index of overall anxiety or arousal, but they may be useful as part of an assessment battery.

Clinical Use

Electromyography has three main clinical uses: to examine the characteristics of clinical populations; to monitor change during treatment; and in biofeedback. In practice there may be considerable overlap in these uses.

Clinical Population Characteristics.   Many applications have been reported, but only a few will be mentioned here. Subjects with reading difficulties show greater electromyographic activity from speech muscles during silent reading than do proficient readers. Patients with high anxiety levels tend to respond in a global "blunderbuss" way to a task (e.g., reaction time), in that activity occurs in muscle groups unrelated to task performance. Similarly, anxious patients display greater residual activity after completion of a response and produce more anticipatory movements. Much attention has been devoted to the relationship between facial muscle activity and mood in recent years. Several reports suggest that experimentally induced mood following instructions to contemplate a variety of emotionally arousing thoughts is accompanied by changes in facial electromyographic activity. The corrugator muscle at the eyebrow is particularly associated with negative mood states. The emotions of happiness, sadness, anger, and fear have been discriminated by computer pattern-recognition of facial muscle activity (Fridlund, Schwartz, & Fowler, 1984). Clinically depressed patients demonstrate similar electromyographic patterns, and it has been suggested that such patterns can be used as predictors and/or measures of response to treatment. The relationship between mood and facial EMG is particularly marked in female subjects.

Several painful clinical conditions are often alleged to be associated with sustained muscular contractions, such as tension headache and low back pain. It might therefore be suggested that electromyographic recording could provide a useful assessment tool in such cases. Evidence indicates that this is not so and that the relationship between electromyographic activity and reported pain is minimal, several studies reporting a zero relationship between head pain and scalp muscle activity. There is some evidence that patients who complain predominantly of a disorder of muscle function respond to stress by changes in muscular activity, whereas patients with heart complaints tend to display cardiovascular stress responses.

Detailed analyses of electromyographic activity also have produced advances in the taxonomy of stuttering and of articulatory disorders in children, in the assessment of tardive dyskinesia, and in the description of type A behaviors.

Monitoring Change. One use of electromyographic recording is to monitor the effects of relaxation training conducted as an ingredient of systematic desensitization or as treatment in its own right. Surprisingly, few studies have examined electromyographic changes during relaxation. A further use is to monitor changes during electromyographic biofeedback treatment (see below) of muscular disorders such as dystonia, blepharospasm, and torticollis.

Biofeedback. Biofeedback is a procedure whereby biological signals are electronically detected and amplified, and converted into a readily discernible signal that is fed back to subjects, enabling them to alter and control the biological state. Electromyography was the first biological signal to be used in clinical biofeedback, being used in physical rehabilitation for several years before it attracted the attention of clinical psychologists. As is generally the case in biofeedback work, electromyographic feedback is particularly useful if the source of the feedback signal is directly related to the underlying pathology. That is, feedback from muscles is most useful when applied to a problem that has a muscular origin. It is less useful when used indirectly, that is, in such problems as general anxiety, in which there is no necessary muscular involvement. Furthermore, electromyographic biofeedback has little or no incremental value relative to relaxation training or even to simple instructions if the goal of treatment is to reduce muscle tension, as in the treatment of tension headaches. However, if the goal of treatment is muscular activation and control, electromyographic biofeedback is effective, perhaps the most predictably effective of all the methods of biofeedback applied to a clinical problem. Firmly established in its value to increase muscle activity in neuromuscular disorders such as hemiplegia, cerebral palsy, and facial nerve injury, it must be noted that progress is often slow and erratic. Its value has also been suggested in a wide variety of areas, such as training in muscle control during childbirth, the development of appropriate facial expressions in the blind, myofacial pain dysfunction, writer's cramp, torticollis, severe tics and tremors, blepharospasm, and insomnia. Other promising applications include those to tinnitus, postoperative pain, Bell's palsy, dysphonia, and low back pain. Finally, electromyographic biofeedback has been used as an ingredient in some treatment packages applied to conditions such as hypertension and hyperkinesia, although its precise role in such packages has not been fully delineated. An excellent account of electromyographic biofeedback is contained in a report by Yates (1980).

Future Directions

Over the last few decades psychophysiological equipment has become increasingly miniaturized, and this trend will likely continue. Smaller and less obtrusive devices that can amplify and store electromyographic activity would permit extensive use of electromyographic recording in natural settings. This could be important in the assessment of dystonia, in which the spasms are often aggravated by full body movements. Moreover, a miniature device could provide electromyographic feedback during real-life activities (e.g., to assist athletes in maintaining relaxation in those muscles not required during the execution of a particular skill). Miniaturization may also lead to greater use of telemetry in electromyographic work, where activity could be transmitted to a remote recording device. Such a device could also receive signals from many subjects simultaneously.

It is also likely that electromyographic work will be applied to a wider range of problems. Its use as an index of attention may help to shed additional light on disorders of attention, and it may prove useful in the analysis of motor skill development in congenital motor disorders and in sports psychology. There have also been some interesting studies examining the interaction between subject variables, situational factors, and treatment procedures. With further research, it may be easier to decide who will benefit for which problem and under what circumstances from electromyographic biofeedback.

Recent biofeedback research has examined the patterning of different psychophysiological responses, combining them into a composite signal to provide feedback reflecting activity from more than one biological system (e.g., EMG and heart rate) or from multiple sites of the same system (e.g., EMG from frontalis, trapezius, and forearm muscles). Linked to this is an increase in the sophistication of electromyographic signal processing, exemplified in the report by Cacioppo et al. (1983). Of particular promise is the use of spectral analysis. Such advances auger well for an increased role for EMG in general behavioral assessment and in biofeedback.

References

Basmajian, J.V. (1979). *Muscles alive: Their functions revealed by electromyography* (4th Ed.). Baltimore: Williams & Wilkins.

Budzynski, T.H., & Stoyva, J.M. (1969). An instrument for producing deep muscle relaxation by means of analog information feedback. *Journal of Applied Behavior Analysis, 2,* 231-237.

Cacioppo, J.T., Marshall-Goodell, B., & Dorfman, D.D. (1983). Skeletal muscular patterning: Topographical analysis of the integrated electromyogram. *Psychophysiology, 20,* 269-283.

Fridlund, A.J., Schwartz, G.E., & Fowler, S.C. (1984). Pattern recognition of self-reported emotional state from multiple-site facial EMG activity during affective imagery. *Psychophysiology, 21,* 622-637.

Yates, A.J. (1980). *Biofeedback and the modification of behavior.* New York: Plenum.

Experience Sampling Method

Aubrey J. Yates

Description

The Experience Sampling Method (ESM) requires the subject to fill out pages in a self-report diary for 1 week in response to signals occurring at random

times during the course of the day. An electronic pager is used for this purpose, signals occurring once every 2 hours between 8 am and 10 pm. On signal, the subject responds to items in the questionnaire relating to where they are, what they are doing, whether they are alone, and what they were just thinking about. Other aspects can readily be investigated. The method is described by Larson and Csikzentmihalyi (1983).

Purpose

The ESM is used to obtain reports on representative samples of moments during a subject's daily activities. When the signal occurs, the subject responds as just indicated. The results may be analyzed in various ways. Johnson and Larson (1982) compared 15 bulimic patients and 24 normal control subjects on four dimensions: overall mood, extent of mood fluctuation, degree of social isolation, and extent of food-related behavior. They were also able to "explore" the impact of binging and purging episodes on various affective states among bulimic persons.

Development

The technique was developed by Csikzentmihalyi, Larson, and Prescott (1977) to explore adolescent activity; it was subsequently employed to investigate solitude.

Psychometric Characteristics

Insufficient data are available to establish the psychometric characteristics of the method. It is essentially a time-sampling technique and therefore has inherent problems of reliability and validity.

Clinical Use

This is a potentially powerful technique for investigating any aspect of functioning in a clinical patient. Johnson and Larson (1982) used it with bulimic patients, but its use is not restricted to particular disorders.

Future Directions

The potential of this method is unlimited. It would serve, for example, as a corrective to the use of open-ended food diaries, because it requires responding at unequivocally specified but uncertain times. It would seem to have wide applicability with respect to some aspects of eating disorders, especially patterns of social/isolated behavior, feelings, and eating habits.

References

Csikzentmihalyi, M., Larson, R., & Prescott, S. (1977). The ecology of adolescent activity and experience. *Journal of Youth and Adolescent, 6,* 281-294.

Johnson, C., & Larson, R. (1982). Bulimia: An analysis of moods and behavior. *Psychosomatic Medicine, 44,* 341-352.

Larson, R., & Csikzentmihalyi, M. (1983). The experience sampling method. In H.T. Reis (Ed.), *Naturalistic approaches to studying social interaction.* San Francisco: Jossey-Bass.

Expired Air Carbon Monoxide Measurement

Joel D. Killen

Description

Expired air (alveolar) carbon monoxide (CO) measurement is a valid procedure for estimating the concentration of carboxyhemoglobin (COHb, the complex of carbon monoxide with hemoglobin in the body) without obtaining blood samples (Goldsmith & Landaw, 1968). The concentration of CO in expired air is directly related to the blood carboxyhemoglobin concentration (Ringold, Goldsmith, Helwig, Finn, & Schuette, 1962). Measurement of expired air CO is increasingly employed in smoking cessation and epidemiology research as a biochemical index of smoking status.

Although there are many environmental sources of CO (e.g., motor vehicle exhaust, home heating, and industry), cigarette smoking is probably the most important source of human exposure (Goldsmith & Landaw, 1968). Carbon monoxide occurs in high concentrations in cigarette smoke. The alveolar CO levels of regular smokers are significantly greater than those of nonsmokers (Goldsmith & Aronow, 1975) and correlate modestly with a variety of smoking behavior variables such as the number of cigarettes smoked per day and the average smoking rate.

Purpose

Until recently, smoking researchers have relied almost exclusively on subjects' self-reports to determine smoking status. However, the validity of self-report data, particularly from smoking prevention and cessation research, has been questioned. Self-reports can be sensitive to demand characteristics and subjects' forgetfulness and misperceptions (McFall, 1978). These findings have led many researchers to call for the use of various biochemical indices of tobacco exposure to verify subjects' self-reports of nonsmoking. Expired air carbon monoxide is easy and relatively inexpensive to collect, and it has been shown to be a useful indirect measure of regular cigarette smoking status in a variety of published reports.

Development

Expired air CO analysis was first shown to be a valid method for determining carboxyhemoglobin levels in the body in the late 1950s and early 1960s by investigators examining the effects of human exposures to air pollution (Ringold et al., 1962).

Carbon monoxide enters the body through inspired air and is bound to hemoglobin forming COHb. The biologic half-life of COHb in the body is relatively short (1 to 4 hours). Therefore, the pool of COHb circulating in the bloodstream can be viewed as a sample of recent exposure to CO. Because the body does not utilize CO in metabolic processes or excrete it through routes other than the lung, expired air CO can be used to estimate COHb concentrations (Ringold et al., 1962).

Because of its presence in heavy concentrations in the atmosphere of urban environments, CO has become a major air pollutant. Measurement and control of environmental CO represent important public health priorities. Studies have shown that elevated CO levels in humans are associated with significant health risks. In particular, CO appears related to increased incidence of coronary heart disease, for which cigarette smoking is a primary risk factor. Persons with COHb levels above 5% have a 20 times greater risk of developing atherosclerosis than do those with levels below 3%. In general, nonsmokers show COHb levels ranging from 0.5 to 2.0%, whereas smokers may show levels approaching 15%.

Carbon monoxide would seem to promote heart disease through its ability to displace oxygen in the bloodstream and its action on the walls of blood vessels (Frederiksen & Martin, 1979). Oxygen is displaced in the process of forming COHb. Excess CO inspiration can produce an oxygen deficit in the cardiovascular system. Carbon monoxide also acts to increase the permeability of blood vessel walls, resulting in decreased resistance to plaque buildup.

Psychometric Characteristics

Expired air measurement has been shown to be an effective method for discriminating regular smokers from nonsmokers in a variety of published reports. Investigators have typically chosen a CO level of 8 parts per million as the cutoff mark separating smokers from nonsmokers.

In a representative study, the sensitivity and specificity for CO testing were 97.4% and 95.8%, respectively (Fortmann et al., 1984). Three hundred seventy-nine persons reporting regular smoking had expired air CO levels greater than 8ppm. Only 10 persons who reported smoking showed levels less than 8ppm. By contrast, 853 nonsmokers showed levels less than 8ppm. Only 37 persons who reported nonsmoking showed levels greater than 8ppm.

Expired air analysis, although useful for determining smoking status, is less desirable as an index of tobacco consumption. Despite its usefulness for identifying regular smokers, the short biological half-life of COHb reduces the sensitivity of expired air assessment in detecting smokers with light or irregular smoking habits. Persons smoking less than 10 cigarettes per day are likely to be misclassified as nonsmokers. In the Fortmann study, 45 smokers reporting light smoking habits showed CO levels below 8ppm.

Other variables may also produce variation of expired air CO concentrations in smokers. Carbon monoxide levels can be affected by physiological variables such as pulmonary ventilation and cardiac activity. There is evidence that variation in construction of cigarette materials may also influence the CO levels of smokers. Behavioral variables also have a role to play in determining CO concentrations. The rate of cigarette smoking, the temporal distribution of smoking, and the depth of inhalation provide additional sources of variation in CO levels among smokers (Frederiksen & Martin, 1979). Therefore, although CO can be used to separate regular smokers from nonsmokers, it is a less reliable measure for (a) identifying those with light or irregular smoking habits, and (b) determining the actual number of cigarettes smoked per day.

Clinical Use

Measurement of expired air CO is typically performed with the Ecolyzer (Energetics Science, Inc., NY), an instrument that measures the rate of conversion of CO to CO2 while it is passed over a catalytically active electrode. Assessments are simple to perform, and the analysis and readout of CO concentrations are immediate.

Those being evaluated are asked to (a) empty their lungs of air; (b) take a deep breath; (c) hold the inhaled air for 10 to 20 seconds; (d) exhale approximately half of the held air; and (e) blow the remaining air into a polyvinyl bag for analysis.

The length of time required for breath holding has varied across studies. Earlier investigations (Ringold et al., 1962) asked persons to hold their breath for 20 seconds. Recent reports (Fortmann et al., 1984) use a 10-second period. Clinical experience suggests that many smokers may have difficulty meeting the 20-second requirement.

Exhalation of half of the held air is requested before measurement is performed, because this portion represents gas from the pulmonary dead space (Ringold et al., 1962).

Future Directions

As noted, expired air CO analysis is a useful measure for identifying regular smoking behavior. However, those smoking at low rates may still escape detection. Inaccurate reporting is of particular concern in smoking prevention and cessation research where demand effects may increase the likelihood of underreporting among trial participants. To improve detection in these situations, CO can be combined with additional measures (i.e., reports by significant others, cotinine, and thiocyanate).

Expired air CO may prove useful as an intervention component in smoking cessation research. Because analysis and readout of information are immediate, program participants receive quick and accurate feedback. The impact of such feedback on participants' behavior change efforts may be significant because of the harmful health effects associated with elevated COHb concentrations.

References

Goldsmith, J.R., & Aronow, W.S. (1975). Carbon monoxide and coronary heart disease: A review. *Environmental Research, 10,* 236-248.

Goldsmith, J.R., & Landaw, S.A. (1968). Carbon monoxide and human health. *Science, 162,* 1352-1359.

Fortmann, S.P., Rogers, T., Vranizan, K., Haskell, W.L., Solomon, D.S., & Farquhar, J.W. (1984). Indirect measures of cigarette use: Expired-air carbon monoxide versus plasma thiocyanate. *Preventive Medicine, 13*, 127-135.

Frederiksen, L.W., & Martin, J.E. (1979). Carbon monoxide and smoking behavior. *Addictive Behaviors, 4*, 703-712.

McFall, R.M. (1978). Smoking cessation research. *Journal of Consulting and Clinical Psychology, 46*, 703-712.

Ringold, A., Goldsmith, J.R., Helwig, H.L., Finn, R., & Schuette, F. (1962). Estimating recent carbon monoxide exposures. *Archives of Environmental Health, 5*, 38-48.

Eyberg Child Behavior Inventory

Carolyn Webster-Stratton

Description

The Eyeberg Child Behavior Inventory (ECBI) (Eyberg & Ross, 1978; Robinson, Eyberg, & Ross, 1980) is a 36-item inventory that describes parental perceptions of specific child problem behaviors. It is designed for use with children 2 to 16 years old. The instrument is easy to administer and score. It yields both an intensity score (frequency of occurrence) and a problem score (degree to which the parent sees a given behavior as undesirable).

Purpose

Although unstructured interviews with parents and direct observations of family interactions and child behaviors are essential assessment procedures, parent-completed behavior checklists such as the ECBI can serve as comprehensive, efficient, practical screening instruments. Most typically, the ECBI could be used during the diagnostic phases of assessment to identify the range of problems being exhibited by the child. The ECBI is a useful measure to determine whether or not the parents' perceptions of their children's behavior problems fall within or outside the realm of "normal" limits. The behavioral specificity of items allows for rapid identification of problem areas that can be explored further during the clinical interview.

Development

The ECBI was constructed from case record data to provide a list of the most typical problem behaviors reported by parents of children with conduct problems. Examples of such behaviors included noncompliance, whining, dawdling, hitting, fighting, and destructiveness. Items that were clearly applicable to a limited age range or to behaviors unobservable to the parent, such as school behaviors, were eliminated.

Psychometric Characteristics

Adequate split-half reliability, test-retest, and internal consistency have been demonstrated (Robinson et al., 1980). Scores on both dimensions of the ECBI (Eyberg & Ross, 1978; Webster-Stratton, 1985a) have been shown to discriminate conduct–disordered children from normal or nonclinic children. The ECBI scores are reported to correlate well with independent observations of children's behaviors (Robinson & Eyberg, 1981; Webster-Stratton, 1985b) and temperamental characteristics of the child (Webster-Stratton & Eyberg, 1982), but to be independent of social desirability factors (Robinson & Anderson, 1983). Normative data for children and adolescents have been presented, and cutoff points for treatment selection have been devised (Robinson et al., 1980).

Clinical Use

The ECBI is useful not only for screening and assessment purposes but also for measuring change in parental perception following intervention. Changes in parental perceptions of child behaviors are at least as important as actual behavior improvements. Treatment outcome studies show the ECBI to be a sensitive measure of change in conduct problem behaviors of children (Webster-Stratton, 1984).

Future Directions

Future research should add prosocial child behaviors to the ECBI inventory. As it exists now, the ECBI focuses solely on deviant child behaviors, and as both an assessment screening measure and a treatment outcome measure, it is equally important to determine whether the child's prosocial behaviors are at normal levels.

References

Eyberg, S.M., & Ross, A.W. (1978). Assessment of child behavior problems: The validation of a new inventory. *Journal of Clinical Child Psychology, 16*, 113-116.

Robinson, E.A., & Anderson, L.L. (1983). Family adjustment, parental attitudes, and social desirability. *Journal of Abnormal Child Psychology, 11*, 247-256.

Robinson, E.A., & Eyberg, S.M. (1981). The dyadic parent–child interaction coding system: Standardization and validation. *Journal of Consulting and Clinical Psychology, 49*, 245-250.

Robinson, E.A., Eyberg, S.M., & Ross, A.W. (1980). The standardization of an inventory of child conduct problem behaviors. *Journal of Clinical Child Psychology, 9*, 22-28.

Webster-Stratton, C. (1984). Randomized trial of two parent-training programs for families with conduct-disordered children. *Journal of Consulting and Clinical Psychology, 52*, 666-668.

Webster-Stratton, C. (1985a). Mother perceptions and mother–child interactions: Comparison of a clinic-referred and a non-clinic group. *Journal of Clinical Child Psychology, 14*, 334-339.

Webster-Stratton, C. (1985b). Comparisons of behavior transactions between conduct disordered children in the clinic and at home. *Journal of Abnormal Child Psychology, 13*, 169-184.

Webster-Stratton, C., & Eyberg, S.M. (1982). Child temperament: Relationship with child behavior problems and parent–child interactions. *Journal of Clinical Child Psychology, 11*, 123-129.

Eysenck Personality Inventory

H. J. Eysenck

Description

This self-report questionnaire was published as part of an on-going series of investigations to measure the personality dimension of neuroticism-stability (N) and extraversion-introversion (E), while also including a dissimulation or lie scale (L). The EPI (Eysenck & Eysenck, 1964) is a development of an earlier instrument, the Maudsley Personality Inventory, from which it was derived by successive factorial analyses of intercorrelations between items. It consists of two parallel forms, thus making possible retesting after experimental treatment without interference from memory factors.

Development

The inventory is of particular interest because it is related to a causal theory and to a large number of experimental investigations that have been carried out to test the causal theories involved (Eysenck & Eysenck, 1985). As regards extroversion, the theory states that extroverted behavior patterns are produced by an interaction between the cortex and the reticular formation, leading to relatively low cortical arousal and arousability, whereas introverted behavior patterns are caused by relatively high states of cortical arousal. Neuroticism is related to biochemical factors like adrenal secretion and generally to the activity of the autonomic system. Both factors are strongly determined by genetic features (Eysenck & Eysenck, 1985), and it may therefore be stated with some confidence that there is a biological basis for these personality patterns (Eysenck, 1967). It is universally accepted by psychologists that man is a biosocial animal, determined in his actions by both biological and social factors. Research on the EPI has explicated to a considerable extent both the biological and the social determinants.

Psychometric Characteristics

The scales are relatively short but have adequate reliability. Repeat reliabilities, with approximately 1 year intervening, are nearer to .9 than .8. Consistency reliabilities are somewhat lower, ranging from .74 to .91 for the individual scales and from .85 to .95 for the combined scales. The L scale has a test-retest reliability of .75 for the single scales and .81 for the combined scales. Considering the shortness of the scales, these reliabilities are satisfactory.

The scales are essentially uncorrelated, as far as E and N are concerned; the L scale is correlated with N (negatively) to a degree that indicates the motivation to dissimulation inherent in the testing situation (Michaelis & Eysenck, 1971). This enables the investigator to determine whether dissimulation has played an important part in a particular study and whether the L scale should be used to correct for dissimulation.

The scales themselves are based on numerous factorial analyses of intercorrelations between items, and these analyses clearly indicate the independent nature of the factors. The factors themselves are conceived as super or second order factors, that is, each combines a number of primaries. The evidence from many different studies is fairly conclusive in showing that these two major dimensions of personality emerge from practically all large scale investigations using questionnaires or rating of personality and are hence of considerable universality (Eysenck & Eysenck, 1985). This is in line with the purpose of the construction of the inventory, namely, to make available a measure of the most firmly established and wide ranging dimensions of personality emerging from psychometric and experimental research.

The psychometric properties of the scales were exhaustively described in a series of empirical studies (Eysenck & Eysenck, 1969) that also used, for comparative purposes, items from the major existing personality scales, such as those of Guilford and Cattell. These studies deal with such questions as the validity of the Minnesota Multiphasic Personality Inventory, giving evidence on both the negative and the positive validity of the scales; the orthogonality of personality structures; and the influence of response sets on the EPI; as well as reporting several joint factorial studies of items in the Eysenck, Cattell, and Guilford Inventories.

Clinical Use

As far as clinical use is concerned, it has been demonstrated repeatedly that neurotic subjects, in particular, tend to have very high N scores and very low E scores; an exception to this rule are persons with hysteria and psychopaths (i.e., extroverted forms of neurosis in which, although N is high, E is relatively normal). N scores can be reduced when suitable therapy produces a remission in the neurotic disorder. Moreover, differences exist in the type of reactions typically shown by high N extroverts and high N introverts. High N extroverts tend to show physical symptoms, such as rapid heart beat, headaches, and dizziness, whereas high N introverts tend to show mental symptoms such as anxiety and worry.

It should be remembered that these scales are not lists of symptoms, attempting to discriminate between normal and neurotic subjects. The intent of the scales is rather to deal with *dimensions* ranging from stability to clinical neurosis, and the scales are applicable not only or even mainly to patients, but also equally, if not more applicable, to normal persons differing in the degrees of neurotic predisposition. Hence, much use of the EPI has been with normal samples in attempts to test aspects of the general personality theory suggested by the author. In clinical samples too, there is still a wide range of differentiation, and it has been shown that knowledge of the particular personality structure of the patient in terms of N and E can be of vital importance in prescribing suitable therapy. Psychotics also tend to have high N scores, and here too marked differences exist between patients with high and low extroversion scores, respectively.

The EPI is the only non-American inventory widely used in the United States, and it has been used perhaps more for research than for clinical purposes. The hundreds of studies based on the theory underlying the construction of these scales have on the whole given positive results, and it has

been suggested that the N and E structure of personality furnishes a very solid basis for personality description, claiming to be a proper paradigm for this purpose (Eysenck & Eysenck, 1985).

Future Directions

For new developments and future directions, readers are referred to the discussion of the Eysenck Personality Questionnaire, which adds to the E and N dimensions a third one, labeled psychoticism (P). Despite this improvement, the detailed standardization of the EPI and the large background material available on it suggest that it is not yet obsolete, but may be used with advantage in studies that are not particularly interested in the contribution of psychoticism.

References

Eysenck, H.J. (1967). *The biological basis of personality.* Springfield: Charles C Thomas.

Eysenck, H.J., & Eysenck, M.W. (1985). *Personality and individual differences: A natural science approach.* New York: Plenum.

Eysenck, H.J., & Eysenck, S.B.G. (1964). *Manual of the Eysenck Personality Inventory.* London: Hodder & Stoughton; San Diego: DIGITS.

Eysenck, H.J., & Eysenck, S.B.G. (1969). *Personality structure measurement.* London: Routledge & Kegan Paul.

Michaelis, W., & Eysenck, H.J. (1971). The determination of personality inventory factor patterns and intercorrelations by change in real life motivations. *Journal of General Psychology, 118,* 223-224.

Eysenck Personality Questionnaire

H. J. Eysenck

Description

The Eysenck Personality Questionnaire (EPQ, Eysenck & Eysenck, 1975) was devised to succeed the Eysenck Personality Inventory by the addition of one further dimension of personality, namely, psychoticism (P). The questionnaire thus attempts to measure three major personality dimensions (psychoticism, extroversion, and neuroticism) and also contains a lie scale to alert the investigator to dissimulation.

The questionnaire is relatively short, containing 90 items, and is written in language that is easy to understand, as it is intended not only or mainly for students, but also for random samples of the population.

Purpose

The purpose of the questionnaire is to measure the major dimensions of personality that have emerged from large numbers of factor analytic descriptive studies of self-ratings and other-ratings in the United States, Europe, Scandinavia, and other countries. The major dimensions of P, E, and N have emerged from many different sources and inventories, such as the Minnesota Multiphasic Personality Inventory, the 16 PF, and the Guilford scales (Eysenck & Eysenck, 1985). They do not cover the whole personality, but are the major second-order or super-factors and cover probably more variance than any other three factors would do.

There are adult and junior versions of the EPQ, the latter constructed to serve children aged 8 to 14 or 15. Standardization data are given in great detail in the manual, as are age trends (there is a decline in P, E, and N from the age of 20 or thereabouts, and an inverse trend from the ages of 7 to 15). Also given are details about the relationship between the scales and neurotic disorders, psychotic disorders, delinquency, and the like. Delinquents tend to score high on P, E, and N, and a special C (criminality) scale has been constructed for which norms are given in the manual.

Development

These scales embody the *dimensional* approach; in other words, the intention is not to diagnose clinical neurosis or psychosis, as opposed to normal, or subvarieties of psychosis and neurosis. The theory underlying the construction of the scale (Eysenck & Eysenck, 1976) is to construct inventories that would measure personality *dispositions* underlying the development, under stress, of neurotic or psychotic disorders. The questionnaires are therefore mainly intended for experimental use (i.e., to investigate the nature of psychotic and neurotic dispositions) rather than for diagnostic purposes, although they have also been widely used in clinics to relate personality with treatment.

The EPQ was developed through a lengthy series of factor-analytic studies, beginning with the items in the Eysenck Personality Inventory (EPI), constructing a separate P scale and then altering concepts and item choice until roughly orthogonal scales were achieved, which in addition fulfill certain validity criteria. The internal consistency of the E, N, and L scales is roughly the same as that for the EPI scales, for P reliabilities are somewhat lower, although test-retest reliabilities are quite satisfactory even for that scale, ranging from .80 to .86. Reliabilities for the P scale tend to be higher for male than female subjects, possibly because male subjects have a significantly higher score on this scale. Female subjects tend to have higher N scores and also L scores, whereas male subjects tend to show slightly higher E scores than do female subjects.

Psychometric Characteristics

The psychometric characteristics of E and N as well as L are similar to those of the EPI (i.e., rather normal distributions, but for P the distribution is skewed and almost J-shaped, possibly because most items are only endorsed by relatively small numbers of people). This distribution may be the result of faulty psychometric test construction, but it is more likely due to the actual distribution of the trait, although at the moment this cannot be asserted with confidence. The scales are reasonably independent, indicating that psychotic and neurotic predisposition is essentially different, as would seem to follow also from the genetic studies that have been performed on these disorders.

All the personality scales give scores that are highly influenced by genetic factors; over 50% of the phenotypic variance, and over 60% of the "true phenotypic variance" is determined by genetic factors (Eysenck & Eysenck, 1985). This suggests that physiological and generally biological theories of individual variation in these factors would be appropriate, and for E and N the theories are similar to those suggested in the EPI. For P, several relationships have been found, beginning with the marked sex difference, which suggest the influence of testosterone. Other studies have implicated serotonin metabolites, MAO, and other substances. The literature is too complex and too recent to arrive at any firm conclusions at this time.

Clinical Use

Clinically, the P scale is related not only to psychosis, which is associated with moderately high P scores and abnormally high L scores (it is important to remember this combination in assessing empirical reports), but also to the general *Erbkreis* of schizophrenia and psychosis generally (i.e., individuals not themselves psychotic, but suffering from psychopathy, who are actively delinquent, alcoholic, drug-taking, or schizoid in their behavior). All of these tend to have very elevated P scores. Different types of psychoses are distinguished by different N and E scores.

Cross-Cultural Features

Research has shown that the P, E, and N factors, at the descriptive level, not only are found in European or North American populations, but also are equally prominent and measurable in African, Indonesian, Chinese, Japanese, and South American populations (Eysenck & Eysenck, 1985). Indices of factor comparison have been calculated for more than 25 different nations, using groups of at least 500 male and 500 female subjects in each country. The coefficients average about .98, indicating almost complete identity of factors in all the different countries concerned (Barrett & Eysenck, 1984). It would therefore seem that the three personality dimensions involved are fundamental and wide-ranging descriptive entities, each of which also is associated with causal theories relating it to the central and autonomic nervous systems.

References

Barrett, P., & Eysenck, S.B.G. (1984). The assessment of personality factors across 25 countries. *Personality and Individual Differences, 5*, 615-632.

Eysenck, H.J., & Eysenck, M.W. (1985). *Personality and individual differences: A natural science approach.* New York: Plenum Press.

Eysenck, H.J., & Eysenck, S.B.G. (1975). *Manual of the Eysenck Personality Questionnaire.* London: Hodder & Stoughton; San Diego: DIGITS.

Eysenck, H.J., & Eysenck, S.B.G. (1976). *Psychoticism as a dimension of personality.* London: Hodder & Stoughton.

Fagerstrom Tolerance Questionnaire

Joel D. Killen

Description

The Fagerstrom Tolerance Questionnaire (TQ) is an 8-item paper-and-pencil measure designed to assess physical dependence on nicotine (Fagerstrom, 1978). The TQ is based on a model of physical dependence that assumes that highly nicotine-dependent smokers will: (a) smoke more than slightly dependent smokers; (b) desire a larger dose of nicotine; (c) use nicotine effectively by regulation of inhalation; (d) smoke soon after awakening

from sleep (because plasma nicotine levels are minimal); (e) rate the first cigarette of the day as most satisfying (as a result of craving relief); and (f) have more difficulty resisting urges to smoke when circumstances forbid or discourage smoking (Fagerstrom, 1981).

Recent research has examined the use of the TQ as a tool for separating highly from slightly dependent smokers (Fagerstrom, 1978) and as a predictor of relapse following smoking cessation (Killen, Maccoby, & Taylor, 1984).

Purpose

As yet, there is no direct experimental support for the hypothesis that smokers consume cigarettes for nicotine. However, research showing that many smokers (a) are beset by a variety of withdrawal symptoms following cessation, and (b) are able to regulate their nicotine intake, is strongly suggestive (Jarvik, 1979).

It is also apparent that the degree of physical dependence varies among smokers. For example, many are able to abstain with minimal physical discomfort. The TQ was developed by Fagerstrom (1978) to help researchers and clinicians categorize smokers according to their degree of nicotine dependence. Accurate measurement of nicotine dependence might then lead to better individualization of treatment (Fagerstrom, 1978).

Development and Psychometric Characteristics

The data base in support of the TQ as a measure of nicotine dependence is small and equivocal. Reliability data are lacking. In a study of 26 smokers, Fagerstrom (1978) reported a correlation of minus .54 between the TQ and changes in body temperature associated with smoking cessation. The body temperature of highly dependent smokers decreased, whereas the temperature of minimally dependent smokers increased.

In an experiment with 19 smokers, a correlation of minus .58 between the TQ and increased heart rate was reported. The more dependent smokers showed smaller increases in heart rate while smoking cigarettes.

Fagerstrom (1978) concluded that the data supported the validity of the TQ as an index of physical dependence because similar changes in body temperature are observed during withdrawal from other drugs. Furthermore, he suggested that smaller increases in heart rate reflect increased tolerance to nicotine.

Killen, Taylor, Maccoby, and Young (1984) examined correlations between the TQ and daily ratings of withdrawal symptoms and urge severity obtained over a 1-week period. Correlations were low ($r = .23$) and not significant.

Attempts to predict relapse with the TQ have not fared well. Killen et al. (1984) reported a nonsignificant correlation (rpb = minus .23) between baseline TQ scores and smoking status 15 weeks after cessation. Fagerstrom (1984) found no differences in baseline TQ scores of abstinent and nonabstinent subjects 6 months after treatment.

Clinical Use

The TQ is easy to administer and score. The instrument has a range of 0 to 11 points, with 0 indicating minimum physical dependence and 11 points maximum dependence. The questions and scoring procedures for the TQ were presented by Fagerstrom in 1978.

The value of the TQ as a tool for individualization of treatment is currently unproven. Fagerstrom (1982) reported that highly nicotine-dependent subjects receiving nicotine gum were more likely to remain abstinent following cessation than were highly dependent subjects receiving a placebo. In contrast, the abstinence rates of minimally dependent subjects in both active gum and placebo conditions were similar. Fagerstrom (1982) therefore suggested that the TQ might be used as a diagnostic tool for prescribing nicotine gum. However, it is unclear how the TQ may contribute to treatment planning because many of those scoring low on the scale may still benefit from use of the gum (Killen, Maccoby & Taylor, 1984).

Future Directions

Most smokers participating in published smoking cessation research relapse following treatment. Research to improve relapse prediction is needed. Current evidence suggests that cigarette smoking may produce nicotine dependence. Although Fagerstrom has provided data suggesting that the TQ measures a dependence process, additional studies focusing on the relationship between the TQ and a wide range of withdrawal phenomena are clearly needed.

The use of the TQ as a clinical tool remains to be demonstrated. Only a few studies have examined the TQ as a predictor of relapse. The results of this

work are not persuasive. However, because cigarette smoking is probably determined by an interaction of many factors reflecting both psychological and pharmacological functions, it is unlikely that any single measure will account for much variation in treatment outcome.

References

Fagerstrom, K.O. (1978). Measuring degree of physical dependence to tobacco smoking with reference to individualization of treatment. *Addictive Behaviors, 3*, 235-241.

Fagerstrom, K.O. (1981). *Tobacco smoking, nicotine dependence and smoking cessation*. Abstracts of Uppsala dissertations from the faculty of social sciences, Uppsala University, Sweden.

Fagerstrom, K.O. (1982). A comparison of psychological and pharmacological treatment in smoking cessation. *Journal of Behavioral Medicine, 5*, 343-350.

Fagerstrom, K.O. (1984). Effects of nicotine chewing gum and follow-up appointments in physician-based smoking cessation. *Preventive Medicine, 13*, 517-527.

Jarvik, M.E. (1979). Biological influences on cigarette smoking. *In Smoking and Health: A report of the surgeon general* (pp. 15[1]15[40], DHEW publication [PHS] 79-50066). Washington, DC: US Government Printing Office.

Killen, J.D., Maccoby, N., & Taylor, C.B. (1984). Nicotine gum and self-regulation training in smoking relapse prevention. *Behavior Therapy, 15*, 234-248.

Killen, J.D., Taylor, C.B., Maccoby, N., & Young, J.W. (1984). *Investigating predictors of relapse: An analysis of biochemical and self-report measures of tobacco dependence*. Unpublished manuscript.

Family Interaction Coding System

Dennis R. Moore

Description

The Family Interaction Coding System (FICS) is a structured, direct observation system for assessing behavior in home settings (Reid, 1978). The system identifies a "target" individual and scores all behavior emitted by the target and all behavior directed to the target. In standard use, observations focus on a given individual for 10 minutes and then rotate to target the next family member. Generally, each family has an identified behavior problem child as the primary target who is observed twice during a given observation, resulting in 10 minutes of data on the problem child and 10 minutes of data on each of the remaining family members. The scoring protocol is based on 30-second time lines in which behaviors are scored approximately every 6 seconds. Observers are cued by an audio beeper to start a new time line at the end of 30 seconds. This scoring format, because of the structure it imposes on the stream of behavior, results in data that approximate the true rate and sequencing of behavior.

The 29 behaviors scored by the FICS are weighted toward aversive behaviors, especially those common to young, behavior problem children. These behaviors include: command negative, crying, disapproval, dependency, destructiveness, high rate, humiliation, ignoring, noncompliance, negativism, physical negative, teasing, whining, and yelling. These aversive codes are often collapsed into a single category, Total Aversive Behavior (TAB), for analysis. Other codes reflect positive or neutral behavior (approval, command, compliance, indulgence, laughing, physical positive, receiving, talking, and touching) and activities (attention, normative, no response, playing, self-stimulation, and working).

The FICS data are collected by observers who have been trained to an 80% agreement criterion with calibrating observers during practice field observations. Training initially requires memorization of behavior definitions and scoring codes and practice with the scoring format. Trainees then practice scoring videotaped scenarios until they reach the accuracy criterion (15 to 20 hours). They then are trained in home settings until they reach the agreement criterion with the calibrating observer. Training typically requires 4 to 6 weeks.

Purpose

The FICS was developed to assess the therapy process and outcome in families receiving treatment for child behavior problems. It also has been used as a primary measure in research describing the development and maintenance of child behavior problems in the family. The FICS data have been prominent in virtually all of the treatment research published by G.R. Patterson and his associates at the Oregon Social Learning Center and were the building blocks for the development of Patterson's (1982) Coercion Theory of deviant family processes.

Development

The FICS was developed and refined over a 10-year period from the mid-1960s to the mid-1970s. Patterson and his colleagues were engaged in the early pioneering work of applying learning theory to describe and explain the development and use of aggressive behavior in children (Patterson, Littman, & Bricker, 1967). This research required direct observation of child behavior in natural settings to reliably document behavior occurrence and its antecedent and consequent events. Because no such measure was available, the researchers assumed the task of developing one. Early observations were comprised of written narratives of behavior. These were followed by a series of observation methods using tape recorded narratives (an early version had observers speaking into face masks containing microphones to prevent the subject from noting what was being said). The enormous time and cost involved in transcribing, coding, and summarizing tapes led researchers to consider more efficient methods of collecting direct observation data while maintaining a sense of the stream of behavior. The result was a structured format for hand recording the 29 defined behavior codes. The basics of this system have remained essentially unchanged since the late 1960s (Patterson, Ray, Shaw, & Cobb, 1969).

Since the early phases of development, research has focused on aggressive children between the ages of 3 and 12 years, their families, and normative comparison children and families. This focus was expanded during the late 1970s and included families with children exhibiting covert behavior problems such as stealing and fire setting, families with adolescent juvenile delinquents, and child abusing families. To date, the observation data have been collected on over 200 families participating in the Oregon studies.

Psychometric Characteristics

Interobserver agreement of the FICS has generally been reported to be between 70 and 80% on the basis of a global computation of agreement. Occurrence agreement for individual categories ranges from 30 to 96% for all 29 codes and from 38 to 91% for the 14 identified aversive behaviors. The level of agreement varies inversely with the difficulty of observation. Correlations between the complexity of an observation and interobserver agreement scores range between −.53 and −.75 in three different studies. In addition, interobserver agreement also varies depending on the subject observed, with observations of children having less agreement (X = 55%) than observations of adults (X = 74%). As expected, child observations also tend to be more complex than adult observations.

The validity of the FICS has been assessed with a variety of methods. Parent ratings of code definitions on an "annoying" to "pleasing" dimension showed that parents identified the 14 aversive codes as being more annoying than the nonaversive codes. The FICS also was shown to correlate moderately well with parent checklists of child aggressive behavior and with parents' daily reports of child problem behavior. Finally, the construct validity of the FICS has been demonstrated in treatment studies by its ability to document behavioral improvements in children following treatment and by its ability to differentiate problem behavior children from normative children.

Clinical Use

The FICS can provide valuable objective information on the severity and type of child behavior disorders, on the quality of adult parenting skills, and on general patterns of family interaction. These areas carry significance for clinical diagnosis and for tracking the process and outcome of therapy. However, FICS data are expensive to collect and analyze and therefore have seldomly been used in strictly clinical settings. Instead, this direct observation measure has mostly been used in clinical research to examine the etiology of child disorders and to test the efficacy of clinical interventions in altering disruptive child and family behavior patterns.

Future Directions

The FICS should continue to function as an important behavioral assessment tool in clinical research with children and families. The richness of the data and the variety of methods in which they can be analyzed (e.g., behavior rates, sequences, and patterns of interaction) provide a place for this measure in both descriptive and experimental studies. Were it not for its prohibitive cost and complexity, the FICS would also be an extremely valuable measure of clinical assessment. Perhaps future research will develop more cost-effective and simple measures that will correlate high enough with the FICS to make them useful for accurate and objective monitoring of client progress in clinical settings.

References

Patterson, G.R. (1982). A social learning approach: Volume 3. Coercive family process. Eugene, OR: Castalia Publishing Company.

Patterson, G.R., Littman, R.A., & Bricker, W. (1967). Assertive behavior in children: A step toward a theory of aggression. Monographs of the Society for Research in Child Development, 32, 1-43.

Patterson, G.R., Ray, R.S., Shaw, D.A., & Cobb, J.A. (1969). Manual of Coding of Family Interactions. New York: Microfiche Publications.

Reid, J.B. (Ed.) (1978). A social learning approach to family intervention: Vol. 2. Observation in home settings. Eugene, OR: Castalia Publishing Company.

Family Ratings of Program Behaviors

Beverly Sandifer

Description

Family members are trained to rate six program behaviors chosen on the criterion of ease of observability (Johnson & Stalonas, 1981; Sandifer & Buchanan, 1983). Observers give dichotomous ratings, indicating only the presence or absence of the following behaviors: (a) limiting of liquids consumed while eating, minimizing "washing down" food quickly; (b) chaining, slowing down the pace of eating by the performance of only one small eating behavior at a time; (c) eating only in a designated food area, structuring the environment to promote stimulus control; (d) eating only one serving of food, limiting the quantity of food eaten; (e) taking a 2-minute pause in the middle of the meal, allowing the subject to futher slow down the pace of consumption and providing an opportunity to focus on bodily cues of hunger or satisfaction or both; and (f) refraining from other activities during the meal, promoting attention to eating behavior as opposed to "automatic eating."

At an orientation meeting, family members are trained to make accurate ratings of these behaviors. Training involves verbal descriptions, modeling of appropriate and inappropriate behaviors, and practice ratings of standardized live vignettes. Observers are trained to a criterion level of 100% accuracy in three successive trials.

At the beginning of each week, the observer selects one meal in the coming week in which to observe the subject's eating behavior. The behavior list is reviewed immediately before the meal, observations are made as unobtrusively as possible, and observations are recorded on the checklist immediately following the meal. The collaboration between observer and subject is assumed to be minimal because, when questioned in individual progress review sessions, subjects are unable to specify correctly at what meal observations had been made. Periodic telephone contacts help to further assure that ratings are being made according to experimental directions. All checklists are returned promptly on a weekly basis in self-addressed envelopes provided by researchers.

Purpose

The purpose of family member ratings is twofold. First, these ratings are used as an independent measure of adherence to program behaviors in relation to weight loss. Second, these ratings serve as reliability checks for a subject's self-report of adherence to prescribed eating behaviors.

Development

The potential value of trained observers in the assessment of behavioral performance has been amply documented in numerous settings. Using individuals who are normally present in the natural environment enhances the unobtrusive quality of the assessment procedures. However, it is also evident from the literature that such individuals may tend to make global judgments based on interpersonal variables or social desirability factors. Therefore, in developing usable procedures of this nature, it is critical that family raters be given a rationale for accuracy of ratings that includes "helping the subject." Behaviors chosen for observation must be fairly unambiguous. Finally, specification of behavioral definitions through description, modeling, and practice ratings are necessary to decrease the probability of response biases.

Psychometric Characteristics

Family member ratings in specific studies have the obvious psychometric drawback of lack of normative data. Their reliability and validity, similar to those of self-report procedures, are suspect because of the interpersonally based response biases that may be present. However, when cross-validated with other objective as well as subjective measures, they can serve a useful function in a thorough assessment of adherence in a behavioral treatment program.

Clinical Use

In addition to the described value of the use of family member observers in assessment, education of a client's "significant others" can enhance the development of an environment supportive of sustained behavioral change (Brownell, Heckerman, Westlake, Hayes, & Monti, 1978). Although such individuals are often eager to help, without specific knowledge of effective change strategies, they are often unable to do so. Furthermore, clinical experience with involvement of family members in weight programs has shown that these persons often lose weight themselves, suggesting that they too have begun engaging in more healthy eating habits. The powerful effect of modeling on behavioral performances is well documented (Bandura, 1977.)

Future Directions

Observation, by family members, of eating behaviors in the naturalistic setting is a promising tool for obtaining data to corroborate subjects' self report of behavioral adherence. Because a family member views a broad sample of a subject's behavior, he or she is in a better position than an outside observer to provide information on actual routine performance. Furthermore, when family members are properly trained to observe and record unobtrusively, these ratings may provide a less reactive assessment tool than would those of an observer who is foreign to the naturalistic environment.

Despite these advantages, several methodological difficulties may be present. Several years ago, precautions were suggested by Wildman and Erickson (1977) to minimize methodological problems in observer ratings, including (a) training observers with samples of typical relevant behaviors occurring in settings similar to those in which the data collection will occur; (b) training all observers together, with ratings being compared to a single standard; (c) using two independent observers of subject behavior, whenever possible; (d) avoiding the communication of experimental hypotheses to observers; (e) minimizing the number of observed variables as well as the complexity of coding procedures; and (f) training observers in specific strategies enhancing the unobtrusiveness of observations.

Although family members may be used effectively as observers of "public eating," many overweight individuals report that it is "in the closet" that they engage in their most inappropriate eating patterns (e.g., binging). Fear of social disapproval enhances somewhat the adherence to program behaviors in the presence of others, whether or not those others have the assigned task of observation. In the Sandifer and Buchanan study (1983), family member ratings and self-reported adherence were strongly positively correlated with each other, and both correlated with weight loss. However, in using family member observations of any addictive behaviors, it is especially important to corroborate these data with objective measures of adherence (e.g., weight and blood alcohol levels).

Family member observers/raters then may be used in any treatment and research program that occurs naturally in the home environment. Assessment of the generalizability of behavior to situations outside the office or laboratory is an essential step in learning whether behavior changes are merely statistically significant or whether they are clinically significant in ameliorating problems in the client's real world."

References

Bandura, A. (1977). *Social learning theory.* Englewood Cliffs, NJ: Prentice-Hall.

Brownell, K.D., Heckerman, C.L., Westlake, R.J., Hayes, S.C., & Monti, P.M. (1978). The effect of couples training and partner cooperativeness in the behavioral treatment of obesity. *Behaviour Research and Therapy, 16,* 323-333.

Johnson, W.G., & Stalonas, P.M. (1981). *Weight no longer.* Gretna, LA: Pelican.

Sandifer, B.A., & Buchanan, W.L. (1983). Relationship between adherence and weight loss in a behavioral weight reduction program. *Behavior Therapy, 14,* 672-688.

Wildman, B.G., & Erickson, M.T. (1977). Methodological problems in behavioral observation. In J.D. Cone & R.P. Hawkins (Eds.), *Behavioral assessment: New directions in clinical psychology.* New York: Brunner/Mazel.

Fear of Negative Evaluation

Robert T. Ammerman

Description

The Fear of Negative Evaluation (FNE) scale is a 30-item true/false format questionnaire measuring social-evaluative anxiety. Specifically, the FNE consists of a series of statements involving concern about other's evaluations, avoidance of evaluative situations, distress about negative evaluation, and

expectation of being negatively evaluated. A scoring key yields a summative score from 0 to 30, indicating the degree of social-evaluative anxiety.

Purpose

A number of investigations have found a positive relationship between interpersonal dysfunction, social anxiety, and psychopathology (Watson & Friend, 1969). Although a variety of global trait anxiety inventories are available, few instruments specifically measure social-evaluative anxiety. To partly remedy this situation, Watson and Friend (1969) developed two self-report tests measuring this construct. The Social Avoidance and Distress Scale (SAD) was designed to assess the experience of distress and discomfort in interpersonal interactions, as well as the deliberate avoidance of social situations. The FNE, conversely, was designed to measure apprehension about negative evaluations.

Development

The FNE was developed and standardized with a college population. One hundred forty-five items were chosen from a larger pool and administered to 297 male and female undergraduates. The Marlowe-Crowne Social Desirability Scale and the first 10 items of Jackson's Infrequency Scale were also administered. The latter items were used to detect pseudorandom responding, and persons who answered one or more of these incorrectly were dropped from further analysis. The Marlowe-Crowne Scale was employed to detect a socially desirable response set. Items endorsed by less than 5% of the sample were omitted from further consideration. Criteria for inclusion in the final inventory were: (a) probability of endorsement of at least 10% and as close to 50% as possible, (b) high item-total correlation after social desirability variance was removed (using Jackson's Differential Reliability Index), and (c) content dissimilarity with other items and representativeness of situations. Using these guidelines, 17 true and 13 false items were chosen.

Psychometric Characteristics

Using an undergraduate sample, Watson and Friend (1969) examined reliability of the FNE. The test yielded a mean biserial item-total correlation of .72. In addition, KR-20 coefficients were .94 and .96, using two separate subgroups. Test-retest correlations after a 1-month interval were .78 (sample

= 154) and .94 (sample = 29). The mean score was 15.47 (SD = 8.62), and the median was 16 (sample = 205). Female subjects had a higher mean score than did male subjects (16.10 and 13.97, respectively; p <.10).

The FNE also has adequate convergent and predictive validity. It correlates .60 with Taylor's Manifest Anxiety Scale and .77 with the Social Approval subscale of Jackson's Personality Research Form (Watson, & Friend, 1969). In addition, persons with high FNE scores (as determined through a median split) tend to avoid potentially threatening social comparisons (Friend & Gilbert, 1973), feel worse about receiving negative evaluations (Smith & Sarason, 1975), and feel nervous in evaluative situations (Watson & Friend, 1969).

Leary (1983) has developed a brief form (12 items) of the FNE. Items with item-total correlations of at least .50 were chosen, and the true/false format was changed to a 5-point Likert scale reflecting how characteristic the statement is of the individual (1 = not at all; 5 = extremely). The brief FNE correlates highly with the original form (.96). It has a Cronbach's alpha of .90, and a 1-month test-retest Pearson product-moment correlation of .75. However, validity data on the brief FNE are unavailable.

Clinical Use

The FNE was designed for use with socially anxious individuals. However, it has been used primarily as a research instrument with nonclinical populations. Until normative data on psychiatric patients are available, caution must be employed when using the FNE with clinical groups.

Future Directions

The excellent psychometric properties of the FNE make it a useful adjunct in the assessment of social anxiety. However, additional research is needed to examine the relationship between fear of negative evaluation and other cognitive and behavioral correlates of anxiety. In addition, factor analysis of the FNE would provide information about the dimensions of evaluative anxiety measured by the instrument. Studies examining ecological validity of the FNE are also warranted. This research, combined with normative data on clinical populations, would greatly enhance the usefulness of the FNE.

References

Friend, R., & Gilbert, J. (1973). Threat and fear of negative evaluation as determinants of locus of social comparison. Journal of Personality, 41, 328-340.

Leary, M.R. (1983). A brief version of the Fear of Negative Evaluation scale. Personality and Social Psychology Bulletin, 9, 371-375.

Smith, R., & Sarason, I. (1975). Social anxiety and the evaluation of negative interpersonal feedback. Journal of Consulting and Clinical Psychology, 43, 429.

Watson, D., & Friend, R. (1969). Measurement of social–evaluative anxiety. Journal of Consulting and Clinical Psychology, 33, 448-457.

Fear Survey Schedule I

Robert T. Ammerman

Description

Lang and Lazovik's (1963) Fear Survey Schedule I (FSS-I) is a 50-item questionnaire measuring the type and intensity of fear-eliciting stimuli. Specifically, it consists of a list of common phobias. Individuals are asked to endorse each item using a 7-point Likert scale indicating the degree to which the stimulus causes fear (1 = not at all; 7 = terror). The FSS-I can be used to identify specific phobic stimuli, or a total score can be derived (ranging from 50 to 350) reflecting overall fearfulness.

Purpose

The FSS-I was originally used to measure self-reported fear in a systematic desensitization outcome study. In particular, it provided the following information: (a) degree of change in reported fear for the stimulus targeted in desensitization training (i.e., snakes) from before to after treatment, and (b) generalization of treatment effects to other fears as reflected by FSS-I total scores.

Development

The FSS-I was adapted from a similar fear survey schedule developed by Akutagawa (1956). Items were chosen using face-valid criteria to reflect common phobias.

Psychometric Characteristics

The FSS-I has been replaced by more extensive (FSS-III) and empirically derived (FSS-II) fear survey schedules. As a result, no investigations of the

FSS-I's psychometric properties are extant. However, given significant overlap in format and content between survey schedules, it is likely that the FSS-I displays similar reliability and validity to those of the FSS-II and FSS-III. The latter instruments exhibit good reliability and internal consistency. Their factor structures are complex and they vary as a function of sex and clinical population. Female subjects tend to report more intense fears than do male subjects. Correlations between fear survey schedule scores and behavioral measures, however, are moderate, as related to the relative lack of descriptive information for stimulus items. For example, when additional descriptors are added, correlations between items and behavioral measures increase (Lick, Sushinsky, & Malow, 1977).

Clinical Use

Fear survey schedules are a useful adjunct to the assessment of phobias and related anxiety disorders. The FSS-I, however, is too brief and inadequately tested to warrant use. Rather, it is recommended that more extensive inventories (e.g., FSS-III) be employed. (See Tasto, 1977, for a detailed discussion of fear survey schedules.)

Future Directions

Given that the FSS-I has been replaced by other inventories, it is unlikely that further research using this test will be conducted.

References

Akutagawa, D. (1956). A study in construct validity of the psychoanalytic concept of latent anxiety and a test of a projection distance hypothesis. Unpublished doctoral thesis, University of Pittsburgh.

Lang, P.J., & Lazovik, A.D. (1963). Experimental desensitization of a phobia. Journal of Abnormal and Social Psychology, 66, 519-525.

Lick, J.R., Sushinsky, L.W., & Malow, R. (1977). Specificity of fear survey schedule items and the prediction of avoidance behavior. Behavior Modification, 1, 195-203.

Tasto, D.L. (1977). Self-report schedules and inventories. In A.R. Ciminero, K.S. Calhoun, & H.E. Adams (Eds.), Handbook of behavioral assessment (pp. 154-193). New York: John Wiley & Sons.

Fear Survey Schedule III

Robert T. Ammerman

Description

Wolpe and Lang's (1964) Fear Survey Schedule (FSS-III) is a 76-item questionnaire measuring the type and intensity of irrational fears. Specifically, it lists common fear-eliciting stimuli (e.g., open wounds, thunder, and dentists). Using face-valid criteria, items are organized into the following stimulus categories: (a) animal, (b) social and interpersonal, (c) tissue damage, illness, and death, (d) noises, (e) other classic phobias (e.g., elevators and enclosed places), and (f) miscellaneous. Individuals are asked to endorse each item using a 5-point Likert scale, indicating the degree to which the object or situation causes fear or discomfort (0 = not at all; 4 = very much). The FSS-III can be used to identify specific anxiety-arousing stimuli, or a total score can be derived (ranging from 0 to 380) reflecting overall fearfulness.

Purpose

With the development of systematic desensitization as an effective treatment of phobic disorders, the usefulness of global trait anxiety measures waned. Behavioral assessment for desensitization training required identification of specific stimuli to be used in the construction of an anxiety hierarchy. The FSS-III was designed to facilitate assessment of fear-eliciting objects or situations in clinical practice or both. It allows for more rapid identification of phobic stimuli as compared with more cumbersome and time-consuming interview techniques. Although originally developed for clinical use, the FSS-III has been widely employed in research. It is one of several fear survey schedules that differ in terms of length, format, and item construction.

Development

The FSS-III was developed using face-valid criteria based on formats employed in other fear survey schedules (Wolpe & Lang, 1964). Items were derived from phobias encountered by the authors in their practice of behavior therapy. Stimuli were chosen because (a) they were relatively common, and (b) it would be maladaptive for a person to display anything more than mild anxiety when exposed to them.

Psychometric Characteristics

Although a variety of studies have examined the reliability of fear survey instruments, few investigations have looked at the FSS-III in particular. In one study, Hersen (1971) administered the FSS-III to 160 male and 191 female psychiatric inpatients. Internal consistency was high, with KR-20 coefficients of .98 for male, female, and total samples. Likewise, all item-total correlations were statistically significant. Furthermore, female subjects (mean = 165.8, SD = 61.2) reported more intense fears than did male subjects (mean = 140.0, SD = 54.5). These findings are consistent with the high reliability found in other fear survey schedules (Tasto, 1977).

Factor analytic studies, however, have yielded more complex results. Studies with college populations consistently derive five to seven interpretable factors, with different factor structures for male and female subjects. Merbaum and Stricker (1972) found the following fear factors for college men: (a) aggression, (b) travel, (c) harmless animals, (d) bodily insults, and (e) unreality. For college women, however, the following factors were extracted: (a) bodily insults, (b) social rejection, (c) harmless animals, (d) public display, (e) aggression, (f) disability, and (g) confinement. More complex factor structures are found in psychiatric populations. Although most studies derived at least 16 factors, most of these account for less than 5% of the variance. For example, Bates (1971) identified 17 factors, accounting for 77.1% of the variance in a sample of male VA patients. Only two factors emerged, which accounted for more than 5% of the variance: (a) tissue damage, medical (35.5%), and (b) interpersonal (7.0%). On the whole, these studies suggest that the FSS-III has a multidimensional factor structure that varies as a function of sex and population.

Validity of the FSS-III (as well as other fear survey schedules) is less than adequate. Correlations between the FSS-III and other anxiety measures are moderate. Hersen (1971) found a coefficient of .46 between the FSS-III and Taylor's Manifest Anxiety scale (.42 for male and .52 for female subjects). Bates (1971) found a coefficient of .57 between the same instruments. Furthermore, Bates (1971) suggests that factor-derived scores are more useful than total scores.

Correlations between the FSS-III and behavioral measures of fear are also moderate. This weak correspondence is partly due to the lack of descriptive information for stimulus items. For example, Lick, Sushinsky, and Malow (1977) administered an abbreviated FSS with three levels of descriptive information. These ranged from no additional descriptors (e.g., "rat") to more elaborate descriptions (e.g., "harmless white laboratory rat in a cage"). Subjects then participated in a Behavioral Avoidance Test (BAT). Correlations between the three levels of descriptive information and behavioral measures on the BAT were .58, .78, and .81, respectively. These results suggest that more detailed items, reflecting encounters with stimuli in the natural environment, would enhance the validity of the FSS-III. However, modest correlations between the FSS-III and other modes of fear assessment may also be a function of the multidimensional nature of anxiety, in which behavioral, cognitive, and physiological measures often vary.

Clinical Use

The FSS-III is well-suited for assessment of phobic and related anxiety disorders. It is particularly useful in the identification of specific fear-eliciting stimuli for the construction of systematic desensitization hierarchies. However, given the FSS-III's questionable validity, it is best employed in conjunction with other fear assessment measures. Interpretation of scores should be made with reference to the type of clinical population and sex.

Future Directions

The FSS-III is one of the most widely used self-report measures of fear. However, further research is required to improve its validity and utility. *First*, more extensive item analyses and factor analytic studies are needed to develop a more homogeneous test. Indeed, several attempts to refine the FSS-III have been made (Tasto, 1977). *Second*, more detailed stimulus descriptors should be added to enhance external validity.

References

Bates, H.D. (1971). Factorial structure and MMPI correlates of a fear survey schedule in a clinical population. *Behaviour Research and Therapy, 9*, 355-360.

Hersen, M. (1971). Fear scale norms for an in-patient population. *Journal of Clinical Psychology, 27*, 375-378.

Lick, J.R., Sushinsky, L.W., & Malow, R. (1977). Specificity of fear survey schedule items and the prediction of avoidance behavior. *Behavior Modification, 1*, 195-203.

Merbaum, M., & Stricker, G. (1972). Factor analytic study of male and female responses to the Fear Survey Schedule. *Journal of Behavior Therapy and Experimental Psychiatry, 3,* 87-90.

Tasto, D.L. (1977). Self-report schedules and inventories. In A.R. Ciminero, K.S. Calhoun, & H.E. Adams (Eds.), *Handbook of behavioral assessment.* New York: John Wiley & Sons.

Wolpe, J., & Lang, P.J. (1964). A fear survey schedule for use in behaviour therapy. *Behaviour Research and Therapy, 2,* 27-30.

Fear Survey Schedule for Children-Revised

Thomas H. Ollendick

Description

The Fear Survey Schedule for Children-Revised (FSSC-R) is a self-report instrument for the assessment of fear in children (Ollendick, 1983). The scale is a revised version of an inventory developed by Scherer and Nakamura in 1968. It consists of 80 fear stimuli to which children are asked to report their level of fear (i.e., none, some, and a lot). The specific fear stimuli are drawn from adult fear survey schedules and from consultation with professionals familiar with children's fears. Representative items include "Being called on by teachers," "Going to bed in the dark," "Getting a cut or injury," "Getting lost in a strange place," and "Having to go to the hospital." A five-factor solution accounting for 77% of the variance associated with responding to these items has been reported: Fear of Failure and Criticism (18 items), Fear of the Unknown (19 items), Fear of Injury and Small Animals (22 items), Fear of Danger and Death (14 items), and Medical Fears (7 items). The five most common fears in boys and girls can be found on the Fear of Danger and Death factor and consist of: "A burglar breaking into our house," "Bombing attacks," "Being hit by a car or truck," "Falling from high places," and "Not being able to breathe." Of interest, two of the next highest fears are reported to be, "Being sent to the principal" and "Being punished by father." In general, girls report a greater number and a greater intensity of fears than do boys.

Purpose

As with other self-report instruments, the FSSC-R was designed to measure the child's own perceptions of the problems at hand. Specifically, it was designed to provide the child an opportunity to indicate her or his level of fear to diverse situations. Although, as will be noted shortly, the instrument is reliable, valid, and useful, it has those limitations attendant on other self-report inventories (Finch & Rogers, 1984). The scale appears particularly useful as an ipsative instrument to identify specific fear sensitivities in individual children, as a normative instrument for selecting fearful children for treatment, and as a before and after measure of therapeutic efficacy.

Development

Revision of the original Scherer and Nakamura 80-item scale was undertaken to develop a response format that took into consideration developmental and cognitive limitations of young children as well as mentally retarded and psychiatrically impaired children. For the original instrument, each fear item was rated on a 1- to 5-point scale (1 = none and 5 = very much). In our research and clinical work, we noted that young children as well as mentally retarded children had difficulty understanding and discriminating responses on the original 5-point scale. Accordingly, the response format was changed to a 3-point scale (none, some, and a lot) consistent with other self-report instruments used with children. Specific items on the measure were not changed, inasmuch as they appeared to tap the large variety of fear stimuli encountered in our clinical practice and research.

Initially, the revised instrument was examined in 211 children between 8 and 11 years of age who resided in midwestern and southeastern communities in the United States. These results indicated that the mean Total Fear Score was higher for girls (mean = 142, SD = 38) than for boys (mean = 142, SD = 26). In a subsequent normative study with 126 midwestern children and adolescents between 7 and 18 years of age (Ollendick, Matson, & Helsel, 1985a), similar gender differences were obtained (mean for girls = 143, mean for boys = 123). Furthermore, it was shown that the mean level of fear for 7- to 9-year olds (127), 10- to 12-year olds (139), 13- to 15-year olds (137), and 16- to 18-year olds (138) was similar. No gender by age interactions were noted. Collectively, these findings suggest that fear levels greater than 180 for girls (142 + 38) and 150 for boys (124 + 26) are both clinically and statistically significant.

Moreover, results of these normative studies indicate that girls reported higher levels of fear than did boys for 73 of the 80 items. Consequently, girls scored higher than boys on the Failure and Criticism factor (means = 35 and 32, respectively), the Fear of the Unknown factor (means = 30 and 26, respectively), the Fear of Injury and Small Animals factor (means = 38 and 30, respectively), the Fear of Danger and Death factor (means = 28 and 25, respectively), and the Medical Fears factor (means = 12 and 10, respectively). We do not know whether these differences in self-report reflect "real" differences in fear or simply the tendency of girls to report more verdically on such scales than boys. Regardless, the findings are consistent with other studies that report higher levels of fear in girls than in boys and provide useful normative data for the interpretation of such differences.

Psychometric Characteristics

Reliability of the FSSC-R has been determined in three ways: internal consistency, test-retest reliability, and stability of scores over 1-week and 3-month intervals (Ollendick, 1983). The internal consistency (coefficient alpha) ranges from .92 to .94 for boys and from .94 to .95 for girls, whereas the test-retest reliability ranges from .81 for boys to .89 for girls for a 1-week interval and from .58 for girls to .62 for boys for a 3-month interval. Although slight decrements in total scores have been noted over these time intervals (between 2 and 5 total scale points), the scores have remained relatively stable. Therefore, at least for normal samples of children, the FSSC-R possesses high internal consistency and is both highly reliable and stable over a 1-week interval and moderately reliable and stable over a 3-month interval. Reliability estimates have not been determined for clinical samples of children, however.

The validity of the FSSC-R has been examined through relationships between the scale and self-report measures of trait anxiety, self-concept, and locus of control (Ollendick, 1983) and through comparison of matched-control groups to clinical samples of visually impaired (Ollendick, Matson, & Helsel, 1985b) and school phobic youngsters (Ollendick & Mayer, 1984). The FSSC-R is positively related to trait anxiety ($r = .46$) and inversely related to both self-concept ($r = -.69$) and internal locus of control ($r = -.60$) in normal children. Therefore, children scoring high on the scale report higher levels of trait anxiety, lower levels of self-concept, and greater externality. The pattern of these relationships supports the convergent and discriminant validity of the FSSC-R.

The validity of the FSSC-R is further demonstrated by significant differences between school phobic girls (mean = 175; SD = 41) and boys (mean = 152; SD = 29) and matched-control girls (mean = 145; SD = 39) and boys (mean = 125; SD = 24). Perhaps of greater interest, specific fear items differentiated youngsters with school phobia apparently related to separation anxiety (e.g., having my parents argue, getting lost, and being alone) from those whose phobia appeared to be due to specific aspects of school (e.g., taking a test, being teased, and making mistakes). The two subgroups, however, did not differ in the overall level of self-reported fear.

Finally, the FSSC-R evinces reliable differences between visually impaired and normally sighted children and adolescents. More specifically, visually impaired youngsters showed greater fear on the Danger and Death factor as well as the Total Fear score than did their normally sighted counterparts. Such differences demonstrate quantitative as well as qualitative differences between these two groups. Collectively, these early findings suggest the validity of the FSSC-R in differentiating known clinical groups.

Clinical Use

As noted earlier, the FSSC-R appears most useful as an ipsative instrument to identify specific fear sensitivities in children and as a normative instrument for selecting fearful children for treatment and in evaluating therapeutic outcome. Of special interest is the Survey's ability to identify subgroups of children in whom fear might be related to specific diagnostic categories. This possibility has been illustrated in the study of school phobia (by Ollendick & Mayer, 1984).

In addition, it would seem possible that the Survey could be used to examine the frequency, intensity, and stability of fears in diverse cultural and socioeconomic groups. As such, it could be used to monitor trends in fears and their development over time. For example, it is of interest that the top fears reported for boys and girls by Ollendick in 1983 were remarkably similar to those reported by Scherer and Nakamura 15 years earlier in 1968.

Future Directions

In addition to studies confirming the general reliability and validity of the FSSC-R, the greatest need appears to be in the area of establishing the factorial invariance (Arrindell, Emmelkamp, & van der Ende, 1984) of the instrument. In simplest terms, factorial invariance refers to constancy in composition of a given dimension or factor structure as one moves across significant subject parameters, such as gender, age, social class, population, or culture. Information on factorial invariance is important because it provides data regarding the practical limits of generalizability that can be used to underscore differences among various groups (clinical as well as normal) in their manifestations of psychopathology. Therefore, it would be desirable to administer the Survey to diverse clinical and normal groups to establish the invariance of the factor structure reported in earlier normative studies.

A second major area of future development concerns the actual utility of the Survey in making important decisions related to clinical assessment and treatment. As a screening tool, the Survey seems eminently justified. However, whether it actually helps streamline the assessment/treatment process remains open for verification. Nonetheless, initial findings suggest that the instrument is a welcome tool in the clinician's armamentarium in working with fearful and anxious children.

References

Arrindell, A., Emmelkamp, P.M.G., & van der Ende, J. (1984). Phobic dimensions: I. Reliability and generalizability across samples, gender and nations. *Advances in Behaviour Research and Therapy, 6,* 207-253.

Finch, A.J., & Rogers, T.R. (1984). Self-report instruments. In T.H. Ollendick & M. Hersen (Eds.), *Child behavioral assessment: Principles and procedures.* New York: Pergamon Press.

Ollendick, T.H. (1983). Reliability and validity of the Revised Fear Survey Schedule for Children (FSSCR). *Behaviour Research and Therapy, 21,* 685-692.

Ollendick, T.H., Matson, J.L., & Helsel, W.J. (1985a). Fears in children and adolescents: Normative data. *Behaviour Research and Therapy, 23,* 465-467.

Ollendick, T.H., Matson, J.L., & Helsel, W.J. (1985b). Fears in visually-impaired and normally-sighted youths. *Behaviour Research and Therapy, 23,* 375-378.

Ollendick, T.H., & Mayer, J.A. (1984). School phobias. In S.M. Turner (Ed.), *Behavioral theories and treatment of anxiety* (pp. 367-411). New York: Plenum Press.

Scherer, M.W., & Nakamura, C.Y. (1968). A fear survey schedule for children: A factor analytic comparison with manifest anxiety. *Behaviour Research and Therapy, 6,* 173-182.

Fear Thermometer

Ronald A. Kleinknecht and Douglas A. Bernstein

Description

The Fear Thermometer (FT) is a self-report technique for assessing the cognitive component of fear in specific fear situations (Walk, 1956). The FT consists of a sheet of paper with a thermometer-like figure sketched on it. There are 10 equally spaced segments on the thermometer, numbered "one" at the bottom to "ten" at the top. The respondent places a mark on the segment that best represents his or her level of fear at the moment.

Purpose

The FT was originally designed to assess situation-specific fear experienced cognitively by parachute trainees preparing to jump from a training tower (Walk, 1956). Because of its conceptual and structural simplicity, the FT is highly adaptable for assessing fear levels of respondents before, during, or after live or imagined exposure to fear-provoking stimuli. As such, the FT and its adaptations have been widely used in assessment, process, and outcome studies of fear behavior and fear reduction (Lang & Lazovik, 1963; Watson & Marks, 1971).

Development

The FT technique was originally developed by Walk (1956) to obtain self-ratings of fear and to study the relationship between these ratings and performance in fearful situations (i.e., parachute jump training). Walk conducted two studies which demonstrated that self-ratings of fear before a jump were related to the number of errors made on the ensuing jump and that high ratings of fear were related to subsequent failure in the airborne training program. Following these initial studies, the technique served as the model for in vivo assessment of subjective fear. Among the first to adopt the technique were Lang and Lazovik (1963), who named it the "Fear Thermometer."

Psychometric Characteristics

Reliability studies on the FT and related instruments have generally found these self-ratings to be relatively stable over varying time periods. Test-retest correlations have ranged from .68 to .98 for immediate retest (Borkovec & Craighead, 1971) and .75 over a period of several weeks (Lang & Lazovik, 1963).

Validity research also has demonstrated significant relationships between FT ratings and other fear indices. Walk (1956) demonstrated concurrent validity by showing significant correlations between FT ratings given by airborne trainees immediately before a training jump and the number of errors made on the jump as judged by instructors. Similarly, Watson and Marks (1971) reported significant correlations among phobic patients' fear ratings in the presence of feared stimuli and ratings of their fear made by therapists ($r = .83$) and independent assessors ($r = .75$). Laboratory subjects' FT ratings of fear experienced during a behavioral avoidance test with snakes were significantly correlated with heart rate ($r = .29$) and degree of approach to the snake ($r = .41$; Craighead, 1973). Predictive validity of FT ratings was also demonstrated by Walk (1956), in that trainees who ultimately failed the airborne training course had rated themselves more fearful during their training jumps than did those who passed.

Therefore, FT responses appear to be relatively stable over time, assuming no therapeutic intervention, and have demonstrated significant relationships (at low to moderate levels) with behavioral and physiological components of anxiety.

Clinical Use

The FT and its variants are highly adaptable for assessing a variety of fears in various clinical settings. Simple ratings can be obtained with imaginal exposure in the consulting office and/or during live exposure to feared objects or situations. Such measures are useful for constructing anxiety hierarchies and for assessing progress and outcome during fear reduction treatments. These ratings are also widely used for self-monitoring fear or anxiety responses outside formal treatment, such as during client's home practice sessions.

Future Directions

Because the FT and related self–rating measures have demonstrated adequate reliability and validity, we see little need for instrument modification per se. However, continued research could enhance its research and clinical utility by explicating more clearly the extent to which nonfear factors (e.g., response sets and situational demands) influence self-ratings of fear.

Clinicians and researchers should remain cognizant of the fact that simple self-ratings of subjective fear comprise only a small portion of the larger construct known as fear or anxiety. These ratings should be supplemented by concurrent assessments of behavioral and physiological components whenever possible. Furthermore, users of the FT and like instruments should be aware that a single self-rating of subjective fear does not capture the complexity of cognitive aspects of fear. Therefore, FT measures should be supplemented by more detailed self-report scales to tap individuals' perceptions and expectations associated with fear stimuli.

References

Craighead, W.E. (1973). The assessment of avoidance responses on the Levis Phobic Test apparatus. *Behavior Therapy, 4*, 235-260.

Borkovec, T.D., & Craighead, W.E. (1971). The comparison of two methods of assessing fear and avoidance behavior. *Behaviour Research and Therapy, 9,* 285-291.

Lang, P.J., & Lazovik, A.D. (1963). Experimental desensitization of a phobia. *Journal of Abnormal and Social Psychology, 66,* 519-525.

Walk, R.D. (1956). Self ratings of fear in a fear-invoking situation. *Journal of Abnormal and Social Psychology, 52,* 171-178.

Watson, J.P., & Marks, I.M. (1971). Relevant and irrelevant fear in flooding: A crossover study of phobic patients. *Behavior Therapy, 2,* 275-293.

Feinstein Weight Reduction Index

Randall Flanery

Description

The Weight Reduction Index (WRI) was proposed by Feinstein (1959) as a method of quantifying an individual's weight loss success in a single, numerical expression. The WRI is constructed such that higher values represent more successful weight loss. The WRI takes into account factors that influence weight loss success, namely, initial level of obesity, target or goal weight, excess weight, and amount of weight loss. The WRI can be defined conceptually as the product of two quantities: WRI = Percent of Excess Weight Loss times the Relative Initial Obesity (Equation 1).

Each quantity is a ratio of simpler elements. Percent of Excess Weight Loss is the amount of weight lost during treatment divided by the amount of excess weight, multiplied by 100. Relative Initial Obesity is the ratio of the individual's weight at the beginning of treatment to the individual's target or ideal weight. Using these terms, the WRI equals weight loss divided by excess weight, multiplied by 100 times the initial weight, divided by the target weight (Equation 2).

Simpler terms may be substituted. Weight loss is initial weight minus final weight. The amount of excess weight is determined by subtracting the initial weight from the target weight. Target weight is usually obtained from an actuarial table (Bray, 1978), which specifies ideal or average weight for men and women according to height. Written in the simplest terms with some rearrangement of elements, the WRI equals initial weight minus final weight, divided by initial weight, minus target weight, times initial weight, divided by target weight, and multiplied by 100 (Equation 3).

This expression shows that the WRI is constructed of three simple, easily obtained values. Initial weight and final weight are obtained by weighing the individual at the beginning and end of treatment. Target weight is given by a height-weight table. Although weight (initial weight, target weight, and final weight) is usually given in kilograms, the units cancel each other (Equation 2). Therefore, no units or dimensions are associated with WRI. Whether weight is measured in kilograms or pounds, if the units used are consistent, the WRI will remain identical.

Initial weight and target weight can be specified at the start of treatment, and Feinstein (1959) recommends grouping them to produce what he calls the Reduction Coefficient (RC), which is defined as follows: Reduction Coefficient equals initial weight divided by initial weight minus target weight, times target weight, multiplied by 100 (Equation 4).

In essence, the RC characterizes an individual's obese status at the start of treatment. The RC is determined by three terms: initial weight, target weight, and initial weight minus target weight, each of which reflects the degree of obesity. More obese individuals have smaller RC values. This may not be obvious because the numerator of Equation 4, initial weight, is larger for heavier individuals. However, the quantity in the denominator, initial weight minus target weight, also increases, resulting in a smaller RC. As an indicator of initial obese status, the RC functions as a "correction factor," by which the amount of weight loss, initial weight minus final weight, is multiplied to produce the WRI: WRI equals initial weight minus final weight times the RC (Equation 5). Therefore, more obese individuals must lose more weight to achieve a WRI comparable to that of a thinner individual. Because the RC can become large for a less obese individual, producing large WRIs, the WRI should be used only with persons more than 20% overweight.

Purpose

The WRI was designed as a quantitative standard against which to evaluate the performance of individuals losing weight. The WRI is most commonly used as a dependent variable in outcome studies of obesity treatment, for which it is well suited. Because it is quantitative, it is amenable to statistical analysis. It is widely recommended (Wilson, 1978) that absolute weight loss and the WRI be reported in all obesity treatment reports.

Although it is most appropriate for group comparison, Feinstein (1959) proposed other innovative uses for the WRI. He proposed that the WRI and the RC be used for cross-study comparisons of treatment. Published treatment studies could be evaluated for effectiveness using a common standard: the WRI. Similarly, the comparability of groups for initial level of obesity could be assessed using the RC.

Another use is to evaluate a single individual's success. Feinstein (1959) argued that, based on comparisons with other weight loss criteria, a WRI score greater than 60 might be used as a standard for success.

Development

The WRI is a rationally developed measure designed to correct biases inherent in other, widely used indices of weight loss treatment. Specifically, it is an alternative to absolute weight loss and percentage of weight goal attained. By way of illustration of some of the difficulties in comparing individuals who differ in several weight-related characteristics, consider an individual 40 kg overweight and an individual 10 kg overweight. A 5-kg weight loss, about the average for published outcome studies, represents very different levels of success for the two individuals. Even a 10-kg loss in the more obese individual, although a significant accomplishment, is not an unmitigated success in light of the amount that needs to be lost. In a similar vein, it is difficult to compare individuals whose initial weight and target weight are 40 kg apart, even if the persons are similar in other respects. Use of absolute weight loss or percentage of weight goal obtained will not adequately reflect the dietary efforts of individuals in these circumstances. Absolute weight loss will favor the more obese who will probably lose more, in part because they have a great deal to lose. Using percentage of weight goal attained is an improvement, but it fails to recognize that the more obese person must lose a great deal of weight to achieve the same percentage as a less obese person.

The WRI attempts to take into account the initial level of obesity, target weight, and actual weight loss in ways that other outcome measures do not. Because the initial level of obesity and target are determined by values found in an actuarial table, factors related to weight, such as sex and height, are accounted for in the WRI, indirectly. Feinstein included elements in the WRI, because on logical grounds they appeared to take account of factors affecting outcome.

Psychometric Characteristics

The WRI is a conceptually simple measure whose behavior is actually fairly complex. The fundamental purpose of the WRI is to make individuals "comparable" who vary in several weight-related characteristics, namely, initial weight, target weight, initial weight minus target weight, and amount of weight loss. It is impossible to systematically vary initial weight or target weight without simultaneously altering initial weight minus target weight. Individuals must necessarily vary in at least two of these parameters. The effect of one of those parameters on the WRI cannot be determined unambiguously. This does not pose a serious problem of interpretation as long as individuals are roughly comparable. Returning to Equation 1, for a given range of obesity, greater weight loss represents more success, as indicated by larger values of WRI. Conversely, the more obese individual (see Equation 2, initial weight/target weight) of two losing the same proportion of weight (weight loss/excess weight) would obtain the higher WRI. The values of terms that constitute the WRI can vary substantially. As the values of initial weight and target weight of individuals being compared diverge, the comparability of the resulting WRI

becomes more questionable. For example, of two persons with the same target weight, the more obese person might have to lose two or three times the amount of the less obese individual to achieve similar values for the WRI.

Despite the oddities just reported, the available data support the validity of the WRI for group comparisons. In his initial report, Feinstein (1959) showed good correspondence between success defined by the WRI and success defined by other criteria. Consistent with this initial finding, when the WRI and another measure of weight loss outcome have been reported, the pattern of results has been comparable. By now, this represents a large body of research. The data strongly suggest that the WRI is an adequate measure of weight loss success; it is not clear that it is superior to supposedly biased measures such as kilograms lost or change in percentage overweight. The reliability of the WRI is not at issue, because the numbers that constitute it are selected from a height-weight table or are read from a weight scale. These values are not subject to much variation over time or from person to person.

The WRI has been reported for use in children, but such use may be inappropriate. Children who grow in stature but maintain a stable weight become less overweight. The WRI will not reflect this fact, because a failure to lose weight results in a WRI of zero.

The validity of the WRI rests on the validity of the RC as a measure of initial obesity. Currently, the relationship of RC to other measures of obesity, such as the body mass index (weight/height 2) or the ponderal index (height/weight 3), is unexamined.

The WRI also can be influenced by other factors, which are especially relevant to cross-study comparisons. Height-weight charts, which determine both target weight and percentage overweight, vary substantially. Some charts are more detailed, specifying weights by sex, body frame, and even age. The WRI will be affected accordingly. Another factor is duration of treatment. Longer treatments tend to produce more weight loss, which will make for larger values of WRI. Therefore, a longer lasting program will appear more effective than a briefer intervention, based on the WRI alone. If these data are not specified, WRI results can be misleading.

In summary, the WRI is fairly useful as an obesity treatment outcome measure, with the following qualifications: (a) It should not be used with individuals less than 20% overweight. (b) As the individuals being compared are increasingly different in initial weight, amount overweight, and target weight, WRI values may be misleading. (c) WRIs for children who grow during treatment may be inaccurate. The use of the WRI for cross-study comparisons is premature. The WRI can readily be influenced by the length of treatment and the method for determining the level of obesity and target weights and by substantial variation in the weight-related characteristics of individuals.

Clinical Use

The WRI is primarily a research tool. Its clinical applications are limited. One might follow Feinstein's (1959) recommendation of using a WRI scale of 60 as a benchmark of treatment success, although dieters are likely to find such a measure irrelevant to their concerns.

Future Directions

Although the WRI has been used with increasing frequency, its psychometric qualities have not been extensively investigated. Several questions exist about the use of the WRI comparisons. The deficiencies in existing measures that Feinstein (1959) attempted to correct remain. The WRI is the best effort to date, but further refinement is warranted. One advance would be for obesity researchers and clinicians to reach a consensus as to what constitutes dietary success. A second advance is to improve the "comparability" of the WRI, perhaps by modification of the mathematical definition of the WRI. A third possibility is to gather some empirical data on the relationship of the WRI to other measures of obesity and treatment outcome. With these advances, it might be possible to conduct legitimate cross-study analyses of obesity treatment outcomes.

References

Bray, G.A. (1978). Definition, measurement, and classification of the syndromes of obesity. *International Journal of Obesity, 2,* 99-112.

Feinstein, A.R. (1959). The measurement of success in weight reduction: An analysis of methods and a new index. *Journal of Chronic Diseases, 10,* 439-456.

Wilson, G.T. (1978). Methodological considerations in treatment outcome research on obesity. *Journal of Consulting and Clinical Psychology, 46,* 687-702.

Fire Emergency Behavioral Situations Scale

Russell T. Jones

Description

The Fire Emergency Behavioral Situations Scale (FEBSS) is a behavioral scale designed to assess children as well as adult functioning in simulated nighttime residential fires (Jones, Kazdin, & Haney, 1981; Jones & Thornton, in press). The instrument is made up of nine different situations consisting of a total of 115 steps and 28 different responses. For example, in each situation, individuals should roll or slide to the edge of their bed on first learning that there is a fire and then roll out and get into a crawl position. During this time, individuals must determine whether they are coughing and their eyes are burning. If so, the individual should not exit through the bedroom door, but should decide whether it is safe to exit through the window without assistance. If not, the individual must take a rug and crawl to the door, cover the crack under the door, crawl to an article of clothing (e.g., shirt), take the shirt and crawl to the window, open the window, wave the shirt out the window, and call for help. Scores for individual responses as well as sequence of responses for each situation can be obtained.

Purpose

The FEBSS was derived to assess an individual's ability to perform effectively in a variety of simulated nighttime fire emergencies. More specifically, the pattern of an individual's responding to a nighttime fire after being awakened by various fire-related stimuli is obtained. Although limited in its external validity, it possesses worthwhile features. Since its inception, it has been found to determine reliably a sample of one's functioning before, during, and after intervention. Performances of normal 7- to 11-year-old black and white children from lower, middle, and upper-middle socioeconomic levels (across semirural and urban communities) have been adequately assessed with this instrument (Jones et al., 1981; Jones & Haney, 1984; Hillman, Jones, & Farmer, 1984). Similarly, the responding of mentally retarded adolescents aged 12 to 16, mildly and moderately retarded adults aged 43 to 55 (Jones & Thornton, in press), blind adolescents aged 11 to 15 (Jones, Van Hasselt, &

Sisson, 1984), and the elderly aged 55 and above (Jones, 1984) has been reliably assessed.

Scores from over 300 subjects indicate that subjects' baseline levels of responding range from 0 to 46%, with a mean of 8%. No significant differences in quality of responding across age, sex, race, intelligence level, socioeconomic levels, or communities have been found, partly because of the stringent scoring system.

More specifically, the scoring system devised takes into account the occurrence of the response as well as the occurrence of the response in the correct sequence. For each situation, the individual receives a *sequence score* and an *occurrence score*. The *sequence score* is made up of correct responses in the correct place in the sequence. For example, the subject must first feel the door before opening it. One point is given for each response that is preceded and followed by correct behaviors (except for the first and last response in a sequence). The *occurrence score* is based on performance of a correct response, whether or not it is in the correct sequence (i.e., feeling the door properly but performing the responses that precede and follow it incorrectly). One point is given when the individual performs the correct response independently of the responses that precede and follow it. The sequence scoring method provides a more stringent measure of mastery of emergency fire skills and is used to evaluate the effects of training.

Development

The appropriate method of responding to fire emergency situations was established in the following manner: First, published materials describing ways of escaping from a burning house were examined (Bete, Inc., Bryson, Burger King, Hartford Insurance Group, International Association of Fire Chiefs and Dictograph Security, International Association of Fire Chiefs and the General Electric Company, National Fire Protection Association, Pennsylvania Department of Health, US Consumer Product Safety Commission, and US Department of Housing and Urban Development). Additionally, information about fire safety skills was obtained from local and national fire agencies and officials (i.e., AT&T and Pittsburgh Fire Department). Second, 42 hypothetical fire emergency situations in which children might find themselves were devised, and suggested responses were derived from the previously obtained information. These 42 situations were then presented to

14 city firefighters at a local station house. A short description of the circumstances surrounding the fire emergency (e.g., when and where the event was taking place) was given, and the firefighters were asked to evaluate individually whether the responses for each situation were correct or incorrect. For each response marked as incorrect, the firefighters were requested to describe briefly what they believed to be the correct response. Following initial administration, those items that were judged as correct by 64% or more of the firefighters were retained. Using the responses recommended by the firefighters, those items not meeting the criterion were revised and administered to 11 firefighters. Items achieving a criterion of 73% approval were retained. Criterion was still not reached on three items. These items were then revised and presented to 10 firefighters, who agreed that the responses to these situations were correct. Third, responses to the questionnaire were used to provide sequences of responses that would lead to safety in each of the nine different situations. These responses served as targets for training. The nine different fire emergency situations differed in the cues that dictated the steps that the child needed to follow to avoid injury. Further validation methods are presently being carried out by the first author.

The final phase of the development of this scale consisted of the informal observation of two 6-year-old and three 7-year-old children to evaluate their ability to respond appropriately without training as well as to discover the effectiveness of the assessment instructions. One of these children was taught the correct responses to the first situation to assess the suitability of the training procedure.

Psychometric Characteristics

No method with known psychometric properties currently exists for establishing levels of competence before, during, or after a fire emergency situation. Because of the nature of this event, much of the information desired cannot be objectively assessed. Therefore, the use of simulation is a necessary first step in assessing baseline levels of such functioning. Although the development of additional psychometric properties awaits future research, test-retest reliability has been obtained. This test-retest reliability is .80. Presently, additional validation is being carried out with the assistance of the Fire Marshall's Association of North America.

Clinical Use

At this time the FEBSS is most appropriately used as a behavioral index of an individual's responding in a simulated fire emergency. The scale has been effective in assessing an individual's functioning in a variety of simulated situations with subjects aged 7 to over 55, across normal, retarded, and blind populations. The dimensions of age, developmental level, intellectual level, race, and sex have yet to be differentially correlated with performance at baseline. This finding is probably due to the lack of specific knowledge concerning emergency functioning. However, data obtained during and after training demonstrate differences in performance as a result of the subjects' ages and their developmental and intellectual levels. No differential responding has been noted with reference to race or sex.

Future Research

Future research should be aimed at further validation of this instrument. Several strategies might be employed. For example, data describing what individuals actually do during fire emergencies and the outcome of such actions (through retrospective reports) are needed to target better evacuation responses. The need for more objective assessment of appropriate modes of functioning in such situations is important to define more accurately those behaviors to be taught. Also, collection of data from individuals who were actually involved in fire emergencies after training are needed to obtain measures of the appropriateness of various learned responses. It is hoped that future research will enable us to devise more sensitive measures of subjects' behavior as well as their thoughts and feelings accompanying such behavior. In summary, given the severity and extensiveness of injury and harm produced by fire, the need for continued systematic research is evident.

References

Hillman, H.S., Jones, R.T., & Farmer, L. (November, 1984). *Memory processing and overlearning in the acquisition and maintenance of fire safety skills.* Presented at the 18th Annual Association for Advancement of Behavior Therapy Convention, Philadelphia, PA.

Jones, R.T. (1984). *Teaching the elderly fire evacuation skills.* Unpublished manuscript, University of Pittsburgh.

Jones, R.T., & Haney, J.I. (1984). A primary preventive approach to the acquisition and maintenance of an adaptive community behavior: Fire emergency responding. *Journal of Community Psychology, 4,* 180-191.

Jones, R.T., Kazdin, A.E., & Haney, J.I. (1981). Social validation and training of emergency fire safety skills for potential injury prevention and life saving. *Journal of Applied Behavior Analysis, 14,* 249-260.

Jones, R.T., & Thornton, J.L. (in press). The acquisition and maintenance of emergency evacuation skills with mildly to moderately retarded adults in a community living arrangement. *Journal of Community Psychology.*

Jones, R.T., Van Hasselt, V.B., & Sisson, L.A. (1984). Emergency fire-safety skills: A study with blind adolescents. *Behavior Modification, 8,* 59-78.

Fire Emergency Dialing Checklist

Russell T. Jones

Description

The Fire Emergency Dialing Checklist (FEDC) is a behavioral assessment measure designed to assess children's ability to make an emergency telephone call in a simulated emergency situation (Jones, 1980). More specifically, this instrument was devised to assess a child's ability to call the operator and provide relevant information concerning home emergencies (e.g., fire and accidents). A total of 14 discrete steps make up the sequence of appropriate behavior. Emergency dialing consists of: (a) picking up the receiver, (b) placing the receiver to the ear, (c) waiting for the dial tone, (d) dialing "0" or "911" (where appropriate) and listening for the operator, and (e) reporting the nature of the home emergency (i.e., fire and injury). The subject then recites his or her full name (first and last) and address (house number, street, and city) in the following manner: (a) giving his or her full name, (b) giving complete address, (c) holding the line for further instructions and/or possible clarification of information before hanging up the receiver, and (d) hanging up the receiver. Scores for individual responses as well as sequence of responses can be obtained.

Purpose

The FEDC was designed to determine objectively a child's competence in performing in a variety of simulated home emergencies. Although the instrument was initially devised to assist children in obtaining help "in case of fire," it has been used to assist children in procuring help in instances in which she or he, a sibling, or a parent has had an accident and requires emergency medical assistance. Additionally, in the event of a discovered burglary, children are taught to contact the police.

While the external validity of this instrument is currently being assessed, it has been found to obtain reliable samples of functioning before, during, and after behavioral intervention in simulated situations. Subject populations that have used this instrument include normal 3-, 4-, 5-, and 6-year-old children from lower to upper-middle socioeconomic levels across semirural and urban communities (Jones, 1980; Jones & Kazdin, 1980; Rivera-Tovar & Jones, in press). Arab, black, oriental, and white children make up the nationalities represented. Scores obtained from over 170 children show that subjects' baseline levels of emergency dialing range from 0 to 33%, with a mean of 1.3%. Although no significant differences have been found in terms of the quality of responding across age, sex, and race, there have been some differences in intellectual level. Those subjects with increased intellectual ability (IQ scores of approximately 130 as measured by standardized intelligence tests) have performed at somewhat higher levels. The extent of differences and the meaning of such differences are currently being examined.

Development

The initial form of the FEDC was devised by Jones (1980), with the checklist consisting of six components: (1) responding to a parent's instructions in an emergency, (2) identifying and approaching the telephone, (3) dialing zero for the operator, (4) reporting the nature of the emergency, (5) providing full name and address, and (6) hanging up the receiver. The content validation of this checklist was achieved through the following means: (1) Initial contact with fire officials from the city's fire department was made to ascertain what information was necessary for preschool children to get help in case of fire. The following steps were offered: (a) respond to a parent's instructions in the emergency situation, (b) approach the telephone, (c) dial zero, (d) report the emergency, (e) give full name and address, and (f) hang up the receiver. (2) A 4-year-old child, capable of making the desired emergency call, was observed carrying out this skill. All observations were recorded by three observers to specify each behavioral step. Following several observations, the chain of required responses was objectively defined and transcribed to a written test sheet. (3) This test sheet was then

given to two specialists in child development as well as to consultants from Bell Telephone and the National Fire Protection Association, whose function was to provide children in classroom settings with information and instruments to learn emergency skills. Three parents with preschool and primary school children were asked for their feedback and approval. Following their suggestions and modifications, a second test sheet was composed and two pilot subjects, aged 4 and 5, were tested to insure its appropriateness for the target population.

This instrument was first revised by Jones and Kazdin (1980), whereby two pilot subjects, aged 4 and 5, were observed carrying out the target skills. Only those responses concerning dialing and reporting pertinent information were retained.

The second and most recent revision was carried out by Rivera-Tovar and Jones (in press), where two group managers (mean years of experience, 19 years) employed by Operator Services, four telephone operators (mean years of experience, 23 years), three grade school teachers (mean years of experience, 13 years), and 13 firefighters from two local firehouses (mean years of experience, 16 years) carried out the following steps: (a) each individual was asked to evaluate the "appropriateness" of several dialing responses using a questionnaire; (b) they were asked to judge each response as either correct or incorrect; and (c) those items judged incorrect were asked to be followed by suggestions advising us as to the most appropriate alternative. Those items agreed upon by no less than 70% of the respondents were used in the final checklist.

Two steps were then added to the emergency dialing sequence: (1) what to do when no dial tone can be heard after bringing the receiver to one's ear, and (2) what to do if the telephone line is in use in case of a party line. This validation procedure followed several guidelines suggested by Kazdin (1977).

Psychometric Characteristics

The children's scores on this assessment scale were found to be stable over time, with test-retest reliability of .80. Presently, additional reliability data are being obtained.

Clinical Use

Although this scale does not possess unique relevance to clinical populations, it has served as a valuable tool in assessing a variety of children's skills in using the telephone in an emergency situation. Children from 3 to 10 years of age have been successfully taught to carry out this valuable set of skills in a variety of simulated situations. No significant differences in baseline responding have been found to result from age, developmental and/or intellectual level, race, or sex. Consistent with the assessment of other emergency skills, significant differences at baseline are rarely reported because of the lack of specific knowledge concerning emergency functioning within this age group.

Future Research

Future research should be aimed at establishing the checklist's external validity. Additionally, empirical demonstration of its use with other emergencies should be demonstrated.

References

Jones, R.T. (1980). Teaching children to make emergency telephone calls. *The Journal of Black Psychology, 6,* 81-93.
Jones, R.T., & Kazdin, A.E. (1980). Teaching children how and when to make emergency telephone calls. *Behavior Therapy, 11,* 509-521.
Kazdin, A.E. (1977). Assessing the clinical or applied importance of behavior change. *Behavior Modification, 1,* 427-452.
Rivera-Tovar, L., & Jones, R.T. (in press). An extension and refinement of telephone emergency skills training: A comparison of training methods. *Behavior Modification.*

Frequency Interaction Recording System

Charles R. Greenwood and Nancy M. Todd

Description

The Frequency Interaction Recording System (FIRS) is a direct observation procedure for recording the reciprocal interaction rates of 3- to 6-year-old preschool children (Greenwood, Walker, Todd, & Hops, 1979; Todd, 1976). The system is designed for the simultaneous recording of up to 10 students' interactions within a peer group. The system is designed for screening and a molar level analysis of social interaction. The system, unlike the Peer Interaction Code (Greenwood, Todd, Hops, & Walker, 1982), does not allow recording of the details within continuing interactive episodes.

In the FIRS, social interaction is defined as the first exchange of observable responses between two children. These responses can be verbal, nonverbal, or physical. Interactions are defined as initiations, either from or to the subject, that result in a response from a peer or the subject. Interactions also continue beyond first initiation and response interchanges. Continuing responses are defined as all interactive behaviors following the original interchange. Termination of interaction is arbitrarily defined as the absence of interchange between a dyad exceeding 5 seconds. In the FIRS, however, only the originating initiation and response components are actually recorded. Observers use an event recording procedure to encode interaction data in the FIRS.

The features of interaction that are obtained include (a) the rate of subject initiations to peers, (b) the rate of peer initiations to the subject, (c) the rate of subject responses to peer initiations, (d) the rate of peer responses to subject initiations, (e) the rate of initiations not receiving a response, (f) the ratio of subject-initiated versus peer-initiated interactions, and (g) who initiates to whom in each interaction.

The system does not differentiate positive or negative valences of responses, nor does it provide specific topographical responses (e.g., share offers and amenities). The system can be used for contrasting interactions between contexts within preschool settings. Specific contexts that have been represented in FIRS include (a) teacher-led, (b) assigned task, and (c) free play.

Purpose

The FIRS system is intended for use in the identification and treatment of socially withdrawn, socially unresponsive children. It was developed for use by preschool teachers and is included as one component of a multimethod social behavior assessment system called the Social Assessment Manual for Preschool Level (SAMPLE) (Greenwood, Todd, Walker, & Hops, 1978). The SAMPLE includes the FIRS and separate teacher ranking and rating procedures. The three procedures are used for screening, identification, problem definition, and monitoring of intervention progress (Hops & Greenwood, 1981).

Development

The FIRS system was developed at the Center at Oregon for Research in the Behavioral Education of the Handicapped (CORBEH) over the course of several federally funded projects that focused on the assessment and treatment of social withdrawal in preschool and elementary school populations (Walker, Hops, & Greenwood, 1984). The FIRS was developed over a 3-year period during which reliability and validity studies were conducted and the system was refined and tested. Normative data collected each year provide a locally derived social comparison norm group.

Psychometric Characteristics

Discriminant Validity. A study was conducted to examine the extent to which students low on the FIRS also performed low in other social behavior measures (Greenwood, Walker, & Hops, 1977). Low, mid, and high interaction-rate student groups on the FIRS were found to differ on (a) teacher rankings of students' interaction frequencies, (b) teacher ratings of specific positive social behaviors, (c) teacher ratings of specific negative social behaviors, and (d) directly observed qualitative aspects of their social repertoires (Greenwood et al., 1982).

Convergent Validity. A study of the FIRS system was conducted in which FIRS interaction rate scores were correlated with scores from teacher ratings and peer-nomination sociometrics (Greenwood et al., 1979). The largest and most uniform correlations between FIRS scores occurred in relationship to teacher rating measures. These relationships remained reasonably stable at both a test and a retest occasion and across free-play and assigned-task contexts of interactions (Greenwood et al., 1979). The range in correlations (Spearman rho) between interaction rate and teacher ratings of verbal frequency was .50 to .63 ($p < .001$). The correlation between social interaction rate and sociometric acceptance ranged from .29 to .39 ($p < .001$).

Reliability. Interobserver agreement: Interobserver agreement with the FIRS has been consistently high. The average percentage agreement score was 97% ($SD = 7\%$) for the number of interactions and 96% ($SD = 9\%$) for who initiated and who responded in interactions in the Greenwood et al. (1979) study. The overall Pearson r for interaction rate in this same study was .99.

Test-retest: The stability of interaction rate scores over a 1-month period was reported to be .75 using an odd-even day procedure for forming test and retest mean scores (Greenwood et al., 1979). A t test indicated no significant difference between test-retest mean scores, .67 versus .66 (t [426] = .493, $p > .10$).

Cross-setting consistency: The correlation between social interaction rate scores derived from free-play and assigned-task preschool contexts was .58 ($p < .001$), indicating a moderate tendency for high rate interactors in one preschool context to be high rate in another context.

Normative Data. Normative FIRS data from 17 preschools, 29 classrooms, and 461 students are available (Greenwood, Walker, Todd, & Hops, 1981). Interaction rate means are available for students broken down by age, ranging from 3 to 7 years, and for male and female children during free play. Significant differences in interaction rates were found for both age and sex factors. Older students demonstrated increasingly higher rates of interaction. Male students had significantly higher rates of interaction at each age level.

Clinical Use

The FIRS system can be used by preschool teachers or by behavioral specialists (e.g., school psychologists, teacher supervisors, behavior therapists, and special education specialists) as one procedure in the identification of withdrawn children and the monitoring of social behavior intervention procedures that they decide to initiate. The system is available as part of the SAMPLE package, which includes a teacher ranking system for screening, a teacher behavior rating for problem identification and pinpointing target skills, and the FIRS for both identification and monitoring the effects of behavioral treatments within single-subject designs.

Future Directions

The FIRS system is a relatively efficient system for obtaining information on the social interaction rates and frequencies of multiple subjects simultaneously. Compared with similar procedures it has excellent reliability and validity characteristics and a locally derived set of normative data. It can be used by agents in the natural setting and does not require extensive training. It does not provide elaborate data on topography, interaction episodes, or specific social skills (e.g., sharing); however, it does assess the incidence of reciprocal social behavior. The FIRS has direct application in socially withdrawn, unresponsive children in preschool settings and potential application in infants and toddler populations in which social behavior is just emerging. However, validation studies remain to be conducted with these latter populations.

References

Greenwood, C.R., Todd, N.M., Hops, H., & Walker, H.M. (1982). Behavior change targets in the assessment and treatment of socially withdrawn preschool children. *Behavioral Assessment, 4, 273-289.*

Greenwood, C.R., Todd, N.M., Walker, H.M., & Hops, H. (1978). *Social Assessment Manual for Preschool Level: (SAMPLE).* Eugene, OR: Center at Oregon for Research in the Behavioral Education of the Handicapped.

Greenwood, C.R., Walker, H.M., & Hops, H. (1977). Some issues in social interaction/withdrawal assessment. *Exceptional Children, 43, 490-499.*

Greenwood, C.R., Walker, H.M., Todd, N.M., & Hops, H. (1979). Selecting a cost-effective screening device for the assessment of preschool social withdrawal. *Journal of Applied Behavior Analysis, 12, 625-638.*

Greenwood, C.R., Walker, H.M., Todd, N.M., & Hops, H. (1981). Normative and descriptive analysis of preschool freeplay interaction rates. *Journal of Pediatric Psychology, 6, 343-367.*

Hops, H., & Greenwood, C.R. (1981). Social skill deficits. In E.J. Mash & L.G. Terdal (Eds.), *Behavioral assessment of childhood disorders* (pp. 347-394). New York: Guilford Press.

Todd, N.M. (1976). *The Frequency Interaction Recording System: (FIRS).* Eugene, OR: Center at Oregon for Research in the Behavioral Education of the Handicapped.

Walker, H.M., Hops, H., Greenwood, C.R. (1984). The CORBEH research and development model: Programmatic issues and strategies. In S. Paine, T. Bellamy, & B. Wilcox (Eds.), *Human services that work* (pp. 57-77). New York: Paul H. Brooks.

Fully Faceted Type A Survey for Students

Paul R. Yarnold, Kim T. Mueser, and Barry W. Grau

Description

The Fully Faceted Type A Survey for Students (FFTAS-S) is an experimental, objective, self-report questionnaire measure of Type A "coronary-prone" behavior. Type A behavior reflects a constellation of response styles, theoretically believed to be elicited by the perception or loss (or threat of loss) of control over psychologically salient events, generally described by the categories: time urgent/impatient, hard-driving/competitive, and/or aggressive/hostile. (See Friedman & Rosenman, 1974, and Glass, 1977, for reviews.) The FFTAS-S was designed to assess an individual's general and specific level of Type A responding in each of these behavioral modes and across all possible combinations of differing task versus nontask situations, in work versus nonwork environments. (See Development.) The mean completion time for undergraduate college students is approximately 15 minutes.

Individuals completing the FFTAS-S may be assigned a total score ranging from 0 (extreme Type B, noncoronary-prone individual) to 52 (extreme Type A) as well as a score on each of nine subscales. The subscales include Type A responding in general, specific, task, and nontask situations and in work and nonwork environments; and separate measures of aggressive, involved, and time urgent responding (independent of mode, situation, or environment). The total and subscale scores may then be used as is currently the case with alternative Type A measures. (See reviews.)

Purpose

The FFTAS-S is used exclusively as a research instrument, to assess an individuals' self-reported levels of Type A responding overall, in specific behavioral modes, and across a variety of situation, environments, and stimulus specificities.

Development and Psychometric Characteristics

Factor analyses of responses to the Student Jenkins Activity Survey (SJAS) generally revealed a two-factor, rather than the hypothesized three-factor, solution perhaps as a consequence of poor item selection and psychometric deficiencies of the items and response alternatives (Yarnold, Mueser, Grau, & Grimm, 1986). Accordingly, Grau, Yarnold, and Grimm (1982) analyzed students' responses using multidimensional scaling, a more appropriate methodology. Grau et al. (1982) first analyzed the responses of a randomly selected sample of 413 undergraduates completing the SJAS, and then attempted a replication with another randomly selected sample of 507 undergraduates (sexes were equally represented in both samples). Because the results replicated virtually exactly, they may be considered concurrently. The results suggested that a four-dimensional solution was most appropriate, and examination of the item ordering revealed an underlying topological structure characteristic of cylindrex. A mapping sentence was constructed to identify the resulting structure, and the 21 scored SJAS items were classified as belonging to one of the categories described by full expansion of the sentence. Items that, as prescribed by the sentence, *should* have been on the SJAS but were not, were then created. The resulting full expansion of the mapping sentence represents the contents of the FFTAS-S. It is because of this fully faceted character that this questionnaire derived its name. No additional research using the FFTAS-S has yet been reported.

Research directly considering the psychometric properties of the FFTAS-S has not yet been reported. The fact that the multidimensional scaling analyses were replicated, however, suggests that at least the SJAS component is relatively precise (Yarnold et al., 1986).

Clinical Use

The FFTAS-S is currently used exclusively for research purposes.

Future Directions

Evaluation of the FFTAS-S should proceed along three avenues: psychometric, behavioral, and physiological. Examples of psychometric research questions of interest include whether the structural relations among the 21 SJAS items are affected by virtue of their inclusion as a subset of the FFTAS-S and whether the FFTAS-S total score, subscale scores, and complete topologies represent temporally reliable measures.

Behavioral studies targeted at validating the FFTAS-S total and subscale scores are clearly necessary, although the most powerful test of the instrument would involve evaluating its fully expanded form. That is, researchers might consider attempting to validate the FFTAS-S in a context defined by each of the specific faceted categories.

Ultimately, assessment of the utility of the FFTAS-S must involve retrospective and prospective studies of its ability to predict cardiopathogenic physiological, neuroendocrine, and biochemical responsiveness of Type A persons, in addition to correspondingly elevated clinical manifestations of disease.

References

Friedman, M., & Rosenman, R.H. (1974). *Type A behavior and your heart.* New York: Knopf.

Glass, D.C. (1977). *Behavior patterns, stress, and coronary disease.* Hillsdale, NJ: Lawrence Erlbaum Associates.

Grau, B.W., Yarnold, P.R., & Grimm, L.G. (May, 1982). *A multi-dimensional scaling of the Student form of the Jenkins Activity Survey.* Presented at the 29th Annual Conference of the Society for Behavioral Medicine, Chicago.

Yarnold, P.R., Mueser, K.T., Grau, B.W., & Grimm, L.G. (1986). The reliability of the Student version of the Jenkins Activity Survey. *Journal of Behavioral Medicine, 9,* 401-414.

General Happiness Rating

Dirk Revenstorf

Description

The General Happiness Rating of a marital relationship is a simple self-report measure: a one-item questionnaire. It usually is presented in graphical form on a 7-point scale with the following instructions: "Mark the dot on the scale line below that best describes the degree of happiness, all considered, in your present marriage. "The midpoint, "happy," represents the degree of happiness that most persons get from their marriage, and the entire scale ranges from those few who are very unhappy in marriage to those few who experience extreme joy or felicity in marriage.

Purpose

This overall rating of happiness is ofen used to supplement more extended instruments for assessing the quality of a marital dyad. It is meant to be free of cultural or subcultural norms about what constitutes a satisfactory relationship, because it appeals to the definition of happiness that the respondent has in mind when he or she thinks about those persons considered happy or unhappy. A rough distributional restriction is imposed, however, as it is implied that most persons are happy and few are very happy or very unhappy.

Development

Whereas most authors have found several aspects of happiness or success in a marriage, this simple type of rating scale has enjoyed continued popularity since it was introduced in 1938 by Terman, Buttenwieser, Ferguson, Johnson, and Wilson in their classic study. In contrast to this unitary concept, two structural dimensions of the success or failure of the relationship have been substantiated most often: cohesion and control. Too much or too little of either is indicative of a troubled relationship (Olson, Sprenkle, & Russel, 1979). Spanier's (1976) rather comprehensive analysis of self-report items revealed four factors of dyadic adjustment: dyadic consensus, dyadic cohesion, dyadic satisfaction, and affectional expression. Another frequently used self-report measure of marital adjustment, the Marital Adjustment Test (Locke & Wallace, 1951), contains simple ratings about the agreement of finances, recreation, affection, friends, sex, conventional matters, philosophy of life, in-laws, outside interests, and going out/staying at home. In addition, each spouse is asked for a general happiness rating and whether she or he preferred not to have married the partner, would marry him or her again, and has confidence in her or him. All 15 scores are summed up to one Marital Adjustment Test score for each spouse.

Similar areas of self-report are covered in Stuart and Stuart's Marital Precounseling Inventory (1972), although they are couched in terms of more objective observations. Other behaviorally oriented surveys of marital satisfaction are those of the Oregon research group (Weiss, Hops, & Patterson, 1973): the Marital-Activity-Inventory and the Spouse Observation Checklist. The latter three questionnaires constituted the pool of items for a recently developed 30-item questionnaire by Hahlweg, Schindler, Revenstorf, and Brengelmann (1984). Factor analysis resulted in three aspects of marital satisfaction and distress: fighting, communication, and tenderness. This questionnaire is also supplemented by the General Happiness Rating. Questionnaires of marital happiness vary in the number of items between 246 (Burgess & Wallin, 1953) and 15 (Locke & Wallace, 1959). It is of theoretical interest that the terms "marital satisfaction," "adjustment," "success," and "happiness" are generally used as if they were synonymous. Reiter and Steiner (1981) have offered some criticism of this; however, as Burgess and Wallin (1953) found, those aspects are highly correlated.

Psychometric Characteristics

Some data on the reliability of the General Happiness Rating are reported. For instance, Hahlweg et al. (1984) report a consistency of .80 between husbands' and wives' estimation of happiness in happy (sample = 85) and unhappy (sample = 25) couples. The correlation between self-rating and rating by friends was .60. Locke and Wallace (1959) found a retest reliability of .90 for their summary score of 15 rating scales, including the General Happiness Rating. The distributional characteristics of the General Happiness Rating are surprisingly stable over cultures and time. Terman et al. (1938) found 85% of couples to be happy (sample = 1,000) and 15% to be more or less unhappy. This was also found by Hahlweg et al. (1984) in a German sample of 150. Among those who apply for therapy, 28% score as happy or better and 72% as unhappy. Validity coefficients (correlations with other questionnaires) range between .70 and .81. In predicting marital success, the validities of the General Happiness Rating are as good or better than those of other questionnaires for short-range prognoses (before and after comparison) and less so for long-range prognoses (follow-up of 6 or 12 months).

Clinical Use

The General Happiness Rating is widely used for a quick overall assessment and an additional criterion of happiness on a subjective level.

Future Directions

Because the General Happiness Rating has good validity and subjective appeal, it will continue to be included in subsequent studies.

References

Burgess, E.W., & Wallin, B. (1953). Engagement and marriage. Chicago: Lippincott.

Hahlweg, K., Schindler, L., Revenstorf, D., & Brengelmann, J.C. (1984). The Munich marital therapy study. In K. Hahlweg & N.S. Jacobson (Eds.), Marital interaction: Analyses and modification. New York: Guilford Press.

Locke, H.J., & Wallace, K.M. (1959). Short marital adjustment and prediction tests: Their reliability and validity. Marriage and Family Living, 21, 251-255.

Olson, D.H., Sprenkle, D.H., & Russel, C.S. (1979). Circumplex model of marital and family therapy. I. Cohesion and adaptability dimensions, family types and clinical applications. Family Process, 18, 3-28.

Reiter, L., & Steiner, E. (1981). Ist eheliche Anpassung ein latentes Therapieziel in der Therapie? Partnerberatung, 18, 78-89.

Spanier, G.B. (1976). Measuring dyadic adjustment. New scales for assessing the quality of a marriage and similar dyads. Journal of Marriage and the Family, 38, 15-28.

Stuart, R.B., & Stuart, F. (1972). Marital pre-counseling inventory. Champaign, IL: Research Press.

Terman, L.M., Buttenwieser, B., Ferguson, L.W., Johnson, W.P., & Wilson, D.P. (1938). *Psychological factors in marital happiness*. New York: McGraw-Hill.

Weiss, R.L., Hops, H., & Patterson, G.R. (1973). Framework for conceptualizing marital conflict. In L.A. Hamerlynck, L.C. Handy, & J. Mash (Eds.), *Behavior change: Methodology concepts and practice* (pp. 309-348). Champaign, IL: Research Press.

Generalized Expectancy for Success Scale

Christopher Layne

Description

The Generalized Expectancy for Success Scale (GESS) was first published by Fibel and Hale (1978). This publication presents not only the scale itself, but also a description of its rationale, construction, statistical properties, and purposes.

The GESS is a 30-item scale. All items begin with the same stem phrase: "In the future I expect that I will...." Responses to the items are in Likert format. Subjects are instructed to circle a number on a 5-point scale. Seventeen items are phrased in the positive or success direction and 13 in the negative or failure direction. The scale is scored additively and in the direction of success such that a high total score indicates a high expectancy for success.

Purpose

The purpose of the scale is to measure generalized, as opposed to specific, expectancies. A generalized expectancy for success is a global optimism about future achievement; it is to be contrasted with a specific expectancy for success, the target of which may be, for example, victory on an upcoming chess game or a favorable reaction to a soon-to-be-published article.

Social learning theory, learned helplessness, and other theories of human behavior have all indicated that people's generalized expectancies for success are important mediators in their behaviors. Low expectations are associated with low motivation, inferior performance, and depression, among other difficulties. The purpose of the GESS is to measure accurately these generalized expectancies for success so that they can be studied and monitored.

Development

One hundred fifty items were originally constructed; these items sampled across situational domains (such as familial and work-related areas). The 150 items were then screened for face validity by three psychologists. Of these, 104 items were selected and then administered to 100 subjects. An item analysis yielded 30 items that were substantially correlated with the total score but not significantly related to social desirability. These 30 items became the current version of the GESS.

Psychometric Characteristics

The GESS is not significantly affected by either the gender of the subject or social desirability. Conversely, it correlates significantly with scores on psychometric measures of depression and hopelessness. Test-retest reliabilities are good: Over a 6-week interval, the reliability coefficient was .83. The GESS enjoys high internal consistency. Factor analysis indicates that its scores are a function of one general factor.

Clinical Use

The GESS is more valuable as a research tool than as a clinical tool. Nevertheless, it can be used as a general measure of pessimism, and the client's individual responses can become a springboard to therapeutic discussions.

Future Directions

The GESS has been used in a variety of research reports, as in an investigation of motivational deficits in depressed persons (Layne, Heitkemper, Roehrig, & Speer, 1985; Layne, Lefton, Walters, & Merry, 1983). Both of these studies indicate that depressed persons have lower generalized expectations for success. A variety of theories of motivation and depression indicate that such pessimism is the root of a number of difficulties with psychiatric patients. In the future, this simple 30-item test may successfully measure the genesis of several psychological disorders.

The test may spawn similar tests. One modification of the GESS is a test that measures the pleasurableness of future successes; a person's valuation of pleasurable events may be another central causative factor in depression (Layne et al., 1983).

References

Fibel, B., & Hale, W.D. (1978). The Generalized Expectancy for Success Scale–a new measure. *Journal of Consulting and Clinical Psychology, 46,* 924-932.

Layne, C., Heitkemper, T., Roehrig, R.A., & Speer, T.K. (1985). Motivational deficit in depressed cancer patients. *Journal of Clinical Psychology, 41,* 139-144.

Layne, C., Lefton, W., Walters, D., & Merry, J. (1983). Depression: Motivation deficit versus social manipulation. *Cognitive Therapy and Research, 7,* 125-132.

Georgia Court Competency Test - Revised

William G. Johnson and Nancy R. Mullett

Description

The Georgia Court Competency Test - Revised (GCCT-R) is a screening instrument used in the assessment of competency to stand trial. Administered in a structured interview format, the test takes 10 to 20 minutes to complete and covers four major components of court competency including: (a) familiarity with the courtroom layout, (b) role of the courtroom participants, (c) ability to assist one's attorney in preparing a defense, and (d) knowledge of pending legal charges and the consequences if convicted. Scoring is achieved using clearly defined criteria with a cutoff score of 70 or above out of 100 possible points indicative of competency.

Purpose

The GCCT-R is designed as a quick, formal assessment instrument to aid in conducting forensic evaluations. Results of the test yield pass/fail scores and specific information regarding the examinee's knowledge of the various components of competency. This information will assist evaluators in determining competency to stand trial in response to requests from the court.

Development

The Court Competency Test was originally developed at the Forensic Services Division, Central State Hospital, Georgia (Wildman et al., 1978). The test was revised at the Forensic Unit, Mississippi State Hospital, to include additional components of competency to stand trial, more specific scoring criteria, and a picture of the courtroom layout to aid administration.

Psychometric Characteristics

Test-retest correlations of .79 and .84 were obtained by Wildman et al. (1978) and Mullett and Johnson (1985), respectively. Also, an interrater reliability coefficient of .96 was obtained by the latter researchers. Using a cutoff score of 70, Wildman et al. showed a strong statistical relationship between court competency test scores and forensic staff decisions with 85% of those scoring 70 or above considered competent, whereas only 15% scoring below 70 were deemed competent. Mullett and Johnson (1985) failed to observe a statistical association between GCCT-R scores and forensic staff decisions regarding competency to stand trial because of a 90% base rate of competency.

Clinical Use

The GCCT-R is designed to aid in the pre-trial evaluation of competency to stand trial for criminal defendants who are typically referred by the courts. Statistically significant associations between GCCT-R scores and staff decisions may be variable because of the differences in high base rates of competency. Regardless, a major attribute of the GCCT-R is its ability to specify a defendant's performance on the various components of competency to stand trial.

Future Directions

The GCCT-R is undergoing continuing study directed towards its refinement and comparison with other measures of competency to stand trial.

References

Wildman, R.W., II, Moore, J.T., Nelson, F.R., Thompson, L., Batchelor, E.S., de Laosa, M., & Patterson, M.E. (1978). *The Georgia Court Competency Test: An attempt to develop a rapid quantitative measure of fitness for trial.* Unpublished manuscript, Forensic Services Division, Central State Hospital, GA.

Mullett, N.R., & Johnson, W.G. (1985). *The assessment of competency to stand trial.* Paper presented at the 30th annual convention of the Southeastern Psychological Association, New Orleans.

Geriatric Assessment Inventory

John F. Schnelle

Description

The Geriatric Assessment Inventory (GAI) is a 70-item behavior checklist designed to monitor behavior of large groups of elderly nursing home patients. Nursing aides rate 10 patient behaviors in each of seven specific areas: self-help general, self-help eating, depression, socialization, communication, locomotion, and cognition memory. Scoring is done on a basis of "+" (behavior occurs most of the time) or "−" (behavior does not occur most of the time). A patient competent in all areas receives a total score of 70. Nursing aides are taught to use the scale in a 30- to 45-minute training session which consists of two major parts: (1) each item is read and briefly discussed, and (2) aides independently rate the same patient and the areas of disagreement are discussed. The rating and discussion of disagreement procedure is continued until two aides can rate a previously unrated patient with 100% reliability. A trained aide can complete the inventory on a patient known to them in approximately 5 minutes.

Purpose

The GAI was specifically designed for three major purposes: (1) to identify patient problems that should be targeted as treatment goals, (2) to track changes in patient behavior over time, and (3) to identify critical behavioral deficits that could be justification for a specific level of nursing care (i.e., intermediate or skilled). To realize these goals it is recommended that nurses complete a GAI on a patient each month. To facilitate the organization of the large amount of data that the monthly rating generates, computer programs were designed to organize the information. Two printouts are produced and include GAI item scores for each patient on admission, the average GAI score for each quarter that the patient is in the nursing home, and a current monthly score. In addition, changes in item scores from the admission month to the current month and from the previous month to the current month and from quarter to quarter are printed. Finally, it is recommended that at least four different patients be rated independently by two aides each month. Interrater reliability between these aides is then calculated. The item number of the specific items for which disagreements occurred is listed in a printout for feedback purposes to the aides.

Development

Items were developed after extensive consultation with nursing facility staff who were asked to list the primary problems the residents displayed. An initial listing of items was obtained and presented to nursing aides who were asked to rate more than 100 patients. The interrater reliability of these initial ratings was computed, and specific items that most frequently resulted in low reliability were identified. These items were revised so that the distribution of agreement for the 70 different items was approximately even and infrequent.

Psychometric Characteristics

Reliability. Interrater agreement was calculated over 100 different occasions after the scale was placed in its final form and averaged 93.4%. In addition, the scale was used for 1 year in three nursing homes. Four agreement checks were calculated each month for each nursing home. There was no trend over time for the reliability to drift downward.

Concurrent Reliability. Direct observations of behavior in 10 randomly selected patients were conducted throughout the day for 8 days. Using the items on the GAI as an observational checklist, two observers independently observed each patient. Both raters independently filled out a complete GAI for each patient at the end of 8 days based on their observational records. Interrater agreement for these completed GAI records was 97%. One of the two geriatric assessment inventory records for each patient was randomly selected and compared with the most recent aide rating of the GAI for that patient. The correlation between the direct observational data and the aide ratings was .98 for overall geriatric assessment score. For the subscales, the correlations were substantial and statistically significant in all cases ($p < .01$).

Discriminant Validity. A comparison of two samples of elderly people who could be expected to differ in behavioral competencies was made to further validate the geriatric assessment inventory.

Twenty elderly persons who attended a community day care center but who lived independently were assessed on the GAI by day care personnel. Interrater reliability was calculated for all 20. The 20 day care patients and the 220 patients in three nursing homes were categorized into the same age groupings. Twenty nursing home patients were randomly selected to match the age groupings of the 20 day care clients. Differences between the two groups on each scale of the GAI were assessed. The overall score on the GAI for the nursing home population was significantly different and lower than the overall score for the day care population. The specific scales contributing to significant differences were self-help general, self-help eating, socialization, and locomotion.

Treatment Sensitivity. Changes in the GAI cognitive memory scale correlated positively with independently documented improvements in patient orientation level, resulting from a therapy program that took place over 9 days. Therapeutic personnel who documented improvements in orientation level were independent of the nursing personnel who documented improvements with the GAI. Five patients who do not respond to the reality orientation program were not rated as different over the same period by the nursing personnel using the GAI.

Clinical Use

The GAI is a general evaluation tool most useful for monitoring the behavior of large groups of nursing home patients over time. The time efficiency of the rating system and the ease with which the inventory lends itself to automated information processing techniques are its particular advantages.

Future Directions

The GAI will be more useful when normative data are collected for large groups of nursing home populations. Such normative data will permit identification of specific nursing homes whose patients show excessive deficits given age norms. Such nursing homes could then be targeted for further analysis and perhaps even remedial intervention.

Global Deterioration Scale

Robert B. Fields and Christopher Starratt

Description

The Global Deterioration Scale (GDS; Reisberg, Ferris, deLeon, & Crook, 1982) is a 7-point rating scale of the severity of dementia. It was developed specifically for use with patients with dementia of the Alzheimer's type (DAT). The scale consists of seven descriptive classifications, or stages, that measure the overall level of cognitive and behavioral impairment along a continuum from normality to severe dementia. Presumably, patients with DAT pass through these stages in an invariant sequence during the course of their illness. The GDS stages can be summarized briefly as follows: Stage 1, No cognitive decline: normal cognitive functioning. Stage 2, very mild cognitive decline: No significant objective deficits, but subjective complaints of forgetfulness that may be normal for age. Stage 3, mild cognitive decline: First objective cognitive deficits that may signal the beginning of DAT. Referred to as the early confusional stage, deficits at this stage may include word finding difficulty, becoming lost in unfamiliar places, and decreased performance in demanding social or occupational situations. Stage 4, moderate cognitive decline: Clear-cut cognitive impairment. Progression to this late confusional stage indicates the presence of DAT and a poor prognosis. Deficits may include deficient memory for recent events, concentration difficulties, and impairment in the ability to travel independently and handle finances. Stage 5, moderately severe decline: At this early dementia stage, patients can no longer survive on their own and demonstrate significant cognitive and memory deficits. Knowledge of personal information and history is often impaired and assistance may be needed in areas such as selection of clothes. Stage 6, severe cognitive decline: In middle dementia, patients require complete supervision. Cognitive and functional behavioral deficits are severe and personality and emotional changes are common. Names of family members are typically forgotten, diurnal rhythm is often disturbed, and hallucinations and delusions are common. Stage 7, very severe cognitive decline: In late dementia, virtually all verbal and psychomotor abilities are lost.

Purpose

The GDS was initially developed as an index of the severity of impairment once the clinical diagnosis of probable DAT had been made. It was designed to be sufficiently global so that stages of dementia could be determined across different assessment strategies and across cultures. The GDS also was designed to be sensitive to the entire range of cognitive and behavioral functioning in order that it be used to assess patients at all levels of impairment. Therefore, as an index of the severity of dysfunction, the GDS can be used with an individual patient to measure deterioration over time. It also can be used more broadly to provide researchers with standardized criteria for the degree of dementia with which patients can be compared across samples.

A secondary purpose of the GDS is to aid in the diagnosis of DAT. Alzheimer's disease is the most common form of irreversible dementia; however, differential diagnosis is often difficult. Diagnosis of early DAT is complicated by the fact that the presentation of many geriatric disorders includes symptoms of mild cognitive dysfunction. In the later stages, DAT may resemble other dementias such as multi-infarct dementia. By specifying the unique progression of patients with DAT, the GDS can be seen as an additional diagnostic tool particularly when diagnosis is based on a reliable history or longitudinal assessment or both.

Development

Before the development of the GDS, there were no established instruments to measure the unique stages of overall deterioration associated with DAT. Previous assessment strategies typically focused on specific areas of functioning and included rating scales for activities of daily living and brief tests of cognitive and memory functioning. Although these measures have been useful in documenting the existence of dysfunction, they have been of limited value in assessing the level of severity of impairment (Fields & Starratt, 1985). The GDS was one of the first scales to combine cognitive and behavioral data obtained in a structured manner to derive a global index of severity of dysfunction.

Descriptions of the GDS states were derived from interview data collected over several years with patients with DAT and their families. Initial concurrent and predictive validity studies were conducted with elderly individuals with probable DAT and with normal elderly subjects. In both the descriptions of the GDS stages and the initial research using this scale, emphasis has been on the clinical characteristics that define particular levels of severity of impairment and that predict prognosis.

Two separate 7-point scales were developed in conjunction with the GDS to assess cognition and functional behavior in a more systematic manner. The Brief Cognitive Rating Scale (BCRS; Reisberg, Schneck, Ferris, Schwartz, & deLeon, 1983; Reisberg, Ferris, deLeon, & Crook, 1985) contains eight areas, or axes, of cognitive functioning. The eight axes, which are each scored on a 7-point scale to correspond with the GDS, are: (1) concentration, (2) recent memory, (3) remote memory, (4) orientation, (5) functioning and self-care, (6) language, (7) motor functioning, and (8) mood and behavior. The Functional Assessment Stages (FAST; Reisberg et al., 1984) are an expansion of axis 5 (functioning and self-care) of the BCRS with particular emphasis on GDS stages 6 and 7 in which cognitive testing is often of little value.

Psychometric Characteristics

The GDS is an invariant sequence scale that presumes an ordinal level of measurement. No interrater reliability data have been reported. However, given the detailed descriptions of each stage it is unlikely that reliability will be a significant problem. Preliminary validity data are impressive. Concerning the scale as a whole, the GDS correlated significantly with psychometric and structural indices of organic impairment. The GDS correlates significantly with dementia screening tests (e.g., the Mini-Mental State Examination, n = 40, $r = -.38$ to $-.64$) (Reisberg et al., 1985), more traditional psychometric tests (e.g., Buschke verbal learning and Memory for Designs) (n = 54, $r = -.38$ to $-.64$) (Reisberg et al., 1982) as well as with computerized tomographic scan (n = 43, ventricular dilation: $r = .62, p < .01$; sulcal enlargement: $r = .53, p < .01$) and PET scan (n = 7, glucose utilization in a variety of cortical areas: $r = .69$ to .83, $p < .05$) findings (Reisberg et al., 1982).

Support for the validity of the specific stages was demonstrated by significant differences in neuropsychological test performance between patients at GDS stage 2 versus stage 4 (sample = 108) and between patients at stage 4 versus stage 5 and 6 (sample = 53) (Reisberg et al., 1985). Use of the GDS for prognosis is based on longitudinal assessment of patients at different levels of severity of DAT. Based on a study of over 100 patients who were followed up 3 to 4 years, GDS stage 4 appears to be the point at which DAT begins and prognosis worsens. Only 7 of 70 patients at GDS levels 2 or 3 deteriorated two or more GDS stages at follow-up. However, 26 of 34 patients initially determined to be at GDS stages 4, 5, or 6 continued to deteriorate further at follow-up (Reisberg et al., 1985).

Clinical Use

The GDS was designed to be used by clinicians and researchers trained in geriatric psychiatry and presupposes a knowledge of psychiatric diagnosis as well as psychometric and functional behavioral assessment. The GDS is recommended for both clinical and research purposes. In clinical settings, sufficient validity data exist to use the GDS to assess the severity of impairment and as a diagnostic aid for establishing probable DAT. Prediction of prognosis over 3 to 4 years also is justified based on the longitudinal studies of patients at different GDS stages. For research purposes, the GDS is recommended in studies of patients with DAT to increase comparability of results across studies and to identify further the specific cognitive and behavioral characteristics that correspond with each stage of the disorder.

Future Directions

As the GDS is a relatively new instrument, several areas of investigation are needed. The first area is interrater reliability. Although reliability should not be a problem with the GDS, currently there are no published reports on the reliability of its use. The second area concerns utility and validity. Increased awareness and use of the GDS by clinicians and researchers in laboratories across the country will determine its acceptability to practitioners in the field and will add to the validity data pool begun by Reisberg and his colleagues. In particular, longitudinal assessment will allow for evaluation of the sequence of deterioration proposed by the scale. A third area of investigation is the notion of specificity to DAT. Long-term follow-up (including autopsy) of patients with DAT and other dementias will help determine if the GDS stages are indeed specific for DAT. One possible addition to the GDS would be supplementary descriptive stages for levels of severity for other types of dementia to aid in differential diagnosis. A final area is assessment. The GDS might be made more reliable and practical with the construction of a structured assessment/interview procedure based on the BCRS and the FAST for patients and their families. Structured interviews generally have increased reliability of several diagnostic classifications and, recently, a specific structured assessment procedure has been used to assess dementia with the Clinical Dementia Rating Scale, an analogous instrument reviewed in this volume.

References

Fields, R.B., & Starratt, C. (1985). *The role of dementia screening tests in the evaluation of cognitive functioning in the elderly.* Paper presented at the Mid-South Conference on Human Neuropsychology, Memphis, TN, May.

Reisberg, B., Ferris, S.H., Anand, R., deLeon, M.J., Schneck, M.K., Buttinger, C., & Borenstein, J. (1984). Functional staging of dementia of the Alzheimer type. *Annals of the New York Academy of Science, 435,* 481-483.

Reisberg, B., Ferris, S.H., deLeon, M.J., & Crook, J. (1982). The global deterioration scale for assessment of primary degenerative dementia. *American Journal of Psychiatry, 139,* 1136-1139.

Reisberg, B., Ferris, S.H., deLeon, M.J., & Crook, J. (1985). Age-associated cognitive decline and Alzheimer's disease: Implications for assessment and treatment. In M. Bergener, M. Ermini, & H.B. Stahelin (Eds.), *Thresholds in aging* (pp. 255-292). London: Academic Press.

Reisberg, B., Schneck, M.K., Ferris, S.H., Schwartz, G.E., & deLeon, M.J. (1983). The brief cognitive rating scale (BCRS): Findings in primary degenerative dementia (PDD). *Psychopharmacology Bulletin, 19,* 47-50.

Goal Attainment Scaling

Deborah C. Beidel

Description

Goal attainment scaling is a procedure whereby individual treatment goals are carefully defined and scaled according to an incremental series of possible treatment outcomes. The technique consists of three steps: (a) goal selection and scaling; (b) random assignment of the patient to one of the available treatment modalities; and (c) a follow-up assessment of the patient with regard to treatment goals established at intake. Although random assignment would seem to be necessary only when the scale is used in a research design, the originators of the Goal Attainment Scale view randomization as an integral part of the procedure and necessary to preserve the integrity of the scale whether used in a clinical setting or for research.

An example of an individualized treatment goal may be "admission into a job training program." Before treatment, an expected treatment outcome is behaviorally defined (e.g., "acceptance into a training program"). This expected outcome is given a weight of 0. Other possible treatment outcomes are then delineated in graded increments using a Likert scale format. According to a standard procedure, at least 2 points on the scale must be behaviorally anchored. For example, the most unfavorable treatment outcome might be "expresses no desire for a training program" and given a scale weight of minus 2. The best anticipated treatment outcome might be "successful job placement" and given a rating of plus 2. Other levels may be included in the scaling procedure within these parameters and graded accordingly. Following treatment, the individual's progress is scored according to the appropriate levels on the scale, yielding a total treatment score. Any number of treatment goals may be scaled in this manner. Although individuals may have entirely different treatment goals, the Likert scale format allows for conversion to standard scores such that treatment comparisons can be made across patients or intervention strategies.

Purpose and Development

Goal attainment scaling was originally proposed by Kiresuk and Sherman (1968) as a method for evaluating comprehensive community mental health programs. This behavioral assessment procedure is designed to reflect the individualized treatment needs of each patient, while allowing for comparability among individuals. It was noted that programs had a tendency to use a fixed battery of measures despite individual demographic characteristics or presenting problems. Use of a standard battery could result in evaluation based on inappropriate variables. Additionally, idiosyncratic problems might not be addressed within a rigid assessment procedure. Goal attainment scaling was proposed as a method in which measurement of treatment outcome could be targeted at the specific need of each individual, yet at the same time provide a quantitative estimate of achievement. These quantitative scores can be used in a comparative evaluation of various intervention strategies. An additional purpose of the Goal Attainment Scale is a program evaluation tool. Within this context, the effectiveness of the program can be assessed by examination of the individual's Goal Attainment Scale scores at the end of treatment intervention. A composite score can be calculated and converted to a standardized t score by use of a mathematical formula.

One difficulty with the Goal Attainment Scale is the necessity to scale goals realistically. Kiresuk and Sherman (1968) note that goals must be scaled so that the expected value and standard deviation of each goal are equal to 0 and 1, respectively, in order for the t score transformation formula to be appropriate. Biased or unrealistic scaling may create other problems as well. Several researchers have noted that final outcome scores on the Goal Attainment Scale may reflect not only the treatment outcome, but also the goal setter's ability to accurately predict treatment outcome. Goal setters may inadvertently subvert the scale in the selection of the predicted level of outcome. If there is overprediction, the patient's score will not reflect the extent of improvement. If the expected outcome is underpredicted, the score will be inflated. A second form of bias is to select goals that favor a particular therapist's expertise, rather than an objective assessment of the patient's needs. Kiresuk and Sherman (1968) suggest that randomization of subjects to treatment conditions will control for some of this bias. Because patients are assigned to a therapist after goal selection is completed, goals cannot be set in line with a particular therapist's expertise, thereby assuring favorable outcome scores. In reality, although randomization is a standard part of goal attainment scaling, in a survey of publications that used the Goal Attainment Scale as an outcome measure, the procedure was frequently violated or ignored (Cytrynbaum, Ginath, Birdwell, & Brandt, 1979).

A second confound in the development of the original scale is the lack of provision for recording the subject's behavior at entry into treatment. Several researchers have modified the Goal Attainment Scale procedure to account for patient behavior at intake. In these instances, outcome is calculated in terms of the direction and magnitude of change during treatment. To address the need for accurate prediction and provide a measure of baseline behavior, the Goal Attainment Scale may be revised whereby the patient's behavior at entry into the program is used as the zero point. The scale format can be expanded to 7- or 9-point, rather than a 5-point, scale to allow finer discriminations to be made in scoring partial attainment of the goal. Increments in the direction of goal attainment can be scaled in a positive direction (+ 2) up to complete goal attainment (+ 4), whereas deterioration of behavior can be scored in a negative direction (− 2) up to complete deterioration (− 4). It should be noted that this revision does not completely eliminate the fallibility of goal setters in setting accurate goals. However, it does assure that any improvement over baseline is scored in a positive direction.

Psychometric Characteristics

The Goal Attainment Scale has become one of the most utilized and popular outcome measures, as will be described. Despite its popularity, the psychometric properties of the instrument have been called into question. The first issue pertains to its reliability. Concepts such as test-retest reliability and internal consistency are not appropriate measures by which to evaluate the Goal Attainment Scale. However, other estimates of reliability, which are appropriate, have not been encouraging. Cytrynbaum et al. (1979) note that when estimates of reliability are reported, interrater reliability estimates range from $r = .51$ to $r = .95$. Interrater stability, the consistency of scores by two raters across rating intervals, has been described as moderate ($r = .60$). Rater stability, which would appear to be very important in Goal Attainment Scaling, has not been investigated. Rater reliability can be affected by any number of variables, including the rater's expectation of improvement, rater training procedures, rating complexity, rater drift, and rater awareness of reliability checks. Comprehensive training procedures and frequent reliability checks, in conjunction with clearly defined behavioral anchors, would strengthen the reliability of the Goal Attainment Scale.

The validity of the Goal Attainment Scale has been a particularly thorny issue. The highly individualized nature of each scale makes comparison with other measures extremely difficult. However, content and concurrent validity issues have been examined. Determination of content validity has been based on evaluation of the appropriateness of the chosen goals for the needs of the particular patient. Concurrent validity also has been frequently investigated. Patient self-report or therapist ratings on variables such as therapist response,

effectiveness of the program, relief from symptoms, progress with respect to the presenting problem, or satisfaction with service (Cytrynbaum et al., 1979) have been the most utilized concurrent measures. Because these measures also are somewhat individualized, their correlation with the Goal Attainment Scale would appear most appropriate. Correlations have been uniformly low to moderate. On the basis of these findings, Cytrynbaum et al. (1979) concluded that the concurrent validity of the Goal Attainment Scale is in doubt. In response to these criticisms, Heavlin, Lee-Merrow, and Lewis (1982) suggest that the Goal Attainment Scale's low validity coefficients may indeed represent poor validity; however, they indicate a second explanation for the low coefficients. Because of its idiosyncratic nature, the Goal Attainment Scale should not be expected to correlate highly with measures that were developed on a normative basis. These authors conclude that the Goal Attainment Scale may measure an aspect of outcome not reflected in other global procedures.

Clinical Use

The Goal Attainment Scale has become one of the most popular mental health outcome measures. Estimates of the number of studies using the Goal Attainment Scale range from 200 to 800 and include the evaluation of treatment interventions, effectiveness of staff training programs, and program evaluation. Patient groups that have been assessed by the Goal Attainment Scale include adult, adolescent, and child psychiatric inpatients, outpatients, and partial hospitalization patients, sexually dysfunctional men, problem drinkers, community mental health center patients, spina bifida adolescents, mentally retarded children and adults, and rehabilitation patients. The Goal Attainment Scale has been used to evaluate staff training programs directed at psychiatric nursing skills, staff therapeutic behaviors, and psychiatric clerks. Finally, rather than focusing on treatment gains made by one particular individual, scores on the Goal Attainment Scale can indicate the effectiveness of a particular treatment intervention or program. Evaluation of training programs incorporating this measure include clinical pharmacy programs, social work services, intensive environmental intervention programs in an inner city setting, special education programs, summer camps for children with psychiatric programs, partial hospitalization programs, drug and alcohol treatment programs, health counseling programs, family therapy, residential treatment programs, and rehabilitation services. It is evident that goal setting procedures are appropriate across a range of programs and populations. The issue of appropriateness for application of the Goal Attainment Scale is more an issue of therapist acceptance rather than patient applicability.

Therapists sometimes object to implementation of goal attainment scaling because of the explicit statement of treatment goals (Choate, Smith, Cardillo, & Thompson, 1981). They express concern that their therapeutic skills were the focus of evaluation, and failure of the patient to meet the goals would reflect poorly on their therapeutic ability. A second source of resistance on the part of therapists is the perception of extra paperwork. A final source of concern on the part of the therapist relates to the ability to set appropriate treatment goals in behavioral terms. Goals such as increased ego strength or resolution of an oedipal complex do not readily lend themselves to scaling of observable behaviors along a Likert scale. Thus, clinicians must be taught to conceptualize problems in behavioral terms. The success of the Goal Attainment Scale depends on the ability to formulate and scale these behaviors appropriately.

Future Directions

Before speculating on future directions, it is important to note that many of the Goal Attainment Scale procedures have already been substantially modified from the classic paradigm. Some innovations include allowing the therapist or patient or both to set the treatment goals, rather than using an independent evaluator; having the therapist rather than an independent evaluator complete the follow-up scoring; ignoring the randomization procedure, which in the classic design, partially controls for inaccurate goal setting; rescaling procedures such that the level of entry is assigned a point value of 0 rather than the expected outcome level; and perhaps the largest violation of the spirit of goal attainment scaling, constructing a "standard" Goal Attainment Scale in which all patients are rated on a series of 38 standard goals. In this instance, the assumptions of the procedures are violated to such an extent that the greatest asset, the ability to measure highly individualized goals while allowing for comparison across subjects, is lost.

Introduction of an innovative procedure, such as goal attainment scaling, into a treatment setting requires changes by the treatment staff. To examine some of the factors that might help insure successful adoption of the Goal Attainment Scale, Glaser and Becker (1980) surveyed 10 programs that had implemented goal attainment scaling. Of those, four were still using the measure 2 years later, whereas six had dropped the procedure. The experience of these programs may be important in assuring successful implementation by future organizations. Factors that differentiated the two groups and seemed to be related to durability included goal attainment scaling procedures well integrated into the standard operating practice of the organization and meeting a clearly recognized and well-defined need acknowledged by the leadership. In addition, when modifications are possible in response to local circumstances, and staff values are congruent with those represented by goal attainment scaling and enthusiastically supported over time, durability of the program will be enhanced. Finally, when the planning and implementation phases include the program staff so that resistance can be dealt with in a constructive manner, successful implementation of the procedures is more likely.

Goal attainment scaling has evolved from an outcome measure to a therapeutic intervention in its own right. Goal setting has been demonstrated to be effective in improving therapeutic interventions. Although deviating radically from the classic procedure, this new use of the Goal Attainment Scale may prove an effective therapeutic tool by clarifying the purpose and extent of the therapeutic interventions. Further use of the procedure in this manner may be effective in improving patient expectations and thereby increasing consumer satisfaction.

References

Choate, R., Smith, A., Cardillo, J.E., & Thompson, L. (1981). Training in the use of goal attainment scaling. Community Mental Health Journal, 17, 171-181.

Cytrynbaum, S., Ginath, Y., Birdwell, J., & Brandt, L. (1979). Goal attainment scaling: A critical review. Evaluation Quarterly, 3, 5-40.

Glaser, E.M., & Becker, T.E. (1980). Durability of innovations: How goal attainment scaling programs fare over time. Community Mental Health Journal, 16, 130-143.

Heavlin, W.D., Lee-Merrow, S.W., & Lewis, V.M. (1982). The psychometric foundation of goal attainment scaling. Community Mental Health, 18, 230-241.

Kiresuk, T.J., & Sherman, R.E. (1968). Goal attainment scaling: A general method for evaluating comprehensive community mental health programs. Community Mental Health Journal, 4, 443-453.

Height Avoidance Test

S. Lloyd Williams

Description

The height avoidance test is a behavioral avoidance (or approach) test of height phobia, the purpose of which is to see how high into a building or other elevated locale an individual can ascend. Ideally, the building chosen for the test should have an exposed landing on every level, and should be at least 7 or 8 floors tall to allow room for improvement and to be sensitive to behavioral changes of more than a few floors. Because persons with height phobia usually have problems only when there is some chance of falling, the test cannot be conducted on landings that are safely enclosed by glass or high fencing, and any protective railing should be no higher than about 4 feet. Height avoidance tests have been conducted on fire escapes (e.g., Marshall, 1985), multilevel parking garages (Williams, Turner, & Peer, 1985), and buildings with balconies at every level (Williams & Watson, 1985). At ground level, the tester instructs the subject to try to ascend to each level in order from lowest to highest or until unable to continue. The tester generally observes the height performance from the ground. Instructions should further specify the criterion performance of the individual on each floor in order to successfully complete the floor. When the subject successfully performs the criterion task on a given level, the assessor signals the person to attempt the next level. When the assessment setting is a fire escape, the test performance usually consists simply of how many steps the individual ascends. In settings other than fire escapes, a stringent test would involve having the testees: (a) lean with their stomach against the railing of each landing or balcony, (b) not hold onto the railing but clasp their hands behind their back or fold their arms in front of them in such a way that the tester can verify that they are not holding on, and (c) look straight down at the ground for a given number of seconds (15 to 30). Because it can be difficult to ascertain whether the individual being tested is actually looking straight down, the subjects are asked to identify a distinctive card placed at the base of the building as they attempted each floor, and only if they were able to correctly identify it were they credited with successful performance on that floor. As with all behavioral avoidance tests, the testee should be allowed only a limited

period of time to achieve the criterion performance (in height tests, 10 to 15 seconds to get into criterion position should be sufficient). In addition, the tester's instructions should not embody any limitations on how anxious subjects become, but should simply state "do as much as you can." Otherwise, the test confounds the behavioral and emotional response modes (Williams, 1985). If the tester wishes to know how anxious persons become during the test, then they can be asked to give their SUDS (anxiety) rating during or immediately after each task of the test. Height avoidance is scored as either the number or the percentage of floors successfully completed.

Purpose

The purpose of the height avoidance test is to obtain a precise estimate of how high a person with height phobia can ascend. This information is useful primarily as a basis for evaluating behavioral progress in a program of height phobia treatment and for evaluating scientific hypotheses in which the experimenter needs an objective measure of phobic behavior. The popularity of height phobia as a target problem in studies of phobic behavior derives in part from the entirely straightforward scaling of height performance scores from height avoidance tests.

Development

Height avoidance tests have been used in many studies of height phobic behavior, including both individual case studies and group experimental designs. The procedures currently used for such tests are essentially the same as those used with the earliest height avoidance tests developed in the early 1960s.

Psychometric Characteristics

The psychometric characteristics of height avoidance tests have not been extensively studied. However, height avoidance tests, like all behavioral tests, possess a high degree of face validity as a measure of the extent of a person's behavioral capabilities for specifically defined activities. The correlations between scores on behavioral tests of phobia and self-report inventories of phobic behavior are often of modest magnitude (Hersen, 1973). The test-retest reliability of height avoidance tests appears to be very high: Williams, Turner, and

Peer (1985) obtained a test-retest reliability coefficient of .95 for height avoidance behavior among 38 persons with height phobia over a 1-month treatment follow-up interval.

Clinical Use

As already described under "Purpose," height avoidance tests are used in clinical applications much as behavioral tests generally are used: to obtain objective and precise measures of phobic behavior in the natural environment. Perhaps the most important clinical use of behavioral tests, in addition to their value as a measure of behavioral capabilities, is that of providing a context for sampling the thoughts and feelings that arise in phobic clients as they attempt to cope in real life with what they fear (Williams, 1985).

Future Directions

Although height avoidance tests will undoubtedly continue to be widely used in research and practice with phobic individuals, their straightforward nature suggests that their basic format and procedures are unlikely to change very much.

References

Hersen, M. (1973). Self-assessment of fear. *Behavior Therapy, 4*, 241-257.

Marshall, W.L. (1985). The effects of variable exposure in flooding therapy. *Behavior Therapy, 4*, 117-135.

Williams, S.L. (1985). On the nature and measurement of agoraphobia. In M. Hersen, R.M. Eisler, & P.M. Miller (Eds.), *Progress in behavior modification: Vol. 19* (pp. 109-144). New York: Academic Press.

Williams, S.L., Turner, S.M., & Peer, D.F. (1985). Guided mastery and performance desensitization treatments for severe acrophobia. *Journal of Consulting and Clinical Psychology, 53*, 237-247.

Williams, S.L., & Watson, N. (1985). Perceived danger and perceived self-efficacy as cognitive determinants of acrophobic behavior. *Behavior Therapy, 16*, 136-146.

Heterosocial Skills Behavior Checklist for Males

Barry Edelstein, Gregory Alberts, and Sharon Estill

Description

The Heterosocial Skills Behavior Checklist (HSBC) contains 17 items divided into four categories:

voice, form of conversation, affect, and motor behavior while seated. "The voice category includes loudness, pitch, inflection, and dramatic effect. Form of conversation involves initiating conversation, following up on female vocalizations, ensuring continued flow of conversation, and verbalizing interest in the female's activities or appearance. Items under affect include appropriate facial expression, eye contact, and appropriate versus inappropriate laughter. Finally, masculine versus feminine motor behavior while seated includes six items from a larger scale used in the assessment of feminine motor behavior in males" (Barlow, Abel, Blanchard, Bristow, & Young, 1977). The authors include the "motor behavior while seated" category in the checklist, while noting that the construct validity of the category has not been established. Rating instructions and definitions of appropriate and inappropriate behaviors are given for each item under each of the four categories. Each item has five blocks beside the description of the inappropriate behavior. These blocks are used to indicate the presence or absence of the behavior described by the item during successive 30-second time periods. The scale is used by raters who observe a 5-minute videotape of the person being rated.

Purpose

The purpose of the HSBC is to identify specific social behaviors which are deficient in a client who apparently demonstrates poor heterosocial skills. It can also be used to monitor progress or assess outcome in skills training. The checklist appears particularly appropriate for use with sexually deviant men with poor heterosocial skills.

Development

The HSBC was developed by Barlow, Abel, Blanchard, Bristow, and Young (1977) to "pinpoint social behaviors important in initiating a heterosocial relationship in males." At the time the checklist was being developed, social skills researchers were attempting to determine the behavioral correlates of successful social skills so that valid assessment and effective training could proceed. The initiation of a heterosocial relationship was seen as one of three skills or competencies that comprised heterosocial skills, the remaining being social skills that precede sexual behavior, and social skills that maintain a heterosocial relationship.

Behaviors intended to discriminate between adequate and inadequate social performance were generated by having several male and female judges observe role-played heterosocial interactions by both black and white socially adequate high school and college students. Subjects were high school and college students chosen by first having counselors nominate five women who were popular and dated frequently. These women then nominated several men whom they judged to be very socially adept and whom they would like to date. Subjects for both the development of the checklist items (behaviors) and examination of the psychometric properties were drawn from this group of nominated men. Several male and female judges observed brief social interactions of several male subjects and identified behaviors that "seemed to discriminate socially adequate subjects from socially inadequate subjects" and that could be agreed upon by two independent raters.

Psychometric Characteristics

Data on the validity of the HSBC are minimal. The developers provided data on the ability of the checklist to discriminate between a group of socially adequate students from a matched group of male subjects referred for evaluation and assessment of sexual deviations. The inadequate or inappropriate subjects were differentiated from the adequate and appropriate subjects on the basis of form of conversation, affect, and voice categories (Barlow et al., 1977). However, in a subsequent study, Alexander and Johnson (1980) found that only the Affect category differentiated sex offenders from normal subjects.

Interobserver agreement for ratings using each of the item categories ranges from .84 to .97 (Barlow et al., 1977) and .90 to 1.00 (Alexander & Johnson, 1980). Split-half reliability ranges from .95 to .97. Test-retest reliability is poor for the overall checklist score and the conversation category ($r = .27$ and $r = .09$, respectively). Test-retest reliability for the voice and affect categories was moderate ($r = .53$ and .74, respectively). For a test with good internal consistency, the split-half reliability may be a better estimate of temporal stability than test-retest reliability.

Clinical Use

The HSBC may be used to identify possible target behaviors for intervention with male clients who are suspected of having poor heterosocial skills and also to monitor the effects of training.

Future Directions

The need for reliable and valid prescriptive assessment measures of social skills is substantial. The HSBC possesses some important psychometric characteristics, such as good interobserver agreement for ratings and good split-half reliability, although it has rather poor test-retest reliability. In addition to being reliable, the HSBC discriminated sex offenders from a normal population. Therefore, the HSBC may prove to be the best available instrument for evaluating the social skills of male subjects, particularly those who have committed sexual offenses.

With the exception of the original article by Barlow et al. (1977) and a study by Alexander and Johnson (1980), few research investigations have addressed the psychometric characteristics of the HSBC. A detailed item analysis might be the next step needed to determine the discrete behaviors that fall under the broad categories, such as affect. This might allow for more objective definitions of the behavioral categories in the checklist.

Perhaps with its continued use the reliability and validity of the HSBC will also be further explored. The HSBC holds considerable promise for those working with socially unskilled sexual offenders as well as other populations with heterosocial skill and gender role problems.

References

Alexander, B.B., & Johnson, S.B. (1980). Reliability of heterosocial skills measurement with sex offenders. *Journal of Behavioral Assessment, 2,* 225-237.

Barlow, D.H., Abel, G.G., Blanchard, E.B., Bristow, A.R., & Young, L.D. (1977). Heterosocial skills behavior checklist for males. *Behavior Therapy, 8,* 229-239.

Home Accident Observations

Allen Marchetti

Description

Home Accident Observations refers to skills necessary for self-preservation in emergency situations within the residential environment of the client. During evaluation, the retarded individual's ability to identify and respond quickly, appropriately, and independently to emergency situations is assessed. Such skills may include self-preservation in the case of fire (Mac Eachron & Janicki, 1983; Mac

Eachron & Krauss, 1985; Matson, 1980) or situations in which an individual is in physical distress, as with injuries or seizures (Matson, 1980).

During assessment, the client is required to role-play his response to simulated emergencies such as fire drills or situations in which the individual is being trained or in which a "confederate" needs medical attention. Performance may be assessed through direct observation or by analysis of tape recordings of training sessions.

Purpose

Self-preservation in the event of fire or in situations involving physical distress is of major concern to individuals serving the substantially impaired. The research literature is scant with regard to methods to assess and train self-preservation skills.

National statistics related to acute illness and injury indicate that there were 212 acute conditions per 100 persons among America's civilian non-institutionalized population in 1975 (U.S. Department of Health, Education, and Welfare, 1975). Although such data are not available for the mentally retarded population, it is assumed that the incident rate among these individuals is at least as high, if not higher, because of their inability to recognize, avoid, and/or react to potentially dangerous situations.

With regard to self-preservation ability during residential fire emergencies, Mac Eachron and Janicki (1983) found that in a study of developmentally disabled persons in New York State, 61% of the clients assessed required no evacuation assistance, 18% required moderate assistance, and 21% required substantial assistance. In a New England state, in a replication of this study (Mac Eachron & Krauss, 1985), in which 8,000 developmentally disabled persons were studied, similiar results were reported with 51% needing no evacuation assistance, 28% requiring moderate assistance, and 20% requiring substantial assistance.

Factors such as potential dangers within the residential environment, the inability of retarded individuals to respond appropriately to such situations, and recent trends related to placing retarded persons into lesser restrictive settings highlight the need for developing such skills in this population. It is essential that more sophisticated techniques be developed for assessing and training retarded persons to identify and respond appropriately to such situations.

Development

Few empirical studies are reported in the applied research literature focus on assessment and training techniques for home accident observations. Studies that have targeted self-preservation skills such as residential fire emergencies (Matson, 1980; Mac Eachron & Janicki, 1983; Mac Eachron & Krauss, 1985) or instances of physical trauma or distress (Matson, 1980) have used simulated emergencies for assessment purposes.

In these studies, assessment consisted of the researcher "staging" various emergency situations, such as activating fire warning mechanisms or simulating a situation in which a "confederate" is injured or needs assistance. The subject is required to respond appropriately to such occurrences.

The appropriate response to these situations has been carefully delineated in task-analyzed sequences of the target behavior. Assessment is completed by the primary trainer or, in more methologically rigorous studies, by independent observers who are blind to the experimental conditions. Subject ratings have included assessment of the client's ability to provide a verbal description of required reactions to each step of the target behavior and/or to role-play these steps.

Assessment has included evaluation of the individual's ability to identify a potentially dangerous situation and to respond appropriately, quickly, and independently to such a situation. The severity, time, and place of such emergencies have also been varied during these simulated emergencies.

Psychometric Characteristics

Because assessment of home accident observations requires that, for the most part, such emergency situations be contrived, it is essential that these "staged" situations approximate actual emergencies if such assessments are to yield valid data. Assessment during an actual emergency has not been reported in the general research literature. Staged emergency situations have not included many stimulus properties of actual emergency situations that may affect client behavior (i.e., smoke and fire in the event of fire).

Reliability data using trained observers have been consistently high in the few reported studies targeting self-preservation skills. Studies reported vary considerably with regard to the rigor with which such studies have collected reliability data.

Few studies have used two or more independent, trained observers to determine reliability.

Clinical Use

Assessment of home accident observations is useful for all mentally retarded individuals regardless of the degree of retardation or the residential setting. Specific populations that have been assessed and have received training in self-preservation skills include clients who reside in both institutional (Matson, 1980) and community settings (Rae & Roll, 1985). The effectiveness of such procedures has been demonstrated with clients at all levels of retardation. Assessment and training of home accident observations are most appropriate for clients who are required to reside independently in less staff-intensive settings. The safety of such home-like settings depends greatly on the client's skill and competency in self-preservation.

Future Directions

Assessment of home accident observations has received only limited attention in the applied research literature. Studies that have been conducted have assessed subjects during staged emergency situations. Such studies were analogue in nature and did not provide information on performance during actual emergency situations. Future studies must incorporate stimulus properties that more closely approximate actual emergency situations if such assessments are to prove valid.

Defining further the client population that would benefit from such assessment and training (i.e., physical and mental abilities) and determining their ability to maintain and generalize treatment effects must be more closely investigated. Determining other adjustment skills that may facilitate self-preservation in emergency situations is also essential. The ability to dial a telephone for assistance or to manipulate various locking mechanisms to escape the home may be considered essential to minimize the effects of emergency occurrences.

References

Mac Eachron, A.E., & Janacki, M.P. (1983). Self-preservation ability and residential fire emergencies. *American Journal of Mental Deficiency, 88*, 157-162.

Mac Eachron, A.E., & Krauss, M.W. (1985). Self-preservation ability and residential fire emergencies: Replication and criterion-validity study. *American Journal of Mental Deficiency, 90*, 107-110.

Matson, J.L. (1980). Preventing home accidents: A training program for the retarded. *Behavior Modification, 4*, 397-410.

Rae, R., & Roll, D. (1985). Fire safety training with adults who are profoundly retarded. *Mental Retardation, 23*, 26-30.

U.S. Department of Health, Education, and Welfare (1975). *Current estimates from the health interviewing survey.* Publication No. (HRA) 77-1543. Washington, DC: US Government Printing Office.

Home Accident Prevention Inventory

Deborah A. Tertinger, Brandon F. Greene, and John R. Lutzker

Description

The Home Accident Prevention Inventory (HAPI) measures the nature and quantity of hazardous items that are accessible to young children in the home. Five categories of hazards can be assessed using the HAPI: fire and electrical hazards, mechanical suffocation, ingested object suffocation, firearms, and solid and liquid poisons. These five categories and their subcategories are among the principal causes of accidental death in children from birth to 4 years of age, the age group most susceptible to home accidents.

The HAPI, when used by trained observers, provides the following information about the home: (a) the location of each accessible hazard, (b) which and how many subcategories of accessible hazards are present, and (c) the absolute number of accessible hazards.

The hazardous items included on the HAPI are considered dangerous only if they are accessible to the target children in the home. Accordingly, hazards are inaccessible if they: (a) are locked up using a childproof or similar locking device, (b) have child-resistant closures (childproof caps on medicines), or (c) are out of reach from either the floor level or a second level on to which the child might climb.

Purpose

The HAPI was designed to contribute to one component of a multifaceted, ecobehavioral program (Project 12 Ways) rendering treatment and prevention services to families referred for child abuse and neglect. Specifically, the HAPI was developed and validated as part of a training package designed to reduce safety hazards that were common sources of injury or death, and that parents could eliminate through simple environmental rearrangements in the home. The development of such a package was particularly important for this at risk population because the poor and unsafe conditions of the homes are often the basis for referral to child protective service agencies.

Development

The hazards included in the HAPI were identified from several different sources, primarily the 1980 edition of *Accident Facts* published by the National Safety Council. Already existing home safety checklists from a variety of organizations also were used.

The validity of the HAPI was further established by individuals associated with pediatric departments, safety commissions, and accident prevention research who completed a questionnaire consisting of 19 descriptions of hazardous situations compiled from the 26 hazards described on the HAPI. Using a scale ranging from 1 (no threat) to 5 (very serious threat), the five experts were asked to rate the 19 hazardous situations. They were also asked if they thought additional items should be included. Virtually all items were considered at least a moderate threat.

Psychometric Characteristics

Reliability of assessment was conducted at each family's home during each condition. On these occasions the reliability and the primary observers went through the home independently and used the HAPI to record the hazards.

Mean interobserver agreement on the frequency of hazards for each separate category of the HAPI (across families and categories) averaged 62%; however, agreement on the overall number of hazards (collapsing across categories of HAPI) averaged 80%.

Clinical Use

The HAPI was used with six families living in rural southern Illinois who were receiving services from Project 12 Ways. The selection criteria for these families were: the primary counselor identified home safety as one of the family's service objectives, at least one child in the home was between 1 day and 4 years old, and a parent consented to participate.

Following the collection of baseline data, parents were presented with a treatment package that included instructions and demonstrations on making hazards inaccessible to their children for each of the five categories that were targeted. This treatment package also provided feedback to the parent about the number and location of hazards within the home.

The first targeted category contained the least number of hazardous items recorded during baseline. The rationale for this was to promote the chances of parents achieving early success. The criterion for advancing to additional categories was a 50% reduction in the number of hazardous items (not subcategories) in the preceding category. If the 50% criterion was not met in the target category, modeling and practice procedures were repeated. Furthermore, if on any home check the number of hazardous items exceeded the original 50% criterion in any previously targeted categories, the parents were given feedback about these hazardous items and were asked to correct the situation; however, in these instances they were not prevented from progressing to new categories of hazards.

Follow-up visits began after the 50% reduction criterion had been met in all categories. During these home visits, parents were asked to restate the methods of making hazards inaccessible and to describe previously targeted categories. If hazardous items were found in the home, the counselor provided feedback. Parents were then asked to locate and eliminate these items while the counselor was in the home. Prompts were provided if the parent had difficulty correcting a situation. The parent received verbal praise for a low number of hazards and for correcting previously identified hazards. These unannounced follow-up checks continued until all services provided by Project 12 Ways were discontinued. The multiple-baseline design across hazardous categories in each family's home showed that the package resulted in decreases in the number of these accessible hazards. These improvements were maintained over an extended period of unannounced follow-up checks.

Future Directions

This research evolved from the findings of Dershewitz and his colleagues (Dershewitz & Williamson, 1977; Dershewitz, 1979) which indicated that parents, even those from higher socioeconomic levels than those in this study, did not make even a limited set of changes that would have made their homes safe for children. Therefore, the merits of this study are based on the demonstration that a program can be provided that has effects on parents in removing or relocating household hazards.

Perhaps the most significant contribution of this research is the demonstration that empirical procedures can be used to treat components of the deviant family systems (Lutzker, 1980) by social workers (Wahler & Graves, 1983) operating in families involved with child abuse and neglect. Indeed, this particular component, home safety, has never received such careful methodological attention and assessment.

References

Dershewitz, R.A. (1979). Will mothers use free household safety devices? *American Journal of Diseases of Children, 133,* 61-64.

Dershewitz, R.A., & Williamson, J.W. (1977). Prevention of childhood household injuries: A controlled clinical trial. *American Journal of Public Health, 67,* 1148-1153.

Lutzker, J.R. (1980). Deviant family systems. In B.B. Lahey & A.E. Kazdin (Eds.), *Advances in clinical child psychology: Vol. III* (pp. 97-148). New York: Plenum Press.

Wahler, R.G., & Graves, M.G. (1983). Setting events in social networks: Ally or enemy in child behavior therapy. *Behavior Therapy, 14,* 19-36.

Home / Clinic Coding System

Nicholas Long and Rex Forehand

Description

Direct observation of behavior is often necessary for the valid assessment of child behavior problems. Objective coding systems have been developed to quantify these types of observational data. This section will focus on one such coding system, developed at the University of Georgia, that can be used for both home- and clinic-based evaluations of noncompliant child behavior, the most prevalent type of child behavior problem (Forehand & McMahon, 1981).

This coding system was designed to assess specific child behaviors, specific parent behaviors, and parent-child interaction. The system is most appropriate for use with children 3 to 8 years old.

Observers use specially designed data sheets, divided into 30-second intervals, for recording their observations. Data are recorded sequentially, thus providing a record of the temporal relationship between behaviors. Three major categories or sequential behaviors are recorded: parental antecedents, child responses, and parental consequences.

Five types of parental antecedent behaviors are coded using this system: rewards, attends, questions, commands, and warnings. Rewards are defined as praise or approval, expressed either verbally or physically. Attends refer to verbal phrases that describe the child's behavior, appearance, or objects related to the child's activity. Questions are defined as interrogatives to which the child's appropriate response is verbal. In this coding system, two types of commands (order, suggestion, question, rule, or contingency) are coded: alpha and beta. Alpha commands refer to clear, specific commands to which the appropriate response is motoric or verbal. Beta commands, however, are commands to which compliance cannot be initiated because they are vague or the parent does not allow the child the opportunity to comply. Finally, warnings refer to "if ... then" statements in which the stated consequence is aversive.

Two types of child responses to parent alpha commands are coded: compliance and noncompliance. Compliance is recorded if the child initiates or inhibits, within 5 seconds, the motoric or verbal response specified in a parental alpha command. Noncompliance is recorded if the child does not initiate compliance within 5 seconds or fails to maintain compliance for 5 seconds.

Three types of parental consequences are recorded in response to child compliance and/or noncompliance: attends, rewards, and time-out. Attends and rewards, which must occur within 5 seconds of a compliance, are coded as previously defined. The use of time-out is coded according to whether or not this procedure was correctly implemented after noncompliance.

In addition to sequential data recording, an interval sampling technique is used to record the general appropriateness of the child's behavior. For each 30-second interval the observer rates the child's behavior as being appropriate or inappropriate. A child's behavior is rated as inappropriate if he or she exhibits whining, crying, yelling, tantrums, aggression, or deviant talk. Appropriate behavior is defined as the absence of such inappropriate behavior.

Purpose

Direct observation of behavior is important for understanding and modifying behavior. The coding system just described allows for the examination of antecedent-behavior-consequence relationships regarding noncompliant child behavior. Coding systems such as this allow information gained from direct observation to be quantified. This allows the clinician to analyze the observational information and to reach conclusions in regard to the need for treatment, the selection of treatment procedures to be used, and improvement during or after treatment. This assessment technique is also useful for researchers requiring a behavioral measure of parent–child interaction.

Development

This coding system was developed as part of a large parent-training research project (Forehand & McMahon, 1981). The parent-training program was based on behavioral formulations concerning the development and maintenance of noncompliant child behavior. The coding system assesses those parent and child behaviors believed to be important in this regard. The data obtained with this coding system were used as a major outcome measure of the effectiveness of the parent-training program.

Psychometric Characteristics

Interobserver reliability varies from .67 to 1.00 using observers who had participated in 20 hours of training in the use of the coding system (Baum & Forehand, 1981; Forehand & Peed, 1979). The coding system also possesses adequate test-retest reliability (Forehand & McMahon, 1981). In regard to validity, data obtained using the coding system have differentiated clinic-referred and nonclinic-referred children (Griest, Forehand, Wells, & McMahon, 1980). The coding system has also been found to be sensitive enough to detect treatment effects (Peed, Roberts, & Forehand, 1977). Finally, data obtained from home observations have been similar to those obtained in clinic observations (Peed et al., 1977).

Clinical Use

The coding system can be used to assess parent-child behavior in both the home and the clinic. Data obtained from these observations can be of assistance in treatment selection. The coding system is also appropriate for use as an outcome measure to evaluate the effectiveness of treatment, parent-training in particular. Data obtained using this approach often have greater validity than do more indirect measures (e.g., parent report) which are more prone to inferences and biases. The major drawback of using the coding system clinically is the length of training (20 to 25 hours) necessary to become competent with the technique.

Future Directions

More normative data are needed to assist clinicians in identifying families in need of treatment. The coding system and training procedure also will have to be modified before it would be practical for most clinicians to learn and use the measure with their clients.

References

Baum, C.G., & Forehand, R. (1981). Long term follow-up assessment of parent training by use of multiple outcome measures. *Behavior Therapy, 12,* 643-652.

Forehand, R., & McMahon, R.J. (1981). *Helping the noncompliant child: A clinician's guide to parent training.* New York: Guilford.

Forehand, R., & Peed, S. (1979). Training parents to modify noncompliant behavior of their children. In A.J. Finch, Jr. & P.C. Kendall (Eds.), *Treatment and research in child psychopathology.* New York: Spectrum.

Griest, D.L., Forehand, R., Wells, K.C., & McMahon, R.J. (1980). An examination of differences between nonclinic and behavior problem clinic-referred children and their mothers. *Journal of Abnormal Psychology, 89,* 497-500.

Peed, S., Roberts, M., & Forehand, R. (1977). Evaluation of the effectiveness of a standardized parent training program in altering the interaction of mothers and their non-compliant children. *Behavior Modification, 1,* 323-350.

Home Report

Arthur L. Robin and Sharon L. Foster

Description

The Home Report (HR) is a 14-item checklist completed daily by mothers, fathers, and adolescents (Prinz, Foster, Kent, & O'Leary, 1979). Items pertain to positive and negative interactive behavior of family members and to dyadic exchanges. Responses to 10 yes/no items in the negative direction are summed to provide an index of family conflict. In addition, family members are asked to rate the overall pleasantness of their conversations on that day on a 5-point scale called the "argument ratio." The remaining three items (fillers) are not scored. As an addendum, family members may be asked to list any specific disputes that arose during the day and to rate the anger intensity of the disputes on a 5-point scale. Each family member is given a set of addressed, stamped envelopes and instructed to complete the HR independently each evening (ordinarily for 1 week) and to mail it to the therapist the next morning. When all the HRs have been received, average scores can be computed for the Daily Conflict and Argument Ratio scores.

Purpose

The HR is designed to provide a daily report of the valence of parent–adolescent interactions to assess overall conflict in the family. It is based on the premise that daily reports of events may prove more accurate than retrospective reports based on longer intervals.

Development

The items for the HR were based on a review of the behaviors that characterized daily conflict and arguments between parents and adolescents.

Psychometric Characteristics

Only a single investigation has explored the discriminant validity of the HR. Prinz et al. (1979) collected HRs from distressed (in treatment for relationship problems) and nondistressed (not in treatment and satisfied with their relationships) mother–adolescent dyads over a 1-week interval. Conflict scores and argument ratios of both mothers and adolescents discriminated distressed from nondistressed dyads, but the degree of discrimination was relatively weak compared with that of other self-report and observational measures. Neither Foster, Prinz, and O'Leary (1983) nor Robin (1981) found the HR to be sensitive to treatment effects of a problem-solving communication skill training intervention reflected in other measures. In both studies, treatment and wait-list groups showed positive changes after the assessment. Because the correspondence between daily HRs and actual behavior has not yet been assessed, it is difficult to determine the source of these reported improvements: test-retest phenomena, acquisition of response biases, inadequate

sampling of behaviors relevant to day-to-day family conflict, or actual improvement in family interactions. It is also possible that reactivity influences the validity of home report data, particularly when HRs are collected daily over fairly long periods.

Clinical Use

The HR appears to have potential clinical use as a measure of daily conflict between parents and adolescents, but the limited validation data to date suggest that the practitioner proceed cautiously in adopting it in routine practice. Compliance can also be a problem, particularly with prolonged use, and the clinician should insure that family members understand the task, agree to complete it, set aside time to do the HR, and so forth. Contingencies for compliance (e.g., therapist praise, use of data in session, amd phone calls for inquiring about missing data) are also important. If supported by further validation research, the HR would be appropriate for use with parents and 10- to 17-year-old children, when the presenting problems involve open conflict and disagreement.

Future Directions

Further discriminant and construct validity research is needed to establish more clearly the psychometric characteristics of the HR, particularly its relationship to actual interactions. In addition, the optimal number of HRs needed to make valid inferences about interaction needs to be determined. Finally, alternative item content and administration formats might be explored. For example, an HR that borrowed 10 items that best discriminated distressed from nondistressed families and had the highest item-total correlations from a retrospective inventory such as the Conflict Behavior Questionnaire might prove superior to the current HR. Innovative administration formats such as structured telephone interviews might also prove useful (Montemayor & Hanson, 1985).

References

Foster, S.L., Prinz, R.J., & O'Leary, K.D. (1983). Impact of problem-solving communication training and generalization procedures on family conflict. *Child and Family Behavior Therapy, 5,* 1-23.

Montemayor, R., & Hanson, E. (1985). A naturalistic view of conflict between adolescents and their parents and siblings. *Journal of Early Adolescence, 5,* 23-30.

Prinz, R.J., Foster, S.L., Kent, R.N., & O'Leary, K.D. (1979). Multivariate assessment of conflict in distressed and nondistressed mother–adolescent dyads. *Journal of Applied Behavior Analysis, 12,* 691-700.

Robin, A.L. (1981). A controlled evaluation of problem-solving communication training with parent–adolescent conflict. *Behavior Therapy, 12,* 593-609.

Hopelessness Scale

Robert T. Ammerman

Description

The Hopelessness Scale (HS) is a 20-item true/false format questionnaire designed to measure negative expectancies and pessimism about the future. It consists of a series of statements concerning one's self and one's future such as, "I look forward to the future with hope and enthusiasm," and "Things just won't work out the way I want them to." A scoring key yields a summative score between 0 and 2, indicating the degree of hopelessness.

Purpose

Hopelessness is a core feature of depression, as well as a correlate of other forms of psychopathology (e.g., schizophrenia and sociopathy). In particular, it is a primary component of suicidal intent (Beck, Kovacs, & Weissman, 1975). Despite its acknowledged importance in a variety of disorders, few empirical investigations have examined the construct. To facilitate research on hopelessness, Beck, Weissman, Lester, and Trexler (1974) designed a scale to measure and quantify negative expectancy. The HS is the product of this endeavor.

Development

Two sources were used to generate items for the HS: (a) a semantic differential test of attitudes about the future, and (b) statements from psychiatric patients who were judged by clinicians as feeling hopeless. To refine the items, the HS was administered to a random sample of depressed and nondepressed patients. In addition, several clinicians reviewed the HS for content validity and comprehensibility. On the basis of these opinions, the final form was constructed with 9 true and 11 false items.

Psychometric Characteristics

To examine the reliability of the HS, Beck et al. (1974) administered the test to 294 psychiatric inpatients who had made recent suicide attempts. Internal consistency was high, with the HS yielding a reliability coefficent (KR-20) of .93. Item-total correlations ranged from .39 to .76. Durham (1982) administered the HS to three groups: (a) male forensic psychiatric inpatients, (b) general psychiatric patients, and (c) college students. Results indicated higher KR-20 coefficients for psychiatric (.83 and .86, respectively) as compared with college (.65) groups. The lower reliability for students was partly attributable to the restricted range employed by the sample.

A principal components factor analysis with varimax rotation yielded three interpretable factors (Beck et al., 1974). The first factor, Feelings About the Future (41.7% of the variance), reflects happiness, enthusiasm, and hope about the future. The second factor, Loss of Motivation (6.2% of the variance), consists of items related to giving up and not trying to get something that is wanted. The third factor, Future Expectations (5.6% of the variance), reflects negative expectancies of what life will be like in the future.

Research supports the concurrent and construct validity of the HS. Correlations between global clinical ratings of hopelessness and the HS are high in psychiatric and suicidal patients (Beck et al., 1974). Likewise, there is a positive correlation between the HS and the pessimism item of the Beck Depression Inventory (.63) and the Stuart Future Test (.60; Beck et al., 1974). The HS also correlates highly with suicidal intent. Indeed, the positive relationship between depression and suicidality is reduced when the effect of hopelessness is statistically controlled (Beck et al., 1975).

Indications are that the HS may be confounded by a socially desirable response set. For example, using a psychiatric sample, Mendonca, Holden, Mazmanian, and Dolan (1983) found a negative correlation (− .71) between the HS and the Desirability Scale of Jackson's Personality Research Form. In addition, when desirability was statistically controlled, differences between suicidal and nonsuicidal patients on the HS were nonsignificant. Nevid (1983), however, pointed out that a negative correlation with social desirability does not necessarily indicate a confound unless it is theoretically inconsistent with the hopelessness construct. Future research examining the discriminability between the HS and desirability is required to determine if a confound exists.

Clinical Use

The HS is appropriate for use with a variety of psychiatric populations in which hopelessness is an important component. It is particularly useful in identifying suicidal patients.

Future Directions

There is a need for continued research on the HS with additional clinical populations. Normative data as well as reliability and validity studies with specific psychiatric groups are required. Likewise, the relationship between hopelessness and demographic characteristics (sex, age, SES, etc.) should be further examined. Such information would help determine the generalizability of the HS.

References

Beck, A.T., Kovacs, M., & Weissman, A. (1975). Hopelessness and suicidal behavior. *Journal of the American Medical Association, 234,* 1146-1149.

Beck, A.T., Weissman, A., Lester, D., & Trexler, L. (1974). The measurement of pessimism: The Hopelessness Scale. *Journal of Consulting and Clinical Psychology, 42,* 861-865.

Durham, T.W. (1982). Norms, reliability, and item analysis of the Hopelessness Scale in general psychiatric, forensic psychiatric, and college populations. *Journal of Clinical Psychology, 38,* 597-600.

Mendonca, J.D., Holden, R.R., Mazmanian, D., & Dolan, J. (1983). The influence of response style on the Beck Hopelessness Scale. *Canadian Journal of Behavioural Science, 15,* 237-247.

Nevid, J.S. (1983). Hopelessness, social desirability, and construct validity. *Journal of Consulting and Clinical Psychology, 51,* 139-140.

Hospital Fears Rating Scale

Barbara G. Melamed and Mark A. Lumley

Description

The Hospital Fears Rating Scale (HFRS) is a self-report measure of situational anxiety related to medical and hospital concerns. This 25-item scale contains eight items from the Medical Fears subscale which was factor analyzed from the Fear Survey Schedule for Children (FSS-FC) designed by Scherer and Nakamura (1968). These items include: (1) sharp objects, (2) having to go to the hospital, (3) going to the dentist, (4) going to the doctor, (5) getting a shot, (6) getting a haircut, (7) getting car sick, and (8) deep water or the ocean. Another eight items with face validity for assessing hospital fears include: (1) germs or getting seriously ill, (2) the sight of blood, (3) being alone without your parents, (4) having an operation, (5) getting a cut or injury, (6) getting sick at school, (7) not being able to breathe, and (8) persons wearing masks. Finally, nine other nonmedically related "filler" fear items are included: (1) spiders, (2) making mistakes, (3) going to bed in the dark, (4) strange or mean looking dogs, (5) flying in an airplane, (6) getting punished, (7) thunderstorms, (8) ghosts or spooky things, and (9) falling from high places. The HFRS is a 5-point Likert scale, and each item is rated as to how fearful the child is of it. A value of 1 equals not afraid at all and 5 equals very afraid. To assist young children in their ratings, a visual aid known as the Fear Thermometer can be used to allow the children to point to one of the five sections of the thermometer corresponding to the level of their fear for the item just presented. The sum of the ratings of the 16 medically related items is the child's total score for the scale.

Purpose

Fear of anxiety is considered to be a multidimensional construct consisting of behavioral, self-report, and psychophysiological manifestations. A thorough assessment of one's fear needs to measure these three domains. The HFRS is intended to assess the self-report or subjective modality of state, or situational, medically related fear in children. When used in conjunction with behavioral observations and, when possible, psychophysiological recordings, a determination of a child's fear regarding hospitals and medical situations can be determined. This assessment can then be used in selecting a fear reduction technique or in evaluating a treatment implemented to reduce fear levels.

Development

Scherer and Nakamura (1968) constructed the FSS-FC using factor analytic techniques, and produced 10 subscales of children's fears, including a factor they called "Medical Fears." Melamed and Siegel (1975) developed a self-report measure of medically related fears to accompany their observational (Observer Rating Scale of Anxiety) and physiological (Palmar Sweat Index) measures of anxiety in children facing hospitalization and surgery. They selected the eight items from the Medical Fears subscale because of their known validity. They then added eight other items that had face validity for fears of the hospital setting. Finally, nine items that were believed to arouse fear and anxiety in children but that were unrelated to the medical setting were included so as to decrease the scale's appearance as a measurement tool of hospital fears alone. The result was the 25-item HFRS.

Psychometric Characteristics

Several studies have made use of the HFRS, and its validity as a measure of situational fear of the medical setting has been demonstrated. Melamed and Siegel (1975) found a significant difference in self-reported fears both preoperatively ($p < .01$) and postoperatively ($p < .01$) between experimental groups that saw a hospital-relevant modeling film and a control group that saw an unrelated film. Moreover, younger children reported greater fear than older children regardless of the experimental condition ($p < .04$). This last observation was also noted by Melamed, Dearborn, and Hermecz (1983), who additionally found that higher fear reports correlated positively with medical outcome, including the number of disruptive behaviors displayed in the operating room ($r = .48$, $p < .06$) and the number of days spent in recovery ($r = .54, p < .008$).

Ferguson (1979) studied two methods of preparing children aged 3 to 7 years for hospitalization. She found the HFRS to be a valid and sensitive measure between groups and across assessment periods ($p < .01$). Furthermore, significant differences were found for age ($p < .01$), time of assessment ($p < .01$), and age-time interaction ($p < .001$).

Finally, Faust and Melamed (1984) found that same-day surgery patients showed a much larger reduction in anticipatory medical concerns, as measured with the HFRS, after viewing an unrelated film as compared with a hospital-relevant film.

Only one study has reported reliability data on the HFRS. Melamed et al. (1983) report test-retest reliability of 0.75 ($p < .004$).

Clinical Use

The HFRS can be used to assess a child's self-report of situational anxiety regarding fears relevant to the hospital or medical setting. The results of this assessment can then be used to determine the necessity and type of fear-reduction techniques useful for the child. The HFRS can also be used in research protocols that seek to determine the variables related to medical fears such as age, sex, and time and type of treatment. Ideally, observational and physiological recordings should be conducted as well.

Future Directions

Research into children's hospital and medical fears should continue to use the HFRS as one of a battery of instruments. In this way, variables that are relevant for fear-reduction interventions can be examined thoroughly. Second, the reliability and validity of this scale (or a slightly modified version with several adult-directed word changes) with adults should be examined.

References

Faust, J., & Melamed, B.G. (1984). Influence of arousal, previous experience, and age on surgery preparation of same day surgery and in-hospital pediatric patients. *Journal of Consulting and Clinical Psychology, 52,* 359-365.

Ferguson, B.F. (1979). Preparing young children for hospitalization: A comparison of two methods. *Pediatrics, 64,* 656-664.

Melamed, B.G., Dearborn, M., & Hermecz, D.A. (1983). Necessary considerations for surgery preparation: Age and experience. *Psychosomatic Medicine, 45,* 517-525.

Melamed, B.G., & Siegel, L.J. (1975). Reduction of anxiety in children facing hospitalization and surgery by use of filmed modeling. *Journal of Consulting and Clinical Psychology, 43,* 511-521.

Scherer, M.W., & Nakamura, C.Y. (1968). A fear survey schedule for children (FSS-FC): A factor analytic comparison with manifest anxiety (CMAS). *Behaviour Research and Therapy, 6,* 173-182.

Hostility and Direction of Hostility Questionnaire

Paul M.G. Emmelkamp

Description

The Hostility and Direction of Hostility Questionnaire (HDHQ) (Caine, Foulds, & Hope, 1967) was designed to sample a wide range of possible manifestations of aggression, hostility, or punitiveness. It consists of 51 items culled from the MMPI and comprises five subscales, namely, urge to act out hostility (AH), criticism of others (CO), projected delusional or paranoid hostility (PH), self-criticism (SC), and delusional guilt (DG). The first three subscales are summed to form an extrapunitive score, and the latter two are summed to yield an intropunitive score. A *direction of hostility* score may be obtained from a formula in which the sum of the three extrapunitive scales (AH + CO + PH) is balanced by substracting it from the sum of *twice* the SC score and the DG score: Direction of Hostility (DH = 2 SC + DG) minus (AH + CO + PH). Positive scores therefore indicate intropunitiveness, whereas scores in a negative direction indicate extrapunitiveness.

Purpose

This questionnaire may be used to study various components of hostility and to evaluate treatment outcome. It does not seem to be particularly suited for diagnostic purposes.

Development

Caine et al. (1967) factor analyzed the data of 169 neurotic persons and found five subscales clearly represented. A modified version of the method of criterion groups was used to validate the questionnaire. Persons with paranoid schizophrenia scored at the extrapunitive end, depressed persons at the intropunitive end, and persons with nonparanoid schizophrenia scored in between. Normal persons were extrapunitive relative to neurotic persons. Paranoid schizophrenic persons appeared to be more extrapunitive than did normal subjects (Caine et al., 1967).

Psychometric Characteristics

Arrindell, Hafkenscheid, and Emmelkamp (1984) factor analyzed the data of approximately 300 psychiatric outpatients. The loadings of the items of the extrapunitive subscales confirmed the original analysis of Caine et al. (1967). However, only 64 and 57% of the items relating to self-criticism and delusional guilt, respectively, were found to load more strongly on their corresponding factors than on conceptually distinct ones. No confirmation was found for the existence of self-criticism and delusional guilt as separate scales. Actually, the interscale correlation was .97. Cronbach's coefficient alpha was employed as an internal consistency estimate of composite scale reliability. The subscale reliabilities attained satisfactory values. The *extra* and *intro* scales' reliabilities proved to be very satisfactory.

To determine construct validity of the HDHQ, its subscales were correlated with other measures. A clear difference in correlational patterns emerged for the *extra* versus *intro* scales. As predicted, the *extra* scale correlated highly (r = .78) with the Anger-Hostility scale of the SCL-90, whereas the *intro* did not. Furthermore, substantial relationships were shown between the *intro* scale on the one hand and the SCL-90 depression scale on the other. Shyness and unassertiveness appeared to be related to the *intro* scale and not to the *extra* scale. Finally, HDHQ scores did not appear to be highly affected by social desirability.

It is questionable whether the delusional guilt scales and self-criticism scales can continue to be used as separate dimensions, because they were found to be highly related. The data of the Arrindell et al. (1984) study do not justify use of a General Hostility Score as an index of treatment effects. It is possible for a total hostility score to be disproportionately influenced by a relatively irrelevant dimension.

Clinical Use

Although this questionnaire may be used to assess the effects of treatment, it is not particularly suited as a diagnostic instrument, except perhaps in a supplementary capacity.

Future Directions

Future research with the HDHQ may follow several avenues that have been outlined by Arrindell et al. (1984). First, studies on changes in hostility levels in clinical samples during treatment may throw light on predictive, concurrent, and some degree of discriminant (construct) validity of the subscales, provided that behavioral measures are gathered as well. Second, related to this, research that might clarify the degree of occasion sensitivity of the HDHQ scales is badly needed. It should be noted that the paranoid hostility and delusional guilt subscales contain symptom-like items. To deal with this problem, rigorous methodology is available. Finally, use of the Campbell and Fiske (1966) multitrait-multimethod matrix for determining convergent and discriminant validity (by means of intercorrelating scales measuring a number of traits and each employing several methods) may contribute to a better understanding of the usefulness of the HDHQ as an assessment technique for clinical and research purposes.

References

Arrindell, W.A., Hafkenscheid, A.J.P.M., & Emmelkamp, P.M.G. (1984). The Hostility and Direction of
Hostility Questionnaire (HDHQ): A psychometric
evaluation in psychiatric outpatients. *Journal of Personality and Individual Differences, 5,* 221-231.

Caine, T.M., Foulds, G.A., & Hope, K. (1967). *Manual of
the Hostility and Direction of Hostility Questionnaire
(HDHQ).* London: University of London Press.

Campbell, D.T., & Fiske, D.W. (1966). Convergent and
discriminant validation by the multitrait-multimethod matrix. In E.I. Megargee (Ed.), *Research in
clinical assessment.* New York: Harper & Row.

Impact of Event Scale

Andrea L. Seidner, Angelynee E. Amick, and Dean G. Kilpatrick

Description

The Impact of Event Scale (IES) (Horowitz,
Wilner, & Alvarez, 1979) is a 15-item self-report
instrument used to measure two key elements of
Post-Traumatic Stress Disorder (PTSD): event-
related intrusion (intrusively experienced ideas,
images, feelings, or dreams) and event-related
avoidance (consciously recognized avoidance of
certain ideas, feelings, or situations). Respondents
indicate the frequency with which they have
experienced each item during the preceding week.
The IES is scored by assigning a value of 0, 1, 3, or 5
to each item for a frequency response of not at all,
rarely, sometimes, or often, respectively. In
addition to a global distress mean, intrusion and
avoidance subscale means are calculated.

Purpose

The purpose of the IES is to provide a psychometrically sound self-report of psychological sequelae of traumatic experiences for both research
and clinical purposes. The measure operationalizes
the Horowitz et al. (1979) information processing
model of posttraumatic stress response and is relevant for experiences such as combat, crime, natural
disasters, personal injury, and death of a significant
other.

Development

Initial scale construction used a clinically based,
rational approach. As Horowitz et al. (1979)
described, the initial pool of items was derived

from descriptions of distress by individuals seeking
treatment for posttraumatic symptoms. Items were
divided into two subgroups, based on clinical judgment, corresponding to the themes of intrusion and
avoidance of event-related thoughts, feelings, and
situations. Various forms of the item list were
adminstered over a period of years to patient and
nonpatient victims of traumatic events, with
appropriate revisions in wording, format, and time
frame of response.

In the next phase of development, a pilot form of
the IES was evaluated to determine: (a) the frequency of item endorsement in a new group of
patients with PTSD, (b) whether the logical subscale division would be empirically supported, and
(c) the internal reliability of the scale (psychometric outcomes of pilot testing are presented in
the section on Psychometric Characteristics). The
pilot form consisted of 9 intrusion and 11 avoidance
items, rated for frequency and intensity of occurrence in the preceding week. The sample consisted
of 66 adults (16 male and 50 female; age range, 29 to
75 years; mean age, 34; lower-middle to middle
social class) referred to an outpatient clinic specializing in stress response symptoms at the University
of California. Thirty-four participants had experienced bereavement secondary to loss of a significant other. The remaining 32 suffered personal
injury from accidents, violence, illness, or surgery.
Subjects completed the IES after an initial interview, with the time elapsed since their event ranging from 1 to 136 weeks (mean = 25 weeks).

A cluster analysis resulted in the identification of
two main clusters composed of 15 of the 20 original
items, which corresponded to the logically derived
subgroups. These 15 items had significant item-to-
subscale correlations ($p < .01$) and were retained
for the final form of the IES. The remaining five
items, which clustered into two residual groups
with nonsignificant item-to-scale correlations,
were deleted. Because frequency and intensity
scores were found to be highly similar, only the frequency rating was retained, based on the authors'
clinical impression of greater subject accuracy on
this variable.

Psychometric Characteristics

On the basis of the administration of the IES to the
bereavement/personal injury sample described
previously, Horowitz et al. (1979) reported a high
split-half reliability for the total scale ($r = .86$) and
internal consistency of the subscales (Cronbach's

alpha: intrusion = .78 and avoidance = .80). The high item endorsement of frequency (38.85%) supported relevancy of item content. A moderate correlation between the subscales ($r = .42, p < .0002$) suggested that related but distinguishable dimensions were being measured. Acceptable test-retest reliability (1-week testing interval) was found upon administration of the IES to a sample of 25 physical therapy students 4 weeks after their first cadaver dissection (total scale, $r = .87$; intrusion, $r = .89$; avoidance, $r = .79$).

The sensitivity of the IES to changes in symptoms over time was demonstrated in a subset of the bereavement/personal injury sample. Following brief therapy to alleviate stress response symptoms, 32 of these patients were readministered the IES (mean = 11 weeks; range, 4 to 31 weeks). Congruent with clinical judgments and subjective reports of positive gains, t tests ($p < .05$) revealed statistically significant pre- and posttreatment improvements on all individual items as well as on global and subscale scores.

The IES was also found to accurately distinguish between reactions to contrasted types of trauma. Thus, the bereavement/personal injury group showed more severe distress on subscale and overall means than did a group of freshmen medical students (75 male and 35 female) exposed to their first cadaver dissection 4 weeks previously.

Zilberg, Weiss, and Horowitz (1982) conducted a cross-validation study of a patient group ($n = 35$) and a field group ($n = 37$) of adults who had recently experienced the death of a parent. The patient group was assessed before 12 weeks of dynamically oriented psychotherapy (mean time since event = 25.7 weeks) and at 4 and 12 months after treatment termination. The field subjects were assessed at entry into the study (mean time since event = 7.7 weeks) and at 7 and 13 months after the event. The groups differed significantly on a number of demographic and event-related variables, including age, marital status, gender composition, and time interval since event. No significant differences were found on socioeconomic status or incidence of the death of the mother versus father.

The ability of the IES to distinguish contrasted groups was supported by significant differences (t tests, $p < .01$) between patient and field groups in the expected direction on most individual items and on both subscale scores. Again, the IES also was found to sensitively reflect changes over time. Correlated t tests ($p < .025$) revealed sensitivity to change across evaluation intervals in both field and patient groups.

Finally, a data-based rationale was presented to support the use of separate subscale scores as opposed to a total distress score. Briefly, a low subscale correlation was found at pretreatment evaluation of the patient group, whereas high correlations were found for the nonpatient and posttreatment groups. The authors indicate this is consistent with Horowitz's (1976) theory of stress response syndromes, which associates most problematic adjustment with asynchrony between event-related cognitive intrusions and avoidance strategies. In contrast, the predicted relationship between appropriate adjustment and cyclical alteration between avoidance and intrusion phases was supported among nonpatient and posttreatment groups. Therefore, to preserve the sensitivity of the scale to both intrusion and avoidance processes, the authors recommend use of separate subscale scores.

Clinical Use

The IES has been an efficacious measure of posttraumatic adjustment in crime victims and other personal injury victims, combat veterans, and bereaved individuals. One of the most extensive applications of the IES has been its use in the assessment and treatment of rape victims. Kilpatrick and Veronen (1984a) employed the IES in a longitudinal assessment of rape-induced trauma (female victims, aged 16 or older, $n = 75$) at 6 to 21 days, 3 months, 6 months, 1 year, and 2 years after rape. They found rape victims to report substantial distress at the initial assessment intrusion (mean = 23.8, avoidance mean = 26.0), reflecting an acute state of PTSD. Over time, scores on both subscales declined but still remained fairly high at 2 years after the assault (intrusion mean = 11.4, avoidance mean = 16.0), suggesting a chronic impact on adjustment.

Kilpatrick and Veronen (1984b) also reported utility of the IES as a treatment outcome measure among adult rape victims ($n = 11$) who participated in a Stress Inoculation Training treatment program. A significant decline in scores on the intrusion subscale was found when a repeated measures ANOVA was performed comparing pretreatment and 3-month follow-up scores.

Wilson, Smith, and Johnson (1985) recently employed the IES in a comparative analysis of victims of various traumatic life events (combat, divorce, violent crimes, natural disasters, and family trauma such as alcoholism, mental illness, and death). Results revealed the use of the IES in significantly differentiating among various trauma groups and in distinguishing persons who lost a significant other from persons who did not experience such a loss.

Future Directions

The IES shows promise both in delineating distress subsequent to a traumatic event and in assessing treatment outcome. One research area of considerable theoretical import is further investigation of the interplay between the intrusion and avoidance processes measured by the scale. For instance, does a particular pattern or style of cognitive processing co-vary with behavioral or physiological indicators of adjustment to trauma? Does the pattern of cognitive processing vary predictably as a function of time since trauma or type of trauma?

Finally, treatment implications of IES data must be explored. Once an appropriate cognitive processing style is defined, then cognitive behavioral interventions might be designed to approximate a healthy intrusion/avoidance balance. For example, a posttraumatic individual assessed as overly avoidant of event-related stimuli might be guided in overt or covert exposure techniques, whereas debilitating event-related intrusions might be brought into an adaptive range through thought-stopping techniques.

References

Horowitz, M.J. (1976). *Stress response syndromes.* New York: Jason Aronson.

Horowitz, M., Wilner, N., & Alvarez, W. (1979). Impact of event scale: A measure of subjective distress. *Psychosomatic Medicine, 41,* 209-218.

Kilpatrick, D.G., & Veronen, L.J. (1984a, March). *Rape and post-traumatic stress disorder: A two-year longitudinal study.* Paper presented at the annual meeting of the American Psychosomatic Society, Hilton Head, SC.

Kilpatrick, D.G., & Veronen, L.J. (1984b). *Treatment of fear and anxiety in victims of rape* (Final Report, Grant No. R01 MH29602). Rockville, MD: National Institute of Mental Health.

Wilson, J.P., Smith, W.K., & Johnson, S.K. (1985). A comparative analysis of PTSD among various survivor groups. In C.R. Figley (Ed.), *Trauma and its wake* (pp. 142-172). New York: Brunner/Mazel.

Zilberg, N.J., Weiss, D.S., & Horowitz, M.J. (1982). Impact of event scale: A cross-validation study and some empirical evidence supporting a conceptual model of stress response syndromes. *Journal of Consulting and Clinical Psychology, 50,* 407-414.

Individualized Behavioral Avoidance Test

Chris M. Adler and David H. Barlow

Description

The Individualized Behavioral Avoidance Test (IBAT) assesses the degree of fear and avoidance exhibited by a patient in his or her own home environment. Before this test, the patient and therapist together develop a 10-item individualized fear and avoidance hierarchy. Following this, the therapist will arrange to conduct a session at the patient's home. During this session, the therapist will ask the patient to attempt to carry out five different fear-eliciting behaviors, selected from their fear and avoidance hierarchy. The five items selected should span the range from mildly to severely anxiety provoking. The therapist assigns tasks in order of their difficulty, with easier tasks (those with lower anxiety ratings) being assigned first. To minimize anticipatory anxiety, the therapist should avoid presenting more than one task at a time. Although patients have the option to refuse any item, they are encouraged to enter each situation and carry out the task unless "undue anxiety" is experienced.

A patient's performance on the IBAT is scored by the therapist on a 3-point scale: refusing to attempt an item (avoidance) = 0; beginning an item and not successfully completing it (escape) = 1; and successfully completing an item (performance to criteria) = 2. The patient's score on each of the five assigned tasks is summed to provide a single behavioral performance score, ranging from 0 to 10. This measure allows direct assessment of behavioral functioning in the patient's own environment.

In addition to the behavioral performance score, the IBAT also provides a measure of subjective anxiety during the test. Immediately after a patient has attempted or completed each of the IBAT items, a SUDS score is recorded, reflecting the patient's self-report of maximum anxiety. A subjective measure of coping ability can also be included to further broaden the IBAT assessment.

Purpose

The primary purpose of the individualized behavioral avoidance test is to allow the simultaneous assessment of subjective and behavioral components of anxiety on exposure to life-relevant anxiety-provoking situations. When used before and after treatment, the IBAT is a particularly useful tool for analyzing the effects of treatment on actual behavioral flexibility as well as on the patient's subjective report. The information obtained in the IBAT is also valuable when designing exposure sessions throughout treatment.

Development

The IBAT was developed by Agras, Leitenberg, and Barlow (1968). Over a period of years, this test has been used and refined by the staff of the Phobia and Anxiety Disorders Clinic, of the State University of New York at Albany. The Clinic is funded by the National Institute of Mental Health to study the classification and treatment of anxiety disorders. The patient instructions and assessment procedures have evolved over several years' experience in the assessment and treatment of agoraphobic patients.

Clinical Use

The IBAT is designed as an in vivo assessment of subjective and behavioral anxiety components in agoraphobic patients. As an assessment tool, the IBAT is of most use with patients who display moderate to severe fear and avoidance in a variety of situations.

Future Directions

With technological advances, such as the vitalog portable monitor, the use of the IBAT can be further broadened by including such physiological measures of anxiety as heart rate, breathing rate, and Galvanic Skin Response.

References

Agras, W.S., Leitenberg, H., & Barlow, D.H. (1968). Social reinforcement in the modification of agoraphobia. *Archives of General Psychiatry, 19,* 423-427.

Instrument to Measure Knowledge of Behavioral Principles as Applied to Children

Stan L. O'Dell

Description

The Knowledge of Behavioral Principles as Applied to Children (KBPAC) instrument is a 50-item multiple forced-choice test designed to assess

understanding of the application of basic behavioral principles with children. Administration requires 30 to 60 minutes. The questions avoid behavioral vocabulary, and most present practical problem situations to which the respondent is to select the response that has the greatest probability of producing the desired effect. Other issues covered include basic behavioral assumptions about behavioral change, principles in the use of reinforcement and punishment, schedules, shaping, counting and recording, differential attention, and extinction.

Purpose

The purpose of the instrument is to help clinicians and researchers assess an adult's verbal understanding of basic behavioral principles as they are applied to children.

Development

The questions were based on a tally of 60 behavioral principles found in the four texts: "Parents Are Teachers" (Becker, 1971), "Managing Behavior 2" (Hall, 1971), "Living With Children" (Patterson & Gullion, 1968), and "Families" (Patterson, 1971). An initial set of 105 questions was written, and each was rated on a 5-point Likert scale by four PhD behavioral psychologists. Questions were rated for clarity and how well each represented one of the principles. The 70 most highly rated questions were selected to be administered to the first group of respondents, and many items were modified according to suggestions made by the raters.

The first sample of 102 respondents included persons whose responses to a self-report questionnaire showed they ranged from never having heard of behavior modification to having taught the subject in graduate school. They primarily included parents in the community plus teachers and university students in undergraduate and graduate classes. Educational level ranged from eighth grade to a doctorate degree, with a median level of high school.

The responses of the subjects were used to select 41 of the 70 items that had the highest point-biserial correlations with the overall test (all over 0.30) and the highest overall ratings. The distribution of responses to incorrect items was analyzed and used to provide information for further improving items by writing better distractors.

An additional set of 64 new items was developed and rated by behavioral psychologists; the 29 most highly rated of these items were added to the aforementioned 41 items to yield a second set of 70 items for further analysis. This set of 70 items was administered to a new sample of 147 persons who were targeted as respondents because of their varied experience with behavior modification. The sample included parents from a local school, parents receiving services at a psychological clinic, members of a civic organization, local teachers, graduate students in psychology, and mental health professionals. There were 109 women, and the median educational level of the sample was two years of college. The mean age of respondents was 30.2 years and ranged from 17 to 65 years. The 50 items with the highest point-biserial correlations with the total score (all >0.30, mean = 0.49) were retained to comprise the final instrument.

Psychometric Characteristics

The data from the second sample of respondents produced the following values: mean = 24.4; SD = 11.75; and SE = .97. The Kuder-Richardson reliability coefficient was 0.94, and the odd-even split-half correlation was 0.93.

Content validity of the instrument is based on the assumption that the texts from which the principles are derived represent the set of behavioral principles most frequently required of persons who will work on behavioral programs with children. All of the 60 principles were represented by at least one question in the initial set of questions. However, elimination of questions by raters and statistical procedures resulted in only approximately 70% of the principles being represented in the final set of 50 questions. Therefore, the instrument is not diagnostic of all individual principles covered in the texts previously mentioned.

Before taking the test, respondents were asked to answer "yes" or "no" to 10 questions related to their past involvement with behavior modification. Examples are: "Have you ever heard the phrase *behavior modification*?," "Have you ever read a book about behavior modification?," and "Have you ever taught behavior modification?" One point was given for each of the 10 questions to which the person answered "yes." The correlation between this self-report measure and the total score on the instrument was 0.63 and decreased to 0.53 when the effect of the educational level was reduced through covariation techniques. Twenty-five parents who volunteered for a child management workshop were administered the instrument before and after training (O'Dell, Flynn, & Benlolo, 1977). Thirty-four were women with a mean age of 35 years; modal educational level was completion of high school, and mean IQ was 102. They were given 5 hours of training in behavioral principles using lectures, films, discussion, and an assignment to read the book "Families" (Patterson, 1971). Their mean percentage correct on odd-even split-halves of the instrument increased pre-post from 48 to 85%. Four other samples of undergraduate university students, approximately one third of whom were psychology majors, yielded an additional sample of 91. They were provided training similar to that of the aforementioned parents; their mean percentage correct on split-halves of the instrument increased pre-post from 57 to 85%.

Clinical Use

This instrument's most likely clinical application is in child intervention, when the therapist believes an adult client should possess a general knowledge of behavioral principles before implementation of the treatment program. The results can provide guidance concerning whether the client will need formal training in such principles and to what extent.

No normative data are yet available on parents who request training or on what score reflects an "acceptable" level of knowledge. It should be stressed that it would not be appropriate to make behavioral inferences from scores on the instrument, because verbal knowledge of behavioral principles may not relate to actual skills with children.

Future Directions

A revised version of this instrument is in progress. The revision will be similar in format but will provide improved content validity and face validity of the questions.

References

Becker, W.C. (1971). *Parents are teachers*. Champaign, IL: Research Press.

Hall, R.V. (1971). *Managing behavior 2*. Lawrence, KS: H. & H. Enterprises.

O'Dell, S., Flynn, J., & Benlolo, L. (1977). A comparison of parent training techniques in child behavior modification. *Journal of Behavior Therapy and Experimental Psychiatry, 8*, 261-268.

Patterson, G.R., & Gullion, M.E. (1968). *Living with children*. Champaign, IL: Research Press.
Patterson, G.R. (1971). *Families*. Champaign, IL: Research Press.

Interaction Coding System (Kategoriensystem fur partnerschaftliche Interaktion)

Kurt Hahlweg

Description

The Interaction Coding System (ICS) (Kategoriensystem fur partnerschaftliche Interaktion; KPI) was developed by Hahlweg et al. (1984) to code marital and family interactions.

The aim of the ICS is to assess empirically the communication skills that are the basis of many communication skills training programs (Hahlweg, Revenstorf, & Schindler, 1984). Although different programs differ somewhat with regard to content and technique, there are some common assumptions. General communication will be enhanced when the family members use the following skills: (a) speaker skills: use "I" messages, describe specific behaviors in specific situations, and stick to the "here and now"; (b) listener skills: listen actively, summarize your partner's remarks and check their accuracy, ask open questions, and give positive feedback. Family members who employ these skills in turn should avoid blaming, criticizing, and side-tracking and should increase their mutual understanding. The core skills are reciprocal self-disclosure of feelings, attitudes, and thoughts and accepting (not necessarily agreeing with) the partner's utterances.

Coding Unit. The basic unit is a verbal response that is homogeneous in content without regard to its duration or syntactical structure. For each content code a nonverbal rating (negative, neutral, and positive) is assigned (Gottman, 1979; Notarius & Markman, 1981). In case of a sequence of codes for one speaker, a listening code (LI) with the nonverbal rating is assigned to the listener, thus guaranteeing alternate coding.

Description of Categories. The following 12 positive, neutral, and negative categories have been derived primarily from the aforementioned communication skills and were supplemented by some of the more salient categories and definitions

from other coding systems, notably the Marital Interaction Coding System (Hops, Wills, Patterson, & Weiss, 1972), Couples Interaction Scoring System (Gottman, 1979), and the coding system for interpersonal communication (Wegener, Revenstorf, Hahlweg, & Schindler, 1979). (1) Self-disclosure (SD): There are two types of SD: (a) direct expression of feelings (e.g., "I am too angry to listen to you at the moment"), and (b) direct expression of wishes and needs (e.g., "I would like to go fishing tomorrow"). (2) Positive solution (PS): (a) specific, constructive proposals (e.g., "I'll sweep the floor if you play with the kids"), and (b) compromises. (3) Acceptance of the other (AC): (a) paraphrase (e.g., "You are saying that the kids are too young to go to the kindergarten"), (b) open questions (e.g., "Are you still unhappy?"), and (c) positive feedback (e.g., "I liked the way you started the discussion"). (4) Agreement (AG): (a) direct agreement (e.g., "Yes, that is right"), (b) acceptance of responsibility (e.g., "I was responsible for the quarrel"), and (c) assent ("yes" or "o.k."). (5) Problem description (PD): This code includes neutral descriptions of the problem (e.g., "I think we have got a problem with the kids") or neutral questions (e.g., "Did the car break down yesterday?"). (6) Meta-communication (MC): (a) clarification requests (e.g., "Would you say that again, please") and (b) meta-communication related to topic (e.g., "We are getting away from the issue"). (7) Rest category (RC): RC is coded when a statement (a) does not fit into any other verbal code or (b) is inaudible. (8) Listening (LI): LI is coded for the listener when double-coding of the speaker occurs. (9) Criticize (CRI): (a) when the speaker's intention is to hurt, demean, or embarrass the listener in a global way (e.g., "You are lazy") and (b) when the speaker expresses his or her dislike or disapproval of a specific behavior of the listener (e.g., "Yesterday you wasted money" or "The car broke down because you forgot to take it to the garage"). (10) Negative solution (NS): NS is coded when the speaker describes something he or she would like the other *not* to do in order to solve a problem (e.g., "You shouldn't sleep all day"). (11) Justification (JU): (a) excuse of own behavior (e.g., "I had a lot of things to do yesterday") and (b) denying of responsibility (e.g., "That is not my job"). (12) Disagreement (DG): (a) direct disagreement (e.g., "No, that is not true"), (b) Yes, but (e.g., "Yes, you are right, but we don't have the money"), and (c) short disagreeing statements (e.g., "No" or "What? ").

Nonverbal Codes. All of the foregoing content categories receive a nonverbal rating (Gottman, 1979; Notarius & Markman, 1981). In a hierarchical order, first the facial cues of the speaker or listener are evaluated as positive, neutral, or negative. If the coder is unable to code the utterance as positive or negative, the body cues are scanned and then the appropriate rating is applied.

Reduction of Categories. To apply sequential analysis, the 12 categories can be collapsed into 6 (reduction I) and 4 (reduction II) summary codes. The reduction is based on content and yields the following codes: Reduction I: Self-disclosure (SD) and positive solution (PS) are collapsed into direct express (DE), acceptance of partner (AC) and agreement (AG), and positive or neutral listening (LI + LIO) into acceptance and agreement (AA). Criticize (CRI) and negative solution (NS) are collapsed into critique (CR), disagreement (DG), justification (JU), and negative listening (LI-) into refusal (RF). Problem description (PD) and metacommunication (MC) are collapsed into neutral information (NI). The rest category (RC) remains uncollapsed. Reduction II: The positive codes DE and AA are collapsed into positive communication (PC), the negative codes CR and RF into negative communication (NC), and NI and RC remain uncollapsed.

When three family members are discussing a family problem, the verbal responses of each family member are coded as described. Whenever double coding occurs or both parents are talking to each other, listening (LIS) plus the nonverbal rating for Identified Patient is coded. In case of double coding for Identified Patient, LIS is coded for the parent to whom Identified Patient is addressing. For the purpose of sequential analysis the responses of mother and father are combined and treated as coming from one person.

Purpose

The ICS was developed for several purposes: (1) Research: To assess marital and family communication patterns in such a way that both frequency and sequential analysis of the data can be applied; (2) Diagnosis: To diagnose and assess individual and family communication and problem-solving skills in order to plan treatment; (3) To evaluate marital and family therapy.

Psychometric Characteristics

Several reliability studies in Germany, England, and the United States yielded satisfactory results. Kappa's were generally well over .80, implying that the interobserver agreement is acceptable for frequency and sequential analysis.

The discriminant validity of the ICS could be established using criterion groups of: (1) distressed and nondistressed couples (Hahlweg et al., 1984a), and (b) depressed patients with relatives high and low on "expressed emotion" (Hooley, 1986). Results of another study investigating the effects of behavioral marital therapy on the couples' Communication Skills showed that the ICS is also a sensitive instrument to monitor change after treatment (Hahlweg et al., 1984).

Clinical Use

Because of the costs involved in coding interactions from the videotape, the ICS is used predominantly in research. However, it seems worthwhile for the clinician working in marital/family therapy to become acquainted with the code definitions to enable him or her to intervene more effectively.

Future Directions

The ICS is currently used in very different research projects investigating the relationship of psychopathology and family interaction, especially in families with a schizophrenic, depressive, manic, or hyperactive child or family member.

References

Gottman, J.M. (1979). *Marital interaction: Experimental investigations.* New York: Academic Press.

Hahlweg, K., Reisner, L., Kohli, G., Vollmer, M., Schindler, L., & Revenstorf, D. (1984a). Development and validity of a new system to analyze interpersonal communication (KPI). In K. Hahlweg & N.S. Jacobson (Eds.), *Marital interaction: Analysis and modification.* New York: Guilford Press.

Hahlweg, K., Revenstorf, D., & Schindler, L. (1984b). The effects of behavioral marital therapy on couples' communication and problem solving skills. *Journal of Consulting and Clinical Psychology, 52,* 553-566.

Hooley, J.M. (1986). Expressed emotion and depression: Interactions between patients and high versus low EE spouses. *Journal of Abnormal Psychology, 95,* 237-246.

Hops, H., Wills, T.A., Patterson, G.R., & Weiss, R.L. (1972). *Marital interaction coding system.* University of Oregon, Oregon Research Institute, Unpublished manuscript. Order from ASIS/NAPS, c/o Microfiche Publications, 305 E. 46th Street, New York, NY 10017.

Notarius, C.I., & Markman, H.J. (1981). The couples'
interaction scoring system. In E. Filsinger (Ed.),
Assessing marriage: New behavioral approaches.
Beverly Hills, CA: Sage.

Interpersonal Attraction Inventory

Terence M. Keane and Kathryn L. Taylor

Description

The Interpersonal Attraction Inventory (IAI) is a
self-report questionnaire designed to measure the
social perception of interpersonal interactions,
particularly assertiveness. The IAI consists of 26
descriptors of interpersonal functioning, each of
which is rated on a 7-point Likert rating scale. To
control for possible response sets, the positive and
negative anchors are reversed for 10 of the items.
Twenty-four adjectives describing various facets of
interpersonal functioning are combined with two
statements regarding a person's interest in socializing and working with the individual being rated.
The inventory is scored by creating factor scores
that are derived from a factor analysis. In virtually
all of the 12 studies that have used the instrument,
the IAI has been independently factor analyzed,
thus creating factors that are unique to the population under study. In general, the factors have
been comparable in these studies. Moreover, the
sample size is typically large in these studies, ranging from 105 to 835 subjects. Therefore, the stability of the factors across the many studies is a definite strength of the instrument and yields a high
degree of confidence in the IAI for evaluations of
interpersonal functioning.

Purpose

Kelly, Kern, Kirkley, Patterson, and Keane (1980)
developed the instrument to standardize the
measurement of attraction, competence, and
likability in studies evaluating a person's subjective
responses to assertion. Before the development of
the IAI, only a few studies had addressed the issue
of subjective reactions to an assertive individual.
Each of these studies employed a different assessment instrument with questionable psychometric
properties. The development of the IAI led to a
progression of studies that systematically evaluated the social impact of assertive communications.

The result of these studies is that we now understand to a much greater extent how people in our
culture respond to assertion.

Development

The IAI was developed by five doctoral level clinical psychologists (Kelly et al., 1980) who rated
adjectives on the basis of their contribution to independent sources of variance for interpersonal
attraction and likability. From a pool of 55 adjectives that had previously been validated for their
capacity to measure personality traits (Anderson,
1968), 24 items were chosen. This content analysis
of the adjectives was completed through consensus
among all five raters. The basis for item selection
was the degree to which the adjective was appropriate for evaluating assertiveness.

In addition to the 24 adjectives that were selected, two other ratings were included in the instrument. First, we were interested in evaluating the
extent to which a respondent wanted to work on a
committee with the person rated. Second, a rating
was included for the degree to which the respondent would like to socialize at a party with the person rated. These two ratings added the dimensions
of both work and play to the ratings of the person
and were judged, therefore, to tap more general
dimensions of personality and interpersonal
functioning.

Psychometric Characteristics

The psychometric properties of the IAI have been
determined primarily through the use of factor
analyses. Two primary sources of variance are
included in the instrument. First are those items
that seem to measure a dimension of competence or
effectiveness. Second is a cluster of items that
seems to measure likability. In each of the many
studies using the IAI, these two factors have consistently emerged in the analyses, and there has
been substantial overlap in the terms that comprise
these factors from study to study.

To date there has not been a direct evaluation of
the test-retest reliability of the IAI, because the
same subjects have not rated the same behavior
twice in any project completed. However, there is
indirect evidence of strong test-retest reliability of
the instrument stemming from the same behavior
being rated very consistently across studies. For
example, Kelly et al. (1980) and Keane et al. (1983)
employed the same videotapes of assertive and
passive behavior. The ratings by subjects were

stable for the model's assertive and passive behavior in each study. These experiments were conducted nearly 1 full year apart and would qualify as one form of test-retest reliability. Because the same instrument was used, very similar results were obtained (as evidenced by the factor structures and factor scores), and a fairly lengthy interval of time between the two studies existed. However, because subjects in each of the studies varied, direct evidence for test-retest reliability of the IAI is lacking.

Clinical Use

Results of studies employing the IAI have helped to bring about a transition in assertion training. Although previous emphasis has been placed primarily on training clients to refuse unreasonable requests and to request behavior change when it is desired, studies using the IAI have found that assertive behavior must be complemented by either empathic or commendatory statements in order for individuals to be viewed as both competent and likable. Additionally, research using the IAI has indicated the importance of providing clients with positive feedback to their newly learned assertion skills so that there is an increased likelihood of skill transfer and maintenance to extra therapy environments. Positive feedback on assertion can be elicited by first teaching patients commendatory skills and only then teaching methods for dealing with criticism and refusing unreasonable requests (St. Lawrence, Hansen, Cutts, Tisdelle, & Irish, 1985).

The IAI, as it was originally designed, was not intended for clinical use. Rather, it was developed as a research tool. Although the instrument has had an effect on our understanding of the mechanisms of action in the generalization of assertion skills, its use as a diagnostic tool or an assessment instrument in the clinical setting awaits documentation.

Future Directions

Further studies on the reliability and validity of this scale need to be conducted. Studies of construct validity wherein the IAI is compared with other indices of likability and competence would be particularly welcomed. Multiple studies of this type would provide incremental evidence supporting the constructs that appear to underlie the IAI.

In addition, concurrent validation of these constructs would also be valuable and feasible. Ratings on the IAI could be evaluated for the degree to which they positively relate to known quantities.

This could be accomplished by having very popular and/or socially effective individuals (obtained through sociometric ratings) behaving in social vignettes and then rated on the IAI by large groups of people. It would be hypothesized that they would be evaluated very highly across the two dimensions of the scale. People who are effective communicators, but unpopular, would be predicted to receive high ratings on the competence dimension and low ratings on the likability dimension. Such concurrent validational strategies would provide further information of the psychometric strength of the IAI.

References

Anderson, N.H. (1968). Likeableness ratings of 555 personality trait words. *Journal of Personality and Social Psychology, 9*, 272-279.

Keane, T.M., Wedding, D., & Kelly, J.A. (1983). Assessing subjective responses to assertive behavior. *Behavior Modification, 7*, 317-330.

Kelly, J.A., Kern, N.M., Kirkley, B.G., Patterson, J.N., & Keane, T.M. (1980). Reactions to assertive versus unassertive behavior: Differential effects for males and females and implications for assertiveness training. *Behavior Therapy, 11*, 670-682.

St. Lawrence, J.S., Hansen, D.J., Cutts, T.F., Tisdelle, D.A., & Irish, J.D. (1985). Situational context: Effects of perceptions of assertive and unassertive behavior. *Behavior Therapy, 16*, 51-62.

Interpersonal Behavior Construct Scale

Carolyn Webster-Stratton

Description

The Interpersonal Behavior Construct Scale (IBCS) (Kogan, 1972; Kogan & Gordon, 1975a) consists of 23 categories of behaviors that are coded as either present or absent for each 40-second segment. Ratings in the 23 categories for all time segments are summed to form eight various dimensions of parent and child interactions (Kogan, 1972). The dimensions include: Positive Affect, Negative Affect, Nonacceptance, Control, Submissiveness, Attention, Vocalization, and Lead-Taking. There are two classes of ratings: Duration Constructs, which refer to certain behaviors that occur during at least 7 of the 10 intervals in any unit, and Frequency Constructs, which are checked if they occur at any time during the 40-second unit. Each of these dimensions is assessed for both the parent and child behaviors with the exception of shared conversation and working together categories.

Purpose

The IBCS is an observational coding system designed to provide detailed analyses of videotaped observations of parent–child interactions. A parent and child are videotaped in a standardized laboratory setting with a specific set of toys, and the tapes are later analyzed in detail by trained coders according to the IBCS. Direct observational analyses of parent and child behaviors can provide baseline assessment information for making treatment recommendations and for evaluating behavioral changes after treatment.

Psychometric Characteristics

The author has reported satisfactory test-retest and interrater reliabilities and validity (Kogan & Gordon, 1975a; Kogan & Wimberger, 1971). These reliability findings were corroborated by more recent research (Webster-Stratton, 1982), which reported reliabilities for each behavior dimension ranging from .89 to .98. The IBCS has discriminated conduct-disordered children and their mothers from normal mother-child interactions on the bases of mother and child positive affect (Webster-Stratton, 1985). Normative data based on 95 children aged 3 to 5 years and their mothers are also available.

Development

The development and refinement of the IBCS has been the focus of several research projects (Kogan, 1972; Kogan & Gordon, 1975a, 1975b). In the initial phases, behaviors were meticulously analyzed in 4-second units but were later modified to 40-second units in the interests of economy and practical applicability. The approach treats the events of social interactions as reflecting a reciprocal relationship and places emphasis on delineation of the unique communication patterns of individual mother–child pairs. The original conceptual scheme was selected to represent three main dimensions having qualities of dominance-submission (states), hostility-warmth (affect), and detachment-involvement.

Clinical Use

The IBCS is useful for baseline assessment of parent–child interactions and for making treatment recommendations. It is also useful for assessing posttreatment changes. Treatment outcome studies have shown the IBCS to be a sensitive measure of change in parent–child interactions (Kogan, 1972; Webster-Stratton, 1982). In particular, this coding system assesses nonverbal behaviors and affect dimensions that are not found in many other behavior coding systems.

Future Directions

Future research needs to validate this measure by correlating it with other standardized coding systems and behavior checklists. It is essential to determine which observational coding systems are best able to discriminate clinic and nonclinic families and provide relevant therapeutic information.

References

Kogan, K.L. (1972). Specificity and stability of mother–child interaction styles. Child Psychiatry and Human Development, 2, 160-168.

Kogan, K.L., & Gordon, B.M. (1975a). Interpersonal behavior constructs: A revised approach to defining dyadic interaction styles. Psychological Reports, 36, 835-846.

Kogan, K.L., & Gordon, B.M. (1975b). A mother-instruction program: Documenting change in mother–child interactions. Child Psychiatry and Human Development, 5, 189-200.

Kogan, K.L., & Wimberger, H.C. (1971). Behavior transactions between disturbed children and their mothers. Psychological Reports, 28, 395-404.

Webster-Stratton, C. (1982). The long term effects of a videotape modeling parent-training program: Comparison of immediate and one-year follow-up results. Behavior Therapy, 13, 702-714.

Webster-Stratton, C. (1985). Mother perceptions and mother–child interactions: Comparison of a clinic-referred and a non-clinic group. Journal of Clinical Child Psychology, 14, 334-339.

Interpersonal Evaluation Inventory

Jeffrey A. Kelly

Description

The Interpersonal Evaluation Inventory (IEI) is a scale consisting of 24 adjectives that can be used to describe the social skills behavior of another person. The items comprising the IEI are: assertive, appropriate, tactful, offensive, truthful, educated, friendly, agreeable, pleasant, considerate, flexible, open-minded, sympathetic, good-natured, attractive, fair, kind, honest, likable, intelligent, thoughtful, socially skilled, warm, and superior. Additional adjective descriptors have occasionally been added to this set of items, depending on the investigator's purposes. The 24 items included in the IEI were selected because they had been validated as sensitive to interpersonal attraction and because they appeared relevant to the evaluation of an individual's social skill. Each item is in the form of a 7-point bipolar rating dimension (1 = extremely assertive to 7 = extremely unassertive).

Purpose

The IEI was first developed by Kelly, Kern, Kirkley, Patterson, and Keane (1980) to serve as a dependent measure in a study examining how people react to assertive behavior shown by others. In the Kelly et al. (1980) project, observers rated assertive and unassertive videotaped models on the IEI; the project found that observers assigned differing IEI ratings to assertive and unassertive models. The IEI, occasionally with item modifications or additions, has also been used in subsequent perception-of-assertiveness studies. The rationale for using this measure is that clinicians often teach clients social skills or assertive behavior. A quantified instrument to assess how observers actually evaluate social skills can help therapists and researchers ensure that they are teaching clients social skills that will be evaluated favorably by others.

Development

The items comprising the IEI were selected from a pool of 555 personality trait descriptions empirically shown to reflect interpersonal attraction (Anderson, 1968). The 24 adjectives appearing in the IEI were those that correlated at high levels with interpersonal attraction and that also appeared, on a face validity basis, capable of describing an individual's social/assertive behavior. The IEI was not developed to serve as a traditional personality or clinical evaluation test; rather, it was developed as a measure evaluating the social impact on observers of an individual's assertive behavior.

Psychometric Characteristics

Data on the reliability of the IEI have not been reported. The validity of the measure has been studied indirectly; observers of assertive models have rated them differently on the IEI than have observers of passive, unassertive models. For example, assertive models are given higher ratings than unassertive models on the IEI items assertive, appropriate, truthful, educated, intelligent, superior, and socially skilled (Kelly et al., 1980).

A factor analytic study of the IEI with a population of 1,258 college student subjects who observed and rated assertive models revealed the presence of four factors underlying the scale. These factors were labeled likability, ability/achievement, honesty, and tactlessness (Kelly et al., 1980).

Clinical Use

The IEI has been used to date only as a research/validation dependent measure, and its use in the clinical evaluation of client social skills has not yet been established. However, the measure may prove useful if a clinician wishes to obtain a quantified assessment made by observers of a client's social skills behavior.

Future Directions

Evaluations of social skills made by observers using the IEI have shown that assertive versus unassertive styles produce different social impacts on the observers. Further research with the IEI and with related instruments may help clinical researchers better determine those social skills styles that result in the most favorable impact on others. This, in turn, will enable therapists to teach skill-deficit clients to engage in social behaviors that can maximize their likelihood of being perceived favorably by others.

References

Anderson, N.H. (1968). Likeability ratings of 555 personality-trait words. *Journal of Personality and Social Psychology, 9,* 272-279.

Kelly, J.A., Kern, J.M., Kirkley, B.G., Patterson, J.N., & Keane, T.M. (1980). Reactions to assertive versus unassertive behavior: Differential effects for males and females, and implications for assertiveness training. *Behavior Therapy, 11,* 670-682.

Intervention Rating Profile

Joseph C. Witt

Description

The Intervention Rating Profile (IRP) was developed to assess teachers' perceptions about the acceptability of classroom intervention strategies. The scale assesses five aspects of intervention acceptability, including: (a) whether or not an intervention is generally acceptable, (b) whether it poses a risk to children upon whom it is implemented, (c) the degree to which the intervention is likely to have negative effects on other children, (d) the degree to which the intervention is acceptable because of excessive requirements in terms of time and material resources, and (e) the degree to which the intervention may be unacceptable because it requires too much teacher skill to be implemented by most teachers.

The scale consists of 20 items that require that the teacher responds in a Likert type format ranging from strongly agree to strongly disagree (Sample Item: This intervention should prove effective in changing the child's behavior problem). The instrument yields a total score, with higher scores denoting more acceptable interventions than lower scores. Modifications of the scale have been developed for both parents and children.

Purpose

The IRP is designed to yield scores on each of five dimensions of intervention acceptability. Although it can be used by school-based consultants to evaluate the acceptability of interventions actually applied in school settings, it has been used primarily as a tool for researchers investigating intervention acceptability.

The other major instrument in this general area is the Treatment Evaluation Inventory (TEI) developed by Kazdin (1980). The difference between these two instruments is that the TEI is a more global measure for assessing the perceptions of a variety of individuals concerning the acceptability of interventions designed for use in a wide variety of applied settings. Instead, the IRP is designed for use by teachers in educational settings.

Development

The IRP was developed for use in intervention acceptability research. Initially, a pool of approximately 100 items was generated. Items within that initial pool were subjected to item analysis and factor analytic procedures. Items were retained if they made a relatively unique contribution to the measurement of intervention acceptability.

Psychometric Characteristics

In most factor analytic studies of the instrument (Witt & Elliott, 1985), the results suggest that the scale is comprised of one major factor, termed general acceptability, which accounts for approximately 40% of the variance. In addition, there are four secondary factors, each of which contributes less than 20% to the total variance. These secondary factors include: (a) risk to the child, (b) teacher time required, (c) negative effects on other children, and (d) teacher skill required.

Reliability of the IRP, as determined by Cronbach's alpha, is in the .90's. Validity of the instrument has been established by correlating it with the evaluative dimension of the Semantic Differential. The correlation between these two instruments is in the high .80's. Further validity evidence can be inferred from the numerous studies that have used the IRP for research purposes (Witt & Elliott, 1985). These studies suggest that the IRP is capable of differentiating between two interventions in terms of the degree to which they are acceptable to a teacher. For example, the scale has indicated that positive interventions are typically much more acceptable than reductive interventions.

Clinical Use

This instrument is primarily for use by researchers and practitioners in schools who need an instrument to assess the acceptability of classroom interventions. Within the context of a consultation model, it is designed to be administered to the consultee rather than the client.

Future Directions

Since the IRP was originally developed, a new, one-factor version of the instrument has appeared. Termed the IRP-15 because it contains only 15 items, this new instrument is designed for the same purpose as the original IRP, but it does not yield the multiple dependent variables inherent in the IRP. Therefore, its use is preferred in many situations.

Another instrument, termed the Children's Intervention Rating Profile, was developed to assess children's perceptions of the acceptability of interventions implemented upon them. This scale contains only seven items, but it is a well-validated and reliable measure of acceptability.

References

Kazdin, A.E. (1980). Acceptability of alternative treatments for deviant child behavior. *Journal of Applied Behavior Analysis, 13*, 259-273.

Witt, J.C., & Elliott, S.N. (1985). Acceptability of classroom intervention strategies. In T.R. Kratochwill (Ed.), *Advances in school psychology*. Hillsdale, N.J.: Lawrence Erlbaum.

Interview Assessment of Adolescent Male Offenders

Steve Sussman and Kim T. Mueser

Description

The Interview Assessment of Adolescent Male Offenders (IAAMO; Spence, 1981a) is an instrument designed to assess the social skills of adolescent male offenders in an employment interview. The IAAMO consists of a 5-minute standardized interview with a previously unknown adult and is followed by a role-play that requires the subject to return a defective article to a shop. Topics in the interview include school life, hobbies, and career ideas. The interview and role-play are videotaped and later rated for 13 behaviors thought to be important to successful job interviewing: gestures (conversation-relevant movements of hands or arms; number/minute); fiddling (conversation-irrelevant movements of hands; seconds/minute); gross body movements (number/minute); smiling (number/minute); conversation-relevant head movements (number/minute); eye contact (seconds/minute); dysfluencies (meaningless noises; number/minute of speech); attention feedback responses (acknowledgments and questions; number/minute); amount spoken (total verbal utterances; number/minute); interruptions (verbal initiations that take over speaker role; number/minute); questions asked (verbal initiations that request new information; number/minute); initiations (speaker role verbal initiations other than questions, interruptions, or responses to interviewer's questions; number/minute); and latency of response to interviewer questions (seconds/response). An event recorder is used to measure discrete behavioral events (e.g., number of head movements), and a cumulative stop watch is used to measure the duration of nondiscrete responses (e.g., eye contact).

Observers rate the videotaped behaviors blindly and independently to establish interrater agreement. A separate group of judges has independently rated the same videotaped conversations on the dimensions of friendliness, social anxiety, social skills performance, and employability using four 10-point rating scales (and interrater agreement is calculated) to evaluate the measures within a social context (Spence, 1981a).

Purpose

The IAAMO was developed to (a) assess social skills response deficits in young adolescent male offenders that are applicable to real-life initial interview situations; (b) validate the social importance of the responses through independent ratings of interview-relevant dimensions (e.g., employability); and (c) serve as a basis for social skills training that would normalize behavior response frequency and duration, presumably to aid adolescent male offenders to achieve employment following discharge from juvenile facilities.

Development

The IAAMO developed from literature stressing the importance of a wide range of verbal and nonverbal responses in different situations (Argyle, 1972) as well as from Spence's work in social skills training with adolescent male offenders (Spence & Marzillier, 1981). Behaviors and social validity dimensions were chosen to represent that wide range of responses relevant to the initial interview situation.

All of the IAAMO results reported stem from a project conducted by Spence and her colleagues (see references), in which Spence herself was the interviewer and two observers performed behavioral ratings of the videotapes.

Psychometric Characteristics

Norms. Differences in behavioral responses and social validity dimensions between adolescent male offenders and nonoffenders have been examined (Spence, 1981b). Offenders exhibited more fiddling and gross body movements and less conversation-relevant head movements, eye contact, and total amount spoken than did nonoffenders. Offenders were rated as higher in social anxiety and lower in social skills performance and employability than were nonoffenders. Finally, social anxiety correlated positively with gross body movements and negatively with conversation-relevant head movements and eye contacts, whereas both social skills performance and employability correlated positively with conversation-relevant head movements and eye contact.

Reliability. Interrater agreement for the 13 behavioral measures (Pearson's r sample = 10 adolescent offenders), based on ratings by two observers (one of whom was blind to study purposes), ranged from .76 (initiations) to 1.00 (gross body movements). Interrater agreement for the four social validity measures (average Pearson's r calculated with Fishers' r-to-z transformation; sample = 70), based on ratings by four observers (all blind to study purposes), was .47 for social anxiety, .61 for friendliness, .62 for social skills performance, and .62 for employability. Intercorrelations among the four scales varied from .65 (friendliness and social anxiety) to .92 (friendliness and employability).

Validity. The validity of the 13 behaviors rated on the IAAMO as well as the 4 social validity scales as predictors of performance of in vivo interviewing skills has not been determined. Some correlations have been reported between the behavioral observations and clinical interventions. Social skills training for adolescent offenders in order to normalize maladaptive behaviors assessed by the IAAMO have resulted in short-term increases in self-esteem and internal locus of control (Spence & Spence, 1980) and fewer self-reported social problems for offenders (Spence & Marzillier, 1981). However, independent ratings of social skills, anxiety, friendliness, employability, social relationship quality, and future offenses have not covaried with changes in those behavioral responses (Spence & Marzillier, 1981). Similarly, the impact of the social skills training program, based on the IAAMO on actual interview performance and job attainment, was not assessed.

Clinical Use

The IAAMO has been used primarily for clinical research by a single group of researchers and has no practical clinical applications at this time. A single person has conducted all the interviews, and two judges have made all the behavioral ratings. Therefore, the feasibility of training additional interviewers and behavioral raters to administer the IAAMO has not been evaluated, and its potential as an assessment instrument is unknown. The initial subject pool studied has been primarily white, adolescent (10 to 15 years), male criminal offenders with low socioeconomic status. When additional validational data are available, the IAAMO could theoretically be used with a wide variety of adolescent and young adult clinical populations, with the limitations that: (a) it is specifically intended to assess initial interview performance; (b) it does not deal with appropriate/inappropriate verbal content of interactions and therefore is most suitable for assessing deficits in nonverbal behavioral expression; and (c) it is inappropriate for individuals who are unable to voluntarily perform all behavioral responses (e.g., physically disabled clients).

Future Directions

Most important, the validity of the 13 behavioral categories obtained from the IAAMO as predictors of in vivo interview performance and job attainment among male adolescent offenders needs to be evaluated. In addition, the trainability of other interviewers and behavioral raters for the IAAMO has not been assessed. More detailed psychometric analyses on larger, more heterogeneous populations are needed. Multivariate techniques relating behavioral responses to social validity ratings obtained from in vitro and in vivo interview situations are needed to best establish the predictive validity of the approach.

References

Argyle, M. (1972). *The psychology of interpersonal behavior.* Harmondsworth: Penguin Books.

Spence, S.H. (1981a). Validation of social skills of adolescent males in an interview conversation with a previously unknown adult. *Journal of Applied Behavior Analysis, 14,* 159-168.

Spence, S.H. (1981b). Differences in social skills performance between institutionalized juvenile offenders and a comparable group of boys without offense records. *British Journal of Clinical Psychology, 20,* 163-171.

Spence, S.H., & Marzillier, J.S. (1981). Social skills training with adolescent male offenders-II. Short-term, long-term, and generalized effects. *Behaviour Research and Therapy, 19,* 349-368.

Spence, A.J., & Spence, S.H. (1980). Cognitive changes associated with social skills training. *Behaviour Research & Therapy, 18,* 265-272.

Interview Schedule for Children

Cynthia G. Last

Description

The Interview Schedule for Children (ISC) (Kovacs, 1978, 1983a) is a semistructured, symptom-oriented psychiatric interview that is suitable for use with youngsters aged 8 to 17. Two parallel forms of the instrument are available: Form C, which focuses on current (intake) symptoms, and the Follow-up version, which is used for reevaluation (follow-up). Both forms cover the following areas: (a) major core symptoms of psychopathology (43 items), (b) severity of current condition (1 item), (c) mental status (8 items), (d) developmental milestones (2 items), (e) behavioral observations (12 items), and (f) clinician's impressions (5 items). In addition, collateral or subsidiary data are collected through the use of additional items when appropriate (e.g., an affirmative response to a particular symptom item may require additional information in regard to duration, content, consequences, and the like).

In the ISC, symptoms/items are accompanied by a set of questions that the clinician asks to elicit necessary information. Replies are recorded directly on the interview schedule, which is precoded. Most symptoms are rated on an 8-point severity scale; i.e., 0 (none) to 8 (severe), although a small number of items are rated on a more global, 4-point scale. Mental status items have their own content-appropriate severity scales, whereas collateral items are rated either on a dichotomous scale (yes or no) or a precoded nominal scale. Generally, data are quantified in a uniform direction, that is, the higher the rating, the greater the psychopathology. Space also is provided to record DSM-III diagnoses, their duration, and the duration of specific symptoms.

In administering the instrument, the parent(s) alone is interviewed first about the child (parent interview data), then the child is interviewed alone about him- or herself (child interview data). Parent and child ratings are recorded separately on the precoded form. Finally, the clinician also records his or her own overall summary rating for each symptom/item based on data supplied by both informants. An intake ISC with the parent(s) usually requires from 1 to 2 hours. The child interview takes from 45 minutes to 1.5 hours to administer.

Purpose

The ISC can be used to delineate specific clinically significant problem areas for children as well as to formulate DSM-III diagnoses. Use of the Follow-up version of the instrument allows continued evaluation of children's psychiatric condition over time.

Development

The instrument was developed in 1978 by Kovacs. Following its initial development (before publication of DSM-III), diagnostic addenda were created to supplement the core instrument in order to achieve correspondence with DSM-III.

Psychometric Characteristics

Kovacs (1983b) has demonstrated that the interrater reliability of the ISC is satisfactory for most of the symptoms/items included in the instrument. More recently, Last, Hersen, Kazdin, and Finkelstein (1985) have obtained excellent testretest reliability for DSM-III diagnoses for a wide variety of psychiatric disorders generated on the basis of ISC data.

Clinical Use

The ISC is intended to be administered by experienced professionals (e.g., child psychiatrist and child clinical psychologist) because clinical judgment plays a role in assigning both clinician summary ratings and DSM-III diagnoses. The instrument can be used with a variety of child populations (e.g., inpatients or outpatients) in a number of settings (e.g., hospital, clinic, school, and private practice).

Future Directions

The reliability of the ISC relative to other available structured and semistructured interview schedules for children remains to be examined. Preliminary data suggest that the ISC is superior to other comparable instruments for reliably diagnosing anxiety disorders in children and adolescents (Last et al., 1985). Its relative merits for other psychiatric disorders remain to be explored.

References

Kovacs, M. (1978). *The Interview Schedule for Children (ISC): Form C, and the follow-up form.* Unpublished manuscript.

Kovacs, M. (1983a). *The Interview Schedule for Children (ISC): Interrater and parent–child agreement.* Unpublished manuscript.

Kovacs, M. (1983b). *The Interview Schedule for Children (ISC): Interrater and parent–child agreement.* Unpublished manuscript.

Last, C.C., Hersen, M., Kazdin, A.E., & Finkelstein, R. (1985). *Reliability and validity of DSM-III anxiety disorders of childhood and adolescence: A preliminary report.* Unpublished manuscript.

In Vivo Cognitive Assessment

Steven D. Hollon and Christopher Vye

Description

In vivo cognitive assessment strategies include a diverse array of methodologies designed to sample cognitive processes at the time and in the situations in which those phenomena actually occur. In general, such strategies seek to eliminate the vagaries of selective recall, cue dependence, and forgetting in the assessment of cognitions.

Several major strategies have been proposed, some relying on the direct assessment of thought content and process, others utilizing various reconstruction strategies. Chief among these strategies, as described by Genest and Turk (1981), are: (a) continuous monologues, (b) thought sampling, (c) event sampling, and (d) reconstruction procedures. In the continuous monologue methodology, the subject is simply instructed to carry on a running dialogue describing everything that runs through his or her stream-of-consciousness. This dialogue is recorded in some fashion, usually with an audiotape recorder, and then examined or scored at a later time. Thought sampling (see Klinger, Barta, & Maxeiner, 1981) typically involves providing a random signal generator that the subject carries throughout his or her day, with prior instructions to write down whatever he or she is thinking about at the time of the signal. Event sampling keys the cognitive assessment to a particular event (e.g., an anxiety attack or instance of unassertive behavior), rather than randomly sampling throughout a given time period. Finally, reconstructive procedures, such as Meichenbaum's (1977) postperformance videotape reconstruction procedure, involve having the subjects view a recorded sample of their behavior in a particular situation in a "think aloud" paradigm, verbalizing their thoughts as in the continuous monologue procedure.

Purpose

The major purpose of the in vivo cognitive assessment strategies is to provide a sampling of cognitive phenomena closely linked to the time and place in which events of interest are occurring. Hollon and Kendall (1981) have argued that clinical scientists have too readily adopted a belief in *cognitive intransigence,* that what a person believes does not vary as a function of time and place. Rather, it is argued that what an individual professes to believe in one situation (e.g., sitting in a therapist's office) may be very different from what he or she actually believes or experiences in his or her stream-of-consciousness in the actual situation of interest (e.g., approaching an elevator for a person with elevator phobia or interacting with a spouse in the heat of an argument). While recognizing the difficulty in establishing the validity of any cognitive assessment, it is believed that sampling thinking in the appropriate circumstances will help minimize threats to the accuracy of assessment based on selective recall and forgetting.

Development

In vivo cognitive assessment has a very short formal history, but a long past (Genest & Turk, 1981). Introspection has long been a major method in psychological research, but one that has fallen in disfavor in recent decades. Interest in in vivo cognitive assessment represents an outgrowth of the renewed concern with cognitive assessment and intervention and can be linked directly to the clinical discovery that subject self-reports vary widely as a function of circumstances (Hollon & Kendall, 1981). Since the category of in vivo cognitive assessment covers a multitude of approaches, the reader is directed to the various articles and chapters that discuss the development of those various systems (Cacioppo & Petty, 1981; Genest & Turk, 1981; Hollon & Kendall, 1981; Klinger et al., 1981; Meichenbaum, 1977).

Psychometric Characteristics

All of these varying assessment strategies depend upon self-report. Because the basic phenomena of interest are not amenable to direct observation, in vivo cognitive assessment strategies share with all other cognitive assessment strategies major difficulties in establishing accuracy and minimizing reactivity (Hollon & Kendall, 1981).

Accuracy refers to the validity of the assessment; are subjects reporting faithfully what they are thinking? Because the phenomena of interest cannot be directly observed, accuracy is typically pursued by efforts to minimize factors that might lead to dissimulation. Efforts to evaluate the accuracy of the assessment have invariably relied on convergent measurement operations.

Reactivity refers to the tendency of a phenomenon to change as a consequence of obtrusive monitoring. The very process of monitoring, relying as it does on introspection, probably influences the nature and content of thinking. Efforts to minimize reactivity have typically involved the careful selection of cues for recording (e.g., the use of random signals by Klinger et al., 1981) and a preference for less obtrusive recording methods, as in the "think aloud" procedures and content-free prompts, as in thought-listing strategies (Cacioppo & Petty, 1981).

More is known about the formal psychometric properties of the various scoring systems developed to code the specific cognitions collected. Although the precise nature of these systems varies with the phenomena of interest, it would appear that coding systems with acceptable psychometric properties can be developed. (See, for example, Cacioppo & Petty's [1981] scoring procedures for thought-listing paradigms or Klinger et al.'s [1981] scoring system for random-thought sampling procedures.) At this time, the psychometric properties of the procedure utilized depend upon the nature of the scoring system adopted or developed, and should be demonstrated anew with each change in systems or judges.

Clinical Use

In vivo cognitive assessment has probably been more extensively used in informal clinical practice than in formal clinical research. Cognitive therapists, such as Beck (1976), Mahoney (1974), and Meichenbaum (1977), have long advocated use of in vivo cognitive assessment as a particularly useful way of getting at idiosyncratic thoughts and beliefs. Such assessments are seen both as providing a means of better understanding the source of distressing affective states and troublesome behaviors and as a starting point for the clinical change process. Procedures such as the Dysfunctional Thought Record (probably originating in Ellis' group but widely used and often modified by Beck and Goldfried, among others), in which clients record beliefs in particular situations, often in conjunction with targeted affective states, have been widely used, as have a host of other idiosyncratic or informal systems or both. Cueing stimuli and recording media have been widely varied to fit the particular clinical situation. In most cases, however, use of these strategies has been embedded within the context of a larger cognitive-behavioral intervention strategy in which cognition is seen as playing a key mediating role in the genesis of both affect and behavior.

Future Directions

There is a clear need for more careful evaluation of the properties of the in vivo cognitive assessment strategies, with particular respect to their twin properties of accuracy and reactivity. In the absence of direct observation of the cognitive phenomena of interest, major reliance will have to be placed on the convergence of multiple methodologies. The rejection of cognitive intransigence, at the core of interest in in vivo cognitive assessment, has rarely received direct empirical scrutiny, with current support deriving largely from clinical anecdotes. Finally, systematic evaluation needs to be made of the impact of variations in prompting cues, recording methods, and scoring systems before any firm conclusion can be drawn about the properties of these systems. Their widespread use in clinical practice suggests that they attempt to fill an important need. How adequately they meet that need remains a subject for empirical investigation.

References

Beck, A.T. (1976). *Cognitive therapy and the emotional disorders*. New York: International Universities Press.

Cacioppo, J.T., & Petty, R.E. (1981). Social psychological procedures for cognitive response assessment: The thought-listing technique. In T.V. Merluzzi, C.R. Glass, & M. Genest (Eds.), *Cognitive assessment* (pp. 309-342). New York: Guilford Press.

Genest, M., & Turk, D.C. (1981). Think-aloud approaches to cognitive assessment. In T.V. Merluzzi, C.R. Glass, & M. Genest (Eds.), *Cognitive assessment* (pp. 233-269). New York: Guilford Press.

Hollon, S.D., & Kendall, P.C. (1981). Current concerns: Assessing therapeutically reliant motivation. In P.C. Kendall & S.D. Hollon (Eds.), *Assessment strategies in cognitive-behavioral intervention* (pp. 319-362). New York: Academic Press.

Klinger, E., Barta, S.G., & Maxeiner, M.E. (1981). Current concerns: Assessing therapeutically reliant motivation. In P.C. Kendall & S.D. Hollon (Eds.), *Assessment strategies for cognitive-behavioral intervention* (pp. 161-195). New York: Academic Press.

Mahoney, M.J. (1974). *Cognition and behavior modification.* Cambridge, MA: Ballinger.

Meichenbaum, D. (1977). *Cognitive-behavior modification: An integrative approach.* New York: Plenum Press.

In Vivo Measurement of Agoraphobia

Paul M. G. Emmelkamp

Description

Several in vivo tests have been developed to assess agoraphobic behavior in fearful situations. Emmelkamp (1982) had agoraphobic patients walk along a preselected route leading to progressively more crowded places; they were instructed to return when they became anxious. Both time and distance walked away from a "safe" place can be measured.

Another behavioral test with agoraphobic persons has been used by Mathews, Gelder, and Johnston (1981). This test consists of a hierarchy of progressively more difficult items. This hierarchy attempts to sample the whole range of phobic situations from very easy to exceedingly difficult. An attempt was made to ensure that before treatment began, the patient could carry out three or four of the items on the hierarchy, thereby allowing room for significant deterioration as well as for improvement. A serious problem with this test is that because of its idiosyncratic nature, different subjects' scores cannot be meaningfully compared with one another.

Purpose

Both in vivo tests were developed to evaluate the effects of treatment for agoraphobia. There is no advantage in using the in vivo tests as a diagnostic instrument, except perhaps in a supplementary capacity.

Development

Behavioral approach tests are a widely used measure to assess phobic behavior in analogue studies. In the early 1970s both Emmelkamp, Mathews, and their colleagues felt the need to develop behavioral measures to assess agoraphobic fears in treatment outcome studies. In recent years other researchers have used slight variations of these in vivo tests (Williams, 1985). Subjective anxiety, psychophysiological arousal, and cognitions have also been assessed during or immediately after the in vivo tests.

Psychometric Characteristics

Few data are available with respect to psychometric characteristics of the in vivo tests. Correlations between Emmelkamp's behavioral measure and phobic anxiety and avoidance ratings have been fairly high. Furthermore, this behavioral measure was relatively stable over time with untreated patients. Finally, this measure could detect significant differences in effectiveness between treatments (Emmelkamp, 1982). Results of the behavioral test of Mathews et al. correlated highly with phobic severity rating by assessors but less so with patients' ratings.

Although demand characteristics have had a substantial influence on the results of behavioral avoidance tests in analog studies, the effects of demand characteristics on behavioral assessment with clinical phobics have not been assessed. Different treatments might create different demands with posttesting. For example, "undue anxiety" might mean something different for a patient who has been treated with gradual exposure in vivo than it means for a patient treated by flooding in vivo. The posttest instruction with patients who have been flooded is rather paradoxical. Obviously, results at posttesting might be influenced to some extent by the implicit demands of the treatment received.

Clinical Use

Both behavioral tests are of little clinical utility. A clear disadvantage of Emmelkamp's measure is that only part of the cluster of agoraphobic fears is measured behaviorally, although presumably the most important part. Although the assessment approach of the Oxford group attempts to encompass all agoraphobic fears and their idiosyncratic patterning by constructing a single hierarchy for each subject, a number of other disadvantages (e.g., Williams, 1985) prevent its clinical use, the most important being that such a test is difficult and expensive to implement. Because both behavioral tests have been found to correlate highly with other measures of agoraphobic fears, there is no need to include these tests in routine clinical practice.

Future Directions

Given the difficulty in implementing in vivo tests and the costs involved, it might be worthwhile to develop less expensive methods to assess in vivo agoraphobic behavior. Probably the most economical approach is to rely on patients' self-reports about their actual behavior in potentially phobic situations. Mathews et al. (1981) had their patients complete diaries of their daily comings and goings and found that time spent away from home was a satisfactory measure. Research needs to be undertaken into the reliability and validity of such behavioral diaries.

For research purposes, in vivo tests may still be required. A potentially fruitful area of future research involves the measurement of thoughts and psychophysiological arousal during behavioral tests.

References

Emmelkamp, P.M.G. (1982). *Phobic and obsessive-compulsive disorders: Theory, research and practice.* New York: Plenum Press.

Mathews, A.M., Gelder, M.G., & Johnston, D.W. (1981). *Agoraphobia: Nature and treatment.* London: Tavistock.

Williams, S.L. (1985). On the nature and measurement of agoraphobia. In M. Hersen, R.M. Eisler, & P.M. Miller (Eds.), *Progress in behavior modification: Vol. 19* (pp. 109-144). New York: Academic Press.

IOWA-Conners Teacher Rating Scale

Marc S. Atkins and Richard Milich

Description

The IOWA-Conners Teacher Rating Scale (Loney & Milich, 1982) is a 10-item scale designed to provide a standard measure of attention deficit disorder and aggression in children. There are two subscales, each consisting of 5 items: Inattention/overactivity (I/O; fidgeting, humming, and making other odd noises, excitable/impulsive, inattentive/distractible, and failing to finish things that are started), and aggression (A; quarrelsome, acting smart, temper outbursts, defiant, and uncooperative). Items are scored by a child's classroom teacher as occurring "not at all," "just a little," "pretty much," or "very much." These descriptors are scored as 0, 1, 2, or 3, respectively. Four subgroups

based on IOWA-Conners scores have been proposed: normal controls (low scores on both the I/O and A scales), exclusively hyperactive (high I/O score and low A score), exclusively aggressive (low I/O score and high A score), and hyperactive/aggressive (high I/O score and high A score).

Purpose and Development

Teacher ratings are commonly used to screen children in need of psychological services. However, to be maximally useful, teacher ratings should be able to discriminate among different types of childhood disorders in addition to making a global distinction between deviance and normality. The differential diagnosis of attention deficit disorder and conduct disorder is of particular importance because hyperactive children who also exhibit aggressive symptoms have been found to exhibit different symptoms at intake. They also have a poorer prognosis at follow-up, as compared with nonaggressive hyperactive children, providing strong support for the utility of this dichotomy (Loney & Milich, 1982).

Following a series of empirical evaluations of clinically diagnosed hyperactive children, the IOWA-Conners Teacher Rating Scale was derived to offer relatively independent scores for hyperactivity and aggression. The items contained on the two rating scales were derived from the Conners Teacher Rating Scale, currently the most common rating scale for research and treatment of hyperactivity and related disorders. The IOWA-Conners Inattention/Overactivity Scale was so labeled to emphasize its focus on both attentional problems and problems in overactivity, as well as to avoid confusion with the widely used Conners Teacher Rating Scale Hyperactivity factor (Loney & Milich, 1982).

Psychometric Characteristics

Considerable psychometric information is becoming available for this instrument, indicating adequate reliability and high concurrence with alternate measures of childhood hyperactivity and aggression. Loney and Milich (1982) reported means and standard deviations for a sample of 50 clinically referred children aged 6 to 12 and for a sample of 120 children from regular elementary classrooms. One week test-retest correlations for the normative sample were $r = .89$ (I/O) and $r = .86$ (A). Internal stability coefficients (coefficient alpha) were .87 (I/O) and .85 (A) for the normative sample, and .80 (I/O) and .87 (A) for the clinic sample. Means, standard deviations, and recommended cutoff scores by grade and sex are provided by Murphy, Pelham, and Milich (1985) for a sample of 617 children from regular elementary classrooms. The cutoff scores are those that identify 6% of their sample as having an extreme score on each scale.

The validity of the IOWA-Conners has been assessed in a number of investigations. Significant correlations were reported for the Inattention/Overactivity Scale with the Hyperactivity factor of the Conners Teacher Rating Scale, and for the Aggression Scale with the Conduct Problems factor of the Conners Teacher Rating Scale. The Aggression Scale, but not the Inattention/Overactivity Scale, was found to correlate significantly with peer ratings of aggression in preschool (Milich, Landau, Kilby, & Whitten, 1982), kindergarten (Milich & Landau, 1984), and elementary-age (Landau & Milich, 1985) samples, supporting the validity of this scale as a measure of aggression and confirming the independence of the IOWA Inattention/Overactivity and Aggression Scales. Similarly, convergent and discriminant validity for the IOWA scales was evidenced with classroom observations of clinic-referred boys (Milich & Fitzgerald, 1985), with classroom observations of non-referred schoolage boys, with measures of academic performance, and with peer ratings (Atkins, Pelham, & Licht, 1986). In these studies, partial correlation coefficients controlling for the interdependence of the two scales demonstrated a unique and independent relationship for each scale on a subset of these measures. Further evidence for the validity of the IOWA-Conners scales was provided by Milich and Pelham (1985) who observed children referred to a summer treatment program for hyperactive and aggressive children. Using the IOWA-Conners to classify children, they found that hyperactive/aggressive children, as compared with hyperactive children, were timed-out by staff more frequently, had higher percentages of negative peer interactions and verbal abuse toward staff, and had significantly lower compliance percentages.

Clinical Use

The clinical utility of the IOWA-Conners appears promising. It is easily administered and easily interpreted with documented reliability and validity for the subtyping of schoolage children with externalizing disorders. Its use as a measure of treatment

outcome is less well researched, but it appears to have considerable utility in this regard as well. In particular, there is evidence that hyperactive and hyperactive/aggressive children may exhibit differential responses to stimulant medication, especially regarding measures relating to aggression. Therefore, the IOWA-Conners scores for inattention/overactivity and aggression would provide useful information regarding assessment for diagnosis or treatment outcome, especially when supplemented by less easily obtained measures such as laboratory assessment of attention or behavioral observations.

Future Directions

Assuming the continued use of rating scale data in research and clinical practice with hyperactive and aggressive children, the IOWA-Conners is likely to be of considerable importance because of the relative independence of its two scales, as compared with other commonly used rating forms, such as the factors derived from the Conners Teacher Rating Scale. Future research needs to validate the IOWA-Conners Teacher Rating Scale as a measure of treatment outcome by determining, for example, that it is sensitive to medication effects for symptoms of inattention or overactivity as well as concurrent effects on symptoms of aggression. In addition, to date, the IOWA-Conners has been used almost exclusively with school age children. Normative data are not as yet available for pre-schoolers or adolescents, and only limited validity data are available for these populations. These data are important for the early identification of children at risk for later problems, for the long-term assessment of target problems, and for the assessment of possible developmental changes for these two symptom clusters.

References

Atkins, M.S., Pelham, W.E., & Licht, M.H. (1986, November). *The differential validity of teacher ratings of hyperactivity and aggression: A correlational analysis with multiple classroom measures.* Paper presented at the 20th Annual Convention of the Association for Advancement of Behavior Therapy, Chicago, IL.

Landau, S., & Milich R. (1985). Social status of aggressive and aggressive/withdrawn boys: A replication across age and method. *Journal of Consulting and Clinical Psychology, 53,* 141.

Loney, J., & Milich, R. (1982). Hyperactivity, inattention, and aggression in clinical practice. In M. Wolraich & D. Routh (Eds.), *Advances in developmental and* behavioral pediatrics: Vol. 3 (pp. 113-147). Greenwich, CT: JAI Press.

Milich, R., & Fitzgerald, G. (1985). A validation of inattention/overactivity and aggression ratings with classroom observations. *Journal of Consulting and Clinical Psychology, 53*, 139-140.

Milich, R., & Landau, S. (1984). A comparison of the social status and social behavior of aggressive and aggressive/withdrawn boys. *Journal of Abnormal Child Psychology, 12*, 277-288.

Milich R., Landau, S., Kilby, G., & Whitten, P. (1982). Preschool peer perceptions of the behavior of hyperactive and aggressive children. *Journal of Abnormal Child Psychology, 10*, 497-510.

Milich, R., & Pelham, W.E. (1985). *Identifying the aggressiveness in hyperactive/aggressive boys.* Paper presented at the 6th annual meeting on Attention Deficit Disorder, San Antonio.

Murphy, D., Pelham, W., & Milich, R. (1985). *Reliability and validity data for the IOWA-Conners Teacher Rating Scale.* Paper presented at the annual meeting of the Association for the Advancement of Behavior Therapy, Houston.

Irrational Beliefs Inventory

Lynn Alden

Description

The Irrational Beliefs Inventory (IBI) is a brief self-report measure of the irrational ideas hypothesized by Albert Ellis (1962) to underlie emotional disturbance. The inventory consists of 11 statements, each reflecting one irrational belief. The items are preceded by a set of simple instructions: "The statements below concern common beliefs. Read each statement, then mark the extent to which you agree or disagree with that statement." Each item is followed by a 9-point bipolar scale ranging from disagree to agree. The scales are summed to yield a total score.

Purpose

The IBI was developed as a research instrument to assess the association between endorsement of irrational beliefs and various aspects of maladaptive emotion and behavior. The IBI has been used primarily in investigations of nonassertiveness, social anxiety, shyness, and other types of dysfunctional social behavior.

More recently, the IBI is being used by clinicians in treatment programs for nonassertive and shy individuals. In this clinical context, the IBI often serves as a stimulus for discussion of Ellis' irrational beliefs to provide a foundation for rational-emotive and other types of cognitive therapy.

Development

In writing statements to reflect the specific beliefs, our intent was to develop scales that would provide maximum variability among research subjects. In the first stage of development, belief statements were taken directly from Ellis' (1962) volume describing rational-emotive theory and therapy. However, the wording of these original items was sufficiently extreme that subjects were reluctant to endorse the beliefs. The original means were low (around 2 on the 9-point scales), and the range of scores was restricted. As a large part of rational-emotive therapy is focused on convincing clients they do hold such beliefs, it seemed unlikely that even individuals with strongly held irrational beliefs would readily endorse these items on first contact. In the second step of item development, the original beliefs were restated in a less extreme manner. For example, Ellis' statement: "One should be thoroughly competent, adequate, and achieving in all possible respects if one is to consider oneself worthwhile," was stated as: "I believe I should be competent at everything I attempt."

The items were readministered to a sample of university students. The mean scores for the majority of items fell closer to the mid-range of the scale, although the means for items 5, 7, and 11 remained somewhat low (means of 3.41, 2.29, and 3.22, respectively). On all but two items, subjects employed the full range of the scale. On items 5 and 7, subjects used all but the top point on the scale.

Most items were stated in the form of a belief (e.g., "I believe I need another person stronger than myself on whom to rely"). However, three items did not fall readily into this format. All of these concerned emotional reactions to situations (e.g., "When things are not the way I want them to be"). When stated in the belief format ("I believe I should become upset when things are not the way I want them to be"), the items did not seem sensible to subjects and were not endorsed. Virtually none of the pilot subjects believed they should become upset, although some individuals recognized that they did indeed experience more emotional distress than was warranted. These items were worded in terms of the individual's reaction, or overreaction, to the situation.

Psychometric Characteristics

Research on the psychometric characteristics of the IBI has focused primarily on internal consistency. Pearson r's computed between the items, although generally positive, are in the low to moderate range (r's from − .19 to .42). The average interitem correlation is .18, suggesting that the specific items do not measure the same content. The average item-whole scale correlation is .35, ranging from .14 to .52, indicating that there is some shared variance among the items.

A principal components analysis was conducted on the interitem correlation matrix, using unities in the diagonals. The components that emerged were rotated to a simple solution following varimax procedures. Four components emerged with eigenvalues greater than 1. These four components accounted for a total of 62% of the variance.

The first component accounted for 28% of the shared variance and was marked by high positive loadings on belief No. 9 (My past history is an important determinant of my present behavior. I believe that once something strongly affects my life it will always affect my behavior), No. 8 (I believe I need another person stronger than myself on whom to rely), and No. 6 (I become very concerned about things that are dangerous and dwell on the possibility of their occurrence). This component appears to reflect a theme of personal powerlessness. The second component, which accounted for 28% of the shared variance, was marked by high positive loadings on belief No. 11 (I believe there is one right solution to any given problem. If I do not find this solution, I feel I have failed), No. 7 (I believe it is better in the long run to avoid some life difficulties and responsibilities than to face them), and No. 1 (I believe it is important to be loved and approved of by most people). These items reflect personal perfectionism and avoidance, perhaps stemming from that perfectionism.

The third component accounted for 23% of the shared variance, and had high loading on two beliefs, No. 2 (I believe I should be competent at everything I attempt) and No. 4 (I become more upset than I should when things are not the way I want them to be). This component also reflects a type of perfectionism, but the sense here is more of a John McEnroe type of perfectionism, where failure to live up to high self-expectations produces emotional distress. The final component accounted for 21% of the shared variance and reflects a theme of concern, perhaps overconcern,

for others. Belief No. 10 (I become more upset than I should about other people's problems and disturbances) displayed a high positive loading, whereas beliefs No. 3 (I believe that there are some people in the world who are bad...) and No. 5 (I believe most human unhappiness is caused by external factors and that people have little ability to control their own sorrows and disturbances) displayed strong negative loadings. Belief No. 1 displayed a moderate positive loading. This factor structure requires replication in other samples, particularly in clinical samples.

Because the IBI was developed in the context of research on dysfunctional social behavior, the standardization sample also completed three other measures of social behavior: The Social Avoidance and Distress Inventory (Watson & Friend, 1969), the Revised Self-Monitoring Scale (Lennox & Wolfe, 1984), and the Concern for Appropriateness Scale (Lennox & Wolfe, 1984). The latter two scales arose from an empirical investigation of the item domain of Snyder's original Self-Monitoring Scale. The Revised Self-Monitoring Scale assesses sensitivity to social behavior and an ability to modify one's own behavior in response to social cues. The Concern for Appropriateness Scale assesses a tendency to conform due to social anxiety and contains two subscales: Cross-situational Variability and Attention to Social-comparison Information. Subjects were divided into high and low irrational beliefs groups based on a median split of their total IBI scores. High scorers reported significantly more social avoidance and discomfort on the Schedule for Affective Disorders and Schizophrenia than did low scorers (t [100] = 2.73, p <.05). The two groups did not differ on the Revised Self-Monitoring measure, but they did differ significantly on the Concern for Appropriateness scale. More specific analyses revealed that this difference was due to the Social Comparison subscale. High scorers on the IBI were significantly more likely to use ongoing social comparison to guide their social activities (t [100] = 4.41, p <.01) than were low scorers. These data suggest that, relative to low IBI scorers, individuals who endorse irrational beliefs experience greater social discomfort, are less trusting of their own social instincts, and are less willing to stand out in a crowd. These findings are consistent with the reasoning behind the development of the IBI.

Male and female subjects were similar on their total belief scores. However, several significant differences emerged in the specific beliefs. Male subjects were significantly more likely to endorse

Belief 3 (I believe that there are some people in the world who are bad and wicked. They should be held responsible for their actions and punished) than were female subjects ($t [100] = 2.31, p < .05$). Apparently, the men either believed or were more willing to report that there are bad people in the world who should be punished for their actions. The mean score for male subjects on this item, 7.3, was the highest obtained by either group. Male subjects obtained significantly higher scores on Belief 5 (I believe that most human unhappiness is caused by external factors and that people have little ability to control their own sorrows and disturbances) than did female subjects ($t [100] = 2.52, p < .05$). Because the means for both groups were below the scale midpoint, this difference may be better interpreted as women disagreeing more strongly with the statement than did men. Female subjects apparently believed that human unhappiness is more controllable than did male subjects. Female subjects obtained significantly higher scores on Belief 10 (I become more upset than I should about other people's problems) than did males ($t [100] = 2.08, p < .05$). It should be noted that although these differences were statistically significant, they were not dramatic. The two groups were within 1 to 2 points on all of the belief scales.

Clinical Use

The IBI has been used in research investigating characteristics of clients reporting socially dysfunctional behavior (Alden, Safran, & Weideman, 1978; Alden & Safran, 1978). This research suggests that clients seeking treatment for social anxiety and for nonassertiveness obtain significantly higher IBI scores than do nonclinical populations. Changes on the IBI are associated with treatment improvement (Alden, Safran, & Weideman, 1978). Therefore, the IBI may prove useful as a measure of treatment effectiveness. An investigation of individuals seeking assertiveness training revealed that those clients with higher IBI scores behaved less assertively and experienced greater discomfort during a laboratory interaction than did clients with lower IBI scores (Alden & Safran, 1978). Furthermore, the high scorers reported greater difficulties with real-life assertion situations, suggesting that the IBI may be useful in identifying clients with greater social impairment.

Although research to date has used the IBI total score, there is some suggestion that the individual belief scores may provide useful information about different client subgroups. For example, nonassertive clients most strongly endorsed three specific beliefs: "I believe I should be competent as everything I attempt," "I become more upset than I should when things are not the way I want them to be"; and "I believe it is important to be loved and approved of by most people." It may prove useful to design cognitive treatment strategies around these particular themes. Similarly, as noted earlier, there were differences between beliefs endorsed by male and female subjects. These differences may provide guidance in designing treatment strategies for male and female clients.

The IBI is a useful stimulus for discussion in assertiveness or shyness groups, and it can be used as a group exercise to introduce concepts of rational-emotive therapy or systematic rational restructuring.

The IBI has been used primarily with clients seeking treatment for different types of interpersonal problems and requires further investigation before being extended to other populations.

Future Directions

If the IBI is to be a useful instrument, more psychometric information must be collected. For example, information about the temporal stability of total and specific belief scores is important. Research is necessary concerning the extent to which conclusions drawn with socially dysfunctional individuals generalize to other populations. For now, the IBI is best viewed as an experimental instrument that may prove useful in research and treatment with clients with socially dysfunctional behavior.

References

Alden, L., & Safran, S. (1978). Irrational beliefs and non-assertive behavior. *Cognitive Therapy and Research, 2,* 357-364.

Alden, L., Safran, J., & Weideman, R. (1978). A comparison of cognitive and skills training strategies in the treatment of unassertive clients. *Behavior Therapy, 9,* 843-846.

Ellis, A. (1962). *Reason and emotion in psychotherapy.* New York: Lyle Stuart.

Lennox, R.D., & Wolfe, R.N. (1984). Revision of the self-monitoring scales. *Journal of Personality and Social Psychology, 46,* 1349-1364.

Watson, D., & Friend, R. (1969). Measurement of social-evaluative anxiety. *Journal of Consulting and Clinical Psychology, 33,* 448-457.

Issues Checklist

Arthur L. Robin and Sharon L. Foster

Description

The Issues Checklist (IC) assesses self-reports of specific disputes between parents and teenagers (Prinz, Foster, Kent, & O'Leary, 1979). It lists 44 issues that may lead to disagreements between parents and adolescents, such as chores, curfew, bedtime, friends, and homework. Parents and adolescents complete identical versions of the IC. Adolescents in two-parent families complete it separately for disputes with their mothers versus those with their fathers.

For each topic, the respondent indicates whether the issue has been broached during the previous 4 weeks. For each topic reported as having been discussed, the respondent rates the affectual intensity of the discussions on a 5-point scale (ranging from calm to angry) and estimates how often the topics come up. The IC yields three scores for each respondent: (a) the quantity of issues (the total number of issues checked as broached); (b) the anger intensity of issues (an average of the anger-intensity ratings for all of the endorsed issues); and (c) the weighted average of the frequency and anger-intensity level of issues (a score obtained by multiplying each frequency estimate by its associated intensity, summing these cross products, then dividing by the total of all the frequency estimates). The weighted average provides an estimate of the anger *per discussion*, whereas the intensity score reflects the average anger *per issue*, regardless of the frequency with which the issue was discussed.

Purpose

The IC was designed to provide specific information on the frequency and content of disputes between parents and adolescents and the perceived anger-intensity level of these disputes. It covers a broad array of possible disputes applicable to 12- to 16-year-old teenagers and their parents.

Development

The IC was constructed by revising a similar instrument developed by the first author, with issues selected on the basis of literature on parent–adolescent relationships and clinical experience. No pilot testing was done before formal validation studies.

Psychometric Characteristics

The reliability, discriminant/criterion-related validity, and treatment sensitivity of the IC were examined in a number of investigations. Estimates of test-retest reliability were computed in two studies. Using small sample data collected over 6- to 8-week intervals from the wait-list groups of two outcome studies (Foster, Prinz, & O'Leary, 1983; Robin, 1981), adolescent reliability ranged from .49 to .87 for the quantity of issues, .37 to .49 for the anger-intensity score, and .15 to .24 for the weighted frequency by intensity score. Parental reliability was higher, averaging .65 and .55 for mother and father quantity of issues, .81 and .66 for mother and father anger-intensity scores, and .90 and .40 for mother and father weighted frequency by anger-intensity scores. Using 33 nonclinic families assessed over 1- to 2-week intervals, Enyart (1984) found somewhat higher reliabilities, particularly for adolescents (range .49 to .80).

Agreement reliability between mothers and adolescents, assessed by examining whether parents and adolescents concurred that an issue either had or had not been discussed, averaged 68% (range 38 to 86%). When the congruence of mother and adolescent responses was examined by way of correlations, results ranged from .10 to .64 (mean $r = .28$). These results raise questions about the accuracy of the IC as a measure of actual discussions at home.

The discriminant/criterion-related validity of the IC was studied by contrasting the responses of distressed parents and adolescents (referred for treatment of family relationship problems) with the responses of nondistressed parents and teenagers (no history of treatment and self-reports of satisfactory relationships). Aggregated data from three assessment and two treatment studies with male and female adolescents aged 10 to 18 revealed that all of the IC scores discriminated between groups, with the most pronounced effects on maternal anger-intensity scores (accounting for 48% of the variance in distress/nondistressed status) and paternal quantity of issues scores (36% of the variance) (Robin & Foster, 1984). Adolescent effects were much weaker, explaining 3 to 19% of the variance (mean 12%). Across all scores, distressed family members reported significantly more frequent, angrier disputes than did nondistressed family members.

When the IC was used as a before and after measure of change, treatment outcome studies of both a problem-solving communication skill training program and a heterogeneous nonbehavioral family therapy revealed significant decrements in anger-intensity and weighted frequency by anger-intensity scores following intervention (Foster et al., 1983; Robin, 1981).

Clinical Use

The clinician can use the IC to pinpoint sources of conflict and to survey which topics are perceived as provoking the greatest amounts of anger. These topics ordinarily are selected by family members as their most important problems and often warrant further assessment through interviews or home data collection or both. Ratings of IC issues can also help the therapist sequence a skill-oriented treatment so that early intervention sessions focus on less intense conflicts and later sessions address more intense problems. Noting discrepancies between parent and adolescent ICs and inquiring further about them can also yield invaluable information about differential perceptions within the family system. Preliminary norms from distressed and nondistressed families are also available (Robin & Foster, 1984). Because the IC was validated on families with adolescents experiencing externalizing behavior disorders (attention deficit disorder, conduct disorder, etc.), its psychometric properties with families in which the adolescents have other presenting problems are unknown. Therefore, it should be interpreted cautiously with such populations.

Future Directions

The most important unanswered question concerning the IC is the extent to which reports of specific disputes correspond to actual disputes. The low reliability suggests that the IC may not be an accurate measure of actual interactions. Correlational studies comparing retrospective IC scores to daily reports and direct observations of family disputes are needed. In addition, a broader-based normative sample, including distressed families with a variety of presenting problems, would be desirable.

References

Enyart, P. (1984). Behavioral correlates of self-reported parent-adolescent relationship satisfaction. Doctoral dissertation, West Virginia University, Morgantown, West Virginia.

Foster, S.L., Prinz, R.J., & O'Leary, K.D. (1983). Impact of problem-solving communication training and generalization procedures on family conflict. Child and Family Behavior Therapy, 5, 1-23.

Prinz, R.J., Foster, S.L., Kent, R.N., & O'Leary, K.D. (1979). Multivariate assessment of conflict in distressed and nondistressed mother–adolescent dyads. Journal of Applied Behavior Analysis, 12, 691-700.

Robin, A.L. (1981). A controlled evaluation of problem-solving communication training with parent-adolescent conflict. Behavior Therapy, 12, 593-609.

Robin, A.L., & Foster, S.L. (1984). Problem solving communication training: A behavioral-family systems approach to parent–adolescent conflict. In P. Karoly & J.J. Steffen (Eds.), Adolescent behavior disorders: Foundations and contemporary concerns (pp. 195-240). Lexington, MA: D.C. Heath.

Jenkins Activity Survey: Student Version (Form-T)

Kenneth E. Hart

Description

The Student Version of the Jenkins Activity Survey (i.e., JAS-Form T) is a 44-item self-administered multiple choice paper-and-pencil questionnaire that ostensibly measures Type A behavior, a psychosocial "risk-factor" for premature coronary heart disease. The inventory yields three scale scores: an overall, composite score (i.e., JAS-A/B), a Speed and Impatience scale score (i.e., JAS-S/I), and a Hard-Driving Competitive scale score (i.e., JAS-H/C). An inspection of the 21 items that comprise the composite JAS-A/B scale reveals that Type A's, compared to Type B's, see themselves as more serious about life, responsible, energetic/active, impatient, competitive, and hard-driving. In addition, Type A's report having leadership qualities, eating rapidly, having had a fiery temper when young, doing a lot of homework, studying during vacations, juggling more than one project at a time, and encountering and setting deadlines and quotas. The JAS-Form T is the college student version of the original JAS, which was designed for and validated on employed adults.

Purpose

The JAS-Form T was originally developed in an attempt to provide university-based researchers with a convenient, low-cost way to quantify the degree of coronary heart disease risk associated with the Type A, coronary-prone behavior pattern. The intent or purpose of the scale, then, is to tap the Type A construct defined by its originators as "a characteristic action-emotion complex which is exhibited by those individuals who are engaged in a relatively *chronic struggle* to obtain an *unlimited number of poorly defined* things from their environment in *the shortest period of time* and, if necessary, against the opposing effects of other things or persons in this same environment" (Friedman & Rosenman, 1969, p. 84).

Development

Originally, the Type A construct was assessed among employed males solely by means of a "structured interview," a face-to-face stressful interpersonal encounter designed to elicit Type A behaviors in susceptible individuals (Rosenman, 1978). In an attempt to make Type A assessment more convenient, objective, and cost-effective, the Adult version of the JAS was developed. The Adult JAS was designed explicitly to mimic or duplicate the interview. To this end, questions contained in the interview were converted into a pool of self-report multiple choice questions and statements. Each item was then analyzed for its empirical ability to discriminate between men previously judged (by the interview) Type A or B. Only those items found to be valid discriminators were retained for the actual scale.

In 1974, Krantz, Glass, and Snyder modified the fourth revision of the Adult JAS to make it applicable to college students. On the Student version of the JAS (i.e., Form T), all items referring to income, job responsibility, and job involvement were either modified or eliminated. In addition, a total of eight items on the 21-item A/B scale were slightly reworded. For example, the question, "Do you ever set deadlines or quotas for yourself at work or at home?" was changed by substituting the words *in courses or other things* for *at work or at home*. Another item on the A/B scale was completely rewritten so that a new question, "Do you maintain a regular study schedule during vacations such as Thanksgiving, Christmas and Easter?" was substituted for the original question, "In the past three years have you ever taken less than your allotted number of vacation days?" One final item that began with "When you were younger, did most people consider you to be. . ." was modified to "Do most people consider you to be . . ."

Psychometric Characteristics

One recent study examined the abstracts of 161 published papers on experimental studies of Type A behavior, and found that 112 (75%) used the JAS,

and of these 85 (76%) used the Student version. Unfortunately, despite the widespread use of Form T, remarkably little is known about its psychometric properties. To date, no normative data exist for the JAS-Form T, and the inventory has yet to be standardized. An analysis of approximately 30 Type A articles revealed that basic descriptive data were reported in only one-quarter of the studies. The mean JAS-A/B score for these 8 studies was calculated to be 7.76 (n = 1694), while the mean standard deviation for those studies reporting this statistic was 3.33 (n = 626). Statistics pertaining to the reliability of the Student JAS are not readily accessible. While these data may have indeed been reported, this author was able to locate only one article addressing the issue. This study reported a split-half reliability of .82. In the Manual for the copyrighted version of the *Adult* JAS, internal consistency reliability coefficients for the 21 item A/B scale are reported to range from .83 to .85, suggesting that among employed men the scale measures a unified, homogeneous construct. The Manual also reports that when the same JAS edition was readministered over a four- to six-month interval, the retest coefficients ranged from .65 to .82. For retest intervals of from one to four years, coefficients fell between .60 and .70.

It should be noted, however, that the fact that the JAS-Form T is scored differently than the Adult JAS provides reason to suspect that the two forms are less comparable than is commonly assumed. On the A/B scale of the JAS-Form T, the scoring system is binary such that on any particular item, a chosen alternative is either "Type A positive" (i.e., given a weight of one) or not. Type B alternatives are weighted zero.

On the copyrighted version of the Adult JAS (i.e., Form C), each of the response alternatives for the 21 items on the A/B scale is associated with a numerical weight that may vary from − 26 to +81. What is noteworthy, and perhaps problematic, is that the JAS-Form C contains a number of items for which response alternatives defined by the JAS-Form T as not "Type A positive" (i.e., weighted zero) are given substantial weightings. As a result, it is possible for a single person to obtain a raw score of zero on the JAS-Form T (i.e., approach *zero percentile*), while at the same time obtain a raw score of 150 on the Adult JAS, which translates into a rank approaching the *20th percentile*. While it is indeed clear that a difference exists between the Adult and Student JAS in terms of how each is scored, the significance of such a lack of inter-test scorer reliability remains unclear.

Overall, the validity of the Student JAS is questionable. One problem stems from the fact that there is widespread disagreement as to how to conceptualize the Type A construct. Since the construct has not been adequately mapped, it is quite likely that the JAS-Form T does not adequately sample the Type A item universe, and that it fails to cover all aspects of the construct in the correct proportions. In particular, the scale does not tap hostile attitudes, angry emotions, or speech stylistics, all of which are thought to be key aspects of the construct.

On the other hand, however, if the issue of construct validity is addressed from the viewpoint of social-psychological laboratory investigations, the Student JAS seems to fare better. Behavioral studies generally show that JAS-Form T defined A's exhibit exaggerated achievement-striving, a rapid pace, impatience, and aggressiveness when confronted by appropriate environmental circumstances.

Over the last 20 years, the Adult JAS has been subjected to repeated factor analyses which have shown that the scale is comprised of three major dimensions. These factors have been labeled: Factor S (speed and impatience), Factor H (hard-driving and competitive), and Factor J (job involvement). In marked contrast to the Adult JAS, only one study could be found in which the factor structure of the JAS-Form was assessed. Glass (1977) reported in passing that he factor analyzed the JAS-Form T responses of 459 male college students and found items loaded on two dimensions which he labelled Factor S (speed and impatience; JAS-S/I), and Factor H (hard-driving and competitive; JAS-H/C). A job related factor did not emerge because most job items were eliminated when the Adult JAS was modified for students. (It might be mentioned here that items appearing on the scoring keys for Factor S and H of the Student JAS were determined by factor analyses of the Adult JAS; in addition, the scoring procedure for the two subscales is different for the Adult versus Student JAS.)

It is a truism that the validity of a test must be determined with reference to the particular use for which the test is being considered. It is possible, then, that the JAS-Form T may be a valid predictor of laboratory behavior, but not a valid predictor of interview defined Type A behavior, or the risk of heart disease. In this regard, recall that the original intent or purpose of the Adult JAS was to duplicate the interview method of assessment. Studies that have attempted to validate the Adult JAS against the interview have generally shown there is a marked lack of agreement. Using the interview as the criterion, the Adult JAS misclassifies 30 to 40% of subjects. Correlation coefficients are reported to fall between .22 and 31. An overall agreement rate (i.e., percent correct classification) of 63% (13% above chance) has also been reported. Other research indicates that the agreement between the Student JAS and the interview is only of the order of 11 to 13% shared variance. It would seem, then, that despite the fact that the Student JAS purports to measure the same construct as the interview, it is in fact tapping only part of the same construct.

A number of studies have validated the Adult JAS against the prevalence of clinical manifestations of coronary heart disease and the severity of arteriosclerosis. The JAS, however, has been found to be a much weaker predictor of these criteria than the interview. For obvious reasons, it has not been possible to concurrently validate the Student JAS against such criteria. However, the validity of the JAS-Form T has been examined using sympathetic nervous system activation as a proxy measure of coronary pathology. Setting the magnitude of stress induced reactivity as the criterion, research has shown that the JAS-Form T is a relatively poorer predictor when compared to the interview. In terms of predictive validity, research has shown that, after controlling for biomedical risk factors, the 21-item A/B scale of the Adult JAS successfully predicted new cases of coronary disease. However, the A/B scale was found to be a relatively poor predictor of this criterion, capturing only one quarter of the predictive ability of the interview. In addition, it has also been found that each of the JAS subscales fails to demonstrate predictive validity. Recent results from two prospective clinical trials (i.e., MRFIT & AMIS) of individuals at risk for CHD fail to support the predictive validity of the Adult JAS. Prospective studies using the JAS-Form T have not been conducted. Since a test may be valid in predicting a particular criterion in one population, and not valid in predicting the same criterion in a different population, the predictive ability of the Student JAS remains to be determined.

Clinical Use

The Student version of the JAS has been employed almost exclusively as a research instrument in social-psychological and psychophysiologic studies with college students. Only one published study could be located in which the JAS-Form T was used in clinical research (Hart, 1984). As pointed out by the authors of the original Adult JAS, a major limitation of this instrument is that it misclassifies too many people to allow its use for evaluating small group or individual heart disease risk in clinical settings. Clinicians are therefore urged not to rely solely on JAS-Form T scores when attempting to estimate behavior pattern related risk of heart disease. Moreover, because the Student JAS taps only a part of the heterogeneous Type A construct, and because our knowledge of the relative pathogenic potential of each component is so meager, it is possible that reductions in JAS-Form T related Type A behaviors may not result in heart disease risk reduction.

Future Directions

Clinicians and researchers are slowly beginning to realize that the Type A concept is multidimensional, and that perhaps the time is ripe for a comprehensive approach to measurement. This being the case, it seems reasonable to suggest that future assessment efforts might be directed toward the development of some sort of comprehensive assessment battery. This battery might consist of measures that include: psychophysiologic records, interview derived clinical ratings of speech stylistics and hostility, self-reported pace of living and competitive achievement striving (i.e., JAS-Form T scores), the experience and expression of anger, and ways of coping with stress.

As far as the JAS-Form T is concerned, considerably more research is needed to establish its reliability, validity, and factor structure. The development of alternative forms would facilitate reliability research. In addition, normative data need to be collected. Some attention also needs to be given to the possibility of developing a more sophisticated scoring system. This might improve the concurrent validity of the scale.

References

Friedman, M., & Rosenman, R.H. (1969). The possible general causes of coronary heart disease. In M. Friedman (Ed.), *The pathogenesis of coronary artery disease* (pp. 75-135). New York: McGraw Hill.

Glass, D.C. (1977). *Behavior patterns, stress and coronary heart disease*. Hillsdale, NJ: Lawrence Erlbaum.

Hart, K.E. (1984). Anxiety management training and anger control for Type A individuals. *Journal of Behavior Therapy and Experimental Psychiatry, 15,* 133-139.

Krantz, D.S., Glass, D.C., & Snyder, M.L. (1974). Helplessness, stress level, and the coronary-prone behavior pattern. *Journal of Experimental Social Psychology, 10,* 284-300.

Rosenman, R.H. (1978). The interview method of assessment of the coronary-prone behavior pattern. In T.M. Dembroski, S.M. Weiss, J.L. Shields, S.G. Haynes, & M. Feinlieb (Eds.), *Coronary-prone behavior* (pp. 55-70). New York: Springer-Verlag.

Job Interview Assessment

Jeffrey A. Kelly

Description

Job interview assessment is a role-played simulation of a preemployment interview. In this social skill assessment, the client is asked to play the part of a candidate seeking employment; the part of the interviewer is played by a confederate. During the assessment, the role-play interviewer directs a series of interview questions to the client, and the client responds to them as she or he would in a genuine job interview situation. A job interview assessment role-play is of approximately the same duration as a genuine interview, because the interaction is intended to simulate a realistic employment interview. The performance is often tape-recorded and closely evaluated to assess strengths and deficits in the client's job interview skills.

Purpose

Research has shown that decisions to hire someone are often based on impressions made by the applicant during an employment interview. Because employers make inferences about a candidate's experience, work habits, reliability, honesty, and personality quickly during an interview (Cohen & Etheridge, 1975), it is important that job-seeking individuals learn to appropriately handle the interview situation. Even if an applicant has sound work skills, the inability to effectively convey this information to an interviewer may produce a failure in job-seeking efforts.

Within the social skills assessment and training literature, role-play enactments are widely used to identify deficits in a client's interpersonal skills repertoire. Job interview role-plays are used for the same purpose. Clients who will soon be seeking a job or clients with a history of unsuccessful job attainment can be asked to role-play job interview interactions. If deficits are observed in the client's handling of the practice interview, social skills training can then be used to teach more effective interview behavior. A job interview role-play can also be used as the practice vehicle for behavior rehearsal in social skills training sessions, and performance improvement following training provides information on the effectiveness of skills training efforts.

Development

Studies that have employed job interview assessment use a "pool" of standard interview questions and comments (Kelly, 1982; Kelly, Laughlin, Claiborne, & Patterson, 1979; Kelly, Urey, & Patterson, 1981; Kelly, Wildman, & Berler, 1980). These might include questions directed to the client about work experience ("Can you tell me about your past experience?"), education ("Why do you want to work here?"), background ("What do you like to do in your spare time?"), and other comments ("Do you have any questions for me?," "Is there anything else you would like to tell me?," etc.). These interviewer questions are arranged in a realistic script, with the client responding to each one. Development of interview assessment role-plays has largely been based on intuitive, face validity criteria, although some investigators developed specific questions by surveying genuine interviewers to determine what questions they typically ask of job applicants (Kelly et al., 1980).

When evaluating client skill in the interview role-play, a number of nonverbal and stylistic behaviors have been observed and related to interview effectiveness. *Appropriate verbal behaviors* targeted for assessment and later training attention include fully describing one's past work experience and accomplishments; job skills and vocational competencies; educational background and training; interest in the position and enthusiasm for work; personal background that connotes responsibility, reliability, and positive personal attributes; and directing appropriate questions to the interviewer. *Nonverbal behaviors* identified as useful in the interview include appropriate affect, eye contact, posture, and voice quality. *Stylistic skills* that can be observed in a client's interviewer role-play include succinct and focused responses to the interviewer's questions; composure and "thoughtful" quality of response; and effective integration of verbal and nonverbal skill elements. (See Kelly [1982] and Kelly et al. [1980] for elaborated descriptions of these target behaviors.)

To date, investigators using job interview skill assessment procedures have employed different methods of rating client skills during the role-play. In some cases, counts are made of the frequency with which the client exhibits a skill behavior during the entire role-play (e.g., the total number of positive "facts" about work experience that the client conveys). Other aspects of skill can be evaluated using global criteria of effectiveness (e.g., rating the client's voice quality using a 7-point scale).

Psychometric Characteristics

As with other forms of role-play assessment, job interview role-plays are likely to yield valid data only if: (a) the staged interaction closely approximates what takes place in real-life job interviews, and (b) the client's behavior in the role-play reflects his or her behavior in genuine job interviews. Direct evaluation of the validity of job interview role-plays has not yet been undertaken. However, indirect correlational evidence supports their validity. For example, experienced personnel managers asked to make "blind" judgments of client job interview assessments have been shown to ascribe higher ratings to role-plays enacted after social skills training than before its implementation (Kelly et al., 1980). Effective job interview role-play performance has also been associated with higher rates of actual success in employment attainment, although these data have relied on small client samples (Kelly et al., 1979). Reliability between trained judges asked to rate job interview skill behaviors exhibited by clients during assessment role-plays has been consistently high in a number of studies.

Clinical Use

Assessment of job interview skills is likely to be useful for clients inexperienced in job interviewing, for clients who are anxious and unable to present themselves effectively in the interview situation, or for clients who are expected to encounter other problems in the job-seeking process. Specific populations that have received assessment attention with this procedure, usually followed by interview skills training, include the chronically unemployed, first-time job seekers, formerly hospitalized psychiatric patients, and developmentally challenged persons who have completed vocational training and are seeking standard employment. (See Kelly [1982] for a review of assessment of these populations.)

Assessment and training of job interview skills are most appropriate clinically for those individuals who have adequate employment skills, will be attempting to gain employment, but are likely to have difficulties in self-presentation. It is also prudent to consider that successful job attainment requires the presence of a variety of other skill competencies, including being able to telephone employers to arrange for an interview, completing job application forms, and once hired, interacting effectively with others on the job. The clinician assessing a client's job interview skills may wish to evaluate behaviorally the client's skills in these related areas as well.

Future Directions

Although researchers and clinicians have used job interview assessment role-plays extensively, relatively little effort has been made to document that the assessment procedure closely approximates the demands and stimulus characteristics of real-life job interviews. Future projects might seek to analyze the content of genuine employment interviews and to study the specific criteria used by personnel interviewers when they evaluate jobseekers; basic data of this kind would better ensure the validity of the assessment procedure.

In addition and in common with other social skill assessments, it will be important to more closely evaluate skill generalization from the role-play assessment to behavior in the actual job interview situation. Presenting clients with novel interview questions during their assessment role-plays, using multiple role-play interviewers, and conducting the assessments in realistic settings similar to those in which genuine interviews will take place are strategies that may improve the generalizability and the validity of this assessment technique.

References

Cohen, B.M., & Etheridge, J.M. (1975). Recruiting's main ingredient. *Journal of College Placement, 35*, 75-77.

Kelly, J.A. (1982). *Social skills training: A practical guide for interventions.* New York: Springer.

Kelly, J.A., Laughlin, C., Claiborne, M., & Patterson, J. (1979). A group procedure for teaching job interviewing skills to formerly hospitalized psychiatric patients. *Behavior Therapy, 10*, 299-310.

Kelly, J.A., Urey, J.R., & Patterson, J. (1981). Small group job interview skills training in the mental health center setting. *Behavioral Counseling Quarterly, 1*, 202-212.

Kelly, J.A., Wildman, B.G., & Berler, E.S. (1980). Small group behavioral training to increase the job interview skills repertoire of mildly retarded adolescents. *Journal of Applied Behavior Analysis, 13*, 461-471.

Kiddie-Schedule for Affective Disorders and Schizophrenia in Present Episode

Francis C. Harris

Description

The Kiddie-Schedule for Affective Disorders and Schizophrenia in Present Episode (K-SADS-P) is a semistructured psychiatric interview instrument administered to a child or adolescent (6 to 17 years old) and his or her parent. The entire proceeding takes approximately 1.5 to 2 hours. First, the parent is interviewed in an unstructured fashion to establish the chronology of a psychiatric disorder and the period of its greatest severity. Next, the parent is questioned about numerous specific features of child psychiatric disorders. The interviewer rates the presence and severity of each feature on the basis of the parents' responses and information from other sources, such as teachers. Next, the child is interviewed regarding the presence or absence of each feature. Following the child interview, the interviewer makes a "summary" judgment of the presence or absence of each feature based on all of the information obtained. The protocol itself is lengthy, but it presents a variety of ways in which questions might be asked. More detailed information on administration also is available (Chambers et al., 1985).

Purpose

The K-SADS-P was designed to assess the presence or absence of four major diagnostic categories of psychiatric disorders as defined by Research Diagnostic Criteria (Spitzer, Endicott, & Robins, 1978) and the DSM-III (American Psychiatric Association, 1980). These categories of psychopathology are affective, anxiety, conduct, and psychotic disorders (Chambers et al., 1985).

Development

The K-SADS-P was designed by Puig-Antich and his colleagues to "mirror" the Schedule for Affective Disorders and Schizophrenia (SADS), which had been developed to assign psychiatric diagnoses to adults. The K-SADS-P was developed initially to assess affective disorders, but it was expanded rapidly to include anxiety, conduct, and psychotic disorders.

Psychometric Characteristics

A preliminary study demonstrated adequate inter-rater reliability of diagnosis, internal consistency for items within symptom groups, and test-retest reliability for depressive, conduct, and psychotic disorders, but not for anxiety/attentional disorders (Chambers et al., 1985).

Clinical Use

The K-SADS-P is a useful clinical tool in that it presents a structure for assessing a wide variety of problem behaviors. It is especially useful in situations that require a "diagnosis." In addition, information gleaned from the interview is useful in selecting problem target behaviors for intervention.

Future Directions

The K-SADS-P represents a major improvement in the assessment of psychopathology in children and adolescents. Although initial reliability data are encouraging, behavioral assessors are likely to be somewhat uncomfortable in relying on a self-report instrument without demonstrated relationships between objective behavioral ratings. Assessment studies that explore the relationships between K-SADS-P responses and direct observations of child behavior in various settings would be of great interest.

References

American Psychiatric Association. (1980). *Diagnostic and statistical manual of mental disorders* (3rd ed.). Washington, DC: American Psychiatric Association.

Chambers, W.J., Puig-Antich, J., Hirsch, M., Paez, P., Ambrosini, P.J., Tabrizi, M.A., & Davies, M. (1985). The assessment of affective disorders in children and adolescents by semistructured interview: Test-retest reliability of the K-SADS-P. *Archives of General Psychiatry, 42,* 696-702.

Spitzer, R.L., Endicott, J., & Robins, E. (1978). Research Diagnostic Criteria: Rationale and reliability. *Archives of General Psychiatry, 35,* 773-782.

Large Scale Integrated Sensor

Leonard H. Epstein

Description

The Large Scale Integrated Sensor (LSI) is a small (3.8 by 4.5 by 2.2 cm), lightweight (51 g) unit completely contained with battery, in a rugged Plexiglas housing. It contains a mercury switch, sensitive to 10 degrees tilt from horizontal, activated by the motion of the wearer. Every 16 closures of the mercury switch produce 1 count on the external counter. A magnet activates the 4-digit display (McPartland, Kupfer, & Foster, 1976).

Purpose

The LSI is designed as an objective measure of activity. One measure that is obtained is the activity count per unit of time observed. In addition, recent research has shown that it is possible to obtain an estimate of energy expenditure from the activity counts based on individual calibration curves for each subject (McGowan, Bulik, Epstein, Kupfer, & Robertson, 1984). The monitor records activity that involves horizontal movement of the body, such as walking, but not such activities as weight lifting or bicycling.

Development

The LSI was developed as a measure of activity to assess activity patterns for psychiatric patients, particularly those with affective illness (Kupfer et al., 1974). These measures were used both to assist in the differential diagnosis of depression and to assess changes in the activity component of depression. They have more recently been used as a more general method of assessing activity, with emphasis on relating activity counts to energy expenditure (LaPorte et al., 1979).

Psychometric Characteristics

The LSI is a very reliable instrument, with a small number of missed readings (LaPorte et al., 1979). In addition, no significant differences were observed in activity counts of subjects over two consecutive days of recording (LaPorte et al., 1979). The LSI counts correlate with self-reported measures of activity (McPartland, Kupfer, Foster, Reisler, & Matthews, 1975). The LSI is best suited to activities that involve movement, such as walking, and not activities in which the person is not moving, such as weight lifting. In addition, when walking, the LSI is responsive to distance and to treadmill speed in controlled investigations (LaPorte et al., 1979), but not to changes in grade. The LSI has been used on the waist, wrist, and ankle, and each position may provide different indications of activity. The wrist measure is often used to assess depression, whereas the waist measure is more closely related to energy expenditure than is the ankle measure (LaPorte et al., 1979).

Clinical Use

The LSI is a general measure of activity that may be of use to any clinician or investigator assessing activity.

Future Directions

The measurement of activity is an important aspect of assessment of many disorders. Although activity counts can serve as an important dependent variable, the activity counts in many cases should be converted to an external standard for comparison among persons who differ in body size, rate of walking, and the like. For this reason, continued research on the relationship between activity counts and energy expenditure is needed. In addition, information classifying the activities that are best measured by the LSI is important to its valid use.

References

Kupfer, D.J., Weiss, B.L., Foster, F.G., Detre, T.P., Delgado, J., & McPartland, R. (1974). Psychomotor activity in affective states. *Archives of General Psychiatry, 30,* 765-768.

LaPorte, R.E., Kuller, L.H., Kupfer, D.J., McPartland, R.J., Matthews, G., & Caspersen, C. (1979). An objective measure of physical activity for epidemiologic research. *American Journal of Epidemiology, 109,* 158-168.

McGowan, C.R., Bulik, C.M., Epstein, L.H., Kupfer, D.J., & Robertson, R.J. (1984). The use of the Large-Scale Integrated Sensor (LSI) to estimate energy expenditure. *Journal of Behavioral Assessment, 6,* 51-57.

McPartland, R.J., Kupfer, D.J., & Foster, F.G. (1976). The movement activated recording monitor: A third-generation motor-activity monitoring system. *Behavior Research Methods and Instrumentation, 8,* 357-360.

McPartland, R.J., Kupfer, D.J., Foster, F.G., Reisler, K.L., & Matthews, G. (1975). *Biotelemetry, 2,* 317-323.

Lehrer-Woolfolk Anxiety Symptom Questionnaire

Paul M. Lehrer and Robert L. Woolfolk

Description

The Lehrer-Woolfolk Anxiety Symptom Questionnaire (Lehrer & Woolfolk, 1982) is a 36-item factor analytically derived instrument designed to measure somatic, cognitive, and behavioral aspects of anxiety. Each item is rated by the examinee on a Likert type scale from 0 (never) to 8 (almost always). The 16 somatic items represent the symptoms of hyperventilation, the 9 behavioral items the symptoms of social avoidance, and the 11 cognitive items a tendency to worry and ruminate.

Purpose

This questionnaire measures separately three dimensions of anxiety that, according to our review of the comparative treatment literature, respond differentially to modality-specific treatments (Lehrer & Woolfolk, 1984). The instrument can be administered with instructions to complete it with reference to an individual's experience with any specific time period (e.g., the past 2 weeks or the past 6 months), and it was specifically designed to be used as an outcome measure in studies of specific treatment for any of the three types of anxiety.

Development

The items were developed from an initial pool of 113 items chosen by the investigators because they reflected one of the three hypothesized types of anxiety: somatic, cognitive, and behavioral. Items were adapted from the Minnesota Multiphasic Personality Inventory, the 16 Personality Factor Questionnaire, and the State–Trait Anxiety Inventory, and were drawn from the clinical experience of the investigators. These items were given to a heterogeneous population, consisting of 253 adult students in collegiate night school introductory psychology classes, 65 participants in a stress workshop at a mental health center, and 67 anxious neurotic outpatients recruited through psychiatrists, psychologists, mental health centers, and other mental health professionals and clinics in the Central New Jersey area.

Only items that, according to a *t*-test, discriminated at the *p* <.05 level between the night school students and the anxious patients were included in the principal components analysis to insure that the derived scales all represent dimensions of neurotic anxiety. In addition, one of each pair of items that correlated at levels >.7 was arbitrarily excluded before the principal components analysis, to prevent the emergence of factors based on semantic equivalence of two or more items. Sixty-eight of the items met the criteria for inclusion in the principal components analysis. The first factor, hyperventilation, accounted for 28.3% of the total variance and had an eigenvalue of 19.3; the second factor, social avoidance, 6.1% of the total variance and an eigenvalue of 4.1; and the third factor, worry and rumination, 3.4% of the total variance and an eigenvalue of 2.3.

Psychometric Characteristics

The correlations between factors range from *r* = .47 to *r* = .66. The cognitive factor is significantly more closely related to the other two factors than the latter are to each other. Split–half reliabilities are .93 for the somatic factor, .91 for the behavioral factor, and .92 for the cognitive factor.

Clinical Use

This scale is designed to assess specific aspects of anxiety in treatment outcome studies. With appropriate caution, it may be used as a clinical tool to help the clinician determine which response domain to address in the course of therapy. The items were specifically designed to discriminate neurotic mental health center clients or psychiatric patients with "primary symptoms of anxiety" from others. The test is therefore most appropriate for this population. Because the overwhelming number of persons in the standardization sample were white middle–class Americans, caution should be exercised when using this instrument with other populations.

Future Directions

To our knowledge, this instrument has thus far been used in only two clinical outcome studies. In a study cited by Lehrer and Woolfolk (1982), anxious college freshmen were given either cognitive therapy or communications skills training. Subjects in the cognitive therapy group improved only on the cognitive scale, whereas subjects in the communications skills training group improved only on the behavioral scale of the Lehrer-Woolfolk Anxiety Symptom Questionnaire. Two other studies, however, found that this scale did not differentiate the effects of progressive relaxation and mantra meditation among anxious volunteers (Woolfolk, Lehrer, McCann, & Rooney, 1982; Lehrer, Woolfolk, Rooney, McCann, & Carrington, 1983), and one study found that it did not differentiate the effects of cognitive therapy, progressive relaxation, and behavior rehearsal among socially anxious adults (McCann, Woolfolk, & Lehrer, 1985).

In the future, greater use of this instrument should be made in clinical outcome studies of modality-specific anxiety treatments. When and if this instrument reliably predicts specific treatment effects, it may be useful as a clinical tool to determine which behavioral treatments may be most useful for a particular anxious individual.

References

Lehrer, P.M., & Woolfolk, R.L. (1982). Self-report assessment of anxiety: Somatic, cognitive, and behavioral modalities. *Behavioral Assessment, 4,* 167-177.

Lehrer, P.M., & Woolfolk, R.L. (1984). Are stress reduction techniques interchangeable, or do they have specific effects?: A review of the comparative empirical literature. In R.L. Woolfolk & P.M. Lehrer (Eds.), *Principles and practice of stress management.* New York: Guilford Press.

Lehrer, P.M., Woolfolk, R.L., Rooney, A.J., McCann, B., & Carrington, P. (1983). Progressive relaxation and meditation: A study of psychophysiological and therapeutic differences between two techniques. *Behaviour Research and Therapy, 21,* 651-662.

McCann, B.S., Woolfolk, R.L., & Lehrer, P.M. (1985). *Specificity in response to treatment: A study of interpersonal anxiety.* Unpublished manuscript, Rutgers University.

Woolfolk, R.L., Lehrer, P.M., McCann, B.S., & Rooney, A.J. (1982). Effects of progressive relaxation and meditation on cognitive and somatic manifestations of daily stress. *Behaviour Research and Therapy, 20,* 461-468.

Leyton Obsessional Inventory

Paul M. G. Emmelkamp

Description

The Leyton Obsessional Inventory (LOI) (Cooper, 1970) consists of 69 questions printed on separate cards, which a respondent puts into either the "Yes" or "No" slots of an answer box. Forty-six questions are concerned with obsessional symptoms and the other 23 with obsessive traits, thus giving *symptom* and *trait* scores. Further questions regarding 35 of the cards provide a *resistance* score (measuring the severity rather than the symptoms) and an *interference* score (measuring the disability caused by the symptoms).

Questions about a wide range of obsessional symptoms are included, with particular emphasis upon domestic topics such as household cleanliness and tidiness. The trait questionnaire contains questions about meanness, moodiness, irritability, stubbornness, pedantry, conscientiousness, punctuality, and hoarding. A disadvantage of the LOI concerns the interdependence of the subscales. All items that might involve resistance and interference and that have been put in the "Yes" box the first time have to be rated a second and a third time for resistance and interference, respectively. Therefore, the scores on the latter scales are not independent from the scores on the symptom and trait scales. Furthermore, the LOI contains neither items concerning unpleasant or abhorrent thoughts, nor items concerning excessive handwashing.

Purpose

Although the questionnaire was originally developed for studying obsessional attitudes and traits in normal families, it is now being used clinically to assess the symptoms and traits of obsessional patients. In addition, it can be used as an outcome measure to assess the effects of treatment of obsessional patients. Finally, this inventory has been widely used as a research instrument to study the nature of obsessional complaints.

Development

Cooper (1970) demonstrated that the scales of the LOI could discriminate among obsessional patients, house-bound housewives, and normal women. The obsessional patients received the highest scores, normal women the lowest, and the house-bound housewives scored between the other groups. Murray, Cooper, and Smith (1979) found that the four subscales discriminated between obsessional patients and normal subjects. In addition, Kendel and diScipio (1970) found that depressed patients with obsessional symptoms and traits gave high symptom and trait scores on the LOI, but scored much lower than obsessional

neurotics on resistance and interference. Therefore, the latter scales distinguish primary obsessional patients from those with primary depression.

A major disadvantage of this inventory is the time taken to administer it. For obsessional patients the time taken may be over 1 hour. Snowdon (1980) compared results on the postbox form with results when the LOI was administered as a questionnaire. Correlations between both versions of the LOI were reasonably good ($r = .72$ to .77), which suggests that the LOI might be used in written questionnaire form.

Psychometric Characteristics

Murray et al. (1979) found distinct distributions of the scores of obsessional and normal subjects. There was almost no overlapping on symptom, resistance, and interference scores, whereas there was considerable overlapping in trait scores. Similar results were reported by Miller (1980).

Several studies have addressed the issue of reliability of the LOI. Test-retest reliability is satisfactory for both the symptom and trait scale (Cooper, 1970). Furthermore, the LOI is rather homogeneous, resulting in a Cronbach's alpha of .93 (Kraaykamp, Emmelkamp, & van der Hout, 1986).

Murray et al. (1979) performed a principal component analysis on the correlation matrix formed from the responses of 73 obsessional patients on the LOI. The first five components that emerged from the analysis accounted for 30% of the variance. Three of the components were unipolar and were labeled (a) household order, (b) personal contamination, and (c) doubting. The other two components were bipolar and concerned (a) checking/parsimony and (b) desire for closure/ unpleasant ruminations. Earlier analysis of normal subjects provided an almost similar picture.

The concurrent validity of the LOI was assessed by comparing scores on this measure with those on the Maudsley Obsessional-Compulsive Inventory, resulting in a correlation of .67 for the total scores of both questionnaires (Kraaykamp et al., 1986).

Clinical Use

The LOI is widely used as an instrument to assist clinicians in the assessment of obsessive-compulsive disorders and for treatment planning and evaluation. The symptom and trait scales do not necessarily discriminate between primary depressed patients and obsessional patients, so caution should be used in interpreting the scores on these scales with depressed patients. Because this questionnaire was not developed for clinical purposes, a number of relevant characteristics of obsessive-compulsive behavior and thoughts cannot be assessed with this questionnaire (e.g., obsessions and handwashing).

Future Directions

Relatively little work has been done to evaluate the LOI psychometrically. The most interesting aspect from a clinical point of view (the resistance and interference scales) has hardly been investigated psychometrically. Researchers interested in developing this questionnaire might first increase the item pool with items representing clinically relevant aspects of obsessive-compulsive disorder, and then by further analyses reduce the item pool to only psychiatric conditions (e.g., depression). The concurrent validity needs to be investigated by comparing LOI scores with behavioral measures of obsessive-compulsive disorder.

References

Cooper, J. (1970). The Leyton Obsessional Inventory. *Psychological Medicine, 1*, 48-64.

Kendel, R., & diScipio, W.J. (1970). Obsessional symptoms and obsessional personality traits in patients with depressive illnesses. *Psychological Medicine, 1*, 65-72.

Kraaykamp, H.J.M., Emmelkamp, P.M.G., & van der Hout, M. (in preparation). The Maudsley Obsessional-Compulsive Inventory: A psychometric evaluation.

Miller, D.G. (1980). A repertory grid study of obsessionality: Distinctive cognitive structure or distinctive content? *British Journal of Medical Psychology, 53*, 59-66.

Murray, R.M., Cooper, J.E., & Smith, A. (1979). The Leyton Obsessional Inventory: An analysis of the responses of 73 obsessional patients. *Psychological Medicine, 9*, 305-311.

Snowdon, J.A. (1980). A comparison of written and post-box forms of the Leyton Obsessional Inventory. *Psychological Medicine, 10*, 165-170.

Likert Scaling

Gail Steketee, Blanche Freund, and Edna B. Foa

Development and Description

The term Likert scaling refers to a method of measuring a subject's responses to a question using a continuous dimension with numerical anchor points. The Likert-like scales presently employed in clinical assessment were based on research on attitude scaling pioneered by Thurstone.

To simplify Thurstone's method of scoring, Likert, Roslow, and Murphy (1934) scaled responses on a 5-point continuum from strongly disagree to strongly agree, assigning extreme choices the number 5 or 1, depending upon its positive or negative valence with respect to the overall dimension being measured. Intermediate alternatives were given values of 2, 3, or 4. Intervals between anchor points were presumed to be equal, and therefore a subject's endorsements of particular attitudes could be summed across scales to yield a total score. This score was treated as interval data for purposes of statistical analysis and interpretation.

Originally used to measure attitudes in clinical research, such scales are now frequently employed to assess the severity of a patient's symptoms. In this context they are commonly referred to as Likert-like or Likert-type scales. The number of intervals on these scales typically ranges from 2 points (dichotomous, e.g., true-false and agree-disagree) to more than 10 points. The scale is divided by "anchors" in which a number on the scale corresponds to a written descriptor. For example, in rating the severity of fear on a 5-point scale the following anchors may be employed: 0 = no fear, 1 = mild fear, 2 = moderate fear, 3 = considerable fear, and 4 = extreme fear. Although equal distances between anchors are implied by the numerical sequence, they may not be reflected in the semantic intervals between the descriptors. A scale requesting the use of percentage points of numerical quantities may yield data that can more confidently be viewed as equal-interval. For example, "How much improvement have you experienced in your target symptom since the beginning of treatment?" can be scored on a scale ranging from 0 to 100% with 11 anchor points, each spanning 10 percentage points.

Purpose

In clinical research, Likert-like scales have been used to quantify information about behaviors or cognitions of interest to the clinician. Such scales may assess the outcome of behavioral interventions using self, therapist, and independent assessor ratings of various target symptoms. For example, Foa and her colleagues have employed 9-point scales adapted from studies by Watson and Marks.

These scales are used by patients and assessors to rate the intensity of the main obsessive fear and time spent ritualizing as well as the severity of depressed and anxious mood and adequacy of general functioning at home and work. Similarly, researchers studying agoraphobia (e.g., Marks, Mathews, and Emmelkamp) have assessed anxiety and avoidance with respect to specific situations; 0 to 8 scales, ranging from "none at all" to "extremely severe" have been completed by patients, their spouses, and therapists. With both patient populations, the use of Likert scaling enabled investigators to study change in target symptoms that were specifically defined for each individual client.

By contrast with the foregoing usage, Marks and Mathews (1979) developed a Fear Questionnaire in which a series of standard behavioral situations associated with phobic avoidance, anxiety, and other psychiatric symptoms were rated on 9-point Likert-like scales. A global rating of the indivdual's main phobic symptoms was also included. Verbal descriptors of the numerical anchor points varied according to the type of symptom being rated. Many of the standardized questionnaires measuring psychiatric symptoms discussed elsewhere in this volume utilize Likert scaling.

Psychometric Characteristics

Reliability.   Test-retest reliability of Likert scales used by Foa and her colleagues to assess obsessive-compulsive symptoms ranged from .40 to .87 for self-ratings and from .20 to .50 for assessor ratings over a mean 60–day interval (Freund, 1985). These relatively low correlations may have resulted from the restricted range of severity and inadequate training of assessors in the use of the scale anchors. By contrast, the test-retest coefficients for the Marks and Mathews (1979) Fear Questionnaire were generally good; the lowest correlation was .79 for the global rating of phobic disturbance. Interrater reliability for this measure has been found to be satisfactory by some investigators but not by others. Emmelkamp (1982) notes that earlier forms of global rating scales using a 5-point interval yielded less satisfactory correlations than did the later 9-point scale versions.

Validity.   With respect to the validity of the summed Likert-like scales used in the Fear Questionnaire, Williams (1985) pointed out that self-ratings of specific fears bore only a moderate relationship to actual phobic behavior as measured

by performance on a behavioral test in a similar situation. Average correlations of main phobia ratings and behavioral test performance after treatment ranged from − .53 to − .59 in several studies.

When used to assess symptoms of obsessive-compulsive behavior, self-rated Likert-like scales correlated moderately (.56 to .59) with a standardized self-rated measure (Maudsley Obsessive-Compulsive Inventory). Similar correlations (.55 to .60) were obtained for assessor-rated Likert-like scales and an assessor-rated standardized measure (Compulsive Activity Checklist). Sensitivity to change following treatment has been reported in several studies using various Likert-like rating scales. However, Williams (1985) has raised concern that such scales tend to overestimate a patient's improvement, thus exaggerating the value of weak treatment and obscuring differences in effectiveness among treatment methods.

Clinical Use

The data just reported focus on the use of individual Likert scales in the assessment of the symptoms and functioning of anxiety-disordered individuals. A review of recent volumes on behavioral assessment techniques suggests that such rating scales are used more frequently in this population. However, they appear appropriate for use in assessing symptoms in any psychiatric population and are presently employed in National Institute of Mental Health studies to rate general impairment in functioning, mania, depression, and psychosis.

There are several advantages to using such scales in clinical treatment. They are relatively easy to administer and the use of identical forms rated by the patient, an independent assessor, the therapist, and/or an informant permits a comparison among observers. Their adaptability for use in rating specific symptoms selected by the investigator is particularly valuable when no standardized measure of the target symptoms is available. For example, in rating the symptoms of obsessive-compulsive subjects, the absence of a standardized measure of obsessions alone (apart from compulsive behaviors) or, conversely, compulsions alone (apart from obsessions) was remedied by the use of separate Likert scales for these two obsessive-compulsive manifestations. These scales permitted the study of the separate effects of behavioral treatment procedures on each type of symptom. As Emmelkamp (1982) points out, however, scores of different patients are not directly comparable when different types of symptoms are assessed. Obviously, the value of measuring specific targets for change must be balanced against the need for comparability of ratings among patients. The latter can only be accomplished if the population is homogeneous with respect to their target problems.

To ensure accuracy and therefore reliability of measurement over time and across raters, anchor points for the intervals on Likert-like scales should be carefully defined with discrete, objective and, if possible, quantitative response choices. Because of the difficulty in assuring equal intervals between anchoring points of a given scale, investigators may wish to be cautious about their application of parametric statistics to data derived from Likert scales.

Future Directions

Their ease of administration and ability to measure highly specific target symptoms render Likert scales a valuable tool for assessing behavior. However, because of concerns about their use as interval data and the relative lack of information regarding reliability and validity, these scales should be used in conjunction with other measures (standardized self-report measures as well as behavioral observations and physiological responses). The need for other measures is further emphasized by Wilson (1982), who noted that "changes of one or two points on a five- or nine-point rating scale. . . provide a very limited view of therapeutic progress" (p. 86).

References

Emmelkamp, P.M.G. (1982). *Phobic and obsessive-compulsive disorders*. New York: Plenum Press.

Freund, B. (1985). *Comparison of obsessive-compulsive symptomatology measures: Standardized versus global rating scales, assessor versus self-rated*. Unpublished manuscript.

Likert, R., Roslow, S., & Murphy, G. (1934). A simple and reliable method of scoring the Thurstone Attitude Scale. *Journal of Social Psychology, 5,* 228-238.

Marks, I.M., & Mathews, A.M. (1979). A brief standard self-rating scale for phobia patients. *Behaviour Research and Therapy, 17,* 263-267.

Williams, L.S. (1985). On the nature and measurement of agoraphobia. In M. Hersen, R.E. Eisler, & P.M. Miller (Eds.), *Progress in behavior modification: Vol. 19* (pp. 109-144). New York: Academic Press.

Wilson, G.T. (1982). Fear reduction methods and the treatment of anxiety disorders. In C.M. Franks, G.T. Wilson, P.C. Kendall, & K.D. Brownell (Eds.), *Annual review of behavior therapy* (pp. 82-119). New York: Guilford Press.

Marital Interaction Coding System

Daniel L. Tennenbaum

Description

The Marital Interaction Coding System (Weiss & Summers, 1983) is used by highly trained raters to give a molecular description of a couples' behavior as they engage in problem-solving discussions as recorded on videotape. The MICS includes 32 carefully defined codes which describe all observed behaviors in such discussions. They include positive verbal and nonverbal behaviors (e.g., Complain, Put Down, Turn Off), problem solving behaviors (e.g., Positive Solution and Compromise), and the two codes, Attend and Not Tracking, that describe listener state rather than discrete behavoirs.

MICS codes are applied sequentially to each new behavioral unit defined as "behavior of homogeneous content, irrespective of duration or formal grammatical accuracy emitted by a single partner" (Weiss & Summers, 1983, p. 89). More than one code may be required to fully describe a specific behavioral unit. Additionally, a simultaneous description of listener behavior is maintained, indicating at a minimum whether the listener is "Attending" or "Not Tracking."

The MICS provides seven summary categories based on code function for the 32 codes, including Problem Description, Blame, Proposal for Change, Validation, Invalidation, Facilitation, and Irrelevant. This simplification of the coding system greatly facilitates the analysis and interpretation of complex interactional data. Subsequently, these summary categories are than used in the creation of dyadic behavior units (DBU). Each DBU contains the behavior of the speaker described by one of the seven category codes, and the concurrent behavior of the listener. The advantage of DBUs is that the sequence of coded behavior is clarified, and a context (i.e., listener behavior) is given for each speech. This allows for the statistical evelution of the contribution of both speaker and listener behavior to the occurrence of subsequent behavior. Software developed within the Oregon Marital Studies program automatically converts raw MICS data into DBUs which can than be analyzed. The availability of this process should greatly facilitate sophisticated analysis of MICS data.

Purpose

The MICS is used to describe the actual behaviors couples engage in during problem-solving discussions. Use of the MICS has also been extended to other family subgroups (e.g., Parent-Child; Jacob, Ritchey, Cvitkovic, & Blane, 1981).

Development

The MICS was developed by Weiss and his colleagues as part of an integrated assessment and treatment approach to marital distress. The behavioral theories which guided its development encouraged a focus on discrete, relatively well-defined behaviors. Patterned after the Family Interaction Coding System (Patterson, Ray, Shaw, & Cobb, 1969), which had been developed within the same theoretical framework to perform the related function of describing family interactions in the home, the MICS resulted in a less inferential description of couples' communication than could be obtained using more traditional self-report procedures. Measures of interaction derived from the MICS could then be used for identifying couples' behaviors, which in turn, could provide a focus for therapy and for evaluation of therapy outcome.

The originally published MICS has been revised three times, leading to the currently used MICS-III (Weiss & Summers, 1983). By far, the MICS has been the most frequently used coding system found within the marital assessment literature.

Psychometric Characteristics

The MICS is a very complex coding system which requires that raters receive extensive training before they can apply it reliably. Training involves new raters memorizing the coding manual, being shown examples of the behaviors described by all of the codes, and engaging in extended practice with training tapes. When their skills improve, trainees are evaluated against precoded criterion tapes. After they reach acceptable levels of ability and start to code real data, raters need to continue attending regularly scheduled meetings to maintain their high levels of performance.

The reliability of MICS raters is assessed by determining interrater agreement (IRA) on a code-by-code basis. Since raters are maintained at better than a 70% IRA level, the mean IRA for a particular study is greater than 70%. Additionally, since MICS codes usually are grouped prior to analysis,

and since rater disagreements often involve disagreements among codes from the same group, the reported IRA is actually an underestimate of the reliability that would be obtained if it were assessed at the unit of analysis.

Another way to address the issue of the reliability of MICS raters is to conduct a generalizability study as was done by Wieder and Weiss (1980). They determined the amount of variance accounted for by coders, couples, and occasions. Among other findings, they reported that the majority of variance in their results was attributable to differences between couples and the interactions of couples by occasions, whereas differences between coders did not contribute to significant amounts of variance. This again suggests that coders can reliably use the MICS.

Validity of the MICS has been demonstrated by its successful use in discriminating distressed and nondistressed marital groups. In such studies the most common finding is that distressed couples engage in more negative behaviors than nondistressed couples and that the patterns of communication in distressed couples include longer chains of negative interactions. The MICS has also served as a sensitive index of changes in marital therapy outcome studies (Jacobson & Anderson, 1980). Additionally, it has been used in several methodolocial investigations which have contributed to the understanding of factors, such as demand characteristics, which affect direct observation assessment procedures.

Clinical Use

The MICS is designed for use in the assessment of marital distress. In the initial phases of therapy it is effective for describing problems in marital communication and in helping pinpoint goals for change. Later in treatment it is of value for the assessment of changes in couples' behaviors. Although most appropriate when the presenting problem is marital distress, the MICS can also be used when the clinician believes that relationship difficulties are importantly related to other presenting problems such as depression or alcoholism in a spouse.

Future Directions

Although an excellent and potentially valuable measure, the MICS is difficult to utilize outside of well-funded research projects because of the large commitment of resources required for its use. By coding videotapes of marital interaction for a fee, the Oregon Marital Studies program has begun to offer the only type of service that could make the MICS a viable instrument in general clinical practice. Finally, although the MICS is a relatively old behavioral assessment tool, continued investigations regarding the relationships of MICS variables to other measures and its utility for assessing relationships given other presenting problems is certainly warranted.

References

Jacob, T., Ritchey, D., Cvitkovic, J., & Blane, H. (1981). Communication styles of alcoholic and nonalcoholic families when drinking and not drinking. *Journal of Studies on Alcohol, 42,* 466-482.

Jacobson, N. S., & Anderson, E. A. (1980). The effects of behavior rehearsal and feedback on the acquisition of problem-solving skills in distressed and nondistressed couples. *Behaviour Research and Therapy, 18,* 25-36.

Patterson, G. R., Ray, R. S., Shaw, D. A., & Cobb, J. A. (1969). *Manual for coding of family interaction.* New York: Microfiche Publications (revised).

Weiss, R. L., & Summers, K. J. (1983). Marital Interaction Coding System-III. In E. Filsinger (Ed.), *Marriage and family assessment.* Beverly Hills, CA: Sage.

Wieder, G. B., & Weiss, R. L. (1980). Generalizability theory and the coding of marital interactions. *Journal of Consulting and Clinical Psychology, 48,* 469-477.

Marks and Mathews Fear Questionnaire

Paul Lelliott

Description

The Fear Questionnaire (FQ; Marks & Mathews, 1979) is a one-page self-rated form designed to monitor the severity of and change in phobic symptoms and anxiety and depression in phobic patients.

The questionnaire yields four scores:

1. Main Target Phobia: Phobia for which the patient is seeking treatment. The phobic object or situation is described in the patient's own words and rated for the extent to which this object or situation is avoided as a result of fear or other unpleasant feelings (0 = not avoided, 8 = always avoided). Exactly the same words are used to describe the Main Target Phobia at subsequent ratings.

2. Total Phobia: Fifteen common phobic situations, each rated 0 to 8 for avoidance, total score

range 0 to 120. The rating form allows for the division of Total Phobia into three subscores: (a) Agoraphobia, (b) Blood-Injury, and (c) Social Phobia, each subscore having a range of 0 to 40. Phobic situations, other than the Main Target Phobia and those included in the Total Phobia Items can be described and rated separately.

3. Global Phobia: An overall rating of the present state of phobic symptoms (0 = no phobias present, 8 = very severely disabling phobias).

4. Anxiety-Depression: Five symptoms of anxiety and depression commonly encountered in phobic patients, each rated from 0 (hardly troublesome at all) to 8 (very severely troublesome). Total score range of the five items is 0 to 40.

Purpose

The FQ was originally conceived as a standard instrument for use in research with phobic patients. It has since been used in routine clinical practice to assess progress of phobic symptoms with behavioral treatment and as a simple screening tool for coexisting depression.

Development

The FQ is based on a schedule completed by 1,020 phobic subjects in a postal survey of members of a phobic club in Great Britain (Marks & Herst, 1970). Factor analyses of a revised schedule used in the assessment of 171 phobic patients treated by nurse therapists (Marks, Hallam, Connolly, & Philpott, 1977) eliminated items with low factor loading and yielded the three subscores of the Total Phobia (Agoraphobia, Blood-Injury, and Social Phobia) and the items comprising the measure of Anxiety-Depression. Items with low test-retest reliability or item/subscore correlation were further excluded from the final questionnaire.

Psychometric Characteristics

When administered on two occasions with an interval of 7 days to 20 phobic patients, the test-retest reliabilities of the scores and subscores ranged from 0.79 for Global Phobia to 0.96 for Blood-Injury. Intercorrelations between the four scores were low, only that between Anxiety-Depression and Total Phobia reaching significance ($r = 0.44, p < .05$) (Marks & Mathews, 1979).

The pretreatment means of the FQ scores in 640 phobic patients assessed for behavior therapy by a group of nurse therapists in London were: Main

Target Phobia 7.1, Total Phobia 43.5, Global Phobia 6.2, Anxiety-Depression 19.4. The patients fell clinically into three categories: agoraphobia, social phobia, and specific phobia (fear and avoidance of animals, heights, thunder, etc.). Total Phobia scores for the three groups were: agoraphobia 58.4, social phobia 41.7, and specific phobia 24.1.

The FQ scores are sensitive to clinical change; significant improvement occurred in all scores and subscores in a group of 45 agoraphobic patients treated in a clinical trial (Marks et al., 1983). Measures were taken before treatment and 6 months after the end of treatment. During this time Total Phobia score decreased from 48.1 to 27.8, most of the change being accounted for by improvement in the Agoraphobia subscore from 25.3 to 11.8. Global Phobia improved from 5.8 to 2.8 and Anxiety-Depression from 18.8 to 10.7.

Clinical Use

The FQ is short, easy to understand, and takes just a few minutes to complete. It is applicable to all types of phobic patients. The Total Phobia items are 15 of the most common phobic situations whereas the Agoraphobia and Social Phobia subscales cover the two categories of phobic illness most commonly met in clinical practice. Phobic situations not included in the Total Phobia items can be incorporated and rated as the Main Target Phobia or as additional items.

The Total Phobia and Anxiety–Depression scores probably reflect the patient's overall clinical status (Marks & Mathews, 1979). The Main Target Phobia, being specific to the patient, is likely to be rated at near maximum pathology before treatment, leaving much scope for improvement with target-directed therapy.

Future Directions

The FQ measures avoidance of phobic situations rather than the fear induced by these situations.

In phobic patients fear and avoidance are highly correlated. However, individual patients do exist who experience fear in certain situations but do not avoid it. Incorporating a rating of fear engendered by each situation may improve the flexibility of the rating scale in clinical practice.

References

Marks, I.M., Grey, S., Cohen, S.D., Hill, R., Mawson, D., Ramm, E., & Stern, R.S. (1983). Imipramine and brief therapist-aided exposure in agoraphobics having self-exposure homework. *Archives of General Psychiatry, 40,* 153-162.

Marks, I.M., Hallam, R., Connolly, J., & Philpott, R. (1977). *Nursing in behavioural psychotherapy.* London: Royal College of Nursing.

Marks, I.M., & Herst, E.R. (1970). A survey of 1200 agoraphobics in Britain. *Social Psychiatry, 5,* 16-24.

Marks, I.M., & Mathews, A.M. (1979). Brief standard self-rating for phobic patients. *Behaviour Research and Therapy, 17,* 263-267.

Maudsley Obsessional-Compulsive Inventory

Paul M. G. Emmelkamp

Description

The Maudsley Obsessional-Compulsive Inventory (MOCI) (Hodgson & Rachman, 1977) consists of 30 questions that have to be answered by drawing a circle around "true" or "false" following each question. The questionnaire provides five scores: total obsessional score, checking, washing, slowness-repetition, and doubting-conscientiousness. High score on the *checking* subscale indicates that a great deal of time is spent every day rechecking things. The obsessional *cleaning* subscale includes items with respect to excessive concerns about germs and cleanliness and worries about contamination and items concerning excessive washing. High score on the obsessional *slowness* scale indicates that the person adheres to a strict routine and often counts when doing a routine task. Finally, persons scoring high on *obsessional-doubting-conscientiousness* have a strict conscience and usually have serious doubts about simple everyday events. A person with this problem often feels that a job has not been completed correctly even when it was performed very carefully. Obsessions are not assessed with this questionnaire.

Purpose

The questionnaire was developed to delineate different types of obsessional-compulsive problems. Hodgson and Rachman did not aim to cover all obsessional problems but only those associated with observable rituals. For the same reason, obsessional personality traits are not assessed with this questionnaire. (See Leyton Obsessional Inventory.) According to the authors the MOCI is less appropriate as a diagnostic instrument. It may be used to investigate the origin, course, and prognosis of different obsessional complaints. The questionnaire has also been used as an outcome measure in treatment research.

Development

From an initial pool of 65 items, which either had been selected from the literature or were assembled after interviewing 30 obsessional patients, 30 questions differentiated neurotic and obsessional groups. A principal components analysis on the responses of 100 obsessional persons revealed five components, namely, checking, cleaning, slowness, doubting-conscientiousness, and ruminating. Because the ruminating component consisted of two items only, the authors ignored it.

To validate the MOCI, Hodgson and Rachman (1977) compared the scores of two of the subscales (checking and washing) with retrospective therapist ratings of 42 obsessional patients.

A satisfactory relationship between therapist rating and questionnaire score was found. Similar results were reported by Kraaykamp, Emmelkamp, and van der Hout (1986). Therefore, patients who were categorized as checkers or cleaners on the basis of their questionnaire score were usually assigned to the respective category by the therapist. To date, two studies found this questionnaire to discriminate reliably between groups of phobic and obsessional patients (Volans, 1976; Hodgson, Rankin, & Stockwell, 1980). Furthermore, Kraaykamp et al. (1986) found this questionnaire to discriminate reliably between obsessional patients on the one hand, and normal control subjects, patients with anorexia nervosa, and anxious patients on the other. However, this questionnaire did not differentiate obsessional patients from depressive patients.

The concurrent validity was assessed by Kraaykamp et al. (1986) by comparing MOCI scores with Leyton Obsessional Inventory (LOI) scores. Apart from the subscale slowness, the total scale and other subscales were found to correlate moderately with the LOI scores.

Hodgson and Rachman (1977) factor analyzed the MOCI and found four factors explaining 43% of the variance. Replicating this analysis on Dutch obsessional patients, Kraaykamp et al. (1986) found that the four factors of the MOCI explained 35% of the variance in their group. Therefore, the four factors of the MOCI appear to be robust. Rachman and Hodgson (1980) reported the results of a principal components analysis of 100 nonobsessional

subjects (50 neurotic patients and 50 night school attenders). The components that emerged were very similar to the checking, cleaning, and doubting components identified in the earlier analyses of obsessional patients. However, no slowness component emerged. Moreover, items that loaded highly on the doubting component also tended to have high loadings on the checking component.

As to test-retest reliability, Hodgson and Rachman (1977) found this satisfactory (Kendall's tau = .80). Kraaykamp et al. (1986) found moderate to good homogeneity (Cronbach's alpha) for the total scale (.89), checking (.79), cleaning (.67), and doubting (.70), but low homogeneity for the slowness subscale (.26).

Clinical Use

Obvious advantages of the MOCI are its easy administration, its discrimination of obsessional from other neurotic patients, and the validation of two subscales (checking and washing). However, the slowness and doubting subscales appear to be less useful. Depressive persons are not easily differentiated from obsessional persons; therefore, results with depressed patients should be interpreted cautiously. The MOCI may be used to evaluate effects of treatment, but simple ratings of obsessive-compulsive behavior for anxiety-discomfort and avoidance for target obsessional problems on 0 to 8 scales appear to be a more sensitive index of change than is the MOCI (Kraaykamp et al., 1986).

Future Directions

Few studies have evaluated the MOCI psychometrically. Further research is needed to establish the value of the doubting and slowness subscales. It might also be worthwhile to investigate whether the addition of two scales to assess resistance and interference of patients may increase the clinical usefulness of this questionnaire. Finally, concurrent validity studies are needed to compare MOCI scores with those of behavioral tests.

References

Hodgson, R.J., & Rachman, S. (1977). Obsessional-compulsive complaints. *Behaviour Research and Therapy, 15,* 389-395.

Hodgson, R.J., Rankin, H., & Stockwell, T.R. (1980). *Introversion, obsessional personality and obsessional-compulsive complaints.* Unpublished manuscript. London, England.

Kraaykamp, H.J.M., Emmelkamp, P.M.G., & van der Hout, M. (in preparation). *The Maudsley Obsessional-Compulsive Inventory: A psychometric evaluation.*

Rachman, S., & Hodgson, R.J. (1980). *Obsessions and compulsions.* Englewood Cliffs, NJ: Prentice-Hall.

Volans, P.J. (1976). Styles of decision-making and probability appraisal in selected obsessional and phobic patients. *British Journal of Social and Clinical Psychology, 15,* 305-317.

McGill Pain Questionnaire

Ronald Melzack

Description

The McGill Pain Questionnaire (MPQ) consists of 78 adjectives arranged into 20 groups that reflect similar pain qualities (Melzack, 1975). Ten groups of words characterize the sensory dimension of pain (e.g., hot, burning, scalding, and searing) and five groups characterize the affective dimension (e.g., punishing, grueling, cruel, vicious, and killing). A single set of words reflects the evaluative dimension of pain and four groups represent miscellaneous qualities. In addition, the overall intensity of pain is designated by an adjective scale that ranges from 1 (mild) to 5 (excruciating).

Purpose

The purpose of the MPQ is to obtain quantitative measures of complex qualitative experiences. The MPQ can be administered to patients already suffering pain (Reading, 1984) or to laboratory subjects who receive painful stimuli such as electric shocks (Klepac, Dowling, & Hauge, 1981). Another purpose of the MPQ is to aid in diagnosis by differentiating among the characteristic descriptors of different pain syndromes (Reading, 1984).

Development

The MPA evolved from a study on the language of pain (Melzack & Torgerson, 1971) which determined the perceived similarity among pain descriptors and the relative intensity assigned to each descriptor by patients, physicians, and university students.

Psychometric Characteristics

Two major kinds of scores are derived from the MPQ. The first consists of the pain-rating index (PRI) obtained separately for sensory, affective,

evaluative, and miscellaneous words in addition to the total PRI for all words. The PRI is obtained by adding the rank values of the words chosen in each set. The second score is called the present pain intensity (PPI) and designates the overall intensity of pain.

The MPQ can be administered by a health professional (or appropriate assistant) or can be given to the patient as a paper-and-pencil test with accompanying instructions.

The MPQ has now been used in many studies and has been shown to provide reliable and valid measures of pain experience. This literature has recently been reviewed by Reading (1984) and in several chapters that deal with the MPQ in a volume of pain measurement and assessment (Melzack, 1983).

Clinical Use

The MPQ has been used with patients suffering virtually every kind of chronic and acute form of pain. It has been used to study the effects of different treatments for pain (biofeedback, analgesic drugs, etc.) as well as to differentiate between different forms of pain, such as low back pain in patients with or without demonstrable organic symptoms.

Future Directions

The MPQ has been used in different formats (interview versus paper-and-pencil tests; words presented in the prescribed sets versus randomly scrambled presentations). The direction of such studies is to increase the discriminant capacity of the MPQ.

References

Klepac, R.K., Dowling, J., & Hauge, G. (1981). Sensitivity of the McGill Pain Questionnaire to intensity and quality of laboratory pain. *Pain, 10,* 199-207.

Melzack, R. (1975). The McGill Pain Questionnaire: Major properties and scoring methods. *Pain, 1,* 275-299.

Melzack, R. (Ed.). (1983). *Pain measurement and assessment.* New York: Raven Press.

Melzack, R., & Torgerson, W.S. (1971). On the language of pain. *Anesthesiology, 34,* 50-59.

Reading, A.E. (1984). Testing pain mechanisms in persons in pain. In Wall, P.D. & Melzack, R. (Eds.), *Textbook of pain.* Edinburgh: Livingstone Churchill.

Measurement of Chronic Aggression: Direct Quantitative Methods

Larry A. Doke

Description

Direct measurement of chronic aggressive behavior may be contrasted to interview methods, projective methods, and personality inventories. Once a category of aggressive behavior (verbal or nonverbal) has been clearly defined, it may be directly quantified with respect to frequency or rate, duration, latency, intensity, and topography. Methods for directly measuring aggressive behavior along these dimensions include: *counting* discrete responses; *spot-checking* or *interval sampling* (observing instantaneously or for brief periods at regular intervals, recording the occurrence or nonoccurrence at each observation); *timing* latency intervals or intervals between responses; scoring changes in the topography of complex aggressive episodes by repeatedly *applying checklists* of movements comprising the aggressive act; and *applying automatic devices* that detect changes in the intensity of a targeted aggressive response. Of these methods, frequency/rate measures and interval sampling have been applied most often to the direct measurement of aggressive behaviors.

Purpose

A major reason for employing direct quantitative methods to the study of aggressive behavior has been to reduce the need for inference. With respect to projective and self-report methods, it is typically necessary to infer a relationship between a client's aggression scores and his overt aggressive behavior outside the test situation. Fewer inferences are called for (aside from those pertaining to generality) when the aggressive behavior of interest is measured directly.

Direct quantitative methods are also applicable to situations that require repeated measurement, the assessment of day-to-day effects of a program designed to control aggressive behavior. Similarly, most direct measurement procedures can be applied in various natural settings in which the aggressive behavior might occur.

Development

Historically, the direct measurement of chronic aggression has paralleled the development of applied behavior analysis and experimental clinical research, as represented in such sources as *Journal of Applied Behavior Analysis, Behavior Therapy, Behavior Modification,* and *Journal of Behavior Therapy and Experimental Psychiatry.* This has been the case primarily because of emphasis in the experimental analysis of behavior on (a) time-series experimental designs employing frequent repeated measures, and (b) behavioral interventions that have typically focused on discrete observable responses (in contrast to, say, "hostile intent").

Psychometric Characteristics

With respect to direct quantitative methods, the issue of measurement reliability or interobserver agreement has received much attention. Research on reliability has resulted from recognition of such common sources of data contamination as observer bias, observer drift (i.e., changes in observer sensitivity or vigilance), errors in data computation, and ambiguity in defining target behaviors.

The reliability of direct measures of aggressive behavior is typically summarized in the form of a percentage-agreement coefficient based on data obtained by two independent observers. For response rate or frequency data, this coefficient is usually calculated by dividing the smaller data value by the larger. For interval or spot-check recordings, the coefficient is usually derived by dividing the number of intervals in which both observers agree by the total number of observation intervals. Published studies employing direct measures of aggressive behavior have typically reported interobserver agreement coefficients exceeding .85. Various other methods for computing the reliability of direct measurement data have been used.

Warranting attention in studies of chronic aggression is the finding that specific behaviors being measured sometimes change as a function of being measured. Commonly referred to as "subject reactivity," this problem may be minimized by using direct measures that are as unobtrusive as possible. Nevertheless, subject reactivity may be even more difficult to eliminate in work with aggressive clients who, more than other clinical groups, might deliberately deceive those who are attempting to measure their behavior.

Clinical Use

The professional journals cited earlier contain reports of clinical studies that represent the application of direct measures to a wide range of aggressive behaviors including self-injury (head banging, self–biting, eye gouging, etc.), aggressive screaming and verbal threats, fighting and various forms of physical battery against others, setting fires, and temper tantrums. These measures have been applied in diverse populations of children and adults (retarded, psychotic, criminal, and delinquent individuals) in many settings (clients' own homes, schools, residential treatment centers, outpatient clinics, and correctional facilities).

To illustrate, a study by Doke, Wolery, and Sumberg (1983) included direct measures of the aggressive behavior of a 7-year-old boy who for several years had exhibited frequent episodes of hitting, pushing, poking, butting, bumping, scratching, or punching others; pulling others' hair; spitting on others; throwing objects not intended to be thrown; jerking objects away; and jerking himself away abruptly when held. In this study, direct measures were also applied concurrently to other categories of behavior (e.g., inappropriate vocalizations and participation in planned activities) as a means of assessing side effects of treatment.

This study illustrates the application of two different direct measurement procedures to a single client's aggressive behavior. First, the investigators used an interval-sampling method in which a primary observer and, occasionally, a second observer scored the occurrence or nonoccurrence of targeted behaviors in consecutive 10-second intervals. These measures were obtained during 20-minute recordings over a period of 104 days, as treatment procedures were systematically introduced and withdrawn. Interobserver agreement coefficients calculated by the standard method for interval time-sampling data on aggression averaged .93.

In the same study, direct measures of rates of aggressive behavior were obtained in a second recording period daily. Discrete aggressive responses (listed above) were counted, and the total response frequencies for each period were divided by the number of minutes comprising each period. In spite of variations in the length of observation periods from day to day, the derived rate measure, aggressive responses per minute, allowed comparison of data values from one session to the next. The reliability coefficients with respect to these rate measures of aggressive behavior averaged .99.

Future Directions

Kazdin (1977) called for more research in which direct measures are used to establish norms for nondeviant populations which can be used in setting treatment goals and assessing the significance of client progress. For example, Patterson (1974) evaluated the effectiveness of a treatment program for deviant boys, which focused on changing a variety of behaviors, including physical aggression. This project included pre- and posttreatment comparisons of direct observational data on the aggressive behavior of treated boys to data obtained through identical direct measures of the aggressive behavior of a nondeviant control group of boys. There are very few other studies illustrating the application of direct quantitative methods to the construction of norms. However, the continuing need to evaluate the significance of treatment effects should prompt the development of expanding pools of normative direct-measurement data on various categories of aggressive behavior for diverse populations. This work will require increasing standardization of procedures for directly measuring aggression.

Because of the paucity of data on the validity of direct measures, it is also predicted that there will be more research comparing direct quantitative methods with other methods for assessing aggression (e.g., projective instruments, self-report inventories, and subjective ratings by independent judges). However, research on the validity of direct measures of discrete behaviors will not be without its problems, because the more subjective measures to which direct measures are compared are likely to be much more susceptible to artifacts and biases (Kazdin, 1977).

References

Doke, L., Wolery, M., & Sumberg, C. (1983). Treating chronic aggression: Effects and side effects of response contingent ammonia spirits. *Behavior Modification, 7*, 531-556.

Kazdin, A.E. (1977). Assessing the clinical or applied importance of behavior change through social validation. *Behavior Modification, 1*, 427-452.

Patterson, G.R. (1974). Interventions for boys with conduct problems: Multiple settings, treatments, and criteria. *Journal of Consulting and Clinical Psychology, 42*, 471-481.

Michigan Alcoholism Screening Test

Arthur I. Alterman

Description

The Michigan Alcoholism Screening Test (MAST) is primarily a screening instrument for alcoholism and problem drinking. The original interview-based version (Selzer, 1971) of the MAST consists of 25 items that are either weighted 0, 1, 2, or 5 points. Each of the 5-point items is considered to be diagnostic of alcoholism (e.g., attended an AA meeting; sought help for drinking problem; hospitalized because of drinking). The MAST takes about 10 minutes to administer by relatively untrained personnel. The items obviously have high face validity. The maximum score of the original MAST is 55. A score of 4 suggests possible or suspected alcohol problems, whereas a score of 5 or higher is indicative of alcoholism. Other versions of the MAST are forthcoming (Jacobson, 1983). Selzer (1971) introduced a 24-item self-administered version of the MAST and also developed a 13-item scale (SMAST), which employs the most sensitive items from the original MAST. Also extant is an expanded 35-item (SAST) self-administered version of the MAST and a brief 10-item version (Jacobson, 1983). A revised MAST (MAST-R), consisting of 24 items and minor modifications in scoring, is also in use.

Purpose

The MAST was developed to provide a convenient, relatively brief, and economical instrument that could provide information to service providers about the presence of problem drinking or alcoholism in individuals not diagnosed as alcoholic addicts. Because knowledge about alcohol-related problems and consequences is somewhat specialized, and problem drinking and alcoholism are believed to be present in significant numbers in a variety of populations, it was believed that screening of the individuals would be of broad utility.

Development

Development of the MAST does not appear to have been guided by any particular theoretical orientation, but it arose out of the author's perception of a need for a simple, quick, and consistently effective means of identifying alcoholism and problem drinkers. Items were drawn from existing batteries; those found to discriminate between alcoholic and nonalcoholic addicts were ultimately included in the instrument. Item weights were determined on the basis of both the author's clinical experience and an analysis of the discriminatory abilities of the items. Selzer's original study compared five groups: hospitalized alcoholics, a control group, drivers convicted of driving under the influence of alcohol, persons convicted of drunk and disorderly conduct, and drivers who had incurred 12 penalty points in 2 years for moving violations and accidents. The proportion of problem drinkers and alcoholics found in the different groups suggested valid and meaningful detection rates. The validity of the MAST was further supported by records of legal, social, and medical agencies and driving and criminal records. The MAST and its variants have now been administered to a variety of populations, including alcoholic addicts, drunk drivers, military personnel, students, prisoners, and members of other societies (Brady, Foulks, Childress, & Pertschuk, 1982). It is believed that some of the MAST items may not be entirely suitable for women and may be biased towards yielding a higher score for members of certain minority groups. Although the MAST is probably the most used and possibly the most useful screening instrument for problem drinking and alcoholism in the United States, considerable question remains and research is being conducted on its psychometric characteristics.

Psychometric Characteristics

Norms for this instrument have not been provided, because it has mainly been used to detect individuals who exceed the threshold for problem drinking or alcoholism. Research has revealed high internal consistency and good test-retest reliability (Skinner & Scheu, 1982; Jacobson, 1983) for the lifetime incidence of alcohol-related problems. Much of the validity evidence derives from differential detection rates in populations with diagnosed or assumed problem drinking/alcoholism rates (i.e., empirical validity). As noted, records have been used to a limited extent to provide validation for MAST scores. However, validity has primarily been established by comparing MAST "hits" and "miss" rates in diagnosed alcoholic patients. Validity of these rates for other groups is inferred from the anticipated incidence of alcoholic problems in that group. Obviously, this is a rather weak and circular form of evidence. The finding of unusually high "hit" rates in some groups indeed raises questions about the interpretation and validity of MAST scores in nondiagnosed populations. For example, one study concluded that approximately 25% of college students were alcoholic. More reasonable rates were apparent when the cutoff threshold for alcoholism was raised from 5 to 11. Several workers (Jacobson, 1983) have argued that the higher threshold for alcoholism is more appropriate. As it is not realistic in large studies to perform extensive testing and diagnostic workups for alcohol-related behaviors and problems, we cannot be sure of actual alcoholism rates. This issue is less problematic if we remind ourselves that the MAST is intended to *detect alcohol problems* in such large groups. Unfortunately, large scale utilization of the MAST by individuals with little training or knowledge of alcholism has sometimes led to the misimpression that the MAST *diagnoses* alcoholism.

A number of investigators have reported high false–positive rates in many populations (Jacobson, 1983). Again, this problem can be resolved by raising the threshold for alcoholism to 11 and recognizing at the same time that the instrument is intended for use by nonspecialists for the detection of alcohol problems. It is reasonable to employ a cutoff score(s) in large population studies. However, in individual cases, it is wiser not to use specific cutoff points and it is more advisable to recognize that the higher the score, the more likely the extent of the individual's alcohol involvement. The occurrence of false–negative outcomes is also a significant problem. The MAST is most effective in individuals who are cognizant of and willing to admit their problems with alcohol. The high validity of the MAST items makes its purpose apparent, so that it is understandable that testees who are unaware of or wish to deny that they have an alcohol problem will yield low MAST scores. Detection rates are usually less satisfactory when abbreviated versions of the MAST are employed.

The differential item weights, which stem largely from Selzer's (1971) conceptualization of alcoholism, may represent another unnecessary complication of the MAST. Noteworthy in this connection is the assumption that three of the items in the MAST are diagnostic of alcoholism and should be assigned 5 points, which automatically places an individual into the designated alcoholic range. At least one study has obtained approximately 15% false–positive rates for each of these "diagnostic" items in nonalcoholic subjects. Skinner and Scheu (1982) also found that unit scoring of the MAST items resulted in essentially the same outcome as the weighted scoring system, and could be quickly converted to regular scores with little loss of information by applying a simple regression formula. Therefore, although the MAST is designed to be time efficient and used by relatively untrained personnel, inclusion of scoring weights increases the time costs and provides an opportunity for scoring error without obvious benefits. A number of factor analytic studies of the MAST have been undertaken. Findings with alcoholic addicts generally have revealed a dominant factor, suggesting a unidimensional instrument. However, findings with other groups, such as driving offenders, have revealed four to five factors, suggesting multidimensionality. On the basis of such findings, Jacobson (1983) concluded that the MAST may prove to have value as an assessment and possibly even as a diagnostic instrument. This reviewer believes that the MAST needs drastic modifications before such levels of measurement could be obtained. The effort to develop the MAST in these directions seems misplaced, because a number of alcoholism assessment and diagnostic instruments that appear more appropriate for these purposes are already available.

Clinical Use

The MAST is designed to detect problem drinking/alcoholism in individuals who are not manifestly suffering from these problems. It seems to have value in screening for such problems in psychiatric and medical populations and in other large populations, as may be found in the military, industry, students, and the like. The MAST also has considerable value in research studies of alcholism and problem drinking. Despite the shortcomings described, the MAST has thus far proven to be as useful a screening instrument for alcohol problems as any test currently existing.

Future Directions

There are as yet few studies in which the MAST scores of individuals (and its various abbreviated versions), not known to be alcoholic, are compared with more detailed information on alcohol involvement patterns (including records) and sociodemographic and personality/psychiatric characteristics. These studies would provide a much clearer indication of what the MAST is and is not measuring and may be of value in developing a more refined and valid instrument. Further research on the relative utility of a unit versus weighted scoring system could also result in an improved scale.

References

Brady, J., Foulks, E., Childress, A., & Pertschuk, M. (1982). The Michigan Alcoholism Screening Test as a survey instrument. *Journal of Operational Psychiatry, 13*, 27-31.

Jacobson, G. (1983). Detection, assessment, and diagnosis of alcoholism: Current techniques. In M. Galanter (Ed.), *Recent developments in alcoholism: Vol. 1.* New York: Plenum Press.

Selzer, M. (1971). The Michigan Alcoholism Screening Test: The quest for a new diagnostic instrument. *American Journal of Psychiatry, 127*, 89-94.

Skinner, H., & Scheu, W. (1982). Reliability of alcohol use indices: The lifetime drinking history and the MAST. *Journal of Studies on Alcohol, 43*, 1157-1170.

Mini-Mental State Exam

Christopher Starratt and Robert B. Fields

Description

The Mini-Mental State Exam (MMSE; Folstein, Folstein, & McHugh, 1975) is a brief cognitive screening test. It contains 11 items that sample across the following areas of function: orientation, attention, immediate and delayed memory, expressive and receptive language, and graphomotor visuoconstruction. The MMSE is an untimed test that usually requires no more than 10 minutes to complete. A maximum of 30 points can be obtained.

Purpose

The stated purpose of the MMSE is that of a simply administered, quantified evaluation of cognitive function as part of a traditional psychiatric mental status examination. It is intended to be used to detect the presence and severity of cognitive impairment as well as to follow changes in cognitive status over time through objective serial evaluation (Folstein et al., 1975). It is most frequently used in geriatric evaluation, both clinically and for research. The MMSE is one of several cognitive screening tests described by the Work Group on

the Diagnosis of Alzheimer's Disease as appropriate for use in the initial screening for the assessment of dementia associated with Alzheimer's Disease (McKhann et al., 1984).

Development

The MMSE grew out of an attempt to standardize the cognitive assessment portion of the traditional mental status examination conducted during a diagnostic psychiatric interview. Folstein et al. (1975) devised a scoring system to apply to the traditional questions asked to evaluate cognitive status. Typical questions included inquiry into the patient's ability to state the date and location, to name and subsequently recall common objects, and to perform serial 7s and follow multi-step commands.

Psychometric Characteristics

Since its initial introduction a decade ago, considerable investigation into the test's reliability, validity, and utility has been conducted. In a recent review of the use of dementia screening tests over the last 5 years, as reported in major psychology, medicine, and geriatric journals, Fields and Starratt (1985) noted that the MMSE represented the most frequently cited cognitive screening test with 36 citations. Of these, six were directly related to reliability, validity, and/or utility of the MMSE. The following test characteristics are based on findings from that review. Although not an exhaustive review of all studies using the MMSE since its inception, it is judged to be a reasonable representation of the research related to the instrument's characteristics.

Test-retest reliability values range from .85 to .99. Interrater reliability values range from .82 to .95. Several concurrent validation studies have been reported with structural, psychometric, and behavioral indices of impairment used as criteria. A significant correlation ($r = -.35$) was found between MMSE and computerized tomography (CT scan) results. Correlations with WAIS VIQ range from .40 to .78 and with WAIS PIQ from .56 to .66. A significant correlation ($r = .58$) between MMSE and the Wechsler Memory Scale score has also been reported. Concerning functional behavior, correlations between MMSE and the behavioral portion of the Blessed Dementia Rating Scale have been reported to range from .66 to .75. Reisberg, Ferris, deLeon, and Crook (1985) also noted a strong relationship between the MMSE and their Global Deterioration Scale score which is used to stage the level of functional impairment associated with Alzheimer's type dementia ($r = -.924$). However, they caution that the MMSE is not as useful in differentiating persons in the later stages of the disorder as are ratings of functional behavior.

Utility studies have also been conducted. Using structured interview for cognitive impairment as the criteria, the sensitivity of the MMSE ranges from 76 to 87%, and the specificity has been reported at 82%. Interestingly, the individual orientation items of the test (e.g., date, year, and hospital name) have a high degree of specificity (92 to 100%) but relatively low sensitivity (15 to 57%). In contrast, the reverse is true for the nonorientation items (e.g., serial sevens, delayed recall: sensitivity is 81 to 100%; specificity is 43 to 74%) (Klein et al., 1985). Specificity is affected by age (92% for subjects less than 60 years of age and 65% for subjects over 60 years) and by education (63% with less than 8 years of education and 100% with over 8 years). Group differences have been reported to be related to socioeconomic status as well as race, with those of lower socioeconomic status and nonwhites obtaining more impaired scores.

Clinical Use

The MMSE represents one of the most extensively researched brief cognitive screening measures currently available. Folstein et al. (1975) have carefully articulated the uses and limitations of this instrument. It has been useful in both clinical and research situations and has the advantage of assessing a broader range of cognitive functions than do many other cognitive screening measures.

For a more thorough evaluation of cognitive decline associated with dementing disorders, the MMSE in combination with additional neuropsychological tests as well as a global rating scale of severity of impairment such as the Global Deterioration Scale (Reisberg et al., 1985) is recommended.

Future Directions

Additional longitudinal studies, similar to those of Reisberg et al. (1985) that investigate the relationship between MMSE score and functional changes over time, will help clarify the role and use of the MMSE in tracking cognitive decline associated with progressive dementing disorders. In addition,

investigations of the utility of developing a weighting procedure to adjust for moderators such as race and socioeconomic status should be pursued.

References

Fields, R.B., & Starratt, C. (1985). The role of dementia screening tests in the evaluation of cognitive functioning in the elderly. Paper presented at the Mid-South Conference on Human Neuropsychology, Memphis, TN, May.

Folstein, M.F., Folstein, S.F., & McHugh, P.R. (1975). "Mini-Mental State": A practical method for grading the cognitive state of patients for the clinician. *Journal of Psychiatric Research, 12,* 189-198.

Klein, L.E., Roca, R.P., McArthur, J., Vogelsand, G., Klein, G.B., Kirby, S.M., & Folstein, M. (1985). Diagnosing dementia: Univariate and multivariate analyses of the mental status examination. *Journal of the American Geriatrics Society, 33,* 483-488.

McKhann, G., Drachman, D., Folstein, M., Katzman, R., Price, D., & Stadlan, E.M. (1984). Clinical diagnosis of Alzheimer's disease: Report of the NINCDS-ADRDA work group under the auspices of the Department of Health and Human Services Task Force on Alzheimer's disease. *Neurology, 34,* 939-944.

Reisberg, B., Ferris, S.H., deLeon, M.J., & Crook, T. (1985). Age-associated cognitive decline and Alzheimer's disease: Implications for assessment and treatment. In M. Bergener, M. Ermini, & H.B. Stahelin (Eds.), *Thresholds in aging* (pp. 255-292). London: Academic Press.

Minnesota Multiphasic Personality Inventory

Ralph E. Tarter

Description

The Minnesota Multiphasic Personality Inventory (MMPI) is currently the most commonly employed standardized psychometric test of emotional adjustment and personality status. The inventory is self-administered and consists of 566 questions or statements requiring either a true or false endorsement (16 of the items are repeated throughout the test as one of the validity checks).

The instrument consists of 4 validity scales and 10 clinical scales. However, from the large item pool, virtually hundreds of additional scales having varying utility and validity have also been derived.

Several test formats have been designed for administration of the MMPI. These include a card-sorting format and six different forms of computerized scoring formats. Although computer scoring is readily available, manual scoring, by using templates that are superimposed on the answer sheet, can also be employed to obtain the score for each scale. The raw score obtained is converted to a standard T score that has a mean of 50 and a standard deviation of 10. Norms for the various scales have been derived separately for male and female subjects. The standard T scores are plotted graphically on a specific profile form. From this psychogram, an interpretation of the person's personality and psychopathological status is made on the basis of the scores obtained on the individual scales as well as on the particular configuration among scales in which there are significant score elevations ($T > 70$).

The MMPI consists of the following scales:

Cannot Say Score. The number of items that the respondent omits and/or doubly answers (answers both true and false) are tabulated and recorded. Items responded to in this manner are generally considered to be either unclear to the individual with regard to their meaning or are intrusive, in that they directly infringe on the person's privacy in areas where strong beliefs or feelings are held (e.g., religious attitudes and sexual practices). The inventory is very "elastic" in that it allows for a large number of "Cannot Say" responses: a T score of 70 (95th percentile) is attained only after 110 items, or 20% of the total number of inventory items, are endorsed doubly or left unanswered.

Lie Scale (L). This 15-item scale was developed to detect intentional deception. The items in this scale consist of mildly negative attributes that a person who is deliberately lying may be inclined to deny (e.g., "I do not always tell the truth").

Infrequent Scale (F). This scale, consisting of 64 items, was developed to identify idiosyncratic or atypical attitudes. There are numerous factors that could influence a nonnormative response pattern, including severe psychopathology as well as strong ideological beliefs and attitudes that are not consensually validated.

Correction Scale (K). This is the fourth and last validity scale. Unlike the previous three scales, which were primarily designed to detect possible reasons for distortions in the protocol, this 30-item scale was empirically derived so as to enhance the sensitivity of the clinical scales. It is for this reason

that several of the clinical scales contain a K correction that is added to the raw score. This scale detects a defensive orientation to the test–taking situation, such that a high score either indicates poor insight or reflects an exaggerated attempt to create an impression of psychological well-being.

Hypochondriasis Scale (Hs). Preoccupation and concern for somatic well-being are assessed by this 33-item scale. Patients with medical illnesses having a confirmed physical basis also, however, score in the disturbed ranges on this scale. Factor analytic studies of the Hs scale reveal that it measures a disposition to deny good health.

Depression Scale (D). This 66-item scale was designed to measure the mood state of depression; that is, feelings and cognitions of self-perceived worthlessness, pessimism, apathy, psychomotor retardation, and sadness.

Conversion Hysteria Scale (Hy). Conversion disorders are evaluated by this 60-item scale. The intent of this scale is to identify individuals who manifest somatic symptoms as a neurotic defense to stressful situations.

Psychopathic-deviate Scale (Pd). The 50 items comprising this scale describe the personality disposition of sociopathy. Factor analytic studies reveal that multiple aspects of personality are, however, encompassed by this scale, including self-esteem, interpersonal hypersensitivity, impulse control difficulties, emotional deprivation, and social maladaptation.

Masculinity–Femininity Scale (Mf). Originally, the 60 items comprising this scale were developed to describe male sexual inversion, that is, a "feminine" personality pattern accompanied by homoerotic behavior. Recent studies indicate that the scale instead measures attitudes and interests in the spheres of work, hobbies, social activity, family life, and religion.

Paranoia Scale (Pa). Cognitions lacking social consensual validation, such as exceptional suspiciousness or grandiosity, are measured by this 40-item scale.

Psychasthenia Scale (Pt). This 40-item scale was initially intended to measure obsessive and compulsive disturbances. Associated features of neurotic behavior, including anxiety, fears, self-deprecation, guilt, and worry, are also tapped by this scale.

Schizophrenia Scale (Sc). The psychotic disorder of schizophrenia, replete with disturbed cognitive, affective, and behavioral functioning, is measured by this 78-item scale.

Hypomania Scale (Ma). An energized behavioral state, featured by emotional excitement and rambling pressed speech, is assessed by this 46-item scale.

Social Introversion Scale (Si). Withdrawal from social interaction or a disposition toward solitary activity is measured by the 70 items comprising this scale. High scores implicate social introversion, whereas low scores point to social extraversion.

The scores obtained from the 4 validity and 10 clinical scales provide valuable information about an individual's current emotional well-being and personality. It should be emphasized that interpretation of the MMPI profile entails analysis of the configuration of scale scores that are markedly elevated. It is not simply a matter of making inferences from individual scale score elevations. The scales that are commonly conjointly elevated ($T > 70$) are described in detail by Dahlstrom, Welsh, and Dahlstrom (1972).

Purpose

The MMPI initially was designed to provide psychologists with a standardized practical instrument that could quantify the severity of personality and emotional disturbance in adults. It was intended for routine clinical practice, particularly for evaluating the outcome of psychotherapy and for monitoring the severity of psychiatric disturbance (Hathaway, 1964).

Development

A guiding principle in developing the inventory was a commitment to establishing its empirical validity. Items were selected based on the type of questions posed by clinicians and from self-descriptions advanced by patients seeking treatment. The

566 items ultimately selected from a pool of over 1,000 statements came from a variety of sources, including case summaries, other scales of personal and social attitudes, psychiatric manuals as well as the developers' own clinical experiences. The items were prepared such that they could be comprehended by a person with a sixth-grade education.

The initial validity sample consisted of patients hospitalized at the University of Minnesota Hospitals. The normative sample consisted of friends or relatives of these patients. The typical normal person was 35 years old, had 8 years of education, was married, lived in a small town, and, if employed, worked at a skilled or semiskilled trade. About 700 normal persons comprised the initial normative sample from which the first published copyrighted version of the MMPI was standardized in 1943. Since then, larger and more heterogeneous samples have been studied to evaluate the validity and reliability of this inventory.

Psychometric Characteristics

No other objective personality test has been as thoroughly researched as the MMPI. Hundreds of journal articles have been published, and although generally regarded to be the most reliable and valid clinical instrument currently available (Dahlstrom et al., 1972), its discriminative validity for differential diagnosis among the various psychiatric disorders is not as good as is generally assumed (Adcock, 1965). In addition, the MMPI is not capable of identifying individuals in the nonhospitalized population who are in need of psychiatric help (Marks & Seeman, 1963). Despite these two shortcomings, the MMPI is nonetheless the most comprehensive psychometric test of personality and psychopathology.

The MMPI is most useful in psychiatric settings. The inventory has less utility in medical and neurological populations in which the onset and origin of emotional disturbance need to be determined in relation to the onset and course of the physical disease in order to ascertain the origin (organic or functional) of the psychopathology. The greatest advantage of the MMPI is that it is a very efficient screening device. It is self-administered, scoring is computerized, and the test can be group administered. Valid actuarial interpretations also can be made (Marks & Seeman, 1963). Hence, when extensive patient contact is not possible, the MMPI can provide useful information about emotional status and personality adjustment.

Future Directions

The MMPI has a number of potentially useful research applications. First, it is important to determine if scales that meet DSM-III criteria for a psychiatric diagnosis can be empirically derived. Second, the MMPI may have value in detecting persons at high risk of developing a psychiatric disorder or during the prodrome, so that preventative interventions can be implemented before florid psychopathology emerges. Third, the usefulness of the MMPI in predicting how a person will react to certain situational conditions or respond to particular treatment procedures remains to be explored. To date, the great majority of studies have focused on dispositional traits; whether the MMPI can assist in predicting person-environment interactions remains to be determined.

The heuristic potential of the MMPI aside, it must be emphasized that this test, its content, and theoretical underpinnings reflect the state of clinical psychological measurement up to about 1940. Since then, major advances have been made in understanding the origin of psychiatric disorders and their classification. Moreover, there has been a theoretical shift in psychology, such that greater emphasis is currently placed on direct behavioral observation and the use of structured interviews. Therefore, although the MMPI still has a place as a screening instrument in the armamentarium of clinical psychologists, its utility and consequently its value in obtaining the type of personality and psychopathology information that is relevant to diagnosis and treatment are rather limited. However, an extensive revision of the MMPI, which reflects some of these aforementioned concerns, will be published shortly.

References

Adcock, C. (1965). Review of the MMPI. In O. Buros (Ed.), *6th mental measurements yearbook*. Highland Park, NJ: Gryphon Press.

Dahlstrom, W., Welsh, G., & Dahlstrom, L. (1972). *An MMPI handbook* (Vols. I and II). Minneapolis: University of Minnesota Press.

Hathaway, S. (1964). MMPI: Professional use by professional people. *American Psychologist, 19*, 204-210.

Marks, P., & Seeman, W. (1963). *The actuarial description of abnormal personality*. Baltimore: Williams & Wilkins.

McPartland, R.J., Kupfer, D.J., Foster, F.G., Reisler, K.L., & Matthews, G. (1975). *Biotelemetry, 2*, 317-323.

Mobility Inventory for Agoraphobia

Dianne L. Chambless

Description

The Mobility Inventory for Agoraphobia (Chambless, Caputo, Jasin, Gracely, & Williams, 1985) is a self-report questionnaire containing two sections. The first section concerns avoidance behavior. Twenty-six situations are rated on a 5-point scale, indicating how much they are avoided because of discomfort or anxiety when the client is alone and again when accompanied by a trusted companion. A score of 1 indicates "never avoid" and 5 "always avoid." The Alone and Accompanied scales are moderately correlated (e.g., $r = .44$). The same items may also be rated for discomfort experienced in these situations. (The revised version of the Mobility Inventory, including the Panic Intensity scale, is available from Dianne Chambless, Ph.D., Department of Psychology, The American University, 4400 Massachusetts, NW, Washington, DC 20016, as is the Discomfort scale.) In practice, however, this is rarely necessary because avoidance behavior and discomfort have been found to be highly correlated before, during, and after treatment (r's range from .87 to .94).

The second section pertains to panic attacks. A definition of panic is provided, and clients are asked to indicate how many panic attacks they have experienced in the last 7 days. This interval was chosen to allow measurement of change in panic with brief treatment, but it correlates highly with the frequency of panic in a longer (3-week) interval: tau (35) = .80. In a revised version of the inventory (Chambless, 1985a), clients are then asked to rate the intensity of the attacks on a 5-point scale ranging from 1 (very mild) to 5 (extremely severe). The Mobility Inventory has been translated into Spanish, Portuguese, French (Canadian), and Dutch.

Purpose

The Mobility Inventory is intended for both research and clinical use. It measures the severity of agoraphobia and may be used as an aid in diagnosis. It should not be used to assign a diagnosis without a clinical interview, because clients may ignore the instructions and rate how much they avoid situations because of depression, delusions, or reality concerns. Moreover, it is not a comprehensive screening measure for all phobias (cf., the Fear Survey Schedule, Wolpe & Lang, 1964), although some specific phobias and social phobias may be evident in ratings. In research the inventory may be used as a measure of change or for selection. The relationships of the scales to a wide range of measures of agoraphobics' functioning have been reported by Chambless (1985b).

Description

The Mobility Inventory was developed and validated on several samples (n = 428) of outpatients with a diagnosis of agoraphobia with panic attacks. Smaller groups of 18 persons with social phobia and 23 normal control subjects were involved in validation as well. Items were constructed on the basis of interviews with agoraphobic persons about situations they avoid and of observation of stimuli for anxiety during in vivo exposure sessions, or they were taken from the Fear Survey Schedule. On the basis of initial analyses, two items were deleted, wordings were revised, and the reliability of the final version was reconfirmed. Analyses showed that the changes did not alter the means on the scales or reduce the reliability.

Psychometric Characteristics

The 26 or 25 items on the Alone and Accompanied Scales, respectively, are averaged to yield total scores. Panic Frequency and Panic Intensity are analyzed as separate items. The avoidance scales and Panic Intensity are normally distributed (Alone: M = 3.35, SD = 1.06; Accompanied. M = 2.64, SD = 0.90; Panic Intensity: M = 3.19, SD = 1.00), but Panic Frequency (M = 2.07) is leptokurtic and positively skewed. Consequently, nonparametric analyses are recommended for the latter.

Reliability. The avoidance scales were found to be highly internally consistent in two reliability samples, rs ranging from .91 to .97, as well as reliable over test-retest intervals of a median of 31 days in one sample and 8 days in the other (rs of .75 to .90). Panic Frequency's reliability is lower, perhaps reflecting the variable nature of panic; tau was .49 and .60. Reliability data are available in only 12 cases for Panic Intensity: r = .66 over a mean test-retest interval of 20.42 days (SD = 16.92). Modest

reliability was obtained; however, it cannot be presumed that the underlying phenomenon would be invariable.

Validity. Validation has been conducted in several ways. First, the two avoidance scales and Panic Frequency were shown to be stable during a period in which no treatment was provided and as predicted, to show significant change with in vivo exposure treatment, which has been repeatedly documented to be effective treatment for phobic avoidance. Therefore, they are sensitive to clinically important alterations in the client's condition. Change data are not yet available on Panic Intensity, but it does remain stable during a period with no treatment. Second, the avoidance scales and Panic Frequency were shown to significantly discriminate agoraphobic clients from groups of socially phobic and normal control individuals. Comparable data are not available on Panic Intensity. Finally, the scales were correlated with other inventories measuring various symptoms hypothesized to be related to the constructs they measure. As predicted, all scales were positively correlated with severity of depression and trait anxiety, and the Alone (r = .68) and Accompanied (r = .44) scales were significantly correlated with the Agoraphobia Factor of the Fear Questionnaire (Marks & Mathews, 1979). The scales were not positively correlated to a theoretically irrelevant scale, the Psychoticism Scale of the Eysenck Personality Questionnaire, indicating that clients are not expressing global psychopathology on the Mobility Inventory. Panic Frequency and Intensity show low, but significant, positive relationships with severity of avoidance and one another.

Clinical Use

It is useful to administer the Mobility Inventory before an intake interview. It is not necessary that the clinician formally score the avoidance scales before the interviews; the items that provide considerable information in abbreviated form may simply be scanned. It is helpful to check with clients to be sure they were rating the items for avoidance due to fear they would become anxious in the situations, as opposed to other factors. Furthermore, some clients will exaggerate their responses to the Panic Frequency item, and such responses (e.g., "All the time" or "Too many to count") can be clarified during the interview. The inventory may be periodically readministered to check for progress in treatment. It often highlights problem areas of which the clinician is unaware.

Future Directions

Further validation on the Mobility Inventory has been undertaken to assess the relationship of the scales to avoidance as measured by behavioral avoidance tests and behavioral diaries. Although such correlations across modalities are not expected to be high, significant relationships, if obtained, will further buttress confidence in the solidity of the scales.

References

Chambless, D.L. (1985a). *Panic intensity on the Mobility Inventory.* Unpublished research.

Chambless, D.L. (1985b). The relationship of severity of agoraphobia to associated psychopathology. *Behaviour Research and Therapy, 23,* 305-310.

Chambless, D.L., Caputo, G.C., Jasin, S.E., Gracely, E.J., & Williams, C. (1985). The Mobility Inventory for Agoraphobia. *Behaviour Research and Therapy, 23,* 35-44.

Marks, I.M., & Mathews, A.M. (1979). Brief standard self-rating for phobic patients. *Behaviour Research and Therapy, 17,* 263-267.

Wolpe, J., & Lang, P. (1964). A fear survey schedule for use in behavior therapy. *Behaviour Research and Therapy, 1,* 27-30.

Modified Fear Survey

Andrea L. Seidner and Dean G. Kilpatrick

Description

The Modified Fear Survey (MFS) (Veronen & Kilpatrick, 1980) is a 120-item self-report inventory of potentially fear-producing items and situations that respondents rate on a 5-point scale indicating the degree of disturbance currently engendered by each item. A rating of 1 indicates the item is "not at all" disturbing and a rating of 5 indicates it is "very much" disturbing. In addition to an overall or total fears score, the following subscale scores are obtained: animal fears, classical fears, social-interpersonal fears, tissue damage fears, miscellaneous fears, failure/loss of self-esteem fears, and rape-related fears.

Purpose

The purpose of the MFS is to provide a psychometrically sound self-report assessment instrument that is useful in the measurement and treatment of rape-induced fear and anxiety. It is intended to be applicable to clinical and research pursuits.

Development

The MFS is based on the original Fear Survey Schedule III (Wolpe & Lang, 1964) and contains all 78 items comprising this measure. The additional 42 items of the MFS were the most frequently cited stimuli generated by a group of five adult rape victims who recalled situations and events that were fear-evoking during and subsequent to the rape (Veronen & Kilpatrick, 1980).

Psychometric Characteristics

Studies have been conducted that provide information on the psychometric characteristics of the MFS. The relevant findings from several studies will be briefly reviewed here. For further information, the reader is referred to the work of the following groups of researchers: Kilpatrick and his colleagues at the Charleston, South Carolina, Crime Victims Research and Treatment Center (Kilpatrick & Veronen, 1984; Kilpatrick, Resick, & Veronen, 1981; Kilpatrick, Veronen, & Best, 1985; Kilpatrick, Veronen, & Resick, 1979; Veronen & Kilpatrick, 1980) and Calhoun and her colleagues in Georgia (Calhoun, Atkeson, & Resick, 1982; Ellis, Atkeson, & Calhoun, 1981); and Resick and her colleagues at the University of Missouri (Resick, 1985).

The individual subscales of the MFS have shown alpha coefficients from .81 to .94, and a value of .98 is reported for the overall score (Kilpatrick et al., 1985). Adequate test-retest reliability has been demonstrated over a 2.5-month interval, with values for the subscales ranging from .60 to .74, a value of .73 being found for the overall score (Kilpatrick et al., 1985).

The ability of the MFS to reliably differentiate rape victims from nonvictims has been repeatedly demonstrated. Kilpatrick and Veronen (1984) reported on the results of a large-scale longitudinal assessment study examining the sequelae of rape in 204 recent adult rape victims (aged 16 or older, raped 6 to 21 days before initial assessment) who were compared with a nonvictim group ($n = 179$)

matched for age, race, and residential neighborhood. Participants were assessed with a battery of instruments at 6 to 21 days, 1 month, 3 months, 6 months, 1 year, 18 months, 2 years, 3 years, and 4 years after the assault. Of the greatest relevance here was the finding that, through the 3-year postassault assessment, the MFS reliably distinguished victims from nonvictims on the rape-related fears subscale at least at the .05 level of significance, except for the 18-month assessment. Too few subjects were available to conduct statistical analyses on the 4-year postassault assessment data, but victims continued to have higher scores on this subscale than did nonvictims. The exact same pattern of findings is reported for the overall fears score, except that the 2-year postrape scores were in the expected direction but did not reach statistical significance. Similarly, Calhoun et al. (1982) assessed 115 adult rape victims aged 15 to 71 years, mean = 25.6) at 2 weeks and at 1, 2, 3, 4, 8, and 12 months after the rape. A comparison group of nonvictims matched for age, race, and socioeconomic status also participated. Briefly, the MFS significantly differentiated victims from nonvictims ($p < .05$) in terms of overall and rape-related fears at all assessment periods, except for overall fears at 12 months after the assault, which only approached significance ($p < .07$).

The ability of the MFS to sensitively reflect spontaneous and treatment-induced change over time has also been supported. Therefore, in the Kilpatrick and Veronen study just described (1984), victims' scores on the MFS (rape and overall fears) showed a significant spontaneous decrease from 6 to 21 days or 1 month (no difference between these two assessments) to 3 months after the assault; no significant change in scores occurred after this up to 2 years after the assault. This suggested that substantial spontaneous improvement does not occur after 3 months after the rape for most victims, which is consistent with a classical-conditioning-followed-by-avoidance-behavior model of fears. In support of these findings, Calhoun et al. (1982) found a significant decline in scores on the MFS over the first 2 months after the assault, with the scores then stabilizing through 12 months after the rape. Treatment-induced change has also been sensitively reflected by the MFS. Kilpatrick and Veronen (1984) also report that the MFS rape-related subscale showed significant pre- to posttreatment decreases in a group of 15 adult rape victims (17 to 75 years old, mean = 32; 3 months to 8 years after the rape, mean = 2.5 years)

who participated in a 20-hour Stress Inoculation Training treatment program focused on overcoming individualized target phobias.

Finally, the MFS was demonstrated to be insensitive to the effects of repeated testing. Calhoun et al. (1982) included three additional groups of victims assessed only 2, 4, or 8 months after the rape (mean = 22, 26, and 24, respectively) to control for testing effects. Their findings revealed no significant differences between each single testing victim group and the group that was assessed repeatedly.

Clinical Use

The MFS was specifically designed for use with a population of rape victims. It is intended to provide an accurate depiction of a victim's current level of fear and anxiety in relation to rape-related and non-rape-related stimuli. Useful clinical information may be derived by examining specific items, subscale scores, and overall fearfulness. Thus, specific phobias to target for intervention, patterns of fear, degree of generalization of specific fears, and overall fearfulness level may be determined. The MFS can also be used by clinicians to assess treatment effectiveness.

As demonstrated in research conducted to date, the MFS is a promising research tool as well as a clinically useful device. Therefore, as examples discussed in the Psychometric Characteristics section of this entry illustrate, patterns of rape-induced fear and anxiety over time have been elucidated, appropriate focus and timing of treatment for such difficulties have been suggested, and effectiveness of specific treatment approaches have been explored with the MFS.

Future Directions

Two future uses of the MFS appear promising. The first is the use of individual items to construct new MFS scales that tap unique fear patterns associated with particular stressful events. One example of this approach is the procedure used in the development of the Rape Symptom Aftermath Test (RAST) as described elsewhere in this volume. A portion of the RAST consisted of items from the MFS that tapped specific fears of rape victims. The second promising future direction is to evaluate the usefulness of the MFS with crimes other than rape or sexual assault. Resick (personal communication, August 1985) found that the MFS was able to detect fears of male and female robbery victims as well as those of female rape victims.

Finally, the MFS should prove useful as a general fear scale to be used for clients with anxiety disorders.

References

Calhoun, K.S., Atkeson, B.M., & Resick, P.A. (1982). A longitudinal examination of fear reactions in victims of rape. *Journal of Counseling Psychology, 29*, 655-661.

Ellis, E.M., Atkeson, B.M., & Calhoun, K.S. (1981). An assessment of long-term reaction to rape. *Journal of Abnormal Psychology, 90*, 263-266.

Kilpatrick, D.G., Resick, P.A., & Veronen, L.J. (1981). Effects of a rape experience: A longitudinal study. *Journal of Social Issues, 37*, 105-122.

Kilpatrick, D.G., & Veronen, L.J. (1984). *Treatment of fear and anxiety in victims of rape* (Final Report, Grant No. R01 MH29602). Rockville, MD: National Institute of Mental Health.

Kilpatrick, D.G., Veronen, L.J., & Best, C.L. (1985). *Factors predicting psychological distress among rape victims*. In C.R. Figley (Ed.), *Trauma and its wake* (pp. 113-141). New York: Brunner/Mazel.

Kilpatrick, D.G., Veronen, L.J., & Resick, P.A. (1979). Assessment of the aftermath of rape: Changing patterns of fear. *Journal of Behavioral Assessment, 1*, 133-148.

Resick, P.A. (1985). *Psychological reaction of victims of rape/robbery* (Grant No. R01 MH37296). Rockville, MD: National Institute of Mental Health.

Veronen, L.J., & Kilpatrick, D.G. (1980). Self-reported fears of rape victims: A preliminary investigation. *Behavior Modification, 4*, 383-396.

Wolpe, J., & Lang, P.J. (1964). A fear survey schedule for use in behavior therapy. *Behaviour Research and Therapy, 2*, 27-30.

Motivation Assessment Scale

V. Mark Durand

Description

The Motivation Assessment Scale (MAS) is a rating scale that assesses the variables maintaining problematic behaviors (e.g., aggression, selfinjurious behavior, and tantrums) in populations with developmental disabilities. The MAS assesses the likelihood that these behaviors will occur in a variety of situations (e.g., as a function of social isolation, denial of rewards, task difficulty, and unstructured settings). For example, a rater may be asked whether a child's self-injurious behavior increases when preferred toys are taken away. Similarly, another question asks whether this behavior increases following a command to perform a difficult task. Raters respond on a 7-point scale, ranging from 0 (never) to 6

(always). A score is obtained for each of four categories of maintaining variables: social attention, tangible consequences, escape from aversive situations, and sensory consequences. High scores in one or more of these categories indicate that these variables may be responsible for maintenance of the problem behavior. Thus, the MAS provides information on the situational determinants of problem behavior.

Purpose

The MAS is an alternative or adjunct to the functional analysis of problematic behavior. It was developed to determine the relative influence of social attention, tangible consequences, escape from aversives, and sensory consequences on these behaviors. These variables were demonstrated to be involved in the maintenance of severe behavior problems in children (Carr & Durand, 1985; Durand & Carr, 1985), and therefore are important to identify for treatment selection and design. The goal in developing this assessment device was to bridge the gap between thorough functional analysis (i.e., manipulating antecedents and consequences) and clinical intuition.

Development

The MAS was developed over a period of 4 years with the help of teachers, parents, and service providers of autistic and other developmentally disabled persons. Questions were added and deleted from the scale based on clarity and predictive value. Questions and wordings were tested until persons involved in the care of developmentally disabled persons could, through the scale, adequately report how these individuals would behave in situations such as difficult tasks, unstructured settings, being denied rewards, and settings with reduced adult attention.

Psychometric Characteristics

Preliminary psychometric data were obtained with a population of 44 developmentally disabled children (Durand & Crimmins, 1983). Interrater and test-retest reliability data were assessed by comparing responses between 18 special education teachers and 18 assistant teachers. The children displayed frequent problem behaviors (aggression, self-injury, tantrums, and stereotyped behaviors). Interrater reliabilities and test-retest reliabilities computed for each category of maintaining variable yielded consistently high correlations.

Preliminary validity data were obtained by comparing these teachers' MAS ratings with observations of their students' behaviors in analogue settings. These settings were patterned after previous assessment research (Carr & Durand, 1985; Durand & Crimmins, 1987; Iwata, Dorsey, Slifer, Bauman, & Richman, 1982). Initial work indicates that teachers' MAS ratings can accurately predict in which situation their student is likely to misbehave. Therefore, a high score on the MAS for Social Attention was predictive of high rates of misbehavior in analogue settings with reduced attention. Similarly, a high score on Tangible Consequences predicted increased rates of misbehavior when favorite tangibles were denied. Escape scores predicted increased misbehavior with increased task difficulty, and Sensory scores predicted increased misbehavior in unstructured situations. Although item analyses, factor analyses, and normative data are not yet available for this instrument, the strength of these validity data suggests its potential for aiding clinical decision-making.

Clinical Use

Clinically, the MAS has been used with a variety of persons with severe handicapping conditions (e.g., infantile autism and mental retardation) as well as with nonhandicapped young children. Problem behaviors assessed with this scale include aggressive behavior, self-injury, tantrums, stereotyped behaviors, and psychotic speech. The information derived from the scale has proven useful in designing effective interventions as well as selecting alternative behaviors (Durand & Carr, 1985). For example, if a client's aggressive behavior is assessed to be maintained by social attention, then a treatment such as time-out would probably reduce this behavior. However, if this aggressive behavior is assessed to be maintained by escape from social demands, then a procedure such as time-out (which involves removing social demands) might result in an *increase* in aggression. Treatment decisions depend on the type of information provided by the MAS.

Although populations and behavioral topographies for which the MAS is applicable appear to be wide-ranging, one limitation involves its use with infrequent behaviors. The MAS is not as successful in predicting maintaining variables for behavior problems that occur only occasionally (e.g., once per month).

Future Directions

Work with the MAS continues in several areas. More extensive psychometric studies of this rating scale are ongoing and are being conducted with a large number of subjects who vary greatly in the type and severity of their problem behavior and in their diagnosis. Future efforts in documenting the validity of this instrument will be focused on demonstrating treatment validity. In other words, does the MAS contribute significantly to the selection and design of effective interventions (Durand & Carr, 1985)? Initial research appears to support this use of the MAS (Carr & Durand, 1985). Finally, work has begun to determine if the MAS can be used to select reinforcers. This research is exploring whether knowledge of the variables maintaining problem behavior (i.e., social attention, tangibles, escape, or sensory consequences) can be translated into classes of reinforcers. Thus, would sensory reinforcers be most effective with persons who frequently misbehave to obtain sensory feedback? Similarly, would social attention, tangible reinforcers, and escape from task demands be most effective with persons displaying behavior problems being maintained by these respective influences? Pilot work suggests that the MAS may indeed be useful in identifying effective classes of reinforcers.

References

Carr, E.G., & Durand, V.M. (1985). Reducing behavior problems through functional communication training. *Journal of Applied Behavior Analysis, 18*, 111-126.

Durand, V.M., & Carr, E.G. (1985). Self-injurious behavior: Motivating conditions and guidelines for treatment. *School Psychology Review, 14*, 171-176.

Durand, V.M., & Crimmins, D.B. (1983). *The Motivation Assessment Scale: A preliminary report on an instrument which assesses the functional significance of children's deviant behavior.* Paper presented at the meeting of the Berkshire Association for Behavior Analysis and Therapy, Amherst, MA.

Durand, V.M., & Crimmins, D.B. (1987). Assessment and treatment of psychotic speech in an autistic child. *Journal of Autism and Developmental Disorders, 17*, 17-28.

Iwata, B.A., Dorsey, M.F., Slifer, K.J., Bauman, K.E., & Richman, G.S. (1982). Toward a functional analysis of self-injury. *Analysis and Intervention in Developmental Disabilities, 2*, 3-20.

Multiple Affect Adjective Check List-Revised

Marvin Zuckerman and Bernard Lubin

Description

The Multiple Affect Adjective Check List (MAACL) consists of 132 adjectives. The trait form asks subjects to check all the words that describe how they "generally" feel, and the state form asks them to check the words describing how they feel "now-today." Because of the simplicity of the check/no check response format, the test usually requires only 3 to 5 minutes to fill out. The words on the test do not exceed an eighth grade reading level. The revised version (MAACL-R, Zuckerman & Lubin, 1985) contains five basic scales and two summary scores: Anxiety (A), Depression (D), Hostility (H), Positive Affect (PA), Sensation Seeking (SS), Dysphoria (Dys = A + D + H), Positive Affect plus Sensation Seeking (PASS = PA + SS). Raw scores on each of the seven scales are converted into standardized T scores within different ranges of the number of items checked. This standardization controls the scores for the acquiescence factor.

Purpose

The purpose of the MAACL-R is to measure the primary dimensions of affect from self-reports. The state form is designed to assess transient affects from periods ranging from minutes to 1 day. The instructions usually are given to designate the time period for which a description is required. The trait form is intended to measure the same dimensions of affects as summaries of reactions over longer periods of time. Research has shown that although a state score on a single day does not correlate very highly with a trait measure, an average of state scores on a number of days correlates highly with the trait measure of the same affect (Zuckerman, 1976). Therefore, a trait is the individual's summary of his or her states over some period of time and over some range of situations.

Development

The first version of the MAACL (Zuckerman & Lubin, 1965) had three empirically developed scales: Anxiety, Depression, and Hostility. Positive affects were not measured separately because the scales were bipolar, and positive affect items were reverse scored on the negative affect scales. The three scales were highly intercorrelated and tended to correlate with the total number of items checked. The new scales (Zuckerman & Lubin, 1985) were developed from factor analyses of the state form (Zuckerman, Lubin, & Rinck, 1983). As in other factor analyses of affect, positive and negative affects tend to emerge as two independent factors. However, smaller factors enabled us to separate three components of negative affect (A, D, & H)

and two of positive affect (PA & SS). The trait form was standardized on a large national probability sample providing extensive data on demographic correlates of trait affect. The state form is standardized only on college students.

Psychometric Characteristics

The manual (Zuckerman & Lubin, 1985) provides reliability and validity data from many large normal and clinical samples. Internal (alpha) reliabilities of the A, D, and H state scales in eight samples range from .74 to .90 with two thirds are in the .8 to .9 range. Alphas for the PA, Dys, and PASS scores are mostly .90 or higher. Only the SS scale shows any unsatisfactory alphas (range .49 to .81, median .65). For the trait form, alphas for A, D, and H are mostly .8 to .9, and those for PA and Dys are mostly .9 or higher. The SS scale had even poorer internal reliability in the trait form, with coefficients exceeding .60 in only three of eight samples.

The trait state model (Zuckerman, 1976) suggests that state affect will have low retest reliability, whereas trait affect will have relatively higher reliability over time. The results generally fit this model. Only the PA state shows any significant reliability over 2- to 5-day periods. Retest reliabilities on the trait form after 8 weeks range from .39 to .64. Dysphoria and its component scales (A, D, & H) show higher reliabilities over 2 to 6 weeks. Standardization within different ranges of the total number of items checked has markedly reduced the correlation of the scales in standard score form with the number checked.

Validity data on the new scales are presented in the form of correlations with self-ratings, peer ratings from other patients in group therapy, counselors' ratings of clients, correlations with the Lorr Profile of Mood States, the trait Sensation Seeking Scale, the Minnesota Multiphasic Personality Inventory (MMPI), and comparison of scores of different diagnostic groups and a matched normal group. The diagnostic study indicates that a simple linear combination of two of the scales (D and PA) effectively discriminates between patients with affective disorders and other types of patients as well as normal subjects. A study of examination anxiety showed that normal subjects demonstrate a significant increase on the Anxiety scale and a significant decrease on the Positive Affect scale just before taking an examination.

Clinical Use

The revised MAACL will certainly be used for the same purposes as the old MAACL. A recent bibliography compiled through August 1983 by Lubin, Zuckerman, and Woodward (1985) lists 716 published articles and doctoral dissertations. Of these, 90 dealt with assessment, 56 with behavioral therapy, 23 with cognitive therapy, 31 with psychotherapy, 9 with biofeedback, 13 with relaxation or meditation, 30 with sensitivity training and encounter groups, 12 with different nursing approaches, 63 with drugs, alcohol, and alcoholism, and 22 with other clinical psychiatric studies. The state MAACL will probably continue to be an instrument of choice for studies of short-term affect changes. The new positive affect scales should make the test even more useful because many treatments aim at restoration of positive affect as well as reduction of negative affect.

The old MAACL trait scale was not used nearly as often as the state scale, probably because of the inadequate standardization. The MAACL-R trait scales should be quite useful for diagnosis of affective disorders and perhaps for anxiety disorders as well. Standardization on a national probability sample offers a solid basis for the standard scores that make scale comparisons and profile analysis possible. The trait scale also may be useful to measure changes over longer periods of time because affect trait measures do change with changes in clinical states.

Future Directions

Clinical researchers will want to explore the diagnostic possibilities for the new trait scales. Combinations of standard scales scores, like the D-PA index for diagnosis of affective disorders, can be evolved for other diagnostic problems like the distinction between affective and anxiety disorders. The simplicity of the MAACL and its short administration time may recommend it for some diagnostic problems over long and difficult instruments like the MMPI.

Apart from the many possible developments of the scales for clinical uses, the MAACL-R should prove invaluable for research or naturalistic studies of stress and stress amelioration. Basic theoretical problems of clinical relevance like those dealing with the role of learned helplessness in depression can also be addressed using the affect scales.

References

Lubin, B., Zuckerman, M., & Woodward, L. (1985). *Bibliography for the Multiple Affect Adjective Check List - August, 1983*. San Diego, CA: Educational & Industrial Testing Service.

Zuckerman, M. (1976). General and situation-specific traits and states: New approaches to assessment of anxiety and other constructs. In M. Zuckerman & C.D. Spielberger (Eds.), *Emotions and anxiety: New concepts, methods, and applications*. Hillsdale, NJ: Erlbaum.

Zuckerman, M., & Lubin, B. (1965). *Manual for the Multiple Affect Adjective Check List*. San Diego, CA: Educational and Industrial Testing Service.

Zuckerman, M., & Lubin, B. (1985). *Manual for the Revised Multiple Affect Adjective Check List*. San Diego, CA: Educational and Industrial Testing Service.

Zuckerman, M., Lubin, B., & Rinck, C.M. (1983). Construction of new scales for the Multiple Affect Adjective Check List. *Journal of Behavioral Assessment, 5*, 119-129.

Munroe Daily Sleep Questionnaire-Revised

L. Michael Ascher and Robert M. Gilligan

Description

The revised Daily Sleep Questionnaire is a self-report measure designed to assess various aspects of sleep-related behaviors. The questionnaire contains two components: (a) self-report of relatively objective sleep measures, and (b) self-report of subjective ratings.

The relatively objective components include: (a) sleep-onset latency as measured by the number of minutes required to fall asleep after entering bed and turning off the lights, (b) number of awakenings during the night, (c) number of nighttime awakenings followed by difficulty returning to sleep, (d) number of hours slept the night before, and (e) current medication intake derived by counting the number of nights per week on which the subject or client took sleep medication.

Subjective measures include: (a) difficulty in falling asleep the previous night, and (b) feelings of restedness upon waking in the morning. Both of these employ ratings on a 7-point scale, with 1 assigned to a great deal of difficulty falling asleep or the experience of a lack of restedness and 7 indicating ease in falling asleep or the experience of being very well rested.

The Daily Sleep Questionnaire is generally completed by the subject or client in the morning upon waking as part of a home-based behavioral assessment of sleep difficulties.

Purpose

The revised Daily Sleep Questionnaire is designed as a self-monitoring device for subjects or clients already diagnosed as having complaints of primary sleep-onset and sleep-maintenance insomnia. It has been used both as an assessment of change after clinical intervention as well as a dependent variable measure in outcome research evaluating the efficacy of various treatments for insomnia.

Development

The Daily Sleep Questionnaire was originally developed as a selection device to differentiate between good and poor sleepers (Munroe, 1967). Large group differences were found between good and poor sleepers on several self-reported quantitative sleep measures such as: (a) number of minutes required to fall asleep, (b) number of times per week that sleep onset latency reaches 30 minutes or more, and (c) number of nights per week awakenings occurred. In addition, large group differences in subjective measures were observed in good and poor sleepers in the percentage of subjects who have: (a) initial difficulty falling asleep, and (b) difficulty returning to sleep when awakened during the night.

Sleep laboratory electroencephalographic evaluations provided some validation for the self-reported objective sleep measures as well as the physiological correlates of sleep. Statistically significant differences between the good and poor sleeper groups were obtained in: (a) total amount of sleep, (b) total time awake, (c) percentage of time in Stage 2 sleep, (d) amount of REM sleep, (e) percentage of time in REM sleep, (f) number of REM awakenings, (g) number of total awakenings, and (h) time to sleep onset.

Good sleepers were differentiated from poor sleepers in that they fell asleep more quickly, averaged considerably more sleep time, had less time awake, and had fewer awakenings. The differences in sleep patterns of good and poor sleepers were accounted for in terms of the differential proportions of Stage 2 and REM sleep. The poor sleeper group averaged significantly more Stage 2 sleep and significantly less REM sleep than did the good sleep group. Munroe's study established that

there is a correspondence between self-reported sleep behaviors and electrophysiological sleep indicators and that these measures discriminate between good and poor sleepers. However, the author cautions that the poor sleep group did not necessarily perceive themselves as having insomnia or a specific sleep disturbance.

Psychometric Characteristics

Test-retest reliability for sleep-onset latency has been assessed in one study, and the average test-retest correlation was + 0.93 for those subjects classified as poor sleepers and + 0.58 for good sleepers. The reliabilities for the number of awakenings were + 0.69 for this same population of poor sleepers and + 0.35 for good sleepers (Coates et al., 1980).

Interobserver reliability has been tested using spouses or roommates to verify a client's estimates of latency to sleep onset in at least three studies. Tokarz and Lawrence (1974) obtained correlations between observer and subject estimates ranging from + 0.91 to + 0.99. Turner and Ascher (1979) found correlations of + 0.84 and + 0.93, respectively, in their assessments of spouse/roommate and client estimates of sleep-onset latency. It appears that there is substantial interobserver agreement for the sleep questionnaire in the measurement of sleep-onset latency.

Measures of validity have focused on cross-validation with physiological measures of sleep behaviors. Although insomniacs are reported to overestimate sleep latency and underestimate total sleep time and the number of awakenings during the night compared with electroencephalographic assessment, they do so in a consistent manner. Substantial correlations have been reported with electroencephalographic sleep laboratory recordings and estimates of subjective sleep behaviors (Bootzin & Engle-Friedman, 1981).

Clinical Use

The Daily Sleep Questionnaire has been employed as a clinical assessment device for patients reporting primary sleep disorders. In addition, it has typically been used as an outcome measure in studies examining the efficacy of various behavioral treatments for insomnia.

Future Directions

Future studies using the Daily Sleep Questionnaire might focus on several dimensions. Of major importance is the lack of standardization. Studies have typically used either different or altered versions of the form, which poses some difficulty for both reliability and validity assessments. In addition, discriminant validity studies need to be conducted which differentiate between self-labeled poor sleepers and clinically diagnosed insomniacs as well as between pseudoinsomnia and idiopathic insomnia. Furthermore, the problems of reactivity (a weakness in all self-report measures), demand characteristics, and cognitive aspects of sleep disorders associated with this assessment device need to be addressed.

A beneficial addition to the Daily Sleep Questionnaire would be inclusion of a report of terminal insomnia (waking up too early) that is not presently included in the assessment. To further validate the sleep questionnaire, future studies might examine the physiological measures that covary with the self-report. Most studies to date have focused on those measures that relate to sleep-onset insomnia while neglecting sleep-maintenance and terminal insomnia.

Compliance with daily self-report recording has been a problem during treatment and especially during follow-up. Strategies need to be devised that improve compliance with self-reports of sleep problems.

References

Bootzin, R.R., & Engle-Friedman, M. (1981). The assessment of insomnia. *Behavioral Assessment, 3*, 101-126.

Coates, T.J., George, J., Killen, J.D., Marchini, E., Silverman, S., & Thoresen, C. (1980). Estimating sleep from self, spouse, and all-night polysomnograms: A multitrait-multimethod analysis. Unpublished manuscript, The Johns Hopkins School of Medicine.

Munroe, L.J. (1967). Psychological and physiological differences between good and poor sleepers. *Journal of Abnormal Psychology, 72*, 255-264.

Tokarz, T., & Lawrence, P. (1974). *An analysis of temporal and stimulus factors in the treatment of insomnia.* Paper presented at the meeting of the Association for Advancement of Behavior Therapy, Chicago.

Turner, R.M., & Ascher, L.M. (1979). Controlled comparison of progressive relaxation, stimulus control and paradoxical intention therapies for insomnia. *Journal of Consulting and Clinical Psychology, 49*, 500-508.

Musical Performance Anxiety Self-Statement Scale

Michael G. Craske, Kenneth D. Craig, and Margaret J. Kendrick

Description

The Musical Performance Anxiety Self-Statement Scale (MPASS) is a 32-item self-report questionnaire designed to permit description of subjective thoughts and feelings concerning musical performance anxiety. Pianists rate the frequency of positive and negative thoughts that occur before, during, and/or after a performance, on a 7-point scale ranging from "never" to "almost continuously." The questionnaire, which is administered after completion of a performance, requires approximately 5 to 10 minutes to complete.

Purpose

The purpose of the questionnaire is to assess the extent to which a performer thinks positively (e.g., "I was confident I would play well"), and focuses his or her attention on the music (e.g., "I was thinking about the music I was going to play—its mood, tempo, and feeling"), as opposed to the extent to which the performer thinks negatively (e.g., "I feel like a complete failure") and is distracted from the music (e.g., "I wished this performance were taking place at another time"). It was designed to measure the cognitive response counterpart to the behavioral and physiological components of the anxiety state for research and clinical purposes (Kendrick, Craig, Lawson, & Davidson, 1982).

Development

The scale was developed on a rational basis. A group of six pianists, who represented a range of musical competence, created a pool of 92 items describing thoughts they believed occur before, during, or after a performance. These items were consensually validated by a second group of 34 musicians. Items that were not rated by at least 80% of the second group as clearly positive or clearly negative were discarded. The remaining 70 items were administered to a third group of 101 pianists, who rated the frequency with which each item occurred in reference to a specific performance. Each item score was correlated with the total score. Sixteen positive and 16 negative items that yielded the highest correlations with the total score were selected to comprise the final scale. Correlation coefficients ranged from .38 to .65. Eighty percent agreement was required to designate an item in the before (16 items), during (25 items), or after (18 items) performance category. Some items occur in more than one category.

Psychometric Characteristics

The MPASS has demonstrated concurrent validity. Kendrick (1979) found that Self-Statement scores correlated with the State Scale of the Spielberger State-Trait Anxiety Inventory ($r = -0.40$) and with the Subjective Stress Scale ($r = -0.50$). The correlation of -0.34 found between self-statements and a behavioral measure (performance quality) by Kendrick, Craig, Lawson, and Davidson (1982) was not replicated by Craske and Craig (1984). Conversely, the correlation of -0.38 found between self-statements and a physiological measure (heart rate) by Craske and Craig (1984) was not obtained by Kendrick et al. (1982). The inconsistency of the correlations between this cognitive measure and behavioral and physiological measures of performance anxiety is perhaps in part a reflection of a natural discordance among those measures. The construct validity of the questionnaire is shown by the difference in scores obtained by highly anxious and mildly anxious pianists. Highly anxious pianists report significantly more negative thoughts and fewer positive thoughts than do mildly anxious pianists (Craske & Craig, 1984; Kendrick, 1979). Scores from the Self-Statement scale obtained 4 weeks apart in reference to different performances were correlated $r = 0.56$. This moderate level of retest reliability should strengthen under comparable performance conditions. An alpha correlation coefficient of 0.92 indicated the high internal consistency of this questionnaire (Kendrick, 1979).

Scores are based on the sums of all frequency ratings (negative items are reverse scored). The average score obtained from three groups of anxious pianists (sample = 48) in Kendrick's study was 199.02 ($SD = 59.35$). Twenty anxious pianists in Craske and Craig's (1984) study reported an almost identical average score of 198.70 ($SD = 70.55$). The average increased to 242.07 ($SD = 55.79$) in Kendrick's study following training in techniques of anxiety reduction. A group of 20 mildly anxious pianists reported an average of 256.80 ($SD = 46.95$) in Craske and Craig's study.

Clinical Use

The MPASS appears to be very useful in the assessment of the positive or negative direction of thought content in reference to musical performances. It is an indicator of performance-anxiety level and treatment-related change. The scale was designed specifically for pianists who perform in public. However, it may easily be modified to suit other musical instruments and performance settings. The questionnaire is appropriate for musicians in a wide range of age, experience, and competence.

Future Research

Future research with this questionnaire should concern its application to other performance situations (musical and nonmusical). Its relationship to behavioral and physiological indices of anxiety also awaits further investigation. In line with current attempts to match treatment approach with individual response style, the potential of this questionnaire to discriminate between musicians who would benefit most and benefit least from cognitive/attentional approaches to performance-anxiety reduction should be examined.

References

Craske, M.A., & Craig, K.D. (1984). Musical-performance anxiety: The three-systems model and self-efficacy theory. *Behaviour Research and Therapy, 22*, 267-280.

Kendrick, M.J. (1979). *Reduction of musical performance anxiety by attentional training and behavioral rehearsal: An exploration of cognitive mediational processes.* Doctoral Dissertation, University of British Columbia, Vancouver.

Kendrick, M., Craig, K.D., Lawson, D., & Davidson, P. (1982). Cognitive and behavioral therapy for musical performance anxiety. *Journal of Consulting and Clinical Psychology, 50*, 333-362.

Novaco Provocation Inventory

Raymond W. Novaco

Description

The Novaco Provocation Inventory (NPI) is an 80-item self-report instrument for assessing anger responsiveness. The inventory consists of brief descriptions of situations of provocation, for which the respondent notes the degree of anger that he or she would experience if that event should occur. The ratings are performed on a 5-point scale of arousal level.

Purpose

The NPI is designed to gauge the range and intensity of anger responses. As a measure of anger problems, it does not assess frequency, duration, or mode of response parameters (Novaco, 1985). It was developed for three purposes: (a) to provide a general index of anger responsiveness across a wide range of situations; (b) to serve as a guide for interview assessments; and (c) to generate an empirical basis for the content of laboratory provocation procedures used by Novaco (1975). The inventory provides information about the types of situation most likely to arouse anger and the overall magnitude of the respondent's proneness to provocation.

Development

The NPI was first reported by Novaco (1975). The items were intuitively derived and partly based on interviews with subjects about situations of anger arousal. The instrument was found to have high internal consistency ($r = .95$), but several items were replaced to incorporate more situations of home life. The resulting 80-item measure was then administered to clinical and nonclinical samples, including university students, industrial workers, police officers, military personnel, mental health workers, psychiatric patients, child abusers, and prison hospital inmates.

Psychometric Characteristics

The principal index for the inventory is the total score, computed by summing the item-intensity ratings. The mean for normal samples ranges from 230 to 255. This approximates endorsing the scale midpoint across the 80 items. The standard deviation is consistently about 45. Internal reliability coefficients are consistently high ($r > .93$) across samples. Test-retest reliabilities with university student samples have ranged from $r = .83$ (sample $= 34$) for a 1-month interval to $r = .89$ (sample $= 39$) and $r = .90$ (sample $= 69$) for 1-week intervals. Correlations with the Buss-Durkee Hostility Inventory (Buss & Durkee, 1957) range from .41 to .48.

One structure for the inventory is the intuitive categorization of the provocation items. Seven primary categories were identified: (1) annoying behavior of others, (2) humiliation/verbal insult, (3) personal injustice, (4) social injustice, (5) frustration, (6) personal clumsiness, and (7) physical assault. Items were sorted into these categories with a 94% rate of agreement between judges (Novaco & Robinson, 1984).

Factor analysis of the inventory was performed with the undergraduate, industrial worker, military, and child abuse samples by means of principal axis analysis rotated to a varimax solution. The factor solution was selected by the "scree" method. Across samples, three factors emerge consistently: injustice/unfairness, frustration/clumsiness, and physical affronts. One departure from this pattern is that for female undergraduates, humiliation/verbal insult emerges as the first factor.

Validational studies on the inventory have found it to be significantly related to laboratory self-report measures of anger (Novaco, 1975). Studies with military samples have found significant associations with the Jenkins measure of Type A behavior ($r = .34$, sample $= 59$) and inverse relationships to job performance evaluations ($r = -.32$, sample $= 59$). Recent research by Selby (1984) has shown a 25–item subset of the NPI to discriminate between violent and nonviolent criminal offenders with 90% accuracy, which far exceeded that for several other alternative instruments.

Clinical Use

The NPI may be used as a dependent measure index for assessing pre- and post-intervention changes in anger propensity, as a preliminary screening instrument in selecting candidates for treatment programs, and as a guide for structuring a clinical interview. In the latter regard, the clinician might select from the respondent's protocol those items endorsed as eliciting high anger. By probing into the nature of the identified situations, asking the client to recall a recent example, one can systematically learn about the situational cues, dispositional states, cognitive structures, and cognitive processes that are entailed in the client's anger patterns.

Future Directions

Although there are several self-report anger instruments in the literature, no instrument has been developed from a theory. Inventories should be distinguished from "scales," and scales should follow from a theory of the dimensions of anger and the deficits linked with anger problems. Hence, the next step is to develop such a theoretically based anger scale and proceed with its systematic validation.

References

Buss, A., & Durkee, A. (1957). An inventory for assessing different kinds of hostility. *Journal of Consulting Psychology, 21,* 343-349.

Novaco, R.W. (1975). *Anger control: The development and evaluation of an experimental treatment.* Lexington, MA: D.C. Heath.

Novaco, R.W. (1985). Anger and its therapeutic regulation. In M.A. Chesney & R.H. Rosenman (Eds.), *Anger and hostility in cardiovascular and behavioral disorders.* New York: Hemisphere.

Novaco, R.W., & Robinson, G.L. (1984). Anger and aggression among military personnel. In R.M. Kaplan, V.J. Konecni, & R.W. Novaco (Eds.), *Aggression in children and youth.* The Hague: Martinus Nijhoff.

Selby, M.J. (1984). Assessment of violence potential using measures of anger, hostility, and social desirability. *Journal of Personality Assessment, 48,* 531-537.

Observational System for Assessing Mealtime Behaviors in Children and Associated Parent Behavior

Robert C. Klesges, Lisa M. Klesges, and Thomas J. Coates

Description

There is increased interest in identifying subtle, microanalytic behaviors that differentiate between normal weight and overweight children (Waxman & Stunkard, 1980). Although techniques such as the 24-hour dietary recall and food records produce reliable estimates of food consumption in children (Frank, Voors, Schilling, & Berenson, 1977), these instruments can neither document the behavioral aspects of mealtime behavior nor identify psychosocial and parental influences on eating behavior. As a result, Bob and Tom's Method of Assessing Nutrition (BATMAN) was constructed to achieve these goals (Klesges et al., 1983).

The BATMAN was designed to record child behaviors at mealtime and related social environmental variables. A time–sampling system in which a 10-second observation is followed by a 10-second record phase is used. Observers first code the child's behavior (e.g., eating, talking, and away from table) and if someone interacts (e.g., food offer, encouragement to eat, and food presentation) with the child, the food being prompted is coded along with the child's response (i.e., eat, cry, and refuse). The BATMAN does not measure the topography of eating but rather mealtime behavior and parental variables that may modify the child's eating behavior.

Purpose

The BATMAN is a specific, microanalytic assessment used to document subtle differences between normal weight and overweight children and differences in parental interactions between these groups.

Development

The BATMAN was developed by initially conducting a comprehensive review of the literature of children's food intake as well as childhood obesity. This was completed to determine meaningful and quantifiable behavioral categories. Potential social, parental, interactional, and environmental factors associated with children's food intake were identified based on a social learning theory model (Bandura, 1978). The initial instrument was then extensively field tested and modified.

Psychometric Characteristics

High levels of interrater reliability can be achieved with the BATMAN (mean = 95%; mean Kappa coefficient = .91). Test-retest correlations over a 1-month period ranged from .61 to .94 (mean r = .84). Most importantly, various parental prompts (food offers and encouragements to eat) significantly correlated with the relative weight of the child.

Clinical Use

The BATMAN has been demonstrated to be useful for descriptive purposes and to identify psychosocial risk factors associated with childhood obesity. The BATMAN's assessment ability could be used for intervention purposes, especially to target parental variables as correlates of child relative weight. The instrument has been validated on a population of 2- to 4-year-old preschoolers. Further research and modifications of the instrument would be needed to extend its age range.

Future Directions

The BATMAN has been used to discriminate normal from overweight children. It is useful for intervention purposes, especially in pinpointing certain types of food that parents encourage or discourage. Future research should attempt to identify psychosocial risk factors for obesity in older, school-aged children.

References

Bandura, A. (1977). *Social learning theory*. Englewood Cliffs, NJ: Prentice-Hall.

Frank, G.C., Voors, A.W, Schilling, P.E., & Berenson, G.S. (1977). Dietary studies of rural school children in a cardiovascular survey. *Journal of the American Dietetic Association, 71,* 31-35.

Klesges, R.C., Coates, T.J., Brown, G., Sturgeon-Tillisch, J., Moldenhauer-Klesges, L.M., Holzer, B., Woolfrey, J., & Vollmer, J. (1983). Parental influences on children's eating behavior and relative weight. *Journal of Applied Behavior Analysis, 4,* 317-378.

Waxman, M., & Stunkard, A.J. (1980). Caloric intake and expenditure of obese boys. *Journal of Pediatrics, 96,* 187-193.

Observational System to Quantify Social, Environmental, and Parental Influences on Physical Activity in Children

Robert C. Klesges, Lisa M. Klesges, and Thomas J. Coates

Description

The accurate and reliable assessment of physical activity in children is important not only to identify physical activity differences in clinical populations (e.g., obesity), but also to evaluate treatment outcome. Furthermore, increased attention is being paid to the psychosocial, environmental, and parental influences of physical activity (Waxman & Stunkard, 1980). Given that both self-report (LaPorte et al., 1978) and actometer/pedometer-like devices (Klesges, Klesges, Swenson, & Pheley, 1985) are unreliable in the assessment of preschool obesity, direct observation of physical activity appears to be the most promising method of quantifying the subtle differences, for example, between overweight and normal weight children. The Fargo Activity Time–sampling Survey (FATS; Klesges et al., 1984) was constructed to begin to address these issues.

The Fargo Activity Time–sampling Survey (FATS) is an observational system that measures children's physical activity and parent-child interactions related to physical activity. An interval time–sampling procedure is used; the subject is

observed for 10 seconds followed by a 10-second recording interval. During the observation phase the child's behavior (e.g., sleeping, crawling, and running) and the intensity of behavior are coded along with any interactions. If someone encourages or discourages the child's activity, the observer records the person interacting (e.g., mother, father, and sibling), the form of the interaction (e.g., verbal or physical), the targeted behavior (e.g, walking or sitting), and the child's response to the interaction. In case of multiple interactions, all are coded.

Purpose

The purpose of the FATS is to microanalytically assess physical activity in children. It was designed to assess physical activity in terms of discriminable body movements and interactions that serve to selectively influence activity. The results of the FATS can be used for descriptive purposes or for potential targets of intervention.

Development

The FATS was developed after thoroughly reviewing the literature on physical activity in children to determine meaningful and quantifiable behavioral categories. Potential social, parental, and environmental influences on child physical activity were developed intuitively based on a social learning model (Bandura, 1977). The instrument was then extensively field tested and modified.

Psychometric Characteristics

High levels of interrater reliability can be achieved with the FATS (proportion agreement = .90 to .96, weighted Kappa coefficients = .87 to .93). One-month test-retest reliability ($r = .59$) is acceptable. Furthermore, parental prompts to be active correlate with children's activity levels ($r = .53$), and overall levels of children's physical activity correlated negatively with the child's relative weight.

Clinical Use

The FATS is useful for descriptive and intervention purposes. Its usefulness in analyzing specific types of behavior versus a global measure of behavior is apparent. The FATS has the ability to assess parental interactions that may be selectively modifying children's activity levels. Because of the sensitive assessment offered by the FATS, it is useful for designing intervention strategies and measuring their effectiveness. The instrument has been validated on a population of 2- to 4-year-old preschoolers. Further research must be conducted before extending it to older, school-aged children.

Future Directions

The FATS has been used to discriminate between normal and overweight children. Its usefulness in other areas such as predicting differences in hyperactive preschoolers or measuring adherence to treatment recommendations could certainly be explored. In the future, normative data could be offered as the populations studied increase. Validating the FATS on a school-aged population is also important.

References

Bandura, A. (1977). *Social learning theory*. Englewood Cliffs, NJ: Prentice-Hall.

Klesges, R.C., Coates, T.J., Moldenhauer-Klesges, L.M., Holzer, B., Gustavson, J., & Barnes, J. (1984). The FATS: An observational system for assessing physical activity in children and associated parent behavior. *Behavioral Assessment, 6,* 333-345.

Klesges, R.C., Klesges, L.M., Swenson, A.M., & Pheley, A.M. (1985). A validation of two motion sensors in the prediction of child and adult physical activity levels. *American Journal of Epidemiology, 122,* 400-410.

LaPorte, R.E., Sandler-Black, R., Cauley, J.A., Kinsey, C.M., Corbett, W., & Robertson, R. (1982). The epidemiology of physical activity in children, college students, middle aged men, menopausal females and monkeys. *Journal of Chronic Diseases, 75,* 787-795.

Waxman, M., & Stunkard, A.J. (1980). Caloric intake and expenditure of obese boys. *Journal of Pediatrics, 96,* 187-193.

Observer Rating Scale of Anxiety

Barbara G. Melamed and Mark A. Lumley

Description

The Observer Rating Scale of Anxiety (OBRSA) is an observational scale comprised of 29 verbal and skeletal motor behaviors thought to represent behavioral manifestations of anxiety or its absence in children. The 29 behaviors are functionally defined and include 24 anxious behaviors, such as crying, trembling hands, playing with hair, talking about separation from mother, and rocking back and forth. The other five behaviors are presumed to indicate low levels of anxiety, and include smiling, speaking spontaneously, laughing, speaking when spoken to, and talking about interests. A time–sampling procedure is employed in which an observer indicates the presence or absence of each response category during consecutive 3-minute intervals, until the observation session is complete. Functional definitions are provided. Behaviors indicative of anxiety are scored in the anxiety direction if they are present during the interval, and the five behaviors indicative of low levels of anxiety are scored in the anxiety direction if they are absent. A final anxiety score is calculated by totaling the number of anxiety-related behaviors per each 3-minute interval and then calculating a mean score across all observation intervals.

Purpose

Anxiety is considered to be a multidimensional construct manifested in three domains: self-report (subjective), overt behavior, and psychophysiological. Moreover, some researchers believe that anxiety falls into two classes: trait anxiety, which is one's characteristic level of anxiety, and state anxiety, which is one's anxiety as revealed in particular situations and settings. The OBRSA is an instrument that measures state anxiety in the overt behavioral domain. Moreover, functionally defined categories are presented to assist in defining behaviors. The purpose of the OBRSA, therefore, is to aid in the determination of the anxiety level of a child when he or she is in a specific, usually stressful, situation.

Development

There has been little research on direct observational measures of children's fear-related behavior during medical procedures. Jay and Elliot (1984) recently provided a measure of behavioral distress, but this is specific to extreme procedures, such as bone marrow aspiration and lumbar puncture.

To aid in the selection of specific items for the OBRSA, available behavior problem checklists were reviewed (Peterson, 1961; Quay & Quay, 1965). Items that were applicable to an age range of 4 to 17 years, were fear-related, and would potentially interfere with medical procedures were chosen. Five items that indicated low anxiety levels were also selected. The result is the 29-item OBRSA.

Psychometric Characteristics

The initial validity data were provided by examination of the sensitivity of the measure to changes between treated and untreated children being prepared for surgery and hospitalization with the use of filmed modeling (Melamed & Siegel, 1975). The anxiety measure provided by the OBRSA not only differentiated between these two groups, but also, as predicted, reflected changes over time from admission to postdischarge 1-month follow-up physical examination ($p < .01$). Parallel findings for self-reported medical concerns (Hospital Fears Rating Scale) and sweating (Palmar Sweat Index) were seen at pre- and postoperational assessments. Moreover, this scale was found to be unbiased by age or sex differences. Melamed, Dearborn, and Hermecz (1983) found that the OBRSA significantly differentiated ($p < .04$) children under the age of 8 who had previous surgery and had seen a hospital-relevant film from those children in this same age and experience group who had seen a control film. Moreover, a child's knowledge of hospital procedures (Hospital Information Test) correlated negatively with the OBRSA score ($r = -.046$, $p < .01$).

Several studies have used the OBRSA, and in all of these cases, children's anxiety was assessed in dental or medical settings. In the Melamed and Siegal (1975) and the Melamed et al. (1983) studies, interrater reliabilities, defined as percentage agreement per total number of observed categories, of 94% and 91%, respectively, were found. Such high reliabilities are probably due to the functional definitions of the behaviors and the simplicity of recording only the presence or absence of a behavior during several 3-minute intervals.

Clinical Use

The greatest value of the OBRSA is its utility as one of several instruments measuring the anxiety of a child in a given situation. Although observational measures of behavior are vital to a valid assessment of anxiety, ideally, self-reports and physiological measures should be obtained as well. Research endeavors of clinical assessments that seek valid observational measures of a child's anxiety in a particular setting and as manifested in the behavioral domain would benefit from the use of this scale. It is important, however, to obtain an accurate baseline level of the child's anxiety using this scale before any interventions, or before one draws conclusions regarding heightened or reduced levels of anxiety being displayed by the child.

Future Directions

More research into the predictive validity of this scale needs to be undertaken. Additional categories that are found to be indicative of anxiety in children should be added, and any categories found to be invalid need to be removed. Moreover, it may be preferable to score the OBRSA using weighted criteria for each behavior as to the behavior's intensity or the degree to which it interferes with adaptive functioning in the setting. Finally, a frequency count for the observed behavior rather than a present/absent dichotomy may provide greater sensitivity in a less aversive situation in which specific stressors are absent.

References

Jay, S.M., & Elliot, C. (1984). Behavioral observation scales for measuring children's distress: The effect of increased methodological rigor. *Journal of Consulting and Clinical Psychology, 52*, 1106-1107.

Melamed, B.G., Dearborn, M., & Hermecz, D.A. (1983). Necessary considerations for surgery preparation: Age and previous experience. *Psychosomatic Medicine, 45*, 517-525.

Melamed, B.G., & Siegel, L.J. (1975). Reduction of anxiety in children facing hospitalization and surgery by use of filmed modeling. *Journal of Consulting and Clinical Psychology, 43*, 511-521.

Peterson, D.R. (1961). Behavior problems of middle childhood. *Journal of Consulting Psychology, 25*, 205-209.

Quay, H.C., & Quay, L.C. (1965). Behavior problems in early adolescence. *Child Development, 36*, 215-220.

Observational Record of Inpatient Behavior

Alexander J. Rosen

Description

The Observational Record of Inpatient Behavior (ORIB) is a practical, sensitive, and reliable time-sampling instrument designed to record eight components of the ward behavior of psychiatric inpatients: body activity (movement of the whole body such as running, walking, bending, and shifting); extremity activity (movement of arms or legs); proximity (within an arm's length of another person); social interaction (verbal or physical interpersonal exchange); scanning (eye or head movements, as distinguished from fixated); laughing/smiling (facial expressions); participation (in ongoing group activity); and idiosyncratic behavior (bizarre behavior, repetitive movements, or self-verbalization).

The ORIB is used in the context of a focal time-sampling procedure in which a target patient is observed for 5 seconds; the occurrence or nonoccurrence of each specific behavior is recorded during the following 20-second interval for a total of nine consecutive observation/recording cycles per patient per day. Places in which observations have been conducted include the dayroom, the gym, and the occupational therapy room. Each target patient is typically observed two to three times a week for about 6 to 8 weeks, although these parameters will depend on the particular interests of the investigator and the questions being asked. Patients are typically observed in random order, and observers are always blind to diagnostic and medication information.

Purpose

The ORIB was designed to test hypotheses regarding pharmacological interventions in severely disturbed patients through analyses of objectively defined, low inference, publicly observable behaviors (Rosen et al., 1980; Rosen, Tureff, Lyons, & Davis, 1981a; Lyons, Rosen, & Dysken, 1985). It has been used to compare hospitalized patients with normal subjects (Rosen et al., 1981a) across different environmental contexts and to assess the relations of various biochemical markers to specific behaviors (Rosen, Wirtshafter, Pandey, & Davis, 1982).

Development

The ORIB was developed in response to the perceived need for an instrument that could be used to measure changes in specific behaviors consequent to pharmacological intervention with ward patients. Observers first recorded all behavior that patients emitted in narrative form. Three significant dimensions emerged from these initial narratives: social interaction, proximity, and idiosyncratic behavior. A review of the available literature supported the viability of these categories and suggested the use of two additional dimensions: visual activity (scanning versus fixation) and facial expression (laughing/smiling versus crying).

Additional pilot work resulted in the inclusion of the participation dimension and the two motor activity dimensions (body and extremity). A primary concern in the development of the instrument was the issue of reliability, and only those behaviors that had interobserver reliabilities of at least .80 were included. Procedures for establishing reliabilities are described in Rosen et al. (1980).

Clinical Use

The ORIB was designed as a research instrument. However, it has proven sensitive to changes in ward behavior over time, and these changes corresponded significantly with clinical evaluations including those of diagnostic category (Rosen et al., 1980) and clinical improvement following drug interventions with depressed patients (Lyons et al., 1985). The ORIB uses within-subject comparisons and could be given to any inpatient population that exhibits the relevant behaviors. Populations that have been observed with the ORIB include: schizophrenic, affective, schizoaffective, anorectic, gerontological, personality-disordered, and anxiety-disordered persons.

Psychometric Characteristics

Interobserver reliability coefficients are uniformly high for all dimensions ($M = .87$: range from .80 for laughing/smiling to .98 for participation) following 3 weeks of training for the observers. Training consists of familiarization with the ward environments, including the nursing station from which the observations are made in the dayroom, as well as the gym and the occupational therapy room. In addition, each trainee is familiarized with the dimensions of the ORIB and the specific definitions of each behavior category. Trainees are then paired with experienced observers until satisfactory reliabilities are obtained. Subsequently, periodic checks on reliability are conducted to insure against decay over time.

The validity of the ORIB is revealed in its ability to discriminate between patients and normal subjects (Rosen et al., 1982), among patient diagnostic categories (Rosen et al., 1980), between drug classes administered to patients (Rosen et al., 1981a), between patient responders to drug therapy and nonresponders (Lyons et al., 1985), and between levels of various biochemical markers (Rosen et al., 1982).

The raw data of the ORIB (frequency counts) are typically combined into mean scores representing a baseline period and comparable postintervention periods. Investigators can use particular dimensions to test hypotheses about specific behavior. The factor structure of the ORIB also permits tests using combined measures. A rotated factor pattern, derived from the frequency counts of 116 patients over a 6- to 8-week period, revealed the existence of three factors: Factor One had a high positive loading on extremity activity and participation and a high negative loading on body activity. This factor has been termed the Instrumental Activity (IA) factor. Factor Two had high positive loadings on social activity, scanning, and laughing/smiling and has been termed the Social Activity (SA) factor. Factor Three had high positive loading on idiosyncratic behavior and high negative loading on proximity; this has been termed the Inappropriate Activity (InA) factor.

Future Directions

Inquiries on the use of the ORIB have been received from investigators studying depressed versus nondepressed chronic pain patients, inpatient adolescents, childhood depression, and other disorders. It was originally conceived as a device that could be used to provide information on behavior change consequent to drug administration in severely disturbed patient populations. The fact that it can be used by paraprofessionals trained to criterion in a relatively short time renders it applicable in almost any context and for any type of investigation in which questions about specific overt behaviors are involved.

References

Lyons, J., Rosen, A.J., & Dysken, M.W. (1985). Behavioral effects of antidepressant drugs in depressed inpatients. *Journal of Consulting and Clinical Psychology, 53,* 17-24.

Rosen, A.J., Tureff, S.E., Daruna, J.H., Johnson, P.B., Lyons, J.S., & Davis, J.M. (1980). Pharmacotherapy of schizophrenia and affective disorders: Behavioral correlates of diagnostic and demographic variables. *Journal of Abnormal Psychology, 89,* 378-389.

Rosen, A.J., Tureff, S.E., Lyons, J.S., & Davis, J.M. (1981), Pharmacotherapy of schizophrenia and affective disorders: Behavioral assessment of psychiatric medications. *Journal of Behavioral Assessment, 3,* 133-148.

Rosen, A.J., Wirtshafter, D.J., Pandey, G.N., & Davis, J.M. (1982). Platelet monoamine oxidase activity and behavioral response to pharmacotherapy in psychiatric patients. *Psychiatry Research, 6,* 49-59.

Open Middle Inventory

Karen Marchione

Description

The Open Middle Interview (OMI) is used to assess children's ability to generate multiple alternative solutions, which is a major component of effective problem solving. The measure consists of four age-relevant, hypothetical peer problems that are read to the children with accompanying pictures of the described situations with a same sexed protagonist. The OMI is typically used with children 8 to 9 years of age. Individual administration is desirable, although it is feasible to administer the OMI in a small group format. The four problems depicted include: (a) two children who want to take home the class gerbil; (b) a child who is teased because of his/her haircut; (c) a child who wants to ride a bike that another child has been using for a long time; and (d) a child who borrows a friend's toy and loses it. Children are requested to identify the problem in each situation and to generate as many solutions as possible.

Children's answers are divided into response units and scored using four basic categories: (a) *Alternative Solutions,* which consist of goal-directed actions by the protagonist in response to the specific problem; (b) *Solutions' Variants,* which consist of variations of previously offered alternatives; (c) *Chained Responses,* which consist of a sequence of four or more connected events, similar to a form of story telling; and (d) *Irrelevant Responses,* which consist of responses that are non-goal-directed or not initiated by the protagonist. Alternative solutions and variants are then rated on a 5-point scale for effectiveness (5 = high effectiveness). This range determines the way in which positive consequences are maximized and negative consequences minimized. Realistic outcome probability for the appropriate age range is also a factor taken into consideration. Alternatives and variants are then classified according to eight content categories which include: compromise, direct action, bargaining, verbal assertion, help-seeking, verbal aggression, and physical and nonconfrontation responses.

Independent raters are required for scoring. A minimum of three sessions consisting of 15 practice forms is necessary. Scoring decisions are compared with those of a criterion judge who is skilled in the

OMI scoring procedures. Ninety percent agreement for unitization and content and 85% for total categorization are the minimum requirements for the interrater agreement between the rater and the criterion judge during the overall training period. A Pearson r of .90 is the minimum requisite of agreement on the effectiveness rating. It is suggested that 15 to 20% of the forms be independently scored and interrater agreement calculated. If a rater falls below a minimum of 85% agreement for the total categorization of 10 to 20 forms, retraining and rescoring are required.

Development

The OMI was developed as a modification of three tests: The Preschool Interpersonal Problem Solving (PIPS) test, developed by Shure and Spivack (1974); the Interpersonal Problem Solving Measure (IPSM) for third graders; and the Open Middle Test (OMT) for second and fourth graders, which were developed by the Rochester Social Problem Solving research group, respectively.

The administration and scoring procedures are direct modifications of the OMT. The OMI and the OMT differ in the following areas: (a) administration of four (OMI) versus two (OMT) stories (before and after) to eliminate error variance, (b) the OMI allows two prompts for additional responses for each story, whereas the OMT suggests only one prompt and that is limited only to the second story, and (c) specific goal statements within the OMI story content versus relatively vague goal descriptions for the OMT. Scoring differs in regard to broadening the area of subordinate conjunctions and subsuming the category of Repetitions into the category of Variants.

Psychometric Characteristics

To date, there is a paucity of research examining the OMI's psychometric properties. Therefore, the psychometric properties of OMT will be discussed, because there are only relatively minor differences between the two tests. The range of interrater agreement for the OMT has been reported as 84 to 90% for scoring and content areas. Pearson correlations for rating effectiveness scores range from .80 to .89 (Kendall & Hollon, 1981; Weissberg et al., 1981). No construct, convergent, predictive, or external validity studies of the OMI or OMT have been reported.

Clinical Use

The OMI provides a clinical assessment, of unknown reliability or validity, regarding the components of problem solving. It has potential clinical research use with regard to assessing problem-solving skills at various developmental levels and evaluating treatment responses following Interpersonal Problem-Solving Training (Marchione, Michelson & Mannarino, 1985).

Future Directions

Research is needed to establish psychometric properties of the OMI. In addition, the OMI's relationship to moderating variables, such as IQ, sex, and race needs to be empirically investigated.

References

Kendall, P., & Hollon, S. (Eds.) (1981). *Assessment strategies for cognitive-behavioral interventions.* New York: Academic Press.

Marchione, K., Michelson, L., & Mannarino, A.P. (1985). Cognitive-behavioral treatments of high risk antisocial youth: Short and long-term outcome. University of Pittsburgh. Unpublished manuscript.

Shure, M., & Spivack, G. (1974). Preschool Interpersonal Problem-Solving (PIPS) test: Manual. Philadelphia: Department of Mental Health Sciences. Hahnemann Community Mental Health Center.

Weissberg, R., Gesten, E., Rapkin, B., Cowen, E., Davidson, E., Flores de Apodaca, R., & McKim, B. (1981). Evaluation of a social-problem-solving training program for suburban and inner-city third-grade children. *Journal of Consulting and Clinical Psychology, 49,* 251-261.

Pain Assessment Questionnaire

Steven H. Sanders

Description

The Pain Assessment Questionnaire is a 32-item, multiple-choice, written questionnaire (Sanders & Webster, 1982) containing eight questions across each of four different areas relating to behavioral methods applied to patients with chronic pain. These areas consist of: (a) basic behavioral principles, terminology, and facts about pain patients, (b) application of behavioral principles to decrease pain behavior, (c) application of behavioral principles to increase well behavior, and (d) when and with which pain patients these behavioral principles should be used. Most of the questions apply to various clinical situations. For example, one such situation reads: Your patient has had back pain for years and finds the pain distressing. At the same time she enjoys being looked after and having errands done for her. Over the past year she has learned that the way to get these things is to produce pain behavior. This patient says to you, "I've got a dreadful headache and I need some cigarettes. Would you mind getting some for me? Here is the money." Given such a situation, one is then asked to select from one of four possible answers the best response to that particular situation. The eight questions for each of the four knowledge areas are randomly distributed throughout the questionnaire, with the entire questionnaire taking approximately 20 to 30 minutes to complete. Scoring is accomplished by computing the percentage of questions answered correctly in each of the four knowledge areas, as well as the total percentage answered correctly across the four knowledge areas.

Purpose

The purpose of the questionnaire is to systematically assess nurses' knowledge base of behavioral methods with chronic pain patients (Sanders, Webster, & Framer, 1980). Therefore, it is somewhat unique in that it is not intended to assess characteristics of chronic pain patients themselves, but rather the knowledge base and understanding of nursing professionals who work with these patients. The questionnaire is specific to behavioral methods with chronic pain patients. It is intended to assess nurses' knowledge base of basic behavioral terminology and principles, as well as the specific understanding of applying such principles to chronic pain patients. Likewise, questions about when and with which patients to use these principles attempt to offer some measure of a nurse's ability to appropriately discriminate when behavioral methods should be applied under various medical circumstances.

Development

Questions and answers in each area of knowledge were constructed by three PhD level behavioral psychologists with specific training in behavioral treatment of chronic pain. Specific clinical situations and possible answers were taken from direct behavioral observation of nurse-patient interactions on a chronic pain inpatient unit. Starting with a pool of 10 to 15 questions per knowledge area, eight questions per area were selected by the three psychologists.

The four knowledge areas (e.g., behavioral principles to decrease pain behavior) were chosen a priori and consensually validated by the three psychologists. Their inclusion was not based upon an initial statistical evaluation of factorial structure. Thus, the questionnaire was developed on a "conceptual" basis, not a statistical basis.

Psychometric Characteristics

To date, the questionnaire's internal structure and consistency, reliability, and content and construct validity have been examined. Psychometric properties were determined using scores obtained from 66 health professionals: 37 licensed or registered nurses with no prior training in behavioral principles, 10 licensed or registered nurses with training in behavioral principles, and 19 MA or PhD behavioral psychologists working at a medical center setting.

Internal structure and item consistency were determined through a varimax rotated factor analysis on the total percentage of correct scores for the 66 health professionals and a point-biserial correlational item analysis between individual item scores (i.e, correct or incorrect) and total percentage of correct scores, respectively. Factor analysis revealed the two main factors that accounted for 82% of the total variance. Factor 1 (behavioral knowledge) accounted for 46% of the common variance, with significant loadings on items concerning behavioral terminology and principles, increasing well behavior, and decreasing pain behavior areas of knowledge. Factor 2 (differential application) accounted for 36% of the common variance, with significant loadings on items in the area of when and with which patients to use. These data suggest that the questionnaire appears to be measuring two distinct factors: (a) basic knowledge of behavioral methods with pain patients, and (b) ability to differentially apply behavioral methods in various medical situations. Item analysis revealed significant positive correlations to total percentage scores for all items except 1, 4, 14, 19, and 21. This finding suggests that the questionnaire has basic internal consistency.

To establish an estimate of reliability, total percentage of correct scores for the 66 health care professionals was subjected to split-half (odd-even) correlational analysis. This analysis yielded a cor-relational coefficient of $r = 0.79$. This was signifi-cant at the 0.001 level and supports the basic reliability of the instrument.

Content validity was inferred, given that the situations contained in the questionnaire were taken directly from actual clinical encounters with chronic pain patients. Likewise, content validity for the behavioral terminology and principles ques-tions was assumed, given that these questions were also taken from a representative pool.

Construct validity was examined by comparing total percentage of correct scores for the 10 nurses trained in behavioral principles, 19 behavioral psychologists, and 37 untrained nurses. It was reasoned that construct validity would be sup-ported if the questionnaire was able to discriminate between those nurses and psychologists trained in behavioral principles and untrained nurses. Specifically, it was predicted that trained nurses and psychologists would achieve significantly higher scores than untrained nurses, with no differ-ence occurring between the trained nurses and psychologists. A one-way analysis of variance and Newman-Keuls test confirmed the predictions. Thus, the instrument's construct validity was supported.

With the exception of those data from the sample used in establishing current psychometric characteristics, no normative data are available for the questionnaire.

Clinical Use

As noted, the primary use is to offer a more struc-tured evaluation of nurses' knowledge of behavioral methods with chronic pain patients. This includes both licensed practical nurses and registered nurses. The instrument could also be applied to nursing students to assess current know-ledge level and to determine areas of strength and weakness for future curriculum planning. With such information, specific training areas could be targeted to enhance the consistency and quality of nursing care regarding behavioral methods with chronic pain patients.

Although no specific data are currently avail-able, the use of this questionnaire to assess the gen-eral knowledge base of other health care pro-fessionals (e.g., physicians, medical psychologists, nursing assistants, orderlies, and physical thera-pists) who might also be involved in the treatment of chronic pain patients should be considered.

Obviously, such application must await further empirical scrutiny.

Without significant revision or empirical dem-onstration, the questionnaire is not intended for use with acute or chronic pain patients or their fam-ily members. Likewise, it is not intended for use in patients with other chronic disorders (e.g., dia-betes). Finally, the questionnaire is intended to assess knowledge level and should not be used as a direct indication of the actual ward behavior of nurses.

Future Directions

There are a number of needs and future directions to consider. Given the item analysis data, additional work in refining specific items con-tained in the questionnaire is needed. Likewise, factor analysis would suggest the possibility of combining items originally categorized in the knowledge areas of behavioral terminology and principles, increasing well behavior, and decreas-ing pain behavior into one basic category. On the whole, further assessment of psychometric charac-teristics is certainly needed before the final form and structure of the questionnaire is established. Likewise, there is obvious need to obtain norma-tive data across various groups of nurses.

Given the establishment of fully scrutinized psychometric characteristics for the questionnaire, consideration should also be given to determining its utility with other health care professionals (e.g., physicians and physical therapists) who are typi-cally involved in the management of chronic pain patients. Likewise, it is not inconceivable to con-sider development of significant others and patient versions of the questionnaire.

References

Sanders, S.H., & Webster, J.S. (1982). An instrument to measure nurses' knowledge of behavioral methods with chronic pain patients. *Journal of Behavior Therapy and Experimental Psychiatry, 13,* 63-68.

Sanders, S.H., Webster, J.S., & Framer, E. (1980). Analy-sis of nurses' knowledge of behavioral methods applied to chronic and acute pain patients. *Journal of Nursing Education, 19,* 46-50

Pain Behavior Observation

Francis J. Keefe

Description

Pain behavior observation is a procedure to record pain behaviors, such as body posturing, guarded movement, and painful facial expressions in patients having persistent pain. Pain behaviors are those overt behaviors that communicate to others that pain is being experienced. Videotaped (Keefe & Block, 1982) and live observation (Keefe, Wilkins, & Cook, 1984) formats can be used to record pain behavior. In videotaped observation, patients are observed while they carry out a standard set of activities (sitting, standing, walking, and reclining). The live observation format involves recording of pain behavior during medical evaluation procedures such as a physical examination. Systematic pain behavior observations have been carried out in patients with low back pain (Keefe & Block, 1982; Keefe & Hill, 1982; Keefe et al., 1984), myofacial pain (temperomandibular joint pain) (Keefe & Dolan, 1986), and pain secondary to rheumatoid arthritis (McDaniel et al., 1986), and head and neck cancer (Keefe et al., 1985).

Purpose

The purpose of the observation is to assist clinicians who need to carry out a behavioral analysis of chronic pain patients. The observation helps the clinician in three ways: (a) to determine the level of specific motor pain behaviors, (b) to examine the level of pain behaviors occurring during movement, and (c) to compare pain behaviors occurring during movement and static activities. Chronic pain patients who exhibit excessive levels of overt pain behaviors, whose pain behavior is inconsistently related to movement, or who display an equal or greater amount of pain behavior during static than movement activities are likely to have a pain problem maintained by operant conditioning factors. In these patients, pain behavior is more likely to be controlled by its reinforcing consequences (social reinforcement, access to habit-forming pain medications, and avoidance of unwanted responsibilities) than by underlying organic pathology.

Development

The initial step in the development of the observation method was to interview pain patients, their spouse, and the nursing and medical staff working with these patients to determine the overt behaviors displayed by the patients when they experienced increased pain. A list of 20 behaviors was generated and preliminary observations of these behaviors were carried out by nurses on an inpatient pain management unit. Certain

behaviors, such as complaining about pain or crying, occurred at a low rate. However, the nurses noted that other pain behaviors occurred frequently and that these behaviors were very salient in that they were likely to elicit a sympathetic reaction or to interrupt the ongoing activity of other individuals. The behaviors included guarded movement, bracing (pain avoidant static posturing), rubbing or touching of the painful area, grimacing, and sighing. An observation method for recording these motor pain behaviors was initially developed for chronic low back patients (Keefe & Block, 1982). Subsequent studies have extended this method to more patients with acute low back pain (Keefe et al., 1984) as well as myofacial pain dysfunction (Keefe & Dolan, 1986), rheumatoid arthritis (McDaniel et al., 1986), and head and neck cancer (Keefe et al., 1985). Detailed information on methods for carrying out the observations has recently been provided by Keefe, Crisson, and Snipes (1987).

Psychometric Characteristics

A number of reliability and validity studies have been conducted. In an initial report by Keefe and Block (1982), four experiments carried out in patients with low back pain are described. Experiment I demonstrated that five motor pain behaviors (guarding, bracing, rubbing of the painful area, grimacing, and sighing) could be reliably observed and that the frequency correlated highly with patients' ratings of pain. Pain behaviors were much more frequent during movement than nonmovement. Experiment II found that the frequency of these pain behaviors decreased significantly in patients who underwent a behavioral pain management program. Changes in pain behavior correlated highly with changes in pain ratings. Experiment III showed that the level of pain behavior was highly correlated with naive observers' judgments as to how much pain the patient was having. Experiment IV supported the discriminant validity of the observation system in that pain behaviors were significantly more frequent in low back pain than in pain-free normal and depressed control subjects. Similar studies supporting the reliability and validity of the observation system have recently been carried out in a rheumatoid arthritis population (McDaniel et al., 1986). Further support for the validity of the observation system is the finding that in a sample of patients with low back pain presenting for neurosurgical evaluation (Keefe et al., 1984), pain behavior levels were clearly related to physical findings. The greater the evidence of lumbar disk disease at the time of examination, the higher the level of pain behavior observed during the examination.

Clinical Use

The observation method can be used: (a) as an outcome measure to evaluate the effects of behavioral psychological, medical, or surgical interventions; (b) as a method to study individual differences in pain presentation that allow behavioral discriminations even among patients who report having the same pain level; (c) as a procedure to objectively evaluate environmental factors (e.g., presence versus absence of spouse and exposure to stress) and psychological factors (depression, anxiety, and somatization) presumed to affect a patient's pain behavior; (d) as a method to collect pretreatment baseline data to make a more rational decision about the appropriateness of medical or surgical treatment for pain; (e) as a technique for identifying specific tasks such as walking, sitting, or movement of a body part likely to elicit pain behavior in a particular patient; (f) as a method for ongoing evaluation of patients being treated on specialized inpatient pain management programs; and (g) as an approach to evaluating patients' behavior in controlled laboratory studies.

Future Directions

Research is needed to extend the use of pain behavior observation methodologies to a much broader range of pain disorders. Practical methods for recording pain behavior in clinical settings need to be developed to enable physicians to make greater use of this more objective pain assessment. The consistency of pain behavior across settings also deserves study. Comparisons of pain behavior in medical versus more naturalistic settings can be potentially valuable.

References

Keefe, F.J., & Block, A.R. (1982). Development of an observation method for assessing pain behavior in chronic pain patients. *Behavior Therapy, 13*, 363-375.

Keefe, F.J., Brantley, A., Manuel, G., & Crisson, J.E. (1985). Behavioral assessment of head and neck cancer pain. *Pain, 23*, 327-336.

Keefe, F.J., Crisson, J.E., & Snipes, M.T. (1987). Observational methods for assessing pain: A practical guide. In J.A. Blumenthal & D.C.McKee (Eds.), *Applications in behavioral medicine and health psychology.* Sarasota, Florida: Professional Resource Exchange.

Keefe, F.J., & Dolan, E. (1986). Pain behavior and pain coping strategies in low back pain and myofascial pain dysfunction syndrome patients. *Pain, 24*, 49-56.

Keefe, F.J., & Hill, R. (1982). An objective approach to quantifying pain behavior and gait patterns in low back pain patients. *Pain, 21*, 153-161.

Keefe, F.J., Wilkins, R.H., & Cook, W.A. (1984). Direct observation of pain behavior in low back pain patients during physical examination. *Pain, 20*, 59-68.

McDaniel, L.K., Anderson, K.O., Bradley, L.A., Young, L.D., Turner, R.A., Agudelo, C.A., & Keefe, F.J. (1986). Development of an observation method for assessing pain behavior in rheumatoid arthritis patients. *Pain, 24*, 165-184.

Pain Behavior Rating Scales

Mary L. Kelley, and Ronald S. Drabman

Description

The Pain Behavior Rating Scales consist of two instruments, both of which are used to rate children's behavior during painful medical procedures. One scale is completed by adult observers (e.g., mothers and medical personnel); the other is a children's self-report instrument.

The adult instrument consists of three 9-point rating scale items for assessing the degree to which a child was fearful, cooperative, and in pain during the medical procedure. The scale is completed immediately following the treatment session. The scale items are: (a) How much pain did the child really feel? (b) How afraid was the child? and (c) How cooperative was the child? Each item is anchored with written descriptors presented under alternating numerals (1, 3, 5, 7, and 9). Anchors for the pain scale are no pain, little pain, hurting, a lot of pain, and extreme pain. The fear scale is anchored with very calm, a little uneasy, afraid, very afraid, and in a panic. Descriptors for the cooperativeness item are very uncooperative, uncooperative, so-so, cooperative, and very cooperative.

The children's scale is a 5-point pictorial rating scale. The scale represents a combination of the arousal and pleasure scales of the Self-Assessment Mannequins developed by Lang (1980). A figure of a person is presented in each picture. The figures vary along two dimensions: facial expression and size of the spot in the abdominal area. Facial expressions range from a wide smile to a deep frown. The abdominal area ranges from a small dot to a large, sun-like spot (which represents intense arousal or pain). When completing the scale, children are required to choose the picture that best represents the way they felt during treatment. In explaining the scale to the child, the administrator points out the differences in the pictures and requires the child to practice using the scale by choosing pictures that reflect his/her feelings during daily activities.

Purpose

The scales are designed to assess children and adult observers' perceptions of children's behavior during painful medical procedures. The scales are completed immediately following treatment and are intended to measure behavior and feelings exhibited during specific situations and not to assess generalized traits. Furthermore, the rating scales are intended to be used in conjunction with and not as an alternative to observational data collection. Although the scales were developed for evaluating behavior exhibited during treatment of burns, the instruments appear applicable to a variety of situations.

Development

The rating scales primarily were developed for assessing the relationship between perceived and observed pain and to socially validate an observational coding system of children's pain behavior (Kelley, Jarvie, Middlebrook, McNeer, & Drabman, 1984). The three dimensions evaluated in the adult scale (pain, fear, and cooperativeness) were included, as each may provide a unique contribution to evaluation of the treatment effects of pain reduction strategies.

Psychometric Properties

Initial examinations of the relationship between physical therapists and mothers' ratings of pain, fear, and cooperativeness, and observational measures of children's pain have been conducted (Kelley et al., 1984). Observational measures of motoric and verbal pain (e.g., thrashing, crying, having a tantrum, and treatment refusal) were obtained using a time-sampling coding procedure of children's behavior while receiving treatment for burns. The results indicated that physical therapists and mothers' ratings of their children's fear, pain, and cooperativeness correlated highly with

observational data. However, the strongest correlation was noted between ratings of cooperativeness and the observational data ($r = -.63$ for physical therapists and $-.58$ for mothers). Thus, a strong, negative correlation was obtained between the adults' ratings of cooperativeness and the percentage of intervals in which the children exhibited pain behavior. Multiple correlation coefficients for the physical therapists' and mothers' ratings with the observational data were .76 and .74, respectively. The R's represent a substantial increase over the largest Pearson correlation coefficients obtained for mothers' and physical therapists' ratings with the observational data. This indicates that the largest independent contribution of the three scales by both raters were the cooperativeness ratings.

Mother and physical therapists' interrater reliability was calculated by obtaining Pearson product-moment correlation coefficients for each of the three scales. The results indicated that mothers and physical therapists' ratings of pain, fear, and cooperativeness were significantly correlated (p). The children's ratings were not correlated with the observational data or with any of the adults' ratings.

Clinical Use

The scales may be used in assessing children's pain behavior during painful medical procedures. The scales are quickly and easily administered and therefore may be well suited for use in clinical settings. Given that children's ratings did not correlate with adults' ratings or with the observational data, information obtained with the children's scale must be interpreted cautiously. It may be that young children (4 and 6 years of age) cannot fully comprehend the purpose of the scale or rate their perceptions of pain. Alternatively, it may be that children rate covert events that were unrelated to the overt behavior evaluated by observers. Finally, anecdotal data suggest that children may rate their perceptions of pain at the time of assessment, rather than report pain experience during the medical procedure.

Future Directions

Only preliminary data on the reliability and validity of the scales have been obtained. Therefore, additional research is needed to examine the interrater and test-retest reliability as well as the convergent, discriminant, and social validity of the instruments. In particular, the reliability and validity of the children's self-report scale need to be examined with children of varying ages, so that lower age limits for using the scale may be established. In addition, the directions for administering the scale should be evaluated to ensure that children report on pain experienced during and not subsequent to the medical procedure. Finally, the sensitivity of adults' ratings to treatment effects has not been established and therefore should be examined in future research.

References

Kelley, M.L., Jarvie, G.J., Middlebrook, J.L., McNeer, M.F., & Drabman, R.S.A. (1984). Decreasing burned children's pain behavior: Impacting the trauma of hydrotherapy. *Journal of Applied Behavior Analysis, 17,* 147-158.

Lang, P.J. (1980). Behavioral treatment and bio-behavioral assessment: Computer applications. In J.B. Sidowski, J.H. Johnson, & T.A. Williams (Eds.), *Technology in mental health care delivery systems* (pp. 119-132). Norwood, NJ: Ablex Publishing Co.

Pain Cuff

Ernest G. Poser

Description

The Pain Cuff consists of an acrylic pain stimulator used in conjunction with a standard clinical sphygmomanometer calibrated to 300 mm Hg. The pain stimulus is delivered by a series of 94 pointed projections, 7 mm in height. The projections arise from a flat acrylic base roughly 4.5 by 2.75 inches in size. The base, consisting of four sections, is sewn onto the sleeve of a sphygmomanometer, so that it comes to rest against the medial surface of the subjects' upper arm when the cuff is applied. The stimulator is in sections rather than in one piece to allow for greater flexibility when the projections are sharp enough to prevent most subjects from tolerating more than 250 mm Hg of pressure, but not so sharp as to cause skin laceration at 300 mm Hg. The instrument should not be used at higher levels of pressure.

Purpose

The original purpose of the instrument was to provide a more convenient and acceptable alternative to thermal and electrical means of establishing pain threshold and tolerance measures. In that context the test was used by Lambert, Libman, and Poser (1960) to examine differences between ethnic groups before and after their response to pain was experimentally manipulated. Also, Tan and Poser (1982) employed the technique in testing for generalization of treatment effects in a study concerned with the preventive attenuation of acute clinical pain.

Subsequently, the test was also found useful in two other ways, both related to clinical applications. One use was a means of thymometry, i.e., matching a patient's subjective pain experience with that of an objective pain stimulus, to measure the intensity of subjective pain. With that aim, the test was helpful in monitoring the effects of behavioral treatment in a patient with psychogenic pain with that delivered by the Pain Cuff. In this way it was possible to quantify fluctuations in the subjectively perceived clinical pain (Poser, 1977). In yet a third application, the Pain Cuff was used as an aversive stimulus in treating patients with socially maladaptive behaviors. Here again the instrument's ability to deliver measurable amounts of pain made it suitable as a stimulus event in aversion therapy.

Development

The idea of producing pressure pain by means of a hard object inserted into a blood pressure cuff did not originate with the present author. At one time a nutmeg grater was used as a pain stimulator, but because such graters are relatively blunt, many subjects were able to tolerate stimulation at 300 mm Hg, thus causing a ceiling effect.

The present method circumvents that difficulty and is adequate for clinical purposes. However, when doing research, it is important to eliminate errors of measurement arising from fluctuations in speed and the grip pressure different examiners use as they inflate the cuff.

Therefore, the sphygmomanometer pressure bulb was replaced by a compressed air tank with a capacity of 2,000 pounds of pressure. The tank is fitted with a one-stage reduction valve and the airflow is regulated by a pressure-compensated flowmeter calibrated to output levels ranging from 0 to 15 liters/min. In this way a constant air supply is delivered to the cuff through an 11.5-ft latex rubber tube with a 6 mm lumen. We have found 1 liter/min to be the optimal rate of air supply for our purposes. At this setting the cuff is inflated at a rate of 12.5 mm Hg/s. Air input is by way of a metal T junction in the rubber tube. To inflate the cuff the examiner simply occludes the outlet from the T junction with his thumb, thereby forcing air into the cuff. Lifting the thumb instantaneously releases pressure from the cuff.

Psychometric Characteristics

Poser (1962) established pain tolerance levels in various groups of university students, obtaining rank-order retest correlations between 0.75 and 0.85 with a mean time interval of 12 days between test and retest. Immediate test-retest reliability of the present device, as reported by Clark and Bindra (1956), varied between 0.86 and 0.91. The same investigators found significant intercorrelations among mechanical, thermal, and electrical means of producing cutaneous pain, somewhat higher at tolerance than at threshold levels.

Clinical Use

To determine pain threshold levels, subjects are simply asked to report when the perceived pressure sensation first changes to pain. A reading is taken whereupon the cuff is immediately deflated. To obtain a pain tolerance measure the cuff is again inflated until the subject reports the point at which pain becomes intolerable. Wording of the instructions is a crucial variable, particularly in the determination of pain tolerance levels.

Used as a thymometric stimulus, the procedure is slightly different in that the subject is instructed to control the airflow until a point is reached at which the pain caused by the cuff appears subjectively equal to the endogenous pain being measured. In our experience, patients learn to do this in one or two sessions.

As an aversive stimulus it is first necessary to establish the person's pain tolerance level in the usual way. The pressure at that point is then increased by a fixed amount, which will vary with the desired duration of the pain stimulus. By allowing the air to escape from the T valve at the same rate at which it comes into the sleeve, it is possible to hold the pressure constant at any desired level.

Future Directions

The instrument in its present form is serviceable for the purposes described. To enhance its effectiveness as a research tool, further parametric studies are needed, especially with respect to the reliability of repeated measures over prolonged periods of time.

It is also desirable to standardize the instructions and then to elaborate norms for various subsets of the population. Sex and ethnic differences in pain tolerance are already known to exist. Age, health status, and medication are other variables that may well affect the response to pain stimulation with this instrument.

Finally, the method of stimulation could be further improved so that even fewer subjects reach the maximal tolerance level of 300 mm Hg. This must be done without courting the risk of tissue damage.

In summary, the pressure cuff, in combination with the air tank, provides a useful and convenient technique for the delivery of experimental pain in a variety of clinical and investigative endeavors.

References

Clark, J.W., & Bindra, D. (1956). Individual differences in pain thresholds. Canadian Journal of Psychology, 10, 69-70.

Lambert, W.E., Libman, E., & Poser E.G. (1960). The effect of increased salience of a membership group on pain tolerance. Journal of Personality, 28, 350-357.

Poser, E.G. (1962). A simple and reliable apparatus for the measurement of pain. American Journal of Psychology, 75, 304-305.

Poser, E.G. (1977). Behavior therapy in clinical practice: Decision making, procedure and outcome. Springfield, IL: Charles C Thomas.

Tan S.Y., & Poser E.G. (1982). Acute pain in a clinical setting: Effects of cognitive-behavioural skills training. Behaviour Research and Therapy, 20, 535-545.

Pain Observation

J. David Hook and Paul M. Cinciripini

Description

Pain may be conceptualized as having a nociceptive-physiological dimension, a behavioral-motoric dimension, and a subjective-cognitive dimension (Cinciripini, Williamson, & Epstein, 1981). In healthy persons with acute pain, a high degree of correlation is observed among the three dimensions, whereas concordance is lower in persons with chronic pain. Information on the physiological dimension is derived from an assessment of the medical etiology of a patient's pain. Biofeedback also can facilitate assessment and treatment of the psychophysiological mechanisms that may mediate changes in subjective pain. The behavioral motoric dimension of the pain response includes observable nonverbal behaviors, such as limping, which may be used to communicate pain. Behavioral measures of physical performance, such as number of miles walked and pounds lifted, are also part of the behavioral motoric dimension. The subjective cognitive dimension reflects the patient's private experience of pain in verbal descriptors and quantifiable ratings. This includes behaviors such as pain-related verbal statements, pro-health talk, and assertion.

Purpose

Observation of the three dimensions of pain is important in the assessment and treatment of patients with chronic pain. The reliable assessment of the problem behavior before intervention is one of the central tenets of applied behavior analysis. Such observation serves as a baseline against which the effectiveness of treatment can be gauged. Establishing reliable, quantifiable indices of a patient's pain in its various dimensions is a critical, although time-consuming matter. Behavioral pain observation can also make a therapeutic contribution when specific pain behaviors are self-monitored and graphed.

The purpose of pain observation is *not* to establish whether pain is "functional" or "real." Such a distinction ignores a patient's learning history, while giving preeminence to the physiological dimension of a patient's pain. Furthermore, patients with frank factitious disorders seldom seek treatment. Therefore, the primary purpose of pain observation is to establish a stable baseline of pain behaviors with which the effects of treatment can be compared across repeated assessments.

Development

Many pain clinics of various orientations have been established, including surgical, pharmacological, multidisciplinary, and behavioral. However, the absence of outcome data makes comparison of treatment efficacy difficult. Development of behavioral strategies for the assessment of the response directly redressess deficits of pain observation systems that rely solely on global rating scales to measure improvement.

Clinical Use

A comprehensive behavioral pain observation system can be used to assess or treat patients with chronic pain. The observation systems may be

roughly divided into four categories: (a) the initial interview; (b) behavioral or self-monitoring; (c) physical performance measures; and (d) psychophysiological.

Initial interview assessment of a patient should address a number of questions including: What is the physiological contribution to the etiology of this patient's pain? Are litigation or disability hearings pending and thus possibly contributing to maintenance of pain at current levels? Is the patient dependent on prescribed or illicit narcotic-analgesic medication? How does the patient communicate his or her pain to others in both behavioral-motoric or subjective-cognitive modes? What is the role of the family or significant others or both? What recent life stressors might contribute to the pain? Is the patient depressed or are other emotions, such as anger, reinterpreted or expressed as pain? Since the behavioral treatment of chronic pain generally focuses on a decrease in pain behavior or an increase in activity or adaptive functioning, not pain relief per se, the preeminence of the patient's demand for relief from subjective pain is a final important question in the initial assessment. The extent to which the patient is willing to suspend this demand is often an important predictor of success in the behavioral treatment of chronic pain.

Following an initial interview assessment, a comprehensive, repeated series of behavioral or self-monitoring assessments of patients suitable for treatment may be conducted (Cinciripini & Floreen, 1982). For example, patients can be taught to self-monitor their own level of subjective pain on an hourly basis while awake, by rating their pain on an ordinal scale ranging from 0 to 5. Each scale value of the subjective pain ratings may be grounded in behavioral terms by specifying the extent to which motor activities are impaired by the pain. The location where the ratings are made as well as concurrent activities may also be recorded. Patients may also be asked to self-monitor a variety of target behaviors that have been chosen for their relevance to treatment outcome. Most importantly, several of these same target behaviors should be rated by an external observer to provide an unbiased assessment and measure of treatment outcome. Samples of a patient's pain behaviors may be obtained during a structured interview (Cinciripini & Floreen, 1983) or, in the case of inpatients, during daily hospital activities. These behaviors are as follows (See Cinciripini & Floreen for implementation): (l) *Verbal Pain Behavior* consisting of statements related to pain, directly or indirectly, such as

"My back hurts" or "I've got to see the doctor today"; (2) *Nonverbal Pain Behavior* including limping, gesturing, grimacing, posturing, rubbing an affected body part, wincing or other nonverbal expressions of discomfort; (3) *Nonpain Complaints* consisting of the patient's expressions of discomfort on subjects other than pain, including dietary services, hospital administration, or physical problems not related to pain; (4) *Pro-health Talk* including positive statements about one's health or well-being, such as "I really accomplished something today" or "I feel good about my exercise"; (5) *Assertive Behavior* including standing up for one's rights, attempts to compromise in a dispute, praise, or other behaviors expressed in a socially appropriate manner: (6) *Socialization* including social interactions with staff or other patients or overlapping with other categories.

Behavioral observation can also include assessment of physical gains, such as the number of miles on the exercycle, daily pedometer readings, weights lifted, or total hours of uptime. A psychophysiological assessment may be used to determine the extent to which measures of sympathetic arousal or nerve and muscle function directly correlate with changes in a patient's subjective or motoric aspects of pain. Thus, measures of heart rate, blood pressure, muscle function (EMG), skin temperature, or aspects of electroencephalography may be obtained simultaneously with subjective pain ratings, observations of physical activity, or measures of affect, to determine any covariation between the response categories. This type of assessment is also useful to determine the physiological system in which the patient is most reactive (e.g., cardiovascular or muscular). Biofeedback may then be used to reduce reactivity in the system showing the most activity during periods of psychological or physical stress.

Psychometric Characteristics

Observations in the initial interview are most reliably obtained when the interview is performed from a standardized format across patients. Validity of conclusions regarding etiology or treatment is augmented by additional sources of information, especially previous medical records, an interview with the family or significant others, or information from standardized assessment devices such as the MMPI. Reliability across physical findings is likely to be high, whereas concordance between physical

findings or the subjective-cognitive dimension frequently decreases with increasing chronicity.

In a behavioral observation system, the efficacy of self-monitoring is facilitated by an introduction giving both oral and written instructions. Patients may be cued to self-monitor at selected intervals using an external device. Reliability of outside ratings of pain behaviors may be directly assessed by comparing the ratings of two independent raters. Reliability may be enhanced by training each rater, beginning with a thorough review of behavioral definitions of target behaviors, followed by assessment or discussion of ratings made using a videotaped vignette of patient behavior. Interrater argument of 80% or greater should be established between raters for each behavior class.

Future Directions

The current system for pain observation might be expanded to place increasingly formal emphasis on the relationship between the subjective-cognitive and behavioral-motoric aspects of pain.

References

Cinciripini, P., Williamson, D., & Epstein, L.H. (1981). Behavioral treatment of migraine headaches. In J.M. Ferguson & C.B. Taylor (Eds.), *The comprehensive handbook of behavioral medicine, Vol 11.* New York: SP Medical.

Cinciripini, P.M., & Floreen, A. (1982). Evaluation of an inpatient behavioral program for chronic pain. *Journal of Behavioral Medicine, 5,* 375-389.

Cinciripini, P.M., & Floreen, A. (1983). An assessment of chronic pain behavior in a structured interview. *Journal of Psychosomatic Research, 27,* 117-123.

Panic Attack Questionnaire

G. R. Norton

Description

The Panic Attack Questionnaire (PAQ) is divided into seven sections. The first obtains demographic information such as age, sex, and marital status. The second section, using a yes/no format, asks respondents to indicate if they have ever had any of a variety of mental disorders, such as depression or anxiety, or physical disorders, including endocrine disorders, heart problems, and different types of headaches. Research suggests that these disorders may be associated with Panic Disorders.

The third section begins with a detailed description of a panic attack which is derived from DSM-III and is followed by a series of questions asking in a yes/no format (a) if any of the respondent's first order relatives have experienced panic attacks, (b) if the respondent has ever had a panic attack, and (c) for respondents who report having experienced panic attacks, how many panic attacks they had during (1) the past year and (2) the past 3 weeks. The third section ends with a yes/no question which asks if panic attacks have occurred more frequently any time in the past, and a fill-in-the-blank question asking how many years/months the respondent has been experiencing panic attacks.

The fourth section asks the respondent to indicate in which of 33 situations panic attacks have occurred. Most of the situations are associated with agoraphobic, social phobic, and blood/injury phobic situations (Marks & Mathews, 1979), but also include other situations such as unpredictable (i.e., spontaneous), exercise, and sleep.

In the fifth section respondents are asked to rate, on a 5-point scale (0 = does not occur; 4 = very severe), the severity with which 23 symptoms are experienced during panic attacks. Fourteen of the symptoms are derived from DSM-III criteria. The remaining items and many of the situations in the fourth section are based on surveys using earlier versions of the PAQ.

Three multiple-choice questions in the sixth section ask: (a) how rapid is the onset of the panic attack, (b) the percentage of attacks with a rapid onset (i.e., less than 10 minutes), and (c) how long the average panic attack lasts. Rapid onset is included as a criterion for Panic Disorder in a proposed revision of DSM-III.

The last section asks respondents to indicate (a) if they have ever been treated for a panic attack, (b) if they have ever used alcohol or nonprescription drugs to prevent or reduce a panic attack, and (c) if they had been experiencing any of five categories of stressors when they experienced their first panic attack.

The questionnaire takes most subjects 10 to 20 minutes to complete. However, most subjects who have completed the questionnaire thus far have been university students. Persons with less education may need assistance with some questions.

Purpose

The PAQ was designed as a research instrument to assess the frequency with which persons experience panic attacks, the characteristics of the panic attacks, and using other instruments, the differences between subjects who do experience panic attacks and those who do not (e.g., Norton, Harrison, Hauch, & Rhodes, 1985).

Development

The PAQ has gone through three revisions. The first two, in addition to measuring the frequency of panic attacks and the associated symptoms, also asked subjects to answer open-ended questions designed to gather additional information about the phenomenon of panic attacks. The final version of the PAQ (a) accommodated projected changes in the DSM-III, (b) used information from a new structured interview designed to produce differential diagnosis of Anxiety Disorders (Di Nardo, O'Brien, Barlow, Waddell, & Blanchard, 1983) and recent findings related to "The Phenomenon of Panic" (Barlow et al., 1985), and (c) reports of subjects who were interviewed/responded to open-ended questions using earlier versions of the PAQ.

Clinical Use

Recent evidence (e.g., Barlow et al., 1985) has shown that patients with different Anxiety Disorders are similar in many ways, but differ in respect to the frequency of panic attacks, the situations in which the attacks occur, and the number, type, and severity of symptoms experienced during a panic attack. The PAQ could be useful in producing differential diagnoses. It might also be useful in planning and measuring the progress of treatment. Respondents' answers to items measuring situations in which panic attacks occur could assist in the planning of exposure-based therapies. Repeated measures of symptoms/situations in which panic attacks have occurred could provide information on the progress of therapy.

Psychometric Characteristics

The PAQ has been given to four groups of approximately 150 university students. The results consistently show that approximately 35% of the respondents have had one or more panic attacks in the last year and that approximately 22% have had a panic attack in the past 3 weeks. In addition, about 3% of the subjects meet the DSM-III frequency criterion (three panic attacks in a 3-week period) for Panic Disorder. The test groups have also produced a consistent picture of types, number, and severity of symptoms that accompany panic attacks. Comparisons between persons who report panic attacks and those who do not have consistently shown that those with panic attacks score significantly higher on measures of anxiety, depression, and other measures of psychopathology. Finally, those who have panic attacks have many characteristics that are similar to those of patients with Panic Disorder and Agoraphobia (Norton, Cox, Dorward, & Brenner, 1985).

Future Directions

Studies are currently under way to determine: (a) the test-retest reliability of the PAQ, (2) the similarity of diagnoses based on structured interviews and the PAQ, and (3) the usefulness of the PAQ in assessing anxiety/panic associated with other disorders (e.g., alcohol abuse and mitral valve prolapse). However, the PAQ might be most useful as a research instrument in epidemiological studies related to the incidence of anxiety disorders and in helping to clarify the most important characteristics for a diagnosis of Panic Disorder. For example, preliminary research suggests that DSM-III diagnostic criteria for Panic Disorder might need to be expanded to include (a) weightings based on the number of panic attacks, symptoms experienced, and severity of symptoms, (b) a larger and more elaborate description of symptoms related to panic attacks and situations evoking panic attacks, and (c) clarification of panic attacks that are or are not appropriate to the diagnosis of panic disorder (e.g., life-threatening situations, predictable panic attacks, and panic attacks during sleep/relaxation).

References

Barlow, D.H., Vermilyea, J., Blanchard, E.B., Vermilyea, B.B., DiNardo, P.A. & Cerny, J.A. (1985). The phenomenon of panic. *Journal of Abnormal Psychology, 94*, 320-328.

DiNardo, P.A., O'Brien, G.T., Barlow, D.H., Waddel, M.T., & Blanchard, E.B. (1983). Reliability of DSM-III anxiety disorder categories using a new structured interview. *Archives of General Psychiatry, 40*, 1070-1075.

Marks, I.M., & Mathews, A.M. (1979). Brief standard self-rating for phobic patients. *Behaviour Research and Therapy, 17*, 263-267.

Norton, G.R., Cox, B.J., Dorward, J., & Brenner, K. (1985). Factors associated with panic attacks in non-clinical subjects. *[Abstract]. Canadian Psychology, 26*, 391.

Norton, G.R., Harrison, B., Hauch, J., & Rhodes, L. (1985). Characteristics of people with infrequent panic attacks. *Journal of Abnormal Psychology, 94*, 216-221.

Parent-Adolescent Interaction Coding System

Arthur L. Robin

Description

The Parent-Adolescent Interaction Coding System (PAICS) is a content-oriented coding system that classifies all verbal behavior by parents and adolescents during audiotaped interaction tasks into 15 mutually exclusive categories of problem-solving and communication (Robin & Fox, 1979). Verbal behaviors are categorized within 30-second time intervals on the basis of homogeneity of content. There is no artificial constraint on the number of verbal behaviors that could be coded separately within each interval. A "verbal behavior" is defined as a statement by one family member that is both homogeneous in content and bound by the statements of other family members. Scores are obtained for the frequency and/or proportion of behavior within each category and across the positive, negative, and neutral categories.

Positive PAICS categories include agree-assent, appraisal, consequential statements, facilitation, humor, problem solution, and specification of the problem. Negative categories include command, complaint, defensive behavior, interruption, and put-down. Neutral categories include no response, problem description, and talk.

Purpose

The PAICS is designed to provide clinicians and researchers with a detailed account of verbal problem-solving communication behavior in audiotaped parent-adolescent discussions. It samples steps of problem-solving (problem definition, solution listing, solution evaluation, and agreement) as well as positive (I statements, reflections, etc.) and negative (accusations, sarcasm, etc.) communication skills.

Development

The PAICS was derived from the Marital Interaction Coding System (MICS) (Weiss & Summers, 1973), which was originally developed for coding videotaped samples of problem-solving communication behavior displayed by marital dyads. The categories of the original MICS were revised, taking into account the nature of parent-adolescent relations and the limitations of audiotaping. A 23-category version, called the Modified MICS, was evaluated in a criterion-related validity study and then further revised, combining infrequent and/or overlapping categories and eliminating categories that failed to discriminate between distressed and nondistressed dyads.

Psychometric Characteristics

The interobserver reliability of the PAICS has been assessed through percentage agreement on individual categories and discussions and correlational reliability on summary scores. Using the Modified MICS, individual category percentage agreement reliability ranged from 0 to 100%, whereas individual discussion reliability ranged from 58 to 86% ($M = 76\%$) (Robin & Weiss, 1980). Using the PAICS, individual discussion reliability ranged from 51 to 81% ($M = 64\%$), whereas correlational summary score reliability ranged from .73 to .92 ($M = .85$) on positive and negative parent and adolescent problem-solving communication behavior (Robin, 1981).

In the Robin and Weiss (1980) criterion-related validity comparison of 14 distressed and 14 nondistressed mother-adolescent dyads, 12 of the 23 Modified MICS categories discriminated between groups; in nine cases the distressed group scored lower than the nondistressed group (accept responsibility, agree, approval, assent, evaluation, humor, laughter, positive solution, and specification of the problem); in three cases the distressed group scored higher than the nondistressed group (command, complaint, and put-down). These results validated the positive valences assigned the nine categories and the negative valences assigned the three categories. A composite score of these 12 categories (sum of the nine positive minus sum of the three negative categories) explained 70% of the between-group variance.

Evidence for the construct validity of the Modified MICS was obtained in a study that compared MICS summary scores with community members' global ratings (Robin & Canter, 1984). Untrained mothers, fathers, adolescents, and mental health professionals completed 7-point Likert ratings of conflict, problem-solving, and communication for eight distressed and eight nondistressed dyads from the Robin and Weiss (1980) study. Ratings correlated with MICS composite scores .80, .90, and .89 for conflict, problem-solving, and communication, with no significant differences among the four groups of community members.

The treatment sensitivity of the PAICS was demonstrated in an outcome study in which parent and adolescent composite summary scores decreased significantly following problem-solving communication training (Robin, 1981).

Clinical Use

The PAICS and its earlier counterpart, the Modified MICS, are extremely useful for pinpointing the nature of problem-solving and communication skills deficits in families, because the clinician obtains a detailed breakdown of the frequencies or proportions of positive and negative behaviors for parents and adolescents. They are also useful for obtaining a summary score of the overall degree of skill deficits and a sequential analysis of the patterning of communication and problem-solving. Because they have been used with samples of families in which the adolescents have externalizing behavior disorders (conduct problems, attention deficit disorders, etc.), their validity in assessing interactions in which the presenting problems are internalizing behavior disorders (depression, anxiety, and somatic concerns) is unknown.

A major disadvantage of these observation codes is the great amount of time and effort involved in training coders and obtaining adequate reliability. It takes 25 to 30 hours of training to teach coders to use the PAICS reliably, and even after such protracted training, percentage agreement reliability is typically no higher than 70 to 80%. Consequently, the PAICS is not practical for the average clinician, although clinical researchers with adequate resources will find it useful.

Future Directions

There is an immediate need to refine the PAICS and improve reliability as well as to simplify coding procedures and decrease training time. The primary factors impeding achievement of higher reliability with less training time have been poor fidelity of audiotapes, ambiguity in category definitions, and unclear coding procedures. In addition, further validation research is needed to establish more carefully the construct and discriminant validity of the most recent version of the PAICS. Finally, the parameters of the interaction task used to collect the behavior sample to be coded need to be explored in greater depth.

References

Robin, A.L. (1981). A controlled evaluation of problem-solving communication training with parent-adolescent conflict. *Behavior Therapy, 12,* 593-609.

Robin, A.L., & Canter, W. (1984). A comparison of the Marital Interaction Coding System and community ratings for assessing mother-adolescent problem solving. *Behavioral Assessment, 6,* 303-313.

Robin, A.L., & Fox, M. (1979). *The parent-adolescent interaction coding system: Coding manual.* Unpublished manuscript, University of Maryland, Baltimore County.

Robin, A.L., & Weiss, J. (1980). Criterion-related validity of behavioral and self-report measures of problem-solving communication skills in distressed and non-distressed parent-adolescent dyads. *Behavioral Assessment, 2,* 339-352.

Weiss, R.L., & Summers, K.J. (1973). Marital Interaction Coding System III. In E.E. Filsinger (Ed.), *Marriage and family assessment.* Beverly Hills, CA: Sage Publications.

Parent's Consumer Satisfaction Questionnaire

Marc S. Atkins

Description

The Parent's Consumer Satisfaction Questionnaire (PCSQ) is a 47-item self-report questionnaire providing information on parental satisfaction with the components of a parent training program to modify child noncompliance. The questionnaire is administered following the parent's successful completion of the treatment program as well as at subsequent follow-up evaluations. It is divided into five parts describing (a) satisfaction with the overall program (e.g., status of the referral problems, current family functioning, and parent's confidence in managing current and future problems); (b) difficulty and usefulness of the teaching format (i.e., lectures, therapist demonstrations, home practice, other homework, and written materials); (c) difficulty and usefulness of the specific parenting techniques (i.e., attends, rewards, ignores, commands, time-out, and the overall group of techniques); (d) satisfaction with the therapists (e.g., teaching ability, preparation, and interest and concern with the family); and (e) overall opinion (e.g., "What part of the program was most helpful to you?" and "What did you like least about the program?"). All items are scored on a 7-point Likert scale containing verbal anchors (e.g., very satisfied to very dissatisfied), with the exception of the last section, which is open-ended.

Purpose and Development

Consumer satisfaction provides information on the social perception or acceptability of treatment programs. Increased satisfaction with treatment regimens may facilitate the maintenance or generalization of treatment (McMahon & Forehand, 1983). The PCSQ, presented by Forehand and McMahon (1981) and described and evaluated by McMahon, Tiedemann, Forehand, and Griest (1984), was developed to assess parental attitudes towards the parent training program developed by Forehand and McMahon (1981) for child noncompliance. The questionnaire provides a broader definition of parental satisfaction than prior efforts by evaluating satisfaction with the components of treatment rather than assessing satisfaction with treatment outcome and therapist only. Although several items are derived from prior parent satisfaction scales (e.g., Eyberg & Johnson, 1974), many of the items are specific to this parent training program.

Psychometric Characteristics

No reliability or validity data have been published for this instrument at this time. The items appear to have high face validity, but there is no documentation of the development of this questionnaire and it is not known if these items sufficiently sample all issues relevant to consumer satisfaction. Some data suggests that the PCSQ is stable over time. Based on a sample of 20 mothers, half of whom received training in specific parenting techniques only and half of whom received this training along with didactic instruction in social learning principles, McMahon et al. (1984) found some evidence for the temporal stability of the PCSQ. They found no significant differences across groups or from posttreatment to 2-months follow-up on parent ratings of overall satisfaction with the program. Analysis of the temporal stability of individual items regarding satisfaction with teaching format, specific parenting techniques, and therapists indicated that about three fourths of these items were not significantly different from posttreatment to follow-up. Means and standard deviations for these items regarding satisfaction with teaching format, usefulness and difficulty items, on parenting skill usefulness and difficulty items, as well as on global scores for overall satisfaction with the program and satisfaction with the therapists (McMahon et al., 1984). Further empirical evaluations are necessary to assess the stability of PCSQ scores over periods longer than 2 months, the internal reliability of the instrument (e.g., split-half reliability or coefficient alpha), and the comparison of this instrument to alternative measures to assess convergent and discriminant validity. These data are necessary to rule out confounding factors that may contribute to PCSQ scores (e.g., demand characteristics) and to provide normative data for general use. Similarly, the open-ended questions on overall satisfaction with the treatment program have not been evaluated statistically and require empirical validation of their utility.

Clinical Use

Although the PCSQ was developed to assess parental satisfaction with a specific parent training program, parts or all of the questionnaire appear to be generalizable to other parent training programs as well. For example, the sections covering the parent's perception of the overall treatment program, the parent's attitudes towards the therapist, and the open-ended questions of the parent's overall opinion of treatment appear applicable to any parent training program. The sections describing the usefulness and difficulty of the teaching formats and the specific parenting techniques are more specific to the social learning model employed by the authors. However, these sections can be modified easily to delete or add components specific to other training models. The questions are well written, clear, and concise. Administration time is not stated but it appears to be under one-half hour.

Future Directions

If adapted for general use, the PCSQ could provide important information on the feasibility and thoroughness of the training procedures used in current parent training programs. This issue is important, especially considering the current lack of knowledge in the maintenance of treatment gains over time and the uncertain generalization of gains across target problems for parent training programs. However, before the systematic use of this instrument in clinical practice or research, thorough psychometric evaluation is necessary, including the collection of normative data,

reliability estimates (e.g., test-retest, split-half), and comparisons with alternative measures of child behavior and parental perceptions. Pending the availability of this information, the PCSQ presents a prototype consumer satisfaction questionnaire with considerable promise for future applications.

References

Eyberg, S.M., & Johnson, S.M. (1974). Multiple assessment of behavior modification with families: Effects of contingency contracting and order of treated problems. *Journal of Consulting and Clinical Psychology, 42*, 594-606.

Forehand, R., & McMahon, R.J. (1981). *Helping the noncompliant child: A clinician's guide to parent training.* New York: Guilford Press.

McMahon, R.J., & Forehand, R. (1983). Consumer satisfaction in behavioral treatment of children: Types, issues, and recommendations. *Behavior Therapy, 14*, 209-225.

McMahon, R.J., Tiedemann, G.L., Forehand, R., & Griest, D.L. (1984). Parental satisfaction with parent training to modify child noncompliance. *Behavior Therapy, 15*, 295-303.

PFB Partnership Questionnaire

Kurt Hahlweg

Description

The PFB Partnership Questionnaire is a 30-item self-report instrument developed in West Germany to measure marital quality. Of the 30 items, 85% are designed to capture the behavior of the *spouse* (e.g., "He/she criticized me in a sarcastic way"); the other 15% are directed to the behavior of the *couple* (e.g., "We make plans for the future together"). Each item is rated on a 4-point scale (very seldom, seldom, often, and very often) according to the frequency of its occurrence.

The PFB consists of three scales with 10 items each. The scales cover three important areas of marital functioning. The first scale (*Quarreling*) deals with aggressive or quarreling behaviors ("He/she blames me when something goes wrong" and "When we quarrel, he/she keeps taunting me"). The second scale (*Tenderness*) includes verbal and nonverbal behaviors indicating tenderness and intimacy ("He/she caresses me tenderly" and "He/she tells me that he/she loves me"). The third scale (*Togetherness/Communication*) includes items such as "We talk to each other for at least half an hour every day" and "We make plans for the future together."

The PFB scales are internally consistent and discriminate reliably between distressed and nondistressed couples. Means and standard deviations are available for groups of happily and unhappily married couples. Moreover, the PFB has been shown to monitor sensitively marital therapy and to predict therapy outcome. Concurrent validity seems to be established because the three scales correlate with categories of a behavioral observation coding system designed to measure marital and family communication (KPI, Hahlweg et al., 1984b).

The original PFB questionnaire is available in the following cross-culturally checked versions: (a) English, in Hahlweg & Jacobson (1984, p. 22-24), (b) German, in Hahlweg, Schindler, and Revenstorf (1982, p. 233-235), (c) French, and (d) Portuguese (both versions are available on request from the author).

Purpose

The PFB was developed (1) to diagnose and assess spouses who apply for marital therapy, and (2) to evaluate couples in therapy, especially couples in Behavioral Marital Therapy (BMT). The PFB can be used in clinical practice and research.

Development

The PFB was developed in several different studies. In the first study a pilot questionnaire including 178 items was completed by 224 distressed and nondistressed spouses. Factor analysis yielded three scales with a total of 45 items. These scales were successfully cross-validated with a sample of 183 distressed and nondistressed partners. To improve the validity of the scales as a measure of therapeutic change, data from 60 couples treated with BMT were used. Items showing no significant change from pretherapy to posttherapy were eliminated, leaving three scales with 10 items each: (a) Quarreling, (b) Tenderness, and (c) Togetherness/Communication.

Psychometric Characteristics

Norms. Means and standard deviations are available for criterion groups of nondistressed (sample = 370) and distressed couples (sample = 175). Distressed couples asked for marital therapy and described their marriage as unhappy on the "General Happiness Rating" (see Revenstorf, this volume). Nondistressed couples did not apply for marital therapy and described their marriage as happy. Statistical analyses (t test) revealed highly significant differences between both groups on every scale.

Reliability. Each scale has a high internal consistency (average Cronbach's alpha = 0.187) and a moderate 6-month test-retest reliability (average $r = 0.75$).

Intercorrelation of scales. Using a sample of 170 spouses in BMT, the three scales were correlated. The correlations generally were low (mean $r = 0.18$) and in the expected direction, indicating that the scales measure different aspects of marital functioning.

Validity. *Discriminant validity:* The three scales discriminate significantly between groups of distressed and nondistressed couples. This result has been replicated in several other studies conducted in West Germany. *Concurrent validity:* The PFB scales correlate significantly with other self-report measures of marital quality (Hahlweg et al., 1984a). They also correlate with a behavioral observation coding system to monitor marital and family communication (KPI = Kategoriensystem fur partnerschaftliche Interaktion, Hahlweg et al., 1984b). In general, the concurrent validity of the PFT seems to be established. *Validity as a measure of change:* In a recent treatment outcome study (Hahlweg et al., 1984a) the PFB was used among other instruments as a measure of change. Results showed that the PFB scales monitored change very reliably.

Clinical Use

The PFB was developed specifically for use in behavioral marital therapy, although it can also be used in other areas (e.g., research). As just discussed, the PFB seems valid for clinical purposes. As a diagnostic tool in therapy, the PFB can be used to assess change following marital therapy. To evaluate outcome in a single case, critical differences are calculated for each of the PFB scales using the scales' internal consistency and standard deviation. A spouse will have improved significantly (5%) when the posttest score is 5 points lower (quarreling scale) or higher (tenderness and communication scales) than the pretest score (Hahlweg et al., 1982).

Future Directions

The PFB is currently used in different research projects analyzing the association of marital quality and psychopathology or psychosomatic disorders. It is also used in a longitudinal study investigating the stability of marital satisfaction. Further research will concentrate on the concurrent validity of the PFB with other self-report instruments of marital quality and cognitive-attitudinal aspects of marriage.

References

Hahlweg, K., Schindler, L., & Revenstorf, D. (1982). *Partnerschaftsprobleme: Diagnose und Therapie. Handbuch fur Therapeuten.* Heidelberg: Springer.

Hahlweg, K., & Jacobson, N.J. (Eds.), (1984). *Martial interaction: Analysis and modification.* New York: Guilford Press.

Hahlweg, K., Reisner, R., Kohli, G., Vollmer, M., Schindler, L., & Revenstorf, D. (1984b). Development and validity of a new system to analyse interpersonal communication (KPI). In K. Hahlweg & N.S. Jacobsen (Eds.), *Marital interaction: Analysis and modification.* New York: Guilford Press.

Hahlweg, K., Revenstorf, D., & Schindler, L. (1984a). The effects of Behavioral Marital Therapy on couples' communication and problem-solving skills. *Journal of Consulting and Clinical Psychology, 52,* 553-566.

Peer and Self-Rating Scale

Roslyn A. Glow and Peter H. Glow

Description

The Peer and Self-Rating Scale is a 50-item yes/no questionnaire prepared for use by upper elementary school children. The items are listed at the left of the page, and a subset of class members is listed across the page. The rater's task is to put a cross under the name of every child to whom each item applies. After rating the group, the child rater goes back over the questions and marks the items that apply to himself or herself. The child's self-ratings are averaged on two or more occasions of ratings and on 4 to 11 items. Peer ratings are computed by averaging across all available raters in the peer group and all items. The instrument consists of scales entitled R1 Shy-Sensitive, R2 Inconsiderate, R3 Hyperactive, R4 Effective, R5 Popular, and R6 Bully. There are 10 additional items.

Purpose

The school context is important in child behavior. Although traditionally teachers have been used as observers, classroom peers present an alternative source of observation of child behavior. Sociometric choice is an established technique, but the capacity of children to judge other elements of behavior, such as characteristics relevant to attention deficit disorder (ADD), has been little studied. Peer rejection in middle childhood predicts adult psychopathology, suggesting that children are sensitive to at least some important aspects of peer behavior.

Peer ratings have a psychometric advantage over single raters because the use of multiple observers reduces rater bias and thus enhances reliability. Additionally, the comparison of peer ratings with teacher and parent ratings allows observer effects to be disentangled from context effects, potentially answering questions about the context generality of child behavior. Self-rating is an established adult technique that has important ethical advantages in a clinical setting. Although children rarely seek help on their own behalf, inclusion of self-assessment in the clinical assessment procedure can help to focus treatment efforts effectively.

Development

Seventh grade children (approximately 12 years of age) rated classroom peers and themselves on 50 yes/no items (see description) (see Glow & Glow, 1980). Item content was based on the Pupil Evaluation Instrument (Pekarik, Prinz, Liebert, Weintraub, & Neale, 1976) with the addition of items in the areas of activity, restlessness, impulsiveness, attention, and their opposites. Items were written so as to be understood by upper school elementary children, using the form "Who is taller than most?," "Who can't sit still?," and the like. No questions likely to be offensive to children or mentions of antisocial behavior were included. Cluster analysis was used to sort the 50-item profiles into groups (clusters). Fourteen clusters were identified. Scores for each cluster were found by aggregating item scores. Correlations among the 14 variables were then examined, and the 14 reduced to 6.

Psychometric Characteristics

Alpha coefficients varied from .87 to .98. Peer and self-ratings on the same characteristic varied from nonsignificant for R5 Popular to .55 for R6 Bully.

Multimethod Multitrait (MMMT) factor analysis showed good convergent and discriminant validity for R3 Hyperactive, whereas Rl Shy-sensitive and R4 Effective met some of the criteria. There generally was failure of convergence between self- and peer-rated behavior that is clearly positively and negatively valued.

When two available teacher ratings on a teacher rating scale (the ATRS) were averaged and correlated with the peer ratings, they ranged up to $r = .93$ for teacher rating T2 Hyperactive-Inattentive with peer ratings R2 Inconsiderate and R3 Hyperactive. MMMT factor analysis showed meaningful overlap, R6 Bully being closely related to Tl Conduct Problem ($r = .90$), Rl Shy-sensitive being closely related to T4 Socially Rejected and T6 Depressed mood ($r = .73$ and .51), and R5 Popular being closely related to T4 Socially Rejected ($r = .65$).

When the peer ratings were compared with parent ratings on the APRS, the relationships were not as strong, ranging up to $r = .77$ for R6 Bully correlated with P6 Antisocial. Once again, MMMT factor analysis was used to assess convergent and discriminant validity. Clear correspondence between peer and parent scales was not expected, because the scales were defined in different studies and the dimensions were not designed to be strictly aligned. Nevertheless, all MMMT criteria for convergent and discriminant validity for one pair of scales were met, and criteria for five were partially met.

Clinical Use

Children can clearly recognize significant behavior such as shyness-sensitivity and hyperactivity in both themselves and others, although self-ratings of popularity are apparently distorted. The use of self-ratings has clear advantages both tactically and ethically when the child is the focus of the clinician's attention. The use of peer ratings presents ethical problems, but these can be overcome by arranging for child consent to be raters and seeking both child and parent consent to be rated. The identity of individual raters can be obscured, only group results being preserved in the target child's record. There are great psychometric advantages in having multiple raters, and peer opinion may be more important predictively than adult opinion about child behavior, subject as it is to individual bias as a result of adult stress and tolerance.

Future Directions

The Peer and Self-Rating Scales is as yet a promising rather than a well-researched instrument. There is a need for research into its suitability for younger children, for the collection of normative data, as well as for further validity studies.

References

Glow, R.A., & Glow, P.H. (1980). Peer and self-rating: Children's perception of behavior relevant to hyperkinetic impulse disorder. *Journal of Abnormal Child Psychology, 8,* 471-490.

Pekarik, E.G., Prinz, R.J., Liebert, D.E., Weintraub, S., & Neale, J.M. (1976). The Pupil Evaluation Inventory: A sociometric technique for assessing children's social behavior. *Journal of Abnormal Child Psychology, 4,* 83-97.

Penile Volume Responses

Neil McConaghy

Description

Freund (1963) developed a transducer to measure a subject's penile volume responses (PVRs) consisting of a specially constructed glass tube that was placed over the penis and rendered airtight by an arrangement of washers. Pressure changes in the glass tube were recorded by a manometer. A simpler device was subsequently introduced by McConaghy (1967). A nipple was soldered into the closed end of the 6-cm wide and 9-cm long cylindrical aluminium can. The blind end of a fingerstall was cut off and the cut end stretched over the open end of the can to provide an airtight seal when the subject placed his penis within the can. A plastic tube attached to the nipple of the can was connected to a standard Grass pressure transducer, enabling pressure changes in the can to be recorded on a polygraph. With both devices fluctuations in pressure reflected increases and decreases in penile volume. Other workers in Western countries have investigated penile responses by measuring circumference changes mainly with strain gauges.

Purpose

Penile volume responses have been used to measure sexual orientation, paraphilic arousal, aversion, and conditionability.

Development

The major developments have been in the stimuli used and the measurement and interpretation of the PVRs to these stimuli. Freund (1963) measured subjects' PVRs to still pictures of male and female nudes ranging in age from 4 to 30 years, to assess the subjects' *sexual orientation* and pedophilic interest. Pictures were exposed for 13 seconds, with intervals of 19 seconds between exposures or longer if the tracing had not returned to near the original level. The greatest positive or negative deflection from the level at onset of each exposure was used as the measure of response. When a positive and negative response occurred to the same picture, which was reported to occur rarely, the negative value was subtracted from the positive one. Freund appeared to treat negative and positive responses as equally significant. He reported a modification he considered more useful in assessing sexual orientation but not pedophilic interest. Subjects were given testosterone and caffeine before being shown pictures of women aged 19 to 25 or men aged 19 to 30 for 12 seconds, followed by the pictures used in the initial method. Responses were measured by the difference in the height of the tracing at the beginning and end of the exposure.

McConaghy (1967) used the simpler transducer just described to investigate the responses of subjects to a moving travelogue film containing (at minute intervals) 10-second segments of moving pictures, alternately 10 of a nude woman and 10 of a nude man. A 10-second segment of a red circle preceded each film of a woman and a 10-second segment of a green triangle preceded those of a man. Responses were measured by the difference in the height of the tracing at the beginning and end of the exposure. The majority of subjects investigated showed negative as well as positive responses to the films of nudes. A series of scoring rules was advanced to obtain results most consistent with the subject's stated sexual preference. When a subject showed mean positive PVRs to films of women and mean negative PVRs to films of men or vice versa, the positive response indicated his sexual orientation, irrespective of whether the positive or negative response was greater. Positive responses to films of both sexes were indicative of bisexuality, with predominant heterosexuality if the greater positive mean responses were to films of women and predominant homosexuality if the reverse. Mean negative PVRs to films of both men and women were shown by 5 of 19 subjects who reported significant homosexual feelings. This unexpected pattern was also taken to indicate bisexuality, with predominant heterosexuality if the greater negative mean PVRs were to films of women and vice versa. This atypical pattern has not so far been found in subjects reporting predominant heterosexual orientation.

The majority of subjects watching the film used by McConaghy (1967) showed *conditioned* PVRs to the circles and triangles similar in direction to the responses to the following nudes. The mean magnitude of the positive conditioned responses (that is, responses to the red circles in the heterosexual subjects and to the green triangles in the homosexual subjects) correlated very strongly (0.92 and 0.86, respectively,) with the magnitude of the corresponding unconditioned responses (that is, those to the female and male nudes). Hence, the magnitude of the conditioned responses was determined largely by the magnitude of the related unconditioned responses, leaving little variance to be determined by a possible general factor of conditionability. To maximize this variance a work ratio assessment of conditioned responses was used. The work ratio is the proportion of total conditioned and unconditioned response achieved by the conditioned response at the moment of unconditioned response onset. Using the work ratio assessment, support was found for the existence of a general factor of conditionability (Barr & McConaghy, 1971), but no attempts appear to have been made to replicate the finding.

Little attention has been given to determining the significance of *negative* PVRs. They occur in most self-defined heterosexual and some homosexual subjects to films of nudes of the nonpreferred sex. Freund reported that such negative PVRs occur to slides of members of the nonpreferred sex only when the slides were preceded by slides of members of the preferred sex. McConaghy (1977) reported evidence refuting this. Negative PVRs also occur to aversive stimuli such as painful electric shocks to the finger and to slides of victims of road accidents. Positive penile conditioned responses based on positive unconditioned responses, like conditioned responses generally, were significantly smaller in magnitude than the related unconditioned responses. Conditioned responses based on negative unconditioned responses were not.

Psychometric Characteristics

McConaghy reported test-retest reliability of Spearman's rho of .60 and .65 in two studies of sexual orientation of 20 bisexual or predominantly homosexual men. These were derived from their PVRs to two presentations (at 3-week intervals) of the film of nude male and female subjects described earlier. In regard to validity, Freund (1963) reported that all of 65 heterosexual and 48 of 58 homosexual subjects shown pictures of male and female nudes were classified correctly by PVRs. Asked to fantasize so as to produce records that misclassified themselves, only 5 of 44 heterosexual and 6 of 24 homosexual subjects were able to do so. McConaghy (1967) reported that as assessed by PVRs to the film described earlier, all of 11 heterosexual men showed a heterosexual orientation and 17 of 22 men reporting homosexual feelings showed a homosexual orientation. Of the remaining five who did not, three reported they were more attracted to women than men, and two of the three reported that they were having regular heterosexual intercourse. With the same assessment of sexual orientation it was possible to significantly discriminate nuclear transsexuals, fetishistic transsexuals, marginal transvestites, and nuclear transvestites (McConaghy, 1982).

Clinical Use

The correlation between sexual orientation as measured by PVR and as assessed by clinical interview is sufficiently high that its assessment by PVR appears unnecessary. Some workers believe that patients who consciously or unconsciously deny anomalous impulses can be shown to demonstrate these by PVR assessment, and this is helpful in their management. Others believe that these patients can be helped as well without this confrontal technique. No treatment of anomalous impulses has been shown to alter the PVR assessment to a significant extent. It has therefore been argued that treatments act by altering not the sexual component of anomalous behaviors but rather the compulsive element they have developed through behavior completion mechanisms (McConaghy, 1982). If this is so, PVR assessment has no clinical application in measuring response to treatment.

Future Directions

Many issues concerning PVRs require resolution. McConaghy's report that they can be opposite in direction to penile circumference responses measured by strain gauge and when they are, they reflect actual penile tumescence requires replication or rejection. The significance of negative

PVRs needs to be established, particularly those occurring with films of both male and female nudes in sexual orientation assessment. The fact that conditioned responses based on negative unconditioned PVRs are equivalent in amplitude to the unconditioned PVRs seems to require explanation. Conflict exists concerning categorization of transsexualism and transvestism. It could be aided by replication or rejection of the findings that subjects belonging to different categories demonstrate different degrees of homosexual/heterosexual balance on PVR assessment of sexual orientation. Workers who believe that treatments that alter sexual orientation exist should use PVR assessment to validate such alteration.

References

Barr, R.F., & McConaghy, N. (1971). Penile volume responses to appetitive and aversive stimuli in relation to sexual orientation and conditioning performance. *British Journal of Psychiatry, 119*, 377-383.

Freund, K. (1963). A laboratory method of diagnosing predominance of homo- or heteroerotic interest in the male. *Behaviour Research and Therapy, 1*, 85-93.

McConaghy, N. (1967). Penile volume change to moving pictures of male and female nudes in heterosexual and homosexual males. *Behaviour Research and Therapy, 5*, 43-48.

McConaghy, N. (1977). Behavioral treatment in homosexuality. In M. Hersen, R.M. Eisler, & P.M. Miller (Eds.), *Progress in behavior modification, Vol. 5*. New York: Academic Press.

McConaghy, N. (1982). Sexual deviation. In A.S. Bellack, M. Hersen, & A. E. Kazdin (Eds.), *International handbook of behavior modification and therapy*. New York: Plenum Press.

Personal Beliefs Inventory

Ricardo F. Munoz and Peter M. Lewinsohn

Description

The Personal Beliefs Inventory (PBI, Form M-1) is a 30-item paper-and-pencil scale consisting of declaratory statements such as, "What others think of you is most important." The respondent is asked to read each statement and indicate the extent of agreement or disagreement with each item by choosing a number from 1 to 5 (1 = I disagree completely, 5 = I agree completely). The directions also state that there are no right or wrong answers.

Purpose

The PBI was designed to test the hypothesis that psychological difficulties, and more specifically depression, stem from certain types of beliefs. Ellis (1962) calls these beliefs "irrational." We prefer to describe them as maladaptive or dysfunctional. The PBI records the degree of agreement with these types of beliefs.

Development

An earlier form of a PBI was developed by Hartman (1968). However, this instrument includes not only beliefs, but also behavioral- and symptom-related items. In addition, this instrument was not specifically designed to assess depression-related beliefs. In constructing the PBI (Form M-1), Munoz (1977) used 30 items judged by the authors to be relevant to depression and depicting only belief statements. Fifteen items were obtained from the Hartman (1968) scale and 15 from unpublished personal beliefs inventories furnished by Dr. Gerald Kranzier of the University of Oregon.

The instrument was developed for a doctoral dissertation (Munoz, 1977) which was, in turn, part of a larger treatment outcome study of depression (Zeiss, Lewinsohn, & Munoz, 1979). The subjects were 219 residents of Eugene, Oregon, and consisted of three groups: The depressed sample (sample = 75; 24 men and 51 women; mean age 33.9 years) consisted of persons applying for treatment for depression, having Minnesota Multiphasic Personality Inventory (MMPI) D scale T scores greater than 80 or greater than 70 if D is greater than all other clinical scales (clinical scales did not include Lie, Test-Taking Attitude, Masculinity and Femininity, Hypomania, or Social Introversion) and meeting clinical criteria for depression based on a clinical interview. (See Zeiss et al., 1979, for details.) The depressed group can be described as suffering from unipolar, nonpsychotic depression. The "high MMPI" group (sample = 66; 27 men and 39 women; mean age 25.8 years) was designed to approximate a psychiatric control group, that is, neither depressed nor "normal." They responded to an adjustment offering a minimum of $20 for participants in a psychology experiment. No expectation of treatment or anything related to depression was mentioned in the ad. They were chosen if their MMPI D scale T score was less than 70 and if at least one other clinical scale was greater than 70. In addition, the clinical

interview had to show no current or past problems with depression. The third group was a "normal" control group (sample = 78; 38 men and 40 women; mean age 29.7 years) consisting of persons with no measurable clinical problem who responded to the same advertisement as the "high MMPI" group, but had MMPI T scores less than 70 on all clinical scales and less than 60 on the Lie scale. They also had to show no current or past problems with depression in the clinical interview.

Our general strategy for hypothesis testing was geared to the identification of cognitive factors uniquely related to depression, that is, to measures in which the depressed sample differed from both high and normal MMPI groups. (In addition to the PBI, two other cognitive measures were developed: The Subjective Probability Questionnaire and the Cognitive Events Schedule. See Munoz [1977] for details.)

Psychometric Characteristics

Scoring. Scores were obtained by adding the ratings made by the respondent for each of the 30 items. Thus, the range was from 30 to 150. All items depict maladaptive or "irrational" beliefs, so the higher the score, the higher the level of maladaptive thinking. The average score (total score/ number of items answered) is also a useful measure, because it can be used even when there are missing items.

Reliability. One-month test-retest correlations on the total scores were significant at the .001 level (depressed: $r = .74$, sample = 34; high MMPI: $r = .69$, sample = 18; normal MMPI: $r = .60$, sample = 24). Correlations between pretest and follow-up results at 2 months ranged from .34 to .65. After 3 months, correlations ranged from .46 to .68. All test-retest correlations were significant at least at the .05 level (Munoz, 1977).

Validity. A significant difference in the predicted direction was found at initial assessment among the three groups studied. The mean score for the normal group was 2.6, the high MMPI group 2.55, and the depressed group 2.93. A one-way ANOVA with age and sex as covariates shows the difference in means to be significant at the .001 level (Munoz, 1977).

The mean PBI score for the depressed sample in the McKnight, Nelson, Hayes, and Jarrett (1984) study was 3.08 (sample =9).

Most Discriminating Items. The depressed group responded differently from the nondepressed control subjects to 13 of the 30 items at a statistically significant level in the predicted direction. These 13 items now comprise Form M-2 of the PBI.

Clinical Use

The instrument can be used to determine the magnitude of the difference between normative and clinical samples. It can also be used to determine the amount of change in these beliefs before, during, and after an intervention for groups in treatment outcome studies as well as for individual patients.

Zeiss et al. (1979) reported significant improvement in the cognitive measures, including the PBI, in depressed patients taking part in a randomized control treatment outcome study. Interestingly, that study used three distinct intervention strategies, focusing on cognitions, interpersonal skills, or increasing pleasant activities. The three strategies produced similar treatment effects on depression levels, and all three also produced effects across all measures related to the various interventions, and not just to the variables specifically targeted by the interventions.

Because all patients were assigned randomly to the three treatments, the Zeiss et al. study did not answer the question whether assignment to specific treatments based on preassessment scores on the PBI would have produced greater improvement in depression levels. A later study begins to provide this information. McKnight et al. (1984) report using the PBI to examine differential effects of treating individually assessed response classes in the amelioration of depression. They assessed patients meeting Research Diagnostic Criteria for depression to determine whether they had problems with irrational cognitions (as measured by the PBI) or with social skills. They then studied the effect of therapy sessions that focused on one or the other of these problem areas. They report greater improvement in depression levels after the sessions that focused on the appropriate problem area.

Future Directions

We are presently studying minority samples and samples of Spanish-speaking and Chinese-speaking persons. Early findings suggest that although depressed persons within these linguistic-cultural groups again score at higher levels than do nondepressed persons, the absolute scores differ from those of English-speaking samples. For example, Spanish-speaking samples score somewhat higher than English-speaking samples. We believe that these differences might be the result of cultural value differences, that is, more individualistic norms for English-speaking samples and more group-oriented norms for the Spanish-speaking sample. Further work is needed to determine normative levels within demographically different samples.

References

Hartman, B.J. (1968). Sixty revealing questions for 20 minutes. *Rational Living, 3,* 7-8.

McKnight, D.L., Nelson, R.O., Hayes, S.C., & Jarrett, R.B. (1984). Importance of treating individually assessed response classes in the amelioration of depression. *Behavior Therapy, 15,* 315-335.

Munoz, R.F. (1977). *A cognitive approach to the assessment and treatment of depression.* (Doctoral dissertation, University of Oregon, 1977). *Dissertation Abstracts International, 38,* 2873B. (University Microfilms No. 77-26, 505, 154.)

Zeiss, A.M., Lewinsohn, P.M., & Munoz, R.F. (1979). Nonspecific improvement effects in depression using interpersonal skills training, pleasant activity schedules, or cognitive training. *Journal of Consulting and Clinical Psychology, 47,* 427-439.

Personal Questionnaire Rapid Scaling Technique

Stan Lindsay

Description

The first step in the Personal Questionnaire Rapid Scaling Technique (PQRST) (Mulhall, 1978) procedure is to elicit descriptions of symptoms experienced by the client. These symptoms are then transcribed onto a record sheet that is inserted into a test booklet. The booklet presents a standard series of pairs of descriptors from "absolutely none" to "very considerable" or "maximum possible." One pair of descriptors is presented on each page. The client then has to select which of the two descriptors better describes the symptom he or she is experiencing at that moment. For example, for "I am feeling uneasy," the client may have to choose between "moderate" and "considerable" on the first page. The client marks the choice on the record sheet opposite the descriptors. On the next page he or she may have to choose whether "maximum possible" or "little" describes the "feeling uneasy."

Once all questions on pages of the descriptors have been answered, the record sheet is removed and a template is used to produce a total score in the range 0 to 9 (or 0 to 13) for the client's experience of the symptom. In addition, the template provides indications of internal consistency in the client's answers. Ten symptoms can be presented to the client and scored in this way at each testing. As many as 10 symptoms can be presented on each page of the booklet, there being 10 pairs of descriptors on each page. At the outset, the tester has to choose which scale, 0 to 9 or 0 to 13, he wants for the symptom being measured. One part of the booklet presents the descriptors for the 14-point scale; the remainder presents the descriptors for the 10-point version.

Purpose

The technique is designed to provide ratings of symptoms described by clients. Any symptom can be rated by the scaling procedure. This may be, for example, "feeling anxious" or "aching in my joints." Two standard scales, consisting of 10 or 14 points, are available according to the number of descriptors chosen. The clinician has to insert the client's record sheet in the appropriate part of the booklet to select the 10- or 14-point scale. The main advantages that have been claimed for the technique are: (a) It enables a standard rating procedure to be applied to whatever symptoms the clinician seeks to rate, even though a given symptom may be unique to the client under investigation. (b) The client needs to consider only two descriptors at a time, and this is probably less confusing than rating scales in which several descriptors have to be considered all at once. (c) The technique provides a check on consistency among the client's answers. (d) The procedure provides a quick, ready constructed method of using personal scaling techniques (Shapiro, 1961).

Psychometric Characteristics

Estimates of the reliability of the client's responses are given by measures of internal consistency. For example, if a client chooses "considerable" rather than "little" to describe a symptom on one page, it would be predicted that he or she would also choose "very considerable" rather than "very little" on another page if he or she were giving consistent answers. Estimates of internal consistency are possible because the descriptors have been selected to be arranged on an ordinal scale from "absolutely none" to "maximum possible." The manual gives guidelines for assessing different types of inconsistency.

Development

The PQRST was developed from Shapiro's (1961) Personal Scaling technique. Further developments of the technique have been described by Phillips (1966, 1970) and Singh and Bilsbury (1982). These developments, unlike the PQRST, require the clinician to construct materials afresh for each client.

Clinical Use

The PQRST can be used to provide ratings of the intensity of any given symptom that can be described by the client. Attitudes and beliefs can also be scaled with the technique. The principal advantage of the technique probably lies in its ability to provide an estimate of internal consistency for each occasion of its application. This is not readily available with the use of orthodox procedures, such as bipolar visual analogue rating scales or single scales with several ordinal descriptors. (See, for example, Marks and Mathews, 1979.)

References

Marks, I.E., Mathews, A. (1979). Brief standard self-rating for phobic patients. *Behaviour Research and Therapy*, *17*, 263-267.

Mulhall, D. (1978). *Manual for Personal Questionnaire Rapid Scaling Technique*. Windsor, England: NFER-Nelson Publishing Co.

Phillips, J.P.N. (1966). On a certain type of partial higher-ordered metric scaling. *British Journal of Mathematical and Statistical Psychology*, *19*, 77-86.

Phillips, J.P.N. (1970). A further type of personal questionnaire technique. *British Journal of Social and Clinical Psychology*, *9*, 338-346.

Shapiro, M.B. (1961). A method of measuring psychological changes specific to the individual patient. *British Journal of Medical Psychology*, *34*, 151-155.

Singh, A.C., & Bilsbury, C.D. (1982). Scaling subjective variables by SPC (Sequential Pair Comparisons). *Behavioural Psychotherapy*, *10*, 128-145.

Personal Report of Confidence as a Performer

Michael G. Craske, Kenneth D. Craig, and Margaret J. Kendrick

Description

The Personal Report of Confidence as a Performer (PRCP) scale is a 30-item self-report questionnaire answered in "true" or "false" format. The items sample different manifestations of anxiety during solo piano performances, including somatic components (e.g., "I perspire and tremble just before performing"), cognitive aspects (e.g., "I am terrified at the thought of performing before a group of people"), and behavioral features (e.g., "I always avoid playing solos in public if possible"). Fifteen items are worked to reflect positive states and 15 are worded negatively. The questionnaire requires approximately 3 to 5 minutes to complete and is administered in reference to the respondent's most recent solo performance.

Purpose

The scale's purpose is a self-report assessment of subjective and behavioral states of anxiety before and during public performances on the piano. It is described as having been designed as "an introspective measure of experienced anxiety" (Appel, 1974, p. 13) and serves as a screening device for identifying clients with high levels of musical performance anxiety for research and clinical purposes (Craske & Craig, 1984; Kendrick, Craig, Lawson, & Davidson, 1982).

Development

The scale was derived by Appel (1974) from Paul's (1966) Personal Report of Confidence as a Speaker scale. The latter is a shortened version of a questionnaire developed by Gilkinson in 1942 (Appel, 1974). Although it was developed explicitly for piano performances, the wording can be varied to apply to other forms of musical performance.

Psychometric Characteristics

Appel (1974) reported a Spearman-Brown reliability coefficient of .94. She reported an average score of 15.53 in a group of 30 anxious pianists (positively worded items are reversed when scored), with individual scores ranging from 6 to 25.

Craske and Craig's (1984) group of 20 anxious pianists reported an almost identical mean score of 15.50 (SD = 4.40), with a range of 11 to 27. In contrast, the 20 nonanxious pianists in their study reported a mean score of 6.50 (SD = 2.99), with a range of 1 to 10. Kendrick et al. (1982), who used only the 15 negatively worded items as a brief screening instrument, obtained a mean score of 9.42 (SD = 2.99) in 53 anxious pianists. A Pearson product moment correlation of .71 was obtained between the PRCP scale and the General Trait Anxiousness scale (adapted for solo piano performance), attesting to the concurrent validity of the scale (Craske & Craig, 1984). Construct validity has also been demonstrated. Appel (1974) found that scores on the PRCP reduced significantly after systematic desensitization. This change was accompanied by reductions in pulse rate and performance errors. Kendrick, Craig, Lawson, and Davidson (1982) selected pianists who scored at least 5 on the negative PRCP items. Their sample reported higher scores on the state scale of the Spielberger State-Trait Anxiety Inventory than those of general medical and surgical patients. They also had high heart rates and frequent errors during performance. Craske and Craig (1984) used a median-split of PRCP scores to identify relatively anxious versus relatively nonanxious pianists. The relatively anxious group made more performance errors and reported higher levels of state anxiety, lower levels of self-efficacy, and more negative self-statements than did the relatively nonanxious group. These differences were enhanced when extreme scorers on the PRCP were compared. In summary, the available evidence indicates the PRCP scale possesses some characteristics of reliability and validity.

Clinical Use

The scale provides a means of assessing levels of performance anxiety during solo piano performance, a serious problem for many performing artists at all levels of musical accomplishment. Craske (1982) noted that some pianists identified by PRCP scores as relatively nonanxious reported high levels of distress during actual performance, suggesting that the incidence of false-negative results needs to be established and that the PRCP needs to be supplemented by other measures of anxiety.

Future Directions

Further research is needed in the psychometric properties of the scale, its relationship to multifactorial models of anxiety, and its extension to other performance settings and musical instruments.

References

Appel, S. (1974). Modifying Solo Performance Anxiety in Adult Pianists. *Dissertation Abstracts International, 35,* 353A.

Craske, M.G. (1982). *The three-systems model and self-efficacy theory: Piano performance anxiety.* Unpublished master's thesis, University of British Columbia, Vancouver.

Craske, M.G., & Craig, K.D. (1984). Musical performance anxiety: The three-systems model and self-efficacy theory. *Behaviour Research and Therapy 22,* 267-280.

Kendrick, M.J., Craig, K.D., Lawson, D.M., & Davidson, P.O. (1982). Cognitive and behavioral therapy for musical performance anxiety. *Journal of Consulting and Clinical Psychology, 50,* 333-362.

Paul, G.L. (1966). *Insight vs desensitization in psychotherapy: An experiment in anxiety reduction.* Stanford, CA: Stanford University Press.

Personal Report of Confidence as a Speaker

Thomas W. Lombardo

Description

The Personal Report of Confidence as a Speaker (PRCS) is a 30-item true-false self-report inventory designed to measure public speaking anxiety in reference to a particular speech. The score is the sum of the number of items marked in the high anxiety direction. Both fear and confidence are represented in item content but are not scored separately.

Purpose

The PRCS was developed by Gilkinson (1942) and later modified by Paul (1966) to measure anxiety during public speaking. Although designed as a research tool, the PRCS is suitable for evaluating clinical speech anxiety.

Development

The original PRCS (Gilkinson, 1942) contained 104 true-false items selected to represent two cognitive/emotional domains, fear and confidence in public speaking, and three temporal domains, anticipatory, concurrent, and postspeech cognitions and emotions. Gilkinson tested 420 male and female speech class students. The students responded to items on the basis of a class speech given within the previous 48 hours. Chi-square tests indicated that most items discriminated among sample quartiles derived from total scores on the scale.

The form of the PRCS in common use today contains 30 items that were selected for their high chi-square values by Paul (1966) from Gilkinson's (1942) original list. Most of the current PRCS items reflect cognitions and emotions during speaking. Eight reflect anticipatory anxiety, and three reflect cognitions after speaking. Discriminability of confidence and fear items was never empirically evaluated. About half the current PRCS items appear to represent fear, although it could be argued that the confidence items also measure fear.

Psychometric Characteristics

Gilkinson's (1942) version of the PRCS had very good internal consistency: odd/even reliability was .93. Test-retest reliability after 4 months was somewhat weaker ($r = .60$, sample = 117), but it was probably deflated by variability in exposure and training effects from speech class participation. Retest scores were significantly lower than initial test scores. Discriminant validity and intra- and cross-modality concurrent validity were good for the original instrument. The PRCS scores predicted teacher ratings on speech quality ($r = .39$) and motor anxiety (e.g., lack of eye contact, facial expression, and "nervousness") and predicted self-ratings of public speaking confidence ($r = .72$) and fear ($r = .69$). Scores were not correlated with high school rank or scholastic aptitude test results.

The current 30-item version of the PRCS also has demonstrated good concurrent and predictive validity. Paul (1966) found PRCS scores significantly decreased following a speech anxiety treatment identified as effective by several other anxiety measures. Also, the PRCS significantly correlated with the S-R Inventory of anxiousness speech item ($r = .62$, sample = 67) and with therapist ($r = .43$, sample = 45) and subject ($r = .46$, sample = 45) ratings of improvement following treatment.

There are no published normative data on the PRCS. However, in a study of 38 public speaking class volunteers (Lombardo & Bellack, 1978), the mean PRCS score was 12 with a standard deviation of 6. Paul's (1966) cutoff score of 16 or higher has been adopted as the standard for speech anxiety studies with high anxiety subjects. Interestingly, the selection of this particular criterion was arbitrary. In our small sample, 13 of 38 subjects or 33% scored 16 or above.

Clinical Use

Although it was developed as a research device, the PRCS is suitable for use with clinically speech anxious populations. As with similar devices, the PRCS could be used clinically in two ways. Total scores on the PRCS could be used to objectively evaluate improvement following treatment. Alternatively, the PRCS could be used to increase the efficiency of assessment. The PRCS could substitute for asking the patient a series of questions. Patterns of anxiety (e.g., anticipatory versus concurrent anxiety) could be ascertained, and positive responses to individual items could be pursued in subsequent interviewing. Because Gilkinson's (1942) 104-item version samples a wider domain of behaviors, it may be more suitable for this latter application.

Future Directions

Paul's version of the PRCS is widely used as a research tool largely because of its demonstrated validity. However, test-retest reliability is unknown. Because its validity is established, it must be reliable. However, it would be useful to know the degree of its reliability. Factor analytic research would be useful for determining whether the PRCS assesses more than one dimension of speech anxiety, as Gilkinson originally intended. Such information would be of interest to both researchers and clinicians.

References

Gilkinson, H. (1942). Social fears as reported by students in college speech classes. *Speech Monographs, 9*, 141-160.

Lombardo, T.W., & Bellack, A.S. (1978, November). *The external validity of laboratory analogue assessments for speech anxiety.* Paper presented at the meeting of the Association for Advancement of Behavior Therapy. Chicago, IL.

Paul, G.L. (1966). *Insight versus desensitization in psychotherapy.* Stanford, CA: Stanford University Press.

Pittsburgh Initial Neuropsychological Testing System

Gerald Goldstein

Description

The Pittsburgh Initial Neuropsychological Testing System (PINTS) is a series of cognitive and neuropsychological tests that are administered in part or in their entirety. Those component tests for which norms are available have their scores converted to T scores with a mean of 50 and a standard deviation of 10. A computer program has been written that displays and profiles these scores. The tests in the series are, for the most part, derived from the Halstead-Reitan battery, the Wechsler Memory Scale, the Wechsler Adult Intelligence Scale, and the Boston Diagnostic Aphasia Examination. Form L of the Peabody Picture Vocabulary Test and the Smith Symbol Digit Modalities Test, which are not part of a standard battery, are administered in their entirety. The component tests are organized into the following categories: (a) general level of performance, (b) memory functions, (c) language functions, (d) motor functions, and (e) spatial constructional functions. The computer printout generated from the test scores provides the user with a readily interpretable profile of commonly employed components of a neuropsychological assessment.

Purpose

The primary purpose of PINTS is to provide a screening instrument covering the major components of a full neuropsychological assessment, but in an abbreviated form. It is intended for use in psychiatric facilities primarily for screening out patients with structural brain damage. It has also been used in research in which brief neuropsychological assessment is required.

Development

The PINTS was developed by neuropsychologists at the University of Pittsburgh in response to the need for a screening procedure covering the major components of a neuropsychological assessment that could be administered in less than an hour and a half. Computerized scoring and profiling were also felt to be desirable. The first step was determination of the areas to be assessed, such as memory or language, following which the specific tests and test components were selected. Tests were abbreviated when necessary to keep the procedure within the hour-and-a-half time limit. Thus, for example, only alternate items from WAIS Block Design are administered. After test selection and modification, normative information was gathered and the computer program was written. Finally, the procedure was validated at a psychiatric facility and cross-validated at a different facility. The results of the validation study were reported by Goldstein, Tarter, Shelly, and Hegedus (1983).

Psychometric Characteristics

Because the procedure as a whole consists of a number of published tests, norms contained in the manuals or similar publications for those tests were used to convert individual test scores to T scores. Only tests with demonstrated validity and reliability were selected for PINTS, but the developers of the procedure had to determine whether the battery as a whole discriminated between brain-damaged and non-brain-damaged patients in a psychiatric facility. A discriminant analysis using a combination of measures derived from the procedure yielded a hit rate of 84.5%. However, cross-validation in another psychiatric facility was not successful mainly because the general level of performance in that facility was different from that at the hospital in which the original validation was done. However, when all cases were combined, with the validation and cross-validation based upon random samples drawn from this combined pool, the cross-validation was satisfactory. The user of PINTS is therefore cautioned to acquire local normative data rather than to accept published cutoff scores for the presence or absence of brain damage. However, the classification coefficients appear to be reasonably stable. Therefore, cutoff scores are likely to be reliable across different samples from the same patient population.

Clinical Use

Considering the limitations just described, PINTS should be applied clinically only after local norms have been established in order to avoid creation of excessive numbers of false-positive false-negative results. However, once that is accomplished, the procedure provides a rapid screening assessment

that yields a readily interpretable neuropsychological profile. In addition to what is yielded by the single instrument screening for brain-damaged procedures, PINTS provides information on specific abilities such as memory or language skills. It therefore should provide the clinician with cues regarding further, more detailed assessment. For example, a pattern of impaired performance on the language tests with relatively intact function elsewhere should alert the clinician to the need for a more detailed aphasia evaluation or a consultation with a speech/language pathologist. Clinicians with a background in neuropsychology should be able to use PINTS in writing brief neuropsychological testing reports.

Future Directions

It would be desirable to develop a neuropsychological screening procedure that is not as dependent as PINTS on local norms. Such development requires further psychometric research aimed at seeking measures that are relatively resistant to population differences. Considering the current state of computer technology, it may be possible to totally computerize procedures such as PINTS, so that tests are administered, scored, and profiled by automated devices. There has been some preliminary exploration of computer-assisted interpretation of neuropsychological tests, and that area will no doubt be vigorously explored in the future in view of the great need for screening devices in psychiatric and other clinical facilities.

References

Goldstein, G., Tarter, R.E., Shelly, C., & Hegedus, A. (1983). The Pittsburgh Initial Neuropsychological Testing System (PINTS): A neuropsychological screening battery for psychiatric patients. *Journal of Behavioral Assessment, 5,* 227- 238.

Pleasant Events Schedule

Peter M. Lewinsohn and Carolyn Alexander

Description

The Pleasant Events Schedule (PES) is a 320-item self-report inventory of the frequency and subjective enjoyability of pleasant activities and events. The instructions call for the subject to rate each item twice, first on a 3-point scale of frequency of occurrence during the last month and then on a 3-point scale of subjective enjoyability. In addition to mean frequency and enjoyability scores, a cross-product score based on the product of the frequency and enjoyability ratings for each item is also computed. The latter is assumed to reflect the obtained pleasure. Several rational, factorial, and empirical scales have been developed. Some of these are based on the relative number of social and nonsocial activities (SSN); the first principal component (G); masculine versus feminine role-related activities (MF); extroverted and stimulus-seeking activities versus introverted and solitude- and quiet-seeking activities; and on items focused on outdoorsmanship and crafts (RB); and sexual activity (C3). There is also a scale based on activities shown to be related to mood fluctuations (mood-related).

Purpose

The PES was developed by MacPhillamy and Lewinsohn in 1974 to assess the rate of occurrence and the degree of enjoyment in pleasant activities. It was intended to be a simple and effective assessment device for measuring positive reinforcers. Ideally, such an instrument not only should possess good reliability and validity in the usual psychometric sense but should also meet the needs of both therapists and researchers. The items in such an instrument should not be restricted solely to those activities and events with obvious stereotyped pleasurable associations, and it should assess the reinforcement value of events that are currently reinforcing as well as events that will be potentially rewarding. Such a schedule should be useful in naturalistic settings, and be capable of identifying events that are effective in maintaining behavior. Most suitably, it would also be useful in identifying classes of functionally related events and in demonstrating that the items on the scale are functionally effective and do not simply reflect the respondent's verbal preferences. The PES was intended to accomplish the aforementioned goals.

Development

The construction of the schedule was described elsewhere (MacPhillamy & Lewinsohn, 1982). The initial item pool for the PES was obtained by asking college students to list events or experiences they found to be pleasant and rewarding. After 66 lists had been obtained, they were found to be highly redundant. The resulting items were categorized into content classes to assure that no class of items was disproportionately represented in the item pool. The items were randomly arranged, and frequency and enjoyability ratings were obtained from a normative sample of 641 university and junior college students. Items found to have virtually no variance were eliminated as were items that were poorly worded. New items were generated by obtaining lists of pleasurable events from a wide variety of persons with diverse educational and social backgrounds ranging in age from 35 to 76 years. After obtaining 70 such lists, 34 new items had been generated and were incorporated into the PES. This relatively empirical item selection procedure and the diverse sample of persons chosen to write items assured that the PES was suitable for a wide variety of individuals and situations.

Psychometric Characteristics

Reliability was assessed by the test-retest method. Three separate samples of subjects of diverse ages and social classes were readministered the PES after periods of 1, 2, and 3 months. Subjects were not asked to recall events of the first month, but they were instructed to take the schedule again, applying it to the events of the current month. Correlation between scores from the first and second administrations are thus attenuated, not only by test unreliability but also by true changes in subjects' activities. Because the correlation coefficients were generally similar across frequency, enjoyability, and cross-product scores, average correlations were reported.

Because behavioral self-report inventories are intended to provide approximations of the types of information gathered by trained observers, observational data were also collected. Thus, it was possible to examine the concurrent validity of the PES by comparing the self-ratings with those of trained observers. The obtained agreement was found to be substantial in all cases. The predictive validity of the PES was tested by having subjects monitor their daily activities for 1 month after taking the PES. The observed correlations were .57 and .62 in two data sets. These correlations are both significant beyond the .001 level and are reasonable figures for a state variable. Current PES activity ratings are therefore good predictors of subsequent activity level as measured by individual daily self-monitoring. Predictive validity using the PES enjoyability ratings to predict subsequent choice behavior was also tested. In a study asking subjects to make choices between paired comparisons and stimuli opportunities to engage in certain pleasant events, the PES enjoyability ratings were found to possess predictive validity with subsequent choice behavior. This finding suggests that the enjoyability ratings of the items on the PES provide useful information about the reward value of their corresponding events.

To test the construct validity of the scores on various scales of the PES, several research studies were conducted. The findings generally support the construct validity of the scales. For example, the mood-related scale was found to discriminate significantly between depressed persons and both normal and psychiatric control groups (Lewinsohn & Amenson, 1978). The G scale also discriminated between subgroups of depressed individuals with different levels of clinical improvement (Lewinsohn, Youngren, & Grosscup, 1979).

For purposes of comparison, means and standard deviations for a sample of 464 normal adult white subjects in the Pacific Northwest are available. However, because the PES items could reasonably be expected to be sensitive to cultural, geographical, and climactic differences and such variations with age have been documented (MacPhillamy & Lewinsohn, 1982), investigators are urged to develop local norms for the populations with which they work.

Clinical Use

The PES has been in clinical use for several years and sufficient data have been accumulated to permit description of its properties in usage. The PES has been used in a variety of clinical and research studies including those on the treatment of depression, the treatment of drug addiction, the relationship of pleasant activities to mood, the rate of engagement in pleasurable activities as a function of age, and the association of attractiveness and success expectancy with obtained pleasure. A study of the PES with older persons demonstrated a significant reduction in activity level with age, but the reported enjoyability of the events remained constant at least until age 70 (MacPhillamy & Lewinsohn, 1974).

The PES has also proven useful in generating individualized activity schedules for monitoring daily reinforcing events in behavior therapy. It is also in clinical use together with the Unpleasant Events Schedule, which assesses aversive events.

Future Directions

In a recent study with depressed adolescents (Clarke, Lewinsohn, & Alexander, 1985), the PES was modified for use with children and adolescents. Other potential uses of the PES might involve patients with medical illnesses that limit their activities, e.g., arthritis.

References

Clarke, G.N., Lewinsohn, P.M., & Alexander, C. (1985). *A psychoeducational approach to the treatment of depressed adolescents.* Paper presented at Western Psychological Association, San Jose, CA, Spring 1985.

Lewinsohn, P.M., & Amenson, C. (1978). Some relations between pleasant and unpleasant mood-related events and depression. *Journal of Abnormal Psychology, 87,* 644-654.

Lewinsohn, P.M., Youngren, M.A., & Grosscup, S.J. (1979). Reinforcement and depression. In R.A. Depue (Ed.), *The psychobiology of depressive disorder: Implications for the effects of stress* (pp. 291-316). NY: Academic Press.

MacPhillamy, D.J., & Lewinsohn, P.M. (1974). Depression as a function of desired and obtained pleasure. *Journal of Abnormal Psychology, 83,* 651-657.

MacPhillamy, D.J., & Lewinsohn, P.M. (1982). The Unpleasant Events Schedule: Studies of reliability, validity and scale intercorrelations. *Journal of Consulting and Clinical Psychology, 50,* 363-380.

Plethysmography

Kimbra L. O'Krinsky and Paul M. Cinciripini

Description

Plethysmography refers to the measurement of volume of an organ or limb. Volume increases as the area fills with blood and decreases as blood is drained. Changes in blood volume occur with each heart beat, as the blood surges through a particular capillary bed. In transmittance photoplethysmography, a light source is placed over a peripheral vascular bed, e.g., the finger, and a light-sensitive electronic device is placed opposite the light source. The amount of light transmitted through the tissue, in this case the finger, is detected by the photocell and varies systematically with the amount of blood in the digit. The transmitters technique is possible only in body parts that are relatively thin, like the earlobe or finger. Reflectance photoplethysmography is an alternative technique in which the light source and photocell are positioned adjacent to each other. The amount of light reflected back through the tissue is proportional to the changes in blood flow. Photoplethysmography is based on the fact that living tissue is transparent to red and infrared radiation (7,000 to 9,000 angstroms), whereas whole red blood is relatively opaque to light of the same wavelength. The interposition of living tissue between the light source and the photocell modulates the electrical output of the photocell as a function of the concentration of blood in the area.

Purpose

Photoplethysmography measures the blood volume and the blood volume pulse within a selected capillary bed. Properly transduced, the photoplethysmograph yields a distinct sinusoidal waveform, reflecting discrete elements within each cardiac cycle. Therefore, the photoplethysmograph can be used to measure both heart rate (blood volume pulse) and overall changes in the amount of blood (blood volume) passing through the bed. Physiologically, the shape of response is controlled by changes in vasomotor activity (smooth muscle in the arterioles). Vasomotor activity refers to the relative amount of vasoconstriction or vasodilation in the vessel at any given moment. The level of vasomotor activity is mediated by the activity of the sympathetic nervous system, mostly through changes in alpha-adrenergic stimulation.

Volumetric measures have also been described using strain gauge plethysmography. In this method, a mercury-filled or resistant strain gauge is placed around the area in which volumetric measures are to be determined. Changes in electrical resistance are reflected by expansion and contraction of the strain gauge, corresponding to changes in volume (blood) in the area of measurement.

Development

Photoelectrical plethysmography originated with the work of Hertzman in this country and Bonsman in Germany. The precision and sensitivity of the technique have been improved by recent advances in the development of new photosensitive materials and with electronics (See Martin & Venables, 1980.)

Psychometric Characteristics

Several factors may affect the reliability and validity of plethysmographic recordings. In general, the requirements for artifact-free and sensitive recordings include: (a) Proper placement of the transducer and restriction of movement. In fingertip recordings, the pickup should be mounted so as to maintain the arm in a position at approximately heart level or slightly below for the seated or reclining subject. In finger, earlobe, or vaginal transduction, any variability of motion will cause artifacts in the recorded values. (b) The observed tissue must be shielded from the heat generated by the light source. Thus, a "cold" light source, such as a neon tube, or electroluminescent elements are recommended because the recordings are more stable over time and the transducers are easier to mount and position. (c) There must be a constant source of direct current to maintain the light source and ambient light must be shielded out. Vasomotor activity will be indistinguishable from fluctuations in ambient light intensity unless the housing of the transducer itself or some other covering, e.g., a black cloth, is used to block outside light. (d) The transducer must also be positioned in such a way as to prevent application of excessive amounts of pressure on the tissue. Too much pressure will cause changes in vasomotor activity independent of the variables of interest. (e) Proper interpretation of plethysmographic data must rely on evaluation of within session changes (relative) as opposed to across-session changes (absolute). Blood volume measures may be digitized using analogue to digital converters, but the resulting numbers should be used to assess changes between a resting baseline and the imposition of some treatment strategy. Because it is almost impossible to standardize placement, absolute changes observed across recording sessions cannot be validly compared. (f) Factors that affect vasomotor activity will affect the height and slope of the blood volume pulse wave, and therefore these factors should be controlled, e.g., room temperature, administration of vasoconstricting or vasodilating drugs, and the like.

Clinical Use

The clinical and research applications of photoplethysmography include the measurement of heart rate, pulse transit time, and peripheral blood flow and volume. The finger photoplethysmograph is a convenient measure of heart rate. The blood volume pulse spikes with each ventricular contraction and can be counted using any voltage detection device. Rate measures can easily be obtained by counting the number of spikes per unit of time. A complete discussion of the clinical uses of heart rate assessment and heart rate biofeedback are beyond the scope of this paper, and the reader is referred to other more complete sources (e.g., Obrist, 1981; Martin & Venables, 1980). Suffice it to say that heart rate is a sensitive index of autonomic arousal, and applications of finger plethysmography have included heart rate biofeedback during stressful cognitive imagery and the assessment of cardiovascular reactivity to mental and physical stressors.

Plethysmographic recording of blood volume pulse waves at two distinct peripheral sites, such as the earlobe and finger, may also be used to measure pulse transit time. Pulse transit time (PTT) refers to the time it takes the arterial pulse wave to propagate down the length of the artery between the two measurement sites. Pulse transit time may also be assessed by determining the time (in milliseconds) between the R wave of the electrocardiogram and the arrival of the peripheral blood volume pulse wave at a distal site, e.g., the finger. Pulse transit time is strongly correlated with systolic blood pressure and less so with distolic pressure (Obrist, 1981). In the absence of peripheral vascular disease, PTT is affected by factors that influence beta-adrenergic stimulation of the cardiovascular system, and as such it is sensitive to changes in the sympathetic driving of the heart. Activities such as exercise and psychological stress produce clear changes in PTT, mostly by increasing the sympathetic tone in cardiac and vascular tissue. Pulse transit time feedback has been used with limited success in biofeedback applications in the treatment of hypertension (Agras & Jacob, 1979).

Strain gauge plethysmography has been applied to the measurement of male sexual arousal. (See Geer, in Martin & Venables, 1980.) In measuring male sexual arousal, a strain gauge is placed around the penis. Changes in electrical resistance are produced by changes in penile circumference corresponding to erection and changes in subjective sexual arousal. The subject may be asked to rate his subjective feelings of arousal to film or slide presentations of erotic stimuli, while simultaneous recordings of penile tumescence are obtained. These findings can then be used by the patient and therapist to explore therapeutic issues with specific attention to possible discrepancies between measures of subjective and objective arousal. Strain gauge assessments have been used to discriminate heterosexuals and homosexuals during exposure to erotic stimuli. This technique has also been useful in assessing sexual arousal to pedophilic stimuli and differential arousal to both violent and nonviolent sexual stimuli. Clinical assessment of physiological responses may be especially important when working with individuals who display sexually deviant behavior, because objective measures of sexual arousal may provide a precise description of the type and nature of the sexual stimuli associated with the deviant behavior (Leiblum, 1982).

Vaginal photoplethysmography has also been used to asess female sexual arousal. A tampon-like acrylic tube of a photocell and light source is used to measure blood volume and pressure pulse changes in the vagina, i.e., vaginal vasocongestion. Many investigators have failed to find a correlation between measures of vaginal blood volume (or temperature) and changes in female subjective sexual arousal, although at least one study did report a significant positive correlation between the two measures (Leiblum, 1982). Other investigators have also found lower levels of vaginal blood volume and pressure pulse in women reporting sexual disinterest (Leiblum, 1982).

Ongoing assessment of arousal may be useful in research and clinical practice when trying to teach women to recognize their own sexual arousal or as outcome measures of the effectiveness of sex therapy. When working with persons exhibiting sexual deviance, objective assessment of sexual arousal would also appear critical.

Future Directions

Future directions in the application of plethysmography may be in two areas: the assessment of cardiovascular reactivity and treatment of deviant sexual arousal or sexual dysfunction. Recent developments applying plethysmographic techniques to measures of forearm blood flow may yield knowledge about the role of sympathetic arousal and psychological stress in the development of hypertension. In addition, physiological assessment of sexual arousal may be used to carefully guide and measure the outcome of behaviorally based programs designed to change deviant patterns of sexual arousal or sexual dysfunction.

References

Agras, S., & Jacob, R. (1979). Hypertension. In O.F. Pomerleau & J.P. Brady (Eds.), *Behavioral medicine: Theory and practice* (pp. 205-232). Baltimore, MD: Williams & Wilkins.

Leiblum, S.R. (1982). Assessment of sexual dysfunction. In J.F. Keefe & J.A. Blumenthal (Eds.), *Assessment strategies in behavioral medicine* (pp. 373-389). New York: Grune & Stratton.

Martin, I., & Venables, P.H. (Eds.) (1980). *Techniques in psychophysiology*. New York: John Wiley & Sons.

Obrist, P.A. (1981). *Cardiovascular psychophysiology: A perspective*. New York: Plenum Press.

Probability Ratings and Liking Category Ratings

Charlene Muehlenhard

Description

Probability ratings and *liking category ratings* are ratings of how interested someone appears to be in dating another person. For example, suppose we want to assess how interested a woman is in dating a man. We would videotape her interactions with him. Raters would then watch and rate the videotapes. For *probability ratings*, raters would answer the question, "If he were to ask her for a date, what is the probability that she would say Yes?." Probability ratings can range from 0 to 100%. High probability ratings indicate that the woman seems interested in dating the man; low probability ratings indicate that she seems uninterested. For *liking category ratings*, raters would answer the question, "Which of the following best describes how she probably feels about him?." They would be given three choices: (a) "She likes him and wants to date him" (positive); (b) "She is being as friendly to him as she would be to anyone; she has not thought one way or the other about dating him" (neutral); or (c) "She dislikes him and does not want to date him" (negative).

Purpose

These ratings were used for several different purposes. One was to identify cues a woman can use to convey her interest in dating a man (Muehlenhard, Koralewski, Andrews, & Burdick, 1986). For example, to assess whether a woman's complimenting a man serves as a cue that she is interested in dating him, two scripts for male-female conversations were written. These two scripts were identical except that in one, the woman complimented the man, and in the other, she did not. We then videotaped a man and woman as they acted out these two scripts. These videotapes were shown to male raters, who made probability ratings indicating how likely the woman would be to accept a date with the man. Their probability ratings were significantly

higher when the woman complimented the man than when she did not. Therefore, it was concluded that giving compliments is a dating cue, because it communicates interest in dating. Cues identified in this manner can be useful for social skills training with female clients who have difficulty conveying their interest in dating men. Note that *men's* probability ratings were used because the purpose of this study was to identify women's behaviors that *men* would interpret as cues.

Probability and liking category ratings have also been used to assess men's cue-reading ability (Muehlenhard, Miller, & Burdick, 1983). We videotaped male-female conversations in which the woman had been instructed to convey either a positive attitude (i.e., that she wanted to date the man) or a neutral attitude (i.e., that she was being friendly but had not thought about dating him). Male subjects then watched these videotapes and made probability and liking category ratings. We used these ratings to evaluate the following: (a) We assessed how well each man could identify which attitudes the women were trying to convey, by calculating the percentage of videotapes on which the man's liking category rating matched what the woman intended to convey. (b) We assessed how well the man's interpretations of the women's behavior corresponded with other men's inter-pretations, by calculating the percentage of tapes on which the man's probability ratings were within 1 standard deviation of the mean. (c) We assessed how positively or negatively the man interpreted the cues, by looking at how high his probability ratings were compared with other men's probability ratings and at the percentage of positive and negative liking category ratings compared with other men's category ratings.

Probability ratings are currently being used to assess women's cue-sending skills (Muehlenhard, Bourg, & Imhof, 1985). We videotaped each woman as she role-played a conversation with a male confederate while imagining that he was someone she was interested in dating. We are now rating these videotapes, using probability ratings to assess how well each woman conveyed her interest in dating a man. We are also rating the appropriateness and attractiveness of each woman's behavior to be sure she is not sending cues that are inappropriate or unattractive.

Development

The development of these measures was straightforward. They are face-valid measures of how interested one person appears to be in dating another person.

Psychometric Characteristics

The means and standard deviations of these ratings vary depending on the behavior and appearance of the persons being rated. Usually a positive liking category rating is associated with a probability rating of 50% or greater, whereas a negative liking category rating is associated with a probability rating of 50% or less. Internal inconsistencies suggest that the rater has misunderstood the instructions or is being careless or uncooperative.

Clinical Use

These measures can be used when a clinician suspects that a client has difficulty sending or reading dating cues. Most clients will not come in complaining of problems with sending or reading cues. Instead, they might seem lonely or depressed caused by social isolation. If they date infrequently, they might have problems with cue sending or cue reading. For example, research on women's dating initiation has shown that unless a woman either asks or hints, she is unlikely to get a date with a man (Muehlenhard & Miller, in press). Hinting obviously involves sending cues of interest. Asking someone out also involves sending cues, because asking someone out without a prior exchange of positive cues between the two persons can seem abrupt and inappropriate. Reading the other person's cues is also an important dating skill because it provides information that can save the client from repeatedly being turned down for dates or from hoping in vain to be asked out by someone who is totally uninterested. Therefore, difficulty with either cue sending or cue reading can lead to problems with dating, which might lead to frustration, loneliness, depression, and other related problems.

To measure cue-sending skills, the clinician could have the client interact with a confederate under instructions to imagine that the confederate was someone the client did versus did not want to date. (It might be most convenient for the clinician to serve as the confederate.) The client's live or videotaped performance could then be rated. Good cue-sending skill would be indicated if the client's performance under the want-to-date instructions received high probability ratings and positive liking category ratings, and if the client's performance under the uninterested-in-dating instructions received lower probability ratings and neutral liking category ratings. Negative liking category ratings suggest a problem because the client usually should not have to behave as if she or he dislikes the other person to convey lack of interest in a date. Clinicians should use these probability and liking category ratings in conjunction with ratings of appropriateness and attractiveness to ascertain that the client is not sending inappropriate or unattractive cues.

To assess a client's cue-reading skills, a clinician could have the client rate tapes of conversations in which one person conveys various levels of interest in dating the other person. The clinician could then assess how well the client can judge the model's intentions and how well the client's judgments coincide with others' judgments.

Future Directions

A standardized videotape for clients to watch and rate, with norms available as to what attitudes about dating the models intended to convey and how most persons interpret the models' behavior, would be useful to help therapists to assess the cue-reading skill of individual clients.

Probability and liking category ratings have already been used to assess the cue-reading skills of high- versus low-frequency daters (Muehlenhard et al., 1983). They could also be used to assess the cue-reading skills of other populations, such as rapists versus nonrapists or women versus men.

References

Muehlenhard, C.L., Bourg, W.J., & Imhof, B. (1985). (Validation of a questionnaire assessing women's ability to initiate interactions with men). Unpublished raw data.

Muehlenhard, C.L., Koralewski, M.A., Andrews, S.L., & Burdick, C.A. (1986). *Verbal and nonverbal cues that convey interest in dating: Two studies. Behavior Therapy, 17,* 404-419. publication.

Muehlenhard, C.L., & Miller, E.N. (in press). *Traditional and nontraditional men's responses to women's dating initiation. Behavior Modification.*

Muehlenhard, C.L., Miller, C.L., & Burdick, C.A. (1983). Are high-frequency daters better cue readers? Men's interpretations of women's cues as a function of dating frequency and SHI scores. *Behavior Therapy, 14,* 626-636.

Problem Identification Checklist

Thomas Kratochwill

Description

Behavioral consultation is an indirect service delivery model in which a consultant-psychologist works with a consultee (e.g., parent or teacher) to assist a client (usually a child) with academic or behavioral problems in applied settings (Bergan, 1977; Bergan & Kratochwill, in press). The behavioral consultation process involves a four-stage model of service delivery in which the consultant moves from identification of the problem to analysis of the problem, and final implementation and evaluation of the treatment plan. During the problem identification phase a problem identification interview is conducted with the consultee. Two *Problem Identification Checklists* have been developed to specify criteria for effective problem identification interviews for both developmental and problem-centered consultation (Tables 1 and 2).

1. Problem-Identification Checklist for Problem-Centered Consultation.
2. Problem-Identification Checklist for Developmental Consultation.

Problem-centered consultation typically focuses on single or a more isolated problem during the consultation process. In contrast, developmental consultation may focus on several or multiple problems of the client that may or may not be inter-related in terms of the target treatment focus. Developmental consultation generally involves much longer contact with the consultee.

Developmental and Psychometric Characteristics

The Problem Identification Checklist allows consultants to score their interviews in terms of required verbal units necessary to conduct consultation interviews. For example, in the problem identification, problem-centered consultation interview, the consultant would be required to emit verbal units related to behavior specifications or individual characteristic specifications elicitors that introduce the discussion, behavior setting specifications elicitors that relate to establishing consequent conditions, and observation summarization emitters that relate to facilitating recall of recording procedures during the interview process (Checklist 1). Once the consultant has completed the interview, the checklist can be scored according to criteria on the frequency of use in each of these categories.

The Problem Identification Checklist has been used in several research investigations in which its reliability and validity have been examined. For example, Bergan and Tombari (1975) examined the reliability of assigning verbalizations to specific units of observation in terms of content, process,

and control during the consultation process. When two raters coded randomly selected verbalizations from consultation interview, 96% agreement on assigned units of observation were obtained (e.g., behavior, behavior setting, observation, specification, and summarization). In addition, interrater reliability for the problem identification interview is reported to be high ($r = .92$).

In the area of content validity, the Problem Identification Checklist allows analysis of verbalizations that occur during the consultation process. Thus, the Problem Identification Checklist provides the categories in which the content of the interview is examined.

Criterion-related validity was also examined in a study by Bergan and Tombari (1976), wherein behavioral consultants provided services to teachers and their child clients. Through multiple regression analyses the authors found the single best predictor of implementing a treatment plan was problem identification ($r = .776$). The authors reported that the consultants' interviewing behaviors had the greatest impact on problem-solving during the problem identification phase. Other research on the psychometric aspects of the consultation process is reviewed by Gresham (1984).

Future Directions

Relative to other areas of behavioral interviewing there is a growing research base on the use of behavioral consultation interviews. A top priority in future research is an examination of the reliability and validity of the interview process. Especially important are validity studies that show that the behaviors analyzed during the interview process relate highly to those described in the natural environment (Gresham, 1984). Finally, the use of consultations formats, particularly those that are standardized for use in applied settings, should facilitate well-controlled behavior interviews in practice (Kratochwill & Van Someren, 1985).

References

Bergan, J.R. (1977). *Behavioral consultation*. Columbus, OH: Charles E. Merrill.

Bergan, J.R., & Kratochwill, T.R. (in press). *Behavioral consultation in applied settings*. New York: Plenum.

Bergan, J.R., & Tombari, M.L. (1975). The analysis of verbal interactions occurring during consultation. *Journal of School Psychology, 13*, 209-226.

Bergan, J.R., & Tombari, M.L. (1976). Consultant skill and efficiency and the implementation and outcomes of consultation. *Journal of School Psychology, 14*, 3-13.

Gresham, F.M. (1984). Behavioral interviews in school psychology: Issues in psychometric adequacy and research. *School Psychology Review, 13*, 17-25.

Kratochwill, T.R., & Van Someren, K.R. (1985). Barriers to treatment implementation in behavioral consultation. *Journal of School Psychology, 23*, 225-239.

Problem List

Kurt Hahlweg

Description

The Problem List (PL) was developed to be used in Behavioral Marital Therapy, especially in the behavior analysis phase. It consist of 17 possible problem areas of marriage (e.g., finances, household management, leisure time, sexuality, tenderness, and social activities).

Each problem area is rated by each partner using the following categories: 0 = no problems; 1 = problems, but we can usually solve them; 2 = problems we cannot find solutions for, and we often quarrel; 3 = problems we cannot find solutions for, and we don't discuss them any more.

During the behavior analysis phase the PB is used as a guideline to structure the interview with the partners. During the problem solution phase of therapy, the list is used to construct a hierarchy of conflict areas for each couple.

For therapy evaluation, categories 2 and 3 are summed by yielding one "Conflict Score" for each person.

English and German versions of the PL are available: English: (Hahlweg, Schindler, Revenstorf, & Brengelmann, 1984). German: (Hahlweg, Schindler, & Revenstorf, 1982).

Purpose

As described, the PL can be used in Behavioral Marital Therapy (a) as a diagnostic tool to structure the behavior analysis, (b) as a therapeutic tool to structure problem-solving discussions, and (c) as a measure of change. Furthermore, the PL can be used in research.

Development

The list was put together using couples' interviews and other assessment devices, including the Marital Happiness Scale (Azrin, Naster, & Jones, 1973), the Marital Precounseling Inventory (Stuart &

Stuart, 1973), and Potential Problem Areas (Patterson, 1976).

Psychometric Characteristics

To test reliability, 50 spouses rated the PL twice over a 6-month interval. The test-retest reliability of the conflict score was $r = 0.66$.

The PL was validated in an experiment with a group of 90 clients in marital therapy and a matched control group of 100 nondistressed partners (Hahlweg et al., 1982). For each area we computed how often the distressed or nondistressed respondents checked category 2 or 3. Within each group the areas were then rank ordered according to the relative frequency of the score.

As expected, distressed and nondistressed groups differed significantly in the total number of conflict areas. Distressed clients on an average checked 7.1 areas as conflict-producing, whereas nondistressed partners checked roughly 1 area. In each of the 17 areas the difference between both groups was highly significant. Obviously, there is a quantitative difference between the two samples, but not a marked qualitative one. Between the two samples a very similar rank ordering of problem areas was found (Spearman's $r = .73, p = .001$). For both distressed and nondistressed partners the most conflict-producing areas were sexuality, affection, leisure time, temperament, and personal habits of the partner. In general, the emotional-interpersonal problems rank at the top, whereas the instrumental problems (household, job, and finances) are of minor importance in both groups.

Clinical Use

The PL can be used in Behavioral Marital Therapy in the following way. During the *behavior analysis phase*, the problem areas rated as 1, 2, or 3 can be used as a guideline to structure the interview with the partners. During the *problem solution phase* of therapy, the list can be used to construct a hierarchy of conflict areas for each couple. Beginning with a problem lowest in the hierarchy, couples can attempt to solve the problem using the acquired problem-solving skills.

For *therapy evaluation*, categories 2 and 3 are summed up yielding one "Conflict Score" for each person. Using the retest reliability coefficient and the standard deviation, a critical difference can be computed. A patient has improved significantly (5%) whenever the difference score is >4 (pre-

and, posttreatment). In the same way a significant deterioration can be assessed.

Future Directions

The clinical use of the PL in family therapy is currently being investigated.

References

Azrin, N.H., Naster, B.J., & Jones, R. (1973). Reciprocity counseling: A rapid learning-based procedure for marital counseling. *Behaviour Research and Therapy, 11,* 365-382.

Hahlweg, K., Schindler, L., Revenstorf, D., & Brengelmann, J.C. (1984). The Munich marital therapy study. In K. Hahlweg & M.S. Jacobson (Eds.), *Marital interaction: Analysis and modification.* New York: Guilford Press.

Hahlweg, K., Schindler, L., & Revenstorf, D. (1982). *Partnerschaftsprobleme: Diagnose und therapie. Handbuch fur therapeuten.* Heidelberg: Springer.

Patterson, G.R. (1976). Some procedures for assessing changes in marital interaction patterns. *Oregon Research Institute Bulletin No. 16.*

Stuart, R.B., & Stuart, F. (1973). *Marital Pre-Counseling Inventory.* Champaign, IL: Research Press.

Procrastination Assessment Scale - Students

Laura J. Solomon and Esther D. Rothblum

Description

Solomon and Rothblum (1984) developed the Procrastination Assessment Scale - Students (PASS) to measure the frequency of cognitive-behavioral antecedents of academic procrastination. The PASS contains two parts. The first part assesses the prevalence of procrastination in six academic areas: (a) writing a term paper, (b) studying for an exam, (c) keeping up with weekly reading assignments, (d) performing administrative tasks, (e) attending meetings, and (f) performing academic tasks in general. Subjects indicate on a 5-point Likert scale the extent to which they procrastinate on each task (1 = never procrastinate; 5 = always procrastinate) and the extent to which procrastination on each task is a problem for them (1 = not at all a problem; 5 = always a problem). Because definitions of procrastination include both behavioral delay and psychological distress, the extent of self-reported procrastination and the extent to which it presents a problem are summed for each academic task (score

ranging from 2 to 10) as well as across the six academic areas (total score ranging from 12 to 60).

The second part of the PASS describes a procrastination scenario (delay in writing a term paper) and then suggests many possible reasons for procrastination in the task, including: (a) evaluation anxiety, (b) perfectionism, (c) difficulty making decisions, (d) dependency and help seeking, (e) aversiveness of the task and low frustration tolerance, (f) lack of self-confidence, (g) laziness, (h) lack of assertion, (i) fear of success, (j) tendency to feel overwhelmed and poorly manage time, (k) rebellion against control, (l) risk-taking, and (m) peer influence. For each of these reasons, two statements are given, and students rate each statement on a 5-point Likert scale according to how much it reflects why they procrastinated the last time they delayed writing a paper. For example, the two perfectionism statements are "You were concerned you wouldn't meet your own expectations" and "You set very high standards for yourself and you worried that you wouldn't be able to meet those standards."

Purpose

Before development of the PASS, assessment of academic procrastination had focused largely on the measurement of study habits; however, procrastination seems to involve more than inadequate time management and study skills. Clinical observations of procrastinators (Burke & Yuen, 1983) suggested other possible reasons for the delay behavior. Yet, there had been no empirical examination of the reasons for procrastination. Additionally, few researchers used behavioral measures in their assessment, and no studies compared the self-report of procrastination with behavioral measures.

Development of the PASS had three purposes: (a) to assess the prevalence of academic procrastination among college students; (b) to examine the reasons for academic procrastination; and (c) to develop a self-report measure of procrastination that could be compared with behavioral indices of procrastination and standardized self-report measures of potentially related constructs (e.g., anxiety, study habits, depression, self-esteem, irrational cognitions, and assertion).

Development

In a pilot study that investigated the relative frequency of procrastination in academic, domestic, and social areas, college students reported that procrastination was most common and presented more of a problem in the academic arena. The six academic areas included on the PASS consist of most of the school tasks students are engaged in and in which procrastination is possible.

The list of antecedents of procrastination was generated in a pilot study in which undergraduate students and clinical psychology faculty were asked to indicate why they procrastinate on academic tasks. An open-ended format was used. Responses were categorized, and two statements were generated reflecting each antecedent. The list of antecedents thus derived was given to a third pilot sample of undergraduates, who were asked to match each statement (e.g., "You had difficulty requesting information from other people") with its correct reason (e.g., "lack of assertion"). Only statements that were identifiable to the majority of subjects were included in the PASS, resulting in 26 statements (two statements reflecting 13 possible antecedents of procrastination).

Psychometric Characteristics

Normative Data.
Normative data on the PASS were obtained from a sample of 323 university students who were enrolled in two sections of Introductory Psychology. The sample included 101 male and 222 female students. Of the subjects 85% were freshmen, 13% sophomores, and the remaining 2% juniors or seniors. Ninety percent of the subjects were 18 to 21 years old.

Frequency of self-reported procrastination data indicated that 46% of the subjects nearly always or always procrastinate on writing a term paper, 27.6% procrastinate on studying for exams, and 30.1% procrastinate on reading weekly assignments. To a smaller degree subjects procrastinate on administrative tasks (10.6%), attendance tasks (23.0%), and school activities in general (10.2%).

Regarding the extent to which subjects felt procrastination created a problem for them, 23.7% reported that it was always or nearly always a problem when writing a term paper, 21.2% said it was a problem when studying for exams, and 23.7% said it was problem when doing weekly readings. Procrastination created less of a problem for the remaining tasks and for school activities in general.

There were no significant gender differences in any area of academic procrastination or total self-reported procrastination.

Factor Structure of Reasons for Procrastination.
Factor analysis of subjects' reasons for procrastination revealed two main factors. The first factor, accunting for 49.5% of the variance, reflects fear of failure. It is composed of items related to anxiety about meeting others' expectations (evaluation anxiety), concern about meeting one's own standards (perfectionism), and lack of self-confidence. The second factor accounts for 18% of the variance and reflects aversiveness of the task and laziness. It includes items indicative of lack of energy and task unpleasantness. No other factors had eigenvalues after the varimax rotation that were greater than 1.50. Therefore, factor analysis suggests that fear of failure and aversiveness of the task are the two independent reasons for academic procrastination.

Analyses of variance of gender differences on the two primary reasons for procrastination revealed a significant difference for the Fear of Failure factor, $F(1,273) = 7.0, p < .001$. Female subjects were significantly more likely to endorse items within this factor than were male subjects. There was no significant gender difference on endorsement of Aversiveness of the Task items.

Comparison of the PASS with Other Self-Report Measures.
The self-report scales that correlated most significantly with the total procrastination score on the PASS were the Beck Depression Inventory ($r = .44, p < .0005$), the Ellis Scale of Irrational Cognitions ($r = .30, p < .0005$), the Rosenberg Self-Esteem Scale ($r = .23, p < .0005$), and the Delay Avoidance Scale of the Survey of Study Habits and Attitudes ($r = .24, p < .0005$). The latter scale measures punctuality and organized study habits. Total procrastination score was significantly correlated with the Spielberger Trait Anxiety Inventory ($r = .13, p < .05$), but the correlation was very small, and there was no significant correlation between procrastination and the College Self-Expression Scale of Assertion.

When the Fear of Failure factor was correlated with the foregoing self-report measures, this factor correlated significantly not only with depression ($r = .41, p < .005$), irrational cognitions ($r = .30, p < .0005$), punctuality, and organized study habits ($r = -.48, p < .005$), but also with anxiety ($r = .23, p < .0005$). To a lesser extent, the Fear of Failure factor was negatively correlated with assertion ($r = -.12, p < .05$).

When the Aversiveness of the Task factor was examined in relation to the other self-report measures, this factor was found to correlate significantly with depression ($r = .36, p < .0005$), irrational beliefs ($r = .36$, $p < .0005$), and punctuality and organized study habits ($r = -.53$, $p < .0005$). However, the Aversiveness of the Task factor was not significantly correlated with anxiety or assertion, and the correlation with self-esteem ($r = -.13$, $p = .013$), although significant, was low.

Test-Retest Reliability. There have been no repeated administrations of the PASS to a subject sample. The PASS has been administered in class (sample = 323) and then readministered to a subsample consisting of one third of the class (sample = 98) who attended a psychology experiment held later in the semester. This yielded a Pearson product-moment correlation coefficient of 0.57 ($p < .005$) on the total frequency score of the PASS.

Validity. *Behavioral measures of procrastination in self-paced quizzes:* Subjects in a self-paced section of Introductory Psychology (samples = 161) took 23 self-paced quizzes during the semester. The number of self-paced quizzes that subjects took during the last third (5 weeks) of the semester was used as a behavioral index of procrastination. Those students who took more quizzes during the final weeks of the semester were considered to be greater procrastinators than were students who took fewer quizzes in those last weeks. A frequency distribution of the number of self-paced quizzes taken by all students during the last 5 weeks revealed a range of 0 to 23 and a median of 12.5.

Significant positive correlations were found between the number of self-paced quizzes and PASS scores of self-reported procrastination on writing a term paper ($r = .24$, $p < .001$), studying for exams ($r = .19$, $p < .01$), and doing weekly readings ($r = .28$, $p < .0005$). Therefore, subjects who reported that they frequently procrastinated on these tasks also delayed taking their quizzes. There were no significant correlations between the number of quizzes taken late in the semester and procrastination on administrative or attendance tasks.

Attendance at extra-credit sessions: One hundred students attended one of three extra-credit sessions held during the early, middle, or late part of the semester. The results revealed a significant effect for sessions with regard to self-reported procrastination on administrative tasks as measured by the PASS, $F(2,99) = 3.4$, $p < .05$. Students who attended the late session reported that they procrastinated on administrative tasks significantly more than did students who attended the earlier sessions ($M = 4.02$, 4.10, and 5.75 for the early,

middle, and late experimental sessions, respectively, for the sum of self-reported procrastination and the degree to which procrastination presented a problem). There were no other significant effects.

Grades: Psychology course grade was not significantly correlated with self-reported procrastination on the PASS. However, subsequent research correlating the PASS with students' total grade point average (GPA) resulted in significant negative correlations between total self-reported procrastination on the PASS and GPA, as well as between Fear of Failure on the PASS and GPA (Rothblum, Solomon, & Murakami, 1985).

Clinical Use

To date, the PASS has been used exclusively with nonclinical populations of college students. The scale not only can help identify procrastinators, but also can help determine the effective, cognitive, and/or behavioral basis for the problem. This information is valuable, as intervention efforts can then be tailored to address the specific reasons for academic procrastination. Finally, the PASS can be used to evaluate the effectiveness of procrastination intervention programs.

Future Directions

Future research with the PASS includes collecting normative data with younger populations as well as with adults in the work setting.

References

Burka, J., & Yuen, L. (1983). *Procrastination: Why you do it, what to do about it.* Reading, MA: Addison-Wesley.

Rothblum, E.D., Solomon, L.J., & Murakami, J. (1985). Behavioral, effective, and cognitive differences between high and low procrastinators as an academic deadline approaches. Paper presented at the annual convention of the Association for Advancement of Behavior Therapy, Houston, TX.

Solomon, L.J., & Rothblum, E.D. (1984). Academic procrastination: Frequency and cognitive-behavioral correlates. *Journal of Counseling Psychology, 31,* 503-509.

Psychophysiological Assessment of Electrodermal Activity

Carlos F. Mendes de Leon and Paul M. Cinciripini

Description

Electrodermal activity (EDA) refers to changes in the electrical activity on the surface of the skin. The measure is associated with activity of the eccrine sweat glands, which are located in the palms of the hand and soles of the feet (Stern, Ray, & Davis, 1980).

There are primarily three types of electrodermal measures: the skin resistance response (SRR), also known as the galvanic skin response (GSR); the skin conductance response (SCR); and the skin potential response (SPR). Skin resistance and conductance are measured using the exosomatic method, in which a small interval current (.75 to 1.0 Volt) is passed through two electrodes on the surface of the skin. This method yields a measure of electrical skin resistance observed between the two active electrodes. Skin resistance is recorded in ohms. The skin conductance response is the reciprocal of the skin resistance response and is expressed in micromhos (;MUmhos). The second technique to measure EDA is the endosomatic method. Unlike the exosomatic method, it measures the electrical activity at the surface of the skin, without imposing an external current. This technique results in a measure of skin potential (SPR) and is expressed in millivolts (mV) (Stern et al., 1980).

Electrodermal responses may be evaluated in terms of both phasic and tonic changes. Phasic responses refer to discrete changes in EDA which follow exposure to an external stimulus (e.g., loud noise). Phasic responses are also known as AC responses and may be quantified by counting the number of criterion responses per unit time or the latency of criterion response (e.g., 5 mV). Tonic changes refer to the absolute level of skin conductance or skin potential at any given moment, and usually reflect the state of the organism during a continuous measurement period.

The standard way to record EDA is to use silver-silver chloride electrodes, attached to the palmar surface of the hands or fingers or the soles of the feet. Electrode cream applied to the electrodes serves as a conductive medium between the electrodes and the skin.

Purpose

Recent formulations of EDA have considered it a measure of general arousal or a measure of the state of the organism's interaction with the environment (Stern et al., 1980). The activity of the eccrine sweat glands primarily reflects responsivity to stimulation of a psychological nature, whereas other sweat glands are more sensitive to changes in temperature. The increase in sweat gland activity as a result of sympathetic nervous stimulation leads to increased levels of conductance (decreased resistance). Emotional arousal and generalized discharge of the sympathetic nervous system are correlated with each other. However, unlike most sympathetic activity, the primary neurotransmitter is acetylcholine, not epinephrine. However, there is no specificity with regard to particular emotions and electrodermal responses. Emotions such as fear, anger, and sexual feelings all produce similar responses.

In general, EDA is regarded as an acute and moderately sensitive measure of sympathetic arousal. The latency of the skin conductance response or skin potential response is between 0.3 and 2.5 seconds (Stern et al., 1980). Therefore, it is often used as a surface physiological measure of stress. Recent stress research has investigated electrodermal events in two ways. Most studies have used electrodermal events as an index of psychological stress, by correlating changes in skin conductance with exposure to potentially emotionally arousing stimuli. A few other studies, however, have explored whether EDA could be brought under voluntary control with the aid of biofeedback procedures. A review of both types of studies may be found in a report by Cinciripini, Hook, Mendes de Leon, and Prichard (1984).

Development

The first studies investigating electrical conductivity of the skin were performed as early as the late 1800s by researchers Vigouroux and Fere (Stern et al., 1980). Fere in 1888 was the first to report a change in skin resistance after exposure to emotional and sensory stimulation. Two Swiss researchers, Mueller and Veraguth, observed similar associations between skin resistance and changes in psychological state. This influenced Jung to examine the use of EDA as a measure of unconscious or mental phenomena in his word-association experiments (Stern et al., 1980). The recording and measurement of EDA have remained popular in psychophysiological research. It can be a sensitive measure of an organisms physiological response to emotional stimuli. However, there are several caveats in making this interpretation, which are described in the next section.

Psychometric Characteristics

The expected values of skin conductance level are between 2 and 100 ;MUmho/cm² and for skin conductance response between 0.01 and 5 ;MUmho/

cm². The expected values for skin potential level range between +10 mV and −70 mV; for the skin potential response, the expected negative component ranges between 2 and 4 mV (Venables & Christie, 1973). Factors affecting the reliability of EDA are: hand washing (enhanced resistance); environmental temperature and humidity; age; sudden inhalation; movement; pressure against the electrodes; and nicotine and alcohol intake (Venables & Christie, 1973). In terms of the validity of the electrodermal response, it should be reiterated that skin conductance responses and skin potential responses are nonspecific measures of general arousal: different emotions generate similar responses. Electrical activity of the skin represents only one of several psychophysiological measures of arousal. Moreover, the neurotransmitter at the postganglionic synapse associated with EDA is acetylcholine, not adrenaline as is generally the case elsewhere in the sympathetic nervous system. This fact is particularly important in understanding the relationship between EDA and other psychophysiological measures of sympathetic origin, e.g., cardiovascular arousal. Generalization to other psychophysiological activity should be interpreted with caution (Stern et al., 1980), because factors that affect acetylcholine transmission do not necessarily affect adrenergic activity (adrenaline).

Clinical Use

Recordings of EDA are mainly used clinically in biofeedback procedures. Modification of electrodermal responses through biofeedback techniques has been examined in only a few clinical populations. For example, electrodermal biofeedback has been combined with relaxation training in the treatment of hypertensive patients. Significant decreases in blood pressure were obtained, with maintenance of the gains at 4 and 7 months follow-up (Patel & North, 1975). Electrodermal biofeedback is also applied in the treatment of anxiety disorders and phobias. Increases in skin conductance are considered as an indication of anxiety, which is incompatible with a relaxation response. Through a counterconditioning procedure, patients are trained to relax while exposed to anxiety-triggering stimuli. Feedback on EDA is presented to help the patient to establish a state of relaxation. This technique has been used successfully in the treatment of specific fears, such as excessive fear of spiders and flying (Olton & Noonberg, 1980). However, only a few case studies have been published, and

not enough evidence is currently available to evaluate the efficacy of electrodermal biofeedback in the treatment of anxiety and phobic disorders.

Future Directions

The clinical usefulness of achieving voluntary control of EDA through biofeedback procedures remains limited. The use of relaxation training and electrodermal biofeedback in the treatment of hypertension is a possibility that certainly deserves replication. Little evidence is available on the efficacy of electrodermal biofeedback in anxiety disorders or phobias. Learned control of EDA might prove to be useful in inducing or maintaining relaxation states in counterconditioning procedures. Generally, however, attempts to control EDA during exposure to stressful stimuli using biofeedback have proven ineffective. In fact, increases in EDA may result from attention to the biofeedback or stress stimulus (Cinciripini et al., 1984). For the immediate future, the widest application of measures of EDA probably involves experimental stress research, in which it may serve as a fairly sensitive surface physiological measure of cholinergic (acetylcholine) sympathetic arousal. It may be particularly important in situations in which adrenergic (epinphrine and norepinephrine) release is considered minimal, as when these responses are blocked by drugs or when stress is subtle, requiring little cardiovascular (adrenergic) adjustment (Cinciripini et al., 1984).

References

Cinciripini, P.M., Hook, J.D., Mendes de Leon, C.F., & Prichard, W.A. (1984). Review of cardiovascular, electromyographic, electrodermal, electrocortical and respiratory measures of psychological stress. NIOSH Monograph, Contract No. 84-257.

Olton, D.S., & Noonberg, A.R. (Eds.) (1980). *Biofeedback. Clinical applications in behavioral medicine.* Englewood Cliffs, N.J.: Prentice-Hall.

Patel, C.H., & North, W.R.S. (1975). Randomized controlled trial of yoga and biofeedback in management of hypertension. *Lancet, ii,* 93-99.

Stern, R.M., Ray, W.L., & Davis, C.M. (1980). *Psychophysiological recording.* New York: Oxford University Press.

Venables, P.M., & Christie, M.L. (1973). Mechanisms, instrumentation, recording techniques and quantification of responses. In W.F. Prohasky & D.D. Rashin (Eds.), *Electrodermal activity in psychological research.* London: Academic Press.

Psychosocial Adjustment to Illness Scale

Leonard R. Derogatis

Description

The Psychosocial Adjustment to Illness Scale (PAIS) is a multidimensional, semistructured clinical interview designed to assess the psychological and social adjustment of medical patients, or members of their immediate families, to the patient's illness. The PAIS is comprised of 46 items designed to be completed in conjunction with a personal interview with the respondent. Although primarily focused on the patient's adjustment to illness, with minor adjustments in format the PAIS may also be used to assess the quality of adjustment of spouses, parents, or other relatives to the patient's illness.

The PAIS is designed to be scored from a clinical interview conducted by a trained health professional or interviewer. When the interview is limited strictly to information scored on the PAIS, it usually takes approximately 20 to 30 minutes to complete. The PAIS items may be integrated into a broader interview; however, if they are, PAIS items must be addressed consecutively without the interjection of other items.

In addition to the PAIS interview, there is also a self-report version of the instrument, the PAIS-SR. Like the PAIS, the PAIS-SR is comprised of 46 items, developed to be as comparable as possible to the 46 items of the interview. The PAIS-SR also takes approximately 20 minutes to complete, and may be used effectively when experienced clinical interviewers are unavailable or when the expense of using such personnel is prohibitive. Although some flexibility is sacrificed in using the PAIS-SR, we have found that this loss is more than compensated for in many situations by the ease and transportability of administration and the reduction in expenses associated with its use.

The PAIS and PAIS-SR both reflect psychosocial adjustment to illness through *primary domains of adjustment*: (a) Health Care Orientation; (b) Vocational Environment; (c) Domestic Environment; (d) Sexual Relationships; (e) Extended Family Relationships (f) Social environment; and (g) Psychological Distress. Interview and self-report items are designed to assess the quality of adjustment in each of the seven primary domains, with each item represented on a 4-point (0 to 3) scale of adjustment. Higher scores represent poorer adjustment, with scale direction alternated on the PAIS-SR to reduce position response biases.

Development

Norming the construct "adjustment to illness" presents special problems, because there are an enormous number of different disorders, and significant stages or variations within each disorder, to attempt to standardize. We have approached this problem with the PAIS and PAIS-SR through the concept of a *normative library*. This strategy involved the programmatic development of norms for the PAIS and PAIS-SR for distinct illness categories as representative cohorts of patients become available. Currently, six norms (four for the PAIS and two for the PAIS-SR) have been completed and are presented in the test manual (Derogatis & Lopez, 1983). The four normative groups for the PAIS involve samples of *lung cancer patients, renal dialysis patients, acute burn patients,* and *patients with essential hypertension.* Norms for the PAIS-SR are currently available for a cohort of *cardiac bypass patients* and a sample of *heterogeneous cancer patients.* We are committed to the continued development of the normative library for the PAIS and PAIS-SR and will continue to publish additional norms for the instruments as soon as they become available.

Prototype versions of the PAIS and PAIS-SR were developed in 1975 and 1977, respectively; however, because of the long development time required for the scales, the test manual was published only recently (Derogatis & Lopez, 1983) and the introductory report on the instruments is about to be published (Derogatis, 1985). Both documents provide extensive details on the psychometric characteristics of the scales, as well as the validation studies that have been performed.

Psychometric Characteristics

Concerning reliability estimates, both internal consistency and interrater agreement coefficients have been developed based on a number of cohorts. Although validation by its nature is programmatic and requires considerable time to establish conclusively, convincing validation studies have been accomplished with the PAIS and PAIS-SR. Derogatis (1985) has reported a consistent and meaningful set of convergent relationships for the PAIS relative to other psychological instruments with a sample of patients with breast cancer, whereas DeNaur (1982) has reported good convergent relationships for the PAIS relative to the MAACL and physicians' clinical judgments. Derogatis (1985) has also reported convincing predictive validity for the PAIS with a sample of 120 patients with lung cancer, as has Kaplan-DeNaur (1982) with renal dialysis patients and judged the quality of overall adjustment. Both Lamping (1981) and Murphy (1982) have also observed strong predictive and convergent relationships for the PAIS with renal dialysis patients relative to such instruments as in the MMPI and the POMS.

Future Directions

Currently, Clinical Psychometric Research (Baltimore, MD), the distributor of the PAIS and PAIS-SR, has made a microcomputer scoring program available for the PAIS that will score and norm PAIS profiles (through T scores) in terms of all currently available PAIS and PAIS-SR norms. Future directions involve expanding the normative library to provide extensive coverage of major illness groups.

References

Derogatis, L.R. (1986). The Psychosocial Adjustment to Illness Scale (PAIS). *Journal of Psychosomatic Research, 30*, 77-91.

Derogatis, L.R., & Lopez, M. (1983). *The Psychosocial Adjustment to Illness Scale Administration & Scoring Manual.* Baltimore, MD: Clinical Psychometric Research.

DeNaur, A.K. (1982). Social adjustment of chronic dialysis patients. *American Journal of Psychiatry, 139,* 97-99.

Lamping, D.L. (1981). *Psychological adaption and adjustment to the stress of chronic illness.* Doctoral dissertation, Harvard University, Cambridge.

Murphy, S.P. (1982). *Factors affecting adjustment and quality of life: A multivariate approach.* Doctoral dissertation, University of Illinois Medical Center, Chicago.

Pupil Evaluation Inventory

Marc S. Atkins and Charlotte Johnston

Description

The Pupil Evaluation Inventory (PEI) is a peer nomination procedure developed for classroom administration in grades one through nine (Pekarik, Prinz, Liebert, Weintraub, & Neale, 1976). It contains 34 items and 1 training item. A shorter version consisting of 17 items is provided for first graders. The PEI is presented to a class as an item-by-peer matrix, with items listed down the left side of the page and the names of each child in that class along the top of the page. Each child rates each other child in that class by placing an "X" in the box corresponding to items descriptive of the child being rated. Same-sex, cross-sex, and self-ratings can be obtained in this way. The score for each child is the percentage of peers nominating that child on each item. More commonly, however, factor scores are derived for Aggression, Withdrawal, and Likability based on Pekarik et al.'s (1976) factor analysis. Factor scores represent the percentage of peers nominating each child averaged across items contained on that factor. Pekarik et al. report that administration time is approximately 30 minutes. However, administration is somewhat longer for nonreading children.

Purpose

The PEI was developed by the Stony Brook High Risk Project to study peer relationships in children at risk for psychopathology (Pekarik et al., 1976). Peer ratings were selected because of the availability of normative data, the stability of peer assessments over time and across raters, and the effectiveness of peer ratings as predictors of adult psychopathology. However, most previous peer rating instruments assessed global peer perceptions such as popularity and rejection. In contrast, the PEI focuses on specific behavioral patterns presumed to relate to maladjustment.

Development

Items selected were based on a review of prior peer rating instruments and of the research literature on correlates of psychopathology. Items with the highest loadings in factor analyses of prior instruments were selected for consideration, resulting in an initial pool of 13 factors and 80 items. Redundant items were eliminated and the remaining items were arranged into rational categories. These items were piloted on 45 third- and fourth-grade children. A factor analysis of these results led to the selection of 39 nonredundant items. These items were presented to a second sample of 74 second- and third-graders, which resulted in the elimination of route items that appeared confusing to the children. The final version contained 34 items and 1 training item. The 17-item version for first graders consisted of items derived from each factor.

Psychometric Characteristics

Pekarik et al. (1976) factor analyzed PEI ratings for children in grades one to nine and extracted three factors labeled Aggression, Withdrawal, and Likeability, which accounted for 65% of the variance. Using a multidimensional scaling technique, Younger, Schwartzman, and Ledingham (1985) found that these three factors became more distinctive across grades one, four, and seven. Factor means and standard deviations for the PEI are presented by Pekarik et al. (1976) and by Johnston, Pelham, Atkins, and Crawford (1986). In both studies, older children received fewer ratings and boys were rated as more aggressive.

Johnston et al. (1986) reported uniformly high internal consistency coefficients for PEI factors in grades two to five. However, on the 16-item grade-one version, the Withdrawal and Likability factors showed unsatisfactory levels of internal consistency. Pekarik et al. (1976) observed 2-week test-retest reliabilities above .80 for each factor in grades three and six. Test-retest reliabilities for the individual items ranged from .71 to .76. Johnston et al. (1976), reporting 4-month test-retest reliabilities, found the Aggression and Withdrawal factors were most reliable over time. Ratings were consistently stable in each of grades two to five; however, the test-retest reliabilities for grade-one children were unsatisfactory. Computing grade-one reliabilities using a larger pool of both-sex raters rather than only same-sex raters resulted in modest improvement in these reliabilities.

Evidence for the concurrent validity of the PEI exists in several studies. Pekarik et al. (1976) reported a median correlation of .57 between teacher and peer ratings on the PEI factors. Johnston et al. (1986) correlated PEI factor ratings and positive and negative nominations and found the Likeability factor and items most strongly related to positive nominations and the Aggression scores most highly correlated with negative nominations. Weintraub, Prinz, and Neale (1978) reported that children, particularly girls, of depressed and schizophrenic mothers were rated by peers as more aggressive, more withdrawn, and less likeable than children of normal mothers. Similarly, Ledingham (1981) found that children rated by peers as extremely aggressive and/or withdrawn were rated by mothers and teachers as having problems similar to those represented by the PEI ratings.

Clinical Use

The PEI assesses peer perceptions on specific items related to children's classroom behavior. This information is particularly important for the diagnosis and assessment of peer deficits. However, despite considerable utility, this information may not be readily available in many clinical settings. Potential problems include difficulty in obtaining entrance into classrooms, reluctance of school officials to allow peer evaluations on negatively worded items because of the purported negative impact on children of these ratings, and time needed for administration and scoring. However, for those clinicians working or consulting in schools, the PEI may be extremely useful, especially in light of recent evidence that negative peer ratings have little or no effect on children's social status (Bell-Dolan, Foster, & Pack, 1985). Similarly, although scoring and administration will be more time-consuming than less comprehensive peer-rating instruments, administration and scoring of the PEI are approximately equivalent to those of other comprehensive assessment instruments for children, such as the WISC-R. For children with suspected peer deficits for whom peer ratings are warranted, the PEI offers an instrument with considerable evidence for reliability and validity.

Future Directions

The PEI has proven to be an important research tool and has considerable potential for clinical application as well. However, although the psychometric properties of the PEI have been reported to be similar across a variety of studies, important differences exist in administration and scoring procedures across these same studies. Weintraub et al. (1978) asked children to rate only one sex of child in each class. Ledingham (1981), using a French translation of the PEI, had both boys and girls rated, but during separate administrations. Johnston et al. (1986) and Pekarik et al. (1976) asked children to rate both sexes at the same time. Some studies requested an unlimited number of nominations for each item (e.g., Pekarik et al., 1976; Johnston et al., 1986); however, other studies (e.g., Ledingham, 1981) have reported allowing only three or four nominations per item. Finally, although Pekarik et al. (1976) and Johnston et al. (1986) used raw factor and item scores for analyses, Ledingham (1981) and Weintraub et al. (1978) employed transformed or standardized scores, or both. No direct comparisons among the data resulting from these different procedures have been made, and such contrasts would undoubtedly facilitate comparisons among studies.

References

Bell-Dolan, D.J., Foster, S.L., & Pack, D.M. (1985). *The effects of peer nominations on peer interactions and loneliness in school.* Paper presented at the annual meeting of the Association for Advancement of Behavior Therapy, Houston.

Johnston, C., Pelham, W.E., Atkins, M.S., & Crawford, J. (1986). *A psychometric study of positive and negative nominations and the Pupil Evaluation Inventory.* Manuscript submitted for publication.

Ledingham, J.E. (1981). Developmental patterns of aggressive and withdrawn behavior in childhood: A possible method for identifying preschizophrenics. *Journal of Abnormal Child Psychology, 9,* 1-22.

Pekarik, E.G., Prinz, R.J., Liebert, D.E., Weintraub, S., & Neale, J.M. (1976). The Pupil Evaluation Inventory: A sociometric technique for assessing children's social behavior. *Journal of Abnormal Child Psychology, 4,* 83-97.

Weintraub, S., Prinz, R.J., & Neale, J.M. (1978). Peer evaluations of the competence of children vulnerable to psychopathology. *Journal of Abnormal Child Psychology, 6,* 461-473.

Younger, A.J., Schwartzman, A.E., & Ledingham, J.E. (1985). Age-related changes in children's perceptions of aggression and withdrawal in their peers. *Developmental Psychology, 21,* 70-75.

Rape Aftermath Symptom Test

Dean G. Kilpatrick

Description

The Rape Aftermath Symptom Test (RAST) is a 70-item self-report inventory of psychological symptoms and potentially fear-producing stimuli that respondents rate on a 5-point Likert scale indicating the degree of disturbance currently associated with each item. A rating of 0 indicates no distress or disturbance, and a rating of 4 severe disturbance. The RAST yields a global distress score that can range from 0 to 280. The RAST was developed by D.G. Kilpatrick, G.A. Ruff, and J.C. Allison.

Purpose

The RAST was developed to provide a relatively brief but sensitive objective measure of fear and other symptoms commonly experienced by female victims after a rape experience. Although other tests have proven capable of detecting the effects of rape, the major objective of the RAST is to increase assessment efficiency by measuring critical symptoms with a much briefer instrument.

Development

The RAST was constructed using items from two assessment instruments that proved most useful in detecting rape-related symptoms, the Derogatis SCL-90-R and the Veronen-Kilpatrick Modified Fear Survey. As described elsewhere in this volume, each of these parent scales has excellent reliability and was sensitive to short- and long-term effects of rape. Together, the parent instruments contain 210 items, and it was reasonable to assume that some items were more useful than others in tapping postrape symptoms. Because previous research had shown no significant improvement in postrape symptoms from 3 months to 3 years after rape (Kilpatrick & Veronen, 1984), test construction efforts focused on the 3-month postrape assessment data from 137 recent rape victims and 139 nonvictims matched for age, race, and neighborhood of residence, who had completed the Modified Fear Survey (MFS) and the SCL-90-R. Victims' and nonvictims' responses to each of the 120 MFS and 90 SCL-90-R items were examined using Cramer's V statistic to determine items that were most effective in distinguishing between the two groups. This process was completed separately for the MFS items and the SCL-90-R items, and the top third of the most discriminating items from each test was determined. Thus, the RAST was constructed using 40 items from the MFS and 30 from the SCL-90-R. Items comprising the RAST can be viewed as reflecting the particular fears and other symptoms that characterize the psychological aftermath of rape.

Some notion of the content of the RAST can be gained by examining the types of items included. The 10 most discriminating MFS items included in the RAST were: persons behind you, being alone, darkness, going out with new people, sound of a doorbell, walking on a dimly lit street, being awakened at night, crowds, sexual intercourse, and sleeping alone. The 10 most discriminating SCL-90-R items in the RAST were: feeling nervous when left alone; having to avoid certain things, places, or activities because they frighten you; feeling afraid to go out of your house alone; being suddenly scared for no reason; having spells of terror or panic; feeling that most people cannot be trusted; feeling fearful; feeling afraid in open spaces or in streets; feeling self-conscious with others; and feeling so restless you cannot sit still.

Psychometric Characteristics

Good internal consistency (alpha = .95) as well as good test-retest reliability (r = .85 over a 2.5-month interval for nonvictims) were demonstrated with the RAST. The high internal consistency of items suggested that the scale was primarily measuring only one symptom dimension, so plans for developing subscales via factor analysis were abandoned.

With respect to the RAST's validity, Kilpatrick et. al. (1985) recently examined the extent to which the RAST could distinguish the symptoms of rape victims from those of nonvictims at several postrape intervals, ranging from 6 to 21 days to 3 years afterrape. That victim and nonvictim RAST scores would differ significantly at 3 months afterrape was virtually certain because the test was constructed on the basis of items that discriminated at that point. However, it remained an open question as to whether the test could discriminate at earlier and later assessment points. Cross-sectional comparisons of victim and nonvictim RAST scores yielded significant differences at 6 to 21 days, 3 months, 6 months, 1 year, 2 years, and 3 years afterrape, with victims having higher scores on all occasions. A repeated measures analysis of variance on the scores of victims and nonvictims having completed all assessments indicated that: (a) nonvictims' scores were not significantly different across assessments, (b) victims' scores were significantly higher than nonvictims' scores at all assessments, and (c) victims' scores declined significantly between 6 and 21 days and 3 months afterrape, but they did not change significantly thereafter. Normative information is available from the authors regarding victim and nonvictim scores at each assessment session.

Clinical Use

The RAST would appear to have substantial clinical utility with rape victims. In addition to the information provided by examination of overall RAST scores, inspection of individual item scores provides substantial, clinically useful data about idiosyncratic fears and other symptoms of given victims. The RAST might also be usefully applied to evaluation of treatment efficacy. Because this test appears to tap the information measured by the

two parent tests but is one-third as long, the RAST's relative brevity should enhance its usefulness.

Future Directions

Currently in progress are three major undertakings with the RAST. The first is a specific examination of the extent to which the RAST is capable of measuring response to treatment intervention for rape-related fear and anxiety problems. The second is an exploration of the RAST's ability to detect the psychological impact of crimes other than rape, such as robbery, burglary, and aggravated assault. The final undertaking is a more thorough investigation of the RAST's concurrent and discriminative validity. We are currently examining the extent to which the RAST correlates with other assessment measures in our assessment battery.

References

Kilpatrick, D.G., Best, C.L., Veronen, L.J., Ruff, M.H., Ruff, G.A., & Allison, J.C. (1985, August). *The aftermath of rape: A 3-year longitudinal study.* Paper presented at the annual convention of the American Psychological Association, Los Angeles.

Kilpatrick, D.G., & Veronen, L.J. (1984). *Treatment of fear and anxiety in victims of rape.* (Final Report, Grant No. RO1 MH 29602). Rockville, MD: National Institute of Mental Health.

Rational Behavior Inventory

Ruth Morelli

Description

The Rational Behavior Inventory (RBI) is a 37-item questionnaire that measures irrational beliefs defined by Ellis (1962) as rigid, antiempirical beliefs that lead to emotional distress and prevent attainment of goals. Items reflect self-statements such as, "I get terribly upset and miserable when things are not the way I would like them to be" or "A person should be thoroughly competent, adequate, talented and intelligent in all possible respects." These items are derived from a 119-item pool of irrational beliefs. Factor analysis also revealed that these items loaded high on 11 factors thought to parallel Ellis' (1962) irrational beliefs. These factors include Catastrophizing, Guilt, Perfection,

Approval, Caring and Helping, Blame and Punishment, Inertia and Avoidance, Independence, Downing Self and Others, Projected Misfortunes, and Control of Emotions.

The person rates the degree of agreement with each statement using a 5-point Likert scale ranging from 1 (strongly agree) to 5 (strongly disagree). Scores are converted to 0 or 1 based on Guttman scale cutting points. Therefore, the total score ranges from 0 to 38, because one item is included on two factors. Lower RBI scores reflect greater irrationality.

Purpose

The RBI was developed by Shorkey and Whiteman (1977) to accurately describe, measure, and compare degrees of rationality in selected populations. Indeed, the RBI is an improvement psychometrically over earlier scales, because it is brief, yet has good reliability and validity. The RBI was also developed to guide rational emotive counselors in the treatment of clients. In fact, the 11 individual factor scores could aid in identifying and treating specific irrational beliefs.

Development

Hartman (1968) and Fox and Davies (1971) created rationality measures that formed the 119-item pool for the RBI, which was initally administered to 235 college undergraduates. Each of the 119 items was assigned to 1 of 14 preconceived factors based on Ellis' irrational beliefs and then factor analyzed. Results showed 70 of the 119 statements loaded high on each of the major irrational beliefs. These 70 statements were again factor analyzed, and 11 interpretable factors emerged that explained 77% of the variance of the total items. Guttman scaling to measure each of the 11 factors resulted in the selection of 37 items with high loadings. These 37 items were processed to find the order of the cutting points and also produced a Guttman scale with a coefficient of reproducibility of at least 0.90 and a coefficient of scalability of at least 0.60 for each factor.

Psychometric Characteristics

In developing the RBI, Shorkey and Whiteman (1977) found that split-half reliability was .72 and test-retest reliability was .82 after 3 days and .71 after 10 days. Another study found the RBI stable over 10 weeks. Initial validity for the RBI was established by Shorkey and Whiteman (1977) when they administered the RBI to mental health providers undergoing brief training in Rational Emotive Therapy. Their scores changed in the direction of greater rationality after the training. Later studies using college students revealed that the RBI was related to personality variables such as neuroticism, extraversion, self-actualization, anomie, authoritarianism, dogmatism, self-esteem, and defensive styles. The RBI was also related to affective measures of depression and anxiety. However, the measure was not related to social desirability and was more related to another rationality measure than to three anxiety measures.

Clinical Use

The original goal in developing the RBI was clinical in nature. It was hoped the measure would guide counselors in treating their clients' irrational beliefs. Aside from using the total RBI score, individual factor scores are also available. These can be useful in identifying and treating specific irrational beliefs rapidly and accurately. Normal as well as clinically diagnosed persons could benefit from the application of this measure. Although most studies using the RBI have examined personality variables among college students, there is evidence that the RBI is also relevant to clinical populations. The RBI distinguished between normal and clinical groups and was sensitive to changes that resulted from therapy in a recent study by Shorkey and Sutton-Simon (1983).

Future Directions

The RBI is the most popular measure of Ellis' irrational beliefs, perhaps because of its greater reliability and validity compared with those of similar instruments. However, studies have revealed the RBI is also related to affective variables such as depression and anxiety. This result calls for more careful conceptualization of rationality and of the distinction between irrational self-statements and emotions.

Endorsement of beliefs on a self-report inventory may not be isomorphic to underlying beliefs or with behaviors. Therefore, there is a need to gather behavioral data as well as self-report data on irrational beliefs before addressing treatment. However, validation of the RBI with more clinical studies is warranted. Assessment of the perceived difficulty in converting the RBI's Likert scores to Guttman scale scores is needed, because this rescoring might prevent more widespread use of the measure.

References

Ellis, A. (1962). *Reason and emotion in psychotherapy.* New York: Lyle Stewart.

Fox, E.E., & Davies, R.L. (1971). Test your rationality. *Journal of Rational Living, 6,* 23-25.

Hartman, B.J. (1968). Sixty revealing questions for 20 minutes. *Journal of Rational Living, 3,* 7-8.

Shorkey, C.T., & Sutton-Simon, K. (1983). Reliability and Validity of the Rational Behavior Inventory with a clinical population. *Journal of Clinical Psychology, 39,* 34-38.

Shorkey, C.T., & Whiteman, V.L. (1977). Development of the Rational Behavior Inventory: Initial validity and reliability. *Educational and Psychological Measurement, 37,* 527-534.

Real-Time Data Acquisition

David Felce

Description

Real-time data acquisition is the most precise form of behavioral measurement involving continuous scoring of responses with the passage of time. A simple definition can be offered. Continous real-time measurement occurs when every onset and offset of codable behavior is recorded and assigned an elapsed time from the beginning of the measurement period.

Purpose

Behavioral measurement generally is conducted to establish certain properties of functioning of an organism. It may be conducted in a structured laboratory setting (which can be adapted to aid data acquisition) or under field conditions in which few such possibilities exist. It may be achieved by some form of electromechanical recording device triggered by the target behavior itself, or more commonly in human research, by an observer trained to discriminate the motor and vocal responses of interest and assign behavioral codes. The basic properties of a defined response that one may wish to establish are its frequency and duration of occurrence. By fixing the beginning and end of each behavioral episode relative to the time frame, real-time data capture provides both of these independent measurement units. For a measurement period of known length, for each coded behavior, the total frequency (number of onsets) and rate per unit of time, the duration of each event (elapsed time between onset and offset), the interval between successive events (elapsed time between offset and next onset), the cumulative duration, and the proportion of total time responding occurred can be established. The order of occurrence of codes in a multiple coding scheme is preserved, and the data obtained will allow sequential analyses for identifying event- or time-related patterns and cycles in the flow of behavior.

Development

When the subject's movement is constrained, as in laboratory and animal research, and when the definition of the behaviors of interest can be restricted to particular topographies that permit automated recording, real-time data acquisition can be achieved electromechanically. However, wider applications of behavioral measurement require the eyes and ears of an observer and a portable means of recording. Real-time data acquisition within the natural environment or where multiple responses are of interest has been technically complicated. If onsets and offsets of behavioral events are noted as they occur using paper-and-pencil methods with a stopwatch or similar device to provide the time frame, the method becomes unwieldy when more than a few behaviors are recorded or if responding is of short duration but high frequency. However, the rapid development of computer technology has brought onto the market machines that, as a result of their portability, can provide a highly flexible means of overcoming some of the problems in generating real-time data from the natural environment.

A computer program (BEHAVIOR) has been developed for one such machine, the Epson HX-20 (Repp, Harman, & Felce, 1983; Felce, de Kock, Harman, & Repp, 1984). A description of the use of this machine can illustrate the advantages of computer assistance, the properties of a data capture program, and its applications. The Epson HX-20 is relatively inexpensive, is small enough to be handheld, is entirely portable (being powered by rechargeable batteries), has a small integral printer and liquid crystal display, and can be fitted with an integral microcassette recorder. It has a full typewriter keyboard and an adequate memory for each to be established as an independent category for encoding. The screen can be used to aid the entry of identifier information and to cue the observer; the printer allows self-contained production of output and the microcassette allows permanent storage of data. Most importantly, the computer has an internal clock that can be used to monitor the elapsed time of every key depression, relieving the observer of any need to measure time independently.

Behavior establishes each of 43 keys as a usable behavioral code. Successive key depressions *of the same key* signal onset and offset of that code, and the elapsed time of each key depression from the point of commencement is recorded in completed seconds. The keys operate independently, and any number can be in the on-mode at the same time, allowing encoding of response concurrent and dyadic interaction (Felce, de Kock, & Repp, in press). Modifications of the basic program have been established (a) for mutually exclusive measurement categories in which a key depression signalling the onset of a category automatically terminates the prior category, (b) to allow the simultaneous recording of up to two environmental variables that may each take any number of defined states (Felce et al., in press), and (c) to record short-duration events by a single key depression.

The BEHAVIOR program outputs summary data in two forms. It gives a record of key depressions (i.e., codes indicated by the symbols on the keys) in temporal order of onset with time of onset, time of offset, and response duration printed against each. It also gives a summary table listing the 43 key symbols and includes the frequency of onset of each, rate of onset per minute, total duration, and percent of total time each code occurred. It then automatically records the data array to cassette, which allows storage and retrieval for subsequent analysis.

Psychometric Characteristics

These are not applicable here.

Clinical Use

The BEHAVIOR program is usable in any research or clinical application in which it is desirable to ascertain the frequency and/or duration of defined events. Of particular relevance is the behavioral responding of an individual subject. It can be used to study response patterns (bout and interbout lengths) and response interactions, establish baselines, and evaluate interventions. Composite group data can be assembled by observing individual subjects for set periods in random rotation. The BEHAVIOR program is independent of any particular set of response definitions, and therefore its use is entirely unconstrained.

Future Directions

A major advantage of this form of measurement over various forms of time-sampling or event-recording measures is that the precise temporal order of responding is preserved. The exciting directions for development come from the use of analyses that exploit fully this unique characteristic of real-time data. One such technique is sequential lag analysis (Sackett, 1978), in which the conditional probability of response A following response B is compared for different lag sizes defined by temporal latency with the unconditional probability of response A. This comparison can show the nature of the dependency of one category of response on another. A similar form of analysis can result in the production of state transition diagrams. A number of mutually exclusive states are defined: say Teacher attends and Student is on-task, Teacher attends and Student is off-task, Teacher does not attend and Student is on-task, Teacher does not attend and Student is off-task. The state transition diagram maps the probabilities of each state persisting (i.e., leading to itself) and of each state changing to each of the others in contrast to the probabilities of each state existing (i.e., occurring). Given the capability of the BEHAVIOR program to record concurrent and overlapping events, the analysis of dyadic interactions by these means has considerable potential.

References

Felce, D., de Kock, U., Harman, M., & Repp, A.C. (1984). Using the Epson HX-20 as a fully self-contained unit for data capture and analysis. Department of Psychology, University of Southampton, Highfield, Southampton, England.

Felce, D., de Kock, U., & Repp, A.C. (1986). An eco-behavioral analysis of small community-based houses and traditional large hospitals for severely and profoundly mentally handicapped adults. *Applied Research in Mental Retardation. 7,* 4, 393-408.

Felce, D., Repp, A.C., de Kock, U., Thomas, M., Ager, A., & Blunden, R. (in press). Staff: client ratios and their effects on staff interactions and client behaviour in twelve facilities for severely and profoundly mentally handicapped adults. *Analysis and Intervention in Developmental Disabilities.*

Repp, A.C., Harman, M.L., & Felce, D. (1983). A real-time parallel entry, portable computer system for observational research. Department of Learning and

Development, Northern Illinois University, Dekalb, Illinois.

Sackett, G.P. (1978). Measurement in observational research. In G.P. Sackett (Ed.), *Observing behavior: Data collection and analysis methods (Vol. 2)*. Baltimore, MD: University Park Press.

Reinforcement Survey Schedule

J.R. Cautela

Description

The Reinforcement Survey Schedule (RSS) is divided into four major sections. In the first three sections the respondent is asked to rate items on a 5-point scale representing the degree to which the stimuli give joy or other pleasurable feelings. The extreme points of the scale are "not at all" and "very much."

Section I consists of items that actually can be presented to a subject or client in many conventional settings, such as food items. There are 10 items in Section I, some of which are further subdivided. The total number of rating decisions in Section I is 33.

Section II consists of items that, for most practical purposes, can be presented only through facsimile or imagination. Usually these items will be presented in imagination. There are 44 items in Section II, eight of which have subcategories. The total number of rating decisions is 106.

Section II items include both active and spectator pursuits and solitary and interpersonal activities. These items encompass objects, persons, and psychological states (such as being perfect). Some items portray the respondent in an initiating role with respect to other persons, whereas other items portray the person in a recipient role.

Section III differs from the preceding section in that it presents situations rather than discrete objects and activities. This section presents six brief "situations I would like to be in." Each situation is constructed from at least three specific reinforcing stimuli. For example, Item 1 combines the satisfaction of having completed a difficult job, praise and appreciation from a superior, and a promise of future reward.

After responding to each situation separately, the subject is asked to indicate which situation most appeals to him or her. The items in Section III are usually presented in imagination.

In Section IV, the subject is asked to list the things she or he does or thinks about at certain designated frequencies (more than 5, 10, 15, or 20 times per day).

The RSS is given either individually or in group sessions. When subjects present problems in comprehension or communication, it is suggested that the size of the group be reduced. The author's experience suggests that administration time for adults is approximately 25 minutes. For certain persons who are illiterate or unable to read the questionnaire for one reason or another, the test must be administered orally. A minimum of seventh-grade education is necessary for fairly good comprehension of the questionnaire.

Purpose

For years, learning theorists have been aware that a behavior can be influenced by both its antecedents and its consequences. Self-report inventories developed in the early 1960s were constructed to identify antecedents that influence behavior. Cautela and Kastenbaum (1967) subsequently developed the RSS to discover possible reinforcing consequences.

Classes of stimuli that are reinforcing to many individuals, such as attention, praise, or food, are called general reinforcers. Idiosyncratic reinforcers are stimuli that are especially pleasurable to one individual; for example, rock music may be highly reinforcing to a teenager while aversive to some adults. The RSS is one way to discover possible idiosyncratic reinforcers.

Development

Although the RSS was developed primarily within a behavior therapy model, other theoretical frameworks and empirical applications need not be excluded. The RSS is also intended to be useful to investigators who favor an eclectic viewpoint. Although terminology may differ from theory to theory, most psychologists recognize the importance of identifying those stimuli that are associated with the probability of response occurrence.

After determining the need for developing a self-report inventory, the authors interviewed adults from 18 to 60 years of age. These adults were asked what thoughts, situations, and experiences gave them joy or pleasure. Frequency counts were obtained to determine the most preferred experiences. A number of individuals also described enjoyable situations as well as particular specific experiences.

It was decided to ask the clients to list the thing they did or thought at various frequencies in order to use the high probability events so as to increase the probability of desirable low-probability events (Premack principle).

Psychometric Characteristics

Keehn, Bloomfield, and Hugh (1970) correlated the percentage of "much" and "very much" responses from themes in Section III with specific items from Sections I and II that were judged to be related to the general themes. A correlation of .96 was computed for data provided by Cautela and Kastenbaum (1967). A second reliability study by Kleinknecht, McCormick, and Thorndike (1973) attempted to determine the stability of responses over time. The experimenters selected 140 items from Sections I and II and administered them to 118 subjects. The resulting correlation coefficients for the 1-week group, 3-week group, and 5-week group were .73, .67., and .70, respectively. Median correlations for each subject were generally higher than those for the items. They were .82 for the 1-week group, .78 for the 3-week group, and .80 for the 5-week group. The authors concluded that the data suggest sufficient stability to use the schedule as a clinical instrument.

Mermis (1971) found a significant correlation between the items chosen on the schedule and the amount of time looking at a slide of each item. He concluded that his research stands as a semivalidation of the RSS.

Cautela and Kastenbaum (1967) found differences in the ways that males and females respond. The schedule has three sections: (a) items that can be presented in a conventional setting, (b) items that can be presented only in imagination, and (c) situations in which the subject might like to be. A comparison of responses for each category (not at all, a little, a fair amount, much, and very much) found female subjects choosing a greater percentage of "very much" responses for each of the three divisions of the scale. A possible explanation presented by the authors suggested less inhibition among women given greater cultural freedom in their expression of affect. A second hypothesis suggested greater dependency on vicarious enjoyment among women through fantasy or wish fulfillment. The average Western man is possibly allowed more overt sources of satisfaction.

Comparisons of Sections I, II, and III of the RSS among juvenile offenders (Cautela & Kastenbaum,

1967) indicated a greater percentage of "very much" responses in Section I over Section II. It appears that immediate, concrete reinforcement (Section I-type items) is more effective in treatment with juvenile offenders than are reinforcers that are delayed or presented through imagination (Section II-type items). The opposite seems to be true of college undergraduates who were tested.

Clinical Use

Data made available through the schedule can be used in developing rapport in the initial interviews, building specific treatment plans for the individual, shaping behavior during therapeutic sessions, reinforcer sampling, and as an aid in assessing progress toward treatment goals.

The RSS can be used to predict cooperation in treatment and treatment outcome. Cleveland (1981) found that subjects with high RSS scores responded better to various treatments of myofacial pain. In my private practice, I have consistently observed that low RSS scores at the beginning of treatment indicate that the clients cooperate poorly in the treatment process.

The value of developing rapport is especially evident with highly anxious clients who are frightened of the therapeutic process. For example, the therapist might initially talk about the topics that the client checked "very much" in regard to their reinforcing value. This seems to be especially important with juvenile offenders, elderly persons, and persons with high anxiety. Aside from establishing rapport, the information made available through survey schedules provides a great deal of background information. Clients' responses are highly idiosyncratic and therefore highlight aspects of lifestyle.

Knowledge of reinforcers is necessary in the use of treatment strategies such as covert conditioning, shaping, response cost, extinction, and token economy.

The use of tokens and money has often been implemented in providing rewards for appropriate behavior. Because logistical and financial concerns, the number of possible reinforcers in a token economy is usually small. For this reason, the reinforcers must be the most effective available. Because reinforcement survey schedules provide an estimate of reinforcing value of each item, the discovery of effective reinforcers can be enhanced by the RSS.

Future Directions

Although the RSS has been useful with a general adult population, implementation with various other populations, such as patients in psychiatric hospitals, the elderly, children, and special needs populations, presents problems concerning the nature of the items and reading level of the subjects. Also, reinforcement survey schedules that elicit information on therapeutic issues have been developed. At least 23 different reinforcement survey schedules have now been constructed for various populations and issues. More development and research are needed on the RSS and these other reinforcement schedules.

Further research could also compare RSS scores with variables such as treatment outcome, physical disability, writer's left hemisphere functions, different diagnostic categories, and activity levels.

References

Cautela, J.R., & Kastenbaum, R. (1967). A reinforcement survey schedule for use in therapy training and research. *Psychological Reports, 20,* 1115-1130.

Cleveland, P.R. (1981). *A comparison of covert conditioning, biofeedback, and a placebo as treatment for myofacial pain dysfunction syndrome.* Unpublished doctoral dissertation, Boston College.

Keehn, J.D., Bloomfield, F.F., & Hugh, M.A. (1970). Uses of the reinforcement survey schedule with alcoholics. *Quarterly Journal of Studies on Alcohol, 31,* 602-615.

Kleinknecht, R.A., McCormick, C.E., & Thorndike, R.M. (1973). Stability of stated reinforcers as measured by the reinforcement survey schedule. *Behavior Therapy, 4,* 407-413.

Mermis, B.J. (1971). *Self-report of reinforcers and looking time.* Unpublished doctoral dissertation, University of Tennessee.

Relaxation Assessment Device

Timothy J. Hoelscher

Description

The Relaxation Assessment Device (RAD: Hoelscher, Lichstein, & Rosenthal, 1984) is a modified tape player with concealed capacity to electronically monitor the amount of taped relaxation practice. A digital wristwatch with a cumulative stopwatch function is surreptitiously placed inside the sealed battery compartment of the tape player. The stopwatch is electronically activated when the play button of the tape player is depressed. The *auto-stop* and *stop* functions freeze the stopwatch.

To prevent use of other cassettes, the relaxation tape is sealed in the tape chamber. Subjects are told to bring their tape players to each session for "routine inspection and inventory purposes." During each visit, a research assistant records relaxation practice time from the RAD stopwatch, tests the timing circuit, and resets the stopwatch. Although the RAD stopwatch reflects only the amount of time the relaxation tape is played, subjects are unaware that their practice is being monitored and therefore have little reason to play the tape without practicing relaxation.

Purpose

The purpose of the RAD is to objectively and unobtrusively monitor the amount of home relaxation practice. It is a valuable tool for monitoring relaxation compliance across time, examining dose-response relationships, and evaluating methods for increasing relaxation compliance.

Development

A number of mechanical and electronic designs can be used for monitoring relaxation compliance. We chose a method that is reliable, relatively inexpensive, and easy to build. The total cost of materials, including the tape player and watch, is about $75 per device. It takes an electronics technician approximately 2 hours to construct each device. Details on the electrical design and construction of the RAD have been published elsewhere (Lichstein & Hoelscher, in press).

In some cases, it may be desirable to use an alternative design. For example, Taylor, Agras, Schneider, and Allen (1983) reported on the development of a microelectronic system that stores a real-time record of taped relaxation practice. Memory storage is large enough so that the tape players only need to be checked once each month. This microelectronic system appears to be the method of choice for at least two types of investigations: (a) studies in which the exact time and date of each relaxation practice are important variables, and (b) long-term compliance studies in which weekly RAD checks are too cumbersome. The disadvantages of the system compared with the RAD concern its technical complexity and higher cost.

Psychometric Characteristics

The reliability of the RAD was assessed by conducting 100 experimental trials. In each trial, the tape player was started, played for varied durations, and stopped. The RAD stopwatch functioned flawlessly and correlated at $r = 1.00$ with an independent stopwatch.

The unobtrusiveness of the RAD was examined in two ways. First, subjects completed a postexperimental questionnaire that contained an embedded question to assess any suspicion that home relaxation practice was monitored. Second, following debriefing, the therapist asked subjects if they suspected that their relaxation practice was monitored. To date, only 1 of 60 subjects suspected that practice was monitored. This finding lends strong support to the unobtrusiveness of the RAD.

Two potential threats to the validity of RAD data should be noted. First, the RAD may underestimate practice time if the subject practices relaxation without the aid of the tape. This problem can be minimized by emphasizing the therapeutic importance of using the tape and by having subjects record self-administered practices on their self-report forms. Second, the RAD may overestimate practice time if the subject turns on the tape but does not practice relaxation. The likelihood of this problem occurring frequently appears small, because subjects are not aware that their practice is being monitored (i.e., they have little reason to play the tape without practicing relaxation). To date, no RAD validity studies have been conducted because of the difficulty in finding an acceptable criterion variable. Perhaps an inpatient setting could be used to collect validity data by corroborating RAD readings with reports of trained observers.

Two studies have presented data on RAD-determined relaxation practice and its relationship to subjects' self-reports. Hoelscher et al. (1984) trained 20 anxious adults in progressive relaxation and instructed them to practice relaxation at least once each day (16 minutes) during a 4-week treatment period. The RAD revealed that subjects averaged 68 minutes of practice per week. Only 25% of the subjects (sample = 5) averaged one practice or more per day. On average, subjects' self-reports overestimated actual practice by 126%. In a 10-week treatment study of 34 hypertensive subjects (Hoelscher et al., 1986), the RAD revealed an average of 100 minutes of practice per week. However, only 32% of the subjects (sample = 11) averaged one practice or more per day. Self-reports exceeded monitored practice by an average of 91%. Based on these preliminary studies, it appears that relaxation noncompliance is common and is frequently obscured by inaccurate relaxation self-reports.

Therefore, these data highlight the importance of using objective measures of relaxation practice.

Clinical Use

The RAD is appropriate for use with any population receiving relaxation training. To date, the RAD has been used in clinical research studies of anxiety (Hoelscher et al., 1984) and hypertensive (Hoelscher, Lichstein, & Rosenthal, 1986) populations.

Because use of the RAD involves deception, clinicians and researchers should be aware of important ethical considerations. The subjects are unaware that their home practice is being monitored until they are debriefed following the conclusion of their participation. This deception is deemed necessary in research applications because it (a) prevents falsification of data (i.e., playing the tape without practicing relaxation in order to appear compliant), and (b) limits reactivity (i.e., practicing relaxation at a higher rate because of the presence of the monitoring system). For strictly clinical purposes, the cue tone tracer method of Martin, Collins, Hillenberg, Zabin, and Katell (1981) appears preferable because it does not involve deception.

Future Directions

The recent development of the RAD and related monitoring systems (Martin et al., 1981; Taylor et al., 1983) focuses attention on several previously neglected areas of relaxation research. First, the critical subject, therapist, and procedural variables controlling relaxation compliance can now be identified, and strategies for increasing compliance can be developed and tested. Second, the therapeutic dosage of relaxation (i.e., amount of practice required to effect clinically meaningful changes) can be empirically determined. Third, the importance of continued relaxation practice during follow-up for maintenance of treatment gains can be examined. Finally, objective monitoring of home relaxation practice will allow researchers and clinicians to separate compliance issues from questions of relaxation efficacy and thereby more precisely determine the effectiveness of relaxation for various clinical disorders.

References

Hoelscher, T.J., Lichstein, K.L., & Rosenthal, T.L. (1984). Objective vs subjective assessment of relaxation compliance among anxious individuals. *Behaviour Research and Therapy, 22,* 187-193.

Hoelscher, T.J., Lichstein, K.L., & Rosenthal, T.L. (1986). Home relaxation practice in hypertension treatment: Objective assessment and compliance induction. *Journal of Consulting and Clinical Psychology, 54,* 217-221

Lichstein, K.L., & Hoelscher, T.J. (1986). A device for unobtrusive surveillance of home relaxation practice. *Behavior Modification, 10,* 219-233.

Martin, J.E., Collins, F.L. Jr., Hillenberg, J.B., Zabin, M.A., & Katell, A.D. (1981). Assessing compliance to home relaxation: A simple technology for a critical problem. *Journal of Behavioral Assessment, 3,* 193-197.

Taylor, C.B., Agras, W.S., Schneider, J.A., & Allen, R.A. (1983). Adherence to instructions to practice relaxation exercises. *Journal of Consulting and Clinical Psychology, 51,* 952-953.

Reprimand Assessment Scale

Ron Van Houten and Ahmos Rolider

Description

The Reprimand Assessment Scale is designed to evaluate the frequency, intensity, and appropriateness of reprimands. This technique involves the use of a partial interval recording procedure over a 20-minute assessment period. This instrument will allow assessment for the presence of various components known to influence the efficacy of reprimands as well as determination of whether reprimands are being employed in appropriate circumstances. The observation period is divided into 8- to 10-second observation intervals. Each 10-second observation interval is followed by a 5-second recording interval. The observer is typically cued to observe and record the target behaviors through instructions played back over an audiocassette (i.e., "observe 1, record 1 ...").

Reprimands are scored within three major categories: verbal, nonverbal, and appropriateness. The verbal and nonverbal categories are further subdivided into several subcategories. A reprimand incident can be scored for more than one subcategory. Verbal aspects can be scored in one of three categories: (a) Specific: Statements instructing someone to cease a behavior or not to repeat it, such as, "Billy, stop hitting your brother" or "Johnny, never touch those papers again." (b) Affective: Statements indicating a dislike for a particular behavior, such as: "Susan, I don't like it when you do that" or "Jim, that makes me mad." (c) Brief Nonspecific: Nonspecific reprimands that are not affective in context, such as "Stop that right now" or "Cut it out." It includes single word utterances, such as, "Hey," "What," or "Stop," which are delivered to stop a behavior.

Verbal reprimands are also scored for tone of voice. A reprimand is scored as firm if the voice pitch is low (relative to the individual's normal pitch) and if the words are spoken distinctly.

Nonverbal disapproval can be scored in one of four categories: (a) Eye Contact: Eye contact is scored whenever the person delivering the reprimand makes eye contact with the target individual for the entire reprimand. (b) Stare: Stare is scored whenever sustained eye contact involves a furrowed brow. Eye contact must be maintained for at least 3 seconds. (c) Firm Grasp: Firm grasp is scored whenever the person delivering the reprimand grasps the persons shoulder(s), arm(s), or head while delivering the reprimand. Holding the chin with finger(s) or grasping the chin is also scored for firm grasp. Soft touches or rubbing is not scored as a firm grasp or is shaking the child or squeezing very hard. (d) Gesture: A gesture is scored whenever the person delivering the reprimand makes any of the following gestures: points a finger, holds up an open palm as to indicate stop, wags the index finger from side to side, or turns their head from side to side.

Each time any of the foregoing categories or verbal or nonverbal reprimands are scored, the observer also indicates whether the reprimand followed inappropriate behavior. Inappropriate behavior may either be jointly defined along with the parent or teacher who is going to be observed before using the scale, or the observer could use his or her own definition of inappropriate behavior based on generally accepted standards for the setting involved. This measure allows assessment of whether the parent or teacher's reprimand responses are under appropriate stimulus control.

Purpose

The Reprimand Assessment Scale was devised to assess both reprimand use as well as whether reprimands were employed effectively. This measure was originally developed to study teacher reprimands to determine what factors influence their effectiveness. Data indicated that disapproval tended to be most effective with children (aged 2 to 12 years) when it was specific, firm, involved eye contact including a hard stare, and firm contact (Van Houten & Doleys, 1983; Van Houten, Nau, MacKenzie-Keating, Sameoto, & Calavecchia, 1982).

Psychometric Characteristics

With this type of observational instrument, independent observers must be able to obtain at least 70% agreement on the occurrence of each category. Independent observers should not influence each other in any way. Both observers must have a clear view of the parent or teacher to score nonverbal behaviors. Van Houten et al. (1982) obtained interobserver agreement scores of 73% and better.

Clinical Use

The Reprimand Assessment Scale can be employed to assess how effectively parents or teachers use reprimands as well as the overall frequency of reprimand use. Measures of verbal content, firmness, and nonverbal aspects allow for assessment of overall skill level, whereas the measure of appropriateness allows assessment of whether the parent or teacher can effectively discriminate the appropriate occasions for reprimand use.

Future Directions

As more is discovered about factors that influence the effective use of reprimands, the scale should be updated to reflect new data.

References

Van Houten, R., & Doleys, D.M. (1983). Are social reprimands effective? In S. Axelrod & S. Apsche (Eds.), *The effects of punishment on human behavior*. New York: Academic Press.

Van Houten, R., Nau, P.A., MacKenzie-Keating, S.E., Sameoto, D., & Calavecchia, B. (1982). An analysis of some variables influencing the effectiveness of reprimands. *Journal of Applied Behavior Analysis, 15*, 65-83.

Resident Disruptive Behavior

V. Mark Durand

Description

Included under the general rubric of Resident Disruptive Behavior is a plethora of problematic behaviors exhibited by persons in residential settings. These include various forms of aggressive behaviors (e.g., hitting, biting, and pushing), self-injurious behaviors (e.g., head banging, hair pulling, and face slapping), stereotyped behaviors (e.g., hand flapping and rocking), tantrums (e.g., screaming and stamping feet), property destruction, pica, psychotic speech, and noncompliance (Durand, 1983). The selection of specific behaviors to be included in this category often depends on the expectations of staff and the environment (Evans & Meyer, 1985). Therefore, stereotyped hand clapping can be seen as "disruptive" if it interferes with academic tasks, but it might be viewed as appropriate if it is in response to music.

Purpose

The presence of disruptive behavior is often a major obstacle to the habilitation and placement of persons with handicaps in community settings (Durand, 1983). Therefore, assessing resident disruptive behavior has been a major focus of a number of research investigations. Resident disruptive behavior has been assessed to correlate its presence with other variables (e.g., age, gender, and communication skills), to evaluate specific treatment interventions (e.g., time-out and dietary changes), and to evaluate global changes in residential environments (e.g., deinstitutionalization and changes in staff use of leave). With recent trends towards removing persons with handicaps from large institutions, accurate assessment of resident disruptive behavior is becoming increasingly important.

Development

In a review of articles between 1965 and 1984 on resident disruptive behavior, a majority of these reports (21 of 32) relied on developing idiosyncratic definitions of disruptive behavior. They used either informal observations or staff reports to develop definitions of disruptive behavior that were presumably unique to their subjects. Less than half (11 of 32) used any standardized measure for assessing disruptive behavior. Therefore, it seems that definitions of resident disruptive behavior have generally been subject to the vagaries of the investigator.

The most frequently cited formal device (6 of 32) used to assess disruptive behavior was the AAMD Adaptive Behavior Scale. Other devices that assess the presence of resident disruptive behavior include the Hand Test, the Disability Assessment Schedule, the New York Developmental Disabilities Information System, and the Vineland Adaptive Behavior Scales.

Psychometric Characteristics

Researchers who rely on idiosyncratic definitions of disruptive behavior calculate interobserver agreement scores for their data, and these have generally been high (Durand, 1983). However, traditional psychometric data (e.g., test-retest reliability) are typically not collected on these measures.

The AAMD Adaptive Behavior Scale (Nihira, Foster, Shellhaas, & Leland, 1974) includes 13 categories of disruptive behavior (e.g., violent and destructive behavior, antisocial behavior, and self-abusive behavior). Reliability data are typically high for this instrument, but no normative data are available for the disruptive behavior scales. A new instrument (Vineland Adaptive Behavior Scales; Sparrow, Balla, & Cicchetti, 1984) has been introduced that assesses resident disruptive behavior and has extensive normative data on these behaviors. The Vineland Adaptive Behavior Scales may be the most useful formal instrument for assessing resident disruptive behavior.

Clinical Use

Idiosyncratic definitions of resident disruptive behavior can be useful in monitoring the effects of treatments on specific client behaviors. However, using these definitions of disruptive behavior can limit comparisons across clients. Investigations employing idiosyncratic definitions are often observing different behaviors, limiting generalizations about the effects of treatments or other manipulations. Including data from a standardized measure such as the Adaptive Behavior Scale provides comparative information on disruptive behavior as well as data on other populations (e.g., nonresidential clients).

Using only standardized definitions for resident disruptive behavior is also limiting, however. Difficulties may arise in interpreting changes from the broad categories of behavior provided by some scales (e.g., Violent and Destructive Behavior). For example, intervention may result in decreases in one form of violent and destructive behavior (e.g., damages other's property), but it may produce a concurrent increase in a second form (e.g., threatens or does physical violence). Although no change would be recorded on the scale in this instance, this does not adequately represent the effect of the intervention. Therefore, specific, idiosyncratic definitions may be useful for more molecular analyses. It is therefore recommended that formal definitions of resident disruptive behavior be used in addition to idiosyncratic definitions.

Future Directions

A limitation of both standardized and idiosyncratic definitions lies in the lack of contextual information provided. These assessment methods do not allow for distinction between acceptable and unacceptable responses to certain settings (Evans & Meyer, 1985). For example, physical aggression is universally considered a form of disruptive behavior. However, pushing other residents to escape from being punched or kicked may be acceptable, whereas pushing staff to escape from daily chores is not. One solution to this problem is to gather information on the *function* of resident disruptive behavior (see Motivation Assessment Scale). Therefore, a determination of acceptability could be based on a behavior's function or use. Similarly, social validity data on the acceptability of certain behaviors would also provide valuable information for researchers and clinicians (Durand, 1982) (see Social Validation). Future work in the behavioral assessment of disruptive behavior should focus on an evaluation of the contextual determinants of these behaviors and the role of this information in treatment selection and success.

References

Durand, V.M. (1982). Analysis and intervention of self-injurious behavior. *Journal of the Association for the Severely Handicapped, 7,* 44-53.

Durand, V.M. (1983). Behavioral ecology of a staff incentive program: Effects on absenteeism and resident disruptive behavior. *Behavior Modification, 7,* 165-181.

Evans, I.M., & Meyer, L.H. (1985). *An educative approach to behavior problems.* Baltimore, MD: Paul H. Brookes.

Nihira, K., Foster, R., Shellhaas, B., & Leland, H. (1974). *Adaptive behavior scale.* Washington, DC: American Association on Mental Deficiency.

Restraint Scale: Assessment of Dieting

Janet Polivy, C. Peter Herman, and Kenneth I. Howard

Description

The Restraint Scale (Restrained Eating Questionnaire) is a 10-item self-report questionnaire assessing weight fluctuations, degrees of chronic dieting, and related attitudes toward weight and eating. All questions are multiple-choice in format, with either four or five possible response options. Each item is scored 0, 1, 2, or 3 (five items) or 0, 1, 3, or 4 (five items), with no reverse-keyed items. Scores may thus range from 0 to 35. In addition, the questionnaire as administered typically contains five additional, unscored items assessing age, sex, height, weight, and maximum weight ever. The scale is easily administered to large groups of individuals and takes 5 minutes or less to complete. The questionnaire is usually entitled the "Eating Habits Questionnaire" to deemphasize its focus on dieting.

Purpose

The Restraint Scale was developed to identify individuals who are chronically concerned about their weight and who attempt (however successfully) to control or reduce it through dieting. The scale does not measure the degree of success at weight reduction, or deviation from a defended (or set-point) for body weight. However, because both current and maximum weight are included, a crude estimate of success at weight loss may be calculated, particularly in light of the last scored question on scale, which assesses how far above ideal weight one's maximum weight is or was. Therefore, the purpose of the Restraint Scale is to assess a *chronic* tendency to think about and try to control one's weight by curtailing intake. The emphasis on "chronic" is intentional, because the scale was developed to measure an enduring disposition; questions are phrased in terms of the respondent's usual behavior, rather than his or her status at the precise moment of administration. Therefore, it is possible that a person's score might not reflect his or her acute concern (or lack of concern) about dieting, although the two tend to be highly correlated. For research purposes, investigators must decide whether a chronic concern with dieting is an adequate discriminator, or whether acute dieting status should also be assessed.

Development

The scale was originally developed in 1973 and was refined in a series of studies (see Herman & Polivy, 1980, for a review) intended to establish parallels between normal weight dieters and obese persons. It was initially assumed that chronic dieting might provide an indirect measure of the extent to which an individual maintained a weight below body-weight set point, but it soon became evident that concern with weight loss and even chronic engagement in dieting did not bear much relation to successful weight loss. Therefore, the scale now is seen more conservatively as a measure of dieting attitudes and behaviors, rather than as a measure of actual weight suppression. Indeed, it has been argued that dieters may occasionally achieve weights well above set point (Polivy & Herman, 1983).

Early versions of the scale varied in the number of items, only some of which were scored in a strict multiple-choice format. Because some items, mainly those involving weight fluctuation, could exert undue influence on total score, the scale was administered to over 500 college students and a series of psychometric analyses was performed to render the scale more uniform and reliable (see below). The current version of the scale, sometimes called the Revised Restraint Scale, incorporates the improvements based on the 1976 psychometric exercise.

Psychometric Characteristics

The original Restraint Scale was administered to 166 male and 348 female college students for purposes of psychometric evaluation. Although the item-total and item-item correlations were good, a new, limited, multiple-choice scoring scheme was developed, and one item, which did not seem to provide true ordinal data, was eliminated. Subjects' scores on each item were converted to the new scoring scheme, and item-total and item-item correlations were computed. Item-item correlations were again good, with only one item (Item 5) correlating negatively with any other items (for males $r = .005$ with Item 3 and .127 with Item 4; for females, $r = .068$ with Item 4). The item-total correlations ranged from .303 to .676 for male subjects and from .413 to .777 for female subjects. The scale thus displays adequate internal reliability.

As an additional test of internal reliability, we placed ones in the major diagonals of a 10 by 10 matrix and factor analyzed the scores for male and female subjects separately. The first unrotated factor accounted for 28% of the variance for male and 32% for female subjects. The fact that the first principal components were so high indicates that the scale may be considered unifactorial (more so for female subjects). Correlations of each item with the first principal component, the equivalent of item-total correlations of each item with an idealized restraint construct, confirm that the first principal component is stable. The loadings of all items on the first principal component are high (for male subjects: .72, .59, .53, .39, .34, .34, .41, .69, .32, and .72; for female subjects: .81, .61, .51, .29, .49, .45, .62, .77, .51, and .74), confirming that the scale may be interpreted as unidimensional.

An orthogonal varimax rotation provided two factors; the second factor accounted for 16% of the variance for male subjects and 14% for female subjects. The two-factor solution was the same for males and females, with the first factor comprising items 1, 5, 6, 7, 8, and 9, and the second factor comprising items 2, 3, and 4, with item 11 loading on both factors. (Note: Item 10 on the questionnaire as usually presented is not scored.) The first factor seems to represent diet-related cognitions, whereas the second factor reflects mainly weight fluctuations. Subsequent factor analyses by various investigators with different samples have confirmed these two factors with only minor variations. Therefore, although the Restraint Scale may be seen (and used) as unifactorial, a two-factor solution is also reliable. Research using the two factors separately as predictors has shown that sometimes one factor predicts "restrained" behavior, whereas sometimes the other does; neither factor alone seems superior to the entire scale.

The test-retest reliability of the Restraint Scale was also evaluated and proved satisfactory ($r = .93$ over the course of 1 week); considering the nature of the questionnaire items, this result is not surprising. In conclusion, the Restraint Scale has demonstrated internal and temporal reliability in addition to its predictive validity. (See Herman & Polivy, 1980, or Polivy & Herman, 1983, for extensive reviews.)

Norms for males and females differ, with males scoring consistently lower than females on average. Most experimental studies contrasting the behavior of restrained and unrestrained subjects have used median splits to differentiate subject groups, with separate medians calculated for males and females. The logic underlying sex-segregated median splits is debatable. In any event, for female college students, the median is typically around 15 or 16. Fewer studies have employed male subjects, but in those that do, the median seems to be about 12.

Clinical Use

The Restraint Scale has been used with anorexic and bulimic patients as well as with obese patients in treatment. Our experience is that more restrained obese patients have more rather than less difficulty in losing weight. Likewise, anorexic and bulimic patients with higher restraint scores seem to be more pathological than those with lower scores. Moreover, we have argued that elevated restraint scores (indicative of chronic dieting) predispose susceptible individuals to bulimia (Polivy & Herman, 1985).

The Restraint Scale is used less frequently with identified clinical populations than as a tool to identify "normal" college students who exhibit the aberrant behavior often associated with "normal" dieting. High scoring students are more likely to: (a) "counter regulate" (i.e., eat more after a large forced preload than after a small load or none), (b) eat more when emotionally stressed, (c) overeat when they feel "intoxicated," (d) overreact emotionally to affective stimuli, and (e) become more easily distracted during cognitive tasks. The latter two effects are exaggerations of normal reactions, but the first three are actually opposite to the pattern found in nondieters.

Future Directions

There are many unanswered questions on the nature of dieters' behavior and how it differs from that of nondieters. Restrained eaters exhibit many unusual behavioral characteristics, some with respect to eating, some more general. Reliable description of these patterns, not to mention adequate theoretical accounts of their "etiology," could keep a researcher busy for the forseeable future. It seems clear that complete understanding of the peculiarities of dieters' eating behavior will require analysis of their cognitive assessment of the eating situation. Accounting for emotional and social reactions will probably require a deeper analysis of a dieter's entire personality structure than has heretofore been attempted. Extensions to clinical populations (e.g., persons with anorexia or bulimia) will perforce require a degree of sophistication commensurate with the subtle blend of pathologies that underly these disorders. Any complete analysis of the "disorders of dieting" will no doubt require an understanding of the social and cultural pressures that are so salient for young women in particular; moreover, the manner in which such pressures are transmitted through family and peer structures must be analyzed. Determining why some persons become obsessed with dieting whereas others do not will require consideration of factors both inside and outside the "victim." Physiological factors may play a contributory role. The problem posed by "dieting disorders" will not lend itself to easy solution until it is better formulated than it currently is and until dieting is recognized as an activity that cannot be undertaken without producing ramifications, some unexpectedly problematic, significantly affecting the dieter's body and mind.

References

Herman, C.P., & Polivy, J. (1980). Restrained eating. In A.J. Stundard (Ed.), *Obesity*. Philadelphia: W.B. Saunders.

Polivy, J., & Herman, C.P. (1983). *Breaking the diet habit: The natural weight alternative*. New York: Basic Books.

Polivy, J., & Herman, C.P. (1985). Dieting and bingeing: A casual analysis. *American Psychologist, 40*, 193-201.

Reward Computation Worksheet

William G. Johnson and April H. Crusco

Description

The Reward Computation Worksheet is a checklist used to monitor performance in a weight reduction program (Johnson & Stalonas, 1981). Initially, six discrete behaviors are monitored daily. Participants progress through the program in a stepwise, criterion-referenced fashion until a total of 16 behaviors are monitored in the final phase. The specific behaviors assessed include: (a) recording food intake, (b) daily exercise, (c) uncontrolled eating episodes (snacks), (d) eating in designated areas, (e) making the designated eating area distinctive, (f) refraining from other activities while eating, (g) separating links of the eating chain into distinctive units, (h) taking a 2-minute pause mid-meal and stopping if full, (i) limiting liquid intake during meals, (j) eating one serving of each food, (k) graphing daily exercise and uncontrolled eating episodes, (l) inhibiting eating urges with aversive imagery, (m) monitoring caloric intake, (n) being assertive in food-related situations, (o) replacing negative cognitions with positive ones, and (p) using strategies to inhibit impulsive or emotional eating.

Point values are associated with each behavior, and criterion point levels are established to evaluate daily and weekly performance. The participant or therapist, or both, can award points, and criterion levels must be met before progressing to the next set of therapeutic recommendations.

Purpose

The Reward Computation Worksheet is used to monitor behavioral progress in a weight reduction program and to evaluate whether weight control is mediated by performing the behaviors targeted in the treatment program. The instrument also offers daily and weekly feedback on performance standards.

Development

The Reward Computation Worksheet was developed over the course of several experimental and clinical studies on the effective components of behavioral weight reduction programs as well as the applicability of such instrumentations in clinical settings (Stalonas, Johnson, & Christ, 1978; Johnson, Stalonas, Christ, & Polk, 1979).

Psychometric Characteristics

Sandifer and Buchanan (1983) correlated 13 behaviors on the Reward Computation Worksheet with weight loss of participants who completed a weight reduction program. All 13 behaviors were significantly correlated with weight reduction. Pausing for 2 minutes at mid-meal, chaining the sequence of eating behaviors, and limiting oneself to one serving reached the highest levels of significance ($p < .001$). Moreover, the results of a stepwise, multiple regression indicated that 11 of the 13 behaviors on the Reward Computation Worksheet accounted for 87.5% of the variance in weight reduction.

Additionally, family members periodically rated six behaviors on the Reward Computation Worksheet, and correlations of these ratings with ratings made by participants achieved significance ($p < .005$). Ratings by family members also correlated with weight reduction ($p < .005$).

Clinical Use

The Reward Computation Worksheet can be used by participants or therapists, or both, to monitor progress. It also provides a medium for feedback on progress using comparison standards. Lastly, the worksheet can identify which specific program behaviors are correlated with weight loss.

Future Directions

Results collected thus far indicate that performance of the treatment program behaviors assessed on the Reward Computation Worksheet is significantly related to weight loss. Currently, a computer program is being written that will generate individual participant profiles with the capacity to analyze performance.

References

Johnson, W.G., & Stalonas, P.M. (1981). *Weight no longer*. Gretna, LA: Pelican.

Johnson, W.G., Stalonas, P.M., Christ, M., & Pock, S. (1979). The development and evaluation of a behavioral weight reduction program. *International Journal of Obesity, 3,* 229-238.

Sandifer, B.A., & Buchanan, W.L. (1983). Relationship between adherence and weight loss in a behavioral weight reduction program. *Behavior Therapy, 14,* 682-688.

Stalonas, P.M., Johnson, W.G., & Christ, M. (1978). Behavior modification for obesity: The evaluation of exercise, contingency management and program adherence. *Journal of Consulting and Clinical Psychology, 46,* 463-469

Reynolds Adolescent Depression Scale

William M. Reynolds

Description

The Reynolds Adolescent Depression Scale (RADS, Reynolds, 1986a) is a self-report inventory designed to measure the depth of depressive symptoms in adolescents aged 12 through 18. The RADS consists of 30 items and uses a 4-point Likert-type ("almost never" to "most of the time") response format. The RADS was developed specifically for use with adolescents. Item content reflects symptoms specified by the Diagnostic and Statistical Manual for Mental Disorder, Third Edition (DSM-III, American Psychiatric Association, 1980) for major depression and dysthymic disorder, as well as additional symptoms described by Carlson and Strober (1979) in their study of unipolar depression in adolescents. The RADS items evaluate somatic, behavioral, cognitive, mood, and vegetative components of depression. Items are worded so that reading is not a confounding variable for normal high school students. In research with learning disabled or mentally retarded adolescents, the RADS can be verbally presented. As a self-report measure, it requires approximately 10 minutes to complete. Overall, the RADS is a quick, easy to administer measure of severity of depressive symptoms in adolescents.

Purpose

The RADS was developed for use in school and clinical settings as both an individual and a screening measure of depression. Epidemiological investigations of depression in adolescents suggest base rates for clinically relevant levels of depressive symptoms ranging from 9 to 16% (Reynolds, 1985). The availability of reliable and valid measures is prerequisite to the systematic study and treatment of this disorder in adolescents. The RADS was designed to meet this need, particularly in school-based populations, in which the lack of identification and self-referral contributes to the problematic nature of this disorder in adolescents.

Development

Development of the RADS was begun in 1981 as a response to the lack of measures designed to assess depression in adolescents. Item development was based on symptoms specified by DSM-III for major depression and dysthmyic disorder as well as additional symptoms delineated by Carlson and Strober (1979). The initial version of the RADS consisted of 32 items. Two items were subsequently removed after field testing because of low item with total score correlations. Validation and normative studies of the RADS were conducted between 1981 and 1985 and included over 7,000 adolescents.

In addition to extensive reliability and validity investigations conducted as part of the development process, development of the RADS also included its utilization in a number of clinical applications. These included formal use as a screening measure in a multiple-stage model for the identification of depressed adolescents in school settings (Reynolds, 1986b). The RADS has also been used as a treatment outcome measure in an experimental treatment study that examined cognitive-behavioral and relaxation training treatments for depression in adolescents (Reynolds & Coats, 1986).

Psychometric Characteristics

Reliability. Reliability of the RADS has been examined from the perspective of internal consistency and temporal stability. Internal consistency estimates (coefficient alpha) have been uniformly high (.92 to .96) with different samples of normal and depressed adolescents ranging in size from 126 to 2,460. In a study of 26 mildly retarded adolescents, the r was .87 (Reynolds & Miller, 1985). Overall, the internal consistency findings support homogeneity of item content on the RADS.

The determination of stability (or replicability) of measurement is more complex, especially when dealing with depression, because depression is not viewed as a trait. However, the expectancy is that over short periods there should be replicability of measurement. The test-retest reliability with a sample of 126 adolescents and a 6-week interval between testings was .84, which is viewed as acceptable given the nature of the construct assessed. A 12-week test-retest reliability coefficient of .81 was also found for the RADS.

Validity. The validity of the RADS has been established in studies using bivariate and multivariate procedures to examine relationships with other depression scales and measures of related constructs. A synopsis of these results is provided in the RADS Manual (Reynolds, 1986a). To summarize, the RADS has been highly correlated with other self-report measures of depression, including the Beck Depression Inventory (BDI), Center for Epidemiological Studies-Depression Scale (CES-D), and the Zung Self-Rating Depression Scale, with r's ranging from .71 to .89. With a sample of 1,054 younger adolescents aged 12 to 14 years, a correlation of .70 was found between the RADS and the Children's Depression Inventory. Although these correlations are high, their interpretation may be somewhat attenuated by their common method variance.

For the measurement of depression, the structured clinical interview is considered the most sensitive and selective assessment methodology. Of the available interview measures for depression, a standard in the field and the most commonly used outcome measure in psychiatric studies of depression is the Hamilton Clinician Rating Scale. In the study of 126 adolescents, individual Hamilton interviews were administered to all subjects with trained interviewers (five) who were blind to subjects' scores on the self-report measures. On the

first assessment with both the RADS and the Hamilton scale, the correlation between the two measures was .83. This can be considered high given that the RADS is a brief paper-and-pencil self-report measure and the Hamilton is a 30- to 40-minute individual interview. Both measures were readministered to subjects 12 weeks later, with interviewers assessing different subjects from time 1 and once again blind to subjects' test scores. On this administration, the correlation between scales was .84, cross-validating the initial finding.

In addition to these analyses, a multiple regression analysis was computed using Hamilton interview scores as the dependent variable and the RADS and BDI as independent variables. Of interest were the beta coefficients for the RADS and BDI. These were meaningful from the perspective of validity, because the BDI has been a standard in self-report assessment of depression in adults. Regression analysis produced betas of .55 between the RADS and Hamilton ($F = 24.87$), and .31 ($F = 7.95$) between the BDI and Hamilton. These results also suggest the validity of the RADS as a measure of depression in adolescents.

Normative Information. Normative data on the RADS was collected in over 8,000 adolescents from the country. Subjects were from senior and junior high schools in surburban/urban and suburban/rural communities, with a wide range of socioeconomic levels and at least one racially integrated community. Because of the nature of the construct assessed, the use of different norm groups is debatable. Norms for the RADS currently consist of percentile ranks for the total sample and grade and sex groups based on the raw score total. For clinical purposes a cutoff score was developed to designate a clinically relevant level of symptom severity. Little variability has been found in mean scores on the RADS across relatively large nonclinical (i.e., school-based) samples of adolescents (samples ranging from 665 to 2,460). In addition, investigation of developmental differences in a sample of 2,460 adolescents aged 12 through 18 found a correlation of .03 between RADS and age. A three-way grade by sex by race ANOVA of RADS scores in a sample of 2,019 adolescents that included 992 male and 1,027 female subjects, 1,610 white and 409 black high school students resulted in significant main effects for grade ($F = 7.86$, $p < .001$) and sex ($F = 72.72$, $p < .001$) but not for race ($F = .01$, $p < .90$). There was also a small but significant grade by sex interaction ($F = 2.21, p < .05$). A consistent sex difference is found on the RADS, with girls endorsing greater depressive symptoms. In summary, a substantial amount of demographic and normative information has been collected on the RADS.

Clinical Use

The RADS has been used in a number of clinical investigations. As noted, Reynolds and Coats (1986) used the RADS as one of several outcome measures to assess the efficacy of psychologically based treatments for depression in adolescents. The RADS also has clinical use as a screening measure for the identification of depressed adolescents in school settings. In this application the RADS is used in the first two stages of a three-tiered assessment procedure for identifying depressed adolescents in school.

It should be noted that the RADS is not designed to provide a formal diagnosis of depression as delineated by DSM-III or Research Diagnostic Criteria. A cutoff score, designed to signify a clinically relevant level of severity of depression, has been developed on the basis of the bivariate distribution of RADS and Hamilton scores. This cutoff provides for the designation of a clinical level of depressive symptom severity and is not considered a classification or diagnostic label.

Future Directions

In addition to studies of reliability and validity, a number of research investigations have been conducted with the RADS. These studies include: epidemiological investigations; studies of descriptive psychopathology examining developmental, race, and sex differences; a longitudinal and cross-sectional (sequential) study of depression now in its third year of data collection; studies of stressful life events and depression in adolescents; a treatment study comparing cognitive-behavior therapy and relaxation training to a wait-list control condition; studies of depression in mentally retarded adolescents; a repeated measures study examining the course of depressive symptoms in adolescents over the academic year; correlational studies examining the RADS and measures of self-esteem, anxiety, loneliness, and related constructs; and other investigations.

Research with the RADS is continuing. The RADS currently is the only measure of depression developed specifically for adolescents. Results obtained so far suggest that the RADS is a reliable and valid measure of depressive symptoms in adolescents. This combined with the substantial normative sample and the increasing research base supports the clinical and research use of the RADS. The RADS is a psychometrically sound measure for which there is a growing need. Future research with the RADS needs to focus on special populations of adolescents, especially emotional and conduct-disordered individuals. In addition, the relationship between depression and substance abuse is a very viable avenue of research with the RADS, given the likelihood that for some adolescents, their drug and/or alcohol use may represent a self-treatment for depression.

References

Carlson, G., & Strober, M. (1979). Affective disorders in adolescence. *Psychiatric Clinics of North America, 2*, 511-526.

Reynolds, W.M. (1985). Depression in childhood and adolescence: Diagnosis, assessment, intervention strategies and research. In T.R. Kratochwill (Ed.), *Advances in school psychology, Vol. 4.* (pp. 133-189). Hillsdale, NJ: Lawrence Erlbaum.

Reynolds, W.M. (1986a). *Reynolds Adolescent Depression Scale.* Odessa, FL: Psychological Assessment Resources.

Reynolds, W.M. (1986b). A model for the screening and identification of depressed children and adolescents in school settings. *Professional School Psychology, 1,* 117-129.

Reynolds, W.M. & Coats, K.I. (1986). A comparison of cognitive behavioral therapy and relaxation training for the treatment of depression in adolescents. *Journal of Consulting and Clinical Psychology, 54,* 653-660.

Reynolds, W.M., & Miller, K.L. (1985). Depression and learned helplessness in mentally retarded and nonretarded adolescents: An initial investigation. *Applied Research in Mental Retardation, 6,* 295-307.

Riboflavin Tracer Technique for Assessment of Medication Compliance

Patricia A. Cluss

Description

This technique for assessing mediation compliance behavior involves the use of a riboflavin tracer or marker that is added to a patient's (or subject's) medication. Riboflavin (vitamin B^2), which is nontoxic, water-soluble, and freely excreted, fluoresces in the urine when a sample is placed under ultra-violet light, making this a safe and effective sub-stance for use in a method designed to test day-to-day compliance behavior.

The vitamin is added to evening doses of pre-scribed medication. The first morning urine samples are collected and tested for fluorescence, its presence indicating compliance with the pre-vious evening's dose. This method may be used by professionals concerned with accurate measure-ment of compliance for clinical or research pur-poses. Moreover, it is simple enough to be employed by parents, using an inexpensive "black light," in behavioral programs aimed at targeting and improving compliance in children with chronic disease.

Purpose

It is well established that adherence to medication regimens among patients requiring long-term treatment is poor: approximately 54% (Sackett & Snow, 1979). Although many researchers have attempted to target and modify compliance prob-lems, a major difficulty in this research has been the lack of accurate compliance assessment methods, because self-report data, data inferred from thera-peutic outcome, pill and bottle counts, and serum and urine assays all have their disadvantages as accurate measures of daily compliance patterns (Epstein & Cluss, 1982).

We have attempted to develop compliance assessment methods that can be employed by parents at home as part of a behavioral treatment package focusing on improving compliance in chil-dren with chronic disease. The home monitoring of medicine compliance facilitates parental decisions about when to provide positive reinforcement for compliance or punishment for noncompliance. In the development of this technique, we specifically focused on the adaptation of a riboflavin tracer method for asthmatic children on regimens of daily theophylline. Riboflavin has been used previously as a tracer substance in several studies (e.g., VA Cooperative Study Group, 1970).

Development

Three studies were designed to determine the applicability of home monitoring methods for use in a home-based behavioral program targeting chil-dren's medication compliance (Cluss & Epstein, 1984). Questions to be answered included what

dose of riboflavin was necessary for accurate assess-ment by inspection of urine specimens, whether the vitamin B^2 present in a regular diet was enough to cause a high percentage of false-positive results, whether inexpensive, easy-to-use equipment was available for use at home, and whether lay adults could detect accurately the presence of riboflavin in urine samples.

The initial study addressed the last question. Six healthy adult volunteers ingested various doses of vitamin B^2 (2.5, 5, 10, 25, and 50 mg) or placebo at night over a 10-day period and collected first morn-ing urine samples each day. These adults were trained briefly in the method of determining fluorescence/nonfluorescence of urine samples with a black light similar to those purchased by ado-lescents to make day-glow posters fluoresce, and then rated their own samples. Subjects were cor-rect in determining fluorescence and nonfluor-escence (verified by the experimenter with a short-wave ultraviolet light) 73% of the time ($p < .025$). Accuracy was higher when larger (10 mg or more) doses of vitamin B^2 had been ingested. "Spillover" of fluorescence from the largest (50 mg) dose into urine collected 2 mornings later appeared to occur in 80% of cases.

Study II was designed to refine further this tech-nique for use with children. Six healthy children who were not taking vitamin supplements con-sumed their normal diet and collected one bedtime urine sample immediately before ingesting a cap-sule containing 10 mg of vitamin B^2. Next morning first void urines were collected, refrigerated, and returned to the experimenter. Eleven samples were available for assessment. All five collected at bedtime after consumption of a normal diet were nonfluorescent, as determined by the experi-menter, indicating the absence of any detectable amounts of riboflavin. All six samples collected the morning after vitamin B^2 ingestion were fluor-escent. Nine lay adults were asked to assess these samples for fluorescence with a black light. Of 99 judgments, 87 were correct (88% accuracy, $p < .001$).

In the third study, the rate of fluorescence spill-over from one 24-hour period to the next in chil-dren taking riboflavin was assessed. Five healthy children who ate their normal diets and who refrained from taking over-the-counter vitamin supplements ingested 10 mg of riboflavin at bed-time on Days 1 and 3 of the study, took nothing on Days 2 and 4, and collected first void urine samples on Days 2 through 5.

Of 19 specimens returned to the experimenter, all but one were fluorescent the morning after B[2] ingestion and nonfluorescent the morning after no B[2] had been ingested. The one "incorrect" sample was still minimally fluorescent when no vitamin had been consumed the night before. Ten lay adults judged fluorescence of the 18 "correct" samples; of 180 judgments, 169 were accurate (94% accuracy, $p < .001$).

These three studies demonstrated that relatively untrained adults can detect the presence of riboflavin in the urine with an inexpensive black light for ingested doses of 10 to 50 mg for adults and 10 mg for children. A 50-mg dose causes spillover of fluorescence in 80% of samples for adults; a 10-mg dose for children produces spillover and therefore, false-positive results for compliance in approximately 5% of cases. A normal diet does not appear to contain enough vitamin B[2] to cause detectable fluorescence in the urine of adults or children.

Psychometric Characteristics

The reliability and validity of this method as a useful assessment tool for determining compliance behavior were studied over a 2-week period with a sample of 22 chronic asthmatic children on daily regimens of theophylline. Ten milligrams of riboflavin were added to bedtime capsules of this medication and fluorescence of first morning urine samples was determined by two independent raters. Interrater agreement on fluorescence and nonfluorescence of these samples was 96%.

The sample was divided into compliant (<79% fluorescent urine samples) and noncompliant (<80% fluorescence) subgroups. Noncompliant subjects reported more wheezing days, showed more variable lung functioning, recorded lower peak flow rates, and were significantly more likely to have been wheezing on the day of an office visit than were their more compliant peers (Cluss, Epstein, Galvis, Fireman, & Friday, 1984), thus demonstrating the validity and clinical relevance of this method of assessment.

Clinical Use and Future Directions

Although this technique was developed as a research tool, its usefulness in determining behavioral differences among asthmatic children that are clinically meaningful has been established. Future refinements of this method could include development of a package to be used by practicing physicians as an in-office method of determining

day-to-day compliance and/or the development of riboflavin doses based on the patient's weight for more accurate detection of compliance and minimization of the risk of spillover.

References

Cluss, P.A., & Epstein, L.H. (1984). A riboflavin tracer method for assessment of medication compliance in children. *Behavior Research Methods, Instruments, and Computers, 16,* 444-446.

Cluss, P.A., Epstein, L.H., Galvis, S.A., Fireman, P., & Friday, G. (1984). Effect of compliance for chronic asthmatic children. *Journal of Consulting and Clinical Psychology, 52,* 909-910.

Epstein, L.H., & Cluss, P.A. (1982). A behavioral medicine perspective on adherence to long-term medical regimens. *Journal of Consulting and Clinical Psychology, 50,* 950-971.

Sackett, D.L., & Snow, J.C. (1979). The magnitude of compliance and noncompliance. In R.B. Haynes, D.W. Taylor, & D.L. Hackett (Eds.), *Compliance in health care.* Baltimore, MD: Johns Hopkins Press.

Veterans' Administration Cooperative Study Group on Antihypertensive Agents (1970). Effects of treatment on mortality in hypertension: Results in patients with diastolic blood pressure averaging 90 through 114 mm Hg. *Journal of the American Medical Association, 213,* 1143-1152.

Role-Playing Assessment Instruments

Stephen B. Fawcett

Description

In role-playing assessment, a consistent set of probes is presented which permits direct observation of target behaviors in a situational context that is replicable. For skills requiring responses to *things,* the probes take the form of standardized materials or objects that set the occasion for appropriate responses. For example, job application forms provide a consistent set of probes for the behaviors involved in completing employment applications.

For skills requiring responses to *persons,* a confederate is trained to deliver statements that set the occasion for appropriate responses. To assess competence in the skill of making a reflection statement, for example, a confederate role plays nonverbal behavior by telling the counselor trainee that she or he is *not* scared in a trembling voice.

Each scripted probe, whether presented verbally or in writing, provides an opportunity to observe for the occurrence or nonoccurrence of a specific target response. For example, a counselor's reflection statement, such as "I noticed that your voice was trembling slightly when you said that you weren't afraid of your husband hitting you again," would be scored following each probe calling for a reflection statement. Written response definitions would be used to score whether or not the specific statement met the criteria of a reflection statement. The percentage of occasions in which appropriate responses are emitted provides a measure of skill acquisition, maintenance, or generalization.

Written role-playing scripts often specify different types of probes. For example, a confederate's script used to play the part of a client in counseling might include: a general probe to start the session (i.e., standing at the counselor's door); a general statement of the problem (e.g., "I have been laid off from my job as a construction worker. I need some food for my family and help finding a new job"); probes setting the occasion for specific behaviors such as reflection statements or summarization statements; and a statement requesting an end to the session (e.g., "I need to get back to my kids."). To make the situation more natural, confederates can be instructed to "make up" responses to trainee questions and otherwise fill in the dialogue to simulate an actual situation. Scripted probes ensure similar opportunities for each participant to display targeted responses.

Role-playing assessment instruments have been used to measure a wide variety of behaviors including: counseling and problem-solving skills (Whang, Fletcher, & Fawcett, 1982); assertiveness (e.g., Bornstein, Bellack, & Hersen, 1977); door-to-door canvassing (Fawcett, Miller, & Braukmann, 1977); program writing (Fawcett & Fletcher, 1977); pedestrian safety (Page, Iwata, & Neef, 1976); job finding (Mathews, Whang, & Fawcett, 1980); and job-related social skills (Whang, Fawcett, & Mathews, 1982). Participants in these studies included elementary school children; normal, learning disabled, adjudicated, and developmentally delayed youths; and employed and unemployed adults.

Purpose

Role-playing assessment is used to measure the level of competence in skills for which in vivo observation is precluded. Observation in such analogue situations may be necessary when conditions calling for skill performance are infrequent or difficult to observe, such as trainee performance in a job

interview situation. Ethical considerations may also preclude repeated exposure of untrained person to actual performance situations, such as in pretraining observations of counseling skills.

Unlike informal simulations, role-playing assessment instruments provide standardized descriptions of probe situations and detailed specification of target behaviors. In the absence of scripted probes specifying confederate behavior, the possibility of systematic variations across evaluation sessions is increased. Therefore, a primary purpose of any role-playing assessment instrument is to ensure measurement consistency over time.

Development

Developing a role-playing assessment instrument for a particular skill requires two general operations: specifying target responses in behavioral terms and specifying probes used to assess performance.

To specify the behaviors involved in a skill, investigators typically review relevant literatures, conduct interviews with experts, and observe appropriate and inappropriate examples of the skill. As a result, broad categories of performance (e.g., opening a counseling session) are identified, and specific responses within each category (e.g., make a greeting statement) are noted in a task analysis.

Descriptions of the topography of each response and examples and nonexamples that illustrate its boundaries are prepared. Observers use these embryonic response definitions and other scoring instructions in field situations to obtain feedback on their clarity and completeness. Written specifications are revised until observations by independent observers show high levels of interobserver agreement. Thus, the target behaviors constituting performance of a particular skill are specified.

To specify the probes or stimulus situations calling for skill performance, a similar development process is followed. Investigators review relevant literature, interview experts and consumers, and observe critical incidents in settings and situations calling for performance of the skill. For example, to develop probes for a job interview situation, the literature on job finding, job training, and personnel selection would be reviewed; experts in job interviewing and personnel selection would be interviewed as would successful and unsuccessful job candidates; and actual job interviews with persons of varied competence would be observed. As a result, broad categories of probes (e.g., the job interview situation and telephoning a potential employer) and specific probes (e.g., "Tell me about your work experience" and "What are your future work plans?") would be identified. Experts review the overall simulated situation for naturalness and completeness and note whether specific probes are representative of the class of stimuli under which responding should occur. Also, confederates use the probes in field situations to determine whether persons competent in the skill emit the specified behaviors in response to the probe.

Psychometric Characteristics

Several types of psychometric considerations are particularly useful in evaluating the quality of a role-playing assessment instrument: reliability, content validity, convergent validity, concurrent validity, and social validity.

Reliability. Reliability denotes the consistency with which observers score data using written behavioral specifications and probe situations. Measures of interobserver agreement on performance indicate the clarity and completeness of written definitions. Interobserver agreement on the occurrence of specific probes for performance provides a measure of the consistency with which the measurement instrument was used. Virtually all published studies using role-playing assessment instruments provide an estimate of reliability for behaviors; reports of reliability for presentation of probes are rare, however.

Content Validity. Content validity refers to an estimate of the adequacy with which the role-playing assessment instrument samples behaviors and stimulus situations of interest. The process for developing behaviors and probes described earlier suggests a model for systematically mapping the context to be represented. A judgment about the adequacy of this development process is the primary basis for assessing content validity (Mathews et al., 1980).

Convergent   Validity. Convergent   validity denotes a procedure for determining the extent to which levels of behavior measured by a role-playing assessment instrument correlate with levels measured by another instrument. For example, Mathews et al. (1980) reported correlations between measures of job interview performance

obtained using an occupational skills assessment instrument and a rating procedure developed by other researchers. Such measures of convergent validity are rarely included in reports of studies using role-playing assessment instruments.

Concurrent   Validity. Concurrent   validity assesses the extent to which measures obtained using a role-playing assessment instrument correlate with other measures of performance taken at a similar time. For example, Bellack, Hersen, and Lamparski (1979) reported comparisons for measures of social skills obtained in role-playing situations and in simulated situations in the natural environment. Measures of generalization from role playing to in vivo situations are common, permitting estimates of concurrent validity for many published studies using this technique.

Social Validity. Social validity is a special type of content validity that has particular relevance to clinical practice. It refers to the extent to which direct observations of behavior correlate with expert ratings of the importance of the specified behaviors and situations. For example, Whang et al. (1982) reported a positive relationship between specified counseling behaviors and expert judges' ratings of evaluative dimensions of performance such as the counselor's understanding, the quality of alternatives considered, and overall satisfaction. Measures of social validity are frequently required for studies in which the social importance of the goals and effects might be informed by expert judgments.

Treatment Validity. Treatment validity refers to evidence, such as obtained in experimental demonstrations, that specific methods of behavioral assessment actually lead to better treatment. For example, results might be obtained showing that those employment rehabilitation clients who received individualized training based on an occupational skills assessment performed better than their counterparts whose pretraining skills were not assessed. Measures of treatment validity for role-playing assessment instruments are virtually nonexistent.

Clinical Use

The three primary uses for role-playing assessment instruments are (a) to identify the need for intervention; (b) to permit performance feedback during training of new responses; and (c) to evaluate the effects of attempts to promote acquisition, maintenance, or generalization of behaviors.

First, role-playing assessments are commonly used to determine the level of the behavior of interest before intervention. In a counseling training program, for example, a role-playing assessment might be used to measure levels of skill for specific behaviors, such as active listening or problem-solving, before training. The results could be used to determine the necessity for training and to target specific skill deficiencies for training.

Second, most behaviorally based training programs include an opportunity to rehearse or practice behaviors specified in instructions or modeled by the instructor. Typically, the instructor, a teaching assistant, or another student uses a role-playing assessment instrument to provide a precise measure of performance. Performance feedback, consisting of descriptions of appropriate and inappropriate aspects of performance, is provided based on these direct observations. (Presumably performance feedback includes both antecedent and consequent events.) Although some form of behavior rehearsal and performance feedback is used in most skill training programs, standardized probes for rehearsal situations are relatively uncommon.

Third, role-playing assessment instruments are also used to evaluate skill acquisition, maintenance, and generalization. Used without performance feedback, role-playing assessments can provide an estimate of performance during and after training for a particular skill. For example, an occupational skills assessment instrument may be used during training to determine whether to continue or conclude training for a particular job-finding skill. As a posttest, it may be used to justify providing additional or alternative training or consequent events. Thus, role-playing asssessment instruments may be used by clinicians to determine the need for intervention, to provide performance feedback during training, or to evaluate the effects of efforts to promote acquisition, maintenance, and generalization of behavior.

Future Directions

Recommendations for future research and development in role-playing assessment parallel those outlined by Nelson and Hayes (1981). They suggest attention to the issues of demonstrating treatment validity, establishing general rules to guide clinical practice, and improving the use of behavioral assessment instruments. First, evidence of the treatment validity of role-playing assessment instruments is almost nonexistent. Experimental analyses of the effects of using such devices on treatment outcome would help establish an empirical basis for their use. Second, clinical judgments, rather than precise decision rules, are typically used to select target behaviors, identify potential controlling variables, and tailor treatments based on individual performance. Further specification of the rules used by clinicians and empirical evidence supporting their effectiveness would provide a more scientific basis for clinical use of role-playing assessment instruments. Finally, the practicality of role-playing assessment instruments might be improved by more systematic consumer input into the design and field testing of assessment instruments and improved standards for reporting costs of their use. Such future contributions may improve the quality of role-playing assessment instruments and may contribute to attempts to promote their widespread adoption and use by clinicians and other change agents.

References

Bellack, A.S., Hersen, M., & Lamparski, D. (1979). Role-playing tests for assessing social skills: Are they valid? Are they useful? *Journal of Consulting and Clinical Psychology, 47,* 335-342.

Bornstein, M.R., Bellack, A.S., & Hersen, M. (1977). Social skills training for unassertive children: A multiple baseline analysis. *Journal of Applied Behavior Analysis, 10,* 183-196.

Fawcett, S.B., & Fletcher, R.K. (1977). Community applications of instructional technology: Training writers of instructional packages. *Journal of Applied Behavior Analysis, 10,* 739-746.

Fawcett, S.B., Miller, L.K., & Braukmann, C.J. (1977). An evaluation of a training package for community canvassing behavior. *Journal of Applied Behavior Analysis, 10,* 504.

Mathews, R.M., Whang, P.L., & Fawcett, S.B. (1980). Development and validation of an occupational skills assessment instrument. *Behavioral Assessment, 2,* 71-85.

Nelson, R.O., & Hayes, S.C. (1981). Nature of behavioral assessment. In M. Hersen & A.S. Bellack (Eds.), *Behavioral assessment: A practical handbook* (2nd Ed., pp. 3-37). New York: Pergamon Press.

Page, T.J., Iwata, B.A., & Neef, N.A. (1976). Teaching pedestrian skills to retarded persons: Generalization from the classroom to the natural environment. *Journal of Applied Behavior Analysis, 9,* 433-444.

Whang, P.L., Fawcett, S.B., & Mathews, R.M. (1982). Teaching job related social skills to learning disabled adolescents. *Analysis and Intervention in Developmental Disabilities, 4,* 29-38.

Whang, P.L., Fletcher, R.K., & Fawcett, S.B. (1982). Training counseling skills: An experimental analysis and social validation. *Journal of Applied Behavior Analysis, 15*, 325-334.

Rosenbaum's Self-Control Schedule

Michael Rosenbaum

Description

The Self-Control Schedule (SCS) is a self-report measure consisting of 36 items. It uses a Likert-type format with six levels of endorsement ranging from +3 (very characteristic of me, extremely descriptive) to -3 (very uncharacteristic of me, extremely nondescriptive). A high composite score, after reversing the direction of scoring for 11 of the items, is indicative of a richer repertoire of self-control skills (resourcefulness).

Purpose

Rosenbaum (1980a) suggested that individuals may differ in the extent in which they have acquired an effective repertoire of self-control behaviors. More recently, Rosenbaum (1983), following Meichenbaum (1977), has applied the term *learned resourcefulness* to describe an acquired repertoire of behaviors and skills (mostly cognitive) by which a person self-regulates internal responses (such as emotions, cognitions, or pain) that interfere with the smooth execution of a desired behavior. The SCS is directed at assessing individual differences in learned resourcefulness.

Development

The specific kinds of self-controlling behaviors that are assessed by the SCS were derived from various coping skills therapies proposed by cognitive behavior therapists. Coping skills therapies are characterized by their emphasis on *general* coping strategies. Self-control behaviors were categorized in the following way: (a) use of cognitions and self-instructions to cope with emotional and physiological responses; (b) application of problem-solving strategies (e.g., planning, problem definition, evaluating alternatives, and anticipation of consequences); (c) ability to delay immediate gratification; and (d) general belief in one's ability to self-regulate internal events.

Items for the scale were generated in the follow-

ing way. We sampled a large number of situations in which self-controlling responses would most likely occur. Thirty items were written in which a direct reference was made to an unpleasant emotional or physiological experience such as anxiety, low mood, boredom, pain, and hunger. Twenty additional items were written that refer to tasks requiring self-controlling responses such as breaking an undesirable habit, carrying out a boring but necessary job, and handling one's limited funds. The situations were described in general terms to make them applicable to a wide range of persons. Ten items were written to represent a general belief in one's ability to self-control (self-regulatory efficacy). With the exceptions of the latter items, each item consisted of a description of a self-controlling response in a specific situation.

The preliminary list of 60 items was given to two experienced, behaviorally oriented clinical psychologists who were well acquainted with the concept of self-control as defined by the author. For the 50 items describing specific kinds of self-controlling behaviors, the psychologists were requested to evaluate each item based on the following criteria: (a) Is the item comprehensible? (b) Does the item describe a situation that could be experienced by a wide range of people? and (c) Does the item reflect an effective use of a self-controlling response? The 10 items describing expectations for self-regulator efficacy were evaluated on the basis of their comprehensibilty as well as on the extent to which the items describe expectations for self-regulatory efficacy. Sixteen items in which there was disagreement on one or more of the foregoing criteria were dropped. The resulting 44 item schedule was then administered to a group of 84 female and 68 male undergraduates for item analysis. Eight items that did not conform to one or more of the following criteria were dropped: (a) all of the points on the Likert scale were endorsed across subjects, (b) the standard deviation of the item was at least 1, and (c) the item contributed to the internal consistency of the items. The final 36-item schedule consists of 12 items that refer to the use of cognitions to control emotional and physiological responses, of 11 items that refer to the use of problem-solving strategies, of 4 items that relate to delay of gratification, and of 9 items that refer to self-regulatory efficacy. Although items were taken from four different content areas, these should not be considered as four subscales of the SCS.

Psychometric Characteristics

The psychometric characteristics of the SCS were discussed in Rosenbaum (1980a) and in Redden, Tucker, and Young (1983). The SCS mean scores for three samples of Israeli students (197 males and 244 females) ranged from 23 to 27 with standard deviations ranging from 21 to 25. Although there was a slight tendency for female students to score higher than the male subjects, no significant differences were noted between male and female subjects. Redden et al. (1983) in American undergraduate students found significant differences between male and female students. The mean score for the 388 males was 22.0 (SD = 21.6) and for the 596 females, 29.9 (SD = 22.3). (In Redden et al. (1983) the mean scores of the items were reported, not the sum of all items. To adjust their scores to ours, we had to multiply their SCS scores by 6). Thus, it appears that although the mean scores were equal in the Israeli and American samples, sex differences were found only in the American samples.

Reliability. Two kinds of reliability measures were reported: test-retest reliability and internal consistency of the items. Rosenbaum (1980a) reported a test-retest correlation after 4 weeks of .86, and Leon and Rosenthal (1984) in the United States reported a correlation of .77 after an interval of 11 months. Thus, the SCS scores are stable over time. However, the SCS scores would be expected to increase following cognitive behavior therapy. The internal consistency of the SCS items was computed on the data obtained from five samples in the Rosenbaum (1980a) study by the use of Kuder-Richardson formula 20. The alpha coefficient obtained ranged from .78 to .81. Redden et al. (1983) reported a Cronbach coefficient alpha of .82.

Validity. Since publication of the SCS in 1980 (Rosenbaum, 1980a) many studies have contributed to its construct validity as a measure of learned resourcefulness (i.e., a repertoire of self-control skills). Some of this research was reviewed by Rosenbaum (1983).

The convergent and discriminant validity of the SCS were examined by comparing scores obtained on the SCS with scores obtained on existing scales. The SCS had low but statistically significant correlations with the following scales: Rotter's I-E Locus of Control Scale, Jones' Irrational Beliefs Test, and the G Factor ("self-control") of Cattell's 16 PF (cf. Rosenbaum, 1980a). In addition, the SCS scores correlated with Fitz's Self-Esteem Scale and with various antidepressant cognitions and behaviors. The SCS is not related to measures of Type A coronary prone personality as assessed by Jenkins' Activity Scale.

The construct validity of the SCS was established in a number of experimental studies. The basic research strategy focused on the differential performance of high and low scores on the SCS (namely, high and low resourceful persons [HR and LR, respectively]) on tasks requiring self-control skills. In comparison with LR persons, HR persons were found to better tolerate laboratory-produced pain as well as clinical pain. The learned helplessness phenomenon, the interference with new learning following exposure to uncontrollable aversive events, appeared more strongly in the LR subjects than in HR subjects. The SCS was found to be related to the ability of dialysis patients to delay immediate gratification.

Clinical Use

The SCS can be appropriately used with an adult population of at least 8 years of education. The SCS has been used effectively in predicting (a) success in self-management treatment programs for modification of habits such as eating habits and nail biting; (b) suitability to cognitive behavior therapy with problems such as depression and hypertension; (c) compliance with medical advice; (d) vulnerability to depression and to the effects of stressful events (Rosenbaum & Palmon, 1984); and (e) predicting ability to cope with physiological reactions such as pain, seasickness, and childbirth. The scale has not been used in patients with severe psychopathologies.

Future Directions

We currently are testing a shorter version of the SCS that consists of 17 items only. The shorter SCS was almost as reliable as the longer scale. However, further validation studies are needed before the shorter version can be used in clincal practice. In addition, we have developed two additional versions of the SCS: one for youth and one for children aged 10 to 14 years. Because children under the age of 10 find it difficult to reliably complete a self-report measure, new assessment methods need to be developed to assess resourcefulness in younger children.

References

Leon, G.R., & Rosenthal, B.S. (1984). Prognostic indicators of success or relapse in weight reduction. *International Journal of Eating Disorders, 3*, 15-24.

Meichenbaum, D. (1977). *Cognitive-behavior modification: An intergrative approach.* New York: Plenum.

Redden, E.M., Tucker, R.K., & Young, L. (1983). Psychometric properties of the Rosenbaum Schedule for Assessing Self-Control. *The Psychological Record, 33*, 77-86.

Rosenbaum, M. (1980a). A schedule for assessing self-control behaviors: Preliminary findings. *Behavior Therapy, 11*, 109-121.

Rosenbaum, M. (1983). Learned resourcefulness as a behavioral repertoire for the self-regulation of internal events: Issues and speculations. In M. Rosenbaum, C.M. Franks, & Y. Jaffe (Eds.), *Perspectives on behavior therapy in the eighties* (pp. 54-73). New York: Springer.

Rosenbaum, M., & Palmon, N. (1984). Helplessness and resourcefulness in coping with epilepsy. *Journal of Consulting and Clinical Psychology, 52*, 244-253.

S-R Inventory of Anxiousness

Thomas W. Lombardo

Description

The S-R Inventory of Anxiousness is a self-report scale for measuring anxiety in a variety of situations. Fourteen items or response modes are rated for each situation. The intensity of responses to each situation is rated on a 5-point scale ranging from "none" to "very much". The response modes include physiological reactions, feelings, approach, or withdrawal and the effect of anxiety on goal-oriented activity. Scores for particular situations are obtained by summing the ratings on the 5-point response items. Although the S-R Inventory was designed to measure anxiety within particular situations, an overall anxiety score can be computed by summing across situations.

Purpose

The S-R Inventory was developed by Endler, Hunt, and Rosenstein (1962) primarily to provide empirical evidence toward the debate on whether persons (i.e., traits) or situations account for more variance in behavior. Because the situations selected for the inventory were for theory testing with college undergraduate populations, clinical use will often require adding relevant situations. The same response mode items are used for all situations, making such adaptations a simple task.

Development

The 11 situations measured by the S-R Inventory were selected intuitively. They represent situations that are directly or vicariously encountered by college freshmen and sophomores and that vary on their valence for anxiety. The 11 response modes were also selected intuitively. Factor analyses indicate that situations encompass three dimensions of danger (i.e., threat to interpersonal status and the achievement of goals, inanimate danger, and an ambiguous dimension) and response modes encompass three dimensions of reactions to situations (i.e., distress, disruption of action and avoidance; exhilaration, enjoyment, and approach; and autonomic reactions). Endler and Hunt (1966) added situations for testing the generalizability of earlier findings on the trait-situation controversy across age groups, socioeconomic and mental health status, geographic location, and sex. These modified forms rarely appear in the literature.

Psychometric Characteristics

Internal consistency of the S-R Inventory is high. Coefficient alphas for the entire test ranged from .95 to .97 in undergraduate samples (Endler et al., 1962). Alpha reliabilities for the 14 response modes ranged from .64 to .89, with all but four above .80. For the 11 situational scales, alpha reliabilities ranged from .55 to .90, with all but two above .73. There are no reports of the temporal stability of the S-R Inventory.

Highly anxious subjects show about three times more situational variability in their behavior than do randomly selected subjects (Endler et al., 1962). This supports the construct validity of the test, because more anxious individuals would be predicted to show more situational consistency because of suppressed behavior and reduced adaptability to environmental demands. Concurrent validity with other self-report measures of anxiety and with motoric measures of anxiety is well established, particularly for the speech anxiety situation. Endler et al. (1962) found the S-R Inventory correlated significantly with several other omnibus anxiety scales, such as the Taylor Manifest Anxiety Scale. Scores on the speech anxiety item correlate ($r = -.63$) with the number of times students speak out in class (D'Zurilla, 1964). In his speech anxiety outcome study, Paul (1966) found the S-R Inventory speech situation correlated significantly with other self-report measures and with Timed

Behavior Checklist ratings of motoric anxiety. Interestingly, significantly lower correlations resulted using other S-R Inventory situations. This suggests that validity depends on the similarity of the test and criterion situations.

Clinical Use

Although it was originally used as a research device, the S-R Inventory is suitable for use with clinically anxious populations. Total scores could be used to objectively evaluate improvement following treatment for specific or diffuse anxiety. Alternatively, the S-R Inventory could be used to increase assessment efficiency by substituting the Inventory for asking the patient a series of questions. Patterns of anxiety could be ascertained and positive responses to individual items could be pursued in subsequent interviewing. Additional situations not included in the S-R Inventory can be assessed by simply creating a new heading for the response mode items.

Future Directions

The S-R Inventory is widely used as a research tool for measuring situation-specific anxiety. There are no published normative data on the Inventory despite the fact that Endler and Hunt have collected an anormous amount of data. Publication of these data would benefit both clinicians and researchers.

Test-retest reliability of the Inventory is unknown. Because predictive validity is established, the Inventory must be reliable. However, it would be useful to know the magnitude of reliability.

References

Endler, N.S., & Hunt, J. McV. (1966). Sources of behavioral variance as measured by the S-R Inventory of Anxiousness. *Psychological Bulletin, 65,* 336-346.

Endler, N.S., Hunt, J. McV., & Rosenstein, A.J. (1962). An S-R inventory of anxiousness. *Psychological Monographs, 76,* (Whole Number 536), 1-31.

Paul, G.L. (1966). *Insight versus desensitization in psychotherapy.* Stanford, CA: Stanford University Press.

D'Zurilla, T.J. (1964). *Effects of behavioral influence techniques applied in group discussion on subsequent verbal participation.* Unpublished doctoral dissertation, University of Illinois.

Scale for Suicide Ideation

Robert A. Steer and Aaron T. Beck

Description

The Scale for Suicide Ideation (SSI) (Beck, Kovacs, & Weissman, 1979) was developed as a clinician-administered scale to measure one of the dimensions that the Task Force for the NIMH Center for Studies of Suicide Prevention proposed for its multiaxial classification of suicidal behaviors. The Task Force identified three categories: (a) completed suicide, (b) suicide attempts, and (c) suicidal ideas. Each category reflected clinical ratings across several dimensions of suicidal behavior. The ratings included, for example, the severity of the intent to die and medical lethality of the contemplated or actual attempt.

The SSI was designed to measure the intensity and definitiveness of suicidal ideas (suicidal ideation) in psychiatric patients. Suicide ideators are individuals who currently have plans or wishes to commit suicide, but have not many recent overt attempts. Because suicidal ideation logically precedes a suicide attempt or completed suicide, it seemed appropriate to focus on the intensity, pervasiveness, and characteristics of the ideation and wishes. Suicidal ideation as an indicator of suicidal risk might predict later suicides.

The SSI quantifies a variety of factors about suicide attempts that are considered to be applicable to suicide ideators. It consists of 19 items for evaluating in a semistructured interview the suicidal ideas in psychiatric patients. Each item consists of three alternative statements that represent an increasing scale of severity ranging from 0 to 2. A total score is computed by adding the individual ratings, and the scores can range from 0 to 39.

Development

The SSI was partially derived from clinical observations and rational deductions made from the psychological literature about suicide. Systematic observations of suicidal patients were made. Lists of these patients' preoccupations, concerns, wishes, thinking, and behavior patterns were developed, and the most frequently observed and mentioned suicidal behaviors were pilot tested during scale construction. A 30-item scale was administered to 35 suicidal patients. Items that had overlapping content with other items or were difficult to score were then eliminated. On the basis of this selection process, a 19-item scale emerged. The items assessed the extent of suicidal thoughts and characteristics as well as the patient's attitudes toward them; the extent of the wish to die, the desire to make an actual attempt, and the details of any plans; internal deterrents to an actual attempt; and subjective feelings of control regarding a proposed attempt.

Psychometric Characteristics

The psychometric characteristics of the SSI that follow are primarily derived from Beck, Kovacs, and Weissman's (1979) original validation study. Wetzel (1977) earlier had reported that there were positive relationships between the SSI and Beck's Hopelessness Scale and Depression Inventory, and Beck et al. (1979) confirmed these relationships.

The internal consistency (KR20) of the SSI, determined with a sample of 90 patients who had been hospitalized for suicide ideation (Beck, Kovacs, & Weissman, 1979), was .89. Another analysis reported by Beck et al. (1979) showed that 16 of the SSI's items had significant positive correlations with its total scores. Preparation of a suicide note, commission of arrangements in anticipation of death, and deception about contemplated suicide were not significantly related to the total scores. These nonsignificant items were retained, however, because previous research had demonstrated that suicide notes and final acts were important in assessing prior suicidal intent in actual suicide attempts. Two clinicians also independently completed the SSI for 25 of the 90 inpatients, and their interrater reliability was .83, p <.00.

The foregoing two clinicians also rated each of the 90 patients using an 0- to 8-point rating scale for immediate and near-future suicidal attempts. The correlation between their clinical ratings and the SSI scores was .49, p <.001. A significant difference was also found between the mean SSI scores of the 90 hospitalized suicidal ideators ($M = 9.43$) and 50 outpatients who were being treated for depression ($M = 4.42$) (p <.001). The SSI was also administered to a subsample of 58 depressed patients before and after treatment (Beck et al., 1979). Treatment consisted of receiving either antidepressant medication, cognitive therapy, or a combination of the two. Patients were tested an average of 88 days after intake. Before therapy the patients' mean SSI score was 6.36; the posttreatment mean SSI score was 1.39 (p <.01).

With respect to the factorial validity of the SSI, Beck et al. (1979) performed a principal components analysis and found three meaningful psychological dimensions which they called (a) Active Suicidal Desire, (b) Preparation, and (c) Passive Suicidal Desire. Wetzel (1977) also conducted a principal components analysis of the SSI with 56 white psychiatric patients who had not made any suicidal attempts within 1 year of their testing. He identified four generalizable factors representing (a) Specificity of Planning Suicide, (b) Desire to Attempt, (c) Trapped by Problems, and (d) Active Behavioral Preparation. None of Wetzel's (1979) factors was significantly related to being diagnosed with either a primary affective disorder or a character disorder.

Finally, Beck, Steer, Kovacs, and Garrison (1985), in a 10-year follow-up study of Beck's original sample of suicidal ideators, found that the SSI did not predict ideators or eventual suicide, whereas the Beck Hopelessness Scale did. However, studies in England and Wales indicated that scales similar to the SSI applied following an attempted suicide were predictive of a completed suicide within 2 years or on the next suicide attempt.

Clinical Use

The SSI requires more evaluation before the range of its predictive power can be established. However, the SSI does provide clinicians with a rapid tool for qualitatively assessing basic psychological and behavioral aspects of their patients' suicidal ideation. A positive rating on any one of the SSI's 19 items should be followed up clinically.

Future Directions

Only a few investigations have employed this instrument in its present form in clinical research, and the SSI needs to be used by more clinicians across a broader spectrum of psychiatric disorders. Persons at different stages of suidical intention need to be evaluated, and the instrument's concurrent validities with other measures of suicidal intent and risk need to be explored more fully. The Center for Cognitive Therapy is currently developing a self-report version of the SSI as well as a computerized version. These versions should prove attractive to a broader audience of clinicians.

References

Beck, A.T., Kovacs, M., & Weissman, A. (1979). Assessment of suicidal intention: The Scale for Suicide Ideation. *Journal of Consulting and Clinical Psychology, 47,* 343-352.

Beck, A.T., Steer, R.A., Kovacs, M., & Garrison, B. (1985). Hopelessness and eventual suicide: A 10-year prospective study of patients hospitalized with suicide ideation. *American Journal of Psychiatry, 142,* 559-563.

Wetzel, R.C. (1977). Factor structure of Beck's suicide intent scales. *Psychological Reports, 40,* 295-302.

Self-Control Questionnaire

Lynn P. Rehm

Description

The Self-Control Questionnaire (SCQ) consists of 40 statements of attitudes and beliefs about self-control behaviors and cognitions related to depression. Instructions require the examinee to indicate the degree to which each statement is characteristic of him or her on a 5-point scale from A (very characteristic of me, extremely descriptive) to E (very uncharacteristic of me, extremely undescriptive). Nineteen items are phrased to reflect positive nondepressive attitudes and 21 to reflect negative, depressed attitudes. Sample items include, "Planning each step of what I have to do helps to get things done well," and " It's no use trying to change most of the things that make me miserable."

Purpose

The SCQ was initially developed to assess the teaching effectiveness of the self-control therapy program for depression (Fuchs & Rehm, 1977). The therapy program is based on the self-control model of depression (Rehm, 1977). Item content is derived from the deficits in self-control behavior that the model posits are contributory causes of depression. The therapy program teaches participants self-management concepts relevant to each of the deficits and instigates homework to remedy the deficits. The SCQ was intended as an outcome measure to assess the effectiveness of the program in accomplishing the specific proximal purpose of acquisition of these concepts by participants, i.e. modification of these attitudes and beliefs.

Development

An initial 25-item scale, termed the Concepts Test, was developed for use in an outcome study of the self-control therapy program (Fuchs & Rehm, 1977). A second 41-item version of the scale was developed to increase and to equalize the number of items related to each self-control deficit. One ambiguous item was dropped and the response form was changed to produce the current SCQ.

Psychometric Characteristics

Internal consistency alpha coefficients of .82 and .88 have been reported in the literature. Test-retest reliability over a 5-week period was reported by O'Hara, Rehm, and Campbell (1982) to be .86. In a sample of 101 clinically depressed community volunteers the scale correlated .42 with the Rosenbaum Self-Control Schedule, a measure of a broad range of self-control skills. In the same sample the SCQ correlated .16 with the Beck Depression Inventory (BDI). In a sample of normal women, O'Hara et al. (1982) found a correlation of .31 with the BDI. In a series of outcome studies of the self-management therapy program for depression, the SCQ consistently showed significant improvement in scores pretherapy to posttherapy (cf., Rehm, 1984). Posttest scores have differentiated self-management patients from patients in waiting list, traditional therapy, and assertion training conditions. Pretreatment scores did not predict depression outcome in these studies. O'Hara et al. (1982) did note that the SCQ contributed significantly to the prediction of postpartum depression when included in a battery administered in the second trimester of pregnancy.

Future Directions

The scale was constructed for a specific purpose and it was written on a purely rational basis with little psychometric development. Although data currently available suggest that it fulfills its initial purpose satisfactorily, further psychometric evaluation is clearly desirable. In addition to its use as an outcome measure for a specific therapy program, the scale may have further use as an assessment of vulnerability to depression.

References

Fuchs, C.S., & Rehm, L.P. (1977). A self-control behavior therapy program for depression. *Journal of Consulting and Clinical Psychology, 45,* 206-215.

O'Hara, M.W., Rehm, L.P., & Campbell, S.B. (1982). Predicting depressive symptomatology: Cognitive-behavioral models and post-partum depression. *Journal of Abnormal Psychology, 91,* 457-461.

Rehm, L.P. (1977). A self-control model of depression. *Behavior Therapy, 28,* 787-804.

Rehm, L.P. (1984). Self-management therapy for depression. *Advances in Behaviour Research and Therapy, 6,* 83-98.

Self-Control Rating Scale

Philip C. Kendall and Rebecca C. Hays

Description

The Self-Control Rating Scale (SCRS) is a 33-item measure that provides an indication of the degree to which a child's behavior can be described as self-controlled (versus impulsive). The scale requires an observer (the rater) to place the child being rated at a point along a continuum. The scale ranges from 1 to 7, where 1 indicates maximum self-control, 7 indicates maximum impulsivity, and 4 indicates a position where the average child might fall. Of the 33 items, 10 are descriptive of self-controlled action (e.g., "Can the child deliberately calm down when he or she is excited or all wound up?"), 13 are indicative of impulsivity (e.g., "Does the child butt into games or activities even when he or she has not been invited?"), and 10 are worded to denote both possibilities (e.g., "Does the child interrupt inappropriately in conversations with peers, or wait his or her turn to speak.") A child's score for the SCRS is the sum of the 33 rating items, with higher scores indicating a greater *lack* of self-control.

Purpose

The SCRS was specifically developed to assess self-control in school children as rated by their classroom teacher, parents, or both. The development of the SCRS was promoted by the absence of an existing measure for assessing self-control in children, and a measure was needed that would be sensitive to and could be used to assess the generalization of treatment-produced changes in meaningful environments. The SCRS was developed so that it would not be hampered by the demands of extensive naturalistic observations, or be restricted to a limited environment. The SCRS was developed to provide a scale that would aid clinicians and researchers in examining the correlates of different levels of self-control and improve

our understanding of the relations between individual variations in self-control and the effects of different types of treatment. Finally, the SCRS was developed to provide an appropriate measure for developmental studies of age-related changes in self-control.

Development

The development of the SCRS was based on a cognitive-behavioral definition of self-control (Kendall & Wilcox, 1979). The cognitive component includes factors such as deliberation, problem-solving, planning, and evaluation, whereas the behavioral factors include the ability to execute the behavior that is chosen or inhibit the behaviors that are cognitively disregarded. When first working on the creation, revision, and selection of final items for the SCRS, we sought to include those features of behavior that had been identified in the literature as associated with a lack of self-controlled (impulsive) behavior. For instance, data suggested that impulsive children showed less persistence, so we prepared an item that would tap observations of persistence (e.g., "Does the child jump or switch from activity to activity rather than sticking to one thing at a time?").

Psychometric Characteristics

Kendall and Wilcox (1979) reported two studies on the reliability and validity of the SCRS. In the first, they had teachers rate 110 children in grades three to six on the SCRS, and from these, randomly chose children to participate in an experimental session. This session included the completion of the Peabody Picture Vocabulary Test (PPVT), Matching Familiar Figures, (MFF), and Porteus Mazes. Additionally, during the experimental session, another observer rated the children on the frequency of these behaviors: Off-Task Verbal Behavior, Off-Task Physical Behavior, Off-Task Attention, Out of Seat, and Interruptions. In a second study (Kendall & Wilcox, 1979), teachers were asked to refer children whom they identified as behavior problems (i.e., those lacking self-control) for an opportunity for self-control training. Each of these children was then matched with a nonselected student and subjected to the same procedure outlined in Study 1.

Kendall and Wilcox (1979) reported both the internal reliability (Cronbach's alpha = .98) and test-retest reliability (r = .84) of the SCRS. It was significantly correlated with self-control measures and total scores of behavioral observations, even after mental age and chronological age were partialed out. Age was negatively correlated with the SCRS, MFF errors, and the Porteus Q score, supporting the developmental concept of self-control, in that an increase in self-control was noted with an increase in age. Additionally, no significant correlation was found between the SCRS and PPVT IQ, providing discriminant validity for the SCRS.

Significant differences were noted between boys and girls, with boys being less self-controlled, a finding that is consistent with data on the general incidence of problem behavior in boys compared with girls. Factor analysis supported a one-factor solution accounting for 71.7% of the total variance. All items loaded meaningfully on the first factor, suggesting that the SCRS provides an assessment of an internally consistent concept labeled "cognitive-behavioral self-control." Finally, additional validation was provided, because analyses revealed significant differences between referred and nonreferred children. The teacher-referred children were rated higher on the SCRS, had shorter MMF latencies, and obtained higher behavior observation totals (indicating a higher frequency of disruptive behaviors during the testing session) than did the nonreferred children.

In more recent research, Kendall, Zupan, and Braswell (1981) examined the behavioral correlates of actual in-class behavior with SCRS ratings and identified other cognitive and behavioral correlates of the SCRS. Their report provided support for the SCRS as an index of self-control in children, noting that children measured as lacking in self-control did engage in a higher rate of off-task disruptive behaviors. It was also noted that the SCRS was significantly related to a measure of "social perspective taking" but not related to a delay of gratification task. The correlation between parents and teachers' rating was .66 (Kendall & Braswell, 1985).

Robin, Fischel, and Brown (1984), using 4- to 18-year-old lower class subjects, demonstrated that parents can be effectively used as raters and that the SCRS discriminated psychologically distressed from nondistressed subjects. Using consecutive admissions to a major children's hospital, parents' ratings on the SCRS were reported to differentiate hyperactivity from other disorders as well as from nondistressed normal scores. Hyperactive subjects obtained the highest mean score, followed by conduct-disordered children, whereas children with other (internalizing) types of problems that did not involve problems of self-control received the lowest mean ratings.

Clinical Use

The SCRS has been useful for discriminating between levels of self-control in children. The SCRS has discriminated referred from nonreferred children (Kendall & Wilcox, 1979; Kendall, Zupan, & Braswell, 1981) and children with various types of pathology, as well as being sensitive to treatment effects (Kendall & Wilcox, 1980; Kendall & Braswell, 1985). The most direct use of the scale is the identification of problems associated with deficits in self-control and in selecting proper cases for treatment. That is, persons scoring at or above 160 to 165 are candidates for cognitive-behavioral treatment (Kendall & Braswell, 1985). In this sense, this scale is useful in matching children with treatment. Generally, the SCRS is a measure for examining pretreatment to posttreatment gains.

Future Directions

Additional research is needed to buttress the existing support for the SCRS. For instance, further details of the psychometric properties of the scale and relationships with other psychological constructs are in order. More detailed examination of the effects of treatment (e.g., examination of specific items) and more focused tests of the matching of children who differ in self-control to different types of treatment will prove useful. The scale has been translated into several languages, suggesting the timeliness of cross-cultural studies.

References

Kendall, P.C., & Braswell, L. (1985). Cognitive-behavioral therapy for impulsive children. New York: Guilford.

Kendall, P.C., & Wilcox, L.E. (1979). Self-control in children: Development of a rating scale. Journal of Consulting and Clinical Psychology, 47, 1020-1029.

Kendall, P.C., & Wilcox, L.E. (1980). A cognitive-behavioral treatment for impulsivity: Concrete versus conceptual training in non-self-controlled problem children. Journal of Consulting and Clinical Psychology, 48, 80-91.

Kendall, P.C., Zupan, B.A., & Braswell, L. (1981). Self-control in children: Further analyses of the Self-Controlled Rating Scale. Behavior Therapy, 12, 667-681.

Robin, A.L., Fischel, J.E., & Brown, K.E. (1984). The measurement of self-control in children: Validation of the Self-Control Rating Scale. Journal of Pediatric Psychology, 9, 165-175.

Self-Efficacy Scale

Robert E. Becker

Description

The Self-Efficacy Scale is a method of assessing a person's sense of self-efficacy as defined by Bandura (1977). There is no one specific "Self-Efficacy Scale" in the traditional sense that you find a single scale with identical items administered to each person. The Self-Efficacy Scale is specific to the particular situation being assessed. A self-efficacy expectation as measured by this scale is defined as the subject's belief that he or she can adequately carry out the necessary behaviors and cognitions required to produce a successful outcome in a specific situation that will unfold in the near future. In this sense, a self-efficacy expectation is a self-generated evaluation of one's own skill in specific circumstances. The usual assessment procedure (Bandura, Adams, & Beyer, 1977) consists of breaking down a complex task intended for treatment into discrete behavioral units that are arrayed into increasingly more difficult steps. This ordering is specific to the disorder being treated and is similar to the construction of a systematic desensitization hierarchy. Once this ordering has been determined, the subject is instructed to designate which of these subtasks he or she expects to perform in the immediately following behavioral test. For each task designated as completable, the subject estimates the strength or certainty of the belief that she or he will successfully carry it out. An identical rating procedure is conducted for an unfamiliar (hypothetical) although conceptually related set of circumstances. From these two rating procedures three types of measures are created. First, a quantity labeled *magnitude* is determined by counting the number of discrete subtasks designated as completable on each of the tests (i.e., the "treatment" test and the hypothetical test). Because subtasks in each test are arranged in order of increasing difficulty, the more items a subject believes she or he can successfully complete the greater the *magnitude* or self-efficacy. *Strength* of self-efficacy is calculated by summing the certainty rating for each completable subtask and dividing this sum by the *magnitude* for each test. The last quantity to be calculated is labeled *generality* and is defined as the difference between the *magnitude* ratings on the two tests. A similar calculation using the *strength* estimates yields a second measure of *generality*.

Purpose

These measurement procedures are derived from Bandura's (1977) paper proposing a cognitive theory to account for behavior change, especially behavior change in anxiety disorders. This theory posits that central nervous system processing of stimulus information is responsible for the acquisition and regulation of behavior. Much human behavior is acquired in ways that traditional operant or classical conditioning cannot predict, for example, observational learning. Learning from reinforcement is seen as largely a cognitive process in that response consequences provide information to the person. Behavior is controlled, not by its immediate consequences, but by the aggregate consequences produced by thought about these events. These aggregate operations are defined in terms of self-efficacy. Self-efficacy expectations are formed as a result of the person making outcome predictions that would be produced from their own behavior and then verifying that predicted outcome. To be sure, behavior is not produced for its own sake, but requires adequate incentives and an appropriate skill level. Once these are given, however, the theory assumes that self-efficacy expectations will be the major predictor of behavior.

Development

To turn the concept of self-efficacy into a testable assumption, Bandura (1977) provided for the definition and quantification of the concept. Information that affects self-efficacy outcome predictions come from four sources: (a) previous performance accomplishments on similar tasks; (b) vicarious experiences (observational learning); (c) verbal persuasion; and (d) personal emotional arousal. These four sources of information combine to produce the three dimensions of a self-efficacy expectation: (a) *magnitude* (b) *strength*, and (c) *generality*.

Psychometric Characteristics

Bandura et al. (1977) provide evidence about the first application of this assessment technique. Their data showed that all three dimensions of self-efficacy (*magnitude, strength,* and *generality*) were sensitive to a modeling treatment procedure with simple phobic subjects. The percentage of accurate predictions of later behavioral performance varied between 82 and 89% agreement depending on the type of treatment provided. During posttreatment assessment, if only predictions of behavior not performed before treatment are considered, then the percentage of agreement is 79%. A prediction that those who performed maximally in treatment would also perform maximally on posttreatment performances was wrong 28% of the time for T tests and 52% for U tests. A prediction that persons expressing maximal self-efficacy expectations will perform maximally was wrong 21% of the time on T tests and only 24% of the time on U tests. Williams and Rappoport (1983) report that female agorophobic patients treated with cognitive techniques generally showed that the higher a subject's self-efficacy the higher the level of performance on the behavioral test (r's ranged from .92 to .63). Beyond this finding, these two investigators showed that the lower a subject's self-efficacy score, the more anxiety the subject anticipated experiencing (r = .92).

Clinical Use

Measurement of self-efficacy as defined by Bandura (1977) has not been used clinically. Williams and Rappoport (1983) report using these procedures in a study examining the cognitive treatment of agoraphobics. In their study, female patients suffering from fears associated with driving were given cognitive and exposure treatments. Self-efficacy was measured before and after treatment.

Future Directions

Assessment of the three components of self-efficacy still appears to be too complicated for the average clinician to easily add such a procedure to his or her regular assessment routine. Each of the three components seems to be clearly defined, but the overall assessment procedure is bulky. Additionally, this set of operations has not been applied to psychopathology other than anxiety-based disorders. Improvements in the time needed to carry out an assessment would be of practical benefit as would more normative information. Theoretically, this approach would benefit from further evidence that predictions over greater time spans can be reliably made. In the intervening time circumstances may have changed to such a degree that the predictions begin to lose their accuracy.

References

Bandura, A. (1977). Self-efficacy: Toward a unifying theory of behavioral change. *Psychological Review*, 84, 191-215.

Bandura, A., Adams, N.E., & Beyer, J. (1977). Cognitive processes mediating behavioral change. *Journal of Personality and Social Psychology*, 35, 125-139.

Williams, S.L., & Rappoport, A. (1983). Cognitive treatment in the natural environment for agorophobics. *Behavior Therapy*, 14, 299-313.

Self-Injurious Behavior Assessment

Johannes Rojahn

Description

Because applied behavior analysis has been the dominating approach to Self-Injurious Behavior (SIB) during the last 25 years, systematic behavior observation has been by far the most frequently used form of SIB assessment. It involves repeated observations of predefined behavior categories across baseline and treatment conditions. Parameters of response frequency, duration, or both are assessed. The unit of measurement depends on the mode of data collection (time sampling or continuous recording). Severity and intensity of SIB cannot be estimated with observation techniques. The data are usually plotted in graphs, which are used for visual interpretations of the findings.

Behavior observation often takes place in special settings and involves the recording of SIB as well as collateral behaviors, such as stereotypes, tantrum behaviors, and aggressive and destructive behaviors, so that possible treatment side effects can be identified. The selection of behavior categories depends largely on the subjects' behavior repertoire. The SIB observation packages have been proposed, which consist of a set of predefined behavioral categories. For example, the ecobehavioral SIB coding system (Schroeder, Rojahn, & Mulick, 1978) consists of more than 20 standard categories, including SIB, appropriate behaviors (e.g., play and work behavior), inappropriate behaviors (e.g., aggressive, disruptive, and stereotypic behaviors), and social behaviors (social approach and social interaction). Additional variables, such as medication, environmental characteristics, and planned activities that are likely to be of importance for the target behavior in a given observation session are also monitored on a cover sheet. The behavior categories are operationally defined. Relevant idiosyncratic behaviors can be added. In contrast to more traditional forms of behavioral assessment, ecobehavioral observations are typically performed in the clients' natural environment to assess treatment effects in interaction with the natural environment. Ecobehavioral data can also be used for post hoc analyses in which the impact of uncontrolled variables on behaviors can be evaluated.

Purpose

Systematic observations are generally used for applied behavior analysis of SIB. This involves the analysis of maintaining conditions of the behavior at hand and the evaluation of behavioral treatment programs. In addition, the effects of other treatment modalities, such as medication, can also be assessed. Singh and Winton (1984) suggested a data graphing system for the assessment of drug effects on SIB in which the data are displayed in two graphs: one showing the *daily* mean rate per minute of SIB responses per minute, and the other one the *hourly* mean rate per minute of the frequency of SIB. The second display can reveal special drug effects relative to the time of drug administration.

Development

The selection of behaviors to be observed is based on interviews with parents, teachers, or others familiar with the client. In addition, nonsystematic observations of the client under circumstances in which SIB is expected to occur (transition periods, demand situations, etc.) should be performed. The SIB categories should be operationally defined for every client to facilitate observer agreement. Observers need to be trained accordingly. Ecobehavioral observations provide a standard set of categories in which only those categories have to be added that are not very frequent but that are important for given persons. The selection of the recording technique (continuous recording, time sampling, etc.) will depend on the resources available and its validity for a given behavior. Simple frequency counts or interval recording techniques are usually the methods of choice.

Psychometric Characteristics

Interobserver agreement is traditionally the only psychometric characteristic assessed in the observation research literature. Validity of behavior categories (construct validity) or other types of validity are generally not estimated in observational data, despite the fact that this has been recognized as an important requirement for years (Johnson &

Bolstad, 1973). The selection of recording techniques can potentially generate accurate estimates of behavior duration, given that the parameters of the behavior and the sampling technique are matched. However, they can lead to severe over- or underestimations as well, if the recording parameters are not chosen on the basis of the behavior's parameters.

Clinical Use

Systematic behavior observation is used for the identification of clinically adequate treatment procedures and for the evaluation of direct and collateral treatment effects. Ecobehavioral observation systems can help to identify extraneous variables which may interact with certain behavioral procedures under certain conditions. Such findings could be critical for the generalization of behavior programs from the treatment setting to the natural environment of the client.

Future Directions

Systematic behavior observation remains the primary source of behavior assessment in applied behavior analysis of SIB. More emphasis should be placed on validity issues, which have been all but ignored in observational SIB research.

References

Johnson, S.M., & Bolstad, O.D. (1973). Methodological issues in naturalistic observation: Some problems and solutions for field research. In L.A. Hamerlynck, L.C. Hardy, & R.J. Mash (Eds.), *Behavior change: Methodology, concepts, and practice* (pp. 7-67). Champaign, IL: Research Press.

Schroeder, S.R., Rojahn, J., & Mulick, J.A. (1978). Ecobehavioral organization of developmental day care for the chronically self-injurious. *Journal of Pediatric Psychology, 3,* 81-88.

Singh, N.N., & Winton, A.S.W. (1974). Behavioral monitoring of pharmacological interventions for self-injury. *Applied Research in Mental Retardation, 5,* 161-170.

Self-Monitoring Analysis System

David G. Schlundt

Description

The Self-Monitoring Analysis System (SMAS) is a set of computer programs along with self-monitoring forms that are used to identify relationships among antecedents, behaviors, and consequences. The user first constructs a self-monitoring form. The form can consist of any number of variables that sample environmental, affective, and behavioral antecedents, motoric, cognitive, or physiological behaviors, and environmental, affective, and behavioral consequences. The variables can be either free response, multiple choice, or numerical.

Four computer programs make up the SMAS. *Setup* is a program that allows the user to define a set of categorical or numerical variables and to design a data entry screen. *Enter* is a data entry program that allows entering to editing self-monitoring records into a computer data base. *Summary* is a program that operates on self-monitoring data bases to produce statistical summaries. The program produces a graphic plot of the probability distribution of a single categorical variable, a plot of the conditional mean of a numerical variable given each level of a categorical variable, a cross-tabulation table of two categorical variables, a graphic plot of the deviation of the conditional probabilities from the unconditional probability of a category of a variable given the categories of a second categorical variable, and the means, standard deviations, and correlations of two numerical variables. The *Summary* program allows the user to exclude observations having specific values on numerical or categorical variables, and to repeat analyses separately for each level of a categorical variable. The fourth program is *Multicon,* a program that performs multivariate log–linear analysis and multivariate information theory analysis of three or four categorical variables. The multicon program can be used to perform sophisticated sequential analyses of the relationship of antecedents and consequences to self-monitored behaviors.

Purpose

The SMAS implements a methodology for performing observational functional analysis, the study of the relationships among antecedents, behaviors, and consequences, as described in detail by Schlundt (1985). The methodology is used to identify associations among antecedents and behaviors, behaviors and consequences, and antecedents and consequences. It provides a way to operationalize many of the concepts of learning theory (e.g., evocative stimuli, inhibiting stimuli, positive reinforcement, negative reinforcement, safety signals, discriminative stimuli) in observational or correlational data sets. The purpose of the methodology is to provide a way to identify the situational variables that may be controlling behavior for both individuals and populations. The SMAS eliminates clinical judgment from the task of finding patterns in self-monitoring records.

Development

The SMAS was developed as part of programmatic research being conducted on the assessment and treatment of bulimia (Johnson, Schlundt, Kelly, & Ruggiero, 1984; Schlundt, Johnson, & Jarrell, l985). We first started by coding free-response self-monitoring records, keypunching these records, and analyzing these data on a mainframe computer. We soon developed a multiple choice version of the self-monitoring form to eliminate the need to code free response data and to lower the response costs involved in the self-monitoring task.

Microcomputer programs *Setup, Enter, Summary,* and *Multicon* were written on an IBM system/23 and used to collect and analyze eating data from bulimic and overweight patients. These data were used to assess environmental, behavioral, and affective variables that induced overeating and self-induced vomiting. Subsequently, the programs were rewritten into Microsoft *C-Basic* to run on a CP/M microcomputer. Version 3 of the SMAS programs were written in *Turbo Pascal* and are designed to run on most 8-bit and 16-bit microcomputer systems.

Psychometric Characteristics

Self-monitoring is a way to sample target behaviors directly in the natural environment over long periods. As such, traditional concepts of reliability and validity are difficult to apply. The major issues are the extent to which subjects or patients will comply with a self-monitoring task, and the accuracy with which they record their behavior.

The high response cost associated with self-monitoring creates great variability in the degree to which subjects will comply with self-monitoring (Schlundt, Johnson, & Jarrell, l985, Schlundt, Levine, & Jeffrey, 1984). Approximately 15% of the subjects will not self-monitor at all, whereas another 10% will provide records from 100% of the days over an 8- to 12-week period. The remainder generally provide data from 65 to 85% of the assigned days.

Levine, Brown, Raney, Russell, and Schlundt (1984) examined the accuracy of self-reported nutrient intake and showed that most subjects were accurate (r's in the 0.80 to 0.90 range) in their computations of nutrient values of foods they had reported eating.

To the extent that an individual subject complies well with the self-monitoring task and has the requisite verbal and mathematical skills for accurate reporting, a self-monitoring record provides a complete behavioral history including information about the situations in which the target behaviors occurred.

Clinical Use

To date, the SMAS has been used to assess and modify eating behavior in bulimia, obesity, and hypertension. Subjects are instructed to self-monitor during their attempts to make changes in their eating habits. These records are computer analyzed to identify problem situations for each individual. These analyses are then used to structure an individual assessment and problem-solving interaction.

Future Directions

The SMAS is a flexible system that can be used with a wide variety of target behaviors. It can be used to collect baseline data, to monitor the effects of treatment, or to conduct follow-up assessments.

References

Johnson, W.G., Schlundt, D.G., Kelley, M.L., & Ruggiero, L. (1984). Exposure with response prevention and energy in the treatment of bulimia. *International Journal of Eating Disorders, 3,* 37-43.

Levine, K., Brown, S., Raney, C., Russell, L., & Schlundt, D.G. (1984). *Accuracy of self-monitored nutrient intake.* Paper presented at the Mississippi Psychological Association, October, Biloxi.

Schlundt, D.G. (1985). An observational method for functional analysis. *Bulletin of the Society for Psychologist in Addictive Behaviors, 4,* 234-249.

Schlundt, D.G., Johnson, W.G., & Jarrell, M.P. (1985). A naturalistic functional analysis of eating behavior in bulimia. *Advances in Behavior Research and Therapy, 7,* 149-162.

Schlundt, D.G., Levine, K., & Jeffrey, R.W. (1984). *Modality and sex differences in adherence to nutritional behavior modification.* Paper presented at the Association for the Advancement of Behavior Therapy, November, Philadelphia.

Self-Monitoring of Cognitions

Robert E. Becker

Description

Randomly sampled, cued, self-monitoring of cognitions is more a set of data collection procedures than an assessment instrument (at least compared with the traditional paper-and-pencil instruments). This method is one set of several procedures devised to monitor the cognitive activity of a subject and is a variant of the think aloud techniques used by other investigators (cf., Pope, 1978).

This method involves having the subject interrupted by a portable electronic random interval signal generator. On hearing the audible signal, subjects are told to record whatever thoughts they have on an audio recorder provided. In more automated uses the signal generator automatically engages the audiorecorder for a limited period (usually around 20 to 30 seconds). Once the thought data have been collected on audiotape, they are usually transcribed and then unitized according to some specific definitional rule, and a count is made of the various categories of thoughts reported. The process of unitization is complex and several techniques have been employed (See Genest & Turk [1981] for a review.) Some analyses attempted to go further than simple counts and try to identify the process of thinking, with less emphasis on the content.

Purpose

This method has been developed to assess the content of cognitive activity while the person is involved in a particular stimulus situation. A typical application was that employed by Williams and Rappoport (1983) in the assessment of treatment effects on agoraphobic patients. These patients were treated with exposure and cognitive coping strategies in various combinations. During the exposure forays, patients were outfitted with a lapel microphone connected to a portable tape recorder. A signal generator produced a "beep" randomly (about every 90 seconds) and then turned on the tape recorder. Patients then said aloud any of their thoughts. Data were unitized into 20-second recording segments and rated for the occurrence of five different thought content criteria.

Development

Randomly sampled, cued, self-monitoring of cognition developed from earlier "think-aloud" procedures (Meichenbaum & Goodman, 1979). The initial "continuous monologue" procedures seemed to have several problems associated with them. A few of these problems are: (a) continuous talking is tiring for the subject; (b) over-learned behavior may never be reported; (c) talking is slower than thinking and continuous talking forces a slow down in or editing of thinking; (d) continuous talking in the presence of others usually heightens the subject's reactivity to the assessment; (e) unitizing these continuous data is very difficult. Because of these problems, both a mechanical recording of self-talk and a random sampling of thoughts were employed along with specific procedures to unitize and categorize the data.

Psychometric Characteristics

The reliability of the unitization and categorization process has been reported by several investigators and typically have r values that range from .80 to .93. Williams and Rappoport (1983) report that agoraphobic subjects displayed the same level of coping thoughts before treatment and that subjects receiving cognitive treatment did display significantly more coping thoughts after treatment. Several other investigators report significant change in self-reported cognitions following a specific cognitive intervention. (See Kendall & Hollon [1981] for a review.)

Clinical Use

This procedure is not routinely used in clinical assessment. This method or some close variant of it may be an economical and easy way (for the patient) to gather cognitive information. The difficulty obviously lies in the "scoring" of the data.

Future Directions

There are two areas in which further work would aid in the enhanced value of this set of procedures. First, some agreed upon "standard" scoring system for the data would aid clinical use greatly, not to mention research use. Second, more data are needed to demonstrate that changes in these targeted cognitions are actually effective in changing the patient's particular malady.

References

Genest, M., & Turk, D.C. (1981). Think aloud approaches to cognitive assessment. In T.V. Merluzzi, C.R. Glass, & M. Genest (Eds.), Cognitive assessment. New York: Guilford Press.

Kendall, P.C., & Hollon, S.D. (1981). Assessing self-referent speech: Methods in the measurement of self-statements. In P.C. Kendall & S.D. Hollon (Eds.), Assessment strategies for cognitive-behavioral interventions. New York: Academic Press.

Meichenbaum, D., & Goodman, S.H. (1979). Clinical use of private speech and critical questions about its study in naturalistic settings. In G. Ziven (Ed.), Development of self-regulation through private speech. New York: John Wiley & Sons.

Pope, K.S. (1978). How gender, solitude, and posture influence the stream of consciousness. In K.S. Pope & J.L. Singer (Eds.), The stream of consciousness. New York: Plenum Press.

Williams, S.L., & Rappoport, A. (1983). Cognitive treatment in the natural environment for agoraphobics. Behavior Therapy, 14, 299-313.

Self-Reinforcement Questionnaire

Elaine M. Heiby

Description

The Self-Reinforcement Questionnaire (SRQ) is composed of 30 true-false questions. A 13-item short form written at the fourth to sixth grade reading level is available (Heiby & Campos, 1985). The self-report questionnaire also has been referred to as the Frequency of Self-Reinforcement Questionnaire (Heiby, 1982) and the Self-Reinforcement Attitudes Questionnaire (Heiby, 1983a). The items reflect three aspects of the self-reinforcement process (self-monitoring, self-evaluation, and self-reward), as well as general attitudes toward engaging in self-reinforcement. Sample items include, "When I succeed at small things, I become encouraged to go on," and "Praising yourself is being selfish."

Purpose

The SRQ is designed to measure individual differences in how frequently one engages in self-administered covert and overt reinforcement and reward. The SRQ is considered to be measuring a construct referred to as the ego-ideal aspect of the superego by the psychoanalytic theorists and as the self-reinforcement aspect of self-control by the behavioral theorists. Deficits in the self-administration of reinforcement and reward have been implicated in theories concerning the etiology and treatment of general psychopathology, depression, anxiety, and compliance to health regimens.

Of these theories implicating the role of self-reinforcement, those concerning depression have been the most fully developed (e.g., Heiby & Staats, in press). Depression theorists have proposed that individuals with deficit self-reinforcement skills are predisposed to depression when faced with a loss of environmentally controlled reinforcement. These individuals are believed to depend on externally controlled sources of reinforcement and reward, which may fluctuate and occur randomly. Consequently, the mood of those deficit in self-reinforcement skills may fluctuate as a function of changes in sources of environmental reinforcement. Conversely, the mood of those with adequate self-reinforcement skills is considered to be determined by both self-controlled and environmentally controlled reinforcement and therefore may be more stable regardless of how sources in the environment change. Deficits in self-reinforcement may reflect inadequate monitoring of one's behavior (i.e., poor self-awareness), excessively high standards for positive self-evaluation (i.e., having aspirations beyond probable attainment), and failure to self-administer rn self-reinforcement may reflect inadequate monitoring of one's behavior (i.e., poor self-awareness), excessively high standards for positive self-evaluation (i.e., having aspirations beyond probable attainment), and failure to self-administer reinforcement and reward (i.e., poor self-esteem). Self-reinforcement skills can be acquired through modeling and direct training, and training in self-reinforcement has been applied to successfully alleviate depression (Heiby & Staats, in press).

Until the development of the SRQ, individual differences in self-reinforcement skills were measured by observing the frequency of overt reinforcement a subject self-administered during a variety of experimental tasks. Because of the apparent importance of individual differences in self-reinforcement skills, it became necessary to develop a measurement tool for this characteristic that is practical in research and clinical settings.

Development

Item construction followed a rational procedure (Heiby, 1983a). The present author constructed 100 items that were reasoned to pertain in varying degrees to aspects of the self-reinforcement process. These items were presented to 10 Master's level clinical psychology graduate students for classification. Students were provided with a definition of self-reinforcement and were asked to select questions that they judged to be representative of self-reinforcement behavior and that could be responded to as "true or false" and subsequently were combined into a total score. Questions with at least 80% agreement were retained for the SRQ. This procedure resulted in 30 true-false items scored so that a higher score reflects a greater tendency to engage in self-reinforcement. Based on item-total correlations, a 13-item short form also has been developed (Heiby & Campos, 1985).

Psychometric Characteristics

Scores on the SRQ range from 0 to 30. Although norms have yet to be developed, several studies based on different samples of educated adults have found it useful to define a deficit in self-reinforcement skills as a score less than the median of 17 on the instrument (Heiby, 1982, 1983a, 1983b). Unless noted otherwise, all psychometric evaluations of the SRQ have been conducted on samples of undergraduate college students.

Reliability has been evaluated in terms of both internal consistency and stability. Using the split-half method with the Spearman-Brown correction, internal consistency evaluations have yielded coefficients ranging from .68 to .87 (Heiby & Campos, 1985), suggesting that the SRQ is measuring a fairly homogeneous construct. The SRQ scores have also been found to be stable across an 8-week interval with a test-retest coefficient of .92 (Heiby, 1983a), indicating that the instrument could be useful for determining experimental or therapeutic change in self-reinforcement skills. Stability of scores has also been evaluated across situations according to whether the situation involves work, pleasure, or routine activity, and whether the individual is alone or with others. Correlations between self-monitored self-reinforcement and SQR scores in each of these situations were comparable, suggesting that the administration of self-reinforcement is a generalized rather than a situation-specific skill (Heiby, 1982).

Validity of the SRQ has been demonstrated in terms of content, criterion-related, and construct validity evaluations. Content validity of the SRQ was demonstrated in the item selection procedure (Heiby, 1983a). Criterion-related concurrent validity was demonstrated by correlating SRQ scores with (a) frequency of reported self-praise during a variety of experimental tasks yielding r coefficients ranging from .65 to .69 (Heiby 1983a); (b) frequency of self-monitored self-reinforcement over a 1-month period yielding an r coefficient of .78 (Heiby, 1982); and (c) experimenter rating of subjects' tendency to engage in self-reinforcement, yielding an r of .42 (Heiby, 1982). All of these coefficients are significant at the .05 level and suggest that scores on the SRQ are indicative of a tendency to engage in self-reinforcement.

Construct validity has been investigated in terms of convergent-discriminant correlations and experimental manipulations. Discriminant validity has been shown in the lack of a significant correlation between SRQ scores and scores on the Marlowe-Crown Social Desirability Scale (Heiby, 1982), suggesting that responses to the SRQ are not strongly influenced by a tendency to provide socially desirable responses.

Convergent validity has been shown in terms of significant correlations between SRQ scores and measures of characteristics that in theory are expected to be positively or negatively associated with the frequency of self-reinforcement. Theories of self-control predict that infrequent self-reinforcement habits may be accompanied by a relatively high frequency of self-punishment, and a significant negative correlation has been demonstrated (Heiby & Campos, 1985). Theories of compliance with health regimens predict that greater skills in self-reinforcement are associated with motivation to adhere to long-term exercise regimens, and such a relation was demonstrated in a sample of members of a running clinic (Heiby & Campos, 1985). Theories of depression (Heiby & Staats, in press) have predicted a moderate positive relation between this construct and self-reinforcement, and this relation also was demonstrated (Heiby, 1982; Heiby & Campos, 1985). Theories of depression have also proposed the role of general cognitive dysfunction in depression, and one study has shown a moderate correlation between measures of general dysfunction and deficit self-reinforcement skills, suggesting that the SRQ is measuring a construct related to dysfunctional interpretations of one's own behavior and of environmental events (Heiby & Campos, 1985).

Construct validity of the SRQ has also been demonstrated in experimental studies. Low (less than 17) SRQ scores were found to be predictive of mood fluctuations (Heiby, 1983b) and depression (Heiby & Campos, 1985) in both undergraduate students and outpatient psychiatric samples. The SRQ scores also were useful in predicting a depressed person's response to treatment matched or unmatched to the presenting deficit (Heiby & Campos, 1985). Finally, SRQ scores were found to increase following training in self-reinforcement, and such training accompanies a decrease in reported depression (Heiby & Campos, 1985).

Clinical Use

There is persuasive evidence suggesting that the SRQ may be useful in identifying individuals who are predisposed to depression and in identifying depressed individuals whose depression is at least partly a function of deficits in self-reinforcement skills. The SRQ can also be used to evaluate the effects of training in self-reinforcement skills. Some data suggest that the SRQ may be useful in identifying individuals who may be vulnerable to non-compliance to a long-term health-related lifestyle regimen.

Future Directions

The SRQ has sufficient evidence of reliability and validity to warrant the development of norms and the establishment of cross-validation support for the application of the instrument to the population at large. We are currently planning a study to establish norms applicable to the US population including the various ethnic groups represented in Hawaii. We are also developing alternate forms of the SRQ to facilitate multiple assessments of self-reinforcement skills.

References

Heiby, E.M. (1982). A self-reinforcement questionnaire. *Behaviour Research and Therapy, 20,* 397-401.

Heiby, E.M. (1983a). The assessment of frequency of self-reinforcement. *Journal of Personality and Social Psychology, 44,* 263-270.

Heiby, E.M. (1983b). Toward the prediction of mood change. *Behavior Therapy, 14,* 110-115.

Heiby, E.M., & Campos, P.E. (1985). Measurement of individual differences in self-reinforcement. Paper presented at the 9th Internal Conference on Personality Assessment, Honolulu, Hawaii, March 10-11.

Heiby, E.M., & Staats, A.W. (in press). Depression and its classification. In I. Evans (Ed.), *Paradigmatic behavior therapy: Critical perspectives on applied social behaviorism.* New York: Springer.

Self-Schema in Depression

Nicholas A. Kuiper

Description

Self-schema in depression can be assessed by a self-reference rating and recall technique developed originally for social cognition research on the self (Kuiper, Derry, & MacDonald, 1982). In this approach, the self-schema is postulated to be a well-organized memory structure that facilitates the efficient processing, storage, and retrieval of personal information. Important self-relevant information is stored in the self-schema in terms of general personality traits and characteristics.

In using the self-reference technique, the respondent first makes a series of yes or no personality judgments on a list of 60 personal adjectives (Cue question: "Does this word describe you?"). Thirty of these adjectives are depressed in content (e.g., bleak and troubled), whereas 30 are nondepressed (e.g., capable and sociable). After the entire set of yes/no judgments have been completed and recorded, the respondent is asked to recall as many of the adjectives as possible, within a 2- to 3-minute period. In a paper-and-pencil format, this technique can easily be administered to either individuals or groups and produces two measures of interest: (a) the number of yes responses to depressed and nondepressed content adjectives, and (b) the recall for the adjectives. A slightly modified version of this technique also allows for the collection of rating times for each yes/no self-referent judgment, but necessitates an individual testing procedure (Derry & Kuiper, 1981). For both forms of the self-reference technique the pattern of yes responses and the recall performance are used as measures of self-schema content (depressed versus nondepressed). The rating times gathered in the individual assessment procedure are employed as a measure of processing efficiency and, in turn, suggest a well-consolidated self-schema (Kuiper & Olinger, in press).

Purpose

The self-reference technique has been used primarily as a research tool to provide converging empirical support for the self-schema model of depression as described in detail elsewhere (Kuiper et al., 1982; Kuiper & Olinger, 1986). The recall and rating time measures associated with this technique generally offer an alternative to an exclusive reliance on self-report measures that may be particularly susceptible to the negative response biases that often characterize depression (Derry & Kuiper, 1981). In addition, the combination of measures involved in the self-reference technique (yes responses, recall, and rating times) allows for the development and empirical investigation of theoretical constructs not easily considered or assessed by traditional self-report measures. As one example, the rating time measure provides a useful index of self-schema processing efficiency, a schema construct not easily addressed by typical self-report measures.

Development

The entire set of 60 personal adjectives employed in the self-referent task, along with normative information, is presented in detail by Kuiper et al. (1982). To briefly summarize, the original pool of nondepressed and depressed content personal adjectives was taken from a wide variety of sources, including Jackson's Personality Research Form, Lubin's Depression Adjective Checklist, and various descriptions of depressed individuals. The final lists of 30 depressed and 30 nondepressed content adjectives were constructed to ensure that possible confounding variables, such as work frequency, word length, and imagery values, were controlled for across the lists. The self-referent cue question and response measures were derived from work in social cognition and cognitive psychology, with particular emphasis on the depth of processing memory models (Derry & Kuiper, 1981). The rating time measure was derived from cognitive psychology approaches that have focused on rating times as an index of information processing efficiency (Kuiper et al., 1982; Kuiper & Olinger, 1986).

Psychometric Characteristics

In terms of face validity, several clinical and university samples (normals, mildly depressed, clinically depressed, and nondepressed psychiatric control groups) have provided content ratings that clearly distinguish the two adjective sets in terms of their depressed versus nondepressed content. With respect to both concurrent and construct validity, individuals have been categorized into depressed or nondepressed groups on the basis of several depression measures, including the Beck

Depression Inventory, the Hamilton Rating Scale for Depression, and the Multiple Affect Adjective Checklist. Across a variety of studies, these groups then displayed the expected content differences for the three response measures associated with the self-reference technique. Furthermore, these measures are also sensitive to variations in the level of depression, with distinctive self-referent patterns being predicted and observed for mild versus clinically depressed subjects (Kuiper et al., 1982; Kuiper & Olinger, 1986).

Research also provides information on discriminant validity, with self-schema effects being restricted to adjectives receiving the self-reference cue question (versus semantic or other-referent cue question). In addition, depressive self-schema effects are not related to MAACL anxiety or hostility ratings, or evident in nondepressed psychiatric control subjects (Derry & Kuiper, 1981). Finally, schematic effects do not appear to be sensitive to other possible confounding variables, such as IQ level or general speed of responding (Derry & Kuiper, 1981; Kuiper et al., 1982).

The reliability or consistency of self-schema responding has been examined using a modified test-retest formula. As one illustration, MacDonald and Kuiper (1984) computed an index of consistency between yes/no self-referent judgments and subsequent 9-point self-ratings. Using this index, both normal and clinically depressed subjects displayed a high degree of response consistency for schema-congruent content (85 to 98%).

Clinical Use and Future Directions

To date, the self-reference technique has been employed primarily as a research tool. The recent advent of microcomputer systems, however, suggests that this technique could easily be adapted to the clinical setting. Testing procedures and scoring could be computerized, thus resulting in an easily administered and relatively quick (10- to 15-minute) measure of the self-schema in depression. This technique could be employed in an initial assessment or used several times throughout the course of therapy, to provide a schema-based measure of therapy effectiveness.

References

Derry, P. A. & Kuiper, N. A. (1981). Schematic processing and self-reference in clinical depression. *Journal of Abnormal Psychology, 90,* 286-297.

Kuiper, N. A., Derry, P. A., & MacDonald, M. R. (1982). Self-reference and person perception in depression: A social cognition perspective. In G. Weary & H. Mirels (Eds.), *Integrations of clinical and social psychology* (pp. 79-103). New York: Oxford University Press.

Kuiper, N. A., & Olinger, L. J. (1986). Dysfunctional attitudes and a self-worth contingency model of depression. In P.C. Kendall (Ed.) *Advances in cognitive-behavioral research and therapy,* Ch. 1, Vol. 5. (pp. 115-142). New York: Academic Press.

MacDonald, M. R., & Kuiper, N. A. (1984). *Self-schema decision consistency in clinical depressives. Journal of Social and Clinical Psychology, 2,* 264-272.

Self-Statement Assessment via Thought Listing

Valerie S. Tarico and Elizabeth M. Altmaier

Description

The "thought-listing" label actually represents a family of self-report techniques for eliciting and quantifying cognitions. These techniques share in common the fact that the researcher or practitioner is interested in obtaining the subject or client's thoughts relevant to some experimental (e.g., persuasion or influence attempt) or clinical (e.g., public speaking) situation. However, the techniques vary in the means by which thoughts are solicited and the format in which they are considered. Cacioppo and Petty (1981) provide an overview of the different forms the procedure may take and discuss their relative advantages and disadvantages.

Most commonly, discrete sentences or meaning units are requested. For example, subjects may be given sheets marked with boxes, one box for each individual thought, to assure this kind of response. Alternately, the subject or client may engage in stream of consciousness expression, which is given an overall rating or broken into units by either the person or a rater at a later time. Another possibility is for persons to keep journals of thoughts about a given topic over a period of days or weeks. Thoughts may be elicited in oral form, which has the advantage of being immediate and easy, or in written form, which permits group assessment and may reduce self-consciousness.

Bounds on the range of thoughts solicited also vary. The researcher or clinician may request thoughts elicited by a specific stimulus, thoughts on a given topic, or all thoughts that occur during a set time period. The first of these is the most restrictive in that it assumes that subjects can discriminate which of their thoughts were triggered by the stimulus. Additionally, some research evidence suggests that it produces more reactive responsès than do the other two types of instructions (Cacioppo & Petty, 1981). The second type of instruction tends to produce balanced thoughts covering both sides of an issue, as opposed to the subject's predominant reaction or feelings. However, the third type of instructions usually produces a more spontaneous, unfiltered reaction to the stimulus situation, including both relevant and irrelevant thoughts. Therefore, in many cases the last type of instructions is to be preferred. However, for particular purposes, one of the first two methods may be more appropriate.

Deciding the form and range of thoughts to be solicited is the first step in implementing a thought-listing procedure. Once obtained, listed thoughts are quantified according to a rating system molded to the questions of interest. In the past, thoughts were rated for realism, function, and origin, to name a few examples. Two of the most popular dimensions are polarity (favorable/neutral or unfavorable) and target (stimulus situation/self-other or on-task/off-task). To illustrate, in scoring thoughts about performance situations (e.g., public speaking), the authors have employed a system in which thoughts are rated for valence or polarity (facilitative/debilitative) and for intensity (ranging from 1 to 3). A thought such as, "When I walk to the front of the room, I'll get light-headed and dizzy," would merit a rating of 3 (debilitative, high intensity). Whatever the rating system, raters need to be provided with instructions and training for placing thoughts in each category. (See Tarico, Van Velzen, Altmaier [in press] for a review of rating systems.)

The raters themselves represent another factor that varies across applications of thought-listing procedures. Trained raters are often used to quantify or classify thoughts. However, Tarico et al. (in press) report that ratings by research participants themselves predicted criterion measures as well as those by trained raters, and were more economical.

Purpose

Growing numbers of psychologists recently have come to acknowledge that a consideration of cognitive processes contributes to our understanding of human behavior. Even among the most staunch behaviorists, thoughts have been called a subset of human behavior, subject to the same laws of learning and environmental determinism as are overt

actions and legitimate as a topic of study. Another prevalent view is the interactionist perspective, in which cognitions are viewed as crucial mediators between the environment and behavior. With increasing attention to thought processes, cognitive assessment has become an important part of the behavioral scientist's repertoire of skills.

In research settings, the thought-listing method has served many different functions. Listed thoughts have served as independent variables, dependent variables, and manipulation checks. The procedure has been used in persuasion research, treatment outcome assessment, and correlational studies relating thoughts to various behaviors, affects, or states. The technique provides a way of gathering data that directly bear on many of the assumptions and hypotheses of the cognitive learning perspective. Altmaier and Tarico (under review) employed the thought-listing technique in a study designed to examine the reciprocal influence of thoughts and behaviors in a speech performance setting among anxious and nonanxious students.

The applications to clinical work are also numerous. Cacioppo and Petty (1981) noted that if maladaptive self-statements are to be changed (which is the stated goal of several cognitive therapies), they must first be identified. The thought-listing procedure can be used to obtain a listing of maladaptive beliefs and self-statements. Research in the cognitive behavioral perspective has produced evidence to suggest that anticipated contingencies predict behavior better than do actual contingencies. So, even if one is attempting to change overt behavior through contingency management, it may be helpful to know the client's idiosyncratic understanding of the rewards or punishers and their relation to behavior. For example, Huber and Altmaier (1983) assessed the thoughts of snake phobic and nonphobic subjects to relate cognitions to avoidance behavior. The thought-listing method may also be used to determine the target of interventions or to assess the effectiveness of interventions once made.

Development

At a broad level, thought-listing emerged out of cognitive-behavioral and cognitive theories and the need for assessment tools that fit these conceptions of human functioning. George Kelly's personal construct theory, for example, postulates that to faciliate change, one must first understand both the content and organization of a person's thoughts. Bandura and Mischel have produced evidence to substantiate their claims that active construing of experience mediates the relationship between person and environment. However, use of the technique has not been limited to the realm of these theories. Researchers and practitioners have adapted dimensions to fit theories from analytic to behavioral and to fit the needs presented by specific practical problems. In some cases, pilot studies have been used to identify categories of thoughts that are characteristic of a target situation. A strength of the technique lies in its flexibility; each user can develop a means of soliciting and categorizing thoughts that best suits his or her purposes.

Psychometric Characteristics

The thought-listing method has generally been found to have reliability comparable to that of other cognitive assessment techniques. Cullin (1968) compared thought-listing to Thurstone and Likert scales for attitude assessment, and found split-half and test-retest reliabilities that were acceptable and intermediate to these other two methodologies. Interrater reliabilities for the system employed by Altmaier and colleagues average .92 (Tarico et al., in press).

Listed thoughts have been found to be sensitive to manipulations of both information processing and environmental influences (Cacioppo & Petty, 1981). They generally correlate moderately with behavioral and other self-report measures of the phenomenon in question. These phenomena cover a broad range and include attitudes, social interaction, and engagement in previously anxiety-provoking action.

Clinical Use

Thought-listing techniques provide an assessment device that clearly fits the therapeutic focus of cognitive therapists, such as Beck and Ellis. Like any diagnostic tool, it may be used to gain a better understanding of the nature and extent of problems, which in these therapies are characterized by maladaptive or irrational thoughts. The technique may also be used during the course of therapy to call attention to remaining problematic cognitions, to underscore change, and to monitor the efficacy of interventions. In Meichenbaum's self-instruction therapy, for example, thought-listing might be

applied in target situations to assess change in self-instructions. Self-statement assessment at the end of therapy can provide a measure of outcome and a source of feedback to the therapist and client.

Future Directions

Two types of change in the thought-listing technique may be expected in the near future. Some researchers, to avoid the difficulties inherent in soliciting and then organizing unstandardized material, are developing inventories of listed thoughts. These typically are constructed after a period of work in an area during which thoughts are solicited in a free format; thoughts commonly elicited are included in the inventory. This format greatly facilitates quantification of thoughts, evaluation of change, and comparison across persons. However, it has the disadvantage of potentially suggesting thoughts not listed on the inventory.

Because of these drawbacks, and the large quantities of data necessary to develop appropriate inventories, it is expected that unstandardized thought-listing will continue to be used widely in research as well as in clinical settings. Currently, most researchers train raters who quantify thoughts that have been attained. However, Cacioppo and Petty (1981) and Tarico et al. (in press) suggest situations in which subject ratings of thoughts may be preferable. It is probable that subject or client rating will become more common as evidence for this method becomes available, and as the thought-listing technique is used more widely in clinical practice.

References

Altmaier, E. M., & Tarico, V. A. (1985). *Reciprocal influence of thoughts and cognitions*. Unpublished manuscript.

Cacioppo, J. T., & Petty, R. E. (1981). Social psychological procedures for cognitive response assessment: The thought-listing technique. In T. V. Marluzzi, C. R. Glass, & M. Genest (Eds.), *Cognitive Assessment* (pp. 309-342). New York: Guilford Press.

Cullin, D. M. (1968). Attitude measurement by cognitive sampling. (Doctoral dissertation, Ohio State University, 1968). *Dissertation Abstracts International, 29*, 159A.

Huber, J. W., & Altmaier, E. M. (1983). An investigation of the self-statement systems of phobic and nonphobic individuals. *Cognitive Therapy and Research, 7*, 355-362.

Tarico, V. S., Van Velzen, D. R., & Altmaier, E. M. (1986). A comparison of thought-listing rating methods. *Journal of Counseling Psychology, 33*, 81-83.

Semantic Differential of Sex Roles

R. Julian Hafner

Description

The original version of the Semantic Differential of Sex Roles (Hafner, 1984) has been superseded by the instrument now to be described. Basically, the instrument comprises 15 scales (e.g., assertive and sympathetic), each to be rated at one of seven equidistant points. The scales are derived from Andrew and Ross' (1981) work on the BEM Sex Role Inventory.

The 15 scales form three subscales: (a) *Power* (Assertive, Strong Personality, Forceful, Dominant, Aggressive, and Acts as Leader); (b) *Empathy* (Sympathetic, Understanding, Compassionate, Warm, Tender, and Gentle); and (c) *Autonomy* (Self-reliant, Independent, and Self-sufficient).

Scoring is simple: each scale point is allocated a score from 1 to 7. *Total* the scores on the individual scales within each subscale and then *divide* by the number of scales to yield a *mean score* for each subscale. Thus, mean scores for each subscale will range from 1 to 7.

Concepts can be selected according to the aim of the researcher or therapist. In *marital work,* the primary role of the instrument, four concepts are used: (a) Myself as I am (actual self); (b) Myself as I would like to be (ideal self); (c) My partner as he/she is (actual spouse); and (d) My partner as I would like him or her to be (ideal spouse). For *each concept,* the instrument is scored as just outlined. In marital work, the instrument should ideally be given to both partners.

Purpose

1. *Measurement of Overt Marital Dissatisfaction* is obtained by substracting Actual Spouse score from Ideal Spouse score on each of the three subscales. The greater the overall difference, the greater is marital dissatisfaction.

2. *Measurement of Dissatisfaction with Self* is obtained by subtracting Actual Self score from Ideal Self score on each subscale, and totalling the three scores.

3. *Measurement of Sex Role Stereotyping.* In women rating the "Myself" concept, a high score on Empathy and lower scores on Power and Autonomy indicate a sex-role stereotyped self-perception. In men, this is indicated by high scores on

Power and Autonomy and relatively low Empathy scores. For both sexes, high scores on all three subscales reflect *androgyny,* and low scores indicate an *undifferentiated* status.

Applied to married couples, the Semantic Differential measures the extent of agreement or disagreement about sex-role stereotyping within the marriage.

4. *Measurement of Denied Conflict.* When one or both partners *deny* martial conflict, the Semantic Differential allows *indirect* assessment. This is achieved by subtracting clients' ratings of their spouses (on each subscale) from spouses self-ratings. Only Actual Spouse and Actual Self measures are used. The greater the difference, the greater is the *spouse perception discrepancy* of each partner. This discrepancy often reflects fundamental marital problems that are usually difficult or impossible to measure directly (Hafner, 1984).

Development

The Semantic Differential in its current form is in the early stages of development. Although some normative data are provided below, and the instrument itself is based on factor analytic studies of the Bem Sex Role Inventory (Andrew & Ross, 1981), reliability and validity remain to be established.

Psychometric Characteristics

These normative data are derived from 68 married couples aged 18 to 60 and free of any significant psychiatric disorder.

Clinical Use

The Semantic Differential is of value in both clinical and research settings. Independently of the present author, Bland and Hallam (1981) found a semantic differential measure of marital adjustment to be the best predictor of the outcome of behavioral therapy for agoraphobia.

Future Directions

As the marital contribution to persisting psychiatric disorders becomes more widely acknowledged, it will be necessary to develop simple, valid, reliable, and relevant measures of marital adjustment in a clinical or research setting.

The Semantic Differential is an efficient and acceptable means of measuring several aspects of marital adjustment that are relevant not just to psychiatric disorders, but also to obesity and other disorders in which psychosocial factors play an important part.

References

Andrew, G.M., & Ross, M.W. (1981). A short form of the Bem Sex Role Inventory. *Journal of Psychiatric Treatment and Evaluation, 3,* 563-566.

Bland, K., & Hallam, R.S. (1981). Relationship between response to graded exposure and marital satisfaction in agoraphobics. *Behaviour Research and Therapy, 19,* 335-338.

Hafner, R.J. (1984). The marital repercussions of behavior therapy for agoraphobia. *Psychotherapy, 21,* 530-542.

Sensation Scale

Stephen A. Maisto and Gerard J. Connors

Description

The Sensation Scale consists of 26 adjectives (items) that describe behavioral, psychological, and physical effects that persons experience when drinking alcohol. Each item is rated on a scale of 0 (not at all) to 10 (a great deal) to indicate the extent to which a particular effect is experienced. The 26 variables are clustered into six dimensions that will be described.

Purpose

The original purpose in developing the Sensation Scale was to advance research on blood alcohol level (BAL) discrimination training, a technique designed to help individuals attain better control over their drinking (Caddy, 1978). In this regard, BAL discrimination training required persons to associate internal and behavioral cues with different BALs. The Sensation Scale provided a structured format to help subjects do this.

Although the Sensation Scale has proved useful in research on BAL discrimination training, it may be used in any basic or applied research or in prevention and treatment programs that involve measurement of behavioral, physiological, and psychological experiences of individuals consuming alcohol.

Development

Original Construction of the Sensation Scale.   The initial sample of adjectives describing sensations and feelings associated with drinking alcohol was obtained empirically.

There were 16 male and 16 female subjects who volunteered to participate in the study. These subjects were selected to be at least 18 years of age and to represent the range of light-to-heavy drinkers. No subject had alcohol problems or reported physical contraindications to the use of alcohol.

Subjects had no food or beverages other than water for 4 hours preceding their experimental sessions.

Subjects were randomly assigned so that half of each sex group received American regular beer and half received brandy served with ice. Subjects received their beverages in a dose divided into three parts and designed to raise the BALs to 0.08% (g of alcohol/100 ml of blood). The three drinks were consumed consecutively; 5 minutes were allowed for consumption of each of the three drinks, which were separated by 15-minute intervals.

The session took place in a bland but comfortable laboratory setting, and reading and other activities that could interfere with subjects' describing their sensations were not permitted.

After subjects consumed their first drink, they were asked to write down any changes they experienced in various modalities (e.g., visual, auditory, gastrointestinal, and mental). Subjects continued to record these changes through the drinking period to the time their BALs peaked and had descended to 0.05% or lower, when they were dismissed from the laboratory.

This procedure resulted in a listing of 179 different adjectives.

Adesso and Lauerman (1975) extracted the most frequently occurring adjectives, collapsed across similar meanings, and finally included 30 different variables. Maisto and Adesso (1977) added "powerful" to this list, and had their subjects report on a scale of 0 to 10 the degree to which they experienced a given sensation, and not merely whether they experienced it.

Adjective sorting.   To reduce the number of variables the 31 adjectives were sorted subjectively on the basis of face validity into the minimum number of categories that would include the most variables.

The adjectives that seemed to go together were listed under one and only one factor. One "other" category also was included. The results of this sorting and the names given to the categories are as follows: (a) *Gastrointestinal:* Nauseous, stomach growling, burning in stomach, and stomach bloated; (b) *Anesthetic:* tongue thicker, face numb, numb all over, lips numb, head numb, relaxed, drowsy, limbs heavy, and heavy; (c) *Central Stimulant:* lightheaded, dizzy, ringing, and buzzing; (d) *Impaired Function:* impaired writing, impaired vision, and difficulty with thinking; (e) *Warmth/ Glow:* warm; (f) *Dynamic Peripheral:* breathing changing, face flush, cheeks warm, heart beat changing, and body rushes; (g) *Other:* powerful, itchy, hands cool, head throbbing, and ears tingling.

Psychometric Characteristics

The reliability of the Sensation Scale was established by assessing interrater agreement with the classification of the scale items. In this study, 18 undergraduate and 7 graduate psychology students were given a list of the (randomly ordered) 31 sensation adjectives and the sensation categories.

Subjects were given a definition for each category as follows: Gastrointestinal: sensations you feel in your stomach; Impaired Function: effects that describe changes in certain abilities or skills; Warmth/Glow: effects associated with blushing sensations; Central Stimulant: sensations involving effects on the brain, or what is commonly called "getting high"; Anesthetic: sensations associated with loss of feeling or with decreased sensitivity to feelings; Dynamic Peripheral: sensations associated with how you would feel when out of breath, frightened, or excited; Other: sensations not logically described by the other six categories.

After receiving this information, subjects were instructed to read over the 31 adjectives and the category headings with their respective descriptions. Subjects then were instructed to "sort the adjectives into whichever category is most appropriate," using the category headings and descriptions as a guide. They were told that the same adjective could not appear under two category headings, and that all 31 adjectives had to be in the "Other" category. No time limit was imposed for these sortings.

The reliability data were analyzed by computing the percentage of sorts that agreed with the a priori category sortings.

Specifically, a variable sort was scored as an agreement if the subject assigned it to the same category heading as it appeared in the a priori classification. The tabulation of the subject sorts showed the following percentages of agreement: Gastrointestinal factor, 97%: Anesthetic factor, 61%; Central Stimulant factor, 80%; Impaired Function factor, 89%; Warmth/Glow factor, 96%; Dynamic Peripheral factor, 76%; Other, 44%.

The validity of the Sensation Scale has been established in studies that have involved the administration of low to moderate doses of alcohol to nonalcoholic subjects. These experiments have shown consistently that the Sensation Scale discriminates between subjects who drink at least a low dose of alcohol (designed to raise the BAL to .035%) and those who drink no alcohol. (For two recent examples, see O'Malley & Maisto, 1984; Sher, 1985).

Clinical Use

The Sensation Scale was originally designed as an aid to training persons who abuse alcohol or who are alcohol dependent to control their drinking. Of course, the Scale still is useful for this purpose, but currently it seems to have widest application in primary prevention in conjunction with providing individuals with self-control techniques to modulate their drinking.

Future Directions

As a research and clinical instrument, the Sensation Scale probably can be improved by studies of the sensations that people experience when consuming doses of alcohol that are higher than that used in previous research. Second, because the scale was developed and has been tested in fairly bland laboratory settings, it is important to see how setting factors affect the sensations that people report.

References

Adesso, V.J., & Lauerman, R. (1975). Unpublished data University of Wisconsin, Milwaukee.

Caddy, G.R. (1978). Blood alcohol concentration discrimination training: Development and current status. In G.A. Marlatt & P.E. Nathan (Eds.), *Behavioral approaches to alcoholism* (pp. 114-129). New Brunswick, NJ: Rutgers Center of Alcohol Studies.

Maisto, S.A., & Adesso, V.J. (1977). Effect of instructions and feedback on blood alcohol level discrimination training in nonalcoholic drinking. *Journal of Consulting and Clinical Psychology, 45,* 625-636.

O'Malley, S.S., & Maisto, S.A. (1984). Factors affecting the perception of intoxication: Dose, tolerance, and setting. *Addictive Behaviors, 9,* 111-120.

Sher, K.J. (1985). Subjective effects of alcohol: The influence of setting and individual differences in alcohol expectancies. *Journal of Studies on Alcohol, 46,* 137-146.

Sensation Seeking Scale-Form VI

Marvin Zuckerman

Description

Previous forms (II, IV, and V) of the Sensation Seeking Scale (SSS: Zuckerman, 1979) used a forced choice type of item. Forms IV and V contain four subscales derived from factor analyses of the items: Thrill and Adventure Seeking (TAS), Experience Seeking (ES), Disinhibition (Dis), and Boredom Susceptibility (BS). Form IV also contains a General scale and Form V has a Total score based on the sum of the four subscales. These scales contain a mixture of items asking about actual experiences or preferences and intentions, or what one would like to do.

Form VI separates the test into two parts: one set of scales based on actual experience of sensation-seeking activities and the other based on intentions for the future, regardless of whether or not one has had any experience with the particular activities. The forced choice format has been replaced by 3-point item responses. In the Experience scales the subjects are asked to indicate for each activity whether they have: (a) never done this; (b) have done this once; or (c) have done this more than once. In the Intention scales the subjects are asked to indicate for each activity whether they: (a) have no desire to do this; (b) have thought of doing it but will probably not do it; and (c) have thought of doing it and will do it if given the chance. The same activities listed in the Experience section are listed again in the Intentions section. Two of the factors contained in Forms IV and V are represented in both Experience and Intentions parts of the SSS VI: TAS and Dis. This results in four scales: (a) *Experience-Thrill and Adventure Seeking* (E-TAS): The weighted scores based on the reports that one has engaged in adventurous and physically risky activities like mountain climbing, parachute jumping, car racing, and swimming far out from shore. (b) *Intentions-Thrill and Adventure Seeking* (I-TAS):

The weighted scores based on the reported intention of doing such activities in the future. (c) *Experience-Disinhibition* (E-Dis): The weighted scores based on assertions that one has engaged in unconventional or uninhibited activities such as going to "wild" parties, having sex with strangers, trying drugs, getting drunk, and shocking older persons just for the fun of it. (d) *Intentions-Disinhibition* (I-Dis): The weighted scores based on the reported intentions of engaging in such activities in the future.

In addition to these content scales there is one validity scale: *Lie.* This consists of seven TAS items in which an assertion that one has had the experience is infrequent and improbable, for example, swimming the English channel, climbing Mount Everest, taking a trip to the moon, or hunting lions and tigers. These items are not scored in the E-TAS scale and any claim to experience of one of these may invalidate the record.

However, the items are scored in the I-TAS, because one may legitimately claim the desire or intention to engage in the activity.

There are 64 items in each of the two parts of the test for a total of 128 items. The test usually takes about 20 minutes to complete.

Purpose

A large body of literature has established the predictive value of previous forms of the SSS in many areas of activity including sexual experience, drug use (even when specific drug items are omitted), volunteering for unusual activities, responses to confinement, gambling, and other (Zuckerman, 1979, 1983). In a study of behavior in actual phobic situations, the TAS subscale predicted approach-avoidance behavior and self-reported anxiety as highly as specific-situation anxiety scales and better than general anxiety scales (Mellstrom, Cicala, & Zuckerman, 1976). The SSS scores are high in antisocial personalities, drug abusers, and manic depressives and low in schizophrenics. Sensation-seeking motives are involved in much normal and abnormal behavior, but this factor is often neglected in selecting predictive measures.

The purpose of separating experience from intention in the SSS is to get an estimate of the discrepancy between sensation-seeking need and actual experience, or changes in sensation-seeking need as reflected in a discrepancy between past experience and future intentions. These discrepancies should make the SSS more useful in studies of depression or mania in which there may be changes in sensation-seeking needs based on the clinical state or in studies of aging in which the discrepancy may reflect physical or motivational decline, or both.

Development

The TAS and Dis items from previous forms that describe activities, rather than attitudes or desires, were shortened and together with newly written items were used in an experimental form of the new SSS (Zuckerman, 1984). The experimental form was given to a sample of 215 undergraduates, and their responses to the items were factor analyzed separately for male and female subjects. Two factors were rotated for each analysis in accordance with the design of the item selection.

Although both sections of the test were factor analyzed separately, only the results of analyses of the Intentions scale were used to select items for both parts, because these items separated clearly into the TAS and Dis factors in both sexes.

Using the criterion of similar loadings for male and female subjects, 42 items were selected for a Dis scale and 22 for a TAS scale. The same 64 items are used in the two parts of the test.

Psychometric Characteristics

As noted in the previous section, items were selected for the two scales using the criterion of loadings on the two relevant factors in both sexes.

Internal reliabilities in the form of alpha coefficients were calculated in a second sample. The coefficients for male and female subjects were: E-TAS .62 and .69; E-Dis .93 and .89; I-TAS .91 and .89; I-Dis .94 and .88. Only the E-TAS scale showed less than optimal internal reliability, probably because of the shorter length of the scale (15 items) and the lower frequency of reports of experience in these physically risky activities.

Retest reliabilities of the four scales over a 7-week test-retest interval ranged from .84 for I-TAS to .93 for both E-TAS and E-Dis.

The E-TAS and E-Dis were correlated at .45 and I-TAS and I-Dis also correlated at .45. These correlations are somewhat higher than those between TAS and Dis in Forms IV and V of the SSS. The E-TAS and I-TAS correlated at .49 and E-Dis correlated at .70, showing substantial relation between reported experience and desires and intentions for the future, particularly for Dis.

Correlations for male and female subjects between the corresponding scales of Forms V and VI were: Form V TAS versus E-TAS .52 and .53; TAS versus I-TAS .79 and .64; Form V Dis versus E-Dis .67 and .61; Dis versus I-Dis .70 and .68. As might be expected, correlations between Forms V and VI are higher for the Intention than for the Experience scale.

Norms are now being calculated for the SSS-VI on a college student population. It is essential that scales be expressed in standard score form to interpret the discrepancies between Experience and Intention scales. Data are being collected by investigators at the National Institute on Aging, which should eventually provide norms for an older normal population.

Clinical Use

The SSS-VI Dis scales should prove valuable in the assessment of antisocial personality and other types of impulse disorder. Discrepancies between standardized Experience and Intention scales should be of value in assessment of affective disorders. If there is a major discrepancy between past experience and future intentions that cannot be accounted for by age, this could be one sign of depression. Scores could also be used to distinguish character traits that are important in therapeutic goals. One does not want to attempt to disinhibit a basically low sensation seeker, but highs may need some counseling as to socially acceptable modes of sensation seeking.

Sensation seeking has shown high correlations between happily married couples and low relationships between those seeking marital therapy (Ficher, Zuckerman, & Neeb, 1981). The SSS-VI may be useful in assessing discrepancy between experience and intention in both partners in a relationship as a possible source of conflict.

Future Directions

Apart from the investigation of clinical applications just described, the SSS-IV should provide reliable scales for investigation of the sensation-seeking motive and its role in basic psychological processes. The Dis scale in Forms IV and V has proved to be the scale most related to certain biological measures including gonadal hormones, augmenting of the critical evoked potential, and heart rate acceleration or deceleration in response to tones of moderate to high intensity.

The SSS-VI Dis scales are more extensive than the one in Form V and provide a more reliable mode for investigations of biological or social phenomena related to sensation seeking.

References

Ficher, I.V., Zuckerman, M., & Neeb, M. (1981). Marital compatibility and sensation seeking trait as a factor in marital adjustment. *Journal of Sex and Marital Therapy, 7*, 60-69.

Mellstrom, M., Cicala, G.A., & Zuckerman, M. (1976). General versus specific trait anxiety measures in the prediction of fear of snakes, heights, and darkness. *Journal of Consulting and Clinical Psychology, 44*, 83-91.

Zuckerman, M. (1979). *Sensation seeking: Beyond the optimal level of arousal.* Hillside, NJ: Erlbaum.

Zuckerman, M. (1983). A biological theory of sensation seeking. In M. Zuckerman (Ed.), *Biological bases of sensation seeking, impulsivity, and anxiety* (pp. 37-76). Hillsdale, NJ: Erlbaum.

Zuckerman, M. (1984). Experience and desire: A new format for Sensation Seeking Scales. *Journal of Behavioral Assessment, 2*, 101-114.

Sexual Experience Scales

Walter Everard

Description

The Sexual Experience Scales (SES) comprise an inventory consisting of four scales intended to measure four aspects of sexual experience, as follows: SES 1: Restrictive sexual morality (rejection versus acceptance), 21 items; SES 2: Psychosexual stimulation (seeking, allowing versus avoidance of symbolic sexual stimuli), 15 items; SES 3: Sexual motivation (approach tendency versus avoidance tendency in sexual interaction with partner), 29 items; SES 4: Attraction to own marriage (low versus high), 18 items.

The SES contains a total of 83 multiformatted questions. In addition to the four major scales, partial aspects of SES scales are measured by 14 relatively independent subscales. The scales originally were developed as research instruments, but have proven to be of use in clinical practice.

Purpose

The scales were developed to study sexual aversion in middle-class married couples (Frenken, 1976). The SES can be used as a research instrument in social and medical sexological research. It can also be used as an additional instrument in the assessment of sexual complaints. In the area of therapy effect research the SES scales also have been useful.

Development

The construction of the scales was part of a larger study into the structure and significance of sexual behavior as experienced within marriage. Special emphasis was placed on the negative and conflict-provoking characteristics of sexuality (Frenken, 1976). Acceptance versus rejection of sexuality was the hypothetical basic dimension of sexual experience. Most hypotheses were formulated within the framework of Rotter's social learning theory.

Operationalization of 182 verbal self-report questions and statements was the starting point of construction. Answers of a random stratified pilot group of married middle-class Dutch men and women up to 50 years of age provided the data base for item selection.

By factor analysis 76 pre-selected items were found to belong to three factors (SES 1, 2, and 3). A further measure was constructed for "attraction to marriage" (SES 4). The construction of the SES scales was initiated in 1968 and resulted after repeated studies in a final presentation in a manual (Frenken & Vennix, 1978, 1981).

Psychometric Characteristics

Internal consistency (coefficient alpha and lamba) and the test-retest reliability of SES 1 to 4 were determined for the random samples of married persons and for two groups of (married) couples who applied for sex therapy. Reliabilities for the four scales varied from .86 to .92. Some of the 14 subscales have a lower reliability.

Construct validity and predictive validity of the scales were acquired in studies, including survey, experimental, and sex-therapy outcome studies.

Construct validity was established for the following hypotheses: (a) The more a person accepts a restrictive moral attitude to sex, the stronger his or her aversion to and inhibition in sexual behavior. (b) The more a person accepts a restrictive sex moral, the stronger his or her rejection of psychosexual stimulation induced by internal and external stimuli and the stronger his or her tendency to increased inhibition of sexual behavioral responses to these stimuli. (c) The stronger a person's rejection of psychosexual stimulation, the stronger his or her aversion to sexual responses. (d) The stronger a person's aversion to sexual behavior with a partner, the lower his or her attraction to marriage. (e) The lower a person's attraction to marriage, the stronger his or her seeking for psychosexual stimulation induced by internal and external stimuli as a means of vicarious gratification.

Norm tables are available for men and women from the random study group and from a clinical sexual dysfunction group. Vennix (1983) reported data of a study on his Intimate Body-Contact Scale and at the same time repeated Frenken's last SES study of 1971. Ten years later the SES 3, at least for Vennix's (1981) Dutch sample, seems to be an inadequate measure. The best solution, after factor analysis, seemed to be the construction of two scales. Item content of the scales is different for men and women, and as a consequence there are separate scales for both sexes. New norm tables are reported for SES 1, 2, and 4 and for the new as well as the old SES 3 scales.

Clinical Use

The SES scales can be used in intake interviews with patients when exact scale scores are not stressed. Some insight can be gained by inspection of individual items and in discussing answers with the patient. For evaluation of a larger group of patients in comparison studies or therapy effect studies, the SES scales have proved to be adequate and useful.

Future Directions

The SES scales have been found to reflect sexual attitudes and sexual experiences, which fluctuate over time. Satisfaction with sex is derived from frequency data in the area of consummatory (coital) behavior and experience.

Vennix (1983) criticized this approach and has proposed that intimacy is a more adequate area for developing satisfaction criteria. However, no data are available on the validity of his Intimate Body Contact Scale to judge his assertions.

References

Frenken, J. (1976). *Afkeer van de seksualiteit* (Sexual Aversion). Deventer: van Loghum.

Frenken, J., & Vennix, P. (1978). *SBS Handleiding*. Amsterdam: Swets and Zeitlinger.

Frenken, J., & Vennix, P. (1981). *SES Manual*. Lisse: Swets and Zeitlinger.

Vennix, P. (1983). De ILKS-fedachte en andere operationalisaties (The IBCS-idea and other operationalisations). Onderzoeksrapport) 37. Zeist: Netherlands Institute of Social Sexological Research.

Situation Role-Play Assessment

Paul E. Bates

Description

Situation role-play assessment refers to an analogue behavioral measure of a person's performance in laboratory type situations that have been created to resemble natural conditions.

Although the format for these assessments has included videotaped, audiotaped, and live presentations, "typical" administration involves a verbal description of realistic social-interpersonal situations and an opportunity for the individual to respond as if he or she were actually in the natural situation. In some cases a narrator describes the situation and another person (role-play confederate) delivers the specific social-interpersonal prompt, whereas in others the narrator both describes and delivers the prompts. The response requirements for situation role-play assessments have varied from single opportunity to multiple opportunities through extended role-play interaction. An example follows:

Narrator: You are watching your favorate TV show. A person you live with changes the channel and says...(Narrator or Role-Play Confederate): "I want to watch my show." (Pause for the person's response or narrator prompt.) "You say." (In the single opportunity method, assessment of this item would cease after the client's first response; in the extended interaction format, the role-play confederate would prompt further.) In most cases a person's responses to role-play situations are videotaped or audiotaped for future scoring by trained observers.

However, if observers are present and the response scoring demands are relatively simple, it is possible to directly evaluate a person's situation role-play performance. Scoring has ranged in complexity from subjective global ratings to specific behavioral measurement of verbal and nonverbal components of specific responses (e.g., eye contact, response latency, and content.)

Purpose

Primarily, situation role-play assessment has been used to measure social skills. This method of assessment emerged as a result of logistical and ethical difficulties associated with measuring interpersonal behavior in naturalistic situations.

Before development of situation role-play assessments, researchers had to rely on self-report data. By recreating natural situations in a controlled setting through role-play interactions, researchers hoped to obtain a more objective measure of a person's social behavior.

Development

Goldfried and D'Zurilla's (1969) description of the behavioral-analytical model for assessment competence identified a 5-step process that has been used by some researchers (Bates, 1980) for developing and evaluating situation role-play assessments. This process included: (a) Situational Analysis (collection of a large representative sample of problematic situations that a person is likely to encounter), (b) Response Enumeration (sample of responses to previously identified situations), (c) Response Evaluation (use of significant others to evaluate the effectiveness of specific responses), (d) Development of Measuring Instrument Format (clarify procedures for conducting the assessments and evaluating performance), and (e) Evaluation of the Measure (investigation of the validity of the assessment). In most cases Goldfried and D'Zurilla's (1969) recommendations have been used to generate role-play items and scoring procedures, but little emphasis has been directed toward a more in-depth evaluation of content and criterion validity of the measure.

Psychometric Characteristics

Initially, situation role-play assessments were viewed as an attractive alternative to self-report measures on the basis of their apparent face validity.

However, more recently professionals have challenged the assumption that role-play behavior corresponds to behavior exhibited in naturalistic situations. Several studies have examined the external validity of situation role-play assessments. Although the results of these studies are not entirely consistent, a few trends emerge: (a) Correlations between specific role-play behavior and specific naturalistic behaviors are low; however, more global measures of role-play performance tend to correspond more closely with general interpersonal competence in natural situations. (b) Variations in role-play format, content, target behaviors, and subjects could yield different conclusions on the usefulness of situation role-play assessments (Bellack, Hersen, & Lamparski, 1979). (c) Assessment situations that most closely approximate the stimulus conditions of real-life are more likely to result in externally valid interpersonal responses.

Clinical Use

Situation role-play assessments have been used with virtually all target populations for whom social skills training has been conducted. These assessments have included children and adults who experience social skills deficits associated with primary disabilities such as mental retardation and behavior disorders. Also, situation role-play assessments have been developed for more common social-interpersonal problems experienced by the general population of youth and adults (e.g., heterosocial interaction and assertiveness).

Future Directions

Although the external validity of situation role-play assessments has been seriously challenged, recent emphasis has shifted toward methods to enhance the generalizability of role-play information and the use of multimodal assessment procedures. Linehan (1980) suggests that more sophisticated sampling of naturally encountered social-interpersonal situations would result in the identification of more content-valid role-play items. According to Linehan and others, situation role-play assessment data are useful to the degree to which the assessment conditions reflect those conditions to which one is interested in generalizing. The guidelines provided by Goldfried and D'Zurilla (1969) offer a useful reference for those interested in more adequately analyzing and sampling the stimulus and response variability associated with social-interpersonal problem situations. By identifying realistic role-play situations and creating more natural role-play conditions (e.g., natural physical conditions, live interpersonal partners, extended role-play interactions, and instructions to behave as if one is actually experiencing the natural consequences of specific actions), the external validity of situation role-play assessments would likely be increased.

Efforts to improve the quality of situational assessments should increase the correspondence between role-play exhibited behaviors and naturally exhibited behaviors. However, because of the subtleties in variation of naturally occurring stimulus and response conditions, this correspondence will never be 100%. As a result, the use of multimodal assessment procedures may be necessary to obtain the most complete and useful data base from which program decisions can be made. These assessments might include carefully selected situation role-play items, a sample of direct observation in naturalistic situations, and other subjective evaluations (e.g., self-report and sociometric ratings). In the context of a multimodal assessment, the value of situation role-play assessment can be further studied to identify those conditions under which it contributes the most useful information. However, in the absence of verification of behavior change in naturalistic settings, situation role-play assessment results should be interpreted very cautiously.

References

Bates, P. (1980). The effectiveness of interpersonal skills training on the social skill acquisition of moderately and mildly retarded adults. *Journal of Applied Behavior Analysis, 13,* 237-248.

Bellack, A.S., Hersen, M., & Lamparski, D. (1979). Role play tests for assessing social skills. Are they valid? Are they useful? *Journal of Consulting and Clinical Psychology, 47,* 335-342.

Goldfried, M.R., & D'Zurilla, T.J. (1969). A behavior-analytic model for assessing competence. In C.D. Speilberger (Ed.), *Current topics in clinical and community psychology,* Vol. 1. New York: Academic Press.

Linehan, M. (1980). Content validity: Its relevance to behavioral assessment. *Behavioral Assessment, 2,* 147-159.

Situational Self-Statement and Affective State Inventory

Ruth Morelli

Description

The Situational Self-Statement and Affective State Inventory (SSASI) is a research inventory designed to assess cognitions and affects across a variety of interpersonal situations. The SSASI consists of five interpersonal situations.

Each situation is followed by five self-statements (All I do is let him or her down. I never seem to be able to help...) and five affective descriptors (dejected/depressed/helpless) that reflect the clinically relevant affective categories of anger, anxiety, suspiciousness, depression, and rationality. The participants are asked to first imagine themselves in a given situation and then rate how characteristic of them are the presented cognitive and affective responses (actor version).

They are also asked to respond to the situation as they believe most other people would, by rating others' imagined affective and cognitive responses (observer version). Responses are scored on a 5-point scale from 1 (extremely uncharacteristic or nondescriptive of me) to 5 (extremely characteristic or descriptive of me). A simple characteristic rating ranging from 1 to 5 can be obtained by averaging the rating for self-statements and for affective descriptors across the five situations of the SSASI. Results then indicate the extent to which anger, anxiety, suspiciousness, depression, and rationality were characteristic of the participant's cognitions and emotions in the five situations. Between the self-statements and the affective descriptors, two validity questions are included to assess if the situations seem realistic and if participants responded as if they would have in real life. The format of the SSASI is similar to a typical cognitive behavioral homework assignment in which the situation, emotions, and automatic thoughts of the person are gathered before cognitive restructuring.

Purpose

The SSASI was developed by Harrell, Chambless, and Calhoun (1981) to assess the relation between thoughts and emotions in various situations. The impetus for this investigation came from the cognitive theories of Ellis (1962) and Beck (1976) which stress that person's thoughts mediate their emotional responses to events. Although Ellis posits 11 irrational beliefs that can lead to general emotional distress, Beck and Emery (1985) are more specific in hypothesizing that certain types of thoughts (of danger) give rise to specific emotions (anxiety). However, studies of irrational beliefs have not been clearly related to emotional arousal using physiological measures, whereas other self-statements have contained emotionally laden words that confound cognitions with affect.

These studies generally ignored situational variables. The SSASI was developed to fill that gap, because it assesses the relation between specific types of thoughts and corresponding emotional states. The SSASI also examines if these relationships are cross-situationally consistent.

Development

The forerunner of the SSASI was the experimental research inventory of LaPointe and Harrell (1978). The actor version of their inventory was presented to 130 undergraduates.

This inventory consisted of 10 hypothesized situations for which 10 self-statements and 10 affective descriptors were present, reflecting the affective categories of anger, anxiety, suspiciousness, depression, and rationality. Three validity questions were included. Of the 130 students, 105 stated the situations were realistic and 70% agreed with the experimentors' categorization of thoughts for 60 of 99 thoughts. In the current SSASI (Harrell et al., 1981), both the actor and observer versions were completed by 400 undergraduates. This inventory consisted of five hypothesized situations, five self-statements, and five affective descriptors reflecting the same relevant affective categories as above. The self-statements all showed greater than 70% agreement between student and experimentor in the LaPointe and Harrell study.

Two validity questions were retained. Both the actor and observer versions were represented to undergraduates. Similar findings in both versions suggest that the participants were expressing their own thoughts and emotions in both versions.

Psychometric Characteristics

In validating the SSASI among 84 normal and 67 psychiatric patients, Thorpe, Barnes, Hunter, and Hines (1983) reported moderate internal consistency with the exception of depression, which was somewhat higher. Thus, for self-statements, internal consistencies were .68 for anger, .82 for depression, .79 for anxiety, .69 for suspiciousness, and .65 for rationality. For affective descriptors, internal consistencies were .66 for anger, .81 for depression, .61 for suspiciouness, and .70 for rationality. The author also noted the SSASI was valid, because it could discriminate normal from clinical groups in three of five alternative descriptors and four of five self-statments. For example, the clinical group endorsed depressed feelings as well as depressed self-statements more strongly than did normal subjects. There was a moderate relationship between thoughts and feelings, which varied

by category. Depressed and rational self-statements seemed more strongly related to their corresponding affective descriptors than were "anxious" thoughts and feelings. Failure to replicate these results in one study could be due to divergent scoring methods. However, results were unclear about the nature of the relation between thoughts and emotions, with support for both Beck's notion of specificity and Ellis' more generalized views.

There also is evidence that the moderate relationships found between thoughts and feelings are a function of cross-situational consistency, in which the relationship between thoughts and emotions is stronger for low cross-situationally consistent persons than for high cross-situationally consistent ones.

Clinical Use

The SSASI is a research inventory designed to examine the relation between cognition and affect as well as the interaction of these variables across situations. The inventory was normed and revised using college students. However, it has the potential to be used experimentally with clinical populations as an assessment and treatment tool. Because of its format, the SSASI would most easily be used by clinicians familiar with cognitive therapies such as rational emotive therapy or cognitive behavioral therapy. However, clinicians of other orientations could also benefit by using the information derived from the SSASI's structured format. A recent study using the SSASI among two groups of normal subjects (college students and paraprofessionals) and two groups of clinical patients (psychiatric outpatients and inpatients) found no significant differences in the relation between their self-statements and affective descriptors, aside from the greater tendency of paraprofessionals to express rational thoughts related to noncorresponding feelings than did other groups. This suggests that data from college students might be generalized to clinical groups such as those with affective disorders. However, severely depressed persons may have difficulty imagining themselves in these situations.

Future Directions

The SSASI is clearly a research inventory and needs more psychometric evaluation, with both normal and clinical populations, to assess its reliability and validity in measuring cognitive, affective, and situational variables as well as their interaction. Some affective categories may be more clearly conceptualized through self-statement and affective descriptors than others (depression and rationality). Therefore, the inventory may benefit from revision as well as the presentation of standardized scoring procedures. Because participants showed highly similar responses in both actor and observer versions of the SSASI, the latter version could be eliminated. The issue of cross-situational consistency as a moderator of thoughts and emotions requires further study.

References

Beck, A.T. (1976). *Cognitive therapy and the emotional disorders*. New York: International Universities Press.

Beck, A.T., & Emery, G. (1985). *Anxiety disorders and phobias; A cognitive perspective*. New York: Basic Books.

Ellis, A. (1962). *Reason and emotion in psychotherapy*. New York: Lyle Stuart.

Harrell, T.H., Chambless, D.L., & Calhoun, J.F. (1981). Correlational relationships between self-statements and affective states. *Cognitive Therapy and Research*, 159-173.

LaPointe, K.A., & Harrell, T H. (1978). Thoughts and feelings: Correlational relationships and cross-situational consistency. *Cognitive Therapy and Research*, 2, 311-322.

Thorpe, G.L., Barnes, G.S., Hunter, J.E., & Hines, D. (1983). Thoughts and feelings: Correlations in two clinical and two nonclinical samples. *Cognitive Therapy and Research*, 7, 565-574.

Skill Survey

Barbara Gershenson and Randall L. Morrison

Description

The Structured Learning Skill Survey was developed by Goldstein, Sprafkin, and Gershaw (1976) to evaluate individuals on the various social skills emphasized by Structured Learning Therapy. There are two forms of the Skill Survey, Form S and Form T. Form S is designed to be used by a staff member or observer. The observer is to rate whether and how adequately a "trainee" or client employs the various social skills. Form S includes 36 skills in the areas of conversational and planning skills as well as alternatives to aggression. Each skill is accompanied by a brief description or definition such as: Starting a Conversation: Talking to someone about light topics and then leading into more serious topics; or Carrying on a Conversation:

Opening the main topic, elaborating on it, and responding to the reactions of the person you are talking to (Goldstein et al., 1976, p. 270). The observer rates the "trainee's" or client's performance on a 5-point scale, from "never good" to "always good" at using that skill. Form T is a self-rating form. The trainee or client rates himself or herself on the 36 skills included on Form S and one additional skill, assertiveness. The skills are accompanied by the same brief descriptions or definitions used in the observer rating form and are to be rated on the same 5-point scale.

Purpose

Structured Learning Therapy was developed to aid psychiatric inpatients in an array of community-relevant daily living skills. The approach involved modeling, role-playing, social reinforcement, and transfer training (Goldstein, Sprafkin, & Gershaw, 1979). The Skill Survey was designed by Goldstein et al. (1976) to identify whether and how potential trainees or clients use the specific social skills. The trainer or leader of the Structured Learning Therapy group asks observers or staff members to rate the social skills of potential clients, using Form S. Self-ratings of social skills are obtained from clients, using Form T. The results can then be used to identify deficits to be targeted in treatment and to track treatment progress. Goldstein et al. (1976) advocate that trainees or clients with similar skill deficits at similar levels should be grouped together.

Development

Items for the Skill Survey were selected based on face validity. The 36 items of Form S and 37 items of Form T correspond to the 37 basic skills defined by Structured Learning Therapy. The Skill Survey includes these 37 skills, with a brief definition or description of each one.

Psychometric Characteristics

Magaro and West (1983) used the Skill Survey to evaluate the efficacy of a 6-month Structured Learning Therapy group with chronic psychiatric inpatients.

Skill Survey scores indicated a significant increase between initial skill levels and those at 3 and 6 months. The authors report that this increase was paralleled by an improvement in measures of psychopathology. No other data are available on the psychometric characteristics of the Skill Survey.

Clinical Use

The Skill Survey has been used in both research and treatment settings. Campbell, Steffen, and Langmeyer (1981) investigated the relationship of psychological androgyny and three self-report indicators of social competence, one of which was the Skill Survey. As part of Structured Learning Therapy, the Skill Survey has been employed in the formation and evaluation of Structured Learning Therapy groups (Goldstein et al., 1976).

Future Directions

The Skill Survey includes a wide variety of social skills and provides brief descriptions of definitions for each skill. The scale was developed so that it could be employed in an inpatient setting and for use by less skilled staff and patients. In addition, there is an observer and a self-report rating form. Goldstein (1981) also provides an alternative form that may be used with adolescents, the Skill Checklist. The format of the Skill Checklist is similar to that of the Skill Survey; 50 skills are listed, each of which is accompanied by a brief description or definition. Skill Checklist categories include: dealing with feelings, alternatives to aggression, skills for dealing with stress, and planning skills. These different forms as well as their close association with a specific treatment approach (Structured Learning Therapy) make the Skill Survey attractive for use in a variety of settings. More psychometric data would make the Skill Survey an even more useful instrument.

References

Campbell, M., Steffen, J.J., & Langmeyer, D. (1981). Psychological androgyny and social competence. *Psychological Reports, 48*, 611-614.

Goldstein, A.P. (1981). *Psychological skill training: The structured learning technique.* New York: Pergamon Press.

Goldstein, A.P., Sprafkin, R.P., & Gershaw, N.J. (1976). *Skill training for community living: Applying structured learning therapy.* New York: Pergamon Press.

Goldstein, A.P., Sprafkin, R.P., & Gershaw, N.J. (1979). Structured learning therapy: Training for community living. *Psychotherapy: Theory, Research and Practice, 16*, 199-203.

Magaro, P.A., & West, A.N. (1983). Structured learning therapy: A study with chronic psychiatric patients and level of pathology. *Behavior Modification, 7*, 29-40.

Skinfolds

Patricia M. Dubbert

Description

Measurement of skinfolds is an indirect and relatively inexpensive method of estimating the percentage of fat in the body. A skinfold refers to the "pinch" of loose tissue that can be grasped at the back of the upper arm, the waistline, and at other places on the body.

Standardized measures of the thickness of these folds of skin, along with the underlying subcutaneous fat, are obtained with one of several types of skinfold calipers.

Although the technique may vary slightly when different sites are used, the procedure generally is as follows. The person making the measurement grasps a fold of skin and subcutaneous tissue with the thumb and forefinger of the nondominant hand, about 1 cm above the skinfold site. The skinfold is then held firmly while calipers are applied and the handle of the caliper is released. Readings should be made 2 to 5 seconds after the calipers are applied. At least two readings from separate caliper applications are recommended to enhance reliability (Selzer & Mayer, 1965).

Different sites have been used for skinfold measurement, commonly the biceps, triceps, subscapular, suprailiac, upper thigh, and abdominal skinfolds (McArdle, Katch, & Katch, 1981; Montoye, 1978). Although the triceps is probably the most popular and easiest to use (Selzer & Mayer, 1965), behavioral researchers have more often relied on the method described by Durnin and his colleagues (e.g., Durnin & Rahaman, 1967) using the sum of four skinfold sites (triceps, biceps, subscapular, and suprailiac).

Measuring four sites may be more representative of various types of fat distribution and a single measurement error is less influential.

All measures are taken on the right side of the body with the subject standing and the arms hanging freely at the sides. Most of the skinfold sites can be measured with a minimum of disrobing. For convenient measurement, women and men should be instructed to wear loose-fitting clothing that can be draped away from the skinfold site. It is almost always necessary for women to unhook their bras to get the subscapular skinfold; therefore, it is recommended that assistants of the same sex be employed to obtain skinfold measurements.

The *triceps* skinfold is located over the midpoint of the belly of the triceps muscle, at the back of the right upper arm, midway between the acromion (bony prominence at the top of the shoulder) and the tip of the elbow. Because the amount of subcutaneous fat varies along the upper arm, a measuring tape should be used to locate and mark the midpoint site.

The *biceps* skinfold is taken over the center of the biceps muscle belly of the right arm. As with the triceps measurement, the arm should be hanging freely during calipering.

The *subscapular* skinfold site is just below the tip of the inferior angle of the scapula. The skinfold is pinched at about a 45°angle to a vertical line up the back.

The *suprailiac* skinfold site is located just above the iliac crest in the midaxillary line. The skinfold is lifted to follow the natural diagonal line at this point.

The *upper thigh* skinfold is measured at the midline of the front of the thigh, twothirds of the distance from the knee cap to the hip.

The *abdominal* skinfold is a vertical fold 1 inch to the right of the umbilicus.

Purpose

Skinfold measures can be used several ways. First, a single skinfold or sum of several skinfolds can be entered into equations that have been developed to predict body density or percentage of body fat. Equations are now available for converting skinfold measures to estimates of body density, each derived from water displacement or hydrostatic weighing of representative individuals from various populations. For investigators who want to avoid calculations, some authors also provide tables that give the percentages of fat corresponding to the skinfold measures (Durnin & Rahaman, 1967; Montoye, 1978).

A second purpose for skinfold measurement is to classify individuals by nutritional status. Simple measurements of body weight can be misleading indicators of body composition because very muscular individuals (such as football players) may appear overweight according to ideal weight standards, whereas apparently thin individuals with underdeveloped muscle mass may actually be overweight. Selzer and Mayer (1965), for example, provide a table showing the minimum triceps skinfold thickness to be used as a criterion for obesity for men and women aged 5 to 50.

A third use of skinfold measures is to assess change following an intervention that is expected to produce changes in body composition, such as a fitness training program or weight reduction program.

Development

By 1930, skinfold calipers were being used to measure subcutaneous fat (McArdle, Katch, & Katch, 1981), but the pressure exerted by the first calipers was not standardized, making comparisons difficult. Standardized C-shaped calipers were developed at the Laboratory of Physiological Hygiene at the University of Minnesota (Montoye, 1978). These calipers were designed to exert a precise jaw pressure of 10 g mm^2 with a contact surface of 20 to 40 mm^2. Two types of skinfold calipers are now most commonly used: Lange calipers are lighter and easier to handle, whereas Harpendon calipers provide a more accurate scale (Montoye, 1978; Selzer & Mayer, 1965). Therefore, Lange calipers are useful for field work, whereas Harpendon calipers are useful when accurate readings are needed to detect small changes.

Many investigators have published data on the relations between pinch caliper skinfolds and other methods of measuring subcutaneous fat, such as underwater weighing, roentgenograms, incision, and ultrasound (Montoye, 1978). These validity coefficients are discussed in the next section.

Psychometric Characteristics

A major drawback of skinfold measures acknowledged by most investigators is that it is difficult to obtain consistent results across time or with different persons measuring the same individuals. Error can be introduced in the selection of the site, method of pinching the skinfold, application and reading of the caliper, and so forth.

There are no standards to compare the results obtained by different investigators. However, it is also agreed that reproducibility of skinfold readings is generally good among the same subjects measured by the same investigator on more than one occasion, with $r = .90$ or better (Montoye, 1978). Straw and Straw (1980) recently evaluated the reliability of skinfold measures at the four sites recommended by Durnin and Rahaman (1967) with inexperienced technicians in the realistic context of assessing obese patients. They also evaluated three different methods: (a) taking skinfold measures until three agree; (b) taking the average of all skinfold measures at one site; and (c) taking the average of the first measures at a site. After only 1 hour of training, investigators were able to obtain very good reliability (.90 to .97) between five pairs of observers measuring different subjects. All methods produced good reliability, and the only site with relatively low reliability was the triceps (.60 to .90).

How well do skinfold readings reflect the actual amount of fat in the body? McArdle, Katch, and Katch (1981) report that estimates of body fat content obtained from skinfold measures are usually within 3 to 5% of the amount estimated from body density determinations by hydrostatic weighing or water displacement (the most valid measures). Montoye (1978) includes a table of 31 studies showing the correlation between body fat as measured by skinfolds and that measured by hydrostatic weighing. In these studies, investigators used 1 to 13 skinfold sites and reported correlation coefficients from .70 to .92. Durnin and Rahaman (1967) reported that total skinfold thickness from four sites (triceps, biceps, subscapular, and suprailiac) correlated with body density with $r = .84$ for young male adults and $r = .78$ for young female adults.

Clinical Use

Skinfold measures can be a valuable addition to the behavioral assessment of body composition. Scale weights give a reliable and objective indication of an individual's weight or the current weight or weight loss is fat rather than lean body mass. Skinfold measures allow estimation of the percentage of body fat change as well as weight change. Because the goal of obesity treatment programs is reduction of body fat, for most clinicians and researchers, skinfolds are the only available, albeit indirect, measure of the desired outcome.

Our clinical experience indicates that skinfold measures may not be reliably sensitive to small body fat changes associated with the 10- to 12-pound weight losses produced by brief behavioral weight control programs. However, we do use skinfold measures whenever the treatment participants are concurrently engaging in exercise training programs. Individuals who begin a vigorous training program increase the amount of lean muscle tissue while decreasing the amount of body fat. Scale weights may not reflect this change in body composition, but decreases in subcutaneous fat can be reflected in skinfold measures even if there is little weight loss.

To obtain the most reliable results, it is advisable to: (a) provide training for those who will be doing the calipering and allow adequate practice on individuals of varying body types: (b) use a measuring tape and mark the skinfold sites; (c) take at least two readings at each site; (d) use more than one site; and (e) plan for the same individuals to perform skinfold calipering on each individual at each measurement occasion. Validity will be improved by selecting an equation or conversion table based on a population similar to the one being assessed.

Future Directions

As is evident in the section on *Psychometric Characteristics*, the reliability of skinfold measures is a severe limitation to their current clinical application. Studies evaluating the reliability of different procedures and the use of various skinfold sites are clearly needed.

References

Durnin, J.V.G.A., & Rahaman, M.M. (1967). The assessment of the amount of fat in the human body from measurements of skinfold thickness. *British Journal of Nutrition, 21,* 681-689.

McArdle, W.D., Katch, F.I., & Katch, V.L. (1981). *Exercise physiology, energy, nutrition, and human performance.* Philadelphia: Lea & Febiger.

Montoye, H.J. (1978). *An introduction to measurement in physical education.* Boston: Allyn & Bacon.

Selzer, C.C., & Mayer, J. (1965). A simple criterion of obesity. *Postgraduate Medicine, 38,* A101-A107.

Straw, R.B., & Straw, M.K. (1980, November). *Generalizability of skinfold measures in obesity treatment outcome studies.* Presented at the annual meeting of the Association for Advancement of Behavior Therapy, New York.

Social Adjustment Scale - Self-Report

Angelynne E. Amick and Dean G. Kilpatrick

Description

The Social Adjustment Scale-Self-Report (SAS-SR) is a self-report adaptation of Weissman and Paykel's structured interview: the Social Adjustment Scale (SAS, Weissman & Paykel, 1974). The 54-item instrument measures role functioning during the previous 2 weeks and requires approximately 15 to 20 minutes to complete. To maximize accuracy, the authors recommend involvement of a technician to clarify instructions and check completion; however, the instrument is self-explanatory.

In addition to yielding a global measure of social functioning, the scale also assesses role performance in six social contexts: (a) relevant occupational performance (i.e., performance as a worker inside or outside the home as a student), (b) social and leisure functioning, (c) relations with extended family, (d) marital role, (e) parental role, and (f) membership in a family unit. Questions comprising the six subscales fall into four qualitative categories: (a) behavioral performance at expected tasks, (b) interpersonal behaviors and skills, (c) interpersonal friction and arguments, and (d) intrinsic satisfaction derived from the role. In answering each question, respondents select a point along a 5-point continuum, ranging from appropriate to impaired functioning. The five anchor points are specifically defined for each question, with highest scores reflecting greatest impairment. Scoring involves computing mean subscale scores for each of the six social contexts and averaging all responses to yield a global estimate of social functioning. Finally, a single item (5-point response continuum) is included to assess financial status.

Purpose

The mental health Zeitgeist of the early 1970s was characterized by expansion of community-based mental health programs and by practitioner rejection of a symptomatic assessment focus in favor of attention to more adaptive aspects of patients' behavior. Partially in response to these trends, Weissman and Paykel designed the SAS interview form to assess adaptive functioning within a variety of social contexts. The scale was originally intended to yield descriptive data as well as to serve as a treatment outcome measure in a study of depressed women. Later, the SAS was converted to the more economical self-report form, which eliminated both the need for interviewer training and the risk of interview bias (Weissman & Bothwell, 1976).

Development

Item content of the SAS-SR was derived completely from the SAS structured interview, which in turn was drawn heavily from the Structured and Scaled Interview for Maladjustment by Gurland,

Yorkston, Stone, Frank, and Fleiss (cited in Weissman & Bothwell, 1976). The SAS-SR was normed with several psychiatric populations (acute and recovered depressed persons, alcoholics, and schizophrenics) as well as with a random community sample (Weissman, Prusoff, Thompson, Harding, & Myers, 1978).

Psychometric Characteristics

Acceptable test-retest reliability of the SAS-SR was demonstrated by Resnick, Calhoun, Atkeson, and Ellis (1981) within a 1-month interval ($r = .74$) and by Edwards, Yarvis, and Mueller (cited in Weissman et al., 1978) across two unspecified time intervals (mean coefficient, $r = .80$). Edwards et al., also reported interval consistency of item content (mean coefficient alpha, $r = .74$). For depressed patients and significant others, interrater reliabilities on subscales ranged between .43 and .62. For recovered patients and significant others, reliabilities ranged between .34 and .74 (see Weissman & Bothwell, 1976).

Supportive of the concurrent validity of the instrument was Weissman and Bothwell's (1976) report of agreement of the SAS-SR with the SAS structured interview criteria. Reliabilities on subscales ranged from .40 to .76 and was .72 on the global assessment measure. Further empirical validation was evidenced by the efficacy of the instrument in statistically differentiating a nonclinical, community sample from three psychiatric populations (alcoholic, depressed, and schizophrenic persons). The scale also distinguished acutely depressed from recovered patients (Weissman & Bothwell, 1976).

Discriminant validity of the instrument was supported by the lack of relationship between SAS-SR scores and such demographic variables as age, sex, social class, and race. Finally, although Edwards et al. reported the instrument to be insensitive to the effects of repeated testing, Resnick et al. (1981) detected some reactivity to the instrument among both untreated rape victims and non-victim control subjects who reported increasing improvement in social functioning across six testing sessions.

Clinical Use

The SAS-SR provides an economical assessment of behavior typically occurring outside the range of clinical observation. In operationalizing social functioning, the instrument yields diagnostic information, is sensitive to pre- posttreatment behavioral changes, and assesses generalization and maintenance of treatment gains. The efficacy of the SAS-SR for clinical study and research is enhanced by the availability of substantial normative data for both nonclinical and several psychiatric populations (Weissman & Bothwell, 1976; Weissman et al., 1978).

In the midst of clinical conjecture on the debilitating effects of sexual assault on a victim's social adjustment, the SAS-SR has shown particular use in operationalizing social functioning. The following provides a brief summary of results to date from the use of the SAS-SR with several assault victims. Unpublished data from a National Institute of Mental Health funded study of psychological sequelae to rape (sample = 204 rape victims, 173 nonvictim-matched controls; Kilpatrick & Veronen, 1984a) found that SAS-SR global scores, as well as the leisure, extended family, and marital subscales, distinguished recent victims (6 to 21 days after rape) from nonvictims. On all scales, victims showed poorer adjustment than did nonvictims. As part of this study's longitudinal assessment protocol (assessment at 6 to 21 days, 3 months, 6 months, 1 year, 18 months, 2 years, 3 years, and 4 years after the assault), the SAS-SR also found that postassault social impairment persisted at later postrape assessments. Contrasted with nonvictims, victims were characterized by global impairment (at 3, 6, and 12 months) as well as by specific deficits in leisure (at 3, 6, 12, and 18 months), extended family (at 3 and 6 months and 4 years), and marital (at 3 and 18 months and 3 years) role performance.

Resnick et al. (1981) investigated adjustment during the first year after rape (sample = 93 victims and 87 matched controls) and reported global and specific impairment (work, economics, leisure, and extended family functioning) persisting several months before stabilizing at nonvictim levels of social functioning. Frank, Turner, and Stewart (1980) related functioning within the immediate family (assessed through the SAS structured interview) to assault characteristics. Most adaptive postassault intrafamilial functioning was related to threatening assault variables (e.g., more than one assailant, weapon, threat to life). Finally, Calhoun, Jackson, and Amick (1985) reported the SAS-SR to differentiate adult victims of childhood incestuous experiences from nonvictim controls on the basis of greater victim impairment in global functioning, with particular difficulty in leisure roles.

The most consistent finding across studies applying the SAS-SR to sexual abuse victims is impaired leisure functioning (operationalized in terms of communication and social activity with friends, dating behavior, feelings of interpersonal hurt, loneliness, and shyness). The SAS-SR also revealed victim difficulty with extended families involving arguments, poor communication, avoidance, anger, worry, and guilt. These findings, along with Kilpatrick and Veronen's (1984a) report of disrupted marital relations (Resnick et al. [1981] had too few married subjects to analyze that subscale separately), suggest the sensitivity of the SAS-SR to postassault relationship disruption, theretofore clinically assessed in a less standardized fashion.

Future Directions

Several avenues for psychometric refinement of the SAS-SR are indicated. First, to remedy the restriction of the scale to literate respondents, the instrument might be tape recorded and possibly adapted for computer-based administration. Second, as the scale currently stands, respondents without particular roles (e.g., marital or occupational) are not rated in any way with regard to those social contexts. To the extent that nonparticipation in typical roles offers information on adjustment, the instrument would be improved by including a method for scoring nonparticipation. Third, having been initially designed for a female population, the SAS-SR includes several items that could be modified to include content more appropriate for male respondents.

Fourth, further work is needed to refine a scoring sytem for the original four qualitative categories (behavioral performance, interpersonal behavior and skills, interpersonal friction and arguments, and intrinsic satisfaction) comprising each subscale. For example, impairment across marital, extended family, and leisure roles (as seen among sexual assault victims) might be mediated by factors such as irritability or withdrawal secondary to a sexual assault. Among some populations, impairment across several social contexts may be mediated by specific social skill deficits. In addition to clarifying the operative factors in social maladjustment, such a scoring scheme would imply specific loci for treatment intervention (i.e, social or communication skills deficits).

Stemming from the demonstrable use of the SAS-SR with sexual assault victims, a particularly exciting future direction is the application of the instrument to other victim populations. Indeed, the SAS-SR provides a means of assessing several essential DSM-III criteria for Posttraumatic Stress Disorder: (a) markedly diminished interest in one or more significant activities, (b) feelings of detachment or estrangement from others, and (c) avoidance of activities. Pioneering in the comparative study of victims of crime a National Institute of Justice funded study (Kilpatrick & Veronen, 1984b) suggests the efficacy of the SAS-SR in distinguishing among various victim groups. Preliminary results from that project suggest sexual assault and aggravated assault victims suffer more postassault social impairment than do victims of robbery or burglary than nonvictims.

In summary, the SAS-SR shows promise with a variety of populations. Further refinement and application of the instrument, with concomitant attention to treatment implication of results, are strongly encouraged.

References

Calhoun, K.S., Jackson, J.L., & Amick, A.E. (1985). *Psychological adjustment of women who experienced childhood intrafamilial sexual abuse.* Manuscript submitted for publication.

Frank, E., Turner, S.M., & Stewart, B.D. (1980). Initial response to rape: The impact of factors within the rape situation. *Journal of Behavioral Assessment, 2,* 39-53.

Kilpatrick, D.G., & Veronen, L.J. (1984a). *Treatment of fear and anxiety in victims of rape* (Final Report, Grant No. RO1 MH29602). Rockville, MD: National Institute of Mental Health.

Kilpatrick, D.G., & Veronen, L.J. (1984b). *The psychological impact of crime* (Grant No. 84-IJ-CX-0039). Washington, DC: National Institute of Justice.

Resnick, P.A., Calhoun, K.S., Atkeson, B.M., & Ellis, E.M. (1981). Social adjustment in victims of sexual assault. *Journal of Consulting and Clinical Psychology, 49,* 705-712.

Weissman, M.M., & Bothwell, S. (1976). Assessment of social adjustment by patient self report. *Archives of General Psychiatry, 33,* 1111-1115.

Weissman, M.M., & Paykel, E.S. (1974). *The depressed woman: A study of social relationships.* Chicago: University of Chicago Press.

Weissman, M.M., Prusoff, B.A., Thompson, W.D., Harding, P.S., & Myers, J.K. (1978). Social adjustment by self-report in a community sample and in psychiatric outpatients. *Journal of Nervous and Mental Disease, 166,* 317-326.

Social Avoidance and Distress Scale and Fear of Negative Evaluation Scale

Richard G. Heimberg

Description and Purpose

The Social Avoidance and Distress Scale (SADS) and the Fear of Negative Evaluation Scale (FNE) are true-false questionnaires developed by Watson and Friend (1969) to measure social-evaluative anxiety, defined by the authors (p. 448) as "the experience of distress, discomfort, fear, anxiety, etc., in social situations; as the deliberate avoidance of social situations; and finally as a fear of receiving negative evaluations from others." The first two components of social-evaluative anxiety, distress and avoidance, are measured by the SADS, whereas the third component is assessed by the FNE. Sample items from the SADS include: "I am usually at ease when talking to someone of the opposite sex" and "I try to avoid talking to people unless I know them well." Sample items from the FNE include: "I am afraid that I may look ridiculous and make a fool of myself" and "When I am talking to someone, I worry about what they may be thinking of me."

Development

The SADS and FNE were developed simultaneously. One hundred forty-five items were constructed on a rational basis. After empirical evaluation, items for both scales were selected from this initial pool. The 145-item set was administered to a sample of 205 college undergraduates. Several criteria were established for the evaluation of items: (a) each item had to show a correlation in excess of .50 with its own scale when variance due to social desirability was controlled, (b) each item had to be endorsed by at least 10% of the sample (as close to 50% as possible), (c) a discriminant relationship between the SADS and the FNE was encouraged, (d) acquiescence response set was controlled, and (e) items were selected to provide a representative sampling of the universe of relevant social situations. The final version of the SADS contains 28 items, whereas the FNE has 30 items.

Psychometric Characteristics

Watson and Friend report the following data in support of the reliability and homogeneity of the SADS and FNE: (a) mean point-biserial item-total correlations of .77 (SADS) and .72 (FNE), (b) KR-20 coefficients of homogeneity of .94 (both scales), and (c) 1-month test-retest coefficients of .68 (SADS) and .78 (FNE) (calculated on an additional sample of 154 subjects). In addition, both scales were correlated −.25 with a measure of social desirability response set, and they were correlated .51 with each other. However, Arkowitz, Lichtenstein, McGovern, and Hines (1975) report a correlation of .71 between the two scales in a sample of high frequency and low frequency daters. The distribution of FNE scores in the sample of 205 was described as skewed, with a mode of 0, a median of 7, and a mean of 9.11 (SD = 8.01). Males subjects (M = 11.20) scored significantly higher than did female subjects (M = 8.24) on the SADS. In samples of 259 male and 302 female students from the State University of New York at Albany, the means were somewhat lower, 7.35 (SD = 6.03) and 6.68 (SD = 5.53), respectively.

Watson and Friend report several experimental studies in support of the validity of the SADS and FNE. High SADS subjects preferred to work alone and tended to avoid social interactions. Participants in a psychology experiment were invited to take part in a second study that would involve either essay writing or participation in a group discussion. High SADS subjects preferred the essay over the discussion group, whereas low SADS subjects preferred the group discussion. High SADS subjects described themselves as more worried, less calm, and more nervous about participation than did low SADS subjects. In additional studies of the SADS, high SADS subjects talked less while participating in a cooperative task with another subject and were more likely to keep appointments for psychology experiments than were low SADS subjects.

Additional validity data for the SADS are available in the work of other experimenters. The SADS scores were negatively correlated with peer ratings of social skill (r = .695) and significantly related to measures of gaze, speech latency, and number of words spoken in two social interaction tasks (Arkowitz et al., 1975). The SADS scores were also significantly related to other measures of heterosexual-social anxiety (r = .52 with the Situation Questionnaire; r = .54 with the Survey of Heterosexual Interactions (Wallander, Conger, Mariotto, Curran, & Farrell, 1980). In addition, high SADS subjects were shown to (a) report more negative self-statements in anticipation of an interaction with someone of the opposite sex (Cacioppo,

Glass, & Merluzzi, 1979), (b) report fewer positive self-statements in anticipation of a similar interaction (Heimberg, Acerra, & Holstein, 1985), (c) rate themselves as more negative, less active, and less potent in a sematic differential task (Cacioppo et al., 1979), and (d) show less ability to discriminate between similar and dissimilar partners in an interpersonal attraction task (Heimberg, Acerra, & Holstein, 1985) than were low SADS subjects.

Watson and Friend report that high FNE subjects become more anxious in social-evaluative situations and work harder to avoid disapproval or gain approval. In a study by Smith and Sarason (1975), high FNE subjects indicated that they would feel worse about it than would low FNE subjects.

Clinical Use

Both the SADS and the FNE have been increasingly used in the evaluation of treatments for social phobia. Heimberg, Becker, Goldfinger, and Vermilyea (1985) treated a group of social phobic patients with a group treatment composed of exposure, cognitive restructing, and homework assignments. The SADS scores averaged 24.43 (SD = 4.39) at pretest and were reduced to 6.83 (SD = 6.34) at 6-month follow-up. The FNE scores averaged 24.57 (SD = 7.19) at pretest and 16.67 (SD = 10.01) at follow-up. Follow-up scores for both scales fell close to the mean of the normative samples reported by Watson and Friend. Butler, Cullinton, Munby, Amies, and Gelder (1984) treated persons with social phobia with exposure, exposure plus anxiety management training (AMT), or a waiting list. After treatment, the group receiving exposure plus AMT showed greater reductions on both the SADS and FNE than exposure alone or waiting list subjects.

Future Directions

The SADS and FNE are valuable scales for the assessment of social anxiety and are often used in clinical research. Sound data are available that support the psychometric adequacy and validity of the scales. However, the majority of these data have been collected on a college student population and extrapolated to clinical settings. There is a need for the conduct of psychometric and validational studies with patients who seek treatment for social anxiety and evaluative fears. Such research will serve to further strengthen these very good instruments.

References

Arkowitz, H., Lichtenstein, E., McGovern, K., & Hines, P. (1975). The behavioral assessment of social competence in males. *Behavior Therapy, 6,* 3-13.

Butler, G., Cullinton, A., Munby, M., Amies, P., & Gelder, M. (1984). Exposure and anxiety management in the treatment of social phobia. *Journal of Consulting and Clinical Psychology, 2,* 642-650.

Cacioppo, J.T., Glass, C.R., & Merluzzi, T.V. (1979). Self-statements and self-evaluations: A cognitive-response analysis of heterosocial anxiety. *Cognitive Therapy and Research, 3,* 249-262.

Heimberg, R.G., Acerra, M., & Holstein, A. (1985). Partner similarity mediates interpersonal anxiety. *Cognitive Therapy and Research, 9,* 446-457.

Heimberg, R.G., Becker, R.E., Goldfinger, K., & Vermilyea, J.A. (1985). Treatment of social phobia by exposure, cognitive restructuring, and homework assignments. *Journal of Nervous and Mental Disease, 173,* 236-245.

Smith, R.E., & Sarason, I.G. (1975). Social anxiety and the evaluation of negative interpersonal feedback. *Journal of Consulting and Clinical Psychology, 43,* 429.

Wallander, J.L., Conger, A.J., Mariotto, M.J., Curran, J.P., & Farrell, A.D. (1980). Comparability of selection instruments in studies of heterosexual-social problem behaviors. *Behavior Therapy, 11,* 548-560.

Watson, D., & Friend, R. (1969). Measurement of social-evaluative anxiety. *Journal of Consulting and Clinical Psychology, 33,* 448-457.

Social Interaction Test

Barbara Gershenson and Randall L. Morrison

Description

The Social Interaction Test (SIT) is a role-play measure designed by Trower, Bryant, and Argyle (1978) to assess social skills. It is a standardized procedure structured as a social encounter between the subject and two strangers, one male and one female. During the SIT the subject is instructed to act as if this encounter were actually occurring outside the confines of the laboratory.

The following instructions are read to subjects at the start of the SIT: As you all know, this is part of an experiment in communication, so I wonder if you (patient) would start the ball rolling by talking about yourself, what you do, where you come from, and so on, and keep the conversation going for 4 minutes (indicate clock), and then would you (woman confederate) do the same for the next 4 minutes? It is not meant to be a speech; the idea is simply to give one person the responsibility for keeping the conversation going, and then another

person so you can talk or ask questions or carry on any kind of conversation you want. Finally, would you (male confederate) chip in whenever you feel like it? (Trower et al., 1978, p. 144).

Unknown to the subject, the behavior of the two confederates is prepared in advance. For the first 2 minutes of the first phase of the SIT, during which the subject has been instructed to "talk about himself," the female confederate gives appropriate attention and feedback. For the second 2 minutes she is silent and looks down for 15-second periods. The male confederate remains silent and disengaged from the interaction. During the next phase the female confederate attempts to keep the conversation going by using appropriate self-disclosure. Her conversation is a rehearsed script. For the first 2 minutes of this phase there are no periods of silence, but during the second 2 minutes the conversation is interrupted with 15-second periods of silence. The male confederate remains silent as before. In the third phase the male confederate questions, implies criticism, disagrees with, and gives advice on the subject's work, hobbies, and time interests. He withholds any positive feedback and discloses little information about himself. Briefings, instructions, physical features of the situation, and the verbal and nonverbal behavior of the confederates are standardized.

The SIT is videotaped and retrospectively rated using a three-part scale. The first part of the rating scale refers to specific behavioral components including verbal and nonverbal responding as well as physical appearance. The specific components of verbal behavior, which are rated, include volume, tone, pitch, clarity, pace, and speech disturbances. Nonverbal behavior categories include proximity, orientation, appearance, gaze, posture tonus, posture position, gesture, and autistic gestures. Other categories that are scored include conversation length, generality, formality, variety, humor, nonverbal grammar, feedback, meshing, turn taking, questions, supportive routines, assertive routines, behavior in public, and situation-specific routines. The second part of the rating scale includes overall ratings on 13 seven-point bipolar adjective scales. The dimensions rated include warm / like-cold / dislike; superior / dominant-inferior / submissive; happy-sad; emotional-unemotional. The third part of the rating scale asks the rater to write behavioral descriptions for two of the general impressions he or she considers most faulty.

Purpose

The purpose of the SIT is to assess a range of social skills, such as listening, speaking, handling silences, and coping with a difficult person. Trower, Bryant, and Argyle (1978) note that this format provides more reliable and comprehensive information than less structured encounters. Trower (1980) makes a distinction between the components and the process of social skills. Specific component skills are single elements or identifiable sequences of elements, such as looks, nods, greetings, and partings, whereas skill processes include the ability to generate skilled behavior according to rules and goals and in response to social feedback. To generate skilled behavior the individual must draw on a repertoire of component skills, as well as organize them into new sequences appropriate to the immediate situation and his or her own plans. Assessment of social skills may benefit by focusing on both deficits in component skills and deficits in organizational ability. Trower, Yardley, Bryant, and Shaw (1978) note that the SIT provides a global measure of social skills organized performance as well as a means of identifying component skill deficits.

Psychometric Characteristics

Trower, Bryant, and Argyle (1978) recommend that all raters familiarize themselves with the scale and the definitions of the elements, through the companion rating guide, and rate some sample films before rating subjects or patients for research or treatment purposes. Without citing data, they note: There will usually be reasonable agreement on the elements and adjectives that most characterize the deficits (Trower, Bryant, & Argyle, 1978, p. 146).

As part of a treatment study, Trower et al. (1978) selected 20 patients whose primary difficulty was social inadequacy and 20 patients whose primary problem was social phobia. Patients were rated on a 5-point scale by an independent clinical assessor and by therapists before, after, and at 6-month follow-up. All patients participated in the SIT. Qualitative ratings of elements of behavior and global impressions were made by treatment-blind lay assessors from videotapes of the SIT using the ratings scale. The sum of scores on the scale correlated .87 with the clinical judgment, and average agreement on each element was .55.

To further evaluate the scale, Trower (1980) compared the performance of two groups of patients (skilled and unskilled) on the SIT. Sixty patients were assigned to one of two groups, a socially skilled and a socially unskilled group, according to ratings by two clinical assessors. Patients were rated on a 9-point skilled-unskilled rating scale by two professional assessors, a psychiatrist and a clinical psychologist. Ratings were based on the patient's behavior during an interview, reported relationships with family, friends, employers, and co-workers, information about social life, group activities, evidence of avoidance of socializing, and type and degree of symptoms. Interrater agreement was .77. All patients took part in the SIT. A lay assessor using the same scale also made ratings based on the patient's performance in the SIT. The correlation between lay and professional ratings was .73.

In assessing the ability of the SIT to differentiate socially skilled and socially unskilled individuals, Trower (1980) predicted that the two groups would differ on both the component and process skills measured by the SIT. The SIT differentiated between skilled and unskilled individuals: skilled patients were observed to speak, look, smile, gesture, and move their posture more than were unskilled patients. The skilled group also showed more variability in behavior in response to situation changes. These results suggest that performance on the SIT identifies deficits in component skills and in the organization or use of these skills in adapting to various situations.

Clinical Use

Trower, Bryant, and Argyle (1978) suggest that the raters should include the two confederates from the interaction test and at least one of the therapists. All raters should familiarize themselves with the scale and definitions of the elements and rate sample films before rating the subject or patient.

The SIT samples only one kind of situation: talking to strangers. Clinicians/researchers should be cautious about making generalizations from the behavior observed during the SIT and applying them to other situations. Therapists should consider the appropriateness of the behavior in the context of the situation being observed. The ratings are intended to reflect an individual's capacity for normal social behavior. Trower, Bryant, and Argyle (1978) recommend that the therapist supplement observations from the interaction test with observations made in other settings and adjust the ratings where necessary. They note that some parts of the raing scale cannot be completed on the basis of the interaction test and information must be obtained elsewhere.

The SIT has been used as a measure of treatment outcome. Beidel, Turner, and Dancu (1985) used the SIT rating scale to evaluate two unstructured role-play interactions and an impromptu speech. Reliability coefficients were adequate, and the ratings appeared to reflect clinical judgments of improvements in social skills after treatment.

Future Directions

Although the SIT appears to be a reliable and valid measure of social skills deficits, it is difficult to use in a strictly clinical setting as it requires a significant amount of time to administer and score. One benefit of using the SIT is that it provides a measure of specific component skills deficits and deficits in the ability to organize and use these skills. It represents a good compromise between unstructured naturalistic observation and highly structured laboratory ratings.

References

Beidel, D.C., Turner, S.M., & Dancu, C.V. (1985). Physiological, cognitive and behavioral aspects of social anxiety. *Behaviour Research and Therapy, 23,* 109-117.

Trower, P., Bryant, B., & Argyle, M. (1978). *Social skills and mental health.* Pittsburgh: University of Pittsburgh Press.

Trower, P., Yardley, K., Bryant, B.M., & Shaw, P. (1978). The treatment of social failure: A comparison of anxiety-reduction and skills acquisition procedures on two social problems. *Behavior Modification, 2,* 41-60.

Trower, P. (1980). Situational analysis of the components and processes of behavior of socially skilled and unskilled patients. *Journal of Consulting and Clinical Psychology, 48,* 327-339.

Social Reaction Inventory - Revised

Kim T. Mueser

Description

The Social Reaction Inventory, Revised (SRI-R) is a self-report questionnaire that is designed to assess social skills in adult psychiatric patients (Curran, Corriveau, Monti, & Hagerman, 1980). The SRI-R is composed of 105 items describing specific different social situations (e.g., giving a speech before a group of relative strangers). Using a 5-point Likert scale, subjects first rate all the situations for the degree of anxiety they would experience, and then they rate how skillfully they would handle each situation (high numbers reflect high anxiety and poor skill). The SRI-R was originally constructed to measure seven different dimensions of social skill and anxiety, but the overall scores may be used as global measures.

Purpose

The SRI-R is a time-efficient questionnaire aimed at identifying performance deficits and subjective discomfort experienced by psychiatric patients in a wide range of social situations.

Development

The SRI-R was constructed on the basis of the Richardson and Tasto (1976) Social Anxiety Inventory (SAI), a 165-item scale designed to measure anxiety in social situations experienced by undergraduate college students. In creating the SRI-R, Curran et al. (1980) selected 65 items with the highest factor loadings on the seven factors chosen for interpretation by Richardson and Tasto, and added 40 more items designed by Richardson and Tasto to further assess these factors. The seven factors include fear of criticism or disapproval, assertiveness and visibility, confrontation and anger/expression, heterosocial contact, intimacy and interpersonal warmth, conflict or rejection by parents, and interpersonal loss. The 105-item SRI-R was normed on a group of psychiatric patients to be described.

Psychometric Characteristics

The psychometric characteristics of the SRI-R were examined in 195 psychiatric patients at a Veterans Administration Hospital (Curran et al., 1980). Principal components analyses were conducted for the anxiety and social skills ratings, rotating seven factors (accounting for 54 and 66% of the variance, respectively), as in Richardson and Tasto. Three of the seven factors were replicated for both the anxiety and social skill data: assertiveness and visibility, heterosexual contact, and intimacy and interpersonal warmth.

The internal validity of the SRI-R was examined by calculating Cronbach's alpha coefficients for the seven scales identified by Richardson and Tasto, and the total anxiety and social skills scores.

Alpha coefficients were high for all the scales (ranging from .875 to .968), even those that had not been replicated in two principal components analyses, and were highest for the total scale scores (9.87 and .983 for anxiety and social skills, respectively). These data suggest that the SRI-R measures a single factor for anxiety and social skills, which are moderately correlated with each other ($r = 57$). The test-retest reliability of the SRI-R over a 5- to 15-week interval was assessed in a group of 28 patients and was high for overall anxiety and social skill (r's = .80 and .71, respectively). The external validity of the SRI-R as a predictor of skill performance and behavioral indicators of anxiety has not been reported.

The psychometric properties of the SRI-R are weak, in part because the psychometric properties of the SAI on which the SRI-R is based are also weak. Evidence suggests that the SAI is unidimensional. For example, a scree test (Cattell, 1966) revealed that a single factor model appeared to be most appropriate. Similarly, the alpha coefficients for the SRI-R aim at assessing multiple dimensions of anxiety and social skill, but actually fit single factor models which may be due in part to the inadequate subject-to-item ratios in both factor analyses: less than half the recommended minimum 5 to 1 ratio (Wade, 1978).

Clinical Use

Because the external validity of the SRI-R has not been reported, its use as a clinical instrument is unknown. One clinical outcome study suggests the SRI-R may reflect role-play skill performance in psychiatric patients (Monti, Curran, Corriveau, DeLancey, & Hagerman, 1980). In this study, social skills training produced greater improvements in the two SRI-R scales as well as in skills and anxiety observed during role-plays assessed with the Simulated Social Interaction Test (SSII) than did sensitivity training. Norms for the SRI-R have only been established for the psychiatric veteran population.

Future Directions

Additional factor analytic studies are needed that adhere more closely to accepted psychometric procedures for the construction of scales (Wade, 1978). Assessment of the external validity of the SRI-R as a predictor of in vivo and role-played skills and anxiety could determine the clinical use of the instrument. Establishing norms on the SRI-R for the nonveteran psychiatric population and normal

subjects is important in assessing the generality of results obtained using the scale in veterans.

References

Cattell, R.B. (1966). The meaning and strategic use of factor analysis. In R.B. Cattell (Ed.), *Handbook of multivariate experimental psychology*. Chicago, IL: Rand McNally.

Curran, J.P., Corriveau, D.P., Monti, P.M., & Hagerman, S.B. (1980). Social skill and social anxiety. *Behavior Modification, 4*, 493-512.

Monti, P.M., Curran, J.P., Corriveau, D.P., DeLancey, A.L., & Hagerman, S.B. (1980). Effects of social skills training groups and sensitivity groups with psychiatric patients. *Journal of Consulting and Clinical Psychology, 48*, 241-248.

Richardson, F.C., & Tasto, D.L. (1976). Development and factor analysis of a social anxiety inventory. *Behavior Therapy, 7*, 453-462.

Wade, T.C. (1978). Factor analytic approaches to the investigation of common fears: A critical appraisal and reanalysis. *Behavior Therapy, 9*, 923-935.

Social Skills Test for Children

Donald A. Williamson and Sandra J. McKenzie

Description

The Social Skills Test for Children (SST-C) is a role-play assessment procedure designed to evaluate children's social behavior. Administration of the SST-C requires videotaping children in 30 role-play situations which require five different social responses: Assertion, Giving Help, Giving Praise, Accepting Help, and Accepting Praise. Each type of role-play has five situations. The child's behavior is assessed using eight behavior categories: desired content, appropriate assertion, effective assertion, gestures, overall skill rating, response latency, duration of eye contact, and duration of speech. For a more complete description of the SST-C and scoring procedures, refer to Williamson et al. (1987).

Purpose

The purpose of the SST-C is behavioral assessment of children's social skills for evaluation of specific social skills deficits. Because the SST-C uses a variety of role-play scenes (both positive and assertive) and a number of specific behavioral components (including content of speech, speech duration and nonverbal components of communication), it allows a very molecular analysis of a child's social behavior. Therefore, the SST-C can be used as a diagnostic tool and as a measure of therapy outcome for social skills training.

Development

The behavior analytic model was used as the principal model for developing the SST-C. As described by Williamson et al. (in press), the development of the SST-C involved six steps (a) Selection of role-play scenes and behaviors, (b) establishment of behavioral definitions for scoring the SST-C, (c) establishment of reliable scoring methods, (d) reliability studies, (e) validity studies, and (f) establishment of norms. As described in the next section, the SST-C has been reliable and valid. Tests for racial bias have shown it to be relatively free of bias. Also, normative data for second-grade and sixth-grade children have been established and are reported in Williamson et al. (1987).

Psychometric Characteristics

Test-retest reliability over a 2-week period has been assessed with a group of 30 children (Williamson et al., 1987). Significant positive correlations were found for all eight behavioral categories. The correlations for each response were: Desired Content (.36), Appropriate Assertion (.59), Effective Assertion (.67), Gestures (.62), Overall Skill Rating (.46), Response Latency (.98), Duration of Eye Contact (.64), and Duration of Speech (.74).

Criterion-related validity of the SST-C was evaluated by Williamson, Moody, Granberry, Letherman, and Blouin (1983). Using teacher ratings, a self-report instrument, and peer nominations as criterion measures, response profiles of the SST-C correlated positively with the criterion measures. Canonical correlational procedures were used for these analyses. Maximum correlation coefficients were found to be above .40.

The social validity of the SST-C was evaluated by Letherman, Williamson, Moody, Granberry, Lemanek, and Bodiford (1984). In this study, untrained observers (33 adults and 30 children) rated children in terms of their subjective impressions of their social skill. These subjective ratings were found to correspond with the objective behavioral ratings yielded by the SST-C. An important finding of this study was that untrained raters most similar to the children being rated perceived the least differences in social behavior among children having high, medium, and low

social skills by the SST-C. The overall pattern of these data suggested that age and racial characteristics of the raters systemically influenced subjective ratings in a manner to suggest some type of racial bias.

Williamson et al. (1987) presented normative data on 49 second-grade children and 55 sixth-grade children. Significant differences in role-play behavior were found as a function of age and race of the children. Older children were generally more assertive and more appropriate in their social behavior. Also, white chilren were generally more socially skilled than were black children.

In a follow-up to the findings of Williamson et al. (in press) of racial differences on the SST-C and the findings of Letherman et al. (1984) of racial influences in subjective ratings by untrained observers, Letherman, Williamson, Moody, and Wozniak (1986) systematically evaluated the influence of race of trained raters on scoring of the SST-C. The results of this study showed systematic effects caused by racial bias.

Clinical Use

A modification of the SST-C was used in a treatment outcome study reported by Lemanek, Williamson, Gresham, and Jensen (1986). This study involved using social skills training with hearing-impaired children. The SST-C was modified to be used with these handicapped children, and social skills training procedures were used to successfully remediate social skills deficits. This investigation is the only published treatment outcome study that has used the SST-C.

Future Directions

The SST-C has been developed as a useful role-play test of children's social skills. Current data support the reliability and validity of this behavioral assessment instrument. Clinical applications of the SST-C have only begun to be reported. Future directions for this behavioral assessment should focus on its ability to discriminate clinical and nonclinical samples and its use as a measure of treatment outcome. Also, tests of the application of the SST-C with younger children are needed.

References

Lemanek, K.L., Williamson, D.A., Gresham, F.M., & Jensen, B.J. (1986). Social skills training with hearing-impaired children and adolescents. *Behavior Modification, 10,* 55-71.

Letherman, V.R., Williamson, D.A., Moody, S.C., Granberry, S.W., Lemanek, K.L., & Bodiford, C. (1984). Factors affecting the social validity of a role play test of children's social skills. *Journal of Behavioral Assessment, 6*, 231-245.

Letherman, V.R., Williamson, D.A., Moody, S.C., & Wozniak, P. (1986). Racial bias in behavioral assessment of children's social skills, *Journal of Psychopathology and Behavioral Assessment, 8*, 329-337.

Williamson, D.A., Moody. S.C., Granberry, S.W., Letherman, V.R., & Blouin, D.C. (1983). Criterion-related validity of a role-play social skills test for children. *Behavior Therapy, 14*, 466-481.

Williamson, D.A., Moody, S.C., Granberry, S.W., Letherman, V.R., Lemanek, K.L., & Bruce, B.K. (1987). Development of a role-play of children's social skills. Manuscript submitted for publication.

Sociometric Measures

Scott R. McConnell and Samuel L. Odom

Description

Sociometric measures are intended to assess the relative social acceptance, desirability, or status of individuals in groups. These measures have been used extensively since the 1930's in a wide variety of disciplines. Developmental psychologists have devised and used sociometric measures to study friendships, social acceptance, and social status of children and adolescents. In addition, sociologists and social psychologists have employed similar measures to describe social networks and group structure. Since the mid-1960's, sociometric measures have been used in behavioral assessment to provide a general criterion for evaluating social behaviors and as a social validity measure for social skills training and other behavioral interventions. Although sociometric measures have most often been used with children, similar procedures can be used with adults. (See Hops & Lewin, 1984; McConnell & Odom, 1986 for reviews.)

The specific definitions of sociometric methodology have varied widely. Originially, Moreno (1934) conceptualized sociometrics as general measures, reflecting the relative social preference of one individual for another in a particular social situation. Since that time, a number of variations of this definition have been offered, leading to considerable ambiguity regarding the critical features of sociometric assessment (McConnell & Odom, 1986). Most recently, however, sociometric procedures have been operationally defined by several reviewers as assessments in which children (or other individuals) are asked to make general and preferential responses regarding peers in their own social group. Given this, social status can be defined as the score received on a given sociometric measure.

Although specific procedures vary widely, sociometric measures are generally one of three types: peer nominations, peer ratings, or paired comparisons. *Peer nominations* are perhaps the most commonly used sociometrics. With these measures, members of a group are asked to identify others within the group whom they feel meet some general criterion (e.g., "Who are your best friends?" or "with whom do you least like to play?"). Peer nominations may request a friend or an unlimited number of nominations from each respondent. In addition, respondents may be asked to weight their nominations (e.g., "Out of all of the children in the class, who is your best friend? Who is your next best friend?"). With peer nomination measures, individual sociometric scores are typically expressed as the total number of nominations received.

Peer ratings have been more frequently used in behavioral assessment. With peer ratings, each member of a particular group (e.g., a classroom) rates every other member of the group along some continuum of attraction-rejection. Like peer nominations, the specific criteria rated by members of given groups vary according to the purpose of assessment; however, all ratings are completed to reflect general statements of preference (e.g., how much a child likes to play or work with a given classmate). Unlike nominations, however, these ratings are completed on a Likert-type scale, ranging from 2 to 9 points. Individual scores for peer rating assessments are generally calculated as the sum of numerical ratings provided by all other members in the group: however, other scoring systems (e.g., sum of ratings by same-sex classmates and number of highest-preference ratings) are occasionally used.

Paired comparisons assessment is perhaps the most homogeneous group of sociometric procedures. Paired comparisons often yield highly reliable scores, but they are also the most labor-intensive sociometric measures to complete. Photographs of each member of a group are paired with every other member of the group, resulting in the formation of all possible dyads, or ([n-l] [n-2]) two pairs. Each rater is shown each of these pairs (or a sample of the possible dyads) and asked to choose one member of the dyad in preference to a specific evaluation criterion. The number of choices received by each member of the group is computed as the social status measure.

Sociometric measures based on any one of these three basic procedures may be used alone or combined with other measures. Frequently, investigators will ask subjects to complete peer ratings with reference to multiple evaluation criteria (e.g., "How much do you like to play with each classmate?" and "How much do you like to work with each classmate?"), or will ask students to complete a peer nomination (e.g., "Name your three best friends") along with peer ratings. Sociometric measures (i.e., those of social preference) may also be combined with peer assessments in which subjects are asked to evaluate the occurrence or quality of peers' behavior. These mixed assessments are frequently used to develop treatment goals for classroom-based treatment programs (McConnell & Odom, 1986).

Purpose

The purpose of using sociometric measures in behavioral assessment vary widely. These procedures generally are used to gather global evaluations on the quality of a given dimension of a child's social performance. For instance, sociometric measures have been used: (a) to provide a general criterion for evaluating observed social behaviors and other characteristics of children, such that critical social skills can be tentatively identified; (b) to identify homogeneous subgroups of children with respect to social status (i.e., accepted, rejected, popular, or neglected children); (c) to identify "friendships" (i.e., those children that reliably rate one another highly) for study and analysis; and (d) to assess the effects of social skills training or other interventions on the social status of individuals in groups.

One of the most controversial uses of sociometric procedures is in the assessment of social competence in children. Some have suggested that sociometrics offer the best available single measure of general competence. However, although considerable face validity may be available for this position, the concurrent and predictive validity of sociometrics for this application are currently limited (McConnell & Odom, 1986). More recently, sociometrics have been conceptualized as a general judgment of the quality of an individual's social behavior (Hops, 1983), with similarities to other measures of social validity. In this context, sociometric procedures have been suggested as one

important component of a multiple-measure model for assessing social competence in children (Hops, 1983; McConnell & Odom, 1986). In this latter application, general evaluations drawn from a child's peers (i.e., sociometrics) are combined with similar evaluations drawn from other social agents (e.g., teacher, parents, and observers) to form a composite performance-based measure of social competence.

Development

Sociometric methodology has developed slowly and somewhat idiosyncratically since the 1930s. Peer nominations were developed first, although weighting methods used with these procedures occasionally yielded rating-like scores. Peer ratings and paired comparisons were developed somewhat later, both coming into more widespread use during the last 20 years.

However, little standardization is apparent in the various uses of sociometric measures. Evaluation criteria and specific procedures (e.g., number of nominations or rating points) often vary from study to study, with methods developed to fit the requirements of a particular investigation. Some procedures are more frequently used than others (e.g., "play with" ratings and "best friend" nominations), and there have been some efforts to develop standardized assessments. However, no carefully developed and fully evaluated sociometric measure is currently available for use in applied settings.

Psychometric Characteristics

Reliability. Estimates of the reliability of sociometric measures have varied widely. The temporal stability of sociometric assessment appears to vary as a function of at least five factors: (a) the specific method employed, with paired comparisons offering the most stable social status scores across time; (b) the age of children completing the assessment, with older children typically providing more stable ratings; (3) the type or number of criteria used in a particular assessment; (d) the length of time between assessments, with stability generally declining as the time between assessments increases; and (e) the scoring procedure applied to individual evaluations (e.g., number of nominations received and number of reciprocal friendship choices). After reviewing stability analyses from a wide array of studies, McConnell and Odom (1986) concluded that reliability estimates should be obtained each time sociometric instruments are used in research and, when possible, clinical applications.

Validity

Sociometric measures have been positively associated with: (a) other measures of social competence completed by peers, teachers, parents, or observers; and (b) stable (e.g., sex, appearance, and handicapping condition) and manipulable (e.g., social behavior and social cognition) characteristics of individual children. A number of investigations have also provided tentative evidence for the predictive validity of sociometrics. Finally, there is some evidence for the treatment validity, or sensitivity to social behavior interventions, of sociometric measures. However, the degree of association between sociometric measures and other measures of social behavior and child competence is frequently low. As a result, there is currently limited information available to support the singular reliance on sociometrics as a measure of social competence in children. Rather, it has been suggested that these measures can be most appropriately used as one source of measurement in a multiple component model for the assessment of social competence in children (Hops, 1983; McConnell & Odom, 1986).

Clinical Use

Although sociometric measures were initially developed and are most commonly used in research applications, several clinical applications can be noted. First, sociometrics can be used in screening for individuals with social interaction deficits. Peer ratings or nominations can be administered to large groups of children, and individuals scoring in the lower quartile can be identified for further assessment. Second, sociometrics can be used for pre- and postassessment of group or individual social interaction skills (or related) interventions. Although these measures are not sufficiently sensitive to be used to evaluate the daily or weekly effects of treatment, sociometrics may prove to be useful secondary measures for evaluating a variety of interventions. Third, sociometrics can be used to evaluate the social validity of clinical interventions. Clinical interventions often focus on behaviors that are related to peer interaction. As a result, sociometrics can be viewed as consumer satisfaction measures of the effects of these interventions.

Future Directions

A review of the rich and varied history of sociometric measures suggests at least three areas in which further research and development are needed. First, a further understanding is needed of the correlates and determinants of sociometric status. A variety of descriptive studies have identified simple correlates of sociometric status, but as yet little is known regarding the causal status of these variables, either alone or in combination. Although significant advances have recently been made in the identification of behavioral determinants of sociometric status, much work remains to be done. Second, further information is needed on the relationship between sociometric measures and other general measures of social performance (e.g., teacher or parent rating and direct observation). Further analysis of the ways in which these measures are related may contribute to the development of a *functional* multiple measure model for the assessment of social competence in children. Third, further efforts are needed to develop standardized, well-validated sociometric procedures for use in behavioral assessment. With the development of procedures of known reliability and utility, the use of sociometric measures in behavioral assessment will increase.

References

Hops, H. (1983). Children's social competence and skill: Current research practices and future directions. *Behavior Therapy, 14*, 3-18.

Hops, H., & Lewin, L. (1984). Peer sociometric ratings. In T. Ollendick & M. Hersen (Eds.), *Child behavioral assessment: Principles and procedures*. New York: Pergamon.

McConnell, S.R., & Odom, S.L. (1986). Sociometrics: Peer-referenced measures and the assessment of social competence. In P.S. Strain, M. Guaralnick, & H.M. Walker (Eds.), *Children's social behavior: Development, assessment, and modification* (pp. 215-284). San Diego, CA: Academic Press.

Moreno, J.L. (1934). *Who shall survive? A new approach to the problem of human interrelations*. Washington, DC: Nervous and Mental Disease Publishing Company.

Spouse Observation Checklist

Randall L. Morrison and Barbara Gershenson

Description

The Spouse Observation Checklist (SOC) is a checklist of marital behaviors that is completed by each spouse about his/her partner. The SOC was developed by Patterson, Weiss, and their colleagues at Oregon (Patterson, 1976) and has undergone several revisions. The current version consists of over 400 items comprising 12 categories of marital behavior: companionship, affection, consideration, sex, communication process, coupling activities, childrearing, household management, financial decision-making, employment-education, personal habits, and self- and spouse independence. The checklist is intended to be completed by each spouse retrospectively regarding his or her partner's behavior during the past 24 hours. Behaviors are rated on an occurrence/nonoccurrence basis. For those behaviors that have occurred, the individaul is also asked to provide a rating of the impact of the behavior (positive, negative, and neutral). Finally, spouses are also asked to rate their overall marital satisfaction for that day on a 9-point Likert scale.

Purpose

Behavioral assessment relies heavily on direct observation of behavior. One difficulty in assessing marital behavior is that the interactions of greatest interest tend to occur infrequently and unpredictably or to be intimate and private. In addition, many behaviors are associated with marital distress. An alternative to direct observation by the clinician/researcher is to use the spouse as a participant observer.

Development

The SOC was developed as a research instrument for use in evaluating treatment and testing hypotheses derived from behavioral models of marital therapy and as a treatment outcome measure. The development of the SOC was closely tied to behavioral marital therapy and related theorizing on the behavioral causes and correlates of marital distress. The most pervasive theoretical basis for behavioral marital therapy and assessment comes from behavior exchange theory. As applied to marital relationships, behavior exchange theory posits that happy marriages are characterized by the maximization of positive reinforcement and the minimization of costs. Reciprocity, the tendency for spouses to reward one another at equivalent rates, is considered to be an important component of marital satisfaction. Dysfunctional marriages are characterized by a paucity of positive reinforcers in the exchanges between spouses. Marital dissatisfaction is considered a function of the couple's exchange of punishers or unpleasant events. According to behavior exchange theory, the ratio of rewards to punishments provides an index of marital distress.

The assessment focus suggested by behavior exchange theory is on the occurrence of positive and negative behaviors during marital interactions. As part of a program to develop a series of instruments for the behavioral assessment of marriage, the Oregon group began the development of the SOC. Items were selected on the basis of interviews with both happy and distressed couples, and were categorized on an a priori basis as either pleasing or displeasing.

Psychometric Characteristics

As a participant observation instrument, the SOC is used by essentially untrained raters to assess interactional behavior that is of considerable significance to the rater. These factors may mitigate against the reliability of the measure. In fact, results from recent studies of interspouse agreement have consistently indicated that the SOC may perhaps best be viewed as a self-report instrument rather than a behavioral observation instrument per se. Reliability studies have been conducted using a self-monitoring form in addition to the SOC. Spouses rate their own and their partner's behavior for the preceding 24-hour period. Although data on interrater agreement between spouses have shown significant correlations on composite scores, percentage agreement on individual items has been much lower and rarely reaches acceptable levels for observational research. Jacobson and Moore (1981) report the mean percentage agreement of couples using the SOC to be 47.8%, with a range of 31 to 78.6%. Christensen and Nies (1980) and Jacobson and Moore (1981) report that the SOC ratings of distressed couples are significantly less accurate than the ratings of nondistressed couples. However, even nondistressed couples typically disagree as often as they agree. Also, displeasing items elicit lower agreement than do pleasing items.

With regard to validity, distressed couples report fewer pleasing items and more displeasing items than do nondistressed couples (Birchler, Weiss, & Vincent, 1975; Margolin, 1981; Barnett & Nietzel, 1979). The SOC is also correlated with ratings of marital satisfaction. Finally, the SOC is sensitive to change in therapy. Data indicate that the ratio of displeasing events to pleasing events decreases from pretreatment to posttreatment.

Clinical Use

The SOC may have greatest clinical usefulness as a measure of spouses' *perceptions* of what is happening on a day-to-day basis in the relationship. Regardless of the objectivity of SOC data in terms of actual frequency of specific behaviors, spouses' perceptions of marital behavior are clearly related to marital satisfaction. However, before using the SOC, the researcher/clinician should be clear as to what it is he or she wishes to measure. Direct observation by trained raters may be used in conjunction with the SOC if data regarding the actual frequency of specific behaviors are required.

The SOC can be used clinically to identify behaviors that are most important to a spouse (those that are most highly correlated with daily satisfaction ratings) and to help couples increase the frequency of pleasing behaviors. It can also be used to monitor the progress of marital therapy and as a treatment outcome measure, providing pre- to posttreatment changes in spouses' ratings of pleasing/displeasing behaviors. As an assessment measure, the SOC can be used with any intervention procedure that is intended to increase positive exchanges, decrease negative exchanges, or both.

When using the SOC, the researcher/clinician should be aware of possible reactivity effects: the act of completing the measure in and of itself appears to influence behavior. The SOC requires a 10th-grade reading level. Although completion of the SOC typically takes less than 20 minutes, that time alone, independent of any other homework assignments, may represent a substantial time commitment for most couples. Midweek phone calls to couples may help to encourage consistent record keeping.

Future Direction

In its present form, the most pertinent data that the SOC provides are the summary scores for total pleasing and total displeasing events. These scores have been demonstrated to have adequate reliability and validity. Further evaluation of the individual items and category subtotals is needed. The appropriateness, representativeness, and possible overlap of the current item sample should be assessed. The differential validity of items and subscores for special populations such as older adults or various subcultures should be investigated.

References

Barnett, L.R., & Nietzel, M.T. (1979). Relationships of instrumental and affectional behaviors and self-esteem to marital satisfaction in distressed and non-distressed couples. *Journal of Consulting and Clinical Psychology, 47,* 946-957.

Birchler, G.R., Weiss, R.L., & Vincent, J.P. (1975). Multimethod analysis of social reinforcement exchange between maritally distressed and nondistressed spouse and stranger dyads. *Journal of Personality and Social Psychology, 31,* 349-360.

Christensen, A., & Nies, D.C. (1980). The Spouse Observation Checklist: Empirical analysis and critique. *The American Journal of Family Therapy, 8,* 69-79.

Jacobson, N.S., & Moore, D. (1981). Spouses as observers of the events in their relationship. *Journal of Consulting and Clinical Psychology, 49,* 269-277.

Margolin, G. (1981). Behavior exchange in happy and unhappy marriages: A family cycle perspective. *Behavior Therapy, 12,* 329-343.

Patterson, G.R. (1976). Some procedures for assessing changes in marital interaction patterns. *Oregon Research Institute Bulletin,* Whole No. 16.

Spouse Verbal Problem Checklist

Kathy Sexton-Radek and Stephen N. Haynes

Description

The Spouse Verbal Problem Checklist (SVPC) is a 27-item questionnaire that asks an individual to describe the verbal behavior of his or her spouse during discussions or arguments. This questionnaire is a modified version of the Verbal Problem Checklist developed by Carter and Thomas (1973). The subject circles a response from "never" (0) to "always" (5) to indicate the spouse's verbal behavior. Examples include "talks too much," "talks too little," and "fails to compliment you."

Purpose

The purpose of the SVPC is that of spouse observational (participant monitoring) measure designed to assess the subject's perceptions of the spouse's communication problems.

Development

The SVPC represents a change in instructions from the original Verbal Problems Checklist developed by Carter and Thomas. The SVPC has been subjected to psychometric investigation.

Psychometric Characteristics

Samuels (1983) reported that the internal consistency of the SVPC (Cronbach's alpha) was .90 for male and .92 for female subjects. In a criterion-validity study, Haynes, Chavez, and Samuels (1984) evaluated the correlation between scores on the SVPC and three additional measures of marital satisfaction. In a sample of 380 married individuals married less than 4 years, the SVPC correlates − 0.67 (p <0001) with the Dyadic Adjustment Scale, − .59 (p <.0001) with a measure of Communication Satisfaction, − 0.05 (not significant) with positive behaviors emitted in an analogue communication situation, and 0.11 (p <.05) with negative behaviors emitted in an analogue communication situation. A mean score of 46.01 and standard deviation of 19.82 were obtained from this sample. No significant between-sex differences were found.

Clinical Use

The SPVC is a useful measure of an individual's perception of his or her spouse's verbal behavior and can be used to pinpoint specific communication behaviors that may require modification during communication training.

References

Carter, R.D., & Thomas, E.J. (1973). Modification of problematic marital communication using corrective feedback and instruction. *Behavior Therapy, 24,* 100-109.

Haynes, S.N., Chavez, R.E., & Samuels, V. (1984). Assessment of marital communication and distress. *Behavioral Assessment, 6,* 315-321.

Samuels, V. (1983). *Validity of the Spouse Verbal Problem Checklist.* Unpublished master's thesis, Southern Illinois University.

Staff Behavior Observation

Alan M. Delamater

Description

This procedure for the measurement of staff behavior employs direct, naturalistic behavioral observation. It has been used in a study of staff training procedures in a child psychiatric inpatient setting (Delamater, Conners, & Wells, 1984). Observers are trained in the observational methods, including operational definitions and the use of interval time-sampling procedures. After meeting criteria for reliability, they observe staff interacting with patients in their natural environments, and code their behavior into one of the following categories: reward, attend, punish, redirect, and ignore/no response. In addition, the staff behavior is coded as having been a vocalization or not, and the patient behavior to which the staff responded is coded as either adaptive or maladaptive. The definitions and observational procedures will be described in detail herein. Observational data can be obtained at several times during the day, such as during free interaction periods in the lounge or dayroom or during meals. Observers should be in a nonintrusive position in the room, or better yet, conduct the observations through a one-way mirror. Each staff member is observed through an interval time-sampling procedure, e.g., observe during a 10-second interval and record for 5 seconds. The first occurring staff response to a patient behavior in the observational interval is coded, and the patient behavior is also coded. If maladaptive behavior occurs during the interval, that behavior and the staff response to it should be coded. Each staff member's behavior should be sampled for as much time as is reasonable, given the resources of the facility. In the Delamater et al. (1984) study, each staff member was observed for up to 8 minutes on each day of the 5-day work week. Practical considerations may make daily recording on every staff member difficult, but attempts should be made to observe each staff member as frequently and for as long as possible. Obviously, the greater the sample, the more representative it will be. It is also important to record the number of staff and patients present during the observational periods. If the staff behavior data are to be used as part of a research study, attempts should be made to keep the staff-to-patient ratio constant.

Purpose

The purpose of this behavioral assessment technique is to quantify the response of staff members as they interact with patients. When staff behavior is operationalized and systematically observed and recorded, it provides information that may be used in performance feedback and program evaluation. The technique described here provides data reflecting the percentage of time staff members engaged in each of the behavioral categories; in addition, it can be used to derive a percentage of appropriate responses (e.g., rewards or attends to adaptive patient behavior) as well as inappropriate responses (e.g., rewards or attends to maladaptive patient behavior). In noting the relative neglect of measuring independent variables in behavioral research, Wodarski, Feldman, and Pedi (1974) pointed out that assessments of staff behavior may provide assurance that interventions are being appropriately implemented.

Development

This technique was developed in conjunction with a research project to determine which of several staff training procedures was most effective in increasing appropriate staff behavior and decreasing inappropriate staff behavior in a child psychiatric inpatient setting. The definitions and procedures were piloted and refined before the actual study. The observational system was designed to operationalize the full range of staff response and patient behavior by considering the most general categories that would provide specific, quantitative information.

Psychometric Characteristics

Reliability was assessed by having two observers independently observe the same staff member simultaneously. As reported in the Delamater et al. (1984) study, reliability was assessed on 20% of the total recorded data. Reliability was determined for each category separately by dividing agreements by agreements plus disagreements on occurrences only. The results revealed mean reliabilities of .78 for reward, .90 for attend, .60 for punish, .38 for redirect, .83 for ignore/no response, .80 for vocalization, .96 for adaptive patient behavior, and .76 for maladaptive patient behavior. The reliabilities for the punish and redirect categories were attenuated because of the low frequency of occurrence of those behaviors in the reliability samples. During the development and training period before the study, acceptable reliabilities for all categories were obtained.

The data obtained with these assessment procedures indicated that staff behavior was affected by certain training procedures and not by others. The differential response of staff to the various training approaches lends support to the validity of the assessment techniques.

Clinical Use

This assessment technique can be used to measure staff response in institutional settings such as child or adult inpatient psychiatric facilities, or residential or day treatment centers or group homes for disadvantaged, delinquent, mentally retarded, or handicapped individuals. Care must be taken in using this technique to ensure that reliability is maintained. Frequent, unobtrusive reliability checks, regular discussions concerning definitions and procedures, and retraining as necessary are critical in preventing observer drift and maintaining adequate reliability. Staff reactivity to observations does not appear to be an issue after staff habituate to the presence of observers (Hagen, Craighead, & Paul, 1975).

Future Directions

Although some studies of staff behavior rely on indirect measures such as rating scales, permanent products (e.g., number of tasks completed), or patient behavior, the technique described here utilizes direct measures of staff behavior and provides objective information that may be used in many ways. The general approach described here may be modified to meet individual needs. For example, Jones, Evans, and Blunden (1984) used 30-second momentary time-sampling to record resident activity and type of staff assistance given. Kissel, Whiteman, and Reid (1983) directly measured appropriate and inappropriate verbal instruction, physical guidance, and reward in conjunction with specific self-care behaviors of retarded residents. In each of these cases, the approach used to measure staff behavior depended on the specific behaviors of interest. The general approach of using direct, naturalistic, behavioral observation can be modified to meet individual needs. Future work should see continued exploration of direct measures of staff behavior in diverse staff-patient interaction as it unfolds in time, rather than "freezing" the behavior in narrow time frames such as 10-second intervals or 30-second momentary samples.

References

Delamater, A.M., Conners, C.K., & Wells, K.C. (1984). A comparison of staff training procedures: Behavioral applications in the child psychiatric inpatient setting. *Behavior Modification, 8,* 39-58.

Hagen, R.L., Craighead, W.E., & Paul, G.L. (1975). Staff reactivity to evaluative behavioral observations. *Behavior Therapy, 6,* 201-205.

Jones, A.A., Evans, G., & Blunden, R. (1984). Introducing a general prompting and recording system: Its effect on client and staff behavior in an institutional ward. *Applied Research in Mental Retardation, 5,* 125-136.

Kissel, R.C., Whiteman, T.L., & Reid, D.H. (1983). An institutional staff training and self-management program for developing multiple self-care skills in severely/profoundly retarded individuals. *Journal of Applied Behavior Analysis, 16,* 395-415.

Wodarski, J.S., Feldman, R.A., & Pedi, S.J. (1974). Objective measurement of the independent variables: A neglected methodological aspect in community-based behavioral research. *Journal of Abnormal Child Psychology, 2,* 239-244

Staff-Resident Interaction Chronograph

Mark H. Licht and Gordon L. Paul

Description

The Staff-Resident Interaction Chronograph (SRIC) is a component instrument of the Computerized TSBC/SRIC Planned-Access Observational Information System (Paul, 1987b). The TSBC/SRIC in toto is the core of a comprehensive assessment paradigm designed to provide all of the common information needed on adult clients, staff, and programs to maximize the quality and rationality of clinical, administrative, professional/legal, and scientific decision-making in public and private mental hospitals and residential schools, inpatient units of mental health centers, community residential facilities, and psychiatric units of general hospitals (Paul, 1986). The component instruments of the TSBC/SRIC System, the SRIC (Paul, 1987a; Power, 1984) and the TSBC (Paul & Licht, this volume), are standardized Direct Observational Coding (DOC) devices applied by full-time, noninteractive technician-level observers who are trained in objective and nonreactive data collection. Observers function as independent support personnel whose only job is to collect and process trustworthy data. In the standard and most cost-effective installation, observers are "on the floor" of a treatment unit about half the time, directly transcribing their immediate observations of the contexts and of the actions, interactions, and/or states of every client and staff member into the categories of the TSBC or SRIC. Each observational session is repeated on multiple occasions, following continuous time-sampling schedules to cover all client waking hours, 16 hours per day, 7 days per week. The same cadre of independent observers typically provides coverage of two or more units, averaging about two full-time equivalent observational staff for each 20- to 50-bed treatment unit.

No ongoing cost increase is usually entailed because of efficency resulting from the documentation and data breadth provided. A computer terminal and video screen or microcomputer on each implementing unit allows daily entry of DOC data into computer files, usually by night shift clinical staff while clients are sleeping. Computer programs retrieve and combine observations over occasions (situations and times), and/or people (clients or staff) and categories within each instrument to provide visual or printed summaries. After clinical, management, and research staff are trained to use summary reports, the TSBC/SRIC System provides printed Standard Weekly Reports for each client and staff member as well as aggregates for the entire client and staff groups on each unit. Unique or "special searches" can be initiated on-unit to answer additional questions about individuals, groups, or subgroups over any specified activity, time period, or variable on the DOC instruments or in biographical files. These special searches may be scanned on the video screen for interactive questioning of the continuous data files, with printed reports obtained when a permanent record is desired. Three Quality Assurance Reports are also provided over any specified time period from 2 weeks to 1 year or more; these reports combine and sort higher level data from the DOC instruments with information on client movement, demographics, staff and client turnover, staffing levels, costs, and the like for total units or small aggregate groups, such as treatment teams.

The SRIC is the primary instrument within the TSBC/SRIC System for providing information on staff functioning, especially staff-client interactions that define the psychosocial treatment received by clientele. Within Paul's nomenclature for DOC encoding devices (Paul, 1986), the SRIC is: (a) a standardized direct multivariate system, providing (b) exhaustive, concurrent-sequential sets of content categories for client behavior and for target staff responses/behavior to define the units of observation, and (c) a fixed-time, successive interval matrix format and direct entry, joint event notational coding scheme to define dichotomous units of measurement, based on (d) continuous chronographic observation of coding techniques with single target staff protocols, collected through (e) individual observation of focal staff and their client interactants in single target sessions, stratified with balanced factorial representation of staff in proportion to their time in the treatment program, applied on (f) hourly time-sampling schedules, further stratified within clock hours and behavior settings over sessions.

As a direct-multivariate system, the entire SRIC is applied on every continuous chronographic (10-minute) observation of a target staff member and resident (client) interactants. Depending on the physical plant and activity level, an average of 15 to 20 minutes is required for an observer to locate, observe, record, and process a complete observation of focal staff, with one or more being observed each hour within a treatment program in proportion to the time on duty during client waking hours. *Collateral categories* specify the facility, unit, observer, shift, and time (date, day, and clock time) of every observation period (session) as well as several aspects of the behavior setting and functional context (location, activity, residents present, residents shared, staff sharing, group composition, and situation specific appropriate resident behavior). *Content categories* specify the nature of: (a) client behavior to which staff might respond, defined in five global "resident categories" (appropriate, inappropriate failure, inappropriate crazy, "straight" requests, and neutral), and (b) staff verbal and nonverbal actions that could be directed to individual residents or groups as well as noninteractive job-relevant and irrelevant activities, defined in 21 detailed "staff categories" (both positive and negative verbal, nonverbal, nonsocial, statement, prompt, and group reference; reflect/clarify; suggest alternatives; instruct/demonstrate; doing with; doing for; physical force; ignore/no response; announce; and attend/record/observe.

Content categories are arranged in 5 by 21 matrices (columns = residents, rows = staff) on recording protocols, with one matrix for each successive 1-minute recording interval. This allows instantaneous/continuous coding of all staff-resident interactions, or absence thereof, by entering initials (or code numbers) of residents and groups in the proper cells of each matrix to record the joint occurrence of an instance of staff behavior in functional relationship to a class of resident behavior; the "neutral" resident column allows coding of staff initiations, rather than responses, and noninteractive activities. Each coding entry provides a dichotomous unit of measurement for actions by residents and by staff, and their functional co-occurrence as well as a permanent record of specific

residents receiving attention. Marginal comments clarify unusual events. A single SRIC observation is prepared for entry in computer files by summing the number of discrete codes in each cell over all 10 minutes of the observation period onto one summary 5 by 21 matrix; the number of staff "commands" and number and identification of residents contacted individually or only as part of a group are also tallied.

The units of measurement from a single SRIC can be retrieved for documentation/feedback, with identification of the synchrony/chronology of elemental categories and interactions within the observation period, but most uses rely on units of analysis (scores) from computer summaries over multiple observations of individual staff or staff groups. The SRIC reports are formatted to produce two summaries for different staff, groups, or time periods. *Standard Weekly Reports* summarize all staff and observations on a treatment unit in the same format as Special Reports for individuals or groups. Each SRIC report provides: (a) the average hourly rates of occurrence (and standard deviations) for each cell of the matrix and for sums over each resident category, each staff category, all interactive cells (total interaction), and all cells (total activity), (b) resident and staff categories as a percentage of total interactions and total interactions as a percentage of total activity, and (c) the average number of residents present and resident/staff ratios, average contacts per hour, interactions/contact, and total attention received by the average resident.

Purpose

The SRIC is designed to provide a continuous time- and situation-specific data base on residental staff psychosocial activities, specifically the nature, amount, content, and distribution of verbal/nonverbal interactions provided to clients. The SRIC summaries are designed to provide comparable information on individual staff and groups for timely concurrent monitoring of planned/unplanned psychosocial interventions and for staff training, development, utilization, and personnel decisions. They are also designed to provide the most trustworthy data on staff psychosocial functioning for placement/disposition decisions, problem identification/description, program evaluation, legal-ethical regulation/documentation, and specific research questions. (For decision problems and information needed in rational operations, see Paul, 1986).

Development

Since the SRIC's introduction to assess independent variables in a long-term comparative treatment study, 18 years of research and development resulted in its incorporation in the TSBC/SRIC System as the most cost-effective way to support rational operations in adult residential facilities and in materials and procedures needed for widespread implementation and dissemination. Multi-institutional normative feasibility studies on more than 600 staff in 36 programs have established its utility in the full range of staff and hospital/community programs (e.g., 8 to 120 beds; PhD/MD-aide level; 1/1, group, and unit-wide modalities; rational-emotive, behavioral, psychodynamic, milieu, biological, social learning, and eclectic models). The implementation package includes self-contained observer training materials (Licht, Paul, Power, & Engel, 1980), instructions for training clinical, administrative, and research staff in SRIC use and interpretation with technical/users manuals (Paul, 1987a 1987b), computer programs, and management procedures.

Psychometric Characteristics

The SRIC interobserver reliabilities (omega squares) are regularly high. For example, over the entire multi-institutional sample, replicabilities from 1 day's observation ranged from $r = .84$ to 1.00 for individual cells of the matrix with the median, and $r > .99$ over all cells. The SRIC data have been free of reactivity, drift, or bias. Validity evidence is extensive for all categories of decisions for which it is designed. Traditional concurrent validity studies are impossible, as non-DOC devices cannot provide any comparable data. Discriminations among public institution programs reflect average staff-client ineractions ranging from 42.66 to 45.23 interactions per hour, with the average staff member being responsible for as few as 4.31 clients or as many as 32.96 clients over a full week. The total attention received by the average client varies more than 1300%; noninteractive job-relevant and -irrelevant activities of staff show 5-fold and 13.5-fold differences. Even greater discriminations are obtained within cells of the SRIC matrix over programs and for individual staff within programs. The SRIC has demonstrated remarkable sensitivity to change in groups and individuals following staff training or feedback, or both, with efficiency increased three- to fivefold in different programs while reducing nonprogrammatic activity to near

zero. Correlations of SRIC data with continuous client data over time have documented relationships (r's in the .50 to .90 range) between how staff interact and client functioning/improvement. Large scale norms provide a basis for comparative interpretations. Local comparisons are usual with desirable patterns based on legal guidelines, theory, or documented effectiveness.

Clinical Use

In addition to the purposes just described with "hard evidence," the SRIC has been used in a host of ways, including protection of staff by defusing unjustified complaints; avoidance of legal suits, and improving morale and judged fairness of salary and personnel actions.

Future Directions

After publication of implementation materials, emphasis will be on dissemination of the TSBC/SRIC System to research and service facilities. This will also allow continuing improvements in clinical, administrative, and research utility and expansion of the normative base. The SRIC will also be used alone in research needing data on psychosocial interactions or environments.

References

Licht, M.H., Paul, G.L., Power, C.T., & Engel, K.L. (1980). The comparative effectiveness of two modes of observer training on the Staff Resident Interaction Chronograph. *Journal of Behavioral Assessment, 2,* 175-205.

Paul, G.L. (Ed.), (1986). *Principles and methods to support cost-effective quality operations: Assessment in residential treatment settings, Part 1.* Champaign, IL: Research Press.

Paul, G.L. (Ed.), (1987a). *Observational assessment instrumentation for service and research - The Staff Resident Interaction Chronograph: Assessment in residential treatment settings, Part 3.* Champaign, IL: Research Press.

Paul, G.L. (Ed.), (1987b). *Observational assessment instrumentation for service and research, The Computerized TSBC/SRIC Planned-Access Observational Information System: Assessment in residential treatment settings, Part 4.* Champaign, IL: Research Press.

Power, C.T. (1984). Assessment of staff and programs in residential treatment settings. In M. Mirabi (Ed.), *The chronically mentally ill: Research and services* (pp 109-122). New York: SP Medical & Scientific Books (Spectrum Publications).

Standardized Observation Codes

M. Angeles Cerezo

Description

The Standardized Observation Coding (SOC) System is a packaged behavior coding procedure devised by Wahler, House, and Stambaugh (1976) and revised by Dunn, Barker, and Wahler (1981). The SOC provides multiple code measures of social exchanges between the target child and other family members, at home within a framework of 15-second time intervals.

The SOC codes are scored in 30-minute sessions limited to one entry per code for each interval, but there is no upper limit to the number of codes that may be scored in a single interval. The observers are cued on time intervals through pre-recorded tape signals delivered by earphone.

The SOC observations are structured as free interchanges among family members with some restrictions, which can be summarized as follows: all family members are required to be within two door opened rooms of one another, all TV sets are turned off, and no extra family persons are in the house.

The system distinguishes between two groups of codes, one describing child behaviors characterized by their duration (e.g., schoolwork and opposition) and the other describing molecular instances (e.g., self-stimulation and social approach). The former grouping of codes is scorable only at the beginning of a 15-second interval, whereas the latter are scorable throughout the interval. A third group of stimulus codes, describing instructions and social attention provided by adults and peers, are likewise scorable throughout the interval. Twenty child behavior codes and nine stimulus codes comprise the three groupings.

Purpose

The SOC has two general purposes: (a) to provide a reliable clinical assessment of a child's in-setting behavior for planning and evaluating a treatment program, (b) to be a research intrument for providing a good picture of parent–child interactions. In fact, the instrument has evolved in new versions because the observational data by themselves pointed out further lines of investigations on the processes involved in family interactions with the target child.

In terms of clinical assessment, the codes provide a profile of child behavior that allows assessment of his or her present functioning and changes over time. Therefore, the coding system allows for a sample of both aversive behavior excesses and deficits and prosocial child behaviors along with contiguous social stimuli produced by family members.

Research uses center on a comprehensive view of family interchanges often pointing to new relationships between parent and child behavior. These new findings have led to published empirical studies.

Development

Over 10 years ago, Wahler and colleagues faced the task of developing a reliable assessment instrument for child problems as presented by parents and teachers.

The subject population at that time included children of both sexes, aged 4 to 14 years, referred to the Child Behavior Institute (CBI) by different institutions: mental health centers, city and county school systems, state hospitals, and juvenile courts.

Two goals were set for the projected coding system: (a) to appropriately reflect the concerns of persons in daily direct association with the problem child, namely, caretakers and teachers; (b) to meet the conventional standards of objective and reliable measurement of behavior. The process of meeting these goals was initiated by interviewing parents and teachers who referred "problem" children to the CBI. Two sets of adult concerns emerged: (a) so-called conduct problems, and (b) behavior deficiencies. The problem behaviors were then assessed through 100 hours of narrative description obtained from a sample of 50 children in home and school settings. A team of clinicians then selected commonly occurring narrative episodes and these became the first set of codes.

The original version consisted of 24 codes that provided a comprehensive picture of interactions between the target child and other relevant adults and peers. The interchanges were observed during 10 seconds and then the code occurrences were recorded in the next 5 seconds.

The original SOC consituted the basic assessment approach at Child Behavior Institute for 5 years. In 1981 the SOC was revised by Dunn et al. Several new codes were introduced, while two codes were removed in this second version. However, the most important change was in regard to the recording method. Now the intervals were consecutive and of 15 seconds' duration. The observer, on hearing the taped announcement "observe," started scoring according to the three groupings of codes described earlier.

Because the focus of the research was moved to child-family interaction rather then child interchanges at school, the revised coding system reflected this by means of several new codes regarding parent and sibling affection. Once the revision of the SOC was accomplished in 1981, this replaced the original version.

Psychometric Characteristics

Given that most of the studies involving the use of the SOC coding system have been aimed at searching for answers to different clinical problems, the reliability data available are mainly for those clinically relevant codes. There is a substantial body of data supporting the reliability of codes reflecting child aversive and prosocial behavior and those summarizing maternal aversive and nonaversive reactions to the child.

Wahler and Dumas (in press) studied all families referred to the Child Behavior Institute from April 1976 to July 1981, for whom complete baseline data were available. The study involved 52 mothers aged 21 to 38 years ($M = 28.37, SD = 5.93$). Their children (21 boys and 10 girls) ranged in age from 2 to 11 years ($M = 6.22; SD = 2.31$). All the observation sessions (twice a week for 4 to 6 weeks) were conducted by trained observers using the original SOC (1976).

Ten of 24 codes were relevant to this study and two measures of observer reliability were obtained: total session score agreement and interval-by-interval agreement. The measure of session reliability was computed through intraclass correlation coefficients on 52 cross-checked baseline observations. Interval-by-interval reliability was based on a random sample of 50% of these observations through Cohen's Kappa. The obtained values for the interclass correlation coefficients ranged from .83 to .98 ($M = .89, SD = .09$), whereas the interval-by-interval Kappa indices ranged from .51 to .86 ($M = .62, SD = .11$). All of them reached statistically significant levels of reliability.

The data generally are congruent with those obtained with a smaller sample (six mother–child dyads) by Wahler and Dumas (in press). Reliability session values (intraclass correlation coefficients) for the mother and child aversive behavior codes

just listed ranged from .77 to .97 ($M = .89, SD = .09$), all of them statistically significant (F tests, $p < .01$). Moreover, the Kappa coefficients (interval-by-interval reliability) for the same codes across three sessions per family ranged from .39 to .56 ($M = .44, SD = .09$), all of them statistically significant.

With respect to the SOC-R, revised version of 1981, the reliability data have been extended to a nonclinic sample of 33 families who met the criteria of disadvantaged and insular mothers. Panaccione and Wahler (in press) assessed the mother–child dyadic interactions through SOC-R for an average of 4.15 sessions per family. Ten of the 29 codes were relevant for study purposes: Child Affection and Child Compliance grouped as Child Prosocial Behavior; Rule Violation, Opposition, Verbal Compliants, and Physical Compliants grouped as Child Aversive Behavior; Mother Physical Affection and Facial and Verbal Affection grouped as Mother Affection; and, finally, Mother Aversive Social Attention and Aversive Instruction grouped as Mother Aversive Behavior. The interobserver agreement was computed as the number of agreements on the occurrence of behavior divided into the total number of agreements plus disagreements. The mean values reported for the four groups of codes ranged from 81.3 to 83.2% ($M = 81.95\%, SD = 1.26$).

These data are congruent with those reported by Wahler, Rogers, Collins, and Dumas (1984) with regard to three clinic-referred mothers of conduct-disordered children. Ten codes of the 29 plus two newly defined codes, added to SOC-R-Child Aversive Instruction and Maternal Compliance, were relevant. The codes were grouped in four clusters, namely, Child Aversive, Child Positive; Mother Aversive, and Mother Positive, the same code groupings used by Panaccione and Wahler (in press).

Two reliability checks were computed as agreement percentages. They ranged from 91 to 97% ($M = 95\%; SD = .03$) for the first reliability check and from 94 to 99% ($M = 96\%, SD = .02$) for the second checking across the three families. Moreover, the two new codes, Child Aversive Instruction and Maternal Compliance, obtained reliabilities of 96 to 99 and 100%, respectively.

In this study the computation of agreement percentages was based on time interval agreements and disagreements in which both occurrences and nonoccurrences of a code group were counted. For this reason the values reported were higher than the aforementioned ones.

Finally, in regard to validity, Moore (1975), using the SOC as a coding system, reported significant differences between deviant and nondeviant children observed in both settings: school and home. Specifically, the results demonstrated behavioral and social interaction differences between teacher-selected normal and conduct-disordered children in both their school and home settings. Oppositional behavior, setting-appropriate sustained behavior (play and work), and social behavior categories significantly differentiated the two groups. According to these findings, the measures derived from the SOC were consistent with teachers' ratings of child deviance. Likewise, the coding system was sensitive to the behavioral changes displayed by the children across settings.

Clinical Use

The population commonly evaluated with the SOC is comprised of conduct-disordered children aged 4 to 11 years who are primarily boys. The SOC allows assessment of the actual behavior of the child and the associated adult behavior in the natural environment. The SOC (in its two versions) has shown itself to be sensitive to changes in child and mother problem behaviors over the course of baseline assessment treatment and follow-up.

Future Directions

The SOC and SOC-R have provided valuable descriptive data which has formed the basis for planning new approaches to the study of family interactions. However, as more complex issues are examined, it is evident that both systems share common limitations, namely, the interval recording method of scoring behavior. Because this method does not permit real-time descriptions of behavior interactions, more fine-grained analyses of family interchanges are not possible.

Accordingly, to facilitate more fine-grained analysis of structural relationships within family interactions, a new version was designed. The Standardized Observation Codes-III devised by Cerezo, Kessler, and Wahler (1985) allow for recording frequency, duration, sequence, and valence in the family interchanges with a given target child.

The redefined behavior codes may be recorded on scoring sheets or by means of a recording device (HP-71B portable data acquisition computer) that notes the time of each occurrence. It should be pointed out that 15-second intervals are still used

for reliability checking, but not to break the scoring of behavioral streams.

Given that the first goal for SOC III was the sequential recording of social interactions in family setting, the codes were defined in mutually exclusive categories. Thus, the occurrence of a code necessarily indicates termination of that immediately preceding code.

The distinction between aversive and nonaversive codes has been segmented into positive, neutral, and aversive. The valences are used only with those codes defined as interactional. The different combinations between contents and valences provide a fine-grained picture of prosocial and nonprosocial behaviors. Finally, the use of alphabetical prefixes allows for identifying up to five family members interacting with the child (i.e., an instruction [I] can be given to the child by the mother [MI], father [FI], sister [SI], etc.).

The initial reliability data on SOC III are very promising. In fact, interval-by-interval agreement computed by Kappa across three families shows the average for all codes is .86 (SD = .09). Likewise the intraclass correlation coefficient has been computed for four groups of codes, namely, child aversive and positive behaviors and maternal aversive and positive behaviors. The obtained values ranged from .80 to .98 (M = .88, SD = .08). With two observers, 70% of 15-second intervals in 60-minute sessions agree in content frequency and sequence; over 60 of the intervals match in content, frequency, sequence, and valences of scores.

We are convinced that the development of observational coding systems is a priority task for researchers and clinicians concerned with family interactions. The third revision of the SOC coding system is based on a behavioral technology sufficiently advanced to permit more fine-grained inspections of family performance.

References

Cerezo, M.A., Keesler, T.Y., & Wahler, R.G. (1985). *Standardized Observation Codes III. SOC-3.* Unpublished manuscript. Child Behavior Institute, University of Tennessee, Knoxville, TN.

Dunn, E.S., Barker, M.L., & Wahler, R.G. (1981). *Standardized Observation Codes-Revised.* Unpublished manuscript. Child Behavior Institute, University of Tennessee, Knoxville, TN.

Moore, D.R. (1975). *Determinants of deviancy: a behavioral comparison of normal and deviant children in multiple settings.* Unpublished Doctoral Dissertation, University of Tennessee, Knoxville, TN.

Panaccione, V.F., & Wahler, R.G. (in press). Child behavior, maternal depression and social coercion as factors in the quality of child care. *Journal of Abnormal Child Psychology*.

Wahler, R.G., & Dumas, J.E. (in press). Indiscriminate mothering is a contextual factor in aggressive-oppositional child behavior: "Damned if you do and damned if you don't." *Journal of Abnormal Child Psychology*.

Wahler, R.G., House, A.E., & Stambaugh, E.E. (1976). *Ecological assessment of child problem behavior*. New York: Pergamon Press.

Wahler, R.G., Rogers, D., Collins, B., & Dumas, J.E. (1984). Maintenance factors in abusive mother–child interactions: The compliance and uncertainty hypotheses. Symposium for Association for Advancement of Behavior Therapy. Philadelphia, November 1984.

Standardized Walk

Chris M. Adler and David H. Barlow

Description

The standardized walk consists of a standard 1.2-mile course, divided by 20 approximately equidistant stopping points or "stations." The course begins at the clinic, continues through an increasingly crowded downtown area, and terminates at a heavily trafficked mid-city concourse. Patients are instructed to walk alone as far as possible on the course, unless undue anxiety is experienced. Patients are provided with instructions, directions, and an easy-to-follow map for the walking course.

In addition to providing a behavioral measure of avoidance (i.e., number of stations completed ranging from 0 to 20), the standardized walk also provides subjective and physiological measures of anxiety. Subjective anxiety (SUDS) is measured by instructing the patients to report their current level of anxiety (using a 0 to 8 scale, in which 0 = no anxiety and 8 = as much anxiety as possible) at each station completed. The patient makes this report by speaking into a lapel microphone, which is attached to a concealed miniature cassette recorder. The physiological component of the anxiety response is assessed by monitoring the patient's heart rate throughout the walk. This continuous monitoring of heart rate is accomplished through the use of a pulsemeter electrode belt (such as the "Exersentry Respironics, Inc), worn around the lower chest, underneath the patient's clothing. The pulsemeter itself can be rewired so that the voltage signal is diverted from the speaker, which normally emits an audible tone with each heart beat, directly to a microcassette recorder.

Each heart beat, therefore, produces a voltage charge that is recorded on the cassette tape. This tape can later be processed through preamplifiers and polygraph tachographs to obtain a graphic display of beats per minute.

Purpose

The primary purpose of the standardized walk is to allow the simultaneous assessment of subjective, behavioral, and physiological components of an agoraphobic's anxiety on exposure to controlled, yet fear-relevant situations. When used before, during, and after treatment, the standardized walk is particularly useful in analyzing the effects of treatment on actual behavioral flexibility as well as on the patient's subjective report.

As a research instrument, the standardized walk has been used to examine desynchrony between self-report of anxiety and heart rate as a prediction of outcome.

Development

The standardized walk was developed by Agras, Leitenberg, and Barlow (1968). Over a period of years this test has been used and further refined by the staff of the Phobia and Anxiety Disorders Clinic of the State University of New York at Albany. The patient instructions and walk procedures have evolved over several years' experience in the assessment and treatment of agoraphobic patients.

Clinical Use

The standardized walk is designed to be used as an in vivo assessment of subjective, behavioral, and physiological components of anxiety in agoraphobic patients. The standardized walk is of most use in the assessment of patients who display global rather than circumscribed fear, as well as moderate to severe avoidance of being alone, in familiar or unfamiliar open areas, and in crowds.

Future Directions

Technological advances, such as the vitalog portable monitor, may overcome many of the difficulties involved with in vivo physiological recording. Use of the vitalog allows for continuous analysis of information from up to eight physiological sensors, for up to 24 hours. The availability of this type of technology will no doubt broaden and further the examination of the interrelationships between subjective, behavioral, and physiological anxiety.

Reference

Agras, W.S., Leitenberg, H., & Barlow, D.H. (1968). Social reinforcement in the modification of agoraphobia. *Archives of General Psychiatry, 19,* 423-427.

State-Trait Anger Scale

Charles D. Spielberger

Description

The State-Trait Anger Scale (STAS), a 20-item psychometric self-report inventory with separate 10-item scales for assessing state and trait anger (Spielberger, 1980; Spielberger, Jacobs, Russell, & Crane, 1983), is analogous in conception and format to the State-Trait Anxiety Inventory (STAI, Spielberger, 1980b). State anger (S-Anger) consists of subjective emotional feelings of irritation, annoyance, fury, and rage, which are associated with activation (arousal) of the autonomic nervous system. S-Anger can vary in intensity and fluctuate over time as a function of perceived injustice, unfair criticism, physical attack, or frustration resulting from the blocking of goal-directed behavior. Trait anger (T-Anger) is defined in terms of individual differences in how often angry feelings are experienced. Individuals high in T-Anger are likely to experience elevations in S-Anger more frequently and under a wider range of circumstances than are persons low in T-Anger.

In responding to the STAS S-Anger items (e.g., "I am furious" or "I feel irritated"), individuals report the *intensity* of their subjective emotional feelings of anger at a *particular moment in time* by rating themselves on the following 4-point scale: (1) not at all; (2) somewhat; (3) moderately so; and (4) very much so. Subjects respond to the STAS T-Anger items by reporting how often they have experienced particular manifestations of anger (e.g., "I am quick tempered" or "I get angry when I am slowed down by others' mistakes") by rating themselves on the following 4-point *frequency* scale: (1) almost never; (2) sometimes; (3) often; and (4) almost always.

Two distinctive but related trait anger concepts have been identified. *Angry temperament* refers to individual differences in a general tendency to

experience feelings of anger in a variety of situations and circumstances. Common descriptions of this tendency refer to "hot headedness" and having a "fiery temper." The second type of T-Anger, *angry reactions,* refer to individual differences in the tendency to experience feelings of anger when criticized, negatively evaluated, or not given adequate recognition. These two types of T-Anger are assessed by 4-item subscales that were derived from factor analyses of the 10 STAS T-Anger items. The *T-Anger Temperament* subscale assesses individual differences in a general disposition to experience anger, irrespective of the provoking circumstances (e.g., "I am a hotheaded person"). The T-Angry Reaction subscale assesses individual differences in a more specific disposition to experience anger when provoked or unfairly criticized (e.g., "I feel annoyed when I am not given recognition for doing good work").

Purpose

Anger, hostility, and aggression are central concepts in many theories of personality and psychopathology, and the maladaptive effects of anger are recognized as important in the etiology of psychiatric and medical disorders (Spielberger & London, 1982). Although much has been written about its negative effects, anger is often used interchangeably with hostility and aggression, resulting in a great deal of conceptual confusion and ambiguity in the research and clinical literature. There is, however, an emerging consensus on the definitions of these terms. Anger generally refers to an emotional state, aggression is used most often to denote behaviors directed toward destroying objects or injuring other persons, and hostility connotes a complex set of negative attitudes and reactions involving angry feelings, cynicism, and aggressive behavior. The STAS was designed to assess the intensity of angry feelings at a particular moment, and individual differences in anger proneness as a personality trait or disposition (Spielberger, 1980a; Spielberger et al., 1983).

Development

To link the STAS to previous research, the first stage of test construction attempted to identify an underlying anger factor in the Buss-Durkee Hostility Inventory (BDHI). When work on the STAS began in 1977, the BDHI was generally regarded as the most carefully developed and best validated instrument for measuring anger and hostility. If an anger factor could be identified in the BDHI, items with the strongest loadings on this factor could be rewritten in state-trait format to provide the nuclei for psychometric scales designed to assess state and trait anger. However, factor analyses of responses to the BDHI items failed to identify an underlying anger factor, revealing instead that the BDHI was factorially complex.

The next step in constructing the STAS was to compile a pool of items based on the definition of trait anger just noted. Items were adapted from the BDHI and other measures of anger and hostility, and new items consistent with this definition were written in the trait format of the STAI T-Anxiety scale (Spielberger, 1980b). This pool of 22 T-Anger items was administered to new samples of university students, along with measures of trait anxiety and trait curiosity (Spielberger et al., 1983). The 15 items with the highest item-remainder correlations and with relatively low correlations with the measures of anxiety and curiosity were selected for the preliminary STAS T-Anger scale. Alpha coefficients for the 15-item T-Anger scale were .87 for both male and female subjects, indicating an acceptable level of internal consistency.

In developing the STAS S-Anger scale, *Roget's International Thesaurus* and several standard dictionaries were consulted to identify synonyms and idioms for describing anger. A pool of 20 items, written in the format of the STAI S-Anxiety scale and given with the same instructions (Spielberger, 1983), was administered to a large sample of Navy recruits, along with a measure of state anxiety. The 15 S-Anger items with the highest item-remainder correlations and the lowest correlations with a state anxiety measure were selected for the preliminary STAS S-Anger scale. The alpha coefficients for the preliminary S-Anger scale were .93 for both male and female subjects.

The high degree of internal consistency reflected in the preliminary STAS S-Anger scales suggested that these constructs could be measured with fewer items. Because it was considered desirable for the anger measures to be relatively independent of anxiety, the psychometric characteristics of each S-Anger and T-Anger item were examined and those items with the highest item-remainder correlations and the lowest correlations with anxiety were retained for the final 10-item STAS S-Anger and T-Anger scales. Because correlations between the 10-item and 15-item scales for large samples of Navy recruits and university students were .95 to .99, the 10-item forms were retained for the STAS S-Anger and T-Anger scales.

Psychometric Characteristics

Norms for the STAS are available for large samples of junior and senior high school students (sample = 3,016), college students (sample = 1,617), military recruits (sample = 2,360) and working adults, aged 18 to 63 (sample = 1,252). The alpha coefficients of the S-Anger scale for the normative samples range from .88 to .95; the alphas for the T-Anger scale range from .81 to .91. The alpha coefficients for the 4-item T-Angry Temperament and T-Angry Reaction subscales were also very high, with a median alpha of .90 and .81 for the T-Angry Temperament and T-Angry Reactions subscales, respectively. Thus, the STAS and its subscales have a surprisingly high degree of internal consistency for a scale with so few items.

There were relatively few differences between male and female subjects in the various samples, although the male military recruits were somewhat higher in state and trait anger than were the female recruits, and female college students and older working adults (33 or older) were higher than their male counterparts. High school students scored substantially higher in T-Anger and its subscales than did other groups. They also scored higher in S-Anger, even though the military recruits were tested at a highly stressful time early in their basic training programs. In general, scores on T-Anger and its subscales were higher for the younger and less educated subjects, and these relationships were stronger for male than female subjects.

The STAS T-Anger scale is moderately to highly correlated with the BDHI and MMPI hostility measures. Low to moderate correlations have also been found between the STAS T-Anger scale and trait anxiety, and much higher correlations have been observed between the STAS S-Anger scale and state anxiety ($r = .63$). The T-Anger scale is also moderately correlated with Eysenck's neuroticism scale ($r = .50$), and small but significant correlations have been found with the EPQ Psychoticism scale for both male and female subjects. The STAS scales, which measure the experience of angry feelings, are moderately correlated with anger expression (anger-out) and are also positively correlated with suppressed anger (Spielberger et al., 1985).

Clinical Use

The STAS provides information on the intensity of angry feelings and individual differences in anger proneness that may be useful in clinical research and in the evaluation of individual clients and patients. The scale has been recently adapted in Dutch, German, Korean, Hungarian, and Japanese, and these adaptations have excellent psychometric properties. The relative ease in developing foreign language adaptations suggests that the STAS measures a universal emotional experience that can be readily assessed because it is clearly reflected in different language systems.

In clinical research with the STAS, hypertensive patients, when compared with a control group of medical and surgical patients, have had higher T-Angry Reaction scores, but do not differ in T-Angry Temperament. They also score higher on S-Anger while performing a mildly frustrating task. Surprisingly, chronic pain patients have relatively low anger scores but are very high in anxiety, suggesting that repressed or denied anger may contribute to higher anxiety and chronic pain reactions.

Future Directions

The STAS may be used in screening candidates for psychotherapy to evaluate the extent to which angry feelings are an important problem for particular patients. Because anger appears to be an important component of the Type-A coronary-prone behavior syndrome (Spielberger & London, 1982), the STAS should prove useful in the rehabilitation of patients with coronary heart disease. It may also be used as an outcome measure in research on counseling and psychotherapy and stress management programs.

References

Spielberger, C.D. (1980a). *Preliminary Manual for the State-Trait Anger Scale.* Tampa: University of South Florida. Unpublished manuscript.

Spielberger, C.D. (1980b). *Manual for the State-Trait Anxiety Inventory, STAI (Form Y) ("Self-Evaluation Questionnaire").* Palo Alto, CA: Consulting Psychologists Press.

Spielberger, C.D., Jacobs, G., Russell, S., & Crane, R.S. (1983). Assessment of anger: The State-Trait Anger Scale. In J.N. Butcher & C.D. Spielberger (Eds.), *Advances in personality assessment,* (Vol. 2). Hillsdale, NJ: LEA.

Spielberger, C.D., Johnson, E.H., Russell, S.F., Crane, R.J., Jacobs, G.A., & Worden, T.J. (1985). The experience and expression of anger: Construction and validation of an Anger Expression Scale. In M.A. Chesney & R.H. Rosenman (Eds.), *Anger and hostility in cardiovascular and behavioral disorders.* New York: Hemisphere/McGraw-Hill.

Spielberger, C.D., & London, P. (1982). Rage boomerangs, a key to preventing coronaries is emerging: Learn to handle anger and avoid seven deadly responses. *American Health, 1,* 52-56.

State-Trait Anxiety Inventory (Form Y)

Charles D. Spielberger

Description

The State-Trait Anxiety Inventory (STAI) is comprised of separate self-report psychometric scales for measuring two distinct but related anxiety concepts (Spielberger, Gorsuch, & Lushene, 1970). State anxiety (S-Anxiety) is conceptualized as a transitory emotional condition characterized by subjective, consciously perceived feelings of tension, apprehension, nervousness, and worry, and heightened activation (arousal) of the autonomic nervous system. Anxiety states may vary in intensity and fluctuate over time as a function of situational stress. Trait anxiety (T-Anxiety) refers to relatively stable differences in anxiety proneness, that is, individual differences in the tendency to perceive or appraise stressful situations as personally dangerous or threatening, and to respond to such situations with elevations in S-Anxiety.

The STAI S-Anxiety scale consists of 20 statements that ask persons to report how they feel *at a particular moment in time* by rating the *intensity* of their subjective feelings of anxiety (e.g., "I feel frightened") on the following 4-point scale: (1) not at all; (2) somewhat; (3) moderately so; and (4) very much so. The STAI T-Anxiety scale consists of 20 statements that require persons to indicate how they *generally* feel. In responding to each T-Anxiety item (e.g., "I have disturbing thoughts"), subjects report how often they have experienced particular symptoms of anxiety by rating themselves on the following 4-point *frequency* scale: (1) almost never; (2) sometimes; (3) often; and (4) almost always.

Purpose

Anxiety is a fundamental explanatory construct in most theories of personality and psychopathology and is generally regarded as the central problem in psychoneurosis. Therefore, measuring anxiety is essential in psychological research and clinical practice. The importance of anxiety as a powerful influence in contemporary life is also widely recognized, and concern with anxiety phenomena is reflected in many facets of our culture, including literature, the arts, and religion, as well as in psychology, psychiatry, and medicine. The STAI was constructed to provide brief, internally consistent, reliable, and valid self-report scales for assessing state and trait anxiety in a variety of populations and settings.

Development

The initial goal in the development of the STAI was to identify a single set of items that could be administered with different instructions to assess either S-Anxiety or T-Anxiety. In 1963, when test construction began, most anxiety scales measured trait anxiety. Therefore, in assembling the preliminary item pool for the STAI, many items were selected from the most widely used T-Anxiety scales. These items were rewritten to form a single scale, STAI (Form A), which could be administered with different instructions for assessing either S-Anxiety or T-Anxiety.

In evaluating the stability and construct validity of the STAI (Form A), it was discovered that key words in a number of items had strong state or trait connotations, making it impossible to use these items as measures of both S-Anxiety and T-Anxiety. Consequently, the test-construction strategy was modified, and items with the best psychometric properties for measuring either state or trait anxiety were selected for the revised STAI (Form X). More than 6,000 high school and college students, approximately 600 neuropsychiatric, medical, and surgical patients, and 200 prison inmates were tested in the construction, standardization, and validation of the first commercially published form of the STAI (Form X). The principal steps and procedures in the test construction process are described in the STAI (Form X) Test Manual (Spielberger et al., 1970).

The STAI was further revised to replace several items, the content of which seemed more closely related to depression than to anxiety. A few items that were ambiguous or difficult to comprehend for persons with limited education or intellectual ability were also replaced. The replacement items all had equal or better psychometric properties than did the original items, i.e., larger factor loadings or item-remainder correlations or both. In

revising the STAI, more than 5,000 additional subjects were tested. The procedures for item selection, standardization, and validation of the STAI (Form Y) are described in the revised Test Manual (Spielberger, 1983).

Psychometric Characteristics

The internal consistency of the STAI S-Anxiety and T-Anxiety scales is relatively high, as measured by alpha coefficients and item-remainder correlations. Alpha coefficients for the S-Anxiety and T-Anxiety scales of the revised STAI (Form Y) are .90 or higher for the normative samples. Stability of the T-Anxiety scale, as measured by test-retest correlation coefficients, were also relatively high, ranging from .73 to .86 for 1 hour to 104 days. Test-retest stability was low for the S-Anxiety scale, as was considered appropriate for a measure designed to be sensitive to fluctuations in anxiety resulting from situational stress. In studies of the factor structure of the STAI, individual S-Anxiety and T-Anxiety items have consistently loaded on distinctive state and trait anxiety factors, and state and trait anxiety-absent and anxiety-present factors have also been consistently identified for both sexes.

Concurrent validity coefficients for the original STAI (Form X) T-Anxiety scale range from .73 to .85 (median = .80), as reflected in correlations with Cattell's Anxiety Scale Questionnaire and Taylor's Manifest Anxiety Scale, the two most widely used T-Anxiety measures before the publication of the STAI (Spielberger et al., 1970). Evidence of the construct validity of the T-Anxiety scale can be seen in substantially higher mean scores for various psychiatric patient groups as compared with normal subjects (Spielberger, 1983). The construct validity of the STAI S-Anxiety scale has been demonstrated in numerous studies in which S-Anxiety was found to fluctuate as a function of situational stress (Spielberger, 1984). For example, surgical patients scored higher before than after successful surgery, and college students were higher in S-Anxiety during examinations and lower after relaxation training, than when these same students were tested in regular classroom settings (Spielberger, 1983, 1985).

Clinical Use

The STAI has been used extensively in research and clinical practice, because it was first introduced some 20 years ago. The populations with which the inventory has been used include high school and college students, working adults, military personnel, prison inmates, and psychiatric, psychosomatic, medical, surgical, and dental patients. Most early studies were concerned primarily with the effects of stress and anxiety on learning and performance, but the STAI has been used increasingly in investigations of stress-related psychiatric and medical disorders. In addition to applications in psychology, psychiatry, and behavioral medicine, the STAI has been used extensively for research in education, counseling and guidance, nursing, criminal justice, speech and hearing, sports psychology, sociology and anthropology, fine arts (e.g., effects of anxiety on musical performance), and political science (e.g., effects of anxiety on voting behavior). The STAI has also been widely used to evaluate outcome in counseling, psychotherapy, biofeedback, and behavioral and cognitive treatment studies. References to more than 300 treatment studies published in the last decade may be found in the comprehensive bibliography of research with the STAI (Spielberger, 1984).

The STAI has excellent psychometric properties for the assessment of anxiety in elderly persons, but larger type may be required in printing the items for this age group because of their diminished visual acuity. Because the key words in most STAI items are at or below the sixth-grade reading level, the inventory can be readily administered to junior high school students. The State-Trait Anxiety Inventory for Children (STAIC) was constructed for testing fourth-, fifth-, and sixth-grade elementary school children (Spielberger, 1973), and appears to have adequate psychometric properties for the assessment of anxiety in second- and third-grade pupils. The STAI has also been used successfully with first graders when the items are read to the children by experienced examiners.

Future Directions

Current trends in research with the STAI, which are noted in the comprehensive bibliography (Spielberger, 1984), indicate that the scale is being used increasingly (a) in measuring outcome in counseling, psychotherapy, behavior therapy, and biofeedback; (b) in research with various psychiatric, psychosomatic, medical, and surgical patients; (c) in studies of alcohol and drug abuse; and (d) in the rapidly growing field of health psychology. Use of the STAI in cross-cultural research

has increased with foreign-language adaptations, which are now available in 39 languages and dialects (Spielberger, 1984). As the use of computers in psychological assessment becomes more commonplace, it seems likely that the STAI will be employed in clinical screening and in test batteries for the comprehensive assessment of patients with all types of psychosomatic, psychiatric, and medical disorders.

References

Spielberger, C.D. (1973). State-Trait Anxiety Inventory for Children: Preliminary Manual. Palo Alto, CA: Consulting Psychologists Press.

Spielberger, C.D. (1983). Manual for the State-Trait Anxiety Inventory (Revised Ed.). Palo Alto, CA: Consulting Psychologists Press.

Spielberger, C.D. (1984). The State-Trait Anxiety Inventory: A comprehensive bibliography. Palo Alto, CA: Consulting Psychologists Press.

Spielberger, C.D. (1985). Assessment of state and trait anxiety: Conceptual and methodological issues. The Southern Psychologist, 2, 6-16.

Spielberger, C.D., Gorsuch, R.L., & Lushene, R.D. (1970). Manual for the State-Trait Anxiety Inventory (Self-Evaluation Questionnaire). Palo Alto, CA: Consulting Psychologists Press.

Strain Gauge

Neil McConaghy

Description

Introduced to measure respiratory movements, strain gauges (SGs) have been used mainly in behavioral assessment to measure penile circumference responses (PCRs). Fisher, Gross, and Zuch (1965) reported that a mercury SG was more sensitive than a water-filled cuff or skin thermometer in assessing penile tumescent changes. Subsequently, many workers used a similar SG-silicone rubber tubing of internal diameter 0.05 to 0.98 cm filled with mercury and plugged at both ends with platinum electrodes. The tubing is placed in a loop around the shaft of the penis. Some gauges are commercially available in loops of various diameters. Alternatively, a sliding mechanism may be placed on the loop to ensure its fit. The resistance of the mercury in the tube is measured and reflects, virtually linearly, changes in penile diameter. Graphite in rubber and mechanical SGs has also been employed.

Purpose

The penile SG was introduced to measure erectile cycles during sleep. However, possibly because it was less cumbersome or more readily available than the transducers used to measure penile volume responses (PVRs), it has also been widely used in awake subjects to record PCRs associated with penile responses smaller than erections. Such PCRs are considered to measure PVRs and hence sexual arousal to visual and auditory heterosexual, homosexual, and paraphilic stimuli.

Development

Bancroft, Jones, and Pullan (1966) assumed that with penile tumescence, penile circumference increase would be proportional to an increase in length and stated that the SG measured true volume changes and hence sexual arousal. On the basis of this belief, he used SGs in a treatment procedure for sexual anomalies. Subjects received painful electric shocks if they showed penile circumference increases to pictures of deviant sex objects.

McConaghy (1974) compared subjects' penile responses measured by volume transducer with those measured by mercury SG to 10-second film segments of nude male and female subjects. The responses were not identical. In some subjects they were similar, but in others they were virtual mirror images: in these subjects PVR increase accompanied penile circumference shrinkage, and the reverse. Freund apparently observed the same phenomenon but attributed it to unexplained malfunctioning of the apparatus. It must result from the fact that in these subjects an increase or decrease in penile length was too rapid in relation to the associated increase or decrease in blood flow into the penis. So, although the length and volume were increasing, the circumference was shrinking and vice versa. Such subjects treated by Bancroft's procedure would receive shocks when they were showing penile detumescence to the deviant stimulus.

McConaghy's demonstration that early PCRs (i.e., those much less than full erections) commonly do not reflect PVRs was not accepted. The SGs are currently widely employed to record such PCRs as measures of sexual arousal and, particularly in single-case designs, to assess homosexuality and paraphilias and their change with treatment. The PCRs are usually recorded over several minutes of exposure to the stimulus. Hence, subjects have a considerable time in which to consciously influence such PCRs. When instructed to attempt to do so, many can reduce them to a marked extent.

The achievement of full or nearly full erection as measured by PSG in response to various stimuli presented over several minutes has been considered evidence that subjects are sexually aroused by these stimuli. For example, with practice, some homosexual men develop the ability to respond with full erections to pictures of nude women. Yet, they may report no increased heterosexual interest.

An independent development of SGs was based on the assumption that unlike organic factors, psychological factors do not influence erections during sleep. If this is correct, nocturnal penile tumescence (NPT) studies of subjects with psychogenic but not organic impotence would show normal erectile cycles. Subjects' NPT was investigated by SG, usually in a sleep laboratory. A "first night effect" of reduced NPT was reported. This evidence of a nonorganic effect on NPT led not to rejection of the assumption but acceptance that subjects should be investigated over two or preferably three nights. It was found that such psychological factors as the stress of imprisonment also could reduce NPT. Reduced NPT was reported in some impotent subjects in whom no organic cause could be demonstrated, and normal NPT in others whose impotence was apparently of organic origin.

Psychometric Characteristics

Presumably because PCRs recorded by SG were identified with PVRs recorded by volume transducers, validation of SG-assessed PCRs as measures of sexual arousal was attempted only some years after they were being used for this purpose. Thirty homosexual men showed mean mercury SG-assessed PCRs to pictures of men significantly greater than those to women. In only 14 were significant correlations ($r = 0.65$) found between their PCRs and subjective ratings of sexual arousal. These 14 subjects were mainly those with mean penile diameter increases over 0.4 mm. As a group, six heterosexual men were discriminated from six homosexual men by their mean mechanical SG-assessed PCRs to 2-minute video stimuli of subjects involved in sexual activity, but not of a nude young woman. Penile pulse amplitude and PCRs of 42 men were assessed by mercury SG to 6- to 8-minute audiotapes of descriptions of erotic, romantic, and nonsexual activity. Pulse amplitude provided significant correlations between response and assessed level of sexual arousal, ranging from $r = 0.4$ to 0.67. Most correlations based on PCRs were insignificant. Studies demonstrating failure of PCRs to validly assess sexual anomalies and paraphilias and their response to treatment have been reviewed or referenced elsewhere (McConaghy, 1977; McConaghy et al., 1985).

As measures of individual sexual orientation or degree of sexual arousal to visual or auditory erotic stimuli, mercury or mechanical SG, assessed PCRs appear to be of low validity in subjects who do not show consistent marked penile tumescence to such stimuli. Paradoxical penile diameter reduction occurring in many subjects with early tumescence is presumably responsible for the low validity. In their original capacity as an index of complete or near complete erection, the validity of the SG should be high in regard to the concomitant penile size increase, although not necessarily to penile rigidity, as significant diameter increase would seem to accompany erection in most subjects.

Strain gauge measures of NPT were obtained in 20 patients: 10 with an established organic cause for impotence and no psychogenic factors, and 10 the reverse. Using cutting points that best discriminated the two groups, 16 of the 20 could be discriminated correctly on the basis of their maximum NPT and 19 of 20 on the frequency of NPT episodes over two nights. The study would need replication using the same cutting points on the responses on a new sample to provide meaningful evidence of the validity of NPT in discriminating psychogenic from organic impotence. Consecutive night reliability of a portable NPT monitor using two SGs was investigated in 77 subjects, 16 with end-stage renal disease and major deficits in sexual performance. Correlations between assessments on the two nights were significant for proportion of sleep time spent with erections, for maximal PCC, and for the number of erections per night. When NPTs were categorized by arbitrary criteria as normal or abnormal, there was agreement between the two nights' categorizations in 61 of the 77 subjects (79.6%). No studies have demonstrated that this expensive and demanding procedure improved outcome of treatment of impotence over that based on an adequate clinical history including data from the patient and his partner concerning the frequency and rigidity of his nocturnal and morning erections.

Clinical Use

The SG measurement of PCR currently has no established clinical value. As an index of other than near complete or complete erections, PSGs are misleading. Unfortunately their widespread use in assessing sexual orientation and paraphilias or response to treatment of individual subjects with sexually anomalous behaviors has persisted despite evidence of their lack of validity for these purposes. The value of the NPT in discriminating psychogenic from organic impotence is not established, although it is widely recommended for this purpose.

Future Directions

The use of PCRs reflecting less than complete or near complete erections as measures of sexual arousal should be abandoned and the large body of findings based on this use reassessed. The significance of the ability of some men to develop PSG-measured complete or near complete erections to various stimuli with repeated exposure needs further investigation. The value of NPT in improving the assessment and treatment of impotent patients should be determined.

References

Bancroft, J., Jones, H.C., & Pullan, B.P. (1966). A simple transducer for measuring penile erections with comments on its use in the treatment of sexual disorders. *Behaviour Research and Therapy, 4*, 239-241.

Fisher, C., Gross, J., & Zuch, J. (1965). Cycle of penile erection synchronous with dreaming (REM) sleep. *Archives of General Psychiatry, 12*, 29-45.

McConaghy, N. (1974). Measurements of change in penile dimensions. *Archives of Sexual Behavior, 3*, 381-388.

McConaghy, N. (1977). Behavioral treatment of homosexuality. In M. Hersen, R. M. Eisler, & P.M. Miller (Eds.), *Progress in behavior modification*, Vol. 5. New York: Academic Press.

Structured Observation System

Karen S. Budd

Description

The structured observation system consists of five brief, structured activities for assessing the behavior of parents and their preschool or primary-grade children. Each standardized situation is oriented toward evaluating parents' use of a specific set of child management techniques for dealing with common behavior problems. Skill areas assessed include: (a) giving and following through with instructions; (b) differential social attention; (c) use of a token system; (d) teaching new skills; and (e) use of timeout. Each structured activity lasts between 5 and 12 minutes.

Structure is imposed on parent-child interactions by the use of specific cues (instructions, signals, materials, or assigned activities) that set the occasion for behaviors of interest to occur. Structure also is obtained by selecting a limited number of pertinent behaviors and a systematic framework for recording the occurrence of behaviors. Based on data obtained from observations, calculations are made of the proportion of desired parent and child responses per opportunity to obtain summary performance scores.

Purpose

The structured observation system is designed for clinical evaluation of behaviorally oriented parent training programs. It is applicable in families of young children with normal development and children with mental or physical handicaps. The system allows for direct observation of parent and child behaviors within the practical constraints of an applied setting. Because specific parent and child responses can be anticipated from the structure, the therapist can obtain maximal information on behaviors and environmental variables found to be relevant in other cases. A consistent structure also allows the therapist to compare findings across families, thus making structured assessment a viable research tool for clinical investigations. The recording procedure (or a simplified form of the procedure) could be used for self-recording by parents as either a training exercise or a means of obtaining supplemental data in additional settings.

Development

The structured observation system was initially developed by Budd, Riner, and Brockman (1983) as one means of evaluating a group parent training program. This research indicated that the system was highly reliable, was applicable across diverse families and behavior problems, and reflected considerable increases in parents' correct performance of child management skills correlated with training. Modifications were made to increase the sensitivity of the system to child behavior change, and further research demonstrated that therapists naive to the development of the system obtained

reliable recording when using the system in clinical evaluation with individual families (Budd & Fabry, 1984).

Psychometric Characteristics

Naive therapists attained mean interobserver agreement levels greater than 90% across all components within structured activities, thus attesting to the interobserver reliability of the structured observation system (Budd & Fabry, 1984). One index of validity was examined by comparing parent performance changes on the observational data to changes on two paper-and-pencil measures: a Child Management Questionnaire, which assesses parents' knowledge of behavior management principles, and a Parent-Child Behavior Inventory, which assesses parents' perceptions on the frequency of appropriate and inappropriate child responses in the home. Parents showed statistically significant changes on both paper-and-pencil measures correlated with increased parent performance in the structured activities following clinic training (Budd, Riner, & Brockman, 1983).

Clinical Use

The focus of the observational system is the behavior of parents and their young children referred because of behavior problems. It is most appropriate for children functioning at a cognitive level between 2 and 5 years and is applicable to children of normal development as well as handicapped children. The structured activities can be carried out either in families' homes or in a simulated home environment in a clinic. Although some measures of child behavior are provided, the system emphasizes recording of parent responses entailed in child management procedures. Application of the system to clinical cases (Budd & Fabry, 1984) indicated that, for many families, a single observation before training and another observation at termination are sufficient to provide the data needed for clinical evaluation. Additional assessments conducted periodically during the course of training can provide supplementary information about parents' acquisition and maintenance of behavior management skills.

Future Directions

Therapist comments indicated that three of the five structured activities (instruction giving, differential social attention, and use of timeout) were particularly useful as clinical tools. Proposed improvements on the other two activities are outlined by Budd and Fabry (1984). Future research could be directed to obtaining normative data on clinic and nonclinic families and comparing data from structured activities to parent-child interactions in unstructured home observations.

References

Budd, K.S., & Fabry, P.L. (1984). Behavioral assessment in applied parent training: Use of a structured observation system. In R.F. Dangel & R.A. Polster (Eds.), *Parent training: Foundation of research and practice* (pp. 417-442). New York: Guilford Press.
Budd, K.S., Riner, L.S., & Brockman, M.P. (1983). A structured observation system for clinical evaluation of parent training. *Behavioral Assessment, 5,* 373-393.

Student Version of the Jenkins Activity Survey

Paul R. Yarnold and Kim T. Mueser

Description

The Student Version of the Jenkins Activity Survey (SJAS) is a self-report measure of Type A coronary-prone behavior. The SJAS was modeled after the Adult Version of the JAS (AJAS), except that items on the AJAS measuring job involvement were modified or deleted in the SJAS (Glass, 1977). The SJAS consists of 44 multiple-choice items having two to four response alternatives, and it requires college undergraduates a mean of 10.2 minutes to complete. In usual practice, a total A/B score is computed using a unit-weighting procedure with 21 of the items, and undergraduates may be located on an A/B continuum ranging from extreme Type B (a score of zero) to extreme Type A (a score of 21). Based on this total A/B score, an individual may be assigned to relative A/B categories. In correlational research, the total A/B score is often used, rather than assigning individuals dichotomous categories. In addition to a total A/B score, two subscale scores may also be computed (using a unit-weighting procedure): speed/impatience (four items) and hard-driving/competitive (seven items).

Purpose

The SJAS is used exclusively as a research instrument to assess an individual's self-reported levels of Type A responding. Research with undergraduates is primarily directed toward validating the behavior pattern, identifying correlated behaviors, and assessing the role of environmental factors.

Development

When constructing the SJAS, Glass (1977) modified or eliminated items in the AJAS that referred to income and job involvement. The AJAS was designed to optimally predict what A/B Type an individual would have been classified had the Structured Interview been used rather than the AJAS. The Structured Interview places primary emphasis on behavioral stylistics rather than contents of verbal reports, and evidence suggests the Structured Interview is a better prospective predictor of clinical coronary artery and heart disease (Glass, 1977). No prospective study of the SJAS has been reported.

Psychometric Characteristics

Despite the relatively widespread use of the SJAS in the literature, relatively little discussion considers its psychometric properties.

Yarnold, Mueser, Grau, and Grimm (1986) reported two types of reliability of the SJAS. The SJAS had high test-retest reliability, ranging from .96 over a 2-week interval to .70 over a 3-month interval, suggesting that individuals tend to remain Type A or Type B over these time intervals. Such temporal consistency of the hypothesized cardiopathogenic behavior pattern is important, given the relatively long time over which coronary artery disease develops. The SJAS has moderate internal consistency, with Cronbach's alpha ranging from .72 (white male subjects on speed/impatience subscale score) to .40 (nonwhite female subjects on A/B total score). Coefficient alpha is an estimate of the degree to which a score measures a single dimension; therefore, it appears that the A/B total score and two subscale scores of the SJAS are not highly internally consistent. However, the Type A response pattern is believed to be a variable constellation of behaviors that are not necessarily highly intercorrelated (Glass, 1977). Race and its interaction with A/B Type were statistically significant predictors of mean differences in A/B total and subscale scores, but effects were small. There was no main or interactive effect of sex.

Despite the modest internal consistency of the SJAS total and subscale scores, factor analyses suggest that it consists of two factors: speed/impatience and hard-driving/competitive. In an exploratory factor analysis of the responses of 459 male undergraduates, Glass (1977) reported finding these two factors. More recently, Yarnold, Bryant, and Grimm (1986) reported a confirmatory factor analysis using a sample of 1,248 male and female undergraduates. The results suggested that although the two-factor Glass model was significantly better than a zero- or one-factor model, the current Glass model is a poor representation of the actual responses, explaining less than half of the common variance.

Nevertheless, research suggests that the SJAS is ecologically valid. That is, individuals classifed as Type A are more time-urgent, aggresssive, dominant, competitive, achievement-oriented, and cardiopathogenically hyperactive (e.g., higher, more rapid increases in heart rate and blood pressure, and neuroendocrine levels) when appropriately stressed, relative to Type B individuals (Glass, 1977).

Clinical Use

The SJAS is currently used exclusively for research. Moreover, until the type of research to be discussed is conducted, it is unlikely that the SJAS will be used in a clinical capacity in the near future.

Future Directions

The establishment of norms for classifying individuals into A/B categories would standardize sample characteristics across studies and eliminate sample differences as a potential explanation of unexpected research findings. Therefore, future research should establish criteria for assigning individuals into A/B categories based on their total A/B AJAS score. Once a normative data set becomes available, an optimizing factor analysis, including method factors (e.g., nature of the items, nature and number of response alternatives, and correlated errors) and demographic factors (e.g., sex, race, and age) should be conducted to obtain a better representation of the actual response patterns or structure (Yarnold, Bryant, & Grimm, 1986) and to determine whether the students respond to the SJAS as the adults respond to the AJAS. Because the two subscales (speed/impatience and hard-driving/competitive) consist of different numbers of items, comparing reliability and validity coefficients between these and other measures is difficult (Yarnold, Mueser, Grau, & Grimm, 1986). Therefore, future research should consider reconstructing the SJAS to more closely match established psychometric guidelines.

Research also suggests that the Student (and Adult) JAS does not adequately measure aggression, whereas medical research suggests that aggressive Type A individuals are at particularly high risk for developing clinical coronary artery and heart disease. Furthermore, a preliminary multidimensional scaling of the SJAS (discussed in Yarnold et al., 1985) suggested that many items that would be created by combining the facets necessary to reproduce a subject's response patterns to the SJAS are not included. Therefore, a future "enhanced" SJAS should include items to completely measure the known (and suspected) domain of Type A behavior. Finally, whereas many procedures for assessing an individual's A/B Type have been developed, research suggests that no single procedure measures the entire constellation of attributes that currently defines Type A responding, and that the various procedures do not produce measures that are highly positively correlated (Byrne, Rosenman, Schiller, & Chesney, 1985). Reconciling these differences and prospectively validating the result represent a major problem for researchers in this area.

Reference

Byrne, D.G., Rosenman, R.H., Schiller, E., & Chesney, M.A. (1985). Consistency and variation among instruments purporting to measure the Type A behavior pattern. *Psychosomatic Medicine, 47*, 242-261.

Glass, D.C. (1977). *Behavior patterns, stress and coronary disease.* Hillsdale, NJ: Lawrence Erlbaum Associates.

Yarnold, P.R., Bryant, F.B., & Grimm, L.G. (1986). Comparing the long and short students Jenkins Activity Survey. *Journal of Behavioral Medicine, 10,* 75-90.

Yarnold, P.R., Mueser, K.T., Grau, B.W., & Grimm, L.G. (1986). The reliability of the student version of the Jenkins Activity Survey. *Journal of Behavioral Medicine, 9,* 401-414.

Yarnold, P.R., Mueser, K.T., & Grimm, L.G. (1985). Interpersonal dominance of Type As in group discussions. *Journal of Abnormal Psychology, 94,* 233-236.

Subjective Anxiety Scale

Joseph Wolpe

Description

The Subjective Anxiety Scale is a method for quantifying felt anxiety. Its unit is the subjective unit of disturbance (sud). It is based on the proposition

that because persons experience emotions at varying intensities, it should be possible to quantify
these experiences.

Purpose

Subjective Anxiety Scale enables patients to indicate how much anxiety they feel in a way that is
more informative than the conventional use of
language, such as pretty anxious and panicky.

Development

The Subjective Anxiety Scale arose in the context
of systematic desensitization in the course of which
the therapist needs to know as precisely as possible
the level of ongoing anxiety as well as the amount of
anxiety particular stimuli evoke. The idea for this
kind of scale arose from studies of the "psycho-
physical law" (Stevens, 1962), which relates the
physical magnitude of stimuli to the perceived
intensity communicated by the subject.

Psychometric Characteristics

A subjective scale relates to the responses of an
individual and provides no information that can be
generalized to other individuals. Even more than
with most other scales, its numerical range is an
arbitrary matter. The standard range that has been
adopted for the sud scale is from 0 (no perceptible
anxiety) to 100 (maximal anxiety). This wide range
is convenient because it provides a great deal of
flexibility; however, any person who prefers a more
compact range (e.g., 1 to 10) can easily be
accommodated.

An interesting question is the extent to which
the subjective scale correlates with psychophysiological indicators of anxiety. Thyer, Papsdorf,
Davis, and Vallecorsa (1984), in 20 subjects, found
significant correlations between the subjective
anxiety scale and two physiological indices, peripheral vasoconstriction and heart rate. This agrees
in general with earlier studies relating autonomic
indices to items of fear hierarchies (Lang,
Melamed, & Hart, 1970; Gray, Sartory, & Rachman, 1979).

Although the foregoing relationships are of great
interest, they should not, from a practical point of
view, be overrated. A patient comes to a therapist
for the alleviation of anxiety that he inappropriately feels in situations in which others are comfortable. The prime target of therapy is to enable him
also to be comfortable in these situations. From the

patient's point of view, experienced anxiety counts
more than its psychophysiological correlates, even
though the latter may be the therapist's objective
target.

Clinical Use

A Subjective Anxiety Scale could profitably be
used in any kind of psychological or psychiatric
practice. It is routinely introduced by the following
statement:

"Think of the worst anxiety you have ever
experienced or can imagine, a state of panic, perhaps, and assign to that the figure 100. Then
imagine that you are completely calm. This is zero
anxiety. The range from 0 to 100 covers all possible
intensities of anxiety. At every moment of your
waking life your anxiety must be somewhere in this
range. How do you rate yourself at this moment?"

Most persons are able to apply the scale to themselves immediately and with practice are able to do
so with increasing assurance.

The Subjective Anxiety Scale has many applications in the practice of behavior therapy. A
patient tutored in the scale, on being asked "How
anxious are you?," will answer 20 or 50, or whatever
other number applies. The patient may also use the
scale to report changes in anxiety in the course of an
hour, a day, or a week. Anxiety levels over a week
may be recorded graphically, often together with
their antecedents.

The scale comes into play in various ways in systematic desensitization programs. In the construction of anxiety hierarchies, one elicits from the
patient how much anxiety he or she would expect
to have in relation to various stimuli on a particular
anxiety-arousing theme. For example, a person
who is made anxious by human blood may have five
suds at seeing a lightly blood-tinged bandage, and
100 suds at the sight of a person with blood-soaked
clothing, with intermediate values at such intermediate stimuli as a syringe full of blood. In making
up a hierarchy, numerical values are used to ensure
relatively even differences between successive
hierarchy items, usually aiming to have items
separated by 5 to 10 suds.

During the desensitization procedure, the Subjective Anxiety Scale is used first to indicate the
baseline level of anxiety. Deep relaxation often
achieves a zero baseline level, but not always.
Nevertheless, desensitization often succeeds with
a baseline of 5 or 10. The sud scale is also employed
to indicate how much anxiety is aroused by each

presentation of a scene. Typically, there is a progressive decline from one presentation to the next (Wolpe, 1982).

Future Directions

The Subjective Anxiety Scale is useful whenever the need to communicate anxiety exists. It is difficult to see how it might evolve from its present form, except in minor ways. The general idea, however, lends itself to application of other categories of feeling. For example, there could be parallel scales for anger, disgust, and sexual arousal as well as for pain.

References

Gray, S., Sartory, G., & Rachman, S. (1979). Synchronous and desynchronous changes during fear reduction. *Behaviour Research and Therapy, 17,* 137-148.

Lang, P.J., Melamed, B.G., & Hart, J. (1970). A psychophysiological analysis of fear modification using an automated desensitization procedure. *Journal of Abnormal Psychology, 76,* 220-234.

Stevens, S.S. (1962). The surprising simplicity of sensory metrics. *American Psychologist, 17,* 29-39.

Thyer, B.A., Papsdorf, J.D., Davis, R., & Vallecorsa, S. (1984). Autonomic correlates of the subjective anxiety scale. *Journal of Behavior Therapy and Experimental Psychiatry, 15,* 3-7.

Wolpe, J. (1982). *The practice of behavior therapy* (3rd Ed). New York: Pergamon Press.

Subjective Probability of Consequences Inventory

Monroe A. Bruch

Description

The Subjective Probability of Consequences Inventory (SPCI) was developed by Fiedler and Beach (1978) as a research instrument to assess expectancies about the likelihood that positive and negative consequences would follow a person's refusal of, or compliance with, an unreasonable request. The SPCI consists of a series of rights assertion situations that in each case are followed by two sets of consequences. The first group consists of five positive and five negative consequences relevant to complying with a request. For example, one positive consequence is, "We will become better friends." The second group consists of five positive and five negative consequences relevant to refusing a request. For example, one positive consequence is, "She/he is less likely to

make further unreasonable requests." Respondents are instructed to read each rights assertion situation and then imagine first that they complied. Having decided to comply, the respondent reads the list of 10 consequences and for each one circles a value on an accompanying scale that ranges from 0 to 100%, in increments of 10, to indicate how likely it is that the consequence will occur. Following this, respondents are instructed to imagine that they decided to refuse and then are to read the second list of 10 consequences. In this part the respondent again circles a value ranging from 0 to 100% to indicate what they think the probability is that each consequence would occur if they refused. The SPCI yields four subscores that result from crossing the variables of response type (i.e., comply or refuse) with consequences type (i.e., positive or negative) in a 2 by 2 design. Each subscore is derived by calculating the mean probability rating for the set of five consequences relevant to one of the four resulting categories.

Purpose

The SPCI was designed by Fiedler and Beach (1978) as a part of their investigation of cognitive components of assertive behavior. These investigators proposed a decision-making model of assertive behavior in which the decision to refuse or comply is based both on a person's expectation that his or her behavior will lead to various consequences and on the value or importance that the person places on these consequences. The SPCI assesses the expectancy component by having the respondent make a subjective estimate of the probability that refusing or complying would result in the occurrence of a particular consequence.

Development

The SPCI contains only assertive situations that involve responding to an unreasonable request. The lists of positive and negative consequences were developed by presenting a group of assertiveness trainer's with three sample refusal situations and asking them to generate lists of positive and negative consequences commonly experienced by clients when they chose to refuse or comply. Based on this procedure a final list of 10 consequences for compliance and 10 consequences for refusal was selected and the same lists of consequences are used with each assertion scene. Therefore, it is important to note that Fiedler and Beach (1978) did not develop lists of consequences that were specific to each situation.

In subsequent use of the SPCI, Kuperminc and Heimberg (1983) did develop unique lists of consequences for each assertion situation that they used. These investigators reasoned that a respondent's probability estimates would be more accurate if they were based on the types of consequences that students consensually viewed as relevant to a particular situation. They assembled scene-specific consequences by asking a sample of college students to generate, for a series of assertion situations, potential consequences that they would think about if they were to comply and then to refuse. After generating the consequences, subjects were instructed to reread the consequences and indicate whether they perceive them as desirable (i.e., positive), undesirable (i.e., negative), or neutral. The most frequently generated positive and negative consequences under conditions of refusing and complying were then selected for each situation.

In testing their model, Fiedler and Beach (1978) found that subjects' probability estimates were a significant predictor of their subsequent decision to either refuse or comply with an unreasonable request. Using their revised form of the SPCI, Kuperminc and Heimberg (1983) replicated these findings, but their study did not include any direct comparisons of the predictive use of the two forms of the SPCI. Although their development of situation-specific consequences is theoretically sound and consistent with behavioral assessment methods, a comparison of their lists of consequences with the lists developed by Fiedler and Beach (1978) shows little difference in the types of consequences covered. The major difference lies in the fact that the Kuperminc and Heimberg (1983) consequences are worded in a manner that makes them more relevant to the specific situation, whereas the latter consequences, in some instances, are written very generally, perhaps making their meaning vague in some situations.

Psychometric Characteristics

Information on the reliability and validity of the SPCI is limited to data from two studies. Bruch, Haase, and Purcell (1984) report an internal consistency reliability of .77 for ratings on the total set of 20 consequences. Also, a principle-components factor analysis using a varimax rotation yielded four factors that accounted for 58.8% of the total

variance, with individual factor loadings of 21.4, 19.6, 12.0, and 5.9%. The substantive basis of the factors closely paralleled the four categories that Fiedler and Beach (1978) intended to assess by crossing two types of response (compliance and refusal) with two types of consequence (positive and negative).

In terms of predictive validity, Kuperminc and Heimberg (1983) found that their revised SPCI correlated with self-perceived assertiveness. Compared with low assertive subjects, subjects classified as being highly assertive, based on both self-report and behavioral response criteria, expected a lower probability that positive consequences would occur and a higher probability that negative consequences would occur following compliance. Also, when instructed to imagine that they refused, high compared to low assertive subjects expected a higher probability of positive consequences and a lower probability of negative consequences to occur. In addition, these investigators report that the correlation between a subject's self-report of discomfort during an assertive encounter and their expectancy of negative consequences when refusing was significantly stronger in the group of low assertive subjects than high assertive subjects. The predictive validity of Bruch et al.'s (1984) factored SPCI scales was tested by regressing a measure of content knowledge of an assertive response on these four scales. The results revealed a greater expectancy of positive consequences when refusal was associated with higher knowledge scores, and both a higher expectancy for positive consequences to follow compliance and negative consequences to follow refusal were related to lower knowledge scores.

Clinical Use

The SPCI was designed as a research instrument for use with college students and therefore has not been employed in clinical practice. Given the evidence to support the theoretical role of perceived consequences in assertive behavior, the SPCI may be useful in assessing unrealistic expectations about consequences that may inhibit a client's willingness to act assertively. However, this assessment strategy would be limited to work with nonpsychotic and nonintellectually impaired clients because this model of assertive behavior assumes that individuals are capable of learning response consequences and that they vary only in the expectancy of their occurrence.

Future Directions

Further development of the SPCI might focus on clarifying whether it is meaningful to average probability estimates across assertion situations or to maintain them as situation-specific estimates of a person's expectancies about consequences. Certainly the latter approach seems more theoretically relevant for separating the situational factors from the person factors that contribute to unrealistic expectations. For some purposes, it may be desirable to have respondents generate their own consequences, which are then evaluated for desirability and the degree to which they are expected to occur. This approach may provide a more ideographic analysis of the types of positive and negative consequences resulting from assertion that are salient to an individual client.

References

Bruch, M.A., Haase, R.F., & Purcell, M.J. (1984). Content dimensions of self-statements in assertive situations: A factor analysis of two measures. *Cognitive Therapy and Research, 8*, 173-186.

Fiedler, D., & Beach, L.R. (1978). On the decision to be assertive. *Journal of Consulting and Clinical Psychology, 46*, 537-546.

Kuperminc, M., & Heimberg, R.G. (1983). Consequence probability and utility as factors in the decision to behave assertively. *Behavior Therapy, 14*, 637-646.

Suicidal Ideation Questionnaire

William M. Reynolds

Description

The Suicidal Ideation Questionnaire (SIQ: Reynolds, in press) is a self-report inventory designed to assess thoughts about suicide in adolescents and young adults. Suicidal ideation is considered a high-risk factor for suicide (Linehan, 1981). It is therefore advantageous to use this aspect of suicidal behavior to screen for the potential of more severe and life-threatening behavior. Although not all who think about killing themselves will engage in self-destructive behaviors, the fact that they are having such cognitions may be considered maladaptive in and of itself as well as being a potential precursor to more serious physical self-injurious behavior.

The standard form of the SIQ consists of 30-items. There is also a 15-item junior high school (grades seven through nine) form of the SIQ (SIQ-JR) designed for use with younger adolescents. The 15 items that appear on the SIQ-JR also appear on the 30-item senior high and college version. The rationale for a shorter version for younger adolescents (aged 12 to 14 years) was based on a slower reading rate for this age group as well as the ability to construct a shorter form that still maintains adequate reliabilty and validity.

Both SIQ forms use the same response format. Each item consists of a cognition to which the adolescent or young adult answers as to the frequency with which the thought has occurred in the last month, if the thought has occurred previously but not in the last month, or if the thought has never occurred. Items are scored on a 0- to 6-point scale, with 0 assigned to never having had the thought, 1 to having had the thought but not in the last month, and 2 to 6 to the frequency of the thought, with the higher score indicating very frequent (almost every day). Based on results from field testing with over 2,200 adolescents, this response format appears to be suitable for this age group. Examination of the variability and dispersion of responses suggests that adolescents and young adults respond to each item individually, using the response format to discriminate between the frequency of occurrence of different suicidal cognitions.

Purpose

The purpose of the SIQ is to assess suicidal ideation in adolescents and young adults. The recent increase in the suicide rate in this age group supports the need for procedures designed to identify individuals at risk for self-destructive behaviors. The use of purely demographic models that rely on retrospective data from previous suicides/attempts, loss/separation, and the like is not a viable or practical methodology for early identification of potentially suicidal persons. Although it is important to note that most of the adolescents and young adults who think about killing or harming themselves will probably not do so, the maintenance of serious suicidal cognitions should be considered maladaptive. The SIQ is viewed as a screening measure for identification of individuals who are serious suicidal ideators and for whom formal individual evaluation of suicide potential is essential. The format of the SIQ allows for individual as well as large group administration with minimal time requirements (5 to 10 minutes).

Development

Development of the SIQ item content was based on domains suggested by published research and clinical data as well as on clinical interviews with depressed adolescents conducted by the author over a 3-year period. In addition to morbid ideation, wishes that one were dead or not around, and specific thoughts of how, when, and where to commit suicide, SIQ content samples domains of suicidal ideation that include: suicide as retribution to others, a way of making others realize one's worth, thoughts that no one cared if he or she lived or died, and suicide as a way of solving one's problems. Although tapping different levels of a continuum of suicidal ideation with varying degrees of seriousness, the items demonstrate a very homogeneous set as will be described in the section on reliability.

The initial form of the SIQ consisted of the current item content, but it used three separate ratings for each item. Ratings assessed the frequency of the cognition, duration, and seriousness with which the individual viewed the thought. This form was field tested with 86 adolescents aged 14 through 19. Although some adolescents could use the three separate rating scales for each item and appeared to differentiate their ratings, this task was confusing for others. Consequently, the format was modified to the present form, which evaluates the frequency of the cognition's occurrence during the last month.

The final development study involved the assessment of 2,279 adolescents aged 12 through 18. Subjects were drawn from three high schools in an urban/suburban community and represented a diverse range of socioeconomic levels. Schools were racially integrated with 78% of the sample white, 19% black, and the remainder hispanic and Asian. Subjects were tested in their classrooms on the SIQ and on measures of depression and related constructs as part of an annual mental health screening in the school. In addition, the SIQ was used in a study of 152 young adults selected from a midwestern university.

Psychometric Characteristics

Reliability. The reliability of the SIQ has been examined using internal consistency (coefficient alpha) methodology. Reliability for the 30-item form was .97 with a sample of 896 adolescents aged 14 through 18, and .96 with a sample of 152 young adults aged 18 through 21 at a midwestern university. Internal consistency reliability of the 15-item form of the SIQ was found to be .93 with a sample of 1,383 adolescents aged 12 through 14. Items with total scale correlations for the SIQ and SIQ-JR are high, with median correlations of .72 and .76,

respectively. These data suggest that the SIQ is a homogeneous measure of suicidal cognitions.

Validity. Validity data on the SIQ is in the form of content validity and construct validity. Content validity is demonstrated by examination of SIQ item content according to a continuum of suicidal cognitions, ranging from morbid ideation and very minor/nonspecific thoughts (e.g., I wish I was never born) to major/specific thoughts (e.g., I thought of when I would kill myself). A consistent sex difference was found, with female subjects endorsing significantly ($p < .0001$) greater suicidal ideation than male subjects. Construct validity was demonstrated by correlations with highly related constructs, particularly depression and hopelessness. Depression was assessed using the Reynolds Adolescent Depression Scale (RADS, Reynolds, 1986), the Beck Depression Inventory (BDI), or the Children's Depression Inventory (CDI). The BDI was used with senior and the CDI with junior high school students. Hopelessness was measured using the Beck Hopelessness Scale (Beck, Kovacs, & Weissman, 1975). Both depression and hopelessness have been significantly related to suicidal behavior. In addition, the relationship between the SIQ and other related constructs was examined, including anxiety, self-concept, and major negative life events (Gersten, Langner, Eisenberg, & Orzeck, 1974). Significant relationships were found between SIQ scores and scores on measures of depression, hopelessness, and other constructs. The correlations found between the SIQ and related constructs in senior high school students were similar to the relationships found with the 15-item form of the SIQ with junior high school students. A multiple regression analysis with SIQ as the dependent variable and the RADS, measures of anxiety, self-concept, negative life events, daily hassles, and social support as independent variables, resulted in an R of .65. The SIQ factor structure has also been examined. A principal components factor analysis of the standard 30-item form of the SIQ with 890 senior high school students resulted in three factors accounting for 67.7% of the total variance, with a strong first factor (eigenvalue = 17.61). When rotated to an orthogonal solution (varimax criterion), 25 of the items had factor loadings of .45 or greater on the first factor. Of the remaining items, three items loaded on the second factor and the two items dealing with morbid ideation on the third factor. Examination of the rotated factor structure indicated that the first factor subsumed 89.6% of the common variance (lambda = 17.27). A factor analysis of the SIQ-JR with 1,120 adolescents produced two factors accounting for 67.3% of the total variance. After orthogonal rotation (varimax criterion), 13 of the items loaded on the first factor, with factor loading ranging from .41 to .89. The two items that loaded on the second factor dealt with morbid ideation and manifested loadings of .86 and .77 with this factor. In terms of the unique variance, the first factor with a lambda of 8.38 accounted for 88.7% of the common variance, with the second factor, a lambda of 1.07, subsuming the remainder of the variance.

Clinical Use

The SIQ is useful for individual assessment and as a screening measure for large group identification of suicide-ideating adolescents. As a brief, self-report method with high content validity, it can be used effectively in identifying adolescents who need psychological attention. It is noted in the literature on suicide that no one has ever committed suicide because they were asked if they contemplated this act. However, not asking a person if they are suicidal may have negative consequences if they are in fact seriously considering suicide. In clinical interviews, adolescents questioned as to their suicidal intent answer in an open and matter of fact manner. The SIQ is viewed as meeting a great need in providing a reliable measure for the identification of adolescents and young adults who are demonstrating serious suicidal ideation and potential for suicide. In school settings, the SIQ can be used in conjunction with depression and/or other measures as a mental health screening battery. It should be noted that in screening studies with large samples of adolescents, adolescents have been identified who endorse significant levels of suicidal ideation but are not depressed, a finding similar to that found in studies with adults. This points to the need to assess both suicidal ideation as well as depression when evaluating the mental health needs of adolescents.

Future Directions

The clinical validity of the SIQ is currently under investigation through examination of SIQ responses and suicidal risk as assessed with a semistructured clinical interview for suicidal behavior. Further research with the SIQ should examine prior history of suicide attempts with current ideation. In addition, further investigation of the psychometric characteristics with college populations is needed, as well as studies with adult populations in general. Because of important ethical responsibilities, predictive validity studies are not recommended, because identification of serious ideators should be followed up with further evaluation and treatment if necessary. Of clinical interest is research with adolescents who are actively engaged in suicidal cognitions but not depressed according to their scores on self-report depression measures. The SIQ should also prove useful in screening out serious ideators from depression treatment studies, particularly studies using a waitlist control group.

References

Beck, A.T., Kovacs, M., & Weissman, A. (1975). Hopelessness and suicidal behavior. *Journal of the American Medical Association, 234.* 1146-1149.

Gersten, J.C., Langner, T.S., Eisenberg, J.G., & Orzeck, L. (1974). Child behavior and life events: Undesirable change or change per se? In B.S. Dohrenwend & B.P. Dohrenwend (Eds.), *Stressful life events: Their nature and effects.* New York: Wiley.

Linehan, M.M. (1981). A social-behavioral analysis of suicide and parasuicide: Implications for clinical assessment and treatment. In J.F. Clarkin & H. Glazer (Eds.), *Depression: Behavioral and directive treatment strategies* (pp. 229-294). New York: Garland Press.

Reynolds, W.M. (in press). *Suicidal Ideation Questionnaire.* Odessa, FL: Psychological Assessment Resources.

Reynolds, W.M. (1986). *Reynolds Adolescent Depression Scale.* Odessa, FL: Psychological Assessment Resources.

Suinn Test Anxiety Behavior Scale

Richard M.Suinn

Description

The Suinn Test Anxiety Behavior Scale (STABS) is a 50 = item self-administered instrument with each item describing behavioral situations that may arouse different levels of test anxiety in clients, such as "On a multiple choice test, seeing a question I cannot answer" (Suinn, 1969). Individuals rate each item in terms of how much anxiety they experience, using a prepared answer sheet. A total test anxiety score is computed by assigning the value of 1 to 5 for each of the increasing levels of anxiety checked. To provide application to a large variety of clients, the items represent a broad sampling of different behaviors and situations. The scale has been translated into Chinese, Indonesian, and Lebanese.

Purpose

The scale was developed to measure anxiety through concrete assessment of actual behavioral settings, rather than simply through asking clients their opinions about how anxious they may be generally. As an added benefit, the scale can also be used as a basis for construction of text anxiety hierarchies for desensitization.

Development

The items were originally constructed by psychologists experienced in behavioral assessment and behavioral theory. The scale was eventually limited to 50 items for ease of administration.

Psychometric Characteristics

In an initial normative study, test-retest reliability afer a 6-week interval was .74 for one sample and .78 for a second sample retested after 1 month.

Validity data have been reported in terms of the scale's correlation with other measures of anxiety and its ability to predict performance on course examinations.

Norms have been collected on a variety of samples totaling over 1,000 subjects. Norms are reported by gender, by year in school (university), and by schools. A revised version has been used with junior high school students.

Clinical Use

The STABS has been used for phobic disordered persons whose specific phobia involves test-taking. In addition, the scale has also been used as a dependent measure in studies of the efficacy of intervention methods, either specifically for test-taking anxiety or when test-taking anxiety is viewed as an analogue for other phobic or anxiety disorders. (Goldfried, Linehan, & Smith, 1978; Harris & Johnson, 1983). Counseling centers have used the instrument to identify students in need of counseling or behavior therapy for underachievement.

Future Directions

The STABS should continue to be one of the more frequently selected objective instruments for use by counseling centers in both universities and eventually high schools. It should also continue to be a valuable instrument in research studies involving intervention or in identifying factors contributing to career choice or academic achievement (Allen, Elias, & Zlotlow, 1980). Cross-cultural studies of differing ethnic groups may be of increased importance.

References

Allen, G., Elias, M., & Zlotlow, S. (1980). Behavioral interventions for alleviating test anxiety: A methodological review of current therapeutic practices. In I. Sarason (Ed.), *Test anxiety: Theory, research, and applications.* Hillsdale, NJ: Erlbaum.

Goldfried, M., Linehan, M., & Smith, J. (1978). Reduction of test anxiety through cognitive restructuring. *Journal of Consulting and Clinical Psychology, 46,* 32-39.

Harris, G., & Johnson, S. (1983). Coping imagery and relaxation instructions in a covert modeling treatment for test anxiety. *Behavior Therapy, 14,* 144-157.

Suinn, R. (1969). The STABS, a measure of test anxiety for behavior therapy: Normative data. *Behaviour Research and Therapy, 7,* 335-339.

Survey of Heterosexual Interactions

Charlene Muehlenhard

Description

The Survey of Heterosexual Interactions, which is for male respondents (SHI, Twentyman, Boland, & McFall, 1981; Twentyman & McFall, 1975), and the Survey of Heterosexual Interactions for Females, which was developed subsequently for female respondents (SHI-F, Williams & Ciminero, 1978), are both self-report questionnaires. They present 20 brief scenarios in which respondents are asked to imagine initiating social interactions with someone of the other sex whom they know only slightly or not at all. On the SHI, respondents indicate how able they would be to engage in these interactions, using 7-point scale ranging from "not able in any case" (1) to "able in every case" (7). Responses are summed, yielding a total score ranging from 20 to 140. The SHI-F has a similar format, but it uses a 5-point scale, yielding a total score ranging from 20 to 100. In addition, both the SHI and SHI-F include a fact sheet asking about (a) dating frequency during the last 4 weeks and during an average month, (b) the number of different persons dated during the last year, and (c) the respondent's amount of heterosocial behavior compared with that of others of the same age. A copy of the SHI appears in the article by Twentyman et al. (1981). A copy of the SHI-F is available from Dr. Carolyn Williams (see references for the address).

Purpose

The SHI originally seemed to measure men's skill in heterosocial interactions. Twentyman and McFall (1975) found that high-frequency daters with high SHI scores were rated as more skillful in role-play interactions with women than were low-frequency daters with low SHI scores. Subsequently, however, Twentyman et al. (1981) suggested that perhaps the SHI measures willingness to approach members of the opposite sex rather than skill during the interaction. In their original study, Twentyman and McFall (1975) had given subjects a choice about whether they wished to engage in role-play interactions; those who avoided the interactions were given the lowest possible score. On reanalyzing Twentyman and McFall's (1975) data, Twentyman et al. (1981) found that when the avoidance responses were omitted from the analysis, there were no significant differences between the skill ratings of men with high versus low SHI scores. Similarly, on a forced interaction test in which men had no choice about whether to interact with the woman, high-frequency daters with high SHI scores and low-frequency daters with low SHI scores showed no significant differences in skill levels. Therefore, the SHI seems to be measuring willingness to approach rather than skill within the interaction.

Twentyman et al. (1981) also found that compared with nondating men who had low SHI scores, men who dated and who had high SHI scores were able to list more cues that a woman was enjoying interacting with them. The cues listed by the daters with high SHI scores were not necessarily valid, however (e.g., a high SHI-scoring man stated, "If I'm having a good time, she's having a good time"). Possibly the high SHI-scoring male subjects were more confident about their ability to read women's cues, although not necessarily more skillful. Consistent with this hypothesis are the results of a study that assessed the cue-reading skills of men with high-, medium-, and low-SHI scores (Muehlenhard, Miller, & Burdick, 1983). Although the high SHI-scoring men were not superior on any measure of cue-reading skill, they were significantly more certain of their ratings.

In a factor analysis of several questionnaires assessing heterosocial problems, the SHI loaded on the same factor as Watson and Friend's Social Avoidance and Distress Scale, Rehm and Marston's Situation Questionnaire, and two items from Christensen and Arkowitz's Social Activity Questionnaire that asked about the subject's degree of discomfort in social situations with girls and ability to talk socially with girls (Wallander, Conger, Mariotto, Curran, & Farrell, 1980). Wallander et al. (1980) concluded that this factor "appeared to represent a 'social anxiety' construct; these measures all addressed how anxious and/or comfortable the subject would be in certain social situations" (p. 555).

In an extended report describing the validation of the SHI-F, Williams and Ciminero (1978) reported the "SHI-F was primarily a measure of heterosocial skill" (p. 16). Women with high SHI-F scores were rated as being more skilled in role-play interactions with male confederates than were women with low SHI-F scores. There also was evidence that the SHI-F related to confidence in heterosocial situations: Women scoring high on the SHI-F rated themselves as more physically attractive than did women scoring low on the SHI-F, even though objective raters evaluated the two groups as equally attractive. Women with high SHI-F scores rated themselves as experiencing relatively more social interactions with the opposite sex than did low-scoring women, even though there were no significant differences between the two groups in the number of dates they reported per month. High-scoring women reported being less anxious during heterosocial interactions than did low-scoring women, even though the two groups showed no significant differences in behavioral or physiological measures of anxiety. Therefore, this SHI-F seems to measure both skill and confidence.

Development

In developing the SHI, Twentyman and McFall (1975) surveyed male introductory psychology students to identify common problematic heterosocial situations. The list of situations they compiled was presented to additional men, who rated how frequently they occurred and how problematic they were. The 20 scenarios retained on the final version of the SHI were those that men experienced frequently and that reflected a cross-section of difficulty.

The scenarios in the SHI-F are similar to those in the SHI, except that some of the initiation skills have been changed to conform to traditional sex roles. For example, the SHI asks men to imagine, "You want to call up a girl for a date"; the SHI-F asks women to imagine, "You want to call a guy you like about a homework assignment." The SHI asks the male respondent to rate his ability to ask a girl to dance; the SHI-F asks the female respondent to rate her ability to walk over to a boy so that he could ask her to dance.

Psychometric Characteristics

Twentyman et al. (1981) presented normative data for the SHI from four samples of male subjects. The mean total scores for these four samples ranged from 85.7 to 92.5 on a scale of 20 to 140, with standard deviations ranging from 9.2 to 18.8. They reported inter-item correlations ranging from .147 to .779, with a median of .345, a split-half reliability of $r = .85$, and a 4-month test-retest reliability of $r = .85$.

For a sample of 256 female undergraduates, SHI-F scores ranged from 32 to 98 on a scale of 20 to 100, with a mean of 68.28 and a standard deviation of 11.78 (Williams & Ciminero, 1978). Test-retest reliability over an unspecified period of time was $r(38) = .62$. Coefficient alpha was .89.

Clinical Use

The SHI and SHI-F could be administered to clients who the clinician suspects have difficulty initiating heterosocial interactions. Such difficulties probably will not be a presenting complaint; instead, such clients might complain of being depressed or lonely, overeating from boredom, and so forth. If the clinician suspects that the client has difficulty initiating heterosocial interactions, having the client complete the SHI or SHI-F would be useful. Whether low scores on the SHI or SHI-F indicate lack of confidence or actual skills deficits in initiating heterosocial interactions, clients with low scores could benefit from social skills training to increase their confidence or skills or both. Twentyman and McFall (1975) described a training procedure that was successful in increasing social skills and decreasing anxiety in male low-frequency daters who had low SHI scores. This treatment procedure used modeling, coaching, rehearsal, and homework assignments with female assistants to help men learn to initiate face-to-face and telephone interactions with women.

Future Directions

Additional research could help determine the extent to which the SHI and SHI-F measure skill versus confidence in initiating heterosocial interactions. Additional research could also identify skills that could be taught to persons in need of heterosocial skills training. For example, what are the best ways to initiate heterosocial interactions? What cues can someone look for to tell if another person is receptive to being approached?

Given current changes in sex-role norms, it might be useful to have a version of the SHI-F that measures women's skill at more direct initiation approaches, such as asking men for dates. It might also be useful to have versions of these questionnaires aimed at assessing homosexual persons' ability to approach members of the same sex.

References

Muehlenhard, C.L., Miller, C.L., & Burdick, C.A. (1983). Are high-frequency daters better cue readers? Men's interpretations of women's cues as a function of dating frequency and SHI scores. *Behavior Therapy, 14*, 626-636.

Twentyman, C., Boland, T., & McFall, R.M. (1981). Heterosocial avoidance in college males: Four studies. *Behavior Modification, 5*, 523-552.

Twentyman, C.T., & McFall, R.M. (1975). Behavioral training of social skills in shy males. *Journal of Consulting and Clinical Psychology, 43*, 384-395.

Wallander, J.L., Conger, A.J., Mariotto, M.J., Curran, J.P., & Farrell, A.D. (1980). Comparability of selection instruments in studies of heterosexual-social problem behaviors. *Behavior Therapy, 11*, 548-560.

Williams, C.L., & Ciminero, A.R. (1978). Development and validation of a heterosocial skills inventory: The Survey of Heterosexual Interactions for Females. *Journal of Consulting and Clinical Psychology, 46*, 1547-1548. (An extended report and a copy of the SHI-F are available from Dr. Carolyn L. Williams, University of Minnesota, School of Public Health, Program in Health Education, Box 197 Mayo Memorial Building, Minneapolis, MN 55455.)

System for Observing Social-Interpersonal Behavior

Stephen W. Armstrong

Description

The System for Observing Social-Interpersonal Behavior (OSIB) is based on a set of 47 operationally defined appropriate and inappropriate social behaviors. These behaviors are measured using event recording, but include aspects of intensity and duration in the operational definitions. Examples include sufficient volume such that it can be heard from 20 feet away and therefore be considered an inappropriate greeting, or waiting for a 2-second pause in a conversation to speak in order to qualify as appropriate. Along with other characteristics, the volume or duration of the behavior determine the parameters that divide the appropriate and inappropriate forms.

The Data Recording Form and Data Conversion Chart are designed to produce two ways to review the results of observation of the behavior. The Recording Form translates the data into social behavior per hour. This seems to be the most workable measure, because many social behaviors are low frequency; according to our investigations the common unit of behavior per minute would result in frequencies considerably less than one. This leads to unnecessary problems in communication and mathematics. The Conversion Chart allows comparison of *matched* inappropriate and appropriate behavior. The percentage of inappropriate behavior and the total of inappropriate and its matched appropriate behavior are calculated.

Both social behavior per hour and the percentage of inappropriate to total matched appropriate and inappropriate behavior for the student/client of interest are compared with those of peers using yoked peer norming (Armstrong & Mulkerne, 1985), a technique adapted from Strain, Steele, Ellis, and Timm (1982). Yoked peer norming involves alternating between the student/client of interest and 15 peers at 1-minute intervals. The behavior being observed with the student/client of interest is also observed in the peers. The sequence is to observe the student/client during odd minutes and a different peer during each even minute. At the end of 30 minutes of observation there would be 15 minutes of behavior of the student/client of interest and an aggregate of 15 minutes of behavior from the peers.

The average of 15 peers' behavior may be the closest approximation to normative data in direct observation. Social behavior seems to be particularly susceptible to influence from the setting. Because this method draws data from peers within the same setting, the comparison may be more valid than to compare student/client behavior to traditional normative data taken from a representative national sample. Specific instructions for a three stage observer training sequence are

included as suggested by Ollendick and Hersen (1984).

Purpose

The OSIB is designed (a) to provide assistance in program placement (i.e., emotionally disturbed, behaviorally disordered); (b) to diagnose specific social deficits and excesses for treatment purposes; (c) to monitor individual progress during treatment; (d) to assist in determining program exit, and (e) as a social skill treatment package evaluation.

Development

The first edition of the OSIB was printed in early 1983. It was field-tested from videotaped samples of elementary school children in grades four and five. It was presented at the national conference of the Council for Exceptional Children in April of that year in Detroit. Data were collected from 60 students and presented at the national conference of the Council for Exceptional Children in April 1984 in Washington, DC. Further field-testing led to a second edition, which was presented at the National Adolescent Conference in Penscola in October 1984, along with data contrasting the social behavior of fourth, fifth, and sixth grade students. The third edition was printed in April 1985 and presented at the national conference of the Council for Exceptional Children that same month. This edition was the first to include the yoked peer norming procedure. A fourth edition is currently being developed, with detailed instructions for observer training, suggestions for translating the results into treatment programs using existing social skill treatment packages, sample data collection formats, and a means of graphically displaying social behavior of the client with the peer average across different settings.

Psychometric Characteristics

Many of the characteristics of the OSIB are unknown because it is an assessment instrument in preparation. Additionally, because there have been four editions, it is inappropriate to compare the results of an earlier edition to the current one. Untrained graduate and undergraduate observers averaged 67% agreement on occurrences of the operationally defined behavior using the first edition. The observations were made from videotapes and included the 47 behaviors in the fourth edition and 23 that have since been deleted.

The training of observers, interobserver agreement studies with trained observers, and comparisons of OSIB results with rating scales and checklists results are being carried out.

Clinical Use

The OSIB should be used cautiously until more investigation establishes the level of interobserver agreement, whether yoked peer norming is a useful procedure, and if it passes what has been referred to as the "reliability and validity tests" (Barton & Ascione, 1984, p. 173). The potential of instruments using direct observation like the OSIB is to improve the decision-making process in the area of social behavior for the purposes previously mentioned. Because social behavior is transitory in nature and does not lend itself to traditional norming procedures, decisions have been made on the basis of subjective and indirect forms of assessment (i.e., rating scales, sociometrics, and self-report measures) or tests of personality that frequently have problems of adequate reliability and validity.

Future Directions

The OSIB should be further refined and its psychometric characteristics more fully established. The usefulness of yoked peer norming will be explored in social and other domains in which traditional normative procedures are improper. Standardized direct observation will probably become a more established tool in assessment. It undoubtedly will be important to avoid too great a reliance on standardized observation and retain the flexibility to adapt operational definitions, observer training, and norming procedures in order to fit the characteristics of populations, setting, and purpose in individual cases.

References

Armstrong, S.W., & Mulkerne, S. (1985, April). *Behaviors for censure and success.* Paper presented at the national conference of the Council for Exceptional Children, Anaheim, CA.

Barton, E.J., & Ascione, F.R. (1984). Direct observation. In T.H. Ollendick & M. Hersen (Eds.), *Child behavioral assessment* (pp. 166-194). New York: Pergamon Press.

Ollendick, T.H., & Hersen, M. (1984). *Child behavioral assessment.* New York: Pergamon Press.

Strain, P., Steele, P., Ellis, T., & Timm, M. (1982). Long-term effects of oppositional child treatment with mothers as therapists and therapist trainers. *Journal of Applied Behavior Analysis, 15,* 163-169.

Target Behaviors in Compliance Training

J. Macon Parrish and Nancy A. Neef

Description

Target behaviors for compliance training consist of responses to both "do" and "don't" requests. Compliance with "do" requests is defined as the independent completion of a specified behavior within 10 seconds of a request to perform the response. Compliance with "don't" requests is defined as the cessation of ongoing behavior within 10 seconds of the corresponding instruction and its continued absence for an additional 10 seconds. Specific behaviors targeted for compliance training assessment are selected individually on the basis of 10- to 15-minute observation sessions in the criterion situation or an analogue setting designed to simulate the criterion situation. During a series of direct observations, the valuator records each request issued, the type of request (do or don't), whether or not compliance occurred, and the consequences delivered for compliance or noncompliance. A percentage of compliance measure along with a record of antecedents/consequences is thereby obtained. Requests most frequently issued but not often complied with are targeted for compliance training. Typically, requests with which the child has complied between 10 and 60% of occasions are targeted for intervention. Once target behaviors are identified, performance assessments are conducted before, during, and after training.

Purpose

The assessment is designed to allow determination of: (a) the effects of an intervention on compliance with target requests (e.g., Neef, Shafer, Egel, Cataldo, & Parrish, 1983), (b) generalization of training effects with a subset of requests to compliance within or between classes of request (e.g., Bucher, 1973; Neff et al., 1983), and (c) the conditions in the natural environment that may be predictive of compliance/noncompliance (e.g., Neff, Shafer, Egel, Cataldo, & Parrish, 1983; Williams & Forehand, 1984).

Development

The development of this method of targeting behaviors for compliance training has been based upon the following four considerations: (a) the type of request issued, (b) the definition of compliance, (c) the ecological validity of the targeted requests, and (d) the discrimination of whether noncompliance is an acquisition or maintenance issue.

Most studies have solely examined compliance with "do" requests. Yet, observational data suggest that "don't" requests are more likely to be issued to clinic-referred children than to comparison children and that the former are often noncompliant with such requests (Green, Forehand, & McMahon, 1979). Neef et al. (1983) first investigated the relationship between compliance with "do" and "don't" requests. They found that generalized compliance occurred only with requests of the same type as the target exemplar, implying that compliance with "don't" as well as "do" requests must be assessed and trained.

Although compliance is typically defined as initiation of an appropriate motoric response within 5 seconds following an instruction, in the natural environment it is likely that greater importance is attached to task completion than to task initiation. Consequently, in the current schema, emphasis is placed on timely completion of a task.

Requests targeted for intervention should be those issued frequently to the client by significant others in the natural environment. A structured interview is often employed to ascertain the requests typically made of the client in the home, school, and community-at-large. Preferably, the requests selected are functional, in that they elicit action resulting in benefit to the client or others or both, and that compliance with them is likely to be maintained by natural consequences.

Before compliance training, it is often necessary to determine whether noncompliance is a problem of acquisition (ability) or maintenance (motivation). Compliance training is frequently predicated upon the assumption that the client possesses the receptive language and motoric skills requisite for task completion. Through a series of direct observations, it is often possible to tease out whether noncompliance is a function of ability or motivation. If, for example, the client complies with the request on one or more trials but typically does not follow through, it can be assumed that the problem is that of maintenance, not acquisition. If, however, the client never complies with a request, the possibility that the skills required to complete the requested action are not contained in the client's repertoire cannot be ruled out, and a skills training program based on the tactics of shaping before compliance training per se is indicated.

Psychometric Characteristics

To date, the psychometric properties of this assessment paradigm have not been investigated extensively. Specifically, few studies have examined the issue of consistency (reliability) through calculation of coefficients of stability or equivalence, a determination of internal consistency, or a measure of homogeneity. Furthermore, the validity (construct, content, and predictive) of this assessment strategy has not been studied frequently.

Clinical Use

Because noncompliance is one of the most prevalent problems presented by clients, an assessment of instruction-following is often warranted within almost all clinical contexts. The paradigm previously described has been found to be particularly useful with clients between the ages of 2 and 11. Such clients frequently have the minimal receptive language skills and motoric abilities that are prerequisite for compliance with one- and two-step requests. If the assessment just outlined is conducted in a clinic-based analogue setting, the procedure will sometimes yield an overestimate of compliance as a consequence of reactive effects to the setting (e.g., presence of evaluator, monitoring, and reduction in competing activities). Such reactive effects also occur in more naturalistic settings, but to a lesser extent. For a detailed description of the clinical use of an assessment paradigm with children similar to that presented here, readers are referred to Forehand and McMahon (1981). For individuals of higher developmental ages, requests typically are related to daily responsibilities such as home chores, self-care routines, long-term medical/behavioral regimens, and/or academic/work assignments.

Future Directions

Research into the psychometric qualities of this assessment paradigm should receive high priority. The reliability and validity of this paradigm have not been determined. For example, it is not known to what extent compliance in one setting is predictive of compliance in another setting or to what extent compliance is stable over time. The data base regarding what antecedents and consequences are most highly associated with compliance/noncompliance remains inconclusive. Elucidation of variables that are most predictive of compliance will have important implications for the content of an optimal assessment protocol. The range of individual differences in performance is also unclear. Furthermore, the impact of request difficulty, number of requests, inter-request interval, presence of competing stimuli, length of the post-request interval for scoring, and other parameters of the assessment procedure are unknown. Finally, as yet there are no widely accepted norms against which to judge an individual client's performance.

References

Bucher, B. (1973). Some variables affecting children's compliance with instructions. *Journal of Experimental Child Psychology, 15,* 10-21.

Forehand, R., & McMahon, R.J. (1981). *Helping the non-compliant child: A clinician's guide to parent training.* New York: Guildor Press.

Green, K.D., Forehand, R., & McMahon, R.J. (1979). Parent manipulation of compliance and noncompliance in normal and deviant children. *Behavior Modification, 3,* 245-266.

Neef, N.A., Shafer, M.S., Egel, A.L., Cataldo, M.F., & Parrish, J.M. (1983). The class specific effects of compliance training with "do" and "don't" requests: Analog analysis and classroom application. *Journal of Applied Behavior Analysis, 16,* 81-99.

Williams, C.A., & Forehand, R. (1984). An examination of predictor variables for child compliance and non-compliance. *Journal of Abnormal Child Psychology, 12,* 491-504.

Target Problems

Paul Lelliott

Description

Target Problems (phobias or rituals) are situations or activities agreed upon between the therapist and patient as targets to be achieved during treatment. The Target Problems are stated briefly but precisely, and ratings are made of the fear (or discomfort) and avoidance engendered by each. The questionnaire can be either assessor- or self-rated and applied to phobic patients and compulsive ritualizers.

For Target Phobias the ratings of fear and avoidance are combined on a single scale of 0 (no uneasiness and no avoidance) to 8 (extreme fear and complete avoidance).

For Target Rituals two ratings are made of each problem: (a) time taken to complete the activity, equivalent to avoidance (0 = same time as a normal person, no avoidance; 8 = five times as long as a normal person, cannot be attempted), and (b) discomfort produced by the activity (0 = no discomfort; 8 = extremely discomforting).

For both phobics and ritualizers, four Target Problems are usually agreed on and the scores averaged and expressed as a Total Target Problems score (range 0 to 8).

Purpose

Target Problems measures are of value in both clinical practice and research. To the clinician they provide a measure of the main presenting phobias or rituals, the targets of treatment. To the researcher, Target Problems are flexible measures of phobias or rituals in that they are tailored to fit each patient. This specificity ensures they are measures of the severity of the most handicapping problems, and as such they tend to be rated at maximum pathology before treatment. It also means that they are sensitive measures of improvement, particularly in response to target-directed therapies (such as exposure in vivo). Target Problems thus complement more general measures of the severity of phobias and rituals, such as the Fear Questionnaire (Marks & Mathews, 1979) and the Compulsions Checklist (Marks, Hallam, Connolly, & Philpott, 1977).

Development

The Target Problems measures are a logical consequence of the development of behavior therapy as an empirical clinical science in which the repeated measurement of symptoms plays such a central role. The nine anchoring points in the Target Problems scale (0, 1, 2, 3...8) are derived from Gelder and Marks, (1966) scale of 1 to 5 (1, 1.5, 2, 2.5... 5).

Psychometric Characteristics

Target Problems tend to be rated at near maximum pathology before treatment and are not good guides to the overall severity of the phobic or obsessive-compulsive problem; they are, however, sensitive markers of change during treatment. Improvement in Target Phobias and Target Rituals (both time and discomfort) from before to after treatment in two clinical trials of agoraphobic (Marks et al., 1983) and obsessive-compulsive subjects were all highly significant ($p < .0001$). For the agoraphobics (sample = 45), Targets improved from 6.5 to 2.9. For the ritualizers (sample = 34)

Targets' time improved from 7.3 to 2.6 and discomfort from 7.4 to 3.1. Interrater reliabilities between independent assessors for Target Problems are high: $r = 0.92$ for Target Phobias (Gelder & Marks, 1966) and $r = 0.86$ for Target Rituals.

Clinical Use

Target Problems are formulated during behavioral analysis (initial clinical interview). They are situations or activities that produce fear (or discomfort) and avoidance. They should be the worst problems (usually four) that the patient encounters and will be used as targets during behavior therapy. A Target Phobia for an agoraphobic might be: "To travel for an hour on a crowded bus." For a compulsive washer a Target Ritual might be: "To wash hands only once after going to the toilet," and for a checker: "To lock the car doors and walk away without checking." The Target Problems are written as far as possible in the patient's own words on the rating sheet; exactly the same words are written onto the questionnaire beside each Target Problem at subsequent ratings. The measure can be both self- and assessor-rated.

Target Phobias can be rated in all groups of phobic patients. Target Rituals cannot be measured in obsessive-compulsive subjects who do not present with rituals (i.e., those with obsessions alone); there are also some rituals that cannot readily be rated for both time and discomfort.

Future Directions

The great specificity of the Target Problems sometimes means that they do not accurately reflect *overall* clinical change. For example, the checker who had the locking of his car door targeted may, after behavior therapy, be able to leave his car without checking but still have a mass of checking rituals in other daily activities. To overcome this difficulty, it might be preferable for Targets to be more general, covering a range of behaviors that have in common a basic feature (in this case compulsive checking).

References

Gelder, M.G., & Marks, I.M. (1966). Severe agoraphobia: A controlled prospective trial of behaviour therapy. *British Journal of Psychiatry, 112,* 309-319.

Marks, I.M., Grey, S., Cohen, S.D., Hill, R., Mawson, D., Ramm, E.M., & Stern, R.S. (1983). Imipramine and brief therapist-aided exposure in agoraphobics having

self exposure homework. *Archives of General Psychiatry, 40,* 153-162.

Marks, I.M., Hallam, R., Connolly, J., & Philpott, R. (1977). *Nursing in behavioural psychotherapy.* London: Royal College of Nursing.

Marks, I.M., & Mathews, A.M. (1979). Brief standard self-rating for phobic patients. *Behaviour Research and Therapy, 17,* 263-267.

Taste Test Assessments

Timothy B. Baker and Dale S. Cannon

Description

In taste tests, subjects sample flavor(s) for the ostensible purpose of making evaluative flavor ratings. Target substances used in taste tests have included alcoholic and nonalcoholic beverages, cigarettes, and foods. Flavor ratings are usually made with semantic differential indices and include such dimensions as tasty-distasteful and harmless-harmful. Although flavor ratings are sometimes analyzed and interpreted, the data of chief interest are the consumption data (i.e., amount consumed and/or number of sips, bites, or puffs). Consumption data are obtained through covert observations using videotape or a one-way videotape or a one-way mirror and by posttest measurement of quantities consumed.

A typical taste test rationale given subjects is as follows (Miller, Hersen, Eisler, & Elkin, 1974): This is a taste experiment. We want you to judge each beverage on the taste dimensions (sweet, sour, etc.) listed on these sheets. Some of the drinks are alcoholic, and some are nonalcoholic. Taste as little or as much as you want of each beverage in making your judgments. The important thing is that your ratings be as accurate as possible (p. 75).

Although early research used only target flavors in taste tests, more recent research used neutral flavors (e.g., water and soft drinks) in an effort to control for intersubject variability in test response set and ingestional style.

Purpose

Taste tests have been used for a variety of reasons that are usually not explicitly stated. In general, researchers appear to have used taste tests for the following reasons: (a) as a measure of stable dispositions that affect target flavor acceptance/rejection, such as an alcoholism diathesis, a durable effect of treatment such as an aversion, and a "restrained eating" style; (b) as a sample of subjects' typical ad lib target consumption patterns; and (c) as a measure of the acute effects of expectancy or motivational manipulations intended to affect target flavor approach/avoidance.

It is obvious that these factors may be conceptually linked, but that they are not functional equivalents. Specific purposes to which taste tests have been applied are the assessment of treatment effectiveness, the effects of stressors on target consumption, the effects of modeling on target consumption, and motivation for treatment. Taste aversion treatments in particular have involved the use of taste tests. Taste tests have been used in alcohol and cigarette aversion therapy studies, in the assessment of the effects of chemo- and radiotherapy on food preferences in oncology patients, and in the experimental investigation of human taste aversion learning in a nonclinical population.

Development

Taste tests apparently originated with Schachter's research on obesity. Applications of taste tests to assess the effects of substance abuse treatments and to investigate expectancy manipulations then developed independently (Marlatt, 1978). The use of taste tests with oncology patients is of recent origin.

Psychometric Characteristics

Little work has been done to evaluate the psychometric characteristics of the taste test; no norms are available for this assessment method. Although some evidence indicates that taste test measures possess some temporal stability (Marlatt, 1978), the best index of their reliability is their concordance with similar measures that tap the same sampling domain. If the purpose of the taste test is to sample subjects' stable approach/avoidance dispositions regarding a target flavor, there is only modest support for its use. In general, taste test measures are only moderately correlated with other concurrent target approach/avoidance measures. For example, taste test cigarette consumption measures are only modestly related to evaluative adjectival flavor ratings of cigarettes, computerized Mehrabian ratings of cigarettes, and urges to smoke (e.g., Erickson, Tiffany, Martin, & Baker, 1983). A similar pattern holds with respect to alcohol (Cannon & Baker, 1981). In addition, the predictive validity of substance ingestion in a taste test as an index of

long-term treatment outcome has not been established.

There is little evidence that taste test consumption constitutes a representative sample of ad lib, extralaboratory self-administration patterns. Although heavy substance users (e.g., alcoholics) may be discriminated from light users (e.g., social drinkers) on the basis of consumption measures (Marlatt, 1978), the reliability of this discrimination is unknown, and there is little evidence that taste tests permit discrimination within such broadly defined user groups (Briddell, Rimm, Caddy, & Dunn, 1979; Erickson et al., 1983).

Not only do taste test measures possess modest validity with respect to tapping enduring approach/avoidance dispositions, but also their use is compromised by the availability of alternative assessments with superior psychometric properties. For example, psychophysiological measures are more sensitive indices of aversion treatment effectiveness (Cannon & Baker, 1981; Erickson et al., 1983), whereas effectance/confidence measures are superior predictors of long-term treatment efficacy (e.g., Erickson et al., 1983). Finally, if the researcher is interested in assessing an individual's current substance use pattern outside the laboratory environment, the most direct and accurate methods are probably self-report or self-monitoring (e.g., Erickson et al., 1983).

Taste tests do appear to reflect, with moderate consistency, the acute effects of motivational treatments such as stress or anxiety-elicitation, modeling of consumption patterns, expectancy manipulations, and target substance preloads.

Clinical Use

To our knowledge, taste tests have been used exclusively for research rather than clinical purposes. Given satisfactory psychometric development, taste tests may be clinically useful in three ways in the future: (a) to gauge the short-term effects of substance abuse treatments on substance ingestion, (b) to assess the effects of antianorexic treatments in oncology patients undergoing chemotherapy, and (c) to assess an individual addict's beliefs about the effects of his or her drug of abuse.

Future Directions

Determinants of taste test consumption need to be better understood. For example, demand effects may be considerable, yet they have not been systematically explored with this measure. Furthermore, neither the credibility of the adjectival rating task as a cover for interest in consumption volume nor the effect of making known the real variable of interest is understood.

With respect to the use of taste test assessments of aversion therapy, it is suggested that two variables influence decreased ingestion following conditioning: lowered palatability and anticipated negative consequences. The relative contribution of these two variables to decreased substance ingestion following aversion therapy should be explored.

References

Briddell, D.W., Rimm, D.C., Caddy, G.R., & Dunn, N.J. (1979). Analogue assessment: Affective arousal and the smoking taste test. *Addictive Behaviors, 4,* 287-295.

Cannon, D.S., & Baker, T.B. (1981). Emetic and electrical shock alcohol aversion therapy: Assessment of conditioning. *Journal of Consulting and Clinical Psychology, 49,* 20-33.

Erickson, L.M., Tiffany, S.T., Martin, E.M., & Baker, T.B. (1983). Aversive smoking therapies: A conditioning analysis of therapeutic effectiveness. *Behaviour Research and Therapy, 21,* 595-611.

Marlatt, G.A. (1978). Behavioral assessment of social drinking and alcoholism. In G.A. Marlatt & P.E. Nathan (Eds.), *Behavioral approaches to alcoholism.* Rutgers Center of Alcohol Studies: New Brunswick.

Miller, P.M., Hersen, M., Eisler, R.M., & Elkin, T.E. (1974). A retrospective analysis of alcohol consumption on laboratory tasks as related to therapeutic outcome. *Behaviour Research and Therapy, 12,* 73-76.

Test Anxiety Inventory

Charles D. Spielberger

Description

The Test Anxiety Inventory (TAI) is a 20-item psychometric self-report that measures individual differences in test anxiety and its major components: worry and emotionality (Spielberger, 1980; Spielberger, Gonzalez, Taylor, Algaze, & Anton, 1978). Respondents report how often they experience symptoms of anxiety during examinations by rating themselves on the following 4-point frequency scale: (1) almost never, (2) sometimes, (3) often, and (4) almost always. The Test Anxiety score is based on all 20 TAI items and measures individual differences in test anxiety as a situation-specific personality trait. Two 8-item subscales assess the Worry (e.g., "Thoughts of doing poorly interfere with my concentration on tests") and Emotionality (e.g., "During tests I feel very tense")

components of test anxiety. Although developed for use with high school and college students, the TAI has been found to have adequate psychometric properties for assessing test anxiety in junior high school students.

Purpose

The TAI was designed to provide a global measure of test anxiety and its worry and emotionality components. Persons high in test anxiety tend to perceive examinations and other evaluative situations as more threatening than do individuals low in test anxiety. Consequently, high test anxious individuals experience more tension, nervousness, emotional arousal, and negative, self-centered worry cognitions during examinations. Research indicates that worry cognitions distract the test-anxious student from attending to test questions and interfere with concentration. Furthermore, worry during tests has greater adverse effects on the performance of test-anxious students than emotionality (Spielberger et al., 1976; Spielberger et al., 1978).

Development

The two major goals in constructing the TAI were: (a) to develop a brief, objective, self-report inventory that would correlate highly with other widely used measures of test anxiety; and (b) to employ factor analysis to construct subscales for measuring worry and emotionality. When construction of the TAI began in 1974, Sarason's Test Anxiety Scale (TAS) was the most widely used global measure of individual differences in test anxiety, and worry and emotionality had been clearly identified as components of test anxiety. Therefore, the first step in the TAI test construction process was to administer the TAS with standard true-false format to 426 undergraduate university students (214 females and 212 males) to determine if worry and emotionality factors could be identified. Of the 37 TAS items, 26 were retained for further study: 22 items had point biserial correlations of .40 or higher with TAS scores and 4 items that did not meet this criterion had clear content validity as measures of either worry or emotionality. The 11 discarded TAS items described correlates of test anxiety, e.g., study habits and attitudes toward teachers and school work, rather than worry and emotionality experienced during examinations.

The next step in test construction was to revise and simplify the retained TAS items and to write additional items with worry or emotionality content for the item pool. To make the TAI a more generic measure of test anxiety, references to specific types of examination (e.g., intelligence tests) were eliminated. The true-false TAS format was also converted to a 4-point frequency rating-scale to make the TAI a more sensitive trait measure. The same format as in the Trait Anxiety Scale of the State-Trait Anxiety Inventory (STAI) was used (Spielberger, 1983).

A preliminary 32-item form of the TAI was administered to a new sample of 300 undergraduates (115 males and 185 females). On the basis of item analysis and separate factor analyses for male and female subjects, 12 items with item-remainder correlations of less than .50 for both sexes, or that did not have a salient loading (.40 or higher) on either the Worry or the Emotionality factor, were discarded. Factor analysis of the 20 remaining items, using a principal components method with varimax rotation, yielded well-defined worry and emotionality factors (Spielberger et al., 1978). On the basis of extensive item analysis and factor analyses of the 20-item TAI with a sample of 1,449 undergraduate university students (654 males and 795 females), eight worry and eight emotionality items were selected for the TAI/W and the TAI/E subscales.

Psychometric Characteristics

The TAI provides operational measures of individual differences in test anxiety, worry, and emotionality. Alpha coefficients and item remainder correlations for five normative samples of high school and college students and Navy recruits provide strong evidence of internal consistency. The alpha coefficients for the TAI Test Anxiety Scale were uniformly high (.92 or higher) for both male and female subjects. Median alphas for the TAI/W and TAI/E subscales are .88 and .90, indicating satisfactory internal consistency for these eight-item measures. The median item-remainder correlations for the TAI Test Anxiety scores in the normative samples range from .61 to .69; the corresponding item remainders for the TAI/W and TAI/E range from .57 to .74. Test-retest stability coefficients for the TAI Test Anxiety score over time periods varying from 2 weeks to 1 month were .80 or higher for both high school and college students, but dropped to .62 for a group of high school students retested after 6 months.

Concurrent validity correlations between the TAI Test Anxiety score and Sarason's TAS were .82 for male and .83 for female subjects. Because these correlations are comparable to the reliability coefficients of each scale, the 20-item TAI and the 37-item TAS are essentially equivalent measures of individual differences in test anxiety. Relatively high correlations ranging from .59 to .84 have also been found between the TAI Worry and Emotionality subscales and the corresponding scales of the Liebert and Morris Worry-Emotionality Questionnaire (WEQ), providing further evidence of the concurrent and discriminative validity of the TAI.

Low to moderate correlations have been found between the TAI and measures of study skills, scholastic aptitude, intelligence, and academic achievement. In general, the correlations with such measures are higher for the TAI/W subscale than for the TAI/E subscale, and higher for male than for female subjects. Significant negative correlations between the TAI/W subscale and academic achievement for both male and female subjects, which are generally stronger for males, have also been found. In contrast, correlations of the TAI/E subscale with achievement are essentially zero for both sexes. The pattern of correlations with various test anxiety and other personality scales, and with measures of aptitude and achievement, provide evidence of the concurrent, predictive, discriminative, and construct validity of the TAI and its subscales.

Clinical Use

The TAI has been used extensively in identifying and screening students with test anxiety problems and as an outcome measure in test anxiety treatment studies (Spielberger, Anton, & Bedell, 1976). Research findings suggest that systematic desensitization, cognitive behavior modification, and rational emotive therapy are successful in reducing test anxiety, and that systematic desensitization in combination with study skills training may be especially effective in reducing and improving academic achievement (Spielberger, Gonzalez, & Fletcher, 1979). However, there is as yet little evidence of the differential effectiveness of various behavioral treatment approaches in reducing the worry and emotionality components of test anxiety. Bright students with effective study skills who experience intense anxiety during examinations are especially likely to benefit from participation in test anxiety treatment programs.

The TAI has been used extensively in cross-cultural research. Arabic, Dutch, German, Hungarian, Portuguese, and Spanish adaptations of the scale are currently available for clinical applications and research.

Future Directions

The TAI may be used as a screening instrument to identify high school and college students who might benefit from participating in test anxiety treatment programs, and in conjunction with standard personality tests and measures of scholastic aptitude and study habits and attitudes in the evaluation of students experiencing a wide range of emotional and academic problems. The inventory should also continue to be useful in evaluating the effectiveness of test anxiety treatment programs for individual clients, and as an outcome measure in studies of the effectiveness of various therapeutic approaches to the treatment of test anxiety.

References

Spielberger, C.D. (1980). *Test Anxiety Inventory: Preliminary professional manual.* Palo Alto, CA: Consulting Psychologists Press.

Spielberger, C.D. (1983). *Manual for the State-Trait Anxiety Inventory (Form Y) ("Self-Evaluation Questionnaire").* Palo Alto, CA: Consulting Psychologists Press.

Spielberger, C.D., Anton, W.S., & Bedell, J. (1976). The nature and treatment of test anxiety. In M. Zuckerman & C.D. Spielberger (Eds.), *Emotions and anxiety: New concepts, methods and applications* (pp. 317-345). New York: LEA/Wiley.

Spielberger, C.D., Gonzalez, H.P., & Fletcher, T. (1979). Test anxiety reduction, learning strategies, and academic performance. In H.F. O'Neil, Jr. & C.D. Spielberger (Eds.), *Cognitive and affective learning strategies.* New York: Academic Press.

Spielberger, C.D., Gonzalez, H.P., Taylor, C.J., Algaze, B., & Anton, W.D. (1978). Examination stress and test anxiety. In C.D. Spielberger & I.G. Sarason (Eds.), *Stress and anxiety* (Vol. 5). New York: Hemisphere/John Wiley & Sons.

Test Meals in the Assessment of Bulimia Nervosa

James C. Rosen

Description

Test Meals in the Assessment of Bulimia Nervosa assesses the amount of food a bulimia nervosa subject is able to eat without vomiting and his or her subjective anxiety in a series of three standard test meals (Rosen, Leitenberg, Gross, & Willmuth, 1985). The food to be used in the test meals may include anything that the subject reports to be anxiety provoking or that is regularly accompanied by self-induced vomiting. In research reports, standard servings of the same food have been used, including: (a) a large dinner served in the clinic consisting of a meat or fish entree (approximately 4 ounces), cooked vegetables (approximately 1/2 cup), tossed salad with dressing (approximately 2 cups), a baked potato, french fries or rice, and two small rolls with butter for a total of 700 to 800 calories; (b) a spaghetti dinner at home alone (approximately 4 cups of spaghetti with meat sauce) which contains approximately 600 calories; (c) a candy snack at home alone consisting of three 1.5-ounce chocolate candy bars which, in total, contain approximately 480 calories.

The subject should be told to eat normally before the test meal, to avoid vomiting for at least 1.5 hours before the test meal, to avoid vomiting for 2.5 hours after the test meal to allow the food to be digested, and to "eat as much of the test meal as you comfortably can keep down knowing in advance that you will not vomit afterwards."

Several measures may be taken during this procedure. The *amount of food consumed* is the primary behavioral measure of anxiety and this is best calculated as the percentage of calories consumed so that in the large dinner, the relative caloric value of the food eaten can be taken into consideration. The clinician records the amount eaten for the in-clinic meal and the subject records the amount eaten in the at-home test meals.

When she is finished eating, the subject rates her *anxiety* on a scale of 0 to 100 in which 0 is no anxiety and 100 is extreme discomfort or anxiety. The subject also rates her *urge to vomit* on a scale of 0 to 100 in which 0 is no urge to vomit and 100 is extreme urge to vomit. A thought-sampling procedure can be conducted in the clinic while the subject is eating and during a rest period after she has finished eating. In our procedure, at the start of the session and every 6 minutes thereafter, an audiotape instructs the subject to turn on a second tape recorder and to "say aloud whatever you are thinking during the next 2 minutes." These remarks can be transcribed for positive, negative, and neutral food and nonfood-related content. Food-related thoughts would include any reference to food, eating, binge-eating, vomiting, dieting, body-image, or weight. This test meal seems to be effective in eliciting the distorted, erroneous, and maladaptive beliefs that may perpetuate the bulimic pattern. (See Leitenberg and Rosen [1985] for the types of beliefs that should be assessed.)

Purpose

Bulimia nervosa has been conceptualized as an anxiety-based disorder in which eating certain amounts of "fattening" foods elicits anxiety, and vomiting after eating initially reduces such anxiety (Rosen & Leitenberg, 1982). The purpose of this test is to provide the clinician with a behavioral measure of eating or food anxiety by using the amount of food consumed as a measure of avoidance. The less food consumed, the more anxiety provoking is the meal for the subject. However, to provoke anxiety and avoidance behavior in the individual with bulimia nervosa, the escape response (vomiting) needs to be prevented. Therefore, the assessment is analogous to the use of behavioral avoidance tests in obsessive-compulsive disorders, in which approach to the feared stimulus or to discriminative stimuli for rituals is measured while the individual is being prevented from engaging in the ritual.

There are two essential eating behaviors to assess in bulimia nervosa: (a) the foods avoided when vomiting is *not* possible, and (b) the type and amount of food consumption that usually result in vomiting. Both of these goals may be reached with eating diaries and careful interviewing. The test meal procedure offers a quantitative measure of anxiety and food avoidance when vomiting is not possible; in contrast to the more free-flowing eating diary, it can be used as a fairly precise measure of improvement following treatment. Another useful function of the test meals is to test different foods for their anxiety-provoking capabilities to select the most appropriate foods for stimuli in therapy sessions if an exposure and response prevention procedure were to be employed. Finally, test meals add to the information that may be gained from more traditional, questionnaire measures, such as the Eating Attitudes Test and Eating Disorders Inventory that are often used with eating-disordered individuals to assess global attitudes about eating, food, and weight. The severity of eating disturbance as measured by direct observation of behavior is not the same as severity of disturbance as measured by these scales. A combination of a behavioral and questionnaire assessment provides a more complete evaluation of bulimia nervosa than does either alone.

Development

Before this measure could be employed as standard practice, it was necessary to determine if women with bulimia nervosa, in fact did eat less food than did normal women in this situation. Also, although it is generally assumed to be the case, there was a related need to empirically determine if women who habitually vomit after eating are unable to eat "normal" amounts of food when they do not plan to vomit afterwards. To answer this question, there must be some objective criteria to define "normal" amounts of food. Hence, the purpose of our first study of test meals (Rosen, Leitenberg, Fondacaro, Gross, & Willmuth, 1985) was to contrast the amount of food eaten by normal control subjects and bulimia nervosa patients in the absence of vomiting. The results indicated that the normal control subjects ate about 70% of all three test meals, whereas patients with bulimia nervosa ate only 27% of the large dinner, 15% of the spaghetti, and 12% of the candy. Bulimia nervosa patients also reported high levels of anxiety and urges to vomit, and their thoughts during and after eating were primarily focused on food and eating and were negative in content. Conversely, normal subjects reported low levels of subjective distress and had relatively few negative food- and weight-related thoughts. Test meals corresponded fairly well with eating diaries. Bulimia nervosa patients who ate little or nothing in the test meals consumed much greater amounts of food and vomited much more at home when they were not constrained from vomiting.

The use of test meals has also been validated as a measure of improvement following exposure plus response prevention therapy (Leitenberg, Gross, Peterson, & Rosen, 1984; Rosen & Leitenberg, 1982). However, there is not *always* a correspondence between decreased avoidance behavior in test meals and decreased vomiting at home.

Clinical Use

In addition to the clinical utility of test meals, the clinician should be aware of some typical patient responses that prevent a valid assessment. Some patients try to minimize the anxiety that they anticipate will occur if they cannot vomit after eating, by choosing "safer" foods. For example, the patient may choose a fish entree instead of beef, the latter triggering a stronger urge to vomit. Some patients carry out the home test meals when they would be constrained from vomiting by the circumstances, as in the presence of friends or just before bedtime. Such efforts to make the behavioral test less threatening can be prevented by carefully specifying the directions, and perhaps even providing the patient with the food.

Other patients eat more food than they can handle without vomiting and as a result are unable to refrain from vomiting. In such cases, the patient may be trying to impress the examiner with just how excessively he or she eats, or if he or she is rarely able to eat without vomiting, the patient may simply be "out of touch" with the amount of food she or he can eat under this condition. It should be emphasized to the patient that he or she is not to push herself to the point where the urge to vomit is very strong or beyond the "safety zone." In fact, it is this boundary between a safe and unsafe amount of food that needs to be determined.

Psychometric Characteristics

The following norms are based on 80 normal weight female subjects with 5.4 years' duration of bulimia nervosa on the average and 2.12 episodes of binge-eating and vomiting per day on the average.

Test Meal = Large Dinner, Mean Consumed = 30.9, SD = 20.2, Range = 0 to 81, % of Ss who consumed 0% = 10.

Test Meal = Spaghetti, Mean Consumed = 21.2, SD = 20.8, Range = 0 to 75, % of Ss who consumed 0% = 20.

Test Meal = Candy, Mean Consumed = 15.9, SD = 20.7, Range 0 to 73, % of Ss who consumed 0% = 40.

Of the foregoing subjects, 45% did not eat anything in one or more of the test meals. Only 19% ate more than half the dinner and 5% ate more than half the spaghetti. Only 8% ate one candy or more.

Future Directions

The use of test meals in bulimia nervosa should be evaluated further by determining how sensitive this measure is to improvement following treatment. Synchrony or dysynchrony between food consumed, subjective anxiety, and cognitions may relate to therapeutic gains. The use of test meals for other eating disorders should be considered.

References

Leitenberg, H., & Rosen, J.C. (1985). A behavioral approach to the treatment of bulimia nervosa. *Annals of Adolescent Psychiatry, 13.*

Leitenberg, H., Gross, J., Peterson, J., & Rosen, J.C. (1984). Analysis of an anxiety model and the process of change during exposure plus response prevention treatment of bulimia nervosa. *Behavior Therapy, 15,* 3-20.

Rosen, J.C., & Leitenberg, H. (1982). Bulimia nervosa: Treatment with exposure and response prevention. *Behavior Therapy, 13,* 117-124.

Rosen, J.C., Leitenberg, H., Gross, J., & Willmuth, M.E. (1985). Standardized test meals in the assessment of bulimia nervosa. *Advances in Behaviour Research and Therapy, 7,* 181-197.

Rosen, J.C., Leitenberg, H., Fondacaro, K.M., Gross, J., & Willmuth, M.E. (1985). Standardized test meals in assessment of eating behavior in bulimia nervosa: Consumption of feared foods when vomiting is prevented. *International Journal of Eating Disorders, 4,* 59-70.

Thought-Listing Procedure

Cynthia G. Last

Description and Purpose

Thought-listing (Cacioppo & Petty, 1981) is a cognitive assessment technique that is used to assess the content and frequency of thoughts. The procedure consists of having clients record their thoughts, in written form, on a sheet provided for this purpose. A time limit for recording thoughts generally is enforced, which typically is 3 minutes. The procedure often is employed during or immediately following: (a) exposure to a stimulus that elicits maladaptive behavior, or (b) maladaptive behavior (i.e., behavior that has been identified as the target for change). Thought-listing should be distinguished from event recording or self-monitoring (Ganest & Turk, 1981), in which clients describe each occurrence of a specific type of thought, rather than all thoughts.

Psychometric Characteristics

Good test-retest reliability has been reported for the thought-listing procedure with normal volunteers (Cullen, 1968). However, with a clinical population of agoraphobics, Last, Barlow, and O'Brien (1984, 1985) found the measure to be unstable over time in the absence of intervention. Moreover, they noted that the procedure may be "reactive" in some cases, in which cognitive improvement may result from repeated administration. In evaluating the congruence of the thought-listing procedure with another cognitive measure (in vivo cognitive assessment), Last, Barlow, and O'Brien (1985) found only modest evidence of a direct or one-to-one correspondence between results obtained from the two measures.

Clinical Use

The thought-listing procedure can be used with any clinical population and age group. The technique has been reported to be particularly useful for identifying maladaptive thoughts in clients with anxiety disorders (i.e., phobias and generalized anxiety disorder) or depression.

Future Directions

The reliability and validity of the thought-listing procedure require further evaluation with different clinical populations.

References

Cacioppo, J.T., & Petty, R.E. (1981). Inductive techniques for cognitive assessment: The thought listing procedure. In T.V. Merluzzi, C.R. Glass, & M. Genest (Eds.), Cognitive assessment. New York: Guilford.

Cullen, D.M. (1968). Attituded measurement by cognitive sampling. Unpublished doctoral dissertation, Ohio State University.

Ganest, M., & Turk, D.C. (1981). Think-aloud approaches to cognitive assessment. In T.V. Merluzzi, C.R. Glass, & M. Genest (Eds.), Cognitive assessment. New York: Guilford.

Last, C.G., Barlow, D.H., & O'Brien, G.T. (1984). Cognitive change during treatment of agoraphobia: Behavioral and cognitive-behavioral approaches. Behavior Modification, 8, 181-210.

Last, C.G., Barlow, D.H., & O'Brien, G.T. (1985). Assessing cognitive aspects of anxiety: Stability over time and agreement between several methods. Behavior Modification, 9, 72-93.

Three-Area Severity of Depression Scales

Allen Raskin

Description

The Three-Area Severity of Depression Scales, often referred to as the Raskin Scale or Raskin Eligibility Scale, were originally developed for use as an entry criterion for patients admitted to a National Institute of Mental Health (NIMH) sponsored collaborative study of drug treatment in hospitalized depressed patients (1970). For entry into this study, patients had to receive a total score

of 9 or higher on three global rating scales measuring severity of depression in verbal report, behavior, and the secondary symptoms of depression. These ratings are made by observers, usually psychiatrists and psychologists, on 5-point intensity scales. Cues are provided for each scale to assist in making these ratings. For example, some of the cues for rating severity of depression on secondary symptoms of depression are insomnia, gastrointestinal complaints, and history of recent suicide attempt.

Purpose

These scales provided an empirical estimate of severity of depression to ensure that patients entering the drug trial were sufficiently depressed to benefit from drug treatment. When they were subsequently used as a patient screen in outpatient drug trials, the entry criterion was dropped from a total score of 9 to a total score of 7, as it was difficult to find depressed outpatients scoring 9 or higher, the criterion used for inpatients. These scales have since been used, primarily in drug trials conducted by the pharmaceutical industry, as change or assessment measures to evaluate drug effects.

Development

Dr. Lino Covi developed an anxiety counterpart to these scales that he labeled Anxiety Scales (Covi). Covi also made some minor modifications in the Three-Area Severity of Depression Scales, which he called Depression Scales (Raskin). These anxiety scales and depression scales are referred to as the Raskin-Covi Scales and have been used primarily as assessment or outcome measures in studies of psychopharmacologic drug efficacy.

Psychometric Characteristics

Data are available on the Three-Area Severity of Depression Scales from 880 depressed inpatients, 94 depressed outpatients, and 239 depressed patients seen in private practice. Intraclass reliability coefficients on the three scales from this data file were all in the high 80s. Both the inpatients and private practice patients scored significantly higher on all three scales than did the outpatients. Finally, these scales have shown sensitivity to treatment effects in numerous studies involving both psychosocial and psychopharmacologic treatments.

Clinical Use

As noted previously, these scales have been used as a screen for entry into clinical studies and as outcome measures of treatment efficacy. As a screen, a convention has been adopted that depressed inpatients should receive total scores of 9 or higher for admittance to a study, whereas depressed outpatients only require scores of 7 or higher. Some studies have used these scales as both a screen for admittance and as an outcome measure.

Future Directions

There currently are no plans for further refinement or development of these scales.

References

Raskin, A., Schulterbrandt, J.G., Reatig, N., & McKeon, J.J. (1970). Differential response to chlorpromazine, imipramine, and placebo: A study of subgroups of hospitalized depressed patients. *Archives of General Psychiatry, 23,* 164-171.

Time Line Drinking Behavior Interview

Timothy J. O'Farrell and James Langenbucher

Description

The Time Line Drinking Behavior Interview is a specialized interviewing method used to gather retrospective data about daily drinking behavior, both quantity and frequency, over a specified time period up to 12 months (Sobell, Maisto, Sobell, & Cooper, 1979). Before the interview, the interviewer administers a breath test to be sure the subject has not been drinking that day. The interviewer shows the subject a Standard Drink Conversion Chart that indicates the equivalent amount of various alcoholic beverages equal to 1 ounce of 86 to 100 proof spirits, an amount defined as one Standard Drink. When starting the Time Line (TL), the interviewer presents the subject with a blank calendar and asks him or her to reconstruct his or her daily drinking behavior over the time period of interest. Specific interview strategies described in detail elsewhere (Sobell et al., 1980) are used to aid the subject's recall. One interview method involves identifying "anchor points"

defined as distinct time-bound events (e.g., holidays, weekends, and birthdays) that facilitate subjects' recall of their drinking before, during, and after the events. Additional techniques include having the subject identify (a) extended periods of relatively invariant drinking behavior (e.g., not drinking at all or drinking every day), and (b) habitual drinking such as weekend or after-work drinking. For each day of the TL period, subjects report the amount of alcohol consumed as well as any time spent in a hospital, jail, or residential treatment center, and the interviewer records this information on the TL calendar.

The daily drinking behavior information obtained from the TL generally is coded into the following mutually exclusive and exhaustive categories (of which the subject being interviewed is not aware): (a) *abstinent days* = no consumption of any alcohol; (b) *light drinking days* = consumption of six Standard Drinks (SDs) or less; (c) *heavy drinking days* = consumption of more than six SDs; (d) *alcohol hospital-incarcerated days* = alcohol-related stays in a hospital often for detoxification, rehabilitation, or treatment of alcohol-caused injuries or illnesses; (e) *nonalcohol hospital-incarcerated days* = stays in a hospital that are not alcohol-related; (f) *alcohol jail-incarcerated days* = days spent in jail for alcohol-related arrests; (g) *nonalcohol jail-incarcerated days* = days spent in jail not alcohol-related; (h) *residential days* = days spent in residential alcohol treatment, e.g., halfway houses or Salvation Army. Two other categories often are used to supplement those just mentioned; (i) *drinking days amount unknown* = respondent is certain of alcohol consumption but cannot specify amount; and (j) *behavior unknown* = days for which the respondent cannot specify which category applies. In addition, some studies have used three categories of alcohol consumption rather than two, light (one to three SDs), moderate (four to six SDs), and heavy (six SDs) drinking days, because these categories have been reported to be associated with different levels of health risks. Finally, several summary categories combining one or more of the foregoing categories have been used including: *total days of drinking,* the sum of light, heavy, moderate, and amount unknown drinking days; *total alcohol-involved days,* the number of days drinking plus days incarcerated in hospital or jail for alcohol-related reasons; and *total days functioning well,* the sum of abstinent and light drinking days.

Purpose

The TL method provides a continuous, quantifiable measure of the drinking behavior of alcoholic addicts and alcohol abusers before and after treatment. The 12-month pretreatment TL interview, which provides a stable baseline against which to measure drinking behavior after treatment, was developed because: (a) clients' pretreatment functioning varies considerably across and within treatment programs, and (b) the frequently used 30-day pretreatment interval does not give a stable representative sample of patients' pretreatment functioning.

Development

The basis of the TL method was derived from work done by Sobell and Sobell for the Individualized Behavior Therapy for Alcoholism (IBTA) study at Patton State Hospital in California in the early 1970s. The IBTA study, which involved controlled drinking, required a more sensitive outcome measure than the traditionally used percentage of patients continuously abstinent over the follow-up period. In the IBTA study, the Sobells used an outcome measure of daily drinking disposition wherein subjects' follow-up data were partitioned into the number of days that drinking occurred at various levels. The Sobells and their colleagues improved and formalized the TL method in further work conducted at Vanderbilt Unversity and in a demonstration project developing a treatment outcome evaluation system for Tennessee's alcohol and drug programs.

Psychometric Characteristics

Test-Retest Reliability. Two studies with college students using TL for the prior 90 days show: (a) high reliability for all TL variables over a 3- to 4-week test-retest period with most r's = $>.87$ (Sobell, Sobell, Klajner, Pavan, & Basian, 1986); and (b) all r's = $>.87$ for all TL categories for a 6-week test-retest interval. In two studies with clinical populations, the level of reliability varied with the type of alcohol abuser and the specific TL variable. Outpatient problem drinkers with moderately severe alcohol problems showed adequate reliability (r = $>.70$) over a 6-week test-retest interval for all TL variables with most r's = $>.85$ for 30, 90, 180, and 360 days before treatment. Using the same TL intervals over a 2-week test-retest interval, two groups of more severe and

chronic alcoholics, consisting of inpatient and residential (Salvation Army) treatment patients, showed: (a) high reliability for days in jail, hospital, or residential centers; (b) adequate reliability for abstinent days for inpatient but not residential patients, and inadequate reliability (r = $<.70$) for both light and heavy drinking days among the inpatient and residential subjects.

Concurrent Validity. Other studies have correlated TL data with information from other sources (e.g., collateral informants or official records) that should agree with TL if the latter is providing accurate data. One-year pretreatment TLs by 73 chronic alcoholic addicts and their wives, who served as collateral informants, showed substantial agreement (r = .88) on the number of days abstinent, drinking, hospitalized, or jailed, but agreement was lower (r = .70) for the amount consumed (i.e., light and heavy drinking days) (O'Farrell, Cutter, Bayog, Dentch, & Fortgang, 1984). For 18 months follow-up, correlations between the TL reports of outpatient alcohol abusers and collaterals were generally high for abstinent (r = .86) and light drinking (r = .95) days and somewhat lower for heavy drinking (r = .68) days. Correlations of TL reports with official record data for 360 days' pretreatment showed adequate agreement (all r's $>.70$) for hospital and residential days for residential alcoholic adults and for jail days for outpatients. Residential subjects did not show good agreement with official records (all but one r $<.70$) for jail days because they tended to report more jail days than did the records.

Three studies of TL and other drinking measures found: (a) alcoholic outpatients' responses to TL and Rand Study questions correlated substantially (all r's $>.79$) in the number of abstinent, drinking, and jail days; (b) for 80 college students about the prior 90 days, TL provided a more sensitive measure of individual differences in drinking behavior and more information than a frequently used Quantity-Frequency measure; (c) for 40 outpatient alcohol abusers, Quantity-Frequency and TL both yielded similar mean daily alcohol consumption, but the Quantity-Frequency masked subjects' actual drinking patterns by failing to identify certain types of consumption thought to be associated with health risks (Sobell, Celluci, Nirenberg, & Sobell, 1982).

Clinical Use

The TL is used primarily in research on alcoholism treatment and on drinking behavior in nonclinic samples. However, we have noted some clinical uses (O'Farrell et al., 1984), particularly in behavioral analyses for treatment planning and for analyzing relapse episodes. The TL can provide a clear, detailed picture of when drinking has occurred before the clinician begins an extensive functional analysis of the specific antecedents and consequences of the drinking. In addition, the clinician can give the patient a summary of the TL data. Such a summary impresses many patients starting treatment with the seriousness of their problem and helps them assess progress after treatment.

Future Directions

A manual for the TL method and a well-documented training program would promote wider use of this innovative and promising assessment method. Studies should examine factors that affect reliability and validity of reports of the amount of alcohol consumed, especially for long, retrospective intervals among chronic, severe alcohol abusers. Other studies could examine: (a) the predictive validity of TL versus other methods in identifying health risks, (b) normal drinkers other than college students, and (c) methods for analyzing the extensive TL drinking records gathered for 1 year before and up to 2 years after treatment. Finally, more clinical uses could be explored.

References

O'Farrell, T.J., Cutter, H.S.G., Bayog, R.D., Dentch, G., & Fortgang, J. (1984). Correspondence between one-year retrospective reports of pretreatment drinking by alcoholics and their wives. *Behavioral Assessment,* 6, 263-274.

Sobell, L.C., Celluci, T., Nirenberg, T.D., & Sobell, M.B. (1982). Do Quantity-Frequency data underestimate drinking-related health risk? *American Journal of Public Health,* 72, 823-828.

Sobell, L.C., Maisto, S.A., Sobell, M.B., & Cooper, A.M. (1979). Reliability of alcohol abusers' self-reports of drinking behavior. *Behaviour Research and Therapy,* 17, 157-160.

Sobell, M.B., Maisto, S.A., Sobell, L.C., Cooper, A.M., Cooper, T., & Sanders, B. (1980). Developing a prototype for evaluating alcohol treatment effectiveness. In L.C. Sobell, M.B. Sobell, & E. Ward (Eds.), *Evaluating alcohol and drug abuse treatment effectiveness: Recent advances* (pp. 129-150). New York: Pergamon Press.

Sobell, M.B., Sobell, L.C., Klajner, F., Pavan, D., & Basian, E. (1986). The reliability of the timeline method of assessing normal drinker college students' recent drinking history: Utility for alcohol research. *Addictive Behaviors* 11, 149-162.

Timeout Assessment

Mark W. Roberts

Description

Timeout Assessment (Roberts, 1982) consists of a direct observation procedure designed for use in a clinic analog. Mothers of noncompliant, clinic-referred, preschool children issue standardized chore-like instructions (e.g., "Johnny, put this block in that box"), praise child compliance (e.g., "Thank you"), warn noncompliance, and use a chair timeout contingent on noncompliance to warnings. (See Forehand & McMahon [1981] for parent training details.) An observer, positioned behind a one-way window, prompts all maternal behavior through a Farrall Instruments "bug-in-the-ear" device and codes child reactions to timeout. The effectiveness of the timeout component is then assessed by measuring three child behaviors: criterion timeouts, timeout duration, and escape efforts. The criterion timeouts index quantifies the number of timeout episodes required to elicit at least 10 consecutive compliant child responses. Thirty instructions are issued. If the child does not obey the last 10 instructions, additional similar instructions are presented until the criterion is met. Timeout duration evaluates the level of child verbal coercion provoked by the timeout routine. Because children are required to be quiet for at least 15 seconds before release from timeout, verbal resistance to timeout is associated with longer timeout durations. The timeout duration interval is measured with a stopwatch, beginning at the onset of timeout and ending when the quiet contingency is met. A 2-minute minimum timeout is required; time elapsing during escape episodes is excluded. Finally, the escape effort measurement quantifies child motoric resistance to the timeout procedure. Escape efforts are counted each time a child leaves the timeout area without prior maternal approval.

Purpose

Timeout assessments can be used to determine if a noncompliant, preschool child is reacting within acceptable limits to a widely used, standardized, chair timeout procedure (Forehand & McMahon, 1981). If the timeout assessment indicates excessive child resistance, a clinician can adjust the standardized timeout procedure to accommodate the behavioral style of the individual child.

Development

Although timeout appears to be a well-defined, empirically validated component of many parent training programs, timeout procedures actually host such a wide variety of options that the term itself is now ambiguous. Moreover, procedural differences are of a substantive nature. For example, optimal duration rules and methods to enforce timeout conditions are unclear. Hobbs and Forehand (1977) have provided a comprehensive review of the many timeout parameters. The timeout assessment measurements were developed to quantify the typical reactions of young, noncompliant children to initial chair timeouts. Although such normative data do not indicate the best procedural alternatives for a given child, the data do provide an empirical framework to quickly judge the adequacy of the standardized routine.

Psychometric Characteristics

The most important psychometric property of timeout assessment measurements is high interobserver reliability. Generalizability indices (e.g., subject reliability and concurrent validation against other measures) have been considered less important than measurement accuracy, because subject change is desirable, sudden, and likely. Two different samples of subjects (Roberts [1982] sample = 32; Roberts [1984] sample = 20) have been evaluated. Interobserver reliability coefficients (r) for escape efforts were .93 and .99, respectively. Timeout duration reliability coefficients were .99 and .98, respectively. Criterion timeouts data were evaluated by observer agreement ratios as to the presence or absence of child compliance, given parental instruction. The two studies yielded agreement ratios for child compliance of 97.9 and 97.6%, respectively. Roberts (1984) did detect correlational relationships among the three measurements. Correspondence between verbal (timeout duration) and motoric (escape efforts) modes of resisting timeout was positive ($r = .67, p < .05$). Interestingly, the number of criterion timeouts was inversely related to timeout duration ($r = .67$, $p < .05$), indicating that

longer timeouts were associated with fewer timeout episodes before criterion responding.

Clinical Use

The interpretation of timeout assessment measurements is limited by the characteristics of the normative sample observed by Roberts (1982). Child referrals should be between 2 and 7 years of age. Timeout assessment is not appropriate for infants, elementary school children, or children with receptive language delays. Presenting problems should include noncompliance to parental instructions. Behaviorally, the population is defined by pretreatment compliance ratios of 60% or less to parental chore-like instructions. (See the Compliance Test in this volume for more detail.) Interpretation of timeout assessment data is also limited by the timeout procedure used by Roberts (1982). Clinicians desiring to evaluate reactions to timeout with conduct-disordered clients should use a 2-minute chair timeout, inhibit escape from timeout, and require 15 seconds of quiet before release from timeout.

By collecting timeout assessment data during the initial compliance training session, a clinician can decide to maintain or alter the standard timeout procedure. If "excessive" is defined to be 1 standard deviation above the mean, then excessive timeout durations in this population are 10 minutes (Roberts, 1982). Therefore, if a child's tantrum lasts more than 10 minutes, a clinician should change the timeout procedure. For example, the clinician could reduce the quiet contingency to the minimum (i.e., 5 seconds), introduce a calm-inducing stimulus (e.g., have the mother silently stand by the timeout chair), or introduce an interest-arousing event (e.g., have the mother play enthusiastically with a toy). Similarly, excessive escape efforts during the initial timeout episode were empirically defined for this population to be six (Roberts, 1982). Therefore, if a child has made six efforts to escape from timeout, the clinician could recommend a holding procedure, a fine or privilege loss system for older children, or the discontinuation of chair timeouts altogether, substituting room timeouts. The normative data collected by Roberts (1982) also indicated that escape efforts should decrease dramatically and quickly to two or less during the second timeout episode. Therefore, if escape efforts continue unabated across timeout episodes, the clinician should also consider changing the timeout routine. Finally, the normative sample of subjects revealed that five or more criterion timeouts should be considered excessive. Therefore, it a child has disobeyed five warnings (and consequently been sent to timeout five times) and has yet to display compliance criterion performance, the clinician should discontinue standard procedures and consider shaping compliance in some other way. For example, the clinician could make the instructions game-like, repetitively model the compliance-praise sequence, or intersperse play periods among instruction-giving periods. In summary, the timeout assessment measurements inform the clinician if a given child is within or beyond normal limits of child reactivity to timeout. If the child is beyond normal limits, a change in procedure is indicated.

Future Directions

Timeout assessment measurements can be used by clinician/researchers to evaluate efforts at reducing timeout resistance (Roberts, 1984), to contrast the efficacy of alternative timeout routines, and, in general, to search for the least punitive method of eliciting behavior change from conduct-disordered children. Although such nomothetic principles are far from available today, the idiographic use of timeout assessment measurements can be employed immediately by any clinician with a stopwatch and a tally sheet. Timeout assessments are strongly recommended, given the prevalence of noncompliant child referrals, the apparent necessity of some form of discipline in their treatment, and the empirically demonstrated emotion-provoking properties of initial timeouts.

References

Forehand, R.L., & McMahon, R.J. (1981). *Helping the noncompliant child: A clinician's guide to parent training.* New York: Guilford Press.

Hobbs, S.A., & Forehand, R. (1977). Important parameters in the use of timeout with children: A re-examination. *Journal of Behavior Therapy and Experimental Psychiatry, 8,* 365-370.

Roberts, M.W. (1982). Resistance to timeout: Some normative data. *Behavioral Assessment, 4,* 237-246.

Roberts, M.W. (1984). An attempt to reduce time out resistance in young children. *Behavior Therapy, 15,* 210-216.

Time-Sample Behavioral Checklist

Gordon L. Paul and Mark H. Licht

Description

The Time-Sample Behavioral Checklist (TSBC) is a component instrument of the Computerized TSBC/SRIC Planned-Access Observational Information System (Paul, 1987b). The TSBC/SRIC System in toto is the core of a comprehensive assessment paradigm designed to provide all of the common information needed on adult clients, staff, and programs to maximize the quality and rationality of clinical, administrative, professional/legal, and scientific decision-making in public and private mental hospitals and residential schools, inpatient units of mental health centers, community residential facilities, and psychiatric units of general hospitals (Paul, 1986). The component instruments of the TSBC/SRIC System — the TSBC (Licht, 1984; Paul, 1987) and the SRIC (Licht & Paul, this volume) — are standardized Direct Observational Coding (DOC) devices applied by full-time, noninteractive technician-level observers who are trained in objective and nonreactive data collection. Observers function as independent support personnel whose only job is to collect and process trustworthy data. In the standard and most cost-effective installation, observers are "on-the-floor" of a treament unit about half of the time, directly transcribing their immediate observations of the contexts and of the actions, interaction, and/or states of every client and staff member into the categories of the TSBC or SRIC. Each observational session is repeated on multiple occasions, following continuous time-sampling schedules to cover all client waking hours, 16 hours per day, 7 days per week. The same cadre of independent observers typically provides coverage of two or more units, averaging about two full-time-equivalent observational staff for each 20- to 50-bed treatment unit.

No ongoing-cost increase is usually entailed, because of the efficiency resulting from the documentation and data-breadth provided. A computer terminal and video screen or microcomputer on each implementing unit allows daily entry of DOC data into computer files, usually by night-shift clinical staff while clients are sleeping. Computer programs retrieve and combine observations over occasions (situations and times), or people (clients or staff), or both, and categories within each instrument to provide visual or printed summaries. After clinical, management, and research staff are trained to use summary reports, the TSBC/SRIC System provides printed Standard Weekly Reports for each client and staff member as well as aggregates for the entire client and staff groups on each unit. Unique or "special searches" can be initiated on-unit to answer additional questions about individuals, groups, or subgroups over any specified activity, time period, or variable on the DOC instruments or in biographical files. These special searches may be scanned on the video screen for interactive questioning of the continuous data files, with printed reports obtained when a permanent record is desired. Three Quality Assurance Reports are also provided over any specified time period from 2 weeks to 1 year or more; these reports combine and sort higher-level data from the DOC instruments with information on client movement, demographics, staff and client turnover, staffing levels, costs, and the like for total units or smaller aggregate groups, such as treatment teams.

The TSBC is the primary instrument within the TSBC/SRIC System for providing information on client functioning and on how and where clients and staff spend their time. Within Paul's nomenclature for DOC encoding devices (Paul, 1986), the TSBC is: (a) a standardized direct-multivariate system, providing (b) taxonomic content categories with exhaustive, concurrent, parallel-level elemental subcategories to define the units of observation, and (c) a checklist format and direct-entry notational coding scheme to define dichotomous units of measurement, based on (d) discrete-momentary observing-coding techniques with multiple-target protocols, collected through (e) sequential observation of all clients and staff on each treatment unit with stratified random-order coverage within multiple-target sessions, applied on (f) hourly time-sampling schedules stratified within clock hours and behavior settings over sessions.

As a direct-multivariate system, the entire TSBC is applied on every discrete-momentary (2-second) observation of each client and staff member. Depending on the physical plant, an average of 20 to 30 seconds is required for an observer to locate, observe, and record each client and staff member during an observational session; 50 to 100 complete hourly observations are obtained on each client during a typical week, whereas observations of staff are proportional to time on-duty during client waking hours. Collateral categories specify the facility, unit, observer, shift, and time (date, day, and clock time) of every observational session as well as aspects of the behavior setting and functional context (activity) for each individual. Content categories specify 69 codes (elemental subcategories) whose presence/absence is immediately recorded following each discrete-momentary observation period, as well as three control codes to account for the absence of a complete scheduled observation (e.g., authorized or unauthorized absence). The elemental codes define action or interaction events and states at a level that possesses social-communicative value (molecular but not microscopic). They are grouped within seven broader categories to taxonomically specify the conceptual content domain: Location: 17 codes (e.g., own bedroom or office); Position: 6 codes (e.g., standing or lying down); Awake-Asleep: 2 codes (e.g., eyes open or closed); Facial Expression: 6 codes (e.g., grimacing-frowning with apparent stimulus, smiling-laughing with no apparent stimulus); Social Orientation: 4 codes (e.g., alone or with staff); Appropriate Concurrent Activities: 17 codes (e.g., talking to others or working); Crazy Behaviors: 17 codes (e.g., verbalized delusions and hallucinations, and posturing).

The units of measurement from a single TSBC observation can be retrieved to identify the location and activity of each individual at a particular time. However, the units of analysis (scores) of interest for most assessment purposes are the absolute and relative rates of occurrence of each code and of higher-order combinations of codes, over multiple observations. Individual Standard Weekly Reports provide rate-of-occurrence scores reflecting current status (rates during the current week) and change scores reflecting the direction and amount of change in rates from the previous week and from the first week of entry to a unit. All scores are provided for higher-order constructs as well as for each elemental code. Higher-order scores are derived on the basis of a hierarchical-cumulative measurement model by summing the incidence of individual codes to obtain rates that index progressively broader areas of functioning. The most global higher-order scores are Total Appropriate Behavior and Total Inappropriate Behavior, respectively, indexing the combined rate of all codes that reflect functioning that is "normal" and appropriate or "abnormal" and inappropriate. More detailed higher-order scores combine codes to reflect rates of narrower conceptually relevant classes of functioning, both appropriate (interpersonal interaction, instrumental activity, self-maintenance, and individual entertainment Indexes) and inappropriate (bizarre motoric behavior, bizarre facial and verbal behavior, and hostile-belligerence indexes). Stereotypy/variability scores reflect the range of performance within the taxonomic categories rather than the amount. In the absence of a complete CFRS (Paul & Licht, this volume), the frequency of assaults is obtained through 100% event-recording by clinical staff and included in TSBC files and reports. The TSBC reports are formatted to identify constituents of higher-order scores and to allow direct incorporation in Problem-Oriented Records. Group Standard Weekly Reports provide means and standard deviations on the total staff and client groups of each unit in the same format. Special Reports for individuals or groups are in the same format, with "current status" scores reflecting the specified time period.

Purpose

The TSBC is designed to provide a continuous time- and situation-specific data base on the assets, deficits, and excesses in functioning of every client in residential treatment programs and on how and where clients and staff spend time. Computer summaries are designed to provide comparable information on individuals and groups for timely concurrent monitoring of treatment programs, psychosocial and biochemical interventions, staff time-management, and affective tenor. They are also designed to provide the most trustworthy data on client functioning for placement/disposition decisions, problem identification/descripton, staff development/utilization, program evaluation, legal-ethical regulation/documentation, and specific research questions. (For decision problems and information needed in rational, operations; see Paul, 1986).

Development

Since the TSBC's introduction to assess dependent variables in a long-term study of institutionalized mental patients, 18 years of research and development resulted in its incorporation in the TSBC/SRIC System as the most cost-effective assessment strategy to support rational operations in adult residential facilities, and in materials and procedures needed for widespread implementation/dissemination. Multi-institutional normative/generalizability studies on more than 1,200 clients in 36 treatment programs have established its use for the full range of hospital/community facilities (e.g., 8 to 120 beds) and residential clients (e.g., 18 to 99 years; 3-day to 59-year stays; alcohol/substance abuse; acute/chronic "MI" and "MR" diagnoses). The implementation package includes self-contained observer training materials (Power, Paul, Licht, & Engel, 1982), instructions for training clinical, administrative, and research staff in TSBC use and interpretation with technical/users

manuals (Paul, 1987a and b), computer programs, and management procedures.

Psychometric Characteristics

The TSBC interobserver reliabilities (omega squares) are regularly high, for example, over the entire multi-institutional sample: 1-day observation, r's $>.90$ ($m > .98$) for all code scores and r's $>.95$ for all higher-order scores; 1-week observation, r's $>.97$ for all code scores and r's $>.99$ for all higher-order scores. The TSBC data have been free of reactivity, drift, or bias. Validity evidence is extensive for all categories of decisions for which it is designed. Discriminations among individuals reflect differences in codes ranging from weekly performances of 0 to 91.7%, with even larger spreads for higher-order scores. Absolute interpretations are possible much of the time, demonstrating remarkable sensitivity to intended and unintended change in individuals and groups with psychosocial or biological interventions. Higher-order scores clearly discriminate among client groups whose level and nature of functioning are well established (e.g., acute/chronic, oriented/disoriented, and organic/nonorganic). Convergent and discriminant validities for TSBC higher-order scores account for most of the reliable variance from concurrently obtained ward rating scales and structured interviews; they also predict successful discharges and level of functioning in the community up to 18 months later (r's in the .60s and .70s). Large sample norms from mental institutions, community facilities, and successful discharge groups provide a basis for comparative interpretations and empirical guidelines to identify assets, deficits, and excesses with measurable goals and triggering of discharge considerations. Local group comparisons are usual and local setting-specific norms can be developed.

Clinical Use

In addition to the purposes just described with "hard evidence," the TSBC has been used in a host of ways, including the identification of prodromal indicators of relapse, goal setting with clients and families, and convincing community agencies to accept clients with "bad reps."

Future Directions

After publication of implementation materials, emphasis will be on dissemination of the TSBC/SRIC System to research and service facilities.

This will also allow continuing improvements in clinical, administrative, and research utility and expansion of the normative base. The TSBC will also be used alone in research needing continuous precision data on client behavior.

References

Licht, M.H. (1984). Assessment of client functioning in residential settings. In M. Mirabi (Ed.), *The chronically mentally ill: Research and services* (pp. 93-207). New York: Spectrum Publications.

Paul, G.L. (Ed.). (1986). *Principles and methods to support cost-effective quality operations: Assessment and residential treatment settings, Part 1.* Champaign, IL: Research Press.

Paul, G.L. (Ed.). (in press a). *Observational assessment instrumentation for service and research - The Time-Sample Behavioral Checklist: Assessment in residential treatment settings, Part 2.* Champaign, IL: Research Press.

Paul, G.L. (Ed.). (in press b). *Observational assessment instrumentation for service and research - The Computerized TSBC/SRIC Planned-Access Observational Information System: Assessment in residential treatment settings, Part 4.* Champaign, IL: Research Press.

Power, C.T., Paul, G.L., Licht, M.H., & Engel, K.L. (1982). Evaluation of self-contained training procedures for the Time-Sample Behavioral Checklist. *Journal of Behavioral Assessment, 4,* 223-261.

Training Proficiency Scale - Parent Version

Alan Hudson

Description

The Training Proficiency Scale (Parent Version) is a 13-item rating scale designed to assess the competence of parents in using behavioral methods to teach their developmentally delayed children. On each item the observer is required to rate the parent on a 7-point dimension ranging from very poorly to very well. The items are: (a) gains child's attention, (b) gives verbal instruction, (c) uses modeling (if appropriate), (d) uses prompts effectively (physical, visual, and verbal), (e) reinforces contingent on appropriate response, (f) reinforces immediately, (g) gives reinforcement enthusiastically, (h) makes trials discrete, (i) makes tasks discrete, (j) controls inappropriate responses, (k) shows adequate patience, (l) organizes teaching materials efficiently, and (m) globally rates teaching ability.

Purpose

The primary purpose of the scale is to give a global measure of a parent's competence in teaching various tasks to their developmentally delayed children. The global measure is a score ranging from 7 to 98 and can be used as a dependent measure in evaluating parent training programs (Hudson, 1982; Smith, Hookes, & Conaghan, 1982).

Development

The Parent Version of the Scale was developed from the original Training Proficiency Scale (Gardner, Brust, & Watson, 1970). The original scale contained 30 items designed to assess teaching competence of staff working with the mentally retarded in schools and institutions. Items on the original scale were either deleted or modified to make the modified scale suitable for use with parents.

A rating scale was preferred to the more traditional behavioral assessment techniques (e.g., interval recording) because of the need to compare the performance of parents who were teaching a diversity of tasks to their children. As Prinz and Kent (1978) have pointed out, the need to compare a diversity of responses prohibits the use of a simple coding system.

Psychometric Characteristics

Interrater reliability was initially assessed by having two trained raters independently assess 40 mothers running teaching sessions with their developmentally handicapped children (Hudson, 1982). An overall interrater reliability of 0.82 was achieved, estimated by calculating the Pearson product-moment correlation between the raters' scores of the parents' teaching performance. Interrater reliability was also calculated for each of the 13 items of the scale. These ranged from 0.41 (makes trials discrete) to 0.80 (reinforces contingent on appropriate response), with a mean of 0.65. Smith et al. (1982) also achieved an overall interrater reliability of 0.82 when assessing the teaching competence of parents of handicapped children.

References

Gardner, J.M., Brust, D.J., & Watson, L.S. (1970). A scale to measure skill in applying behavior modification techniques to the mentally retarded. *American Journal of Mental Deficiency, 74,* 633-636.

Hudson, A.M. (1982). Training parents of developmentally handicapped children: A component analysis. *Behavior Therapy, 13*, 325-333.

Prinz, R.J., & Kent, R.N. (1978). Recording parent-adolescent interactions without the use of frequency on interval-by-interval coding. *Behavior Therapy, 9*, 602-604.

Smith, F., Hookes, R., & Conaghan, J. (1982). *Training parents of retarded children in language teaching skills.* Paper presented at the Fifth National Conference of the Australian Behaviour Modification Association, Surfers Paradise, Queensland.

Treatment Evaluation Inventory

Alan E. Kazdin

Description

The Treatment Evaluation Inventory (TEI) is a self-report measure designed to reflect how acceptable persons view a particular treatment technique. The measure consists of 15 items, each of which is rated on a Likert-type scale from 1 to 7. Separate items ask people to rate how acceptable, fair, humane, and reasonable treatment is, how willing they would be to carry out or undergo the treatment, and in general how much they like the procedure.

Purpose

The purpose of the inventory is to measure the *acceptability* of treatment. Acceptability refers to judgments about the treatment procedures by paraprofessionals, lay persons, clients, and other potential consumers of treatment. Such judges provide information about how treatment conforms to conventional and/or reasonable notions of what treatment should be and whether treatment is intrusive or objectionable. The TEI is designed to evoke an overall evaluation of the treatment procedures, rather than the therapeutic effects that treatment might exert.

Development

The TEI was developed initially in the context of research designed to evaluate the acceptability of alternative treatments as applied to children (Kazdin, 1980, 1981). A large set of items was generated based on "face validity" in relation to the notion of acceptability. The final set of items was selected based on their psychometric characteristics, to be described, and their relevance to issues that emerge in the treatment of children.

Initial evaluations of the TEI were made in analogue studies, i.e., laboratory-based studies in which college students rated descriptions of alternative techniques such as positive reinforcement, time-out, response cost, medication, and electric shock. The task of the subjects was to complete the TEI for each of the several different treatments as applied to children with different sorts of clinical problems including aggressive, oppositional, and "hyperactive' behaviors. Comparisons were made of the acceptability of alternative treatments.

Psychometric Characteristics

The TEI has been evaluated in three separate ways that bear on the internal consistency or validity of the instrument. First, factor analyses have been completed with separate samples and have shown, with some exceptions, that the items load on a single factor (Kazdin, 1980). These data reflect the unidimensional nature of the overall evaluation of the treatment procedures. Second, a positive relationship of the TEI to the evaluative scale of the Semantic Differential has frequently been demonstrated. The TEI items and bipolar evaluative ratings of the Semantic Differential consistently load on the same factor, providing convergent evidence for the construct of the nature of acceptability ratings. Finally, treatments have differed in their acceptability in predictable ways. Also, the TEI has revealed differences in acceptability for different treatments and populations and has revealed treatment characteristics that influence acceptability (e.g., presence of side effects and child involvement in the negotiation of treatment).

Clinical Use

Early studies focused on evaluations of alternative treatments among college students rather than among patient populations or other consumers of the treatments. Extensions were made to include evaluations by child psychiatric patients, parent, hospital staff, and teachers (e.g., Kazdin, French, & Sherick, 1981; Martens, Witt, Elliott, & Darveaux, 1985). These studies demonstrated that diverse types of consumers can evaluate and distinguish among alternative treatments. However, the demonstrations have continued to be restricted to laboratory-based evaluations in which consumers are exposed to verbal, audio- or videotaped, or written descriptions of treatment. The acceptability of a given treatment might be different if the person actually experiences the treatment.

The instrument can be used for different populations. Parents, teachers, clinicians, and others could readily use the instrument to evaluate the acceptability of given treatment or the relative acceptability of alternative treatments. A child's version has also been developed in which item content was simplified and a 3-point rather than 7-point scale is used (Kazdin, 1984). When alternative treatments might be selected for a particular clinical problem, treatment selection might be based on how alternative parties involved in treatment evaluate treatment acceptability.

Future Directions

Research has shown repeatedly that the TEI differentiates alternative treatments. However, four major areas need particular attention in the next few years. First, it is not clear to what extent acceptability of treatment procedures is related to the impact that treatment exerts on client behavior. Evaluations of acceptability have not been elaborated among persons who have experienced the benefits (or costs) of the treatment they are evaluating.

Second, a major reason for looking at treatment acceptability in the first place is the idea that the more acceptable the treatment, the more likely are the clients to agree to participate in, to carry out, and to adhere to treatment. To date, evidence has not been provided to relate acceptability of treatment to client performance before, during, or after treatment.

Third, the TEI or other measures of acceptability have not been widely extended to traditional forms of psychotherapy. Although current discussions of alternative forms of psychotherapy continue to focus on outcome, information on differences in the acceptability of various procedures for particular types of clients who seek treatment would be important as well.

Finally, research needs to identify the factors that contribute to acceptability. A long-term goal is to understand those factors that contribute to acceptability of treatment. Ideally, such factors might be added or augmented in treatments whose efficacy is known so that these latter treatments will be more widely applied and sought among clients in need of treatment.

References

Kazdin, A.E. (1980). Acceptability of alternative treatments for deviant child behavior. *Journal of Applied Behavior Analysis, 13,* 259-273.

Kazdin, A.E. (1981). Acceptability of child treatment techniques: The influence of treatment efficacy and adverse side effects. *Behavior Therapy, 12,* 493-506.

Kazdin, A.E. (1984). Acceptability of aversive procedures and medication as treatment alternatives for deviant child behavior. *Journal of Abnormal Child Psychology, 12,* 289-302.

Kazdin, A.E., French, N.H., & Sherick, R.B. (1981). Acceptability of alternative treatments for children: Evaluations by inpatient children, parents, and staff. *Journal of Consulting and Clinical Psychology, 49,* 900-907.

Martens, B.K., Witt, J.C., Elliott, S.N., & Darveaux, D.X. (1985). Teacher judgments concerning the acceptability of school-based interventions. *Professional Psychology, 16,* 191-198.

Type A Structured Interview

Kim T. Mueser and Paul R. Yarnold

Description

The Structured Interview (SI) is a 22-question assessment instrument that measures an individual's propensity to exhibit Type A behavior, a pattern that is predictive of the development of coronary artery and heart disease (CAHD; Dembroski, Weiss, Shields, Haynes, & Feinleit, 1978). The SI requires 10 to 15 minutes to administer, and ratings are based mainly on speech stylistics (e.g., loudness, rate, pressure, and interruptions) and behavior observations (e.g., firmness of handshake, facial expressions, and fist clenching), and, to a lesser extent, content (e.g., responses to questions such as "Do you take work home with you?").

The Type A behavior pattern is characterized by hard-driving competitiveness, anger, speed, and a sense of time urgency, and is hypothesized to be elicited by environmental stressors (Glass, 1977). Therefore, the SI is designed to impose a moderate stress on the subject to assess the presence of the behavior pattern. Usually, subjects assessed with the SI are categorized dichotomously (A/B: A reflects the presence of the Type A pattern and B reflects the absence of the pattern) or into four categories (A [fully developed]; A [incompletely developed]; B [incompletely developed]; and B [fully developed]). An "X" category is sometimes used to denote neither A nor B. Subjects may also be located on an A/B continuum as well.

Purpose

The SI assesses the level of subject's Type A responding, a behavior pattern presumed to increase risk for the development of CAHD. The instrument has been used primarily for research purposes aimed at validating the behavior pattern, identifying correlated behaviors, and assessing the role of environmental factors. It is not a standard clinical instrument at this time.

Development

Based on anecdotal reports of cardiologists and psychiatrists working with CAHD patients, the SI was originally constructed by Friedman and Rosenman to measure Type A behavior in the Western Collaborative Group Study (WCGS), a prospective study of risk factors in the development of CAHD. Over 3,000 predominantly white, employed men (39 to 59 years old) were followed in the WCGS over approximately 8.5 years. Subjects diagnosed as Type A were almost twice as likely to develop clinical CAHD *after* statistically adjusting for known medical risk factors (familial CAHD, cigarette smoking, blood pressure, diabetes, serum levels of triglycerides, cholesterol, and beta/alpha lipoprotein). The SI has been modified slightly since the WCGS and is briefer than the original version. Although several self-report measures of Type A behavior have been developed and prospectively validated (e.g., the JAS or Framingham), evidence suggests that the SI has greater predictive use because of its emphasis on vocal stylistics and psychomotor behavior than content.

Psychometric Characteristics

The reliability and validity of the SI have been studied most extensively in the population of white men working in middle income jobs.

Reliability. Percentage of agreement of Type A/B category between different trained raters of SI tapes has been good, usually between 75 and 90%. The test-retest reliability of the SI is also good. Eighty percent of over 1,000 subjects were classified in the same A/B category over a 12- to 20-month interval. Furthermore, behavioral subcomponents of the SI (e.g., interruptions, latency, and potential for hostility) have been reported to be stable over a 4-month period (Blumenthal, O'Toole, & Haney, 1984).

Validity. The predictive validity of the SI for later development of CAHD independent of other risk factors has been documented in several studies. The SI classification is also related to the degree of atherosclerosis determined by coronary angiography.

Construct validity of the Type A behavior pattern assessed by the SI has been provided by a wide variety of research avenues. Type A individuals show greater physiological reactivity (e.g., heart rate, blood pressure, skin conductance, norepineprine, epinephrine, and cortisol excretion) when responding to a challenging task (e.g., cognitive task and competition). Type As also differ from Type Bs in many different behavioral domains, such as provocation to aggression, work speed, time perception, and achievement motivation. In addition, the SI has been cross-culturally validated.

The intercorrelations between the SI and other (self-report) instruments that measure Type A behavior (e.g., JAS) are moderate to low (Matthews, Krantz, Dembroski, & MacDougall, 1982). The SI is the only instrument designed to elicit Type A behavior, and its emphasis on behavior rather than content makes it a comprehensive measure of the behavior pattern (Byrne, Rosenman, Schiller, & Chesney, 1985).

Clinical Use

The SI has been used exclusively in clinical research, and it is unlikely that it will become a useful, practical clinical instrument in the near future. The SI is very expensive to administer. Interviewers receive extensive training at the Harold Brown Institute in San Francisco, and the feasibility of training the large number of raters necessary for widespread application of the SI has not been evaluated. For this reason, self-report measures of the behavior pattern have been constructed to predict SI score.

Future Directions

Evidence suggests that different measures of the behavior pattern have unique contributions to the prediction of CAHD. A multimethod assessment of Type A behavior over time should improve prediction and clarify the interrelationships among the different instruments.

Given that a person has been evaluated with the SI, assuming that no clinical or educational manipulations have taken place, test-retest reliabilities indicate good temporal stability. However, it appears unreasonable to assume that the SI or the persons who are being evaluated are insensitive to clinical procedures that enlighten subjects about the nature and function of the various behaviors being measured. Therefore, future research should consider how to evaluate the impact of interventions on manifest Type A behavior once the subject is no longer blind to the purpose of the interview.

Additional directions for research include adaption and validation of the SI for other populations (e.g., women, students, and children), prospective analysis of the etiology and development of the rated components of the SI, and the identification of clinically relevant behavioral dimensions of CAHD that are not assessed by the SI.

References

Blumenthal, J.A., O'Toole, L.C., & Haney, T. (1984). Behavioral assessment of the Type A behavior pattern. *Psychosomatic Medicine, 46,* 415-423.

Byrne, D.G., Rosenman, R.H., Schiller, E., & Chesney, M.A. (1985). Consistency and variation among instruments purporting to measure the Type A behavior pattern. *Psychosomatic Medicine, 47,* 242-261.

Dembroski, T.M., Weiss, S.M., Shields, J.L., Haynes, S.G., & Feinleit, M. (1978). *Coronary prone behavior.* New York: Springer.

Glass, D.C. (1977). *Behavior patterns, stress and coronary disease.* Hillsdale, NJ; Lawrence Erlbaum Associates.

Matthews, K.A., Krantz, D.S., Dembroski, T.M., & MacDougall, J.M. (1982). Unique and common variance in structured interview and Jenkins Activity Survey measures of the Type A behavior pattern. *Journal of Personality and Social Psychology, 42,* 303-313.

Unpleasant Events Schedule

Peter M. Lewinsohn and Carolyn Alexander

Description

The Unpleasant Events Schedule (UES) is a 320-item scale for assessing the rate of occurrence and the experienced aversiveness of stressful life events. The UES assesses both the frequency of occurrence and experienced aversiveness of events within a 1= month time frame. The UES calls for the respondent to rate each of the 320 items twice, first on a 3-point scale of frequency, then again on a 3-point scale of subjective aversiveness. In addition to the frequency and aversiveness cores, a cross-products score is also computed and summed across items. This cross product score is assumed to be a measure of the level of experienced aversiveness. Several rational, empirical, and factor analytically derived scales have been developed for the UES. Of these, nine are recommended for clinical and research use because they are statistically independent, have good internal reliability, and access aspects of stress of clinical interest. These scales are labeled: All Items, Major versus Minor, Self versus Other, Controllable versus Uncontrollable, Life Changes, Death Related, Legal, Sexual-Marital-Friendship, and Most Discriminating. A short form consisting of 53 items is available. The UES was designed to be applicable across the age span beginning with the age of 12.

Purpose

The purpose of the UES was to develop a psychometrically sound instrument that would assess both the frequency and the subjective impact of a wide range of stressful life events. There have been other attempts to develop psychometric instruments to quantify the occurrence of aversive events in people's lives, but most of these have serious methodological and conceptual problems. In constructing the UES a conscious effort was made to surmount some of these problems. For example, in most currently available life events inventories, the criteria for inclusion of specific events have been arbitrary, with strong emphasis on very stressful and very infrequently occurring events. For the development of the UES it was assumed that a large universe of events exists that are experienced as aversive by many individuals and that this universe be adequately sampled. It was also assumed that there are important and consistent individual differences in the subjective impact of events. Hence, it was judged important that stress inventories measure not only the rate of occurrence but also the experienced aversiveness of events.

Development

The UES has undergone three revisions. The initial item pool was generated as follows: First, a short survey was mailed to a large and heterogeneous group of persons who were asked to list nine events that had happened to them, selecting three that had been very unpleasant, three that had been moderately unpleasant, and three that had been only slightly unpleasant. Second, a group of 24 subjects stratified by age and sex were asked to monitor unpleasant events that had happened to them during a 7-day period. The items from the two sources were grouped into seven initial key word categories. Items were eliminated on the basis of three criteria: redundancy, having only cognitive components, and symptoms. From the resulting pool, 320 items were selected to constitute UES Form I. On the basis of item analyses, items with very low frequency or aversiveness ratings were eliminated. In addition a few grammatical changes were made, and a few items that had been repeated were identified. A total of 17 new items from the item pool were added. The 320 items were thoroughly randomized to constitute UES Form II. Another item analysis was conducted and 37 items were eliminated because of extremely low variance and poor test-retest reliability or high correlation with other items. These 37 items were replaced with items generated by a sample of 72 subjects, 34 of whom were adolescents and 38 elderly. The final form of the UES, Form III, may be considered to consist of items that constitute a good sample of the total domain of aversive events for individuals over the age of 12.

Psychometric Characteristics

Test-retest reliability coefficients for the UES scales for intervals of 1, 2, and 3 months were computed for three diagnostic groups: depressed, nondepressed psychiatric control subjects, and normal control subjects. Test-retest reliability coefficients varied, being lowest for the frequency ratings on scales dealing with very infrequent events. Their test-retest reliability would be expected to be lower. To measure intrascale homogeneity, coefficient alpha was computed for all scales. Alpha coefficients ranged from .60 to .96. The correlation between the UES frequency ratings and the daily monitoring totals was used as a measure of predictive validity of the UES frequency ratings. This correlation was .44, indicating that the self-reported daily occurrence of aversive events can be predicted to some extent from the person's UES frequency ratings for the preceding month.

The correlation between the UES scales and the Social Readjustment Rating Scale (SRRS, Holmes & Masuda, 1974) was small, with a mean of .10 and a range of .03 to .21. The lack of relationship between the UES and the SRRS was not unexpected. Most of the SRRS items refer to very infrequent events, and inspection of the life change unit scores indicated that their distribution was extremely skewed, with most of the subjects obtaining 0 to very low

scores on the SRRS. Construct validity for the UES was studied by comparing depressed groups (who are known to have elevated stress scores on other measures) and nondepressed groups. The expected differences were found, and a Most Discriminating item scale was constructed based on items found to be highly discriminating between depressed and nondepressed subjects. The UES correlates with the Beck Depression Inventory ($r = .34$), and the Most Discriminating Items scale correlates .43 with the Center for Epidemiology Depression scale.

Means and standard deviations for the scales based on a sample of 1,186 subjects are available. Because the UES items can reasonably be expected to be sensitive to cultural, geographic, and climatic differences and some definite variations with age have been observed (Lewinsohn, Tursky, & Arconad, 1980), users of the schedule would do well to develop local norms for the population with which they work.

Clinical Use

The UES has been used in a variety of clinical contexts. The rationally derived scales can be used in treatment to identify specific actual or potential areas of distress and discomfort. The UES may also be used as a before and after measure in treatments aimed at reducing the frequency and experienced aversiveness of unpleasant events. One advantage of the UES is the availability of individualized ratings of aversiveness, which allow for the assessment of individual differences in the perception of events. Another advantage of the UES as a measure of stressful life events is the availability of subscales. The UES is distinguished by its inclusion of both relatively minor daily hassles and of major life events. The UES has been used to develop individualized unpleasant activities lists for patients for daily monitoring. A significant association was found between the daily rate of occurrence of aversive events and daily mood. Finally, shortened versions of the UES have specifically been developed for use with the elderly (Teri & Lewinsohn, 1985) and adolescents (Carey, Kelley, Buss, & Scott, in press).

Future Directions

Several future research directions may be suggested. Although the results of reported studies indicate that responses to the UES do not simply reflect a negative response style, further work needs to be done on this question. The UES should also prove useful in future research on the differential impact of daily stressors and major life events on physical and mental disorders. The availability of various scales allows for the investigation of theoretically interesting and clinically important questions about relations between specific stressful life events and particular illnesses. Also, modifying the time frame for some of the items and scales such as those involving major versus minor events may enhance the validity of the instrument.

Further adaptations and refinements to make the test more compatible with the experiences of children and adolescents may also prove useful.

References

Carey, M.P., Kelley, M.L., Buss, R.R., & Scott, W.O.N. (in press). The relationship between activity and depression in adolescents: Development of the Adolescent Activities Checklist. *Journal of Consulting and Clinical Psychology.*

Holmes, T.H., & Masuda, M. (1974). Life changes and illness susceptibility. In B.S. Dohrenwend & B.P. Dohrenwend (Eds.), *Stressful life events: Their nature and effects* (pp. 45-72). New York: John Wiley & Sons.

Lewinsohn, P.M., Mermelstein, R., Alexander, C., & MacPhillamy, D. J. (in press). The Unpleasant Events Schedule: A scale for the measurement of aversive events. *Journal of Clinical Psychology.*

Lewinsohn, P.M., Tursky, S., & Arconad, M. (1980). *The relationship between age and the frequency of occurrence and the subjective impact of aversive events.* Unpublished mimeo, University of Oregon.

Teri, L., & Lewinsohn, P.M. (1985). *Geropsychological assessment and treatment: Selected topics.* New York: Springer.

Visual Analogue Scale

Olof Nyren

Description

The Visual Analogue Scale (VAS) was designed to circumvent some of the problems associated with verbal reports, and it has proven to be a useful tool for the rating of subjective phenomena. It is a straight line, the ends of which are taken to represent the minimum and maximum extremes of the variable to be rated. Raters are required to mark the line at a point corresponding to estimates of the variable under consideration, thereby conveying assessments nonverbally.

The length of the line is not crucial, but the error variance tends to be greater when a line shorter than 10 cm is used (Revill, Robinson, Rosen, & Hogg, 1976). However, if the line is too long, it cannot be grasped as a unit. The performance of a 20-cm VAS seems to be fully satisfactory (Revill et al., 1976), but most authors advocate the use of a 10-cm line. The VAS may be oriented either horizontally or vertically. Because scores from a horizontal VAS tend to be slightly lower than those from a vertical one (Scott & Huskisson, 1976), the scale should remain identical during any one study.

The most appropriate design seems to be a scale with "stops" at each end, at right angles to the line, and anchoring descriptive phrases *beyond* these stops (Huskisson, 1983). The selection of suitable descriptive terms is not an easy task, and the performance of the scale depends very much on how the anchoring phrases are formulated. Firstly, the sensation or response to be rated should be carefully defined. If a feeling to be rated has more than one dimension, care must be taken to ensure that only one is rated at a time. Bipolar scales (e.g., a mood scale ranging from depression through normal mood to elation) are generally more difficult to understand than unipolar ones; it is not obvious to all where to position normal mood. Only universally understood phrases should be used, and although they are to reflect the extremes of the variable, they should not be so extremely worded as never to be employed. Furthermore, the situation in which the scale is to be used should also be considered.

A VAS with additional descriptive phrases distributed along the line is termed Graphic Rating Scale (GRS). This scale is probably easier to understand, and the failure rate seems to be slightly lower than that with the VAS (Scott & Huskisson, 1976). There is, however, a tendency for the scores to be clumped near the descriptive terms, and most individuals who are not familiar with this kind of scale use the GRS as a simple fixed-point verbal rating scale. In a study by Huskisson (1974), only 27% of the patients who rated their pain on a GRS used the spaces between the descriptive phrases, taking advantage of the extra freedom of choice.

Careful instructions are crucial for the successful use of the VAS, especially when employed for self-rating by patients outside a clinic.

At the end of the experiment, the distance from one of the endpoints to the marking is measured, either to the millimeter or in classes by the use of a stencil.

Purpose

It should be kept in mind that the VAS is not a complete assessment method, but a tool to make it possible for raters to convey their estimates with greater freedom. By the nonverbal nature of the scale the need for them to rate in categories is avoided, and the opportunities for widely differing interpretations of the verbal descriptive phrases in simple fixed-point scales should be reduced. In theory, the VAS circumvents the well-known difficulty of equalizing the intervals on a fixed-point scale, and there is sufficient resolution in measurement to provide continuous rather than discrete scores.

Psychometric Characteristics

Reliability. One must distinguish between reliability of an assessment method and reliability of the rating scale. In the latter case reliability depends primarily on the raters' ability to carry out the perceptual-motor task of putting the marking accurately where they intend it to be.

In an experiment reported by Revill et al. (1976), young adult volunteers were asked to make vertical marks one-fifth from the end of a 15-cm line repeatedly at 10-second intervals. The mean error was 0.19%. The 95% confidence limits for the group was + 2% and for an individual mark + 7%. Therefore, most individuals seem to be able to express their opinion relatively accurately using the VAS. However, Dixon and Bird (1981) have shown that the accuracy with which a subject can reproduce a given marking varies along the length of the line; the most accurate estimates seem to be for markings near the apices. Estimates for markings on the first two-thirds of a horizontal VAS are invariably too short. With a 10-cm line there is a swing from estimating too short to estimating too long, which occurs at about 6 cm from the left end (Dixon & Bird, 1981). When subjects are requested to repeat a random mark on a VAS after 5 minutes, the product-moment correlation coefficient is in the order of 0.95, and it remains virtually unchanged even when 24 hours elapse between the markings (Revill et al., 1976).

It is more complicated to establish reliability in assessments of subjective states. If the correlation between repeated measurements is calculated, there is no reason to expect that the feeling would remain constant even from one minute to the next. Moreover, it will be unknown as to how much such a correlation reflects only the subject's "set" to communicate feelings. When the VAS was used for self-rating of mood, the within-patient odd-even day's test-retest reliability coefficient was 0.32 to 0.48 (Folstein & Luria, 1973), and when used for self-rating of epigastric pain in nonulcer dyspepsia, the corresponding coefficient was 0.42 = 0.60 (Nuren et al., in press).

Validity. Several authors have found good correlation between VAS ratings and results obtained from verbal rating scales (Huskisson, 1974; Folstein & Luria, 1973). In a factor analysis the factor loadings were similar, indicating that there are no real calibration differences between the scales (Downie et al., 1978). Conversely, Downie, Leatham, Rhind, Pickup, and Wright (1978) found poor correlation between the objectively measured and subjectively assessed values of grip strength. It seems reasonable to assume that factors within the subject are more important for the validity of assessments than is the scaling method in itself.

Sensitivity. The VAS has been claimed to be more sensitive to small changes in perceived sensation than are simple verbal scales, because the mean number of units of change tend to be greater with the former (Scott & Huskisson, 1976). There is, however, reason to call this claim in question. Studies of these matters are mostly concerned with pain assessments, and comparisons have been made with simple 4-point verbal scales. However, four categories are probably inadequate because most individuals have a greater discriminative power for pain (Wolff, 1978), and a clearly discernible change may take place within one grade of such a scale. Therefore, a fixed-point verbal scale with an adequate number of steps might prove to be as sensitive as the VAS. Moreover, the variance in measurements should be taken into account.

With the VAS the need for assuming the intervals between descriptive terms has been eliminated. This seems to be an important advantage, and the use of parametric statistical tests has been claimed to be more legitimate with VAS data than with data derived from ordinary fixed-point scales. However, no real evidence supports the assumption that the change in a subjective response, which causes a 2-cm shift of the markings along the lower half of the VAS, equals the change that corresponds to 2 cm elsewhere on the scale. Furthermore, VAS data do not fulfill the parametric requirement of constancy of measurement error variance (Dixon & Bird, 1981). Therefore, the powerful parametric tests should be used with as much caution as are fixed-point scales.

Clinical Use

A wide variety of applications has been documented during the last 70 years. Clinically, the VAS has been used mainly to assess pain, but mood, depression, anxiety, and quality of sleep are other examples of subjective feelings for which VAS ratings have been successfully employed. Great interindividual differences in ways of communicating feelings make assessments of this kind unsuited for direct comparisons between subjects. It is preferable to obtain serial ratings to ascertain changes in responses. In this situation the availability of previous recordings might have an impact on the results.

Future Directions

The use of VAS to assess subjective states is limited only by difficulties in formulating suitable anchoring phrases. Indeed, the VAS is a convenient method for conveying feelings or opinions nonverbally, and the scale will probably defend its position as one of the most popular methods of measuring of subjective responses in clinical trials. However, its superiority over other types of rating scales with respect to psychometric and statistical properties should not be overemphasized.

References

Dixon, J.S., & Bird, H.A. (1981). Reproducibility along a 10 cm vertical visual analogue scale. Annual of Rheumatic Disease, 40, 87-89.

Downie, W.W., Leatham, P.A., Rhind, V.M., Pickup, M.E., & Wright, V. (1978). The visual analogue scale in the assessment of grip strength. Annual of Rheumatic Disease, 37, 382-384.

Downie, W.W., Leatham, P.A., Rhind, V.M., Wright, V., Branco, J.A., & Anderson, J.A. (1978). Studies with pain rating scales. Annual of Rheumatic Disease, 37, 378-381.

Folstein, M.F., & Luria, R. (1973). Reliability, validity and clinical application of the visual analogue mood scale. Psychological Medicine, 3, 479-486.

Huskisson, E.C. (1974). Measurement of pain. Lancet, 11, 1127-1131.

Huskisson, E.C. (1983). Visual analogue scales. In R. Melzack (Ed.), Pain measurement and assessment (pp. 33-37). New York: Raven Press.

Nuren, O., Adami, H.O., Bates, S., Bergstrom, R., Gustavsson, S., Loof, L., & Sjoden, P.O. (in press). Self-rating of pain in gastroenterological practice. A methodological study comparing a new fixed point scale and the Visual Analogue Scale applied to patients with non-ulcer dyspepsia. Journal of Clinical Gastroenterology.

Revill, S.I., Robinson, J.O., Rosen, M., & Hogg, M.I.J. (1976). The reliability of a linear analogue for evaluating pain. Anaesthesia, 31, 1191-1198.

Scott, J., & Huskisson, E.C. (1976). Vertical or horizontal visual analogue scales. Annual of Rheumatic Disease, 38, 560.

Wolff, B.B. (1978). Behavioural measurement of human pain. In R.A. Sternbach (Ed.), The psychology of pain (pp. 129-168). New York: Raven Press.

Willoughby Personality Schedule

Gail Steketee and Blanche Freund

Description

The Willoughby Personality Schedule (WPS) is a 25-item self-rated inventory that assesses mainly interpersonal sensitivity. All items are positively worded and are rated on a 5-point scale. Each numerical point is anchored with written descriptors arrayed on a continuum ranging from 0 (no, never, and not at all) to 4 (practically always, and entirely). Sixteen of the questions refer specifically to situations involving other persons and four request information about dysphoric mood. The remaining five items inquire about fears of falling, frequency of daydreaming, self-confidence, giving help at an accident, and decision-making difficulties. A total score is obtained by summing across all items. The inventory requires 10 to 15 minutes to complete.

Purpose and Development

The WPS was developed as a shortened form of the Thurstone Personality Schedule, with an expanded rating scale for each item (Willoughby, 1932). The WPS was intended to measure common areas of neurotic reactivity with a particular focus on interpersonal anxieties. Such social hypersensitivity was viewed as the source of inadequate social functioning and possibly of more general neurotic behavior patterns. A revised version of the questionnaire (Wolpe, 1973) elaborated on the wording of many of the original items, presumably in pursuit of greater clarity and hence increased reliability and validity. The psychometric properties of this revised version relative to the original have not been tested. Since its development, the scale has been largely ignored as a clinical or research assessment tool, with the exception of

Wolpe's interest in the measure. However, recent studies have employed the original or revised version as a diagnostic tool to differentiate high and low assertive individuals and to assess the outcome of treatment for socially anxious patients.

Psychometric Characteristics

Reliability. Willoughby (1934) reports a high split-half reliability coefficient of .91 and a test-retest correlation of .89 with an interval of 2.5 months. Coefficient alpha for internal consistency was .82 for the 25 items of the revised WPS (Turner, DiTomasso, & Murray, 1980).

Construct Validity. A factor analysis of the 25 items conducted by Turner et al. (1980) for combined male and female subjects (sample = 437) yielded three common factors: Factor 1 represented 40% of variance and was labeled "hypersensitivity to interpersonal stress"; Factor 2, "labile affect," accounted for 6.8% of the variance; and Factor 3, which accounted for 4.8% of the variance, was identified as "fear of criticism." The authors suggested that Factors 2 and 3 represented subcomponents of Factor 1, "interpersonal anxiety."

Discriminant Validity. Willoughby (1934) reported a mean score of 32.5 for a college student population (sample = 262), with female subjects tending to score higher (m = 36.1, SD = 15.8) than males (m = 28.9, SD = 13.7). Examining WPS scores of 55 male (mean age 28.6 years) and 45 female subjects (mean age 31.3) from a college and community sample, Hestand, Howard, and Gregory (1971) found no significant difference between the means of their sample and those of Willoughby. A hospital worker control group had a similar mean score of 31.2 (SD = 12.89) (Turner, Meles, & DiTomasso, 1983).

In studying the discriminant validity of the WPS for subgroups of clinical psychiatric outpatients, Turner and his colleagues reported the following mean scores: simple phobia, 34.7; agoraphobia, 54.0; obsessive-compulsive behavior, 54.04; social phobia, 64.2; and sexual disorders, 43.0 (sample sizes ranged from 22 to 32). A discriminant analysis indicated that scores on the WPS correctly classified control subjects and social phobics 88% of the time. However, Eisler, Miller, and Hersen (1973) found that the WPS failed to discriminate between high and low assertive hospitalized male psychiatric patients, calling into question the validity of the WPS as a measure of assertiveness.

With respect to its relationship to depression, Turner, Freund, Leibowitz, and Strauss-Zerby (1983) observed that WPS scores were higher for depressed social phobics (64.7, SD = 8.5) than for nondepressed ones (42.0, SD = 9.8). The WPS was sensitive to change following treatment only for the nondepressed group; posttreatment scores were 62.9 (SD = 3.0) and 31.5 (SD = 17.2), respectively. Sensitivity to change after behavioral treatment has also been reported by Wolpe (1973) for "neurotic" patients. It should be noted, however, that the WPS was found to correlate significantly with the Crowne-Marlowe Social Desirability Scale (.31), suggesting a potential problem with response bias.

Clinical Use

Turner and his colleagues have provided data indicating that the WPS can be used to identify socially anxious individuals. In discussing assertiveness training procedures, Wolpe (1973) suggested that the WPS be used as a diagnostic measure of the need for such training. However, the findings of Eisler and his colleagues just reported cast some doubt on this proposition. Wolpe has further proposed that the WPS may aid in elucidating specific information from patients about situations that involve interpersonal fears and that it may be useful, along with the Fear Survey Schedule and interview information, in providing "raw data" for hierarchy construction for desensitization. In view of its good reliability, construct validity, internal consistency, and sensitivity to change, it appears that the WPS is a reasonable choice for measurement of change following treatment for social anxiety.

Future Directions

The WPS is a brief, easy to administer questionnaire. Although many of its psychometric properties have been examined to date and found satisfactory, its use as a predictor of outcome following behavioral treatment and its convergent/divergent validity with other measures have not been fully studied. With respect to the latter, it is essential at this point to determine whether the WPS represents the best available measure of social anxiety relative to other similar self-report questionnaires. Its utility as a measure of assertiveness requires further study. If it is viewed as a means of assessing general neuroticism, its relationship to other such measures (e.g., Eysenck Personality Questionnaire) should be examined.

References

Eisler, R.M., Miller, P.M., & Hersen, M. (1973). Components of assertive behavior. *Journal of Clinical Psychology, 29*, 295-299.

Hestand, R., Howard, D., & Gregory, R. (1971). Components of assertive behavior. *Journal of Clinical Psychology, 29*, 295-299.

Turner, R.M., DiTomasso, R.A., & Murray, M.R. (1980). Psychometric analysis of the Willoughby Personality Schedule. *Journal of Behavior Therapy and Experimental Psychiatry, 11*, 185-194.

Turner, R.M., Freund, B., Leibowitz, J., & Strauss-Zerby, S. (1983). *The interaction of client's degree of depression with success in social anxiety treatment.* Paper presented at the World Congress on Behavior Therapy. Washington, DC, December 9, 1983.

Turner, R.M., Meles, D., & DiTomasso, R. (1983). Assessment of social anxiety: A controlled comparison among social phobics, obsessive-compulsives, agoraphobics, sexual disorders, and simple phobics. *Behaviour Research and Therapy, 21*, 181-183.

Willoughby, R.R. (1932). Some properties of the Thurstone Personality Schedule and a suggested revision. *Journal of Social Psychology, 3*, 401-424.

Willoughby, R.R. (1934). Norms for the Clark-Thurstone Inventory. *Journal of Social Psychology, 5*, 91-97.

Wolpe, J. (1973). *The practice of behavior therapy.* New York: Pergamon Press.

Written Assertiveness Knowledge Test

Monroe A. Bruch

Description

The Written Assertiveness Knowledge Test (WAKT) was designed to evaluate an individual's knowledge of the content of an effective rights assertion response. The WAKT contains four conflict situations that vary in the type of unreasonable request and in the type of target person making the request. Each situation is followed by a blank space in which the person writes a role-play response using the exact words they would say to the requester in the situation. The four assertion situations were selected from McFall and Lillesand's (1971) Conflict Resolution Inventory (CRI items 6, 16, 21, and 29). The scoring of the WAKT involves a two-step procedure. First, each written response is rated for its effectiveness using McFall and Lillesand's (1971) 5-point refusal scale (i.e., 1 = unqualified acceptance; 5 = unqualified refusal). Second,

because the WAKT was designed to assess cross-situational knowledge of effective assertive responses, a qualitative scoring procedure is used to derive a single score. Specifically, each of the four responses is classified as "effective" if it receives an initial rating of 4 or 5 (i.e., qualified or unqualified refusal) or "ineffective" if it receives a rating of 1, 2, or 3 (i.e., unqualified acceptance to ambiguous). The number of effective responses is then added to yield a total score ranging from 0 to 4.

Purpose

The WAKT was designed to assess knowledge of the critical content dimensions that should be included when formulating a response to refuse another person's unreasonable request. As a test of assertion skills knowledge in refusal situations, it requires that the person actually produce the appropriate response rather than merely recognize an effective response among a list of alternative actions. When the goal of measurement is to tap the upper level of a person's knowledge of effective behavior in a particular domain, it is important that the method selected to conduct the assessment does not constrain a person's capacity to demonstrate such knowledge. Therefore, the WAKT uses a written response format with no time limit rather than a behavioral role-play format in which the person must respond orally within a few seconds to simulate a social interaction. The latter procedure presumably can engender negative emotions of anxiety and embarrassment and therefore may inhibit a person's capacity to concentrate on the full range of their knowledge when formulating a response.

Development

The original procedure from which the WAKT was adopted was developed by Schwartz and Gottman (1976). Their measure was used to test whether assertive as compared to nonassertive individuals differed in both their knowledge of an effective response and their ability to actually deliver a verbal response or just in their ability to deliver a refusal response. Their measure, which is entitled the Assertiveness Knowledge Test (AKT), differs from the WAKT in two respects. First, the directions for the AKT require that respondents provide what they think is an ideal assertive response for the situation. In contrast, the WAKT does not include instructions that are high in experimental demand, but it elicits a sample of reponses that constitute the typical manner in which an individual applies their knowledge to formulating a response. Second, the AKT is scored by adding the rating given to each response, whereas the WAKT's score is based on the absolute number of effective responses that were produced. This difference in scoring probably has its greatest effect when interpreting the meaning of a mid-range score. Because the AKT scoring method treats an ambiguous response (i.e., McFall and Lillesand's rating of 3) as more effective than a qualified acceptance (rating = 2), a moderate as compared to a low score may reflect little real difference in skills knowledge. However, because the WAKT score is based on the absolute number of effective responses, the conceptual distinction among high, moderate, and low scores should be maintained.

Psychometric Characteristics

In its use as a research instrument, both measures evidence very acceptable interrater reliability and validity. The reliability of both measures essentially rests on the interrater reliability of the McFall and Lillesand rating criteria, which have been found to be highly interpretable. For the AKT, two studies (Bruch, 1981; Schwartz & Gottman, 1976) revealed that interrater reliability ranged from .89 to .93, whereas for the WAKT one study revealed an interrater reliability of .91 (Bruch, Haase, & Purcell, 1984). In terms of validity, the AKT was found to correlate with self-perceived assertiveness (Bruch, 1981), suggesting that greater knowledge is associated with self-perceived assertiveness. Also, the AKT was found to correlate with a measure of cognitive complexity (Bruch, Heisler, & Conroy, 1981), suggesting that greater knowledge is related to the tendency to be more differentiated when processing information about social conflict situations. For the WAKT, Bruch et al. (1984) found that content knowledge was positively correlated with a greater frequency of thoughts about the positive consequences resulting from assertive behavior, and inversely correlated with thoughts about possible negative consequences (e.g., "I was concerned that the person would think I was selfish if I refused") associated with assertion.

Clinical Use

Because the WAKT was developed to test research questions involving how the component of skills knowledge contributes to an individual's assertive behavior, it has not been employed as an assessment tool in clinical practice. As a research measure, it has been used only in studies involving samples of college students and consequently contains items involving rights assertion conflicts typical to the college environment.

With only minor modification it could be used in counseling work with low assertive student clients. As part of a pretreatment screening battery, the WAKT might assist the counselor in deciding whether the client possesses adequate knowledge about the content of an effective response to determine what sequence of treatments might be most beneficial.

Future Directions

The WAKT is currently not a fully developed measure with a static set of items and scoring criteria for either research or clinical purposes. One limitation is that the McFall and Lillesand rating criteria place singular emphasis on an explicit statement of "no" to the requestor and do not include other components of an effective assertive response, such as requests that the person change his or her behavior. In the future this measure could be modified or expanded to assess content knowledge about a greater variety of response components as well as to evaluate knowledge about various classes of assertive behavior (e.g., ability to express positive feelings toward others, to initiate an interaction, and to accept compliments). Assessing knowledge about these different types of assertive expression will require the existence of specific rating criteria.

From a clinical perspective, it should be relatively easy to assemble a set of assertion situations that are relevant to a variety of adult outpatient groups to use this instrument to assess general knowledge level. Thus, a modified form of the WAKT could provide an economical means for a preliminary evaluation of a client's rudimentary content knowledge of an effective assertive response.

References

Bruch, M.A. (1981). A task analysis of assertive behavior revisited: Replication and extension. *Behavior Therapy, 12,* 217-230.

Bruch, M.A., Heisler, B.D., & Conroy, C.G. (1981). Effects of conceptual complexity on assertive behavior. *Journal of Counseling Psychology, 28,* 377-385.

Bruch, M.A., Haase, R.F., & Purcell, M.J. (1984). Content dimensions of self-statements in assertive situations: A factor analysis of two measures. *Cognitive Therapy and Research, 8,* 173-186.

McFall, R.M., & Lillesand, D.B. (1971). Behavior rehearsal with modeling and coaching in assertive training. *Journal of Abnormal Psychology, 77,* 313-323.

Schwartz, R.M., & Gottman, J.M. (1976). Toward a task analysis of assertive behavior. *Journal of Consulting and Clinical Psychology, 44,* 910-920.

Zung Self-Rating Anxiety Scale

Robert E. Becker

Description

The Zung Self-Rating Anxiety Scale (Zung, 1971 a, b), is a 20-item list of symptoms of anxiety disorder as derived from DSM-II. It contains five questions aimed at the patient's affective state and 15 questions aimed at somatic symptoms. Each item requires the patient to make a judgment of the frequency of occurrence of the symptom, which ranges from "none or a little of the time" to "most or all of the time." Each item is scored on a scale of 1 to 4 and then summed to yield a total score. This total score is divided by the highest possible score, and the quotient is multiplied by 100 to produce a result called an Index (see below). The index score for a particular patient is then compared to norms provided by Zung (1974) to assess the severity of the symptoms.

Purpose

The purpose of this paper-and-pencil instrument is to assess the number of symptoms of anxiety as a psychiatric disorder and also to provide a measure of the magnitude of the anxiety symptom constellation. The original design was based on the symptoms of anxiety as delineated in DSM-II. With this diagnostic base, individual items were selected to be inclusive of the symptoms of anxiety disorder, and at the same time the scale was to be short and simple to administer. This scale was also to be available in two forms. The Anxiety Status Inventory (ASI) was designed to be rated by a clinician after a clinical interview, whereas the Self-Rating Anxiety Scale (SAS) was designed to be equivalent to the clinician's assessments but collected from the patient by self-report. Both forms employ the same scoring system and yield total scores called a Z-score for the ASI and an Index for the SAS.

Development

The definition of an anxiety disorder was taken from DSM-II, and additional information about the symptoms was taken from three standard psychiatry textbooks current at the time of test construction. (See Zung, 1974, for more detail.) These sources served as the basis for the nosology of the disorder and led to a descriptive approach to the creation of each question. The guiding philosophy in the construction of each item was that anxiety neurosis is characterized by anxious overconcern, which is associated with specific somatic symptoms. Of the 20 items used in the scale, some are worded symptomatically positive and others are symptomatically negative to prevent patients from answering questions in a biased fashion. Patients are instructed to make judgments of symptoms as they appeared during the previous week.

Psychometric Characteristics

Reliability, calculated on a sample that included both normal subjects and subjects with a wide range of psychopathology, is reported as a correlation of $r = .66$ between the ASI and the SAS. When the sample is reduced to include only those patients with a diagnosis of anxiety disorder, the correlation increases to $r = .74$. Validity was determined on a sample of 225 patients and 253 normal subjects. These data suggested a cutoff score of 50, where all the age-matched normal subjects scored below this level and all the anxiety disorder patients scored above it. Mean scores for other patients with a psychiatric diagnosis showed some overlap of scores, with the diagnosis of personality disorder having the greatest overlap. Based on these data the recommended cutoff score for morbidity is 50, with higher scores indicating more severe pathology.

Clinical Use

Although this scale is designed in the traditional manner of most psychological assessment devices, and there appear to be adequate norms and psychometric data, it has not been popularly used in clinical practice or clinical research. The administration and scoring of this device are straightforward and would not appear costly. The basic difficulty with the scale is most likely its conceptualization of the disorder of anxiety, which may now be seen as less adequate in light of more recent diagnostic sophistication.

Future Directions

This scale represents one aspect of assessment of an anxiety disorder. More recent conceptualizations of anxiety include elements from three different domains: behavioral, cognitive, and somatic. Additionally, added sophistication in diagnostic procedure and conceptual understanding of anxiety disorders include more situational factors in the production of anxiety responses (for example, the environmental cues involved in agoraphobia). This scale still captures part of the phenomenon of anxiety disorder, but it would benefit from a revision and extension in recognition of the newer knowledge about the nature of this class of disorders.

References

Zung, W.W.K. (1971a). The differentiation of anxiety and depressive disorders: A biometric approach. *Psychosomatics, 12,* 380-384.

Zung, W.W.K. (1971b). A rating instrument for anxiety disorders. *Psychomatics, 12,* 372-379.

Zung, W.W.K. (1974). The measurement of affects: Depression and anxiety. In P. Pichot & R. Olivier-Martin (Eds.), *Psychological measurements in psychopharmacology.* Basel, Switzerland: S. Karger, AG.

Zung Self-Rating Depression Scale

Robert E. Becker

Description

The Zung Self-Rating Depression Scale (SDS) is a 20= item scale designed to measure the symptoms of depression. Patients are asked to rate the frequency of occurrence of each symptom on a scale ranging from "none or a little of the time" to "most or all of the time." Ten items are worded symptomatically positive and 10 symptomatically negative. Scoring of the instrument is accomplished by summing the 1 to 4 possible score for each item. An Index is created by taking the raw score sum, dividing it by the highest possible score (80), and expressing this result as an integer. The possible score range is 25 at the nonsymptomatic end to 100 at the most symptomatic end. The norms provided by Zung (1965) suggest that scores under 50 indicate little or no depression; scores from 50 to 59, mild to moderate depression; scores from 60 to 69, moderate to severe depression; and scores over 70, severe depression.

Purpose

The Zung Self-Rating Depression Scale was created to provide a qualitative and quantitative assessment of depressive disorder so that rater bias would be diminished or eliminated. The scale was conceived of as a way to reflect the current thinking about the psychopathology of depression and to make the assessment of such psychopathology simple, reliable, and valid. It was also hoped that this scale could be applied to clinical studies of depression, be employed cross-culturally, and correlate highly with an interviewer-rated scale of similar design. Additionally, it was designed so that the scale could provide normative data against which to judge the severity of a patient's symptoms.

Development

Selection of items for the scale was based on the clinical diagnostic criteria most commonly used at the time of scale development and consists of four areas: pervasive affect disturbances, physiological disturbances, psychomotor disturbances, and psychological disturbances. The initial 20-item scale offered four choices of response in order that patients could not find "a middle ground" to look average. The four columns had labels on only the two inner columns, leaving the extreme columns undefined. Initial experience with the scale led to a revision of the column labeling, so that all four columns are not labeled. The revised scale has been used in clinical and cross-cultural studies and in studies of the incidence of depression in the normal population. (See Zung, 1974, for a review.) These studies have provided norms, demonstrated the scale's sensitivity to changes produced by clinical treatment, and suggested cutoff scores for morbidity. The self-report version has also spawned the Depression Status Inventory (DSI), also a 20-item scale but designed as a semistructured interviewer-rated instrument.

Psychometric Characteristics

The split-half reliability of the SDS is .73. The SDS correlates significantly with the Hamilton Rating Scale for Depression, the Beck Depression Inventory, and the D scale of the Minnesota Multiphasic Personality Inventory. Three studies by Zung (1965, 1967) and his colleagues (Zung et al., 1965) provide data that show that the SDS can consistently discriminate between depressive disorders and other psychopathology. Studies on normal populations suggest an SDS Index of 50 as the cut-off for morbidity, and this score correctly classifies 88% of depressed patients and 88% of the normal subjects. Cross-cultural studies conducted in Japan, Australia, Czechoslovakia, England, West Germany, and Switzerland indicate that patients in these countries diagnosed as having a depressive disorder obtained scores comparable to those of their depressed American counterparts. Less data are available on the DSI; however, the DSI and the SDS correlate $r = .81$.

Clinical Use

The Zung SDS is an easy to use measure of the severity of clinical depression and has been used both clinically and in clinical research. In more recent years its popularity has been eclipsed by the Beck Depression Inventory. The Beck Inventory tends to measure more of the psychological symptoms of depression, whereas the SDS tends to measure more of the somatic symptoms.

Future Directions

The SDS has been in use since 1972 and has an extensive literature behind it, but it seems to suffer because of the lesser emphasis on psychological symptoms as compared with the Beck Depression Inventory and because it has not been updated to reflect the greater sophistication currently available in diagnosis.

References

Zung, W.W.K. (1965). A self-rating depression scale. *Archives of General Psychiatry, 12,* 63-70.

Zung, W.W.K. (1967). Factors influencing the self rating depression scale. *Archives of General Psychiatry, 16,* 543-547.

Zung, W.W.K. (1974). The measurement of affects: Depression and anxiety. In P. Pichot & R. Oliver-Martin (Eds.), *Psychological measurements in psychopharmacology.* Basel, Switzerland: S. Karger, AG.

Zung, W.W.K., Richards, C., & Short, M.J. (1965). Self-rating depression scale in an outpatient clinic. *Archives of General Psychiatry, 13,* 508-515.

Author Index

499

About the Editors

ABOUT THE EDITORS

Michel Hersen is Professor of Psychiatry and Psychology at the University of Pittsburgh School of Medicine. He is Past-President of the Association for Advancement of Behavior Therapy. His research interests include assessment and treatment of a variety of child populations, including multihandicapped children and their families, and family violence. Dr. Hersen is the recipient of several research grants from the National Institute of Mental Health, The Department of Education, the National Institute of Disabilities and Rehabilitation Research, and the March of Dimes Birth Defects Foundations. He is the co-author or co-editor of 50 books and has published more than 155 journal articles and is co-editor of several psychological journals.

Alan S. Bellack is Professor of Psychiatry at the Medical College of Pennsylvania and Adjunct Professor of Psychology at Temple University. He is Past-President of the Association for Advancement of Behavior Therapy, and a Fellow of Division 12 of APA. He has published over 90 journal articles and is co-author and co-editor of 18 books as well as co-editor of two journals. Dr. Bellack has received numerous NIMH research grants on social skills, behavioral assessment, and schizophrenia. He has served on the editorial boards of numerous journals and has been consultant to a number of publishing companies and mental health facilities as well as NIMH.

Pergamon General Psychology Series

Editors: Arnold P. Goldstein, Syracuse University
Leonard Krasner, Stanford University &
SUNY at Stony Brook